Please remember that this is a library book,
and that it belongs only temporarily to each
person who uses it. Be considerate. Do
not write in this, or any, library book.

Blackwell Handbook of Social Psychology:
Interpersonal Processes

D1545266

WITHDRAWN

GARY LIBRARY
VERMONT COLLEGE
36 COLLEGE STREET
MONTPELIER, VT 05602

Blackwell Handbook of Social Psychology

Series editors: Miles Hewstone and Marilynn Brewer

Each of the four volumes of this authoritative handbook draws together 20–30 newly commissioned chapters to provide a comprehensive overview of specific topics in the field of social psychology. Designed to have considerable depth as well as breadth, each of the volumes encompasses theory and research at the intraindividual, interpersonal, intergroup, and group levels. Editors have been chosen for their expertise and knowledge of the subject, making *The Blackwell Handbook of Social Psychology* an invaluable companion for any serious social psychology scholar.

Intraindividual Processes, edited by Abraham Tesser and Norbert Schwarz

Interpersonal Processes, edited by Garth J. O. Fletcher and Margaret S. Clark

Intergroup Processes, edited by Rupert Brown and Samuel Gaertner

Group Processes, edited by Michael A. Hogg and Scott Tindale

Blackwell Handbook of Social Psychology: Interpersonal Processes

Edited by

Garth J. O. Fletcher and Margaret S. Clark

Blackwell Publishing

302
B632f
2003

© 2001, 2003 by Blackwell Publishers Ltd
a Blackwell Publishing company
except for editorial material and organization © 2001, 2003 by Garth J. O. Fletcher and
Margaret S. Clark.

350 Main Street, Malden, MA 02148-5018, USA
108 Cowley Road, Oxford OX4 1JF, UK
550 Swanston Street, Carlton South, Melbourne, Victoria 3053, Australia.
Kurfürstendamm 57, 10707 Berlin, Germany

The right of Garth J. O. Fletcher and Margaret S. Clark to be identified as the Authors of
the Editorial Material in this Work has been asserted in accordance with the UK
copyright, Designs, and Patents Act 1988.

All rights reserved. No part of this publication may be reproduced, stored in a retrieval
system, or transmitted, in any form or by any means, electronic, mechanical,
photocopying, recording or otherwise, except as permitted by the UK Copyright,
Designs, and Patents Act 1988, without the prior permission of the publisher.

First published 2001
First published in paperback 2003

Library of Congress Cataloging-in-Publication Data

Blackwell handbook of social psychology. Interpersonal processes / edited by Garth
Fletcher and Margaret Clark.
     p.   cm.
  Includes bibliographical references and index.
   ISBN 0–631–21228–0 (hb : alk. paper); ISBN 0–631–21229–9 (pb : alk. paper)
   1. Interpersonal relations.   2. Social psychology.   I. Fletcher, Garth J. O.
 II. Clark, Margaret Sydnor.

 HM1106.B53 2000
 302—dc21

                            00–025852

A catalogue record for this title is available from the British Library.

Typeset in 10½ on 12½ pt Adobe Garamond
by Ace Filmsetting Ltd, Frome, Somerset
Printed and bound in the United Kingdom
by T.J. International Ltd, Padstow, Cornwall

For further information on
Blackwell Publishing, visit our website:
http://www.blackwellpublishing.com

Contents

Series Editors' Foreword   viii

Preface   x

Part I   Cognition/Attribution   1

1   Attributions in Close Relationships: From Balkanization to Integration   3
Frank D. Fincham

2   Cognition and the Development of Close Relationships   32
Benjamin R. Karney, James K. McNulty, and Thomas N. Bradbury

3   Cognitive Representations of Attachment: The Content and Function of
Working Models   60
Nancy L. Collins and Lisa M. Allard

4   The Structure and Function of Ideal Standards in Close Relationships   86
Jeffry A. Simpson, Garth J. O. Fletcher, and Lorne Campbell

5   Seeking a Sense of Conviction: Motivated Cognition in Close Relationships   107
Sandra L. Murray

Part II   Social Motivation   127

6   Integrating Social Psychological Research on Aggression within an
Evolutionary-based Framework   129
Neil M. Malamuth and Tamara Addison

7   Helping and Altruism   162
John F. Dovidio and Louis A. Penner

8   The Death and Rebirth of the Social Psychology of Negotiation   196
Max H. Bazerman, Jared R. Curhan, and Don A. Moore

9   Motivational Aspects of Empathic Accuracy   229
     William Ickes and Jeffry A. Simpson

Part III   Affect/Emotion   251

10   Understanding People's Perceptions of Relationships is Crucial to
     Understanding their Emotional Lives   253
     Margaret S. Clark, Julie Fitness, and Ian Brissette

11   Emotional Intelligence: Conceptualization and Measurement   279
     Peter Salovey, Alison Woolery, and John D. Mayer

12   Emotional Experience in Close Relationships   308
     Ellen Berscheid and Hilary Ammazzalorso

13   The Status of Theory and Research on Love and Commitment   331
     Beverley Fehr

Part IV   Social Influence and Comparison   357

14   Interdependence in Close Relationships   359
     Caryl E. Rusbult, Ximena B. Arriaga, and Christopher R. Agnew

15   Social Comparison and Close Relationships   388
     Bram P. Buunk and Frans L. Oldersma

Part V   Self and Identity   409

16   An Evolutionary-Psychological Approach to Self-esteem: Multiple Domains
     and Multiple Functions   411
     Lee A. Kirkpatrick and Bruce J. Ellis

17   Is Loving the Self Necessary for Loving Another? An Examination of Identity
     and Intimacy   437
     W. Keith Campbell and Roy F. Baumeister

18   The Self We Know and the Self We Show: Self-esteem, Self-presentation,
     and the Maintenance of Interpersonal Relationships   457
     Mark R. Leary

19   Self-expansion Model of Motivation and Cognition in Close Relationships
     and Beyond   478
     Arthur Aron, Elaine N. Aron, and Christina Norman

Part VI   Methods   503

20   A Statistical Framework for Modeling Homogeneity and Interdependence
     in Groups   505
     Richard Gonzalez and Dale Griffin

Part VII Applications   535

21   Attachment Style and Affect Regulation: Implications for Coping with Stress and Mental Health   537
Mario Mikulincer and Victor Florian

22   Marital Therapy and Social Psychology: Will We Choose Explicit Partnership or Cryptomnesia?   558
Steven R. H. Beach and Frank D. Fincham

Subject Index   587
Author Index   602

Series Editors' Foreword

The idea for a new international handbook series for social psychology was conceived in July 1996 during the triannual meeting of the European Association of Experimental Social Psychology in the idyllic setting of Gmunden, Austria. Over a glass of wine and pleasant breezes from the Traunsee, Alison Mudditt (then Psychology Editor for Blackwell Publishers) engaged the two of us in a "hypothetical" discussion of what a multi-volume handbook of social psychology at the start of the twenty-first century might look like. By the second glass of wine we were hooked, and the project that has culminated in the publication of this four-volume *Blackwell Handbook of Social Psychology* was commissioned.

The EAESP meeting provided a fitting setting for the origin of a project that was intended to be an international collaborative effort. The idea was to produce a set of volumes that would provide a rich picture of social psychology at the start of the new millennium – a cross-section of the field that would be both comprehensive and forward-looking. In conceiving an organizational framework for such a venture, we sought to go beyond a simple topical structure for the content of the volumes in order to reflect more closely the complex pattern of cross-cutting theoretical perspectives and research agendas that comprise social psychology as a dynamic enterprise. Rather than lengthy review papers covering a large domain of social psychological research, we felt that a larger number of shorter and more focused chapters would better reflect the diversity and the synergies representative of the field at this time.

The idea we developed was to represent the discipline in a kind of matrix structure, crossing levels of analysis with topics, processes, and functions that recur at all of these levels in social psychological theory and research. Taking inspiration from Willem Doise's 1986 book (*Levels of Explanation in Social Psychology*), four levels of analysis – intrapersonal, interpersonal, intragroup, and intergroup – provided the basis for organizing the *Handbook* series into four volumes. The content of each volume would be selected on the basis of cross-cutting themes represented by basic processes of social cognition, attribution, social motivation, affect and emotion, social influence, social comparison, self and identity, as they operate at each level. In addition, each volume would include methodological issues and areas of applied or policy-relevant work related to social psychological research at that level of analysis.

Armed with this rough organizational framework as our vision for the series, our role was to commission editors for the individual volumes who would take on the challenging task of turning this vision into reality. The plan was to recruit two experts for each volume, who would bring different but complementary perspectives and experience to the subject matter to work together to plan, commission, and edit 20–30 papers that would be representative of current and exciting work within their broad domain. Once selected, co-editors were encouraged to use the matrix framework as a heuristic device to plan the coverage of their volume, but were free to select from and embellish upon that structure to fit their own vision of the field and its current directions.

We have been extremely fortunate in having persuaded eight exceptionally qualified and dedicated scholars of social psychology to join us in this enterprise and take on the real work of making this *Handbook* happen. Once they came on board, our role became an easy one: just relax and observe as the project was brought to fruition in capable hands. We are deeply indebted and grateful to Abraham Tesser and Norbert Schwarz, Garth Fletcher and Margaret Clark, Michael Hogg and Scott Tindale, Rupert Brown and Samuel Gaertner for their creative leadership in producing the four volumes of this series. Through their efforts, a rough outline has become a richly textured portrait of social psychology at the threshold of the twenty-first century.

In addition to the efforts of our volume editors and contributors, we are grateful to the editorial staff at Blackwell Publishers who have seen this project through from its inception. The project owes a great deal to Alison Mudditt who first inspired it. When Alison went on to new ventures in the publishing world, Martin Davies took over as our capable and dedicated Commissioning Editor who provided guidance and oversight throughout the operational phases. Our thanks to everyone who has been a part of this exciting collaborative venture.

Miles Hewstone
Marilynn Brewer

Preface

The term "handbook" tends to conjure up a vision of long and sometimes tedious reviews of the literature, which long-suffering graduate students are forced to read. None of that here. Instead, the diversity and breadth of social psychology (in the interpersonal domain) is represented in a smorgasbord of short focused chapters. We believe this approach has worked well, and the volume accurately represents contemporary social psychological theorizing and research at the cusp – and what an invigorating cusp it is.

This particular volume of the *Blackwell Handbook of Social Psychology* follows, at least roughly, the kind of framework suggested and described by the series editors (Miles Hewstone and Marilynn Brewer). The chapters, in order, deal with the role of social cognition in interpersonal settings (5 chapters), social motivation (4 chapters), affect and emotion (4 chapters), social influence and comparison (2 chapters), the self (4 chapters), methods and data analysis (1 chapter), and, finally, applications of the field to real-world issues and domains (2 chapters).

These *Blackwell Handbook* volumes represent snapshots of a dynamic and broad field. The picture revealed by this volume on interpersonal processes is no exception. Many themes are apparent, but we will mention just a few that we were struck by. First, there is a groundswell of interest in the social psychology of intimate sexual relationships, from dealing with processes of initial mate selection to investigating how dyadic relationships develop, flourish, and dissolve. Second, an increasingly common theoretical tack adopted is to focus on the goals and functions of lay judgments, beliefs, and behavior. Third, the role of affect and emotions has moved further towards center stage, and treatments of it can be found in many chapters. Fourth, evolutionary psychology is increasingly (but not uncritically) exerting a profound impact on social psychology. Fifth, the study of social cognition remains a pivotal focus in social psychology – it is everywhere in these chapters. Sixth, the breadth and scope of research methods (and associated data analyses) found in these chapters suggests that social psychology has moved on from its obsession with laboratory experiments using stripped-down stimuli and the use of ANOVA designs – not that there is anything wrong with such methods, of course, except when their use is mandated as the only way of practicing "good science." Social psychology has become ecumenical in its research methods, and is in the vanguard of using powerful new statistical and causal modeling methods such as Structural Equation Modeling.

In short, the picture of social psychology revealed by this volume is an exciting and dynamic one, with social psychologists both drawing from and contributing to other related domains of scientific inquiry. We heartily thank the authors who contributed to the volume (with remarkably little arm-twisting involved), the series editors (Miles Hewstone and Marilynn Brewer) and Martin Davies and the staff at Blackwell. This volume was a remarkable pleasure to edit.

Garth Fletcher
Margaret Clark
October 1999

PART I

Cognition/Attribution

1 Attributions in Close Relationships: From Balkanization to Integration   3
    Frank D. Fincham

2 Cognition and the Development of Close Relationships   32
    Benjamin R. Karney, James K. McNulty, and Thomas N. Bradbury

3 Cognitive Representations of Attachment: The Content and Function
    of Working Models   60
    Nancy L. Collins and Lisa M. Allard

4 The Structure and Function of Ideal Standards in Close Relationships   86
    Jeffry A. Simpson, Garth J. O. Fletcher, and Lorne Campbell

5 Seeking a Sense of Conviction: Motivated Cognition in Close Relationships   107
    Sandra L. Murray

PART I

Chapter One

Attributions in Close Relationships: From Balkanization to Integration

Frank D. Fincham

Following Kelley's (1967) and Jones and Davis's (1965) important elaboration and systematization of Heider's (1958) seminal ideas about the perceived causes of behavior, attribution research replaced dissonance as the major research topic in social psychology, accounting for 11 percent of all published social-psychological research during the 1970s (Pleban & Richardson, 1979). Although the focus of attention shifted to social cognition in the 1980s, the number of articles indexed with the term attribution as a descriptor continued to rise, tripling in number between 1974 and 1984 (Smith, 1994). The publication rate has not abated in the 1990s although it appears to have plateaued at approximately 300 articles per annum (1990–8; mean = 322.8, range = 291–366).

What the numbers do not reveal, however, is a shift in the nature of research on attribution that might account for the continued prodigious output. One shift has been increasing attention to Heider's broad concern with how a perceiver links observables to underlying stable or dispositional properties ("invariances") of the world to give meaning to phenomenal experience. From this perspective, attribution is synonymous with perception and comprehension of the environment, and draws on a variety of domains (e.g., text comprehension, world knowledge) that might help elucidate the perceiver's causal construction of events. This emphasis fits well with social cognition research that also assumes continuity between inferences made about the social and nonsocial environment, and it places

The preparation of this manuscript was supported by a grant from the Templeton Foundation. The author thanks Steve Beach for his comments on an earlier draft of the manuscript. Correspondence concerning this chapter should be addressed to Frank Fincham, Department of Psychology, Park Hall, SUNY at Buffalo, Buffalo, NY 14260-4110 (e-mail: fincham@buffalo.edu) attribution in a broader framework of research on how people construct mental models of the world.

The second shift has concerned the narrower and more traditional focus on linking a person's behavior to underlying properties of the person (e.g., traits, motives). Basic attribution research on this topic, stimulated by the classic attribution statements of Kelley (1967) and Jones and Davis (1965), began to wane in the 1980s. However, the application of an attributional framework in emerging areas of inquiry such as close relationships, and to numerous applied problems (e.g., depression), maintained a steady output of research on this topic (see Hewstone & Fincham, 1996; Weiner, 1995).

The continued vitality of attribution research has, however, brought with it increased balkanization of the literature. The lack of interplay between the two new lines of attribution research just mentioned is striking. But even more striking is the relative isolation of research within closely related areas of inquiry. For example, the impact of attributions on individual and relational outcomes has been investigated but the literatures relating to each type of outcome remain distinct.

Like the broader literature on attribution, research on attributions in close relationships has continued to flourish. Although initially focused on marital relationships, the research has broadened to embrace other relationships. But this growth has again brought with it balkanization as there is limited cross-fertilization of attributional research on different topics within the same relationship (e.g., marital violence, distressed marriages) and across research on different types of relationships (e.g., marital, parent–child and peer/friendship relationships).

It is just over 20 years since the inception of marital attribution research in social (Orvis, Kelley, & Butler, 1976) and clinical (Wright & Fichten, 1976) psychology. As the field entered its adolescence, concerns were expressed about its "lack of focus and direction" (Baucom, Epstein, Sayers & Sher, 1989, p. 31). With the onset of adulthood, it behooves us to take stock of its development. In what ways have earlier expectations for the field come to fruition? Conversely, what promises remain unfulfilled and how might they now be realized? At a minimum, we need to recognize the price of balkanization and explore how integration among various domains of attribution research, and how links with a broader psychological literature, might enhance the study of attributions in marriage.

The chapter begins with a brief historical introduction to the study of attributions in marriage. It then evaluates the current state of the art in marital attribution research, paying particular attention to developments in the past decade. This serves as a springboard for examining the marital literature in relation to the two shifts in attribution research that have balkanized the literature. The chapter concludes with a summary of the main points.

Historical Context

A vast body of research on attributions for behavior existed at the time researchers turned to study attribution in close relationships. However, they did not build on this research.

Why? One reason is that basic attribution research concerned attributions made about a stranger or hypothetical other on the basis of highly restricted information and for the purpose of complying with experimenter instructions. These characteristics cast doubt on the relevance of such research for understanding attributions in relationships. Empirical findings supported this doubt. For example, Knight and Vallacher (1981) showed that attributers who believed that they were interacting with another person showed the opposite pattern of attributions for that person's positive (situationally attributed) versus negative (disposition attributed) behavior compared to attributers who only expected to interact with the person at a later time. Detached observers did not make different attributions for these two forms of behavior. In a similar vein, persons tend to make stronger internal attributions for positive behavior performed by a friend or a spouse than for an acquaintance (Taylor & Koivumaki, 1976).

Interestingly, the discontinuity between the basic attribution research and research that emerged on attributions in close relationships extended to theory. Thus, for example, a seminal volume on close relationships published in the early 1980s (Kelley et al., 1983) makes no reference to Jones and Davis (1965) or to Kelley (1967). Reference to these works is also absent in recent, comprehensive overviews of the field (e.g., Berscheid & Reis, 1998; Hinde, 1997). This disjuncture is particularly surprising as both fields have an influential common ancestor in Hal Kelley.

What then were the historical antecedents of attributional research in marriage? Two general roots can be traced. In social psychology Kelley was struck by the frequency with which intimates mentioned stable, general properties of the partner (usually dispositions) when describing relationship problems (see Kelley, 1979). This led to the investigation of attributional conflict or disagreement between a person and their partner about the cause of the person's behavior (Orvis et al., 1976; Passer, Kelley, & Michela, 1978; see also Harvey, Wells, & Alvarez, 1978)[1]. A major finding to emerge from this research was that actors preferred explanations for their negative behavior that reflected a positive attitude to the partner, whereas partners preferred explanations that reflected the actor's negative attitudes and/or traits. The characterization of attributions along an evaluative dimension suggested that satisfaction experienced by the partners may covary with attributions, a possibility which turned out to be the wellspring of marital attribution research in clinical psychology.

The origins of marital attribution research in clinical psychology did not, however, build on Kelley's work, even though Kelley had focused on marital conflict (see Braiker & Kelley, 1979), a topic that was central to clinical research (marital dysfunction was seen to result from a couple's ineffective response to conflict, Jacobson & Margolin, 1979). Instead, the attribution perspective was brought to bear on the dominant pursuit of the time, the attempt to understand what differentiates distressed from nondistressed spouses so as to better understand the determinants of marital satisfaction and thereby improve marital therapy. Accordingly, the focus of most studies tended to be some variant of the hypothesis that attributions are associated with marital satisfaction. Interestingly, this hypothesis was later shown to be consistent with Heider's (1958, pp. 207, 258) observations linking the liking of a person to the attributions made for his/her behavior (see Bradbury & Fincham, 1990).

Interest in the attribution–satisfaction association was facilitated by two factors. At the global level, it was stimulated by dissatisfaction with the limits of a behavioral account of marriage and a subsequent shift in research emphasis from the study of observed behavior to examination of intraindividual factors (cognition, emotions) that might enrich understanding of overt behavior. At a more specific level, excitement was generated by the implicit causal assumption that attributions for marital events (e.g., spouse arrives home late from work) can promote marital satisfaction (e.g., "s/he is working hard to make us financially secure") or distress (e.g., "s/he only cares about work and not about me," see Bagarozzi & Giddings, 1983).

Although originating in social and clinical psychology, the applied concerns of clinical researchers soon dominated the marital attribution literature. Before turning to this literature, it is worth noting some legacies of these historical origins as they inform the evaluation offered in the next section of the chapter.

First, marital researchers drew upon causal attribution dimensions in clinical psychology (e.g., Abramson, Seligman, & Teasdale's, 1978, attributional analysis of learned helplessness) rather than in social psychology (e.g., Weiner, Russel, & Lerman's, 1978, attributional analysis of emotion). This affected both the types of attributions initially investigated (causal attributions) as well as the manner in which they were investigated (in most research spouses rated causal dimensions). Ironically, however, it was not recognized that the locus, stability, and globality dimensions in the attributional reformulation of learned helplessness theory can be directly linked to Kelley's (1967) criteria of consensus, consistency, and distinctiveness.

Second, the evaluative implications of attributions in relationships were underscored by clinical observations that couples "typically view therapy as a way to demonstrate . . . that they are blameless and the other is at fault" (Jacobson & Margolin, 1979). This led to the suggestion that issues of responsibility and blame are particularly germane in relationships (Fincham, 1983). Whereas causal attributions concern who or what produced an event, responsibility entails assessment of who is accountable for the event once a cause is known. Blame, in turn, entails an assessment of responsibility (see Fincham & Jaspars, 1980; Shaver, 1985). As a consequence, responsibility attribution dimensions (e.g., intent, motivation) and blame attributions, in addition to causal attributions, became the subject of study in the marital literature. Figure 1.1 illustrates schematically the attribution hypothesis investigated in the marital literature showing that the pattern of attributions expected varies as a function of the valence of the event and the marital satisfaction of the attributer.

Third, the fact that attribution theory is one element of Heider's (1958) attempt to systematize common sense ("naïve psychology"), means that, as intuitive or lay psychologists, everyone has access to the ideas informing attribution theory. As a result, one can "set up studies without being very explicit about the attribution process" (Kelley in Harvey, Ickes, & Kidd, 1978, p. 375). This is particularly evident in marital attribution research. It manifested itself most obviously in the need to uncover unarticulated assumptions and build basic theory (Thompson & Snyder, 1986) and in measurement where dependent measures sometimes had nothing to do with attributions (e.g., estimates of behavioral frequency for assessment of causal stability, Holtzworth-Munroe & Jacobson, 1985, p. 1402). The upshot is remarkable variety in work that appears under the attribution rubric in the marital literature.

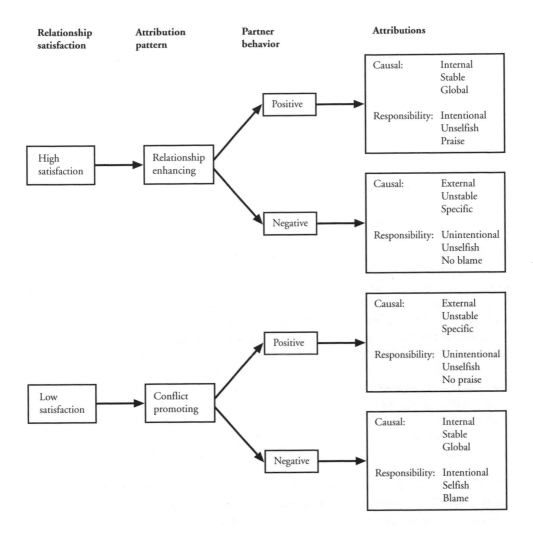

Figure 1.1   The attribution hypothesis in research on close relationships

Attributions and Marriage: A Synopsis and Critique

The purpose of the present section is threefold. The first goal is to identify themes in marital attribution research that might reveal underlying coherence in the literature. The second is to provide a synopsis of the literature. As several earlier reviews are available (e.g., Bradbury & Fincham, 1990; Baucom, 1987; Harvey, 1987; Thompson & Snyder, 1986), the focus is on research that has appeared in the last decade. This leads naturally to the third goal, to evaluate progress by identifying both actualized and forgone opportunities as well as new lines of inquiry suggested by extant research. This, in turn, sets the stage for the next section of the chapter in which links are drawn with research outside of the marital area.

Taking stock

The attribution–satisfaction association.   Early on Thompson and Snyder (1986, p. 136) concluded that "research has supported a strong association between attributional processes and relationship satisfaction." Although perhaps premature, this conclusion was prescient. By the turn of the decade there were 23 relevant studies and across attributional dimensions an average of 80 percent of them supported the attribution hypothesis (Fincham, Bradbury, & Scott, 1990). Support for the attribution hypothesis has continued to accrue in the past decade and no data have emerged to contradict the hypothesis.

This is not to suggest that results obtained across measures and methodologies are identical. For example, Sabourin, Lussier, & Wright (1991), in a successful cross-cultural replication of the attribution hypothesis, found that attributions for marital difficulties and for hypothetical partner behaviors were only moderately correlated, with the former more often accounting for unique variance in satisfaction. They called for a standardized attribution measure to facilitate greater comparison of findings across studies, and the measurement of attributions is a topic that has received increased attention (see the section, "Delineating the domain of attributions," below). Although the relations among attributions obtained using different methodologies (e.g., thought listing, couple conversations, questionnaires) remain unknown, the association with satisfaction is robust. Indeed, the evidence for an association between attribution and marital satisfaction is overwhelming, making it possibly the most robust, replicable phenomenon in the study of marriage.

Threats to the validity of the attribution–satisfaction association.   Concern about the validity of the attribution–satisfaction association has long been evident. Early work ruled out possible methodological artifacts (e.g., independent assessment of attributions and satisfaction, common method variance) and examined depression as a theoretically relevant variable that might account for the association (see Bradbury & Fincham, 1990). As the number of potentially relevant third variables can never be exhausted, it is not surprising to find continued work on this front throughout the 1990s.

Senchak and Leonard (1993) showed that demographic variables and anger did not account for the association and provided further evidence to show that the association was independent of depressive symptoms. They extended prior findings by demonstrating that with affect (anger and depression) of both self *and* partner controlled, attributions accounted for unique variance in satisfaction. In a similar vein, attributions for partner behavior have not been associated with the status of spouses as clinically depressed versus nondepressed (Bauserman, Arias, & Craighead, 1995; Bradbury, Beach, Fincham, & Nelson, 1996). It also appears that negative affectivity more generally (as indexed by neuroticism and depressive mood) does not account for the attribution–satisfaction relation; the association has emerged after controlling for the negative affectivity of both spouses and is independent of measurement error (Karney, Bradbury, Fincham, & Sullivan, 1994). Finally, the demonstration that the attribution–satisfaction association is independent of depression is consistent with findings obtained using dating couples (Fletcher, Fitness & Blampied, 1990).

A new third variable explanation for the attribution–satisfaction relation was raised in a study of marital violence. Holtzworth-Munroe and Hutchinson (1993) found that while violent husbands were more likely to attribute blame, negative intent, and selfish motivation to their wives than satisfied, nonviolent men, the attributions of maritally dissatisfied, nonviolent men did not differ from either of these two groups. If replicated, this finding would show that marital attribution phenomena may be attributable to the high rates of aggression and violence found in some married couples. However, the attribution–satisfaction association has been demonstrated in a sample of nonviolent husbands and also remains significant when marital violence is partialed out of the association (Fincham, Bradbury, Arias, Byrne, & Karney, 1997).

Ruling out threats to validity does not document the importance of attributions in marriage. Although robust, the attribution–satisfaction association may be unimportant for understanding marriage. Alternatively, it may simply reflect what Weiss (1980) has labeled "sentiment override" – the hypothesis that spouses respond noncontingently to partner behavior or questions about the marriage. In other words, spouses simply respond in terms of their dominant feeling or sentiment about the marriage and this is reflected "in as many tests as one chooses to administer" (Weiss & Heyman, 1990, p. 92). Belief in this position is so strong that attempts to explain variance in marital quality using self-reports have been characterized as "invalid from a scientific standpoint" (Gottman, 1990, p. 79). A fundamental task for the field therefore has been to show that attributions increase understanding of marriage and are not simply a proxy index of marital sentiment.

Documenting the importance of attributions in marriage.   One way to address the importance of attributions in marriage is to provide evidence for the assumption that attributions influence marital satisfaction. Such evidence raises the question of how attributions might exert any causal influence. Although any effect may be direct, it may also occur indirectly through spouse behavior. Thus, certain attributions for partner behavior (e.g., rejection of a sexual advance) may be conflict promoting (e.g., "you don't really love me"). This highlights a second important assumption that stimulated interest in spousal attributions, the possibility that attributions may influence marital behavior. For example, attributions might explain interaction patterns (e.g., negative reciprocity) identified with marital distress. Each assumption is addressed in turn.

Attributions and marital satisfaction: A causal association?   A possible causal association between attributions and satisfaction has been investigated primarily through longitudinal studies. Because only the variance that attributions do not share with marital quality is used to predict changes in marital quality, it is difficult to account for significant findings by arguing that attributions simply index marital quality.

Four new longitudinal studies supplement early findings showing that attributions predict later satisfaction in dating (Fletcher, Fincham, Cramer, & Heron, 1987) and married couples (Fincham & Bradbury, 1987a). In established marriages (mean length = 9.4 years) causal attributions predicted satisfaction 12 months later for both husbands and wives

(Fincham & Bradbury, 1993). However, husbands' initial satisfaction also predicted change in their attributions suggesting a possible bidirectional causal relation between attributions and satisfaction. This study also ruled out depressive symptoms as a factor responsible for the longitudinal association and showed that the findings did not change when those who were chronically depressed or distressed were excluded from the sample. In a sample of newlywed husbands, conflict-promoting responsibility attributions contributed to declines in reported satisfaction 12 months later but not vice versa (Fincham, Bradbury, et al., 1997), thereby showing that the longitudinal pattern of findings extends beyond the population of established married couples.

The longitudinal association between attributions and satisfaction has also been replicated over an 18-month period and appears to be mediated by the impact of attributions on efficacy expectations which, in turn, influenced satisfaction (Fincham, Harold, & Gano-Phillips, 2000). In this study, evidence was also obtained to support bidirectional effects in that satisfaction predicted attributions for both husbands and wives.

Finally, Karney and Bradbury (2000) provided novel data on the longitudinal relation through the application of growth curve modeling to eight waves of data collected over the first four years of marriage. They found intraindividual changes in attribution and in marital satisfaction covaried but found no evidence to suggest that either attributions or satisfaction were causally dominant. However, a different picture emerged at the between-subjects level of analysis. Controlling for within-subject covariation, initial attributions had greater effects on the trajectory of marital satisfaction than Time 1 satisfaction had on the trajectory of attributions. Specifically, more conflict-promoting attributions at Time 1 were associated with lower initial marital satisfaction, steeper declines in satisfaction, and satisfaction that covaried less with subsequent changes in attributions. Finally, wives' attributions improved prediction of marital dissolution and both husbands' and wives' changes in attributions were more strongly associated with deviations from the trajectory of marital satisfaction in marriages that dissolved.

In sum, there is a growing body of evidence consistent with the view that attributions influence marital satisfaction and increasing evidence that any causal relation between the two variables is bidirectional. Perhaps not surprisingly, attributions continue to be emphasized in newer, therapeutic interventions for couples (e.g., by offering a "formulation," an element of integrative couples therapy designed to promote non-blaming, Jacobson & Christensen, 1996, pp. 41–58). This highlights the opportunity to gain experimental evidence on the causal role of attributions but interest in such research appears to have evaporated (for an exception see Davidson & Horvath, 1997) following early demonstrations that supplementing standard therapies with an attribution intervention module did not improve therapeutic outcome (see Bradbury & Fincham, 1990). Unfortunately, the impact of attributions on therapeutic outcome has not been directly evaluated and nor has the importance of attributional change as a precursor to progress and positive change in marital therapy (see Fincham, Bradbury, & Beach, 1990). These considerations suggest that intervention research remains a potential source of important information (see the section, "Expressed emotion," below).

Attributions and behavior.   Despite its theoretical and applied significance, few studies have investigated the attribution–behavior link. Moreover, early attempts to do so were quite limited (see Bradbury & Fincham, 1990, p. 24). With the exception of an early experimental study in which manipulated attributions influenced subsequent observed behavior in distressed but not nondistressed spouses (Fincham & Bradbury, 1988), evidence bearing on the attribution–observed behavior relation is quite recent.

Five studies report data relating attributions to behavior observed during marital interaction (Bradbury, Beach, et al., 1996; Bradbury & Fincham, 1992, Study 1 & 2; Fincham & Bradbury, 1992, Study 3; G. E. Miller & Bradbury, 1995). Across 28 tests of the attribution–behavior association found in these studies, the mean effect size was .34; the "fail safe" number or number of unretrieved null findings that would allow one to attribute this effect size to sampling bias was 1,527. This moderate effect size, however, reflects a heterogeneous set of findings (chi-square (27) = 47, $p < .01$). One clear source of heterogeneity was spouse gender which was strongly associated with effect size ($r = .57$); the average effect size for men (mean $z = .23$) was smaller than that for women (mean $z = .45$). Although encouraging, these meta-analytic findings should be viewed with caution as they use a database that includes simple, bivariate correlations between attributions and rates of behavior. In view of earlier comments about sentiment override and the documented association between spousal satisfaction and behavior (Weiss & Heyman, 1997), it is important to show that an attribution–behavior association is independent of marital satisfaction.

With marital satisfaction partialed from the attribution–behavior relation, it has been shown that conflict-promoting responsibility attributions are related to: (1) wives' less effective problem-solving behaviors (Bradbury & Fincham, 1992, Study 1); (2) more negative behaviors during problem-solving and support-giving tasks (G. E. Miller & Bradbury, 1995) and that this association is independent of level of depression (Bradbury, Beach, et al., 1996); (3) specific affects (whining and anger) displayed during problem solving (Fincham & Bradbury, 1992, Study 3); and (4) husbands' and wives' conflict-promoting attributions are related to increased rates of negative behavior during a problem-solving discussion (Bradbury & Fincham, 1992, Study 2). There is some evidence to suggest that the attribution–behavior association is moderated by marital quality in that it is stronger for distressed spouses and tends to occur more consistently for responsibility attributions (e.g., Bradbury & Fincham, 1992; G. E. Miller & Bradbury, 1995).

A recent study by Fletcher and Thomas (2000) provided the first longitudinal data on the relation between attributions and observed behavior. Using a sample of couples randomly selected from the New Zealand electoral rolls, they found that both husbands' and wives' conflict-promoting attributions for marital problems were associated with more negative interaction behavior over a 12-month period. Interestingly, earlier behavior was not related to later attributions, a pattern of findings consistent with the view that attributions influence behavior. A second important finding from this study was that attributions mediated the relation between marital satisfaction and behavior for both husbands and wives at Time 1 and again for husbands at Time 2. These mediational effects were shown to be independent of length of marriage and the seriousness of the problems from which observational data were obtained and for which spouses made attributions.

In sum, available evidence is consistent with the view that attributions influence behavior. This conclusion, however, rests on an important assumption. Because attributions are assessed at a global level rather than for the specific behaviors in the observed interaction, implicit is the view that these global attributions determine attributions for specific behaviors. It therefore remains to demonstrate that global attributions shape attributions for specific behaviors which, in turn, influence responses to the behavior (for a discussion of the issues in relating cognition to interactional behavior, see Fletcher & Kininmonth, 1991). Finally, the correlational nature of the data should not be overlooked.

Delineating the domain of attributions.   Delineation of the domain to which the term attribution applies has been identified as the "single most significant barrier to progress" (Fincham, 1985, p. 205) in marital attribution research. Progress is facilitated on this task to the extent that attention is given to identifying the basic dimensions underlying causal explanations in marriage, the measurement of these dimensions, and the types of attributions important in marriage.

Sayers and Baucom (1995) have attempted to identify underlying dimensions of causal explanations for marital problems. Using explanations offered by spouses, they employed college students' perceptions of the causes for a multidimensional scaling analysis to select a subset of causes to employ in a second multidimensional scaling analysis using spouses' perceptions of the causes. The use of college students is unfortunate as it undermines the study's attempt to document dimensions that are psychologically meaningful for spouses, and the solution they report for spouses is necessarily a function of the stimuli that were selected using student perceptions. The resulting complex set of findings with different, four-dimensional solutions for husbands and for wives, nonetheless identified a dimension in both spouses' solutions (relationship schism and disharmony versus other factors [husband]/family factors [wife]) that is consistent with one of Passer et al.'s (1978) dimensions (positive versus negative attitude towards partner). This finding again emphasizes the implicit evaluative aspect of explanation in close relationships. Sayers and Baucom (1995) concluded that attributional assessment should move beyond assessment of traditional causal dimensions, a feature that is evident in progress to develop attribution measures.

Sabourin et al.'s (1991) earlier noted call for a standardized attribution measure has met with two quite different responses. One has been to develop measures to assess specific attributional content. For example, the development of a measure of dysfunctional attributions includes a subscale that assesses the extent to which partner behavior reflects "lack of love" (Pretzer, Epstein, & Fleming, 1991). Similarly, in their attributional assessment of problems in 12 domains of relationship functioning (e.g., finances, leisure) Baucom, Epstein, et al. (1996) inquire about attributional content (e.g., boundaries: "we disagree about how much of our lives to share with each other in this area of the relationship") and underlying attribution dimensions (as well as self-reported emotional and behavioral responses). Perhaps the most obvious problem with this approach is that it gives rise to nonindependent assessment of attributions and marital satisfaction (disagreement is assessed in both measures, see Fincham & Bradbury, 1987b), making reported associations (see Baucom, Epstein et al., 1996) tautologous. Second, there is a potentially vast domain of attributionally relevant content, a problem that led early attribution researchers to derive (both empirically and rationally) underlying attribution dimensions. Finally, this approach reinforces the earlier noted balkanization of the attribution literature as it militates against developing an attributional perspective that might transcend relationship type.

In contrast, the second response to the need for a broadly accepted, standard measure has been limited to assessment of attribution dimensions. However, it has also addressed the issue of attribution type by building on distinctions among causal, responsibility, and blame attributions documented in basic research. In fact, the presupposition or entailment model in which a blame attribution presupposes a judgment of responsibility, which, in turn, rests upon the determination of causality, was strongly supported among 206 cohabiting couples when they made judgments about relationship conflict (Lussier, Sabourin, & Wright, 1993). Unfortunately this study used single item measures of each attribution type. The use of multiple item measures has revealed that partners do not distinguish readily between responsibility and blame (Fincham & Bradbury, 1992). Although it is possible to imagine circumstances under which such distinctions may be made, only the distinction between causal (locus, stability, and globality) and responsibility dimensions (intent, motivation, blame) are incorporated in the measure resulting from this line of research – the *Relationship Attribution Measure* (RAM; Fincham & Bradbury, 1992). Advantages of this measure include its demonstrated relation to satisfaction and observed behavior, its brevity, its simplicity for respondents, the provision of indices for different types of attributions, and the potential to modify the scale in order to obtain analogous measures across relationship types (cf. *Children's Relationship Attribution Measure*, Fincham, Beach, Arias, & Brody, 1998). Although cause and responsibility attributions yielded by this measure are highly correlated (r = .7–.8), recent research confirms that a two-factor measurement model provides a significantly better fit to the data than a single-factor model (Davey, Fincham, Beach, & Brody, 1999).

In sum, there has been some progress in delineating the domain of attributions in marital research. However, this progress is largely a function of the attempt to develop measures and has been isolated from developments in a broader literature on attributions, leaving unresolved the importance of earlier, identified distinctions (e.g., interpersonal attributions, dyadic attributions, see Newman, 1981).

Some other developments. The foregoing themes capture much of the recent activity in the marital attribution literature. However, without mentioning two further themes the picture painted of developments over the past decade would be incomplete.

The first theme can be characterized in terms of the domain specificity of attributional phenomena. In marriage research it is manifest by the emergence of a quasi-independent literature on attributions for marital violence (for a review see Eckhardt & Dye, 2000). Thus, for example, attributions for violent versus nonviolent partner behavior appear to differ (Holtzworth-Munroe, Jacobson, Fehrenbach & Fruzzetti, 1992), hostile attributions are evoked more readily in specific content domains (jealousy, spousal rejection, and potential public embarrassment) among violent men (Holtzworth-Munroe & Hutchinson, 1993), and are more likely to be spontaneously verbalized in this group (Eckhardt, Barbour, & Davison, 1998). Although the focus has been primarily on violent men, causal and responsibility attributions also correlate with wife-to-husband aggression (Byrne & Arias, 1997), mediate the relation between increased violence and wives' intentions to leave the relationship (Pape & Arias, 2000), and responsibility attributions moderate the association between husband violence and wives' marital dissatisfaction (Katz, Arias, Beach, & Brody, 1995). Explicit recognition of possible domain specificity in relationship attribution phenomena is important. A move from content free to content specific inference rules would link marital attribution research to the broader cognitive literature in which specific knowledge of the world is central to understanding cognitive functioning.

A second theme, particularly evident in the early 1990s, was the development of general theoretical frameworks. These not only focused on the study of attribution/cognition in marriage (e.g., Epstein & Baucom, 1993; Fletcher & Fincham, 1991) but also integrated such study into a broader organizational framework for researching close relationships (e.g., Bradbury & Fincham, 1991). In these frameworks explicit links were drawn to broader literatures, particularly the social cognition literature, and we return to them in the section, "Social cognition," below.

Critique

The themes reviewed have already been critiqued and the present section therefore highlights some of the opportunities forgone in the marital attribution literature. In doing so, however, it is important to acknowledge the potential realized during the field's adolescence: confirmation of a robust attribution–satisfaction association, demonstration that this phenomenon is not an artifact, accumulation of systematic evidence that speaks to two central causal hypotheses, progress in identifying the types and underlying dimensions of attributions and how to measure them, careful theoretical specification of the role of attributions in understanding marriage, and attempts to locate marital attributional phenomena in broader, more comprehensive frameworks. Notwithstanding these achievements, a number of important topics received little or no attention in the 1990s.

Revisiting the beginnings of attributional research in close relationships is instructive. Orvis et al. (1976) studied attributions not as private events but as public behaviors. The implications are profound but remain relatively unexplored (see Bradbury & Fincham, 1990, p. 26–28). Three of these are highlighted. First, attributional understanding in relationships can result from dyadic interaction. However, we know relatively little about how spouses negotiate particular explanations to achieve a shared understanding of relationship events, yet such negotiated understanding is central to some accounts of marriage (see Berger & Kellner, 1970). Here a broader literature on accounts and their communication in relationships is relevant (e.g., Fincham 1992; Weber, Harvey, & Orbuch, 1992) but has not been tapped in marital attribution research possibly because the narratives studied in the accounts literature transcend the level of analysis found in attribution research.

Second, the identification of attributions as public events raises the question of their relation to attributions as private events. Early on, the relation between these two types of events was identified as an important issue (e.g., Bradbury & Fincham, 1988) along with the need to study public attributions (e.g., Holtzworth-Munroe & Jacobson, 1988) but neither have received attention in the marital attribution literature in the past decade.

Third, Orvis et al.'s (1976) work focused on self–partner discrepancies in attribution. Despite early evidence suggesting that discrepancies in attributions for self and partner behavior might advance understanding of the attribution–satisfaction association (e.g., Kyle & Falbo, 1985), self–partner attribution differences have not gained attention over the 1990s. Consideration of the relation between self and partner attributions highlights a further gap that is endemic to close relationships research, the need to study phenomena at the dyadic level. Although several studies have controlled for partner influence in examining the outcomes related to a spouse's attributions (e.g., Senchak & Leonard, 1993; Karney et al., 1994), evidence has only recently emerged to demonstrate the necessity of a dyadic model in examining attribution phenomena (Davey et al., 1999). Finally, study of attributions for self-behavior alerts one to the possibility that self-processes require consideration in a complete attributional account of marriage. Indeed, Kelley (1979, p. 109) notes attributions for partner behavior have implications for the self creating interdependence at the level of inferred dispositions of partners. In any event, it is clear that relating marital attribution research to research on self-processes is long overdue.

Perhaps more important than the relative lack of attention to the above implications, is the failure to systematically explore the assumption that spouses exhibit a tendency to make particular attributions "across different situations and across time" (Metalsky & Abramson, 1981, p. 38). As Karney and Bradbury (2000) point out, the presumed causal role of attributions in maintaining marital dissatisfaction, and attention to attributions in therapy, only make sense to the extent that spouses exhibit an "attribution style." Shifting attention from mean scores to consistency in attributions gives rise to an interesting variant of the attribution hypothesis in which variability in responses on attribution dimensions and patterns of responses across attributional dimensions is related to satisfaction. Although inconsistent findings have emerged for variability in responding on attribution dimensions, there is consistent evidence relating patterns in attributions across dimensions to marital satisfaction (Baucom, Sayers, & Duhe, 1989; Horneffer & Fincham, 1995). However, Karney and Bradbury's (2000) intraindividual analysis showed that attribution responses were not constant across time; wives' attributions became more conflict-promoting over the first four years of marriage and significant interindividual variability among husbands supported a linear change model even though group mean scores did not change. These findings suggest that attributional style does not operate as a trait. However, the conceptual status of "attributional style" is far from resolved.

Finally, a general feature of the marital attribution research is worth noting because it draws attention to a domain of inquiry that has yet to be exploited. Broadly speaking, marital researchers have been concerned with the consequences of attributions and can be said to have developed an attribution based approach to study marriage. Kelley and Michela (1980) distinguish such "attributional theory" from a second genre of attribution research that focuses on the antecedents and processes that lead to attributions. Although attention to this latter type of research is not entirely absent from the marital domain, attribution antecedents and processes have not been studied systematically. However, the events studied in marital attribution research may be important. For example, the feature-positive bias in which inferences about own attitude are influenced more by reactions to stimuli than by failures to react (Fazio, Sherman, & Herr, 1982) suggests that partner behaviors that prompt a reaction may be more likely to instigate attributional processing than those that do not prompt a reaction. In a similar vein, basic attribution research showing that people are considered more responsible for commissions than omissions (Fincham & Jaspars, 1980), may have implications for the demand–withdraw pattern of interaction. Specifically, attributions for demand behaviors (commissions) may differ from those for withdrawal behaviors (omissions).

This critique, like the review preceding it, is not intended to be exhaustive. Rather it serves as a springboard for the remainder of the chapter, which is intended as an antidote to the balkanization noted at the outset. As will soon be evident, the broader literature is relevant to many of the concerns noted in this critique and suggests several new directions for marital attribution research.

From Myopia to Presbyopia: Setting the Stage for an Attributional Analysis of Close Relationships

In its youthful zest, marital attribution research has been somewhat egocentric, a characteristic that has served it well in focusing energy on establishing replicable phenomena, documenting their relevance, and so on. As it enters adulthood, however, the area has the opportunity to look further afield and fashion its identity in new ways. The purpose of this section is to draw connections with domains of inquiry that have the potential to enrich the study of attributions in marriage and contribute to an integrative, attributional account of close relationships. This will be done in relation to three domains of increasing generality, namely, relevant attribution research in family relationships, attribution research and adaptational outcomes, and research on social cognition.

Balkanization on the home front

Perhaps the most obvious starting point for enriching marital research is to examine overlooked areas of attributional research involving family relationships. Two examples with quite different origins and implications for the study of marriage are examined.

Expressed emotion.   In the late 1950s English researchers noted that the success of psychiatric patients released into the community was related to the kind of living group to which they returned, with those returning to the parental or matrimonial home faring worse than those who went to live in lodgings or with siblings (e.g., Brown, Carstairs, & Topping, 1958). Subsequent research identified the emotion expressed toward the patient by key relatives at the time of hospital admission, particularly hostility and criticism, to be a reliable predictor of the patient's relapse following hospital discharge (e.g., Vaughn & Leff, 1976; see Bebbington & Kuipers, 1994, for a review).

Attempts to understand the mechanism underlying the expressed emotion (EE)–relapse association led to an attributional analysis. Vaughn and Leff (1976) suggested that EE was associated with attributing patient behavior to personal characteristics of the patient rather than to the illness. Others went on to identify as critical the patient's perceived control over the causes of the symptoms (e.g., Hooley, 1987); undesirable patient behavior attributed to causes potentially under the patient's control were hypothesized to result in high EE whereas those attributed to the illness would lead to greater tolerance (low EE). Hooley, Richters, Weintraub, & Neale (1987) provided initial, indirect evidence consistent with this formulation in that spouses of patients with "positive" symptoms (those most easily attributed to illness, e.g., hallucinatory behaviors) were more maritally satisfied than those whose spouses displayed "negative" symptoms (behavioral deficits, e.g., lack of emotion). Direct assessment of attributions has confirmed the above predicted attributional difference in high and low EE relatives (Barrowclough, Johnston, & Tarrier, 1994; Brewin, MacCarthy, Duda, & Vaughn, 1991; Hooley & Licht, 1997).

Why is this research relevant? In addition to providing further, converging evidence that attributions may be important for understanding relationship behavior, it points to a major deficit in the marital attribution literature, the emotional dimension of marriage. It is difficult to imagine a comprehensive account of marriage that fails to accord emotion a central role, yet the marital attributional literature has little to say about emotion. This is all the more surprising given Weiner's (1986) attributional theory of emotion which again serves to underline discontinuity between marital and basic attribution research and theory.

One obvious implication is to consider how Weiner's theory can contribute to an understanding of marriage. According to Weiner, the valence of an event determines the initial emotional response (if positive, happy; if negative, frustrated and sad), but the perceived dimensions underlying the causes of the event determine the specific affect experienced. The focus on specific affect accords with developments in the marital domain where specific affects play a prominent role (Gottman, 1994). Specifically, Gottman (p. 184) contends that what makes marital conflict dysfunctional is "the response to one's partner with criticism, disgust, contempt, defensiveness and stonewalling" and he goes on to argue that his data support a chained effect in which complain/criticize → contempt → defensiveness → stonewalling.

An attributional analysis may facilitate an understanding of entry into, and initial movement along, this chain. Weiner's (1986) theory is helpful in understanding the initiation of overt conflict through the generation of anger towards the other (it follows the same logic outlined above in regard to EE). Anger, in Weiner's (1995, p. 18) writing is seen as an accusation that reflects the belief that the person could and should have behaved differently and "provides a bridge between thinking and conduct." Thus Weiner's analysis gets us to the point where overt conflict may arise but there is a subtle difference between disagreement and the initial step towards dysfunctional conflict.

It seems likely that it is the interplay among causal dimensions that may result in the shift from an initial complaint to criticism. Thus, prior experience with the partner in relation to the complaint or in related areas (which is likely to be reflected in causal globality and stability attribution ratings), would produce the shift from complaint to more global criticism. The further shift to contempt may reflect crossing a certain threshold in the configuration of responses on the causal dimensions. Although Gottman (1994, p. 415) believes the specific emotion cascade outlined above fits well "as a behavioral counterpart to attribution theories of marriage," the ultimate viability of the attributional analysis suggested here is less important than the goal of identifying a much needed integration. An integration of emotion and attribution research clearly transcends the scope of the present chapter.

Before leaving the topic of EE, it behooves us to note that this domain may provide one of the best opportunities to obtain experimental evidence on attributions and relationship outcomes. This is because intervention studies that reduce EE among relatives show significant decreases, relative to controls, in patient relapse rates at 6, 9, and 24 months and greater compliance with a medication regime (see Mari & Streiner, 1994, for a review).

Such studies address only indirectly the attributional account of EE but it seems to be a small step to examine whether changes in relatives' attributions predict patient outcome. Brewin (1994) has made a promising start in showing that changes in relatives' hostility following intervention were associated with changed attributions and that these changes could not be ascribed to changes in the patient's behavior.

Parent–child relationships.   Unlike EE research, attributional analyses of parent–child relationships are rooted in attribution theory in social psychology. Thus, for example, Dix and Grusec (1985) offer an exemplary application of Kelley (1967) and Jones and Davis's (1965) models in their analysis of parent attributions in the socialization of children. Since then a substantial literature has emerged on attributions in parent–child relationships. As reviews of this literature are available elsewhere (e.g., Bugental & Goodnow, 1998; Joiner & Wagner, 1996; S. A. Miller, 1995), only selected aspects of this literature are highlighted to illustrate a potential interplay with marital attribution research.

Perhaps the most obvious point to make in linking the two literatures is that study of the parent–child relationship provides further evidence supporting phenomena documented in the marital literature. Thus, for example, it is well established that parental attributions are linked to parent satisfaction (e.g., Sacco & Murray, 1997) and to parenting behavior (e.g., Bugental & Shennum, 1984). Indeed, this literature provides much-needed experimental data to show that attributions influence behavior. Slep and O'Leary (1998) showed that mothers led to believe that their children were misbehaving voluntarily, and with negative intent, were overreactive in observed discipline and reported somewhat more anger compared to mothers who believed the misbehavior was due to the experimental situation. More recently, children's attributions for parent behavior have also been shown to relate to their satisfaction with the parent and to behavior observed with the parent (Fincham, Beach, et al., 1998). The consistency of findings across relationship types is unusual and speaks to the need to document pan-relational phenomena for a science of close relationships (Berscheid, 1994). Unfortunately, "thus far there has been little attempt to integrate findings from the two literatures" (S. A. Miller, 1995, p. 1579).

Turning to the parent–child literature does more than provide additional evidence for the themes studied by marital researchers; it also identifies new lines of inquiry as well as the need to revisit exactly what is studied in attribution research. This can be illustrated by focusing on two features of the parent–child relationship. First, there is a clear imbalance in status and power that necessarily shapes attributional research on this relationship. The specifics of the research are less important in the present context than the fact that power and status have been ignored in marital attribution research. This oversight is emphasized by Heider's (1958, p. 259) observation that "the power of o is an important determinant of p's general evaluation and reaction to an act of harm or benefit. Not only will p's perception of who is responsible for the act be influenced, but also his understanding of the reasons motivating the act."

Attention to power provides a different perspective on sex differences in marital attributions. For example, the stronger association between wives' attributions and their behavior may reflect the fact that women have typically commanded less power in marriage. This could explain the attribution–behavior sex difference because, relative to less powerful actors, more powerful actors are seen to be exerting their will and hence attributions for their behavior are particularly diagnostic (and presumably can be more safely used to guide behavior). If this account is correct, one might also postulate that wives are more likely to be attentive to, and make attributions for, partner behavior.

Power and status are equally important for attributions in egalitarian marriages. This is because making certain attributions for a partner behavior (e.g., "he's offering to help because he thinks I'm incompetent") may imply a change in the power relation. As emphasized by the extension of self-evaluation maintenance process to marriage (e.g., Beach & Tesser, 1995), the implication may be more or less important depending on the relevance of the domain to the self and partner (e.g., for high partner/low self relevance it should have minimal impact). One resulting hypothesis is that acts with real or symbolic implications for status and power will be subject to close attributional analysis and that one class of such acts that can readily evoke issues of power/status are those that benefit another. Thus, contrary to the accepted view that only negative events evoke attribution processing (Weiner, 1985), in relationships certain positive events may also do so. The resulting attributions are likely to be critical for understanding why benefits may be rejected or have minimal impact (for an attributional analysis of social support, see Fincham & Bradbury, 1990).

A second, obvious feature of the parent–child relationship is that one partner is immature and constrained by developmental limitations. This necessarily draws attention to preconditions that have to be met before a child can be held responsible for their actions. For example, what mental capacities need to be present? Although marital researchers have paid attention to dimensions underlying responsibility, the parent–child literature invites us to revisit this attribution type. The issue of capacities necessary for inferring responsibility finds its analogue in marital relationships where a partner lacks the requisite skills or knowledge to act appropriately (e.g., be intimate, communicate freely). Such capacity criteria are utilized in clinical interventions where it is not uncommon to use a cognitive restructuring procedure called relabeling (e.g., Jacobson & Margolin, 1979). Hence a distressing spouse behavior that prompts a conflict-promoting attribution (e.g, "he won't tell me about his worries because he doesn't trust me") is reframed as a skill deficit (e.g., "he has never learned how to share things that he sees as weaknesses"). A good deal might be learned by determining what influences the criteria underlying responsibility attributions in marriage.

The more general and important point, however, is that it is timely to reconsider the study of responsibility in the marital domain. The discontinuity with basic attribution research has tended to isolate the study of responsibility in the marital literature from recent advances in the analysis of this construct (e.g., Schlenker, Britt, Pennington, Murphy, & Doherty, 1994; Shaver, 1985; Weiner, 1995). In this regard, it is worth noting that any analysis of responsibility in marriage will be enriched to the extent that it accords Heider's "ought forces" a central role. This is because partner behavior that violates expected standards is often experienced as upsetting the objective order or perceptions of the way things should work in the relationship even, and perhaps particularly, when spouses are unaware of the expectations that give rise to this response. As a result, attributed responsibility may not be seen as an interpretation regarding partner behavior but as something that is intrinsic to the behavior. General analyses of responsibility that fail to explicitly consider this element (e.g., Weiner, 1995), may nonetheless be helpful in relationship research (e.g., application to EE, see Hooley & Licht, 1997) to the extent that the behaviors studied implicitly violate generally accepted standards of behavior. However, making this assumption explicit allows it to be examined systematically.

To summarize, an attempt was made in this section to illustrate the value of linking marital attribution research and closely related, but independent, areas of inquiry. One outcome of this exercise is the potential to develop a more general attributional perspective that spans different close relationships. Success in achieving this ambitious goal is likely to be facilitated by willingness to benefit from developments outside of the field of close relationships. The remainder of the chapter is devoted to considering two such developments.

Leaving home

In moving further afield, we first visit an area that could be considered a family relative in that it arose from research on learned helplessness and investigates attributions and adaptational outcomes.

Attributions and adaptational outcomes.   Research on attributions and adaptational outcomes need only be briefly considered for the lessons to be learned are obvious, simple ones. Five characteristics of this literature are briefly considered.

First, in an interesting account of the evolution of research emanating from learned helplessness, Peterson, Maier, and Seligman (1993) accord the use of language an important role. The change in terminology from "attributional style" to "explanatory style" to "optimism" bears consideration. Although one can question the motivation to use "vivid language" and to distinguish the study of causal attribution in this literature "from any of a number of others with 'attributional' labels" (p. 302), the fact remains that the linguistic lens one uses as a researcher can have profound effects.

This point can be succinctly illustrated in the marital field. Because marital research has focused on the attributional analysis associated with helplessness, and because attributions tend to occur for negative events (Weiner, 1985), marital research has focused heavily on what could be labeled "pessimistic explanatory style." This highlights two points. First, explicit use of the term "style" crystallizes the often implicit view in marital research that the subject of study is a personality trait (see Karney & Bradbury, 2000). Second, the descriptor, "pessimistic," draws attention to its opposite, "optimistic." Thinking in terms of optimism frees us from focusing on the negative. As marital researchers embrace study of how spouses link positive marital events to Heider's underlying "invariances," it is worth avoiding an assumption about psychological structure relating to optimism and pessimism implicit in the use of bipolar assessment scales. There is already evidence that marital quality, like affect and attitudes in general, comprises distinct and somewhat independent positive and negative dimensions (Fincham & Linfield, 1997), and similar structural independence may characterize explanatory optimism and pessimism.

A second general lesson to be drawn for the broader attribution/adaptational outcome literature is the variety of adaptational outcomes studied. Thus, for example, explanatory style has been shown to be related to such outcomes as performance (e.g., in sports, in insurance sales, in academic tasks), death from coronary disease, victory in presidential elections, and physical health (see Buchanan & Seligman, 1995). The scope of outcomes studied contrasts with the limited range investigated in the marital domain. Investigation of additional relationship (e.g., commitment, intimacy) and individual (e.g., physical health, self-concept) outcomes represents an important avenue of future attributional research in marriage.

Third, the predictive power of the attributional style studied in the broader literature raises an important question for marital research. Is this attributional style sufficient to predict spouses' marital satisfaction? Stated differently, are the attributions studied in marriage simply a subset of a more generic attributional style rendering superfluous a distinct model of attributions in marriage? The single study to address this issue showed that marital attributions provided unique information in predicting both depressive symptoms and marital satisfaction and were significantly more powerful than general attributions in predicting marital satisfaction (Horneffer & Fincham, 1996). Although in need of replication, this study points to the potential value of marital attributions for understanding individual as well as relationship outcomes.

Fourth, the ubiquitous link between attributions and adaptational outcomes raises questions about the mechanisms that might account for this link. Although this is not the context in which to explore such mechanisms, there is an important, relevant lesson to be drawn. Specifically, there is a clear conceptual commitment to attributional style as a risk factor which forces consideration of what potentiates this risk. The resulting diathesis-stress framework in which attributional style is clearly situated as a moderating variable is instructive for marital researchers who have studied attributions independently of stressful events. Not surprisingly, the status of attributions in the marital literature as a mediating versus moderating variable has been unclear. On the one hand, attributions are treated as a mediating variable that "explain[s] how external physical events take on internal psychological significance" (Baron & Kenny, 1986; p. 1176), yet the standard means for testing a mediating variable have not been applied. On the other hand, attributions have also been treated as an individual difference factor that might function as a moderating variable, yet most studies examine only its "main effects." Clarifying the conceptual status accorded attributions in a study is therefore important in assessing the appropriateness of its methodology. One hypothesis worth exploring is whether attributions serve as a moderating variable when assessed globally via questionnaires and as a mediating variable when they pertain to inferences made in situ for partner behavior.

The fifth implication to be considered concerns measurement. Although the past decade has witnessed attention to attribution measurement in the marital domain, this effort has focused on questionnaire development with no attempt to follow up on earlier attention paid to unsolicited attributions (e.g., Holtzworth-Munroe & Jacobson, 1985). Questionnaire development has, however, been accompanied by development of the Content Analysis of Verbatim Explanations (CAVE) in the broader explanatory style literature (see Peterson, Schulman, Castellon, & Seligman, 1992; Reivich, 1995). The CAVE requires coders to identify and then rate causal attributions on the three dimensions (locus, stability, globality) represented in questionnaires. This has the advantage of allowing investigation of the convergence between questionnaire and coded attributions, although it should be noted that convergence is not a prerequisite. Each approach provides a legitimate perspective and source of data on attributions. It is also worth noting that a similar coding measure, the Leeds Attribution Coding System (LACS), has been more fully developed in the 1990s through its application in clinical, work, and consumer settings (see Munton, Silvester, Stratton, & Hanks, 1999). However, the LACS derives from a slightly different theoretical framework than the CAVE and provides a viable alternative to it.

These developments again highlight the need for a second strand to marital attribution research that focuses on coded attributions. This would allow the accrual of much-needed data on unsolicited and on spontaneous attributions that could allow for comparison of attributions that are made spontaneously with those that occur more deliberately (Berscheid & Reis, 1998). Developing a database on such attributions in relationships poses numerous challenges. These were discussed some time ago and that discussion remains pertinent (see Bradbury & Fincham, 1988). The need for developing such a database may not be apparent given the earlier noted link between the marital attribution literature and social cognition research. After all, the study of spontaneous attribution inferences is well represented in social cognitive research and hence the call for research on spontaneous attributions in marriage may appear anomalous. In turning to consider links with the field of social cognition that might advance marital attribution research, it will be seen that this anomaly is more apparent than real.

Social cognition.   Recall that at the beginning of the 1990s several conceptual analyses in the marital domain were influenced by ideas drawn from the social cognition literature (e.g., Fincham, Bradbury, & Scott, 1990; Fletcher & Fincham, 1991). For example, the distinction between automatic and controlled processes was used to deal with the observation that much interactional behavior unfolds rapidly and without mindful cognitive processing. As a result, one might reasonably have expected research on the spontaneous attribution inferences represented in social cognition research (e.g., Bassili, 1989) to be represented in the marital literature. However, during the 1990s clinical and social investigations of cognition in relationships began to diverge (Fincham & Beach, 1999), which may account for the virtual absence of marital research that moves beyond the focus on conscious attributional content. Thus, there is no anomaly in calling for the development of a database on spontaneous attributions in marriage.

In light of the above observation, one purpose of this section is to reiterate the rallying call of the early 1990s for a rapprochement between the study of marital attributions and social cognition. In this regard, it takes its place alongside several similar calls for integrating a social cognitive perspective in the study of close relationships. For example, Reis and Knee (1996, p. 181) noted that relationship cognition research has focused "almost exclusively on 'what' questions" concerning conscious cognitive content and point to the need for research "to consider processes that occur outside of conscious awareness" (p. 175). Similarly, there is limited evidence of such research in a recent comprehensive survey of the close relationship literature where the section on automatic cognitive processes has the status of a promissory note (Berscheid & Reis, 1998). Lest it appear otherwise, one must hasten to add that there are a number of notable exceptions to these summary conclusions (see Chapter 2, by Karney et al., below) that augur well for the future. For the present, however, the social cognitive analyses of marriage offered earlier in the decade remain relevant (see Fincham, Bradbury, & Scott, 1990; Fletcher & Fincham, 1991; Scott, Fuhrman, & Wyer, 1991). Rather than repeat the observations made in them, the remainder of the section highlights two implications of social cognition research that have been overlooked in these analyses.

First, social cognition research shows that people access and use specific knowledge in making social judgments (e.g., Smith & Zarate, 1992). The implication is that marital attributions may vary depending on the stored knowledge that is accessed when the attribution is made. In the social cognition domain this is readily demonstrated through priming or making accessible a construct and then examining the effects of such priming. Although discussed in prior analyses, the complexity of priming effects in marriage has not been recognized. For example, Fincham and Beach (1999) report studies in which priming marital satisfaction did not influence subsequent judgments, whereas priming hostility did affect judgments of partner behavior, but in the direction opposite to that predicted. Spouses who had been primed rated subsequent partner behavior as *less* hostile. It is likely that a variety of such contrast effects, as well as assimilation effects, will be found as marital researchers examine the effects of stored knowledge on spouses' attributions. It will therefore be important to accommodate to the impact of a number of influences on priming effects, including the recency, frequency, and blatancy of the priming, awareness of the priming, exact relation between primed and target materials, and so on (see Higgins, 1996). It has been somewhat simpler to document the importance of chronically primed material; the attribution–marital satisfaction association has been shown to be significantly larger among spouses whose marital satisfaction was more accessible than among spouses where it was less accessible (Fincham, Garnier, Gano-Phillips, & Osborne, 1995).

A final, but important, point regarding the potential impact of accessing stored knowledge on attributions concerns domain specificity. Simply stated, the relevance of accessed knowledge for the event, subject to an attributional analysis, may influence its impact. From this perspective, further and perhaps more subtle, attribution phenomena may emerge from investigations that examine domain specific effects. There is initial evidence to suggest such phenomena. For example, Collins (1996) has found that internal working models of attachment are related to attributions independently of relationship satisfaction among dating students, but only for attachment-relevant partner behaviors. Documenting such domain-specific effects is consistent with the earlier call to broaden the correlates of attributions studied in marriage.

A second implication of social cognition research worth highlighting is the emphasis on goals. The impact of goals on information processing is ubiquitous in social cognition studies and is evident in basic research on spontaneous attribution – in contrast to other goals (e.g., remembering stimulus material), the goal of forming an impression results in spontaneous trait inferences (Smith, 1994). It is also apparent, however, that trait inferences can occur without a causal analysis of the behavior (cf. Smith & Miller, 1979, where trait inferences occur more rapidly than causal inferences), emphasizing the need to examine explicitly the impact of information processing goals on causal and responsibility attributions in marriage. Vorauer and Ross (1996) specifically address the role of information goals in close relationships thereby both extending the range of goals considered and providing a goal analysis specific to the relationship domain. They suggest that the goal of obtaining information about issues relevant to the perceiver leads to a diagnosticity bias that influences attributions; i.e., partner behavior is more likely to be attributed to the self. Their analysis identifies a number of factors likely to influence information goals (e.g., shifting circumstances, relationship development, coordination of partners' goal) that could profitably be used to examine the impact of information goals on attributions.

The value of pursuing a goal-based approach in marital attribution research is enhanced when it is recognized that goal obstruction or interruption may be critical to understanding the instigation of attribution processing. From this perspective, negative events occasion attributions because they are generally inimical to the goals people pursue, but it is the thwarting of the goal that is more fundamental. If correct, this raises a variety of questions about how different elements of goals may influence attributions. At the simplest level one could examine whether thwarting of approach versus avoidance goals are associated with different attributional outcomes in a manner analogous to attributions for commissions versus omissions. Similarly, does the generality of the goal constrain acceptable attributions? For example, is a conversational interruption (e.g., while a couple is trying to locate their destination) adequately explained by an attribution that speaks to goal content (e.g., "I just wanted to let you know I don't like asking for directions") when a relational goal (e.g., to experience mutual respect and equality) is seen to be thwarted? Goals have been found to vary along a number of dimensions that might be examined in relation to attributions (e.g., level of consciousness, importance-commitment, difficulty, specificity, temporal range and connectedness; see Austin & Vancouver, 1996).

Again the specific form of the link between goals and attributions is less important than its potential to yield integrative theory. First, the goal-thwarting hypothesis offered above is cut from the same cloth as Berscheid's (1983) theory of emotion in close relationships where interrupted goal pursuit gives rise to emotion. Goals may be a vehicle for minting the coin that displays affect and cognition on each side. Second, a goal analytic framework has been applied to marital conflict, the topic that simulated marital attribution research (Fincham & Beach, 1999). As this analysis attempts to incorporate research on marital phenomena, marital prevention, and intervention under a single goal theoretic framework, placing marital attribution research in the same framework represents a step towards increased theoretical integration that has been the legacy of social cognition in basic attribution research (Smith, 1994).

Conclusion

The chapter began by noting the continued vitality of attribution research and offered two reasons to account for this phenomenon. One was a broader study of attribution consistent with continuity between social and nonsocial cognition, and the second was the application of an attribution perspective to many new, and especially applied, areas. This provided a context for understanding the emergence and evolution of marital attribution research. An updated review of this field showed that it has realized a great deal of its early potential and several clear themes were evident. However, it was equally apparent that the balkanization accompanying the prodigious output of attribution research was also evident in the marital domain. Accordingly, links were made with other areas of research and with the broader social cognition literature. This analysis identified gaps in the marital attributional literature and pointed to ways in which these new avenues of inquiry might be pursued. The importance of pursuing this research is emphasized by the promise of yielding a more integrated theoretical account of attributions in close relationships.

Note

1. Harvey, Wells, and Alvarez's (1978) study of attribution for conflict and separation in relationships was also an important early influence. However, it gave rise to a broader literature on accounts that was not limited to attributions or relationship events but instead focused on the narratives that arise in reaction to severe stress (see Harvey, Weber, & Orbuch, 1990).

References

Abramson, L. Y., Seligman, M. E. P., & Teasdale, J. (1978). Learned helplessness in humans: Critique and reformulation. *Journal of Abnormal Psychology, 87*, 49–74.

Austin, J. T, & Vancouver, J. B. (1996). Goal constructs in psychology: Structure, process, and content. *Psychological Bulletin, 120*, 338–375.

Bagarozzi, D. A., & Giddings, C. W. (1983). The role of cognitive constructs and attributional processes in family therapy. In L. R. Wolberg & M. L. Aronson, (Eds) *Group and family therapy 1983*. New York: Brunner/Mazel.

Baron, R. M., & Kenny, D. A. (1986). The moderator-mediator variable distinction in social psychological research: Conceptual, strategic, and statistical considerations. *Journal of Personality and Social Psychology, 51*, 1173–1182.

Barrowclough, C., Johnston, M., & Tarrier, N. (1994). Attributions, expressed emotion, and patient relapse: An attributional model of relatives' response to schizophrenic illness. *Behavior Therapy, 25*, 67–88.

Bassili, J. N. (1989). Trait encoding in behavior identification and dispositional inference. *Personality and Social Psychology Bulletin, 15*, 285–296.

Baucom, D. H. (1987). Attributions in distressed relations: How can we explain them? In S. Duck & D. Perlman (Eds.), *Intimate relationships: Development, dynamics, and deterioration* (pp. 177–206). London: Sage.

Baucom, D. H., Epstein, N., Duito, A. D., Carels, R. A., Rankin, L. A., & Burnett, C. K. (1996). Cognitions in marriage: The relationship between standards and attributions. *Journal of Family Psychology, 10*, 209–222.

Baucom, D. H., Epstein, N., Sayers, S., & Sher, T. G. (1989). The role of cognitions in marital relationships: Definitional, methodological, and conceptual issues. *Journal of Consulting and Clinical Psychology, 57*, 31–38.

Baucom, D. H., Sayers, S. L., & Duhe, A. (1989). Attributional style and attributional patterns among married couples. *Journal of Personality and Social Psychology, 56*, 596–607.

Bauserman, S. A., Arias, I., & Craighead, W. E. (1995). Marital attributions in spouses of depressed patients. *Journal of Psychopathology and Behavioral Assessment, 17*, 231–249.

Beach, S. R. H., & Tesser, A. (1995). Self-esteem and the extended self-evaluation model: The self in social context. In M. Kernis (Ed.), *Efficacy, Agency, and Self-esteem* (pp. 145–170). New York: Plenum.

Bebbington, P., & Kuipers, L. (1994). The predictive utility of expressed emotion in schizophrenia: An aggregate analysis. *Psychological Medicine, 21*, 1–11.

Berger, P., & Kellner, H. (1970). Marriage and the construction of reality. In H. P. Dreitzel (Ed.), *Recent sociology: Patterns of communicative behavior*. New York: Macmillan.

Berscheid, E. (1983). Emotion. In H. H. Kelley, E. Berscheid, A. Christensen, J. H. Harvey, T.L. Huston, G. Levinger, E. Mclintock, L. A. Peptan, & D. R. Peterson (Eds.), *Close Relationships* (pp.110–168). New York: W. H. Freeman.

Berscheid, E. (1994). Interpersonal relationships. *Annual Review of Psychology, 45,* 79–129.

Berscheid, E., & Reis, H. T (1998). Attraction and close relationships. In D. T. Gilbert, S. T. Fiske & G. Lindsey (Eds.), *Handbook of Social Psychology* (Vol. 2, pp. 193–281). New York: McGraw Hill.

Bradbury, T. B., Beach, S. R. H., Fincham, F. D., & Nelson, G. M. (1996). Attributions and behavior in functional and dysfunctional marriages. *Journal of Consulting and Clinical Psychology, 64,* 569–576.

Bradbury, T. N., & Fincham, F. D. (1988). Assessing spontaneous attributions in marital interaction: Methodological and conceptual considerations. *Journal of Social and Clinical Psychology, 7,* 122–130.

Bradbury, T. N., & Fincham, F. D. (1990). Attributions in marriage: Review and critique. *Psychological Bulletin, 107,* 3–33.

Bradbury, T. N., & Fincham, F. D. (1991). A contextual model for advancing the study of marital interaction. In G. J. O Fletcher & F. D. Fincham (Eds.), *Cognition in close relationships* (pp. 127–147). Hillsdale, NJ: Erlbaum.

Bradbury, T. N., & Fincham, F. D. (1992). Attributions and behavior in marital interaction. *Journal of Personality and Social Psychology, 63,* 613–628.

Braiker, H. B. & Kelley, H. H. (1979). Conflict in the development of close relationships. In R. L. Burgess & T. L. Huston (Eds.), *Social exchange in developing relationships* (pp. 135–168). New York: Academic Press.

Brewin, C. R. (1994). Changes in attribution and expressed emotion among the relatives of patients with schizophrenia. *Psychological Medicine, 24,* 905–911.

Brewin, C. R., McCarthy, B., Duda, K., & Vaughn, C. E. (1991). Attribution and expressed emotion in the relatives of patients with schizophrenia. *Journal of Abnormal Psychology, 100,* 546–554.

Brown, G. W., Carstairs, G. M., & Topping, G. C. (1958). The post hospital adjustment of chronic mental patients. *The Lancet, ii,* 685–689.

Buchanan, G. M., & Seligman, M. E. P. (Eds.). (1995). *Explanatory style.* Hillsdale, NJ: Erlbaum.

Bugental, D. B., & Goodnow, J. J. (1998). Socialization processes. In N. Eisenberg (Ed.), *Handbook of child psychology. Volume 3: Social, emotional, and personality development.* New York: Wiley.

Bugental, D. B., & Shennum, W. A. (1984). "Difficult" children as elicitors and targets of adult communication patterns: An attributional-behavior transactional analysis. *Monographs of the Society for Research in Child Development, 49* (1, Serial No. 205).

Byrne, C. A., & Arias, I. (1997). Marital satisfaction and marital violence: Moderating effects of attributional processes. *Journal of Family Psychology, 11,* 188–195.

Collins, N. L. (1996). Working models of attachment: Implications for explanation, emotion, and behavior. *Journal of Personality and Social Psychology, 71,* 810–822.

Davey, A., Fincham, F. D., Beach, S. R. H., & Brody, G. (1999). *Does a dyadic conceptualization expand our understanding of marital cognition?* Manuscript submitted for publication.

Davidson, G. N. S., & Horvath, A. O. (1997). Three sessions of brief couples therapy: A clinical trial. *Journal of Family Psychology, 11,* 422–435.

Dix, T. H., & Grusec, J. E. (1985). Parent attribution processes in the socialization of children. In I. E. Sigel (Ed.), *Parental belief systems* (pp. 201–234). Hillsdale, NJ: Erlbaum.

Eckhardt, C. I., Barbour, K. A., & Davison, G. C. (1998). Articulated thoughts of maritally violent and nonviolent men during anger arousal. *Journal of Consulting and Clinical Psychology, 66,* 259–269.

Eckhardt, C. I., & Dye, M. L. (2000). The cognitive characteristics of maritally violent men: Theory and evidence. *Cognitive Therapy and Research, 24,* 139–158.

Epstein, N., & Baucom, D. H. (1993). Cognitive factors in marital disturbance. In K. S. Dobson, and P. C. Kendall (Eds.), *Psychopathology and cognition. Personality, psychopathology, and psychotherapy series* (pp. 351–385). San Diego: Academic Press.

Fazio, R. H., Sherman, S. J., & Herr, P. M. (1982). The feature-positive effect in the self-perception process: Does not doing matter as much as doing? *Journal of Personality and Social Psychology, 42,* 404–411.

Fincham, F. D. (1983). Clinical applications of attribution theory: Problems and prospects. In M. Hewstone (Ed.), *Attribution theory: Social and functional extensions* (pp. 187–205). Oxford: Blackwell.

Fincham, F. D. (1985). Attributions in close relationships. In J. H. Harvey & G. Weary (Eds.), *Attribution: Basic issues and applications* (pp. 203–234). New York: Academic Press.

Fincham, F. D. (1992). The account episode in close relationships. In M. L. McLaughlin, M. Cody, & J. S. Read (Eds.), *Explaining one's self to others: Reason-giving in a social context* (pp. 167–182). Hillsdale, NJ: Erlbaum.

Fincham, F. D., & Beach, S. R. (1999). Marital conflict: Implications for working with couples. *Annual Review of Psychology, 50,* 47–77.

Fincham, F. D., & Beach, S. R. (1999). Marriage in the new millennium: Is there a place for social cognition in marital research? *Journal of Social and Personal Relationships, 16,* 685–704.

Fincham, F. D., Beach, S. R., Arias, I., & Brody, G. (1998). Children's attributions in the family: The Children's Relationship Attribution Measure. *Journal of Family Psychology, 12,* 481–493.

Fincham, F. D., & Bradbury, T. N. (1987a). The impact of attributions in marriage: A longitudinal analysis. *Journal of Personality and Social Psychology, 53,* 481–489.

Fincham, F. D., & Bradbury, T. N. (1987b). The assessment of marital quality: A reevaluation. *Journal of Marriage and the Family, 49,* 797–809.

Fincham, F. D., & Bradbury, T. N. (1988). The impact of attributions in marriage: An experimental analysis. *Journal of Social and Clinical Psychology, 7,* 147–162.

Fincham, F. D., & Bradbury, T. N. (1990). Social support in marriage: The role of social cognition. *Journal of Social and Clinical Psychology, 9,* 31–42.

Fincham, F. D., & Bradbury, T. N. (1992). Assessing attributions in marriage: The Relationship Attribution Measure. *Journal of Personality and Social Psychology, 62,* 457–468.

Fincham, F. D., & Bradbury, T.N. (1993). Marital satisfaction, depression, and attributions: A longitudinal analysis. *Journal of Personality and Social Psychology, 64,* 442–452.

Fincham, F. D., Bradbury, T. N., Arias, I., Byrne, & C. A., Karney, B. R. (1997). Marital violence, marital distress and attributions. *Journal of Family Psychology, 11,* 367–372.

Fincham, F. D., Bradbury, T. N., & Beach, S. R. (1990). To arrive where we began: A reappraisal of cognition in marriage and in marital therapy. *Journal of Family Psychology, 4,* 167–184.

Fincham, F. D., Bradbury, T. N., & Scott, C. K. (1990). Cognition in marriage. In F. D. Fincham & T. N. Bradbury (Eds.), *The psychology of marriage: Basic issues and applications* (pp. 118–149). New York: Guilford.

Fincham, F. D., Garnier, P. C., Gano-Phillips, S., & Osborne, L. N. (1995). Pre-interaction expectations, marital satisfaction and accessibility: A new look at sentiment override. *Journal of Family Psychology, 9,* 3–14.

Fincham, F. D., Harold, G., & Gano-Phillips, S. (2000). The longitudinal association between attributions and marital satisfaction: Direction of effects and role of efficacy expectations. *Journal of Family Psychology, 14,* 267–285.

Fincham, F. D., & Jaspars, J. M. (1980). Attribution of responsibility: From man the scientist to man as lawyer. In L. Berkowitz (Ed.), *Advances in experimental social psychology* (Vol. 13, pp. 81–138). New York: Academic Press.

Fincham, F. D., & Linfield, K. J. (1997). A new look at marital quality: Can spouses feel positive and negative about their marriage? *Journal of Family Psychology, 11,* 489–502.

Fletcher, G. J. O., & Fincham, F. D. (1991). Attribution processes in close relationships. In G. J. O. Fletcher & F. D. Fincham (Eds), *Cognition in close relationships* (pp. 7–35). Hillsdale, NJ: Erlbaum.

Fletcher, G. J. O., Fincham, F. D., Cramer, L., & Heron, N. (1987). The role of attributions in the development of dating relationships. *Journal of Personality and Social Psychology, 53,* 510–517.

Fletcher, G. J. O., Fitness, J., & Blampied, N. M. (1990). The link between attributions and happiness in close relationships: The roles of depression and explanatory style. *Journal of Social and Clinical Psychology, 9,* 243–255.

Fletcher, G. J. O., & Kininmonth, L. (1991). Interaction in close relationships and social cognition. In G. J. O. Fletcher & F. D. Fincham (Eds.), *Cognition in close relationships* (pp. 235–256). Hillsdale, NJ: Erlbaum.

Fletcher, G. J. O., & Thomas, G. (2000). Behavior and on-line cognitions in marital interaction. *Personal Relationships, 7,* 111–130.

Gottman, J. M. (1990). How marriages change. In G. R. Patterson (Ed.), *Depression and aggression in family interaction* (pp. 75–102). Hillsdale, NJ: Erlbaum.

Gottman, J. M. (1994). *What predicts divorce?* Hillsdale, NJ: Erlbaum.

Harvey, J. H. (1987). Attributions in close relationships: Research and theoretical developments. *Journal of Social and Clinical Psychology, 5,* 420–434.

Harvey, J. H., Ickes, W., & Kidd, R. F. (1978). A conversation with Edward E. Jones and Harold H. Kelley. In J. H. Harvey, W. Ickes, & R. F. Kidd (Eds.), New directions in attribution research (Vol. 2, pp. 371–388). Hillsdale, NJ: Erlbaum.

Harvey, J. H., Weber, A. L., & Orbuch, T. L. (1990). *Interpersonal accounts: A social psychological perspective.* Cambridge, MA: Blackwell.

Harvey, J. H., Wells, G. L., & Alvarez, M. D. (1978). Attribution in the context of conflict and separation in close relationships. In J .H. Harvey, W. J. Ickes, & R. F. Kidd (Eds.)*New directions in attribution research* (Vol. 2, pp. 235–260). Hillsdale, NJ: Erlbaum.

Heider, F. (1958). *The psychology of interpersonal relations.* New York: Wiley.

Hewstone, M. R. H., & Fincham, F. D. (1996). Attribution theory and research. In M. Hewstone, W. Stroebe, & G. M. Stephenson (Eds.), *Introducing social psychology* (pp. 167–204). Oxford: Blackwell.

Higgins, E. T. (1996). Knowledge activation: Accessibility, applicability, and salience. In E. T. Higgins & A .W. Kruglanski (Eds.), *Social psychology: Handbook of basic principles* (pp. 133–168). New York: Guilford.

Hinde, R. A. (1997). *Relationships: A dialectical perspective.* Hove: Psychology Press.

Holtzworth-Munroe, A., & Hutchinson, G. (1993). Attributing negative intent to wife behavior: The attributions of maritally violent versus nonviolent men. *Journal of Abnormal Psychology, 102,* 206–211.

Holtzworth-Munroe, A., & Jacobson, N. S. (1985). Causal attributions of married couples: When do they search for causes? What do they conclude when they do? *Journal of Personality and Social Psychology, 48,* 1398–1412.

Holtzworth-Munroe, A., & Jacobson, N. S. (1988). Toward a methodology for coding spontaneous causal attributions: Preliminary results with married couples. *Journal of Social and Clinical Psychology, 7,* 101–112.

Holtzworth-Munroe, A., Jacobson, N. S., Fehrenbach, & P. A., & Fruzzetti, A. (1992).Violent married couples' attributions for violent and nonviolent self and partner behaviors. *Behavioral Assessment,14,* 53–64.

Hooley, J. M. (1987). The nature and origins of expressed emotion. In M. J. Goldstein & K. Hahlweg (Eds.), *Understanding major mental disorder: The contribution of family interaction research* (pp. 176–194). New York: Family Process Press.

Hooley, J. M., & Licht, D. M. (1997). Expressed emotion and causal attributions in the spouses of depressed patients. *Journal of Abnormal Psychology, 106,* 298–306.

Hooley, J. M., Richters, J. E., Weintraub, S., & Neale, J.-M. (1987). Psychopathology and marital distress: The positive side of positive symptoms. *Journal of Abnormal Psychology, 96,* 27–33.

Horneffer, K. J., & Fincham, F. D. (1995). The construct of attributional style in depression and marital distress. *Journal of Family Psychology, 9,* 186–195.

Horneffer, K. J., & Fincham, F. D. (1996). Attributional models of depression and marital distress. *Personality and Social Psychology Bulletin, 22,* 678–689.

Jacobson, N. S., & Christensen, A. (1996). *Integrative couple therapy: Promoting acceptance and change.* New York: Norton.

Jacobson, N. S., & Margolin, G. (1979). *Marital therapy: Strategies based on social learning and behavior exchange principles.* New York: Brunner/Mazel.

Joiner, T. E., & Wagner, K. D. (1996). Parent, child-centered attributions and outcomes: A meta-analytic review with concepetual and methodological implications. *Journal of Clinical Child Psychology, 24,* 37–52.

Jones, E. E., & Davis, K. E. (1965). From acts to dispositions: The attribution process in person perception. In L. Berkowitz (Ed.), *Advances in experimental social psychology* (Vol. 2, pp. 219–266). New York: Academic Press.

Karney, B. R., & Bradbury, T. N. (2000). Attributions in marriage: State or trait? A growth curve analysis. *Journal of Personality and Social Psychology, 78,* 295–309.

Karney, B. R., Bradbury, T. N., Fincham, F. D., & Sullivan, K. T. (1994). The role of negative affectivity in the association between attributions and marital satisfaction. *Journal of Personality and Social Psychology, 66,* 413–424.

Katz, J., Arias, I., Beach, S. R. H., & Brody, G. (1995). Excuses, excuses: Accounting for the effects of partner violence on marital satisfaction and stability. *Violence & Victims, 10,* 315–326.

Kelley, H. H. (1967). Attribution theory in social psychology. In D. Levine (Ed.), *Nebraska symposium on motivation* (pp. 192–238). Lincoln, NE: University of Nebraska Press.

Kelley, H. H. (1979).*Personal relationships: Their structures and processes* Hillsdale, NJ: Erlbaum.

Kelley, H. H., Berscheid, E., Christensen, A., Harvey, J. H., Huston, T. L., Levinger, G., McClintock, E., Peplau, L. A., & Peterson, D. R. (Eds.). (1983). *Close relationships.* New York: W. H. Freeman.

Kelley, H. H., & Michela, J. L. (1980). Attribution theory and research. *Annual Review of Psychology, 31,* 457–501.

Knight, J. A., & Vallacher, R. R. (1981). Interpersonal engagement in social perception: The consequences of getting into the action. *Journal of Personality and Social Psychology, 40,* 990–999.

Kyle, S.O., & Falbo, T. (1985). Relationships between marital stress and attributional preferences for own and spouse behavior. *Journal of Social and Clinical Psychology, 3,* 339–351.

Lussier, Y., Sabourin, S., & Wright, J. (1993). On causality, responsibility, and blame in marriage: Validity of the entailment model. *Journal of Family Psychology, 7,* 322–332.

Mari, J., & Streiner, D. L. (1994). An overview of family interventions and relapse on schizophrenia: Meta analysis of research findings. *Psychological Medicine, 24,* 565–578.

Metalsky, G. I., & Abramson, L. Y. (1981). Attributional style: Toward a framework for conceptualization and assessment. In P. Kendall & S. Hollon (Eds.), *Assessment strategies for cognitive-behavioral interventions* (pp. 13–58). New York: Academic Press.

Miller, G. E., & Bradbury, T. N. (1995). Refining the association between attributions and behavior in marital interaction. *Journal of Family Psychology, 9,* 196–208.

Miller, S. A. (1995). Parents' attributions for their children's behavior. *Child Development, 66,* 1557–1584.

Munton, A. G., Silvester, J., Stratton, P., & Hanks, H. (1999). *Attributions in action: A practical approach to coding qualitative data.* Chichester, England: Wiley.

Newman, H. M. (1981). Communication within ongoing intimate relationships: An attributional perspective. *Personality and Social Psychology Bulletin, 7,* 59–70.

Orvis, B. R., Kelley, H. H., & Butler, D. (1976). Attributional conflict in young couples. In J. H. Harvey, W. Ickes, & R. F. Kidd (Eds.)*New directions in attribution research* (Vol. 1, pp. 353–386). Hillsdale, NJ: Erlbaum.

Pape, K. T., & Arias, I. (2000). The role of perceptions and attributions in battered women's intentions to permanently end their violent relationships. *Cognitive Therapy and Research, 24,* 201–214.

Passer, M. W., Kelley, H. H., & Michela, J. L. (1978). Multidimensional scaling of the causes for negative interpersonal behavior. *Journal of Personality and Social Psychology, 36,* 951–962.

Peterson, C., Maier, S. F., & Seligman, M. E. P. (1993). *Learned helplessness: A theory for the age of personal control.* New York: Oxford University Press.

Peterson, C., Schulman, P., Castellon, C., & Seligman, M. E. P. (1992). The explanatory style scoring manual. In C. P. Smith (Ed.), *Handbook of thematic analysis* (pp. 383–392). New York: Cambridge University Press.

Pleban, R., & Richardson, D .C. (1979). Research and publication trends in social psychology: 1973–7. *Personality and Social Psychology Bulletin, 5,* 138–141.

Pretzer, J., Epstein, N., & Fleming, B. (1991). Marital Attitude Survey: A measure of dysfunctional attributions and expectancies. *Journal of Cognitive Psychotherapy, 5*, 131–148.

Reis, H. T., & Knee, C. R. (1996). What we know, what we don't know and what we need to know about relationship knowledge structures. In G. J. O. Fletcher & J. Fitness (Eds.), *Knowledge structures in close relationships: A social psychological approach* (pp. 169–194). Hillsdale, NJ: Erlbaum.

Reivich, K. (1995). The measurement of explanatory style. In G. M. Buchanan & M. E. P. Seligman (Eds.), *Explanatory style*. Hillsdale, NJ: Erlbaum.

Sabourin, S., Lussier, Y., & Wright, J. (1991). The effects of measurement strategy on attributions for marital problems and behaviors. *Journal of Applied Social Psychology, 21*, 734–746.

Sacco, W. P., & Murray, D. W. (1997). Mother-child relationship satisfaction: The role of attributions and trait conceptions. *Journal of Social and Clinical Psychology, 16*, 24–42.

Sayers, S. L., & Baucom, D. H. (1995). Multidimensional scaling of spouses' attributions for marital conflicts. *Cognitive Therapy and Research, 19*, 667–693.

Schlenker, B. R., Britt, T. W., Pennington, J., Murphy, R., & Doherty, K. (1994). The triangle model of responsibility. *Psychological Review, 101*, 632–652.

Scott, C. K., Fuhrman, R. W., & Wyer, R. S. (1991). Information processing in close relationships. In G. J. O Fletcher & F. D. Fincham (Eds.), *Cognition in close relationships* (pp. 37–68). Hillsdale, NJ: Erlbaum.

Senchak, M., & Leonard, K. E. (1993). The role of spouses' depression and anger in the attribution–marital satisfaction relation. *Cognitive Therapy and Research, 17*, 397–409.

Shaver, K. G. (1985). *The attribution of blame: Causality, responsibility, and blameworthiness*. New York: Springer-Verlag.

Slep, A. M. S., & O'Leary, S. G. (1998). The effects of maternal attributions on parenting: An experimental analysis. *Journal of Family Psychology, 12*, 234–242.

Smith, E. R. (1994). Social cognition contributions to attribution theory and research. In P. Devine, D. L., Hamilton, & T. M. Ostrom (Eds.), *Social cognition: Impact on social psychology*. New York: Academic Press.

Smith, E. R., & Miller, F. D. (1979). Attributional information processing: A response time measure of causal subtraction. *Journal of Personality and Social Psychology, 37*, 1723–31.

Smith, E. R., & Zarate, M. A. (1992). Exemplar-based model of social judgment. *Psychological Review, 99*, 3–21.

Taylor, S. E., & Koivumaki, J. H. (1976). The perception of self and others: Acquaintanceship, affect, and actor–observer differences. *Journal of Personality and Social Psychology, 33*, 403–406.

Thompson, J. S., & Snyder, D. K. (1986). Attribution theory in intimate relationships: A methodological review. *American Journal of Family Therapy, 14*, 123–138.

Vaughn, C., & Leff, J. (1976). The influence of family and social factors on the course of psychiatric illness: A comparison of schizophrenic and depressed neurotic patients. *British Journal of Psychiatry, 129*, 125–137.

Vorauer, J. D., & Ross, M. (1996). The pursuit of knowledge structures in close relationships: An informational goals analysis. In G. J. O. Fletcher & J. Fitness (Eds.), *Knowledge structures in close relationships: A social psychological approach* (pp. 369–396). Hillsdale, NJ: Erlbaum.

Weber, A. L., Harvey, J. H., & Orbuch, T. L. (1992). What went wrong: Communicating accounts of relationship conflict. In M. L. McLaughlin, M. J. Cody, & S. J. Read (Eds.), *Explaining oneself to others*. Hillsdale, NJ: Erlbaum.

Weiner, B. (1985). "Spontaneous" causal search. *Psychological Bulletin, 97*, 74–84.

Weiner, B. (1986). *An attributional theory of motivation and emotion*. New York: Springer-Verlag.

Weiner, B. (1995). *Judgments of responsibility*. New York: Guilford Press.

Weiner, B., Russel, D., & Lehrman, D. (1978). An attributional model of achievement strivings, attributions and affective intensity. In J. H. Harvey, W. Ickes, & R. F. Kidd (Eds.) *New directions in attribution research* (Vol. 2, pp. 59–90). Hillsdale, NJ: Erlbaum.

Weiss, R. L. (1980). Strategic behavioral marital therapy: Toward a model for assessment and intervention. In J. P. Vincent (Ed.), *Advances in family intervention, assessment and theory* (Vol. 1, pp. 229–271). Greenwich, CT: JAI Press.

Weiss, R. L., & Heyman, R. E. (1990). Observation of marital interaction. In F. D. Fincham &

T. N. Bradbury (Eds.), *The psychology of marriage* (pp. 87–117). New York: Guilford.

Weiss, R. L., & Heyman, R. E. (1997). A clinical-research overview of couple interactions. In W. K. Halford & H. J. Markman (Eds.), *The clinical handbook of marriage and couples interventions* (pp. 13–42). New York: Wiley.

Wright, J., & Fichten, C. (1976). Denial of responsibility, videotape feedback and attribution theory: Relevance for behavioral marital therapy. *Canadian Psychology Review, 17,* 219–230.

Chapter Two

Cognition and the Development of Close Relationships

Benjamin R. Karney, James K. McNulty, and Thomas N. Bradbury

Introduction

Although close relationships generally begin with each partner feeling positive and optimistic about the future, most nevertheless end with one or both partners deciding that the relationship is no longer rewarding. The disparity between initial and final evaluations is particularly dramatic in marriage. Although newlyweds presumably approach marriage as a source of satisfaction and fulfillment, nearly two thirds of all first marriages end in divorce or permanent separation (Castro-Martin & Bumpass, 1989), and the dissolution rate for remarriages is even higher (Cherlin, 1992). Thus, the modal course of relationship development indicates that partners in close relationships experience a significant cognitive shift. Somehow the thoughts and feelings that initially draw two people together transform, in a majority of cases, into thoughts and feelings that eventually push those same two people apart. This pattern suggests that a fundamental question for relationships researchers is a cognitive one: how do partner's initially positive evaluations of their relationships so frequently deteriorate and become negative?

For social psychologists, this question is especially perplexing, because a broad tradition of research on social cognition demonstrates that people possess effective techniques for maintaining beliefs that are rewarding to them (for a review, see Kunda, 1990). To protect a desired belief, people tend to ignore evidence that contradicts that belief (Miller, 1997a), generate narratives that support their belief (Murray & Holmes, 1993), and demonstrate better memory for events that are consistent with that belief (Sanitioso, Kunda, & Fong, 1990). Furthermore, people have been shown to adhere to desired beliefs even when confronted with evidence that logically should undermine those beliefs (Nisbett & Ross, 1980). The results of this work suggest that partners' initially positive beliefs about their close relationships, being highly desirable, should be especially resistant to change.

This does not appear to be the case. Despite the often remarkable ability of people to believe what they wish to believe, partners in close relationships are frequently unable to avoid the decline of their initial satisfaction. Examining how evaluations of relationships change or remain stable is thus interesting not only for what it may reveal about the success and failure of close relationships, but also for how it may illuminate broader issues in the way strongly held beliefs can deteriorate despite powerful motivations to maintain them.

Addressing these issues requires understanding the role of cognitions and cognitive processes in the development of close relationships. Accordingly, the last two decades of the twentieth century witnessed a burgeoning interest in the study of cognition in interpersonal contexts (e.g. Baucom, Epstein, Sayers, & Sher, 1989; Berger & Roloff, 1982; Berscheid, 1994; Fincham, Bradbury, & Scott, 1990; Fletcher & Fincham, 1991; Fletcher & Fitness, 1996). Our goal in this chapter is to organize and review recent developments in this literature, with an explicit emphasis on research that has implications for how close relationships change or remain stable over time. We acknowledge at the outset that a focus on cognition alone is unlikely to provide a complete explanation of relationship development. Undoubtedly, interpersonal and environmental factors also play important parts in the success or failure of relationships and so need to be included in any comprehensive explanation of how they change (see Karney & Bradbury, 1995b). Nevertheless, a critical step towards understanding relationship development is to understand the nature of the associated cognitions and cognitive processes.

Chapter overview

Although researchers have examined cognition in close relationships for a relatively short time, already the field has grown to encompass a wide range of variables. As an organizing principle, this chapter divides the field into three aspects of cognition that may affect how close relationships develop and change. The first section addresses the *content* of cognition, i.e., the beliefs and values that make up an individual's mental representation of the relationship. The second section addresses the *structure* of cognition, i.e., how relationship-relevant knowledge is organized. The third deals with the *process* of cognition, i.e., the pursuit, integration, and assimilation of knowledge. Clearly, these three categories are not mutually exclusive. We do not propose them as definitive, but merely as a guide to this broad and complex literature. The last section ends the chapter by suggesting ways that future research might integrate these three areas to better explain how close relationships develop over time.

When possible, we review longitudinal research on aspects of cognition that have been shown to predict relationship outcomes over time. In most cases, however, research in this area has been cross-sectional, identifying the kinds of cognitions associated with satisfying and dissatisfying relationships, but neglecting to explain how disappointment comes about in relationships that begin as satisfying. As a result, many theoretical propositions linking cognition to relationship development have not yet been tested directly. In these cases, cross-sectional work will be reviewed, with suggestions for research still needed to support developmental hypotheses.

The Content of Cognition in Close Relationships

The overwhelming majority of research on cognition in close relationships has examined the content of partners' cognitions. This includes research on partners' enduring attachment models and beliefs, their perceptions of each other's traits and behaviors, and their specific and global impressions of the relationship. As a useful framework to organize this domain, Fletcher and Thomas (1996) distinguished between individuals' theories and beliefs about relationships in general and their theories and beliefs about specific relationships that they have experienced or are experiencing. Global evaluations of a given relationship are the primary dependent variable in this literature and are themselves cognitions that fall into the latter category. In exploring how cognitive content affects the development of relationships, the underlying issue is how general and specific knowledge structures account for change in one particular knowledge structure: a person's global evaluation of a relationship.

Theoretical perspectives

Early models of cognition in close relationships were concerned not with how evaluations of a relationship change but with how individuals integrate their evaluations of specific aspects of the relationship with their global impressions of the relationship. This question arose as a result of early research on marriage that obtained spouses' reports of specific behaviors that occur in the relationship. This research found that spouses who were generally satisfied with their relationships tended to report more positive behaviors and fewer negative ones, whereas spouses who were less satisfied tended to report fewer positive behaviors and more negative ones (e.g., Birchler, Weiss, & Vincent, 1975; Wills, Weiss, & Patterson, 1974). Such findings were taken as support for strictly behavioral models of relationship functioning, until comparisons between spouses' reports revealed that spouses were unreliable observers of what had actually occurred in the relationship (Christensen & Nies, 1980; Jacobson & Moore, 1981). To explain the discrepancies between spouses' reports, relationship researchers drew from existing social psychological models of person perception (e.g., Asch, 1946; Thorndyke, 1920) and suggested that partners rely on their global impressions when asked to evaluate specific aspects of the relationship (Weiss, 1980). As a result of a process of "sentiment override," partners who are generally satisfied with their relationships should tend to evaluate specific aspects of the relationship positively, whereas partners in generally distressed relationships should tend to evaluate specific aspects of the relationship negatively. This line of thinking indicated a need for further work on how partners perceive and interpret each other's behaviors (e.g., Bradbury & Fincham, 1987; Fincham & O'Leary, 1983; Weiss, 1984a), but by itself it said more about the cognitive consequences of global impressions than about the determinants of those impressions.

A subsequent line of thinking about cognition in close relationships shifted the focus from partners' perceptions of the relationship to their beliefs about how relationships function. Drawing from models of rational emotive therapy (Ellis & Grieger, 1977) and cognitive theories of depression (e.g., Abramson, Seligman, & Teasdale, 1978; Seligman, Abramson, Semel, & Von Baeyer, 1979), Epstein and his colleagues (Eidelson & Epstein,

1982; Epstein & Eidelson, 1981) were among the first to argue that certain beliefs about relationships may be dysfunctional. For example, individuals who hold the unrealistic belief that all disagreements are destructive to a relationship are likely to experience disappointment when disagreements arise in their own relationships. To evaluate these ideas, researchers have developed a number of self-report inventories that assess partners' general beliefs and theories about relationship functioning (e.g., Baucom, Epstein, Rankin, & Burnett, 1996; Eidelson & Epstein, 1982; Fletcher & Kininmonth, 1992; Hendrick & Hendrick, 1986; Knee, 1998; Sprecher & Metts, 1989). To date, evidence for a main effect of general beliefs on satisfaction in a particular relationship has been mixed. For example, a number of studies using Eidelson and Epstein's Relationship Belief Inventory (RBI) have found that married spouses who endorse more unrealistic beliefs about relationships also report lower marital satisfaction (e.g., Bradbury & Fincham, 1993; Epstein & Eidelson, 1981; Kurdek, 1992). In contrast, research with the Inventory of Specific Relationship Standards (ISRS), developed by Baucom and his colleagues (1996), found that spouses who endorse higher standards for relationships tend to report higher marital satisfaction. Furthermore, research on dating couples that has used other instruments to assess relationship theories and beliefs has failed to find any direct associations between beliefs and relationship satisfaction (e.g., Fletcher & Kininmonth, 1992; Knee, 1998). The inconsistency of the results across measures and populations suggests that general relationship beliefs may be associated with evaluations of a particular relationship only under certain conditions.

The nature of those conditions was finally suggested by models that integrated the two earlier lines of thinking. The roots of these models lie in Thibaut and Kelley's interdependence theory of interpersonal relationships (Kelley & Thibaut, 1978; Thibaut & Kelley, 1959). In this view, a specific relationship event or outcome will be perceived as satisfying or costly only to the extent that it exceeds or falls short of an individual's enduring values, or comparison level (CL), for relationships. Because standards for relationship functioning and perceptions of specific aspects of relationships vary across individuals, neither category of judgment should directly affect relationship satisfaction. Rather, general beliefs and values for relationships should *moderate* the impact of partners' perceptions of specific aspects of the relationship on their impressions of the relationship as a whole. In other words, a specific perception will have different effects on global evaluations of a relationship depending on the beliefs and values of the perceiver (cf. Kelley et al., 1983; Bradbury & Fincham, 1989, 1991).

Thus, current theories of cognition in close relationships emphasize the interplay between cognitive content and specific experience. To the extent that beliefs are confirmed and standards are met, then initially positive evaluations of a relationship should remain high. Satisfaction should decline, however, when partners' experiences do not coincide with their enduring beliefs and values. It is not the content of cognition itself, but rather the way cognitive content affects interpretations of specific events that determines the development of global relationship satisfaction.

Methodological considerations

Before reviewing empirical research on these issues, two methodological considerations should be noted. First, the reliance on self-report measures, common to much of this research, raises the potential problem of item overlap. For example, frequently used measures of relationship satisfaction, such as the Marital Adjustment Test (Locke & Wallace, 1959) and the Dyadic Adjustment Test (Spanier, 1976), include items assessing a wide range of constructs. In cases where instruments measuring cognitive constructs overlap with these measures, it is entirely possible that significant associations may result from the same construct being measured twice, rather than from an empirical relationship between independent constructs (see Fincham & Bradbury, 1987).

This problem may be exacerbated by a second methodological concern. The wide array of terms used to describe different aspects of cognitive content (e.g., beliefs, assumptions, standards, expectations, ideals, values, theories, etc.) have usually been defined vaguely and in ways that do not clearly distinguish one construct from another (see Baucom et al., 1989). For example, expectations have been described variously as standards for the relationship (e.g., "This is what I expect to receive and I will not settle for less") and as predictions for the relationship (e.g., "I expect that we will have children in a couple of years").

In this chapter, we distinguish between two broad classes of cognitive content: beliefs and values (see Baucom et al., 1996; Kurdek, 1992). Consistent with the distinction offered by Fletcher and Thomas (1996), beliefs can represent general ideas, theories, and assumptions about relationships, or they can represent specific expectations, narrowly defined as predictions for the future, about the functioning of a particular relationship. These types of cognition will be discussed together because both affect the specific experiences that individuals anticipate in their relationships (cf. Baldwin, 1992). In contrast, values encompass standards and ideals, which represent what individuals believe should occur and wish would occur, respectively. Although conceptual distinctions between standards and ideals have been articulated (e.g., Higgins, 1997), these constructs will be discussed together here because both affect how individuals evaluate their specific experiences in relationships (see Tangney, Niedenthal, Covert, & Barlow, 1998, for research that fails to find consequential differences between standards and ideals).

Empirical research

Beliefs.   Researchers have demonstrated at least two ways in which beliefs interact with specific experiences to affect relationship satisfaction. First, certain beliefs may motivate relationship maintenance behaviors that can bolster initial satisfaction. Early evidence for this idea came from experimental research on self-fulfilling prophecies. In a classic study by Snyder, Tanke, and Berscheid (1977), male participants engaged in a telephone conversation with a woman that they believed was either attractive or unattractive. Participants expected that attractive conversation partners would be more sociable, and so they were: those who believed they were conversing with attractive partners led their partners to behave in a more sociable manner. Correlational research on expectancies in close relationships has obtained similar results. For example, the burgeoning literature on adult attachment suggests that people's internal working models of relationships affect the way they approach and maintain their own relationships (e.g., Klohnen & Bera, 1998; Shaver, Collins, & Clark, 1996). Similarly, marital research has shown that spouses with high expectations of personal efficacy (i.e. spouses who believe that they have the ability to affect desired changes in their lives; see Doherty, 1981; Fincham, Bradbury, & Grych, 1990) exchange more positive behaviors during problem-solving discussions and maintain higher marital satisfaction over a one-year period, controlling for their initial satisfaction, compared to spouses who have lower expectations of personal efficacy (Bradbury, 1989). Downey, Freitas, Michaelis, and Khouri (1998) demonstrated more specifically, through daily diary reports and observations of conflict discussions in dating couples, that individuals who expect to be rejected in their personal relationships lead their partners to behave in a more rejecting manner towards them.

Which beliefs motivate relationship maintenance behaviors and which beliefs discourage them? The answer is not entirely clear because, as noted earlier, some positive beliefs, such as expectations of personal efficacy, are associated with efforts to maintain the relationship, whereas other positive beliefs, such as the expectation that partners can read each other's minds, are not. Research on behavior in other domains offers a possible explanation, suggesting that expectations of achievement through effort and expectations of achievement without effort have very different implications for goal-directed behavior (e.g., Henderson & Dweck, 1990; Pham & Taylor, 1999). To date, this distinction has not been examined directly in the context of close relationships.

A second way that beliefs and theories may affect the development of relationship satisfaction is through their effects on how partners interpret specific experiences in the relationship. The same experiences may have different implications for an individual's relationship satisfaction depending on the individual's beliefs about how relationships function. For example, Downey and Feldman demonstrated that individuals who expect to be rejected in their personal relationships are more likely to label an ambiguous interaction with a confederate as rejecting, compared to individuals who do not expect to be rejected. Ruvolo and Rotondo (1998) compared the association between specific views of a partner and overall relationship satisfaction among dating couples with varying beliefs about the malleability of personality. For individuals who believed that people's personalities are fixed and unlikely to change, specific impressions of the partner were strongly associated with global impressions of the relationship. However, for individuals who believed that people's personalities are malleable, the association between specific impressions of the partner and global impressions of the relationship was significantly weaker. In a related line of research, Knee (1998) examined dating partners who endorsed different theories about whether relationship outcomes were destined (i.e., determined by fate and the immutable characteristics of the partners) or grown (i.e., developed through effort and communication). Neither type of belief had any direct associations with relationship satisfaction. However, in response to relationship stressors, those who endorsed destiny beliefs reported reacting with disengagement and restraint, whereas those who endorsed growth beliefs reported reacting with more active coping strategies. Furthermore, for individuals who endorsed destiny beliefs, initial relationship satisfaction predicted the longevity of the relationship across six months, whereas for individuals endorsing a low belief in destiny, initial satisfaction was unrelated to the longevity of the relationship. In other words, the long-term implications of relationship stressors and initial relationship satisfaction may depend on whether partners believe that relationship outcomes can be affected by their own efforts.

A central issue may be whether a given experience is consistent with expectations or a violation of expectations (e.g., Afifi & Metts, 1998; Burgoon, 1993). Experiences that are consistent with general beliefs about how relationships function should require less adjustment than experiences that are inconsistent with those beliefs. To examine this idea, Helgeson (1994) examined relationship beliefs among dating couples coping with long-distance relationships. Not surprisingly, partners who endorsed positive beliefs about the relationship were more likely to stay together over the course of three months. However, for those couples who did not stay together, those initially endorsing positive relationship beliefs experienced greater distress, controlling for initial levels of distress and for which partner initiated the breakup. As Helgeson concludes: "Positive relationship beliefs might facilitate adjustment to a relationship stressor when beliefs are confirmed . . . but impede adjustment to a relationship stressor when beliefs are disconfirmed" (p. 254). Vanzetti, Notarius, & NeeSmith (1992) obtained additional evidence of an interaction between expectancies and experiences within the context of marital interactions. In this study, married couples who were high or low in perceptions of relational efficacy were asked to predict their partners' behaviors during an upcoming marital interaction, and then to make attributions for the behaviors that actually occurred during the interaction. The key analysis compared the two groups of couples on their attributions for the unpredicted negative behaviors of their partners. Spouses who reported low relational efficacy were likely to make dispositional attributions for their partners' unexpected negative behaviors during the interaction, thereby blaming their partners for the negative experiences. In contrast, spouses who reported high relational efficacy were significantly less likely to make dispositional attributions for their partners' unexpected negative behaviors during the interaction. Together, these studies suggest that individuals' beliefs about relationships affect the development of their satisfaction by determining whether specific negative experiences are expected, and thus likely to motivate adequate coping strategies, or unexpected, and thus likely to give rise to maladaptive coping strategies.

Values   The standards and ideals that partners use to evaluate experiences in their close relationships may affect their satisfaction in the same ways that beliefs and theories do. Specifically, relationship-relevant values should moderate the impact of specific experiences such that experiences consistent with an individual's values should enhance satisfaction, whereas experiences inconsistent with an individual's values should diminish satisfaction. A number of studies have supported this view. For example, Fletcher and Kininmonth (1992) examined standards, satisfaction, and self-reports of behavior in a sample of college students. Standards had no direct association with satisfaction, but standards did moderate the association between satisfaction and behavior. For individuals who held that a specific type of behavior was an important part of a good relationship, reports of that behavior were highly correlated with satisfaction. For individuals who held that a specific behavior was less important, reports of that behavior were less strongly associated with satisfaction (see also Fletcher et al., Chapter 4 of this volume). Baucom et al. (1996) elaborated on the role of standards by assessing perceptions of whether or not those standards were being met among spouses in established marriages. Not surprisingly, spouses who perceived that their standards were being met were more satisfied with their relationships than spouses who did not perceive their standards being met. Kelley and Burgoon (1991) assessed violations of standards more directly by comparing spouses' standards for various specific aspects of a relationship with their perceptions of those aspects of their own relationships. The greater the discrepancy between standards and perceptions, the lower the spouses' satisfaction with the relationship.

Two limitations of these studies are that all have been cross-sectional and none have separated the main effects of high or low standards from the main effects of discrepancies between standards and perceptions. Ruvolo and Veroff (1997) addressed these limitations by using multiple regression to examine the unique effects of perceptions of the relationship, relationship-relevant ideals, and real–ideal discrepancies, on change in satisfaction over the first year of marriage. For wives, real–ideal discrepancies, but not perceptions or ideals by themselves, predicted change in satisfaction over the first year. None of these variables predicted changes for husbands, perhaps because husbands experienced relatively little change in their satisfaction over the study period.

The finding that discrepancies between perceptions of the relationship and standards for the relationship predict declines in satisfaction over time raises a provocative question: is it beneficial or harmful for individuals to hold high relationship standards? On one hand, Epstein and his colleagues (Eidelson & Epstein, 1982; Epstein & Eidelson, 1981) have argued that unrealistically high standards place initially satisfied partners at greater risk for disappointment. This logic has led some to argue (e.g., Miller, 1997b) that relationships would be more stable if partners lowered their standards and learned to accept less than their ideal relationships. On the other hand, Murray, Holmes, and Griffin (1996) have argued that high standards act as self-fulfilling prophecies, leading to happier relationships over time. The research reviewed in this section suggests that neither position is completely accurate. These studies support the view that the standards and ideals that individuals use to evaluate experiences in their relationships have negligible direct effects on the development of their marital satisfaction. Rather, high standards support the relationship only to the extent that the individual perceives these standards as being met. Modest standards protect the relationship only if the relationship provides experiences that surpass those standards. Rather than focusing on the cognitions themselves, current research suggests that it is the interaction between partners' values and their experiences that is likely to account for changes in satisfaction over time.

Agreement between partners.   Several researchers have raised the possibility that, in addition to the content of each partner's cognitions, the compatibility between partners' cognitions plays an important role in the development of their relationship. This is a possibility worth considering carefully, because research on cognition in relationships, as can be seen from the studies described above, has focused mostly on intrapsychic, rather than dyadic, analyses.

Despite the potential value of dyadic analyses, to date research that has examined the compatibility of spouses' cognitions has demonstrated few noteworthy effects compared with the effects of perceived discrepancies between values and perceptions within each partner. For example, Baucom et al. (1996) reported that between-spouse differences in relationship standards were negatively associated with relationship satisfaction. However, these associations were notably weaker than the main effects of standards and perceived discrepancies within each spouse. Using multiple regression, Kelley and Burgoon (1991) directly compared agreement between spouses and real–ideal discrepancies within each spouse for their ability to account for variance in spouses' relationship satisfaction. For both spouses, real–ideal discrepancies within each spouse accounted for significantly more variance than agreement between spouses. Finally, Acitelli, Kenny, and Gladstone (1996) noted that any two partners' standards are likely to agree with each other to some extent due to the general agreement among most people about certain values (see Kenny & Acitelli, 1994). Controlling for the stereotypical beliefs held by all couples, Acitelli et al. found no significant associations between spousal agreement on their ideals for marriage and their concurrent marital satisfaction.

Summary and critique

How does cognitive content affect the development of relationship satisfaction? The research and theory reviewed in this section suggest that cognitive content moderates the association between specific information and global evaluations of a relationship. A given experience or perception can contribute to or detract from an individual's initially positive evaluations depending on whether or not that experience or perception is consistent with the individual's beliefs and values. Relationships should remain satisfying to the extent that experiences in the relationship meet or exceed partners' standards for how relationships function. However, satisfaction should decline to the extent that experiences in the relationship fall short of partners' standards or fail to confirm their positive expectations.

An important limitation of this view is that it assumes that, compared to global impressions of the relationship, beliefs and values are relatively enduring aspects of each partner. This may be an accurate assumption, but to date there has been no empirical research to support it. As noted earlier, most of the research in this domain has been cross-sectional, and thus incapable of assessing the stability of cognitive content over time. The few longitudinal studies described in this section have measured cognitive content only at Time 1, using that assessment to predict changes in relationship satisfaction over time. In the absence of longitudinal data on the stability of relationship-relevant beliefs and values, the possibility remains that these cognitions are not stable, but rather may themselves change as a reaction to changes in the quality of the relationship. In other words, rather than beliefs and values determining the global meaning of specific experiences, it is equally likely that specific experiences may affect the development of beliefs and values within the individual. Within the literature on attachment models, there is at least tentative evidence that this can occur (Davila, Karney, & Bradbury, 1999; Kirkpatrick & Hazan, 1994). Before definitive statements can be made about the causal role of cognitive content in close relationships, longitudinal data are needed to evaluate this alternative possibility.

The Structure of Cognition in Close Relationships

There has been far less research on the structure of cognitions in close relationships than there has been on the content of those cognitions. Nevertheless, the way people organize relationship-relevant knowledge may have particular significance for explaining how evaluations of the relationship change or remain stable over time. For example, maintaining globally positive evaluations in the face of the specific challenges and vicissitudes of daily life requires the capacity to assimilate discordant information and respond appropriately to new situations (Raush, Barry, Hertel, & Swain, 1974). As Burgess, Wallin, and Schultz (1954) pointed out in their early research on marriage, "the ability to adjust to one's mate and to the responsibilities of the married state might be regarded, from one standpoint, as the most important factor of all in determining the success or failure of a marriage" (p. 313). The structure of partners' cognitive representations of the relationship may account for this ability.

In other areas of social psychology, research on cognitive structure is well developed (e.g., Scott, Osgood, & Peterson, 1979; Tetlock, 1983). Why has there been so little research on the structure of cognition in close relationships? One reason may be that structure has not played a large role in the theories guiding research in this field. Just as various aspects of cognitive content have been studied without regard to how these aspects may be organized and related to each other, so has the organization of relationship-relevant knowledge within the individual been all but overlooked as a topic of research interest. Another reason may be that studying cognitive structure requires a different repertoire of methods than are commonly employed in research on close relationships. Rather than relying on partners' direct reports of how their cognitions are organized, research on cognitive structure tends to use more indirect techniques, inferring aspects of cognitive structure through thought-listing tasks and assessments of reaction time.

Despite these theoretical and methodological obstacles, a number of researchers have explored the implications of how cognitions are structured for the development of close relationships. In this section, we review theory and research on two dimensions of cognitive structure that have been studied within this context: the complexity of partners' beliefs about the relationship, and the accessibility of certain beliefs and evaluations.

Cognitive complexity

Theoretical perspectives. As noted earlier, relationship-relevant cognitions can vary from global beliefs about how relationships function to perceptions of specific partner characteristics (e.g., Fletcher & Thomas, 1996; Srull & Wyer, 1989; see also Baldwin, 1992). Cognitive complexity (also referred to as conceptual or integrative complexity) draws attention to how individuals differentiate and integrate these distinct cognitions (e.g., Crockett, 1965; Schroder, 1971). Differentiation refers to the number of categories or kinds of information taken into account in evaluating persons or events. For example, people with relatively undifferentiated beliefs about their relationship might evaluate their partners' behaviors by categorizing them as either selfish or unselfish. A person with a more differentiated set of beliefs would recognize that a specific behavior can be evaluated in multiple or even contradictory ways. Integration refers to the degree and quality of the connections among differentiated characteristics. For example, people with less integrated beliefs about their relationships may acknowledge differences of opinion with their partners, but people with highly integrated beliefs should both acknowledge differences and recognize the multiple levels at which different positions on an issue connect and interact. It follows that differentiation is a prerequisite for integration (Tetlock & Suedfeld, 1988).

A premise of research on cognitive complexity in close relationships is that more complex representations of a relationship, independent of the content of those representations, allow partners more flexibility in assimilating specific information about the relationship (R. W. Martin, 1991; Neimeyer, 1984). Thus, an initially complex view of the relationship may allow partners to distinguish their globally positive views of the relationship from the specific challenges of everyday life. In contrast, an initially simple view of the relationship may be more fragile and more likely to deteriorate in response to specific setbacks. In this way, greater cognitive complexity should be associated with more resilient relationship satisfaction over time (cf. also Linville, 1987; Showers, 1992a, 1992b, for similar ideas in research on self-concepts).

Empirical research.   Cross-sectional research suggests that the complexity of partners' cognitions about their relationships is associated with important relationship processes. For example, two studies have examined the association between cognitive complexity and satisfaction in established marriages (Crouse, Karlins, & Schroder, 1968; Neimeyer, 1984). Crouse et al. measured the complexity of spouses' beliefs about their marriage by asking each spouse to continue a series of sentences beginning with relationship-relevant phrases (e.g., "When my mate does not agree with me . . ."). The resulting paragraphs were then rated for differentiation and integration. Neimeyer used a different procedure, asking spouses to complete Kelly's (1955) Role Construct Repertory Test, an instrument that assesses spouses' views of their own families for level of differentiation only. In both studies, complexity scores were moderately associated with marital satisfaction. However, the lack of longitudinal data leaves the precise interpretation of these findings unclear. Although the findings raise the possibility that spouses with more complex views of the marriage are also more satisfied with their relationships, Tetlock and Suedfeld (1988) argue that the complexity of a set of cognitions at any one time should be independent of the content of those cognitions. An alternative explanation of these findings is that complexity predicts rates of change in satisfaction over time and that spouses in these established marriages had experienced different changes in their relationships by the time they were studied. Distinguishing between these possible effects requires longitudinal data and analyses capable of separating effects on levels of satisfaction from effects on rates of change (Karney & Bradbury, 1995a), but such data have not been reported in this area.

More recent research suggests that cognitive complexity may affect the development of close relationships through its association with the way partners communicate with each other. Spouses whose cognitions about relationships are more complex may possess a broader range of potential responses to specific experiences and so should be more likely to exchange adaptive behaviors during problem-solving discussions. Cross-sectional research offers some support for this idea. For example, Tyndall and Lichtenberg (1985) used Budner's (1962) Intolerance of Ambiguity Scale to measure how spouses in established marriages approached ambiguous or inconsistent information in their environments. Spouses describing themselves as more tolerant of ambiguity reported their interactions with their partners to be more adaptive and less rigid than spouses who described themselves as intolerant of ambiguity. Moving beyond self-report data, R. Martin (1992) assessed the complexity of spouses' open-ended descriptions of important relationships and then recorded spouses engaging in problem-solving discussions. The complexity of husbands, but not of wives, was associated with behavior during these discussions, such that husbands who were more complex tended to be more supportive than husbands who were less complex.

A limitation of both of these studies, however, is that neither one examined the simultaneous associations between relationship satisfaction and behavior, leaving open the possibility that associations between satisfaction and both complexity and behavior accounts for the previous findings. Denton, Burleson, and Sprenkle (1995) addressed this possibility by assessing marital satisfaction, cognitive complexity, and problem-solving behavior in a study of established marriages. Analyses indicated that the composite satisfaction of the couple moderated the association between cognitive complexity and problem-solving behaviors. In marriages where both partners were satisfied, complexity scores were unrelated to the quality of the interaction. However, in distressed marriages, spouses who were rated as more cognitively complex proved to be more effective communicators in that the intent of their behaviors matched the impact of those behaviors on the partner.

Summary. Researchers examining cognitive complexity have yet to reach consensus on the appropriate operationalization of the construct. Thus, it is noteworthy that the findings of these studies have been fairly consistent so far. More complex representations of relationships in general appear to be associated with a more flexible and adaptive repertoire of problem-solving behaviors, and possibly with higher satisfaction in established marriages. Still to be addressed is the question of how the complexity of partners' representations of their relationships may influence the way those representations change or remain stable over time.

Accessibility

Theoretical perspectives. In contrast to work on cognitive complexity, which examines the structure of a set of cognitions, research on accessibility examines the ease with which a particular cognition can be brought to mind (Bruner, 1957). A premise of research in this area is that different cognitions vary along this dimension (e.g., Higgins & King, 1981). For example, some beliefs and values are likely to be easily accessible. These cognitions may be chronically activated, or they may be so frequently activated that their reactivation is relatively automatic. Highly accessible cognitions should significantly affect interpretations of relevant specific experiences, increasing the likelihood that new information is assimilated to existing knowledge structures. Thus, highly accessible cognitions should be more stable over time. In contrast, some beliefs and values will be relatively inaccessible. To the extent that certain cognitions are difficult to bring to mind, those cognitions should be less likely to affect interpretations of new data. In this case, existing cognitions are more likely to accommodate to new information, and so should be more likely to change over time. In sum, this view suggests that the accessibility of a particular cognition should moderate the impact of the cognition on the interpretation of specific experiences and on the stability of the cognition over time.

Among relationship-relevant cognitions, satisfaction has been assumed to be highly accessible for most people and thus likely to influence perceptions of specific events across a variety of contexts (Weiss, 1980). Nevertheless, research in other domains has documented significant individual differences in the accessibility of even highly accessible beliefs (e.g., Markus & Smith, 1981). To measure these differences, some researchers have operationalized accessibility as the speed with which an individual uses a particular belief or value to judge a particular object, adjusted for individual differences in speed of responding (see Fazio, 1990). Research participants are typically presented with a range of stimuli and asked to judge whether each one is relevant or irrelevant to a particular cognition. The time to react to the stimulus, also called the response latency, is considered a measure of the accessibility of the cognition in question. Measured in this way, individual differences in construct accessibility tend to be small, a matter of milliseconds or less. Nevertheless, individual differences in accessibility have been associated with a number of important outcomes (e.g., Fazio, 1995).

Empirical research.   Does the accessibility of relationship-relevant cognitions moderate the effects of those cognitions on the relationship? Research conducted by Fincham and his colleagues offers preliminary evidence that it does. In this study, spouses in established marriages reported on their marital satisfaction, attributions, and expectations for their partners' behavior immediately prior to a marital interaction. Spouses also participated in a series of computer tasks in which the time to judge a series of relationship-relevant words (e.g., "your spouse," "your husband") as positive or negative was measured. For husbands, but not for wives, response latencies on the computer task were associated with the strength of the correlation between marital satisfaction and preinteraction expectations. In husbands whose marital satisfaction was highly accessible, marital satisfaction and preinteraction expectations were more strongly correlated than in husbands whose marital satisfaction was less accessible, controlling for overall levels of marital satisfaction. For both spouses, accessibility also moderated the association between marital satisfaction and attributions, such that satisfaction and attributions were more strongly associated in spouses for whom marital satisfaction was more accessible. Additional analyses of this data set (Fincham, 1998) revealed that the accessibility of spouses' marital satisfaction moderated the association between satisfaction and the actual behaviors that spouses exchanged during marital interactions. Behavior and satisfaction were significantly associated only for those spouses whose marital satisfaction was highly accessible. Finally, these effects appear to have implications for the development of relationship satisfaction over time. Through retrospective analyses of these couples, Fincham demonstrated that the accessibility of one spouse's marital satisfaction moderates the stability, measured by a test–retest correlation, of the other spouse's marital satisfaction over the previous 18 months, such that marital satisfaction is more stable for spouses whose partners' marital satisfaction is more accessible. It should be noted that all of these findings await replication in an independent sample. Yet the consistent pattern across dependent measures supports the idea that individual differences in the accessibility of relationship-relevant cognitions may moderate the effect of those cognitions on other relationship processes.

To the extent that this idea receives further confirmation, these data raise an additional important question: how do individual differences in the accessibility of these cognitions come about? Some have suggested that the accessibility of a belief or value is associated with its strength or extremity (e.g., Fazio, 1995). To evaluate this possibility, Fletcher, Rosanowski, and Fitness (1994) measured response latencies in a sample of dating partners with either strong or weak beliefs about the importance of intimacy and passion in relationships. Half of the individuals engaged in the response latency task while distracted by an irrelevant memory task, and half engaged in the task without distraction. For partners who endorsed strong beliefs, the addition of the memory task had no effect on response latencies, suggesting that the beliefs of these individuals could be activated automatically. In contrast, for partners who endorsed weak beliefs, the memory task significantly increased response latencies, suggesting that the beliefs of these individuals were less accessible and therefore more difficult to activate under conditions of distraction. These findings suggest that the cognitions of individuals with more extreme beliefs and values may also be highly accessible and thus likely to influence interpretations of specific experiences.

As an alternative explanation for individual differences in the accessibility of relationship cognitions, Baldwin and his colleagues (Baldwin, 1994; Baldwin, Carrell, & Lopez, 1990; Baldwin, Keelan, Fehr, Enns, & Koh-Rangarajoo, 1996) focused on the ability of different contexts to activate, or prime, specific beliefs and values from among the many that a person might apply to a given situation. For example, Baldwin and Fehr (1995) argued that individuals possess not one attachment model, as has been assumed in most research on attachment, but rather many models that are activated at different times depending on the specific context. In a study that supports this view, Baldwin et al. (1996) demonstrated that randomly assigning participants to be primed with a particular type of attachment experience significantly affected their attraction to different potential dating partners. Their explanation for this finding is that priming a specific attachment model made that model more accessible, thus allowing that model to exert a greater influence over subsequent evaluations. Presumably, different social environments are more or less likely to prime different available relationship cognitions.

Summary.   To the extent that aspects of cognitive content affect how an individual interprets and responds to specific experiences, the research reviewed in this section suggests that relatively accessible cognitions will exert a greater effect than relatively inaccessible ones. Yet research on the determinants of accessibility indicates that the same cognition may be more or less accessible in different contexts. Thus, a task for future research in this area is to determine the natural conditions under which important relationship-relevant cognitions are more or less accessible, and thus more or less likely to affect relationship development.

General critique

Research on the structure of cognitions in close relationships is still in its early stages. The two dimensions reviewed in this section – complexity and accessibility – have only begun to be examined in detail. Furthermore, there remain potentially important aspects of cognitive structure that have yet to be studied with respect to close relationships (Baldwin, 1992; Beach, Etherton, & Whitaker, 1995). For example, individuals may vary in the strength of the covariance between their global evaluations about their relationships and their perceptions of specific aspects of the relationship over time. A strong covariance between global evaluations and specific perceptions may indicate satisfaction that is relatively fragile and sensitive to negative experiences, whereas a weak covariance may indicate satisfaction that is robust to specific negative experiences. In addition, relationships among dimensions of cognitive structure are of potential interest. For example, the complexity of individuals' representations of their relationships may have implications for the accessibility of specific aspects of that representation. Within a more complex representation, the accessibility of any specific cognition may be diminished, leading to less schematic processing for those with more complex representations.

To understand the effects of any of these aspects of cognitive structure on the development of close relationships, longitudinal research is crucial for two reasons. Most obviously, such research is necessary to address the key hypothesis of this research: that the structure of individuals' cognitions about their close relationships affects the resiliency of those cognitions over time. Less obviously, longitudinal research is needed to answer important questions about the origins and development of cognitive structures. With respect to complexity and accessibility, for example, it seems likely that certain representations (such as my image of my spouse during an argument) may become more or less complex, and certain beliefs and values (such as the importance of intimacy and passion in a relationship) may become more or less accessible, depending on the experiences of each partner in the relationship over time.

The Process of Cognition in Close Relationships

Each aspect of cognitive content and cognitive structure reviewed so far can be seen as the product of cognitive processes. These processes include all of the ways in which individuals pursue, integrate, explain, evaluate, and recall general and specific information about their relationships. As many researchers have recognized, the nature of these processes may affect relationships independent of the products of these processes (e.g., Baucom et al., 1989; Fincham, Bradbury, & Scott 1990). The way spouses make attributions for each other's behaviors, for example, has been the most extensively studied cognitive process in this domain. A well-developed literature demonstrates that the nature of partners' attributions has important implications for how their global relationship satisfaction changes or remains stable over time (for reviews, see Baucom, 1987; Bradbury & Fincham, 1990; Harvey, 1987.

Aside from attributions, however, research on close relationships has not focused much attention on the details of specific cognitive processes and how they operate. Instead, this research has focused on the broad motives that may influence the processing of specific information (Kunda, 1990). A premise of this research is that the processing of relationship-relevant information is not strictly rational but rather biased towards the fulfillment of an individual's hopes and aspirations for themselves and their relationships. For example, most people strongly desire to be in a relationship that they perceive as satisfying. Thus, research on close relationships has identified specific cognitive processes that allow individuals to maintain and enhance their perceptions of satisfaction. Other processing goals have also been proposed, and some evidence suggests that these goals also affect the processing of relationship-relevant information. In this section, we review the evidence that the motivated processing of specific information in close relationships may affect the development of global satisfaction.

Maintenance and enhancement

One of the challenges of a long-term relationship is to preserve a positive global evaluation of the relationship despite the specific problems and disappointments that are likely to arise over time. For people who are constrained to remain in their relationships regardless of their satisfaction (e.g., by the presence of children or the lack of available alternatives), this challenge is especially poignant. Rather than confront the possibility that they are trapped in an unsatisfying situation, most people should be highly motivated, regardless of the objective quality of their relationships, to maintain the general belief that their relationships are rewarding and worth pursuing. Research on cognition in close relationships has identified a number of specific processes through which individuals might accomplish this goal.

Social comparison.   One way to justify remaining in an imperfect relationship is to engage in self-serving social comparisons (e.g., Wood & Taylor, 1991) and decide that one's own relationship, whatever its problems, is better than other people's relationships. Indeed, a number of researchers have shown that most people do believe their own relationships to be more supportive (Taylor, Wood, & Lichtman, 1983), more equitable (Buunk & Van Yperen, 1989), and less likely to end (Weinstein, 1980) than the relationships of other people. Buunk and van der Eijnden (1997) demonstrated that the degree of perceived superiority is associated with satisfaction, such that unsatisfied individuals are less likely than satisfied individuals to perceive their relationships as superior (cf. also Fowers, Lyons & Montel, 1996). Nevertheless, even in this study, a perception of superiority was reported by all but the most distressed individuals.

How might the perception of superiority come about? To explore processes that might give rise to the perception of superiority, van Lange and Rusbult (1995) asked undergraduates to list their spontaneous thoughts about their own dating relationships and those of unspecified others. When thinking about their own relationships, people tended to report more positive thoughts than negative ones. However, when thinking about the relationships of others, people tended to report more negative thoughts than positive ones. Furthermore, people were able to generate more positive thoughts about their own relationships than about other people's relationships, and more negative thoughts about other people's relationships than their own. To understand these findings, the authors proposed that people have a "tendency to focus selectively on attributes that make one's own relationship appear advantaged" (1995, p. 43). In other words, out of all the specific dimensions upon which people may compare their relationships to others, people may choose to make comparisons on the specific dimensions that will support the general conclusions they wish to reach.

Derogation of alternatives.   Another process that may contribute to the perception that one's own relationship is superior to others is the derogation of alternative relationship partners. Even for people in satisfying, committed relationships, the presence of an attractive alternative partner can be threatening, potentially raising questions about the value of one's own partner. To avoid having to face these questions, Thibaut and Kelley (1959) proposed that people can eliminate the threat "by taking a 'sour grapes' attitude toward the rewarding aspects of the [alternative] or by emphasizing the negative, cost-increasing aspects of it" (p. 175). Johnson and Rusbult (1989), in one of a series of studies, evaluated this idea by asking people in dating relationships to evaluate photographs of members of the opposite sex, ostensibly for use in a computer dating service. Half were told that their ratings would be used to match them with partners through the service (high threat condition); the other half were told that they would not be participating in the service (low threat condition). People's attitudes towards their own relationships were not generally associated with their ratings of the targets. However, when the targets were attractive and potentially threatening, people who were more committed to their own relationships rated the targets as significantly less desirable than people who were less committed to their own relationships (for replications and extensions of this work, see Lydon, Meana, Sepinwall, Richards, & Mayman, 1999; Simpson, 1987). These findings suggest that people may have considerable latitude in how they evaluate potential alternative partners. The desire to perceive one's own relationship as superior may lead individuals to evaluate alternatives in the most negative way possible.

Selective attention.   Baucom et al. (1989) suggested that one of the fundamental ways in which individuals maintain positive global impressions of their relationships is by selectively attending only to specific information consistent with that impression. In other words, the desire to believe that one is in a rewarding relationship should lead partners to focus on the positive aspects of the relationship and ignore the negative ones. This is a provocative suggestion, but to date there has been little research directly exploring this idea. The one relevant study that we are aware of examined selective attention not for positive and negative aspects of one's own relationship, but for attractive alternatives outside of one's relationship. Miller (1997a) asked subjects to review, at their own pace, a series of slides featuring attractive members of the opposite sex. People who were in relationships where they felt committed and close spent significantly less time reviewing the slides than people who did not feel committed and close to their partners, or who were not in relationships. These findings were interpreted as support for the idea that one way to maintain positive feelings about a relationship is to pay less attention to information, like the availability of attractive alternatives, that might threaten those feelings.

Rationalization.   Similar to the process of attending to positive aspects of a relationship and ignoring negative ones, people motivated to protect their globally positive impressions of their relationships may construct narratives that discount negative aspects of the relationship and augment positive ones. In a sophisticated program of research, Murray and Holmes (1993, 1994) have demonstrated that, when faced with specific threatening information about their relationship partners, people tell stories that minimize the impact of that information. In one study, members of satisfied dating couples who had rated their relationships as low in conflict were informed (falsely) that conflict was actually a sign of a healthy relationship. Participants were then given an opportunity to describe their relationships in an open-ended narrative. Compared to a control group who had not been given the false information, partners who believed conflict was a sign of strength told stories that exaggerated instances of conflict and discounted the conflict avoidance they had reported earlier. These findings suggest that people selectively recruit and weave together specific information to construct narratives that support the general impressions they desire to maintain.

Temporal comparison.   Most research on comparison processes in close relationships has focused on social comparisons. However, it is also possible that relationships are evaluated through temporal comparisons, i.e., through comparisons between the current state of the relationship and the state of the relationship at some point in the past (Albert, 1977). Carver and Scheier (1990) have suggested that the perceptions of change that arise from such comparisons drive people's affective responses to their current state, such that the perception of growth is rewarding and the perception of stagnation and decline is distressing (see also Aronson & Linder, 1965). With respect to relationships, one implication of this idea is that people should be motivated to perceive their relationships as growing more satisfying over time, and their recollections of the past may be biased in order to maintain this perception. Karney and Coombs (2000) evaluated this possibility in a longitudinal study of wives' perceptions of the emotional quality of their marriages. Prospective ratings of the relationship across ten years indicated that wives' perceptions of their marriages grew significantly less positive over time, consistent with other longitudinal research (e.g., Johnson, Amoloza, & Booth, 1992; Vaillant & Vaillant, 1993). However, retrospective reports indicated that the wives believed that their marriages had become significantly more positive over the same interval, and they justified this belief by negatively biasing their recollections of the past. This process had important implications for the future of the relationship, such that wives who did not perceive the present as an improvement over the past were more likely to divorce over the subsequent ten years. Together with other research on the malleability of memory in close relationships (Sprecher, 1999), these findings suggest that the way individuals recall the past may be influenced by the desire to preserve and enhance positive evaluations of the present.

Accuracy and verification

Supporting positive impressions is not the only goal that may drive the processing of information in close relationships. As partners in developing relationships grow more dependent on one another, their need to understand and predict each other's behavior should lead to a desire for accurate information about the relationship, regardless of whether that information is positive or negative (Newman & Langer, 1988). For individuals in unsatisfying relationships, this motive should lead individuals to process information very differently from those whose thinking is driven by the enhancement or maintenance motive. A number of researchers have explored specific implications of this idea. For example, Swann and his colleagues (e.g., de la Ronde & Swann, 1998; Swann, 1983; Swann, De La Ronde, &

Hixon, 1994), in a lengthy program of research, have suggested that people attempt to verify their strongly held beliefs about themselves and their intimates, even when those beliefs are negative. Comparing partners' ratings of each other's specific attributes (Pelham & Swann, 1989), these researchers have shown that people feel closer to their partners when their partners view them as they view themselves (Swann et al., 1994) and that people tend to reject feedback that is inconsistent with their own views of their partners (de la Ronde & Swann, 1998). Vorauer and Ross (1996), adopting a similar position, have suggested that the desire for accurate information may vary at different stages of development, waxing during periods of transition or crisis and waning during periods of stability. Paradoxically, they propose that the desire for accurate information may at these times lead to a diagnosticity bias, i.e., the belief that specific information is more informative than it may actually be (Vorauer & Ross, 1993). To date, research on accuracy and verification motives has focused more on partners' preferences for different kinds of information than on the specific cognitive processes involved in pursuing these goals. Thus, it is not clear whether the specific processes these goals invoke are the same or different from the processes that support maintenance and enhancement goals.

Summary and critique

With few exceptions, there has been little longitudinal research on cognitive processes in close relationships. Therefore, understanding the role of these processes in the development of close relationships requires extrapolating from cross-sectional research. As our review indicates, this research emphasizes top-down or schematic processes, demonstrating how general goals and aspirations for a relationship determine the processing of specific relationship-relevant information. Regardless of the particular goal, each of the processes identified here serves to assimilate new information to existing cognitive structures. By diminishing the impact of inconsistent information and augmenting the impact of supportive information, these various processes protect and maintain rewarding beliefs and evaluations. Thus, the processes identified in this section should contribute to the stability of those beliefs and evaluations over time.

The problem with this conclusion is that it fails to account for the way close relationships actually develop. For most people, initially positive beliefs about a relationship do not endure over time. As noted at the outset of this chapter, the normative course of a close relationship is for cherished beliefs about the relationship to change and deteriorate. Although new information may be assimilated to existing beliefs in the short term, the fact that relationships change indicates that existing beliefs must accommodate to new information in the long term. Research on cognitive processes in close relationships has neglected to consider such bottom-up processes, and this oversight currently limits the ability of this research to contribute to an understanding of how close relationships develop over time.

One way to address this gap would be to explore factors that account for when individuals may be more or less likely to engage in top-down or bottom-up processing. For example, motives to protect existing beliefs may vary in strength at different stages of the relationship. During periods of stability, the preservation of current beliefs and evaluations may be a powerful motive, and so the processes described above may be more likely to occur. During periods of crisis or transition, however, the desire for accurate information may become more relevant, and so bottom-up processing might be more likely (Vorauer & Ross, 1996). Similarly, the motive to protect globally positive beliefs about the relationship may be more powerful for people who are constrained to remain in their relationships than for those who are not so constrained (Thibaut & Kelley, 1959). To the extent that contextual factors are associated with changes in the relative strength of different processing motives at different times, then such factors may also account for when global evaluations of a relationship should be maintained and when they may change in response to specific contradictory information.

Another avenue worth pursuing is the possibility that different individuals may differ in their ability to engage in motivated processes. To date, most research on cognitive processes in close relationships demonstrates merely that motivated reasoning does occur and is associated with relationship satisfaction. By this reasoning, people who are better at protecting their beliefs (e.g., more skilled at rationalization, derogating alternatives, etc.), should over time experience more stable satisfaction. People who are not as skilled should engage in less schematic processing, and so their global impressions of the relationship should be more responsive to specific information that contradicts their beliefs.

Towards an Integrated Theory of Cognition in Close Relationships

To the extent that most social phenomena involve individuals either processing, interpreting, or storing data, there are very few aspects of human behavior that are not in some way cognitive (Berkowitz & Devine, 1995). For researchers examining cognition in the development of close relationships, the vastness of this domain represents a strength and a potential limitation to research. The strength is that research on cognition in close relationships has the potential to integrate what have widely been viewed as disparate areas of investigation. Issues of culture, personality, stress, and behavior unite in that they are likely to influence close relationships through their effects on cognition. Cognitions and cognitive processes may indeed prove to be the "final common pathway" (Jacobson, 1985; Karney & Bradbury, 1995b) through which these other variables affect the outcomes of close relationships. The potential limitation, however, is that this domain may prove so vast that researchers examining particular aspects of cognition fail to recognize their common interests. In order to shed meaningful light on this field, most researchers have chosen to define their topic areas rather narrowly, identifying and examining specific types of beliefs, structures, or processes. The resulting research describes many dimensions of cognition in close relationships, but does not accumulate to support a coherent theory that explains how close relationships develop or remain stable over time (Baucom & Epstein, 1989; Sillars, 1985).

Furthermore, for want of a focus on the larger domain, important parts of this landscape remain unmapped. Researchers have described the elements of cognitive content in relationships, but it is unknown where beliefs and evaluations come from and how they may change over time. Research on the implications of cognitive structure is advancing in other domains (e.g., Read, Vanman, & Miller, 1997; Thagard, 1992), but research on the structure of cognitions in relationships is only beginning. Researchers have identified motives that may drive cognitive processes in relationships, but it remains unclear when different motives are more or less likely to operate. Finally, as we have repeated throughout this chapter, cross-sectional research is an important first step, but additional longitudinal and experimental research is critical to understanding the causal role of cognitions in close relationships. In its absence, the possibility remains that all of these variables do not predict changes in relationship satisfaction but merely follow from them.

Thus, it may be too early to propose an integrative theory of how initially positive beliefs about relationships remain stable or deteriorate over time. Constructing such a theory requires research that fills the gaps in our current knowledge, as well as research that spans the different aspects of cognition reviewed in this chapter. For example, Fincham, Garnier, Gano-Phillips, & Osborne (1995) have speculated that there may be important interactions between cognitive content and cognitive structure. Specifically, they suggest that the accessibility of particular cognitions may be more important for global beliefs about a relationship than for beliefs about more specific characteristics. Such ideas raise the possibility that the effects of different kinds of cognitive content may depend on how those cognitions are structured.

Similarly, research in other areas of social psychology offers evidence for interactions between cognitive content and cognitive processes. In a well-developed line of research, Dunning and his colleagues (e.g., Dunning, Leuenberger, & Sherman, 1995; Dunning & McElwee, 1995; Dunning, Meyerowitz, & Holzberg, 1989) have demonstrated that self-serving motives operate more strongly on perceptions of traits that are ambiguous than on traits that are concrete. Extrapolating to close relationships, these findings suggest that the cognitive processes reviewed here may have stronger effects on global evaluations of a relationship than on perceptions of specific aspects of a relationship. In response to negative experiences, specific perceptions of the relationship may change even when global evaluations do not. Thus, over time, specific negative perceptions may accumulate and ultimately overwhelm global satisfaction. In this way, exploring the interaction between levels of cognitive content and types of cognitive processes may help to explain how globally positive evaluations of a relationship so frequently change despite people's best efforts to maintain them.

Key Readings

Berscheid, E. (1994). Interpersonal relationships. *Annual Review of Psychology, 45,* 79–129.
Fincham, F. D., Bradbury, T. N., & Scott, C. K. (1990). Cognition in marriage. In F. D. Fincham & T. N. Bradbury (Eds.), *The psychology of marriage* (pp. 118–149). New York: Guilford.
Fletcher, G. J. O., & Fincham, F. D. (1991). *Cognition in close relationships.* Hillsdale, NJ: Erlbaum.
Fletcher, G. J. O., & Thomas, G. (1996). Close relationship lay theories: Their structure and function. In G. J. O. Fletcher & J. Fitness (Eds.), *Knowledge structures in close relationships: A social psychological perspective* (pp. 3–24). Mahwah, NJ: Erlbaum.

Acknowledgements

Preparation of this chapter was supported by a Research Development Award from the College of Letters and Science at the University of Florida, by Grant 4-4040-19900-07 from the Committee on Research of the UCLA Academic Senate, and by Grant MH 48674 from the National Institute of Mental Health. The authors wish to express their appreciation to Jennifer Brown for her assistance in gathering references, and to Nancy Frye and Lisa Neff, for helpful comments on a previous draft of this chapter.

References

Abramson, L. Y., Seligman, M. E. P., & Teasdale, J. F. (1978). Learned helplessness in humans: Critique and reformulation. *Journal of Abnormal Psychology, 87*, 49–74.

Acitelli, L. K., Kenny, D. A., & Gladstone, D. (1996). *Do relationship partners embrace the same ideals for marriage? (Yes, but their images of each other don't agree).* Paper presented at the International Network on Personal Relationships, Seattle, WA.

Afifi, W. A., & Metts, S. (1998). Characteristics and consequences of expectation violations in close relationships. *Journal of Social and Personal Relationships, 15*, 365–392.

Albert, S. (1977). Temporal comparison theory. *Psychological Review, 84*, 485–503.

Aronson, E., & Linder, D. (1965). Gain and loss of esteem as determinants of interpersonal attractiveness. *Journal of Experimental Social Psychology, 1*, 156–171.

Asch, S. E. (1946). Forming impressions of personality. *Journal of Abnormal and Social Psychology, 41*, 258–290.

Baldwin, M. W. (1992). Relational schemas and the processing of social information. *Psychological Bulletin, 112*, 461–484.

Baldwin, M. W. (1994). Primed relational schemas as a source of self-evaluative reactions. *Journal of Social and Clinical Psychology, 13*, 380–403.

Baldwin, M. W., Carrell, S. E., & Lopez, D. F. (1990). Priming relationship schemas: My advisor and the pope are watching me from the back of my mind. *Journal of Experimental Social Psychology, 26*, 435–454.

Baldwin, M. W., & Fehr, B. (1995). On the instability of attachment style ratings. *Personal Relationships, 2*, 247–261.

Baldwin, M. W., Keelan, J. P. R., Fehr, B., Enns, V., & Koh-Rangarajoo, E. (1996). Social-cognitive conceptualization of attachment working models: Availability and accessibility effects. *Journal of Personality and Social Psychology, 71*, 94–109.

Baucom, D. H. (1987). Attributions in distressed relations: How can we explain them? In S. Duck & D. Perlman (Eds.), *Intimate relationships: Development, dynamics, and deterioration* (pp. 177–206). London: Sage.

Baucom, D. H., & Epstein, N. (1989). The role of cognitive variables in the assessment and treatment of marital discord. In M. Hersen, R. M. Eisler, & P. M. Miller (Eds.), *Progress in behavior modification* (Vol. 24, pp. 223–248). Newbury Park: Sage.

Baucom, D. H., Epstein, N., Rankin, L. A., & Burnett, C. K. (1996). Assessing relationship standards: The Inventory of Specific Relationship Standards. *Journal of Family Psychology, 10*, 72–88.

Baucom, D. H., Epstein, N., Sayers, S., & Sher, T. G. (1989). The role of cognitions in marital relationships: Definitional, methodological, and conceptual issues. *Journal of Consulting and Clinical Psychology, 57*, 31–38.

Beach, S. R. H., Etherton, J., & Whitaker, D. (1995). Cognitive accessibility and sentiment override – Starting a revolution: Comment on Fincham et al. (1995). *Journal of Family Psychology, 9*, 19–23.

Berger, C. R., & Roloff, M. E. (1982). Thinking about friends and lovers: Social cognition and relational trajectories. In M. E. Roloff & C. R. Berger (Eds.), *Social cognition and communication* (pp. 151–192). Beverly Hills: Sage.

Berkowitz, L., & Devine, P. G. (1995). Has social psychology always been cognitive? What is "cognitive" anyhow? *Personality and Social Psychology Bulletin, 21*, 696–703.

Berscheid, E. (1994). Interpersonal relationships. *Annual Review of Psychology, 45*, 79–129.

Birchler, G. R., Weiss, R. L., & Vincent, J. P. (1975). Multimethod analysis of social reinforcement exchange between maritally distressed and nondistressed spouse and stranger dyads. *Journal of Personality and Social Psychology, 31,* 349–360.

Bradbury, T. N. (1989). *Cognition. emotion and interaction in distressed and non-distressed couples.* Unpublished dissertation, University of Illinois, Urbana-Champaign.

Bradbury, T. N., & Fincham, F. D. (1987). Affect and cognition in close relationships: Towards an integrative model. *Cognition and Emotion, 1,* 59–87.

Bradbury, T. N., & Fincham, F. D. (1989). Behavior and satisfaction in close relationships: Prospective mediating processes. *Review of Personality and Social Psychology, 10,* 119–143.

Bradbury, T. N., & Fincham, F. D. (1990). Attributions in marriage: Review and critique. *Psychological Bulletin, 107,* 3–33.

Bradbury, T. N., & Fincham, F. D. (1991). A contextual model for advancing the study of marital interaction. In G. J. O. Fletcher & F. D. Fincham (Eds.), *Cognition in close relationships* (pp. 127–147). Hillsdale, NJ: Erlbaum.

Bradbury, T. N., & Fincham, F. D. (1993). Assessing dysfunctional cognition in marriage: A reconsideration of the Relationship Belief Inventory. *Psychological Assessment, 5,* 92–101.

Bruner, J. S. (1957). On perceptual readiness. *Psychological Review, 64,* 123–152.

Budner, S. (1962). Intolerance of ambiguity as a personality variable. *Journal of Personality, 30,* 29–50.

Burgess, E. W., Wallin, P., & Shultz, G. D. (1954). *Courtship, engagement, and marriage.* New York: Lippincott.

Burgoon, J. K. (1993). Interpersonal expectations, expectancy violations, and emotional communication. *Journal of Language and Social Psychology, 12,* 13–21.

Buunk, B. P., & van der Eijnden, R. J. J. M. (1997). Perceived prevalence, perceived superiority, and relationship satisfaction: Most relationships are good, but ours is the best. *Personality and Social Psychology Bulletin, 23,* 219–228.

Buunk, B. P., & Van Yperen, N. W. (1989). Referential comparisons, relational comparisons and exchange orientations: Their relation to marital satisfaction. *Personality and Social Psychology Bulletin, 17,* 710–718.

Carver, C. S., & Scheier, M. F. (1990). Origins and functions of positive and negative affect: A control-process view. *Psychological Review, 97,* 19–35.

Castro-Martin, T., & Bumpass, L. (1989). Recent trends in marital disruption. *Demography, 26,* 37–51.

Cherlin, A. J. (1992). *Marriage, divorce, remarriage* (2nd ed.). Cambridge, MA: Harvard University Press.

Christensen, A., & Nies, D. C. (1980). The spouse observation checklist: Empirical analysis and critique. *American Journal of Family Therapy, 8,* 69–79.

Crockett, W. H. (1965). Cognitive complexity and impression formation. In B. A. Maher (Ed.), *Progress in experimental personality research* (Vol. 2, pp. 47–90). New York: Academic Press.

Crouse, B., Karlins, M., & Schroder, H. (1968). Conceptual complexity and marital happiness. *Journal of Marriage and the Family, 30,* 643–646.

Davila, J., Karney, B. R., & Bradbury, T. N. (1999). Attachment change processes in the early years of marriage. *Journal of Personality and Social Psychology, 76,* 783–802.

de la Ronde, C., & Swann, W. B. (1998). Partner verification: Restoring shattered images of our intimates. *Journal of Personality and Social Psychology, 75,* 374–382.

Denton, W. H., Burleson, B. R., & Sprenkle, D. H. (1995). Association of interpersonal cognitive complexity with communication skill in marriage: Moderating effects of marital distress. *Family Process, 34,* 101–111.

Doherty, W. J. (1981). Cognitive processes in intimate conflict: II. Efficacy and learned helplessness. *American Journal of Family Therapy, 9,* 35–44.

Downey, G., & Feldman, S. (1996). Implications of rejection sensitivity for intimate relationships. *Journal of Personality and Social Psychology, 70,* 1327–1343.

Downey, G., Freitas, A. L., Michaelis, B., & Khouri, H. (1998). The self-fulfilling prophecy in close relationships: Rejection sensitivity and rejection by romantic partners. *Journal of Personality and*

Social Psychology, 75, 545–560.

Dunning, D., Leuenberger, A., & Sherman, D. A. (1995). A new look at motivated inference: Are self-serving theories of success a product of motivational forces? *Journal of Personality and Social Psychology, 69,* 58–68.

Dunning, D., & McElwee, R. O. (1995). Idiosyncratic trait definitions: Implications for self-description and social judgment. *Journal of Personality & Social Psychology, 68,* 936–946.

Dunning, D., Meyerowitz, J. A., & Holzberg, A. D. (1989). Ambiguity and self-evaluation: The role of idiosyncratic trait definitions in self-serving assessments of ability. *Journal of Personality and Social Psychology, 57,* 1082–1090.

Eidelson, R. J., & Epstein, N. (1982). Cognition and relationship maladjustment: Development of a measure of dysfunctional relationship beliefs. *Journal of Consulting and Clinical Psychology, 50,* 715–720.

Ellis, A., & Grieger, R. (1977). *Rational-emotive therapy: A handbook of theory and practice.* New York: Springer.

Epstein, N., & Eidelson, R. J. (1981). Unrealistic beliefs of clinical couples: Their relationship to expectations, goals, and satisfaction. *American Journal of Family Therapy, 9,* 13–22.

Fazio, R. H. (1990). A practical guide to the use of response latency in social psychological research. *Review of Personality and Social Psychology, 11,* 74–97.

Fazio, R. H. (1995). Attitudes as object-evaluation associations: Determinants, consequences, and correlates of attitude accessibility. In R. E. Petty & J. A. Krosnik (Eds.), *Attitude strength: Antecedents and consequences* (Vol. 4, pp. 247–282). Hillsdale, NJ: Erlbaum.

Fincham, F. D. (1998). *Construct accessibility in marital research: Does it matter?* Paper presented at the Association for the Advancement of Behavior Therapy, Washington, DC.

Fincham, F. D., & Bradbury, T. N. (1987). The assessment of marital quality: A reevaluation. *Journal of Marriage and the Family, 49,* 797–809.

Fincham, F. D., Bradbury, T. N., & Grych, J. H. (1990). Conflict in close relationships: The role of intrapersonal phenomena. In S. Graham & V. S. Folkes (Eds.), *Attribution theory: Applications to achievement, mental health, and interpersonal conflict* (pp. 161–184). Hillsdale, NJ: Erlbaum.

Fincham, F. D., Bradbury, T. N., & Scott, C. K. (1990). Cognition in marriage. In F. D. Fincham & T. N. Bradbury (Eds.), *The psychology of marriage* (pp. 118–149). New York: Guilford.

Fincham, F. D., Garnier, P. C., Gano-Phillips, S., & Osborne, L. N. (1995). Preinteraction expectations, marital satisfaction, and accessibility: A new look at sentiment override. *Journal of Family Psychology, 9,* 3–14.

Fincham, F. D., & O'Leary, K. D. (1983). Causal inferences for spouse behavior in maritally distressed and nondistressed couples. *Journal of Social and Clinical Psychology, 1,* 42–57.

Fletcher, G. J. O., & Fincham, F. D. (1991). *Cognition in close relationships.* Hillsdale, NJ: Erlbaum.

Fletcher, G. J. O., & Fitness, J. (Eds.). (1996). *Knowledge structures in close relationships: A social psychological approach.* Mahwah, NJ: Erlbaum.

Fletcher, G. J. O., & Kininmonth, L. (1992). Measuring relationship beliefs: An individual differences scale. *Journal of Research in Personality, 26,* 371–397.

Fletcher, G. J. O., Rosanowski, J., & Fitness, J. (1994). Automatic processing in intimate contexts: The role of close-relationship beliefs. *Journal of Personality and Social Psychology, 67,* 888–897.

Fletcher, G. J. O., & Thomas, G. (1996). Close relationship lay theories: Their structure and function. In G. J. O. Fletcher & J. Fitness (Eds.), *Knowledge structures in close relationships: A social psychological perspective* (pp. 3–24). Mahwah, NJ: Erlbaum.

Fowers, B. J., Lyons, E. M., & Montel, K. H. (1996). Positive marital illusions: Self-enhancement or relationship enhancement? *Journal of Family Psychology, 10,* 192–208.

Harvey, J. H. (1987). Attributions in close relationships: Research and theoretical developments. *Journal of Social and Clinical Psychology, 5,* 420–434.

Helgeson, V. S. (1994). The effects of self-beliefs and relationship beliefs on adjustment to a relationship stressor. *Personal Relationships, 1,* 241–258.

Henderson, V. L., & Dweck, C. S. (1990). Motivation and achievement. In S. S. Feldman & G. R. Elliot (Eds.), *At the threshold: The developing adolescent* (pp. 308–329). Cambridge, MA: Harvard University Press.

Hendrick, C., & Hendrick, S. (1986). A theory and method of love. *Journal of Personality and Social Psychology, 50*, 392–402.

Higgins, E. T. (1997). Beyond pleasure and pain. *American Psychologist, 52*, 1280–1300.

Higgins, E. T., & King, G. (1981). Accessibility of social constructs: Information processing consequences of individual and contextual variability. In N. Cantor & J. Kihlstrom (Eds.), *Personality, cognition, and social interaction* (pp. 69–121). Hillsdale, NJ: Erlbaum.

Jacobson, N. S. (1985). The role of observational measures in behavior therapy outcome research. *Behavioral Assessment, 7*, 297–308.

Jacobson, N. S., & Moore, D. (1981). Spouses as observers of the events in their relationship. *Journal of Consulting and Clinical Psychology, 49*, 269–277.

Johnson, D. J., & Rusbult, C. E. (1989). Resisting temptation: Devaluation of alternative partners as a means of maintaining commitment in close relationships. *Journal of Personality and Social Psychology, 57*, 967–980.

Johnson, D. R., Amoloza, T. O., & Booth, A. (1992). Stability and developmental change in marital quality: A three-wave panel analysis. *Journal of Marriage and the Family, 54*, 582–594.

Karney, B. R., & Bradbury, T. N. (1995a). Assessing longitudinal change in marriage: An introduction to the analysis of growth curves. *Journal of Marriage and the Family, 57*, 1091–1108.

Karney, B. R., & Bradbury, T. N. (1995b). The longitudinal course of marital quality and stability: A review of theory, method, and research. *Psychological Bulletin, 118*, 3–34.

Karney, B. R., & Coombs, R. H. (2000). Memory bias in long-term close relationships: consistency or improvement? *Personality and Social Psychology Bulletin, 26*, 959–970.

Kelley, D. L., & Burgoon, J. K. (1991). Understanding marital satisfaction and couple type as functions of relational expectations. *Human Communication Research, 18*, 40–69.

Kelley, H. H., Berscheid, E., Christensen, A., Harvey, J. H., Huston, T. L., Levinger, G., McClintock, E., Peplau, L. A., & Peterson, D. R. (1983). Analyzing close relationships. In H. H. Kelley, E. Berscheid, A. Christensen, J. H. Harvey, T. L. Huston, G. Levinger, E. McClintock, L. A. Peplau, & D. R. Peterson (Eds.), *Close relationships* (pp. 20–67). New York: W. H. Freeman and Company.

Kelley, H. H., & Thibaut, J. W. (1978). *Interpersonal relations: A theory of interdependence*. New York: Wiley-Interscience.

Kelly, G. (1955). *The psychology of personal constructs*. New York: Norton.

Kenny, D. A., & Acitelli, L. K. (1994). Measuring similarity in couples. *Journal of Family Psychology, 8*, 417–431.

Kirkpatrick, L. A., & Hazan, C. (1994). Attachment styles and close relationships: A four-year prospective study. *Personal Relationships, 1*, 123–142.

Klohnen, E. C., & Bera, S. (1998). Behavioral and experiential patterns of avoidantly and securely attached women across adulthood: A 31-year longitudinal perspective. *Journal of Personality and Social Psychology, 74*, 211–223.

Knee, C. R. (1998). Implicit theories of relationships: Assessment and prediction of romantic relationship initiation, coping and longevity. *Journal of Personality and Social Psychology, 74*, 360–370.

Kunda, Z. (1990). The case for motivated reasoning. *Psychological Bulletin, 108*, 480–498.

Kurdek, L. A. (1992). Assumptions versus standards: The validity of two relationship cognitions in heterosexual and homosexual couples. *Journal of Family Psychology, 6*, 164–170.

Linville, P. W. (1987). Self-complexity as a cognitive buffer against stress-related illness and depression. *Journal of Personality and Social Psychology, 52*, 663–676.

Locke, H. J., & Wallace, K. M. (1959). Short marital adjustment prediction tests: Their reliability and validity. *Marriage and Family Living, 21*, 251–255.

Lydon, J. E., Meana, M., Sepinwall, D., Richards, N., & Mayman, S. (1999). The commitment calibration hypothesis: When do people devalue attractive alternatives? *Personality and Social Psychology, 25*, 152–161.

Markus, H., & Smith, J. (1981). The influence of self-schemata on the perception of others. In N. Cantor & J. F. Kihlstrom (Eds.), *Personality, cognition, and social interaction* (pp. 233–262). Hillsdale, NJ: Erlbaum.

Martin, R. (1992). Relational cognition complexity and relational communication in personal relationships. *Communication Monographs, 59,* 150–163.

Martin, R. W. (1991). Examining personal relationship thinking: The Relational Cognition Complexity Instrument. *Journal of Social and Personal Relationships, 8,* 467–480.

Miller, R. S. (1997a). Inattentive and contented: Relationship commitment and attention to alternatives. *Journal of Personality and Social Psychology, 73,* 758–766.

Miller, R. S. (1997b). We always hurt the ones we love: Aversive interactions in close relationships. In R. M. Kowalski (Ed.), *Aversive interpersonal interactions* (pp. 13–30). New York: Plenum.

Murray, S. L., & Holmes, J. G. (1993). Seeing virtues in faults: Negativity and the transformation of interpersonal narratives in close relationships. *Journal of Personality and Social Psychology, 65,* 707–722.

Murray, S. L., & Holmes, J. G. (1994). Story-telling in close relationships: The construction of confidence. *Personality and Social Psychology Bulletin, 20,* 663–676.

Murray, S. L., Holmes, J. G., & Griffm, D. W. (1996). The benefits of positive illusions: Idealization and the construction of satisfaction in close relationships. *Journal of Personality and Social Psychology, 70,* 79–98.

Neimeyer, G. J. (1984). Cognitive complexity and marital satisfaction. *Journal of Social and Clinical Psychology, 2,* 258–263.

Newman, H. M., & Langer, E. J. (1988). Investigating the development and courses of intimate relationships. In L. Y. Abramson (Ed.), *Social cognition and clinical psychology* (pp. 148–173). New York: Guilford.

Nisbett, R. E., & Ross, L. (1980). *Human inference: Strategies and shortcomings.* Englewood Cliffs, NJ: Prentice-Hall.

Pelham, B. W., & Swann, W. B. (1989). From self-conceptions to self-worth: On the sources and structure of global self-esteem. *Journal of Personality and Social Psychology, 57,* 672–680.

Pham, L. B., & Taylor, S. E. (1999). From thought to action: Effects of process- versus outcome-based mental simulations on performance. *Personality and Social Psychology, 25,* 250–260.

Raush, H. L., Barry, W. A., Hertel, R. K., & Swain, M. A. (1974). *Communication, conflict, and marriage.* San Francisco: Jossey-Bass.

Read, S. J., Vanman, E. J., & Miller, L. C. (1997). Connectionism, parallel constraint satisfaction processes, and Gestalt principles: (Re)Introducing cognitive dynamics to social psychology. *Personality and Social Psychology Review, 1,* 26–53.

Ruvolo, A. P., & Rotondo, J. L. (1998). Diamonds in the rough: Implicit personality theories and views of partner and self. *Personality and Social Psychology Bulletin, 24,* 750–758.

Ruvolo, A. P., & Veroff, J. (1997). For better or worse: Real–ideal discrepancies and the marital well-being of newlyweds. *Journal of Social and Personal Relationships, 14,* 223–242.

Sanitioso, R., Kunda, Z., & Fong, G. T. (1990). Motivated recruitment of autobiographical memories. *Journal of Personality and Social Psychology, 59,* 229–241.

Schroder, H. M. (1971). Conceptual complexity and personality organization. In H. M. Schroder & P. Suedfeld (Eds.), *Personality theory and information processing* (pp. 240–273). New York: Ronald Press.

Scott, W. A., Osgood, D. W., & Peterson, C. (1979). *Cognitive structure: Theory and measurement of individual differences.* Washington, DC: Winston and Sons.

Seligman, M. E., Abramson, L. Y., Semel, A., & Von Baeyer, C. (1979). Depressive attributional style. *Journal of Abnormal Psychology, 88,* 242–247.

Shaver, P. R., Collins, N., & Clark, C. (1996). Attachment styles and internal working models of self and relationship partners. In G. J. O. Fletcher & J. Fitness (Eds.), *Knowledge structures in close relationships: A social psychological perspective* (pp. 25–62). Mahwah, NJ: Erlbaum.

Showers, C. (1992a). Compartmentalization of positive and negative self-knowledge: Keeping bad apples out of the bunch. *Journal of Personality and Social Psychology, 62,* 1036–1049.

Showers, C. (1992b). Evaluatively integrative thinking about characteristics of the self. *Personality and Social Psychology Bulletin, 18,* 719–729.

Sillars, A. L. (1985). Interpersonal perception in relationships. In W. Ickes (Ed.), *Compatible and incompatible relationships* (pp. 277–305). New York: Springer-Verlag.

Simpson, J. A. (1987). The dissolution of romantic relationships: Factors involved in relationship stability and emotional distress. *Journal of Personality and Social Psychology, 53*, 683–692.

Snyder, M., Tanke, E. D., & Berscheid, E. (1977). Social perception and interpersonal behavior: On the self-fulfilling nature of social stereotypes. *Journal of Personality and Social Psychology, 35*, 656–666.

Spanier, G. B. (1976). Measuring dyadic adjustment: New scales for assessing the quality of marriage and similar dyads. *Journal of Marriage and the Family, 38*, 15–28.

Sprecher, S. (1999). "I love you more today than yesterday": Romantic partners' perceptions of changes in love and related affect over time. *Journal of Personality and Social Psychology, 76*, 46–53.

Sprecher, S., & Metts, S. (1989). Development of the "Romantic Beliefs Scale" and examination of the effects of gender and gender-role socialization. *Journal of Social and Personal Relationships, 6*, 387–411.

Srull, T. K., & Wyer, R S. (1989). Person memory and judgment. *Psychological Review, 96*, 58–83.

Swann, W. B. (1983). Self-verification: Bringing social reality into harmony with the self. In J. Suhls & A. G. Greenwald (Eds.), *Psychological perspectives on the self, Volume 2* (pp. 33–66). Hillsdale, NJ: Erlbaum.

Swann, W. B., De La Ronde, C., & Hixon, J. G. (1994). Authenticity and positivity strivings in marriage and courtship. *Journal of Personality and Social Psychology, 66*, 857–869.

Tangney, J. P., Niedenthal, P. M., Covert, M. V., & Barlow, D. H. (1998). Are shame and guilt related to distinct self-discrepancies? A test of Higgins' (1987) hypothesis. *Journal of Personality and Social Psychology, 75*, 256–268.

Taylor, S. E., Wood, J. V., & Lichtman, R. R. (1983). It could be worse: Selective evaluation as a response to victimization. *Journal of Social Issues, 39*, 19–40.

Tetlock, P. E. (1983). Accountability and complexity of thought. *Journal of Personality and Social Psychology, 45*, 74–83.

Tetlock, P. E., & Suedfeld, P. (1988). Integrative complexity coding of verbal behavior. In C. Antaki (Ed.), *Analyzing everyday explanation: A casebook of methods* (pp. 43–59). London: Sage.

Thagard, P. (1992). *Conceptual revolutions*. Princeton, NJ: Princeton University Press.

Thibaut, J. W., & Kelley, H. H. (1959). *The social psychology of groups*. New York: Wiley.

Thorndyke, E. L. (1920). A constant error in psychological ratings. *Journal of Applied Psychology, 4*, 25–29.

Tyndall, L. W., & Lichtenberg, J. W. (1985). Spouses' cognitive styles and marital interaction patterns. *Journal of Marital and Family Therapy, 11*, 193–202.

Vaillant, C. O., & Vaillant, G. E. (1993). Is the U-curve of marital satisfaction an illusion? A 40-year study of marriage. *Journal of Marriage and Family, 55*, 230–239.

van Lange, P. A. M., & Rusbult, C. E. (1995). My relationship is better than – and not as bad as – yours is: The perception of superiority in close relationships. *Personality and Social Psychology Bulletin, 21*, 32–44.

Vanzetti, N. A., Notarius, C. I., & NeeSmith, D. (1992). Specific and generalized expectancies in marital interaction. *Journal of Family Psychology, 6*, 171–183.

Vorauer, J. D., & Ross, M. (1993). Making mountains out of molehills: An informational goals analysis of self- and social perception. *Personality and Social Psychology Bulletin, 19*, 620–632.

Vorauer, J. D., & Ross, M. (1996). The pursuit of knowledge in close relationships: An informational goals analysis. In G. J. O. Fletcher & J. Fitness (Eds.), *Knowledge structures in close relationships: A social psychological perspective* (pp. 369–396). Mahwah, NJ: Erlbaum.

Weinstein, N. D. (1980). Unrealistic optimism about future life events. *Journal of Personality and Social Psychology, 39*, 806–820.

Weiss, R. L. (1980). Strategic behavioral marital therapy: Toward a model for assessment and intervention. In J. P. Vincent (Ed.), *Advances in family intervention, assessment, and theory* (Vol. 1, pp. 229–271). Greenwich, CT: JAI Press.

Weiss, R. L. (1984a). Cognitive and behavioral measures of marital interaction. In K. Hahlweg & N. S. Jacobson (Eds.), *Marital interaction: Analysis and modification* (pp. 232–252). New York: Guilford.

Weiss, R. L. (1984b). Cognitive and strategic interventions in behavioral marital therapy. In K. Hahlweg & N. S. Jacobson (Eds.), *Marital interaction: Analysis and modification* (pp. 337–355). New York: Guilford.

Wills, T. A., Weiss, R. L., & Patterson, G. R. (1974). A behavioral analysis of the determinants of marital satisfaction. *Journal of Consulting and Clinical Psychology, 42*, 802–811.

Wood, J. V., & Taylor, K. L. (1991). Serving self-relevant goals through social comparison. In J. Suhls & T. A. Wills (Eds.), *Social comparison: Contemporary theory and research* (pp. 23–49). Hillsdale, NJ: Erlbaum.

Chapter Three

Cognitive Representations of Attachment:
The Content and Function of Working Models

Nancy L. Collins and Lisa M. Allard

As individuals enter new relationships, they bring with them a history of social experiences and a unique set of memories, beliefs, and expectations that guide how they interact with others and how they construe their social world. Of course, these representations continue to evolve as individuals encounter new people and develop new relationships throughout their lives. Nevertheless, attachment theory suggests that cognitive models that begin their development early in one's personal history are likely to remain influential. First proposed by Bowlby (1973), and then refined by other scholars (Bretherton, 1985; Collins & Read, 1994; Main, 1991; Main, Kaplan, & Cassidy, 1985), internal "working models" of attachment are thought to be core features of personality that shape the manner in which the attachment system is expressed by directing cognitive, emotional, and behavioral response patterns in attachment-relevant contexts. Furthermore, individual differences in "attachment style" observed between children and adults are attributed to systematic differences in underlying models of self and others, and whatever continuities exist in these styles across the lifespan are proposed to be largely a function of the enduring quality of these models.

The purpose of this chapter is to provide a review and analysis of working models with regard to adult attachment. We begin by considering the content and structure of these models, including how they may differ for adults with different attachment styles. Next, we consider how these models function, and the processes through which they shape cognitive, emotional, and behavioral response patterns in adulthood.

Preparation of this chapter was supported by National Science Foundation Grant No. SBR-9870524 to the first author. Please address correspondence to Nancy L. Collins, Department of Psychology, University of California, Santa Barbara, CA 93106-9660. Electronic mail may be sent via internet to ncollins@psych.ucsb.edu.

The Content and Structure of Working Models

What are working models? What are they composed of? How are they structured in memory? These are all critical questions for attachment scholars. To answer these questions, we begin by briefly reviewing the major propositions outlined by Bowlby and others on the early development and nature of working models.[1] Our goal is not to review the developmental literature, but to use that literature as a point of departure for understanding how working models may be characterized in adulthood. Next, we specify the components of working models and discuss how these components can be useful for mapping out differences in adult attachment styles. Finally, we discuss how working models are likely to be structured in memory, focusing on some important issues regarding the complex and multidimensional nature of attachment representations.

Working models from infancy to adulthood

Bowlby (1973) used the term "working models" to describe the internal mental representations that children develop of the world and of significant people within it, including the self. These representations evolve out of experiences with attachment figures and center around the regulation and fulfillment of attachment needs – namely, the maintenance of proximity to a nurturing caregiver and the regulation of felt security (Bretherton, 1985; Sroufe & Waters, 1977). Of course, not all infants will have access to caretakers who respond to their attachment needs in a consistent and loving manner. Thus, the quality of the infant–caretaker relationship, and hence the nature of one's working models, are expected to be largely determined by the caregiver's emotional availability and responsiveness to the child's needs. Working models are hypothesized to include two complementary components, one referring to the attachment figure and the other referring to the self. The former characterizes whether the caregiver will be available, sensitive, and responsive when needed, and the latter characterizes the self as either worthy or unworthy of love and care. For example, children whose caretakers are sensitive and consistently available when needed should develop a working model in which others are characterized as responsive and trustworthy and the self is characterized as lovable and worthy of care. In contrast, children who have inconsistent or rejecting caregivers are likely to develop a working model in which others are characterized as unresponsive and the self is characterized either as unworthy of care or as self-sufficient and not in need of such care.

Early working models are thus composed of schemata that reflect a child's attempts to gain comfort and security along with the typical outcome of those attempts (Main, Kaplan, & Cassidy, 1985). That is, working models contain a summary of the child's interactions with the caregiving environment and are expected to be fairly accurate reflections of social reality as experienced by the developing child (Bowlby, 1973). One central aspect of working models adopted by Bowlby is the idea that working models are used to predict the behavior of others and to plan one's own behavior in social interaction. Working models shape the nature in which the attachment behavioral system is expressed, and are dynamic and functional. For this reason, individual differences in infant *behavioral* patterns, as displayed in diagnostic situations, are used to infer underlying differences in internal working models (Main et al., 1985), and serve as the basis for categorizing infants into secure and various forms of insecure attachment styles (Ainsworth, Blehar, Waters, & Wall, 1978).

In early childhood, attachment models appear to be relatively open to change if the quality of caregiving changes (Egeland & Farber, 1984; Thompson, Lamb, & Estes, 1982; Vaughn, Egeland, Sroufe & Waters, 1979). However, given a fairly consistent pattern of caregiving throughout childhood and adolescence, working models are expected to become solidified through repeated experience and increasingly generalized over time. Thus, what begins as a schema of a specific child–caretaker relationship results in the formation of more abstract representations of oneself and the social world (Shaver, Collins, & Clark, 1996). Once formed, these representations are likely to operate automatically and unconsciously, thereby making them resistant to dramatic change (Bowlby, 1979). As such, working models of self and others that take root in childhood are carried forward into adulthood where they continue to shape social perception and behavior in close relationships.

On the basis of this assumption, attachment theory has become a widely used model for understanding interpersonal behavior and romantic experience in adult close relationships. Inspired by Hazan and Shaver's (1987) seminal paper on romantic love as an attachment process, much of the empirical work in social psychology has focused on individual differences in adult attachment style. These styles reflect chronic differences in the way individuals think, feel, and behave in close relationships and they are believed to be rooted in systematic differences in working models of self and others.

Adult attachment researchers typically define four prototypic attachment styles (secure, preoccupied, dismissing, fearful) derived from two underlying dimensions – *anxiety* and *avoidance* (Bartholomew & Horowitz, 1991; Brennan, Clark, & Shaver, 1998; Fraley & Waller, 1998). The anxiety dimension refers to one's sense of self-worth and acceptance (vs. rejection) by others, and is believed to reflect the positive or negative nature of one's model of self. The avoidance dimension refers to the degree to which one approaches (vs. avoids) intimacy and interdependence with others and is believed to reflect the positive or negative nature of one's model of others. *Secure* adults are low in both attachment-related anxiety and avoidance; they are comfortable with intimacy, willing to rely on others for support, and confident that they are valued by others. *Preoccupied* adults (also called *anxious-ambivalent*) are high in anxiety and low in avoidance; they have an exaggerated desire for closeness and dependence, coupled with a heightened concern about being rejected. *Dismissing avoidant* individuals are low in attachment-related anxiety but high in avoidance; they view close relationships as relatively unimportant and they value independence and self-reliance. Finally, *fearful avoidant* adults are high in both attachment anxiety and avoidance; although they desire close relationships and the approval of others, they avoid intimacy because they fear being rejected. Although this four-category typology (Bartholomew & Horowitz, 1991) is widely used, many attachment researchers rely on the original three-category typology (Hazan & Shaver, 1987), which includes a single avoidant category.

Attachment styles represent theoretical prototypes that individuals can approximate to varying degrees (Bartholomew & Horowitz, 1991), and they are most often assessed through self-report scales or semi-structured interviews.[2] Although there are a number of unresolved issues concerning how best to conceptualize and measure individual differences in adult attachment style, attachment researchers agree that these styles are rooted in fundamental differences between people in the content and nature of their working models of self and others. Until recently, however, the concept of working models has remained vague and ill-defined, and the precise mechanisms through which they operate have not been well understood. Fortunately, attachment scholars have begun to develop more detailed theories about the nature of working models, and have employed more sophisticated techniques for studying them (e.g., Baldwin, Keelan, Fehr, Enns, & Koh-Rangarajoo, 1996; Collins & Read, 1994; Shaver, Collins, & Clark, 1996). We begin our discussion of working models by identifying their components and suggesting how these components can be useful for mapping out differences in adult attachment styles.

Building blocks of working models

Internal working models of attachment are similar in many ways to other cognitive structures studied by social psychologists, including schemas, scripts, and prototypes. Like all such constructs, working models are hypothetical structures that are presumed to be stored in long-term memory. They organize past experience and provide a framework for understanding new experiences and guiding social interaction.

Although working models share many features with other social-cognitive structures, they are also unique in some respects (Shaver, Collins, & Clark, 1996). First, unlike traditional approaches to schemas, which tend to focus on semantic knowledge and verbal propositions, attachment theory places greater emphasis on the representation of motivational elements (needs and goals) and behavioral tendencies. Second, because working models are formed in the context of emotional experiences and center around the fulfillment of emotional needs, they are more heavily affect-laden than other knowledge structures typically studied by cognitive social psychologists. Third, working models differ from other schemas in that they are explicitly interpersonal and relational in nature (Baldwin, 1992). Finally, working models of attachment are thought to be broader, more multidimensional, and more complex than other social representations typically studied by social psychologists.

What are working models composed of? Because working models are built within the context of the attachment behavioral system, they should contain the history of experiences of that system, beliefs about the self and others based on those experiences, and the resulting motivational and behavioral strategies that have evolved for the expression of this system. Collins and Read (1994) propose that working models include four interrelated components: (1) memories of attachment-related experience; (2) beliefs, attitudes, and expectations about self and others in relation to attachment; (3) attachment-related goals and needs; and (4) strategies and plans associated with achieving attachment goals. Below we describe the four components of working models in greater detail. In doing so, we suggest some ways in which the contents of each might differ for adults with different attachment styles and we review recent empirical work where available.

Attachment-related memories.   An important component of working models is memories and accounts of attachment-related experiences. These should include not only representations of specific interactions and concrete episodes, but also constructions placed on those episodes, such as appraisals of experience and explanations for one's own and others' behavior. Because these memories should be based, in part, on actual experience, we would expect that secure and insecure adults would represent their attachment experiences differently. In general, secure adults should be more likely than insecure adults to report positive relationship experiences with key attachment figures (parents, peers, romantic partners). Some preliminary evidence for this idea has been obtained in studies involving retrospective reports of relationships with parents. For example, Hazan and Shaver (1987) found that secure adults remembered their relationships with their parents as more affectionate and warm than did avoidant or anxious adults; avoidant adults were especially likely to report their mothers as having been cold and rejecting (see also Feeney & Noller, 1990).

More recently, Mikulincer and his colleagues have used a response latency paradigm to explore attachment style differences in the cognitive accessibility of emotional memories. In one study (Mikulincer & Orbach, 1995), young adults were asked to recall childhood experiences in which they felt a particular emotion (anger, sadness, anxiety, and happiness). The time taken to retrieve each episode was then recorded. When comparisons were made across groups, avoidant adults showed the lowest accessibility (slowest responding) to sadness and anxiety memories, whereas anxious-ambivalent adults showed the highest accessibility (fastest responding). When comparisons were made within groups, secure individuals were faster to retrieve positive memories than negative memories, whereas anxious-ambivalent individuals showed the opposite pattern. In another study, Mikulincer (1998b, Study 1) asked young adults to recall a series of positive and negative experiences related to trust (e.g., "remember a time when your mother behaved in such a way that she increased the trust you felt toward her"). Secure individuals were quicker to retrieve positive trust-related memories whereas avoidant and anxious adults were quicker to retrieve negative memories.

Attachment-related beliefs, attitudes, and expectations.   A person's knowledge about self, others, and relationships is likely to be extremely complex in adulthood. It will include not only static *beliefs* (e.g., "relationships require a lot of work"), but also *attitudes* (e.g., "relationships are not worth the effort") and *expectations* (e.g., "I am unlikely to find someone who will love me completely"). This knowledge is abstracted, in part, from concrete experiences during childhood, adolescence, and adulthood, and may be altered through reflection and reevaluation. Beliefs about oneself and others can also vary in level of abstraction. Some will be associated with particular attachment figures (e.g., "my mother is emotionally distant"), others will be broader generalizations about relationships (e.g., "friends can be counted on for support") or about people (e.g., "people are trustworthy").

Although empirical work is still in its early stages, important links have been found between self-reported attachment style and general beliefs about the self and the social world. For example, Hazan and Shaver (1987) reported that secure adults viewed themselves as having fewer self-doubts and as being better liked by others compared to anxious and avoidant adults. They were also more likely to think that other people are generally well-intentioned and good-hearted. In a more extensive study, Collins and Read (1990) found that individuals with a secure attachment style viewed people in general as trustworthy, dependable, and altruistic. Anxious adults thought that others were complex and difficult to understand and that people have little control over the outcomes in their lives. Avoidant adults reported largely negative beliefs about human nature; they were suspicious of human motives, viewed others as not trustworthy and not dependable, and doubted the honesty and integrity of social role agents such as parents. Important differences were also found in participants' self-concepts. Secure adults were higher in self-worth, saw themselves as more confident in social situations, more interpersonally oriented, and more assertive as compared to anxious individuals. Avoidant individuals did not differ from the secure group in their self-worth or assertiveness, but they did view themselves as less confident in social situations and as not interpersonally oriented.

In addition to identifying the content of one's beliefs about self and others, secure and insecure adults are also likely to differ in the way their social knowledge is organized. Consistent with this idea, Clark, Shaver, and Calverley (1994; described in Shaver & Clark, 1996) found that adults with different attachment styles differed in the degree to which positive and negative features of the self were central or peripheral in their self-schema. For instance, although secure adults reported both positive and negative features in their self-concept, their positive features were more central and their negative features were more peripheral; fearful avoidant individuals showed the opposite pattern. In an impressive series of studies, Mikulincer (1995) provided further evidence for attachment style differences in the structure of self-models by using a variety of measures developed in the self-concept literature. Among the many interesting findings, secure participants were found to have more balanced, complex, and coherent self-structures than anxious and avoidant participants. Secure individuals also reported fewer discrepancies between their *actual* self and their *ideal* self, and between their actual self and their *ought* self.

Finally, Baldwin, Fehr, Keedian, Seidel, and Thomson (1993) have shown that attachment-related beliefs may be stored as "if–then" propositions that reflect a person's expectations about their social interactions with others (e.g., "If I trust others, they will hurt me"). In one study, they asked participants to consider a number of hypothetical, attachment-relevant behaviors (e.g., "If I depend on my partner") and then to rate the likelihood that their partner would respond in various positive and negative ways (e.g., "then my partner will leave me" or "then my partner will support me"). Results indicated that secure participants held more positive if–then expectancies than did avoidant or anxious-ambivalent participants. In a second study, they used a response latency paradigm and a lexical decision task to extend their findings beyond self-reports and to examine spreading activation between elements of relational schemas. Reaction times provided further evidence that insecure adults hold more pessimistic interpersonal expectations than secure adults. For example, when participants with an avoidant attachment style were given a prime that involved trusting a romantic partner, they showed particularly quick reactions to the negative outcome word "hurt."

Response latency paradigms, such as those used by Baldwin et al. and by Mikulincer and his colleagues are especially useful because they provide opportunities to uncover implicit or unconscious aspects of working models that might not be accessible through self-report. Other methods for investigating implicit mental representations that are being developed in the social cognition literature (e.g., Greenwald, McGhee, & Schwartz, 1998) may also prove useful for attachment scholars.

Attachment-related goals and needs.   Although the attachment behavioral system serves the broad goal of maintaining felt-security, a person's history of achieving or failing to achieve this goal is expected to result in a characteristic hierarchy of attachment-related social and emotional needs. For example, individuals differ in the extent to which they are motivated to develop intimate relationships, avoid rejection, maintain privacy, seek approval from others, and so on. As such, the goal structures of secure and insecure individuals should differ considerably. For example, secure adults are likely to desire intimate relationships with others and, within relationships, to seek a balance of closeness and autonomy. Preoccupied (anxious-ambivalent) adults also desire close relationships but their additional need for approval and fear of rejection may lead them to seek high levels of intimacy and lower levels of autonomy. Avoidant adults are guided by a need to maintain distance; dismissing avoidants seek to limit intimacy in the service of satisfying their desire for autonomy and independence, but fearful avoidants do so to avoid rejection (Bartholomew & Horowitz, 1991). Avoidant adults may also place greater weight on non-attachment-related goals, such as achievement in school or in a career (Brennan & Bosson, 1998; Brennan & Morris, 1997; Hazan & Shaver, 1990). Individuals with different attachment styles may also differ in the extent to which certain goals are salient or chronically accessible. For example, although most people are presumed to have a need for acceptance by others, the chronic accessibility of this need should differ considerably between people, being most chronically activated for preoccupied adults.

There is little empirical work that directly assesses the goal structures of adults with different attachment styles, but a few studies point to some potentially important patterns. Collins and Allard (1999) asked participants in dating relationships to rate the importance of their romantic partner fulfilling specific attachment-related needs (e.g., "how important is it that your partner comfort you when you are feeling down?"). They found that attachment-related anxiety was positively associated with importance ratings whereas avoidance was negatively associated with these ratings.

In a series of studies, Mikulincer (1998b) found evidence of attachment style differences in the accessibility of interpersonal goals related to trust. In one study (Study 2) he asked young adults to describe the benefits associated with trusting one's partner. These narratives were then coded for the presence of specific trust-related goals. Secure adults were most likely to spontaneously mention increases in intimacy as a trust-related goal; anxious-ambivalent adults were most likely to mention increases in security; and avoidant adults were most likely to mention increases in the attainment of control. In another study (Study 4), Mikulincer used a lexical decision task to explore the accessibility of trust-related goals. Following a trust-related prime, anxious-ambivalent individuals reacted more quickly to the word "security," whereas avoidant adults reacted more quickly to the word "control."

Plans and strategies.   Plans and strategies are organized sequences of behavior aimed at the attainment of some goal. Individuals are expected to have encoded as part of their working models a set of plans and strategies for regulating their attachment-related social and emotional needs, and these strategies should be contingent upon a person's history of experiences with key attachment figures (Main, 1981). Thus important attachment-style differences are expected in one's plans and strategies for managing socio-emotional needs and goals and maintaining felt security. Among many behavioral strategies, this should include strategies for regulating emotional distress (Kobak & Sceery, 1988), obtaining comfort when needed, maintaining autonomy, developing intimacy with others, giving comfort to others, and so on.

Identifying individual differences in plans and strategies poses some difficulties because such representations are likely to be stored as procedural knowledge, which may be difficult to articulate and which may operate largely outside of awareness. One way to identify different plans and strategies is to examine how individuals behave in response to the *same* social stimuli. For example, in a series of studies, Collins (Collins, 1996; Collins & Allard, 1999) asked respondents to imagine a series of attachment-relevant events in which their partner behaved in a potentially negative manner (e.g., "imagine that your partner didn't respond when you tried to cuddle"). Respondents were then asked to describe in detail how they would behave in response to each event. Content coding of these descriptions revealed important individual differences in behavioral strategies. Relative to insecure adults, secure adults tended to choose behavioral strategies that were less punishing toward their partner and less likely to lead to conflict. (These patterns remained even after controlling for relationship satisfaction.) In another study, Ognibene and Collins (1998) asked young adults to describe how they would cope with a series of hypothetical stressful life events. Results revealed systematic difference in the coping styles of adults with different attachment styles. For example, secure and preoccupied adults were more likely than avoidant adults to seek social support as a coping strategy.

Another useful research strategy is to employ response latency paradigms to uncover differences in the *accessibility* of specific behavioral strategies. For example, Mikulincer (1998b, Study 5) used a lexical decision task to study attachment style differences in the way individuals cope with trust violations. When participants were presented with a prime that involved a violation of trust, secure and anxious-ambivalent adults responded more quickly than avoidant adults to the word "talk," and avoidant adults responded more quickly to the word "escape".

Of course, another method for identifying differences in plans and strategies is to observe actual behavior in attachment-relevant contexts. Although observational research is still somewhat rare in the adult attachment literature, a growing number of studies reveal differences in a variety of attachment-relevant behaviors including support seeking and caregiving (Collins & Feeney, 2000; Simpson, Rholes, & Nelligan, 1992), conflict and problem solving (Feeney, Noller, & Callan, 1994; Simpson, Rholes, & Phillips, 1996), self-disclosure (Mikulincer & Nachshon, 1991), and responses to separation from one's partner (Fraley & Shaver, 1998).

Summary.   In summary, internal working models are attachment-related knowledge structures concerning the self and the social world that include cognitive as well as affective components. They are developed through attachment experience and stored in long-term memory. Working models are composed of a number of elements including episodic memories, beliefs, goals, and plans. Finally, individual differences in attachment styles can be defined in terms of characteristic configurations of these various components. In the section that follows, we continue our discussion of working models by considering how multiple models may be structured in memory.

The structure of working models: a complex representational network

There is a strong tendency to discuss working models and attachment style in the singular, as if an individual can have only one. However, there are good reasons to question this assumption. Because adult representations of attachment are based on a variety of relationships both within and outside the family, they are apt to be complex and multifaceted (Baldwin et al., 1996; Bretherton, Biringen, Ridgeway, Maslin, & Sherman, 1989; Crittenden, 1990; George & Solomon, 1989). Moreover, it is unreasonable to assume that a single, undifferentiated working model can effectively guide the full range of attachment behavior in adulthood. Multiple models of attachment are necessary for adults to function adaptively in diverse circumstances and to satisfy their attachment goals across a variety of relationships.

For these reasons, Collins and Read (1994) have suggested that adult representations of attachment are best considered as a network of interconnected models that may be organized as a *default hierarchy*. At the top of the hierarchy is the default model that corresponds to the most general representations about people and the self, abstracted from a history of relationship experiences with caretakers and peers. This default model can apply to a wide range of relationships and situations, although it may not describe any one of them very well. Further down in the hierarchy are models that correspond to particular kinds of relationships (parent–child relationships, friendships, romantic relationships), and lowest in the hierarchy are the most specific models corresponding to particular partners and particular relationships ("my husband Michael," "my friend Sandra"). It is important to note that models within the network are probably linked through a rich set of associations and are likely to share many elements. Thus, although each model may be somewhat distinct, we would expect a fair amount of overlap between various models.

Consistent with these ideas, a number of recent studies provide evidence for the multidimensional nature of attachment representations in adulthood. Bartholomew and Horowitz (1991, Study 2) compared adult representations of attachment with parents and with peers using a set of parallel interviews. Scores derived from the two interviews were only moderately correlated with each other, and each uniquely contributed to the prediction of interpersonal problems involving warmth. Similar findings were obtained by Crowell and Owens (1996) who developed an interview to assess security of attachment in a specific romantic relationship (the Current Relationship Interview, CRI). The CRI was designed to parallel the Adult Attachment Interview (AAI; George, Kaplan, & Main, 1984), which assesses adults' representations of their attachment experiences with parents. In a sample of young adults who were about to be married, they found a moderate correlation between security scores on the CRI and the AAI. Furthermore, in a series of studies (summarized in Crowell, Fraley, & Shaver, 1999) in which both assessments were used to predict relationship functioning over time, each assessment accounted for unique variance in outcomes. For example, premarital CRI scores uniquely predicted feelings of commitment, intimacy, and aggression 18 months later, and AAI scores uniquely predicted intimacy, threats to abandon the partner, and partner's physical aggression.

Evidence for the multidimensional nature of attachment representations has also been found using self-report measures of attachment style. Baldwin et al. (1996, Study 1) asked young adults to report their general attachment style in romantic relationships and their attachment orientation in their ten most significant relationships. Consistent with the idea of multiple models, the vast majority of participants reported two or more different attachment patterns across their ten relationships. At the same time, however, people with different general styles reported more individual relationships that matched their general style. For example, compared to their secure counterparts, anxious-ambivalent adults were more likely to report having experienced relationships that matched the anxious-ambivalent prototype. These data are consistent with the idea that individuals possess a complex associative network of working models that contains abstract representations (a general model or style) as well as specific exemplars (relationship-specific models or orientations). Further support for this idea was provided in a study by Beer and Kihlstrom (1999) in which they used a cognitive priming procedure to examine how various working models are encoded in long-term memory. Cognitive models of relationships with parents showed evidence of being stored in terms of abstract traits, whereas models of a current relationship showed evidence of being more episodic and autobiographical.

Given the multidimensional nature of attachment representations, how can we predict which model(s) will be activated and used to guide social perception and behavior? As summarized by Collins and Read (1994), activation is likely to depend on characteristics of the models themselves and features of the prevailing social situation. Some models will be more accessible than others, where accessibility depends on a variety of factors including the amount of experience on which the model is based, the number of times it has been applied in the past, and the density of its connections to other knowledge structures. This implies that general working models (which are abstracted from a history of relationship experiences and are likely to be densely connected) are likely to be highly accessible. Consistent with this speculation, Baldwin et al. (1996, Study 2) asked people with different chronic attachment styles (general orientations in romantic relationships) to think of *specific* relationships that matched each of the three attachment style prototypes. Participants then rated how easy it was for them to think of these specific exemplars. Although most participants reported relationships that matched all three attachment prototypes, the ease with which a person could generate a specific exemplar was predicted by their general attachment style. For example, relative to their secure counterparts, adults who rated themselves as avoidant (in general) found it much easier to think of specific relationships in which they were avoidant. Baldwin et al. suggest that although most individuals possess multiple attachment models (or *relational schemas*) a person's general attachment style may represent their best-articulated and most accessible knowledge structure.

Whether or not features of the situation match features of the working model will also affect its likelihood of use. Among the features that should be important are characteristics of the interaction partner, the nature of the relationship, and the goals that are salient in the situation. For instance, characteristics of the interaction partner such as gender and physical appearance should be important cues in matching. In support of this idea, Collins and Read (1990) have shown that in romantic relationships, one's model of the opposite sex parent is a better predictor of aspects of the relationship than is the model of the same sex parent. Presumably the nature of one's current relationship should also be an important cue. For example, models based on relationships with parents may be more relevant when interacting with one's own children than when interacting with one's peers. This functional specificity was illustrated in a study by Kobak and Sceery (1988) in which young adults' representations of their childhood experiences with parents predicted the extent to which they perceived that social support was currently available from their family, but did not predict their judgments about available support from their friends.

The specificity of the match should also be important in determining which models are activated and used. All other things being equal, more specific models should be preferred because they provide more accurate guides for responding to particular partners and relationships. However, a recent study in our lab suggests that the tendency to prefer specific models may differ for people with different attachment styles (Collins & Allard, 1999). We asked respondents to provide attributions for a series of potentially negative partner behaviors. The attributional patterns of secure adults were strongly predicted by their relationship-specific expectations (a relationship-specific working model), such that individuals in better functioning relationships endorsed more benign attributions, whereas those in poorly functioning relationships endorsed more negative attributions. In contrast, insecure adults tended to endorse the negative attributions regardless of the quality of their current relationship. These preliminary findings suggest that adults with insecure chronic models may find it difficult to set aside their doubts and may rely on their pessimistic chronic models even when a more positive relationship-specific model is available.

As the above discussion makes clear, attachment researchers will need to be more precise in specifying which aspect of the attachment network they are concerned with in a given line of research. Just as it is incorrect to speak of a single model of self or others, it may also be incorrect to speak of a single corresponding attachment style. Although this idea has not been made explicit in the literature, it is already reflected in the various approaches used to measure individual differences in adult attachment styles (e.g., Bartholomew & Horowitz, 1991; Brennan, Clark, & Shaver, 1998; George, Kaplan, & Main, 1984; Kobak & Hazan, 1991; Crowell & Owens, 1996). These approaches differ in the particular content that they target (e.g., parents, peers, romantic partners), and in the general versus specific nature of that content (e.g., relationships in general versus one specific relationship). We believe that no one approach is more or less "correct," but that each approach assesses a different aspect of the attachment network. Nevertheless, the notion that someone has a particular attachment "style" in close relationships implies that they are predisposed to think, feel, and behave in certain ways in all such relationships. Thus, Collins and Read (1994) suggest that the term "attachment style" should be reserved for models that are more general (abstract) and chronic. The term "attachment quality" can then be used to describe the model one develops within a specific close relationship: a *relational schema* in Baldwin's (1992) terms. A more detailed understanding of the interrelationships between attachment style and attachment quality will be facilitated by empirical studies that employ multiple methods of assessing adult attachment orientations.

Summary.   In summary, individuals possess multiple models of attachment that differ in their level of specificity and accessibility, and which may be structured in memory as a hierarchical network that provides maximum flexibility in regulating attachment needs. In the next section of the chapter, we turn our attention to the mechanisms through which working models guide social perception and behavior. In doing so, we limit our discussion to a consideration of attachment style as studied by most social psychologists, who define attachment styles in terms of one's general orientation toward intimate relationships. However, the processes we describe below should also be applicable to relationship-specific working models.

The Functions of Working Models in Adulthood

Every situation we meet with in life is construed in terms of the representational models we have of the world about us and of ourselves. Information reaching us through our sense organs is selected and interpreted in terms of those models, its significance for us and for those we care for is evaluated in terms of them, and plans of action conceived and executed with those models in mind. On how we interpret and evaluate each situation, moreover, turns also how we feel.

(Bowlby, 1980, p. 229)

As reflected in Bowlby's statement, working models are central components of the attachment behavioral system that are expected to play an important role in shaping how individuals operate in their relationships and how they construe their social world. Empirical support for this assumption is beginning to accumulate as a growing body of research finds that adults with different attachment styles differ markedly in the nature and quality of their close relationships (see Feeney, 1999, for a comprehensive review of this literature). Although the correlational nature of these studies prevents us from drawing firm conclusions about causality, the underlying assumption throughout this research is that working models of attachment directly contribute to relationship outcomes by shaping cognitive, emotional, and behavioral response patterns. Unfortunately, the specific mechanisms through which this occurs remain poorly understood. In this section of the chapter, we turn our attention to this issue by considering some of the important ways in which working models function. In doing so, we use current research and theory in cognitive social psychology as a guide for suggesting how each process will be shaped by working models, and we review attachment research where available.

Framework for studying the functions of working models

How do working models operate? One way to approach this question is to consider working models of attachment as part of a broader system of cognitive, affective, and behavioral processes that enable people to make sense of their experiences and to function in ways that meet their personal needs. Based on existing research and theory in personality and social psychology, Collins and Read (1994) proposed a very general model for understanding how such a system might operate. They argue that working models of attachment are highly accessible cognitive constructs that will be activated automatically in memory whenever attachment-relevant events occur. Once activated, they are predicted to have a direct impact on both the cognitive processing of social information and on emotional appraisal. The outcome of these processes will then determine one's choice of behavioral strategies.

In short, the impact of working models on *behavior* in any given situation is likely to be mediated by the *cognitive interpretation* of the situation along with the person's *emotional response*. Moreover, we need not assume that people are consciously directing these processes, or even that they are aware of them. In fact, we expect that much of this system will operate "automatically"; that is, spontaneously, with little effort, and outside of awareness (Bargh & Chartrand, 1999).

This model is intended to be a general framework for exploring a number of more specific cognition–emotion–behavior linkages. Our task in the following sections is to specify these links in greater detail. To accomplish this, we discuss each component separately, keeping in mind the broader model that ties them together.

Cognitive response patterns

Working models of attachment contain a rich network of memories, beliefs, and goals that should play a critical role in shaping how individuals think about themselves and their relationships. Although cognitive processes are only just beginning to be studied in the adult attachment literature, support for these ideas is provided by a large body of research in social psychology on the role of prior knowledge in social information processing and social judgment. Empirical work in social psychology clearly demonstrates that social perception is heavily influenced by top-down, theory-driven processes in which existing goals, schemas, and expectations shape the way people view new information. Although most of this research involves thinking about strangers, these processes are increasingly being explored in the context of close relationships (e.g., Fletcher & Fincham, 1991; Fletcher & Fitness, 1996; Martin, 1991; Holmes & Rempel, 1989). Below, we consider three processes that should be strongly influenced by working models and should have important implications for personal and interpersonal functioning: (a) selective attention, (b) memory, and (c) social construal.

Selective attention.   Empirical as well as anecdotal evidence indicates that two people viewing or experiencing the same event rarely agree about what took place. This tendency toward divergent perceptions suggests that perceivers are predisposed to attend to particular features of their environment and to disregard others. Indeed, Bargh (1984) concludes that social perception "involves an interaction between the environmental stimuli that are currently present and the individual's readiness to perceive some over others" (p. 15). But what determines a person's readiness to attend to particular information? One important factor is one's currently active goals. Goals and personal needs provide an orienting framework for the direction of cognitive resources, and evidence indicates that people become highly sensitized to goal-related stimuli (Srull & Wyer, 1986). Individuals are also more likely to notice information that can be easily assimilated into their existing knowledge about self and others (Cohen, 1981; Markus, 1977; Roskos-Ewoldsen & Fazio, 1992), especially when that knowledge is chronically accessible (Bargh, 1984; Higgins, King, & Mavin, 1982). As a result, people are apt to attend to information that is relevant to their goals and consistent with their existing beliefs or attitudes about self and others.

This literature suggests that working models of attachment will play an important role in directing cognitive resources in attachment-relevant situations. For example, anxious-ambivalent (preoccupied) adults are expected to have "seeking approval" and "avoiding rejection" as chronically active goals. As a result, they are likely to have a threat- or rejection-oriented attentional focus that keeps them vigilant for signs of disapproval by others. In addition, because they expect the worst, they will easily notice evidence that confirms their fears. The attentional focus of avoidant adults should be characterized by a very different pattern. Their motivation to maintain autonomy should make them highly sensitive to signs of intrusion or control by others. In addition, their desire to minimize attachment concerns will tend to direct their attention away from features of the environment that make attachment needs salient (Fraley, Davis, & Shaver, 1998). In sum, at the earliest stages in the perceptual process attachment style differences in working models will direct attention toward certain features of the environment and away from others. As a result, information available for further processing may tend to be biased in a goal-relevant and expectation-consistent manner.

Although these specific hypotheses have not yet been tested, a study by Mikulincer (1997) provides preliminary evidence that attachment-related goals can shape information seeking. In this study (1997, Study 2), participants were asked to evaluate a new product and were given the opportunity to select how much information they wanted to hear about the product. In addition, they were told that time spent listening to this information would affect how much time they had left for a second task. Half of the participants were told that this second task was a social interaction, and the other half were told that it was a sensory test. Within-group comparisons revealed that avoidant adults selected more information during the first task when the second task was social than non-social; anxious-ambivalent adults showed the opposite pattern. In contrast, secure adults requested the same amount of information regardless of the second task. These data suggest that insecure participants allocated their attention in ways that served their personal goals. Anxious-ambivalent adults – who value social connection and social approval – limited their attention to a competing task when it interfered with a social task. In contrast, avoidant adults – who value social distance – increased their attention to a non-social task, thereby decreasing their available attention for a social task.

Memory.   One of the most robust findings in the social cognitive literature is that existing knowledge structures shape what gets stored in memory, and what is later recalled or reconstructed. In general, aspects of experience that can be interpreted in terms of easily accessible concepts are more likely to be encoded into memory than aspects that cannot be easily assimilated (Srull & Wyer, 1989). As a result, strong, well-established schemas bias memory toward schema-relevant, and often schema-consistent, information (Hastie, 1981; Higgins & Bargh, 1987). In addition, once information is stored in memory, further processing gives consistent material an advantage over inconsistent material (Srull & Wyer, 1989; Tesser, 1978).

While existing representations improve memory for relevant features of an experience, they may also lead one to recall or reconstruct features that never took place. One reason for this effect is that, as memory for an event fades over time, people may rely more on their generic schemas and less on the particular encounter (Graesser & Nakamura, 1982). As a result, people will sometimes reconstruct experiences and "remember" schema-consistent material that was never encountered. For example, Andersen and her colleagues (Andersen & Cole, 1990; Andersen, Glassman, Chen, & Cole, 1995) have shown that people can mistakenly remember characteristics of a new person when that person resembles someone close to them.

Research on schema-driven memory has clear implications for working models of attachment. Because their social knowledge and prior experiences differ, adults with different attachment styles will be predisposed to remember different kinds of information. In general, individuals should be more likely to store, recall, and reconstruct attachment-related experiences in ways that are consistent with their existing models of self and others.[3]

Support for this idea was provided in a series of studies conducted by Mikulincer and Horesh (1999), who adapted Andersen's (Andersen & Cole, 1990) transference paradigm to explore how models of *self* influence memory for other people. In two studies, participants were presented with descriptions of targets persons who were systematically varied (idiographically) to be similar to or different from the participants' actual self and unwanted self. The ease with which the targets were recalled (Study 2), and false-positive memory intrusions (recalling a characteristic that was not actually presented; Study 3), were measured. Both studies revealed that insecure adults projected their own self-models onto their memory for new people. Avoidant individuals found it easier to remember the target who resembled their *unwanted* self, and they also made more false-positive memory errors for that target. Anxious-ambivalent individuals found it easier to remember the target who resembled their *actual* self, and they also made more false-positive errors for that target. Secure adults showed no memory biases. Mikulincer and Horesh (1999) suggest that these patterns may result from "defensive-projection" on the part of avoidant adults (heightened awareness of a feared self) and "projective identification" on the part of anxious-ambivalent adults (similarity in the search for connection to others).

Mikulincer and Horesh's findings raise the possibility that attachment style differences in memory may be partly due to schema-driven processes and partly due to strategic or motivational processes. Further support for these dual processes is provided by Miller and Noirot's (1999) study in which participants were asked to remember a story after being primed with a supportive or a rejecting friendship memory. Secure attachment was associated with better recall of positive story events, but only when participants were primed by rejecting memories prior to reading the story. Fearful attachment was associated with better recall of negative story events regardless of the prime. These data suggest that secure adults may have been motivated to attend to and remember positive events in an effort to manage or repair the threat presented by the rejecting prime. However, the pattern for fearful participants is more consistent with a schema-driven interpretation. Although these interpretations are speculative, they highlight the importance of exploring both schema-driven and motivational processes – both of which are important to understanding the impact of working models on memory. (See also Fraley & Shaver, 1997.)

Social construal.   A large body of research in social psychology indicates that people's existing concepts and expectations play an active role in shaping the way they perceive others and interpret their social experiences. Social information is filtered through existing knowledge structures, such as social stereotypes and self-schemas, which then guide social inference processes. Although these processes are only just beginning to be explored in the context of close relationships (Fletcher & Fitness, 1993; Holmes & Rempel, 1989; Pierce, Sarason, & Sarason, 1992), these studies illustrate how interpersonal expectations, once established, may be difficult to overcome.

Like other social knowledge structures, working models of attachment should play an important role in guiding how individuals make sense of their relationships. One process that is especially important for relationship functioning, and which is expected to be strongly influenced by working models, is the construction of explanations and attributions (Bradbury & Fincham, 1990). Because adults with different attachment styles hold very different models of themselves and others, they should be predisposed to explain and interpret events in characteristic ways. In a series of studies, Collins (1996; Collins & Allard, 1999) tested this idea by examining attachment style differences in patterns of explanation for relationship events. In these studies, participants were presented with a set of potentially negative partner behaviors (e.g., "imagine that your partner didn't comfort you when you were feeling down") and were asked to provide explanations and attributions for their partner's behavior. Overall, secure adults tended to provide more benign and more relationship-enhancing attributions than their insecure counterparts. For example (Collins, 1996, Study 1), the explanations provided by secure participants reflected stronger perceptions of love and security in their relationship, greater confidence in their partner's responsiveness, and stronger belief in their partner's warmth and desire for closeness. In contrast, anxious-ambivalent participants were more likely to explain events in ways that revealed low self-worth and self-reliance, less confidence in their partner's love and in the security in their relationship, less trust, and a belief that their partner was purposely rejecting closeness. Effects such as these emerged even after controlling for relationship satisfaction (Collins, 1996, Study 2), depressed mood, and attributional style (Collins & Allard, 1999).

By presenting participants with a controlled set of social stimuli, these initial studies provided strong evidence that social construal was colored by existing expectations about self and others. Nevertheless, because participants in these studies were asked to explain hypothetical events on the basis of very little information, the results may not generalize to more natural settings. To address this limitation, Collins and Feeney (1999; 2000) examined biased perceptions in the context of actual social interactions between romantic partners. In one study (Collins & Feeney, 2000) they videotaped couples while one member of the couple (the support-seeker) disclosed a personal problem or worry to his or her partner (the support-provider). Both members of each couple then evaluated the quality and supportiveness of their interaction. Two independent observers also rated each interaction. Results indicated that support-providers who were higher in attachment-related anxiety and avoidance perceived their interactions more negatively (relative to those who were lower in anxiety and avoidance), even after controlling for their partner's perceptions of the interaction and ratings made by independent observers. Although support-seekers' perceptions were not predicted by their general attachment models, they were predicted by their *relationship-specific* working models. Support-seekers who felt closer to their partner and more satisfied with their relationship perceived their interactions as more supportive (relative to those who had less positive models of their current relationship), even after controlling for their partner's perceptions and ratings made by independent observers.

In another series of studies, Collins and Feeney (1999) brought couples into the lab and asked one member of the couple to engage in a stressful task (giving a speech). While preparing alone for their speech task, participants were given a note written by their partner in another room. In the first study, the content of this note was manipulated by asking partners to copy a specific message designed to be either supportive or mildly unsupportive. In the second study, partners were allowed to write a genuine note, which was then rated by the participant and by three independent coders. Results from both studies provided further evidence for biased perceptions; insecure participants perceived their partner's note less favorably than did secure participants.

Taken together, these studies offer compelling evidence that insecure working models pose a cognitive vulnerability; they predispose insecure individuals to construe their social interactions in pessimistic ways, which may have important implications for relationship functioning. At the same time, secure working models appear to offer a cognitive strength or resource that enables secure individuals to arrive at more generous interpretations of their partner's behavior.

In addition to schema-driven processes such as those illustrated above, it is also important to explore *motivated* construal processes. Evidence for attachment style differences in strategic social construal is beginning to accumulate. For example, after receiving failure feedback, avoidant adults tend to inflate their self-views while anxious-ambivalent adults tend to emphasize their negative self-aspects (Mikulincer, 1998a). Along similar lines, under conditions of threat, anxious-ambivalent individuals increase their perceptions of self–other similarity, whereas avoidant individuals decrease self–other similarity (Mikulincer, Orbach, & Iavnieli, 1998). Mikulincer suggests that these strategic patterns reflect chronic emotion-regulation strategies: avoidant adults manage threat by avoiding recognition of personal weaknesses and by distancing self from others; anxious-ambivalent adults manage threat by becoming overly attentive to inner sources of distress and by seeking closeness and connection to others. (See also Fraley & Shaver, 1997; Mikulincer, 1997.) Studies such as these point to the dynamic and functional nature of working models, and they highlight the importance of studying *motivated* social construal processes in close relationships.

Emotional response patterns

The second general function of working models is to guide affective response patterns. Emotional processes are a central feature of attachment theory and individual differences in attachment style are associated with variations in emotion regulation and emotional expression (e.g., Kobak & Sceery, 1988; Shaver, Collins, & Clark, 1996). Collins and Read (1994) suggest that working models of attachment may shape emotional responses through two different pathways. The first is a direct path, which they label primary appraisal, and the second is an indirect pathway, which they label secondary appraisal.

Primary appraisal.   When an attachment-related event occurs, working models are likely to initiate an immediate emotional response. Two primary mechanisms are proposed to operate here. First, attachment representations are heavily affect-laden and this affect should be automatically evoked whenever working models are activated in memory, a process referred to as "schema-triggered affect" (Fiske & Pavelchak, 1986; see also Andersen & Baum, 1994). The second mechanism linking working models and emotional appraisal involves goals and needs. In general, individuals respond with positive emotions when a goal is achieved or facilitated, and negative emotions when a goal is blocked (Berscheid, 1983). Collins and Read (1994) suggest that events are initially appraised for the extent to which they fulfill one's currently active attachment-related goals and needs. Because adults with different attachment styles have different personal and interpersonal goals, they will tend to respond to the same event with different emotions. For example, an avoidant individual is likely to feel pleased when their partner desires to be alone for the evening because it facilitates their own need for distance. In contrast, an anxious-ambivalent individual may feel angry and frustrated because being left alone is inconsistent with their desire for closeness and interdependence. Thus, understanding attachment style differences in emotional response patterns will be facilitated by mapping out the goal structures of secure and insecure adults. Consistent with this idea, Collins and Allard (1999) asked young adults to imagine a series of potentially negative partner behaviors (e.g., "your partner left you standing alone at a party"). They found that attachment style differences in emotional distress in response to the vignettes were mediated by the importance of the needs/goals being violated by their partner.

The outcome of the primary appraisal process is especially important because of its impact on further information processing. Affect has been shown to influence information processing in several ways. First, affect appears to influence what is attended to in the environment. For example, negative arousal will alert one to potential threat and will create a negatively biased search process. Mood will also make mood-congruent events more easily noticed and more salient (Forgas, Bower, & Krantz, 1984). Affect has also been shown to influence memory. In general, people tend to better encode material that is consistent with their current mood (Bower, Monteiro, & Gilligan, 1978). In addition, memory will be enhanced when our mood while storing the material is matched to our mood when retrieving it (Gilligan & Bower, 1984). Finally, high levels of arousal may have a general effect on information processing by restricting cognitive resources (Sarason, 1975). This will make readily retrieved material from memory even more accessible (Eysenk, 1977; Kihlstrom, 1981), and may reduce the likelihood that individuals will do an adequate search of internal and external cues in explaining and interpreting a partner's behavior (Bradbury & Fincham, 1987). As a result, strong emotional responses may lead to a tendency to rely on over-learned schemas at the expense of conducting more "controlled" and effortful processing of information (Kim & Baron, 1988).

Consistent with these ideas, two recent studies suggest that attachment-related anxiety may interfere with information processing. Miller and Noirot (1999) found that, when participants were asked to write about a rejecting (versus a supportive) friendship experience, fearful avoidance was associated with impaired performance on a subsequent (non-attachment-relevant) task. In a second study, Miller (1996) tested the hypothesis that a rejection prime would interfere with insecure adults' ability to effectively solve social problems. In this study, participants read a series of scenarios describing difficult interpersonal interactions and then rated the likelihood of using different strategies. Results revealed that anxious attachment was associated with less problem-solving flexibility, but only after writing about a negative friendship experience. Taken together, these findings provide preliminary evidence that the activation of chronic worries about rejection (for fearful and anxious-ambivalent adults) can interfere with effective problem solving.

Secondary appraisal.   An individual's initial emotional response to an event can be maintained, amplified, or altered depending on how the experience is construed (Lazarus & Folkman, 1984; Weiner, 1986). Collins and Read (1994) suggest that people respond to attachment experiences not just on the basis of whether or not they like the outcome, but also on what the outcome means, at a symbolic level, for themselves and their relationship (Kelley, 1984). And, because adults with different attachment styles will tend to differ in the way they interpret events, they should also differ in the way they feel in response to them.

Consistent with this idea, Collins (1996; Collins & Allard, 1999) found that participants who interpreted their partner's behavior as caused by a lack of responsiveness and caring were much more likely to respond with feelings of anger and distress. Moreover, path analysis indicated that attachment style differences in emotional distress were largely mediated by attributions. These data suggest that individuals who were high in attachment-related anxiety experienced greater distress, in part, because they interpreted their partner's behavior in more threatening ways.

Behavioral response patterns

Thus far we have proposed a number of ways in which working models of attachment direct information processing and emotional response patterns. Although these outcomes are themselves important for understanding social experience, they are also the key to understanding interpersonal behavior. Collins and Read (1994) have suggested that working models shape behavior primarily by shaping the way people think and feel about themselves and their relationships. That is, adults with different attachment styles behave differently precisely *because* they think and feel differently.

Consistent with this idea, Collins (1996) found that attachment style differences in behavioral strategies (in response to hypothetical relationship events) were mediated by the attributions people made for these events and by their emotional responses to them. For example, in two studies, path analyses indicated that individuals who were higher in attachment-related anxiety (relative to those low in anxiety) tended to write explanations that were more negative and to respond to the events with greater emotional distress; these explanatory patterns and emotional responses then strongly predicted their tendency to engage in more conflictual behavior. These patterns emerged even after controlling for relationship satisfaction, and were replicated in a third study using similar methodology (Collins & Allard, 1999). Although these studies did not involve behavioral observations, they provide preliminary evidence for the role that social construal and emotional response patterns may play in explaining attachment style differences in interpersonal behavior. These findings also point to the need for more work that incorporates cognition, emotion, and behavior in ways that allow for the exploration of mediational processes.

What are the specific mechanisms through which working models shape behavioral responses? First, working models contain a rich source of knowledge that can be used to plan one's behavior in social interaction. Indeed, Bowlby (1982) suggested that working models can be used to run "small scale experiments within the head" for making predictions about how attachment goals can be achieved. Thus, once activated in memory, individuals can rely on their social knowledge, along with their construal of the current situation, to develop a plan of action. Because individuals with different attachment styles will draw from different social knowledge, they will tend to develop different plans and strategies for meeting their attachment-related needs.

Of course, planning requires time and cognitive resources, which are not always readily available. Individuals are often required to react immediately and under conditions of high stress and arousal (such as during an argument), when processing capacity is limited. Evidence suggests that under such conditions, individuals may rely on readily accessible, over-learned strategies and behavioral scripts (Clark & Isen, 1982; Ellis, Thomas, & Rodrigues, 1984; Kihlstrom, 1981). In these circumstances, working models may guide behavior by providing ready-made plans and behavioral strategies for the attainment of attachment-related goals. It is important to remember that adults with different attachment styles will draw from different behavioral repertoires and will be motivated to achieve different interpersonal goals. Moreover, it is likely that particular social construals and particular emotions are linked directly to particular plans and strategies. That is, behavioral strategies may be stored in terms of "if–then" contingencies (Baldwin, 1992) that specify which strategies to use in particular circumstances (e.g., if stressed, seek support; if hurt, seek emotional distance). As a result, once a social situation is appraised, a person's behavioral response may be largely over-determined.

The idea that behavioral strategies can be automatically evoked raises the possibility that the mere activation of an attachment model is sufficient for eliciting a behavioral response, without having to posit an intervening cognitive and emotional mediator. To be sure, some situations are so familiar, and some behaviors so over-learned, that behavioral responses can be elicited by particular features of the environment alone (Bargh, Chen, & Burrows, 1996). This may be especially likely to occur in long-term relationships for which people have highly elaborate and strongly held relational schemas. Nevertheless, we suspect that this is unlikely to represent the majority of interpersonal behavior. Many social situations are ambiguous and require at least some degree of cognitive processing to identify the nature of one's social environment. This processing could be as minimal as categorizing the situation as threatening or benign, forming a rapid impression of another's personal goals and motives, or retrieving a past experience from memory. All of these processing activities are likely to occur rapidly and outside awareness, yet they play an important role in determining behavior. We also believe that emotional appraisals are highly influential in guiding behavior and critical to understanding attachment style differences in social interaction.

Attachment style differences in behavior, then, result from a combination of biased cognitive processing and emotional response tendencies. However, under some conditions, behaviors may be evoked automatically when working models are activated in memory. There may also be individual differences in the relative importance of cognition and emotion in directing behavior. We might speculate, for example, that secure adults are better able to integrate cognitive and emotional cues when planning their behavior. In contrast, anxious adults may tend to weight emotional cues more heavily, whereas avoidant adults may over-rely on cognitive cues.

Summary

Working models of attachment operate as part of a broader system of cognitive, emotional, and behavioral response processes that help individuals understand their social world and behave in ways that meet their personal needs. The specific mechanisms are undoubtedly complex, but we have highlighted a few that can be studied using existing methodologies in social and cognitive psychology. Such investigations include studying the role of attachment representations in selective attention, memory encoding and retrieval, social construal, and emotional response tendencies. Future research should also investigate the dynamic and reciprocal relationship between cognitive and emotional processes, and the ways in which these processes work together to guide behavior.

Concluding Comments

Many of the ideas presented in this chapter remain untested and we suspect they will be elaborated, refined, and modified as empirical work on attachment representations continues to grow. Our goal has been to encourage attachment researchers to think about working models in a more precise and systematic way, and to stimulate interesting and thoughtful research on the topic. We hope also to develop links between attachment theory and the literature in cognitive social psychology, which offers research methodologies that might prove useful for attachment scholars. As our review makes clear, a number of attachment scholars have already begun to use these methodologies to uncover important features of working models and to explore their role in social information processing.

As we have highlighted throughout this chapter, individuals do not enter relationships as *tabulae rasae*. Instead they bring with them a rich network of representations that shape how they construct their lives and how they find meaning in their personal and interpersonal experiences. Of course, features of the environment and qualities of particular interaction partners will also make an important contribution to one's social experience, and a full understanding of social functioning requires that we consider the ways in which these factors interact with already existing personal strengths and vulnerabilities. Our intention was not to minimize the importance of situations, or unique person-by-situation interactions, but to clarify some of the ways in which working models operate on an *intra*personal level, and thereby contribute to what are surely very complex *inter*personal systems. Attachment theory reminds us that close relationships in adulthood cannot be fully understood without reference to the long history of social and emotional experiences that precede such relationships.

Notes

1. The interested reader is directed to Bowlby (1973) for a more complete discussion of working models in infancy and childhood, and to the following sources for comprehensive reviews and

elaborations on these original ideas: Bretherton (1985); Bretherton & Munholland (1999); Crittendon (1990); and Main, Kaplan, & Cassidy (1985).

2. A full discussion of measurement issues is beyond the scope of this chapter, but excellent reviews can be found in several recent chapters (Bartholomew & Shaver, 1998; Brennan, Clark, & Shaver, 1998; Crowell, Fraley, & Shaver, 1999).

3. Although our discussion of attention and memory has focused on schema-consistent effects, people are also likely to attend to and remember events that are highly inconsistent with their prior expectations. Improved memory may occur because unexpected events require explanation, which results in more effortful processing of social information. This deeper processing, in turn, facilitates encoding and retrieval (see Fiske & Taylor, 1991, for a more complete discussion of this issue). Thus, attachment style differences in attention and memory may result, in part, from differences in the type of social information that is surprising or unexpected for people with different working models.

References

Ainsworth, M. D., Blehar, M. C., Waters, C., & Wall, S. (1978). *Patterns of attachment: A psychological study of the strange situation*. Hillsdale, NJ: Erlbaum.

Andersen, S. M., & Baum, A. (1994). Transference in interpersonal relations: Inferences and affect based on significant-other representations. *Journal of Personality, 62*, 459–497.

Andersen, S. M., & Cole, S. W. (1990). "Do I know you?": The role of significant others in general social perception. *Journal of Personality and Social Psychology, 59*, 384–399.

Andersen, S. M., Glassman, N. S., Chen, S., & Cole, S. W. (1995). Transference in social perception: The role of chronic accessibility in significant-other representations. *Journal of Personality and Social Psychology, 69*, 41–57.

Baldwin, M. W. (1992). Relational schemas and the processing of social information. *Psychological Bulletin, 112*, 461–484.

Baldwin, M. W., Fehr, B., Keedian, E., Seidel, M., & Thomson, D. W. (1993). An exploration of the relational schemas underlying attachment styles: Self-report and lexical decision approaches. *Personality and Social Psychology Bulletin, 19*, 746–754.

Baldwin, M. W., Keelan, J. P. R., Fehr, B., Enns, V., & Koh-Rangarajoo, E. (1996). Social cognitive conceptualization of attachment working models: Availability and accessibility effects. *Journal of Personality and Social Psychology, 71*, 94–104.

Bargh, J. A. (1984). Automatic and conscious processing of social information. In R. S. Wyer & T. K. Srull (Eds.), *Handbook of social cognition* (Vol. 3, pp. 1–44). Hillsdale, NJ: Erlbaum.

Bargh, J. A., & Chartrand, T. L. (1999). The unbearable automaticity of being. *American Psychologist, 54*, 462–479.

Bargh, J. A., Chen, M., & Burrows, L. (1996). Automaticity of social behavior: Direct effects of trait construct and stereotype activation on action. *Journal of Personality and Social Psychology, 71*, 230–244.

Bartholomew, K., & Horowitz, L. M. (1991). Attachment styles among young adults: A test of a four-category model. *Journal of Personality and Social Psychology, 61*, 226–244.

Bartholomew, K., & Shaver, P. R. (1998). Methods of assessing adult attachment: Do they converge? In J. Simpson & W. S. Rholes (Eds.), *Attachment theory and close relationships* (pp. 25–45). New York: Guilford Press.

Beer, J. S., & Kihlstrom, J. F. (1999). *Representations of self in close relationships: A test of continuity in internal working models in child and adult attachment*. Unpublished manuscript, University of California at Berkeley.

Berscheid, E. (1983). Emotion. In H. H. Kelley, E. Berscheid, A. Christensen, J. Harvey, T. Huston, G. Levinger, E. McClintock, L. A. Peplau, & D. Peterson (Eds.), *Close relationships* (pp. 110–168). San Francisco: Freeman.

Bower, G. H., Monteiro, K. P., & Gilligan, S. G. (1978). Emotional mood as a context for learning and recall. *Journal of Verbal Learning and Verbal Behavior, 17,* 573–585.

Bowlby, J. (1973). *Attachment and loss, vol. 2: Separation: Anxiety and anger.* New York: Basic Books.

Bowlby, J. (1979). *The making and breaking of affectional bonds.* London: Tavistock.

Bowlby, J. (1980). *Attachment and loss, vol. 3: Loss.* New York: Basic Books.

Bowlby, J. (1982). *Attachment and loss, vol. 1: Attachment* (2nd edition). New York: Basic Books.

Bradbury, T. N., & Fincham, F. D. (1987). Affect and cognition in close relationships: Towards an integrative model. *Cognition and Emotion, 1,* 59–87.

Bradbury, T. N., & Fincham, F. D. (1990). Attribution in marriage: Review and critique. *Psychological Bulletin, 107,* 3–33.

Brennan, K. A., & Bosson, J. K. (1998). Attachment-style differences in attitudes toward and reactions to feedback from romantic partners: An exploration of the relational bases of self-esteem. *Personality and Social Psychology Bulletin, 24,* 699–714.

Brennan, K. A., Clark, C. L., & Shaver, P. R. (1998). Self-report measurement of adult attachment: An integrative overview. In J. Simpson & W. S. Rholes (Eds.), *Attachment theory and close relationships* (pp. 46–76). New York: Guilford Press.

Brennan, K. A., & Morris, K. A. (1997). Attachment styles, self-esteem, and patterns of seeking feedback from romantic partners. *Personality and Social Psychology Bulletin, 23,* 23–31.

Bretherton, I. (1985). Attachment theory: Retrospect and prospect. *Monographs of the Society for Research in Child Development, 50,* 3–35.

Bretherton, I., Biringen, Z., Ridgeway, D., Maslin, C., & Sherman, M. (1989). Attachment: The parental perspective. *Infant Mental Health Journal, 10,* 203–221.

Bretherton, I., & Munholland, K. A. (1999). Internal working models in attachment relationships. In J. A. Cassidy & P. R. Shaver (Eds.), *Handbook of attachment: Theory, research, and clinical applications* (pp. 434–465). New York: Guilford Press.

Clark, M. S., & Isen, A. M. (1982). Toward understanding the relationship between feeling states and social behavior. In A. Hastorf & A. Isen (Eds.), *Cognitive social psychology.* New York: Elsevier North-Holland.

Cohen, C. E. (1981). Person categories and social perception: Testing some boundaries of the processing effects of prior knowledge. *Journal of Personality and Social Psychology, 40,* 441–452.

Collins, N. L. (1996). Working models of attachment: Implications for explanation, emotion, and behavior. *Journal of Personality and Social Psychology, 71,* 810–832.

Collins, N. L., & Allard, L. M. (1999). *Working models of attachment and social construal processes in romantic relationships.* Unpublished manuscript, University of California at Santa Barbara.

Collins, N. L., & Feeney, B. C. (1999). *Attachment style and social construal processes in dyadic interaction: Biased perceptions of social support.* Unpublished manuscript, University of California at Santa Barbara.

Collins, N. L., & Feeney, B. C. (2000). A safe haven: An attachment theory perspective on support-seeking and caregiving in intimate relationships. *Journal of Personality and Social Psychology, 75,* 1053–1073.

Collins, N. L., & Read, S. J. (1990). Adult attachment, working models, and relationship quality in dating couples. *Journal of Personality and Social Psychology, 58,* 644–663.

Collins, N. L., & Read, S. J. (1994). Cognitive representations of attachment: The structure and function of working models. In K. Bartholomew & D. Perlman (Eds.), *Attachment processes in adulthood* (pp. 53–90). London: Jessica Kingsley.

Crittenden, P. M. (1990). Internal representational models of attachment relationships. *Infant Mental Health Journal, 11,* 259–277.

Crowell, J. A, Fraley, R. C., & Shaver, P. R. (1999). Measurement of individual differences in adolescent and adult attachment. In J. A. Cassidy & P. R. Shaver (Eds.), *Handbook of attachment: Theory, research, and clinical applications* (pp. 434–465). New York: Guilford Press.

Crowell, J. A., & Owens, G. (1996). *Current relationships interview and scoring system.* Unpublished manuscript, State University of New York at Stony Brook.

Egeland, B., & Farber, E. (1984). Infant-mother attachment: Factors related to its development and change over time. *Child Development, 55,* 753–771.

Ellis, H. C., Thomas, R. L., & Rodrigues, I. A. (1984). Emotions, mood states and memory: Elaborative encoding, semantic processing, and cognitive effort. *Journal of Experimental Psychology: Learning, Memory, and Cognition, 10,* 470–482.

Eysenk, M. W. (1977). *Human memory: Theory, research, and individual differences.* Elmsford, NY: Pergamon.

Feeney, J. A. (1999). Adult romantic attachment and couple relationships. In J. A. Cassidy & P. R. Shaver (Eds.), *Handbook of attachment: Theory, research, and clinical applications* (pp. 355–377). New York: Guilford Press.

Feeney, J. A., & Noller, P. (1990). Attachment style as a predictor of adult romantic relationships. *Journal of Personality and Social Psychology, 58,* 281–291.

Feeney, J. A., Noller, P., & Callan, V. J. (1994). Attachment style, communication and satisfaction in the early years of marriage. In K. Bartholomew & D. Perlman (Eds.), *Attachment processes in adulthood* (pp. 269–308). London: Jessica Kingsley.

Fiske, S. T., & Pavelchak, M. A. (1986). Category-based versus piecemeal-based affective responses: Developments in schema-triggered affect. In R. M. Sorrentino & E. T. Higgins (Eds.), *Handbook of motivation and cognition: Foundations of social behavior* (pp. 167–203). New York: Guilford Press.

Fiske, S. T., & Taylor, S. E. (1991). *Social cognition.* New York: McGraw-Hill.

Fletcher, G. J. O., & Fincham, F. D. (1991). *Cognition in close relationships.* Hillsdale, NJ: Erlbaum.

Fletcher, G. J. O., & Fitness, J. (1993). Knowledge structures and explanations in intimate relationships. In S. Duck (Ed.), *Individuals in relationships* (pp. 121–143). Newbury Park, CA: Sage.

Fletcher, G. J. O., & Fitness, J. (Eds.). (1996). *Knowledge structures in close relationships: A social psychological approach.* Mahwah, NJ: Erlbaum.

Forgas, J. P., Bower, G. H., & Krantz, S. E. (1984). The influence of mood on perceptions of social interactions. *Journal of Experimental Social Psychology, 20,* 497–513.

Fraley, R. C., Davis, K. E., & Shaver, P. R. (1998). Dismissing-avoidance and the defensive organization of emotion, cognition, and behavior. In J. A. Simpson & W. S. Rholes (Eds.), *Attachment theory and close relationships* (pp. 249–279). New York: Guilford Press.

Fraley, R. C., & Shaver, P. R. (1997). Adult attachment and the suppression of unwanted thoughts. *Journal of Personality and Social Psychology, 73,* 1080–1091.

Fraley, R. C., & Shaver, P. R. (1998). Airport separations: A naturalistic study of adult attachment dynamics in separating couples. *Journal of Personality and Social Psychology, 75,* 1198–1212.

Fraley, R. C., & Waller, N. G. (1998). Adult attachment patterns: A test of the typological model. In J. A. Simpson & W. S. Rholes (Eds.), *Attachment theory and close relationships* (pp. 77–114). New York: Guilford Press.

George, C., Kaplan, N., & Main, M. (1984). *Attachment interview for adults.* Unpublished manuscript, University of California at Berkeley.

George, C., & Solomon, J. (1989). Internal working models of caregiving and security of attachment at age six. *Infant Mental Health Journal, 10,* 222–237.

Gilligan, S. G., & Bower, G. H. (1984). Cognitive consequences of emotional arousal. In C. E. Izard, J. Kagan, & R. B. Zajonc (Eds.), *Emotions, cognition, and behavior* (pp. 547–588). Cambridge, England: Cambridge University Press.

Graesser, A. C., & Nakamura, G. V. (1982). The impact of a schema on comprehension and memory. In G. H. Bower (Ed.), *The psychology of learning and motivation* (Vol. 16, pp. 60–109). New York: Academic Press.

Greenwald, A. G., McGhee, D. E., & Schwartz, J. L. K. (1998). Measuring individual differences in implicit cognition: The implicit association test. *Journal of Personality and Social Psychology, 74,* 1464–1480.

Hastie, R. (1981). Schematic principles in human memory. In E. T. Higgins, C. P. Herman, & M. P. Zanna (Eds.), *Social cognition: The Ontario symposium* (Vol. 1, pp. 39–88). Hillsdale, NJ: Erlbaum.

Hazan, C., & Shaver, P. (1987). Romantic love conceptualized as an attachment process. *Journal of Personality and Social Psychology, 52,* 511–524.

Hazan, C., & Shaver, P. (1990). Love and work: An attachment theoretical perspective. *Journal of*

Personality and Social Psychology, 59, 270–280.

Higgins, E. T., & Bargh, J. A. (1987). Social cognition and social perception. In M. R. Rosensweig & L. W. Porter (Eds.), *Annual review of psychology* (Vol. 38, pp. 369–425). Palo Alto, CA: Annual Reviews.

Higgins, E. T., King, G. A., & Mavin, G. H. (1982). Individual construct accessibility and subjective impressions and recall. *Journal of Personality and Social Psychology, 43,* 35–47.

Holmes, J. G., & Rempel, J. K. (1989). Trust in close relationships. In C. Hendrick (Ed.), *Review of personality and social psychology: Vol. 10. Close relationships* (pp. 187–220). London: Sage.

Kelley, H. H. (1984). Affect in interpersonal relations. In P. Shaver (Ed.), *Review of personality and social psychology* (Vol. 5, pp. 89–115). Beverly Hills, CA: Sage.

Kihlstrom, J. F. (1981). On personality and memory. In N. Cantor & J. Kihlstrom (Eds.), *Personality, cognition, and social interaction* (pp. 123–149). Hillsdale, NJ: Erlbaum.

Kim, H., & Baron, R. S. (1988). Exercise and the illusory correlation: Does arousal heighten stereotypic processing? *Journal of Experimental Social Psychology, 24,* 366–380.

Kobak, R. R., & Hazan, C. (1991). Attachment in marriage: The effects of security and accuracy of working models. *Journal of Personality and Social Psychology, 60,* 861–869.

Kobak, R. R., & Sceery, A. (1988). Attachment in late adolescence: Working models, affect regulation, and perception of self and others. *Child Development, 59,* 135–146.

Lazarus, R. S., & Folkman, S. (1984). *Stress, appraisal, and coping.* New York: Springer.

Main, M. (1981). Avoidance in the service of attachment: A working paper. In K. Immelmann, G. Barlow, L. Petrinovich, & M. Main (Eds.), *Behavioral development: The Bielefeld interdisciplinary project* (pp. 651–693). New York: Cambridge University Press.

Main, M. (1991). Metacognitive knowledge, metacognitive monitoring, and singular (coherent) vs. multiple (incoherent) model of attachment. In C. M. Parkes, J. Stevson-Hinde, & P. Marris (Eds.), *Attachment across the life cycle* (pp. 127–159). London: Tavistock/Routledge.

Main, M., Kaplan, N., & Cassidy, J. (1985). Security in infancy, childhood, and adulthood: A move to the level of representation. *Monographs of the Society for Research in Child Development, 50,* 66–104.

Markus, H. (1977). Self-schemata and processing information about the self. *Journal of Personality and Social Psychology, 35,* 63–78.

Martin, R. (1991). Examining personal relationship thinking: The relational cognition complexity instrument. *Journal of Social and Personal Relationships, 8,* 467–480.

Mikulincer, M. (1995). Attachment style and the mental representation of the self. *Journal of Personality and Social Psychology, 69,* 1203–1215.

Mikulincer, M. (1997). Adult attachment style and information processing: Individual differences in curiosity and cognitive closure. *Journal of Personality and Social Psychology, 72,* 1217–1230.

Mikulincer, M. (1998a). Adult attachment style and affect regulation: Strategic variations in self-appraisals. *Journal of Personality and Social Psychology, 75,* 420–435.

Mikulincer, M. (1998b). Attachment working models and the sense of trust: An exploration of interaction goals and affect regulation. *Journal of Personality and Social Psychology, 74,* 1209–1224.

Mikulincer, M., & Horesh, N. (1999). Adult attachment style and the perception of others: The role of projective mechanisms. *Journal of Personality and Social Psychology, 76,* 1022–1034.

Mikulincer, M., & Nachshon, O. (1991). Attachment styles and patterns of self-disclosure. *Journal of Personality and Social Psychology, 61,* 321–331.

Mikulincer, M., & Orbach, I. (1995). Attachment styles and repressive defensiveness: The accessibility and architecture of affective memories. *Journal of Personality and Social Psychology, 68,* 917–925.

Mikulincer, M., Orbach, I., & Iavnieli, D. (1998). Adult attachment style and affect regulation: Strategic variations in subjective self–other similarity. *Journal of Personality and Social Psychology, 75,* 436–448.

Miller, J. B. (1996). Social flexibility and anxious attachment. *Personal Relationships, 3,* 241–256.

Miller, J. B., & Noirot, M. (1999). Attachment memories, models and information processing. *Journal of Social and Personal Relationships, 16,* 147–173.

Ognibene, T. C., & Collins, N. L. (1998). Adult attachment styles, perceived social support and coping strategies. *Journal of Social and Personal Relationships, 15,* 323–345.

Pierce, G. R., Sarason, B. R., & Sarason, I. G. (1992). General and specific support expectations and stress as predictors of perceived supportiveness: An experimental study. *Journal of Personality and Social Psychology, 63,* 297–307.

Roskos-Ewoldsen, D. R., & Fazio, R. H. (1992). On the orienting value of attitudes: Attitude accessibility as a determinant of an object's attraction to visual attention. *Journal of Personality and Social Psychology, 63,* 198–211

Sarason, I. G. (1975). Anxiety and self-preoccupation. In I. G. Sarason & C. D. Spielberger (Eds.), *Stress and Anxiety, Vol 2.* New York: Wiley.

Shaver, P. R., & Clark, C. L. (1996). Forms of adult romantic attachment and their cognitive and emotional underpinnings. In G. G. Noam & K. W. Fischer (Eds.), *Development and vulnerability in close relationships* (pp. 29–58). Mahwah, NJ: Erlbaum.

Shaver, P. R., Collins, N. L., & Clark, C. L. (1996). Attachment styles and internal working models of self and relationship partners. In G. J. O. Fletcher & J. Fitness (Eds.), *Knowledge structures in close relationships: A social psychological approach* (pp. 25–61). Mahwah, NJ: Erlbaum.

Simpson, J. A., Rholes, W. S., & Nelligan, J. S. (1992). Support-seeking and support-giving within couple members in an anxiety-provoking situation: The role of attachment styles. *Journal of Personality and Social Psychology, 62,* 434–446.

Simpson, J. A., Rholes, W. S., & Phillips, D. (1996). Conflict in close relationships: An attachment perspective. *Journal of Personality and Social Psychology, 71,* 899–914.

Sroufe, L. A., & Waters, E. (1977). Attachment as an organizational construct. *Child Development, 48,* 1184–1199.

Srull, T. K., & Wyer, R. S., Jr. (1986). The role of chronic and temporary goals in social information processing. In R. M. Sorrentino & E. T. Higgins (Eds.), *Handbook of motivation and cognition: Foundations of social behavior* (pp. 503–549). New York: Guilford Press.

Srull, T. K., & Wyer, R. S., Jr. (1989). Person memory and judgement. *Psychological Review, 96,* 58–83.

Tesser, A. (1978). Self-generated attitude change. In L. Berkowitz (Ed.), *Advances in experimental social psychology* (Vol. 11, pp. 289–338). New York: Academic Press.

Thompson, R. A., Lamb, M. E., & Estes, D. (1982). Stability of infant-mother attachment and its relationship to changing life circumstances in an unselected middle-class sample. *Child Development, 53,* 144–148.

Vaughn, B., Egeland, B., Sroufe, L. A., & Waters, E. (1979). Individual differences in infant-mother attachment at twelve and eighteen months: Stability and change in families under stress. *Child Development, 50,* 971–975.

Weiner, B. (1986). Attribution, emotion, and action. In R. Sorrentino & E. T. Higgins (Eds.), *Handbook of motivation and cognition: Foundations of social behavior* (pp. 281–312). New York: Guilford Press.

Chapter Four

The Structure and Function of Ideal Standards in Close Relationships

Jeffry A. Simpson, Garth J. O. Fletcher, and Lorne Campbell

> Sometimes the most extreme passion is aroused – not by real-life love objects – but by partners who are barely known . . . or who exist only in imagination.
> (Berscheid & Walster, 1978, p. 152)

As this quotation suggests, romantic relationships often contain "hidden others" – real or ideal persons besides the two partners – who have a bearing on the nature, the quality, and perhaps even the stability of the relationship. At present, very little is known about whom these hidden others are or the dimensions on which they are evaluated. In addition, almost nothing is known about how ideal images affect the thoughts, feelings, and behaviors of partners in close relationships, and how ideal standards are associated with the satisfaction and long-term stability of relationships.

It is surprising that these issues have received relatively little attention in social psychology. Of course, there has been a great deal of theorizing about the functions, development, and possible content of ideal standards from many different theoretical perspectives, including psychodynamic approaches (e.g., Freud, 1961), humanistic approaches (e.g., Maslow, 1954; Rogers, 1961), sociological approaches (e.g., Waller & Hill, 1951), and social psychological approaches (see Berscheid & Walster, 1978). However, in-depth research examining ideals and idealization processes in relationships has

The writing of this chapter was supported by a grant from the New Zealand Marsden Foundation (M1032) to Garth Fletcher and Jeffry Simpson. Correspondence about this article should be addressed to either Jeffry A. Simpson, Department of Psychology, Texas A&M University, College Station, TX, 77843-4235 (e-mail: jas@psyc.tamu.edu); or Garth Fletcher, Department of Psychology, University of Canterbury, Christchurch, New Zealand (e-mail: g.fletcher@psyc.canterbury.ac.nz).

been meager until very recently. One major aim of this chapter is to redress these short-comings.

The chapter is divided into three major sections. In the first section, we review how perceptions of ideal partners and ideal relationships – the "hidden others" that can enter into dyads – have been conceptualized and measured by Interdependence Theory (Thibaut & Kelley, 1959; Kelley & Thibaut, 1978). We then review past theory and research that has focused on "self-based" ideals (particularly Higgins's, 1987, self-discrepancy theory), which has informed the development of more recent theory and research on "partner" and "relationship" ideals. In the second section, we present a new model of ideal standards in relationships. The Ideal Standards Model, which has been developed in a preliminary form by Fletcher, Simpson, Thomas, and Giles (1999), specifies the content and function of partner and relationship ideal standards. We then summarize the results of a series of recent studies that have tested basic tenets of this model. In the final section, we discuss some important, unresolved issues regarding how individuals establish and adjust their ideal standards over time, how relationship-discrepancy models are similar to and different from self-discrepancy models, and how relationships ought to complicate the functioning of ideal standards.

Previous Theories and Research on Ideal Standards in Relationships

Interdependence Theory

The idea that individuals evaluate their partners and relationships based on the perceived consistency between a priori standards or expectations and perceptions of the current partner/relationship is hardly novel. The first major theory to address this topic was Interdependence Theory, as originally formulated by Thibaut and Kelley (1959). According to Interdependence Theory, individuals make judgments about their relationships according to two standards: (1) the degree to which they believe they are receiving the benefits they "deserve" from their current partner/relationship (assessed by the Comparison Level or CL), and (2) the degree to which the current partner/relationship provides outcomes that exceed those available from the best available alternative partner (assessed by the Comparison Level for Alternatives or Clalt).

Interdependence Theory proposes that individuals who think they are receiving less than they "deserve" should become dissatisfied with their partner/relationship, and those with superior alternatives should be less likely to remain in the relationship over time. By postulating the existence of global cognitive standards, Interdependence Theory can explain why some people leave apparently rewarding relationships while others remain in dismal ones. However, the theory does not address the possibility that individuals may evaluate their partners/relationships on content-specific standards or dimensions. Indeed, as we shall see, recent theorizing and research suggests that individuals routinely make cognitive comparisons between their ideal standards (or expectations) and perceptions of their current partner/relationship on multiple dimensions. In addition, Interdependence Theory does not adequately deal with the processes involved in making these cognitive comparisons. Our new model rectifies both of these shortcomings.

Self-discrepancy theories

Several major theoretical perspectives posit that individuals use "actual–ideal" or "actual–ought" discrepancies to make important judgments and regulate their behavior. The earliest theories focused on discrepancies between one's actual and one's ideal self-concept. James (1892), Cooley (1902), and Rogers (1961) believed that feelings of self-worth stem from the degree of disparity between an individual's actual self-concept and his or her ideal self-concept. However, the most detailed and influential self-discrepancy theory has been developed by Higgins (1987, 1989).

Higgins contends that the self has three basic domains (the actual self, the ideal self, and the ought self) which can be assessed from two perspectives (one's own standpoint, and the inferred standpoint of a significant other). According to his theory, the emotions an individual experiences should depend on the nature and magnitude of different kinds of discrepancies. Although many discrepancies are possible, Higgins focuses primarily on four: actual self versus ideal self (i.e., what the self aspires to), actual self versus ideal other (i.e., what one thinks others ideally want him or her to be), actual self versus ought other (i.e., how one thinks others think he or she should behave, in a moral sense), and actual self versus ought self (i.e., how the self thinks he or she should behave morally). Both the cognitive availability (i.e., representation in memory) and the accessibility (i.e., likelihood of activation) of each ideal should determine the extent to which each discrepancy influences an individual's thoughts, feelings, and behavior.

Higgins's model proposes that larger perceived discrepancies on a given dimension ought to produce more intense emotional reactions associated with that dimension. In particular, actual–ideal discrepancies are conjectured to reflect the absence of positive outcomes (because individuals have not fully reached the goals to which they aspire), whereas actual–ought discrepancies purportedly indicate the presence of negative outcomes (because individuals have not lived up to goals they believe they should maintain). As a result, Higgins postulates that individuals with larger actual–ideal discrepancies should feel dejection-related emotions such as disappointment, dissatisfaction, and shame. In contrast, individuals with larger actual–ought discrepancies should feel agitation-related emotions, including resentment, fear, and threat (see Higgins, 1989, for a review of this research). The theory also posits that individuals monitor the size of discrepancies for two purposes: (1) to *regulate* their most important personal attributes (e.g., their appearance, demeanor, behavior) in order to maintain or reduce discrepancies between actual–ideal or actual–ought selves, and (2) to *evaluate* how well they are maintaining or reducing these disparities (see Higgins, 1989).

There are some important differences between the processes that are likely to govern self-based and relationship-based ideal standards, which we shall discuss later. Nevertheless, we have incorporated certain components of self-discrepancy theory into our Ideal Standards Model. For example, we have borrowed Higgins's basic notions about the possible functions of ideals (and have slightly expanded them). We also believe that some of the basic cognitive processes that Higgins has described as applying to self-discrepancies may also apply to relationship-discrepancies. We are less convinced, however, about the merits of other aspects of self-discrepancy theory, which have not been incorporated into our model. Distinctions between ideal standards and ought standards, for instance, are often subtle and murky (e.g., is my personal standard of being a caring, supportive person an ideal standard or an ought standard?). This might explain why some of the theory's basic predictions regarding ideal vs. ought standards and the different emotions that should be produced by different comparisons have not always been confirmed (see, for example, Tangney, Niedenthal, Covert, & Barlow, 1998).[1]

A Model of Ideal Standards in Close Relationships

To date, very little research has examined either the content of partner and relationship ideals or the processes by which such standards might influence the happiness and stability of romantic relationships. Although a few studies have explored these issues, they have been mostly descriptive and atheoretical (see, for example, Rusbult, Onizuka, & Lipkus, 1993; Sternberg & Barnes, 1985).

The structure and content of partner and relationship ideals

According to our model (and consistent with self-discrepancy theory), partner and relationship ideals should operate as chronically accessible knowledge structures that probably predate – and may causally influence – important judgments and decisions in relationships (see Fletcher et al., 1999). However, departing from self-discrepancy theory, we propose that relationship-based knowledge structures should involve three interlocking components: the self, the partner, and the relationship (see Baldwin, 1992; Fletcher & Thomas, 1996). Figure 4.1 depicts the relations among these components and provides prototypic examples of each one.

Goals, expectations, and beliefs about ideals should exist where the self and the partner or relationship intersect (areas e, g, and f in figure 4.2). Ideal standards, therefore, meld elements of the self, the ideal partner, and the ideal relationship. Ideal standards also entail expectations, beliefs, hopes, and aspirations that are relational in character. As shown in the figure, we propose that ideal partner and ideal relationship standards should be stored and represented as separate, semi-independent constructs. However, ideal partner and ideal relationship categories are likely to overlap because people should prefer ideal partners who can help them achieve their ideal relationships (see Fletcher et al., 1999). For example, individuals who believe that laughter and humor are important features of an ideal relationship should also value a sense of humor in their ideal mates, who in turn should be more capable of creating a relationship filled with laughter and humor.

This cognitive framework offers guidelines about the structure of partner and relationship ideals, but it does not illuminate their possible content. To our knowledge, only one previous study has explored the content of relationship ideals (see Rusbult et al., 1993), and just one has investigated partner ideals (see Regan, 1998). Over the years, a considerable amount of research has examined other types of relationship-based knowledge structures, including concepts of love (Aron & Westbay, 1996; Fehr & Russell, 1991), the

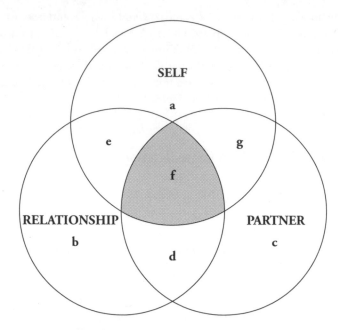

Examples of Cognition
(a) I am intelligent
(b) Relationships fail without good communication
(c) Men are aggressive
(d) Relationships work well when one partner is dominant
(e) I want an exciting relationship
(f) I want an honest relationship with a partner I can trust
(g) I am suited to someone who is sporting and athletic

Figure 4.1   General model of relationship cognition (taken from Fletcher et al., 1999)

perceived causes of relationship success (Fletcher & Kininmonth, 1992), and the concept of a "good" relationship (Hassebrauck, 1997). However, these knowledge structures differ from ideal standards in some crucial respects. Research on love, for instance, has used a prototype approach in which exemplars of love are viewed as prototypical of the construct if they are similar to modal (i.e., average) values on particular dimensions or they are similar to members of the same family of categories (see Aron & Westbay, 1996; Fehr & Russell, 1991). Ideal standards, on the other hand, lie at the positive end of evaluative dimensions rather than near the average or mode (Barsalou, 1985).

   Constructs such as the perceived causes of relationship success (Fletcher & Kininmonth, 1992) and what makes a "good" relationship (Hassebrauck, 1997) tend to be more similar to ideal standards than is true of global relationship concepts like love. However, ideal standards and conceptions of a "successful" or "good" relationship are unlikely to be isomorphic. An individual who believes that strong passion is critical to successful relationships for most people, for example, might opt for a less passionate relationship if he or she has a self-perceived low sex drive. In addition, if certain individuals believe that their ideals may be difficult to achieve, their conceptions of a "successful" or "good" relationship may reflect what they believe they can expect to obtain in a romantic partner or relationship. According to our model, ideal standards should be more firmly connected to the self-concept than beliefs or attitudes about relationships in general.

Principles derived from evolutionary theories offer a rich source of predictions about the possible content of ideal partner dimensions. Recent work by Simpson and Gangestad (see Campbell, Simpson, & Orina, 1999; Gangestad & Simpson, 2000; Simpson & Gangestad, 1992) suggests that people ought to judge ideal partners on three basic dimensions: (1) the prospective partners' capacity for intimacy and commitment, (2) their attractiveness and general health, and (3) their social status and resources.

These three dimensions make good theoretical sense in light of recent evolutionary models that integrate good-provider and good-genes theories of human mating (see Gangestad & Simpson, in press). Each dimension represents a different "route" to obtaining a mate and promoting one's own reproductive fitness (see Buss & Schmitt, 1993). Theory and research on mate selection (Simpson & Gangestad, 1992) and mating strategies (Buss & Schmitt, 1993; Gangestad & Simpson, 2000) suggest that all three domains are highly relevant to successful mating. By being attentive to a partner's capacity for intimacy and commitment, for example, an individual should increase his or her chances of finding a cooperative, committed partner who is likely to be a devoted parent. By focusing on attractiveness and health, an individual is more likely to acquire a mate who is younger, healthier, and perhaps more fertile (especially in the case of men choosing women). And by considering a partner's resources and status, an individual should be more likely to obtain a mate who can ascend social hierarchies and form coalitions with other people who have – or can acquire – valued social status or other resources.

The major dimensions that should underlie relationship ideals are more difficult to predict. Considering the paramount importance of intimacy in relationships (Fletcher & Thomas, 1996), one relationship ideal dimension should center on intimacy and commitment in relationships (paralleling the hypothesized ideal partner intimacy dimension). However, the other hypothesized partner dimensions (attractiveness/health and status/resources) do not have clear conceptual analogues at the relationship level. Recent evolutionary models of human mating have noted that both sexes engage in both short-term and long-term mating strategies (see Gangestad & Simpson, 2000). It seems reasonable to hypothesize that holding high ideal standards for relationship intimacy and commitment should facilitate (and may reflect a preference for) long-term mating. Having high ideal standards for passion and excitement in a relationship, in contrast, should facilitate (and might signal a preference for) short-term mating. Hence, dimensions similar to intimacy and passion might underlie relationship ideals.

The functions and flexibility of ideal standards

Melding principles from Higgins's (1987) self-discrepancy theory, from Carver and Scheier's (1982, 1990) control theory, and adding some elements of our own, our Ideal Standards Model proposes that partner and relationship ideals should serve three functions: *evalua-*

tion, explanation, and *regulation.* More specifically, the magnitude of discrepancies between ideal standards and perceptions of the current partner/relationship should be used by individuals to: (1) estimate and evaluate the quality of their partners and relationships (e.g., to assess the appropriateness of potential or current partners/relationships), (2) explain and better understand what is happening in their relationships (e.g., to give causal accounts explaining relationship satisfaction, problems, or conflicts), and (3) regulate and make adjustments in their relationships (e.g., to predict and possibly control current partners/relationships).

The flexibility of ideal standards (i.e., the degree to which partners can fall below an ideal standard and still be considered acceptable) also should affect how partners and relationships are evaluated, explained, and regulated. The setting of both ideal standards and ideal flexibility should be influenced, at least in part, by self-assessments on the same dimensions. For example, individuals who perceive themselves as being highly physically attractive typically should set higher ideal standards on this dimension and should expect that their partners will come reasonably close to matching these ideals. However, the flexibility of ideal standards may be more labile and responsive to current circumstances than are ideal standards per se. Individuals who have just been rebuffed by a series of prospective romantic partners, for instance, may expand the range of "acceptability" lying below their ideal standards. If rejections are experienced repeatedly, an individual's ideal standards should gradually decline as flexibility increases; conversely, if new partners eagerly accept an individual's romantic overtures, ideal standards should gradually rise over time and flexibility should decline. According to this line of reasoning, shifts in flexibility therefore might act as a barometer of an individual's most recent romantic experiences. Despite the fact that people occasionally might extend their degree of flexibility in order to maintain their ideal standards, they should alter their ideals when discrepancies become chronic and large.

Although not examining the flexibility of ideals directly, some research has shown that individuals display differential flexibility in different relationship contexts. Kenrick, Groth, Trost, and Sadalla (1993) and Regan (1998), for example, have found that men and women apply their standards more flexibly (i.e., they are more tolerant) when evaluating potential partners for short-term relationships than for serious, long-term relationships. Even though men typically exhibit more flexibility than women when evaluating short-term sexual relationships (Buss & Schmitt, 1993), both sexes want romantic partners to match their ideal standards as closely as possible for long-term relationships. Thus, in certain contexts, both men and women seem to be willing to "extend" their acceptability criteria for potential mates while still maintaining their core relationship standards.

Enhancement versus accuracy in relationships

We argue that two fundamental motives guide how individuals evaluate, explain, and regulate their relationships: (1) partner/relationship enhancement or idealization motives, and (2) accuracy motives. The emotional, cognitive, and behavioral consequences of discrepancies between ideals and perceptions of the current partner or relationship should depend (in part) on which motivational set tends to be predominant in a given situation.

According to many self theorists, the self-enhancement motive is a powerful force that leads people to view the social world through rose-colored glasses, to exaggerate their own positive attributes and the control they wield over social outcomes, and to be unduly optimistic about future events. When not carried to ridiculous extremes, these pollyannaish tendencies are associated with a variety of positive outcomes, including greater personal happiness, improved relationships, higher motivation and persistence, better psychological adjustment, and superior mental health (see Taylor & Brown, 1988, for a review). Moreover, individuals who have more realistic, non-illusory views of themselves tend to be more depressed and display poorer adjustment and well-being (Alloy & Abramson, 1979; but see also Colvin & Block, 1994). Various explanations have been offered for why the self-enhancement motive tends to be so powerful and pervasive. Most explanations are based on the general premise that positive illusions promote confidence and persistence, which increase the chances of success at major life tasks (Taylor, 1989) or improve coping with difficult or stressful life events (Steele, 1988).

Relationship theorists have also proposed that people have a basic need to idealize and enhance their romantic partners and relationships (see chapter 5, below). Indeed, there is abundant evidence that individuals often do perceive their partners and relationships in an excessively positive light, and that the tendency to idealize one's partner is associated with greater relationship satisfaction (Spanier, 1972) and lower rates of relationship dissolution (Murray, Holmes, & Griffin, 1996b).

Murray and Holmes have conducted the most systematic and in-depth research on partner idealization processes. They have found that the most satisfied dating and marital partners usually project the features of their ideal partners onto their own partners, effectively seeing in their partners the person they ideally wish to find (Murray, Holmes, & Griffin, 1996a). When confronted with their partners' faults or limitations, the most satisfied individuals often transform their partners' drawbacks into virtues by refuting or discounting their limitations (Murray & Holmes, 1993, 1994) or by cognitively linking their partners' faults with some of their stellar virtues (Murray & Holmes, 1996). In a recent cross-sectional study, Murray et al. (1996a) found that, in both dating and marital relationships: (a) individuals' impressions of their partners tend to be more similar to their own self-images and their own images of an ideal partner than with how their partners actually perceive themselves, (b) more satisfied individuals have more idealized images of their partners, and (c) individuals are more satisfied when their partners idealize them in return. In a recent one-year longitudinal study involving both dating and married couples, Murray et al. (1996b) found that: (a) relationships are more likely to remain stable the more partners idealize each other, (b) partners who idealize each other more early in the year tend to experience larger increases in satisfaction and larger decreases in relationship conflict and doubts by the end of the year, and (c) over time, individuals gradually come to share their partners' idealized images of them.

It is not difficult to understand why people are motivated to idealize their partners and relationships. Individuals' self-concepts often are inextricably intertwined with the perceptions they have of their partners and relationships (Murray et al., 1996a). Thus, any self-serving bias or motive that is used to maintain optimistic, positive self-views should also be used to enhance views of the current partner and relationship, especially since the fate of the self and one's partner/relationship frequently coincide. In addition, the costs associated with relationship conflict and dissolution should motivate most individuals to see the best in their partners and relationships, when possible. From a rational standpoint, most people probably are aware that approximately 50 percent of marriages end in divorce, at least in Western countries (see Singh, Mathews, Clarke, Yannicos, & Smith, 1995). Despite this realization, the vast majority of men and women get married and have children at some point in their lives (Singh et al., 1995). Committing to a long-term relationship, therefore, requires a leap of faith and a level of confidence that may be difficult to justify on purely rational grounds. As a result, the psychological pressure to make charitable and positive judgments about one's partner and relationship needs to be strong to counteract these forces. This might explain the power of the enhancement motive in relationships.

In considering the omnipotence of the relationship-enhancement motive, we are reminded of a quote by Thomas Huxley: "The great tragedy of Science [is] the slaying of a beautiful hypothesis by an ugly fact." In this case, the hypothesis is the presumed pervasiveness and dominance of the relationship-enhancement motive; the ugly fact is that the vast majority of romantic relationships eventually break up. Apparently, the relationship-enhancement motive is either inoperative or is displaced by other basic motives in certain contexts. We contend that partner and relationship idealization processes will sometimes conflict with accuracy aims, including the effective prediction, explanation, and control of partners and relationships. People will often experience difficulties in maintaining overly optimistic views of their partners and relationships, especially when such views are clearly detached from reality. Attempting to accurately understand and attribute motives and beliefs to others should be highly adaptive in certain situations (such as when deciding whether or not to start or to remain in a relationship or when figuring out how to best predict and control the behavior of others). Indeed, evolutionary pressures should have selected humans to figure out and face the truth, no matter how bleak and depressing, in situations where it was dangerous or extremely costly to do otherwise.

How can the coexistence and operation of these two motives be understood? We believe that, in many situations, the motive to bend reality in an enhancing fashion is likely to produce mild distortions that do not twist the truth enough to cause serious problems in most relationships. Moreover, the accuracy and enhancement motives can both be operative, but under different conditions (Gollwitzer & Kinney, 1989). Some people, for example, may have cognitive styles that are better suited to achieving accuracy goals, whereas others may have styles that facilitate the enhancement of cherished views of themselves and their partners/relationships. In addition, relationship interactions that are threatening should increase the accessibility and power of esteem-maintenance goals, often subverting accurate attributions about the partner or the relationship (cf. Simpson, Ickes, & Blackstone, 1995). Different relationship stages or major decision points should also be associated with systematic changes in the salience and importance of the two motives. For example, when the need to make accurate, less biased judgments becomes critical in relationships (such as when individuals must decide whether or not to date someone, to get married, or to have a child), the accuracy motive should assume precedence. On the other hand, when couples are settled into a comfortable relationship maintenance phase, the enhancement motive should be ascendant.

Consequences of discrepancies between ideals and perceptions

According to our model, the consequences of large discrepancies between ideals and perceptions of the current partner/relationship should vary depending on the accessibility and relative strength of relationship enhancement versus accuracy motives. As already noted, relationship enhancement and partner/relationship idealization processes should be dominant when the relationship has stabilized, has reached relatively high levels of commitment, or after major decisions have been made. When enhancement motives predominate, people should handle ideal-perception discrepancies (and the evaluations that stem from them) using cognitive strategies that involve (1) changing perceptions of the current partner/relationship so they more closely match one's ideal standards, (2) changing one's ideal standards so they more closely match one's perception of the partner/relationship, or (3) discounting the importance of ideal standards that one's partner is not likely to meet. We suspect that these processes typically occur automatically and largely outside of conscious awareness.

Many intriguing questions remain about the way in which cognitive idealization processes are likely to work. First, the extent of idealization might depend on the specific ideal standard under consideration. Previous research implies that individuals are most likely to idealize their partners on attributes that (1) are central to what they need or value in a mate (Stephan, Berscheid, & Walster, 1971), (2) are subjective or ambiguous (i.e., are difficult to verify because objective rules or standards for verification do not exist: Lambert & Wedell, 1991; Sedikides & Showronski, 1993), and (3) promote closeness and intimacy in the relationship (Levinger & Breedlove, 1966).

Second, several different cognitive strategies may help individuals protect and sustain their positive partner illusions. For instance, individuals might defend idealized views of their partners by making internal attributions for their partners' successes and external attributions for their failures (Hall & Taylor, 1976), by finding flaws in information that portrays partners unfavorably (Pyszczynski, Greenberg, & Holt, 1985; Wyer & Frey, 1983), by restricting the amount of time spent thinking about negative information associated with partners (Baumeister & Cairns, 1992), by forgetting or selectively misremembering negative information about partners (Crary, 1966; Mischel, Ebbesen, & Zeiss, 1976), or by comparing partners to individuals with less desirable attributes (Crocker & Major, 1989; Wills, 1981). Idealized images also might be buffered by engaging in biased memory searches designed to find or highlight partners' most valued traits (Murray & Holmes, 1993, 1994; Sanitioso, Kunda, & Fong, 1990), by believing that partners' best traits are atypical while their worst traits are common (Campbell, 1986; Marks, 1984), by perceiving partners' ambiguous traits in aggrandized ways (Dunning, Meyerowitz, & Holzberg, 1989), by derogating attractive alternatives (Buunk, Collins, Taylor, Van Yperen, & Dakof, 1990; Johnson & Rusbult, 1989; Simpson, Gangestad, & Lerma, 1990; Van Lange & Rusbult, 1995), by embellishing partners' most endearing attributes (Johnson & Rusbult, 1989), or by inaccurately inferring partners' damaging thoughts and feelings in relationship-threatening situations (Simpson et al., 1995).

On the other hand, in situations that call for greater accuracy (e.g., when important relationship decisions must be made, when attractive alternative partners become available, when difficult relationship problems emerge), moderate to large discrepancies should motivate individuals to engage in more in-depth analysis and information processing about the partner or the relationship. One consequence of engaging in more systematic, in-depth processing might be that individuals will use current perception versus ideal discrepancies to explain their relationship problems more often (e.g., "My ideal partner is very warm, and you are cold and aloof, which explains why I am unhappy"). In-depth processing also may lead individuals to try to alter their own behavior, their partner's behavior, or both. If in-depth processing leads individuals to the conclusion that perception-ideal discrepancies are important but cannot be reduced, individuals may opt to leave the relationship, look for new partners, or seek solace in other activities (e.g., through job satisfaction).

Empirical evidence for the model

To date, much of our theoretical work remains speculative. However, we are currently conducting a program of research that has tested some of the model's basic postulates. We now review this research.

The structure and content of partner and relationship ideals.   To identify the structure and content of partner and relationship ideals, Fletcher et al. (1999) conducted six separate studies. Participants in these studies were heterosexual individuals (usually college students) between the ages of 18 and 30. Adopting an inductive approach to identifying the ideals dimensions that people naturally possess, we asked men and women in Study 1 to list all of the traits or characteristics that described their ideal romantic partners and their ideal romantic relationships. After removing redundant items, we created two extensive lists of attributes that described ideal partners and ideal relationships. In Study 2, another sample of men and women rated each item in terms of its importance for their *own* standards concerning ideal partners and ideal relationships. A factor analysis of the ideal partner items revealed the three factors we expected: (1) partner characteristics relevant to intimacy, warmth, trust, and loyalty (labeled Partner Warmth/Trustworthiness), (2) personality and appearance characteristics concerning how attractive, energetic, and healthy the partner was (labeled Partner Vitality/Attractiveness), and (3) characteristics relevant to the partner's social status and resources (labeled Partner Status/Resources). The relationship ideal items produced two factors: (1) the importance of intimacy, loyalty, and stability in a relationship (labeled Relationship Intimacy/Loyalty), and (2) the importance of excitement and passion in a relationship (labeled Relationship Passion). All five scales possessed good internal consistency and adequate test-retest reliability.

Study 3 tested the factor structure of the ideal partner and ideal relationship scales using Confirmatory Factor Analysis (CFA). In a new sample of men and women who completed all of the ideals scales, two higher-order factors were identified (see figure 4.2) which we labeled Warmth/Loyalty and Vitality/Status/Passion. As predicted, individuals who placed more importance on Passion than Intimacy/Loyalty in their relationships desired ideal partners with attributes that would logically promote the development of such ideal relationships (e.g., partners who scored higher on the partner vitality/attractiveness ideals scale). Further CFA tests revealed that the model shown in figure 4.2 produced a better fit than did other plausible models and, importantly, that a model in which all items loaded di-

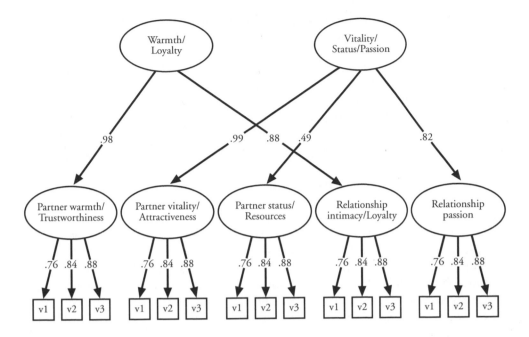

Figure 4.2   Confirmatory factor analysis of the ideal partner and ideal relationship scales (taken from Fletcher et al., 1999)

rectly on the two higher-order factors fit poorly. Moreover, the factor structure shown in the figure replicated across different samples and across men and women. Intriguingly, these higher-order factors are similar to the two basic forms of love identified by Berscheid and Walster (1978): passionate love and companionate love.

Study 4 provided validation evidence for the ideals scales. Convergent validation tests, for example, indicated that individuals who had stronger beliefs about the importance of intimacy in successful relationships rated Partner Warmth/Trustworthiness and Relationship Intimacy/Loyalty ideals as relatively more important. Individuals who rated passion as a primary cause of relationship success, on the other hand, placed more emphasis on the Partner Vitality/Attractiveness and Relationship Passion ideals. Those who rated external factors (e.g., a nice house) as more important in influencing relationship success placed more weight on the Partner Status/Resources ideal. Individuals with a more unrestricted sociosexual orientation (i.e., those who are more willing to have sex without closeness and emotional bonding) rated the Partner Warmth/Trustworthiness and Relationship Intimacy/Loyalty ideals as less important than did individuals with a more restricted sociosexual orientation. Finally, individuals who were involved in more satisfying and longer-term relationships placed more emphasis on the Relationship Intimacy/Loyalty ideal. Discriminant validation tests confirmed that the ideals scales were not correlated with various response biases.

Study 6 tested the basic functional postulate that people will evaluate their current partners and relationships by comparing them against their ideal standards. According to our model, the more closely perceptions of the current partner/relationship match individuals' ideal standards, the more positively they should evaluate their relationships. To test this hypothesis, a new sample of men and women ranked the importance of various ideal attributes along with their perceptions of their current partner/relationship on items taken from the ideal partner and ideal relationship scales. As predicted, individuals who had smaller perception-ideal discrepancies rated their relationships more favorably, even when the perceived difficulty of finding a good alternative partner/relationship was statistically controlled.

Changes in ideal standards across time.   Although the Fletcher et al. (1999) studies provide initial support for our model, all six studies were cross-sectional in design. To test and make inferences about possible causal relations, cross-sectional designs are obviously problematic. Thus, Fletcher, Simpson, and Thomas (1998) conducted a longitudinal study. A large sample of individuals in newly formed dating relationships completed a battery of measures assessing perceptions of their current partner/relationship, the quality of their relationship, and their ideal standards once a month for three months. They then completed the same scales nine months later (unless they had broken up with their partners). The first wave of measurement typically occurred three weeks after individuals had started dating someone.

Using cross-lagged analyses, we were able to test a crucial prediction from our model – that comparisons between ideals and perceptions of the current partner should, in fact, have a causal impact on relationship evaluations. We also tested a balance model, which proposes that ideals, current perceptions, and relationship evaluations all constrain one another equally. The cross-lagged analyses supported our causal hypothesis, but refuted the balance model. Changes in ratings over time occurred in only one direction, with greater consistency between ideals and perceptions of the current partner/relationship (assessed at earlier times in the relationship) predicting increases in evaluations of the partner and the relationship over time, but not vice versa. Because these analyses are correlational, third variables could be generating these effects. Nevertheless, the current evidence suggests that cognitive comparisons between ideal standards and perceptions of the current partner/relationship influence the way in which partners and relationships are evaluated over time, at least in the early stages of relationship development.

We also examined links between ideals and perceptions of the partner/relationship across time. As expected, more positive perceptions of the partner/relationship at earlier points in time predicted more importance being placed on similar ideal dimensions over time, but not the reverse. This finding may be attributable to the fact that ideals tend to be subjective, personally held standards that are similar to preferences. Consequently, ideals may be less constrained by reality than is true of perceptions of the partner and relationship. For example, an individual may want to believe that his or her partner is loyal, considerate, and committed to the relationship, but this belief may be difficult to sustain in the face of incontrovertible evidence that the partner is interested in someone else.

Ideal standards, flexibility, and relationship quality.   To determine how ideal standards and their flexibility jointly affect relationship evaluations, Campbell, Simpson, Kashy, and Fletcher

(2001) had a large sample of individuals involved in dating relationships rate themselves and their ideal partners on all of the items comprising the three ideal partner scales. Individuals also rated how flexible each of their ideals were (that is, how far below each ideal standard a prospective partner could be and still remain a viable partner) and how closely their current partner matched their ideal standards on each scale. Individuals who rated themselves higher on each scale had higher ideal standards that were less flexible. Corroborating past research, the quality of their relationships was higher if individuals' current partners more closely matched their ideal standards. However, this effect was moderated by the degree of flexibility individuals displayed on two ideals dimensions – warmth/trustworthiness and status/resources. For these dimensions, individuals who thought their partners more closely matched their ideals and who had less flexible standards reported the highest relationship quality.

The magnitude of perception-ideal discrepancies not only should affect how individuals evaluate their relationships; such discrepancies also might affect how the partners of the individuals feel about the relationship. Thus, in a second study, Campbell et al. (2001) asked both members of a large sample of dating couples to report their ideal standards, how closely their partners matched their ideals, and their degree of flexibility on each ideals dimension. Smaller perception-ideal discrepancies predicted greater relationship quality as reported by both members of the dyad (i.e., both the "actor" and the "partner"). In other words, individuals whose partners more closely matched their ideals reported that their relationships were better, as did the partners of the individuals. This "partner" effect suggests that individuals may sense how well they are "living up to" their partners' ideal standards. Over time, those who are faring poorly may feel threatened or insecure about the long-term status of the relationship or their position within it, which should lower their evaluations. Replicating the first study, individuals with partners who more closely matched their ideals, and who possessed less flexible standards, also reported the highest relationship quality (i.e., flexibility of ideals moderated the relation between perception–ideal discrepancies and relationship quality).

Unresolved Questions and Issues

Several important questions remain concerning how individuals establish and adjust their ideal standards over time, the ways in which relationship-discrepancies are similar to and different from self-discrepancies, and how dyad-level processes are likely to complicate the operation of ideal standards in relationships. In the final section, we address these issues, all of which require further research and theoretical development.

The establishment and adjustment of ideal standards

Why do some individuals have high standards for their ideal partners and relationships while others possess humble standards? At present, relatively little is known about what factors influence how individuals set and adjust their ideal standards. Greater experience with romantic relationships, along with the reality-checks imposed by occasional romantic rejections, might lower lofty, unrealistic ideal aspirations in some people. For individuals whose parents had a poor marriage, however, greater personal experience in romantic relationships might actually elevate their ideal aspirations. Supply and demand considerations also may affect the level of an individual's ideal standards. Persons who are in relatively "short supply," for example, should be able to command more from prospective mates, slowly raising their own ideal standards. Those not in demand may have to gradually lower their standards (see Guttentag & Secord, 1983). Moreover, as we have seen, individuals with less flexible ideal standards tend to have higher ideals (Campbell et al., 2001). Being less flexible in terms of ideals may encourage individuals to aspire to loftier ideal standards, and vice versa.

Two variables, however, have particularly clear and theoretically important ties to the calibration of ideal standards. First, as Bowlby (1982) hypothesized, partners with more positive self-views (i.e., higher relationship-relevant self-esteem) tend to hold higher ideal standards (Murray et al., 1996a, 1996b). Second, partners who think they have more to offer others (i.e., those with higher self-perceived mate value) should have higher ideal standards, at least concerning their ideal partners (Regan, 1998). Indeed, recent research has documented that individuals who rate themselves higher on the three partner ideals scales (warmth/trustworthiness, vitality/attractiveness, and status/resources) tend to have higher self esteem and higher ideal standards (Campbell et al., 2001). Consistent with our previous theorizing, Campbell et al. (2001) also found that people who have more positive perceptions of their own standing on specific dimensions (e.g., vitality/attractiveness) possess less flexible ideal standards.

How might relationship-based self-esteem and self-perceived mate value be related in the establishment or adjustment of ideal standards over time? One possibility is that increases in self-perceived mate value may gradually increase self-esteem, which in turn might elevate ideal standards. Wright (1994), for instance, has suggested that self-esteem should be a reliable gauge of how an individual is perceived by others as a mate. Among other things, higher self esteem tends to foster enhanced social competence, heightened expectations for success, greater optimism, more self-efficacy, and stronger motives to achieve important goals (Leary, Tambor, Terdal, & Downs, 1995). These attributes should have a direct bearing on how high individuals set their ideal standards. On the other hand, increases in self-esteem could slowly increase self-perceived mate value, which might then increase ideal standards. This prediction could be derived from the sociometer model (see Leary et al., 1995), which claims that self-esteem is a barometer reflecting the degree to which individuals feel included and approved of by significant others. Increases in self-esteem may lead to elevated assessments of one's "worth" as a mate, thereby raising ideal standards. Regardless of which model eventually receives support (and perhaps both will), relations among self-esteem and self-perceived mate value are likely to be stronger on ideal dimensions that are more important to individuals.

Similarities and differences between self-discrepancy and relationship-discrepancy processes

There are important similarities and differences between self-discrepancy processes and relationship-discrepancy processes. As noted earlier, it is often difficult to make clear distinctions between purely self-based cognitions and relationship-based cognitions, primarily because both tend to occur in the same contexts and the self-concept is often closely integrated with intimate partners and relationships. Nevertheless, it is possible to discern some key similarities and differences.

One similarity is that both self-discrepancy and relationship-discrepancy models postulate the operation of the same basic underlying cognitive processes. Both self-based and relationship-based ideals, for example, should exert maximal influence when they are made salient or are chronically accessible. Both models also predict that large, chronic discrepancies between important ideal standards and related perceptions of the self and partner/relationship should draw the individual's attention, increase in-depth processing, and produce negative affect. In addition, the basic perceiver goals of evaluation, explanation, and regulation, as well as the motivating drives of enhancement versus accuracy, are present in both models. These similarities are not surprising given the abstract level at which many of these principles and processes are hypothesized to operate. However, at a more fine-grained process level, and in terms of content, there are some major differences between the two kinds of models.

As we have seen, there are specific categories of partner and relationship ideals that are not present in models of self ideals. We believe that the three categories of partner ideals might reflect specific and unique evolutionary adaptations that may differ in many ways from those associated with self ideals. The cognitive, affective, and behavioral consequences of large perception–ideal discrepancies are also likely to be different in self-discrepancy versus relationship-discrepancy models. For example, individuals might react to large discrepancies by leaving their relationship, by attempting to modify their partner's behavior, or by pursuing a different relationship. None of these actions seem likely to resolve or reduce self–ideal self discrepancies.

Perhaps the major difference between self-discrepancy models and relationship-discrepancy models, however, is that two people are involved – and must be taken into account – in relationship-discrepancy models. When individuals' actual self-views are discrepant from their ideal standards, and changes in behavior could reduce these discrepancies, individuals have to focus only on altering their own actions. However, when individuals' perceptions of their current partners/relationships diverge from their ideal partner and relationships standards, behavior change is likely to involve not only the self but also the partner. As we shall see, this should complicate the operation and functioning of relationship-discrepancies in significant ways. To date, only one study has examined how the ideal standards held by each partner in a relationship affect the relationship outcomes experienced by each partner. Campbell et al.'s (1999) finding that individuals with smaller relationship-relevant perception–ideal discrepancies have partners who also report being more satisfied with the relationship highlights the potential importance – as well as the potential complexity – involved in examining dyadic processes in relation to relationship ideals.

Dyad-level processes and effects

As previously noted, relationship-discrepancy models, unlike self-discrepancy models, take on an added layer of complexity when the thoughts, feelings, perceptions, and behavior of the relationship partner are considered. Partners can influence or manipulate how individuals view themselves, the level of their ideal standards, what individuals can expect from their partners, and even how they view their partners. For example, if individuals have large perception–ideal discrepancies for which they think their partners are primarily responsible, such individuals by themselves may not be in a position to make the behavioral changes necessary to reduce these discrepancies. If a wife is unhappy about the lack of sexual activity in her marriage and blames her husband, the husband's steadfast refusal to have sex should sustain her discrepancies, perhaps regardless of what she says or does.

Moreover, in regulating their own discrepancies, individuals may have to take into account the magnitude and origins of their partners' perception–ideal discrepancies. There may be times when individuals find it difficult to reduce their own discrepancies because their partners refuse to alter their own behavior, or because their partners might threaten to leave the relationship (or worse) if individuals try to reduce their own discrepancies. Consider, for example, how dyadic processes might influence what happens when an individual is motivated to be accurate and is highly committed to his or her relationship, but is experiencing large, persistent perception-ideal discrepancies that are, in part, due to the partner's undesirable actions. Initially, the individual might try to change his or her partner's behavior. However, if the partner simply will not or cannot change the undesirable behaviors, the individual may be forced to shift away from purely behavioral strategies. At first, the individual may try to increase the flexibility of his or her ideal standards. If this proves to be an ineffective solution, but the individual remains committed to the relationship, he or she may shift away from an accuracy motivation set and begin using one or more of the enhancement-based perceptual strategies discussed earlier (such as lowering ideal standards, enhancing perceptions of the partner, or downplaying the importance of formerly valued ideal standards). If these perceptual strategies all fail, the individual eventually may decide to terminate the relationship.

Important dyad-level effects also may exist if relationship partners have different motives when discussing or thinking about important issues in their relationship. For instance, when deciding whether or not to end a relationship, the less-invested (weak-link) partner in a dyad should adopt an accuracy motivational set when contemplating the pros and cons of remaining in the relationship. The more-invested (strong-link) partner, on the other hand, should adopt an enhancement motivational set, struggling to see the best in his or her partner and the dyad in an effort to maintain the relationship. By viewing the same general issue through very different motivational sets, partners are likely to identify further disparities, dissimilarities, and incompatibilities in their relationship. If these new areas of difference grow, the partner who is more motivated to maintain the relationship (most likely the strong-link partner: see Attridge, Berscheid, & Simpson, 1995) may gradually shift to an accuracy motivational set, rendering the relationship even less stable.

Many intriguing questions remain about how dyad-level processes might influence the operation and use of ideal standards. We know very little, for instance, about how one partner's ideal standards are communicated or conveyed to the other partner, or what happens when one partner is motivated to be accurate in situations when the other partner is motivated to enhance the relationship. We also know almost nothing about whether possessing ideal standards that are similar to those held by one's partner facilitates relationship functioning and quality, or how partners might influence one another concerning the timing and extent of in-depth processing of ideal standards.

Conclusions

Berscheid and Walster (1978) were prescient: idealized images of romantic partners – and even romantic relationships – do play important roles in close relationships. However, we are just beginning to understand the underlying functions and processes associated with ideal standards.

In this chapter, we have presented a new model and some supporting data that elucidate the content and structure of partner and relationship ideal standards, the basic functions that ideals serve, and how they may operate at the level of cognitive processing. In addition, we have described the way in which perception–ideal discrepancies are associated with how both partners in a relationship evaluate relationship quality. We have also outlined how the two motivational sets of relationship-enhancement versus accuracy might be related to ideals and related processes, and we have described the differences and similarities between ideals as they function within the self and within dyadic relationships.

The Ideal Standards Model, of course, is still under construction and, therefore, portions of it remain frankly speculative. Nevertheless, some central tenets of the model have received empirical support, and we believe that our theorizing points the way toward fertile possibilities for future research.

Notes

1. The methodology typically used to test self-discrepancy theory also is problematic in that discrepancies between actual–ideal or actual–ought standards are calculated using difference scores. The use of difference scores in correlational studies can produce interpretation problems that render results essentially uninterpretable because main effects are confounded with interactions (Evans, 1991). Consider a study in which individuals' ideal self scores (on positive dimensions) are subtracted from their actual self scores to generate discrepancy scores. These scores might be correlated with self-esteem, resulting in a hypothetical correlation of $-.50$ (that is, smaller discrepancies are associated with higher self-esteem). Unfortunately, this correlation could be driven entirely by the relation between self-esteem and actual self-ratings, having nothing to do with the discrepancy per se. Under these circumstances, a large correlation involving discrepancy scores would emerge even if ideal scores were randomly generated. In testing our model, we measured discrepancies in ways that avoid the problems associated with the use of raw difference scores.

References

Alloy, L. B., & Abramson, L. Y. (1979). Judgment of contingency in depressed and nondepressed students: Sadder but wiser? *Journal of Experimental Psychology: General, 108*, 441–485.
Aron, A., & Westbay, L. (1996). Dimensions of the prototype of love. *Journal of Personality and Social Psychology, 70*, 535–551.

Attridge, M., Berscheid, E., & Simpson, J. A. (1995). Predicting relationship stability from both partners versus one. *Journal of Personality and Social Psychology, 69*, 254–268.

Baldwin, M. W. (1992). Relational schemas and the processing of social information. *Psychological Bulletin, 112*, 461–484.

Barsalou, L. W. (1985). Ideals, central tendency, and frequency of instantiations as determinants of graded structure in categories. *Journal of Experimental Psychology: Learning, Memory, and Cognition, 11*, 629–654.

Baumeister, R. F., & Cairns, K. J. (1992). Repression and self-presentation: When audiences interfere with self-deceptive strategies. *Journal of Personality and Social Psychology, 62*, 851–862.

Berscheid, E., & Walster, E. H. (1978). *Interpersonal attraction* (2nd ed.). Reading, MA: Addison-Wesley.

Bowlby, J. (1982). *Attachment and loss: Vol. 1. Attachment*. London: Hogarth Press.

Buss, D. M., & Schmitt, D. P. (1993). Sexual strategies theory: A contextual evolutionary analysis of human mating. *Psychological Review, 100*, 204–232.

Buunk, B. P., Collins, R. L., Taylor, S. E., Van Yperen, N. W., & Dakof, G. A. (1990). The affective consequences of social comparison: Either direction has its ups and downs. *Journal of Personality and Social Psychology, 59*, 1238–1249.

Campbell, J. D. (1986). Similarity and uniqueness: The effects of attribute type, relevance, and individual differences in self-esteem and depression. *Journal of Personality and Social Psychology, 50*, 281–294.

Campbell, L. J., Simpson, J. A., Kashy, D. A., Fletcher, G. L. O. (2001). Ideal standards, the self, and flexibility of ideals in close relationships. *Personality and Social Psychology Bulletin, 27*, 447–462.

Campbell, L. J., Simpson, J. A., & Orina, M. (1999). Sex and mating: Sexual strategies, trade-offs, and strategic pluralism. In D. H. Rosen & M. Luebbert (Eds.), *Evolution of the psyche* (pp. 34–61). Westport, CT: Greenwood.

Carver, C. S., & Scheier, M. F. (1982). Control theory: A useful conceptual framework for personality-social, clinical, and health psychology. *Psychological Bulletin, 92*, 111–135.

Carver, C. S., & Scheier, M. F. (1990). Origins and functions of positive and negative affect: A control-process view. *Psychological Review, 97*, 19–35.

Colvin, C. R., & Block, J. (1994). Do positive illusions foster mental health? An examination of the Taylor and Brown formulation. *Psychological Bulletin, 116*, 3–20.

Cooley, C. H. (1902). *Human nature and the social order*. New York: Scribner's.

Crary, W. G. (1966). Reactions to incongruent self-experiences. *Journal of Consulting Psychology, 30*, 246–252.

Crocker, J., & Major, B. (1989). Social stigma and self-esteem: The self-protective properties of stigma. *Psychological Review, 96*, 608–630.

Dunning, D., Meyerowitz, J. A., & Holzberg, A. (1989). Ambiguity and self-evaluation: The role of idiosyncratic trait definitions in self-serving assessments of ability. *Journal of Personality and Social Psychology, 57*, 1082–1090.

Evans, M. G. (1991). The problem of analyzing multiplicative composites: Interactions revisited. *American Psychologist, 46*, 6–15.

Fehr, B., & Russell, J. A. (1991). The concept of love viewed from a prototype perspective. *Journal of Personality and Social Psychology, 60*, 425–438.

Fletcher, G. J. O., & Kininmonth, L. (1992). Measuring relationship beliefs: An individual difference scale. *Journal of Research in Personality, 26*, 371–397.

Fletcher, G. J. O., Simpson, J. A., & Thomas, G. (1998). The role of ideals in early relationship development. Unpublished manuscript, University of Canterbury, New Zealand.

Fletcher, G. J. O., Simpson, J. A., Thomas, G., & Giles, L. (1999). Ideals in intimate relationships. *Journal of Personality and Social Psychology, 76*, 72–89.

Fletcher, G. J. O., & Thomas, G. (1996). Lay theories in close relationships: Their structure and function. In G. J. O Fletcher & J. Fitness (Eds.), *Knowledge structures in close relationships: A social psychological approach* (pp. 3–24). Mahwah, NJ: Erlbaum.

Freud, S. (1961). On narcissism: An introduction. In J. Strachey (Ed. and Trans.), *The standard edition of the complete psychological works of Sigmund Freud* (Vol. 14, pp. 69–102). London: Hogarth

Press. (Original work published 1914)

Gangestad, S. W., & Simpson, J. A. (2000). The evolution of human mating: Trade-offs and strategic pluralism. *Behavioral and Brain Sciences, 23*, 573.

Gollwitzer, P. M., & Kinney, R. F. (1989). Effects of deliberative and implemental mind-sets on illusion of control. *Journal of Personality and Social Psychology, 56*, 531–542.

Guttentag, M., & Secord, P. F. (1983). *Too many women? The sex ratio question.* Beverly Hills, CA: Sage.

Hall, J. A., & Taylor, S. E. (1976). When love is blind: Maintaining idealized images of one's spouse. *Human Relations, 29*, 751–761.

Hassebrauck, M. (1997). Cognitions of relationship quality: A prototype analysis of their structure and consequences. *Personal Relationships, 4*, 163–185.

Higgins, E. T. (1987). Self-discrepancy: A theory relating self and affect. *Psychological Review, 94*, 319–340.

Higgins, E. T. (1989). Self-discrepancy theory: What patterns of self-beliefs cause people to suffer? In L. Berkowitz (Ed.), *Advances in experimental social psychology* (Vol. 22). New York: Academic Press.

James, W. (1892). *Psychology.* Cleveland, OH: World Publishing.

Johnson, D. J., & Rusbult, C. E. (1989). Resisting temptation: Devaluation of alternative partners as a means of maintaining commitment in close relationships. *Journal of Personality and Social Psychology, 57*, 967–980.

Kelley, H. H., & Thibaut, J. W. (1978). *Interpersonal relations: A theory of interdependence.* New York: Wiley.

Kenrick, D. T., Groth, G. E., Trost, M. R., & Sadalla, E. K. (1993). Integrating evolutionary and social exchange perspectives on relationships: effects of gender, self-appraisal, and involvement level on mate selection. *Journal of Personality and Social Psychology, 64*, 951–969.

Lambert, A. J., & Wedell, D. H. (1991). The self and social judgment: Effects of affective reaction and "own position" on judgments of unambiguous and ambiguous information about others. *Journal of Personality and Social Psychology, 61*, 884–897.

Leary, M. R., Tambor, E. S., Terdal, S. K., & Downs, D. L. (1995). Self-esteem as an interpersonal monitor: The sociometer hypothesis. *Journal of Personality and Social Psychology, 68*, 518–530.

Levinger, G., & Breedlove, J. (1966). Interpersonal attraction and agreement: A study of marriage partners. *Journal of Personality and Social Psychology, 3*, 367–372.

Marks, G. (1984). Thinking one's abilities are unique and one's opinions are common. *Personality and Social Psychology Bulletin, 10*, 203–208.

Maslow, A. H. (1954). *Motivation and personality.* New York: Harper and Row.

Mischel, W., Ebbesen, E. B., & Zeiss, A. R. (1976). Determinants of selective memory about the self. *Journal of Consulting and Clinical Psychology, 44*, 92–103.

Murray, S. L., & Holmes, J. G. (1993). Seeing virtues in faults: Negativity and the transformation of interpersonal narratives in close relationships. *Journal of Personality and Social Psychology, 65*, 707–722.

Murray, S. L., & Holmes, J. G. (1994). Story-telling in close relationships: The construction of confidence. *Personality and Social Psychology Bulletin, 20*, 663–676.

Murray, S. L., & Holmes, J. G. (1996). The construction of relationship realities. In G. J. O. Fletcher & J. Fitness (Eds.), *Knowledge structures in close relationships: A social psychological approach* (pp. 91–120). Mahwah, NJ: Erlbaum.

Murray, S. L., Holmes, J. G., & Griffin, D. W. (1996a). The benefits of positive illusions: Idealization and the construction of satisfaction in close relationships. *Journal of Personality and Social Psychology, 70*, 79–98.

Murray, S. L., Holmes, J. G., & Griffin, D. W. (1996b). The self-fulfilling nature of positive illusions in romantic relationships: Love is not blind, but prescient. *Journal of Personality and Social Psychology, 71*, 1155–1180.

Pyszczynski, T., Greenberg, J., & Holt, K. (1985). Maintaining consistency between self-serving beliefs and available data: A bias in information processing. *Personality and Social Psychology Bulletin, 11*, 179–190.

Regan, P. C. (1998). What if you can't get what you want? Willingness to compromise ideal mate selection standards as a function of sex, mate value, and relationship context. *Personality and Social Psychology Bulletin, 24*, 1294–1303.

Rogers, C. R. (1961). *On becoming a person*. Boston: Houghton Mifflin.

Rusbult, C. E., Onizuka, R. K., & Lipkus, I. (1993). What do we really want? Mental models of ideal romantic involvement explored through multidimensional scaling. *Journal of Experimental Social Psychology, 29*, 493–527.

Sanitioso, R., Kunda, Z., & Fong, G. T. (1990). Motivated recruitment of autobiographical memory. *Journal of Personality and Social Psychology, 59*, 229–241.

Sedikides, C., & Showronski, J. J. (1993). The self in impression formation: Trait centrality and social perception. *Journal of Experimental Social Psychology, 29*, 347–357.

Simpson, J. A., & Gangestad, S. W. (1992). Sociosexuality and romantic partner choice. *Journal of Personality, 60*, 31–51.

Simpson, J. A., Gangestad, S. W., & Lerma, M. (1990). Perception of physical attractiveness: Mechanisms involved in the maintenance of romantic relationships. *Journal of Personality and Social Psychology, 59*, 1192–1201.

Simpson, J. A., Ickes, W., & Blackstone, T. (1995). When the head protects the heart: Empathic accuracy in dating relationships. *Journal of Personality and Social Psychology, 69*, 629–641.

Singh, G. K., Mathews, T. J., Clarke, S. C., Yannicos, T., & Smith, B. L. (1995). Annual summary of births, marriages, divorces, and deaths: United States, 1994. *Monthly Vital Statistics Report* (Vol. 43, No. 13). Hyattsville, MD: National Center for Health Statistics.

Spanier, G. B. (1972). Romanticism and marital adjustment. *Journal of Marriage and the Family, 34*, 481–487.

Steele, C. M. (1988). The psychology of self-affirmation: Sustaining the integrity of the self. In L. Berkowitz (Ed.), *Advances in experimental social psychology* (Vol. 21, pp. 261–302). New York: Academic Press.

Stephan, W., Berscheid, E., & Walster, E. (1971). Sexual arousal and heterosexual perception. *Journal of Personality and Social Psychology, 20*, 93–101.

Sternberg, R. J., & Barnes, M. L. (1985). Real and ideal others in romantic relationships: Is four a crowd? *Journal of Personality and Social Psychology, 49*, 1586–1608.

Tangney, J. P., Niedenthal, P. M., Covert, M. V., & Barlow, D. H. (1998). Are shame and guilt related to distinct self-discrepancies? A test of Higgins's (1987) hypothesis. *Journal of Personality and Social Psychology, 75*, 256–268.

Taylor, S. E. (1989). *Positive illusions: Creative self-deception and the healthy mind*. New York: Basic Books.

Taylor, S. E., & Brown, J. D. (1988). Illusion and well-being: A social psychological perspective on mental health. *Psychological Bulletin, 103*, 193–210.

Thibaut, J. W., & Kelley, H. H. (1959). *The social psychology of groups*. New York: Wiley.

Van Lange, P. A. M., & Rusbult, C. E. (1995). My relationship is better than – and not as bad as – yours is: The perception of superiority in close relationships. *Personality and Social Psychology Bulletin, 21*, 32–44.

Waller, W., & Hill, R. (1951). *The family: A dynamic interpretation* (2nd ed.). New York: Holt, Rinehart, and Winston.

Wills, T. A. (1981). Downward comparison principles in social psychology. *Psychological Bulletin, 90*, 245–271.

Wright, R. (1994). *The moral animal*. New York: Vintage.

Wyer, R. S., & Frey, D. (1983). The effects of feedback about self and others on the recall and judgments of feedback-relevant information. *Journal of Experimental Social Psychology, 19*, 540–559.

Chapter Five

Seeking a Sense of Conviction: Motivated Cognition in Close Relationships

Sandra L. Murray

Love is a gross exaggeration of the difference between one person and everybody else.

The idea that individuals in satisfying, trusting relationships idealize their romantic partners permeates lay conceptions of love, as Shaw's quip illustrates. Such references usually seem tongue in cheek as they typically warn individuals of the risks of putting imperfect partners on pedestals. In fact, many psychologists argue that relationship well-being and stability depend on individuals relinquishing such seemingly naïve perceptions in favor of more accurate and realistic appraisals of their partners' true virtues and faults (e.g., Brickman, 1987; Brehm, 1992).

Such admonitions ignore a curious phenomenon that emerges as relationships develop. Declines in satisfaction consistently accompany individuals' keener insight into the negative aspects of their partners and relationships (e.g., Clark & Grote, 1998; Huston & Vangelisti, 1991). How then are individuals to resolve the tension between the practical necessity of insight and their hopes for happiness? Should they simply try to minimize the risk of disappointment by resigning themselves to their partners' weaknesses early on? Or does lasting happiness actually necessitate benevolent transformations of a partner's perceived virtues and faults? This chapter attempts to answer these questions by examining the nature and structure of relationship representations that foster well-being and stability without sacrificing insight into a partner's or relationship's more obvious flaws.

This chapter was prepared with the support of a NIMH B/START grant awarded to S. Murray. Please address correspondence to Sandra Murray, Psychology Department, Park Hall, State University of New York, Buffalo, NY, 14260-4110. Electronic mail may be sent via the Internet to smurray@acsu.buffalo.edu.

The Need for Gross Exaggeration: An Uncertainty-Reduction Model

Few decisions are as important or as life-altering as the decision to commit to an imperfect romantic partner (Brehm & Cohen, 1962; Brickman, 1987). In perhaps no other context do adults voluntarily tie the satisfaction of their hopes, goals, and wishes so completely to the good will of another (Braiker & Kelley, 1979; Drigotas & Rusbult, 1992). Given the vulnerability that such dependence implies, individuals need to possess a sense of conviction in the belief that the relationship really is a good one and that the partner can be counted on to be caring and responsive across time and situations (Holmes & Rempel, 1989).

This sense of conviction in the partner's and relationship's continued value and availability seems to require the absence of significant nagging doubts or uncertainties (Murray & Holmes, 1993, 1994). Even in the closest relationships, though, doubts inevitably arise because few partners are perfect and people inevitably transgress in their relationships no matter how well-intentioned they are (Braiker & Kelley, 1979). Conflicts are also virtually guaranteed because so few individuals marry or commit themselves to partners who are compatible on even basic personality dimensions (Lykken & Tellegen, 1993). In the face of such imperfect realities, then, the continuing challenge in maintaining relationship well-being may be to prevent serious doubts from arising and undermining a sense of conviction (e.g., Brickman, 1987; Fletcher, Fincham, Cramer, & Heron, 1987; Johnson & Rusbult, 1989; Murray & Holmes, 1993, 1994).

In this chapter, I outline the processes of motivated construal or relationship-enhancement that seem to foster a sense of conviction in the face of less-than-perfect partners and relationships. I first discuss the content or surface features of conviction, focusing on the positive illusions that predict relationship well-being and stability. I then discuss the structural foundation of conviction, focusing on the organization of relationship representations that successfully contain the implications of negativity. I conclude by discussing self-protection motives that might exacerbate doubt and interfere with relationship-enhancement processes, focusing on the vulnerabilities imposed by dispositional insecurities, such as low self-esteem.

A Leap of Faith: The Surface Features of Conviction

If the imperatives of conviction are such that individuals cannot comfortably tolerate salient, nagging doubts, and the reality of interdependence is such that occasions for doubt inevitably arise, how do individuals resolve this romantic conundrum? The existing evidence suggests that individuals in satisfying, trusting dating and marital relationships find a sense of conviction by overstating the case for commitment – by seeing partners and relationships in the best, or most positive, light possible (e.g., Fletcher, Simpson, Thomas, & Giles, 1999; Martz et al., 1998; Murray, Holmes, & Griffin, 1996a, 1996b; Van Lange & Rusbult, 1995).

This hypothesis rests on the general assumption that the process of dispelling doubt is likely to shape the nature of the motivated perceptions intimates construct. For instance, individuals might strengthen the perception that they really have found the "right" partner by projecting their images of the ideal partner onto the partners they possess (e.g., Murray et al., 1996a; Murstein, 1967, 1971). They might also quell any concerns about potential personality incompatibilities by projecting their own self-images onto their partners, assuming greater similarity than actually exists (e.g., Murray et al., 1996a; Thomas, Fletcher, & Lange, 1997). Second, the possibility or actual occurrence of conflict may heighten intimates' need to believe that they can control or ward off future difficulties. And third, the risk of dissolution might heighten intimates' need to believe that their future is rosy, even if most couples face an uncertain future (Helgeson, 1994).

Given these general sources of uncertainty, the perceptions that foster the sense of conviction critical for well-being might involve benevolent, even idealized, images of the partner, considerable feelings of efficacy or control in resolving differences, and unequivocally positive forecasts for the future. My colleagues and I examined the evidence for this general proposition in a series of studies exploring the existence and consequences of positive illusions in romantic relationships (Murray et al., 1996a, 1996b; Murray & Holmes, 1997).[1]

Because most dictionaries define illusions as perceptions that have no basis in reality, the term "positive illusions" may be raising an eyebrow or two among some readers. In adopting this metaphor, though, we are not arguing that romantic partners' perceptions are patently false. Instead, we prefer to use the term "illusion" in a looser sense, one that implies that individuals base their perceptions on a kernel of truth, but construe this reality in the most positive light possible. The reasons for this looser definition are both conceptual and practical. First, at a conceptual level, obvious distortions of fact, such as deciding a tone-deaf partner is a musical genius, are not likely to instill confidence or conviction. After all, even the most motivated perceivers need to feel as though their perceptions are warranted by the available evidence (e.g., Kunda, 1990). Second, at a practical level, arguing that romantic perceptions are truly illusory requires definitive benchmarks for objective reality.

In the realm of social perception, such objective standards for reality are difficult (if not impossible) to obtain. Recognizing this difficulty, the traditional definition of positive illusions centers around logical impossibilities (e.g., Taylor & Brown, 1988). For instance, it seems at least possible that some couples are being overly optimistic if the vast majority of newlyweds state that they are less vulnerable to divorce than the typical or average couple (e.g., Helgeson, 1994). Similarly, it seems unlikely that the majority of individuals possess partners who are more virtuous than the average partner (e.g., Van Lange & Rusbult, 1995). Although such perceptions provide suggestive evidence of idealism, impressions of the typical relationship do not provide a perfect reality benchmark because intimates might be depicting their own relationships accurately and derogating the typical relationship (cf. Colvin & Block, 1994).

Romantic relationships, though, provide the unique opportunity of using an interpersonal (although still imperfect) benchmark for reality. That is, the convergence between each intimate's perceptions of the same relationship provides a possible benchmark or proxy for the kernel of truth underlying romantic perceptions (e.g., Funder, 1987; Murray & Holmes, 1997; Murray et al., 1996a). Using this consensus criterion for reality, particular types of motivated divergences in judgment provide a potential indicator of positive illusions. For instance, impressions of romantic partners might be cast as motivated, perhaps even illusory, if individuals see virtues in their partners that their partners do not see in themselves (a residualized measure of illusion).[2] Individuals' perceptions might also be cast as overly idealistic if they are more optimistic about the future than their partners' level of optimism seems to warrant.

To pinpoint positive illusions using these reality benchmarks, we asked large samples of dating and married couples to describe themselves, their partners, their hopes for an ideal partner, and their impressions of the typical partner on a series of interpersonally-oriented virtues and faults (e.g., kind and affectionate, critical and judgmental, thoughtless, sociable). These measures provided an index of partner idealization. Participants' estimates of the amount of joint control they (and typical others) possess over positive and negative events in their relationships provided an index of efficacy (e.g., "Through our joint efforts, my partner and I can resolve any problem in our relationship"). And participants' ratings of the likelihood of a variety of positive and negative events occurring in their relationships relative to the typical relationship provided an index of optimism (e.g., "The love my partner and I share continuing to grow"; "My partner and I discovering areas in which our needs conflict in a serious way").

Idealization of the partner.   If conviction depends on intimates overstating the case for commitment, the motivated construals that predict satisfaction are likely to be benevolent ones. After all, not much comfort can be gained by exaggerating a partner's stubbornness. Instead, a sense of security may be better found by seeing a partner's qualities through the generous filters provided by images of the ideal partner. In fact, such processes of wish-fulfillment might even result in individuals seeing virtues in their partners that their partners do not see in themselves.

Consistent with this hypothesis, dating and married intimates who possessed rosier hopes or templates for an ideal partner perceived greater virtue in their own partners (Murray et al., 1996b). Moreover, this assimilation effect emerged in analyses where we controlled for the reality of the partner's self-perceptions. Thus, the motivated aspects of perception – the qualities that perceivers see in their partners that their partners do not see in themselves – seem to reflect the tendency to/see romantic partners through the generous interpretive filter provided by images of the ideal partner.[3] Perhaps because of such tendencies toward idealization, individuals also described their partners more positively than the typical partner (Murray & Holmes, 1997) and even more positively than their partners described themselves (Murray et al., 1996a).

Supporting the hypothesized benefits of conviction, dating and married individuals were more satisfied in their relationships, the more they idealized their partners. In other words, relationship well-being was associated with a particular type of benevolence or generosity in perception – seeing virtues in romantic partners that they did not see in themselves. This claim may confound some readers' intuitions about the importance of insight or understanding. After all, understanding a partner's actual, or at least self-perceived, qualities seems like a practical necessity for negotiating the demands of day-to-day life. However, individuals who idealized their partners the most were not any less insightful than individuals who idealized their partners the least. The correlation between the perceiver's perceptions of the partner and the partner's self-perceptions (i.e., a measure of insight) did not differ as a function of idealization. Moreover, insight itself was not associated with greater well-being. The match between the perceiver's perceptions of the partner and the partner's self-perceptions did not predict satisfaction in either the dating or the married sample.

Efficacy and optimism. Overstating the case for commitment involves more than just projecting images of the ideal partner onto actual partners. Dating and married intimates also optimistically reported that the negative events that threatened others' relationships, such as poor conflict resolution skills or personality incompatibilities, were unlikely to threaten their own relationships (Murray & Holmes, 1997). And if they did, these intimates perceived greater feelings of control or efficacy in redressing such difficulties than they attributed to most other couples (Murray & Holmes, 1997). Such efficacious and optimistic perceptions were also critical for concurrent well-being. Dating and married intimates reported greater satisfaction in their relationships the greater the control they perceived and the more optimism they professed. Crucially, and attesting to the motivated nature of these perceptions, this sense of conviction was not completely warranted by the partner's perceptions of the relationship. The cross-gender or "kernel of truth" correlations were only modest. For instance, the female's level of optimism was only moderately related to the male's level of optimism. Moreover, the perceiver's feelings of optimism and efficacy still predicted satisfaction even after controlling for the component of conviction that was rooted in the reality of the partner's perceptions of the relationship.

The long-term consequences of positive illusions

The sense of conviction that predicts concurrent satisfaction thus seems to depend on individuals going beyond the available evidence, seeing their partners and relationships in the best, most positive, light possible. However, some readers may be left with the lingering suspicion that positive illusions only leave individuals vulnerable to long-term disappointment (although they may instill a false sense of security in the present). After all, the conclusion that satisfaction declines over the first years of marriage because newlyweds idealize one another too much early on seems difficult to resist (Huston & Vangelisti, 1991; Kelly, Huston, & Cate, 1985).

To explore the long-term consequences of positive illusions, my colleagues and I followed a large sample of established dating couples over the course of a year (Murray et al., 1996b; Murray & Holmes, 1997). We did not find any evidence that positive illusions put couples at risk for disillusionment. Instead, individuals who were initially the most optimistic and perceived the greatest control were involved in more stable and ultimately more satisfying relationships (Murray & Holmes, 1997). Individuals who initially idealized their partners the most were also involved in more stable relationships and they reported greater increases in satisfaction and declines in conflict and ambivalence as the year progressed (Murray et al., 1996b). In fact, seeing the best in their partners seemed to protect dating men from suffering any ill effects of the conflicts and doubts they did experience (Murray et al., 1996b). That is, early experiences with conflict and doubt forecast later dissolution for men who idealized their partners the least, but not for men who idealized their partners the most.

The self-corrective nature of idealization.   How is it the case that such motivated and be-nevolent construals of reality actually seem to ward off disappointment rather than ensur-ing it? Part of the answer may lie in the self-corrective and self-fulfilling nature of the idealization process. In the Murray et al. (1996b) study, individuals did accommodate their perceptions to the reality of their partners' self-perceived virtues and faults over the year. However, this increased level of insight was not necessarily coupled with decreased idealization. Why? Because individuals responded to this potential threat to conviction by refashioning their ideals in their partners' images – by deciding that the qualities they perceived in their partners were the ones they desired. In fact, intimates in satisfying, stable relationships did more than just convince themselves that their partners mirrored their hopes. They also seemed to convince their partners. Basking in the warm glow of a part-ner's rosy regard left individuals feeling more secure in their own sense of self-worth as these relationships developed.[4]

The Ties that Bind: The Structure of Conviction

Despite the popular caricature, positive illusions do not seem to be the root of all relation-ship evils. In fact, the opposite appears to be the case. Why might the strong sense of conviction reflected in positive illusions have such short- and long-term benefits? Maybe popular wisdom that admonishes intimates to acknowledge and accept (or at least tolerate) the negative aspects of their relationships is simply wrong. Maybe ignorance really is bliss. However, individuals who possess the strongest illusions still understand their partners' self-perceived virtues and faults (Murray et al., 1996a); they can still point to weaknesses in their relationships (Murray & Holmes, 1999), and they accommodate their perceptions to incorporate such frailties as time passes (Murray et al., 1996b). Given such evidence of reality-monitoring, it seems unlikely that the benefits of positive illusions stem from simple forms of denial.

Perhaps, though, positive illusions have the benefits they do because perceiving so many virtues effectively masks or compensates for faults. That is, acknowledging faults may pose little threat to well-being as long as the positive features of the relationship outnumber the negative. For instance, Gottman (1994) argued that married individuals are likely to re-main committed and happy as long as positive interactions outweigh negative ones by a ratio of at least five to one. Similarly, Huston and Chorost (1994) reported that newlywed wives are less disturbed by their husbands' complaints when they occurred in the context of a warm, affectionate relationship.

Although this "bank account" logic undoubtedly provides a foundation for conviction and well-being, simply perceiving virtue may not be sufficient to inoculate intimates against doubt. In fact, the existing evidence suggests that it is precisely those individuals who are happiest (and presumably perceive the most evidence of virtue in their partners) who are most reluctant to attribute fault to their partners. For instance, satisfied individuals misin-terpret their partners' possible attraction to others (Simpson, Ickes, & Blackstone, 1995) and attribute their partners' negative behaviors to specific, unstable features of the situa-tion (Bradbury & Fincham, 1990) rather than make more threatening attributions to dispositional weaknesses. Moreover, satisfied individuals are unlikely to think about or even look at attractive alternative partners (Miller, 1997) and they derogate available partners in efforts to support idealized views of their own partners (Buunk & Van Yperen, 1991; Johnson & Rusbult, 1989; Simpson, 1987).

If perceiving virtues is not sufficient to foster acceptance of faults, how do intimates sustain a sense of conviction in the face of an inexpressive, stubborn, or childish partner? Perhaps the key to conviction lies in the structure of thought rather than simply being based on the content of mental representations (Murray & Holmes, 1999). Consistent with this hypothesis, self-theorists argue that self-esteem depends on both the content and structure of beliefs about the self (e.g., Pelham, 1991; Pelham & Swann, 1989; Showers, 1992a, 1992b). Although the existing literature on relationship cognition has essentially ignored the question of structure, this perspective raises the possibility that positive illusions may have the benefits they do because such seemingly naïve perceptions actually mask considerable sophistication in thought.

If that is the case, what kinds of representation structures might best sustain conviction and inoculate individuals against doubt? Traditionally, attitude theorists have characterized confidently held attitudes as ones that possess an unequivocal or internally consistent evaluative core (e.g., Chaiken & Yates, 1985; Fazio, 1986; Zanna & Rempel, 1988). In such structures, positive and negative beliefs about an attitude object are reconciled in ways that support an unconflicted overall evaluation, whether positive or negative. In contemplating how individuals might achieve such internal consistency or structural coherence among their relationship beliefs, Murray and Holmes (1999) adopted the metaphor of associative networks used in recent models of impression formation (e.g., Kunda, Sinclair, & Griffin 1997; Kunda & Thagard, 1996). From this perspective, coherent or internally consistent models of others are characterized as interrelated networks where constructs activated at higher, more abstract levels in the hierarchy constrain the meaning of lower-level constructs.

Three elements to structural coherence?

In romantic relationships, positive, evaluatively consistent impressions may depend on individuals organizing representations in ways that elevate the significance of virtues and downplay the significance of faults (Murray & Holmes, 1999). In such representation hierarchies, faults might be interpreted only in light of their links or ties to greater virtues. If that is the case, the motivated organizational processes that sustain such integrated hierarchies ought to underlie the sense of conviction that is so critical for relationship well-being and stability.[5]

As a primary mechanism for elevating virtues, individuals might forge selective and explicit links between beliefs about specific virtues (but not faults) and more abstract, overall evaluations of their relationships. For instance, a satisfied spouse might ascribe greater importance to his partner's sense of humor than her stubbornness, attributing his feelings of closeness to this virtue in particular. Thus, individuals may construct idiosyncratic, personal theories about the criteria for successful relationships that are colored by the virtues (or faults) their partners happen to possess. Consistent with this hypothesis, individuals seem to maintain personal feelings of self-esteem by ascribing greater importance to their own virtues than faults (e.g., Pelham, 1991; Pelham & Swann, 1989; Showers, 1992a).

Simply elevating the significance of virtues, however, may not be sufficient to defuse doubts about a partner's or relationship's more serious weaknesses. Instead, processes of evaluative integration that diminish the significance of particular faults within the representation hierarchy may provide a second structural element supporting internally consistent perceptions. As one means to this end, individuals might try to find evidence of redeeming features in apparent faults (while still acknowledging these frailties). For instance, a satisfied wife might be less concerned about her husband's inexpressiveness if she regards it as the least positive aspect of his strong and silent nature. Such evaluative integration does seem to occur when dating individuals try to cope with experimentally induced concerns about their partners' faults (Murray & Holmes, 1993). In that study, we first led dating individuals to believe that their partners were impeding intimacy by rarely initiating conflicts over the choice of joint activities. Threatened individuals then diminished the significance of this apparent fault by finding evidence of their partners' competing virtues around engaging conflicts in other domains.

Some faults, though, have few redeeming features. In such instances, evaluative integration might depend on intimates constructing "Yes, but . . ." refutations that acknowledge the fault, yet downplay its prominence in the representation hierarchy (e.g., Chaiken & Yates, 1985). Such "Yes, buts . . ." may often involve a type of compensatory or trade-off thinking where intimates directly link faults to greater partner or relationship virtues. We first found evidence for such integrative ties in the open-ended narratives of threatened participants in the Murray and Holmes (1993) study described above. For example, one threatened participant countered his partner's reluctance to initiate conflicts by stating, ". . . *on the other hand, she is very receptive to my needs and willing to adapt if necessary. . . .*" Conceptually similar patterns of thought appear to underlie high self-esteem individuals' feelings about their own greatest faults. Relative to low self-esteem individuals, the thoughts of high self-esteem individuals are more evaluatively integrated, countering negative with positive beliefs (Showers, 1992b). Similarly, Tetlock (1986) argues that integrative complexity in reasoning, defined as a type of balanced thinking that counters negative with positive thoughts, allows individuals to reduce any value conflicts imposed by holding two opposing beliefs.

Organizing general or overall models of a partner's character in ways that temper faults with virtues may provide a third possible foundation for coherent (and thus resilient) representation structures. In other words, lasting conviction may depend on individuals integrating their partners' faults within more significant, positive aspects of their partners' characters. Supporting the possible existence of these ties, reminders of a close other's negative characteristics can actually elicit signs of positive facial affect when individuals perceive these faults in a new acquaintance (Andersen, Reznik, & Manzella, 1996). Similarly, high trust individuals evaluated their partners' behavior and motives in a laboratory interaction most positively when they had just recalled a threatening situation where their partners had disappointed them (Holmes & Rempel, 1989). Perhaps it is precisely the potential for this type of evaluative integration in thought that allows individuals to sustain conviction while still acknowledging their partners' weaknesses.

Readers familiar with Showers's (1992a) work on the compartmentalization of self-knowledge might counter this hypothesis with the notion that linking faults to virtues within integrated representations could actually contaminate virtues rather than blunting faults. For instance, high self-esteem individuals protect important virtues by compartmentalizing less important faults within isolated aspects of their characters, essentially keeping the "good apples out of the bad" (Showers, 1992a). Refuting the implications of weaknesses might also prevent individuals from effectively coping with the negative aspects of their relationships. If that is the case, the type of cognitive organization described above might set the stage for long-term disappointment, although it might provide a false sense of security in the present.

The opposite argument is that actively linking positive and negative beliefs may actually facilitate active and constructive responses to negativity (e.g., Taylor & Armor, 1996). This argument is based on the assumption that because "Yes, but . . ." links are motivated, they are likely to be asymmetrical in nature, such that signs of a fault call the compensatory virtue to mind, but signs of this same virtue do not call the fault to mind. For individuals with more integrated representations, signs of their partners' stubbornness may also remind them of their greater generosity or warmth. The increased perspective gained from such balanced thinking might then facilitate constructive responses to transgressions. For individuals who possess more compartmentalized representations, the same signs of a partner's stubbornness might only remind them of their partner's selfishness. The narrowed focus resulting from such one-sided thinking might then trigger more destructive complaints and criticisms in response to negativity.

A longitudinal investigation of the ties that bind

We reasoned that examining individuals' open-ended descriptions of their relationships provides one of the best, and perhaps least reactive, means of uncovering the structure of their representations (e.g., Baumeister & Newman, 1994, 1995; Murray & Holmes, 1994; Schank & Abelson, 1995). Therefore, we asked our participants to write narratives describing the development of their relationships and mini-narratives describing their partners' greatest faults. We then coded these stories for both the content and structure of thought (see Murray & Holmes, 1999 for further details). We also obtained a more direct index of representation structure by adapting Showers's (1992a) measure of self-compartmentalization. Participants completed a card-sort description on their partners, sorting virtues and faults into meaningful aspects of their partners' characters. In this task, the tendency to sort virtues and faults into the same (vs. separate) groups indexes integrative thinking. Positive illusions again served as a proxy for conviction and reports of satisfaction, trust, conflict, and ambivalence served as our measures of well-being. We contacted participants twelve months after the initial session and established the relationship's status to provide a behavioral proxy for conviction – relationship stability.

Our analyses explored the hypothesis that a resilient sense of conviction depends on the structure of relationship representations rather than being a simple function of the content (i.e., valence) of their constituent elements. Demonstrating such unique effects of structure required analyses that controlled for the evaluative content of the narrative and card-sort measures. Accordingly, we created an index of representation content for each measure. The proportion of partner and relationship features described as faults indexed the evaluative tone of the attributes described in the intimacy narratives. The participant's and coder's ratings of the severity of the partner's greatest fault indexed the evaluative content of this attribute and the proportion of negative attributes in the card-sort provided the index of representation content for the compartmentalization data. We then correlated each structural index (e.g., refutations) with the criteria, controlling for the appropriate index of representation content. The findings we present thus represent relatively pure effects of structure itself rather than any possible content artifacts, such as the benefits of perceiving fewer or less serious faults or being involved in less problematic relationships.

These analyses yielded strong support for the hypothesized structural elements underlying a sense of conviction, as reflected in both concurrent measures of positive illusions and long-term relationship stability. First, the intimacy narratives revealed considerable evidence of intimates' efforts to elevate the importance of virtues over faults. For instance, one person elevated the significance of her partner's supportiveness with the words, "... *I don't think I will ever have to doubt his love for me* because he is always making me feel good about myself ...". Similarly, another participant commented on his partner's patience by saying, "... her ability to realize this and not force me into revealing things about myself that I don't want to, *attracts me to her even more*. ..." Individuals who attached such differential significance to their partners' virtues reported greater conviction (i.e., positive illusions) and relationship well-being. Moreover, elevating the importance of virtues predicted greater relationship stability over the year.

Second, the narratives data also revealed many signs of individuals' efforts to downplay the importance of specific faults through processes of evaluative integration, further supporting our structural perspective on conviction. Consider their thoughts about their partners' greatest fault as but one example. Almost everyone pointed to a feature of their partners' personality as the greatest fault they perceived. The most common complaints included references to a partner's jealousy, concerns about a partner's inexpressiveness, and hesitations around a partner's immaturity. As these examples illustrated, the faults these dating individuals generated were not trivial ones. In fact, the vast majority of participants described this flaw in their partners' character as having more negative than positive effects on their relationships.

Despite (or perhaps because of) these generally negative appraisals, some participants simultaneously found some redeeming features in these apparent imperfections. For instance, one individual described her partner's jealousy as a marker of "... *how important my presence is in his life*. ..." Another found virtue in her partner's obstinacy by remarking, "... *I respect him for his strong beliefs and it helps me to have confidence in our relationship.* ..." And more dramatically still, one individual commented on his partner's "short-fused judgment of people" by saying, "... *at first I thought she was crazy; now I think I'd miss it in her if it were to stop and I also think that the relationship would suffer if this attribute were to disappear*. ..." As we expected, individuals who found such redeeming qualities or silver linings in their partners' greatest fault reported greater concurrent conviction and well-being.

Not all faults were easily turned into partial virtues, though, and many participants responded to this potential threat by constructing "Yes, but . . ." refutations that linked specific faults to virtues in the representation hierarchy. As one example of this type of evaluative integration, one person refuted his partner's inexpressiveness by saying, ". . . I don't place any blame on her; to me, it is just *because she works things out differently in her mind.* . . ." Similarly, another participant excused her partner's reticence on key issues by saying, ". . . I don't think this weighs too heavily on the relationship because *he has no problem discussing other important problems with me.* . . ." As we expected, downplaying the significance of faults within such integrative "Yes, buts . . . " predicted significantly greater conviction and relationship well-being. More impressive still, refuting the importance of a partner's greatest fault predicted greater relationship stability over the year (even though it was only a binary index of a single behavior).

We believe that refutations protect conviction and foster stability in part because they most often involve putting a fault in a broader perspective – one that ties a specific frailty to mental reminders of a partner's or relationship's greater strengths. We found direct evidence of the relationship benefits of such integrative thought when we explicitly asked participants whether their partners' greatest faults reminded them of any other qualities. Individuals who reported the greatest conviction and well-being were more likely to link their partners' greatest fault to a related virtue. In contrast, individuals with the weakest sense of conviction were most likely to tie this specific fault to yet another frailty.

Not surprisingly, then, the mental ties that bind romantic relationships also appear to link qualms about a partner's frailties to comforting thoughts of greater virtues in more general, overall mental models. Supporting the third hypothesized element of representation coherence, individuals who possessed more integrated views of their partners' virtues and faults on the card-sort were more likely to be in stable relationships by the end of the year (independent of the number of faults they perceived initially). Integrated overall representations might foster conviction because linking faults to virtues colors or blunts the meaning of faults (Asch, 1946; Asch & Zukier, 1984; Kunda et al., 1997). In a sense, stubbornness combined with caring may not be the same attribute as stubbornness combined with selfishness. Consistent with this hypothesis, constructing integrative ties on the card-sort seemed to involve finding such competing evidence of virtue in a partner's faults. Individuals with more integrative representations rated the most negative aspects of their partners' personalities more positively than those with more compartmentalized representations.[6]

Integrating a partner's faults within groups of related virtues may also create built-in "Yes, buts . . ." that contain or blunt the implications of faults and transgressions (when they arise). For individuals with more integrated representations, signs of their partners' stubbornness may remind them of their greater generosity or warmth (e.g., Holmes & Rempel, 1989). The perspective gained from such balanced thinking might then facilitate constructive, accommodative responses to occasional transgressions. Apart from regulating behavioral responses, linking faults to virtues may also help regulate the course of potentially destructive emotions. For instance, individuals draw on positive recollections and self-aspects to regulate negative moods (e.g., Boden & Baumeister, 1997; McFarland & Buehler, 1997; Smith & Petty, 1995). Integrated relationship representations may facilitate this type of emotional regulation in response to feelings of annoyance or anger, particularly if signs of a partner's faults automatically prime thoughts about compensatory virtues (e.g., Showers & Kling, 1996). As interdependence increases, integrated, internally consistent representations may also provide the cognitive foundation for inoculation effects that confer resistance against any future threats to conviction (e.g., McGuire & Papageorgis, 1961).

The inverse hierarchy?   The findings thus far suggest that elevating virtues and downplaying faults within integrated representations is the structural prescription for conviction. If that is the case, ruminating about the importance of faults, finding evidence of fault in virtues, and creating pockets of nagging doubt by compartmentalizing faults within negative aspects of a partner's character should be the prescription for distress. Organized in this inverse fashion, virtues are less likely to take the sting away from faults (due to their lesser status). Instead, faults are likely to contaminate virtues, leaving intimates much less confident of their convictions, less satisfied in their relationships, and more vulnerable to dissolution.

The relationship narratives and greatest faults data revealed considerable evidence for this proposition. For instance, individuals who reported less conviction and well-being elevated the significance of faults (e.g., "... *I think that if he really loved me then what I had to say would always be important to him* ...") and found evidence of fault in virtues (e.g., "... no one makes me laugh the way he does, *but it is not enough for a serious relationship* ..."). Elevating faults and downplaying virtues in such ways also put intimates at significantly greater risk for break-up by year end. More generally, responding to the dilemma of a less-than-perfect partner by compartmentalizing faults within pockets of doubt on the card-sort also predicted less stability.

Perception or reality?   Is it possible, though, that the apparent benefits of a hierarchical and integrative structure simply mask the benefits of possessing more virtuous partners? For instance, maybe individuals who encapsulate their partners' greatest faults within "Yes, buts ..." are happier because they actually possess partners with less important faults. After all, perceptions are not created in a vacuum and even the most motivated individual will have difficulty turning a frog into a princess or a prince (Murray et al., 1996a). However, the current findings provide compelling support for the unique effects of structure.

First, at an operational level, the application of a structure code, such as an elevating virtue or refutation code, required statements that explicitly qualified the meaning or importance of the attribute. Simple statements about the extremity of the virtue or fault were not sufficient to warrant these codes. Second, in terms of the nature of partner representations, the number of virtues individuals attributed to their partners on the card-sort task was only weakly related to the number of faults they perceived. Virtuous partners, then, are not necessarily perfect ones. Third, and most crucially, the effects of structure persisted in analyses where we controlled for the proportion or severity of the faults perceived. Moreover, constructing refutations also had its greatest, protective effect when individuals perceived the most, not the least, serious faults. These findings suggest that the benefits of motivated, integrative thinking cannot simply be attributed to satisfied, secure individuals' possession of more perfect partners.

Idealization necessitates insight?

Given that lovers are often chastised for wearing rose-colored glasses, it is ironic that intimates who possess the strongest illusions are best able to contend with the reality of a less-than-perfect partner. These individuals respond to this potential threat to conviction by linking faults to greater virtues within hierarchically structured representations. In this sense, individuals with the strongest sense of conviction are not naïve at all. Instead, they show a certain wisdom in their struggle to accept their partners' faults by gaining a broader, more balanced, perspective on these weaknesses. In fact, the very stability of relationships rests in part on the capacity to create such motivated and integrative mental ties.

Self-Protection Motivations and Constraints on the Quest for Conviction

The considerable benefits of conviction suggest that the need to dispel doubt is a relatively fundamental motive in romantic relationships. Individuals most successful in this quest – those who contain faults within positive, seemingly idealized, representations of their relationships – report greater concurrent well-being, and eventually, greater relationship stability. The opposite is true for individuals less successful in this quest. What might distinguish individuals who find this much-needed sense of conviction from those who do not?

Writers in both the symbolic interactionist and attachment traditions argue that perceptions of the self as worthy of love are strongly tied to beliefs about others and their dispositions in relationship contexts (see Baldwin, 1992). Such reasoning suggests that dispositional insecurities on the part of the perceiver might interfere with intimates finding the sense of conviction they seek. For instance, low self-esteem individuals idealize their partners less than highs (Murray et al., 1996a) and they also experience greater difficulty sustaining illusions as time passes (Murray et al., 1996b). Similarly, low self-esteem individuals are less likely than highs to elevate the importance of virtues and minimize the significance of faults within relationship representations (Murray & Holmes, 1999). Dating individuals high on anxiety or fear of rejection (i.e., a more negative model of self) also interpret their partners' imagined and actual transgressions in suspicious ways that are likely to undermine a sense of conviction (e.g., Collins, 1996; Collins & Allard, 1997; Simpson, Rholes, & Phillips, 1996).

Why do negative models of self pose such a threat to conviction? After all, low self-esteem individuals are most in need of others' acceptance to bolster their tenuous sense of self-worth (e.g., Kernis, Cornell, Sun, Berry, & Harlow, 1993; Leary, Tambor, Terdal, & Downs, 1995; Nezlek, Kowalski, Leary, Blevins, & Holgate, 1997). In fact, low self-esteem individuals report wanting their romantic partners to see them much more positively than they see themselves, suggesting that they see relationships as a resource for self-affirmation (Murray, Holmes, & Griffin, 2000). Moreover, this resource is readily available – the romantic partners of lows see them much more positively than lows see themselves (Murray et al., 2000). Given their great need for this available resource, then, it seems more than a little ironic that low self-esteem individuals are less likely than highs to find the sense of conviction they seek in relationships.

Perhaps, though, it is precisely their dependency on relationships for a sense of self-worth that makes lows so cautious. Low self-esteem individuals typically pursue self-enhancement goals in a self-protective fashion, taking those opportunities for self-enhancement that seem sure to affirm the self and avoiding those that pose a potential threat to the self (see Baumeister, 1993, for a review). Maybe lows approach romantic relationships in a similarly self-protective fashion – regulating their quest for conviction in ways that safeguard the self against threat.

Consistent with this dependency regulation hypothesis, individuals are more likely to make the leap of faith that conviction requires when they feel confident of their partners' reciprocated affections and commitment (e.g., Berscheid & Fei, 1977; Holmes & Rempel, 1989; Kelley, 1983). For instance, dating and married individuals are more likely to idealize their partners when they believe that their partners also see special virtues in them (Murray et al., 2000). This level of confidence in a partner's reflected appraisals comes readily to high self-esteem individuals because they correctly assume that their partners see them just as positively as they see themselves. But the same tendency toward naïve realism makes a sense of confidence in a partner's acceptance elusive for lows. That is, lows dramatically underestimate how positively their partners see them because they *incorrectly* assume that their partners see them just as negatively as they see themselves (Murray et al., 2000).

The tendency to self-verify thus leaves lows caught in a vulnerable position in romantic relationships, needing their partners' positive regard and acceptance, but doubting its existence. Such doubts about their partners' regard are likely to be particularly troublesome for lows because they believe that others' acceptance depends on them living up to certain standards (Baldwin & Sinclair, 1996; Roberts, Gotlib, & Kassel, 1996). In the minds of lows, then, relationships may pose more potential threats than boosts to the self because the possibility of their partners' disaffection or rejection is ever-present (e.g., Downey & Feldman, 1996). Initial correlational data that my colleagues and I collected suggest that low self-esteem individuals protect against the threat of rejection (and the loss to the self it represents) by maintaining a safe distance in their relationships, seeing their partners and relationships in a less idealized light than highs (Murray et al., 2000). In contrast, high self-esteem individuals are more confident of their partners' regard and feeling affirmed, see their partners in a more idealized light than lows.

These correlational data suggest that self-protection motives may interfere with relationship-enhancement motives for low, but not high, self-esteem individuals. If this dynamic really does occur, my colleagues and I reasoned that it should be most evident in situations where a threat to the self is made salient (Murray, Holmes, MacDonald, & Ellsworth, 1998). In a series of experiments designed to explore this possible tension, we first posed a threat to low and high self-esteem individuals' feelings of self-worth (e.g., feelings of guilt over a past transgression, fears of being an inconsiderate partner, fears of being intellectually inept). We then assessed their confidence in their dating partners' positive regard and acceptance (as a measure of reflected appraisals) and perceptions of their partners (as a measure of conviction).

The results of these experiments revealed that low self-esteem individuals react to acute self-doubt by expressing greater insecurity about their partners' positive regard and acceptance. For instance, lows reacted to doubts about their intellectual abilities by concluding that their partners would not forgive them if they transgressed in their relationships. Lows then defended themselves from the prospect of rejection by devaluing their partners, effectively safeguarding the self from the loss of this threatened resource. In contrast, high self-esteem individuals reacted to similar self-doubts by becoming more convinced of their partners' positive regard, essentially using their relationships as a resource for self-affirmation (e.g., Steele, 1988). Such findings suggest that a sense of conviction may prove to be elusive for low self-esteem perceivers because they cannot find the sense of security in a partner's regard that highs so readily perceive.

Summary and Conclusions

The research reviewed here suggests that lasting satisfaction and relationship stability depend on individuals overstating the case for commitment – interpreting and structuring the available evidence in ways that support the most positive possible views of their relationships. For instance, satisfied dating and married intimates seem to project hopes for an ideal partner onto the partners they possess, seeing virtues they wish to see, but their partners do not see in themselves. Satisfied intimates also optimistically believe that the difficulties affecting others' relationships are unlikely to trouble their own, and that if they did, they anticipate coping with such problems more effectively than most couples.

Such seemingly naïve perceptions may foster relationship resiliency because they actually mask (and perhaps require) a considerable degree of integrative complexity in thought. That is, motivated perceivers seem to resolve the tension posed by the practical necessity of insight and their hopes for happiness by elevating the importance of virtues and downplaying the significance of faults within coherent, evaluatively-integrated relationship representations. For instance, individuals with the strongest sense of conviction seem to dispel doubts by ascribing special significance to virtues, countering negative with positive beliefs about specific faults, and by organizing more general mental models in ways that link faults to greater virtues. The broader perspective on negativity gained from such balanced thinking may be what allows motivated, satisfied individuals to sustain their illusions in the face of their knowledge of their partners' more obvious flaws.

Certain realities, though, do constrain these processes of motivated construal and organization. Low and high self-esteem individuals both regulate relationship perceptions in a self-protective fashion, seeing the best in their partners only when they believe their partners also see special qualities in them. However, enduring insecurities about the likelihood and conditions underlying others' acceptance make this level of confidence in a partner's regard more difficult for low than high self-esteem individuals to obtain. Lows then seem to protect themselves against the possibility of rejection by reserving judgment about their relationships, whereas highs can more readily make the leap of faith that seeing the best in their relationships necessitates.

Most poets, philosophers, and psychologists simply assume that relationship well-being and stability depend on intimates relinquishing idealized, seemingly naïve, perceptions. The goal of this chapter was to argue the opposite. Growing evidence now suggests that processes of motivated construal that allow romantic partners to dispel doubts and protect a sense of conviction are critical for sustaining satisfying dating and marital relationships.

Notes

1. This trilogy of perceptions should seem familiar to most readers. Taylor and Brown (1988) argued that similar illusions about the self, including idealized self-perceptions, exaggerated perceptions of control, and unrealistic optimism, appear to function as buffers, protecting self-esteem from the threats posed by negativity.

2. In using the partner's self-perceptions as a "reality" benchmark, we are not arguing that individuals possess true insight into the actual nature of their own attributes. Instead, numerous studies suggest that individuals' self-perceptions are colored by some degree of positive illusions (e.g., Alicke, 1985; Brown, 1986; Greenwald, 1980; Taylor & Brown, 1988). But given this evidence of self-aggrandizement, self-perceptions may prove a very conservative benchmark for indexing a partner's illusions.

3. This evidence for idealization was not simply an artifact of method variance or general tendencies toward Pollyanna-ism. Images of the ideal partner still predicted perceptions of the actual partner when proxies for these artifacts (i.e., perceptions of the typical partner and global self-esteem) were controlled.

4. Despite the evidence of the long-term benefits of positive illusions, some readers may still be questioning our decision to characterize illusions as a measure of conviction. For some, this resistance may stem from the belief that positive illusions depend on naïve forms of denial (a belief I aim to dispel in this chapter). For others, this resistance may stem from a preference for more traditional measures, such as satisfaction or commitment. However, the results of our longitudinal research suggest that positive illusions capture a *prospective* sense of confidence in the continued value availability and availability of the partner and relationship (our definition of conviction) that is not necessarily captured by more traditional indicators of well-being, such as satisfaction. For instance, positive illusions are more stable features of dating relationships, whereas traditional indicators of well-being, such as satisfaction, capture more ephemeral feelings. Moreover, positive illusions appear to have uniquely prophetic (and perhaps self-fulfilling) effects. They predicted changes in satisfaction (and trust and love) over the year, but initial well-being did not predict changes in positive illusions (Murray & Holmes, 1997).

5. In using the term representation, we are referring to the constellation of beliefs, both positive and negative, specific and more abstract that individuals possess about their partners and relationships. We believe that such networks are organized in a hierarchical fashion, such that specific beliefs (e.g., "My partner is honest") provide the substructure underlying core, more abstract evaluations (e.g., "My relationship is a good one"). We use this terminology primarily for heuristic and metaphoric purposes as our data cannot show that such hierarchical structures actually exist in memory.

6. Again, this effect emerged in analyses where we controlled for the number of faults individuals perceived in their partners.

References

Alicke, M. D. (1985). Global self-evaluation as determined by the desirability and controllability of trait adjectives. *Journal of Personality and Social Psychology, 49,* 1621–1630.

Andersen, S. M., Reznik, I., & Manzella, L. M. (1996). Eliciting facial affect, motivation, and expectancies in transference: Significant-other representations in social relations. *Journal of Personality and Social Psychology, 71,* 1108–1129.

Asch, S. E. (1946). Forming impressions of personality. *Journal of Abnormal and Social Psychology*, *41*, 258–290.

Asch, S. E., & Zukier, H. (1984). Thinking about persons. *Journal of Personality and Social Psychology*, *46*, 1230–1240.

Baldwin, M. W. (1992). Relational schemas and the processing of social information. *Psychological Bulletin*, *112*, 461–484.

Baldwin, M. W., & Sinclair, L. (1996). Self-esteem and "if . . . then" contingencies of interpersonal acceptance. *Journal of Personality and Social Psychology*, *71*, 1130–1141.

Baumeister, R. F. (1993). *Self-esteem: The puzzle of low self-regard*. New York: Plenum Press.

Baumeister, R. F., & Newman, L. S. (1994). How stories make sense of personal experiences: Motives that shape autobiographical narratives. *Personality and Social Psychology Bulletin*, *20*, 676–690.

Baumeister, R. F., & Newman, L. S. (1995). The primacy of stories, the primacy of roles, and the polarizing effects of interpretive motives: Some propositions about narratives. In R. S. Wyer (Ed.), *Advances in social cognition* (Vol. 8, pp. 1–88). Hillsdale, NJ: Erlbaum.

Berscheid, E., & Fei, J. (1977). Romantic love and sexual jealousy. In G. Clanton & L. G. Smith (Eds.), *Jealousy* (pp. 101–109). Englewood Cliffs, NJ: Prentice Hall.

Boden, J. M., & Baumeister, R. F. (1997). Repressive coping: Distraction using pleasant thoughts and memories. *Journal of Personality and Social Psychology*, *73*, 45–62.

Bradbury, T. N., & Fincham, F. D. (1990). Attributions in marriage: Review and critique. *Psychological Bulletin*, *107*, 3–23.

Braiker, H. B., & Kelley, H. H. (1979). Conflict in the development of close relationships. In R. L. Burgess & T. L. Huston (Eds.), *Social exchange in developing relationships* (pp. 135–168). New York: Academic Press.

Brehm, S. S. (1992). *Intimate relationships*. New York: McGraw-Hill.

Brehm, J. W., & Cohen, R. A. (1962). *Explorations in cognitive dissonance*. New York: Wiley.

Brickman, P. (1987). *Commitment, conflict, and caring*. Englewood Cliffs, NJ: Prentice-Hall.

Brown, J. D. (1986). Evaluations of self and others: Self-enhancement biases in social judgment. *Social Cognition*, *4*, 353–376.

Buunk, B. P., & Van Yperen, N. W. (1991). Referential comparisons, relational comparisons, and exchange orientation: Their relation to marital satisfaction. *Personality and Social Psychology Bulletin*, *17*, 709–717.

Chaiken, S., & Yates, S. (1985). Affective-cognitive consistency and thought-induced attitude polarization. *Journal of Personality and Social Psychology*, *49*, 1470–1481.

Clark, M. S., & Grote, N. K. (1998). Why aren't indices of relationship costs always negatively related to indices of relationship quality? *Personality and Social Psychology Review*, *2*, 2–17.

Collins, N. L. (1996). Working models of attachment: Implications for explanation, emotion and behavior. *Journal of Personality and Social Psychology*, *71*, 810–832.

Collins, N. L., & Allard, L. M. (1997). *Attachment style differences in patterns of attribution, emotion, and behavior*. Unpublished manuscript, State University of New York at Buffalo.

Colvin, C. R., & Block, J. (1994). Do positive illusions foster mental health? An examination of the Taylor and Brown formulation. *Psychological Bulletin*, *116*, 3–20.

Downey, G., & Feldman, S. I. (1996). Implications of rejection sensitivity for intimate relationships. *Journal of Personality and Social Psychology*, *70*, 1327–1343.

Drigotas, S. M., & Rusbult, C. E. (1992). Should I stay or should I go? A dependence model of break-ups. *Journal of Personality and Social Psychology*, *62*, 62–87.

Fazio, R. (1986). How do attitudes guide behavior? In R. M. Sorrentino & E. T. Higgins (Eds.), *The handbook of motivation and cognition: Foundations of social behavior* (pp. 204–243). New York: Guilford Press.

Fletcher, G. J. O., Fincham, F. D., Cramer, L., & Heron, N. (1987). The role of attributions in the development of dating relationships. *Journal of Personality and Social Psychology*, *53*, 481–489.

Fletcher, G. J. O., Simpson, J. A., Thomas, G., & Giles, L. (1999). Ideals in intimate relationships. *Journal of Personality and Social Psychology*, *76*, 72–89.

Funder, D. C. (1987). Errors and mistakes: Evaluating the accuracy of social judgment. *Psychologi-

cal Bulletin, 101, 75–95.

Gottman, J. M. (1994). *What predicts divorce? The relationship between marital processes and marital outcomes.* Hillsdale, NJ: Erlbaum.

Greenwald, A. G. (1980). The totalitarian ego: Fabrication and revision of personal history. *American Psychologist, 35*, 603–618.

Helgeson, V. S. (1994). The effects of self-beliefs and relationship beliefs on adjustment to a relationship stressor. *Personal Relationships, 1*, 241–258.

Holmes, J. G., & Rempel, J. K. (1989). Trust in close relationships. In C. Hendrick (Ed.), *Review of personality and social psychology: Close relationships* (Vol. 10, pp. 187–219). Newbury Park, CA: Sage.

Huston, T. L., & Chorost, A. F. (1994). Behavioral buffers on the effect of negativity on marital satisfaction: A longitudinal study. *Personal Relationships, 1*, 223–240.

Huston, T. L., & Vangelisti, A. L. (1991). Socioemotional behavior and satisfaction in marital relationships: A longitudinal study. *Journal of Personality and Social Psychology, 61*, 721–733.

Johnson, D. J., & Rusbult, C. E. (1989). Resisting temptation: Devaluation of alternative partners as a means of maintaining commitment in close relationships. *Journal of Personality and Social Psychology, 57*, 967–980.

Kelley, H. H. (1983). Love and commitment. In H. H. Kelley, E. Berscheid, A. Christensen, J. H. Harvey, T. L. Huston, G. Levinger, E. McClintock, L. A. Peplau, & D. R. Peterson (Eds.), *Close relationships* (pp. 265–314). New York: W. H. Freeman.

Kelly, C., Huston, T. L., & Cate, R. M. (1985). Premarital relationship correlates of the erosion of satisfaction in marriage. *Journal of Social and Personal Relationships, 2*, 167–178.

Kernis, M H., Cornell, D. P., Sun, C. R., Berry, A., & Harlow, T. (1993). There's more to self-esteem than whether it is high or low: The importance of stability of self-esteem. *Journal of Personality and Social Psychology, 65*, 1190–1204.

Kunda, Z. (1990). The case for motivated reasoning. *Psychological Bulletin, 108*, 480–498.

Kunda, Z., Sinclair, L., & Griffin, D. (1997). Equal ratings but separate meanings: Stereotypes and the construal of traits. *Journal of Personality and Social Psychology, 72*, 720–734.

Kunda, Z., & Thagard, P. (1996). Forming impressions from stereotypes, traits, and behaviors: A parallel-constraint-satisfaction theory. *Psychological Review, 103*, 284–308.

Leary, M. R., Tambor, E. S., Terdal, S. K., & Downs, D. L. (1995). Self-esteem as an interpersonal monitor: The sociometer hypothesis. *Journal of Personality and Social Psychology, 68*, 518–530.

Lykken, D. T., & Tellegen, A. (1993). Is human mating adventitious or the result of lawful choice? A twin study of mate selection. *Journal of Personality and Social Psychology, 65*, 56–68.

Martz, J. M., Verette, J., Arriaga, X. B., Slovik, L. F., Cox, C. L., & Rusbult, C. E. (1998). Positive illusion in close relationships. *Personal Relationships, 5*, 159–182.

McFarland, C., & Buehler, R. (1997). Negative affective states and the motivated retrieval of positive life events: The role of affect acknowledgment. *Journal of Personality and Social Psychology, 73*, 200–214.

McGuire, W. J., & Papageorgis, D. (1961). The relative efficacy of various types of prior belief-defense in producing immunity against persuasion. *Journal of Abnormal and Social Psychology, 62*, 327–337.

Miller, R. S. (1997). Inattentive and contented: Relationship commitment and attention to alternatives. *Journal of Personality and Social Psychology, 73*, 758–766.

Murray, S. L., & Holmes, J. G. (1993). Seeing virtues in faults: Negativity and the transformation of interpersonal narratives in close relationships. *Journal of Personality and Social Psychology, 65*, 707–722.

Murray, S. L., & Holmes, J. G. (1994). Story-telling in close relationships: The construction of confidence. *Personality and Social Psychology Bulletin, 20*, 663–676.

Murray, S. L., & Holmes, J. G. (1997). A leap of faith? Positive illusions in romantic relationships. *Personality and Social Psychology Bulletin, 23*, 586–604.

Murray, S. L., & Holmes, J. G. (1999). The mental ties that bind: Cognitive structures that predict relationship resilience. *Journal of Personality and Social Psychology, 77,* 1228–1244.

Murray, S. L., Holmes, J. G., & Griffin, D. (1996a). The benefits of positive illusions: Idealization and the construction of satisfaction in close relationships. *Journal of Personality and Social Psychology, 70,* 79–98.

Murray, S. L., Holmes, J. G., & Griffin, D. W. (1996b). The self-fulfilling nature of positive illusions in romantic relationships: Love is not blind, but prescient. *Journal of Personality and Social Psychology, 71,* 1155–1180.

Murray, S. L., Holmes, J. G., & Griffin, D. (2000). Self-esteem and the quest for felt-security: How perceived regard regulates attachment processes. *Journal of Personality and Social Psychology, 78,* 478–498.

Murray, S. L., Holmes, J. G., MacDonald, G., & Ellsworth, P. (1998). Through the looking glass darkly? When self-doubts turn into relationship insecurities. *Journal of Personality and Social Psychology, 75,* 1459–1480.

Murstein, B. I. (1967). Empirical tests of role, complementary needs, and homogamy theories of marital choice. *Journal of Marriage and the Family, 29,* 689–696.

Murstein, B. I. (1971). Self–ideal–self discrepancy and the choice of marital partner. *Journal of Consulting and Clinical Psychology, 37,* 47–52.

Nezlek, J. B., Kowalski, R. M., Leary, M. R., Blevins, T., & Holgate, S. (1997). Personality moderators of reactions to interpersonal rejection: Depression and trait self-esteem. *Personality and Social Psychology Bulletin, 23,* 1235–1244.

Pelham, B. W. (1991). On confidence and consequence: The certainty and importance of self-knowledge. *Journal of Personality and Social Psychology, 60,* 518–530.

Pelham, B. W., & Swann, W. B. (1989). From self-conceptions to self-worth: On the sources and structure of global self-esteem. *Journal of Personality and Social Psychology, 57,* 672–680.

Roberts, J. E., Gotlib, I. H., & Kassel, J. D. (1996). Adult attachment security and symptoms of depression: The mediating roles of dysfunctional attitudes and low self-esteem. *Journal of Personality and Social Psychology, 70,* 310–320.

Schank, R. C., & Abelson, R. P. (1995). Knowledge and memory: The real story. In R. S. Wyer (Ed.), *Advances in social cognition* (Vol. 8, pp. 1–88). Hillsdale, NJ: Erlbaum.

Showers, C. (1992a). Compartmentalization of positive and negative self-knowledge: Keeping bad apples out of the bunch. *Journal of Personality and Social Psychology, 62,* 1036–1049.

Showers, C. (1992b). Evaluatively integrative thinking about characteristics of the self. *Personality and Social Psychology Bulletin, 18,* 719–729.

Showers, C. J., & Kling, K. C. (1996). Organization of self-knowledge: Implications for recovery from sad mood. *Journal of Personality and Social Psychology, 70,* 578–590.

Simpson, J. A. (1987). The dissolution of romantic relationships: Factors involved in relationship stability and emotional distress. *Journal of Personality and Social Psychology, 53,* 683–692.

Simpson, J. A., Ickes, W., & Blackstone, T. (1995). When the head protects the heart: Empathic accuracy in dating relationships. *Journal of Personality and Social Psychology, 69,* 629–641.

Simpson, J. A., Rholes, W. S., & Phillips, D. (1996). Conflict in close relationships: An attachment perspective. *Journal of Personality and Social Psychology, 71,* 899–914.

Smith, S. M., & Petty, R. E. (1995). Personality moderators of mood congruency effects on cognition: The role of self-esteem and negative mood regulation. *Journal of Personality and Social Psychology, 68,* 1092–1107.

Steele, C. M. (1988). The psychology of self-affirmation: Sustaining the integrity of the self. In L. Berkowitz (Ed.), *Advances in experimental social psychology* (Vol. 21, pp. 261–302). New York: Academic Press.

Taylor, S. E., & Armor, D. A. (1996). Positive illusions and coping with adversity. *Journal of Personality, 64,* 873–898.

Taylor, S. E., & Brown, J. D. (1988). Illusion and well-being: A social psychological perspective on mental health. *Psychological Bulletin, 103,* 193–210.

Tetlock, P. E. (1986). A value pluralism model of ideological reasoning. *Journal of Personality and Social Psychology, 50,* 819–827.

Thomas, G., Fletcher, G. J. O., & Lange, C. (1997). On-line empathic accuracy in marital interactions. *Journal of Personality and Social Psychology, 72,* 839–850.

Van Lange, P. A. M., & Rusbult, C. E. (1995). My relationship is better than – and not as bad as – yours is: The perception of superiority in close relationships. *Personality and Social Psychology Bulletin, 21*, 32–44.

Zanna, M. P., & Rempel, J. R. (1988). Attitudes: A new look at an old concept. In D. Bar-Tal & A. W. Kruglanski (Eds.), *The social psychology of knowledge* (pp. 315–334). Cambridge, England: Cambridge University Press.

PART II

Social Motivation

6   Integrating Social Psychological Research on Aggression within an
    Evolutionary-based Framework   129
    Neil M. Malamuth and Tamara Addison

7   Helping and Altruism   162
    John F. Dovidio and Louis A. Penner

8   The Death and Rebirth of the Social Psychology of Negotiation   196
    Max H. Bazerman, Jared R. Curhan, and Don A. Moore

9   Motivational Aspects of Empathic Accuracy   229
    William Ickes and Jeffry A. Simpson

Chapter Six

Integrating Social Psychological Research on Aggression within an Evolutionary-based Framework

Neil M. Malamuth and Tamara Addison

The Perspective of This Chapter

An integrative perspective

In this chapter we review some recent social psychological research on the topic of aggression. To this task we bring the view that there is much to be gained from jointly applying evolutionary and more traditional social approaches to this phenomenon, as has been successfully done in some other areas of scholarship (e.g., Barkow, 1989; Fletcher, Simpson, Thomas, & Giles, 1999). Unfortunately, our view is not yet widely shared. This is evident in another recent review of the aggression literature, in which Geen (1998a) accurately notes that most researchers have largely ignored or dismissed evolutionary models. He further concluded that "it is too soon to tell whether social psychologists and psycho-evolutionists will eventually find much common ground" (1998a, p. 318). Since we believe that achieving such common ground would be exceptionally fruitful in aggression research, we will devote considerable attention to this issue.

Social learning theories typically have emphasized that "people are not born with preformed repertoires of aggressive behaviors; they must learn them in one way or another" (Bandura, 1973, p. 61). As Tremblay et al. (1999) note, this is an image dating back to Rousseau's (1762/1911) model that children are born good and become bad under the influence of the environment. The integrative evolutionary-based approach we emphasize in this chapter uses a different conceptual framework. People are born neither "good" nor "bad." They are born with evolved psychological modules that were "selected" by evolutionary forces because they helped solve the adaptive problems of our ancestors. These modules include those underlying the use of aggressive tactics. This is no more "biological pessimism" than the recognition that humans are also born with innate modules underlying characteristics such as empathy and morality (e.g., Buck & Ginsburg, 1997; Darwin, 1871) is "biological optimism" (DeWaal, 1996). As emphasized here, most of these innate modules are relatively open or facultative programs that are also shaped in critical ways by social learning experiences.

The view of many social psychologists

The view of many social scientists is illustrated by Tedeschi and Felson's (1994) discussion of so-called "biological" perspectives:

> Although lower organisms may inherit instinctual behavior, humans do not. Furthermore, the development of language and culture by humans has transformed, redirected, and obscured whatever biological tendencies that may be coded in the genes . . . Biological capacities do not provide an adequate explanation for complex human actions . . . In general, we view biological factors as playing a remote causal role . . . (1994, p. 36)

While there appear to be a number of reasons (with which we generally disagree) why researchers such as Tedeschi and Felson have adopted such a view, two are particularly noteworthy. First, much of the research conducted by social psychologists has focused on the role of symbolic concepts, such as justice, revenge, honor, etc., which seem to play central roles. These researchers find no connection between such concepts and biologically relevant factors (e.g., physiological processes, evolved mechanisms, cross-species comparisons, etc.). Second, many researchers equate "biological" explanations with outdated models (see Buss, 1999, for a fuller discussion of this issue) and have little knowledge of recent theoretical formulations. In particular, they erroneously think of evolutionary-based approaches as necessarily suggesting inflexible behavior. After discussion of some key issues pertaining to the social psychology of aggression, we will summarize a recent evolutionary-based approach and then illustrate its utility for advancing aggression research.

Some Key Issues in the Social Psychological Literature

Defining and understanding aggression

Silverberg and Gray (1992) note that exasperation with adequately defining the concept of aggression has led many social scientists ". . . to accept the term as polythetic and to define it by adopting Justice Stewart's 'I know it when I see it' stance on pornography" (1992, p. 3). Most social psychologists define aggression as a behavior directed toward the goal of harming or injuring another living being, who is motivated to avoid that harm (e.g., Baron and Richardson, 1994). This definition includes several key elements, wherein (1) aggression is a behavior, not an attitude, motive, or emotion; (2) an intention exists to cause harm to the victim; (3) some type of aversive consequences occur; (4) the victim is a living being; and (5) the victim is motivated to avoid the harm (Baron, 1977; Berkowitz, 1993).

Aggression as tactic

Quigley and Tedeschi (1996) note that even though researchers typically "settle" on the type of definition given above, their actual research procedures are not well linked to the definition. For example, they note that researchers have not developed any measures of the intentions of the aggressors, even though intention has been a key feature of the typical definition. In their work Tedeschi and colleagues have reconceptualized aggression and have preferred to avoid using the word in favor of the term *coercive actions*, which they define as "an action taken with the intention of imposing harm on another person or forcing compliance" (Tedeschi & Felson, 1994, p. 168). They further note that actors expect that their coercive actions will lead to some valued proximate goal, either a tangible benefit to the coercer or a value such as justice, which is primarily based on retribution.

Although our perspective differs in key ways from that of Tedeschi and associates, in certain respects we agree with their critique of existing definitions. We particularly welcome their emphasis on understanding aggression as a tactic of influence. Our interchangeable use of the terms "aggression" and "coercive tactics" will reflect this perspective. We see this conceptualization as a positive step to better integrating the aggression literature within related work on social relations, both in humans and among other primates. For example, in relevant research employing such a "tactics conceptualization" in non-human primates, Humphrey (1976) has noted that ". . . the life of social animals is highly problematic. In a complex society, such as those we know exist in higher primates, there are benefits to be gained for each individual member both from preserving the overall structure of the group, and at the same time from exploiting and out-maneuvering others within it" (pp. 303–317). Coercive influence is one of the various tactics that can be used in such a social context. In research on humans, there has been a growing literature on the use of various social tactics that one person (the agent) exerts on someone else (the target) to induce a change in the target: reward, coercive, legitimate, referent, expert, and informational tactics (Raven, 1999). This research highlights the conditions under which one type of influence may be more effective than others. For example, if reward and coercion are used in relatively long-term interactions, they require the agent's effective surveillance of the target's behavior to insure compliance. In contrast, none of the other four influencing tactics requires such surveillance because the targets "internalize" this influence (e.g., when a person's behavior has been changed via information or persuasion) (also see Molm, 1997).

Other social psychologists have also recognized, at least to some degree, the tactical functions of some aggressive acts in the context of the widely used distinction between *hostile* and *instrumental* aggression (Baron, 1977; Geen, 1998a). Similar distinctions have been successfully used to distinguish among various types of aggressors (e.g., Dodge & Coie, 1987). Definitions of *instrumental* aggression emphasize that any harm is primarily a tactical means of attaining other goals, such as social status, or money (e.g., Berkowitz, 1993). Such behavior has been described as a "learned" behavior (Berkowitz, 1998) involving relatively conscious, calculated analysis. Typically, the definition of the *hostile* aggression emphasizes that harm or injury to the target is the primary goal of the behavior. Berkowitz (1993) suggests that in contrast to instrumental aggression, hostile (also called impulsive or emotional) aggressive acts involve little conscious analysis or calculation:

> Many social scientists and mental health specialists have neglected impulsivity in emotional aggression. They seem to believe that virtually every act of aggression follows a more or less deliberate calculation of the action's possible costs and benefits. I argue that such considerations and evaluations are at times short-circuited, especially under the heat of intense feelings. The failure to recognize this factor . . . results in a seriously incomplete understanding of human aggression. (Berkowitz, 1993, p. 17)

Berkowitz (1993) particularly links hostile aggression with anger in response to frustration, but emphasizes the distinction between aggressive behavior and other correlated responses, such as emotions. He makes the following point (also see Richardson & Green, 1997):

> *Anger* . . . doesn't necessarily have any particular goal . . . and doesn't serve any useful purpose for the individual in that particular situation . . . In my hypothetical example of the abusive husband . . . the man might or might not have an anger experience at this time, but if he does, this experience only goes along with his aggressive inclination and does not directly create it. (Berkowitz, 1993, pp. 20–21)

Berkowitz's model is based on the network theory of emotion which argues that emotions, cognitions, and even action tendencies are connected in memory through association. The activation of one element (e.g., anger) can spread to other "nodes" in the associative network, such as aggression. He and other social scientists do not question "why" many people's psychology would include behavior that does not seem to take into consideration the costs and benefits of their acts. Interestingly, Berkowitz (1994) incorporates in his description the observation that impulsive aggressors can be stimulated to increased violence by viewing the "pain cues" of their victims. Berkowitz here draws an analogy with hunger: "In a sense, the 'pain cues' function much like a hungry person's first bite of food and tell the aggressors that they are approaching their goal; they are coming close to satisfying their appetite; getting an adequate meal or, in the latter case, hurting their victim sufficiently" (p. 35). In the section below where we discuss the concepts of proximate and ultimate functions, the feeding system will also be used. It will hopefully illustrate how incorporating such concepts provides a better understanding of the evolved psychology of emotional (or hostile) aggression.

Rather than considering hostile and instrumental aggression as distinct entities, some researchers have argued that both types of aggression actually share some common underlying mechanisms (e.g., Dodge & Coie, 1987). For instance, Huesmann (1998) suggests that a key distinguishing element is the degree to which emotional anger underlies the aggressive response. He proposes that a continuum is the most suitable conceptualization, with instrumental and hostile aggression being at opposite ends of this emotional anger continuum. We believe that embedded in these types of ideas are evolutionary-based concepts about the functional design of the mind's architecture which would be enhanced considerably if social psychologists were to anchor their models more explicitly in the evolutionary literature regarding such concepts as the proximate and ultimate causes and functions of emotions. We discuss these concepts below.

Aggression in social relationships

It is important not only to recognize that coercive tactics are one of several influence strategies, but also that in other species it is evident that they are often embedded in the larger context of social relationships:

> It must be obvious that war and violence are not human inventions in the same sense as are, say, the wheel and parliamentary government. Aggressive patterns are too transcultural and too similar to patterns observed throughout the animal kingdom. Neither can peacemaking be regarded as a uniquely human capacity. Over the past decade, my research team and several other primatologists have documented powerful behavioral mechanisms of social repair after aggressive disturbance among monkeys and apes. These mechanisms allow aggressive behavior to become a well-integrated part of relationships, so much so that it is fruitless to discuss this behavior outside the relational context. We need to think of aggression as one way in which conflicts of interest are expressed and resolved, and to be open to the possibility that its impact on future relationships ranges all the way from harmful to beneficial. (DeWaal, 1992, p. 37)

In anticipation of the model we will present below, we argue that humans and members of many other species inherit evolved modules (or specific psychological mechanisms) that *potentiate* the use of coercive tactics in response to particular environmental stimuli. Support for this point includes the observation that aggression occurs universally in all cultures (Segall, Ember, & Ember, 1997), that aggression-related emotions such as anger are universal (Ekman & Davidson, 1994), that they are evident in infants generally at very young ages (Sternberg & Campos, 1990; Lemerise & Dodge, 1993), that most children have had their "onset" of physical aggression by the time they are two years old (Tremblay et al., 1999) and that there are neural circuits in human brains that clearly appear designed to orchestrate affective attack (Panksepp, 1998). As emphasized below, although the capacity to aggress may reflect the workings of inherited mechanisms, this does not imply that aggressive behavior is justified or inevitable. Such coercive tactics are clearly one of several delimited alternative responses (see the earlier discussion of various tactics or bases of power) to a specific set of adaptive problems that were recurrent in our ancestors' environments. As Lore and Schultz (1993) note in their review of the extensive literature supporting the existence of evolved mechanisms potentiating aggression in various primate species: ". . . Even in so-called violence-prone animals, aggression is always an optional strategy . . . All organisms have co-evolved equally potent inhibitory mechanisms that enable them to use an aggressive strategy selectively or to suppress aggression when it is in their interest to do so" (p. 16).

Although we believe that cross-species comparisons can be very useful in developing understanding of the use of coercive tactics, we also suggest that some unique features of humans' cognitive capacities enable forms of social learning, particularly via social imitation and complex reasoning, that provide options for social influence that differ substantially from mechanisms of influence in other species. Similarly, humans' technological advances in weaponry (e.g., guns, nuclear weapons, etc.) have created a high risk of lethality from what some may describe as "common aggressive tendencies." Therefore, tolerating some aggression as an integral part of normal social relationships, a phenomenon common in many other species, is not tenable for humans in their personal and international interactions. In consequence, a comprehensive understanding of the causes and effective preventative strategies of human aggression is much needed.

A Comprehensive Framework

A multi-level model

Tedeschi and Felson (1994) correctly note that research relevant to the topic of aggression has often failed to be well integrated among various disciplines and approaches and they call for bridge-building across some social science disciplines. However, as noted earlier, they largely exclude so-called "biological" approaches from this enterprise. We strongly support a more comprehensive integration of different levels of scientific analysis. This bridge should transcend traditional disciplinary boundaries by integrating knowledge derived from various "embedded" analysis levels, including evolutionary, genetic,[1] cultural, and developmental levels. These, in turn, should be used to examine how their interactions affect the characteristics of the individual today. Such an integrative framework in turn enhances understanding of the role of the more proximate "person by situation" interactional level that social psychologists often use to analyze behaviors.

Figure 6.1 illustrates critical elements that might be integrated within a multilevel model designed to explain human behaviors. In this case, it focuses on the factors leading to the enactment of various alternative influence tactics, including coercive tactics (i.e., aggression). This model, which incorporates both ultimate and proximate causal levels, includes some ideas from Malamuth and Malamuth (1999) and Geary (1998). This figure is designed to emphasize the interrelationships and interactions among different levels of analysis, with arrows indicating "causal" influences. This model incorporates (1) psychological mechanisms resulting from evolutionary-based adaptation at the species level, (2) the calibration of these mechanisms resulting from individual life-history adaptation, and (3) the activation of these evolved, calibrated mechanisms via proximate environmental input.

We suggest that the impact of each level on behavior can be better conceptualized by considering it within the framework of the other levels. A key starting point is at the level of the evolved psychological mechanisms or "mental organs" of humans. These include social, biological, and physical modules (Geary, 1998). Such evolved psychological mechanisms underlie the development of cultures and individuals, which we have subsumed in the section of figure 6.1 labeled Mechanism Calibration.[2] A focus on the interaction between cultural environments and individual developmental histories can greatly enhance analyses of the current characteristics of people and how they select, shape, and are affected by particular situational dynamics. The social psychological literature has particularly centered on variables we would classify within this figure's Mechanism Calibration and Mechanism Activation levels (particularly the "person by situation" interactional level).

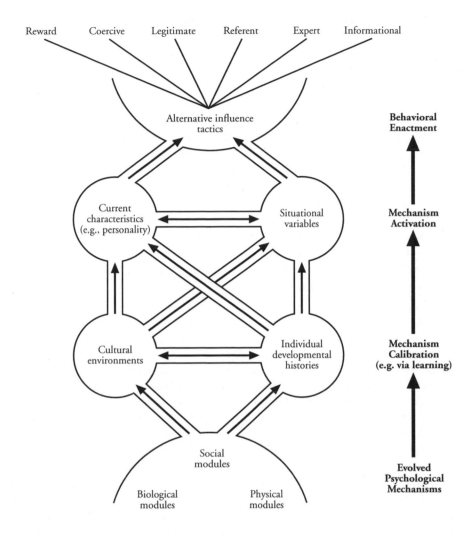

Reward   Coercive   Legitimate   Referent   Expert   Informational

Alternative influence tactics

Current characteristics (e.g., personality)

Situational variables

Cultural environments

Individual developmental histories

Social modules

Biological modules

Physical modules

Behavioral Enactment

Mechanism Activation

Mechanism Calibration (e.g. via learning)

Evolved Psychological Mechanisms

Figure 6.1   Conceptual framework showing how evolved modules are calibrated and activated to affect the enactment of alternative influence tactics.

The evolutionary model and computational theory

We would like to apply the framework outlined in figure 6.1 to an integration of the social psychological research on aggression with evolutionary psychology and associated computational theories of the mind (Buss, 1999; Cosmides & Tooby, 1995; Pinker, 1997). Such a perspective understands all human and other animal behavior as a function of the interrelated blend of "nature and nurture," with each species possessing some unique evolved psychological mechanisms.

This approach clearly places emphasis differently than some reviews of the social psychological research on aggression. For example, Geen (1994) states that "social psychological approaches to aggression begin with the assumption that aggression is a reaction to situations . . . Other antecedents of aggression, whether genetic, temperamental, social or cultural in origin, are usually considered to act as moderators of situational effects but not to motivate aggression in and of themselves" (p. 51). Embedded in this conceptualization must be the recognition that some psychological mechanisms in the mind cause an aggressive reaction. How else could "situations" cause aggression? In our view, conceptualizing this issue as "aggression as human nature versus aggression as response" (Geen, 1998a, p. 317) obscures a critical point: a better understanding of the features of situations that may elicit an aggressive response can be gained by first understanding the nature of the psychological mechanisms that process the relevant situational information.

In his recent book, Pinker (1997) gives an excellent presentation of the evolutionary/ computational approach. The following quote illustrates some central concepts particularly relevant to social psychologists:

> Most intellectuals think that the human mind must somehow have escaped the evolutionary process. Evolution, they think, can fabricate only stupid instincts and fixed action patterns . . . But if evolution equipped us not with irresistible urges and rigid reflexes but with a neural computer, everything changes. A program is an intricate recipe of logical and statistical operations directed by comparisons, tests, branches, loops, and subroutines embedded in subroutines . . . Human thought and behavior, no matter how subtle and flexible, could be the product of a very complicated program, and that program may have been our endowment from natural selection . . . The mind, I claim, is not a single organ but a system of organs, which we can think of as psychological faculties or mental modules. (1997, p. 27)

Pinker notes that the computational theory of the mind explains how such abstract concepts as beliefs, attitudes, and desires are coded in the neurons of the brain, thus providing the link between symbols and physical states. In turn, this theory reveals how symbols affect our information processing mechanisms to influence behavior. We believe this is very important for social scientists to appreciate since some have rejected so called "biological models" largely because of difficulties in understanding how symbolic information can be related to "biological" entities. As Pinker notes, although brains differ in some key respects from computers (e.g., brains are parallel, doing millions of things at once, whereas computers are serial, doing one thing at a time), they share some important properties that illustrate how "symbolic information" can be coded in physical matter. This integrative theory demonstrates that the same fundamental neural tissue underlies the programs which guide the behavior of all species. It also demonstrates how differences in the connections and patterns of activity among neurons represent differing mind programs within and between species (Cosmides & Tooby, 1995).

In defining instincts as specialized programs (or decision rules), Pinker (1997) notes that humans actually have more of these than other species and that "our vaunted flexibility comes from scores of instincts assembled into programs and pitted in competitions"

(p. 184). In trying to better understand such a program, the focus of social psychologists may be described as centering primarily on:

1 "inputs" to the program (e.g., understanding what types of "content situations" are more likely to activate it);
2 calibration of the relevant mechanisms via social experiences (i.e., relatively long-term alteration in various information processing elements, such as the encoding and decoding of stimuli that can affect the way individuals respond to their environments);
3 making explicit the decision rules involved in the various stages of the program.

To illustrate the utility of the evolutionary-grounded approach, let us consider the typical definition of aggression used by most social psychologists (see above). We believe that a shortcoming has been the definition's emphasis on the goal of harming another without understanding, particularly in the context of hostile aggression, the functions of such harm for the aggressor. Many researchers continue to adopt this definition (e.g., Gustafson, 1994) without asking why such a seemingly "sadistic" decision rule might be embedded as part of the mind's architecture.

We suggest that understanding aggression within the framework of evolved underlying decision rules sheds light on why causing harm may have become an embedded heuristic, an agent's response to certain environmental inputs, such as perceived threats. Consider the possible utility of the following decision rule: (1) When threatened, identify the source of the threat, (2) cause losses (i.e., harm) to those people responsible for the threat. A psychological mechanism using this simple decision rule might have been selected because the losses of one's competitors or combatants often may be considered gains for the aggressor. When rapid responding was favored by selection pressures, it may have been more advantageous to be primed to cause harm to any perceived adversaries (i.e., as in hostile or emotional aggression) than to more deliberately evaluate the actual gains or losses from an aggressive action. Under some conditions, natural selection may have favored the efficiency of building in a simple "satisficing algorithm" which could often perform as well as more complex evaluating procedures (Gigerenzer & Goldstein, 1996; Ketelaar & Goddie, 1998).

Proximate and ultimate causes

A comprehensive understanding of any behavior requires attention to both proximate causes (in the person's lifetime) and ultimate functions (i.e., what the mechanism was designed to do, based on the consequences on survival and reproductive success in ancestral environments). Daly and Wilson (1994) nicely illustrate this distinction with feeding behavior. The proximal "goal" may be described as the inhibition of a central motivational mechanism, such as gut-load messages and blood sugar cues. But it is also essential to understand that the "ultimate" function of this system is to extract utilizable energy from food and to maintain energy balance.

While the mind was designed by natural selection processes operating in ancestral environments as a function of fitness, people are not presumed to strive consciously to achieve the goal of fitness (Alcock, 1984). Rather, the types of mind mechanisms which evolved in ancestral environments and which can be "activated" in current environments were naturally selected because in those earlier environments they had fitness-favoring consequences.

The architecture of the mind

The evolutionary approach can be particularly helpful by focusing researchers' attention on the evolved architecture of the mind.[3] It is composed of many information processing psychological mechanisms or algorithms. These were designed by selection processes largely as evolved "solutions" to adaptive problems recurrently faced by our ancestors.[4] There is often confusion in equating evolutionary psychology with some form of genetic determinism. Although genes obviously play a role in enabling and limiting the range of all human behaviors, the algorithms underlying human development in different domains differ in the extent to which they are open to influence by environmental conditions. A *facultative developmental* algorithm is a relatively open mental program that directs development via interaction with particular features of the environment, whereas an *obligative developmental* algorithm is a mental program that is minimally affected by variations in environmental conditions (Alcock, 1984). The degree of genetic contribution to individual differences in various domains is a function of the extent to which the mental programs are facultative or obligative. Geary (1998) has described the former (which he labels open genetic systems as contrasted with closed genetic systems) as representing "skeletal knowledge" wherein domain-relevant experiences during development are essential for full adult competence. The underlying evolved "programs" include what may be described as "subroutines" that motivate children to seek out domain-relevant experiences encountered in emotionally stimulating environments (e.g., rough and tumble play) and to rehearse social scripts (e.g., playing "cops and robbers," engaging in relevant fantasy). Although understanding the evolved structure of the cognitive modules underlying behavior is essential, Geary rejects the idea suggested by some early ethologists that human behavior is reflexively driven by such modules in response to their eliciting environments. Instead, Geary and other evolutionary models (e.g., see Malamuth, 1998) have emphasized the calibrating or modulating effects of various other psychological mechanisms and experiences.

Facultative (or open) developmental programs may also differ. Geary distinguishes between two types of open genetic programs. One is where the genetic program codes for a finite list of possibilities, while experience during a sensitive period activates or deactivates subsets of the possibilities. It is exemplified by language learning. The other type of program is even more open. Although it biases the processing of domain-relevant information and influences the categorization processes, extensive experience is required. The latter type of cognitive model is quite common, and Geary suggests that an important function of relatively long pre-adult stages in our species is to enable the development of adult competencies adapted to local conditions based on the set of skeletal open genetic programs.

Evolution typically is a very slow process that requires many generations to modify the psychological architecture of the mind. Compared to our ancestral environments, current environments may share some features, but may also radically differ in others. It is therefore important to recognize that the complex psychological adaptations developed in ancestral environments are likely to have undergone only minor transformations despite the changes that have occurred in the environments (Cosmides & Tooby, 1987). Evolutionary forces operate "indirectly" on current behavior by having forged the architecture of the mind which interacts with proximate factors, including socialization and situational contingencies (Fletcher et al., 1999). While in some areas the computational problems underlying the evolution of psychological mechanisms may not be very different from those faced by our ancestors (e.g., some perceptual tasks), in areas such as aggression, there are enormous differences. For example, the aggression our ancient ancestors commonly viewed in their everyday experiences provided them with veridical information regarding the frequency and consequences of such behavior in their environments. By contrast, the technologically produced environments people occupy today (e.g., where television violence is common fare) frequently provide highly skewed information. This conceptualization helps to explain why media violence and other forms of conflict viewed through mass media have become such common fare. They "parasitize" evolved attention mechanisms of psychological programs evolved in ancestral environments to be particularly alert to signals of threatening events, imminent danger, and violence or conflict (Posner & DiGirolamo, 1998).[5]

Understanding aggressive responses therefore requires them to be embedded within a model of the psychological architecture of the human mind that underlies decision making, which is based on both conscious and subconscious processes. As noted earlier, this architecture of the mind is composed of many psychological mechanisms. These need to be considered as interrelated "packages" of information processing devices designed to process certain types of inputs, using particular decision rules, and to emit certain types of outputs. Psychological mechanisms and the type of environmental input (e.g., features of situations) they can process, and are responsive to, are not two separable causal processes, but rather elements of the same evolved package (Tooby & Cosmides, 1990). The fact that aggression is often associated with particular situational inputs (e.g., goal blocking, threats, etc.), and internal emotions and cognitions (anger, negative affect, hostility, etc.) is because aggressive tactics evolved as one of a delimited set of optional behaviors within the context of an evolved "package" of psychological mechanisms.

Yet social psychologists have often stressed the relative independence of aggression as a behavior distinct from the various "emotions (e.g., anger) and cognitions (e.g., hostility) that happen to be associated with harmful actions" (Richardson & Green, 1997, p. 172). Such distinctions do enable important differentiation between the activation of psychological mechanisms that may lead to aggression as contrasted with the behavior itself (which is clearly not an inevitable consequence of the activation of these mechanisms). However, conceiving of aggression as an "evolved package" that allows for consideration of ultimate functions points to a rather different conclusion. From an evolutionary perspective, characteristics such as emotions are adaptations[6] which function to alert the person to threats and opportunities and to prepare the organism for strategic behaviors (Nesse, 1990; Tooby & Cosmides, 1990). Without requiring relatively slower conscious processing, emotions may relatively quickly prime action tendencies: the emotion's hedonic component may prime approach or avoidance while the intensity may serve as an indication of the relative significance of the eliciting stimulus.

Emotions are not organized into one general emotional system but each type of emotion (e.g., anger, affection, etc.) is designed as part of a response to a particular set of delimited conditions (or adaptive problems) as input, and transform that input into physiological and behavioral output specifically addressing that type of condition (Ellis & Malamuth, 2000; LeDoux, 1996). For example, inputs perceived as strategic interference elicit anger. Anger produces output changes in information processing (e.g., increased sensitivity to cost-inflicting behaviors), the release of certain hormones, and increased arousal (heightened autonomic activity). These outputs prepare the organism to potentially respond with rapid "fight or flight" actions that reduce interference (Buss, 1989; Malamuth, 1998). Anger is not only an energizer of behavior but it can also serve as an organizer of behavior and as a social signal (e.g., communicating threat) to others. Evolutionary-based theories regarding the motivational functions of affect systems can also be well integrated with the role of cultural expectations and the impact of social, cognitive, and moral motives (e.g., Buck, 1999). Similarly, an evolutionary perspective also incorporates the idea that the experience, display, and consequences of emotions such as anger are strongly affected by socialization by caregivers and the larger social context (Lemerise & Dodge, 1993). Finally, learning experiences may also reverse the causal sequence so that individuals come to seek out experiences that lead to positive emotions and avoid those that have become associated with negative emotions (Nesse, 1990).

The "deep structure" underlying aggression

Consideration of the human mind as shaped by evolutionary mechanisms suggests that social psychologists have overemphasized the extent to which people function as rational decision makers who consciously weigh the various costs and benefits of possible actions (for examples, see Raven, 1965; Tedeschi & Felson, 1994). Aggressive behavior should not be understood as the result of decision rules that are always accessible to conscious processing. Rather, aggression can more generally be conceptualized as a behavior whose most central function is coercive influence. It is one of several individual tactics of influence (for addressing problems of social conflict) that evolved as part of evolutionary stable strategies (Dawkins, 1986; Maynard Smith, 1982).

Applying such an analysis reveals the functional "deep structure" underlying aggressive tactics:

> The relationship-specificity of human violence bespeaks its functionality: circumstances eliciting it are threats to fitness, and the targets of violence are generally not merely those available but those with whom assailants have substantive conflict . . . and hence have something to gain by subduing them. Threats to fitness as a result of others' actions depend not only on the nature of the threats but also on the relationship and the reproductive value of the parties, and on the alternative avenues to fitness of each. The utility of using violence to protect, defend or promote fitness in past environments can be discerned by an analysis of the complex functionality of morphology and psychology . . . (Daly & Wilson, 1994, pp. 260–261)

Consider, for example, the fact that in several North American cities the most frequently occurring motive for homicide is labeled in police reports as "trivial altercations," which often amount to "face" and "status" disputes (Wilson & Daly, 1985, 1993). Moreover, this finding is not confined to North American cities but has been shown to be true elsewhere, including Israel (Landu & Drapkin, 1968) and Japan (Hiraiwa-Hasegawa, 1998).

Relying only on a proximate analysis, it is difficult to conceptualize such aggression as anything but pathological, largely because the eliciting events appear so trivial. However, Daly and Wilson (1988) argue that within the evolutionary framework, these events may actually have considerable importance due to their potential influence on a person's reputation as someone "not to be messed with." They note that "conflicts of interest are endemic to society, and one's interests are likely to be violated by competitors unless those competitors are *deterred*" (p. 128). One effective means of deterring competitors in ancestral environments was to maintain a credible threat of violence but its utility in modern societies has been mitigated because the government has assumed the exclusive legitimate right to use force (although they may allow it in some special circumstances, such as in immediate self-defense). Daly and Wilson note that "wherever that monopoly is relaxed – whether in an entire society or in a neglected underclass – then the utility of that credible threat becomes apparent" (p. 28).

Humans, particularly young males, may therefore have evolved psychological mechanisms attuned to "face saving" and reputation maintenance. Therefore, what may be perceived by an observer as a trivial offense may be experienced by both perpetrator and target as a major affront. In the evolutionary environment where interactions with strangers were relatively rare, the willingness to fight may indeed have been important as a means of maintaining one's reputation with significant others. In current environments where interactions often take place among strangers, there may be less discernible consequences, with no visible lessening on the agent's ability to maintain a reputation and deter potential competitors. But protective mechanisms evolved to particularly function in small social groups may be activated currently even in stranger interactions using ancestrally evolved decision rules. Therefore, in examining the functionality of mechanisms that may increase the likelihood of aggressive responding (e.g., anger and shame) in current environments, it is not sufficient to examine the underlying logic in proximate terms only. It is also necessary to understand the development of these mechanisms (and the information they are designed to process) in terms of ultimate functions.

Frank (1988) presents a model of emotions that advances such understanding. He suggests that the function of emotion is to recalibrate assessments of self-interest to take future costs (or benefits) into account. Emotional predispositions evolved partly because, on average, they resulted in behaviors that appeared irrational in terms of short-term cost and benefit consequences but actually had beneficial consequences on fitness in the long term (on average, in the ancestral environments that shaped the mind's evolution).

Let us consider how Frank's commitment model might relate to our example of face and status disputes. One of two young men in a conflict situation aggressively pushes the other. What are the victim's alternative courses of action? He might walk away. Logically this often seems the best course of action. The damage or cost of being pushed has already been incurred. The benefit of walking away is that no further bodily harm is likely. A second option would be to act aggressively. As this is likely to cause more bodily harm (an obvious cost to fitness which should be avoided), and because there appear to be no immediate benefits in such an action, it seems irrational. However, as we discussed above, one effective means of deterring competitors is to maintain a "credible threat of violence."

The emotion of anger not only makes aggression more likely but also has characteristic facial expressions, changes in voice and posture. Thus anger initially may serve to signal a "threat of danger" to the competitor and may effectively deter the violator. However, if the threat does not act as a deterrent there must be a subsequent aggressive act or the credibility of the threat is eliminated (Daly & Wilson, 1988). After a reputation has been established, there may be little need for aggression, but until this occurs or in situations where the reputation is tested, aggression may maintain the credibility of this threat.

To reiterate, anger, which typically communicates threat and makes aggressive behavior more likely, may be the result of evolutionary-based "computation" which can serve "long-term interests" (at least within some ancestral environments) that the individual is not consciously aware of (Frank, 1988). This, of course, presents a somewhat different perspective than suggested by the quote presented earlier from Berkowitz (1993) regarding anger not having "a particular goal." However, it is more in keeping with Berkowitz's (1998) more recent description of the "automaticity" of some aggressive responses. The evolutionary framework also helps explain why certain mechanisms have "automatic" features. These developed for situations wherein quick and relatively fixed actions would have been advantageous. Some neural pathways mediating the "computation" by the relevant psychological mechanisms at subconscious levels have been described by LeDoux (1996). This work indicates that certain stimuli trigger information processing in two directions: one path activates behavior without conscious processing, while the other simultaneously sends information to "higher centers" that enable conscious analysis.

Aggression Research in Humans and Other Animals

Cross-species comparisons

Some social psychologists have emphasized the limitations of "biological" approaches and cross-species comparisons because of the unique aspects of human aggression (e.g., see Baron, 1977; Baron & Richardson, 1994; Tedeschi & Felson, 1994). We share the view that there are some evolved psychological mechanisms in humans which cannot be understood by simplistic inferences from other species. At the same time, we are convinced that some of the mechanisms often thought by social psychologists to be unique to humans exist in varying degrees in some other species and can be better understood within the framework of evolved mind mechanisms. For instance, Baron (1977), Baron and Richardson (1994), and Tedeschi and Felson (1994) repeatedly illustrate the uniqueness of human motives by pointing to retribution or revenge motives and emotions. Recent research actually demonstrates close parallels in other species. For example, in studying captive bonnet macaques, Silk (1992) found that males, in particular, join aggressive coalitions against specific individuals who had in the past been part of coalitions against them. Smuts and Smuts (1993) similarly concluded that male baboons engage in vicious punishing acts against females who have not associated or mated with them. The evolutionary logic underlying such acts has been explicated by Clutton-Brock and Parker (1995), who note that although positive reciprocity (reciprocal altruism) has been focused on extensively in evolutionary biology, negative reciprocity (retaliatory infliction of fitness reduction) has been largely ignored: "In social animals, retaliatory aggression is common, individuals often punish other group members that infringe their interests, and punishments can cause subordinates to desist from behavior likely to reduce the fitness of dominant animals. Punishing strategies are used to establish and maintain dominance relationships, to discourage parasites and cheats, to discipline offspring or prospective sexual partners and to maintain cooperative behavior" (p. 209). Clutton-Brock and Parker (1995) note the similarity of such punishing acts to human revenge motives. Indeed, such punishing strategies are often directed not only at the principal protagonists but also at their kin and they often appear "spiteful" – they appear to result in considerable cost to the punisher, at least in the more immediate context (Clutton-Brock & Parker, 1995). This result is similar to the costly outcome (in the short run) of reciprocal altruism (Trivers, 1971), although in negative retribution in the long run, there may be clearer evidence of reciprocity (Trivers, 1971). In the long run and in terms of ultimate, evolutionary-stable strategies, some game-theory modeling studies analyzing the logic of retributive behavior in many social species (Clutton-Brock and Parker, 1995) suggest the evolution of specific psychological algorithms underlying such behavior. Other modeling studies point to the evolution of psychological algorithms favoring cooperating, punishing non-cooperators, and punishing those who do not punish non-cooperators (Boyd & Richerson, 1992).

Human uniqueness

We believe that cross-species comparisons may be useful not only because they help shed light on evolved mechanisms and associated decision rules, but also because currently, our ethical system allows the study of other species in ways not permitted with humans, e.g., experimentally manipulating the effects of early deprivation on later aggression. While appreciating the benefits of examining other species, we also hold that certain features of our human psychological mechanisms are importantly unique, particularly those underlying the development of complex cultures and of social learning. As evolutionary anthropologists Boyd and Silk (1998, p. 633) note:

> The idea that culture is separate from biology is a popular misconception that cannot withstand scrutiny. Culture cannot transcend biology because it is as much a part of human biology as bipedal locomotion. Culture is generated from organic structures in the brain that were produced by the processes of organic evolution. However, cultural transmission leads to novel evolutionary processes. Thus, to understand the whole of human behavior, evolutionary theory must be modified to account for the complexities introduced by these, as yet poorly understood processes.

It appears that more than any other species, humans have evolved specialized psychological mechanisms that are particularly adapted to enhance observational learning from other humans. As Henrich and Boyd (1998) suggest, "cultural transmission mechanisms represent a kind of special purpose adaptations constructed to selectively acquire information and behavior by observing other humans and inferring the mental states that give rise to their behavior" (p. 217). This tendency may be easily observed in infants, who typically imitate spontaneously much of what they observe in other humans. Modeling others creates what has been termed a "second system of inheritance," whereby in addition to inheriting genes, humans "inherit" values and norms from others around them via processes that may even share some elements with genetic transmission (Dawkins, 1986). Such "conformist" mechanisms enable the development of gradual, cumulative knowledge transmitted culturally (e.g., strategies that evolve across generations and are adopted via observational learning of others rather than through direct individual experience). The role of media violence and other potential modeling influences in calibrating humans' evolved "aggression-relevant mechanisms" (see discussion below) can be better understood by looking more closely at "conformist" mechanisms.

Calibration/Modulation of Psychological Mechanisms

A primary emphasis of social psychological research on aggression can be described as focusing on how such "conformist" or social learning mechanisms affect various aspects of the development, alteration, maintenance, and activation of evolved modules pertaining to aggressive tactics. As discussed earlier, the underlying programs that potentiate the use of various cooperative, manipulative, and/or aggressive influence tactics are relatively open modules calibrated by relevant environmental experiences. We consider below examples of how these mechanisms are calibrated through social learning. First, we will discuss the social learning processes underlying the modulation of aggressive behavior (observational learning and enactive learning). Second, we will consider some of the known sources of social learning. Third, we will describe how individuals' cognitions and cultural norms moderate the impact of social learning.

Social learning and coercive tactics

The success of influence tactics is expected to vary from person to person in connection with environmental contingencies. One relevant piece of information in deciding which strategy to use is the potential consequences of behavior. According to the social learning paradigm, children acquire knowledge about behaviors and their consequences through two learning processes: (1) through the observation of others, and (2) through enactive learning (instrumental and classical conditioning) (Bandura, 1986).

Observational learning.   From various sources, the child will observe numerous instances of aggressive behavior (as well as other influence tactics) and their consequences. Through observation the child gradually builds a repertoire of knowledge or mental models of different types of social situations, possible behavioral responses to those situations and possible outcomes resulting from the behavior. Thus, the form of the behavior, the situations in which the behavior occurs, its appropriateness for these situations, and the probabilities of various consequences can be learned by the child. The organized mental representations of this learned information are called scripts (Huesmann, 1988).

Observation enables one to learn the consequences of behaviors without taking personal risks. This type of learning has obvious benefits in situations where there is a high probability that enacting behavior will produce severe and irreversible consequences. The observer also benefits from knowledge already acquired by others. Such learning, though, may be guided by evolved modules that "prepare" the organism for particular information (see Gallistel, 1995, for a general discussion of evolutionary-based models of learning). For example, in a series of well-known studies, Susan Mineka and her associates (Mineka, Davidson, Cook, & Keir, 1984; Mineka & Cook, 1993) showed that laboratory-reared monkeys having no experiences with or initial fear of snakes would quickly learn to fear this stimulus after watching a videotape of another member of their species reacting with fear to a snake. However, there was no evidence of similar observational learning when the monkeys saw the same fear response to a flower.

However, simply observing behavioral consequences for others does not ensure equal success when the observer employs the same tactics. The decision-making mechanisms need to be calibrated to relevant information for that individual (e.g., social status, physical size). In situations where the actor and the observer have relevant attributes in common there may be more utility in observational learning. Indeed research indicates that when the actor and observer share more in common, the information is encoded faster (Huesmann, 1986).

A recent series of studies have provided some intriguing early glimpses into possible neurological mechanisms, sometimes referred to as "mirror neurons," underlying observational learning in monkeys and humans (e.g., Rizzolatti & Arbib, 1998; Fadiga, Buccino, Craighero, & Fogassi, 1999). These researchers described certain parts of the brain where neurons are activated in very similar ways when an individual observes the actions of someone with whom they identify or when they engage in the same actions, or even when they simply imagine the same actions. Other associated neurons are activated only when the actor himself/herself engages in the behavior. Although clearly in its early stages, this work may help explain why observing others can be such a powerful influence, since some of the same mind "rehearsal" seems to occur during observation as in actual behavior enactment.

Enactive learning. Although observing others contributes in important ways to the calibration of psychological mechanisms, critical learning occurs when a child actually enacts and rehearses scripts. Depending upon how the child's own actions are reinforced, the probability that he will engage in similar actions increases or decreases. According to Bandura (1986) rewards and punishments for aggression are represented by anticipated consequences of the aggressive act for the individual and the utility or value that the potential outcome has for that individual. The positive consequences can include tangible rewards such as obtaining desired objects, positive self-evaluations, and favorable social reactions from others (e.g., increased status among peers, control or dominance over others, etc.). Similarly, if a child anticipates that negative consequences are likely to result from his or her aggressive behaviors, they are less likely to behave aggressively. Negative consequences might include physical punishment, social disapproval, harm or injury to another person, and disruption of social relationships.

Thus, according to the social learning paradigm, the child will initially learn aggressive behavior through observation of others. (Our evolutionary-based framework, however, conceptualizes such early experiences in terms of the calibration or modulation of already evolved psychological mechanisms.) Depending on what consequences are perceived for his/her own behaviors, the script may become more or less easily activated in subsequent similar situations. Studies supporting this model do indicate that aggressive children are more likely to predict that aggressive acts will result in tangible rewards and increased status among their peers and that such acts are more likely to stop others from behaving aversively towards them (Perry, Perry, & Rasmussen, 1986; Guerra & Slaby, 1990). In addition, Guerra and colleagues (Guerra, 1989; Slaby & Guerra, 1988) have shown that recurrent aggressive behavior during adolescence correlates with lower expectations of negative consequences for aggressive behavior.

Sources of social learning

There are various sources for observational learning. In addition to observing the behaviors of parents, siblings, teachers, and peers, the child receives information about the social environment from books, television, the internet, and films.

Media violence.   Investigators have consistently documented that viewing violence in the media can influence viewers' aggressive tendencies (e.g., the number of aggressive behaviors committed by the viewer) and shape their perceptions and attitudes toward violence in the real world (Smith & Donnerstein, 1998). Some evolutionary theorists have criticized social learning theories for placing too much emphasis on observational learning from television and media sources. They note that violence and aggressive tendencies are prevalent in societies in which such media violence is not available (i.e., Chagnon, 1990). While it is true that in tribal societies, such as the Yanomamo, violence is pervasive without media sources for observational learning, there are certainly many other sources for observational learning in such societies (e.g., from witnessing violence and hearing stories about war raids).

We believe that the media is simply one of many sources from which information about the social environment can be gathered (consciously and unconsciously), but is one that is becoming an increasingly frequent source in modern societies. For example, studies have shown that 57 percent of television programs contain some violence (Kunkel et al., 1996) and that by the age of 13, children will have viewed 100,000 violent scenes on television (Huston et al., 1992). Importantly, however, not all portrayals pose the same risk to viewers. The context in which the violence is portrayed may increase or decrease the risk of increased aggressive tendencies in viewers (Kunkel et al., 1996).

Smith and Donnerstein (1998) reviewed nine different contextual cues that influence learning of aggression, fear, and emotional desensitization. Several of these contexts suggest that the more that this violence is judged "real" and relevant to the individual the more likely it is to affect future aggressive tendencies. For example, several studies have found that increasing the degree of realism raised aggressive responding in children and adults (Atkin, 1983; Berkowitz & Alioto, 1973; Geen, 1975; Thomas & Tell, 1974). The degree of perceived similarity between the perpetrator and viewer also influences the degree of impact on aggression (Berkowitz & Geen, 1966, 1967; Hicks, 1965; Huesmann, 1986; Josephson, 1987). In addition, people are more likely to attend to, identify with, and learn from attractive role models than from unattractive ones (Bandura, 1986, 1994). Aggression research shows that exposure to violent perpetrators with good or heroic natures increases the risk of aggressive behaviors from both child and adult viewers (Leyens & Picus, 1973; Liss, Reinhardt, & Fredrikson, 1983; Perry & Perry, 1976; Turner & Berkowitz, 1972). Viewers become emotionally and physiologically desensitized when the duration of a violent act or its graphic portrayal are increased (Cline, Croft, & Courrier, 1973; Lazaraus & Alfert, 1964, Mullin & Linz, 1995). Perhaps more graphic acts appear to be more realistic. Studies also indicate that portrayed justification or social acceptance of violence increases viewers' aggressive tendencies (Berkowitz & Geen, 1967; Paik & Comstock, 1994). In contrast, viewing socially unjustified violence may cause a decrease in viewers' aggressive responding (Geen, 1981).

Interestingly, media research has documented reliable effects even when subjects are clearly aware that they are reading fictional portrayals. For instance, in a recent study by Strange and Leung (1999), it was found that both true and fictional news stories had similar influences in changing participants' judgments about the causes and solutions for societal problems (education and health care). In addition, the authors found that the greater the extent to which the stories (news or fictional) evoked participants' memories of related experiences, the more likely they were to influence the participants' subsequent judgments.

These and similar data fit in well with recent theorizing and integration of the available scientific literature regarding how people comprehend and validate social information. For example, Wyer and Radvansky (1999) describe a model that views comprehension as a process of constructing "situation models." They note that in modern societies, a major source of the models people construct is the mass media, particularly television. They further note than an important feature of human information processing is the ability to add "tags" to representations (such as situation models) to denote their falsity (e.g., no matter how many times you see Santa Claus on television, you still perceive him as a fictitious character). However, they argue that because information acquired from television is typically not extensively thought about, situation models constructed about fictitious people and events via the mass media are unlikely to be tagged as such. These models may therefore be stored in similar ways as models of events that have occurred in real life and not be often subject to source monitoring (Johnson, Hashtroudi, & Lindsay, 1993). Consequently, the models of fictitious events may be used as a basis for inference without discounting based on the context in which they were formed.

The extent of fictional influence via experiencing an event in the mass media may be related to the fact that although humans have some ability to "decouple" fiction and reality, our evolutionary environments did not have selection pressure to develop highly attuned mechanisms for such distinctions. For instance, even though in some ancestral environments storytellers may have told fictional tales, it was much easier to discriminate between such narrative and the "real world" than to distinguish real events from those depicted via the sophisticated technology of current times. Therefore, we did not evolve strong mechanisms to be immune from fictional portrayals in the media and those motivated to minimize potential impact (e.g., parents) may have to stimulate "extra" cognitive effort by adding "tags" of falsity when observing television and other media.

Direct exposure to family violence.   A variety of studies indicate that there is a positive relationship between direct exposure to familial violence in childhood and aggressive behavior in adulthood. For example, recurrently witnessing parental aggression as a child and/or being the victim of parental abuse is positively correlated with use of violence in dating (Foshee, Bauman, & Fletcher, 1999; Malamuth, Sockloskie, Koss, & Tanaka, 1991). Childhood victims of aggression also committed greater amounts of spouse abuse in adulthood (Hotaling & Sugarman, 1990) and inflicted more physical abuse on their own children (Zaidi, Knutson, & Mehm, 1989). Widom (1989) compared a group of children who were physically or sexually abused to another group that was matched on age, sex, race, and social class but who had not experienced child abuse. The author found that both physical abuse and neglect were strong predictors of adult criminal violence.

Studies also indicate that direct exposure to familial conflict is related to differences in children's aggressive tendencies toward their peers. For example, in several studies Cummings and his colleagues have shown that witnessing angry interactions between parents may contribute to aggression against other children (Cummings, Ianotti, & Zahn-Waxler, 1985; Cummings, Hennessy, Rabideau, & Cichetti, 1994; Davies & Cummings, 1994). In a study by Zaidi, Knutson, and Mehm (1989) subjects read hypothetical vignettes in which a child misbehaved. Those subjects who experienced severe physical punishment as children were more likely to recommend physical punishment for the transgressing child than those who had experienced little or no physical punishment.

Clearly, many studies support the hypothesis that witnessing and experiencing familial violence is related to aggressive tendencies but fewer studies have attempted to identify the mechanisms that may underlie this relationship. According to social learning theory, witnessing familial violence could lead to increased use of aggression in at least two ways. First, because aggression is more likely to be used when positive outcome expectancies are formed for using the behavior, children of violent parents may be more likely to use aggression when they have observed that parental use of aggression leads to more positive outcomes for the aggressive parent than negative outcomes. And second, there may be a lack of opportunities for the child to observe constructive strategies for conflict resolution. A recent study by Foshee et al. (1999) serves to illustrate the type of data gathered in this area. The researchers examined the mediators of the relationship between exposure to family violence in childhood and later dating violence using retrospective assessment of a large number of adolescents. The authors compared variables expected to mediate aggression according to social learning models as compared with social control theories. The social learning mediators are exemplified by variables such as acceptance of dating violence and an aggressive conflict style. The social control variables included parental attachment as well as commitment and belief in conventional rules of society. Support for some, but not all, of the social learning mediating variables was found for both males and females. For the social control variables, support for mediation was only found with male adolescents.

Directly experiencing violence as a child may cause the formation of hostile attribution biases (the tendency to "over attribute" to others hostile intentions). Several studies indicate that aggressive boys are more likely to attribute aggressive intent to others even when intentions are benign or ambiguous (Dodge, 1980; Nasby, Hayden, & DePaulo, 1979). Why should aggressive boys be more likely to infer harmful intent from others? Dodge and Coie (1987) suggest that a history of having to defend oneself against others might increase the probability that one will attribute hostile attributions to the actions of others. Thus, repeatedly experiencing aggression early in life (as is often true in cases of familial violence) may calibrate decision-making mechanisms in such a way that one is more likely to attribute hostile intention to others in social interactions. Perceptions of hostile intentions may then increase the likelihood that aggressive tactics are used in the social interaction. Gouldner (1960) suggests that if someone thinks that they are the victim of aggression, they are more likely to feel justified in retaliating aggressively. Supporting this view, Brown and Tedeschi (1976) found that the initiator of a hostile action is perceived as behaving unfairly, but that an aggressive response to such provocation is judged to be fair. Gouldner proposes that the justification of retaliatory aggression is a norm present in many societies. As noted earlier, retaliatory aggression is also common in various other social species.

Growing up in families with high levels of aggression may also result in the lack of opportunities to learn how to understand and regulate various emotions, such as anger (Dunn & Brown, 1994). For example, exposure to violence in childhood is correlated with heightened emotional reactivity (Davies & Cummings, 1998) and more anxiety, distraction, and withdrawal (Gordis, Margolin, & John, 1997) to staged and naturally-occurring anger episodes. It should be noted that although these types of findings support social learning formulations, it is difficult to disentangle the possible contributions to such individual differences of shared genetic factors underlying both parental violence and children's emotional and behavioral responses from the influences of being in such family environments. Research also indicates both the independent and mutually exacerbating influences of genetic vulnerabilities and risky family environments on the genesis of children's aggressivity and conduct disorders (Cadoret et al., 1995; Repetti, Taylor, & Seeman, 1999).

Moderators of aggression

Individuals' cognitions and perceived norms.   According to the social learning model, children learn aggressive behaviors through observation of aggressive acts and through reinforcement of their own aggressive behaviors. The social scripts, which guide behavior, are modified during the learning process and become less flexible in adulthood. However, even after scripts or decision rules underlying the increased potential for aggression have been activated, the actual implementation of aggression may be moderated by other factors, particularly certain cognitions and beliefs. It has been suggested that normative beliefs, which are those held about what constitutes acceptable and unacceptable behavior (Guerra, Huesmann, & Hanish, 1994), act as filters influencing the likelihood that an activated script will be enacted in aggressive responses. Researchers have shown that the normative beliefs of children and adults who are more aggressive are more accepting of aggression (Guerra, Huesmann, & Hanish, 1994; Huesmann & Guerra, 1997). However, these are correlative data and it remains to be convincingly shown that such beliefs actually have a causal role in the use of coercive tactics.

Bandura (1986) suggests that normative beliefs that do not condone violence can be disengaged in three ways: (1) by altering perceptions of the behavior itself, (2) through misrepresenting the effects that the harmful act has on others, or (3) by altering perceptions of the victim of the act. Moreover, Bandura, Barbaranelli, Caprara, and Pastorelli (1996) contend that "people do not ordinarily engage in reprehensible conduct until they have justified to themselves the rightness of their actions" (p. 365). These investigators examined the causal pathway by which a tendency for moral disengagement affects aggressive and antisocial behavior. The authors measured subjects' inclination to resort to various cognitions related to the three ways described by Bandura (1986). Their findings suggested that moral disengagement mechanisms act upon aggressive tendencies directly and also indirectly by influencing guilt, prosocial behavior, and cognitive reactions conducive to aggression.

Cultural norms.   The transformation of harmful conduct through moral justifications may be a particularly effective means of eliminating self-deterrents if it is supported by significant others in one's group, thereby promoting self-approval (Bandura et al., 1996). Under these conditions aggression may be seen as an acceptable and even socially desirable behavior and may become a part of social norms. Such norms do not typically condone the indiscriminate use of aggression (which may threaten group cohesion) but may have certain identifiable decision rules regarding when aggression is or is not appropriate to use (e.g., against out-group but not in-group members).

Nisbett and Cohen (1996) suggest that cross-cultural consistency and variability in the shaping of evolved mechanisms of the mind can be conceptualized in the context of distinctions between adaptive problems that humans have had to solve in all environments (e.g., rearing offspring that are relatively helpless for long periods of time) and those that differ in varied ecologies and social environments (e.g., variations in availability of food or parasites). Such commonalities and differences in environments interact with the underlying evolved psychological mechanisms shared by members of our species to produce cross-cultural universality in certain phenotypic characteristics and cross-cultural variability in others. Once certain norms and values have emerged and are supported by various cultural institutions, they may be transmitted and maintained across generations even if the environments that originally led to their development have changed considerably.

The American South has long been regarded as more violent than the North (Fischer, 1989). Nisbett and colleagues (Nisbett, 1993; Cohen & Nisbett, 1994; Nisbett & Cohen, 1996) have shown that it is not violence in general that is more common in the South, but more specifically violence relating to self-protection, punishment of disobedient children and in response to insults. For example, Cohen, Nisbett, Bowdle, and Schwartz (1996) investigated differences in aggressive tendencies between Northern and Southern men in the laboratory. In order to invoke possible aggressive tendencies, a confederate of the experimenter bumped into each unsuspecting participant and then continued walking down the hall, verbally insulting the research participant. Whereas Northerners were affected little by these insulting actions, Southerners showed behavioral, physiological, emotional, and cognitive signs of aggressivity. In comparison to the insulted Northerners, insulted Southerners had higher levels of cortisol, increased testosterone levels, were more likely to believe that the insult damaged their masculine status and reputation, were more likely to behave aggressively in a subsequent "chicken" game, were more likely to behave in a domineering fashion with the experimenter, and were more likely to complete an ambiguous story plot with themes of violence. In contrast, there were no differences in the attributions, behaviors, and physiology of those Northern and Southern participants who were not insulted.

The authors (Cohen & Nisbett, 1994) suggested that acceptance of violence, particularly in response to insult, arose as a form of self-defense of property and person. They postulate that a "culture of honor" has arisen in the Southern US because this area has historically been composed of herding communities in which there was inadequate or unjust law-enforcement. They further state that "such conditions perpetuated the culture of honor in the South, as it became important to establish one's reputation for toughness – even on matters that might seem trivial on the surface. If one had been crossed, trifled with, or affronted, retribution had to follow as a warning to the community" (Cohen et al., 1996, p. 946). This analysis is reminiscent of Daly and Wilson's (1994) point, noted earlier in this chapter, that whenever the State's monopoly on the use of violence is relaxed, then the credible threat of aggression as a deterrent is likely to become more important.

Cultural norms may increase or restrain various forms of violence, depending on whether the particular types of aggressive acts are condoned or disapproved of by the particular culture. Moreover, the degree to which the norms supporting or condemning violence influence members of the culture may vary as a function of such factors as the cohesiveness of the family, community, and religious institutions. Support for this type of model was reported by Cohen (1998) who examined various indices of violence as a function of different norms and community cohesiveness in various regions of the United States.

Situational Activation of Psychological Mechanisms

Social psychologists have provided a rich literature on a variety of situational variables that interact with people's psychological mechanisms to affect the probability of aggressive behavior. We will illustrate here the role of such situational factors by considering both (a) situational inputs that activate psychological mechanisms because their content is part of the "package" of those mechanisms, and (b) environmental stimuli that prime the psychological mechanisms because of their learned associations with particular aggression-related concepts. Due to space constraints, we will not consider other research, such as on the effects of alcohol consumption (e.g., Bushman, 1993, 1997; Lipsey, Wilson, Cohen, & Derzon, 1997) or heat (Anderson & Anderson, 1998) that concern situational variables modifying the functioning of psychological mechanisms.

Content situations likely to elicit aggressive tactics

As Buss (1999) has emphasized, evolutionary psychological models propose ". . . a specific interactional model – aggression as evoked by particular adaptive problems confronted in particular cost-benefit contexts. In principle, the mechanisms producing aggression could remain dormant for the entire life of an individual, if the relevant contexts are not encountered" (p. 285). Buss and Shackelford (1997) describe several of the recurrent "adaptive problems" to which aggression is likely to be an evolved "solution." These include the following: (1) to co-opt resources from others, (2) to defend against assault, (3) to inflict costs on competitors, (4) to gain status and power, (5) to discourage competitors from using aggressive tactics, (6) to deter long-term mates from sexual infidelity, and (7) to reduce the amount of resources expended on unrelated offspring. Knowing some of the interpersonal conflicts that our ancestors would have recurrently faced over evolutionary history is valuable information because the evolved mental mechanisms are expected to be activated in current environments by contextual cues inherent to these types of interpersonal conflicts. In these situations, the mechanisms underlying various types of influence tactics are activated, making the use of aggression more likely. It is important to stress that the psychological mechanisms or "decision rules" are not static programs, but instead are designed by evolutionary processes to be "open" and flexible to relevant environmental stimuli. For example, decision-making processes are expected to be flexible to life history variables (e.g. previous success or failures using such tactics), and situational variables (e.g., a novel stimuli that become associated with certain concepts).

Priming of mechanisms

The evolutionary-based framework suggests that aggression may be triggered (i.e., activation of the relevant modules) by specific contextual stimuli, particularly those that ". . . resemble those in which our ancestors confronted certain adaptive problems and reaped particular benefits" (Buss, 1999, p. 284). In keeping with the computational theory of the mind, modern environments may present novel stimuli that also activate aggression-relevant psychological mechanisms. They do so because they are coded in the mind as part of "aggression-related" concepts, even though they do not correspond to a stimulus which appeared in ancestral environments. This is well demonstrated by research on the "weapons effect" using stimuli such as guns, which obviously did not exist in ancestral environments, but can become embedded in our evolved modules pertaining to aggression because the mind's programs have the flexibility to integrate novel stimuli and images within a conceptual framework (Pinker, 1997).

Social psychological research indicates that the presence of common weapons, such as guns or knives, significantly increases aggressive responding both in the laboratory (Berkowitz & LePage, 1967) and in the real world (Turner, Layton, & Simons, 1975). It has been suggested that the presence of weapons or pictures of weapons may prime aggression-related thoughts and may increase the probability of aggressive behaviors (Berkowitz, 1990;

Carlson, Marcus-Newhall, & Miller, 1990). Direct support for the hypothesis in terms of thought has been recently provided by Anderson, Anderson, and Deuser (1996) and by Anderson, Benjamin, and Bartholow (1998). In the latter experiment, for example, subjects were presented (using words or pictures) with a prime stimulus (weapon or nonweapon) followed by a target word (aggressive or nonaggressive) that was to be read as quickly as possible. The findings clearly showed that the mere identification of a weapon primes aggression-related thoughts. Although such effects on cognitive processes have been demonstrated with both unprovoked and provoked individuals, studies focusing on actual aggressive behavior generally indicate that provocation is a necessary precursor of the weapons priming effect (e.g., Turner et al., 1975).

Concluding Remarks

Recent research by Tremblay et al. (1999) and other studies (e.g., Nagin & Tremblay, 1999) indicate that physical aggression is actually a normative behavior in young infants. The majority of children have learned to inhibit their physical aggression by the time they enter kindergarten and to use alternative tactics of influence. Such research supports the existence of a common decision rule to use oppositional and/or aggressive response to blocked goals (what Buss, 1994, has labeled strategic interference). Perhaps in some respects this decision rule may even function as an evolved "default" response, unless learning experiences foster and shape the "preferred" use of alternative tactics (potentiated by aspects of our evolved social modules). Learning experiences may be essential to countermand this "default" response and to encourage the use of other influence tactics potentiated by our evolved psychology. Research suggests that such learning is particularly critical in the early period of life (Tremblay et al., 1999). This finding is consistent with other recent studies (e.g., Pakaslahti, Spoof, Asplund-Peltola, & Keltikangas-Jaevinen, 1998). They indicate that parents of nonaggressive children are more likely to actively teach their offspring problem-solving strategies. By contrast, parents of aggressive children are not only more likely to avoid discussing problems with them but they are also more likely to divert them to other sources for solutions and to generally show indifference to helping them develop problem-solving strategies. In keeping with these findings, the integrative, evolutionary-based framework we have presented in this chapter suggests that if we want to minimize the use of coercive tactics by individuals, groups, and nations (Hall & Whitaker, 1999), then we must actively anticipate the potential use of aggression and promote early behavioral experiences as well as environmental conditions throughout life that inhibit aggression and encourage the use of other influence strategies.

Acknowledgments

We thank Eugenie Dye, Margo Wilson, Eugene Volokh, L. R. Huesmann, and Carlos D. Navarrete for their helpful comments on earlier drafts of this paper.

Notes

1. There is often confusion in equating an evolutionary approach with genetic contribution to behavior. Evolutionary psychologists generally study species-typical psychological mechanisms, whereas genetic behavioral researchers focus on the extent to which individual differences in genetic makeup contribute to various behaviors.
2. The concept of calibration is used here to refer to relatively long-term alteration in various information processing elements, such as the encoding and decoding of stimuli.
3. Some might argue that this type of theorizing is not amenable to systematic testing. Ketelaar and Ellis (2000) present an excellent discussion and defense of the testability of evolutionary psychological concepts.
4. Note that this does not mean that even for our ancestors, these adaptations had beneficial consequences in all or even most circumstances, but that everything else being equal, on average those of our ancestors who had this characteristic survived and reproduced more successfully than those who did not.
5. Consider the commonly used example of taste buds for sweetness, which evolved in ancestral environments as a way to increase the likelihood that we would jump at the opportunity to eat scarce substances that provided nutritional value (e.g., the sweetness in ripe fruit). In today's environments, these taste buds have been capitalized on to develop substances such as processed sugar, which also activates our sweetness mechanisms, but which may actually be harmful rather than beneficial to our health. In a modern environment with an overabundance of artificial sweets, the craving stimulated by the sight of candies may create difficulties in maintaining good health. This is an example of using our knowledge to create products that in the long run make our environments more difficult. But it can work the opposite way – just as we have created buildings, warm coats, and nutritional guidelines to enable our bodies to live comfortably in environments that they were not designed for (as were species with deep furs for living in cold environments), knowledge of our mind mechanisms can help us function more effectively in our social lives.
6. The wide consensus among scholars that the basic or simple emotions (such as anger, disgust, sadness, and fear) are universal is supportive of this perspective (Ekman & Davidson, 1994).

References

Alcock, J. (1984). *Animal Behavior: An evolutionary approach*. Sunderland, MA: Sinauer.

Alexander, R. D. (1979). *Darwinism and human affairs*. Seattle, WA: University of Washington Press.

Anderson, C. A., & Anderson, K. B. (1998). Temperature and aggression: Paradox, controversy, and a (fairly) clear picture. In R. G. Geen & E. Donnerstein (Eds.), *Human aggression: Theories, research, and implications for social policy* (pp. 248–298). San Deigo, CA: Academic Press.

Anderson, C. A., Anderson, K. B., & Deuser, W. E. (1996). Examining an affective aggression framework: Weapon and temperature effects on aggressive thoughts, affect, and attitudes. *Personality and Social Psychology Bulletin, 22,* 366–376.

Anderson, C. A., Benjamin, A. J. Jr., & Bartholow, B. D. (1998) Does the gun pull the trigger? Automatic priming effects of weapon pictures and weapon names. *Psychological Science, 9,* 308–314.

Atkin, C. (1983). Effects of realistic TV violence vs. fictional violence on aggression. *Journalism Quarterly , 60,* 615–621.

Bandura, A. (1973). *Aggression: A social learning analysis.* Englewood Cliffs, NJ: Prentice Hall.

Bandura, A. (1983). Psychological mechanisms of aggression. In R. G. Geen & E. I. Donnerstein

(Eds.), *Aggression: Theoretical and empirical reviews* (Vol. 1, pp. 1–40). New York: Academic Press.

Bandura, A. (1986). *Social foundations of thought and action: A social cognitive theory.* Englewood Cliffs, NJ: Prentice Hall.

Bandura, A. (1991). Social cognitive theory of moral thought and action. In W. M. Kurtines & J. L. Gewirtz (Eds.), *Handbook of moral behavior and development: Theory, research, and applications* (Vol. 1, pp. 71–129). Hillsdale, NJ: Erlbaum.

Bandura, A. (1994). Social cognitive theory of mass communication. In J. Bryant & D. Zillimann (Eds.), *Media effects* (pp. 61–90). Hillsdale, NJ: Erlbaum.

Bandura, A., Barbaranelli, C., Caprara, G. V., & Pastorelli, C. (1996). Mechanisms of moral disengagement in the exercise of moral agency. *Journal of Personality and Social Psychology, 71,* 364–374.

Barkow, J. H. (1989). *Darwin, sex, and status: Biological approaches to mind and culture.* Toronto: University of Toronto Press.

Barnett, O. W., Fagan, R. W., & Booker, J. M. (1991). Hostility and stress as mediators of aggression in violent men. *Journal of Family Violence, 6,* 217–241.

Baron, R. A. (1977). *Human aggression.* New York: Plenum.

Baron, R. A., & Richardson, D. (1994). *Human Aggression.* New York: Plenum.

Berkowitz, L. (1970). Aggressive humor as a stimulus to aggressive responses. *Journal of Personality and Social Psychology, 16,* 710–717.

Berkowitz, L. (1990). On the formation and regulation of anger and aggression: A cognitive neo-associationistic analysis. *American Psychologist, 45,* 494–503.

Berkowitz, L. (1993). Towards a general theory of anger and emotional aggression: Implications of the cognitive-neo-associationistic perspective for the analysis of anger and other emotions. In Wyer, R. S. & Srull, T. K. (Eds.), *Perspectives on anger and emotion: Advances in social cognition,* (Vol. 6, pp. 1–46). Hillsdale, NJ: Erlbaum.

Berkowitz, L. (1994). On the escalation of aggression. In M. Portegal & J. F. Knutson (Eds.), *The dynamics of aggression: Biological and social processes in dyads and groups* (pp. 33–41). Hillsdale, NJ: Erlbaum.

Berkowitz, L. (1998). Affective aggression: The role of stress, pain, and negative affect. In R. G. Geen & E. Donnerstein (Eds.), *Human aggression: Theories, research, and implications for social policy.* San Diego, CA: Academic Press.

Berkowitz, L., & Alioto, J. T. (1973). The meaning of an observed event as a determinant of its aggressive consequences. *Journal of Personality and Social Psychology, 28,* 206–217.

Berkowitz, L., & Geen, R. G. (1966). Film violence and the cue properties of available targets. *Journal of Personality and Social Psychology, 3(5),* 525–530.

Berkowitz, L., & Geen, R. G. (1967). Stimulus qualities of the target of aggression: A further study. *Journal of Personality and Social Psychology, 5,* 364–368.

Berkowitz, L., & LePage, A. (1967). Weapons as aggression eliciting stimuli. *Journal of Personality and Social Psychology, 7,* 202–207.

Boyd, R., & Richerson, P. (1992). Punishment allows the evolution of cooperation (or anything else) in sizable groups. *Ethology and Sociobiology, 13,* 171–195.

Boyd, R., & Silk, J. B. (1998). *How humans evolved.* New York: Norton.

Brock, T. C., & Buss, A. H. (1962). Dissonance, aggression and evaluation of pain. *Journal of Abnormal Social Psychology, 65,* 197–202.

Brown, R. C., & Tedeschi, J. T. (1976) Determinants of perceived aggression. *Journal of Social Psychology, 100,* 77–87.

Bryant, J., Carveth, R. A., & Brown, D. (1981). Television viewing and anxiety: An experimental examination. *Journal of Communication, 31,* 106–119.

Buck, R. (1999). The biological effects: a typology. *Psychological Review, 106,* 301–336.

Buck, R., & Ginsburg, B. (1997). Communicative genes and the evolution of empathy. In W. J. Ickes (Ed.), *Empathic accuracy* (pp. 17–43). New York: Guilford Press.

Bushman, B. J. (1993). Human aggression while under the influence of alcohol and other drugs: An integrative research review. *Current Directions in Psychological Science, 2,* 950–960.

Bushman, B. J. (1997). Effects of alcohol on human aggression: Validity of proposed explanations. In D. Fuller, R. Dietrich, & E Gottheil (Eds.), *Recent developments in alcoholism: Alcohol and violence* (Vol. 13, pp. 227–243). New York: Plenum.

Buss, D. M. (1988). The evolution of human intrasexual competition: Tactics of mate attraction. *Journal of Personality and Social Psychology, 54*, 616–628.

Buss, D. M. (1989). Conflict between the sexes: Strategic interference and the evocation of anger and upset. *Journal of Personality and Social Psychology, 56*, 735–747.

Buss, D. M. (1994). Personality evoked: The evolutionary psychology of stability and change. In T. F. Heatherton, & J. L. Weinberger (Eds.), *Can personality change?* Washington, DC: American Psychological Association.

Buss, D. M. (1995). Evolutionary psychology. *Psychological Inquiry, 6*, 1–30.

Buss, D. M. (1999). *Evolutionary psychology: The new science of the mind.* Boston, MA: Allyn & Bacon.

Buss, D. M., & Shackelford, T. K. (1997). Human aggression in evolutionary perspective. *Clinical Psychology Review, 17*, 605–619.

Cadoret, R. J., Yates, W. R., Troughton, E.,Woodworth, G., & Stewart, M. A. (1995). Genetic-environmental interaction in the genesis of aggressivity and conduct disorders. *Archives of General Psychiatry, 52*, 916–924.

Carlson, M., Marcus-Newhall, A., & Miller, N. (1990). Effects of situational aggression cues: A quantitative review. *Journal of Personality and Social Psychology, 58*, 622–633.

Carmelli, D., Rosenman, R. H., & Swan, G. E. (1988). The Cook and Medley Hostility Scale: A heritability analysis in adult male twins. *Psychosomatic Medicine, 50*, 165–174.

Carmelli, D., Swan, G. E., & Rosenman, R. H. (1990). The heritability of the Cook and Medley Hostility Scale revisited. *Journal of Social Behavior and Personality, 5*, 107–116.

Chagnon, N. A. (1990) Reproductive and somatic conflicts of interest in the genesis of violence and warfare among tribesmen. In J. Haas (Ed.), *The anthropology of war* (pp. 77–104). Cambridge, England: Cambridge University Press.

Cline, V. B., Croft, R. G., & Courrier, S. (1973). Desensitization of children to television violence. *Journal of Personality and Social Psychology, 27*, 360–365.

Clutton-Brock, T. H.. and Parker, G. A. (1995). Punishment in animal societies. *Nature, 373*, 209–216.

Cohen, D. (1998). Culture, social organization, and patterns of violence, *Journal of Personality and Social Psychology, 75*, 408–419.

Cohen, D., & Nisbett, R. E. (1994). Self-protection and the culture of honor: Explaining southern violence. *Personality and Social Psychology Bulletin, 20*, 551–567.

Cohen, D., Nisbett, R. E., Bowdle, B. F., & Schwartz, N. (1996). Insult, aggression, and the Southern culture of honor: An "experimental ethnography." *Journal of Personality and Social Psychology, 70*, 945–960.

Cosmides, L., & Tooby, J. (1987). From evolution to behavior: Evolutionary psychology as the missing link. In J. Dupre (Ed.), *The latest on the best: Essays on evolution and optimality* (pp. 277–306), Cambridge, MA: MIT Press.

Cosmides, L., & Tooby, J. (1995). From function to structure: The role of evolutionary biology and computational theories in cognitive neuroscience. In M. S. Gazzaniga (Ed.), *The cognitive neurosciences* (pp. 1199–1210). Cambridge, MA: MIT Press.

Cummings, E. M., Hennessy, K. D., Rabideau, G. J., & Cichetti, D. (1994); Coping with anger involving a family member in physically abused and non-abused boys. *Development and Psychopathology, 6*, 31–41.

Cummings, E. M., Ianotti, R. J., & Zahn-Waxler, C. (1985). Influence of conflict between adults on the emotions and aggression of young children. *Developmental Psychology, 21*, 495–507.

Daly, M., & Wilson, M. (1988). *Homicide.* Hawthorne, NY: Aldine de Gruyter.

Daly, M. & Wilson, M. (1990). Killing the competition: Female/female and male/male homicide. *Human Nature, 1*, 81–107.

Daly, M., & Wilson, M. (1994). Evolutionary psychology of male violence. In J. Archer (Ed.), *Male violence* (pp. 253–288). London: Routledge.

Darwin, C. (1871). *The descent of man and selection in relation to sex.* London: John Murray.

Davies, P. T., & Cummings, E. M. (1994). Marital conflict and child adjustment: An emotional security hypothesis. *Psychological Bulletin, 116,* 389–411.

Davies, P. T., & Cummings, E. M. (1998). Exploring children's emotional security as a mediator of the link between marital relations and child adjustment. *Child Development, 69,* 124–139.

Dawkins, R. (1986). *The blind watchmaker: Why the evidence of evolution reveals a universe without design.* New York: Norton.

DeWaal, F. B. M. (1992). Aggression as a well-integrated part of primate social relationships: A critique of the Seville Statement on Violence. In J. Silverberg and J. P. Gray (Eds.), *Aggression and peacefulness in humans and other primates* (pp. 37–56). New York: Oxford.

DeWaal, F.B. M. (1996). *Good natured: The origins of right and wrong in humans and other animals.* Cambridge, MA: Harvard University Press.

Diener, E., Dineen, J., Endresen, K., Beaman, A. L., & Fraser, S. C. (1975). Effects of altered responsibility, cognitive set, and modeling on physical aggression and deindividuation. *Journal of Personality and Social Psychology, 31,* 328–337.

Dodge, K. A. (1980) Social cognition and children's aggressive behavior. *Child Development, 51,* 162–170.

Dodge, K. A., & Coie, J. D. (1987). Social information processing factors in reactive and pro-active aggression in children's peer groups. *Journal of Personality and Social Psychology, 53,* 1146–1158.

Dodge, K. A., & Newman, J. P. (1981). Biased decision making processes in aggressive boys. *Journal of Abnormal Psychology, 90,* 375–379.

Dunn, J., & Brown, J. (1994). Affect expression in the family, children's understanding of emotions, and their interactions with others. *Merrill-Palmer Quarterly, 40,* 120–137.

Ekman, P., & Davidson, R. J. (1994). Afterword: How is evidence of universals in antecedents of emotion explained? In P. Ekman & R. J. Davidson (Eds.), *The nature of emotion: Fundamental questions* (pp. 176–179). New York: Oxford.

Eley, T. C. (1997). General genes: A new theme in developmental psychopathology. *Current directions in psychological science, 6,* 90–95.

Ellis, B., & Malamuth, N. M. (2000). Love and anger in romantic relationships: An independence model. *Journal of Personality, 68,* 525–556.

Fadiga, L., Buccino, G., Craighero, L., & Fogassi, L. (1999). Corticospinal excitability is specifically modulated by motor imagery: A magnetic stimulation study. *Neuropsychologia, 37,* 147–158.

Ferguson, T. J., & Rule, B. G. (1983). An attributional perspective on anger and aggression. In R. G. Geen, & E. I. Donnerstein (Eds.), *Aggression: Theoretical and empirical reviews* (Vol. 1, pp. 41–74). New York: Academic Press.

Fischer, D. H. (1989). *Albion's seed: Four British folkways in America.* New York: Oxford University Press.

Fletcher, G. J. O., Simpson, J. A., Thomas, G., & Giles, L. (1999). Ideals in intimate relationships. *Journal of Personality and Social Psychology, 76,* 72–89.

Foshee, V. A., Bauman, K. E., & Fletcher, L. (1999). Family violence and the perpetration of adolescent dating violence: Examining social learning and social control processes. *Journal of Marriage and the Family, 61,* 331–342.

Frank, R. H. (1988). *Passions within reason: The strategic role of the emotions.* New York: W. W. Norton.

Gallistel, C. R. (1995). The replacement of general-purpose theories with adaptive specializations. In M. Gazzaniga (Ed.), *The cognitive neurosciences* (pp. 1255–1267). Cambridge, MA: MIT Press.

Geary, D. C. (1998). *Male and female: Evolution of human sex differences.* Washington, DC: American Psychological Association.

Geen, R. G. (1975). The meaning of observed violence: Real vs. fictional violence and consequent effects on aggression and emotional arousal. *Journal of Research in Personality, 9,* 270–281.

Geen, R. G. (1981). Behavioral and physiological reactions to observed violence: Effects of prior exposure to aggressive stimuli. *Journal of Personality and Social Psychology, 40,* 868–875.

Geen, R. G. (1994) Social psychological. In M. Hersen, R. T. Ammerman, & L. Sisson (Eds.), *Hand-*

book of aggressive and destructive behavior in psychiatric patients (pp. 51–64). New York: Plenum.

Geen, R. G. (1998a). Aggression and antisocial behavior. In D. T. Gilbet, S. T. Fiske, and G. Lindzey (Eds.), *The handbook of social psychology* (Vol. 2, pp. 317–356). Boston, MA: McGraw-Hill.

Geen, R. G. (1998b). Processes and personal variables in affective aggression. In R. G. Geen & E. Donnerstein (Eds.), *Human aggression: Theories, research, and implications for social policy* (pp. 1–48). San Deigo, CA: Academic Press.

Geen, R. G., & Stonner, D. (1973). Context effects in observed violence. *Journal of Personality and Social Psychology, 25*, 145–150.

Gigerenzer, G., & Goldstein, D. G. (1996). Reasoning the fast and frugal way: Models of bounded rationality. *Psychological Review, 103*, 650–669.

Gordis, E. B., Margolin, G., & John, R. S. (1997). Marital aggression, observed parental hostility, and child behavior during triadic family interaction. *Journal of Family Psychology, 11*, 76–89.

Gouldner, A. (1960). The norm of reciprocity: a preliminary statement. *American Sociological Review, 47*, 73–80.

Gouze, K. R. (1987). Attention and social problem solving as correlates of aggression in preschool males. *Journal of Abnormal Child Psychology, 15*, 181–197.

Guerra, N. G. (1989). Evaluative factors in social problem solving by aggressive boys. *Journal of Abnormal Child Psychology, 17*, 277–289.

Guerra, N. G., Huesmann, L. R., & Hanish, L. (1994). The role of normative beliefs in children's social behavior. In N. Eisenberg (Ed.), *Social Development* (pp.140–158). Newbury Park, CA: Sage.

Guerra, N. G., & Slaby, R. G. (1990). Cognitive mediators of aggression in adolescent offenders: II. Intervention. *Developmental Psychology, 26*, 269–277.

Gustafson, R. (1994). Alcohol and aggression. *Journal of Offender Rehabilitation*, 21, 41–80.

Hall, H. V., & Whitaker, L. C. (1999). *Collective violence: Effective strategies for assessing and interviewing in fatal group and institutional aggression.* New York: CRC Press.

Henrich, J., & Boyd, R. (1998). The evolution of conformist transmission and the emergence of between-group differences. *Evolution and Human Behavior, 19*, 215–241.

Hicks, D. J. (1965). Imitation and retention of film-mediated aggressive peer and adult models. *Journal of Personality and Social Psychology, 2*, 97–100.

Hiraiwa-Hasegawa, M. (1998). An evolutionary study of homicide: Universal patterns and cultural differences. Plenary address presented at the 10th annual meeting of the Human Behavior and Evolution Society, University of California Davis, Davis, California.

Hotaling, G. T., & Sugarman, D. B. (1990). A risk marker analysis of assaulted wives. *Journal of Family Violence, 5*, 1–13.

Huesmann, L. R. (1986). Psychological processes promoting the relation between exposure to media violence and aggressive behavior by the viewer. *Journal of Social Issues, 42*, 125–139.

Huesmann, L. R. (1988). An information processing model for the development of aggression. *Aggressive Behavior, 14*, 13–24.

Huesmann, L. R. (1998). The role of social information processing and cognitive schema in the acquisition and maintenance of habitual aggressive behavior. In R. G. Geen & E. Donnerstein (Eds.), *Human aggression: Theories, research, and implications for social policy* (pp. 73–109). San Diego, CA: Acedemic Press.

Huesmann, L. R., & Guerra, N. G. (1997). Childrens' normative beliefs about aggression and aggressive behavior. *Journal of Personality and Social Psychology, 72*, 408–419.

Humphrey, N. K. (1976). The social function of intellect. In P. P. G. Bateson and R. A. Hinde (Eds.), *Growing points in ethology* (pp. 303–317). Cambridge, England: Cambridge University Press.

Huston, A. C., Donnerstein, E., Fairchild, H., Feshbach, N. D., Katz, P. A., Murray, J. P., Rubinstein, E. A., Wilcox, B. L., & Zuckermann, D. (1992). *Big world, small screen: The role of television in American Society.* Lincoln, NE: University of Nebraska Press.

Johnson, M. K., Hashtroudi, S., & Lindsay, D. S. (1993). Source monitoring. *Psychological Bulletin, 114*, 3–28.

Josephson, W. L. (1987). Television violence and children's aggression: Testing and priming, social script, and disinhibition predictions. *Journal of Personality and Social Psychology, 53*, 882–890.

Kaufman, J., & Zigler, E. (1987). Do abused children become abusive parents? *American Journal of Orthopsychiatry, 57*, 186–192.

Ketelaar, T., & Ellis, B. J. (2000). Are evolutionary explanations unfalsifiable? Evolutionary psychology and the Lakatosian philosophy of science. *Psychological Inquiry, 11*, 1–21.

Ketelaar, T., & Goddie, A. S. (1998). The satisficing role of emotions in decision-making. *Psykhe, 7*, 63–77.

Kunkel, D., Wilson, B. J., Linz, D., Potter, W. J., Donnerstein, E., Smith, S. L., Blumenthal, E., & Gray, T. (1996). *Violence in television programming overall.* University of California, Santa Barbara, Scientific Papers, National Television Violence Study. Studio City, CA: Mediascope.

Landau, S. F., and Drapkin, I. (1968). Ethnic patterns of criminal homicide in Israel. Unpublished paper, Hebrew University of Jerusalem, Jerusalem, Israel.

Lazaraus, R. S., & Alfert, E. (1964). Short-circuiting of threat by experimentally altering cognitive appraisal. *Journal of Abnormal and Social Psychology, 69*, 195–205.

LeDoux, J. (1996). *The emotional brain: The mysterious underpinnings of emotional life.* New York: Simon & Schuster.

Lemerise, E. A., & Dodge, K. A. (1993). The development of anger and hostile reactions. In M. Lewis and J. M. Haviland (Eds.), *Handbook of emotions.* New York: Guilford.

Leyens, J. P., & Picus, S. (1973). Identification with the winner of a fight and name mediation: Their differential effects upon subsequent aggressive behavior. *British Journal of Social and Clinical Psychology, 12*, 374–377.

Lipsey, M. W., Wilson, D. B., Cohen, M. A., & Derzon, J. H. (1997). Is there a causal relationship between alcohol use and violence? In D. Fuller, R. Dietrich, & E. Gottheil (Eds.), *Recent developments in Alcoholism: Alcohol and violence* (Vol. 13, pp. 245–282). New York: Plenum.

Liss, M. B., Reinhardt, L. C., & Fredriksen, S. (1983). TV heroes: The impact of rhetoric and deeds. *Journal of Applied Developmental Psychology, 4*, 175–187.

Lore, R. S., & Schultz, L. (1993). Control of human aggression: A comparative perspective. *American Psychologist, 48*, 16–25.

Malamuth, N. M. (1998). An evolutionary-based model integrating research on the characteristics of sexually coercive men. In J. Adair, K. Dion, & D. Belanger (Eds.), *Advances in psychological science* (Vol. 2): *Personal, social, and developmental aspects* (pp. 151–184). Hove, UK: Psychology Press.

Malamuth, N. M. & Malamuth, E. (1999). Integrating multiple levels of scientific analysis and the confluence model of sexual coercers. *Jurimetrics: Journal of Law, Science and Technology, 39*, 157–179.

Malamuth, N. M., Sockloskie, R. J., Koss, M. P., & Tanaka, J. S. (1991). Characteristics of aggressors against women: Testing a model using a national sample of college students. *Journal of Consulting and Clinical Psychology, 59*, 670–681.

McGue, M., Bacon, S., & Lykken, D. T. (1993). Personality stability and change in early adulthood: a behavioral genetic analysis. *Developmental Psychology, 29*, 96–109.

Maynard Smith, J. (1982). *Evolution of the theory of games.* Cambridge, England: Cambridge University Press.

Mednick, S. A., Gabrielli, W. F., & Hutchings, B. (1984). Genetic influences in criminal convictions: Evidence from an adoption cohort. *Science, 224*, 891–894.

Milgram, S. (1974). *Obedience to authority: An experimental view.* New York: Harper & Row.

Mineka, S., & Cook, M. (1993). Mechanisms involved in the observational conditioning of fear. *Journal of Experimental Psychology: General, 122*, 23–38.

Mineka, S., Davidson, M., Cook, M., & Keir, R. (1984). Observational conditioning of snake fear in rhesus monkeys. *Journal of Abnormal Psychology, 93*, 355–372.

Molm, L. D. (1997). Risk and power use: Constraints on the use of coercion in exchange. *American Sociological Review, 62*, 113–133.

Mullin, C. R., & Linz, D. (1995). Desensitization and resensitization of violence against women: Effects of exposure to sexually violent films on judgements of domestic violence victims. *Journal of Personality and Social Psychology, 69,* 449–459.

Nagin, D., & Tremblay, R. E. (1999). Trajectories of boys' physical aggression, opposition, and hyperactivity on the path to physically violent and non-violent juvenile delinquency. *Child Development, 70,* 1181–1196.

Nasby, W., Hayden, B., & DePaulo, B. M. (1979). Attributional bias among aggressive boys to interpret unambiguous social stimuli as displays of hostility. *Journal of Abnormal Psychology, 89,* 459–468.

Nesse, R. M. (1990). Evolutionary explanations of emotions. *Human Nature, 1,* 261–289.

Nisbett, R. E. (1993). Violence and US regional culture. *American Psychologist, 48,* 441–449.

Nisbett, R. E., & Cohen, D. (1996). *Culture of honor: The psychology of violence in the South.* Boulder, CO: Westview Press.

Paik, H., & Comstock, G. (1994). The effects of television violence on antisocial behavior: A meta-analysis. *Communications Research, 21,* 516–546.

Pakaslahti, L., Spoof, I., Asplund-Peltola, R., & Keltikangas-Jaevinen, L. (1998). Parents' social problem-solving strategies in families with aggressive and non-aggressive girls. *Aggressive Behavior, 24,* 37–51.

Panksepp, J. (1998). *Affective neuroscience: The foundations of human and animal emotions.* New York: Oxford University Press.

Perry, D. G., & Perry, L. C. (1976). Identification with film characters, covert aggressive verbalization, and reactions to film violence. *Journal of Research in Personality, 10,* 399–409.

Perry, D. G., Perry, L. C., & Rasmussen, P. (1986). Cognitive social learning mediators of aggression. *Child Development, 57,* 700–711.

Pinker, S. (1997). *How the mind works.* New York: Norton.

Posner, M. I., & DiGirolamo, G. J. (1998). Executive attention: Conflict, target detection, and cognitive control. In R. Parasuraman (Ed.), *The attentive brain* (pp. 401–423). Cambridge, MA: MIT Press.

Quigley, B. M., & Tedeschi, J. T. (1996). Mediating effects of blame attributions on feelings of anger. *Personality and Social Psychology Bulletin, 22,* 1280–1288.

Raven, B. H. (1965). Social influence and power. In I. D. Steiner and M. Fishbein (Eds.), *Current studies in social psychology* (pp. 371–382). New York: Holt.

Raven, B. H. (1999). Reflections on interpersonal influence and social power in experimental social psychology, In A. Rodrigues and R. V. Levine (Eds.), *Reflections on 100 years of experimental social psychology* (pp. 114–134). New York: Basic Books.

Repetti, R. L., Taylor, S. E., & Seeman, T. E. (1999). Risky families: Family social environments and the mental and physical health of offspring. Unpublished manuscript, University of California, Los Angeles.

Richardson, D. R., & Green, L. R. (1997). Circuitous harm: Determinants and consequences of nondirect aggression.In R. Kowalski (Ed.), *Aversive interpersonal behaviors* (pp. 171–188). New York: Plenum.

Rizzolatti, G., & Arbib, M.A. (1998). Language within our grasp. *Trends in Neurosciences, 21,* 188–194.

Rousseau. J. J. (1911). *Emile.* London: J. M. Dent (original work published 1762).

Rushton, J. P., Fulker, D. W., Neale, M. C., Nias, D. K. B., & Eysenck, H. J. (1986). Altruism and aggression: The heritability of individual differences. *Journal of Personality and Social Psychology, 50,* 1192–1198.

Sanders, G. S., & Baron, R. S. (1975) Pain cues and uncertainty as determinants of aggression in a situation involving repeated instigation. *Journal of Personality and Social Psychology, 32,* 495–502.

Sanford, N., & Comstock, C. (1971). *Sanctions for evil.* San Francisco, CA: Jossey-Bass.

Segall, M. H., Ember, C. R., & Ember, M. (1997). Aggression, crime and warfare. In J. W. Berry, M. H. Segall, & C. Kagitçibasi (Eds.), *Handbook of cross-cultural psychology: vol. 3: Social behavior and applications* (pp. 213–254). New York: Allyn-Bacon.

Silk, J. B. (1992). The patterning of intervention among male bonnet macaques: Reciprocity, revenge and loyalty. *Current Anthropology, 33,* 218–225.

Silverberg, J., & Gray, J. P (Eds.) (1992). *Aggression and peacefulness in humans and other primates.*

New York: Oxford.

Slaby, R. G., & Guerra, N. G. (1988). Cognitive mediators of aggression in adolescent offenders: 1. Assessment. *Developmental Psychology, 24*, 580–588.

Smith, L., & Donnerstien, E. (1998). Harmful effects of exposure to media violence: Learning of aggression, emotional desensitization and fear. In R. G. Geen & E. Donnerstein (Eds.), *Human aggression: Theories, research, and implications for social policy* (pp. 167–202). San Diego, CA: Academic Press.

Smuts, B., & Smuts, R. (1993). Male aggression and sexual coercion. *Advances in the Study of Behavior, 22*, 1–63.

Sternberg, C. R. & Campos, J. (1990). The development of anger expressions in infancy. In N. L. Stein & B. Leventhal (Eds.), *Psychological and biological approaches to emotion* (pp. 247–282). Hillsdale, NJ: Erlbaum.

Strange, J. J., & Leung, C. C. (1999). How anecdotal accounts in news and in fiction can influence judgments of a social problem's urgency, causes and cures. *Personality and Social Psychology Bulletin, 25*, 436–449.

Tedeschi, J. T., & Felson, R. B. (1994). *Violence, aggression, & coercive actions.* Washington, DC: American Psychological Association.

Thomas, M. H., & Tell, P. M. (1974). Effects of viewing real versus fantasy violence upon interpersonal aggression. *Journal of Research in Personality, 8*, 153–160.

Thornhill, R., & Thornhill, N. W. (1992). The evolutionary psychology of men's coercive sexuality. *Behavioral and Brain Sciences, 15*, 363–421.

Tinbergen, N. (1951). *The study of instinct.* London: Oxford University Press.

Tooby, J. & Cosmides, L. (1990). On the universality of human nature and the uniqueness of the individual: The role of genetics and adaptation. *Journal of Personality, 58*, 17–68.

Tooby, J., & Cosmides, L. (1992). The past explains the present: Emotional adaptations and the structure of ancestral environments. *Ethology and Sociobiology, 11*, 375–424.

Tremblay, R. E., Christa, J., Perusse, D., McDuff, P., Boivin, M., Zoccolillo, M., and Montplaisir, J. (1999). The search for the age of "onset" of physical aggression: Rousseau and Bandura revisited. *Criminal Behaviour and Mental Health, 9*, 8–23.

Trivers, R. L. (1971). The evolution of reciprocal altruism. *Quarterly Review of Biology, 36*, 35–36.

Trivers, R. L. (1972). Parental investment and sexual selection. In B. Campbell (Ed.), *Sexual selection and the descent of man* (pp. 1871–1971). Chicago, IL: Aldine.

Turner, C. W., & Berkowitz, L. (1972). Identification with film aggressor (covert role taking) and reactions to film violence. *Journal of Personality and Social Psychology, 21*, 256–264.

Turner, C. W., Layton, J. P., & Simons, L. S. (1975). Naturalistic studies of aggressive behavior: Aggressive stimuli, victim visibility, and horn honking. *Journal of Personality and Social Psychology, 31*, 1098–1107.

Wash, G., & Knudson-Martin, C. (1994). Gender identity and family relationships: Perspectives from incestuous fathers. *Contemporary Family Therapy: An International Journal, 16*, 393–410.

Widom, C. S. (1989). Does violence beget violence? A critical examination of literature. *Psychological Bulletin, 106*, 3–28.

Wilson, M. I. (1989). Marital conflict and homicide in evolutionary perspective. In R. W. Bell & N. J. Bell (Eds.), *Sociobiology and the Social Sciences* (pp. 45–62). Lubbock, TX: Texas Tech University Press.

Wilson, M., & Daly, M. (1985). Competitiveness, risk taking, and violence: The young male syndrome. *Ethology and Sociobiology, 6*, 59–73.

Wilson, M., & Daly, M. (1993). Lethal confrontational violence among young men. In N. J. Bell & R. W. Bell (Eds.), *Adolescent risk taking* (pp. 84–106), Newbury Park, CA: Sage.

Wyer, R. S. & Radvansky, G. A. (1999). The comprehension and validation of social information. *Psychological Review, 106*, 89–118.

Zaidi, L. Y., Knutson, J. F., & Mehm, J. G. (1989). Transgenerational patterns of abusive parenting. *Aggressive Behavior, 15*, 137–152.

Zimbardo, P. G. (1995). The psychology of evil: A situationist perspective on recruiting good people to engage in anti-social acts. *Research in Social Psychology, 11*, 125–133.

Chapter Seven

Helping and Altruism

John F. Dovidio and Louis A. Penner

Introduction

Prosocial behavior represents a broad category of actions that are "defined by society as generally beneficial to other people and to the ongoing political system" (Piliavin, Dovidio, Gaertner, & Clark, 1981, p. 4). This category includes a range of behaviors that are intended to benefit others, such as helping, sharing, cooperating, comforting, and donating to charity. The present chapter focuses on two subcategories of prosocial behavior: helping and altruism. We examine the nature of these concepts and review the current state of research on these topics. Specifically, we address three questions: When do people help? Why do people help? Who helps? (see also Batson, 1998; Piliavin & Charng, 1990; Schroeder, Penner, Dovidio, & Piliavin, 1995).

Helping and altruism defined

Helping and altruism are two fundamental types of prosocial behavior. *Helping* represents an intentional action that has the outcome of benefiting another person. Attempts to identify essential characteristics of helping have suggested several key dimensions involving, for example, the type of assistance needed and the potential consequences of helping and of not helping (McGuire, 1994; Pearce & Amato, 1980; Shotland & Huston, 1979).

Whereas the concept of helping concerns the outcomes of an action, the concept of *altruism* concerns the motivation underlying the behavior. Classic definitions in psychology (cf. Sober, 1988, 1992) have included internal motivation as a defining feature of altruistic helping. For example, altruism was defined as a special type of helping in which the benefactor provides aid to another person *without anticipation of rewards from external sources for providing assistance* (Macaulay & Berkowitz, 1970) while incurring some personal costs for taking this action (Krebs, 1982; Wispé, 1978). More recent perspectives have emphasized the importance of further distinguishing the different types of internal motivations involved in helping. For Batson (1991, 1998), altruism refers not to the prosocial act *per se* but to the underlying goal of the act: "Altruism is a motivational state with the ultimate goal of increasing another's welfare" (Batson, 1991, p. 6). In contrast, egoistic helping is motivated by the ultimate goal of improving one's own welfare.

When Do People Help?

Many of the earlier studies of when people help focused on nonemergency situations and thus considered helping to be guided by many of the same external factors (e.g., norms of reciprocity) and internal influences (e.g., need for social approval) as other forms of socially valued behaviors. By the mid-1960s, stimulated by dramatic incidents in the news about failures of bystanders to intervene to save the lives of others, empirical attention turned to emergency situations and to the relatively unique nature of helping behavior. Much of this research was shaped by the pioneering ideas reflected in Latané and Darley's (1970) decision model of bystander intervention.

A decision model of intervention

The Latané and Darley (1970) decision model of bystander intervention proposes that whether or not a person helps depends upon the outcomes of a series of prior decisions. Although the model was initially developed to understand how people respond in emergencies that require immediate assistance, aspects of the model have been successfully applied to many other situations, ranging from preventing someone from driving drunk to making a decision about whether to donate a kidney to a relative (Borgida, Conner, & Manteufel, 1992; Rabow, Newcomb, Monto, & Hernandez, 1990).

According to Latané and Darley, before a person initiates a helping response, that person goes through five decision-making steps. The person must: (1) notice that something is wrong, (2) define it as a situation that requires some sort of intervention, (3) decide whether to take personal responsibility, (4) decide what kind of help to give, and (5) decide to implement the chosen course of action. The decision made at any one step has important implications for the bystander's ultimate response – a "no" response at *any* step means the victim will not be helped.

With respect to the first step of the model, noticing the event, bystanders are more likely to notice events that are inherently more vivid and attention-getting. As a consequence, they are more likely to intervene. Beyond the characteristics of the potential helping situations themselves, aspects of the physical environment (e.g., noise; Mathews & Canon, 1975) and the social environment (e.g., population density; Levine, Martinez, Brase, & Sorenson, 1994) may influence whether people notice an event and respond in helpful ways. For example, in studies conducted in several different countries (e.g., the United States, the United Kingdom, Saudi Arabia, and Sudan) people in urban environments tend to be less helpful than residents in rural settings (Hedge & Yousif, 1992; Yousif & Korte, 1995). One explanation of this rural–urban difference is that in order to cope with stimulus overload (Milgram, 1970) urban residents restrict their attention mainly to personally relevant events. Strangers, and thus their situations of need, may therefore go unnoticed.

Another factor that may influence whether or not people notice that something is wrong is their mood or other transitory feelings or states. There is considerable evidence that when individuals are in a good mood, they are more likely to help (Salovey, Mayer, & Rosenhan, 1991) due, at least in part, to increased attentiveness to others (McMillen, Sanders, & Solomon, 1977). Pleasant environments, such as those with appealing aromas, also facilitate helping (Baron, 1997), mediated in part by positive mood. Conversely, environmental stressors usually have a negative impact on people's moods (Bell, Fisher, Baum, & Greene, 1996).

In terms of the second step of the model, one basic factor that can influence whether a situation, once noticed, is interpreted as a situation requiring assistance is the nature of the event itself. Across a range of studies, bystanders are more inclined to help victims who make their need clear with overt distress cues (e.g., screams) than victims in similar situations who do not scream (Piliavin et al., 1981). The social environment can also influence whether an event is interpreted as requiring help. When bystanders notice an event but the nature of the event is unclear, the reactions of other witnesses may shape their assessment of the situation. Thus, although the presence of others typically inhibits intervention (Latané, Nida, & Wilson, 1981), others' expressions of concern or alarm can facilitate helping (Wilson, 1976).

In the third step of Latané and Darley's model, once the need for assistance is determined, bystanders must decide who is responsible for helping. When a person is the only potential helper, the decision is obvious. In contrast, when a bystander believes that other people are also witnessing the event and that these other people can help, *diffusion of responsibility* may occur. That is, the belief that others will take action can relieve a bystander from assuming personal responsibility for intervention, because it can be reasoned that assistance is no longer necessary (Darley & Latané, 1968; Otten, Penner, & Waugh, 1988). Diffusion of responsibility thus does not occur when the other bystanders are believed to be incapable of intervening (Korte, 1969). It is more likely to occur when personal danger is involved in helping, when other witnesses are perceived as better able to help, and when norms permit or support it (Dovidio, Piliavin, Gaertner, Schroeder, & Clark, 1991; Piliavin et al., 1981).

Whereas the first three steps of the Latané and Darley model have received careful empirical scrutiny and support, the fourth and fifth steps, deciding what to do and implementing the chosen course of action have not been the focus of substantial research. Nevertheless, the work that does exist is generally supportive. People with first aid training, for instance, offer more medically effective help than do people without relevant training (Shotland & Heinold, 1985).

Overall, the Latané and Darley decision model of intervention provides a valuable broad framework for understanding when bystanders will or will not help others in need. The next model to be considered allows a more detailed analysis of how the nature of the situation and characteristics of the victim influence helping.

A cost–reward framework

A cost–reward analysis of helping assumes an economic view of human behavior – people are motivated to maximize their rewards and to minimize their costs (Piliavin et al., 1981). From this perspective, people are relatively rational and mainly concerned about their self-interest. In a potential helping situation, a person analyzes the circumstances, weighs the probable costs and rewards of alternative courses of action and then arrives at a decision that will result in the best personal outcome. There are two categories of costs and rewards: those for helping, and those for *not* helping. Costs for helping can involve effort and time, danger, embarrassment, and disruption of ongoing activities. Costs for not helping include feelings of guilt or shame and public censure. Rewards for helping may include money, fame, self-praise, avoidance of guilt, thanks from the victim, and the intrinsic pleasure derived from having helped. Current research is consistent with the central tenet of the cost–reward approach. Situational factors that decrease the net costs (costs minus rewards) for helping or increase the costs for not helping facilitate intervention (Dovidio et al., 1991).

The cost–reward perspective also assumes that both the negative values attached to costs and the positive values associated with rewards are subjective ones. They are influenced by factors such as characteristics of the person in need, the nature of the relationship between that person and a potential benefactor, and the personal attributes of a potential benefactor. For example, costs for not helping are perceived as lower when the person is seen as responsible for his or her plight (e.g., due to immoral actions) than when the cause is beyond the person's control (e.g., illness; Otten et al., 1988). Physical attractiveness and interpersonal attraction may promote helping because they increase potential rewards associated with opportunities to initiate a relationship. More positive attitudes towards and feelings for a person in need also may increase costs for not helping (e.g., stronger feelings of guilt), decrease costs for helping (e.g., less anxiety about how the person will respond to help), or increase rewards for helping (e.g., more value associated with the recipient's gratitude) – and thereby increase helping. For instance, people who desire a communal relationship with another person experience elevated positive affect when they choose or even are required to help that person. In contrast, those who do not desire a relationship react with negative affect when they are required to help (Williamson & Clark, 1992). Finally, studies of individuals dispositionally inclined to act prosocially provide indirect and direct evidence that these people estimate the costs of such interventions as lower than do individuals not so inclined (Colby & Damon, 1992; Oliner & Oliner, 1992; Penner & Fritzsche, 1993; also see the later section of this chapter, Who Helps? Dispositional Variables).

Similarity, in terms of dress style, nationality, personality, attitudes, and shared group membership or social identity is also positively associated with helping (Dovidio, 1984; Dovidio et al., 1997). Although the general tendency to help members of one's own group more than members of other groups occurs cross-culturally, the effect is stronger in collectivist societies (e.g., Japan and China) than in individualistic cultures (e.g., the United States; see Moghaddam, Taylor, & Wright, 1993). One reason that similarity promotes helping in general is that it leads to interpersonal attraction (Byrne, 1971), which can increase costs for not helping and rewards for helping (Williamson & Clark,

1992). In addition, people who are seen as dissimilar are typically perceived as unpredictable, holding different beliefs and values, and threatening. From a cost-reward perspective, therefore, the benefits for helping a similar other are higher and the costs are lower.

Whereas positive attitudes promote helping, negative attitudes can decrease it. Stigmatized persons are typically less likely to receive help than non-stigmatized persons (Edelmann, Evans, Pegg, & Tremain, 1983; Walton et al., 1988). However, because negative social attitudes, such as racial prejudice, are themselves sanctioned and stigmatized, the effects of race on helping can be complex (Gaertner & Dovidio, 1986). Indeed, whereas some studies show that Whites are less likely to help African Americans than Whites, other studies demonstrate that Whites are as likely or are even more likely to help African Americans than Whites. Gaertner and Dovidio offered a framework to account for these seemingly contradictory results. Because discrimination violates current social norms and may violate most people's self-image of being fair, there are special costs associated with Whites discriminating against African Americans. As a consequence of these costs, Whites may help African Americans as often, and sometimes more often (Dutton & Lennox, 1974), than they help Whites in situations in which a failure to help could be interpreted as bias. However, when Whites can rationalize not helping on the basis of some factor *other* than race (as in the belief that someone else will help), their self-image is no longer threatened, these costs do not apply, and they are then less likely to help African Americans than Whites (e.g., Gaertner & Dovidio, 1977).

In general, then, helping is more likely to occur when the rewards for helping outweigh the costs. Nevertheless, because costs and rewards are subjectively determined, there is considerable individual variation in response to similar situations. In addition, costs and rewards are not necessarily weighed equivalently: costs are normally weighed more heavily (Dovidio et al., 1991). Under highly arousing conditions, because of a more narrow focus of attention, not all costs and rewards may be considered (Piliavin et al., 1981). In the next section, we examine the underlying psychological processes that can shape perceptions of costs and rewards and produce different motivations for helping.

Why Do People Help?

Approaches to the question of why people help have focused on three types of mechanisms: (1) learning, (2) arousal and affect, and (3) social and personal standards. The learning explanation applies general principles from learning theories to the acquisition of helping skills and of beliefs about why these skills should be used to benefit others. Arousal and affect theories focus on emotionally based motivations but generally share a guiding principle with learning theory that people are motivated to behave in ways that bring them some kind of reward – in this case, feeling better. However, there are some theorists who argue that under some very special circumstances people may be motivated by the primary goal of making another person feel better, by true altruism. Finally, there is the social and personal standards approach that considers how people's personal values can motivate helping by affecting both cognitive and affective processes.

Learned helpfulness

Two basic processes have been implicated in the application of learning theory to helping behavior: operant conditioning and social learning. Consistent with the principles of operant learning, people are more likely to help others when their previous helping responses have been positively reinforced (see Staub, 1979). Conversely, people may learn *not* to help others because helping has led to negative consequences (see Grusec, 1991; Staub, 1978).

Social learning, either through modeling or direct instruction, can also be an effective way to facilitate helping. Consistent with more general research on attitudes and behavior, the effectiveness of persuasion is related to the nature of the message and characteristics of the audience and the persuader. Social learning through observing models has both immediate and long-term effects on helping (see Grusec, 1981). Again consistent with general principles, the consequences to the model (e.g., positive, neutral, negative), characteristics of the model (e.g., status, attractiveness, similarity), and relationship between the observer and the model (e.g., attachment between a child and parent) mediate the influence of prosocial models. Furthermore, temporary states or moods, such as positive affect, that may increase the salience of positive, previously learned behaviors can increase the likelihood of helping (Isen, 1993; Salovey et al., 1991).

Parental models can have a strong and prolonged impact on helping. Fabes, Eisenberg, and Miller (1990) found that primary school girls who were sympathetic to children in distress had mothers who also were sympathetic in such situations, suggesting that the children were in part modeling their mothers' reactions. There is also an association between prosocial parental models and the behavior of their children in adulthood (Clary & Miller, 1986; Oliner & Oliner, 1988; Piliavin & Callero, 1991; Rosenhan, 1969).

The relationship between the nature of rewards and helpfulness, however, varies developmentally. According to Bar-Tal and Raviv's (1982) cognitive learning model, very young children are usually motivated by specific material rewards and punishments, older children are motivated by social approval, and adolescents are motivated by self-satisfaction and personal conviction. Similarly, the work of Eisenberg and her colleagues (Eisenberg et al., 1987; Eisenberg, Miller, Shell, McNalley, & Shea, 1991) suggests that prosocial moral reasoning proceeds developmentally. Preschool children engage mainly in hedonistic and self-centered moral reasoning, whereas older children demonstrate more sophisticated and other-oriented kinds of reasoning – and generally more helpfulness. Furthermore, Grusec (1991) suggests that reliance on direct or material rewards may undermine the internalization of helping tendencies for older children. Children who help in order to receive material rewards may be less likely to assist others when these rewards are unlikely (e.g., for anonymous help) and may be less likely to develop intrinsic motivations for helping (Fabes, Fultz, Eisenberg, May-Plumlee, & Christopher, 1989).

Arousal and affect

In addition to the cognitive processes involved in direct and vicarious learning, arousal and affect play important roles in helping and altruism. People are aroused by the distress of others (see Eisenberg & Fabes, 1991). This reaction appears even among very young children and occurs across cultures. In fact, this phenomenon is so strong and universal some researchers have proposed that empathic arousal, arousal generated vicariously by another person's distress, has a biological and evolutionary basis (Cunningham, 1985/6; Hoffman, 1990).

Empathy and emotion.   Although most researchers agree that empathic arousal is important and fundamental in helping (see Dovidio, 1984), there is much less agreement about the nature of this emotion and how it actually motivates people to help. Empathic arousal may produce different emotions. In severe emergency situations, bystanders may become upset and distressed; in less critical, less intense problem situations, observers may feel sad (Cialdini, Schaller, et al., 1987), tense (Hornstein, 1982), or concerned and compassionate (Batson, 1991). How arousal is interpreted can shape the nature of prosocial motivation.

What determines the specific emotion that a person experiences in response to another's problem? Weiner (1980, 1986) suggests that another's need for help stimulates a search for causes by the observer. People seek to understand why the person needs assistance. The perceived causes are then analyzed (with attribution of responsibility and controllability being particularly important dimensions). These attributions, in turn, create an affective experience that motivates action. Weiner suggests, for example, that attribution to uncontrollable causes produces sympathy that motivates helping. Attribution to controllable causes may generate anger, which may inhibit helping. Thus, "attributions guide our feelings, but emotional reactions provide the motor and direction for behavior" (Weiner, 1980, p. 186).

The roles of empathy and emotional experience in prosocial motivation are the focus of several models of helping that rely on arousal and affect as primary motivational constructs underlying helping and altruism. Negative emotions, such as guilt, can be powerful motivators of helping. People are more likely to help others when they feel they have harmed these individuals in some way (Salovey et al., 1991). One explanation is that when people feel that they have unfairly harmed others, their self-esteem suffers. Therefore, they try to make amends. This image-reparation hypothesis suggests that by making a positive social response, people's self-esteem is restored and their self-image is repaired. It is also possible that simply anticipating guilt can motivate helping. That is, within relationships where help is normative – such as parent–child, romantic, or other types of communal relationships – people may offer assistance because they believe, probably through past experience, that they will feel guilty if they do not help. Such guilt is most strongly and commonly experienced in communal relationships (Baumeister, Stillwell, & Heatherton, 1994).

The notion that people are motivated to repair their self-images and avoid feelings of guilt for not helping when it is expected explains some but not all of the data on negative affect and helping. They cannot explain why people who simply witness a transgression against someone else also become more helpful. Cialdini and his colleagues have proposed a broader model, the *negative state relief model* (Cialdini, Kenrick, & Baumann, 1982; Cialdini et al., 1987) to explain such reactions.

Negative state relief model.   According to the negative state relief model, harming another person or witnessing another person being harmed can produce negative feelings such as guilt or sadness. People who experience these negative states are then motivated to reduce them. Through socialization and experience, people learn that helping can serve as a secondary reinforcer (Williamson & Clark, 1989; Yinon & Landau, 1987); the good feelings derived from helping may therefore relieve their negative mood. Thus, negative moods such as guilt and sadness may motivate people to help because helping produces the reward of making them feel better. In contrast to the image-reparation hypothesis, the negative state relief model proposes that people are motivated primarily to feel good rather than to look good. In both theories, however, the motivation for helping is essentially egoistic. That is, the primary motive for helping another person is that helping improves the helper's own situation.

Three fundamental assumptions of the negative state relief model have received some support. The first assumption is that the negative state that motivates a person to help can originate from a variety of sources. Guilt from having personally harmed a person and sadness from simply observing another person's unfortunate situation, because they are negative experiences, can both motivate helping (Cialdini, Darby, & Vincent, 1973). Moreover, these effects seem to motivate *helping* in response to requests in particular; negative moods do not increase compliance in general (Forgas, 1998). The second assumption is that other events besides helping may just as effectively make the person feel better, and exposure to these events can relieve the motivation to help caused by negative states. Consistent with this aspect of the model, if some other event that improves the potential helper's mood precedes the opportunity to help (e.g., receiving praise; Cialdini et al., 1973) or if the person anticipates a less costly way of improving their mood (e.g., listening to a comedy tape; Schaller & Cialdini, 1988), the potential helper is no longer particularly motivated to provide assistance. A third assumption of this model is that negative moods motivate helping only if people believe that their moods can be improved by helping. Negative feelings will *not* promote helping if people are led to believe that these feelings cannot be relieved (Manucia, Baumann, & Cialdini, 1984) or if, as with younger children, the self-rewarding properties have not yet developed (Cialdini & Kenrick, 1976; Cialdini et al., 1982). (For a critique of the negative state relief model as an explanation of helping see Carlson & Miller, 1987.)

Arousal: cost–reward model. Whereas the negative state relief model is based directly on principles of operant conditioning and on virtually the sole concern with one's own well-being, other affective models focus more on the assessment of and reaction to another person's problem, plight, or distress. Arousal is a central motivational concept in the Piliavin et al. (1981) *arousal: cost–reward model* (see also Dovidio et al., 1991). Arousal motivates a bystander to take action, and the cost–reward analysis shapes the direction that this action will take. Specifically, this model proposes that empathic arousal is generated by witnessing the distress of another person. When the bystander's empathic arousal is attributed to the other person's distress, it is emotionally experienced by the observer as unpleasant and the bystander is therefore motivated to reduce it. One normally efficient way of reducing this arousal is by helping to relieve the other's distress.

There is substantial evidence for the fundamental proposition of this model that people are emotionally responsive to the distress of others (see Fabes, Eisenberg, & Eisenbud, 1993). Adults and children not only report feeling empathy, but they also become physiologically aroused by the pain and suffering of others. Moreover, observers may not just feel bad about the pain or distress of another person, but they may also begin to experience what the other person is feeling (Vaughan & Lanzetta, 1980). Preschool children also spontaneously show signs of facial concern and physiological arousal at the distress of others (Fabes et al., 1993), and there is evidence that even one- and two-day-old infants will respond with crying to the distress of another infant (Sagi & Hoffman, 1976).

Also supportive of the arousal: cost–reward model, empathic arousal attributed to the other person's situation motivates helping. Facial, gestural, and vocal indications of empathically induced arousal, as well as self-reports of empathically induced anxiety, are consistently positively related to helping (see Dovidio et al., 1991; Eisenberg & Miller, 1987; Marks, Penner, & Stone, 1982). Consistent with the hypothesized importance of attributing this arousal to the other's situation, people are more likely to help when arousal from extraneous sources such as exercise (Sterling & Gaertner, 1984), erotic films (Mueller & Donnerstein, 1981), and aggressive films (Mueller, Donnerstein, & Hallam, 1983) are attributed to the immediate need of another person. People are less likely to help when arousal generated by witnessing another person's distress is associated with a different cause (e.g., misattributed to a pill; Gaertner & Dovidio, 1977). In addition, work by Eisenberg and her associates (e.g., Eisenberg & Fabes, 1998; Fabes et al., 1993) suggests that extreme empathic overarousal or the inability to regulate empathic arousal, which may interfere with the attribution process, can also reduce helpfulness.

Although the arousal: cost–reward model and the negative state relief model both posit egoistic motivations for helping, there are at least two important differences between them. First, attribution of arousal plays a central role in the arousal: cost–reward model; only arousal attributed to the plight of the other person will motivate helping. In contrast, the negative state relief model posits that, regardless of their attributed source, negative states (particularly guilt and sadness; see Cialdini et al., 1987) can motivate helping. The second major distinction between the two models concerns the goal of the help that is given. The arousal: cost–reward model is a tension-reduction model that assumes that the victim's need produces an arousal state in the potential benefactor and that the goal of the benefactor's intervention is to alleviate his or her own aversive state by eliminating the distress of the victim. According to the negative state relief model, however, people in negative moods are looking for ways to eliminate or neutralize their negative mood. Thus, any event that might improve the emotional state of the observer, including events that have nothing whatsoever to do with benefiting the person in distress, may serve this purpose equally well.

Empathy-altruism hypothesis.   In contrast to egoistic models of helping, Batson and his colleagues (see Batson, 1991) present an *empathy-altruism hypothesis*. Although they acknowledge that egoistically motivated helping occurs, Batson and his colleagues argue that true altruism also exists. Altruism is defined as helping with the primary goal of improving the other person's welfare. Specifically, according to the empathy-altruism hypothesis, witnessing another person in need can produce a range of emotional experiences, such as sadness, personal distress (e.g., upset, worry), and empathic concern (e.g., sympathy, compassion). Whereas sadness and personal distress produce egoistic motivations to help, empathic concern creates altruistic motivation.

The primary mechanism in Batson's empathy-model is the emotional reaction to another person's problem. Batson suggests that under some circumstances, for example if there is a special bond between the potential helper and the person in need, it can elicit empathy or empathic concern, which he defines as "an other-oriented emotional response (e.g., sympathy, compassion) congruent with the . . . welfare of another person" (Batson & Oleson, 1991, p. 63). In contrast to sadness and personal distress which, as noted above, generate an egoistic desire to reduce one's own distress, Batson (1987, 1991) proposes that empathic concern produces an altruistic motivation to reduce the other person's distress. The altruistically motivated person will then help if (a) helping is possible, (b) helping is perceived to be ultimately beneficial to the person in need, and (c) helping personally will provide greater benefit to the person in need than would assistance from another person also able to offer it. Thus, empathic concern is hypothesized to produce greater concern for the welfare of the other person.

In numerous experiments, conducted over a 20-year period, Batson and his colleagues have produced impressive empirical support for the empathy-altruism hypothesis (Batson, 1991, 1998). Participants who experience relatively high levels of empathic concern (and who presumably are altruistically motivated) show high levels of helpfulness even when it is easy to avoid the other person's distress, when they can readily justify not helping, when helping is not apparently instrumental to improving the benefactor's own mood, and when mood-improving events occur prior to the helping opportunity (see Batson, 1991, 1998; Batson & Oleson, 1991). However, several researchers have proposed alternative explanations that challenge Batson's contention that helping may be altruistically motivated. The controversy surrounding the empathy-altruism hypothesis centers on *why* these effects occur.

The *empathy-specific punishment* explanation suggests that feeling empathic concern may generate additional costs for not helping that make these people likely to help even when helping requires moderate effort. From this perspective, the motivation that Batson and his colleagues described as altruistic may represent a subtle form of egoism based on the social costs associated with what *other* people's negative evaluations might be (Archer, 1984; Archer, Diaz-Loving, Gollwitzer, Davis, & Foushee, 1981) or *self-imposed* costs for violating one's personal standards (Schaller & Cialdini, 1988). However, inconsistent with these egoistic interpretations, evidence of altruistic motivation has been obtained even when social evaluation is not possible (Fultz, Batson, Fortenbach, McCarthy, & Varney, 1986); and when information is provided that gives them a reason for not helping that preserves their personal standards of behavior. For example, people who experience empathic concern still help after being told about the inaction of previous potential helpers or about people's general preference for a less helpful option (Batson, Dyck, et al., 1988, Study 2 & 3).

The *empathy-specific reward* interpretation, another alternative explanation for evidence of altruistic motivation, is closely related to the punishment explanations. It proposes that people help others because they expect a reward from the recipient, from others who observe the act, or from themselves. Several specific versions of this alternative egoistic explanation have been proposed and tested. One involves the desire to share in the other's joy – "empathic joy." Another concerns the helper's reactions to the relief of the other person's need.

The evidence with respect to empathic joy is mixed. In support of the egoistic perspective, Smith, Keating, and Stotland (1989) found that participants who were high in empathy helped more when they believed that they would learn of the consequences for helping than when they believed they would not. But in a subsequent study, Batson and his colleagues also varied the likelihood of learning about the consequences of helping and produced support for the empathy-altruism hypothesis (Batson, Batson, Slingsby, et al., 1991). Participants who experienced low levels of empathic concern and were presumably egoistically motivated were more likely to help when they believed they would learn of the benefits of their intervention, particularly when there was a high likelihood it would improve the other person's situation (and thus produce "empathic joy"). In contrast, those who reported high levels of empathic concern and were presumably altruistically motivated exhibited high levels of helping regardless of whether they would have the opportunity to experience "empathic joy." The desire to share in the other's joy, therefore, does not account for helping by these empathically-aroused participants. Overall, this version of the empathy-specific reward explanation, although still possible, does not definitely disprove the existence of altruism.

The other explanation concerns how people respond to the person in need being helped. If empathically concerned people are primarily motivated by a personal desire for reward, they should feel better if *they* help the person in need (and earn the reward) than if someone else does it. In contrast, if people are altruistically motivated, they should feel better just knowing that the person in need is helped, regardless of who the helper is. Empathically concerned people seem to care for others in this latter way. Their moods improve when they learn that the other person's need has been relieved, regardless of the source of relief (Batson, Dyck, et al., 1988). In addition, people experiencing empathic concern respond in ways that maximally benefit the other person's long-term welfare more than their own immediate needs, for example by withholding assistance when it will undermine the other person's subsequent performance and ultimate well-being. Sibicky, Schroeder, and Dovidio (1995), for example, found that participants experiencing higher levels of empathic concern gave fewer hints to help a partner with a problem-solving task when they were led to believe that providing hints would impair the person's performance on a subsequent task with aversive consequences (greater likelihood of being shocked). When they were not informed of these subsequent negative consequences of providing hints, participants experiencing higher levels of empathic concern offered more hints. In general, then, the weight of the evidence is on the side of the empathy-altruism hypothesis. The behavior that Batson and his colleagues identify as altruistic cannot fully be explained by a desire to obtain personal rewards.

Another egoistic interpretation for findings that support the empathy-altruism hypothesis was proposed by Cialdini and his colleagues (Cialdini et al., 1987; Schaller & Cialdini, 1988). They have argued that empathic people may have a greater motivation to help because empathy has aroused sadness as well as empathic concern, and it is the egoistic need to relieve this sadness that is really motivating helping. The data relevant to this argument are inconsistent and controversial. Indicative of egoistic motivation, Cialdini and his colleagues found that empathy produced high levels of sadness as well as empathic concern (Cialdini et al., 1987, Study 1) and that empathically concerned people showed high levels of helpfulness *only* when they believed that their sad mood could be improved by helping (Cialdini et al., 1987, Study 2). In contrast, in two subsequent studies, Batson et al. (1989) demonstrated, consistent with altruistic motivation, that anticipating a mood-enhancing event did *not* lead people high in empathic concern to be less helpful. Other studies have revealed that empathically aroused participants exhibit a high level of helping even when they are led to believe that helping could not improve their mood (Schroeder, Dovidio, Sibicky, Matthews, & Allen, 1988) and that their motivation is directed at helping the particular person for whom they feel empathy, not helping just anyone (which would also presumably improve their mood; Dovidio, Allen, & Schroeder, 1990). Apparently, these individuals' primary goal was not to make themselves feel better; regardless of whether their own moods would soon be improved, they were highly motivated to help the other person.

The most recent egoistic challenge of results that apparently show an altruistic motivation for helping also comes from Cialdini and his associates. Cialdini, Brown, Lewis, Luce, and Neuberg (1997) have argued that the manipulation typically used to induce empathic concern for another person may also create a greater sense of self–other overlap, or "oneness" between the potential helper and the recipient of the help. This raises the possibility that empathy-related helping may not be selfless, because helping would also indirectly improve at least the psychological well-being of the helper. In support of this contention, Cialdini et al. carried out path analyses of participants' responses to helping requests from different individuals and found that empathic concern did not directly lead to helping; rather, it was correlated with "oneness" between the helper and the victim, which did directly affect helping. In response to this challenge, Batson et al. (1997) conducted a series of studies in which they directly manipulated empathy and shared group membership (which presumably affects self–other overlap). Contrary to Cialdini's argument, Batson et al. reported that the empathy helping relationship was "unqualified by group membership" (p. 495). (For further discussion of these studies see also Batson, 1997; Neuberg et al., 1997.)

The extremely large number of conflicting experimental results regarding the question of altruism versus egoism as the motivational basis for prosocial actions makes it quite difficult to draw any firm conclusions about any specific motive responsible for any particular set of results. Certainly, some behaviors labeled as "altruistic" by one researcher may, in fact, be motivated by egoistic concerns and vice versa. However, the preponderance of evidence from the 20 or so years of experimentation on this question strongly suggests that truly altruistic motivation may exist and all helping is not necessarily egoistically motivated.

Social norms and personal standards

Both cognitive (learning) and affective factors are likely involved in the third motivational perspective, social norms and personal standards. Normative theories of helping emphasize that people help others because they have expectations based on previous social learning or the current behavior of others that it is the socially appropriate response. That is, helping is viewed as "a function of the pressure to comply with shared group expectations about appropriate behavior that are backed by social sanctions and rewards" (Schwartz &

Howard, 1982, p. 346). For example, one of the most common reasons people give for becoming involved in volunteer work is to satisfy others' expectations of them (Reddy, 1980). Researchers have identified two classes of social norms involving in helping. One class relates to feelings of fairness and involves perceptions of reciprocity (Gouldner, 1960), equity (Walster, Walster, & Berscheid, 1978), and social justice (Lerner, 1980). The other class of norms relates to very general norms of aiding, such as the social responsibility norm (Berkowitz, 1972). Because it is often difficult to identify all of the relevant social norms in a situation and assess their relative salience, research has also focused on the role of personal standards in helping.

Social responsibility.   According to the *norm of social responsibility*, people are expected to help others who are dependent on them, even when there is no tangible gain for the benefactor (Berkowitz & Daniels, 1963). In general, the greater the need, the more likely people are to help (Piliavin et al., 1981), and, as the research on physical attraction suggests (Dovidio, 1984), this effect may be particularly pronounced when helping increases the likelihood of a desired long-term interdependent relationship, such as a romantic one. There are, however, exceptions and limits to this rule. People are less obligated to adhere to the social responsibility norm if the interdependent relationship is unwanted or threatens feelings of personal freedom and choice (Berkowitz, 1973). This norm also exerts less influence if the person in need is responsible for creating his or her own plight through a lack of effort (Frey & Gaertner, 1986) or through immoral conduct (Weiner, Perry, & Magnusson, 1988). There are also cultural differences, with individualistic cultures having weaker social responsibility norms than collectivistic cultures (Ma, 1985).

Personal norms, goals, and self-concept.   Whereas general norms of social responsibility may provide only a vague guide for behavior in concrete situations, the use of personal norms and standards is valuable for accounting how a particular person will behave in a specific situation. Internalized moral values and personal norms can motivate helping both cognitively and affectively. The cognitive component involves expectations of behavior that are based on personal standards; the affective component concerns the emotional reaction (e.g., pride, guilt) associated with meeting or not meeting one's standards. Personal norms typically predict helping better than general social norms (Schwartz & Howard, 1982), particularly when attention is focused inward on these personal standards (Hoover, Wood, & Knowles, 1983).

Perhaps because of similar cognitive and affective mechanisms, people who are led to make dispositional self-attributions for their helpfulness and to develop the self-concept that they are helpful people subsequently show relatively high levels of helpful behavior (Grusec, 1991; Swinyard & Ray, 1979). In contrast, those who are offered money to help or are pressured externally to help perceive themselves to have helped less altruistically than if they helped without such inducements (Batson, Fultz, Schoenrade, & Paduano, 1987; Thomas & Batson, 1981; Thomas, Batson, & Coke, 1981), which may make them less helpful in the future.

Similarly, with respect to nonspontaneous helping such as volunteering (see Piliavin & Charng, 1990), helping may be functional in fulfilling personal needs and motives (Clary & Snyder, 1991). For example, the most frequent reasons cited for donating blood are humanitarian or altruistic concerns (Piliavin & Callero, 1991). As with spontaneous help-ing, external pressure to volunteer, such as mandatory volunteer programs within colleges, can undermine these motives and make previously committed volunteers less likely to give their time freely in the future (Stukas, Snyder, & Clary, 1999).

Also like spontaneous helping, self-interest can be directly involved in volunteer activi-ties. People may donate money to achieve personal recognition, to get ahead in their ca-reers, to gain the respect of others, or even because they may expect some financial reward for their "charity" (e.g., tax benefits). Two in-depth studies of volunteerism conducted over 30 years apart (Daniels, 1988; Sills, 1957) both found that concern for others co-occurred with personal interest, a feeling of power, feelings of obligation, identification with the goals of the organization, the desire for social contact, and other self-centered motives (see also Chambre, 1987; Pearce, 1983). Thus, although people often report "al-truistic" reasons for helping, personal needs and goals also appear to be very important. (The issue of people's specific motives for helping will be addressed in greater detail in the next major section of this chapter, Who Helps? Dispositional Variables.)

The consequences of action or inaction for one's self-concept, values, and needs may be directly related to cost–reward considerations and affective reactions to opportunities to help. Thus, the issues of when people help and why they help may be closely interrelated.

Regular and public commitments to helping, such as donating blood or volunteering for charities, can lead to the development of a role-identity consistent with those behaviors (Grube & Piliavin, 2000; Penner & Finkelstein, 1998; Stryker, 1980). For example, not only are one's own feelings of moral obligation and personal identity important in decid-ing whether to donate blood, but also the perceived expectations of significant others (e.g., friends, family) are critical. Students who believe that others expect them to continue giving blood express stronger intentions to give blood in the future, and as a consequence, they are more likely to donate blood (Callero, 1985/6; Charng, Piliavin, & Callero, 1988; Piliavin & Callero, 1991). Thus, one's self-identity, which can itself motivate people to donate blood, can become more publicly formalized in terms of social roles and others' expectations. Similarly, people may perform volunteer work in hospitals or for charity because it has become a part of their own identity and what others expect of them (Deaux & Stark, 1996). These influences continue to develop across an entire lifetime. Older volunteers who help others, for example, report that they are motivated to fulfill a "mean-ingful role" (Bengtson, 1985; Midlarsky & Hannah, 1989).

Fairness. The second class of norms for helping relates to issues of perceived fairness. One facet is the norm of reciprocity. According to this norm, people should help those who have helped them, and they should not help those who have denied them help for no legitimate reason (Gouldner, 1960). Consistent with this proposition, people normally reciprocate assistance to others who have helped them. This is particularly true when the person expects to see the helper again (Carnevale, Pruitt, & Carrington, 1982), although it can also occur when there is no expectation of future interaction (Goranson & Berkowitz, 1966). Also, the more assistance a person receives, the more help he or she subsequently gives (Kahn & Tice, 1973). Reciprocity involving the repayment of specific benefits is particularly strong for most casual relationships, but may be weaker in more intimate com-munal relationships (Clark & Mills, 1993). In communal relationships, however, a broader type of reciprocity may be involved in which people are generally mutually responsive to the needs of the other person, if needs arise. People involved in such relationships are primarily concerned about the welfare of their partner and anticipate that kindnesses will be reciprocated if such actions are ever needed (Webley & Lea, 1993). Consequently, they monitor the needs of their partner more closely than the immediate exchange of assistance, and thus helping is tied more directly to responsiveness to these needs than to a desire to repay specific assistance previously received. However, these circumstances notwithstanding, the norm of reciprocity appears to be a basic and fundamental aspect of human social exchanges. However, the work of Miller and her colleagues (e.g., Miller & Bersoff, 1994) does suggest that in different cultures there may be different reasons why people feel obligated to return favors.

The concern for fairness and balance that underlies the reciprocity norm also relates to the principle of *equity*. Equity exists when people in a relationship believe that their input and output – what they contribute to and what they get out of the relationship – are balanced (Walster et al., 1978). When people perceive an imbalance, they are motivated to restore equity. There is considerable evidence of equity motives in helping. People who have unfairly received benefits – for example, those who receive too much reward based on their contribution to the group activity – often freely choose to give up some of their reward (Schmitt & Marwell, 1972). Conversely, if people feel that they have been undercompensated, they will be less helpful to coworkers or the company for which they work (Organ & Ryan, 1995). In addition, when people have transgressed they are less likely to help others if equity has been restored by retribution, and they are more likely to help others if they are simply forgiven, which increases feelings of indebtedness (Kelln & Ellard, 1999). Helping or withholding assistance is therefore instrumental in restoring balance and achieving equity.

The need to see the world as fair and just is also central to the *just-world hypothesis* (Lerner, 1980). Like equity theory, the just-world hypothesis suggests that people will be motivated to help others who have been treated unfairly – to make the world fair and just again. For instance, people are more likely to support federal disaster assistance for people and communities that take appropriate precautions against flood damage than for those that do not take responsibility for preparing for a flood (Skitka, 1999). People who have stronger beliefs in a just-world are also more strongly motivated to achieve positions of power that will enable them to share resources to help compensate others for perceived injustices (Foster & Rusbult, 1999). However, if a person cannot be helped, the just-world hypothesis suggests that people will disparage the victim, thus making the world right again but decreasing the likelihood of helping that person in the future, as well (Lerner & Simmons, 1966).

Biological "motives" for helping and altruism.   Although biologists and ethologists have long argued for a biological basis of helping and altruism, the extension of these arguments to prosocial actions among humans is a relatively recent development. Three things seem responsible for the greater acceptance of a biological view of helping and altruism. First, in general, explanations of human social behaviors that rely on evolutionary theory have become more socially and scientifically acceptable in recent years (see Buss & Kenrick, 1998). Second, it is generally agreed that empathy plays a critical role in helping and altruism and it appears that there is a specific part of the human brain – the limbic system – that gives humans the capacity to empathize with other people (Carlson, 1998). Moreover, this brain structure was present very early in human evolutionary history (MacLean, 1985). Indeed, it may have been present in the earliest mammals, over 180 million years ago. Further, studies of identical twins have consistently suggested the heritability of empathy (Davis, Luce, & Kraus, 1994; Rushton, Fulker, Neale, Nias, & Eysenck, 1986; Zahn-Waxler, Robinson, & Emde, 1992). Thus, although there may be individual differences, people appear to be generally inherently empathic. Finally, there is the fact that in all known cultures the principle of reciprocity exists in some form (Moghaddam et al., 1993), suggesting to some researchers that there is a biological basis for this behavior (Sober & Wilson, 1998).

Trivers (1971), for example, used the term *reciprocal altruism* to refer to a genetic tendency for mutual helping that increases inclusive fitness, the likelihood that one's genes will be transmitted to future generations. One important component of inclusive fitness is a form of helping known as kin selection. A well-documented phenomenon among animals, *kin selection* refers to the strong positive association between biological (i.e., genetic) relatedness and the incidence of mutual helping (Alcock, 1989). Kin selection makes evolutionary sense because saving the lives of relatives (sometimes even at the sacrifice of one's own life) can increase the incidence of one's own genes in subsequent generations (Buss & Kenrick, 1998). Cunningham (1985/6) reviewed the research on kin selection and reciprocal altruism in humans and found, supportive of the biological perspective, that the closer the kinship relationship the greater the expectations that help would be given to them, the greater the resentment if help were withheld, the greater the willingness to provide aid to the other person, and the more they expected that help would be reciprocated. More recently, Burnstein, Crandall, and Kitayama (1994) found that, consistent with the notion of kin selection, biological relatedness has a much greater impact on life-saving help than on mundane helping. Moreover, the impact of relatedness on life-saving help (but not mundane helping) was substantially reduced or eliminated if the recipient relative was unlikely to produce offspring.

Simon (1990) has used the literatures from evolutionary theory, behavioral genetics, and economic theory to develop a model that accounts for both kin selection and reciprocal altruism. In essence, Simon argues that because "altruistic" individuals contribute more to the common good than do "selfish" individuals, they are more valued by and receive more benefits from other members of their group. As a result, they are more likely to survive and to pass their altruistic genetic predispositions on to their offspring.

Comparisons between fraternal and identical twins also point to a genetic basis for altruism. Specifically, there is evidence of greater cooperation among identical than fraternal twins (Segal, 1993). For example, Segal (1984) presented identical and fraternal twins with a joint completion puzzle task. Relative to fraternal twins, identical twins demonstrated much greater cooperation on this task, as shown by measures such as a higher proportion of successful puzzle completions and more equidistant placement of the puzzle pieces between the twins. And in a later study, Segal (1991) found that in a Prisoners' Dilemma game, identical twins chose cooperative strategies more often than did fraternal twins.

On the other side of this issue, Batson (1998) has provided perhaps the most cogent criticism of the evolutionary approach to helping and altruism. It is the absence of any hard or direct information on the mechanisms that mediate the relationship between genes and behavior. That is, it is unlikely that humans are genetically "hardwired" to help others, as is almost certainly the case with insects and other "lower" animals. Thus, in humans certain genes (or gene combinations) must make certain affective and cognitive processes more likely, and these processes are the proximal and direct causes of helping and altruism. At present, however, we can only speculate as to how genetics might make these processes more or less likely to occur by genetic factors.

In summary, the reasons why people help involve both cognitive and affective influences. Cognitively, people learn that helping is a positively valued social behavior and learn when it is appropriate to help. Affectively, the distress of another person can elicit empathic arousal. Depending on how this arousal is interpreted, it can inhibit intervention, facilitate egoistic helping, or produce altruistic motivation. As many models emphasize (e.g., Piliavin et al., 1981), the affective and cognitive processes are not independent. Moreover, individual, developmental, and cultural differences can occur for both the cognitive and affective processes (Fiske, 1991). The next section examines how individual differences moderate the effects of these processes on helping.

Who Helps? Dispositional Variables

Dispositions, situations, and helping

Prosocial dispositional variables are enduring personal attributes that are, across time and situations, associated with consistencies in the tendency to engage in helpful or altruistic acts. The dispositional variables we will consider include demographic characteristics, personal motives, and personality traits.

Over 70 years ago, Hartshorne and May (1928) concluded that prosocial actions are largely situationally determined rather than the result of enduring personal characteristics. This led to the conventional wisdom that dispositional variables are weak and unreliable predictors of helping and altruism. Further, when interest in helping was rekindled in the late 1960s and early 1970s (Dovidio, 1984), the research findings were consistent with the situationist perspective – the notion that social actions such as helping are primarily determined by the characteristics of the situation in which the action occurred (Mischel, 1973). Gergen, Gergen, and Meter (1972) succinctly described the data on the personality correlates of helpful or altruistic actions as a "quagmire of evanescent relations among variables, conflicting findings, and low order correlations" (p. 113). In the same vein, Piliavin et al. (1981) concluded that "[t]he search for the 'generalized helping personality' has been futile" (p. 184).

One likely reason for the absence of strong or consistent relationships between personality measures and measures of prosocial actions was the context in which the dispositional correlates of helping were studied. A substantial portion of the research on helping in the 1960s and 1970s used some variant of the bystander intervention paradigm, measuring a single decision to help or not help in a situation in which strong situational variables had been effectively manipulated (e.g., the severity or clarity of the emergency). However, the impact of traits (or any other dispositional variable) on behavior is most likely to be observed in behavioral consistencies across time and situations rather than in one specific situation. Also, the greater the strength of situational cues or demands, the less likely it is that dispositional variables will influence a person's behavior in that situation. Thus, the failure of dispositional variables to account for meaningful amounts of variance in the bystander intervention experiments is not surprising, and may say as much about the characteristics of the research paradigms employed as about the relationship between dispositional variables and helping (Penner, Escarrez, & Ellis, 1983).

In recent years there has been somewhat of a resurgence of interest in dispositional correlates of helping and altruism. The more recent research generally supports the interactionist perspective on social behavior – situational and dispositional variables jointly explain more of the variance in a measure of interest than either class of variable does individually. However, within this context empirical findings indicate a much more important role for dispositional variables than was suggested by the earlier studies. We now turn to some of dispositional variables that are related to helping and altruism.

Demographic characteristics

Demographic variables are background characteristics related to a person's physical or social status. Among the demographic characteristics that have been studied in relation to prosocial actions are age, ethnicity, socioeconomic status, religion, and gender. Most studies of the demographic correlates of helping have been surveys of the incidence of financial donations to and volunteering for service organizations, including religious, educational, and health organizations. While strong with regard to external validity, surveys, of course, are limited in their capacity to identify causal relationships. Another limitation of these data is that they come almost exclusively from the United States; some of the relationships reported might vary across different countries and cultures. Nonetheless, the results of these studies are informative and useful.

In the United States, at least, there is a curvilinear relationship between age and charitable contributions and volunteering. People in their late fifties and early sixties donate more than other age groups (Independent Sector, 1997). This pattern likely reflects the greater resources available to people at this time in their lives than to people who are younger or older. Indeed, there is generally a positive association between socioeconomic status and charitable actions (Independent Sector, 1997; Weismann & Galper, 1998). The same process may explain why, in the United States, the percentage of African Americans and Hispanic Americans who report engaging in volunteer activities is lower than the percentage of European Americans (Independent Sector, 1997). That is, because members of these ethnic minorities are overrepresented in lower socioeconomic classes, they may have less time and money to give to charities (Schroeder et al., 1995).

However, these associations may not be solely due to wealth. Education relates to charitable actions in ways that cannot be simply explained by greater resources. For example, in the United States blood donors are most likely to be people with at least some college education and who hold professional jobs (Piliavin & Callero, 1991). Bellah and his colleagues (1985) concluded that among wealthy, well-educated people, prosocial actions may also serve personal growth needs. That is, having attained many of their material goals, these people may turn to goals that give more meaning to their lives.

There is also a strong association between religiosity and both donations and volunteerism. People who report a religious affiliation contribute a greater percentage of their household income than people with no religious affiliation (Independent Sector, 1997). It is likely that part of the reason for this is that in the United States religious institutions are the most frequent recipients of donations of time and money (Galper, 1998).

Turning to gender, although national surveys consistently show that a larger percentage of women than men serve as volunteers (Independent Sector, 1997), early laboratory research on gender differences in helping indicated that men were more likely to help than women. Reconciling these apparently conflicting findings, Eagly and Crowley (1986) concluded from their review of the literature that men and women do not differ in *how much* they help but rather in the *kinds of help* they offer. Moreover, the kinds of help men and women will provide is largely determined by whether the helping action is consistent or inconsistent with the actor's gender role, a set of norms about how people should behave based on their biological sex.

Gender-role expectations relate to both cognitive and affective factors in helping. The female gender role is often associated with the trait of "communion" – being caring, emotionally expressive, and responsive to others (Ashmore, Del Boca, & Wohlers, 1986), and being supportive and nurturant, especially to their friends and family (Eagly & Crowley, 1986). In addition, although both men and women experience physiological arousal when they observe distress in others, women are more likely to interpret this arousal as a positive empathic response to the other person's needs (Eisenberg & Lennon, 1983). In accord with these findings, women are more likely than men to provide their friends with personal favors, emotional support, and informal counseling about personal or psychological problems (Eagly & Crowley, 1986; Eisenberg & Fabes, 1991).

The male gender role is more consistent with the trait of "agency" – being independent and assertive (Ashmore et al., 1986). Perhaps because of this, there is a greater expectation that men will engage in *heroic* helping, in which they risk their own well-being in order to help others, even strangers; and *chivalrous* helping, in which they protect individuals who are less able and powerful than them. Systematic reviews of the literature (Eagly & Crowley, 1986; Piliavin & Unger, 1985) strongly support this gender-role explanation of male–female differences in helping. That is, people tend to offer the kinds of help that are most consistent with and appropriate for their gender roles. And the more salient the person's gender role, the stronger is this relationship (Eagly & Crowley, 1986).

It is also likely that gender roles affect perceptions of the costs and rewards associated with various kinds of helping. In particular, women, because of how they have been socialized, may find the rewards associated with nurturant forms of helping and the costs for not helping to be greater, and the costs for helping to be lower, than do men. Otten et al. (1988), for example, demonstrated that in response to a friend's request for psychological support, women reported that they would feel worse than men for not visiting the friend (a higher cost for not helping) and perceived the visit to be less of an imposition on their time (a lower cost for helping). Analogous socialization processes may cause men to see the costs of failing to act "heroically" as greater than women would and the cost for intervening (e.g., personal harm) to be lower (Eagly & Crowley, 1986).

Motives and helping

People may also systematically differ in their personal goals that underlie helping. Snyder, Clary, and their associates (e.g., Clary & Snyder, 1991; Clary et al., 1998; Omoto & Snyder, 1990) have made this idea the cornerstone of their approach to helping and altruism. More specifically, they have employed a "functional analysis" to explain long-term, sustained prosocial actions, such as volunteering. This approach attempts to identify the "personal and social needs, plans, goals, and functions that are being served by . . . [these] actions" (Clary & Snyder, 1991, p. 123).

According to these researchers, there are six primary needs or motives that may be served by volunteering (Clary et al., 1998; Clary & Snyder, 1991). They are: (1) value-expressive – expressing values related to altruistic and humanitarian concerns; (2) understanding – gaining knowledge or exercising existing knowledge, skills, and abilities; (3) social – being among friends and engaging in activities that might win their approval; (4) career – pursuing activities that might directly or indirectly benefit one's career; (5) protective – protecting one's ego from negative features of the self and helping to address personal problems; and (6) enhancement – enhancing positive feelings about oneself and furthering personal growth and development.

Consistent with this functional analysis, surveys of volunteers (e.g., Allen & Rushton, 1983; Anderson & Moore, 1978; Independent Sector, 1997) suggest that different people have different reasons for engaging in this activity. For example, national surveys in the United States find that the most common reason for volunteering seems to be value-expressive – volunteers are concerned about the welfare of other people – but respondents report other, more self-centered motives, as well. For example, in one survey 33 percent of the people who reported making charitable contributions said that keeping their taxes down was one of the reasons for their charitable contributions; and 14 percent of the volunteers said that they did this for career-related reasons (Independent Sector, 1997; see also Anderson & Moore, 1978; Frisch & Gerard, 1981; Jenner, 1982).

Omoto and Snyder (1995; see also Snyder & Omoto, 1992) have conducted longitudinal studies of the motives of volunteers at organizations that serve people with the HIV infection or AIDS. Omoto and Snyder (1995) found that three self-serving motives – understanding, personal development, and esteem enhancement – were all positively associated with tenure as a volunteer, but the value-expressive motive was not. These findings were consistent with earlier findings by Snyder and Omoto (1992), and led Omoto and Snyder (1995) to conclude: "it appears that the opportunity to have personal, self-serving, and perhaps even selfish functions served by volunteering was what kept volunteers actively involved" (p. 683).

Other studies have also found that personal motives play a significant role in volunteerism, but sometimes these are not the same motives identified by Omoto and Snyder. For example, Penner and Finkelstein (1998) also studied AIDS volunteers but did not find any significant relationships involving the self-serving or selfish motives. However, among male volunteers they did find significant positive correlations between the value-expressive motive and level of commitment to the organization, and willingness to directly help a person with HIV and/or AIDS. Similarly, Clary and Orenstein (1991) found a positive association between altruistic motives and the length of service of crisis counseling volunteers. And Deaux and Stark (1996) found a positive correlation between the value-expressive motive and intention to donate time to a conflict resolution program for prisoners, as well as a positive correlation with an egoistic motive. More recent research suggests that motives, including value-expressive ones, may also play a role in sustained prosocial activities ("Organizational Citizenship Behavior") within private, for-profit organizations (Rioux & Penner, 1999; Tillman, 1998).

Overall, although the primary motives for helping appear to vary across situations and studies, there is consistent evident that helping serves many important functions and that different people have different motives for helping.

Personality correlates of helping and altruism

Graziano and Eisenberg (1997) have identified three kinds of evidence supporting the conclusion that personality traits can account for significant amounts of variance in prosocial actions. The first is that, as noted earlier, differences in empathy, a characteristic that is strongly linked with helping and altruism, may be at least in part inherited (Davis et al., 1994). The second kind of evidence is consistency of prosocial actions across situations and across time. For instance, Oliner and Oliner (1988) found that 40 years after World War II ended, people who had risked their lives to save Jews from the Nazis were still more helpful than people with comparable demographic characteristics (e.g., age, nationality) who had not rescued Jews (see also Colby & Damon, 1992; Marwell, Aiken, & Demerath, 1987; Reddy, 1980; Savin-Williams, Small & Zeldin, 1981). The third kind of evidence relates to replicable associations between "prosocial behavior and those personality characteristics conceptually linked to (helping and) altruism" (Graziano & Eisenberg, 1997, p. 813). We briefly consider some of these personality characteristics; and consistent with the approach we have taken in this chapter, focus on how these personality variables relate to the cognitive and affective processes that generally underlie helping.

Personality characteristics associated primarily with cognitive processes may relate to individual differences in how people perceive and weigh the various costs and rewards for helping and to the steps involved in making a decision to help. For instance, individual differences in the propensity to accept responsibility for helping have been identified as an important personality characteristic (Schwartz & Howard, 1982). In their work with the rescuers, the Oliners also found that this trait also distinguished rescuers from nonrescuers. Studies of other kinds of helping, including medical donations and short-term interventions on behalf of a person in trouble, also find a positive association between ascription of responsibility and helping (Schwartz & Howard, 1982; Staub, 1986, 1996).

A sense of self-efficacy and feelings of confidence, which also relate to the subjective assessment of costs and rewards and perceptions of the ability to help successfully, are also consistent personality correlates of helpful and altruistic actions (see Graziano & Eisenberg, 1997). For example, the Oliners identified self-efficacy as an important attribute of the rescuers. And according to Colby and Damon (1992), one of the most salient attributes of the 22 life-long altruists they interviewed was that the altruists welcomed the challenges to achieving their goals and were unlikely to be discouraged by the obstacles that stood in the way of helping others – they were individuals with a strong sense of their own self-efficacy. More direct evidence for the impact of personality traits on cost assessments comes from Penner and his associates (Penner, Fritzsche, Craiger, & Freifeld, 1995). They developed a measure of prosocial personality characteristics, the Prosocial Personality Battery. One of the two factors on this measure is called Helpfulness (a self-reported history of being helpful and an absence of egocentric responses to distress in others). Helpfulness is correlated with a broad range of helpful actions, including emergency intervention, helping peers and friends in nonemergency situations, sustained volunteering, and informal prosocial activities among employees within a large organization (Penner & Finkelstein, 1998; Penner et al., 1995; Penner, Midili, & Kegelmeyer, 1997). And it also is negatively correlated with estimates of the costs of helping distressed others (Penner et al., 1995).

Other personality characteristics that are consistently associated with helping relate directly or indirectly to arousal. Dispositional empathy is one of the most important of these characteristics. Affective empathy involves the tendency to experience affect or emotion in response to others' emotional experiences. Cognitive empathy relates to the tendency or ability to see things from another person's perspective (Davis, 1994). There is substantial consistency in the literature regarding the positive association between dispositional empathy and a broad range of prosocial actions. For example, Oliner and Oliner (1988) identified empathy as one of the personality characteristics that differentiated people who rescued the Jews from those who did not. Turning to less dramatic forms of helping, Davis (1983) found that empathy was correlated with the amount of money donated to a charity telethon, and Rushton (1984) reported that community volunteers were more empathic than nonvolunteers. Otten, Penner, and Altabe (1991) found that even among a group of professional helpers (psychotherapists), helping (in this case, allowing a person to interview them about their work) was positively associated with self-reports of dispositional empathy.

Personality measures also represent characteristics that reflect closely intertwined configurations of both cognitive and affective factors. Penner and his associates (Penner & Craiger, 1991; Penner et al., 1995) have found that empathy, social responsibility, and concern for the welfare of others are all strongly related to one another. Indeed, they form the other factor of their prosocial personality measure, which is called Other-Oriented Empathy – the tendency to experience empathy for, and to feel responsibility and concern about, the well-being of others; in other words, prosocial thoughts and feelings. Scores on this factor correlate with cost estimates and affective reaction to distress in others.

The Other-Oriented Empathy factor is associated with a rather broad range of prosocial actions in emergency and nonemergency situations and involves formal and informal forms of helping. The measures of helping have included the likelihood a person will intervene in an emergency and the speed with which the intervention occurs (Harter, personal communication, April 8, 1997; also see Carlo, Eisenberg, Troyer, Switzer, & Speer, 1991), intention to volunteer (Sibicky, Mader, Redshaw, & Cheadle, 1994), actually volunteering (Penner & Fritzsche, 1993), length of service as a volunteer (Penner & Fritzsche, 1993; Penner & Finkelstein, 1998), the amount of direct contact that male (but not female) volunteers had with people who were HIV positive or who had AIDS (Penner & Finkelstein,

1998), and self-reports and peer reports of informal prosocial activity among retail store workers, municipal employees, and college students who worked in a wide variety of different jobs (Midili & Penner, 1995; Negrao, 1997; Rioux & Penner, 1999; Tillman, 1998).

Personality and helping: some caveats

Before concluding the discussion of dispositional factors and helping and altruism, several caveats must be offered. First, a comprehensive understanding of helping involves an appreciation not only of personality (and situational) factors separately but how they interact to produce helping. Second, although personality is now recognized as an important factor in helping, personality traits typically play a less substantial role in helping than do situational factors (e.g., Oliner & Oliner, 1988; see also Piliavin & Charng, 1990). Third, in many of the studies on personality and helping causal inference is difficult. For instance, sustained volunteering may shape one's self-concept as an empathic, responsible, and efficacious person rather than these characteristics be the causes of helping. Finally, personality studies need to speak even more directly to the mechanisms that mediate the relationship between a particular personality trait and a helpful or altruistic act. That is, people do not help because they score high on, say, a measure of empathy, but rather because their empathic tendencies elicit some sort of affective or cognitive reaction, which, in turn, leads to a certain behavior. Further consideration of these processes may not only help to answer the question about who helps more definitively but also contribute to an understanding of when people help and why.

Integration and Conclusions

In this chapter, we have reviewed a range of causes, moderating influences, and mediating mechanisms involved in helping and altruism. We conclude with a brief, integrative discussion of the processes relating to the answers to the three fundamental questions we posed: When do people help? Why do people help? Who helps? A conceptual model of these processes and how they affect helping and altruism is presented in figure 7.1.

At the model's base are the most distal causes of a prosocial action; the causes become progressively more proximal as we move toward the top. Thus, the model begins with the evolutionary processes associated with natural selection and inclusive fitness. Among humans' ancestors, helping was a behavior that, under many circumstances, served to increase inclusiveness fitness, and thus it is a characteristic that is likely to be reflected in prosocial genetic predispositions among contemporary humans. This should be especially likely for helping biological relatives because this action directly increases the likelihood that one's own genes will be transmitted to future generations. But, in addition, even helping others who are unrelated may ultimately be beneficial to one's own survival or the survival of relatives through processes of reciprocity.

Humans are both feeling and thinking organisms. Thus, the model suggests that affective and cognitive processes provide mechanisms for translating genetic predispositions

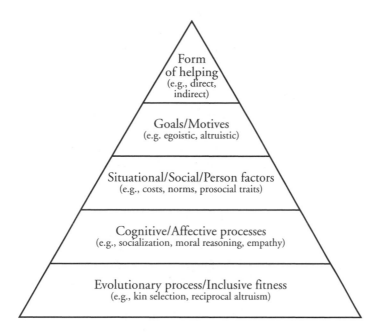

Figure 7.1 Conceptual processes in helping and altruism.

into prosocial actions. With respect to affect, Zajonc (1980) proposed, "Affect is the first link in the evolution of complex adaptive functions" (p. 156). As we noted earlier in this chapter, the capacity to experience empathy and empathic arousal is universal. The neurological structures that are responsible for feelings and emotions (i.e., the limbic system) are among the oldest in the human brain. Moreover, consistent with an evolutionary perspective, empathy is a highly heritable characteristic and empathic arousal increases with closeness to the person in need. From a cognitive perspective, people learn about helping and how to be helpful in the same ways that they learn other social behaviors, through direct or vicarious rewards and punishments. Socialization experiences and culture also affect the way they think about helping (Miller & Bersoff, 1994). Affect and cognitive processes are, of course, reciprocally intertwined. For example, recognition of a discrepancy between one's self-concept and actions may generate unpleasant emotional arousal. In addition, arousal may influence how different costs and rewards for helping are attended to and ultimately how they are weighed in decisions to help.

Reflecting plasticity, and thus adaptiveness, in response, the characteristics of the situation, the victim, and the potential helper may cause particular affective and cognitive mechanisms to be activated selectively and to varying degrees. For example, situations of greater clarity and severity produce higher levels of empathic arousal and are associated with stronger norms supporting intervention and greater guilt for not helping. People have higher levels of cognitive and affective empathy with others who are similar to them, with whom they share group membership, and with whom they are closer. Personal dispositions may also affect affective and cognitive factors and thus produce individual differences in helpfulness. For example, people who are higher in traits such as Other-Oriented Empathy and who are more confident and higher in self-efficacy display affective and cognitive responses that typically produce helpful actions.

How affective and cognitive processes operate as a function of the situational, personal, and interpersonal context determines the nature of the motivation for helping and the ultimate objectives of the action. Helping can be egoistically motivated. In such instances, the primary objective with respect to affect might be to improve one's mood or relieve one's own empathic distress. With regard to cognition, egoistically-motivated helping may reaffirm one's positive self-image or satisfy a wide range of personal goals (e.g., job advancement, distraction from personal problems). Helping may even be used strategically to gain advantage over another person by making them dependent on assistance, by undermining their self-confidence, or by shaping more negative impressions of them by others (Gilbert & Silvera, 1996). However, helping can also be altruistically motivated, with the ultimate goal of improving the other person's welfare. As Batson (1991) has argued, demonstration of truly altruistic motivation provides a broader and different perspective on behavior for a discipline that has been traditionally considered virtually exclusively the effect of personal consequences for behavior (e.g., the Law of Effect or drive reduction models).

Finally, we note that the behavioral outcome of these processes can come in various forms. Helping may be direct or indirect (e.g., calling the police). It may be short-term or involve long-term commitments. Helping may also be reflected in inaction when helping has negative social consequences (e.g., stigmatization for providing academic assistance; Major & Crocker, 1993) or personal consequences (e.g., the failure to develop important skills; Sibicky et al., 1995) that outweigh the immediate benefits of intervention or in the refusal to acquiesce to a request for assistance that might ultimately cause another harm (e.g., an alcoholic's request for a drink).

In conclusion, although many manifestations of helping, particularly those that are commonly studied in the laboratory, appear simple and straightforward, helping is a complex, multidetermined behavior. Whether it is spontaneous and short-term or planned and sustained, helping is an evolutionarily important behavior that is shaped by fundamental cognitive and affective processes, involves self- and other-directed motives, and has consequences that are central to one's self-image and social relationships. Thus, an understanding of the processes underlying helping can illuminate a wide range of other behaviors while offering genuinely unique insights to human motivation.

References

Alcock, J. (1989). *Animal behavior* (4th ed.). Sunderland, MA: Sinauer Press.

Allen, N., & Rushton, J. P. (1983). The personality of community volunteers. *Journal of Voluntary Action Research, 9,* 1183–1196.

Anderson, J. C., & Moore, L. (1978). The motivation to volunteer. *Journal of Voluntary Action Research, 7,* 232–252.

Archer, R. L. (1984). The farmer and the cowman should be friends: An attempt at reconciliation with Batson, Coke, and Pych. *Journal of Personality and Social Psychology, 46,* 709– 711.

Archer, R. L., Diaz-Loving, R., Gollwitzer, P. M., Davis, M. H., & Foushee, H. C. (1981). The role of dispositional empathy and social evaluation in the empathic mediation of helping. *Journal of Personality and Social Psychology, 46,* 786–796.

Ashmore, R., Del Boca, F., & Wohlers, A. J. (1986). Gender stereotypes. In R. Ashmore & F. L. Del Boca (Eds.), *The social psychology of female–male relations* (pp. 69–119). Orlando, FL: Academic Press.

Bar-Tal, D., & Raviv, A. (1982). A cognitive-learning model of helping behavior development: Possible implications and applications. In N. Eisenberg (Ed.), *The development of prosocial behavior* (pp. 199–217). New York: Academic Press.

Baron, R. A. (1997). The sweet smell of . . . helping: Effects of pleasant ambient fragrance on prosocial behavior in shopping malls. *Personality and Social Psychology Bulletin, 23,* 498–503.

Batson, C. D. (1987). Prosocial motivation: Is it ever truly altruistic? In L. Berkowitz (Ed.), *Advances in experimental social psychology* (Vol. 20, pp. 65–122). New York: Academic Press.

Batson, C. D. (1991). *The altruism question: Toward a social-psychological answer.* Hillsdale, NJ: Erlbaum.

Batson, C. D. (1997). Self–other merging and the empathy–altruism hypothesis: Reply to Neuberg et al. (1997). *Journal of Personality and Social Psychology, 73,* 517–522.

Batson, C. D. (1998). Altruism and prosocial behavior. In D. T. Gilbert, S. T. Fiske, & G. Lindzey (Eds.), *The handbook of social psychology* (4th ed., Vol. 2, pp. 282–315). New York: McGraw-Hill.

Batson, C. D., Batson, J. G., Griffitt, C. A., Barrientos, S., Brandt, J. R., Sprengelmeyer, P., & Bayly, M. J. (1989). Negative-state relief and the empathy-altruism hypothesis. *Journal of Personality and Social Psychology, 56,* 922–933.

Batson, C. D., Batson, J. G., Slingsby, J. K., Harrell, K. L., Peekna, H. M., & Todd, R. M. (1991). Empathic joy and the empathy-altruism hypothesis. *Journal of Personality and Social Psychology, 61,* 413–426.

Batson, C. D., Dyck, J. L., Brandt, J. R., Batson, J. G., Powell, A. L., McMaster, M. R., & Griffitt, C. (1988). Five studies testing two new egoistic alternatives to the empathy-altruism hypothesis. *Journal of Personality and Social Psychology, 55,* 52–77.

Batson, C. D., Fultz, J., Schoenrade P. A., & Paduano, A. (1987). Critical self-reflection and self-perceived altruism: When self-reward fails. *Journal of Personality and Social Psychology, 53,* 594–602.

Batson, C. D., & Oleson, K. C. (1991). Current status of the empathy-altruism hypothesis. In M. S. Clark (Ed.), *Review of personality and social psychology: Vol. 12. Prosocial behavior* (pp. 62–85). Newbury Park, CA: Sage.

Batson, C. D., Sager, K., Garst, E., Kang, M., Rubchinsky, K., & Dawson, K. (1997). Is empathy-induced helping due to self-other merging? *Journal of Personality and Social Psychology, 73,* 495–509.

Baumeister, F. F., Stillwell, A. M., & Heatherton, T. F. (1994). Guilt: An interpersonal approach. *Psychological Bulletin, 115,* 243–267.

Bell, F. A., Fisher, J. D., Baum, A., & Greene, T. (1996). *Environmental psychology.* (4th ed). New York: Harcourt.

Bellah, R. N., Madsen, R., Sullivan, W. M., Swidler, A., & Tipton, S. M. (1985). *Habits of the heart: Individualism and commitment in American life.* Berkeley: University of California Press.

Bengtson, V. (1985). Diversity and symbolism in grandparental roles. In V. Bengtson & J. Robertson (Eds.), *Grandparenthood* (pp. 11–25). Beverly Hills, CA: Sage.

Berkowitz, L. (1972). Social norms, feelings, and other factors affecting helping behavior and altruism. In L. Berkowitz (Ed.), *Advances in experimental social psychology* (Vol. 6, pp. 63–108). New York: Academic Press.

Berkowitz, L. (1973). Reactance and the unwillingness to help others. *Psychological Bulletin, 79,* 310–317.

Berkowitz, L., & Daniels, L. R. (1963). Responsibility and dependency. *Journal of Abnormal and*

Social Psychology, 66, 429–436.

Borgida, E., Conner, C., & Manteufel, L. (1992). Understanding living kidney donation: A behavioral decision-making perspective. In S. Spacapan & S. Oskamp (Eds.), *Helping and being helped* (pp. 183–212). Newbury Park, CA: Sage.

Burnstein, E., Crandall, C., & Kitayama, S. (1994). Some neo-Darwinian decision rules for altruism: Weighing cues for inclusive fitness as a function of the biological importance of the decision. *Journal of Personality & Social Psychology, 67,* 773–789.

Buss, D. M., & Kenrick, D. T. (1998). Evolutionary social psychology. In D. T. Gilbert, S. T. Fiske, & G. Lindzey (Eds.), *Handbook of social psychology.* (4th ed., Vol. 2, pp. 982–1026). Boston: McGraw-Hill.

Byrne, D. (1971). *The attraction paradigm.* New York: Academic Press.

Callero, P. L. (1985/6). Putting the social in prosocial behavior: An interactionist approach to altruism. *Humboldt Journal of Social Relations, 13,* 15–34.

Carlo, G., Eisenberg, N., Troyer, D., Switzer, G., & Speer, A. L. (1991). The altruistic personality: In what contexts is it apparent? *Journal of Personality and Social Psychology, 61,* 450–458.

Carlson, N. R. (1998). *Physiology of behavior.* Boston: Allyn Bacon.

Carlson, M., & Miller, N. (1987). Explanation of the relation between negative mood and helping. *Psychological Bulletin, 102,* 91–108.

Carnevale, P. J. D., Pruitt, D. G., & Carrington, P. I. (1982). Effects of future dependence, liking, and repeated requests for help on helping behavior. *Social Psychology Quarterly, 45,* 9–14.

Chambre, S. M. (1987). *Good deeds in old age: Volunteering by the new leisure class.* Lexington, MA: Lexington Books.

Charng, H. W., Piliavin, J. A., & Callero, P. L. (1988). Role-identity and reasoned action in the prediction of repeated behavior. *Social Psychology Quarterly,* 51, 303–317.

Cialdini, R. B., Brown, S. L., Lewis, B. P., Luce, C., & Neuberg, S. L. (1997). Reinterpreting the empathy-altruism relationship: When one into one equals oneness. *Journal of Personality and Social Psychology, 73,* 481–494.

Cialdini, R. B., Darby, B. K., & Vincent, J. E. (1973). Transgression and altruism: A case for hedonism. *Journal of Experimental Social Psychology, 9,* 502–516.

Cialdini, R. B., & Kenrick, D. T. (1976). Altruism as hedonism: A social development perspective on the relationship of negative mood state and helping. *Journal of Personality and Social Psychology, 34,* 907–914.

Cialdini, R. B., Kenrick, D. T., & Baumann, D. J. (1982). Effects of mood on prosocial behavior in children and adults. In N. Eisenberg (Ed.), *The development of prosocial behavior* (pp. 339–359). New York: Academic Press.

Cialdini, R. B., Schaller, M., Houlihan, D., Arps, K., Fultz, J., & Beamen, A. L. (1987). Empathy-based helping: Is it selflessly or selfishly motivated? *Journal of Personality and Social Psychology, 52,* 749–758.

Clark, M. S., & Mills, J. (1993). The difference between communal and exchange relationships: What is and what is not. *Personality and Social Psychology Bulletin, 19,* 684–691.

Clary, E. G., & Miller, J. (1986). Socialization and situational influences on sustained altruism. *Child Development, 57,* 1358–1369.

Clary, E. G., & Orenstein, L. (1991). The amount and effectiveness of help: The relationship of motives and abilities to helping behavior. *Personality and Social Psychology Bulletin, 17,* 58–64.

Clary, E. G., & Snyder, M. (1991). A functional analysis of altruism and prosocial behavior: The case of volunteerism. In M. Clark (Ed.), *Review of personality and social psychology: Vol. 12. Prosocial behavior* (pp. 119–148). Knobbier Park, CA: Sage.

Clary, E. G., Snyder, M., Ridge, R., Copeland, J., Haugen, J., & Miene, P. (1998). Understanding and assessing the motivations of volunteers: A functional approach. *Journal of Personality and Social Psychology, 74,* 1516–1530.

Colby, A., & Damon, W. (1992). *Some do care.* New York: Free Press.

Cunningham, M. R. (1985/6). Levites and brother's keepers: A sociobiological perspective on prosocial behavior. *Humboldt Journal of Social Relations, 13,* 35–67.

Daniels, A. K. (1988). *Invisible careers: Women civic leaders from the volunteer world.* Chicago: University of Chicago Press.

Darley, J. M., & Latané, B. (1968). Bystander intervention in emergencies: Diffusion of responsibility. *Journal of Personality and Social Psychology, 8,* 377–383.

Davis, M. H. (1983). Empathic concern and muscular dystrophy telethon: Empathy as a multidimensional construct. *Personality and Social Psychology Bulletin, 9,* 223–229.

Davis, M. H. (1994). *Empathy: A social psychological approach.* Madison, WI: Brown & Benchmark.

Davis, M. H., Luce, C., & Kraus, S. J. (1994). The heritability of characteristics associated with dispositional empathy. *Journal of Personality, 62,* 369–391.

Deaux, K., & Stark, B. E. (1996, May). *Identity and motive: An integrated theory of volunteerism.* Ann Arbor, MI: Society for the Psychological Study of Social Issues.

Dovidio, J. F. (1984). Helping behavior and altruism: An empirical and conceptual overview. In L. Berkowitz (Ed.), *Advances in experimental social psychology* (Vol. 17, pp. 361–427). New York: Academic Press.

Dovidio, J. F., Allen, J., & Schroeder, D. A. (1990). The specificity of empathy-induced helping: Evidence for altruism. *Journal of Personality and Social Psychology, 59,* 249–260.

Dovidio, J. F., Gaertner, S. L., Validzic, A., Matoka, A., Johnson, B., & Frazier, S. (1997). Extending the benefits of recategorization: Evaluations, self-disclosure, and helping. *Journal of Experimental Social Psychology, 33,* 401–420.

Dovidio, J. F., Piliavin, J. A., Gaertner, S. L., Schroeder, D. A., & Clark, R. D., III (1991). The Arousal: Cost-Reward Model and the process of intervention: A review of the evidence. In M. S. Clark (Ed.), *Review of personality and social psychology: Vol. 12. Prosocial behavior* (pp. 86–118). Newbury Park, CA: Sage.

Dutton, D. G., & Lennox, V. L. (1974). Effect of prior "token" compliance on subsequent interracial behavior. *Journal of Personality and Social Psychology, 29,* 65–71.

Eagly, A. H., & Crowley, M. (1986). Gender and helping behavior: A meta-analytic view of the social psychological literature. *Psychological Bulletin, 100,* 283–308.

Edelmann, R. J., Evans, G., Pegg, I., & Tremain, M. (1983). Responses to physical stigma. *Perceptual and Motor Skills, 57,* 294.

Eisenberg, N., & Fabes, R. A. (1991). Prosocial behavior and empathy: A multimethod developmental perspective. In M. S. Clark (Ed.), *Review of personality and social psychology: Vol. 12. Prosocial behavior* (pp. 34–61). Newbury Park, CA: Sage.

Eisenberg, N., & Fabes, R. (1998). Prosocial development. In W. Colby (Ed.), *Handbook of child psychology* (5th ed., Vol. 3, pp. 701–798). New York: Wiley.

Eisenberg, N., & Lennon, R. (1983). Sex differences in empathy and related capacities. *Psychological Bulletin, 94,* 100–131.

Eisenberg, N., & Miller, P. (1987). The relation of empathy to prosocial and related behaviors. *Psychological Bulletin, 101,* 91–119.

Eisenberg, N., Miller, P., Shell, P., McNalley, S., & Shea, C. (1991). Prosocial development in adolescence: A longitudinal study. *Developmental Psychology, 27,* 849–857.

Eisenberg, N., Shell, R., Pasternack, J., Lennon, R., Beller, R., & Mathy, R. M. (1987). Prosocial development in middle childhood: A longitudinal study. *Developmental Psychology, 23,* 712–718.

Fabes, R. A., Eisenberg, N., & Eisenbud, L. (1993). Behavioral and physiological correlates of children's reactions to others in distress. *Developmental Psychology, 29,* 655–664.

Fabes, R. A., Eisenberg, N., & Miller, P. A. (1990). Maternal correlates of children's vicarious emotional responsiveness. *Developmental Psychology, 26,* 639–648.

Fabes, R. A., Fultz. J., Eisenberg, N., May-Plumlee, T., & Christopher, F. S. (1989). Effects of rewards on children's prosocial motivation: A socialization study. *Developmental Psychology, 25,* 509–515.

Fiske, A. (1991). The cultural relativity of selfish individualism: Anthropological evidence that humans are inherently sociable. In M. S. Clark (Ed.), *Review of personality and social psychology: Vol. 12. Prosocial behavior* (pp. 176–214). Newbury Park, CA: Sage.

Forgas, J. P. (1998). Asking nicely? The effects of mood on responding to more or less polite requests. *Personality and Social Psychology Bulletin, 24,* 173–185.

Foster, C. A., & Rusbult, C. E. (1999). Injustice and powerseeking. *Personality and Social Psychology Bulletin, 25*, 834–849.

Frey, D. L., & Gaertner, S. L. (1986). Helping and the avoidance of inappropriate interracial behavior: A strategy that perpetuates a nonprejudiced self-image. *Journal of Personality and Social Psychology, 50*, 1083–1090.

Frisch, M. B., & Gerard, M. (1981). Natural helping systems: A survey of Red Cross volunteers. *American Journal of Community Psychology, 9*, 567–579.

Fultz, J., Batson, C. D., Fortenbach, V. A., McCarthy, P. M., & Varney, L. L. (1986). Social evaluation and the empathy-altruism hypothesis. *Journal of Personality and Social Psychology, 50*, 761–769.

Gaertner, S. L., & Dovidio, J. F. (1977). The subtlety of white racism, arousal, and helping behavior. *Journal of Personality and Social Psychology, 35*, 691–707.

Gaertner, S. L., & Dovidio, J. F. (1986). The aversive form of racism. In J. F. Dovidio & S. L. Gaertner (Eds.), *Prejudice, discrimination, and racism* (pp. 61–90). Orlando, FL: Academic Press.

Galper, J. (1998). *An exploration of social capital, giving and volunteering at the United States county level.* (Working paper). Washington, DC: Urban Institute.

Gergen, K. J., Gergen, M. M., & Meter, K. (1972). Individual orientations to prosocial behavior. *Journal of Social Issues, 8*, 105–130.

Gilbert, D. T., & Silvera, D. H. (1996). Overhelping. *Journal of Personality and Social Psychology, 70*, 678–690.

Goranson, R., & Berkowitz, L. (1966). Reciprocity and responsibility reactions to prior help. *Journal of Personality and Social Psychology, 3*, 227–232.

Gouldner, A. (1960). The norm of reciprocity: A preliminary statement. *American Sociological Review, 25*, 161–178.

Graziano, W. G., & Eisenberg, N. (1997). Agreeableness: A dimension of personality. In R. Hogan, J. A. Johnson, & S. Briggs (Eds.), *Handbook of personality* (pp. 795–825). San Diego, CA: Academic Press.

Grube, J. A., & Piliavin, J. A. (2000). Role-identity, organizational commitment, and volunteer performance. *Personality and Social Psychology Bulletin, 26*, 1108–1119.

Grusec, J. E. (1981). Socialization processes and the development of altruism. In J. P. Rushton & R. M. Sorrentino (Eds.), *Altruism and helping behavior: Social, personality, and developmental perspectives* (pp. 65–90). Hillsdale, NJ: Erlbaum.

Grusec, J. E. (1991). The socialization of empathy. In M. S. Clark (Ed.), *Review of personality and social psychology: Vol. 12. Prosocial behavior* (pp. 9–33). Newbury Park, CA: Sage.

Hartshorne, H., & May, M. A. (1928). *Studies in the nature of character: Vol I. Studies in deceit.* New York: Macmillan.

Hedge, A., & Yousif, Y. H. (1992). Effects of urban size, urgency, and cost of helpfulness: A cross-cultural comparison between the United Kingdom and the Sudan. *Journal of Cross-Cultural Psychology, 23*, 107–115.

Hoffman, M. L. (1990). Empathy and justice motivation. *Motivation and Emotion, 14*, 151–172.

Hoover, C. W., Wood, E. E., & Knowles, E. S. (1983). Forms of social awareness and helping. *Journal of Experimental Social Psychology, 18*, 577–590.

Hornstein, H. A. (1982). Promotive tension: Theory and research. In V. J. Derlega & J. Grezlak (Eds.), *Cooperation and helping behavior: Theories and research* (pp 229–248). New York: Academic Press.

Independent Sector (1997). *The American volunteer.* Washington, DC: Author.

Isen, A. M. (1993). Positive affect and decision making. In M. Lewis & J. M. Haviland (Eds.), *Handbook of emotion* (pp. 261–277). New York: Guilford Press.

Jenner, J. R. (1982). Participation, leadership, and the role of volunteerism among selected women volunteers. *Journal of Voluntary Action Research, 11*, 27–38.

Kahn, A., & Tice, T. (1973). Returning a favor and retaliating harm: The effects of stated intention and actual behavior. *Journal of Experimental Social Psychology, 9*, 43–56.

Kelln, B. R. C., & Ellard, J. H. (1999). An equity theory analysis of the impact of forgiveness and retribution on transgressor compliance. *Personality and Social Psychology Bulletin, 25*, 864–872.

Korte, C. (1969). Group effects on help-giving in an emergency. *Proceedings of the 77th Annual Convention of the American Psychological Association, 4*, 383–384.

Krebs, D. (1982). Psychological approaches to altruism: An evaluation. *Ethics, 92*, 447–458.

Latané, B., & Darley, J. M. (1970). *The unresponsive bystander: Why doesn't he help?* New York: Appleton-Century-Crofts.

Latané, B., Nida, S. A., & Wilson, D. W. (1981). The effects of group size on helping behavior. In J. P. Rushton & R. M. Sorrentino (Eds.), *Altruism and helping behavior: Social, personality, and developmental perspectives* (pp. 287–313). Hillsdale, NJ: Erlbaum.

Lerner, M. J. (1980). *The belief in a just world: A fundamental delusion*. New York: Plenum.

Lerner, M. J., & Simmons, C. H. (1966). Observers' reactions to the "innocent victim." *Journal of Personality and Social Psychology, 4*, 203–210.

Levine, R. V., Martinez, T. S., Brase, G., & Sorenson, K. (1994). Helping in 36 U. S. cities. *Journal of Personality and Social Psychology, 67*, 69–82.

Ma, H. (1985). Cross-cultural study of altruism. *Psychological Reports, 57*, 337–338.

Macaulay, J. R., & Berkowitz, L. (Eds.). (1970). *Altruism and helping behavior*. New York: Academic Press.

MacLean, P. D. (1985). Evolutionary psychiatry and the triune brain. *Psychological Medicine, 15*, 219–221.

Major, B., & Crocker, J. (1993). Social stigma: The consequences of attributional ambiguity. In D. M. Mackie & D. L. Hamilton (Eds.), *Affect, cognition, and stereotyping: Interactive processes in group perception* (pp. 345–370). San Diego, CA: Academic Press.

Manucia, G. K., Baumann, D. J., & Cialdini, R. B. (1984). Mood influences in helping: Direct effects or side effects? *Journal of Personality and Social Psychology, 46*, 357–364.

Marks, E., Penner, L. A., & Stone, A. V. (1982). Helping as a function of empathic responses and sociopathy. *Journal of Research in Personality, 16*, 1–20.

Marwell, G., Aiken, M. T., & Demerath, N. J., III. (1987). The persistence of political attitudes among 1960s civil rights activists. *Public Opinion Quarterly, 51*, 359–375.

Mathews, K. E., & Canon, L. K. (1975). Environmental noise level as a determinant of helping behavior. *Journal of Personality and Social Psychology, 32*, 571–577.

McGuire, A. M. (1994). Helping behaviors in the natural environment: Dimensions and correlates of helping. *Personality and Social Psychology Bulletin, 20*, 45–56.

McMillen, D. L., Sanders, D. Y., & Solomon, G. S. (1977). Self-esteem, attentiveness, and helping behavior. *Personality and Social Psychology Bulletin, 3*, 257–261.

Midili, A. R., & Penner, L. A. (1995, August). *Dispositional and environmental influences on Organizational Citizenship Behavior*. Annual meeting of the American Psychological Association, New York.

Midlarsky, E., & Hannah, M. E. (1989). The generous elderly. *Psychology and Aging, 4*, 346–351.

Milgram, S. (1970). The experience of living in cities. *Science, 167*, 1461–1468.

Miller, J. G., & Bersoff, D. M. (1994). Cultural influences on the moral status of reciprocity and the discounting of endogenous motivation. *Personality and Social Psychology Bulletin, 20*, 592– 602.

Mischel, W. (1973). Toward a cognitive social learning reconceptualization of personality. *Psychological Review, 80*, 252–283.

Moghaddam, F. M., Taylor, D. M., & Wright, S. C. (1993). *Social psychology in cross-cultural perspective*. New York: W. H. Freeman.

Mueller, C. W., & Donnerstein, E. (1981). Film-facilitated arousal and prosocial behavior. *Journal of Experimental Social Psychology, 17*, 31–41.

Mueller, C. W., Donnerstein, E., & Hallam, J. (1983). Violent films and prosocial behavior. *Personality and Social Psychology Bulletin, 9*, 83–89.

Negrao, M. (1997). *On good Samaritans and villains: An investigation of the bright and dark side of altruism in organizations*. Unpublished manuscript, University of South Florida, Tampa, Florida.

Neuberg, S. L., Cialdini, R. B., Brown, S. L., Luce, C., Sagarin, B. J., & Lewis, B. P. (1997). Does empathy lead to anything more than superficial helping? Comment on Batson et al. (1997). *Journal of Personality and Social Psychology, 73*, 510–516.

Oliner, S., & Oliner, P. (1988). *The altruistic personality: Rescuers of Jews in Nazi Europe.* New York: Free Press.

Oliner, P. M., & Oliner, S. P. (1992). Promoting extensive altruistic bonds: A conceptual elaboration and some pragmatic implications. In P. M. Oliner & S. P. Oliner (Eds.), *Embracing the other: Philosophical, psychological, and historical perspectives on altruism* (pp. 369–389). New York: New York University Press.

Omoto, A. M., & Snyder, M. (1990). Basic research in action: Volunteerism and society's response to AIDS. *Personality and Social Psychology Bulletin, 16,* 152–166.

Omoto, A., & Snyder, M. (1995). Sustained helping without obligation: Motivation, longevity of service, and perceived attitude change among AIDS volunteers. *Journal of Personality and Social Psychology, 68,* 671–687.

Organ, D. W., & Ryan, K. (1995). A meta-analytic review of attitudinal and dispositional predictors of organizational citizenship behavior. *Personnel Psychology, 48,* 775–802.

Otten, C. A., Penner, L. A., & Altabe, M. N. (1991). An examination of therapists' and college students' willingness to help a psychologically distressed person. *Journal of Social and Clinical Psychology, 10,* 102–120.

Otten, C. A., Penner, L. A., & Waugh, G. (1988). That's what friends are for: The determinants of psychological helping. *Journal of Social and Clinical Psychology, 7,* 34–41.

Pearce, J. L. (1983). Participation in voluntary associations: How membership in a formal organization changes the rewards of participation. In D. H. Smith (Ed.), *International perspectives on voluntary action research* (pp. 148–156). Washington, DC: University Press of America.

Pearce, P. L., & Amato, P. R. (1980). A taxonomy of helping: A multidimensional scaling analysis. *Social Psychology Quarterly, 43,* 363–371.

Penner, L. A., & Craiger, J. P. (1991, August). *The altruistic personality.* Paper presented at the annual meeting of the American Psychological Association, San Francisco, CA.

Penner, L. A., Escarrez, J., & Ellis, B. (1983). Sociopathy and helping: Looking out for number one. *Academic Psychology Bulletin, 5,* 209–220.

Penner, L. A., & Finkelstein, M. A. (1998). Dispositional and structural determinants of volunteerism. *Journal of Personality and Social Psychology, 74,* 525–537.

Penner, L. A., & Fritzsche, B. A. (1993, August). *Measuring the prosocial personality: Four construct validity studies.* Paper presented at the annual meeting of the American Psychological Association. Toronto, Canada.

Penner, L. A., Fritzsche, B. A., Craiger, J. P., & Freifeld, T. R. (1995). Measuring the prosocial personality. In J. Butcher & C. D. Spielberger (Eds.), *Advances in personality assessment* (Vol. 10, pp. 147–163). Hillsdale, NJ: Erlbaum.

Penner, L. A., Midili, A. R., & Kegelmeyer, J. (1997). Beyond job attitudes: A personality and social psychology perspective on the causes of Organizational Citizenship Behavior. *Human Performance, 10,* 111–131.

Piliavin, J. A., & Callero, P. (1991). *Giving blood: The development of an altruistic identity.* Baltimore: Johns Hopkins University Press.

Piliavin, J. A., & Charng, H. W. (1990). Altruism: A review of recent theory and research. *Annual Review of Sociology, 16,* 27–65.

Piliavin, J. A., Dovidio, J. F., Gaertner, S. L., & Clark, R. D., III. (1981). *Emergency intervention.* New York: Academic Press.

Piliavin, J. A., & Unger, R. K. (1985). The helpful but helpless female: Myth or reality? In V. O'Leary, R. K. Unger., & B. S. Wallston (Eds.), *Women, gender and social psychology* (pp. 149–186). Hillsdale, NJ: Erlbaum.

Rabow, J., Newcomb, M. D., Monto, M. A., & Hernandez, A. C. R. (1990). Altruism in drunk driving situations: Personal and situational factors in helping. *Social Psychology Quarterly, 53,* 199–213.

Reddy, R. D. (1980). Individual philanthropy and giving behavior. In D. H. Smith & J. Macaulay (Eds.), *Participation in social and political activities* (pp. 370–399). San Francisco: Jossey-Bass.

Rioux, S., & Penner, L. A. (1999, April). *Assessing personal motives for engaging in Organizational Citizenship Behavior: A field study.* Paper presented at the Annual Meeting of the Society for

Industrial and Organizational Psychology, Atlanta, GA.

Rosenhan, D. (1969). The kindnesses of children. *Young Children, 25,* 30–44.

Rushton, J. P. (1984). The altruistic personality: Evidence from laboratory, naturalistic and self-report perspectives. In E. Staub, D. Bar-Tal, J. Karylowski, & J. Reykowski (Eds.), *Development and maintenance of prosocial behavior.* New York: Plenum.

Rushton, J. P., Fulker, D. W., Neale, M. C., Nias, D. K. B., & Esyenck, H. J. (1986). Altruism and aggression: The heritability of individual differences. *Journal of Personality and Social Psychology, 50,* 1192–1198.

Sagi, A., & Hoffman, M. L. (1976). Empathic distress in the newborn. *Developmental Psychology, 12,* 175–176.

Salovey, P., Mayer, J. D., & Rosenhan, D. L. (1991). Mood and helping: Mood as a motivator of helping and helping as a regulator of mood. In M. S. Clark (Ed.), *Review of personality and social psychology: Vol. 12. Prosocial behavior* (pp. 215–237). Newbury Park, CA: Sage.

Savin-Williams, R. C., Small, S., & Zeldin, R. S. (1981). Dominance and altruism among adolescent males: A comparison of ethological and psychological methods. *Ethology and Sociobiology, 2,* 167–176.

Schaller, M., & Cialdini, R. B. (1988). The economics of empathic helping: Support for a mood management motive. *Journal of Experimental Social Psychology, 24,* 163–181.

Schmitt, D. R., & Marwell, G. (1972). Withdrawal and reward reallocation as responses to inequity. *Journal of Experimental Social Psychology, 8,* 207–221.

Schroeder, D. A., Dovidio, J. F., Sibicky, M. E., Matthews, L. L., & Allen, J. L. (1988). Empathy and helping behavior: Egoism or altruism. *Journal of Experimental Social Psychology, 24,* 333–353.

Schroeder, D. A., Penner, L. A., Dovidio, J. F., & Piliavin, J. A. (1995). *The psychology of helping and altruism: Problems and puzzles.* New York: McGraw-Hill.

Schwartz, S. H., & Howard, J. A. (1982). Helping and cooperation: A self-based motivational model. In V. J. Derlega & J. Grzelak (Eds.), *Cooperation and helping behavior: Theories and Research* (pp. 327–353). New York: Academic Press.

Segal, N. L. (1984) Cooperation, competition, and altruism within twin sets: A reappraisal. *Ethology and Sociobiology, 5,* 163–177.

Segal, N. L. (1991, April). *Cooperation and competition in adolescent MZ and DZ twins during the Prisoners' Dilemma Game.* Paper presented at meeting of Society for Research in Child Development, Seattle, WA.

Segal, N. L. (1993). Twin sibling, and adoption methods: Test of evolutionary hypotheses. *American Psychologist, 48,* 943–956.

Shotland, R. L., & Heinold, W. D. (1985). Bystander response to arterial bleeding: Helping skills, the decision-making process, and differentiating the helping response. *Journal of Personality and Social Psychology, 49,* 347–356.

Shotland, R. L., & Huston, T. L. (1979). Emergencies: What are they and how do they influence bystanders to intervene? *Journal of Personality and Social Psychology, 37,* 1822–1834.

Sibicky, M., Mader, D., Redshaw, I., & Cheadle, B. (1994, May). *Measuring the motivation to volunteer.* Paper presented at the annual meeting of the Midwestern Psychological Association, Chicago, IL.

Sibicky, M. E., Schroeder, D. A., & Dovidio, J. F. (1995). Empathy and helping: Considering the consequences of intervention. *Basic and Applied Social Psychology, 16,* 435–453.

Sills, D. L. (1957). *The volunteers.* Glencoe, IL: Free Press.

Simon, H. A. (1990, December 21). A mechanism for social selection and successful altruism. *Science, 250,* 1665–1668.

Skitka, L. J. (1999). Ideological and attributional boundaries on public compassion: Reactions to individuals and communities affected by a natural disaster. *Personality and Social Psychology Bulletin, 25,* 793–808.

Smith, K. D., Keating, J. P., & Stotland, E. (1989). Altruism reconsidered: The effect of denying feedback on a victim's status to empathic witnesses. *Journal of Personality and Social Psychology, 57,* 641–650.

Snyder, M., & Omoto, A. M. (1992). Who helps and why? In S. Spacapan & S. Oskamp (Eds.), *Helping and being helped* (pp. 213–239). Newbury Park, CA: Sage.

Sober, E. (1988). What is evolutionary altruism? [Special Issue] *Journal of Philosophy* [M. Matthen & B. Linsky (Eds.), Philosophy and biology], *14*, 75–100.

Sober, E. (1992). The evolution of altruism: Correlation, cost and benefit. *Biology and Philosophy, 7*, 177–188.

Sober, E., & Wilson, D. S. (1998). *Unto others: The evolution and psychology of unselfish behavior.* Cambridge, MA: Harvard University Press.

Staub, E. (1978). *Positive social behavior and morality: Vol. 1. Social and personal influences.* New York: Academic Press.

Staub, E. (1979). *Positive social behavior and morality: Vol. 2. Socialization and development.* New York: Academic Press.

Staub, E. (1986). A conception of the determinants and development of altruism and aggression: Motives, the self, and the environment. In C. Zahn-Waxler, E. M. Cummings, & R. Ianotti (Eds.), *Altruism and aggression: Biological and social origins* (pp.135–164). Cambridge, England: Cambridge University Press.

Staub, E. (1996). Responsibility, helping, aggression, and evil: Comment. *Psychological Inquiry, 7*, 252–254.

Sterling, B., & Gaertner, S. L. (1984). The attribution of arousal and emergency helping: A bidirectional process. *Journal of Experimental Social Psychology, 20*, 286–296.

Stryker, S. (1980). *Symbolic interactionalism: A social structural version.* Menlo Park, CA: Benjamin/Cummings.

Stukas, A. A., Snyder, M., & Clary, E. G. (1999). The effects of "mandatory volunteerism" on intentions to volunteer. *Psychological Science, 10*, 59–64.

Swinyard, W. R., & Ray, M. L. (1979). Effects of praise and small requests on receptivity to direct-mail appeals. *Journal of Social Psychology, 108*, 177–184.

Thomas, G., & Batson, C. D. (1981). Effect of helping under normative pressure on self-perceived altruism. *Social Psychology Quarterly, 44*, 127–131.

Thomas, G. C., Batson, C. D., & Coke, J. S. (1981). Do Good Samaritans discourage helpfulness? Self-perceived altruism after exposure to highly helpful others. *Journal of Personality and Social Psychology, 40*, 194–200.

Tillman, P. (1998). *In search of moderators of the relationship between antecedents of Organizational Citizenship Behavior and Organizational Citizenship Behavior: The case of motives.* Unpublished master's thesis. University of South Florida.

Trivers, R. L. (1971). The evolution of reciprocal altruism. *Quarterly Review of Biology, 46*, 35–37.

Vaughan, K. B., & Lanzetta, J. T. (1980). Vicarious instigation and conditioning of facial expressive and autonomic responses to a model's expressive display of pain. *Journal of Personality and Social Psychology, 38*, 909–923.

Walster, E., Walster, G. W., & Berscheid, E. (1978). *Equity: Theory and research.* Boston: Allyn & Bacon.

Walton, M. D., Sachs, D., Ellington, R., Hazlewood, A., Griffin, S., & Bass, D. (1988). Physical stigma and the pregnancy role: Receiving help from strangers. *Sex Roles, 18*, 323–331.

Webley, P., & Lea, S. E. G. (1993). The partial unacceptability of money in repayment for neighborly help. *Human Relations, 46*, 65–76.

Weiner, B. (1980). A cognitive (attribution)-emotion-action model of motivated behavior: An analysis of judgments of help-giving. *Journal of Personality and Social Psychology, 39*, 186–200.

Weiner, B. (1986). *An attributional theory of motivation and emotion.* New York: Springer-Verlag.

Weiner, B., Perry, R. P., & Magnusson, J. (1988). An attributional analysis of reactions to stigmas. *Journal of Personality and Social Psychology, 55*, 738–748.

Weismann, R. X., & Galper, J. (1998). The grid. *American Demographics, December*, 46–47.

Williamson, G. M., & Clark, M. S. (1989). Effects of providing help to another and of relationship type on the provider's mood and self-evaluation. *Journal of Personality and Social Psychology, 56*, 722–734.

Williamson, G. M., & Clark, M. S. (1992). Impact of desired relationship type on affective reactions to choosing and being required to help. *Personality and Social Psychology Bulletin, 18,* 10–18.

Wilson, J. P. (1976). Motivation, modeling, and altruism: A person x situation analysis. *Journal of Personality and Social Psychology, 34,* 1078–1086.

Wispé, L. (Ed.). (1978). *Altruism, sympathy, and helping.* New York: Academic Press.

Yinon, Y., & Landau, M. O. (1987). On the reinforcing value of helping behavior in a positive mood. *Motivation and Emotion, 11,* 83–93.

Yousif, Y., & Korte, C. (1995). Urbanization, culture, and helpfulness: Cross-cultural studies in England and the Sudan. *Journal of Cross-Cultural Psychology, 26,* 474–489.

Zahn-Waxler, C., Robinson, J. L., & Emde, R. N. (1992). The development of empathy in twins. *Developmental Psychology, 28,* 1038–1047.

Zajonc, R. B. (1980). Feeling and thinking: Preferences need no inferences. *American Psychologist, 35,* 151–175.

Chapter Eight

The Death and Rebirth of the Social Psychology of Negotiation

Max H. Bazerman, Jared R. Curhan, and Don A. Moore

Introduction

In the 1970s, social psychology was one of the best-represented disciplines in negotiation research (Druckman, 1977; Pruitt, 1981; Rubin & Brown, 1975). Yet, as the social cognitive movement took hold within psychology during the 1980s, the study of negotiations did not fit readily into the changing field and largely disappeared from social psychology. In business schools, by contrast, negotiation was perhaps the fastest growing topic of research in that decade. However, the dominant research perspective of negotiation that emerged during the 1980s was grounded in behavioral decision research and emphasized the systematic and predictable mistakes that negotiators make (i.e., departures from rationality). It left the social variables in negotiations largely unexamined. At the beginning of the twenty-first century, we see the reemergence of the social psychological study of negotiation. This reemergence has been affected profoundly by the behavioral decision theory perspective of the 1980s and 1990s. Yet it also highlights social phenomena that were ignored by investigators with a more cognitive orientation.

In this chapter, we present a brief history of the life and death of negotiation research in social psychology during the 1970s and 1980s as well as the behavioral decision theory perspective that prevailed in business schools during the 1980s and the early 1990s. The

The authors received support for this research from the Dispute Resolution Research Center at Northwestern University, the Dean's office of the J. L. Kellogg Graduate School of Management at Northwestern University, and Faculty Research Support from Harvard Business School. The second author was supported by a National Science Foundation Graduate Research Fellowship. The third author held a visiting position at the Harvard Business School for much of the time spent writing this paper. The paper benefited from excellent feedback obtained from Margaret Clark, Margaret Neale, Susan Rees, Hannah Riley, Rob Robinson, Lee Ross, Katie Shonk, and Leigh Thompson.

chapter also reviews current research heralding the rebirth of the social psychology of negotiations and highlighting important new directions in this area of study.

Negotiations research before 1980

Throughout the 1960s and 1970s, the study of negotiations in social psychology consisted of two main streams of research – the study of individual differences among negotiators and the study of situational factors that facilitate or impede the negotiation process. The dominant psychological research on negotiations emphasized individual difference variables (Rubin & Brown, 1975), including both demographic characteristics (such as gender) and personality variables (such as risk-taking tendencies). Gender, race, age, risk-taking tendencies, locus-of-control, cognitive complexity, tolerance for ambiguity, self-esteem, authoritarianism, and Machiavellianism were all research topics in the 1960s negotiation literature (Lewicki, Weiss, & Lewin, 1988; Neale & Bazerman, 1992; Rubin & Brown, 1975).

Since bargaining is clearly an interpersonal activity, it seems logical that the participants' dispositions should exert significant influence on the process and outcomes of negotiations. However, despite hundreds of studies on individual differences such as those mentioned above, such factors typically do not explain much variance in negotiator behavior (Thompson, 1990). Furthermore, and consistent with findings from the broader field of social psychology (Ross & Nisbett, 1991), slight changes in situational or contextual features often swamp any individual difference effects.

Research on gender differences in negotiation provides a good example of a failed attempt to find individual differences in negotiator behavior. Across hundreds of studies, there has been no consistent evidence to support a main effect for gender differences in negotiator performance (Lewicki, Litterer, Minton, & Saunders, 1999). Thompson (1990) argued that the findings that do support gender effects must be viewed skeptically. She asserted that studies have reported gender differences inconsistently, often as a secondary analysis. The implication is that there may be an even larger number of studies that have never reported findings on gender differences because of the lack of a statistically demonstrable effect. Walters, Stuhlmacher, and Meyer (1998), in their meta-analysis of 62 studies of gender and negotiator competitiveness, concluded that gender differences account for less than 1 percent of the variance in competitiveness. Furthermore, based on a review of 34 research studies conducted since 1975, Watson (1994) asserted that situational factors, such as situational power, are better predictors of negotiation behavior and outcomes than is gender. Walters et al. (1998) concluded: "It appears that even small variations in experimental conditions can eliminate these differences entirely, or more surprisingly, cause them to change direction. Considering all of the factors that shape our decision to be competitive or cooperative in interpersonal bargaining, our gender accounts for but a small fraction" (p. 23).

Although the debate continues (Barry & Friedman, 1998), a number of authors have reached the conclusion that individual differences offer little insight into predicting negotiator behavior and negotiation outcomes (Lewicki et al., 1999; Pruitt & Carnevale, 1993). Lewicki et al. concluded that ". . . there are few significant relationships between personality and negotiation outcomes." Similarly, Hermann and Kogan (1977) argued: "From what is known now, it does not appear that there is any single personality type or characteristic that is directly and clearly linked to success in negotiation." While to have searched and largely not found predictive value in individual difference variables might be considered a discovery unto itself, it is not a particularly rewarding one.

In addition to the lack of predictability of individual difference findings, the individual difference literature also has been criticized for its lack of relevance to practice. Bazerman and Carroll (1987) argued that individual differences are of limited value because of their fixed nature – i.e., they are not under the control of the negotiator. Of course, one could argue that knowing both the personal characteristics of one's counterpart and the effects of those characteristics might have practical implications. However, individuals, even so-called experts, are known to be poor at making clinical assessments about another person's personality in order to accurately formulate an opposing strategy (Bazerman, 1998; Morris, Larrick, & Su, 1998; Morris, Leung, & Sethi, 1998). Cultural differences in negotiation may be an exception to this generalization in that an understanding of such differences might help negotiators formulate strategies (Bazerman, Curhan, Moore, & Valley, 2000).

The second stream of research on negotiation in social psychology during the 1960s and 1970s was the study of situational variables, or relatively fixed, contextual components that define a negotiation. In the language of game theory, situational characteristics define the game. Situational factors include the presence or absence of a constituency (Druckman, 1967), the form of communication between negotiators (Wichman, 1970), the outcome payoffs available to the negotiators (Axelrod & May, 1968), the relative power of the parties (Marwell, Ratcliff, & Schmitt, 1969), deadlines (Pruitt & Drews, 1969), the number of people representing each side (Marwell & Schmitt, 1972), and the effects of third parties (Pruitt & Johnson, 1972). Research on situational variables has contributed to our understanding of the negotiation process and has directed both practitioners and academics to consider important structural components of negotiations. For example, the presence of observers has been shown to produce greater advocacy on behalf of previously announced positions (Lamm & Kogan, 1970) and to foster a more competitive bargaining atmosphere (Vidmar, 1971).

However, from an applied perspective, research on situational factors shares a critical shortcoming with research on individual differences. Situational factors represent aspects of the negotiation that are usually beyond the control of an individual negotiator. Drawing upon the example above, politicians cannot wish away the presence of their constituents. In organizational settings, participants' control over third-party intervention is limited by their willingness to make the dispute publicly visible. If and when the participants do make their disputes public, their managers typically are the ones who determine how and when to intervene (Murnighan, 1986; Pinkley, Brittain, Neale, & Northcraft, 1995). This lack of control applies to other situational factors as well, such as the relative power of the negotiators and prevailing deadlines. While negotiators can be advised to identify ways in which to manipulate their perceived power, obvious power disparities that result from resource munificence, hierarchical legitimacy, or expertise are less malleable. Negotiators are often best served by developing strategies for addressing these power differentials instead of trying to change them.

Our view is that negotiation is most usefully studied from an interpretive perspective. Consistent with social psychology's principle of construal (Nisbett & Ross, 1980; Ross & Nisbett, 1991), we believe that the effects of objective, external aspects of a situation depend on the way the negotiator perceives these features and uses those perceptions to interpret and screen information. This view follows directly from the work of Kelley and

Thibaut (1978), who suggested that negotiators psychologically transform the structure of the negotiation to create the "effective" game that is to be played. The 1960s and 1970s situational research in the negotiation literature suffered from a prescriptive void because it failed to consider this interpretive process.

In summary, the dominant social psychological approaches of the 1960s and 1970s research suffered from critical shortcomings. The individual difference literature from hundreds of studies yielded few consistent findings and thus failed to produce a compelling theory of negotiator behavior that could move the field ahead. The situational literature did not consider the importance of the negotiator's construal in interpreting the negotiation situation. Both literatures were limited in their practical usefulness by a prescriptive silence because they focused on aspects of the process that are beyond the negotiator's control. Moreover, these characteristics of the negotiation field proved inconsistent with the social cognitive movement in social psychology. Thus, in the 1980s and early 1990s, the study of negotiation lost its social psychological focus.

The behavioral decision theory perspective

During the 1980s, scholars in business schools, perhaps influenced by the social cognitive movement, began to recognize ways in which the expanding body of research on decision making might inform negotiation theory. If the typical negotiator is confronted with a situation and an opponent, and has relatively little power to change either one, then the only important feature of the negotiation situation that is routinely within the negotiator's control is how he or she makes decisions. The marriage of negotiation and decision-making research meant that individual axioms of decision making could be applied to negotiation research, lending theoretical rigor to the study of negotiation. Thus, the dominant perspective practiced by negotiation researchers became behavioral decision theory.

Decision researchers from various disciplines have offered a variety of theoretical perspectives on how to improve decision making (Bell, Raiffa, & Tversky, 1989). One aspect that differentiates these perspectives is the descriptive/prescriptive distinction. Behavioral researchers (e.g., psychologists, sociologists, and organizational behaviorists) tend to focus on describing how people *actually* make decisions, while more analytic fields (e.g., economics and decision analysis) typically prescribe how people *ought* to make decisions. Unfortunately, too little interaction has occurred between the descriptive and prescriptive camps.

A central premise of our perspective is that the most useful model of negotiation, and the individual decision making that occurs within it, will include both description and prescription (Lax & Sebenius, 1986). Raiffa made an important theoretical connection between these two camps when he advocated an "asymmetrically prescriptive/descriptive" approach (1982). This approach describes how decision analysis can be used to help individual negotiators ("asymmetric") predict the behavior of their counterparts ("descriptive") and then develop appropriate strategies to deal with those behaviors ("prescriptive").

Raiffa's work represents a turning point in negotiation research for a number of reasons. First, in the context of a prescriptive model, he explicitly acknowledged the importance of developing accurate descriptions of the opponent, rather than assuming the opponent to be fully rational. Second, his realization that negotiators need advice implicitly acknowledges that negotiators themselves do not intuitively follow purely rational strategies. Most importantly, Raiffa initiated the groundwork for dialogue between prescriptive and descriptive researchers. The focal negotiator must use descriptive models to anticipate the likely behavior of the opponent but must also rely on prescriptive advice to overcome his or her own decision biases.

Recently, Bazerman and Neale (1992; Bazerman, 1998; Neale & Bazerman, 1991) and Thompson (1990, 1998) introduced a body of research that addresses some of the questions that Raiffa's work left unexamined. For example, if the negotiator and his or her opponent do not act rationally, what systematic departures from rationality can be predicted? Building on work in behavioral decision theory, a number of deviations from rationality that can be expected in negotiations have been identified. Specifically, research on two-party negotiations suggests that negotiators tend to: (1) be inappropriately affected by the positive or negative frame in which risks are viewed (Bazerman, Magliozzi, & Neale, 1985); (2) anchor their number estimates in negotiations on irrelevant information (Northcraft & Neale, 1987; Tversky & Kahneman, 1974); (3) rely too heavily on readily available information (Neale, 1984); (4) be overconfident about the likelihood of attaining outcomes that favor themselves (Bazerman & Neale, 1982); (5) assume that negotiation tasks are necessarily fixed-sum and thereby miss opportunities for mutually beneficial trade-offs between the parties (Bazerman et al., 1985); (6) escalate commitment to a previously selected course of action when it is no longer the best alternative (Bazerman & Neale, 1983; Diekmann, Tenbrunsel, Shah, Schroth, & Bazerman, 1996); (7) overlook the valuable information that can be obtained by considering the opponent's cognitive perspective (Bazerman & Carroll, 1987; Samuelson & Bazerman, 1985); and (8) reactively devalue any concession that is made by the opponent (Ross & Stillinger, 1991).

The primary contribution that prescriptive models make to descriptive research is to provide a benchmark of optimality. Indeed, the growth and expansion of behavioral decision research has been fueled by the usefulness of performance standards based on perfect rationality, against which actual performance can be compared (Kahneman, Slovic, & Tversky, 1982) and improved (Bazerman, 1998).

In sum, the negotiation research of the 1980s and early 1990s was largely influenced by a behavioral decision theory perspective. This new perspective, informed by Raiffa's "asymmetrically prescriptive/descriptive" approach (1982), prompted a large body of research that outlines systematic departures from rationality in negotiator cognition. Thus, recent descriptive research informs a prescriptive approach by providing necessary information on the impediments to individual rationality.

The rebirth of negotiations research in social psychology

While the behavioral decision perspective has had a significant influence on the scholarship and practice of negotiation, it missed several key social components that are critical to the practical task of negotiating more effectively. In recent years, research has incorporated these missing social factors within the behavioral decision perspective. In the remainder of this chapter we review this set of previously underrepresented topics in the social psychological study of negotiation. Specifically, we focus on work dealing with social relationships, egocentrism, attribution and construal processes, motivated illusions, and emotion. Importantly, we examine this research within the context of a descriptive/prescriptive, decision perspective, highlighting how social factors can create shortcomings that need to be managed.

Social Relationships in Negotiation

Although the importance of relationships in negotiation has been cited repeatedly throughout the history of the negotiation field (e.g., Rubin & Brown, 1975; Rubin, Pruitt, & Kim, 1994; Walton & McKersie, 1965), the late 1980s and early 1990s, in particular, have witnessed a proliferation of studies on the topic (for reviews, see Greenhalgh & Chapman, 1996; Valley, Neale, & Mannix, 1995). The majority of these studies are influenced by the prescriptively descriptive focus of the behavioral decision theory perspective.

For the most part, the study of relationships and negotiation has occurred within three basic domains – the individual, the dyad, and the network. The first domain includes studies of how the judgments and preferences of individual negotiators are influenced by their social context (e.g., Clark, Mills, & Corcoran, 1989; Messick & Sentis, 1985; Morgan & Sawyer, 1967; Polzer, Neale, & Glenn, 1993; Thompson, Valley, & Kramer, 1995; for a review, see Clark & Chrisman, 1994). The second domain explores how social relationships within dyads can influence negotiation processes and outcomes (e.g., Greenhalgh & Chapman, 1996; Halpern, 1992, 1994, 1997a, 1997b; Schoeninger & Wood, 1969; Thompson & DeHarpport, 1990, 1998; for a review, see Valley et al., 1995). Finally, the third domain is concerned with the influence of relationships on the functioning of organizational networks (e.g., Baker, 1984, 1990; Halpern, 1996; Shah & Jehn, 1993; Sondak & Bazerman, 1989; Valley, 1992). Each of these domains is further described below, with a particular focus on the ways in which social relationships help or hinder the negotiation process.

Influence of relationships on the judgment and preferences of individual negotiators

There is evidence to support the argument that individual negotiators evaluate their own outcomes relative to outcomes obtained by their counterparts (Loewenstein, Thompson, & Bazerman, 1989; Thompson et al., 1995). For example, Loewenstein et al. found that disputants' preferences for hypothetical monetary payoffs are greatly influenced by payoffs to their hypothetical counterparts. Disputants generally were found to prefer equal payoffs to unequal payoffs, even when unequal payoffs slightly favored themselves. Such a socially influenced preference structure has been called "social utility" (Loewenstein et al., 1989; Messick & Sentis, 1979). However, when participants were instructed to imagine a negative relationship with their counterparts, they prefered inequality that favored themselves. This result suggests that the impact of social utility on negotiator preferences depends on the relationships among negotiators.

There has been some controversy over which distribution rule, in general, governs interactions that occur in close relationships (Clark & Chrisman, 1994). The controversy has centered on three rules in particular: equity, equality, and need (Deutsch, 1975). The question not only concerns which rule is followed, but also which rule tends to be preferred by individuals in close relationships.

Studies using self-reports from intimate couples have found that serious marital relationships tend to be characterized by equity (i.e. proportionality between contributions and benefits) rather than equality (i.e. absolute equality of benefits) (Sabatelli & Cecil-Pigo, 1985; Utne, Hatfield, Traupmann, & Greenberger, 1984). However, a number of laboratory studies (e.g., Austin, 1980; Greenberg, 1983a; Morgan & Sawyer, 1967; Polzer et al., 1993; Thompson et al., 1995) have found the opposite result: namely that equality is preferred over equity in close relationships. For example, Austin (1980) had participants allocate $5 between themselves and a stranger or a roommate (presumably representing a close personal tie) after receiving false feedback on a word-find task. Strangers were guided primarily by self-interest, allocating the money equally when they believed they had done poorly on the task and equitably when they believed they had done well on the task. Roommates, on the other hand, almost always divided the money equally regardless of differences in task performance.

Clark and Chrisman (1994) argue that these two seemingly contradictory perspectives – equity and equality – can be reconciled through the principle of need (i.e. proportionality between exigency and benefits). The studies supporting the use of an equity allocation rule are based on correlation between self-reported measures, making them subject to a great number of alternative explanations. Studies that have found support for the equality rule typically do not provide participants with information about needs, leaving participants to apply the equality rule as a reasonable substitute for need (Clark & Chrisman, 1994).

A study by Sondak, Pinkley, and Neale (1994) supports Clark and Chrisman's (1994) assertion. Sondak et al. manipulated the scarcity of a jointly held resource and found that, while strangers often use an equity rule in their negotiations, roommates allocate according to equality when resources are available but according to need when resources are scarce. Therefore, an equality rule seems to be used by roommates only in the absence of information about needs. Whenever roommates' needs are made salient, they allocate according to need.

When compared against a standard of rationality, allocation according to need may appear to demand undue concessions on the part of less needy parties. However, this conclusion ignores the inter-temporal nature of a long-term relationship and the possibility of integrative trade-offs over time (Mannix, Tinsley, & Bazerman, 1995). For example, Clark and Chrisman described need-based allocation in the context of an ongoing intimate relationship: "Each person should benefit the other in response to that other's needs without expecting specific repayments but reasonably expecting the other to be responsive to his/her needs if and when those needs arise and if the other has the ability to do so" (1994, p. 75).

Influence of relationships on negotiation processes and outcomes within dyads

In the previous section, we described research on how individuals evaluate and apply distribution rules within social relationships. Inherent in this approach is the assumption that the preferences and actions of individuals, at least to some degree, influence negotiations. However, Bazerman, Gibbons, Thompson, and Valley (1998) argued that certain behaviors that appear irrational from the individual perspective may be rational from the perspective of the dyad. For example, given the opportunity to communicate freely, negotiators often appear irrational in their individual decision making yet reach dyadic outcomes that *outperform* game theoretic models (Valley, Moag, & Bazerman, 1998, Bazerman et al., 1998). That is, individuals negotiating face-to-face routinely divulge more high-quality information than a prescriptive analysis would say they should (i.e., individuals do not fully exploit each other), however, because of the nature of the simulation (cf., Akerlof, 1970), such revelation makes profitable agreement possible for both parties where it would not otherwise be. Consequently, an alternative approach to the study of relationships and negotiation is to view the *dyad* and its relationship as the critical unit of analysis (Greenhalgh & Chapman, 1995). In this tradition, researchers have asked how the relationship within a dyad influences that dyad's joint process and outcome.

A substantial number of studies have examined whether close relationships (social, collegial, or romantic) help or hinder dyadic negotiations. Although one might expect that close relationships would *improve* the overall quality of negotiations, the results of studies suggest that effects of relationships on negotiations are quite complex (Valley et al.,1995). In terms of negotiation process, close relationships are associated with more information sharing (Fry, Firestone, & Williams, 1983; Greenhalgh & Chapman, 1996), less coercive behavior (Fry et al., 1983; Greenhalgh & Chapman, 1996), less demanding initial offers (Halpern, 1992, 1994, 1997a, 1997b; Schoeninger & Wood, 1969; Thompson & DeHarport, 1998), and faster completion of agreements (Schoeninger & Wood, 1969). However, most studies indicate that close dyadic relationships do *not* directly improve joint outcomes (Greenhalgh & Chapman, 1996; Thompson & DeHarport, 1990, 1998).

In fact, in some cases, close relationships may contribute to a *reduction* in joint outcomes (Fry et al., 1983; Schoeninger & Wood, 1969). For example, Fry et al. compared the performance results of 74 dating couples with 32 mixed-sex stranger dyads on a three-issue negotiation simulation with integrative potential. Although dating couples exchange more truthful information and engage in less contentious behavior, they reach less integrative final agreements (i.e., lower joint profit; Pruitt, 1983). This effect is strongest for couples who rate themselves as highest on Rubin's love scale (1970) – i.e., couples who are defensive or possessive in their orientation toward one another.

Data from studies on the impact of close relationships on negotiation among dyads seems inconsistent until one considers that relationships are defined differently across studies – some studies used participants who were friends or colleagues while other studies used romantic partners. In their 1995 review of the relationships and negotiation literature, Valley, Neale, and Mannix noted that the few studies finding a reduction in integrativeness among close dyads (Fry et al., 1983; Schoeninger & Wood, 1969) used *lovers*, rather than friends, as participants. Therefore, Valley et al. (1995) proposed a curvilinear model to describe the association between relationship closeness and outcome integrativeness, suggesting that strangers and lovers fare worse than friends and colleagues. However, no study has demonstrated that friends and colleagues reach better joint outcomes than do strangers. The reason for this may lie in the nature of the outcomes measurable by conventional negotiation simulations. As Valley et al. explain: "Two friends coming to a laboratory to negotiate an artificial scenario cannot be expected to find the issues in the negotiation as important as maintaining their actual relationship" (1995, p. 87).

This explanation for the lack of association between relationship closeness and integrativeness is supported by research on the moderating effects of pressures to reach a *good* agreement. Ben-Yoav and Pruitt (1984) found that when participants are encouraged to have high aspirations, those who are led to expect cooperative future interaction achieve more integrative outcomes than do those who are not. Conversely, when participants are not encouraged to have high aspirations, expectations of future interaction are associated with less integrative outcomes. To the extent that anticipation of presumably cooperative future interaction is a feature of close relationships (Greenhalgh & Chapman, 1996; Greenhalgh & Gilkey, 1993), these findings suggest that high aspirations might be the key to realizing the benefits of friendly and collegial relationships. If supported by future research, this notion qualifies Valley et al.'s (1995) theory of the curvilinear relationship between closeness and integrativeness.

Influence of relationships on the functioning of organizational networks

Many contexts involve the availability of multiple potential negotiation partners. Therefore, a substantial body of research has addressed the question of how relationships influence negotiations in networks. For example, social networks have been found to predict stock market trading patterns (Baker, 1990), market ties between corporations (Baker, 1984), organizational allocations within a newspaper newsroom (Valley, 1992), and business relationships among senior real estate agents (Halpern, 1996).

While the existence of friendships within pre-existing small groups has been found to produce efficient decision-making and motor skills (Shah & Jehn, 1993), larger groups tend to be less efficient (Roth, 1982; Sondak & Bazerman, 1989, 1991), particularly when their member-to-member matching patterns are influenced by social relationships (Tenbrunsel, Wade-Benzoni, Moag, & Bazerman, 1998). Just as negotiator dyads in especially close relationships might choose to preserve their long-term relationships by making concessions rather than painstakingly searching for the most fully integrative outcomes, so too do individuals "satisfice" (March & Simon, 1958) by making deals with people they already know rather than seeking out new partners (Tenbrunsel et al., 1998).

Tenbrunsel et al. simulated a real estate market and examined the influence of pre-existing relationships. The results of their experiment demonstrate not only the clear sub-optimality of negotiators' partner selection (or "matching") process, but also how this sub-optimality is greatest when social relationships guide negotiator partner selection. In a follow-up study involving a more qualitative analysis, Tenbrunsel et al. determined a number of reasons why negotiators are influenced by social relationships, even though their doing so leads to sub-optimality. First, participants unwittingly abbreviate their partner-search activity in favor of matching with a person with whom they have a close personal tie. As in the dyad studies, negotiators place a value on non-scored factors such as fairness, trust, exchange of information, and ease of transaction. However, giving weight to these criteria does not pay off monetarily in terms of the actual negotiations. Instead, negotiators who deal with persons with whom they have close ties are more modest in their reservation prices and aspiration levels. In other words, in an attempt to enhance non-monetary payoffs such as friendship or ease of transaction, negotiators often search for negotiation partners with whom they share personal relationships, even when such partnering preferences reduce their expected monetary payoff.

Summary

Taken together, these three domains of research provide converging evidence of the potential positive *and* negative impact of relationships on negotiations. The literature on networks suggests that negotiators place value on the non-monetary benefits of relationships, leading to sub-optimal matching from a standpoint of monetary concerns and point payoffs (Tenbrunsel et al., 1998). However, research on dyadic interaction provides a potential alternative explanation for this apparent lack of rationality. That is, especially when pressures to reach good outcomes are weak (Ben-Yoav & Pruitt, 1984), dyads in laboratory studies are likely to prioritize maintaining or improving their real relationships over the substance of hypothetical role-play situations (Valley et al., 1995). Moreover, the tendency for dyads to achieve low joint outcomes could be a result of their reliance on the need rule (Sondak et al., 1994). Such use of the need rule, while seemingly irrational in one-shot negotiations, might prove to facilitate inter-temporal logrolling or integrativeness *across* negotiations (Mannix et al., 1995).

Egocentrism in Negotiation

Whether or not they have close relationships with their negotiating partners, negotiators care about fairness. Indeed, fairness arguments play powerful roles in negotiation (Loewenstein et al., 1989; Messick & Sentis, 1979, 1985; Roth & Murnighan, 1982), even when enforcing standards of fairness results in a reduction of material payoffs to the individual (Loewenstein, Babcock, Issacharoff, & Camerer, 1993). However, as we shall see below, ambiguities in determining what is fair make room for egocentric or self-serving interpretations of fairness.

Evidence on egocentrism in negotiation

Walster, Walster, and Berscheid (1978) proposed that parties' interest in fairness is not purely objective, but that people may tend to overweigh the interpretations or fairness rules that favor themselves (see Diekmann, Samuels, Ross, & Bazerman, 1997). The result is that even though people display a preference for fairness, the desire for fairness in negotiated outcomes is easily biased in their own favor (for recent reviews, see Babcock & Loewenstein, 1997; Wade-Benzoni, Tenbrunsel, & Bazerman, 1997). This self-serving bias in assessment or interpretation has been referred to in the literature as egocentrism.

Thompson and Loewenstein (1992) found evidence of egocentrism in reports of fairness, and that egocentrism reduced negotiators' ability to come to agreement. In their first experiment, a negotiation over wages, participants played the role of either management or union. Participants in both roles prepared with the same case information. Before the negotiation, but after receiving their role assignments, parties were asked what they believed a fair outcome to be. These estimates were egocentrically biased: representatives of the union tended to believe that a higher wage was fairer, whereas representatives of management tended to report that a lower wage was fairer. Parties then proceeded to trade bids until they converged on an agreement. Delay was costly to both parties because it meant that the union would go on strike. Thompson and Loewenstein found that the amount of egocentric bias displayed in these pre-negotiation assessments of fairness predicted the length of time it would take parties to reach agreement. The greater egocentricity seen in the partie's *ex ante* perceptions of fairness, the longer strikes tended to last. (See also replications by Babcock, Loewenstein, Issacharoff, & Camerer, 1995; Camerer & Loewenstein, 1993, Loewenstein et al., 1993.)

In their second experiment, Thompson and Loewenstein varied the amount of information provided to participants. Some participants received only the bare facts about the case, whereas others received detailed background information that had been rated as "neutral" in pre-testing. It might be expected that more information should reduce uncertainty and facilitate agreement (Priest & Klein, 1984). However, Thompson and Loewenstein found that more information is associated with greater egocentrism. Those participants who received the background information tended to make more extreme self-serving estimates of a fair outcome (see also Camerer & Loewenstein, 1993). Furthermore, when participants were later tested for recall of the background information, they showed a self-serving recall bias in their tendency to best remember those facts that favored themselves. This self-serving recall effect has been replicated elsewhere (Camerer & Loewenstein, 1993; Loewenstein et al., 1993), and suggests that memory biases contribute to egocentrism during either encoding or retrieval.

Babcock et al. (1995) provided a clever demonstration of the biasing effect of self-interest on the encoding of information. The investigators varied the point at which the participants in the experiment learned which negotiation role they were to play. In particular, all participants received the same case background information, but some read it knowing their roles while others read it without knowing their roles. The results of this subtle manipulation were dramatic. Parties who know their roles before they read the case materials are four times as likely to reach impasse as are dyads who do not know their roles when they read that information. Those who know their roles from the outset also are significantly more egocentric both in their estimations of a fair solution and in their predictions of what a judge will determine to be the just outcome.

Participants in the studies cited here did not make their fairness judgments public. As such, these judgments could not be expected by the parties to influence the other participants' negotiation behavior and thus were unlikely to be "strategic misrepresentations." However, two studies (Babcock et al., 1995; Loewenstein et al., 1993) offered a specific incentive for participants to be accurate in these private fairness judgments. Participants were told that the individual whose fairness assessments came closest to the determinations of an objective third party would be given an extra cash award. This incentive did not eliminate egocentrism in participants' interpretations of fairness, suggesting that their fairness reports reflect actual beliefs.

Wade-Benzoni, Tenbrunsel, and Bazerman (1996) extended this work on egocentrism to a four-party social dilemma. All participants in their experiment were given identical information to prepare for the negotiation and were asked to report, both before and after negotiation, what they believed to be a fair allocation of limited resources among the four parties. The investigators report two important findings. First, communication reduces egocentrism, a result that replicates Thompson and Loewenstein's (1992) finding that disputants' interpretations of fairness are significantly closer after negotiation than before. Second, asymmetry in available payoffs increases egocentrism. When the four parties face identical payoffs, they tend to share common perceptions of fairness; when payoffs are varied among the four parties, perceptions of fairness are divergent. This finding replicates the highly consistent pattern observed elsewhere (Babcock & Olson, 1992; Camerer & Loewenstein, 1993; Diekmann, 1997; Diekmann et al., 1997; Messick & Sentis, 1983) that ambiguity in problem solving creates an opening in the decision-making process in which egocentrism can develop via differential interpretation of the facts and application of the relevant fairness rules.

Consequences of egocentrism in negotiation

A number of researchers have used egocentric interpretations of fairness to explain the vexing problem of impasse in negotiation (Babcock & Loewenstein, 1997; Babcock et al., 1995; Babcock & Olson, 1992; de Dreu, Nauta, & van de Vliert, 1995; Thompson & Loewenstein, 1992). Evidence on egocentrism can help account for why disputants pay the high costs of strikes, litigation, delay, stalemate, and deadlock, despite strong incentives to reach agreement. If both parties seek a fair outcome, yet their self-serving interpretations of fairness are incommensurable, the ironic result is that negotiators may impasse despite a positive bargaining zone and motivation to be fair (Babcock & Loewenstein, 1997; Drolet, Larrick, & Morris, 1998; Thompson & Loewenstein, 1992).

There are two ways to understand how this clash could result in impasse. First, self-serving interpretations of fairness may result in an equitable agreement being perceived as unfair and exploitative. Perceptions of exploitation by another party may give rise to a desire for vengeance. The resulting motivation to punish the opponent for unfair behavior can lead to rejection of otherwise profitable agreements. This motive can be seen most clearly in ultimatum bargaining experiments where recipients reject profitable offers they perceive to be unfair (Ochs & Roth, 1989; Pillutla & Murnighan, 1996). Blount (1995) has shown that uneven allocations are more likely to be accepted when they are simply uneven (generated by a random device) than when they are unfair (generated by a person who benefits from the unevenness).

A second, simpler way to understand how egocentrism leads to impasse is to assume that negotiators have a utility for fairness – that they would prefer a moderately profitable, but equal, alternative to a highly profitable alternative involving inequality that favors the other side. Data supporting this point of view come from work on social utility (Loewenstein et al., 1989; Messick & Sentis, 1985) – people care very much about how their outcomes compare with others' and they display a powerful disutility for disadvantageous inequality (Neale & Bazerman, 1991). In negotiation, social utility may be magnified because negotiator aspirations tend to mirror their fairness judgments (Drolet et al., 1998). In this way, egocentric interpretations of fairness can lead to unrealistic aspirations, which in turn are likely to increase contentious behavior and delay settlement. De Dreu, Nauta, and van de Vliert (1995) offered correlational evidence from actual negotiations, suggesting that egocentric evaluations are associated with escalation of conflict. The cumulative result of these effects is that impasses exact high costs from individuals, businesses, and societies (Pruitt, Rubin, & Kim, 1994).

The practical question is, how can egocentrism be reduced? Bazerman and Neale (1982) were able to successfully debias negotiators by providing them with facts about overconfidence and egocentrism in negotiation. Thus, negotiators may inoculate themselves against egocentric biases by learning about their dangers. While some have argued that egocentrism may help negotiators claim value, we advise negotiators to strive to obtain the most accurate perceptions possible. One may certainly choose a contentious strategy or an extreme bargaining position, but negotiators are best prepared when they have the best information. Critics of research on egocentrism have argued that these effects are likely to be exaggerated in a laboratory situation with minimal context and naïve negotiators. However, others have found the familiar pattern of self-serving biases and egocentrism in real conflicts involving experienced professionals (Babcock & Olson, 1992; Babcock, Wang, & Loewenstein, 1996), including professional negotiators (de Dreu, Nauta, & van de Vliert, 1995). Indeed, evidence suggests that the more a partisan is involved in and cares about a dispute, the more biased he or she is likely to be (Thompson, 1995).

Motivational forces

Although some have argued that egocentrism can arise through unbiased psychological processes (Ross & Sicoly, 1979), the data presented here clearly suggest motivated processing. The general pattern of motivational forces that emerges from studies of fairness in negotiation is that individuals behave as if they are attempting to maximize a complex function made up of three variables of concern. First, people obviously care about their own outcomes. Diekmann (1997) argued that self-interest is a ubiquitous motivation, and that it will tend to bias all judgments in which the decision maker holds a stake. Messick and Sentis (1983) proposed that preferences are basic and immediate, but that we must determine through reflection what is fair, and that this process is vulnerable to bias. When the situation becomes more complex, fairness becomes ambiguous (Messick & Sentis, 1983), and parties in a dispute tend to interpret fairness and invoke fairness rules in ways that favor themselves (de Dreu, 1996; Diekmann et al., 1997; Messick & Sentis, 1979).

Second, people work to manage the way they are perceived by others. It is desirable to be perceived as fair by others (Greenberg, 1990). Diekmann (1997) found that people tend to reach egocentric fairness judgments and allocate accordingly when they are allocating in private. Egocentrism is eliminated, however, in public allocations to the self.

Third, people work to manage their own self-perceptions. People prefer to imagine themselves to be fair, even generous (Greenberg, 1990; Messick, Bloom, Boldizar, & Samuelson, 1985). By having some of his participants make allocation decisions in a room filled with mirrors, Greenberg (1983b) heightened self-awareness and demonstrated the importance of self perception in egocentrism. While participants assigned to the no-mirror control group evaluate disadvantageous inequality as more unfair than the same inequality when it favors them, those participants who are made self-aware by being in a room filled with mirrors do not exhibit this egocentric bias in their fairness judgments.

Summary

While fairness concerns play an important role in negotiation, partisans tend to offer ego-centric assessments of fairness, even when the assessments are private and therefore not motivated by any conscious strategic intent (Loewenstein et al., 1993). Ambiguity and information richness make room for biased interpretations of fairness (Thompson & Loewenstein, 1992), which can occur through differential weighting of available informa-tion (Diekmann et al., 1997) or selective encoding and retrieval (Babcock et al., 1995). Egocentrism grows from individuals' tendency to be self-interested (Messick & Sentis, 1983), but it is moderated by the desire to appear fair both to themselves (Greenberg, 1983b) and to others (Diekmann, 1997).

Attributions and Construal in Negotiation

Two reasons why negotiation outcomes deviate from the predictions of classical game theory are the attributions negotiators make about their counterparts and the construals negotiators form about their situations. While the literature on attributions in negotiation is quite broad, in this section we review only literature that relates directly to the behavioral decision perspective outlined earlier. As a result, we omit a number of significant contribu-tions that do not meet this criterion (e.g., Baron, 1985, 1988, 1990a; Betancourt & Blair, 1992; Bies, Shapiro, & Cummings, 1988; Bradbury & Fincham, 1990; de Dreu, Carnevale, Emans, & van de Vliert, 1994, 1995; Forgas, 1994; Friedland, 1990; Johnson & Rule, 1986; Kette, 1986; Lord & Smith, 1983).

Attributions negotiators make about their counterparts

Work by Robinson and colleagues has shown that partisans to conflict tend to exhibit a false polarization effect. That is, they exaggerate the distance between opposing groups in a conflict. Robinson, Keltner, Ward, and Ross (1995) demonstrated this false polarization effect on a variety of social and political issues (Keltner & Robinson, 1996; Robinson et al., 1995; Robinson & Keltner, 1996). For example, participants, who had identified them-selves as either pro-life or pro-choice, responded to a variety of questions surveying their own attitudes about abortion, as well as the attitudes they believed to be held by the aver-age pro-life or pro-choice advocate. The results clearly demonstrate that participants over-estimate the degree of ideological difference between themselves and their opponents and caricature their ideological opponents as being more extreme than they actually are.

Participants even perceive their *own* group as being more extreme than it actually is. Moreover, this effect is exacerbated for groups that represent the more powerful status quo position (Robinson & Keltner, 1997).

In a similar vein, Kramer (1994) found participants remarkably ready to attribute sinister motivations to others when the basis for their behavior is ambiguous. Kelley (1972) has argued that disputants readily attribute the causes of others' behavior to malevolent ulterior motives where such explanations are plausible. Benign explanations for behavior that are provided by the opponent will be discounted to the extent that more sinister explanations are plausible (Robinson & Friedman, 1995). If parties attribute to their opponents more extreme positions than their opponents actually hold, conflict resolution becomes more difficult (Robinson et al., 1995). Both Kramer's sinister attribution error and Robinson and Keltner's false polarization increase the likelihood that disputants will assume that their interests are opposed, even when they are not (Thompson & Hrebec, 1996). Such attributions are likely to engender blame and hostility that make agreement difficult (Keltner & Robinson, 1993).

What prescriptions can be offered to the negotiator? Rubin et al. (1994) expressed pessimism about the ability of negotiators to counteract the effects of attributional conflict. They argued that selective perceptions will limit the opportunities for parties to correct sinister and fanatical attributions of opponents in three ways. First, partisans tend to be biased in their evaluation of behaviors by the disputants (Hastorf & Cantril, 1954; Oskamp, 1965). Second, confirmation biases in the search for information about other parties magnifies the likelihood that disputants will only reconfirm their prior suspicions (Snyder & Swann, 1978). Third, evidence on attributional distortion has shown that, consistent with the fundamental attribution error (Ross, 1977), people are more likely to attribute opponents' behavior to stable aspects of their personalities than to situational pressures (Morris, Larrick, & Su, 1998), especially when behavioral evidence confirms prior beliefs about the disposition of the opponent. Disconfirming behavioral evidence is more likely to be attributed to situational pressures (Hayden & Mischel, 1976; Regan, Straus, & Fazio, 1974).

Consistent with this logic, Kramer found that careful reflection did not ameliorate the tendency to commit the sinister attribution error. On the contrary, Kramer found that both self consciousness and rumination *increase* the tendency to ascribe malevolent motivations to others (Kramer, 1994). Fortunately, the data on attenuating false polarization offer more hope. Keltner and Robinson (1993) found that when both negotiators disclose their ideological views in a non-contentious way prior to negotiation, outcomes are more complete and more integrative. Qualifying these results, subsequent research by Puccio and Ross (1998) found that disclosure of one's own views is less effective at reducing false polarization than describing the "most legitimate and convincing" arguments on the other side.

Negotiators' construals of their situations

Just as negotiators make attributions about their counterparts, so do they form interpretations or construals about their situations. The principle of situationism in social psychology (Lewin, 1935) asserts that seemingly insignificant aspects of situations can represent potent forces in determining individual behavior. Negotiators not only see and act in biased ways, they misattribute the source of this bias to the malevolence or extremism of the other side rather than the more mundane tendency for people to construe the world in light of their expectations and self-interest (Ross & Ward, 1996). However, as stated earlier, the 1960s and 1970s negotiation literature failed to consider the negotiator's interpretive construal process (Kelley & Thibaut, 1978; Nisbett & Ross, 1980; Ross & Nisbett, 1991). A negotiator responds not only to objective features of his or her situation, but also to his or her *construal* of those features.

One way to study negotiators' construal processes is to examine their pre-existing modes of viewing conflict situations. For example, Pinkley and Northcraft (1994) studied the degree to which individual conflict frames, measured prior to negotiation (Pinkley, 1990), predicted negotiation behavior. Both task orientation (i.e., lack of concern for relationship) and cooperative frame (i.e., lack of competitiveness) are associated with higher individual and joint profit. Although certainly intriguing, the results of this study are correlational, and therefore subject to a number of alternative explanations.

Other studies have mitigated such alternative explanations by *manipulating*, rather than measuring, conflict frame. Ross and Samuels (1993) found that the behavior of participants in a prisoner's dilemma game could be drastically influenced by the name assigned to that game. Participants who played "The Community Game," cooperated approximately twice as frequently as participants who played the identical game entitled "The Wall Street Game" (Ross & Ward, 1995). A similar study by Larrick and Blount (1997) found that manipulating the presentation of an ultimatum game influences the behavior of participants. When the identically structured game is described as a social dilemma (mutual "claiming" of a shared resource) rather than an ultimatum game (a "proposed division" followed by "accepting" or "rejecting"), those who propose the division ("first movers") are more generous in their allocations and those who "accept" or "reject" the division ("second movers") are more tolerant of inequalities that favor the other player. In fact, second movers are approximately three times more likely to accept allocations of zero for themselves when the game is described as a social dilemma ("claiming") rather than an ultimatum game ("rejecting"/"accepting") (Larrick & Blount, 1997).

Still other studies have examined whether these patterns generalize from decision games like the prisoner's dilemma game and the ultimatum game to negotiations (Bottom & Paese, 1997; O'Connor & Adams, 1998; Thompson & DeHarpport, 1998). The results seem to depend on specific features of the manipulations. For example, those for whom a negotiation task is framed as problem solving ("two people face a common problem") rather than as bargaining ("each person is trying to get what he or she wants") are found to expect higher individual profit, more cooperation, and a more collaborative process yielding a fairer outcome. However, the problem-solving task frame does not correlate with actual outcomes (Thompson & DeHarpport, 1998).

In contrast, O'Connor and Adams (1998) found that framing the negotiation task as a joint search for the one and only solution to a problem, or framing it as a negotiation situation in which both parties are trying to reach agreement, influences both pre-negotiation expectations and joint profit. Furthermore, those who are instructed to view the conflict as a joint search for one solution have a more accurate assessment of their counterparts' interest and reach more integrative outcomes.

Although more research is necessary to clarify the specific situational attributions that lead to differences in negotiation behavior, the existing research demonstrates that negotiators' responses to situations do depend on their interpretations or construals of those situations. As noted earlier, situations represent relatively fixed aspects of negotiations unlikely to be under the control of the individual negotiator (Murnighan, 1986; Pinkley et al., 1995). However, the implication of the studies just described is that negotiators may be able to influence their own or their counterparts' construals of those situations and, in doing so, affect negotiation outcomes. More research is necessary to test this assertion.

Summary

The assumptions negotiators make about their counterparts and the ways they construe their situations are important predictors of negotiator attitudes and outcomes. Such attributions can reduce or magnify conflict between parties. For example, although partisans tend to assume that their opponents are more fanatical and extreme than they actually are, certain types of mutual disclosure seem to mitigate harmful attributions about one's counterpart. Although comparatively less researched, strategic re-framing of otherwise fixed conflict situations by individual negotiators may influence negotiator attitudes and outcomes. We consider a negotiator's management of these attributional and construal processes, through these and other means, to be a critical factor in the resolution of conflict.

Motivated Illusions and Negotiation

Beginning in the mid-1980s, a new set of biases entered the social psychology arena: positive illusions (Messick et al., 1985). Evidence on positive illusions suggests that most people view themselves, the world, and the future in a considerably more positive light than reality can sustain (Taylor, 1989). Taylor and Brown (1988) argued that these illusions can enhance and protect self-esteem, increase personal contentment, encourage individuals to persist at difficult tasks, and help people cope with aversive and uncontrollable events. Taylor (1989) even argued that positive illusions are beneficial to physical and mental health. This research is related to the self-serving nature of the egocentric interpretations described earlier. However, while egocentrism tends to be specifically related to judgments of fairness, positive illusions have a broader effect. We highlight four types of motivated illusions of particular relevance to negotiation: (1) unrealistically positive views of the self, (2) unrealistic optimism, (3) the illusion of control, and (4) self-serving attributions. We review each of these motivated illusions and discuss their impact on negotiation.

Unrealistically positive views of the self

We tend to perceive ourselves as being better than others on desirable attributes (Brown, 1986; Messick et al.,1985), causing us to have unrealistically positive self-evaluations (Brown,

1986). For example, people perceive themselves as being better than others across a number of traits, including honesty, cooperativeness, rationality, driving skill, health, and intelligence (Kramer, 1994).

Unrealistic optimism

Unrealistic optimism refers to a tendency to believe that our futures will be better than those of other people (Kramer, 1994, Taylor, 1989). Taylor provided evidence that students expect that they are far more likely to graduate at the top of the class, to get a good job with a high salary, to enjoy their first job, to get written up in the newspaper, and to give birth to a gifted child than reality suggests. Similar results have emerged for groups other than students. Taylor pointed out that we persist in expecting that we can achieve more in a given day than is possible, and that we are immune to the continued feedback that the world provides on our limitations. More directly relevant to negotiation, Kramer (1991) found that 68 percent of the MBA students in a negotiation class predicted that their bargaining outcomes would fall in the upper 25 percent of the class. These students also expected that they would learn more than their classmates would learn, with more unique results, and that they would contribute more to the class experience.

The illusion of control

We also falsely believe that we can control uncontrollable events (Crocker, 1982) and overestimate the extent to which our actions can guarantee a certain outcome (Miller and Ross, 1975). Gamblers believe that "soft" throws of dice are more likely to result in lower numbers being rolled (Taylor, 1989). These gamblers also believe that silence by observers is relevant to their success. Langer (1975) found that people have a strong preference for choosing their own lottery card or numbers, even when this has no effect on improving the likelihood of winning. Many superstitious behaviors are the result of an illusion of control. Kramer (1994) and Bazerman (1998) suggest that negotiators are likely to falsely believe that they have greater control of the behavior of adversaries, the timing of negotiation, and the broader context of their negotiations than is true in reality.

Shafir and Tversky (1992), and Morris, Sim, and Girotto (1998) provided evidence that parties in a prisoner's dilemma act as if their decision will control the decision of the other party, even when doing so is logically impossible. Essentially, this work suggests that one reason that parties cooperate in one-shot prisoner dilemma games is the illusion that their cooperation will create cooperation in the other party. Shafir and Tversky had participants make decisions about whether to cooperate or defect in a prisoner's dilemma game: (1) when the decision of the other party was unknown, (2) when it was known that the other party had cooperated, and (3) when it was known that the other party had defected. Interestingly, many participants cooperate under the first of these conditions, but defect under the latter two.

Shafir and Tversky (1992) argue that this behavior violates Savage's (1954) "sure thing" principle, which states that if you would defect regardless of the decision of the other party, it logically follows that you should defect if you do not know their decision; Morris, Sim, and Girotto (1998) developed this one step further by noting that this result is only common when the other party has not yet made their decision. If the other party has made their decision, participants are much more likely to defect in the unknown condition. Morris, Sim, and Girotto concluded that the illusion of control explains this pattern. When the decision of the other party has already been made, it is no longer intuitively plausible that the participant can control the decision of the other party.

Self-serving attributions

Finally, returning to the theme of attributions developed earlier, people are biased in how they explain the causes of events. We tend to take a disproportionately large share of the credit for collective successes and to accept too little responsibility for collective failures (Kramer, 1994). John F. Kennedy understood this when he said: "Victory has a thousand fathers, but defeat is an orphan." Similarly, when negotiators are asked why they are so successful, they tend to give internal attributions – reasons related to the decisions they made. However, when asked about a failure, they tend to give external attributions – they explain the failure as the result of the unfortunate situation in which they found themselves (Bazerman, 1998). Self-serving biases also play a role in the assignment of blame for a variety of problems. Consider an environmental dispute: What is the cause of global warming? The US blames emerging economies for burning the rain forests and for overpopulation. Emerging nations blame the West for pollution caused by industrialization and excessive consumption. The problem is that in the process of attributing the blame to others, parties reduce their motivation to change their own behaviors so as to contribute to a solution (Wade-Benzoni, Tenbrunsel, and Bazerman, 1997).

We also see the reverse of positive illusions in the context of judgments about opponents. Salovey and Rodin (1984) found that individuals tend to denigrate others who are more successful than they are. Kramer (1994) shows that less-successful MBA students downgrade the performance of more-successful students in negotiation simulations. These MBA students are more likely to attribute the success of other students to uncooperative and unethical bargaining tactics, to ascribe more negative motivations to successful negotiators, and to rate these other students as excessively competitive and self-interested. Both Diekmann (1997) and Tenbrunsel (1995) have found that while students rate themselves above the mean of their class on a variety of positive attributes, they rate their specific negotiation opponent below the mean on these attributes. Kramer (1994), basing his argument partially on Janis's (1962) analysis of political events, tied this pattern of behaviors to tragic mistakes made in politics. Kramer (1994) argued that the mismanagement of the Watergate embarrassment by the Nixon administration was partially the result of denigrating the competence and motivation of their opponents.

The dysfunctional consequences of motivated illusions in negotiation

The self-serving illusions we have reviewed have obvious implications for the negotiation process. For example, Kramer, Newton, and Pommerenke (1993) pointed out that opponent denigration has important negative implications for the process of negotiation. The authors maintained that negotiators' willingness to reveal information about their own interests may be contingent upon their expectation that the other party will reciprocate such disclosures. Individuals' judgments regarding such attributes as the other party's cooperativeness, fairness, and trustworthiness might be expected to play an important role in their negotiations. With the combined effects of self-enhancement and the denigration of opponents, negotiators who see themselves as better than others may undermine their ability to appreciate or fully empathize with the perspective of the other party. This may help explain why negotiators are not very good at understanding the cognitions of the other party (Bazerman & Carroll, 1987). Both parties to a negotiation may feel that they tried harder to reach agreement and offered more substantial concessions than the other party, and that it was only the recalcitrance of the other that forestalled agreement. In a group decision-making study, Polzer, Kramer, and Neale (1997) found that positive illusions about individual performance in a group are positively correlated with the level of conflict in that group.

Motivated illusions also may lead to dysfunctional behaviors for the broader society. Specifically, motivated illusions are argued to lead to defection in large-scale social dilemma problems (Wade-Benzoni, Thompson, & Bazerman, 1998). Positive illusions may lead people to think that, in comparison to others, their behaviors and attitudes are environmentally sensitive, and that they are doing their fair share of sacrificing and working toward the resolution of environmental problems, even though their self-assessments may, in reality, be inflated (Wade-Benzoni et al., 1998). Consistent with Allison, Messick, and Goethals (1989), Wade-Benzoni et al. found self-assessment of environmental sensitivity to depend on how much ambiguity surrounds the self-assessment. Specifically, individuals maintain unrealistically positive beliefs about their degree of environmental sensitivity when their self-evaluation is difficult to disconfirm, but possess more realistic assessments of themselves when they are constrained by the objectivity of the evaluation (cf. Kunda, 1990). For example, assessments of general beliefs such as one's awareness of, concern for, understanding of, and interest in environmental issues and problems are difficult to confirm or disconfirm. However, beliefs about how well one performs on specific activities such as recycling, donating money to environmental organizations, and using energy-saving light bulbs can be checked against objective measures. If individuals define their environmental sensitivity in terms of general (not easily confirmable) behaviors instead of specific (objectively measurable) behaviors, their self-evaluations are likely to be inflated.

Taylor (1989) argued that positive illusions are adaptive. These illusions are said to contribute to psychological well-being by protecting an individual's positive sense of self (Taylor & Brown, 1988). In addition, Taylor and Brown argued that positive illusions increase personal commitment, help individuals persist at difficult tasks, and facilitate coping with aversive and uncontrollable events. Certainly, it is reasonable to argue that positive illusions help create entrepreneurs who are willing to discount risks. Positive illusions help people maintain cognitive consistency, belief in a just world, and perceived control (Greenwald, 1980). Seligman (1991) advocated the selection of salespeople based on the magnitude of their positive illusion – what he calls "learned optimism." He argued that unrealistically high levels of optimism are useful for maintaining persistence in a sales force.

We believe that each of these findings is true and that, in some specific situations (e.g., severe health conditions), positive illusions may prove beneficial. In addition, positive illusions may be useful for coping with tragic events, particularly when the individual has no other alternatives and is not facing any major decisions. However, we also believe that this evidence leads to an incomplete and dangerous story in most decision-making and negotiation environments. Countries go to war because of their positive illusions about the strength of their side. The opportunity to reach agreement with significant others, business partners, and negotiation opponents is lost because of these illusions. We believe that one cannot maintain positive illusions without reducing the quality of decisions that one makes.

In the context of negotiation, the logic of the impact of positive illusions on negotiation success is clearly affected by the choice of the dependent variable. Positive illusions increase the quality of agreements for the party possessing the bias, if an agreement is reached (Loewenstein et al., 1993; Riley, 1999; Riley and Robinson, 1998). However, positive illusions also increase the likelihood of impasse – even when a positive bargaining zone exists (Bazerman, 1998; Bazerman and Neale, 1982; Thompson and Loewenstein, 1992). On balance, we clearly recommend against the acceptance of positive illusions as a positive influence on negotiators. We want a more reasoned trade-off between the claiming of value and the risk of impasse than is possible under the effect of positive illusions.

Our negative reaction to positive illusions in negotiation is shared by a growing number of scholars. These scholars argue that positive illusions are likely to have a negative impact on learning, the quality of decision making, personnel decisions, and responses to organizational crises ("the oil in the water isn't really that big a problem"). Positive illusions can also contribute to conflict and discontent (Brodt, 1990; Kramer, 1994; Kramer et al., 1993; Tyler & Hastie, 1991).

Summary

Substantial evidence demonstrates that many errors made in negotiation result from motivational biases. In contrast to the cognitive biases that dominated the earlier negotiation literature, recent research has highlighted the importance of biases that stem from the desire to see oneself or one's world in a positive light. Although such biases serve a psychological function, we believe that resulting decisions lower the overall benefit to the decision maker and are inconsistent with what the individual would prefer for him- or herself when acting more reflectively.

Out-of-control Behavior and Emotion in Negotiation

The final aspects of social behavior that we seek to integrate into a decision theoretic perspective of negotiation are emotions and out-of-control behavior. Most of us know intuitively that emotions are critical to negotiator behavior, and researchers have a growing sense that emotions in negotiation have been underexplored (Barry & Oliver, 1996; Keltner, 1994; Thompson, Nadler, & Kim, 1999). However, the negotiation literature is not very informative about how emotion affects negotiator performance. Thompson et al. (1999) attributed this void to the cognitive revolution in general, and more specifically to the cognitive tilt of the decision analytic perspective to negotiation. Davidson and Greenhalgh (1999; Greenhalgh & Okun, 1998) argued more strongly that the laboratory/cognitive approach that has dominated negotiation research in the 1980s and 1990s excludes the most important variables for the convenience of the laboratory experimentalist.

Much of the prescriptive writings on negotiation imply that emotions should be controlled (Fisher & Ury, 1981). Emotions generally are viewed as forces that lead negotiators to act against their long-term self-interest (Bazerman, Tenbrunsel, & Wade-Benzoni, 1998). In contrast, Keltner and Kring (1998) described a functional view of emotions. They argued that emotions perform an informative function by signaling information about feelings and intentions. In addition, they argued that emotions serve an incentive function by rewarding or punishing the behavior of the other side. Barry (1999) and Thompson et al. (1999) described how emotions can be used by negotiators for tactical and strategic advantage. Thompson et al. (1999) argue that negotiators learn to maintain what they perceive to be a happy mood in others, and change what they perceive to be a negative mood. They also argue that when people anticipate a negative reaction, they attempt to reduce the negativity by adjusting their own emotional expression.

Emotion in negotiation

There have been a small number of studies directly examining the role of mood on negotiation outcomes. Carnevale and Isen (1986) showed that negotiators in positive moods were less likely to adopt contentious behaviors and more likely to obtain integrative outcomes. Similarly, Baron (1990b) showed that negotiators in good moods make more concessions and are less likely to engage in dysfunctional, competitive behaviors. Kramer et al. (1993) also found that positive moods lead negotiators to believe that they perform better than their opponents and better than other negotiators playing the same role. Forgas (1998) found that good mood enhances, and bad mood reduces, the tendency to select a cooperative strategy in negotiation. Furthermore, Forgas argued that negotiators in a positive mood negotiating against negotiators in a negative mood get more than half of the pie of available resources. Forgas interprets this as resulting from the tendency of a good mood to lead to positive expectations, which as noted earlier, increases the distributive success of the negotiator.

There is less evidence about the effect of negative moods on negotiator performance. This is partly a result of the complexity and ethical concerns of inducing negative moods in controlled experimentation. However, Allred, Mallozi, Matsui, and Raia (1997) did find that angry negotiators are less accurate in judging the interests of opponent negotiators and achieve lower joint gains. Loewenstein et al. (1989) found that negative emotions arising from a negative relationship make negotiators more self-centered in their preferences about the allocation of scarce resources. Loewenstein et al. found that, while those in neutral or positive moods are willing to pay a personal price for equality, those in a negative mood are far less concerned with the outcomes of another party. Pillutla and Murnighan (1996) showed that anger is a key explanatory factor in the rejection of ultimatums in the ultimatum game. That is, when an ultimatum makes people angry, they are likely to reject that ultimatum even when rejection leads to a worse outcome than acceptance.

The good news for these researchers was that, throughout this research, fairly mild manipulations were able to create moderately strong effects. The bad news is that the nature of the emotion/affect manipulations was too "cold" (Janis, 1982) to capture the essence of why people find the role of emotion in negotiation so compelling. When we think about emotion in negotiation, we think of the out-of-control marital argument or the angry customer, instead of the more muted emotions associated with receiving a trivial gift in advance of a negotiation. Thus, ease of experimentation has biased research toward exploring positive and "cold" emotions, rather than the negative, "hot" emotions that we intuitively believe to be the most prevalent emotions in negotiation. Despite the lack of direct evidence, the rest of this section explores the role of "hot" emotions, or out-of-control behaviors, on negotiation.

Out-of-control behavior in conflict situations

Following work on multiple selves by Schelling (1984) and Thaler and Shefrin (1981), Bazerman, Tenbrunsel, and Wade-Benzoni (1998) see emotion as playing a critical role in negotiation. Emotion can create a divide between what people think that they *should* do (cognitive) versus what they *want* to do (emotion). According to this view, people involved in conflicts deal with internal inconsistencies between transient concerns and long-term self-interest. They want to tell their boss what they really think of the recent budget allocation decisions but think that they should keep these insights to themselves. This conflict between cognition and emotion is broadly consistent with Loewenstein's (1996) perspective of visceral responses (emotion) overpowering self-interest (cognition). Loewenstein pointed out that success in many professions is achieved with the skill of manipulating emotions in other people. Salespeople and real estate agents try to close deals by targeting the customer's emotional desire for a commodity, while encouraging them to ignore other options and long-term financial issues. Con men capitalize on the greed of their potential victims. To defend people against their own emotions, many states try to protect consumers from impulses brought on by transient concerns by legislating periods of revocability for high-priced items, such as condominium share purchases (Loewenstein, 1996).

In a study that asked participants to think of a real world episode where they experienced internal conflict between what they wanted versus what they thought that they should do, O'Connor, de Dreu, Schroth, Barry, Liturgy, & Bazerman (1999) found that actual behavior is more closely related to their emotional response (want response) than to their cognitive assessment (should response). Consistent with Loewenstein (1996), this research also showed that study participants are more emotional at the moment of decision than when they are either looking back on the conflict or looking ahead to a future conflict. We posit that these differences in preferences occur because the cognitive self dominates when decision makers are looking toward the future but that emotions, triggered by the immediacy of rewards, often dominate at the point of the decision.

Summary

What research there is on emotion in negotiation has been limited by the practical and ethical difficulties associated with inducing the sorts of powerful emotions that are important in many actual negotiations. It appears that mild positive moods increase cooperative behavior and decrease competitive behavior, improve negotiators' perceptions of their own performance, and actually may improve negotiators' abilities to obtain integrative joint outcomes. Mild negative moods, on the other hand, seem to reduce insight into one's opponents' interests, reduce concern with one's opponents' outcomes, and are associated with the rejection of offers. The "multiple selves" problem explores emotional behavior that is beyond the control of the more deliberative part of the self. Impulsiveness appears to be strongest in the heat of conflict.

Conclusions

The negotiation literature of the 1980s was dominated by a strong cognitive tilt, leaving many important social psychological issues underexplored. This situation was in part due to the failure of the social psychology literature of the 1960s and 1970s to answer prescriptive questions of great importance to negotiators. Behavioral decision research in negotiation of the 1980s and early 1990s emphasized a prescriptive approach to negotiation. In particular, it provided guidance to negotiators about how their own behavior and the behavior of their negotiation opponents might deviate from a rational model. However, this research stream has ignored several key social variables.

This paper has charted the rebirth of the social psychology of negotiations. Relationships between negotiators, concerns for fairness, attribution and construal processes, motivated illusions, and emotions are among the most critical social-psychological variables in this re-emerging literature. We have selectively reviewed each of these variables with a particular focus on their relevance to negotiators.

Negotiation research, especially over the past three decades, has been fueled by concerns of practical relevance. As a result, more negotiation research has taken place in professional schools than in psychology departments. We have attempted to position the new social psychology of negotiation in a way that will preserve this practical relevance by helping us understand, predict, and give advice to a focal negotiator, including advice on how to anticipate the behavior of others. In addition to its practical value, however, the rebirth of the social psychology of negotiation is important because of its theoretical significance. Negotiation – the interpersonal process of conflict resolution – is one of the most basic and most important forms of social interaction. Research on negotiation is an essential step in the process of building a complete understanding of social and organizational behavior.

The beginning of the twenty-first century should be an important period in the development of the social psychology of negotiation. The demand for more social-psychological insights is strong, and many fruitful research directions have begun. We believe a critical determinant of the success of future social psychological research will be the degree to which it provides insights that make negotiators wiser. This value was deficient in early research on the social psychology of negotiations, but has been incorporated in its rebirth. We hope this pattern continues into the next decade and beyond.

References

Akerlof, G. (1970). The market for lemons: Qualitative uncertainty and the market mechanism. *Quarterly Journal of Economics, 89*, 488–500.

Allison, S. T., Messick, D. M., & Goethals, G. R. (1989). On being better but not smarter than others: The Mohammad Ali effect. *Social Cognition, 7*, 275–296.

Allred, K., Mallozi, J. S., Matsui, F., & Raia, C. P. (1997). The influence of anger and compassion on negotiation performance. *Organizational Behavior and Human Decision Processes, 70*, 175–187.

Austin, W. (1980). Friendship and fairness: Effects of type of relationship and task performance on choice of distribution rules. *Personality and Social Psychology Bulletin, 6*, 402–408.

Axelrod, S., & May, J. G. (1968). Effect of increased reward on the two-person non-zero-sum game. *Psychological Reports, 23*, 675–678.

Babcock, L., & Loewenstein, G. (1997). Explaining bargaining impasse: The role of self-serving biases. *Journal of Economic Perspectives, 11*, 109–126.

Babcock, L., Loewenstein, G., Issacharoff, S., & Camerer, C. (1995). Biased judgments of fairness in bargaining. *American Economic Review, 85*, 1337–1343.

Babcock, L., & Olson, C. (1992). The causes of impasses in labor disputes. *Industrial Relations, 31*, 348–360.

Babcock, L., Wang, X. H., & Loewenstein, G. (1996). Choosing the wrong pond: Social comparisons in negotiations that reflect a self-serving bias. *Quarterly Journal of Economics, 111*, 1–19.

Baker, W. E. (1984). The social structure of a national securities market. *American Journal of Sociology, 89*, 775–811.

Baker, W. E. (1990). Market networks and corporate behavior. *American Journal of Sociology, 96*, 589–625.

Baron, R. A. (1985). Reducing organizational conflict: The role of attributions. *Journal of Applied Psychology, 70*, 434–441.

Baron, R. A. (1988). Attributions and organizational conflict: The mediating role of apparent sincerity. *Organizational Behavior and Human Decision Processes, 41*, 111–127.

Baron, R. A. (1990a). Countering the effects of destructive criticism: The relative efficacy of four interventions. *Journal of Applied Psychology, 75*, 235–245.

Baron, R. A. (1990b). Environmentally induced positive affect: Its impact on self-efficacy, task performance, negotiation, and conflict. *Journal of Applied Social Psychology, 20*, 368–384.

Barry, B. (1999). The tactical use of emotion in negotiation. In R. J. Lewicki, R. J. Bies, & B. H. Sheppard (Eds.), *Research on negotiation in organizations* (Vol. 7). Greenwich, CT: JAI Press.

Barry, B., & Friedman, R. A. (1998). Bargainer characteristics in distributive and integrative negotiation. *Journal of Personality and Social Psychology, 74*, 345–359.

Barry, B., & Oliver, R. L. (1996). Affect in dyadic negotiation: A model and propositions. *Organizational Behavior and Human Decision Processes, 67*, 127–143.

Bazerman, M. (1998). *Judgment in managerial decision making.* New York: Wiley.

Bazerman, M. H., & Carroll, J. S. (1987). Negotiator cognition. *Research in Organizational Behavior, 9*, 247–288.

Bazerman, M. H., Curhan, J. R., Moore, D. A., & Valley, K. L. (2000). Negotiation. *Annual Review of Psychology, 51*, 279–314.

Bazerman, M. H., Gibbons, R., Thompson, L., & Valley, K. L. (1998). Can negotiators outperform game theory? In J. J. Halpern & R. N. Stern (Eds.), *Debating rationally: Nonrational aspects in organizational decision making.* Ithaca, NY: ILR Press.

Bazerman, M. H., Magliozi, T., & Neale, M. A. (1985). The acquisition of an integrative response in a competitive market. *Organizational Behavior and Human Performance, 34*, 294–313.

Bazerman, M. H., & Neale, M. A. (1982). Improving negotiation effectiveness under final offer arbitration: The role of selection and training. *Journal of Applied Psychology, 67*, 543–548.

Bazerman, M. H., & Neale, M. A. (1983). Heuristics in negotiation: Limitations to dispute resolution effectiveness. In M. H. Bazerman & R. J. Lewicki (Eds.), *Negotiating in organizations*. Beverly Hills, CA: Sage.

Bazerman, M. H., & Neale, M. A. (1992). *Negotiating rationally*. New York: Free Press.

Bazerman, M. H., Tenbrunsel, A. E., & Wade-Benzoni, K. A. (1998). Negotiating with yourself and losing: Understanding and managing conflicting internal preferences. *Academy of Management Review, 23*, 225–241.

Bell, D. E., Raiffa, H., & Tversky, A. (1989). *Decision making: Descriptive, normative and prescriptive interactions*. Cambridge, England: Cambridge University Press.

Ben-Yoav, O., & Pruitt, D. G. (1984). Resistance to yielding and the expectation of cooperative future interaction in negotiation. *Journal of Experimental Social Psychology, 20*, 323–335.

Betancourt, H., & Blair, I. (1992). A cognition (attribution)-emotion model of violence in conflict situations. *Personality and Social Psychology Bulletin, 18*, 343–350.

Bies, R. J., Shapiro, D. L., & Cummings, L. L. (1988). Causal accounts and managing organizational conflict: Is it enough to say it's not my fault? *Communication Research, 5*, 381–399.

Blount, S. (1995). When social outcomes aren't fair – the effect of causal attributions on preferences. *Organizational Behavior and Human Decision Processes, 63*, 131–144.

Bottom, W. P., & Paese, P. W. (1997). False consensus, stereotypic cues, and the perception of integrative potential in negotiation. *Journal of Applied Social Psychology, 27*, 1919–1940.

Bradbury, T. N., & Fincham, F. D. (1990). Attributions in marriage: Review and critique. *Psychological Bulletin, 107*, 3–33.

Brodt, S. E. (1990). Cognitive illusions and personnel management decisions. In C. L. Cooper & I. T. Robertson (Eds.), *International Review of Industrial and Organizational Psychology* (Vol. 5, pp. 229–279). New York: Wiley.

Brown, J. D. (1986). Evaluations of self and others: Self-enhancement biases in social judgments. *Social Cognition, 4*, 353–376.

Camerer, C., & Loewenstein, G. (1993). Information, fairness, and efficiency in bargaining. In B. A. Mellers & J. Baron (Eds.), *Psychological perspectives on justice* (pp. 155–181). Boston: Cambridge University Press.

Carnevale, P. J., & Isen, A. M. (1986). The influence of positive affect and visual access on the discovery of integrative solutions in bilateral negotiations. *Organizational Behavior and Human Decision Processes, 37*, 1–13.

Clark, M. S., & Chrisman, K. (1994). Resource allocation in intimate relationships: Trying to make sense of a confusing literature. In M. J. Lerner & G. Mikula (Eds.), *Entitlement and the affectional bond*. New York: Plenum.

Clark, M. S., Mills, J., & Corcoran, D. (1989). Keeping track of needs and inputs of friends and strangers. *Personality and Social Psychology Bulletin, 15*, 533–542.

Crocker, J. (1982). Biased questions in judgment of covariation studies. *Personality and Social Psychology Bulletin, 8*, 214–220.

Davidson, M. N., & Greenhalgh, L. (1999). *The role of emotion in negotiation: The impact of anger and race*. Unpublished manuscript.

de Dreu, C. K. W. (1996). Gain-loss frame in outcome-interdependence: Does it influence equality or equity considerations? *European Journal of Social Psychology, 26*, 315–324.

de Dreu, C. K. W., Carnevale, P. J. D., Emans, B. J. M., & van de Vliert, E. (1994). Effects of gain-loss frames in negotiation: Loss aversion, mismatching, and frame adoption. *Organizational Behavior and Human Decision Processes, 60*, 90–107.

de Dreu, C. K. W., Carnevale, P. J. D., Emans, B. J. M., & van de Vliert, E. (1995). Outcome frames in bilateral negotiation: Resistance to concession making and frame adoption. In W. Stroebe & M. Hewstone (Eds.), *European review of social psychology, 6*, 97–125.

de Dreu, C. K. W., Nauta, A., & van de Vliert, E. (1995). Self-serving evaluations of conflict behavior and escalation of the dispute. *Journal of Applied Social Psychology, 25*, 2049–2066.

Deutsch, M. (1975). Equity, equality, and need: What determines which value will be used for distributive justice? *Journal of Social Issues, 31*, 137–150.

Diekmann, K. A. (1997). "Implicit justifications" and self-serving group allocations. *Journal of Organizational Behavior, 18*, 3–16.

Diekmann, K. A., Samuels, S. M., Ross, L., & Bazerman, M. H. (1997). Self-interest and fairness in problems of resource allocation: Allocators versus recipients. *Journal of Personality and Social Psychology, 72*, 1061–1074.

Diekmann, K. A., Tenbrunsel, A. E., Shah, P. P., Schroth, H. A., & Bazerman, M. H. (1996). The descriptive and prescriptive use of previous purchase price in negotiations. *Organizational Behavior and Human Decision Processes, 66*, 179–191.

Drolet, A., Larrick, R., & Morris, M. W. (1998). Thinking of others: How perspective taking changes negotiators' aspirations and fairness perceptions as a function of negotiator relationships. *Basic and Applied Social Psychology, 20*, 23–31.

Druckman, D. (1967). Dogmatism, prenegotiation experience, and simulated group representation as determinants of dyadic behavior in a bargaining situation. *Journal of Personality and Social Psychology, 6*, 279–290.

Druckman, D. (Ed.). (1977). *Negotiations: Social-psychological perspectives.* Beverly Hills, CA: Sage.

Fisher, R., & Ury, W. (1981). *Getting to YES: Negotiating agreement without giving in.* New York: Houghton Mifflin.

Forgas, J. P. (1994). Sad and guilty? Affective influences on the explanation of conflict in close relationships. *Journal of Personality and Social Psychology, 66*, 56–68.

Forgas, J. P. (1998). On feeling good and getting your way: Mood effects on negotiator cognition and bargaining strategies. *Journal of Personality and Social Psychology, 74*, 565–577.

Friedland, N. (1990). Attribution of control as a determinant of cooperation in exchange interactions. *Journal of Applied Social Psychology, 20*, 303–320.

Fry, W. R., Firestone, I. J., & Williams, D. L. (1983). Negotiation process and outcome of stranger dyads and dating couples: Do lovers lose? *Basic and Applied Social Psychology, 4*, 1–16.

Greenberg, J. (1983a). Equity and equality as clues to the relationship between exchange participants. *European Journal of Social Psychology, 13*, 195–196.

Greenberg, J. (1983b). Overcoming egocentric bias in perceived fairness through self-awareness. *Social Psychology Quarterly, 46*, 152–156.

Greenberg, J. (1990). Looking fair versus being fair: Managing impressions of organizational justice. In B. M. Staw & L. L. Cummings (Eds.), *Research in Organizational Behavior* (Vol. 12). Greenwich, CT: JAI Press.

Greenhalgh, L., & Chapman, D. I. (1995). Joint decision making: The inseparability of relationships and negotiation. In R. M. Kramer & D. M. Messick (Eds.), *Negotiation as a social process* (pp. 166–185). Thousand Oaks, CA: Sage.

Greenhalgh, L., & Chapman, D. I. (1996). *Negotiator relationships: Construct measurement. and demonstration of their impact on the process and outcomes of negotiations.* Unpublished manuscript, Dartmouth College.

Greenhalgh, L., & Gilkey, R. W. (1993). The effect of relationship orientation on negotiators' cognitions and tactics. *Special Issue: Relationships in group decision and negotiation. Group Decision & Negotiation, 2*, 167–183.

Greenhalgh, L., & Okun (1998). Negotiation and conflict resolution. In H. S. Friedman (Ed.), *Encyclopedia of mental health.* San Diego, CA: Academic Press.

Greenwald, A. G. (1980). The totalitarian ego: Fabrication and revision of personal history. *American Psychologist, 35*, 603–618.

Halpern, J. J. (1992). The effect of friendship on bargaining: Experimental studies of personal business transactions. In J. L. Wall and L. R. Jauch (Eds.), *Best paper proceedings* (pp. 64–68), Las Vegas, NV: Academy of Management.

Halpern, J. J. (1994). The effect of friendship on personal business transactions. *Journal of Conflict Resolution, 38*, 647–664.

Halpern, J. J. (1996). The effect of friendship on decisions: Field studies of real estate transactions. *Human Relations, 49*, 1519–1547.

Halpern, J. J. (1997a). Elements of a script for friendship in transactions. *Journal of Conflict Resolution, 41*, 835–868.

Halpern, J. J. (1997b). The transaction index: A method for standardizing comparisons of transaction characteristics across different contexts. *Group Decision and Negotiation, 6*, 557–572.

Hastorf, A. H., & Cantril, H. (1954). They saw a game: A case study. *Journal of Abnormal and Social Psychology, 49*, 129–134.

Hayden, T., & Mischel, W. (1976). Maintaining trait consistency in the resolution of behavioral inconsistency: The wolf in sheep's clothing? *Journal of Personality, 44*, 109–132.

Hermann, M. G., & Kogan, N. (1977). Effects of negotiators' personalities on negotiating behavior. In D. Druckman (Ed.), *Negotiation: Social psychological perspectives.* Beverly Hills, CA: Sage.

Janis, I. (1962). Psychological effects of warnings. In G. W. Baker & D. W. Chapman (Eds.), *Man and society in disaster.* New York: Basic Books.

Janis, I. L. (1982). *Groupthink: Psychological studies of policy decisions and fiascoes.* Boston: Houghton Mifflin.

Johnson, T. E., & Rule, B. G. (1986). Mitigating circumstance information, censure, and aggression. *Journal of Personality and Social Psychology, 50*, 537–542.

Kahneman, D., Slovic, P., & Tversky, A. (1982). *Judgment under uncertainty: Heuristics and biases.* New York: Cambridge University Press.

Kelley, H. (1972). Attribution in social interaction. In E. E. Jones, D. E. Kanouse, H. H. Kelley, et. al. (Eds.), *Attribution: Perceiving the causes of behavior* (pp. 1–26). Morristown, NJ: General Learning Press.

Kelley, H. H., & Thibaut, J. W. (1978). *Interpersonal relations: A theory of interdependence.* New York: Wiley.

Keltner, D. (1994). *Emotion, nonverbal behavior, and social conflict.* Paper presented to the Harvard Project on Negotiation.

Keltner, D., & Kring, A.M. (1998). Emotion, social function, and psychopathology. *Review of General Psychology, 2*, 320–342.

Keltner, D., & Robinson, R. J. (1993). Imagined ideological differences in conflict escalation and resolution. *International Journal of Conflict Management, 4*, 249–262.

Keltner, D., & Robinson, R. J. (1996). Extremism, power, and the imagined basis of social conflict. *Current Directions in Psychological Science, 5*, 101–105.

Kette, G. (1986). Attributions restore consistency in bargaining with liked/disliked partners. *European Journal of Social Psychology, 16*, 257–277.

Kramer, R. M. (1991). Intergroup relations and organizational dilemmas: The role of categorization processes. *Research in Organizational Behavior, 13*, 191–228.

Kramer, R. M. (1994). The sinister attribution error: Paranoid cognition and collective distrust in organizations. *Motivation and Emotion, 18*, 199–230.

Kramer, R. M., Newton, E., & Pommerenke, P. L. (1993). Self-enhancement biases and negotiator judgment: Effects of self-esteem and mood. *Organizational Behavior and Human Decision Processes, 56*, 110–133.

Kunda, Z. (1990). The case for motivated reasoning. *Psychological Bulletin, 108*(3), 480–498.

Lamm, H., & Kogan, N. (1970). Risk taking in the context of intergroup negotiations. *Journal of Experimental Social Psychology, 6*, 351–363.

Langer, E. (1975). The illusion of control. *Journal of Personality and Social Psychology, 32*, 311–328.

Larrick, R. P., & Blount, S. (1997). The claiming effect: Why players are more generous in social dilemmas than in ultimatum games. *Journal of Personality and Social Psychology, 72*, 810–825.

Lax, D. A., & Sebenius, J. K. (1986). *The manager as negotiator.* New York: Free Press.

Lewicki, R. J., Litterer, J. A., Minton, J. W., & Saunders, D. W. (1999) *Negotiation* (3rd cd.). Burr Ridge, IL: Irwin.

Lewicki, R. J., Weiss, S., & Lewin, D. (1988). *Models of conflict, negotiation, and third party intervention: A review and synthesis.* Working Paper Series (WPS 88–33). College of Business, Ohio State University.

Lewin, K. (1935). *Dynamic theory of personality.* New York: McGraw-Hill.

Loewenstein, G. (1996). Out of control: Visceral influences on behavior. *Organizational Behavior and Human Decision Processes, 65,* 272–292.

Loewenstein, G., Babcock, L., Issacharoff, S., & Camerer, C., (1993). Self-serving assessments of fairness and pretrial bargaining. *Journal of Legal Studies, 22,* 135–159.

Loewenstein, G., Thompson, L., & Bazerman, M. H. (1989). Social utility and decision making in interpersonal contexts. *Journal of Personality and Social Psychology, 57,* 426–441.

Lord, R. G., & Smith, J. E. (1983). Theoretical, information processing, and situational factors affecting attribution theory models of organizational behavior. *Academy of Management Review, 8,* 50–60.

Mannix, E. A., Tinsley, C. H., & Bazerman, M. H. (1995). Negotiation over time: Impediments to integrative solutions. *Organizational Behavior and Human Decision Processes, 62,* 241–251.

March, J. G., & Simon, H. A. (1958). *Organizations.* New York: Wiley.

Marwell, G., Ratcliff, K., & Schmitt, D. R. (1969). Minimizing differences in a maximizing difference game. *Journal of Personality and Social Psychology, 12,* 158–163.

Marwell, G., & Schmitt, D. R. (1972). Cooperation in a three-person prisoner's dilemma. *Journal of Personality and Social Psychology, 21,* 376–383.

Messick, D. M., Bloom, S., Boldizar, J. P., & Samuelson, C. D. (1985). Why we are fairer than others. *Journal of Experimental Social Psychology, 21,* 480–500.

Messick, D. M., & Sentis, K. P. (1979). Fairness and preference. *Journal of Experimental Social Psychology, 15,* 418–434.

Messick, D. M., & Sentis, K. P. (1983). Fairness, preference, and fairness biases. In D. M. Messick & K. S. Cook (Eds.), *Equity theory: Psychological and sociological perspectives.* New York: Praeger.

Messick, D. M., & Sentis, K. P. (1985). Estimating social and nonsocial utility functions from ordinal data. *European Journal of Social Psychology, 15,* 389–399.

Miller, D. T., & Ross, M. (1975). Self-serving biases in attribution of causality: Fact or fiction? *Psychological Bulletin, 82,* 213–225.

Morgan, W., & Sawyer, J. (1967). Bargaining expectations and the preference for equality over equity. *Journal of Personality and Social Psychology, 6,* 139–149.

Morris, M. W., Larrick, R. P., & Su, S. K. (1998). *Misperceiving negotiation counterparts: When situationally determined bargaining behaviors are attributed to personality traits.* Unpublished manuscript.

Morris, M. W., Leung, K., & Sethi, S. (1998). *Person perception in the heat of conflict: Perceptions of opponents' traits and conflict resolution choices in two cultures.* Unpublished manuscript.

Morris, M. W., Sim, D. L. H., & Girotto, V. (1998). *Distinguishing sources of cooperation in the one-round prisoner's dilemma: Evidence for cooperative decisions based on illusion of control.* Unpublished manuscript.

Murnighan, J. K. (1986). The structure of mediation and intravention: Comments on Carnevale's strategic choice model. *Negotiation Journal, 4,* 351–356.

Neale, M. A. (1984). The effect of negotiation and arbitration cost salience on bargainer behavior: The role of arbitrator and constituency in negotiator judgment. *Organizational Behavior and Human Performance, 34,* 97–111.

Neale, M. A., & Bazerman, M. H. (1991). *Cognition and rationality in negotiation.* New York: Free Press.

Neale, M. A., & Bazerman, M. H. (1992). Negotiator cognition and rationality: A behavioral decision theory perspective. *Organizational Behavior and Human Decision Processes, 51,* 157–175.

Nisbett, R., & Ross, L. (1980). *Human inference: Strategies and shortcomings of social judgement.* Englewood Cliffs, NJ: Prentice Hall.

Northcraft, G. B., & Neale, M. A. (1987). Expert, amateurs, and real estate: An anchoring-and-adjustment perspective on property pricing decisions. *Organizational Behavior and Human Decision Processes, 39,* 228–241.

Ochs, J., & Roth, A. E. (1989). An experimental study of sequential bargaining. *American Economic Review, 79,* 335–385.

O'Connor, K. M., & Adams, A. A. (1998). *Debiasing negotiators' cognitions: The impact of task construal on negotiators' perceptions, motives, and outcomes.* Working paper, Johnson Graduate School of Management, Cornell University.

O'Connor, K., de Dreu, C., Schroth, H., Barry, B., Liturgy, T., & Bazerman, M. H. (1999). *Intrapersonal conflict across time.* Manuscript submitted for publication.

Oskamp, S. (1965). Attitudes towards U.S. and Russian actions: A double standard. *Psychological Reports, 16*, 43–46.

Pillutla, M. M., & Murnighan, J. K. (1996). Unfairness, anger, and spite: Emotional rejections of ultimatum offers. *Organizational Behavior and Human Decision Processes, 68*, 208–224.

Pinkley, R. L. (1990). Dimensions of conflict frame: Disputant interpretations of conflict. *Journal of Applied Psychology, 75*, 117–126.

Pinkley, R. L., Brittain, J. W., Neale, M. A., & Northcraft, G. B. (1995). Managerial third party dispute intervention: An inductive analysis of intervenor strategy selection. *Journal of Applied Psychology, 80*, 386–402.

Pinkley, R. L., & Northcraft, G. B. (1994). Conflict frames of reference: Implications for dispute processes and outcomes. *Academy of Management, 37*, 193–205.

Polzer, J. T., Kramer, R. M., & Neale, M. A. (1997). Positive illusions about oneself and one's group. *Small Group Research, 28*, 243–266.

Polzer, J. T., Neale, M. A., & Glenn, P. O. (1993). The effects of relationships and justification in an interdependent allocation task. *Special Issue: Relationships in group decision and negotiation. Group Decision & Negotiation, 2*, 135–148.

Priest, G., & Klein, B. (1984). The selection of disputes for litigation. *Journal of Legal Studies, 13*, 1–55.

Pruitt, D. G. (1981). *Negotiation Behavior.* New York: Academic Press.

Pruitt, D. G. (1983). Achieving integrative agreements. In M. H. Bazerman & R. J. Lewicki (Eds.), *Negotiating in organizations.* Beverly Hills, CA: Sage.

Pruitt, D. G., & Carnevale, P. J. (1993). *Negotiation in social conflict.* Pacific Grove, CA: Brooks-Cole.

Pruitt, D. G., & Drews, J. L. (1969). The effect of time pressure, time elapsed, and the opponent's concession rate on behavior in negotiation. *Journal of Experimental Social Psychology, 5*, 43–69.

Pruitt, D. G., & Johnson, D. F. (1972). Mediation as an aid to face saving in negotiation. *Journal of Personality and Social Psychology, 14*, 239–246.

Pruitt, D. G., Rubin, J. Z., & Kim, S. H. (1994). *Social conflict: Escalation, stalemate, and settlement,* 2nd edn. New York: McGraw-Hill.

Puccio, C., & Ross, L. (1998). *Attenuating false polarization: Debiasing the social presentation of partisans.* Working paper, Stanford University.

Raiffa, H. (1982). *The art and science of negotiation.* Cambridge, MA: Belknap.

Regan, D. T., Straus, E., & Fazio, R. H. (1974). Liking and the attribution process. *Journal of Experimental Social Psychology, 10*, 385–397.

Riley, H. C. (1999). *Optimism and performance in negative-sum negotiation.* Working paper, Harvard Business School.

Riley, H. C., & Robinson, R. J. (1998). *How high can you go? Preliminary findings on the peril and benefits of negotiator confidence in distributive bargaining.* Working paper. Harvard Business School.

Robinson, R. J., & Friedman, R. A. (1995). Mistrust and misconstrual in union–management relationships: Causal accounts in adversarial contexts. *International Journal of Conflict Management, 6*, 312–327.

Robinson, R. J., & Keltner, D. (1996). Much ado about nothing? Revisionists and traditionalists choose an introductory English syllabus. *Psychological Science, 7*, 18–24.

Robinson, R. J., & Keltner, D. (1997). Defending the status quo: Power and bias in social conflict. *Personality and Social Psychology Bulletin, 23*, 1066–1077.

Robinson, R. J., Keltner, D., Ward, A., & Ross, L. (1995). Actual versus assumed differences in construal: Naïve Realism in intergroup perception and conflict. *Journal of Personality and Social*

Psychology, 68, 404–417.

Ross, L. (1977). The intuitive psychologist and his shortcomings: Distortions in the attribution process. In L. Berkowitz (Ed.), *Advances in experimental social psychology, 10*, 173–220. New York: Academic Press.

Ross, L., & Nisbett, R. E. (1991). *The person and the situation: Perspectives of social psychology.* New York: McGraw-Hill.

Ross, L., & Samuels, S. M. (1993). *The predictive power of personal reputation vs. labels and construal in the Prisoner's Dilemma game.* Unpublished manuscript, Stanford University, Palo Alto, CA.

Ross, L., & Sicoly, F. (1979). Egocentric biases in availability and attribution. *Journal of Personality and Social Psychology, 37*, 322–336.

Ross, L., & Stillinger, C. (1991). Barriers to conflict resolution. *Negotiation Journal, 7*, 389–404.

Ross, L., & Ward, A. (1995). Psychological barriers to dispute resolution. *Advances in Experimental Social Psychology, 27*, 255–303.

Ross, L., & Ward, A. (1996). Naïve realism in everyday life: Implications for social conflict and misunderstanding. In T. Brown, E. Reed, & E. Turiel (Eds.), Values and knowledge (pp. 103–135). Hillsdale, NJ: Erlbaum.

Roth, A. E. (1982). The economics of matching: Stability and incentives. *Mathematics of Operations Research, 7*, 617–628.

Roth, A. E., & Murnighan, J. K. (1982). The role of information in bargaining: An experimental study. *Econometrica, 50*, 1123–1142.

Rubin, J. Z., & Brown, B. R. (1975). *The social psychology of bargaining and negotiation.* New York: Academic Press.

Rubin, J. Z., Pruitt, D. G., & Kim, S. H. (1994). *Social conflict: Escalation, stalemate, and settlement.* New York: McGraw-Hill.

Rubin, Z. (1970). Measurement of romantic love. *Journal of Personality and Social Psychology, 16*, 265–273.

Sabatelli, R. M., & Cecil-Pigo, E. F. (1985). Relational interdependence and commitment in marriage. *Journal of Marriage and the Family, 47*, 931–937.

Salovey, P., & Rodin, J. (1984). Some antecedents and consequences of social comparison jealousy. *Journal of Personality and Social Psychology, 47*, 780–792.

Samuelson, W. F., & Bazerman, M. H. (1985). The winner's curse in bilateral negotiations. In V. Smith (Ed.), *Research in Experimental Economics, 3* (pp. 105–137). Greenwich, CT: JAI Press.

Savage, L. J. (1954). *The foundations of statistics.* New York: Wiley.

Schelling, T. C. (1984). *Choice and consequence: Perspectives of an errant economist.* Cambridge, MA: Harvard University Press.

Schoeninger, D., & Wood, W. (1969). Comparison of married and ad hoc mixed-sex dyads negotiating the division of a reward. *Journal of Experimental Social Psychology, 5*, 483–499.

Seligman, M.E.P. (1991). *Learned optimism.* New York: Pocket Books.

Shafir, E., & Tversky, A. (1992). Thinking through uncertainty: Nonconsequential reasoning and choice. *Cognitive Psychology, 24*, 449–474.

Shah, P. P., & Jehn, K. A. (1993). Do friends perform better than acquaintances? The interaction of friendship, conflict, and task. *Special Issue: Relationships in group decision and negotiation. Group Decision & Negotiation, 2*, 149–165.

Snyder, M., & Swann, W. B., Jr. (1978). Behavioral confirmation in social interaction: From social perception to social reality. *Journal of Experimental Social Psychology, 14*, 148–162.

Sondak, H., & Bazerman, M. H. (1989). Matching and negotiation processes in quasi-markets. *Organizational Behavior and Human Decision Processes, 44*, 261–280.

Sondak, H., & Bazerman, M. H. (1991). Power balance and the rationality of outcomes in matching markets. *Organizational Behavior and Human Decision Processes, 50*, 1–23.

Sondak, H., Pinkley, R., & Neale, M. (1994). *Relationship, input, and resource constraints: Determinants of individual preferences and negotiated outcomes in resource allocation decisions.* Working paper, Duke University.

Taylor, S. E. (1989). *Positive Illusions.* New York: Basic Books.

Taylor, S. E., & Brown, J. D. (1988). Illusion and well-being: a social psychological perspective on mental health. *Psychological Bulletin, 103*, 193–210.

Tenbrunsel, A. E. (1995). *Justifying unethical behavior: The role of expectations of others' behavior and uncertainty.* Unpublished doctoral dissertation. Northwestern University.

Tenbrunsel, A. E., Wade-Benzoni, K. A., Moag, J., & Bazerman, M. H. (1998). *The social aspect of the matching process: Relationships and partner selection.* Unpublished manuscript.

Thaler, R., & Shefrin, H. M. (1981). An economic theory of self control. *Journal of Political Economy, 89*, 392–406.

Thompson, L. (1990). Negotiation behavior and outcomes: Empirical evidence and theoretical issues. *Psychological Bulletin, 108*, 515–532.

Thompson, L. (1995). "They saw a negotiation": Partisanship and involvement. *Journal of Personality and Social Psychology, 68*, 839–853.

Thompson, L. (1998). *The mind and heart of the negotiator.* Upper Saddle River, NJ: Prentice Hall.

Thompson, L. L., & DeHarpport, T. (1990). Negotiation in long-term relationships. Paper presented at the International Association for Conflict Management, Vancouver, Canada.

Thompson, L., & DeHarpport, T. (1998). Relationships, goal incompatibility, and communal orientation in negotiations. *Basic and Applied Social Psychology, 20*, 33–44.

Thompson, L., & Hrebec, D. (1996). Lose-lose agreements in interdependent decision making. *Psychological Bulletin, 120*, 396–409.

Thompson, L., & Loewenstein, G. (1992). Egocentric interpretations of fairness and interpersonal conflict. *Organizational Behavior and Human Decision Processes, 51*, 176–197.

Thompson, L., Nadler, J., & Kim, P. H. (1999). Some like it hot: The case for the emotional negotiator. In L. Thompson, J. Levine, & D. Messick (Eds.), *Shared cognition in organizations: The management of knowledge* (pp. 139–161). Hillsdale, NJ: Erlbaum.

Thompson, L., Valley, K. L., & Kramer, R. M. (1995). The bittersweet feeling of success: An examination of social perception in negotiation. *Journal of Experimental Social Psychology, 31*, 467–492.

Tversky, A., & Kahneman, D. (1974). Judgment under uncertainty: Heuristics and biases. *Science, 185*, 1124–1131.

Tyler, T., & Hastie, R. (1991). The social consequences of cognitive illusions. In M. H. Bazerman, R. J. Lewicki, & B. Sheppard (Eds.), *Handbook of negotiation research: Research on negotiation in organizations* (Vol. 3). Greenwich, CT: JAI Press.

Utne, M. K., Hatfield, E., Traupmann, J., & Greenberger, D. (1984). Equity, marital satisfaction, and stability. *Journal of Social and Personal Relationships, 1*, 323–332.

Valley, K. L. (1992). *Relationships and resources: A network exploration of allocation decisions.* Unpublished dissertation, Northwestern University.

Valley, K. L., Moag, J., & Bazerman, M. H. (1998). "A matter of trust": Effects of communication on the efficiency and distribution of outcomes. *Journal of Economic Behavior & Organization, 34*, 211–238.

Valley, K. L., Neale, M. A., & Mannix, E. (1995). Friends, lovers, colleagues, strangers: The effects of relationships on the process and outcomes of dyadic negotiations. *Research on Negotiation in Organizations, 5*, 65–93.

Vidmar, N. (1971). Effects of representational roles and mediators on negotiator effectiveness. *Journal of Personality and Social Psychology, 17*, 48–58.

Wade-Benzoni, K. A., Tenbrunsel, A. E., & Bazerman, M. H. (1996). Egocentric interpretations of fairness in asymmetric, environmental social dilemmas: Explaining harvesting behavior and the role of communication. *Organizational Behavior and Human Decision Processes, 67*, 111–126.

Wade-Benzoni, K. A., Tenbrunsel, A. E., & Bazerman, M. H. (1997). Egocentric interpretations of fairness as an obstacle to just resolution of environmental conflict. In R. J. Lewicki, R. J. Bies, & B. H. Sheppard (Eds.), *Research on Negotiation in Organization* (Vol. 6). Greenwich, CT: JAI Press.

Wade-Benzoni, K. A., Thompson, L. L., & Bazerman, M. H. (1998). *The malleability of environmentalism.* Working paper.

Walster, E., Walster, G. W., & Berscheid, E. (1978). *Equity: Theory and research*. Boston: Allyn & Bacon.

Walters, A. E., Stuhlmacher, A. F., Meyer, L. L. (1998). Gender and negotiator competitiveness: A meta-analysis. *Organizational Behavior and Human Decision Processes, 76*, 1–29.

Walton, R. E., & McKersie, R. B. (1965). *A behavioral theory of labor negotiation*. New York: McGraw-Hill.

Watson, C. (1994). Gender versus power as a predictor of negotiation behavior and outcomes. *Negotiation Journal, 10*, 117–127.

Wichman, H. (1970). Effects of isolation and communication on cooperation in a two-person game. *Journal of Personality and Social Psychology, 16*, 114–120.

Chapter Nine

Motivational Aspects of Empathic Accuracy

William Ickes and Jeffry A. Simpson

"I want the truth!"
"You can't handle the truth!!"

Dialogue from the film A Few Good Men

As desirable as the truth may be as a theoretical ideal, the hard reality is that sometimes the truth hurts. Sometimes we just can't handle the truth. Sometimes we are even motivated to avoid it. But sometimes, knowing that the truth will hurt, we are motivated to seek it out anyway – even if we have to pay a very painful price for this knowledge.

These abstract propositions have a special force and immediacy when they are viewed within the context of close relationships. With regard to the first proposition, achieving a true understanding of a relationship partner is not only a theoretical ideal; it has considerable practical value as well. To ensure that their close relationship will continue to "work" over any extended period of time, partners must effectively coordinate their individual and shared motives and actions. Such coordination requires that they must be relatively accurate, much of the time, when inferring the specific content of each other's thoughts and feelings. As a general rule, then, partners who can accurately infer each other's thoughts and feelings should be more successful in maintaining satisfying and stable relationships than partners who cannot.

There are times, however, when relationship partners suspect – or even know for certain – that understanding the truth about the other's thoughts and feelings could have a devastating impact on their relationship. Rather than confront the truth about the other's thoughts and feelings in these relationship-threatening situations, one or both partners may avoid this knowledge and thereby attempt to spare themselves and their relationship the pain and injury that might otherwise occur. In such cases, the partners' motivated inaccuracy may provide an important exception to the more general rule that partners seek an accurate understanding of each other in order to make their relationship work. In the short run at least, the use of motivated inaccuracy in relationship-threatening situations may actually be an effective strategy for protecting the partners and their relationship from the threat of impending pain and injury.

However, for some partners, and in some circumstances, even the threat of impending pain and injury may not be a sufficient deterrent. There are cases in which a person's need to confront the truth is so strong that an accurate knowledge of the partner's thoughts and feelings is sought even when this knowledge comes at a very high cost – a cost that can include damage to self-esteem, to esteem for the partner, and to the strength and stability of the relationship. Such cases constitute another important exception to the rule that relationship partners will typically seek to make accurate, rather than inaccurate, inferences about each other's thoughts and feelings in order to help the relationship "work" more effectively. Although perceivers do seek to be accurate in such cases, their accuracy is sought at the expense of – rather than in the service of – relational stability and satisfaction.

In this chapter we consider the motivational implications of empathic accuracy in terms of the general rule and the two important exceptions described above. We first summarize the findings from studies that are consistent with the general rule that motivated accuracy usually helps close relationships to work effectively, resulting in moderate to high levels of relationship satisfaction and stability. We next examine the findings from a recent study that provides preliminary support for the first exception to the rule, i.e., that there are cases in which partners will use motivated inaccuracy to protect themselves and their relationships from personal and relational distress (Simpson, Ickes, & Blackstone, 1995). We then consider findings from a follow-up study that provides preliminary support for the second exception to the rule, i.e., that there are cases in which partners are motivated to "read" each other accurately even though they are likely to pay a high price for this knowledge in both personal and relational terms (Simpson, Ickes, & Grich, 1999). Finally, we integrate these sets of findings within our developing theoretical model (Ickes & Simpson, 1997) of how empathic accuracy might be "managed" in close relationships.

The Rule: Motivated Accuracy Helps Relationships

Many studies in the *marital adjustment literature* have documented a positive association between marital adjustment and understanding of the attitudes, role expectations, and self-perceptions of one's spouse (see Sillars & Scott, 1983, for a review). This claim is based on the results of studies by Dymond (1954), Corsini (1956), Luckey (1960), Stuckert (1963), Laing, Phillipson, and Lee (1966), Taylor (1967), Murstein and Beck (1972), Christensen and Wallace (1976), Newmark, Woody, and Ziff (1977), Ferguson and Allen (1978), Noller (1980, 1981), Noller and Venardos (1986), and Guthrie and Noller (1988). Additional evidence for a positive association between marital adjustment and understanding has been reported by Katz (1965), Navran (1967), Kahn (1970), Gottman et al. (1976), Knudson, Sommers, and Golding (1980), Gottman and Porterfield (1981), Madden and Janoff-Bulman (1981), and Neimeyer and Banikiotes (1981).

Collectively, these studies support the view that, as a rule, more understanding (i.e., greater empathic accuracy) is good for relationships. The generality of this rule has recently been questioned, however, in articles by Noller (Noller, 1984; Noller & Ruzzene, 1991) and by Sillars (Sillars & Scott, 1983; Sillars, Pike, Jones, and Murphy, 1984; Sillars, 1985). For example, in some of the early studies that focused on judgments of spouses' self-rated traits, attitudes, and role expectations, the relationship between understanding and marital adjustment held only when the wife was the respondent and the husband's perceptions were being predicted (Stuckert, 1963; Murstein & Beck, 1972; Corsini, 1956; Kotlar, 1965; see also Barry, 1970). Similarly, research examining the judgments of spouses' intentions has found evidence that distressed wives may display less understanding than nondistressed wives and husbands (Noller & Ruzzene, 1991). Such findings suggest that the association between understanding and marital adjustment is more complicated than earlier theorists and researchers supposed.

Although there are fewer relevant studies available in the recent *empathic accuracy literature*, the results of these studies also suggest that, as a general rule, the partners' accuracy in inferring each other's thoughts and feelings is associated with positive relationship outcomes. For example, in their study of empathic accuracy in a sample of newly married couples, Kilpatrick, Bissonnette, and Rusbult (1999) reported that empathic accuracy was significantly correlated at the couple level with such variables as commitment to the relationship (.42), willingness to accommodate the partner's bad behavior (.60), and dyadic adjustment (.58). These effects, which were found when the couples were in the first 12–18 months of their marriages, generally declined in strength across time, so that only the couple-level correlation between empathic accuracy and dyadic adjustment was still significant (.35) two years later.

Kilpatrick and her colleagues speculated that empathic accuracy might have its greatest effect on positive relationship outcomes early in the course of close relationships because this is a time when the partners' attitudes, values, and behaviors are still relatively unpredictable and difficult to anticipate and accommodate. Accordingly, partners who can successfully infer each other's thoughts and feelings will achieve better relational outcomes during this early period of adjustment than will couples who cannot. With the passage of time, the positive effects of empathic accuracy on relational outcomes may decrease for couples who, having learned each other's idiosyncratic cognitive, emotional, and behavioral predilections, have developed habits that automatically accommodate them. On the other hand, for the (presumably smaller) subset of couples who do not develop such habits – either because of a continuing ignorance of each other's predilections or an unwillingness to accommodate them – empathic accuracy may continue to play an important role in promoting positive relationship outcomes.

A complementary interpretation was proposed in an earlier study by Thomas, Fletcher, and Lange (1997), who studied a larger sample of New Zealand couples who had been married for an average of over 15 years. Thomas and his colleagues also found that couple-level empathic accuracy decreased as the length of the marriage increased (–.31), but discovered that this relationship was mediated by the extent to which the content of the individual partners' thoughts and feelings was divergent. In other words, couples who had been married for longer periods of time tended to have fewer shared thoughts and feelings (and, by implication, more idiosyncratic ones) during their interactions than did more recently married couples; and it was this difference in the level of "shared cognitive focus" that accounted for the lower levels of empathic accuracy attained by couples married for longer periods of time. Thomas and his colleagues suggested that "partners in long-standing relationships become complacent and overly familiar with each other" (p. 840). They therefore lack the motivation to actively monitor each other's words and actions and attain the kind of common, intersubjective focus in their thoughts and feelings that facilitates empathic accuracy.

If the link between empathic accuracy and positive relationship outcomes is likely to be most evident in the earlier stages of a relationship, it makes sense that empathic accuracy was significantly related to marital adjustment in Kilpatrick et al.'s (1999) newlywed sample but was not significantly related to marital satisfaction in Thomas et al.'s (1997) sample of longer-married couples. It may not be surprising, therefore, that Ickes, Stinson, Bissonnette, and Garcia (1990) found that opposite-sex strangers were more accurate in inferring each other's thoughts and feelings to the extent they found each other physically attractive, because – like the recently married couples in the Kilpatrick et al. (1999) and Thomas et al. (1997) studies – they were presumably highly motivated to monitor each other closely and to try to achieve a "shared cognitive focus." In general, then, the available studies suggest that motivated accuracy can contribute to positive relationship outcomes, particularly during the formative stages of close relationships.

The First Exception: Sometimes Motivated Inaccuracy Helps Relationships

As we have just seen, there is support for the commonsense belief that, as a general rule, greater understanding is associated with greater stability and satisfaction in close relationships. It would be a serious mistake, however, not to recognize that there are important exceptions to this rule.

The first exception occurs whenever relationship partners suspect (or know for certain) that their partner harbors thoughts and feelings that they might be better off *not* knowing – thoughts and feelings that, if accurately inferred, could have a devastating effect on their relationship. Rather than confront the painful knowledge of what the other person thinks and feels, one or both partners may be motivated to *mis*infer this knowledge and thereby spare themselves and their relationship the pain and injury that might otherwise occur. In such cases, the partners' *motivated inaccuracy* may provide an important exception to the more general rule that partners seek an accurate understanding of each other in order to keep their relationship happy and stable.

In a recent study (Simpson et al., 1995), we found some preliminary evidence that partners may indeed use motivated inaccuracy to ward off an impending threat to their relationship. The participants in this study were 82 heterosexual dating couples. In each other's presence, the members of each couple took turns rating and discussing with their partner the physical and sexual attractiveness of a set of opposite-sex persons as "potential dating partners." About half of the couples were randomly assigned to view and rate slides of highly attractive people, whereas the remaining couples viewed and rated slides of less attractive people. After the male (or the female) partner rated aloud on a 10-point scale the attractiveness and sexual appeal of each opposite-sex stimulus person, both partners discussed what they liked or disliked about each person for 30 seconds.

Each couple's interaction during this rating-and-discussion task was covertly videotaped. Immediately afterwards, we informed the partners about the taping and obtained their written consent to let us code the videotapes for subsequent analysis. We also asked them to participate in the next phase of the study – a phase in which the actual thoughts and feelings they had experienced during the rating-and-discussion task were assessed.

The partners were seated in different rooms, where each partner viewed a copy of the videotape of the couples' interaction over the entire course of the rating-and-discussion task. Consistent with the experimenter's instructions, each partner made a written record of each of his or her thoughts and feelings as well as the "tape stops" (i.e., the specific times during the interaction) at which each thought or feeling occurred. Each partner then viewed the tape again, this time with the assigned task of attempting to accurately infer the specific content of each of their *partner's* thoughts and feelings at their respective "tape stops" (for additional methodological details, see Ickes, Bissonnette, Garcia, & Stinson, 1990; and Simpson et al., 1995). Four months later, both partners were telephoned to determine whether or not they were still dating.

The purpose of this study was to see if we could identify conditions in which relationship partners would exhibit motivated *in*accuracy and thereby minimize the relational instability and dissatisfaction that might otherwise result. As we predicted, we found that the *least* empathic accuracy during the rating-and-discussion task was displayed by dating partners who were closer (i.e., more interdependent), who were less certain about the stability of their relationship, and who rated attractive (vs. less attractive) "potential dating partners" in each other's presence. We also found that the relation between these last three variables and empathic accuracy was mediated by the perceiver's level of self-reported threat. That is, the partners who were the most interdependent, the least certain about the stability of their relationship, and who rated highly attractive others reported feeling the most threatened, and these high levels of threat in turn predicted their lower (near-chance) levels of empathic accuracy. Even more impressive, the partners in this category were all still dating at the four-month follow-up, whereas the remaining couples in the study had a significantly higher breakup rate of 28 percent.

In general, the pattern of behavior displayed by these close-but-uncertain partners who rated and discussed attractive others provides good preliminary evidence for what we have termed "the first exception to the rule" – that *sometimes motivated inaccuracy helps relationships*. Apparently, there are cases in which partners use motivated inaccuracy in relationship-threatening situations to protect themselves and their relationship from the pain and injury that might result from a more accurate understanding of what the other is thinking or feeling. That such a strategy might help to protect relationships is suggested by Simpson et al.'s finding that the least accurate couples were the most likely to still be together four months later. For a review of the evidence that supports our "motivated inaccuracy" interpretation of this effect, see Simpson et al. (1995).

The Second Exception: Sometimes Motivated Accuracy Hurts Relationships

Within the ranks of relationship researchers, Alan Sillars and his colleagues were among the first to note that an accurate understanding of a partner's thoughts and feelings is not always associated with positive outcomes. After reviewing the literature that was available in the early 1980s, Sillars and his colleagues concluded that there are conditions in which greater understanding is associated with greater personal and relational distress (Sillars, 1981, 1985; Sillars & Parry, 1982; Sillars, Pike, Jones, & Murphy, 1984; Sillars, Pike, Jones, & Redmon, 1983; Sillars & Scott, 1983).

In general, these conditions were found in *conflict paradigms* – experimental situations in which married or dating couples were required to discuss one or more issues that had previously been a source of major conflict in their relationships (Sillars & Parry, 1982; Sillars et al., 1984; Sillars, et al., 1983). Ideally, the partners' successive goals in such discussions should be (1) to identify their respective differences in opinions, values, motives, etc., (2) to clarify the reasons for these differences, and (3) to successfully resolve them. Surprisingly, however, the more successful the partners were in understanding each other's respective positions, the *less* satisfied they felt with the outcome of their attempted conflict-resolution and with the current state of their relationship. Ironically, the more the couples succeeded in achieving their first two goals, the less they succeeded in achieving the third. How could this seemingly paradoxical outcome have occurred?

Sillars (1985) proposed a partial answer to this question by suggesting that when couples attempt to identify and clarify the reasons for their differences, they often wind up making some unpleasant discoveries. In some cases, they discover that their differences are apparently irreconcilable, so that extended discussion and clarification of their respective viewpoints does not improve the relationship but only seems to make things worse (Aldous, 1977; Kursh 1971). In other cases, they discover that "benevolent misconceptions" which they have previously held about each other's viewpoints are false and can no longer be sustained (Levinger & Breedlove, 1966). And, in still other cases, they uncover blunt, unpleasant truths about each other's private thoughts and feelings that could undermine their views of each other and of their relationship (Aldous, 1977; Rausch, Barry, Hertel, & Swain, 1974; Watzlawick, Weakland, & Fisch, 1974).

Granting the importance of all of those processes, we think another important factor is that the partners in such studies do not choose to initiate their conflict discussions but are instead *required* to initiate them. In their daily lives, many of these couples would probably avoid, or at least repeatedly postpone, major confrontations over such high-conflict issues, recognizing them as potential "danger-zone topics" and doing their best to steer clear of them. However, in the special context of laboratory conflict paradigms, couples are essentially compelled to express and defend their respective points of view, and to do so publicly and "for the record" (because their interactions are recorded in some form). Even if their assigned goal is to resolve the conflict(s) in some way, individual face-saving should be an important motive as well – one that could plausibly promote both increased understanding (through the forceful presentation and defense of the partners' respective viewpoints) and decreased satisfaction with the current state of the relationship. Thus, although requiring couples to argue might increase their understanding of each other by making their individual perspectives more explicit (Sillars, 1998), the understanding they gain may be of a type that they find aversive – and therefore usually seek to avoid in the absence of any strong situational constraints (Berger, 1993).

The conflict paradigm studies reported by Sillars and his colleagues provide examples of cases in which increased empathic accuracy can hurt relationships. However, because these studies imposed strong situational constraints, they cannot be regarded as clear-cut examples of cases in which *motivated* accuracy hurts relationships. This observation raises an important question: If relationship partners tend to avoid confronting the more unpleasant truths to be found in each other's thoughts and feelings, would there ever be cases in which *motivated* accuracy hurts relationships, as our second proposed exception to the rule suggests? When, if ever, would partners be motivated to gain such painful knowledge, if the consequences are so predictably aversive?

Perhaps the most obvious answer is that they would do so whenever the alternative (i.e., *not* knowing their partner's actual thoughts and feelings) is perceived as even *more* aversive. Thus, given a choice between learning that a partner does not really love you or spending the rest of your life in an "empty shell" marriage in which you suspect that to be true, you might be motivated to more accurately infer your partner's thoughts and feelings, despite the potential damage to your relationship. Similarly, if you have any reason to believe that your engagement-partner might be less in love with you than with the concept of a quick divorce and a healthy share of your inherited fortune, you might also be motivated to achieve greater empathic accuracy in the face of potential relationship loss. Perceivers in such cases are, in the final analysis, acting rationally; their motive to be accurate derives from a calculated decision to risk an immediate relationship loss in order to avoid a potentially greater one in the future.

A less rational basis for such behavior might also exist, however, in the form of a strong and enduring dispositional motive to accurately infer a partner's private thoughts and feelings. We (Simpson et al., 1999) recently found some preliminary evidence for such a dispositionally-based *accuracy motive* when we re-analyzed the data from our original dating couples study (Simpson et al., 1995) with respect to the partners' scores on the anxiety and avoidance attachment dimensions (see Simpson, Rholes, & Phillips, 1996). Highly anxious partners (particularly highly anxious women) did not display the motivated inaccuracy that we observed in partners with other attachment orientations in the relationship-threatening situation we created. On the contrary, the more anxious they were, the more accurate they were at inferring their partners' relationship-threatening thoughts and feelings. At the same time, however, the more anxious they were, the more they also felt distressed, threatened, and jealous, and the more they displayed other signs of relationship dissatisfaction and instability. In its overall pattern, the behavior of these highly anxious individuals provides intriguing evidence for what we have termed "the second exception to the rule" – that *sometimes motivated accuracy hurts relationships*.

Complementing this evidence that highly anxious partners have a strong "accuracy motive," we also found evidence of what appears to be a contrasting motive in highly avoidant partners. In this case, the more avoidant the partners were, the more likely they were to leave slots on the empathic inference form blank, thereby declining to make certain inferences about their dating partner's potentially threatening thoughts and feelings at certain "tape stops." Taken together, these findings for the anxiety and avoidance attachment dimensions suggest that there may be substantial individual differences in the motive to accurately infer one's partner's thoughts and feelings in relationship-threatening situations, and that this motive may be especially pronounced in highly anxious individuals.

A Theoretical Integration of the Rule and Its Exceptions

Conventional wisdom suggests that understanding a relationship partner's thoughts and feelings should be good for relationships. As we have just seen, however, this widely held belief is overly simplistic and does not account for the entire pattern of available findings. Although greater empathic accuracy tends to be associated with more relationship satisfaction and greater stability in situations that pose little or no threat to relationships (e.g., Kahn, 1970; Noller, 1980; Noller & Ruzzene, 1991), it is associated with *less* satisfaction and *less* stability in relationship-threatening situations (e.g., Sillars et al., 1984; Simpson et al., 1995). At first glance, the findings from the studies involving relationship-threatening situations seem counterintuitive, if not completely paradoxical, in light of the widely held assumption that threats to relationships are more easily defused if partners can gain a greater understanding of each other's respective thoughts and feelings.

To help resolve this apparent paradox, we have proposed a theoretical model of how partners might "manage" their levels of empathic accuracy in relationship-threatening versus nonthreatening situations (Ickes & Simpson, 1997). A description of this model, elaborated in certain respects from its original presentation, is provided below. The goal of the model is to specify the conditions in which (1) empathic accuracy should help relationships (the general rule); (2) empathic *in*accuracy should help relationships (the first exception to the rule); and (3) empathic accuracy should hurt relationships (the second exception to the rule).

The empathic accuracy model

Our model starts by assuming that the range of empathic accuracy (the upper and lower boundaries) that can be attained in a given interaction is set by (1) the partners' respective levels of "readability" (the degree to which each partner conveys cues that reflect his or her true internal states), and (2) the partners' respective levels of empathic ability (the degree to which each partner can accurately decipher the other's valid behavioral cues). Within these broad constraints, however, the model presumes that empathic accuracy should be "managed" very differently depending on a number of factors. The factors we regard as most fundamental are represented in the portion of our model that is depicted in figure 9.1.

It is important to note that figure 9.1 characterizes behavior at the individual, rather than the dyadic, level of analysis. According to this model, each partner makes his or her own preliminary assessment of whether or not the current situation is likely to lead to a *danger zone* in the partners' relationship. As we define it, the term "danger zone" is a convenient shorthand. It denotes having to confront an issue that could potentially threaten the relationship by revealing thoughts and feelings harbored by one's partner that one might personally find distressing and upsetting.

Of course, what one partner might find distressing and upsetting might not be viewed in a similar way by the other partner (for example, male partners might find a revelation of sexual infidelity more threatening than a revelation of emotional infidelity, whereas the reverse might be true for female partners; cf. Buss et al., 1999). A broader and more de-

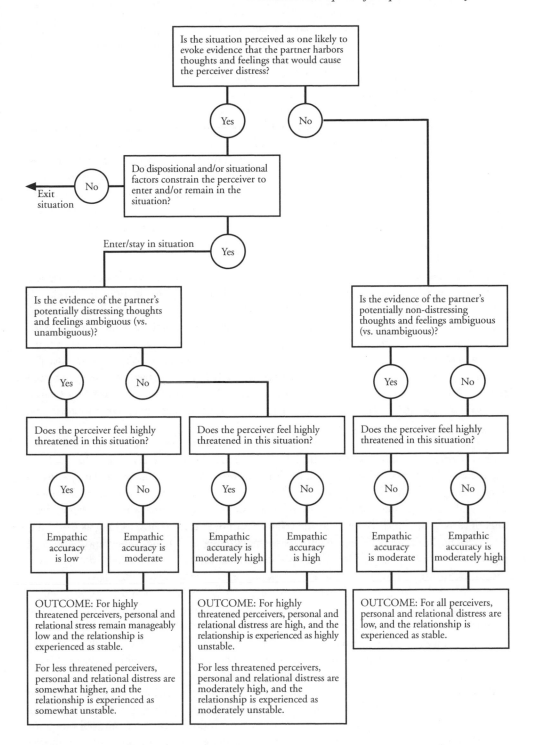

Figure 9.1   The empathic accuracy model

tailed version of our model would therefore begin by acknowledging that individual relationship partners could assign themselves to different "paths" or trajectories if one partner anticipated a danger zone in the current situation whereas the other partner did not. Although developing the various theoretical implications of this broader, more complex "dyadic" model is beyond the scope of the present chapter, we will consider a few of these implications below. In addition, we encourage researchers who are interested in this topic to routinely assess both partners' danger zones (the specific forms they take and how threatening they are perceived to be) at both the individual and the dyadic levels of analysis.

At the first branching point in our model, each individual anticipates either a situation in which a danger-zone issue is likely to present itself or one in which no danger-zone issue is likely to emerge. To "walk through" the possible subsequent outcomes, let us first consider the part of the model that applies when an individual perceives that a situation is nonthreatening (i.e., that no danger-zone issue is likely to emerge that might force the partners to confront each other's relationship-threatening thoughts and feelings).

Empathic accuracy in nonthreatening contexts.   When perceivers expect to deal with issues that do not have threatening implications for their relationship (see the right-hand portion of figure 9.1), the model predicts that they should be at least somewhat motivated to accurately infer their partners' thoughts and feelings. Because experience should have taught them that mutual understanding often facilitates their ability to coordinate their actions and thereby pursue both individual and common goals more effectively, and because the behaviors needed to attain such understanding typically become habitual through repeated reinforcement (Bissonnette, Rusbult, & Kilpatrick, 1997), perceivers should be motivated to attain at least minimal levels of accuracy when inferring their partners' thoughts and feelings.

Accordingly, in nonthreatening situations in which no danger zones are perceived (e.g., everyday conversations concerning trivial or mundane issues), perceivers should display a habit-based "accuracy" orientation. This orientation should help them to clarify misunderstandings over nonthreatening issues, keep minor conflicts from escalating into major ones, and gain a deeper understanding of their partner, all of which should enhance feelings of satisfaction and closeness in the relationship over time. Thus, as long as the situation does not lead the perceiver to anticipate the emergence of issues that could evoke and potentially reveal a partner's relationship-threatening thoughts and feelings, the perceiver should be motivated to attain at least a moderate level of empathic accuracy.

On the other hand, the perceiver's motivation to be accurate should be attenuated to some degree by the routine, taken-for-granted nature of such mundane, nonthreatening interactions (cf. Thomas & Fletcher, 1997; Thomas, Fletcher, & Lange, 1997). The level of empathic accuracy displayed by perceivers in nonthreatening interactions should therefore be moderate to moderately high rather than high (see the lower right portion of figure 9.1). Finally, the levels of relationship satisfaction and stability should correlate positively with the level of empathic accuracy in these nonthreatening situations, consistent with the rule that, in general, *motivated accuracy is good for relationships*. These positive correlations may be small, however, because they are likely to be attenuated by the truncated ranges of both the empathic accuracy and the relationship-outcome variables in most nonthreatening interaction contexts.

Empathic accuracy in threatening contexts.   Inevitably, perceivers will at times encounter situations in which "danger zones" are anticipated – situations that might destabilize their close relationships (see the left-hand portion of figure 9.1). When these situations arise, the model predicts that the perceiver's first impulse should be to avoid or escape from them if it is possible to do so. The strategy of avoiding or escaping from danger-zone situations is the first "line of defense" that perceivers can use to manage their empathic accuracy and keep themselves from having to confront their partners' relationship-threatening thoughts and feelings.

The use of this strategy presumes, of course, that perceivers can recognize – and even anticipate – potential "danger zone" areas in their relationships, that is, the areas in which painful insights or revelations about their partners' private thoughts and feelings might occur (e.g., positive feelings about old flames or lustful thoughts about other attractive people). Over time, perceivers in most (but not all) relationships should learn to identify and avoid such danger-zone areas in order to protect their own self-esteem, their partners' self-esteem, and their positive views of the relationship. In doing so, perceivers can avoid dealing with danger-zone topics directly, acting as if it is better (and easier) to avoid confronting one's worst fears than it is to have one's worst fears confirmed and then be forced to deal with them.

Avoiding or escaping danger-zone issues is not always possible, however, and the section of our model that is relevant to these cases is depicted in the left and middle portions of figure 9.1. When perceivers feel obliged to remain in a relationship-threatening situation, the model predicts that their second "line of defense" should be *motivated inaccuracy* – a conscious or unconscious failure to accurately infer the specific content of their partner's potentially hurtful thoughts and feelings. The success of this strategy should vary, however, depending on the degree to which the inferred content of the partner's potentially distressing thoughts and feelings is perceived to be ambiguous versus unambiguous.

If the content of the partners' potentially threatening thoughts and feelings is perceived as ambiguous (see the left-hand portion of figure 9.1), perceivers should be free to use motivated inaccuracy as a defense. By using subception and other defense mechanisms (e.g., denial, repression, rationalization) to avoid having to deal with the most threatening implications of their partners' potentially destructive thoughts and feelings, perceivers should display low levels of empathic accuracy. Their perceptual-inferential defenses should provide them with an important payoff, however, in helping to minimize their personal and relational distress, and in helping to keep their relationship stable. Thus, the left-hand portion of our model illustrates the "first exception to the rule" – that *sometimes motivated inaccuracy helps relationships.*

What happens when perceivers feel obliged to remain in a relationship-threatening situation but are precluded from using motivated inaccuracy as a secondary strategy for warding off relationship threat? The middle portion of figure 9.1 depicts one case of this type. In this case, the relationship-threatening content of the partner's thoughts and feelings is perceived to be clear and unambiguous (e.g., the partner openly admits that s/he loves someone else). The sheer clarity of this information should force the perceiver to achieve at least moderately high levels of empathic accuracy, accompanied by very low relationship satisfaction and stability. Obviously, this case is one in which increased empathic accuracy hurts relationships. However, because the perceiver is forced to be accurate by virtue of the clarity of the available information, it does not illustrate a case in which true *motivated accuracy* hurts relationships.

Such a case should occur, however, if the perceiver has a strong personal need to confront the truth about the partner's relationship-relevant thoughts and feelings. We were first alerted to such a case when we discovered that the more anxiously attached dating partners in the Simpson et al. (1995) study displayed motivated accuracy, rather than motivated *in*accuracy, in response to relationship threat (Simpson et al., 1999). This finding suggests that a strong, dispositionally based accuracy motive can override such tendencies as avoiding danger-zone situations or using motivated inaccuracy to ward off their threatening implications. Preliminary evidence that motivated accuracy can hurt relationships in cases like this has already been presented in our review of the findings of Simpson et al. (1999). These findings can be used to illustrate the second exception to the rule, i.e., that *sometimes motivated accuracy hurts relationships.*

Toward a revised empathic accuracy model

How should our empathic accuracy model be revised to take such individual differences in accuracy motives into account? We think that, at each level of the model, two individual difference factors should be considered. The first factor concerns how much threat each partner experiences in the situation at hand. To some extent, this factor is already represented explicitly in the figure 9.1 version of the model, although it is treated as a within-individual variable rather than as a within-dyad variable.

The second factor, yet to be included in the model, concerns the strength of each partner's accuracy motive. If figure 9.1 were revised to include only this second factor (ignoring the first factor for the moment to simplify things), the resulting predictions would reflect an overall main effect of the within-dyad difference in the partners' accuracy motives on their ability to accurately read each other's thoughts and feelings (that is, in general, the partner with the stronger accuracy motive should display the higher level of empathic accuracy).

With regard to the right-hand portion of the figure 9.1 model, we would predict that, in mundane, nonthreatening situations, the partner with the stronger accuracy motive should be more empathically accurate than the partner with the weaker accuracy motive. Moreover, because greater accuracy should enhance relationship quality in such situations, strong accuracy motives exhibited by one or both partners should generally lead to greater relationship stability and satisfaction. We should note, however, that as partners become increasingly "mismatched" in their accuracy motives (i.e., when one partner's accuracy motive is very high and the other's is very low), additional dynamics may emerge that complicate the prediction of individual and relational outcomes in this case (for evidence suggesting such dynamics, see Ickes, 1993; Simpson et al., 1995; Stinson & Ickes, 1992).

With regard to the left and middle portions of figure 9.1, differences in the strength of the partners' accuracy motives should lead them down different "paths" in the model. At the second branching point near the top of the model, the partner with the weaker accuracy motive should be more likely to avoid or escape the relationship-threatening situation, whereas the partner with the stronger accuracy motive should be more likely to confront it directly.

If escape/avoidance is either not possible or not chosen (see the next level of the figure 9.1 model), the partner with the weaker accuracy motive should be more likely to use motivated inaccuracy to evade the impending threat when the partner's thoughts and feelings are perceived to be ambiguous, but should be forced to make at least moderately accurate inferences when they are perceived to be clear and unambiguous. In contrast, the other partner's stronger accuracy motive should be more likely to counter or even override the tendency to use motivated inaccuracy, resulting in relatively higher levels of empathic accuracy in both the ambiguous and the unambiguous conditions.

Given these predictions, it should be evident that partners with weak accuracy motives can minimize the threat to their relationships by taking either of the two paths in the model (avoidance/escape or motivated inaccuracy) that are not available to partners with strong accuracy motives. In contrast, partners with strong accuracy motives must directly confront these threats, which they should find difficult to avoid or escape.

Let us now summarize the implications of *both* of the within-dyad differences that we have just considered (i.e., level of perceived threat and accuracy motivation) for the processes depicted in the left and middle portions of the model in figure 9.1. Occasionally, a situation will arise that evokes an initial feeling of threat in the perceiver. This feeling should be based on the conscious or unconscious perception that the unfolding situation might present a danger-zone issue that could potentially threaten the relationship. The strength of this initial feeling should vary substantially, however, depending on (1) the degree to which the perceiver is anxious (i.e., easily threatened) in a dispositional sense, and (2) the strength of the perceiver's accuracy motivation.

Highly threatened perceivers with weak accuracy motives should be the most likely to avoid or exit potentially relationship-threatening situations. In contrast, highly threatened perceivers with strong accuracy motives (e.g., the highly anxious women in the Simpson et al., 1999, study) should be highly *ambivalent*. On the one hand, they should find these situations so threatening that they would ideally prefer to leave them, if they could; on the other hand, their level of accuracy motivation is so high that it tends to override their anxiety and compels them to remain in the situation and confront their "worst fears." Weakly threatened perceivers, regardless of whether their accuracy motives are weak or strong, should also be inclined to stay in relationship-threatening situations. Their responses are likely to diverge not at this point but at the *next* branching point of the model, as we shall see below.

As the situation unfolds, the perceiver's feeling of threat should increasingly reflect the degree to which the developing situation has either clarified the presence of a danger-zone issue (in the unambiguous case) or has failed to clarify its presence (in the ambiguous case). If highly threatened perceivers with weak accuracy motives have not already avoided or escaped from the situation, but have remained in it instead (perhaps because of strong situational constraints), they should follow the path of motivated inaccuracy in the ambiguous case and display only moderate accuracy in the unambiguous case. In contrast, highly threatened perceivers with strong accuracy motives should eschew the path of motivated inaccuracy and display higher levels of empathic accuracy in both cases, but particularly when the potential for threat is unambiguous.

How should weakly threatened perceivers react at this "level" of the model? Weakly threatened perceivers with weak accuracy motives should be more likely to follow the path of motivated accuracy than should weakly threatened perceivers with strong accuracy motives. However, this difference should be less extreme than that observed in these perceivers' more highly threatened counterparts.

Assessing the strength of perceivers' accuracy motives

If perceivers' levels of threat can be measured by a self-report index such as that used by Simpson et al. (1995), how might the strength of their accuracy motives be assessed? To some extent, perceived threat and accuracy motivation may be naturally confounded in relationship-threatening situations, according to the findings of Simpson et al. (1999). Their data suggest that such confounding might be particularly evident in highly anxious women, who appeared to have an exceptionally strong need to accurately infer their partner's thoughts and feelings in the relationship-threatening situation that Simpson et al. (1995) created.

From the standpoint of attachment theory (Bowlby, 1973; Cassidy & Berlin, 1994), this confounding of perceived threat and accuracy motivation makes sense in the case of anxiously attached individuals. Attachment theory proposes that highly anxious individuals are chronically uncertain about the availability and dependability of their relationship partners (Bowlby, 1973). They are chronically worried about the possibility of losing their partners/relationships, and are therefore motivated to monitor their partners closely – a phenomenon that Cassidy and Berlin (1994) have characterized as *hypervigilance* (see also Kobak & Sceery, 1988; Mikulincer, Florian, & Weller, 1993).

These considerations suggest that, to the extent that perceived threat and accuracy motivation are naturally confounded for anxiously attached individuals, perceivers' scores on the anxiety attachment dimension might be used as a single proxy measure that captures the combined influence of both variables. On the other hand, because the natural confounding of perceived threat and accuracy motivation might prove to be relatively limited (e.g., applying primarily to anxiously attached women in relationship-threatening situations), it might be a serious conceptual mistake to assume any general tendency for these two factors to covary. The best strategy, therefore, would be to obtain separate measures of perceived threat and accuracy motivation so that predictions of the type we have outlined above could be tested more impartially.

This strategy would require us to complement our existing measure of perceived threat with one or more new measures specifically designed to assess the strength of individuals' accuracy motives. We are currently pursuing this strategy, which has forced us to confront an important question: Should the accuracy motive be measured at a global level (i.e., generalizing across all types of relationship partners and all categories of their thought/ feeling content), or should it be measured in a more differentiated way (i.e., assessing the strength of the accuracy motive for specific categories of relationship partners and/or their thought/feeling content)?

We would expect, for example, that the strength of the motive to accurately infer a partner's *relationship-threatening* thoughts and feelings would be especially relevant to the paths in the left and center portions of the model depicted in figure 9.1. This expectation has led us to develop the MARTI (*Motive to Acquire/Avoid Relationship-Threatening Information*) scale – a self-report measure that assesses the strength of perceivers' motives to apprehend versus avoid their partners' relationship-threatening thoughts and feelings in dating or marital relationships. Two research investigations using the MARTI scale with samples of dating couples are currently in progress.

Managing Empathic Accuracy in Close Relationships

Given the importance of controlling what one knows and does *not* know about a partner's thoughts and feelings, how should individuals deal with the delicate problem of "managing" their level of empathic accuracy in their close relationships? Any attempt to answer this question must begin by acknowledging that relationship partners have multiple – and sometimes competing – goals in their interactions (Sillars, 1998). When the goal of achieving a good understanding of a partner's thoughts and feelings does not compromise the goal of protecting the relationship from threatening information, empathic understanding should remain relatively high. However, when these goals clash, the first goal (achieving better understanding) may often be sacrificed for the sake of the second one (sheltering relationship partners from painful insights or revelations that could damage their relationship).

Because the relative strength of these two goals cannot be assessed at each branching point in our model without interfering with the very processes we are attempting to predict, our model relies on the use of less proximal predictors. We assume that perceivers' strategies for dealing with both relationship-threatening and nonthreatening situations are guided by the combined influences of relevant situational factors (e.g., whether perceivers think their partner may be having relationship-threatening thoughts or feelings and the ambiguity of the evidence on which this belief is based), and relevant dispositional factors (i.e., their level of relational anxiety and their accuracy motivation).

We suggest that the dispositional factors will influence partners' perceptions at each of the branching points in our model – affecting, for example, the degree to which certain people (e.g., anxiously attached individuals) are prone to infer that their partner might be having damaging thoughts or feelings, "find" evidence supporting these concerns, and therefore feel threatened. Because such dispositions can color and constrain individuals' perceptions through the entire course of a given interaction, it may often be unclear whether the management of empathic accuracy is more strongly governed by situational or by dispositional influences. This blurring of situational and dispositional influences should be especially characteristic of highly anxious individuals, who are chronically predisposed to expect and find the worst in relationship-threatening settings (Bowlby, 1973; Simpson & Rholes, 1994). It may also characterize individuals who are more emotionally invested in their relationship than their partners are (i.e., the "strong-link" partner in each relationship: see Ickes & Simpson, 1997).

Relational implications of motivated inaccuracy and motivated accuracy

Our model has several implications for how the management of empathic accuracy should affect the quality and functioning of relationships, both in the short term and over a longer period of time. In this section, we speculate about how the two "exceptions" to the general rule should affect both short-term and long-term relationship outcomes. We further suggest how certain dyad-level effects (such as the degree of discrepancy between partners' levels of empathic accuracy) may also effect their long-term relational outcomes. Finally, we consider the possible consequences for the partners' relationship of (1) treating "exception-to-the-rule" situations as if they were "general rule" cases and (2) treating "general rule" situations as if they were "exception-to-the-rule" cases.

Implications of motivated inaccuracy.   For individuals who "turn a blind eye" to their partners' potentially distressing thoughts and feelings in relationship-threatening situations, motivated inaccuracy should help to maintain the stability of their relationships in the short term, especially if the threats they "ignore" are temporary, beyond their control, or not likely to reoccur. However, when the threats they ignore involve important, recurrent problems in the relationship, motivated inaccuracy should become an increasingly less effective strategy, particularly if problems that could be resolved are allowed to grow or worsen. Over time, partners who fail to address and solve their chronic problems should experience increased personal and relational distress, ultimately resulting in greater relationship instability.

From this perspective, motivated inaccuracy is best employed as a "stopgap" defensive strategy, freeing individuals from having to ponder and worry about the implications of relational threats that are temporary or largely beyond their control. But when motivated inaccuracy is repeatedly used to avoid or circumvent recurrent, solvable problems, it should have pernicious and damaging long-term effects on most relationships.

Implications of motivated accuracy.   For individuals who cannot "turn a blind eye" to what their partners might be thinking and feeling in relationship-threatening situations, the heightened empathic accuracy they experience should have destabilizing effects on their relationships, particularly in the short term. Acute empathic accuracy in these situations may reflect the operation of substantive information processing (Forgas, 1995), which occurs when individuals are motivated to engage in active, on-line processing in order to observe and interpret the behavior of others very carefully. Substantive processing tends to be elicited when interactions are personally relevant or ambiguous, and when individuals have a strong need to understand what is happening at the moment (see Forgas, 1995). Persons engaged in substantive processing typically think about both new (current) and old (former) information relevant to their interaction partners, and their current emotional states (either positive or negative) are more likely to infuse the judgments and inferences they make about their partners and related events.

Highly anxious individuals may automatically shift to this mode of information processing in relationship-threatening situations, particularly those that might portend relationship loss. This would explain why, in many relationship-threatening contexts, highly anxious individuals (1) become hypervigilant (Mikulincer et al., 1993; Simpson et al., 1999), (2) allow old and often irrelevant relationship issues to invade current discussions with their partners (Simpson et al., 1996), and (3) base their judgments of their partners and relationships on their current emotional states (Tidwell, Reis, & Shaver, 1996). Over time, the tendency to "infer the worst" about what one's partner might be thinking or feeling should produce distrust and suspicion in relationships. This process could explain why highly anxious individuals experience higher rates of relationship dissolution than less anxious individuals do (Kirkpatrick & Davis, 1994; Simpson et al., 1999).

Empathic accuracy over time within relationships

Recent research using conflict resolution tasks indicates that empathic accuracy decreases over the first few years of marriage (e.g., Thomas & Fletcher, 1997; Thomas, Fletcher, & Lange, 1997). A number of factors might help to explain this trend. First, partners in newly formed relationships are probably more motivated to track each other's changing thoughts and feelings by listening to each other carefully, making frequent eye contact, and monitoring the changes in each other's facial expressions and body language. This motivation could reflect the newlyweds' tendency to dote on each other, their desire to get to know each other as well as possible, or their desire to avoid offending each other during the early stages of adjusting to their new life together (Bissonnette et al., 1997; Thomas & Fletcher, 1997). Second, because they have probably not yet settled into familiar interdependent routines (Kelley & Thibaut, 1978), partners in newly formed relationships should approach many recurring interactions as if they were novel ones, at least until they discover ways to maximize their joint reward/cost outcomes (Rusbult & Arriaga, 1997). Third, because they are less certain about how their partners are likely to think, feel, and react in various situations, newlywed partners may be more careful to avoid using premature stereotypes of what their partner is "like" to guide their empathic inferences.

As time passes, the degree of disparity in the partners' general levels of empathic accuracy should play an increasingly important role in their relationship. If one partner consistently understands the other partner well but feels poorly understood in return, the relationship should have a greater potential to become unstable than if both partners are evenly matched in their levels of empathic accuracy (see Ickes, 1993; Simpson et al., 1995; Stinson & Ickes, 1992, for supportive evidence). Glaring, persistent inequities in feeling understood by one's partner could generate increasing feelings of resentment in the more accurate (i.e., the more misunderstood) partner, whereas feeling vulnerable to exploitation by the more accurate partner could generate increasing feelings of resentment in the less accurate (i.e., the better understood) partner. Pronounced asymmetries in the partners' levels of understanding may also signify a flawed intersubjectivity in their relationship – an inability of the partners to bring their individual understandings into synchrony with each other in their day-to-day interactions. For all of these reasons, partners who have "mismatched" levels of empathic accuracy may be at higher risk than more "evenly matched" partners of experiencing greater relational instability over time.

Misapplications of the general rule and its exceptions

In this chapter, we have reviewed the research evidence relevant to a general rule (that motivated accuracy helps relationships) and its two exceptions (that motivated *in*accuracy sometimes helps relationships, and that motivated accuracy sometimes hurts them). What happens when individuals "misapply" either the general rule or its two major exceptions? More specifically, what happens when individuals apply the general rule in situations in which invoking one of the exceptions would be more appropriate? And what happens when individuals apply one of the exceptions when subscribing to the general rule would be more appropriate?

Misapplying the general rule when motivated inaccuracy is the more appropriate response can have potentially devastating consequences for close relationships. Partners who, out of misplaced idealism or naïveté, believe that they should always have free and total access to each other's thoughts and feelings may repeatedly insist on knowing things about each other's private experiences that they might be better off not knowing. By failing to overlook danger-zone issues that are temporary, uncontrollable, and otherwise inconsequential, perceivers may repeatedly make mountains out of molehills, and thereby experience considerable personal and relational distress. On the other hand, if the danger-zone topics involve long-standing, recurrent, and potentially resolvable issues, misapplying the general rule could yield positive long-term outcomes. By providing opportunities for perceivers to finally understand how their partners *really* think and feel about such issues, individuals may come to realize – perhaps for the very first time – that these issues can indeed be resolved. This understanding may, in turn, motivate them to address such issues directly and eventually solve the underlying problems, thereby eliminating the need for motivated inaccuracy to "contain" the danger-zone topic in future interactions.

Mistakenly employing a motivated inaccuracy strategy (the first exception to the rule) in cases when the general rule ought to be followed can also have negative consequences for relationships, particularly if danger-zone issues are recurrent and can be resolved. Besides failing to see and potentially solve these chronic problems, individuals who display motivated inaccuracy when general accuracy should prevail are likely to (1) experience larger disparities in empathic accuracy relative to their partners, and (2) offend or upset their partners by not showing proper empathy and understanding in situations that the partner correctly views as mundane and nonthreatening. These deleterious effects have their origin in dyad-level processes that are triggered by the negative attributions that a perceiver's *partner* makes for the perceiver's apparent lack of empathy and understanding in situations in which the partner justifiably expects more of both.

At first glance, it might appear that adopting a motivated accuracy orientation when the general rule should be applied can never be an inappropriate response, because the consequence in both cases is apparently the same – enhanced empathic accuracy. An excessively high level of empathic accuracy that is motivated by anxiety can be problematic and inappropriate, however, when hypervigilance leads individuals to focus narrowly on, ruminate about, and reach exaggerated, overly generalized conclusions about the nature of their partner's relationship-threatening thoughts and feelings. By basing their subsequent behaviors on such exaggerated and overly generalized inferences, hypervigilant perceivers might engender negative relationship outcomes that would *not* have occurred if the more general "mundane accuracy" rule had governed their behavior. If hypervigilance leads perceivers to search for evidence that might validate their "worst case" fears and concerns each time a danger-zone issue arises, their resulting suspicion – and their partners' awareness of it – could engender a pattern of reciprocated suspicion and hypervigilance laden with strong negative affect (cf. Forgas, 1995). As this process escalates in its intensity, it should amplify both partners' personal and relational distress, lead them to seriously question the quality and viability of their relationship, and engender increased relational instability. Ironically, then, "too much" accuracy can create problems in situations in which a more mundane level of accuracy is appropriate.

Final note

There is an old bromide which holds that greater understanding is a sovereign cure for the various ills that plague close relationships. As we have seen, however, this bromide is not – as it purports to be – an all-purpose panacea. In fact, in some circumstances it is a prescription for disaster.

In this chapter, we have tried to specify the general conditions in which motivated accuracy can help relationships and the exception-to-the rule conditions in which motivated *in*accuracy can help relationships and in which excessive (hypervigilant) accuracy can hurt them. Although relationship partners typically seek to understand the "truth" about each other's thoughts and feelings, there are occasions when the truth can carry a very big price. Knowing when to pay this price, and when to avoid paying it, may be the beginning of wisdom for the partners in close relationships.

Acknowledgment

The preparation of this chapter was supported in part by National Science Foundation grant no. SBR 9732476 to the authors.

References

Aldous, J. (1977). Family interaction patterns. *Annual Review of Sociology, 3*, 105–135.
Barry, W. A. (1970). Marriage research and conflict: An integrative review. *Psychological Bulletin, 73*, 41–54.
Berger, C. R. (1993). Goals, plans, and mutual understanding in relationships. In S. Duck (Ed.), *Individuals in relationships* (pp. 30–59). Newbury Park, CA: Sage.
Bissonnette, V., Rusbult, C., & Kilpatrick, S. D. (1997). Empathic accuracy and marital conflict resolution. In W. Ickes (Ed.), *Empathic accuracy* (pp. 251–281). New York: Guilford Press.
Bowlby, J. (1973). *Attachment and loss*, Vol. 2: *Separation: Anxiety and anger*. New York: Basic Books.
Buss, D. M., Shackelford, T. K., Kirkpatrick, L. A., Choe, J. C., Lim, H. K., Hasegawa, M., Hasegawa, T., & Bennett, K. (1999). Jealousy and the nature of beliefs about infidelity: Tests of competing hypotheses about sex differences in the United States, Korea, and Japan. *Personal Relationships, 6*, 125–150.
Cassidy, J., & Berlin, L. J. (1994). The insecure/ambivalent pattern of attachment: Theory and research. *Child Development, 65*, 971–991.
Christensen, L., & Wallace, L. (1976). Perceptual accuracy as a variable in marital adjustment. *Journal of Sex and Marital Therapy, 2*, 130–136.
Corsini, R. J. (1956). Understanding and similarity in marriage. *Journal of Abnormal and Social Psychology, 52*, 327–332.
Dymond, R. (1954). Interpersonal perception and marital happiness. *Canadian Journal of Psychology, 8*, 164–171.

Ferguson, L. R., & Allen, D. R. (1978). Congruence of parental perception, marital satisfaction, and child adjustment. *Journal of Consulting and Clinical Psychology, 46,* 345–346.

Forgas, J. (1995). Mood and judgment: The affect infusion model (AIM). *Psychological Bulletin, 116,* 39–66.

Gottman, J. M., Notarius, C., Markman, H., Bank, S., Yoppi, B., & Rubin, M. E. (1976). Behavior exchange theory and marital decision making. *Journal of Personality and Social Psychology, 34,* 14–23.

Gottman, J. M., & Porterfield, A. L. (1981). Communicative competence in the nonverbal behavior of married couples. *Journal of Marriage and the Family, 43,* 817–824.

Guthrie, D. M., & Noller, P. (1988). Married couples' perceptions of one another in emotional situations. In P. Noller & M. A. Fitzpatrick (Eds.), *Perspectives on marital interaction* (pp. 153–181). Cleveland, OH: Multilingual Matters.

Ickes, W. (1993). Empathic accuracy. *Journal of Personality, 61,* 587–610.

Ickes, W., Bissonnette, V., Garcia, S., & Stinson, L. (1990). Implementing and using the dyadic interaction paradigm. In C. Hendrick & M. Clark (Eds.), *Review of personality and social psychology: Research methods in personality and social psychology* (Vol. 11, pp. 16–44). Newbury Park, CA: Sage.

Ickes, W., & Simpson, J. A. (1997). Managing empathic accuracy in close relationships. In W. Ickes (Ed.), *Empathic accuracy* (pp. 218–250). New York: Guilford Press.

Ickes, W., Stinson, L., Bissonnette, V., & Garcia, S. (1990). Naturalistic social cognition: Empathic accuracy in mixed-sex dyads. *Journal of Personality and Social Psychology, 59,* 730–742.

Kahn, M. (1970). Nonverbal communication and marital satisfaction. *Family Process, 9,* 449–456.

Katz, M. (1965). Agreement on connotative meaning in marriage. *Family Process, 5,* 64–74.

Kelley, H. H., & Thibaut, J. W. (1978). Interpersonal relations: A theory of interdependence. New York: Wiley.

Kilpatrick, S. D., Bissonnette, V. L., & Rusbult, C.E. (1999). *Empathic accuracy among newly married couples.* Manuscript submitted for publication.

Kirkpatrick, L. A., & Davis, K. E. (1994). Attachment style, gender, and relationship stability: A longitudinal analysis. *Journal of Personality and Social Psychology, 66,* 502–512.

Knudson, R. A., Sommers, A. A., & Golding, S. L. (1980). Interpersonal perception and mode of resolution in marital conflict. *Journal of Personality and Social Psychology, 38,* 251–263.

Kobak, R. R., & Sceery, A. (1988). Attachment in late adolescence: Working models, affect regulation, and representations of self and others. *Child Development, 59,* 135–146.

Kotlar, S. L. (1965). Middle-class marital role perceptions and marital adjustment. *Sociology and Social Research, 49,* 284–291.

Kursh, C. O. (1971). The benefits of poor communication. *Psychoanalytic Review, 58,* 189–208.

Laing, R. D., Phillipson, H., & Lee, A. R. (1966). *Interpersonal perception: A theory and a method of research.* New York: Springer.

Levinger, G., & Breedlove, J. (1966). Interpersonal attraction and agreement. *Journal of Personality and Social Psychology, 3,* 367–372.

Luckey, E. B. (1960). Number of years married as related to personality perception and marital satisfaction. *Journal of Marriage and the Family, 28,* 44–48.

Madden, M. E., & Janoff-Bulman, R. (1981). Blame, control, and marital satisfaction: Wives' attributions for conflict in marriage. *Journal of Marriage and the Family, 43,* 663–674.

Mikulincer, M., Florian, V., & Weller, A. (1993). Attachment styles, coping strategies, and posttraumatic psychological distress: The impact of the Gulf War in Israel. *Journal of Personality and Social Psychology, 64,* 817–826.

Murstein, B. I., & Beck, G. D. (1972). Person perception, marriage adjustment, and social desirability. *Journal of Consulting and Clinical Psychology, 39,* 396–403.

Navran, L. (1967). Communication and adjustment in marriage. *Family Process, 6,* 173–184.

Neimeyer, G. J., & Banikiotes, P. G. (1981). Self-disclosure flexibility, empathy, and perceptions of adjustment and attraction. *Journal of Counseling Psychology, 28,* 272–275.

Newmark, C. S., Woody, G., & Ziff, D. (1977). Understanding and similarity in relation to marital satisfaction. *Journal of Clinical Psychology, 33,* 83–86.

Noller, P. (1980). Misunderstandings in marital communication: A study of couples' nonverbal communication. *Journal of Personality and Social Psychology, 39,* 1135–1148.

Noller, P. (1981). Gender and marital adjustment level differences in decoding messages from spouses and strangers. *Journal of Personality and Social Psychology, 41*, 272–278.

Noller, P. (1984). *Nonverbal communication and marital interaction.* Oxford: Pergamon.

Noller, P., & Ruzzene, M. (1991). Communication in marriage: The influence of affect and cognition. In G. J. O. Fletcher & F. D. Fincham (Eds.), *Cognition in close relationships* (pp. 203–233). Hillsdale, NJ: Erlbaum.

Noller, P., & Venardos, C. (1986). Communication awareness in married couples. *Journal of Social and Personal Relationships, 3*, 31–42.

Rausch, H. L., Barry, W. A., Hertel, R. K., & Swain, M. A. (1974). *Communication conflict and marriage.* San Francisco: Jossey-Bass.

Rusbult, C. E., & Arriaga, X. B. (1997). Interdependence processes in close relationships. In S. Duck et al. (Eds.), *Handbook of personal relationships: Theory, research, and interventions.* (2nd ed., pp. 221–250). Chichester, UK: Wiley.

Sillars, A. L. (1981). Attributions and interpersonal conflict resolution. In J. H. Harvey, W. J. Ickes, & R. F. Kidd (Eds.), *New directions in attribution research* (Vol. 3). Hillsdale, NJ: Erlbaum.

Sillars, A. L. (1985). Interpersonal perception in relationships. In W. Ickes (Ed.), *Compatible and incompatible relationships.* (pp. 277–305). New York: Springer-Verlag.

Sillars, A. L. (1998). (Mis)understanding. In B. H. Spitzberg and W. R. Cupach (Eds.), *The dark side of close relationships* (pp. 73–102). Mahwah, NJ: Erlbaum.

Sillars, A. L., & Parry, D. (1982). Stress, cognition, and communication in interpersonal conflicts. *Communication Research, 9*, 201–226.

Sillars, A. L., Pike, G. R., Jones, T. S., & Murphy, M. A. (1984). Communication and understanding in marriage. *Human Communication Research, 10*, 317–350.

Sillars, A. L., Pike, G. R., Jones, T. J., & Redmon, K. (1983). Communication and conflict in marriage. In K. Bostrom (Ed.), *Communication yearbook* (Vol. 7). Beverly Hills, CA: Sage.

Sillars, A. L., & Scott, M. D. (1983). Interpersonal perception between intimates: An integrative review. *Human Communication Research, 10*, 153–176.

Simpson, J. A., Ickes, W., & Blackstone, T. (1995). When the head protects the heart: Empathic accuracy in dating relationships. *Journal of Personality and Social Psychology, 69*, 629–641.

Simpson, J. A., Ickes, W., & Grich, J. (1999). When accuracy hurts: Reactions of anxiously-attached dating partners to a relationship-threatening situation. *Journal of Personality and Social Psychology, 76*, 754–769.

Simpson, J. A., & Rholes, W. S. (1994). Stress and secure base relationships in adulthood. In K. Bartholomew & D. Perlman (Eds.), *Advances in personal relationships: Vol. 5. Attachment processes in adulthood* (pp. 181–204). London: Kingsley.

Simpson, J. A., Rholes, W. S., & Phillips, D. (1996). Conflict in close relationships: An attachment perspective. *Journal of Personality and Social Psychology, 71*, 899–914.

Stinson, L., & Ickes, W. (1992). Empathic accuracy in the interactions of male friends versus male strangers. *Journal of Personality and Social Psychology, 62*, 787–797.

Stuckert, R. (1963). Role perception and marital satisfaction: A configuration approach. *Marriage and Family Living, 25*, 415–419.

Taylor, B. A. (1967). Role perception, empathy, and marriage adjustment. *Sociology and Social Research, 52*, 22–34.

Thomas, G., & Fletcher, G. J. O. (1997). Empathic accuracy in close relationships. In W. Ickes (Ed.), *Empathic accuracy* (pp. 194–217). New York: Guilford Press.

Thomas, G., Fletcher, G. J. O., & Lange, C. (1997). On-line empathic accuracy in marital interaction. *Journal of Personality and Social Psychology, 72*, 839–850.

Tidwell, M. O., Reis, H. T., & Shaver, P. R. (1996). Attachment, attractiveness, and social interaction: A diary study. *Journal of Personality and Social Psychology, 71*, 729–745.

Watzlawick, P., Weakland, J., & Fisch, R. (1974). *Principles of problem formation and problem resolution.* New York: Norton.

PART III

Affect/Emotion

10 Understanding People's Perceptions of Relationships Is Crucial
    to Understanding their Emotional Lives   253
    Margaret S. Clark, Julie Fitness, and Ian Brissette
11 Emotional Intelligence: Conceptualization and Measurement   279
    Peter Salovey, Alison Woolery, and John D. Mayer
12 Emotional Experience in Close Relationships   308
    Ellen Berscheid and Hilary Ammazzalorso
13 The Status of Theory and Research on Love and Commitment   331
    Beverley Fehr

Chapter Ten

Understanding People's Perceptions of Relationships Is Crucial to Understanding their Emotional Lives

Margaret S. Clark, Julie Fitness, and Ian Brissette

Psychological research on emotion has been flourishing. However, as relationship theorists, we find something strikingly odd about the resulting literature. What is striking is that this literature almost all focuses on the experience and expression of emotions *within a single individual*. We know much about how our moods and emotions influence our processing of information, how we represent our own emotional experiences in our minds, what causes our own experiences of emotion, what our facial expressions of emotion look like, how our temperaments contribute to our emotional experiences, and how our emotions drive our liking for and behavior toward others. The list of work focusing squarely on individuals could go on. This work does have relevance to understanding relationships. However, as Ekman and Davidson (1994) have aptly noted, the interpersonal aspects of emotion have been given "short shrift" by psychologists.

Is there anything about the nature of relationships that can inform our understanding of people's emotional lives? We along with Berscheid and Ammazzalorso (chapter 12, below) would respond with a resounding, yes. Berscheid and Ammazzalorso make a case for one variable that can only be understood in relationship terms, that is, the degree of interdependence between two people, being a variable which is crucial for purposes of understanding people's emotional lives. We make a case for a different variable that also can only be understood in relationship terms as being crucial for understanding people's emotional lives. This variable is relationship members' felt responsibility (or lack thereof) for one another's needs.

We acknowledge NSF grant SBR9630898 and a grant from the Fetzer Foundation which supported Margaret Clark's participation in this project. We also acknowledge graduate training grant T32MH19953 which supported Ian Brissette's participation in this project.

Our arguments will be based upon four straightforward assumptions. The first is that emotions function not only to communicate one's own needs to oneself (Frijda, 1993; Simon, 1967), but also to communicate one's needs to others in one's social environment (Fridlund, 1991; Jones, Collins, & Hong, 1991; Levenson, 1994; Miller & Leary, 1992). This helps others to address our needs and helps us to mobilize external resources (Buck, 1984, 1989; Clark & Watson, 1994; Scott, 1958, 1980). The second assumption is that our emotions communicate both to ourselves and to others the extent to which we care about the needs of those others. The third assumption is that any one person's social relationships can be distinguished from one another on the basis of the extent to which members feel responsible for one another's needs. Sometimes we feel very little responsibility for another's needs. Sometimes we feel a moderate amount. Sometimes we feel a great deal of responsibility. The fourth and final assumption is that there are chronic individual differences in terms of the extent to which people feel responsible for other people's needs and in terms of the extent to which people believe others feel responsible for their own needs. For instance, attachment researchers would argue that insecure/avoidant people have enduring models of other people as being unresponsive to their needs. Or, to give another example, Clark, Ouellette, Powell, and Milberg (1987) have noted that there exist individual differences in communal orientation such that people differ in their tendencies to be responsive to others' needs and to expect others to be responsive to their own needs.

Putting the assumptions together leads us to the simple prediction that, to the extent to which people believe others will be responsive to their needs and to the extent to which they, themselves, feel responsible for their partner's needs, more emotion will be expressed. In some cases, we will argue, more emotion will be experienced in the first place. Moreover, what emotion is expressed will be reacted to more favorably.

Although there is considerable evidence for all these assertions, to our knowledge this evidence has not been pulled together in a single place. The evidence is of two broad types. First, there is what we would call "within" person evidence. That is, it appears that any given person will be more emotional (and will react more positively to partners' expressions of emotion) when the emotion occurs within the context of relationships in which that person expects his or her needs to be met than within the context of other relationships in which that person does not hold such expectations. Second, there is much, quite parallel, "between" person evidence for our propositions. That is, it appears that some people are more emotionally expressive (and react more positively to partners' expressions of emotion) than are other people *because* they are more confident, in general, that their needs will be met by others and/or more willing to meet the needs of others. In other words, some types of relationships seem to be characterized by more emotionality than others and some types of people seem to be characterized by more emotionality than others.

Consider the "within" person evidence first. This is evidence that beliefs about responsiveness to needs vary by type of relationship and that emotions covary with those beliefs.

Types of Relationships and Emotion

Clark, Mills, and their colleagues (Clark & Mills, 1979, 1993; Mills & Clark, 1982) have drawn distinctions between social relationships based upon the implicit rules governing the distribution of benefits in relationships. In most of their papers they have distinguished between communal relationships and exchange relationships. In communal relationships members feel an obligation to demonstrate concern for the other's welfare. Thus benefits are given to fulfill the other person's needs or simply to signal or express a general concern for the other person. In these relationships when a benefit is given to a person, that person does not incur a specific debt which must be repaid with a comparable benefit. Clark and Mills point to friendships, romantic relationships and family relationships as relationships which often exemplify communal relationships.

Clark and Mills have distinguished communal relationships from other relationships in which members feel no special sense of responsibility for the other's welfare. Their most frequently used example of such other relationships are exchange relationships in which benefits are given on the basis of comparable benefits received in the past or with the expectation of being repaid with comparable benefits in the future. Exchange relationships are often exemplified by relationships between people who do business with one another (e.g., a store owner and a customer), and by acquaintances (e.g., parents who work out a car pool to transport their respective children to and from soccer practices). However, exchange relationships are not the only example of non-communal relationships. Exploitative relationships in which the members are primarily concerned with their own needs, and are willing to act in unjust ways so as to extract benefits for themselves, are another kind of non-communal relationship.

Distinctions between social relationships based upon whether or not members feel responsible for the other's needs are important to understanding emotion because emotional expression carries information about needs. Sad people have generally lost something. They may need help in regaining it or help in coping with the loss. Angry people feel unjustly treated. They may need help in ascertaining whether their feelings are justified or help in figuring out a way to rectify the situation. Happy people generally are not needy. Those who feel responsible for them may help them celebrate whatever made them happy but need not address any particular need beyond that. As a consequence of people feeling a special responsibility to meet the other's needs, expressing emotions should be more important to communication within the context of communal relationships than to communication in other types of relationships. Therefore, we would expect emotions to be expressed more frequently within communal than within other, non-communal, relationships.

Expressing emotions more frequently or more intensely when one believes the other feels responsible for one's needs

That emotions are, indeed, expressed more often in communal than in other relationships is supported by the results of at least two studies (Clark & Taraban, 1991, Study 2; Barrett, Robin, Pietromonaco, & Eyssell, 1998). Pairs of same-sex friends were recruited for the

Clark and Taraban (1991) study. They were told they would have a discussion with their friend or with a member of a different pair of friends who was a stranger to the participants. The experimenter commented that when people are told to talk, they sometimes have a problem finding something to talk about. To make things easier, a form suggesting conversation topics was being handed out. Each participant was to rank-order the topics in terms of his or her preferences and the experimenter would then pick a topic both partners seemed to like. The form listed fifteen topics. Five were intrinsically emotional in nature (i.e., "times you have felt especially serene," "your fears," "things that make you sad," "things that make you angry," and "what makes you happy"). The rest were not (e.g., "your future plans," "your favorite restaurants," "your opinions of Carnegie Mellon"). Topics were ordered randomly on the form. After all four participants completed the topic choice forms, the study was complete. The results were clear. All five emotional topics were ranked as more preferable in the Friends than in the Strangers condition with four of those differences reaching traditional levels of significance and one being marginally significant.

Barrett, Robin, Pietromonaco, and Eyssell (1998) also report data linking the existence and strength of communal relationships with emotion expression. They had college students, both males and females, keep daily diaries of happiness, sadness, nervousness, surprise, anger, embarrassment, and shame experienced and expressed within the context of any interaction lasting for ten minutes or longer. They did this for seven days. Participants also indicated the closeness of their ongoing relationships with other people. (Barrett et al. did not define closeness for their participants, but we would argue that most people interpret that term in a communal sense, that is, in terms of mutual caring). The intensity of participants' emotional experiences and the degree to which they expressed those emotions was positively and significantly associated with the rated closeness of their relationship with the other person. Interestingly, Barrett et al. also had participants rate the closeness they felt with the other *within* each individual interaction. This measure also was associated with greater experience and expression of emotion overall. Shimanoff (1988) has reported similar findings.

Although Clark and Mills began their theoretical work with a simple, qualitative, distinction between communal and non-communal relationships, they have also described a quantitative dimension to communal relationships (Mills & Clark, 1982). Specifically, communal relationships vary in the degree to which members feel responsible for the other person's needs – a dimension Clark and Mills refer to as the strength of the communal relationship. In weak communal relationships members feel a small amount of responsibility for the other person's needs and will give some benefits (i.e., those that are not very costly to them) on a communal basis. An example of a low-strength communal relationship would be the relationship a person has with a stranger whom the person is meeting for the very first time. If that stranger asked for the time, the person probably would give it, thereby meeting a need of the stranger undoubtedly without expecting anything in return. However, the person would be unwilling to provide benefits on a communal basis that were much more costly or effortful than telling the time.[1] In increasingly stronger communal relationships members feel greater amounts of responsibility for the other's needs. Communal relationships with friends are stronger. Most people would not only give their friend the time, but also would do such things as treat the friend to lunch, run an errand for the friend, and comfort the friend if he or she was feeling down. Most people have even stronger, indeed very strong, communal relationships with their children. Many parents would do almost anything to meet their children's needs.

The implications of the strength dimension of communal relationships for emotional expression are straightforward. As a result of emotions very often signaling one's own needs or one's concern for one's partner's needs, the expression of one's own emotions and emotional experience and expression in response to one's partner's needs ought to increase in close conjunction with the strength of communal relationships. Thus people presumably express more emotion to spouses than to casual friends and more emotion to casual friends than to mere acquaintances.

A questionnaire study recently conducted by Brissette and Clark (1999) provides evidence that more emotion is expressed as communal relationships grow stronger. Forty-two people in this study rated the communal strength of a number of their existing relationships, as well as the likelihood that they would express a variety of emotions in each of those relationships. To measure communal strength, a communal relationship was first defined as one in which the other responds to the participant's needs without requiring or expecting a comparable benefit in return. We added that, in these relationships, people do not keep track of who has provided what to whom, but they do keep track of who needs what. Then we asked each person to rate eighteen relationships on nine-point Likert scales anchored by − 4 (indicating that the relationship was "Not at all communal") to + 4 (indicating that the relationship was "Very strongly communal"). Participants rated their relationships with: a stranger, their mother, a casual friend, a sister or brother, their boss at work, their professor, a neighbor, a close friend, a member of a sports team (along with them), a classmate, their cousin, a member of their church or temple, their priest, minister, or rabbi, a fellow employee at work, their father, a member of their fraternity or sorority, and their roommate.[2]

All participants received instructions for rating their emotions on a separate sheet. The instructions began with the statement that, "We experience many, many emotions from day to day. Sometimes we freely express the emotions we are feeling to others; sometimes we do not – choosing to suppress them instead." Then the participants were asked to rate their willingness to express happiness, contentment, hurt, sadness, anger, disgust, guilt, and fear (both when each emotion was caused by the person to whom the emotion would be expressed and when it was caused by someone or something else). They used seven-point Likert scales to do this. The scales ranged from −3 (indicating that they would be very likely to suppress the emotion) to +3 (indicating that they would be very likely to express the emotion).

As expected, there were positive, within-subject correlations between each person's rating of how communal a particular relationship was and that person's rating of willingness to express each of the emotions within their relationship. When the emotions were caused by the other those correlations were .23 for anger, .27 for disgust, .40 for fear, .39 for guilt, .39 for hurt, .43 for sadness, .43 for contentment, and .48 for happiness. When the emotions were caused by someone or something else the correlations were .45 for anger, .48 for disgust, .57 for fear, .45 for guilt, .54 for hurt, .51 for sadness, .43 for contentment, and .49 for happiness. All reached statistical significance with the exception of the correlations between how communal one's relationship was and willingness to express anger and disgust when those emotions were caused by one's partner.[3]

The means for willingness to express the various emotions across relationships clearly indicated that although people were willing to express positive emotions to some extent in almost all relationships, they were more willing to do so the stronger the communal nature of the relationship. Moreover, although people were willing to express negative emotions within moderately strong to quite strong communal relationships, they reported being likely to *suppress* negative emotions in relationships low in communal strength. Other findings, consistent with the idea that more emotion will be expressed the stronger the communal nature of a relationship, have been reported by Fitness (2000), Pennebaker (1995), and Rime (1995). Rime and Pennebaker have found that when people experience emotional events, they seek support from their friends and families. Fitness (2000) found that 83 percent of people who reported experiencing an angry incident at work also reported having expressed those feelings to their close friends and family members not only to "let off steam" but also for purposes of reassurance.

In sum, there is clear evidence that the more concerned people are with one another's needs, the more likely they are to express emotions. We turn now to a related point. That is, not only does it appear that more emotion will be expressed the more communal a relationship is, it is also apparent that expressing emotion will be *viewed as more appropriate* and will be *reacted to more positively* to the extent that the relationship in question is communal. We review evidence supporting this next.

Reacting positively to others' emotional expressions when one feels responsible for those other's needs

Two studies support the contention that expressions of emotion will be reacted to more positively when one is oriented toward meeting the other's needs than when one is not. In the first (Clark & Taraban, 1991, Study 1), the impact of expressing irritability, happiness, and sadness on liking for another person, with whom one had been led to desire a communal or a non-communal relationship, was examined. Students participated in this study one at a time, but were led to believe another participant was involved in the study at the same time. When the participant arrived, he or she was seated in front of a monitor and could see another participant (his or her supposed partner) seated at a similar desk. In fact, the monitor showed a videotape of a male or female, attractive, undergraduate confederate. At this point the experimenter turned off the monitor and told the participant the study actually dealt with impression formation. The experimenter went on to explain that the first person to arrive (i.e., the one shown on the monitor) was always designated as the stimulus person and that that person continued to believe the study was about word games. However, the second person to arrive, the actual participant, (being addressed) was to form an impression of the stimulus person – first on the basis of a background information sheet, supposedly filled out by that other person, and later on the basis of a brief interaction.

A manipulation of desire for a communal as opposed to an exchange or no particular relationship was included on this form. In the communal condition, the partner was described as new to the university and quite interested in meeting new people. In the exchange condition, the other was described as married and busy. This person was obviously unavailable for new friendships or romantic relationships. Most importantly for the present point, a manipulation of the partner's expressed emotion appeared on the bottom half of the form. There, the other person indicated either that he or she currently was in no particular mood (the control condition) or that he or she was currently feeling happy, sad, or angry. Finally, the participant rated the other on a number of dimensions (e.g., agreeableness, pleasantness, likeability). These ratings were summed to form an overall measure of likeability. The results were clear.

When no emotion was expressed, liking ratings in the communal and in the non-communal condition were identical. However, when happiness, sadness, or irritability was expressed, liking was greater when participants had been led to desire a communal relationship with the other than when they had not. It appears that expressions of emotion are more appropriate in communal than in other relationships. Moreover, it is notable that within the communal conditions, expression of emotions, *even* negative emotions did not cause significant drops in liking. In contrast, within the non-communal condition, expressing irritability did decrease liking. Why might negative emotions be reacted to more negatively within non-communal than within communal relationships? We think the answer is that negative emotions indicate some level of neediness on the part of the other person. When our sense of obligation for the other's needs and desire to respond to those needs is low, we do not want to deal with the other's irritability or sadness. We may even be irritated ourselves at being forced to witness the emotion. To the extent to which we do feel responsible for the other's needs, or desire the opportunity to assume such responsibility, expressions of the same emotions will be less off-putting. Indeed, if such expressions open up a chance to respond to the other's needs and build a desired relationship, these expressions may even be welcomed.

The second study supporting the idea that expressions of emotion will be reacted to more positively in the context of a communal than in the context of a non-communal relationship has been reported by Clark, Ouellette, Powell, and Milberg (1987). In this study people were recruited for an investigation of links between moods and creativity. Participants were informally told there was another person participating at the same time. However, that person supposedly had left the room briefly. Then the participant filled out a questionnaire which asked, among other things, why he or she had signed up for the study and also what his or her current mood was. The participant's picture was also taken – supposedly as another way to judge mood. The participant was given instructions for his or her painting task and it was casually mentioned that the other person had filled out his or her questionnaire, had had his or her picture taken, and would be returning shortly to complete a balloon sculpture task. In preparation for the other's task, the experimenter casually commented, that other would have to blow up balloons. The actual participant could help if he or she wished but did not have to do so and could just begin painting. Then the experimenter left the room telling the participant to place his or her picture and questionnaire on top of the other participant's materials.

As hoped, the participants looked at the other's completed materials and, depending upon their experimental condition, found out that the other either was feeling no particular mood or sad. They also found out the other was available and anxious to form new communal relationships (e.g., a friendship or romantic relationship), or was quite busy, occupied in other communal relationships, and presumably not interested in forming new communal relationships. The dependent variable was helping. Our question was, how long would the participant spend (if any time) helping the other person to blow up balloons? The results, shown in figure 10.1, were clear.

As expected, participants helped more in the communal than in the non-communal condition. Most interesting for present purposes, though, is the fact that the impact of the other's sadness depended upon the nature of the desired relationship. When a communal relationship was desired, the other's sadness significantly increased the time participants spent helping. When no communal relationship was desired, the other's sadness had no impact on the time participants spent helping.

We actually suspect that, had scores on the measure of helping not been so low in the non-communal condition in the absence of the sadness cue (leaving no room on our measure of helping for them to drop further), they may have dropped when the non-communal other expressed sadness. Fitting with our own speculation that expressions of sadness may be reacted to negatively in non-communal settings are some comments by Hoover-Dempsey, Plas, and Strudler-Wallston (1986). They argue that a woman weeping in work settings results in embarrassment for the woman and confusion and even anger on the part of others around her. However, they note, such negative reactions to weeping do *not* occur in what they call "intimate" or "personal" relationships (and what we might characterize as communal relationships). Miss Manners (aka Judith Martin) (1982) also provides an example of expressing sadness in non-communal relationships leading to annoyance. She reports a boss's reaction to his employees expressing sadness generated by their personal problems. This man says, "I consider myself a reasonable boss. I know that people might have down cycles in their work, and I try to allow for that." However, he adds, he really does not want them expressing their sadness to him saying, "Frankly, it just makes me angry when they try to enlist my sympathies about how they feel bad . . . " (p. 244). Miss

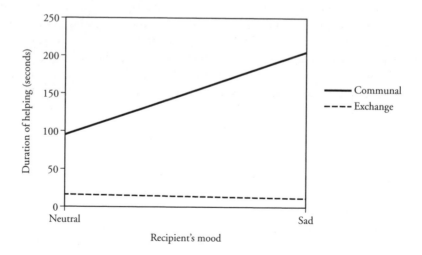

Figure 10.1   Mean duration of helping as a function of relationship manipulation and recipient mood.

Manners agrees with him and also with us when she notes that such expressions should be reserved for "people with whom they have close ties of blood or affection," or, as we would put it, people who feel responsibility for our personal needs.

The view that negative emotions will be reacted to more positively in more communal relationships also helps to explain some otherwise seemingly discrepant findings in the literature. Specifically, when researchers have asked people to evaluate a person *whom they have never met* (and thus with whom they do not have a communal relationship), finding out that that person is feeling a negative emotion (irritated, angry, gloomy, frustrated) causes the person to be judged to be unsociable, unpopular, and non-conventional (Sommers, 1984, Study 3). In contrast, when *spouses* (who typically show a strong desire to follow communal norms in their relationship, cf. Grote & Clark, 1998), have been asked to evaluate messages from their mates, messages that include unpleasant emotions, disclosures of vulnerabilities, and hostilities toward persons other than the spouse often prompt more positive responses and attitudes than do messages devoid of such negative elements (Shimanoff, 1988).

In sum, it is evident that expressing emotion is more commonplace within the context of communal relationships, and is very often reacted to with more liking and more responsiveness in communal than in non-communal relationships. We think expressions of emotion lie at the very heart of communal relationships. They communicate our needs to others. They allow others to be responsive to our needs. Being willing to express emotions indicates that we trust the other with information about our vulnerabilities – that is, we trust the person to use that information to support us rather than to take advantage of our weaknesses. On the other hand, emotions are not central to interacting with another on an exchange or economic basis. Indeed, to the extent to which they do reveal our weaknesses and neediness, expressing emotions in non-communal interactions makes us vulnerable and easy to exploit.

Experiencing more emotion in response to others' needs the more one feels responsible for those needs

To this point, we have argued that people are more willing to express emotion the more they feel they are in a relationship in which the partner feels responsible for their needs. Moreover, we have argued, emotional expressions generally are reacted to more positively in such relationships. Going beyond this, it is important to note that most communal relationships are mutual – not only do we assume the other cares about our needs and should and will respond to those needs on a communal basis, so too do we care about that other's needs and feel we should respond to those needs on a communal basis. In addition, there are certain asymmetric communal relationships in which one feels greater responsibility for the welfare of the other than one expects the other to feel for the self (e.g., a mother's relationship with her own young child). Feelings of responsibility for the *other's* welfare not only have clear implications for expressing certain emotions (i.e., those experienced in response to the other's needs – emotions such as guilt, empathic sadness, and empathic happiness), they also have implications for experiencing these emotions in the first place.

Consider the experience of these emotions first. An example is empathic sadness. One should feel this emotion when one's partner has experienced a loss and, holding the loss constant, one should feel more sadness the more responsibility one feels for the welfare of the other. Is there any evidence for this? Yes. In two separate studies Batson, Duncan, Ackerman, Buckley, and Birch (1981) manipulated how similar college females felt to another college female by providing feedback that the other had answered a personal profile and interest inventory either in very much the same way as the participant or in quite a different way. Later on participants in the highly similar conditions reported feeling more similar to the other and also, importantly for our present arguments, feeling that they valued the other's welfare (on an index that included ratings of valuing the other's welfare, wanting the other to be happy, and not wanting the other to suffer). Following the similarity manipulation, Batson et al. exposed all participants to a person in need and measured the extent to which participants reported feeling sympathetic, compassionate, softhearted, and tender. As they expected, and fitting with our current arguments, people in the high similarity conditions who reported caring more about the other's welfare also experienced more empathic compassion than did those in the low similarity conditions. Analogous results have been reported by Batson, Turk, Shaw, and Klein (1995) and by Krebs (1975). What is important here for our purposes is the clear link between feelings of responsibility for another and the experience of empathic compassion. The fact that similarity was an important elicitor not only of a sense of communal responsibility but also of feelings of communal compassion is intriguing and fits well with the well-established links between similarity and the formation of friendships (Byrne & Nelson, 1965; Newcomb, 1961).

Next consider empathic happiness. There is evidence that this too is experienced more frequently within the context of relationships in which we feel responsible for our partner's needs than in other relationships. Specifically, Williamson and Clark (1989, Study 3; 1992) reported two studies in which they measured positive and negative moods at the beginning of the studies, then manipulated desire for a communal versus an exchange relationship with another "participant." Later, the true participants were either induced to help (or were not induced to help) the other "participant." Finally the experimenters measured mood again. In both studies helping the other was associated with improvements in mood *only* when a communal relationship was desired. Moreover, in the 1992 study, participants were led to feel that they had to help the other or that they had chosen to help the other. The improvement in mood when a communal, but not when an exchange, relationship was desired occurred whether or not the help was freely given or was required. This suggests that the fact that the needy other was benefited was key to the improvement in mood rather than the improvement in mood being dependent upon the helper seeing him or herself as a good person for having chosen to help the other (as might be suggested by Bem's self-perception theory, 1972).[4]

Finally, consider guilt. Guilt usually implies that one feels badly about having not met another's needs or that one has harmed the other's welfare in some way. It is straightforward to argue that this should occur primarily within the context of relationships in which one feels responsible for the other person's needs.[5] It is also straightforward to argue that the stronger one's feelings of responsibility for the other's welfare, the more guilt should be felt for the same neglectful behavior. For example, one should feel more guilty if one forgets one's mother's birthday than if one forgets a friend's birthday and more guilty if one forgets a friend's birthday than if one forgets an acquaintance's birthday.

There is evidence to support the idea that guilt is, indeed, an emotion that is closely associated with communal relationships – work by Baumeister, Stillwell, and Heatherton (1994, 1995). Baumeister et al. had college students describe, in writing, two situations in which they had angered someone. The situations were to be important and memorable, and preferably chosen from the past two or three years. Participants described the incident taking care to include the background, the incident itself, and the consequences. One of the descriptions was to be of an incident after which the student "felt bad or suffered from a feeling of having done something wrong." The other description was to be of an incident after which the participant "did not feel bad or suffer from a feeling of having done something wrong." After collecting the stories, the researchers coded them "for whether the victim was depicted as someone with whom the subject had a communal relationship (defined as involving norms of mutual concern for each other's welfare, such as in family or romantic relationships)" or not (Baumeister et al., 1995, p. 181).

As the investigators predicted, the incidents chosen as examples of times the participants had felt bad, or suffered from feelings of having done something wrong, were more likely to have taken place in the context of a communal relationship than were the incidents chosen to represent times participants did not feel bad or suffer from a feeling of having done something wrong (see also Baumeister et al., 1995, Study 2; Vangelisti, Daly, & Rudnick, 1991). Thus, guilt seems to have been experienced more often in the context of communal than non-communal relationships.

The evidence on empathic sadness, happiness, and guilt taken together suggests that any emotion that indicates to oneself that one cares about the welfare of another person should occur more frequently and more intensely the more communal in nature one's relationship with another person. Asch (1952) noted that "Emotions are our ways of representing to ourselves the fate of our goals" (p. 110). Emotion researchers have long acknowledged the truth of this statement when the goals relate to our personal welfare (Frijda, 1993; Simon, 1967). What this research suggests is that our goals sometimes include other people's welfare as well. Thus we would argue that our emotions also represent to us the fate of the goals of others about whose welfare we care.

Interestingly this evidence also suggests that experiencing emotion in response to the need states of another may be taken as a signal to oneself that the relationship is a communal one (if one feels good when another's needs are met or bad when they are not) or, indeed, that the relationship is not a communal one (if one feels bad when another's needs have been met or good when they have not been met). That people do, indeed, infer that they care about another person when they feel good upon the other's needs being met, and bad upon the other's needs not being met or upon the other actually being harmed, is supported by a number of studies (Aderman, Brehm, & Katz, 1974; Batson, Turk, Shaw, & Klein, 1995; Mills, Jellison, & Kennedy, 1976; Zillmann & Cantor, 1977).

Expressing more emotion when another *has a need the more one feels responsible for those needs*

Our theoretical position also suggests, of course, that not only should one experience more guilt, empathic compassion, and empathic happiness within the context of relationships in which one feels responsible for a partner's needs, one also should express these emotions more often within such relationships. The experience of these emotions communicates to oneself that one cares about the other; but it is the expression of these emotions that is important to communicating this caring to the other. There is less empirical data to back up this idea. However, we would note that Baumeister et al. (1995) found that not only was guilt experienced more often in the context of communal relationships, it was expressed more often within those relationships as well. Of course, these results could be accounted for by simply arguing that one must experience an emotion before it can be expressed. In fact, in our own study, described above in connection with expressing emotions conveying one's own needs, we did include one emotion indicating concern for the other's welfare – namely, guilt. Within that study, we asked our participants to tell us, when they did experience guilt, the extent to which they expressed it to others. The results for guilt caused by neglecting that other's needs were clear. Our participants said they would be far less likely to express guilt feelings to others with whom they had weak communal relationships (e.g., strangers, coworkers, neighbors, professors, and classmates) than they would be to express their guilt to those with whom they had stronger communal relationships (e.g., roommates, siblings, close friends, mothers, and fathers).

Summing up our points thus far

We have argued that, to predict and to understand the expression of emotions conveying information about one's needs, it is crucial to take relationship context into account. Just as experiencing our own emotions alerts us to our own needs and the necessity of doing something about those needs (Frijda, 1986, 1993; Simon, 1967), so too can emotional expression alert our relationship partners about our needs and the necessity of responding to those needs (Buck, 1984, 1989). However, whereas we are all presumably concerned about our own needs (one could say we have a communal relationship with ourselves), not everyone else is concerned about our needs and those who are concerned about them are concerned to differing degrees. This suggests that we will be selective in expressing emotions to others – choosing to express more emotions conveying our needs to those who care most about our welfare. Existing research supports these claims.

Moreover, we have argued, to understand fully the experience and expression of emotions which we experience in response to other people's need states (empathic happiness and sadness as well as guilt), one also must take relationship context into account. Our feelings of responsibility for the needs of others differs dramatically from relationship to relationship. We should experience more empathic emotions and guilt the more we care for another. We should also choose to express these emotions more the more we care for the other. Existing research supports these contentions as well.

At this point we would like to add a caveat to our arguments. We have suggested that the existence (or lack thereof) of communal relationships makes a difference to experiencing guilt and empathic emotions but not to experiencing our own happiness, sadness, anger, and so forth. We have said this because we assume everyone feels responsible for attending to their own needs whereas people are selective in feeling responsible for other people's needs. However, we do not wish to suggest that being in the presence of others who feel responsible for our own needs is completely irrelevant to the experience of our own emotions. Here is why. As we have argued, people should express more emotions conveying their own needs in communal than in other relationships. Others have argued that the very act of expressing emotion provides feedback that intensifies that emotion (Laird, 1974; Laird & Bresler, 1992; Riskind & Gotay, 1982; Riskind, 1984). By choosing to express more emotion in communal relationships we may experience feedback which causes us to actually experience more emotion in those relationships as well. Moreover, not only may expression of emotion intensify that emotion through intrapersonal feedback, it may also influence the experience of the emotion through interpersonal feedback. In some cases such interpersonal feedback may intensify the emotion. For example, when we express emotion our relationship partners may encourage us to express more emotion or to talk more about the emotional experience thereby intensifying or prolonging the experience of emotion. In other cases interpersonal feedback may diminish the experience. When we express emotion our relationship partner may calm us down, reassure us, or redirect our attention elsewhere. When our partner is living up to the norms of a communal relationship, which type of interpersonal strategy he or she chooses should be determined by what that partner believes to be in our best interests.

Types of People and Emotion

To this point we have argued that emotional expression will occur primarily within the context of relationships in which one believes the other feels a responsibility for one's needs and/or in which one feels a responsibility for the other's needs. To some extent we have also argued that emotional experience will follow the same pattern. We have further argued that everyone has a variety of relationships which vary in the extent to which such responsibilities are felt and that those felt responsibilities modulate their emotional lives. Moving ahead in our analysis it is also important to point out that beliefs that others will be responsive to one's own needs and feelings of responsiveness to other's needs vary not just by relationship context. There are also chronic individual differences in such beliefs. Some people are chronically high in the tendency to believe that others will be responsive to their needs and in the tendency to turn to others for help. Others are chronically more cynical. They do not believe others will "be there" for them and they do not tend to turn to others for help. The positions we have taken thus far in this chapter carry the further implication that our emotional lives also will vary according to these chronic individual differences.

Differences in beliefs that others care about one's welfare are captured in a variety of concepts in the extant literature – secure versus insecure attachment styles (Hazan & Shaver, 1987; Bartholomew & Horowitz, 1991), high communal versus low communal orientation (Clark et al., 1987), and chronic tendencies to perceive that one does have social support available to one versus perceptions that one does not have such support available (Cohen & Hoberman, 1983; Cutrona & Russell, 1987). Thus, we would expect people's emotional lives to covary with such established individual differences between people. Existing literature suggests that they do.

Expressing more emotions when one has a chronic tendency to believe partners feel responsible for one's needs

In discussing relationship types we noted that studies by Clark & Taraban (1991), Barrett, Robin, Pietromonaco, and Eyssell, 1998, and Brissette and Clark (1999) all support the idea that people express more emotion in the context of relationships in which they believe the other bears a special responsibility for their needs. Is there parallel evidence that people who are chronically high in the belief that others will be responsive to their needs also express more emotion to their relationship partners? The answer, drawn from the attachment literature, is yes (Feeney, 1995, 1999).

In one study Feeney (1995) examined emotional expression within young adults' dating relationships. Dating couples completed a 15-item measure of attachment based on Hazan and Shaver's (1987) original measure. From this, measures of Comfort (Secure to Avoidant) and Anxiety were extracted. In addition members of the couple completed a measure of emotional control based on the Courtauld Emotional Control Scale (Watson & Greer, 1983). They completed this with regard to emotions experienced in relation to their current dating partner. The scale tapped willingness to express/suppress feelings of anger, sadness, and anxiety.

For our purposes the interesting question is whether secure people, who tend to believe that others will be responsive to their needs, were *less* likely to suppress expressions of these negative feelings to their partners than were insecure people. The results were clear. The more securely attached members of the couples were, the less likely they reported they were to suppress expressions of anxiety (−.31 for females; −.44 for males) and to suppress expressions of sadness (−.38 for females, −.26 for males). In addition, the more securely attached females were, the less likely they were to suppress anger (−.29), but this effect was not obtained for males. All the reported correlations reached significance. Importantly, they remained significant after the researchers controlled for the reported frequency of the emotion in question being experienced. Thus, chronic individual differences in tendencies to perceive that one's partner will be responsive to one's needs do parallel situational/relationship differences in tendencies to believe the other should be responsive to one's needs.[6]

In her later, 1999, study, Feeney again linked Comfort (indicative of security as opposed to avoidance) with willingness to express emotion. This time members of married couples were asked about their willingness to express anger, sadness, anxiety, happiness, love, and pride to their partner when those emotions were caused by their partners, as well as when these emotions were caused by something not involving the partner. As in the 1995 study, feelings of security (comfort in her terms) were negatively linked with controlling/suppressing each of these emotions both when the emotion had been caused by the partner and when it had not. For husbands, the relevant correlations were −.19 and −.22 for anger (partner-related first, other second), −.27 and −.22 for sadness, −.20 and −.26 for anxiety, −.36 and −.28 for happiness, −.35 and −.23 for love, and −.33 and −.31 for pride. All were significant and remained significant after the reported frequency and intensity of experiencing each of these emotions were partialled out. For wives, the correlations were −.29 and −.17 for anger, −.24 and −.22 for sadness, −.31 and −.22 for anxiety, −.14

and −.15 for happiness, −.21 and −.21 for love, and −.12 and −.17 for pride. All correlations except the correlation of Comfort with willingness to express partner-related pride were significant. Importantly, all those correlations that were significant remained significant after the reported frequency and intensity of experiencing each of these emotions were partialled out (except for the negative correlation between Comfort and control of expressing partner-related love.)

Other work supporting the notion that people's perceptions that their partner cares for them will be associated with greater expressions of emotions has been reported by Collins (Collins, 1994; Collins & Di Paula, 1997). These researchers interviewed 92 HIV-infected men. During the interview the men filled out Sarason, Sarason, Shearin, & Pierce's (1987) Social Support Questionnaire (short form) with regard to up to five members of their close social network.[7] They also filled out a ways of coping index (Folkman, Lazarus, Dunkel-Schetter, DeLongis, & Gruen, 1986). For our purposes, what is important about the latter index taps the tendency to suppress expressing distress when in the presence of others. (This scale includes items such as, "I tried to avoid letting others know how bad my situation was," and "I tried to put up a happy front when around others.") Consistent with our current theoretical analysis, the authors observed a negative relationship between the average level of receipt of support their participants perceived, and suppression of distress ($r = −.21, p < .07$), a relationship that, while marginal in significance, became significant when they controlled for physical health in the analyses ($r = −.24, p < .05$).[8]

Reacting more positively to others' emotional expressions when one feels responsible for those others' needs

In discussing how relationship type influences reactions to others' expressions of emotions, we noted evidence that the more people desire a communal relationship with the other the more positively they react to the other's expression of emotion (Clark & Taraban, 1991; Clark et al., 1987). This effect, too, has a parallel in the individual difference literature.

In particular, Clark et al. (1987) have developed a measure of communal orientation which taps chronic individual differences in people's tendencies to feel responsible for others' needs. It includes such items as "When making a decision, I take other people's needs and feelings into account," and "I believe it's best not to get involved taking care of other people's personal needs" (reverse scored). Clark et al. (1987, Study 1) administered this scale to a group of college students at the beginning of a semester. Later on in the same semester, some of these students were recruited to participate in a study ostensibly on creativity. Each participant arrived individually at a psychology faculty member's office. The faculty member greeted the participant and said a research assistant actually would conduct the study. She would take the participant to the relevant lab.

On the way, the faculty member led some participants to believe the research assistant was feeling sad whereas other participants were given no information about the assistant's emotional state. Next they encountered the research assistant, seated at a cluttered desk and the faculty member left. The research assistant, who was unaware of her own alleged mood, was obviously not only not ready to run the study but also clearly worried about her own work. She told the participant she had to get some materials for the creativity study and, as she left the room to get them, she asked the participant for some personal help. Specifically, she asked the participant to alphabetize a stack of 116 index cards with references written on them. The measure of interest was the amount of help, if any, the participants would give the "research assistant" and whether responsiveness to her sadness would depend upon the potential helper's level of communal orientation (a variable which was unknown to both the experimenter and "research assistant" at the time the study was run). The pattern of results is shown in figure 10.2.

As can be seen, people high in communal orientation helped more than those low in communal orientation. More importantly for the present point, though, communal orientation appears to have an impact on reactions to sadness, with the research assistant's sadness garnering increased help from high communal persons but actually resulting in less help from those low in communal orientation. The interaction only approached significance in this case. However, the parallel between the observed pattern found in this study and that in Figure 10.1 (obtained when desire for a communal relationship was manipulated) is striking and the marginal interaction is clearly consistent with the thesis of the present chapter.

Believing others will be responsive to one's needs and coping with one's own emotional states

An important part of one's emotional life, particularly when dealing with negative emotions such as distress, fear, anxiety, and anger is how one reacts to one's own emotional states. Such reactions are a part of the knowledge structures regarding emotions that people have stored in memory. For instance, prototypes of sadness aggregated across people include reacting in the following ways: "talking to someone about sadness," "crying, tears,

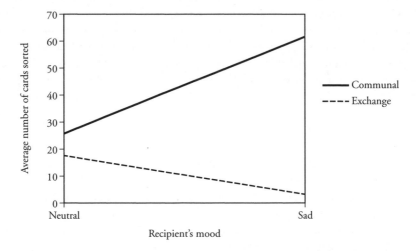

Figure 10.2   Number of cards sorted as a function of donor relationship orientation and recipient mood.

whimpering," and "saying sad things" as well as "suppressing feelings," "acting happy," "withdrawing from social contact," "talking little or not at all." Their prototypes of fear include: "crying, whimpering," "screaming, yelling" and "pleading, crying for help" as well as "acting unafraid, hiding the fear," "comforting self, trying to keep calm" (Shaver, Schwartz, Kirson, & O'Connor, 1987). But what determines whether one really does talk to someone else about one's sadness as opposed to withdrawing from social contact? Again, we would argue, an important determinant will be one's judgment that the person with whom one is with holds a positive attitude regarding being responsive to one's needs. To the extent to which one perceives that the other does hold such a positive view, emotion will be expressed; to the extent to which one does not, emotion will be suppressed.

Several studies offer support for this contention. Some have come out of the attachment literature, some from work on communal orientation and coping with stress. They all support the idea that people who hold a chronically higher tendency to believe others will be responsive to their needs will react to emotion by seeking others out; whereas those who do not hold such beliefs will not seek others out.

Simpson, Rholes, and Nelligan (1992) report one study supporting these ideas. In their study dating couples filled out an attachment style questionnaire and then the female member of each couple was exposed to an anxiety induction procedure. Specifically, an experimenter took her pulse and said, "In the next few minutes, you are going to be exposed to a situation and set of experimental procedures that arouse considerable anxiety and distress in most people. Due to the nature of these procedures, I cannot tell you any more at the moment." The experimenter also casually showed the woman the room that would be used for the study. It was dark, windowless, and contained what appeared to be psychophysiological equipment. Then the woman was led back to a waiting room where her partner (who did not undergo the anxiety provoking situation) was seated. The couple was left alone for five minutes and their interactions were videotaped.

Individual differences in security versus avoidance were not related to the levels of anxiety which observers rated the women as showing. However, how women reacted to their anxiety was dependent upon whether they were secure or not. Secure women, who presumably had high expectations of their partner's responsiveness to their needs, sought more comfort and support from their partners. Insecure women, who presumably had low expectations of their partner's responsiveness to their needs, reacted in a very different fashion. They did not seek much support from their partners. Instead they did such things as trying to distract themselves by thumbing through magazines in the waiting room.

Three additional studies supporting the idea that beliefs about the responsiveness of others to one's needs influence one's own reactions to distress have been reported recently by Brissette and his colleagues (Clark, Brissette, & Grote, 1998; Brissette, Clark, & Scheier, 1999). In all three studies, participants filled out the communal orientation scale (Clark et al., 1987). In two studies people were simply asked the extent to which they tended to react to being in need by seeking out support from close others versus coping with the problem themselves. Then they were asked how becoming especially distressed when they had a need for help influenced these tendencies. In both studies, those high in communal orientation (i.e., those who presumably feel others are responsive to their needs) said they responded to especially high distress by being more likely to rely on others for help and by seeking out more help from others. This is not surprising. After all, when one is especially distressed one is likely to be especially in need of help. What is more surprising is that people low in communal orientation not only reported being less likely to seek out help from others in general but also reported reacting to feeling especially distressed by becoming less likely to seek help. In other words, they reported reacting to their negative emotions by withdrawing from others. The third study was a longitudinal study. College students filled out measures of communal orientation, perceived stress, and perceived support at the beginning of a semester and then again at the end of the semester. Increases in stress led to declines in perceived support among those low in communal orientation, but were not associated with perceptions of support among those who were high in communal orientation.

The overall point of describing these studies is to suggest that the importance of differences in perceived responsiveness to needs for understanding people's emotional lives appears to extend beyond the experience and expression of emotion to styles of coping with emotion as well. Those who view others as responsive to needs not only freely express more emotion and, as a result, probably experience more emotion, they also react to emotional experiences by seeking others out. Those who view others as low in responsiveness to needs are less likely to express emotion, may experience more pallid emotions, and they appear to react to aversive emotional experiences by withdrawing from others.

Possible Interactions between Types of People and Types of Relationships

To this point, we have argued that two very important relationship variables are crucial to understanding individuals' experiences and expressions of emotions: (1) the degree to which one believes one's relationship partner cares about one's own welfare, and (2) the degree to which one cares about one's relationship partner's welfare. We began making a case for this thesis by using data suggesting that people's emotional experiences and expressions vary according to relationship context. More emotion and more intense emotions are experienced and expressed within communal than within other relationship contexts. Then we made a case for the same thesis using data suggesting that people's emotional experiences and expressions vary according to individual differences in the extent to which they expect others to be responsive to their needs. However, relationship context and individual differences are unlikely to have entirely independent effects on people's emotional lives. Rather, we hypothesize that relationship context and individual differences interact (even though we know of no relevant empirical evidence).

First, we suspect that almost everyone, regardless of attachment style, communal orientation, or chronic individual differences in perceived social support, understands (implicitly) and draws distinctions between stronger, weaker communal relationships and non-communal relationships. Moreover, we believe that almost everyone, no matter how secure, or how communally oriented, or how much perceived support they believe they have, suppresses emotional expression when they are in non-communal relationships. For example, people on the whole simply do not go around expressing their fears, sadness, and happiness when in formal business settings. Moreover, on the rare occasions when they do, other people, on the whole, view their behavior as inappropriate. To put it another way, individual differences in both the tendencies to view others as responsive to one's needs and to feel responsible for other's needs probably make little difference to people's emotional lives within the context of clear-cut, non-communal relationships.

Instead, we suspect the individual differences that we have discussed as being relevant to people's emotional lives are going to have their biggest impact within the context of relationships that our culture dictates ought to be communal and intimate in nature – relationships with friends, family, and romantic relationships. Indeed, it is within the actual (or imagined) context of such relationships that the effects cited above have been observed. It may also be the case that chronic individual differences in beliefs about responsiveness to needs make a difference within relationships in which norms regarding such responsiveness are not clearly set by the culture – for instance, in relationships with people one has just met who *might* become friends or romantic partners.

Responsiveness to Needs and Expression of Emotion: Reciprocal Effects

To this point we have emphasized how perceiving that another person will be responsive to one's needs will influence expression and, to some extent, experiences of emotion. We have also emphasized how feeling responsible for another person's needs will influence the experience and expression of certain emotions. However, to talk of perceptions of responsibility for needs driving emotional experience and expression is too simple. Just as perceptions of responsiveness to needs are likely to have an impact on experiences and expressions of emotion so too, we believe, does emotional expression have an impact on the quality of relationships, on responsiveness to needs and, eventually, on perceptions of responsiveness to needs.

Why? There are many reasons. First, the expression of emotions enables others to better meet our needs, which in turn should enhance positive feelings and the communal nature of the relationship. Beyond this, the communication function of emotions goes beyond just conveying information about needs. When emotions are expressed to a person, not only does the person to whom they are expressed learn something about the needs of the person expressing them, he or she also learns that the other is willing to communicate those needs. Expressions of emotion should indicate that the emotional person is open to the formation, maintenance, or deepening of a communal relationship. In turn, this may strengthen the communal relationship not only through enhanced responsiveness to the emotional person's needs but also by enhancing liking, willingness to express emotions in return, and comfort with the relationship. Moreover, when one experiences empathic happiness, sadness, or guilt in response to another person's needs, one may infer from those experiences and expressions that one really does care for the other person. This too may result in the creation or the strengthening of a communal relationship.

The idea that expressing emotion in relationships may strengthen those relationships is supported by some recent findings reported by Feeney (1999) linking willingness to express emotion with marital satisfaction. As we have described already, she measured the extent to which married couples reported suppressing anger, sadness, anxiety, happiness, love, and pride in their relationships, and she linked insecure attachment to greater control of all these emotions. Relevant to the present point is the fact that she also measured marital satisfaction in her study using Norton's (1983) measure. Regression analyses revealed that, *after* controlling for own attachment styles, control of one's own negative and positive emotions and one's partner's control of negative and positive emotions were all negatively associated with marital satisfaction. Moreover, these negative associations reached statistical significance in five of the eight cases.[9] Some similar findings have been reported by Feeney, Noller, & Roberts (1998) and by Laurenceau et al. (1998, Study 2).

In addition, several studies support the idea that experiencing emotion in response to another person's need states (or lack thereof) may strengthen communal relationships. For instance, long ago Mills, Jellison, and Kennedy (1976) reported two studies in which participants received feedback via a meter regarding their feelings when another person experienced good or bad fortune. Those people receiving feedback that they felt badly when another experienced a negative outcome, or that they felt positively when another experienced a good outcome, inferred that they liked that other more.[10]

More recently, Batson, Turk, Shaw, and Klein (1995) have provided another demonstration that if one feels badly when another is feeling needy one may infer that one cares about that person. In two studies Batson and his colleagues directly manipulated the extent to which participants felt empathy for a confederate in need. Then they measured the inferences these people drew about the nature of their relationship with the needy person. In the first study females either were assigned: (1) to a control condition in which they neither heard about another participant's troubles nor were induced to feel empathy for that participant, (2) to a high empathy condition in which they imagined how another participant (who had just been dropped by a boyfriend) felt, or (3) to a low empathy condition in which participants were exposed to the same information about the other person's troubles but were instructed to take an objective perspective and not to get caught up in how the other felt. A manipulation check on empathic feelings supported the effectiveness of the manipulation. More importantly for the point we are making, participants also inferred that they had a stronger communal relationship with the other after they had experienced enhanced empathy with that person. Specifically, participants were given the following instructions: "Think of someone whose welfare you value highly (e.g., a best friend or favorite family member). Now think of someone whose welfare you do not value highly (e.g., someone you know nothing about at all). Compared to these two extremes, how much do you value the welfare of (the other participant)." Mean responses to this question were lowest in the control condition, medium high in the low empathy condition and highest, by a significant amount relative to the low empathy condition, in the high empathy condition. Analogous findings were obtained in a second study in which the perception that participants were feeling empathy with another person in need were manipulated by providing participants in the high empathy condition with false physiological feedback indicating that they had (or had not) experienced arousal upon hearing of another's plight. Again, those participants believing that they had experienced empathy upon hearing of another's plight were especially likely to infer that they had a communal relationship with the other.

As Martin and his colleagues have pointed out, we appear to use our moods and emotions as inputs in processing information (Martin, Ward, Achee, & Wyer, 1993; Martin & Stoner, 1996; Martin & Davies, 1998). Here we emphasize that, as a result of experiencing and expressing emotion in response to another's needs we may strengthen the communal nature of the relationship through coming to care for that person more and, to the extent to which the other notices our empathic reactions, communicating that care to the other. Since liking begets liking (Kenny & LaVoie, 1982; Curtis & Miller, 1986) and, we presume, since caring begets caring, we would expect the expression of empathic emotions to one's relationship partner to feed back and to strengthen communal relationships.

Concluding Comments

We noted at the outset of this chapter that, although psychological research on emotion has been flourishing, most of it has focused on intrapersonal aspects of emotion. In this chapter we have tried to make a case that a variable that can *only* be understood in relationship terms, perceptions of relationship members' responsiveness to one another's needs, is crucial to fully understand people's emotional lives. This is a factor that varies as a function of relationship type and by person. It is also a factor that is central to relationship research although its importance even in that domain is often obscured by the fact that it comes cloaked in different terminologies in different investigators' research programs (e.g., communal versus exchange relationships, communal orientation, perceived social support, secure versus insecure attachment styles). It is the fact that perceptions of responsiveness to needs varies by relationship and *in combination with* the fact that expressing emotions carries information about our need states to others that makes perceptions of responsiveness to needs a crucial factor for emotion researchers to consider. We hope we have convinced the reader of this point.

There is another point we hope we have conveyed to our readers, one that is more relevant to the domain of relationship research than to the domain of emotions research. It is, simply, that our research tends to be fragmented by research groups and theory – there's attachment research, social support research, emotions research, communal/exchange research, and so forth. Each such program of research is valuable in its own right. Yet sometimes it is well worth while to take a step back and see the common themes and sets of findings that run through different, apparently independent, programs of research. In this case, the common theme we have pointed to is that perceptions of responsiveness to needs are closely linked with people's emotional lives.

Notes

1. Exceptions may occur in emergency situations in which another person's need is very great relative to the cost a person would incur to help the other, and in which help from someone with stronger communal ties is unavailable. For instance, a person might call an ambulance for a stranger who has collapsed in front of that person's house and even wait outside with the person until the ambulance arrives.
2. Participants had most of these relationships, but not every one in every case. Thus, a few ratings made by participants were hypothetical and participants were told that this was OK in the initial instructions.

3.   We believe the correlations for anger and disgust caused by the other were smaller than the remaining correlations because, as a mutual communal relationship grows in strength, *both* members' responsibilities for one another's needs grow. Thus, when another with whom one has a mutual communal relationship causes one to feel disgust or anger, one must be concerned not only with one's own needs but also with those of one's partner. As a result of the latter concern, one may suppress expressions of disgust and anger when those emotions have been elicited by one's partner so as not to hurt the partner's feelings.

4.   The Williamson and Clark (1989, 1992) results also can be explained in terms of participants feeling good about promoting the development of communal relationships. Even so, the results are consistent with our overall arguments that feeling positive emotions in response to improving another's welfare is something that occurs primarily when we care about the other's needs. Moreover, experiencing empathic happiness when benefiting another and being pleased to have promoted the relationship are not incompatible processes.

5.   One may also feel guilt in a non-communal relationship if one has broken the norms for that relationship. For instance, one may feel guilt in an exchange relationship for having not paid back a debt. However, we believe the primary source of guilt for most people is failure to demonstrate adequate concern about the welfare of those with whom they have communal relationships.

6.   The dimension of anxious attachment was not associated with significant tendencies to suppress versus express emotion.

7.   We are choosing to report this study on perceived support in the section of our chapter dealing with individual differences. We do this despite the fact that some researchers feel that perceptions of social support are determined primarily by support that is currently and objectively available in one's environment whereas others believe perceptions of support are determined by personality. In fact, our belief is that perceived social support is determined by both factors. Thus our placement of this study in the individual differences section of the chapter is somewhat arbitrary.

8.   Although we are choosing to emphasize the support this finding provides for perceptions of another's responsiveness to needs resulting in greater tendencies to express emotion, it is, of course, possible that the effects go in the opposite direction. That is, it may be that expressing distress elicits support which, in turn, causes perceived support to rise. Our actual belief is that both effects occur.

9.   Interestingly, the effects of attachment styles and of emotional control on marital satisfaction appeared to be largely independent in this study with the exception of some evidence that the negative relationship between husbands' security and satisfaction did seem to be mediated by suppression of emotional expression.

10.   Interestingly, the same set of studies also demonstrated that feeling badly when another experiences good outcomes and good when another experiences bad outcomes can lead to an inference that one does not like that other.

References

Aderman, D., Brehm, S. S., & Katz, L. B. (1974). Empathic observation of an innocent victim: The just world revisited. *Journal of Personality and Social Psychology, 29*, 342–347.

Andersen, P. A., & Guerrero, L. K. (1998). Principles of communication and emotion in social interaction. *Handbook of Communication and Emotion: Research, Theory, Applications, and Contexts* (pp. 49–96). San Diego, CA: Academic Press.

Asch, S. (1952). *Social psychology*. Englewood Cliffs, NJ: Prentice Hall.

Balswick, J., & Avertt, C. P. (1977). Differences in expressiveness: Gender, interpersonal orientation, and perceived parental expressiveness as contributing factors. *Journal of Marriage and the Family, 39*, 121–127.

Barrett, L. F., Robin, L., Pietromonaco, P. R., & Eyssell, K. M. (1998). Are women the "more emotional" sex? Evidence from emotional experiences in social context. *Cognition and emotion, 12*, 555–578.

Bartholomew, K., & Horowitz, L. M. (1991). Attachment styles among young adults: A test of a four-category model. *Journal of Personality and Social Psychology, 61*, 226–244.

Batson, C. D., Duncan, B. D., Ackermann, P., Buckley, T., & Birch, K. (1981). Is empathic emotion a source of altruistic motivation? *Journal of Personality and Social Psychology, 40*, 290–302.

Batson, C. D., Turk, C. L., Shaw, L. L., & Klcin, T. R. (1995). Information function of empathic emotion: Learning that we value the other's welfare. *Journal of Personality and Social Psychology, 68*, 300–313.

Baumeister, R. F., Stillwell, A. M., & Heatherton, T. F. (1994). Guilt: An interpersonal approach. *Psychological Bulletin, 115*, 243–267.

Baumeister, R. F., Stillwell, A. M., & Heatherton, T. F. (1995). Personal narratives about guilt: Role in action control and interpersonal relationships. *Basic and Applied Social Psychology, 17*, 173–198.

Bem, D. J. (1972). Self-perception theory. In L. Berkowitz (Ed.), *Advances in experimental social psychology* (Vol. 6, pp. 1–62). New York: Academic Press.

Brissette, I., & Clark, M. S. (1999). *Emotional expression in social relationships: The type of relationship matters*. Unpublished manuscript.

Brissette, I., Clark, M. S., & Scheier, M. (1999). *Heightened stress as a determinant of perceptions of social support: The moderating role of communal orientation*. Unpublished manuscript.

Buck, R. (1984). *The communication of emotion*. New York: Guilford Press.

Buck, R. (1989). Emotional communication in personal relationships: A developmental-interactionist view. In C. Hendrick (Ed.), *Review of personality and social psychology: Vol. 10. Close relationships* (pp. 144–163). Beverly Hills, CA: Sage.

Byrne, D., & Nelson, D. (1965). Attraction as a linear function of positive reinforcement. *Journal of Personality and Social Psychology, 1*, 659–663.

Clark, L., & Watson, D. (1994). Distinguishing functional from dysfunctional affective responses. In P. Ekman & R. J. Davidson (Eds.), *The Nature of Emotion: Fundamental Questions* (pp. 131–136). New York: Oxford University Press.

Clark, M. S., Brissette, I., & Grote, N. (1998, June). *Perceptions of social support as a function of relationship orientation and arousal*. Paper presented at the meetings of the International Society for the Study of Personal Relationships, Skidmore College, Saratoga, New York.

Clark, M. S., & Mills, J. (1979). Interpersonal attraction in exchange and communal relationships. *Journal of Personality and Social Psychology, 36*, 1–12.

Clark, M. S., & Mills, J. (1993). The difference between communal and exchange relationships: What it is and is not. *Personality and Social Psychology Bulletin, 19*, 684–691.

Clark, M. S., Ouellette, R., Powell, M., & Milberg, S. (1987). Recipient's mood, relationship type, and helping. *Journal of Personality and Social Psychology, 53*, 94–103.

Clark, M. S., & Taraban, C. B. (1991). Reactions to and willingness to express emotion in two types of relationships. *Journal of Experimental Social Psychology, 27*, 324–336.

Cohen, S., & Hoberman, H. M. (1983). Positive events and social supports as buffers of life change stress. *Journal of Applied Social Psychology, 13*, 99–125.

Collins, R. L. (1994). Social support provision to HIV-infected gay men. *Journal of Applied Social Psychology, 24*, 1848–1869.

Collins, R. L., & Di Paula, A. (1997). Personality and the provision of support: Emotions felt and signaled. In G. R. Pierce, B. Lakey, I. G. Sarason, & B. R. Sarason (Eds.), *Sourcebook of social support and personality* (pp. 429–443). New York: Plenum.

Curtis, R. C., & Miller, K. (1986). Believing another likes or dislikes you: Behaviors making the beliefs come true. *Journal of Personality and Social Psychology, 51*, 284–290.

Cutrona, C. E., & Russell, D. W. (1987). The provisions of social relationships and adaptation to stress. In W. H. Jones & D. Perlman (Eds.), *Advances in personal relationships* (Vol. 1, pp. 37–67). Greenwich, CT: JAI Press.

Ekman, P., & Davidson, R. J. (1994). Afterword: What is the function of emotions? In P. Ekman & R. J. Davidson (Eds.), *The Nature of Emotion: Fundamental Questions* (pp. 137–139). New York: Oxford University Press.

Feeney, J. A. (1995). Adult attachment and emotional control. *Personal Relationships, 2,* 143–159.

Feeney, J. A. (1999). Adult attachment, emotional control, and marital satisfaction. *Personal Relationships, 6,* 169–185.

Feeney, J. A., Noller, P., & Roberts, N. (1998). Emotion, attachment, and satisfaction in close relationships. In P. A. Andersen & L. K. Guerrero (Eds.), *The handbook of communication and emotion* (pp. 473–505). San Diego, CA: Academic Press.

Fitness, J. (2000). Anger in the workplace: An emotion script approach to anger between workers and their superiors, co-workers, and subordinates. *Journal of Organizational Behavior, 21,* 147–162.

Folkman, S., Lazarus, R., Dunkel-Schetter, C., DeLongis, A., & Gruen, R. (1986). Dynamics of a stressful encounter. Cognitive appraisal, coping, and encounter outcomes. *Journal of Personality and Social Psychology, 50,* 992–1003.

Fridlund, A. J. (1991). Sociality of solitary smiling: Potentiation by an implicit audience. *Journal of Personality and Social Psychology, 60,* 229–240.

Frijda, N.H. (1986). *The emotions.* Cambridge, England: Cambridge University Press.

Frijda, N. H. (1993). Moods, emotion episodes, and emotions. In M. Lewis and J. M. Haviland (Eds.), *Handbook of emotions* (pp. 381–404). New York: Guilford Press.

Goldberg, S., MacKay-Soroka, S., & Rochester, M. (1994). Affect, attachment, and maternal responsiveness. *Infant Behavior and Development, 17,* 335–339.

Grote, N. K., & Clark, M. S. (1998). Distributive justice norms and family work: What is perceived as ideal, what is applied and what predicts perceived fairness? *Social Justice Research, 11,* 243–269.

Hazan, C., & Shaver, P. (1987). Romantic love conceptualized as an attachment process. *Journal of Personality and Social Psychology, 52,* 511–524.

Hoover-Dempsey, K.V., Plas, J. M., & Strudler-Wallston, B. (1986). Tears and weeping among professional women: In search of new understanding. *Psychology of Women Quarterly, 10,* 19–34.

Jones, S. S., Collins, K., & Hong, H. (1991). An audience effect on smile production in 10-month-old infants. *Psychological Science, 2,* 45–49.

Kenny, D. A., & LaVoie, L. (1982). Reciprocity of interpersonal attraction: A confirmed hypothesis. *Social Psychology Quarterly, 45,* 54–58.

Krebs, D. (1975). Empathy and altruism. *Journal of Personality and Social Psychology, 32,* 1134–1146.

Laird, J. D. (1974). Self-attribution of emotion: The effects of expressive behavior on the quality of emotional experience. *Journal of Personality and Social Psychology, 29,* 475–486.

Laird, J. D., & Bresler, C. (1992). The process of emotional experience: A self-perception theory. In M. S. Clark (Ed.), *Emotion* (pp. 213–234). Newbury Park, CA: Sage.

Laurenceau, J., Barrett, L. F., & Pietromonaco, P. R. (1998). Intimacy as an interpersonal process: The importance of self-disclosure, partner disclosure, and perceived partner responsiveness in interpersonal exchanges. *Journal of Personality and Social Psychology, 74,* 1238–1251.

Levenson, R. W. (1994). Human emotion: A functional view. In P. Ekman & R. J. Davidson (Eds.), *The nature of emotion: Fundamental questions* (pp. 123–126). New York: Oxford University Press.

Martin, J. (1982). *Miss Manners' guide to excruciatingly correct behavior.* New York: Atheneum.

Martin, L. I., Achee, J. W., Ward, D. W., & Harlow, T. F. (1993). The role of cognition and effort in the use of emotions to guide behavior. In R. S. Wyer, Jr., & T. K. Srull (Eds.), *Perspectives on anger and emotion* (pp. 147–157). Hillsdale, NJ: Lawrence Erlbaum.

Martin, L. L., & Davies, B. (1998). Beyond hedonism and associationism: A configural view of the role of affect in evaluation, processing, and self-regulation. *Motivation and Emotion, 22*(1), 33–51.

Martin, L. L., & Stoner, P. (1996). Mood as input: What people think about how they feel moods determines how they think. In L. L. Martin & A. Tesser (Eds.), *Striving and feelings: Interactions between goals, affect, and self-regulation* (pp. 279–301). Hillsdale, NJ: Erlbaum.

Martin, L. L., Ward, D. W., Achee, J. W., & Wyer, R. S. (1993). Mood as input: People have to interpret the motivational implications of their moods. *Journal of Personality and Social Psychology, 64,* 317–326.

Miller, R. S., & Leary, M. R. (1992). Social sources and interactive functions of emotion: The case of embarrassment. In M. S. Clark (Ed.), *Emotion and social behavior* (pp. 202–221). Newbury Park, CA: Sage.

Mills, J., & Clark, M. S. (1982). Exchange and communal relationships. In L. Wheeler (Ed)., *Review of Personality and Social Psychology* (Vol. 3, pp. 121–144). Beverly Hills, CA: Sage.

Mills, J., Jellison, J. M., & Kennedy, J. (1976). Attribution of attitudes from feelings: Effect of positive or negative feelings when the attitude object is benefited or harmed. In J. Harvey, W. Ickes, & R. Kidd (Eds.), *New Directions in Attribution Research* (Vol. 1, pp. 271–289). Hillsdale, N. J.: Erlbaum.

Newcomb, T. M. (1961). *The acquaintance process.* New York: Holt, Rinehart, & Winston.

Norton, R. (1983). Measuring marital quality: A critical look at the dependent variable. *Journal of Marriage and the Family, 45,* 141–151.

Pennebaker, J. (1995). Emotion, disclosure, and health: An overview. In J. Pennebaker (Ed.), *Emotion, disclosure, and health* (pp. 3–10). Washington, DC: American Psychological Association.

Rime, B. (1995). The social sharing of emotion as a source for the social knowledge of emotion. In J. Russell & J. Fernandez-Dols. (Eds.), *Everyday conceptions of emotions* (pp. 475–489). Dordrecht: Kluwer Academic.

Riskind, J. H. (1984). They stoop to conquer: Guiding and self-regulatory functions of physical posture after success and failure. *Journal of Personality and Social Psychology, 47,* 479–493.

Riskind, J. H., & Gotay, C. C. (1982). Physical posture: Could it have regulatory or feedback effects on motivation and emotion? *Motivation and Emotion, 6,* 273–298.

Sarason, I. G., Sarason, B. R., Shearin, E. N., & Pierce, G. R. (1987). A brief measure of social support: Practical and theoretical implications. *Journal of Social and Personal Relationships, 4,* 497–510.

Scott, J. P. (1958). *Animal behavior.* Chicago: University of Chicago Press.

Scott, J. P. (1980). The function of emotions in behavioral systems: A systems theory analysis. In *Emotion: Theory, Research, and Experience: Vol. 1. Theories of Emotion* (pp. 35–56). New York: Academic Press.

Shaver, P., Schwartz, J., Kirson, D., & O'Connor, C. (1987). Emotion knowledge: Further exploration of a prototype approach. *Journal of Personality and Social Psychology, 52,* 1061–1086.

Shimanoff, S. B. (1988). Degree of emotional expressiveness as a function of face-needs, gender, and interpersonal relationship. *Communication Reports, 1,* 43–59.

Simon, H. A. (1967). Motivational and emotional controls of cognition. *Psychological Review, 74,* 29–39.

Simpson, J. A., Rholes, W. S., & Nelligan, J. S. (1992). Support seeking and support giving within couples in an anxiety-provoking situation: The role of attachment styles. *Journal of Personality and Social Psychology, 62,* 434–446.

Sommers, S. (1984). Reported emotions and conventions of emotionality among college students. *Journal of Personality and Social Psychology, 46,* 207–215.

Sroufe, L. A., & Waters, E. (1977). Attachment as an organizational construct. *Child Development, 48,* 1184–1199.

Thoits, P. A. (1989). The sociology of emotions. *Annual Review of Sociology, 15,* 317–342.

Timmers, M., Fischer, A. H., & Manstead, A. S. R. (1998). Gender differences in motives for regulating emotions. *Personality and Social Psychology Bulletin, 24,* 974–985.

Vangelisti, A. L., Daly, J. A., & Rudnick, J. R. (1991). Making people feel guilty in conversations: Techniques and correlates. *Human Communication Research, 18,* 3–39.

Watson, M., & Greer, S. (1983). Development of a questionnaire measure of emotional control *Journal of Psychosomatic Research, 27,* 299–305.

Wessman, A. E., & Ricks, D. F. (1966). Mood and personality. New York: Holt, Rinehart, & Winston.

Williamson, G. M., & Clark, M. S. (1989). Providing help and desired relationship type as determinants of changes in moods and self-evaluations. *Journal of Personality and Social Psychology, 56*, 722–734.

Williamson, G. M., & Clark, M. S. (1992). Impact of desired relationship type on affective reactions to choosing and being required to help. *Personality and Social Psychology Bulletin, 18*, 10–18.

Zillmann, D., & Cantor, J. R. (1977). Affective responses to the emotions of a protagonist. *Journal of Experimental Social Psychology, 13*, 155–165.

Chapter Eleven

Emotional Intelligence: Conceptualization and Measurement

Peter Salovey, Alison Woolery, and John D. Mayer

> The emotions are of quite extraordinary importance in the total economy of living organisms and do not deserve being put into opposition with "intelligence." The emotions are, it seems, themselves a higher order of intelligence.
>
> (Mowrer, 1960, p. 308)

Given recent popular interest in the idea of an emotional intelligence, including mentions by comic strip characters from Zippy-the-Pinhead to Dilbert, it is hard to believe that the term *emotional intelligence* was first formally defined in a 1990 article that appeared in a relatively obscure journal (Salovey & Mayer, 1990). Salovey and Mayer described emotional intelligence as a form of social intelligence that involves the ability to monitor one's own and others' feelings and emotions, to discriminate among them, and to use this information to guide one's thinking and action. They used this term to provoke intelligence theorists to contemplate an expanded role for the emotional system in conceptual schemes of human abilities and to challenge traditional approaches in the emotions field that view the arousal of feelings as disrupting normal cognitive activity. In the spirit of Charles Darwin, who in his 1872 book *The Expression of the Emotions in Man and Animals* viewed the emotional system as necessary for survival and as providing an important signaling system within and across species, Salovey and Mayer emphasized the functionality of feelings and described a set of competencies that might underlie the adaptive use of affectively charged information. After the publication of a best-selling trade book on the topic of emotional intelligence by *New York Times* science writer Daniel Goleman in 1995, the concept of emotional

Preparation of this manuscript was facilitated by the following grants: American Cancer Society (RPG-93–028–05–PBP), National Cancer Institute (R01–CA68427), and National Institute of Mental Health (P01–MH/DA56826). Please address correspondence concerning this chapter to Peter Salovey, Department of Psychology, Yale University, P.O. Box 208205, New Haven, CT 06520–8205, USA.

intelligence gained enormous popular appeal and attracted considerable media attention.

This chapter first presents a framework that organizes the skills and abilities relevant to a theory of emotional intelligence. The challenges of measuring emotional intelligence are described next, along with a review of ability-based instruments and self-report scales. We conclude with a brief discussion of the growing interest in emotional intelligence among educators and business executives.

A Framework

A person's ability to adapt and cope in life depends on the integrated functioning of his or her emotional and rational capacities. "Out of the marriage of reason with affect there issues clarity with passion. Reason without affect would be impotent, affect without reason would be blind" (Tomkins, 1962, p. 112). Interpersonal success depends on one's ability to reason about emotional experiences and other affect-laden information and to respond in emotionally adaptive ways. In our most recent theorizing, we have described emotional intelligence as the ability to perceive and express emotions, to understand and use them, and to manage emotions in oneself and other people (Mayer & Salovey, 1997; Salovey & Mayer, 1990). More formally, however, we define emotional intelligence by the specific competencies it encompasses, including the ability to perceive, appraise, and express emotion accurately; the ability to access and generate feelings when they facilitate cognitive activities; the ability to understand affect-laden information and make use of emotional knowledge; and the ability to regulate emotions to promote emotional and intellectual growth and well-being. This model of emotional intelligence is presented in table 11.1). The model is composed of four branches, each of which represents a class of skills, ordered hierarchically according to their complexity. The subskills of each branch are further organized according to their complexity, such that the more sophisticated subskills of each branch increasingly depend on skills from the other branches of the model.

Perception, appraisal, and expression of emotion

The following competencies represent some of the abilities associated with the first branch of emotional intelligence: perceiving, appraising, and expressing emotions.

Appraising and expressing one's own emotions.   Individuals can be more or less skilled at attending to, appraising, and expressing their own emotional states. These competencies are basic information processing skills in which the relevant information consists of feelings and mood states. For example, some individuals, called *alexithymic,* are unable to express their emotions verbally, presumably because they have difficulty identifying those feelings (Apfel & Sifneos, 1979). Alexithymic individuals have difficulty distinguishing between different emotions, verbally expressing emotions, and realizing that some physical sensations can be the manifestation of emotions (Kooiman, 1998). They are thought to have limited imagination and fantasy life and a concrete, externally-oriented cognitive style.

Table 11.1   The Emotional Intelligence Framework (adapted from Mayer & Salovey, 1997)

Perception, appraisal, and expression of emotion
    Identifying emotions in one's own subjective states
    Identifying emotion in other people
    Expressing emotions accurately
    Discriminating between feelings; between honest and dishonest expressions of feelings
Emotional facilitation of cognitive activities
    Redirecting and prioritizing thinking based on feelings
    Using emotions to facilitate judgment
    Capitalizing on feelings to take advantage of the perspectives they offer
    Using emotional states to facilitate problem solving and creativity
Understanding and analyzing emotional information and employing emotional knowledge
    Understanding how different emotions are related
    Understanding the causes and consequences of various emotions
    Interpreting complex feelings, such as blends and contradictory states
    Understanding transitions between emotions
Regulation of emotion
    Being open to feelings that are pleasant and unpleasant
    Monitoring and reflecting on emotions
    Engaging with or detaching from emotional states
    Managing emotions in self
    Managing emotions in other people

Alexithymia has been assessed with numerous measures, which vary greatly in the degree to which they have demonstrated reliability and validity. In a comprehensive review of most of these measures, Linden, Wen, and Paulhus (1995) concluded that the Toronto Alexithymia Scale (TAS) and the Beth Israel Hospital Questionnaire (BIQ) are psychometrically the best alexithymia measures; other measures (e.g., the Schalling Sifneos Personality Scale, the Revised Schalling Sifneos Personality Scale, and the MMPI Alexithymia Scale) have less well established psychometric properties (see also Bagby, Parker, & Taylor, 1993a, 1993b; Taylor, Ryan, & Bagby, 1985).

Original conceptions of alexithymia focused on deficiencies in handling symbols and abstractions and the presumed neurological abnormalities underlying these deficits. Nemiah and Sifneos (1970) posited that the overt manifestations of alexithymia reflect an abnormal affective style; the alexithymic individual experiences emotion but provides only limited and undifferentiated descriptions of his or her inner state. Some investigators have speculated that this deficiency has been attributed to inefficiencies in the interhemispheric transfer of information (Hoppe & Bogen, 1977; Zeitlin, Lane, O'Leary, & Schrift, 1989). A more recent view, and one that complements our model of emotional intelligence, is that alexithymia represents a deficit in emotional information processing and, subsequently, the conscious experience of emotion (Lane, Ahern, Schwartz, & Kaszniak, 1997).

Lane and Schwartz (1987) propose that the ability to recognize and describe emotion in oneself and others, which they call *emotional awareness*, develops in interaction with cognitive capacities. Their model posits five ascending levels of emotional awareness: physical sensations, action tendencies, single emotions, blends of emotion, and the capacity to appreciate complexity in the emotional experience of self and others. Alexithymia is associated with impaired verbal and nonverbal recognition and understanding of emotion (Lane, Sechrest, Reidel, Weldon, Kaszniak, & Schwartz, 1996). Lane et al. (1997) describe alexithymia as the emotional equivalent of blindsight. Environmental events trigger emotional responses that alexithymic individuals cannot consciously experience fully; they manifest behavioral and autonomic responses, but either say that they do not feel anything or do not know how they feel. There is a dissociation between emotional experience and the visceral concomitants of emotional arousal (Friedlander, Lumley, Farchione, & Doyal, 1997; Wehmer, Brejnak, Lumley, & Stettner, 1995).

Some researchers have suggested that alexithymia might affect the course of various illnesses. Kauhanen, Kaplan, Julkunen, and Salonen (1994) found that alexithymia predicted all-cause mortality after five years, even controlling for demographic and medical risk factors. Associations between alexithymia and hypertension have been reported (Kauhanen, Kaplan, Cohen, Salonen, & Salonen, 1994; Nordby, Ekeberg, & Knardahl, 1995; Osti, Trombini, & Magnani, 1980). Alexithymic individuals have high and stable levels of autonomic reactivity both at baseline and under stress, a pattern of arousal that may be associated with the internalization of emotional experiences (Infrasca, 1997). Although this evidence points to an association between alexithymia, autonomic reactivity, and illness, it does not explain whether reactivity results from unregulated affect or from unhealthy behaviors associated with alexithymia. Alexithymia may influence illness behavior, including the experience and reporting of symptoms and the tendency to seek medical care, rather than disease-relevant physiology (Goldman, Kraemer, & Salovey, 1996; Lumley, Stettner, & Wehmer, 1996; Lumley, Tomakowsky, & Torosian, 1997). The undifferentiated arousal associated with affect may be sensed, amplified, and reported as physical symptoms, as, for example, when the anxious individual perceives butterflies in the stomach as cramps signifying a likely ulcer (Stretton & Salovey, 1998).

Other recent studies support a link between alexithymia and immunocompetence. Highly alexithymic men, for example, had significantly lower numbers of natural killer cells, a measure of immune system functioning, even when controlling for possible effects of smoking and alcohol intake (Dewaraja et al., 1997). These findings suggest that the negative modulation of cellular immunity, combined with other factors that have negative effects on the immune system such as stress, results in the association between alexithymia and illness.

Appraising the emotions of others.   For adaptive social interaction, individuals also must appraise the emotions of others accurately. There are individual differences in people's ability to perceive accurately, understand, and empathize with others' emotions (reviewed in Buck, 1984). Individuals who are best able to do so may also respond flexibly to changes in their social environments and build supportive social networks (Salovey, Bedell, Detweiler, & Mayer, 1999).

Various measures of individual differences in non-verbal receiving of others' emotion have been developed. The Affect Sensitivity Test (Campbell, Kagan, & Krathwohl, 1971; Kagan, 1978) presents videotaped interactions between pairs of individuals; individuals respond by indicating the emotions and thoughts that targets are expressing. This test has moderate internal consistency and a good test-retest reliability, although different versions of it have had surprisingly low intercorrelations (Kagan, 1978). The Communication of Affect Receiving Ability Test (CARAT) consists of a videotape of people watching scenic, unpleasant, unusual, or sexual slides (Buck, 1976). Participants must guess what slide the target is observing by studying the target's facial expressions. The Profile of Nonverbal Sensitivity (PONS; Rosenthal, Hall, DiMatteo, Rogers, & Archer, 1979) has one of the best item samples of emotional expression, including face, body, and face and body combined. Another scale oriented to a more general class of stimuli combines faces, colors, and designs, and finds they define a unifactorial construct of emotional receiving (Mayer, DiPaulo, & Salovey, 1990). Several other scales or procedures exist including, for example, measures of the recognition of tachistoscopically presented facial expressions (e.g., Archer & Akert, 1977; Ekman & Friesen, 1975).

Differences in nonverbal perceptions of emotion have been associated with various criteria. CARAT scores are higher among artists than scientists, and they correlate with Rotter's (1966) interpersonal trust scale. More accurate perceptions may relate to effective mental-health counseling (Campbell et al., 1971). The unifactorial faces, colors, and designs scale correlates moderately with self-reported empathy (Mayer et al., 1990). A number of investigators have found that women are generally better in recognizing emotions (other than anger) in facial expressions than are men (Boucher & Carlson, 1980; Ekman, 1982; Hall, 1978; Kirouac & Doré, 1983, 1985; Wagner, MacDonald, & Manstead, 1986).

A particularly exciting communality between emotional appraisal and expression is that they both appear related to empathy, the ability to comprehend another's feelings and to re-experience them oneself. Empathy seems to depend on subsidiary abilities similar to appraising and expressing emotion (cf. Batson, Fultz, & Schoenrade, 1987; Wispé, 1986): understanding another person's point of view (Dymond, 1949; Hogan, 1969), identifying accurately another's emotions (Buck, 1984), experiencing the same or other appropriate emotion in response to them (Batson & Coke, 1981, 1983; Mehrabian & Epstein, 1972), and finally, communicating and/or acting on this internal experience (Batson, O'Quin, Fultz, Vanderplas, & Isen, 1983; Krebs, 1975).

Empathy may be a central characteristic of emotionally intelligent behavior. As social support researchers have made clear, a person's relatives, friends, and neighbors are critical contributors to his or her well-being (Kessler, Price, & Wortman, 1985; Thoits, 1986). When people relate positively to one another, they experience greater life satisfaction, and lower stress (Mayer, Gottlieb, Hernandez, Smith, & Gordis, 1988). Empathy is also a motivator for altruistic behavior (Batson, 1987). People who behave in an emotionally intelligent fashion should have sufficient social competence to surround themselves with supportive interpersonal relations. Clearly, the greater the number of emotionally intelligent friends, relatives, and coworkers, the more empathic and supportive one's social structure.

Much of the work on empathy has treated it as a dispositional variable (Chlopan, McCain, Carbonell, & Hagen, 1985). Two scales examining empathy were developed by Hogan (1969) and Mehrabian and Epstein (1972). Hogan's scale was constructed according to judges' ratings of California Q-sort items that were intended to reflect empathic and unempathic individuals. The complexity of the scale development techniques reported in Hogan (1969) make it clear that broad attributes other than empathy were considered as part of the criterion including humor, imaginative play, and insight into motives. Although we are sympathetic to this approach, which is similar to emotional intelligence in its generality, the scale may for this reason lack discriminant validity for empathy, as more narrowly considered here. A scale developed by Mehrabian and Epstein more specifically measures emotional responsiveness to others and includes such subscales as emotional contagion, appreciation of distant others' feelings, and being moved by others' positive and negative emotional experiences (e.g., "It makes me sad to see a lonely stranger in a group"; "I like to watch people open presents"). Other empathy scales have been reported but are less widely used (e.g., Dymond, 1949; Kerr & Speroff, 1954), and there is growing concern that all of these self-reported empathy scales are not strongly related to actual empathic abilities (Ickes, 1993).

Another concept that seems to have important implications for the ability to understand the emotions of other people is ambivalence over emotional expression (King, 1998; King & Emmons, 1990). Ambivalent individuals experience conflict over their style of emotional expression; they may be inexpressive because they inhibit the desire to express, or expressive and regretful of their expressiveness (King, 1998). Such individuals are more likely to experience psychological distress and negative affect than people who are comfortable with their emotional expression (King & Emmons, 1990). Especially relevant here is that ambivalent individuals report confusion reading others' emotions. Ambivalent individuals who are inexpressive tend to overinterpret emotional scenarios and facial expressions (King, 1998). These individuals seem to have multifaceted yet confused perceptions of emotion; their confusion is intensified by the fact that they cannot receive effective social feedback about the accuracy of their interpretations because they do not express themselves. Such confusion may prevent ambivalent inexpressive people from being sensitive to the needs of others and gauging their emotional reactions accurately. Consequently, they have problems in their interpersonal relationships. It appears that ambivalence over emotional expression places individuals at risk for problems with alcohol consumption, marital dissatisfaction, and discontent with social support (King, 1998).

Emotional facilitation of cognitive activities

Emotions can facilitate cognitive activities in a number of ways. The arousal of emotions can redirect attention to problems deserving greatest priority (Easterbrook, 1959). Individuals can capitalize on mood swings to view situations in a new way and avoid functional fixedness. People might even simulate emotional states in order to gain access to particular autobiographical memories. The greatest research attention in this area, however, has been focused on the ways in which emotions influence problem-solving and creative activities.

A number of investigators have argued that various emotions create different mental sets. These different sets may be more or less adaptive for solving certain kinds of problems (e.g., Chaiken, Wood, & Eagly, 1996; Isen, 1987; Palfai & Salovey, 1993; Schwarz, 1990; Schwarz, Bless, & Bohner, 1991; Schwarz & Clore, 1996). That is, different emotions create different information processing styles. Happy moods facilitate a mental set that is useful for creative tasks in which one must think intuitively or expansively in order to make novel associations. Sad moods generate a mental set in which problems are solved more slowly with particular attention to detail using more focused and deliberate strategies. Palfai and Salovey (1993) argued that these two different information processing styles (i.e., intuitive and expansive versus focused and deliberate) should be effective for two different kinds of problem-solving tasks: inductive problems like analogical reasoning and deductive logical tasks, respectively.

Mood may also assist problem solving by virtue of its impact on the organization and use of information in memory. For example, individuals may find it easier to categorize features of problems as being related or unrelated while they experience positive mood (Isen & Daubman, 1984). This clarity in categorizing information may have a positive impact on creative problem solving (Isen, Daubman, & Nowicki, 1987). Standard creativity tasks such as the remote associates task and cognitive categorization tests have commonly been used as the dependent variables in this research. For example, Isen, Daubman and Nowicki (1987) demonstrated that positive mood can facilitate more creative responses to Duncker's (1945) candle task. It seems that people experiencing positive mood are more likely to give especially unusual or creative first associates to neutral cues (Isen, Johnson, Mertz, & Robinson, 1985). Moreover, happy individuals may be more likely to discover category-organizing principles and use them to integrate and remember information (Isen, Daubman, & Gorgoglione, 1987).

Emotionally intelligent individuals may also be able to harness the motivational qualities of emotion. For example, a student may focus purposefully on the negative consequences of failing to submit a term paper on time in order to self-induce a state of fear that will spur him to get an early start on the paper. Another student may remind herself of all her successes before sitting down to write the paper. The self-induced positive mood that results bolsters her confidence in writing the paper, and she may be more likely to persevere when faced with a particularly challenging section of it.

Emotional states can be harnessed by individuals toward other ends. For example, positive moods make positive outcomes appear more likely, whereas negative moods make negative outcomes appear more likely (e.g., Johnson & Tversky, 1983; Mayer, Gaschke, Braverman, & Evans, 1992). Thus, addressing a problem while in different moods may enable individuals to consider a wider range of possible actions and outcomes (Mayer & Hanson, 1995). Mood swings may assist people in breaking set when thinking about the future and consider a variety of possible outcomes. As a consequence, they may be more likely to generate a larger number of future plans for themselves and thereby be better prepared to take advantage of future opportunities (Mayer, 1986).

Understanding and analyzing emotional information and employing emotional knowledge

A third branch of emotional intelligence concerns essential knowledge about the emotional system. The most fundamental competency at this level concerns the ability to label emotions with words and to recognize the relationships among exemplars of the affective lexicon. The emotionally intelligent individual is able to recognize that the terms used to describe emotions are arranged into families and that groups of emotion terms form fuzzy sets (see Ortony, Clore, & Collins, 1988). For instance, individuals learn that words such as *rage, irritation,* and *annoyed* can be grouped together as terms associated with anger. Perhaps more importantly, the relations among these terms are deduced – that annoyance and irritation can lead to rage if the provocative stimulus is not eliminated, or that envy is often experienced in contexts that evoke jealousy, but jealousy is less likely to be part of envy-provoking situations (Salovey & Rodin, 1986, 1989).

To understand the emotions, individuals must learn what emotions convey about relationships. Lazarus (1991), for example, describes how core relational themes – the central harm or benefit in adaptational encounters that underlies each emotion – are associated with different kinds of feelings. Anger results from a demeaning offense against the self, guilt from transgressing a moral imperative, and hope from facing the worst but yearning for better (Lazarus, 1991).

Increased complexity in this domain of emotional intelligence is represented by knowledge that emotions can combine in interesting and subtle ways. At a high school reunion, nostalgic conversation can give rise to wistful feelings, a blend of both joy and sorrow. Startled surprise at the wonders of the universe combined with fear about one's insignificant place in it may give rise to awe.

Finally, understanding and analyzing emotions includes the ability to recognize transitions among emotions. For example, Tangney and her colleagues have written extensively about how shame but not guilt can turn quickly to rage. The loss of self-esteem in situations that evoke shame can induce anger, as a kind of coping response and attempt to reestablish a sense of self. These transitions are rarely observed with guilt. Individuals can literally be shamed into rage (Tangney & Salovey, 1999; Tangney, Wagner, Fletcher, & Gramzow, 1992).

Regulation of emotion

Emotional knowledge also contributes to the fourth component of emotional intelligence, emotion regulation. However, individuals must develop further competencies in order to put their knowledge into action in this domain. They must first be open to the experience of mood and emotion and then practice and become adept at engaging in behaviors that bring about desired feelings. These emotion-regulatory skills enable individuals to engage in mood-repair strategies such as avoiding unpleasant activities or seeking out activities that they typically find rewarding. Individuals who are unable to manage their emotions are more likely to experience negative affect and remain in poor spirits.

Self-regulation of emotion.   Through the self-reflective experience of emotion, individuals acquire knowledge of the correlates and causes of their emotional experiences. Knowledge of emotion thus enables individuals to form theories of how and why emotions are elicited by different situations. This ability to understand and analyze emotional experiences translates into the ability to understand one's self and one's relation to the environment better, which may foster effective emotional regulation and greater well-being. In the psychotherapy literature, this has been termed *emotional literacy* (Steiner & Perry, 1997).

Individuals often react emotionally toward their direct experiences of various feelings, and these meta-emotional experiences either can facilitate or impede functioning (Gottman, 1997; Mayer & Gaschke, 1988). For example, a person can feel ashamed for having felt or expressed anger toward a loved one. The meta-emotion in this case is shame, which takes as its object the individual's direct experience of anger, and it may motivate the individual to inhibit anger or at least suppress angry behavior in the future. This type of learned emotional restraint can be highly advantageous to parents, children, between lovers, and in most other social relationships. To date, there have been very few investigations of meta-emotion (although see Gottman, 1997), in part because studying emotional responses to direct emotional experiences is a complex affair. However, meta-emotion is a fascinating instance of how humans take themselves and their experiences as objects and respond to these objects in a higher-order manner.

The emotionally intelligent individual can repair her negative moods and maintain positive moods when doing so is appropriate (it is sometimes desirable to maintain negative moods). This regulatory process comprises several steps. Individuals must (1) believe that they can repair negative moods when they arise (self-efficacy of regulation), (2) monitor their mood states accurately, (3) identify and discriminate those mood states that require regulation, (4) employ strategies to alleviate negative moods and maintain positive ones, and (5) assess the effectiveness of those strategies. Individuals differ in the expectancy that they can alleviate negative moods. Some people believe that when they are upset they can do something that will make them feel better; others insist that nothing will improve their negative moods. Individuals who believe they can successfully repair their moods engage in active responses to stress, whereas people low in self-efficacy of regulation display avoidance responses, as well as depressive and mild somatic symptoms (Catanzaro & Greenwood, 1994).

Although people must attend to their moods in order to identify those moods that require regulation, the mere act of attention may not always be adaptive. Attention to one's mood correlates positively with physical symptom reporting, depression, and neuroticism (Goldman et al., 1996; Nolen-Hoeksema, Morrow, & Fredrickson, 1993; Salovey, Mayer, Goldman, Turvey, & Palfai, 1995). High mood monitors have lower self-esteem and tend to experience more intense affective states and greater negative affect (Swinkels & Giuliano, 1995). These people agree that their moods are important and influence their behavior, but they report less success at mood regulation. Although monitoring in general may be a neutral activity, it can lead to increased rumination and subsequent prolonged negative affect when an unpleasant mood is encountered (Nolen-Hoeksema, 1991).

People differ in how well they can identify, discriminate, and understand their moods (Salovey et al., 1995). Whereas some people claim that they can clearly describe their feelings, other people report that they never know how they feel. Clarity in discriminating moods is associated with lower social anxiety, depression, and physical symptom reporting, as well as optimism and satisfaction with interpersonal and family relationships (Salovey et al., 1995; Salovey, Stroud, Woolery, & Epel, 2000). Individuals who can discriminate clearly among their emotions are less responsive to laboratory stressors, as measured by salivary cortisol secretions (Salovey et al., 2000). They also ruminate less following a negative event than individuals who report being unclear about their moods (Salovey et al.,

1995). Individuals who know what they are feeling tend to be extraverted and less socially anxious, seek and are satisfied with social rapport, experience higher self-esteem, and express greater global life satisfaction (Swinkels & Giuliano, 1995).

Whereas mood monitoring promotes rumination, mood labeling allows people to develop productive strategies for dealing with their moods. People must attend to their moods in order to discriminate among them. Once people can categorize and know their moods, they can work to prolong or change them. Without this process of discrimination, attending to moods becomes a maladaptive process that can lead to rumination – people focus excessively on their mood states and are unable to understand why they are experiencing them. Such rumination may intensify depression and, in turn, leads to difficulties in coping with stressful events. Most recent research has focused on attempts to repair bad moods, rather than maintain positive ones. Individuals who report that they attempt to repair negative moods are less likely to experience social anxiety, depression, and physical symptoms, but are more optimistic and satisfied with interpersonal and family relationships than individuals who do not attempt to repair their moods (Goldman et al., 1996; Salovey et al., 1995).

When individuals do attempt to regulate their moods, they employ a broad range of techniques. Thayer, Newman, and McClain (1994) believe that physical exercise is the single most effective strategy for changing a bad mood, among those under one's own control. Eighty-five percent of the studies on the acute mood effects of participation in a single session of exercise found some degree of improved mood (Yeung, 1996). Exercise also alleviates laboratory-induced anxiety (Yeung, 1996). Other commonly reported mood regulation strategies include listening to music, social interaction, and cognitive self-management, such as giving oneself a "pep talk." Pleasant distractions (chores, hobbies, fun activities, shopping, reading, and writing) are also effective. Less effective strategies include passive mood management (e.g., television viewing, caffeine, food, and sleep), direct tension reduction (e.g., drugs, alcohol, and sex), spending time alone, and avoiding the person or thing that caused a bad mood. In general, the most successful regulation methods involve expenditure of energy; active mood management techniques that combine relaxation, stress management, cognitive effort, and exercise may be the most effective strategies for changing bad moods (reviewed by Thayer et al., 1994).

A major aspect of emotional self-regulation is the ability to reflect upon and manage one's emotions; emotional disclosure provides one means of doing so. Pennebaker (1989, 1993, 1997) has studied the effects of disclosure extensively and finds that the act of disclosing emotional experiences in writing improves individuals' subsequent physical and mental health. The benefits of disclosure include fewer visits to the doctor (Pennebaker, Colder, & Sharp, 1990), enhanced immunological functioning (Pennebaker, Kiecolt-Glaser, & Glaser, 1988), and decreases in self-reported physical symptoms, distress, and depression (Greenberg & Stone, 1992). Text analyses based on these studies indicate that those individuals who benefit most from writing tend to use relatively high rates of positive emotion words, a moderate number of negative emotion words, and an increasing number of cognitive or thinking words from the first to last days of writing (Pennebaker & Francis, 1996; Pennebaker, Mayne, & Francis, 1997). Pennebaker (1997) suggests that these improvements result from the mediating role of language. When individuals experience trauma, they seek to understand the meaning and significance of their events.

If they can label their emotions, they will impose structure on their experiences. This structure helps people assimilate and understand their experiences, thus reducing associated emotional arousal.

Regulating the emotions of others.   The ability to help others enhance their moods is also a valued skill as individuals often rely on their social networks to provide not just a practical but emotional buffer against negative life events (Stroebe & Stroebe, 1996). Moreover, individuals appear to derive a sense of efficacy and social worth from helping others feel better and by contributing to the joy of loved ones. The ability to manage others' emotional experiences also plays a significant role in impression management and persuasion (Goffman, 1959). Although this skill sometimes is employed unscrupulously by sociopaths, cult leaders, and advertisers, impression management and persuasion often are employed prosocially as well. Thus, individuals who are able to regulate effectively the emotions of others are better able to act prosocially and build and maintain solid social networks. One literature that may provide a helpful starting point to investigators in this area is that concerning charismatic leadership (e.g., Wasielewski, 1985), which points out some of the strategies used by especially influential individuals to motivate others toward common goals.

Measuring Emotional Intelligence

Although the construct of emotional intelligence has generated considerable interest, the measurement of it is emerging rather slowly, and validity data are especially scarce. There is a converging sense among researchers of what emotional intelligence is – a set of competencies concerning the appraisal and expression of feelings, the use of emotions to facilitate cognitive activities, knowledge about emotions, and the regulation of emotion. There is less consensus on how best to measure emotional intelligence. Although there are distinct advantages to task-based measures and behavioral assessments, various self-report scales have also appeared that may measure important aspects of individuals' perceptions of their competencies in this domain. Such self-assessments may or may not correlate with actual skills and abilities. Some tests available commercially claim to measure emotional intelligence, but their content usually reflects a more generic focus on social skills, self-esteem, or personality characteristics.

Some investigators in the area of emotional intelligence have become demoralized at the primitive state of measurement in this domain at present. A recent article by Davies, Stankov, and Roberts (1998) concluded, after reviewing extant measures, most of which were earlier versions of instruments and some of which were gleaned from websites and articles in the popular press (e.g., Goleman, 1995b), that there is nothing empirically new in the idea of emotional intelligence – that these measures have no discriminant validity. Our view is that such a conclusion is incredibly premature. We are reminded of how during the Enlightenment, scientists wished to distinguish their thinking from a more medieval, superstitious, style of interpreting facts. In 1769, these scientists directed their skepticism toward the idea, within astronomy, that meteorites are small objects that enter the earth's

Table 11.2

Summary of Measures that have been Used to Assess Emotional Intelligence

Scale	Citation	Subscales	Number of items	Alpha	Convergent validity reported
Task-based scales					
Levels of Emotional Awareness	Lane, Quinlan, Schwartz, Walker, & Zeitlin (1990)		20	.81	Loevinger Sentence Completion Task ($r = .40$) Parental Descriptions Scale ($r = .35$) Openness to Experience ($r = .33$) Denied Emotions (DES) ($r = -.27$)
Emotional Creativity	Averill & Nunley (1992) Averill & Thomas-Knowles (1991)	Emotional Creativity Inventory	32	.89	SAT-V ($r = -.21$) SAT-M ($r = .04$) GPA ($r = .26$)
		Emotional Triads Test	4	.66	Affect Intensity ($r = .58$)
		Emotional Consequences Test	4	.71	Affective Communication ($r = .47$)
Thoughts and Emotions	Mayer & Geher (1996)		8	.53	Empathy ($r = .24$) Fantasy Scale ($r = .23$) Authoritarianism ($r = -.14$) Marlow-Crowne ($r = -.14$) SAT ($r = .26$)
MEIS	Mayer, Caruso, & Salovey (1998), Mayer, Salovey, &	I. Identification of emotion			Verbal IQ ($r = .36$) Empathy ($r = .33$) Life satisfaction ($r = .11$)
		1. faces	48	.89	
		2. sounds	48	.94	

			Parental warmth ($r = .23$)
Caruso (1999)	3. images	48	.90
	4. stories	42	.85
	II. Using emotions		
	1. synesthesia	60	.86
	2. feeling biases	28	.71
	III. Understanding emotions		
	1. blends	8	.49
	2. progressions	8	.51
	3. transitions	24	.94
	4. relativity	40	.78
	IV. Regulation of emotion		
	1. others	24	.72
	2. self	24	.70

Self-report scales

EI scale	Tett, Wang, Thomas, Griebler & Martinez (1997)	1. Recognition of emotion	146	.77 to .88 not reported
		2. Nonverbal emotional expression		
		3. Empathy		
		4. Regulation of emotion		
		5. Flexible planning		
		6. Creative thinking		
		7. Mood redirected attention		
		8. Motivating emotions		
		9. Delay of gratification		
		10. Emotional appropriateness		

Scale	Citation	Subscales	Number of items	Alpha	Convergent validity reported
Schutte EI scale	Schutte, Malouff, Hall, Haggerty, Cooper, Golden & Dornheim (1998)	1. Appraisal and expression 2. Regulation 3. Utilization for cognition	33	.87 to .90	TAS ($r = -.65$) TMMS Attention ($r = .63$) Clarity ($r = .52$) Repair ($r = .68$) Life Orientation Test optimism ($r = .52$) pessimism ($r = -.43$) Zung Depression ($r = -.37$)
Goleman EI scale	Goleman (1995b)		10	.00 to .20	Empathy Emotional control
Emotional Quotient Inventory (EQ$_i$)	Bar-On (1997)	1. Emotional self-awareness 2. Assertiveness 3. Self-regard 4. Self-actualization 5. Independence 6. Empathy 7. Interpersonal relationships 8. Social responsibility 9. Problem solving 10. Reality testing 11. Flexibility 12. Stress tolerance 13. Impulse control	133	.79 .76 .86 .76 .72 .74 .76 .69 .77 .73 .70 .80 .80	Beck Depression ($r = -.56$) Zung Depression ($r = -.66$) Emotional stability ($r = .51$ to .72) Apprehension ($r = -.47$ to $-.55$) Social boldness (r = .49 to .51) Social warmth ($r = .26$ to .51)

Measure	Author	Subscales	n	Reliability	Validity
		14. Happiness 15. Optimism		.79 .79	not reported
Emotional Quotient Inventory (EQI)	EQ Japan, Inc. (1998)	1. Intrapersonal intelligence 2. Interpersonal intelligence 3. Judgment abilities (these 3 domains further broken into 8 abilities and 24 subcategories)		not reported	not reported
Style in the Perception of Affect Scale (SIPOAS)	Bernet (1996)	1. Body-Based 2. Emphasis on Evaluation 3. Looking to Logic	93		Body-based: improved mental health, awareness of small bodily changes, social skill, contentment, creativity
Trait Meta-Mood Scale (TMMS)	Salovey, Mayer, Goldman, Turvey, & Palfai (1995)	1. Attention 2. Clarity 3. Repair	48	A: .78–86 C: .80–88 R: .62–85	Clarity: Ambivalence Over Emotional Expression ($r = -.25$) CES depression ($r = -.27$) Attention: Private self-consciousness ($r = .42$) Public self-consciousness ($r = .36$) Repair: CES depression ($r = -.37$) Optimism (LOT) ($r = .57$) Negative Mood Regulation ($r = .53$)

Scale	Citation	Subscales	Number of items	Alpha	Convergent validity reported
Trait Meta-Mood Scale for Elementary School Children (TMMS-C)	Rockhill & Greener (1999)	1. Attention 2. Clarity 3. Repair	16	A: .73 C: .58 R: .76	Repair and Clarity: Children's Depression Inventory ($r = -.26$ and $-.17$) Optimism (LOT) ($r = .38$ and $.37$)
Mood Awareness Scale (MAS)	Giuliano & Swinkels (1992)	1. Mood monitoring 2. Mood labeling	10	.79	Empathy ($r = .34$) Extroversion ($r = .29$) Self-consciousness ($r = .44$) Affect intensity ($r = .26$) Social anxiety ($r = -.23$) Alexithymia ($r = -.52$)
Negative Mood Regulation Scale	Catanzaro & Mearns (1990)		30	.86–.92	Sadness (DES) ($r = -.28$) Beck Depression men ($r = -.58$) women ($r = -.39$)
Emotional Expressiveness Questionnaire	King & Emmons (1990)		16	.70	Positive affect ($r = .40$) Confusion in reading emotion ($r = -.20$)
Ambivalence Over Emotional Expression Questionnaire	King & Emmons (1990)		28	.91	Negative affectivity (NA) ($r = .44$) Intense ambivalence (RIA) ($r = .36$) Confusion in reading emotion ($r = .26$)

atmosphere and fall to earth. An investigative body of the French Academy of Sciences, including the famous chemist Lavoisier, concluded that meteorites did not exist. Their rationale? Essentially, that because meteorites were "heavenly bodies," and heaven did not exist, neither must meteorites. This spurious line of reasoning had unfortunate consequences, as certain museums throughout Europe threw out their precious collections of meteorites (Bowers, 1976).

Despite such skepticism, measures of emotional intelligence have begun to emerge, though studies of predictive validity are still in their infancy. We divide these measures into two types. The first is those that engage participants in exercises that assess competencies relevant to emotional intelligence as skills. We call these *task-based measures*. We also review measures of beliefs about one's competencies in the domain of emotional intelligence and label these as *self-report measures*. Table 2 summarizes all of these measures and provides some data with respect to their psychometric properties including concurrent and discriminant validity.

Task-based scales

Emotional intelligence is likely to be measured with greatest validity when it is assessed as a set of competencies or skills. Self-reported assessments in this domain may not be especially accurate or even available to conscious introspection. It is unlikely that test items such as "I think I'm a pretty smart person" would make for a valid measure of IQ; the usefulness of analogous questions about one's emotional intelligence is also doubtful, unless the construct that one is trying to measure concerns beliefs about emotional intelligence such as emotional intelligence self-efficacy.

Levels of emotional awareness.   One approach to measuring emotional intelligence is to observe how individuals describe their feelings in response to a standard stimulus set. Lane, Quinlan, Schwartz, Walker, and Zeitlin (1990) devised the Levels of Emotional Awareness Scale (LEAS) as a measure of the articulation of emotional experiences. Participants are asked to describe their own anticipated feelings, and those of another person, in each of 20 scenarios such as:

> You and your best friend are in the same line of work. There is a prize given annually to the best performance of the year. The two of you work hard to win the prize. One night the winner is announced – your friend. How would you feel? How would your friend feel?

Standardized scoring criteria are used to evaluate the degree of differentiation and integration in the language used to describe the responses to each scenario. Low scores indicate a limited awareness of emotion and higher scores indicating high awareness. The rating procedure is based entirely on the denotative structure of the language used to describe emotional responses. Interrater reliability has been consistently high, and women perform significantly better on the LEAS than men, even after controlling for differences in verbal intelligence (for details see Lane, Kivley, DuBois, Shamasundara, & Schwartz, 1995; Lane et al., 1990; Lane et al., 1996).

Emotional creativity.   In another test of emotional understanding, Averill and Nunley (1992) presented participants with three emotions and asked them to write brief descriptions of situations in which they would feel the three emotions together. For example, in response to the emotional triad "joy/relief/distress," one participant wrote about the joy of being at the top of a mountain, the distress at imagining falling off, and the relief of not actually falling. Scoring is according to an expert criterion. Success at this task is moderately correlated with analytic intelligence as well as creativity (see also Averill & Thomas-Knowles, 1991).

Connecting thoughts and emotions.   Mayer and Geher (1996) created a test that specifically measures individual differences in the ability to connect thoughts to emotions. Participants read eight thought samples from a target group of people and estimated what these individuals were likely feeling. Various criteria were used to evaluate the participants' emotional recognition abilities, including agreement with the group consensus and agreement with the targets' report. Participants who agreed more highly with the group consensus and target scored higher than other participants on self-reported empathy and on the Scholastic Aptitude Test, but lower on a measure of emotional defensiveness.

The Multifactor Emotional Intelligence Scale (MEIS).   Arguably the most comprehensive task-based measure of emotional intelligence is the Multifactor Emotional Intelligence Scale (Mayer, Caruso, & Salovey, 1998). The MEIS comprises twelve ability measures that are divided into four branches, reflecting the model of emotional intelligence presented earlier: (1) perceiving emotions, (2) using emotions to guide thought and other cognitive activities, (3) understanding emotion, and (4) regulating emotion (Mayer & Salovey, 1997). Branch 1 tasks measure emotional perception in Faces, Music, Designs, and Stories. The second branch measures Synesthesia Judgments (e.g., "How hot is anger?") and Feeling Biases. Branch 3's four tasks examine the understanding of emotion. Sample questions include, "Optimism most closely combines which two emotions?" A participant should choose "pleasure and anticipation" over less specific alternatives such as "pleasure and joy." Branch 4's two tests measure Emotion Management in the Self and in Others. These tasks ask participants to read scenarios and then rate reactions to them according to how effective they are as emotion management strategies focused on the self or on others.

Investigations using the MEIS are in rather preliminary stages, but some findings have emerged. In general, the data collected support the theoretical model of emotional intelligence described earlier (Mayer, Salovey, & Caruso, 1999). In a normative sample of 503 adults, MEIS tasks were generally positively intercorrelated with one another, but not highly. As well, the test's factorial structure recommended two equally viable factorial models: (a) a three- to four-factor solution that separated out factors of emotional perception, understanding, management, and, at times, using emotions in cognitive activities, or (b) a hierarchical structure that first describes a general factor, g_{ei}. The MEIS as a whole correlates positively with verbal intelligence, self-reported empathy, and parental warmth, and negatively with social anxiety and depression. Controlling for verbal intelligence (i.e., vocabulary), MEIS scores were associated with verbal Scholastic Achievement Test (SAT) – Verbal scores among students at an Ivy League college. A refined and better normed successor to the MEIS, called the Mayer, Salovey, and Caruso Emotional Intelligence Test (MSCEIT) is presently being prepared for publication.

Self-report scales

In recent years, many self-report instruments purporting to measure aspects of emotional intelligence have appeared in the literature. Some of these scales are based on Salovey and Mayer's (1990) original conceptualization of emotional intelligence, others attempt only to operationalize one or another facet, and still others represent general measures of beliefs about social competencies now repackaged under the emotional intelligence rubric.

Scales based on Salovey and Mayer (1990). Several researchers have developed self-report measures based on the original model of emotional intelligence. For example, Tett, Wang, Thomas, Griebler, and Martinez (1997) devised a 146-item measure with 10 scales representing explicitly the original model components and subcomponents: recognition of emotion in the self and others, nonverbal emotional expression, empathy, regulation of emotion in the self and others, flexible planning, creative thinking, mood redirected attention, and motivating emotions (Salovey & Mayer, 1990). In addition, subscales measuring delay of gratification and emotional appropriateness, constructs not described by Salovey and Mayer (1990), were included. The scales have reasonable internal consistency and show moderate to strong associations with conceptually related personality measures and relatively weak relations with conceptually unrelated measures, as indicated in table 11.2.

As with all of the measures described in this section, Tett et al.'s (1997) scale is limited by its self-report nature. Moreover, several items lack face validity with respect to the constructs that they are attempting to operationalize, for example, "I design and make my own furniture" (Motivating Emotions) and "When eating hard candies, I usually chew them soon after putting them in my mouth" (Delay of Gratification). Other items seem particularly prone to self-presentational biases, such as, "I am not a very creative person" and "I have an inventive mind" (Creative Thinking).

Schutte et al. (1998) have also developed a self-report measure of emotional intelligence based on the three most general dimensions delineated by Salovey and Mayer (1990): appraisal and expression of emotion, regulation of emotion, and utilization of emotions in problem solving and other cognitive activities. The 33-item scale is internally consistent and has high test-retest reliability. The Schutte et al. scale correlates with measures of theoretically related constructs, including the Toronto Alexithymia Scale, the Attention, Clarity, and Repair subscales of the Trait Meta-Mood Scale, the Life Orientation Test, the Zung Depression Scale, and measures of openness to experience from the Big Five model of personality. Scores on the scale are positively associated with first-year college grades and were higher for therapists than for therapy clients or prisoners. Females score more highly on this scale than males. Emotional intelligence scores on this measure were associated with supervisor ratings of student counselors working at various mental health agencies (Malouff & Schutte, 1998). The strengths of the Schutte et al. scale include promising reliability, some reported validity, and concise representation of three aspects of emotional intelligence in just 33 items. However, the scale is limited by the small number of negatively-keyed items (3 out of 33).

Scales based on other models of emotional intelligence.   There are numerous measures of emotional intelligence not based on the original Salovey and Mayer (1990) framework. The most intensely marketed of these measures is the Emotional Quotient Inventory (EQ$_i$) developed by Bar-On (1996, 1997). Bar-On's personal effectiveness model of emotional intelligence is intended to represent personality characteristics that are associated with life success, including: Problem Solving, Self Regard, Interpersonal Relationships, Social Responsibility, Independence, Self Actualization, Assertiveness, Flexibility, Happiness, Stress Tolerance, Impulse Control, and Reality Testing. In general, subscales based on these characteristics have adequate internal consistence and good test-retest reliability (Bar-On, 1997).

A cross-national administration of the EQ$_i$ and the 16PF indicated that the EQ$_i$ is positively correlated with emotional stability, social boldness, and social warmth, and negatively correlated with apprehension (Bar-On, 1997, pp. 110–111). In cross-national samples, the EQ$_i$ differentiates among individuals high or low in subjective well-being (Bar-On, 1997, p. 26). Neither the overall scale nor any of its subscales are associated with the intelligence test embedded in the 16PF; a study correlating the EQ$_i$ with the WAIS (Wechsler Adult Intelligent Scales) yielded a negligible correlation (Bar-On, 1997, pp. 137–138). Total EQ$_i$ scores are negatively correlated with depression.

Goleman (1995b) has compiled a rather different test of emotional intelligence for articles in the popular media and elsewhere. The Goleman scale is composed of 10 items; for each item, people state their response to a hypothetical situation. Although the scale was probably never intended for scientific use, it does bear some content overlap with the fourth branch of our model (Emotional Regulation). Goleman's scale correlates highly with self-reported empathy (Davies et al., 1998). The scale also correlates with a measure of emotional control (Roger & Najarian, 1998). However, the psychometric properties of this scale, especially its internal consistency, are unacceptably weak (Davies et al., 1998).

A new measure of self-reported emotional intelligence was developed in Japan, the Emotional Quotient Inventory (EQI) (EQ Japan, Inc., 1998). The EQI operationalizes emotional intelligence in three domains: (1) intrapersonal intelligence (self-concept), (2) interpersonal intelligence (social skills), and (3) judgment intelligence (monitoring ability). These three intelligences are further subdivided into a set of eight abilities, which in turn yield 24 "types of [emotion] knowledge" (EQ Japan, Inc., 1998). For example, self-recognition of emotion is one of the abilities that comprise intrapersonal intelligence; the specific "types of knowledge" that contribute to self-recognition are personal self-awareness, social self-awareness, depression, and anxiety. The EQI provides a detailed guide to interpreting individual profiles, as well as "hints for self-development" for people who score high, average, or low on the various scales (EQ Japan, Inc., 1998). Like Bar-On's EQ$_i$ (Bar-On, 1997), EQ Japan's EQI measures a broad range of perceived personal attributes that extend beyond what is conventionally understood to comprise emotional intelligence. Depression, anxiety, self-assertion, and optimism are important aspects of personal effectiveness, certainly, but they are constructs that transcend emotional intelligence as we have defined it.

In contrast to these scales that measure a broad array of attributes that are then described as emotional intelligence, there are some narrower-gauge measures concerned with aspects of emotion-relevant information processing. An interesting approach to measuring emotional perception, for example, is Bernet's (1996) 93-item Style in the Perception of Affect Scale (SIPOAS), developed on the premise that being able to attend rapidly, appropriately, and effortlessly to feelings is the basis of emotional intelligence. The SIPOAS measures respondents' preferences for three styles. The "Body-Based" (BB) scale assesses attention to the bodily changes that accompany feelings and emotions. The "Emphasis on Evaluation" (EE) scale reflects effortful attempts at understanding one's own emotions in terms of outsiders, ideals, or expectations. The "Looking to Logic" (LL) scale involves favoring intellect and avoiding feeling. Body-based perception has been associated with better mental health, awareness of small bodily changes, social skill, contentment, and creativity (Bernet, 1996).

Other self-report scales measure reflective aspects of affective experiences. The Trait Meta-Mood Scale (TMMS) is a 48-item self-report measure designed to assess a person's general beliefs about attending to moods, the clarity of their own experiences of mood, and their efforts to repair mood states (Salovey et al., 1995). It consists of three subscales: Attention to Mood (Attention), Clarity in the Discrimination of Feelings (Clarity), and Mood Repair (Repair). In several studies involving six independent samples (Salovey et al., 1995; Salovey et al., 2000), internal consistency of the three scales was adequate, and intercorrelations among the subscales were relatively low.

High scores on Repair and Clarity have been associated with lower social anxiety, depression, and physical symptom reporting, as well as optimism and satisfaction with interpersonal and family relationships. Clarity and Attention have been associated with less intense physiological reactions to laboratory stressors, as measured by cortisol release and blood pressure changes (Salovey et al., 2000). Individuals high in Clarity tend to show greater declines in ruminative thought over time following a negative event than individuals who report being unclear about their moods (Salovey et al., 1995).

A recent variation on the TMMS is the Trait Meta-Mood Scale for Elementary School Children (TMMS-C) (Rockhill & Greener, 1999). The TMMS-C includes items adapted from the TMMS and the Life Orientation Test (LOT), which measures the tendency to have optimistic expectancies about future events (Scheier & Carver, 1985). The language of both the items and the rating scales have been simplified from the original measures. In a representative sample of 691 third- through seventh-grade elementary school students, children were reliable reporters of their own emotional Attention, Clarity, and Repair. Cronbach's alphas for these subscales were reasonably good. Correlations among subscales were similar to those found in the adult measures (Salovey et al., 1995). Clarity and Repair correlated-negatively with depression and positively with dispositional optimism.

Another scale measuring the experience of reflecting on one's moods was developed by Giuliano and Swinkels (1992). Their 10-item Mood Awareness Scale (MAS) is composed of two factors, mood monitoring ("I find myself thinking about my mood during the day") and mood labeling ("Right now I know what kind of mood I'm in"). Across 12 independent samples, internal consistency was very good. The full scale is positively associated with empathy, extroversion, private self-consciousness, and affect intensity, and negatively associated with social anxiety and alexithymia. Mood labeling is positively associated with extroversion, nonverbal expressiveness, and positive affect, and negatively associated with neuroticism and social anxiety. Mood monitoring is associated with neuroticism, negative affect, low self-esteem, and ruminative thinking (Swinkels & Giuliano, 1995).

The MAS dimensions of mood monitoring and labeling are very much like the TMMS Attention and Clarity subscales. Another measure, the Negative Mood Regulation (NMR) scale (Catanzaro & Mearns, 1990) resembles the TMMS Repair subscale. The NMR scale is a 30-item questionnaire that asks participants to indicate the strength of their belief that they can alter negative moods. All items begin with the stem "When I'm upset, I believe that . . . " and refer to expectancies regarding the outcomes of attempts to alleviate a negative mood state ("I can do something to feel better"; "I'll feel okay if I think about more pleasant things"). The NMR scale has demonstrated good internal consistency and test-retest reliability. Depression and somatic symptoms and the use of avoidant coping responses are associated with low NMR scores. Higher scores are positively associated with active coping responses (Catanzaro & Greenwood, 1994).

Other scales have been developed to measure aspects of emotional expression. The Emotional Expressiveness Questionnaire (EEQ; King & Emmons, 1990) includes 16 items that pertain to the tendency to express a variety of positive and negative emotions ("People can tell from my facial expressions how I am feeling"). Items are rated on a 7-point scale, with high scores indicating a tendency to express emotion. The scale demonstrates good internal consistency and has been found to correlate with peer ratings of expression and with other measures of emotional expressiveness (King & Emmons, 1990).

The Ambivalence Over Emotional Expressiveness Questionnaire (AEQ; King & Emmons, 1990), is a 28-item scale that measures conflict over one's emotional style. Items pertain to wanting to express emotion and being unable to do so, as well as expressing emotion and later regretting it ("I want to express my emotions honestly but I am afraid that it may cause me embarrassment or hurt"; "After I express anger at someone, it bothers me for a long time"). The scale has excellent internal consistency and correlates with measures of negative affect and confusion in reading emotion. Individuals who are both inexpressive and ambivalent over emotional expression have great difficulty making accurate inferences about the emotions conveyed to them (King, 1998).

The need for studies of predictive validity

This chapter has summarized a model of emotional intelligence and then described various ways that emotional intelligence has been operationalized. This story, however, does not have a typical ending – we know what emotional intelligence is, we have some idea how to measure it, but we do not yet understand whether it matters. At present, there are precious few studies showing that these competencies are related directly to life success, despite exaggerated claims in popular media reports to the contrary. Occasionally, one hears emotional intelligence discussed rather dismissively in scientific circles (e.g., Davies et al., 1998), because there are so few data establishing its predictive validity. As far as we are aware, prospective studies of the relation between emotional intelligence and outcomes that matter in the world – career success, marital satisfaction, subjective well-being, physical health – controlling for potentially related constructs like analytic (traditional) intelligence and Big Five personality attributes simply have not been published. This is where future effort must be directed.

Implications for Education and Business

Despite the paucity of studies measuring the predictive validity of emotional intelligence, in recent years, there is increasing interest in applying this construct in educational and business settings. In schools, the popularity of programs designed to encourage social and emotional learning (Cohen, 1999; Elias et al., 1997) or character education (Lickona, 1991) has led to the search for a unifying idea bridging interest in the development of morality and acquisition of social problem-solving skills. For some, emotional intelligence has provided this unifying framework. Similarly, individuals interested in encouraging managers in corporate settings to cultivate a broader range of skills than just those relevant to the technical aspects of one's job, have seized on emotional intelligence as the construct capturing these diffuse competencies (Cooper & Sawaf, 1996; Goleman, 1998; Ryback, 1998; Salerno, 1996; Weisinger, 1998).

While we cannot help but be pleased by the attention paid to emotional intelligence by forward-thinking educators and managers, we are a bit troubled by the profusion of concepts now thought to be captured by the term. The refining of theory and measurement is derailed by the attempt to include any construct anyone feels is important to success (and not measured by standard intelligence tests) under the emotional intelligence rubric (e.g., optimism, zeal, conscientiousness, innovation, service orientation). Human competencies must be defined separately from the uses to which those competencies can be applied. Emotional intelligence may be a building block of good character or be used effectively in management, but mere possession of these skills does not guarantee honesty and altruism in our children or higher earnings for shareholders.

Conclusion

The notion of an emotional intelligence provides a provocative challenge to traditional descriptions of intelligence as a set of analytic abilities and to the idea that the arousal of passion is incompatible with the maintenance of reason. Now that this gauntlet has been thrown down, however, we must begin to be more precise about the competencies that are encompassed by the concept of emotional intelligence and how to measure them. Our view is that it will be difficult to continue conceptualizing emotional intelligence as a kind of intelligence and impossible to demonstrate its discriminant validity from personality constructs if the field continues to rely on self-report instruments as the way to assess it (Mayer, Caruso, & Salovey, 2000). At the same time, the development of a psychometrically sound set of ability scales to assess emotional intelligence has been rather slow in coming, and even now that it is available, predictive validity data are scarce. Nonetheless, these research challenges have not attenuated the interest in emotional intelligence among educators and human resource managers and consultants. Nor have they inhibited the making of rather outrageous claims in trade books and the popular press. There is a pressing need for high-quality, prospective research on this construct to determine with more confidence what it predicts and what it does not predict. We hope that this chapter inspires others to join us in this endeavor.

References

Apfel, R. J., & Sifneos, P. E. (1979). Alexithymia: Concept and measurement. *Psychotherapy and Psychosomatics, 32,* 180–190.

Archer, D., & Akert, R. M. (1977). Words and everything else: Verbal and nonverbal clues in social interpretation. *Journal of Personality and Social Psychology, 35,* 443–449.

Averill, J. R., & Nunley, E. P. (1992). *Voyages of the heart: Living an emotionally creative life.* New York: Free Press.

Averill, J. R., & Thomas-Knowles, C. (1991). Emotional creativity. In K. T. Strongman (Ed.), *International Review of Studies on Emotion* (Vol. 1, pp. 269–299). Chichester, England: Wiley.

Bagby, R. M., Parker, J. D. A., & Taylor, G. J. (1993a). The twenty-item Toronto Alexithymia Scale—I. Item selection and cross-validation of the factor structure. *Journal of Psychosomatic Research, 38,* 23–32.

Bagby, R. M., Parker, J. D. A., & Taylor, G. J. (1993b). The twenty-item Toronto Alexithymia Scale—II. Convergent, discriminant, and concurrent validity. *Journal of Psychosomatic Research, 38,* 33–40.

Bar-On, R. (1996, August). *The era of the "EQ": Defining and assessing emotional intelligence.* Paper presented at the annual meeting of the American Psychological Association, Toronto, Ontario.

Bar-On, R. (1997). *Bar On Emotional Quotient Inventory: A measure of emotional intelligence – Technical manual.* Toronto, ON: Multi-Health Systems, Inc.

Batson, C. D. (1987). Prosocial motivation: Is it ever truly altruistic? In L. Berkowitz (Ed.), *Advances in experimental social psychology* (Vol. 20, pp. 65–123). New York: Academic Press.

Batson, C. D., & Coke, J. S. (1981). Empathy: A source of altruistic motivation for helping? In J. P. Rushton & R. M. Sorrentino (Eds.), *Altruism and helping behavior* (pp. 167–187). Hillsdale, NJ: Erlbaum.

Batson, C. D., & Coke, J. S. (1983). Empathic motivations of helping behavior. In J. T. Cacioppo & R. E. Petty (Eds.), *Social psychophysiology: A sourcebook* (pp. 417–433). New York: Guilford Press.

Batson, C. D., Fultz, J., & Schoenrade, P. A. (1987). Distress and empathy: Two qualitatively distinct vicarious emotions with different motivational consequences. *Journal of Personality, 55,* 19–39.

Batson, C. D., O'Quin, K., Fultz, J., Vanderplas, M., & Isen, A. (1983). Self-reported distress and empathy and egoistic versus altruistic motivation for helping. *Journal of Personality and Social Psychology, 45,* 706–718.

Bernet, M. (1996, August). *Emotional intelligence: Components and correlates.* Paper presented at the annual meeting of the American Psychological Association, Toronto, Ontario.

Boucher, J. D., & Carlson, G. E. (1980). Recognition of facial expression in three cultures. *Journal of Cross-cultural Psychology, 11,* 263–280.

Bowers, K. S. (1976). *Hypnosis for the seriously curious.* New York: Norton.

Buck, R. (1976). A test of nonverbal receiving ability: Preliminary studies. *Human Communication Research, 2,* 162–171.

Buck, R. (1984). *The communication of emotion.* New York: Guilford Press.

Campbell, R. J., Kagan, N. I., & Krathwohl, D. R. (1971). The development and validation of a scale to measure affective sensitivity (empathy). *Journal of Counseling Psychology, 18,* 407–412.

Catanzaro, S. J., & Greenwood, G. (1994). Expectancies for negative mood regulation, coping, and dysphoria among college students. *Journal of Consulting Psychology, 41,* 34–44.

Catanzaro, S. J., & Mearns, J. (1990). Measuring generalized expectancies for negative mood regulation: Initial scale development and implications. *Journal of Personality Assessment, 54,* 546–563.

Chaiken, S., Wood, W., & Eagly, A. H. (1996). Principles of persuasion. In E. T. Higgins & A. W. Kruglanski (Eds.), *Social psychology: Handbook of basic principles* (pp. 702–742). New York: Guilford Press.

Chlopan, B. E., McCain, M. L., Carbonell, J. L., & Hagen, R. L. (1985). Empathy: Review of available measures. *Journal of Personality and Social Psychology, 48,* 635–653.

Cohen, J. (Ed.). (1999). *Educating minds and hearts: Social emotional learning and the passage into adolescence*. New York: Teachers College Press.

Cooper, R. K., & Sawaf, A. (1996). *Executive EQ: Emotional intelligence in leadership and organizations*. New York: Grosset/Putnam.

Darwin, C. (1965). *The expression of the emotions in man and animals*. Chicago: University of Chicago Press. (Original work published 1872)

Davies, M., Stankov, L., & Roberts, R. D. (1998). Emotional intelligence: In search of an elusive construct. *Journal of Personality and Social Psychology, 75*, 989–1015.

Dewaraja, R., Tanigawa, T., Araki, S., Nakata, A., Kawamura, N., Ago, Y., & Sasaki, Y. (1997). Decreased cytotoxic lymphocyte counts in alexithymia. *Psychotherapy and Psychosomatics, 66*, 83–86.

Duncker, K. (1945). On problem solving. *Psychological Monographs* (Whole No. 270), 1–113.

Dymond, R. F. (1949). A scale for the measurement of empathic ability. *Journal of Consulting Psychology, 13*, 228–233.

Easterbrook, J. A. (1959). The effects of emotion on cue utilization and the organization of behavior. *Psychological Review, 66*, 183–200.

Ekman, P. (1982). *Emotions in the human face*. New York: Cambridge University Press.

Ekman, P., & Friesen, W. V. (1975). *Unmasking the face: A guide to recognizing the emotions from facial clues*. Englewood Cliffs, NJ: Prentice Hall.

Elias, M. J., Zins, J. E., Weissberg, R. P., Frey, K. S., Greenberg, M. T., Haynes, N. M., Kessler, R., Schwab-Stone, M. E., & Shriver, T. P. (1997). *Promoting social and emotional learning: Guidelines for educators*. Alexandria, VA: Association for Supervision and Curriculum Development.

EQ Japan, Inc. (1998). *Emotional Quotient Inventory*. Tokyo, Japan: Author.

Friedlander, L., Lumley, M. A., Farchione, T., & Doyal, G. (1997). Testing the alexithymia hypothesis: Physiological and subjective responses during relaxation and stress. *Journal of Nervous and Mental Disease, 185*, 233–239.

Giuliano, T., & Swinkels, A. (1992, August). *Development and validation of the Mood Awareness Scale*. Paper presented at the annual meeting of the American Psychological Association, Washington, DC.

Goffman, E. (1959). *The presentation of self in everyday life*. New York: Doubleday Anchor Books.

Goldman, S. L., Kraemer, D. T., & Salovey, P. (1996). Beliefs about mood moderate the relationship of stress to illness and symptom reporting. *Journal of Psychosomatic Research, 41*, 115–128.

Goleman, D. (1995a). *Emotional intelligence*. New York: Bantam.

Goleman, D. (1995b). *What's your EQ? The Utne Lens, Utne Reader* [On-line]. Available: *http://www.utne.com/lens/bms/eq.html/*.

Goleman, D. (1998). *Working with emotional intelligence*. New York: Bantam.

Gottman, J. M. (1997). *Meta-emotion: How families communicate emotionally*. Mahwah, NJ: Erlbaum.

Greenberg, M. A., & Stone, A. A. (1992). Emotional disclosure about traumas and its relation to health: Effects of previous disclosure and trauma severity. *Journal of Personality and Social Psychology, 63*, 75–84.

Hall, J. A. (1978). Gender effects in encoding nonverbal cues. *Psychological Bulletin, 85*, 845–857.

Hogan, R. (1969). Development of an empathy scale. *Journal of Consulting and Clinical Psychology, 33*, 307–316.

Hoppe, K. D., & Bogen, J. E. (1977). Alexithymia in twelve commissurotomized patients. *Psychotherapy and Psychosomatics, 28*, 148-155.

Ickes, W. (1993). Empathic accuracy. *Journal of Personality, 61*, 587–610.

Infrasca, R. (1997). Alexithymia, neurovegetative arousal, and neuroticism. *Psychotherapy and Psychosomatics, 66*, 276–280.

Isen, A. M. (1987). Positive affect, cognitive processes, and social behavior. In L. Berkowitz (Ed.), *Advances in experimental social psychology* (Vol. 20, pp. 203–253). San Diego: Academic.

Isen, A. M., & Daubman, K. A. (1984). The influence of affect on categorization. *Journal of Personality and Social Psychology, 47*, 1206–1217.

Isen, A. M., Daubman, K. A., & Gorgoglione, J. M. (1987). The influence of positive affect on cognitive organization: Implications for education. In R. Snow & M. Farr (Eds.), *Aptitude, learning, and instruction: Affective and conative factors*. Englewood Cliffs, NJ: Prentice Hall.

Isen, A. M., Daubman, K. A., & Nowicki, G. P. (1987). Positive affect facilitates creative problem solving. *Journal of Personality and Social Psychology, 52*, 1122–1131.

Isen, A. M., Johnson, M. M. S., Mertz, E., & Robinson, G. (1985). The influence of positive affect on the unusualness of word associations. *Journal of Personality and Social Psychology, 48*, 1413–1426.

Johnson, E. J., & Tversky, A. (1983). Affect, generalization, and the perception of risk. *Journal of Personality and Social Psychology, 15*, 294–301.

Kagan, N. (1978, August). *Affective sensitivity test: Validity and reliability*. Paper presented at the annual meeting of the American Psychological Association, San Francisco, CA.

Kauhanen, J., Kaplan, G. A., Cohen, R. D., Salonen, R., & Salonen, J. T. (1994). Alexithymia may influence the diagnosis of coronary heart disease. *Psychosomatic Medicine, 56*, 237–244.

Kauhanen, J., Kaplan, G. A., Julkunen, J., & Salonen, J. T. (1994). The association of alexithymia with all-cause mortality: Prospective epidemiological evidence. *Psychosomatic Medicine, 56*, 149.

Kerr, W. A., & Speroff, B. J. (1954). Validation and evaluation of the empathy test. *The Journal of General Psychology, 50*, 269–276.

Kessler, R. C., Price, R. H., & Wortman, C. B. (1985). Social factors in psychopathology: Stress, social support, and coping processes. *Annual Review of Psychology, 36*, 531–572.

King, L. A. (1998). Ambivalence over emotional expression and reading emotions in situations and faces. *Journal of Personality and Social Psychology, 74*, 753–762.

King, L. A., & Emmons, R. A. (1990). Conflict over emotional expression: Psychological and physiological correlates. *Journal of Personality and Social Psychology, 58*, 864–877.

Kirouac, G., & Doré, F. (1983). Accuracy and latency of judgment of facial expression of emotion. *Perceptual and Motor Skills, 57*, 683–686.

Kirouac, G., & Doré, F. (1985). Accuracy of the judgment of facial expression of emotions as a function of sex and level of education. *Journal of Nonverbal Behavior, 9*, 3–7.

Kooiman, C. G. (1998). The status of alexithymia as a risk factor in medically unexplained physical symptoms. *Comprehensive Psychiatry, 39*, 152–159.

Krebs, D. L. (1975). Empathy and altruism. *Journal of Personality and Social Psychology, 32*, 1134–1146.

Lane, R. D., Ahern, G. L., Schwartz, G. E., & Kaszniak, A. W. (1997). Is alexithymia the emotional equivalent of blindsight? *Biological Psychiatry, 42*, 834–844.

Lane, R. D., Kivley, L. S., Dubois, M. A., Shamasundara, P., & Schwartz, G. E. (1995). Levels of emotional awareness and the degree of right hemispheric dominance in the perception of facial emotion. *Neuropsychologia, 33*, 525–538.

Lane, R. D., Quinlan, D. M., Schwartz, G. E., Walker, P., & Zeitlin, S. B. (1990). The levels of emotional awareness scale: A cognitive-developmental measure of emotion. *Journal of Personality Assessment, 55*, 124–134.

Lane, R. D., & Schwartz, G. E. (1987). Levels of emotional awareness: A cognitive-developmental theory and its application to psychopathology. *American Journal of Psychiatry, 144*, 133–143.

Lane, R. D., Sechrest, L., Reidel, R., Weldon, V., Kaszniak, A., & Schwartz, G. E. (1996). Impaired verbal and nonverbal emotion recognition in alexithymia. *Psychosomatic Medicine, 58*, 203–210.

Lazarus, R. S. (1991). *Emotion and adaptation*. New York: Oxford University Press.

Lickona, T. (1991). *Educating for character: How our schools can teach respect and responsibility*. New York: Bantam.

Linden, W., Wen, F., & Paulhus, D. L. (1995). Measuring alexithymia: Reliability, validity, and prevalence. *Advances in Personality Assessment, 32*, 153–164.

Lumley, M. A., Stettner, L., & Wehmer, F. (1996). How are alexithymia and physical illness linked? A review and critique of pathways. *Journal of Psychosomatic Research, 41*, 505–518.

Lumley, M. A., Tomakowsky, J., & Torosian, T. (1997). The relationship of alexithymia to subjective and biomedical measures of disease. *Psychosomatics, 38*, 497–501.

Malouff, J., & Schutte, N. (1998, August). *Emotional intelligence scale scores predict counselor per-*

formance. Paper presented at the Annual Convention of the American Psychological Society, Washington, DC.

Mayer, J. D. (1986). How mood influences cognition. In N. E. Sharkey (Ed.), *Advances in cognitive science* (Vol. 1, pp. 290–314). Chichester, England: Ellis Horwood.

Mayer, J. D., Caruso, D., & Salovey, P. (1998). *The Multifactor Emotional Intelligence Scale.* Unpublished scale available from the authors; contact John D. Mayer, Department of Psychology, University of New Hampshire, Conant Hall, Durham, NH 03824, for details.

Mayer, J. D., Caruso, D., & Salovey, P. (2000). Competing models of emotional intelligence. In R. Sternberg (Ed.), *Handbook of human intelligence* (pp. 396–420). New York: Cambridge University Press.

Mayer, J. D., DiPaulo, M. T., & Salovey, P. (1990). Perceiving affective content in ambiguous visual stimuli: A component of emotional intelligence. *Journal of Personality Assessment, 54,* 772–781.

Mayer, J. D., & Gaschke, Y. N. (1988). The experience and meta-experience of mood. *Journal of Personality and Social Psychology, 55,* 102–111.

Mayer, J. D., Gaschke, Y., Braverman, D. L., & Evans, T. (1992). Mood-congruent judgment is a general effect. *Journal of Personality and Social Psychology, 63,* 119–132.

Mayer, J. D., & Geher, G. (1996). Emotional intelligence and the identification of emotion. *Intelligence, 22,* 89–113.

Mayer, J. D., Gottlieb, A. N., Hernandez, M., Smith, J., & Gordis, F. (1988). *Mood and mood-related communication during advice.* Unpublished manuscript, University of New Hampshire.

Mayer, J. D., & Hanson, E. (1995). Mood-congruent judgment over time. *Personality and Social Psychology Bulletin, 21,* 237–244.

Mayer, J. D., & Salovey, P. (1997). What is emotional intelligence? In P. Salovey & D. J. Sluyter (Eds.), *Emotional development and emotional intelligence* (pp. 3–31). New York: Basic Books.

Mayer, J. D., Salovey, P., & Caruso, D. (1999). Emotional intelligence meets traditional standards for an intelligence. *Intelligence, 27,* 267–298.

Mehrabian, A., & Epstein, N. (1972). A measure of emotional empathy. *Journal of Personality, 40,* 525–543.

Mowrer, O. H. (1960). *Learning theory and behavior.* New York: Wiley.

Nemiah, J. C., & Sifneos, P. E. (1970). Affect and fantasy in patients with psychosomatic disorder. In O. W. Hill (Ed.), *Modern trends in psychosomatic medicine* (Vol. 2, pp. 26–34). New York: Appleton-Century-Crofts.

Nolen-Hoeksema, S. (1991). Responses to depression and their effects on the duration of depressive episodes. *Journal of Abnormal Psychology, 100,* 569–582.

Nolen-Hoeksema, S., Morrow, J., & Fredrickson, B. L. (1993). Response styles and the duration of episodes of depressed mood. *Journal of Abnormal Psychology, 102,* 20–28.

Nordby, G., Ekeberg, O., & Knardahl, S. (1995). A double-blind study of psychosocial factors in 40-year old women with essential hypertension. *Psychosocial Psychosomatics, 63,* 142–150.

Ortony, A., Clore, G. L., & Collins, A. (1988). *The cognitive structure of emotions.* Cambridge, England: Cambridge University Press.

Osti, R. M. A., Trombini, G., & Magnani, B. (1980). Stress and distress in essential-hypertension. *Psychotherapy and Psychosomatics, 33,* 193–197.

Palfai, T. P., & Salovey, P. (1993). The influence of depressed and elated mood on deductive and inductive reasoning. *Imagination, Cognition, and Personality, 13,* 57–71.

Pennebaker, J.W. (1989). Confession, inhibition, and disease. In L. Berkowitz (Ed.), *Advances in experimental social psychology* (Vol. 22, pp. 211–244). New York: Academic Press.

Pennebaker, J. W. (1993). Putting stress into words: Health, linguistic, and therapeutic implications. *Behavior Research and Therapy, 31,* 539–548.

Pennebaker, J. W. (1997). Writing about emotional experiences as a therapeutic process. *Psychological Science, 9,* 162–166.

Pennebaker, J. W., Colder, M., & Sharp, L. K. (1990). Accelerating the coping process. *Journal of Personality and Social Psychology, 58,* 528–537.

Pennebaker, J. W., & Francis, M. E. (1996). Cognitive, emotional, and language processes in disclosure. *Cognition and Emotion, 10*, 601–626.

Pennebaker, J. W., Kiecolt-Glaser, J., & Glaser, R. (1988). Disclosure of traumas and immune function: Health implications for psychotherapy. *Journal of Consulting and Clinical Psychology, 56*, 239–245.

Pennebaker, J. W., Mayne, T. J., & Francis, M. E. (1997). Linguistic predictors of adaptive bereavement. *Journal of Personality and Social Psychology, 72*, 863–871.

Rockhill, C. M. & Greener, S. M. (1999, April). *Development of the Trait Meta-Mood Scale for elementary school children.* Presented at the biennial meeting for the Society for Research in Child Development, Albuquerque, NM.

Roger, D., & Najarian, B. (1998). The construction and validation of a new scale for measuring emotional control. *Personality and Individual Differences, 10*, 845–853.

Rosenthal, R., Hall, J. A., DiMatteo, M. R., Rogers, P., & Archer, D. (1979). *Sensitivity to nonverbal communication: A profile approach to the measurement of individual differences.* Baltimore: Johns Hopkins University Press.

Rotter, J. B. (1966). Generalized expectancies for internal versus external control of reinforcement. *Psychological Monographs, 80* (1, Whole No. 609).

Ryback, D. (1998). *Putting emotional intelligence to work: Successful leadership is more than IQ.* Boston: Butterworth-Heinemann.

Salerno, J. G. (1996). *Emotional quotient (EQ): Are you ready for it?* Oakbank, Australia: Noble House of Australia.

Salovey, P., Bedell, B., Detweiler, J. B., & Mayer, J. D. (1999). Coping intelligently: Emotional intelligence and the coping process. In C. R. Snyder (Ed.), *Coping: The psychology of what works* (pp. 141–164). New York: Oxford University Press.

Salovey, P., & Mayer, J. D. (1990). Emotional intelligence. *Imagination, Cognition, and Personality, 9*, 185–211.

Salovey, P., Mayer, J. D., Goldman, S. L., Turvey, C., & Palfai, T. P. (1995). Emotional attention, clarity, and repair: Exploring emotional intelligence using the Trait Meta-Mood Scale. In J. W. Pennebaker (Ed.), *Emotion, disclosure, and health* (pp. 125–154). Washington, DC: American Psychological Association.

Salovey, P., & Rodin, J. (1986). Differentiation of social-comparison jealousy and romantic jealousy. *Journal of Personality and Social Psychology, 50*, 1100–1112.

Salovey, P., & Rodin, J. (1989). Envy and jealousy in close relationships. *Review of Personality and Social Psychology, 10*, 221–246.

Salovey, P., Stroud, L., Woolery, A., & Epel, E. (in press). Perceived emotional intelligence, stress reactivity and symptom reports: Further explorations using the Trait Meta-Mood Scale. *Psychology and Health.*

Scheier, M. F., & Carver, C. S. (1985). Optimism, coping and health: Assessment and implication of generalized outcome expectancies. *Health Psychology, 4*, 219–247.

Schutte, N. S., Malouff, J. M., Hall, L. E., Haggerty, D., Cooper, J. T., Golden, C. J., & Dornheim, L. (1998). Development and validation of a measure of emotional intelligence. *Personality and Individual Differences, 25*, 167–177.

Schwarz, N. (1990). Feelings as information: Informational and motivational functions of affective states. In E. T. Higgins & E. M. Sorrentino (Eds.), *Handbook of motivation and cognition* (Vol. 2, pp. 527–561), New York: Guilford Press.

Schwarz, N., Bless, H., & Bohner, G. (1991). Mood and persuasion: Affective states influence the processing of persuasive communications. In M. Zanna (Ed.), *Advances in experimental social psychology* (Vol. 24, pp. 161–199). San Diego, CA: Academic Press.

Schwarz, N., & Clore, G. L. (1996). Feelings and phenomenal experiences. In E. T. Higgins & A. W. Kruglanski (Eds.), *Social psychology: Handbook of basic principles* (pp. 433–465). New York: Guilford Press.

Steiner, C., & Perry, P. (1997). *Achieving emotional literacy: A personal program to increase your emotional intelligence.* New York: Avon.

Stretton, M. S., & Salovey, P. (1998). Cognitive and affective components of hypochondriacal concerns. In W. F. Flack & J. D. Laird (Eds.), *Emotions in psychopathology: Theory and research* (pp. 265–279). New York: Oxford University Press.

Stroebe, W., & Stroebe, M. (1996). The social psychology of social support. In E. T. Higgins & A. W. Kruglanski (Eds.), *Social psychology: Handbook of basic principles* (pp. 597–621). New York: Guilford Press.

Swinkels, A., & Giuliano, T. A. (1995). The measurement and conceptualization of mood awareness: Monitoring and labeling one's mood states. *Personality and Social Psychology Bulletin, 21*, 934–939.

Tangney, J. P., & Salovey, P. (1999). Problematic social emotions: Shame, guilt, jealousy and envy. In R. M. Kowalski & M. R. Leary (Eds.), *The social psychology of emotional and behavioral problems: Interfaces of social and clinical psychology* (pp. 167–195). Washington, DC: American Psychological Association.

Tangney, J. P., Wagner, P. E., Fletcher, C., & Gramzow, R. (1992). Shamed into anger? The relation of shame and guilt to anger and self-reported aggression. *Journal of Personality and Social Psychology, 62*, 669–675.

Taylor, G. J., Ryan, D., & Bagby, M. (1985). Toward the development of a new self-report alexithymia scale. *Psychotherapy and Psychosomatics, 44*, 191–199.

Tett, R., Wang, A., Thomas, M., Griebler, J., & Martinez, A. (1997). Development of self-report measures of emotional intelligence. Paper presented at the Annual Convention of the Southeastern Psychological Association, Atlanta, Georgia.

Thayer, R. E., Newman, J. R., & McClain, T. M. (1994). Self-regulation of mood: Strategies for changing a bad mood, raising energy, and reducing tension. *Journal of Personality and Social Psychology, 67*, 910–925.

Thoits, P. (1986). Social support as coping assistance. *Journal of Consulting and Clinical Psychology, 54*, 416–423.

Tomkins, S. S. (1962). *Affect, imagery, and consciousness: Vol. 1. The positive affects*. New York: Springer.

Wagner, H. L., MacDonald, C. J., & Manstead, A. S. R. (1986). Communication of individual emotions by spontaneous facial expression. *Journal of Personality and Social Psychology, 50*, 737–743.

Wasielewski, P. L. (1985). The emotional basis of charisma. *Symbolic Interaction, 8*, 207–222.

Wehmer, F., Brejnak, C., Lumley, M., & Stettner, L. (1995). Alexithymia and physiological reactivity to emotion-provoking visual scenes. *Journal of Nervous and Mental Disease, 183*, 351–357.

Weisinger, H. (1998). *Emotional intelligence at work: The untapped edge for success*. San Francisco: Jossey-Bass.

Wispé, L. G. (1986). The distinction between sympathy and empathy: To call forth a concept, a word is needed. *Journal of Personality and Social Psychology, 50*, 314–321.

Yeung, R. R. (1996). The acute effects of exercise on mood state. *Journal of Psychosomatic Research, 40*, 123–141.

Zeitlin, S. B., Lane, R. D., O'Leary, D. S., & Schrift, M. J. (1989). Interhemispheric transfer deficit and alexithymia. *American Journal of Psychiatry, 146*, 1434–1439.

Chapter Twelve

Emotional Experience in Close Relationships

Ellen Berscheid and Hilary Ammazzalorso

Close interpersonal relationships are the setting in which people most frequently experience intense emotions, both the positive emotions, such as joy and love, and the negative emotions, such as anger and fear. No other context in which people customarily live their lives appears to be as fertile a breeding ground for emotional experience as close relationships are. Most emotion theorists recognize that emotions are most frequently and intensely experienced in the context of close relationships (see Ekman & Davidson, 1994). Lazarus, for example, states that "most emotions involve two people who are experiencing either a transient or stable interpersonal relationship of significance" (1994, p. 209).

It is not surprising, therefore, that many of the questions people ask about close relationships concern the emotions they experience in them. When young adults are asked to list the things they wish to understand about close relationships, for example, emotional phenomena invariably figure high on their lists (Berscheid, 1998). They often ask: "Can you both love and hate your partner?"; "Is it abnormal to feel jealous?"; "How can one prevent anger at outside sources from carrying over into anger at a relationship partner?"; "How can I get my partner to feel more passion?"; "Does separation increase passion and love?"; "Can the butterflies in the stomach and other feelings of love reoccur throughout the relationship, 10 or 20 years later?"

Overview of Chapter

This chapter addresses the strong connection between close relationships and emotional experience from the perspective of the Emotion-in-Relationships Model (ERM) (Berscheid, 1983, 1986, 1991; Berscheid, Gangestad, & Kulakowski, 1984). We begin by outlining how the infrastructure of a close relationship differs from that of casual and superficial relationships. Following a brief discussion of the nature of emotional experience and the conditions that appear to trigger intense emotion, we discuss why these emotion triggers are often present in the infrastructure of close relationships but tend to be absent in superficial relationships. Evidence supporting ERM from a study of the emotional effects of separation of close romantic partners is presented next. Then, we differentiate between emotional experiences whose origins lie entirely within the relationship as opposed to emotional experiences occurring in association with the partner but whose precipitating sources lie outside the relationship; the latter is commonly referred to as "emotion spillover." Finally, we discuss some implications of ERM for the experience of jealousy and other negative emotions in the relationship, as well as its implications for current therapeutic approaches to the treatment of negative emotions that dissatisfied relationship partners frequently experience.

The Infrastructure of a Close Relationship

People sometimes wonder if their relationship with another is a close one. At times, they even wonder if they have any relationship at all. Unable to answer this question themselves, some turn to their partner and ask, "Do we still have a relationship?" Other people simply assume that their relationships are close but later events force recognition that their partners did not share their view. As Weber observes in her analysis of breakups of nonmarital romantic relationships: "Indeed, one partner's 'breakup' is the other partner's dead end: The latter may reasonably claim that, in his or her mind, there was no 'breakup' because there was no relationship to break up!" (1998, p. 272). Still other people assume their relationship is not close but when the relationship dissolves, they experience surprisingly intense emotions, causing them to wonder if the relationship wasn't much closer than they ever realized.

Relationship scholars, too, have questioned what relationship closeness means. Their efforts to conceptualize the construct of closeness resulted from their intuitive belief that differences in closeness would help explain many important relationship phenomena (see Clark & Reis, 1988), a belief now confirmed. Relationship scholars initially approached their task by recognizing that the term "close" is a descriptive adjective that modifies the noun "relationship"; that is, "closeness" simply refers to a property of a relationship. Thus before addressing the question of closeness, they first had to confront the even more basic question, "What is a relationship?"

Relationship

Most relationship scholars view the *interaction* that takes place between two people to be the living tissue of an interpersonal relationship (see Berscheid & Reis, 1998). Two people are "interacting" when the behavior of one influences the behavior of the other and vice versa. As this implies, the essence of a relationship is the oscillating rhythm of influence that appears in the partners' interactions. If two people have never interacted, they do not have a relationship; if they seldom interact, they probably do not have much of a relationship; but if they often interact, and if each partner's behavior is influenced by the other partner's behavior, then, from the perspective of most relationship scholars, they are in a relationship with each other. The concept of relationship thus refers to two people whose behavior is *interdependent* in that a change in behavior of one is likely to produce a change in behavior of the other.

The relationship scholar's view may not agree with the views of the relationship partners. One or both partners may believe that a close relationship exists when, from the relationship scholar's perspective, it does not; that is, neither has appreciable influence on the other's activities. "Parallel" or "empty-shell" marriages, where the partners move through time and space together but have little or no impact on the other, are an example. Conversely, some partners may believe that they do not have a relationship with another although they do; that is, there exists a strong pattern of mutual influence in the partners' activities. Partners who are in a relationship are most likely to believe they are not when they dislike each other (see Berscheid, Snyder, & Omoto, 1989).

Closeness

If the essence of a relationship lies in the partners' interaction pattern, then it follows that the descriptor "close" must refer to some property, or collection of properties, of their interaction pattern. Most relationship scholars use the adjective "close" to refer to an interaction pattern in which each partner's behavior is highly dependent on the other partner's behavior. Thus a *close* relationship usually is viewed as one in which the partners are *highly interdependent*.

Although the partners may be highly interdependent, it is unlikely that their degree of dependence on each other is equal. Most relationships, even close relationships, are somewhat asymmetrical in that one partner's activities are more influenced by the other partner's activities than vice versa. A parent–child relationship is an example of an asymmetrical relationship because the child is more influenced by the parent's activities than the parent is influenced by the child's activities (although mothers of "colicky" infants might disagree).

Assessment of the closeness of a relationship, then, requires an assessment of the degree of dependence the partners exhibit in their interaction with each other. Kelley et al. (1983) observe that most relationship scholars regard at least four properties of the partners' interaction pattern to be indicative of high interdependence and thus closeness. First, the interaction pattern reveals that the partners *frequently* influence each other's behaviors; second, they influence a *diversity* of each other's behaviors (i.e., they influence many different kinds of their partner's activities, not simply their leisure activities, for example); third, the magnitude of influence they exert on their partner on each occasion observed is *strong*; and, finally, these three properties have characterized the couple's interaction pattern for a relatively *long duration* of time.

In sum, the infrastructure of a relationship refers to the recurrent patterns of influence that the partners exert on each other's behavior, whether deliberately or unintentionally. The kinds of behaviors the partners influence may include: cognitive behaviors, such as thoughts and feelings; physiological behaviors, such as heart rate and blood pressure; as well as more easily observable motor and verbal behaviors. Examination of the infrastructure of a close relationship, as opposed to a less close or superficial relationship, will reveal that one partner's behavior can be reliably predicted from the other partner's behavior. It is this highly interconnected behavioral infrastructure that appears to be the soil in which the experience of intense emotion flourishes.

Intense ("Hot") Emotion

In the early 1960s, Stanley Schachter and his associates experimentally demonstrated that emotional experience has both a physiological component and a cognitive component (e.g., Schachter & Singer, 1962). The physiological component refers to visceral arousal and the cognitive component refers to the individual's cognitive interpretation of the internal event of arousal and the external circumstances in which it occurs as an "emotional" experience. Schachter demonstrated that people are unlikely to report that they are experiencing an emotion unless they also perceive that they are experiencing peripheral physiological arousal (e.g., a pounding heart, sweaty palms, and other physiological events usually associated with autonomic nervous system [ANS] discharge) and also have cognitively interpreted both the internal event of arousal and the external context in which it has occurred to mean that they are experiencing an emotion.

Following Schachter's studies, the topic of emotion experienced a renaissance in psychology (see Lewis & Haviland, 1993). In fact, since Schachter presented evidence supporting his "two-component" theory of emotion, the task of answering the many questions associated with human emotional experience seems to have attracted as many workers as the task of constructing the Tower of Babel did – and with much the same result: emotion theorists and researchers have had a great deal of trouble communicating with each other. Controversy clouds the answers to even the most fundamental questions about the antecedents and consequences of emotional phenomena (see Ekman & Davidson, 1994). Few emotion theorists and researchers even agree on just exactly what an emotion is (see Berscheid, 1990; Plutchik, 1994). As a result, those who wish to pursue a better understanding of emotional experience in close relationships must choose among a bewildering variety of theoretical approaches to emotion but they have few guideposts to make their choice.

Differing views of emotion

Some theorists contend that there are certain "basic" emotions, whereas others, "constructionists," repudiate that notion and believe that each emotional experience is formed afresh, or "on-line," from the elements present in a particular situation. Because no situation is ever likely to repeat itself in all its particulars, constructionists thus take the position that there are innumerable emotional states which, although they bear similarities to each other, are never precisely the same from one occasion to the next.

Even within these two opposing camps, there is disagreement. For example, those who argue that some emotions are basic – and thus that other emotions are simply a "blend" of a smaller number of basic emotions – do not agree on precisely which emotions are basic nor, as this suggests, do they agree on how many basic emotions there are. Ortony and Turner (1990), for example, estimate that the number of basic emotions currently proposed by theorists who take the position that some emotions are more basic than others ranges from 2 to 18.

Adding to the confusion is the fact that emotion theories frequently have different foci. For example, some theories focus on the expression of emotion once it is experienced (e.g., Ekman, 1982); some theories attempt to describe the neurological circuitry associated with emotional experience (e.g., Panksepp, 1994); some emphasize the coping behavior often associated with emotional experience (e.g., Lazarus, 1991); some emphasize the cognitive circuitry of emotion (e.g., Oatley & Johnson-Laird, 1987); and others highlight still other facets of emotion (e.g., its evolutionary history; Plutchik, 1980).

Because emotion theories differ widely in the phenomena they address, and thus in many of their particulars, it is not surprising that they differ also in their definitions of emotion. When one attempts to impose some order on the plethora of views of what an emotion is, it becomes clear that they can be arrayed along a dimension of inclusiveness – or the range of events the theorist regards as instances of emotional experience.

Inclusiveness.   At the highly inclusive end of the dimension are those emotion theorists who regard an emotion to be any experienced state that carries *positive or negative valence*. For these emotion theorists, preferences (e.g., for vanilla over chocolate), values (e.g., liberal vs. conservative), as well as attitudes, appraisals, evaluations, and other cognitive states that carry positive or negative valence, are viewed as "emotional" states. Even boredom, lassitude, or ennui – usually regarded as negative states by the individual experiencing them – are regarded as emotional states by some theorists.

At the other, more restricted, end of the spectrum are those theorists who argue that such inclusive definitions of emotion include far too much to be useful. They contend that by defining emotional events so broadly, virtually all of human experience becomes defined as "emotional" experience, a far too large and unwieldy array to provide special insight into the kinds of emotional events in which most people are interested (for a discussion of this point, see Mandler, 1997). Supporting their argument are the results of factor analytic studies of human language, which consistently reveal that affective valence (positive–negative) is the primary dimension underlying people's symbolic representations of the external world, including representation of animate and inanimate objects, events, and experiences (Osgood, Suci, & Tannenbaum, 1957). These theorists argue, then, that if the cognitive evaluations of all the objects, persons, and events that people typically encounter carry some degree of positive or negative valence, then people are always in some sort of "emotional" state.

Thus, some theorists of emotion restrict the kinds of events they are willing to call an emotion. Many, for example, restrict emotion to events that are accompanied by ANS arousal. Although they recognize that several other physiological systems are involved in emotional experience, they believe that the experience of ANS arousal is a necessary condition for people to perceive that they are experiencing an emotion (e.g., Schachter & Singer, 1962; Mandler, 1997).

Arousal as a component of emotional experience.   When people talk about the intense emotions they experience in their close relationships, they usually are not talking about states of boredom, or even mildly favorable or unfavorable appraisals of their partner's behavior or attributes. To the contrary, laypersons appear to be Schachterians: when they talk about the emotions they experience in their close relationships, they usually are talking about experiences in which their knees tremble, their faces flush, their heart pounds, and – as will be recalled from one person's question about close relationships – they feel "butterflies" in their stomachs. In other words, they are usually talking about states in which they experience the symptoms of peripheral physiological arousal. It is experiences such as these – often termed "hot" emotions by emotion theorists and researchers, as opposed to milder feelings, attitudes, and appraisals – that many relationship partners say they wish to better understand.

It is, in fact, precisely this kind of experience that Aristotle, the first theorist to treat the subject of emotion, wished to know more about; that William James (e.g., 1884), who introduced the topic of emotion to psychology, wished to know more about; that Stanley Schachter, whose demonstrations that physiologically unaroused individuals are unlikely to report that they are experiencing an emotion, wanted to know more about; and what such contemporary theorists as George Mandler (e.g., 1997) wish to know more about. These theorists view peripheral (ANS) arousal as an essential component of emotional experience and thus they exclude positively or negatively valenced states unaccompanied by such arousal from the realm of their theories of emotion. They also often argue that ANS arousal is in itself – and apart from its contribution to self-reports of emotional experience – an important event for the human. Mandler (e.g., 1975), for example, argues that it is such an important event that the individual is likely to be aware of it – that the perception that one is experiencing the internal event of arousal has high priority status for representation in consciousness.

Relatedly, those emotion theorists who restrict their definitions of emotion to experiences that carry *both* arousal and valence, as opposed to those who define emotion inclusively *only* with respect to valence, believe that the antecedents and consequences of the former events are different from the latter and, thus, that these two types of experiences demand different theoretical approaches. They also argue that the consequences of experiences that involve both arousal and valence, and lead to people's reports that they are experiencing an emotion, more frequently make a significant difference to the people experiencing them, as well as to those who interact with those people, than do experiences that involve valence alone (see Berscheid, 1990).

The thesis that arousal is an important event for the human, and that arousal states differ in their consequences from non-arousal states, has been supported by recent neuroscientific findings. Arnsten (1998), for example, has reviewed neurobiological evidence suggesting that during stressful experiences often associated with self-reports of emotion, catecholamine neuromodulators released in the peripheral and central nervous systems activate opposing actions in the brain – actions that turn on the amygdala (long associated with the expression of emotion) and turn off the prefrontal cortex (associated with working memory and also with the inhibition of inappropriate responses and distractions, both of which contribute to effective problem solving). Moreover, it long has been observed that emotional events are better remembered than valenced events unaccompanied by arousal. Gold (e.g., 1992) has identified one possible mediator of improved memory for emotional events. He finds that the arousal accompanying emotional states may affect neuroendocrine processes regulating memory storage; specifically, Gold has demonstrated that epinephrine release appears to modify brain function and enhance memory storage through an increase in blood glucose level. These recent findings at the neurophysiological level of analysis are consistent with previous findings of relationship researchers at the psychological level of analysis. For example, Knapp and Clark (1991) have shown that people interacting in bad moods make poor problem-solvers whereas good moods do not have a commensurate beneficial effect.

The Emotion-in-Relationships Model (ERM)

The view of emotional experience taken by ERM is consistent with that taken by most laypersons and those emotion theorists who view peripheral arousal as an essential component of emotional experience. ERM thus addresses "hot," or intense, emotions rather than cooler, or milder, valenced feelings, appraisals, and evaluations. Moreover, it adopts the general position taken by Mandler on the antecedents and consequences of such emotions.

ERM adopts Mandler's theory of emotion for two reasons: First, the aim of ERM is to better understand *why* intense emotions more frequently occur in the context of close relationships than in other contexts and, second, it attempts to predict *when* such emotions are likely to occur in relationships. What makes Mandler's theory of emotion especially useful for thinking about the experience of emotion in the context of close relationships, is that, unlike most other theories of emotion, it attempts to identify the precipitating conditions of emotional experience. Most other theorists pick up the thread of emotional experience *after* it has been precipitated by some event. For example, William James's examination of emotional experience began after the individual perceived the "exciting fact" (as he termed it) – the barrel of a gun, a snake in the path, or a threatening husband. In contrast, Mandler directly confronts the question of the nature of the "exciting fact," or the nature of events that are likely to cause emotion. Moreover, in addition to addressing the question of *when* an emotion will be experienced, Mandler also considers the question of the probable intensity of the emotional experience and its duration.

Mandler's theory of emotion

Mandler begins by observing that one of the human's most important evolutionary inheritances – one that has been essential to the survival of *Homo sapiens* – is our innate ability to detect whether the state of the world around us is the "same" as before or "different" from before. If our world has changed – if it is unfamiliar and different from that we expected and have adapted to – it is potentially dangerous and thus we may need to take action to protect our well-being. Our changed environment, however, may also present us with new opportunities to enhance our well-being; if so, action also may be required to take advantage of those opportunities. In either case, the detection of a discrepancy between the world as we currently perceive it and the world as we have known it in the past signals that new ways of living, adapting, and behaving may be required to protect or to enhance our welfare.

Mandler thus believes that humans have evolved in such a way as to be cognitively sensitive to the *detection of a discrepancy* between the world as we expected it to be and the world as we currently perceive it to be, and to automatically undergo bodily changes to help us take survival-promoting actions when a discrepancy is detected. In sum, Mandler theorizes that the detection of a discrepancy provides the occasion for arousal (the initiation of "excitation") that combines with a positive or negative valenced cognitive evaluation of the situation (e.g., as one that presents a threat to well-being or an opportunity to enhance well-being) to produce emotional experience. Thus, in Mandler's theory of emotion, discrepancy detection fulfills a necessary condition for the experience of "hot" emotion.

The arousal-producing and attention-orienting nature of unexpected events has been demonstrated by Stiensmeier-Pelster, Martini, and Reisenzein (1995), who found that expectancy-disconfirming events were more likely to elicit intense feelings of surprise and lead to causal thinking to resolve the discrepancy than events that did not violate prior expectations. Similarly, Gendolla (1997) found that it is unexpected events, rather than attributions of luck, that lead to feelings of surprise in the context of achievement situations. Moreover, Meyer, Reisenzein, and Schutzwohl (1997) demonstrated that schema-discrepant events lead to delayed execution of a simple action previously routinely performed after the event, as well as to subjective feelings of surprise and involuntary attention to the event. In yet another study, when MacDowell and Mandler (1989) experimentally manipulated degree of cognitive discrepancy, they found that heart rate showed larger increases after unexpected events than after expected, and that ANS arousal and subjective reports of emotion were most highly correlated when their respondents had experienced a discrepant event.

Cognitive expectancies about the nature of our social and physical environments have appeared in at least some theories of emotion since Hebb (1946) published his influential theoretical analysis of fear. As a consequence of his experiments with monkeys, Hebb declared, in opposition to conventional psychological wisdom at the time, that "no amount of analysis of the stimulating conditions alone can be expected to elucidate the nature of fear, or lead to any useful generalization concerning its causes . . . " (1946, p. 274). Fear, rather than being generated by the properties of the stimulus alone (e.g., a snake), was theorized to be a joint product of the nature of the stimulus and what Hebb called "autonomous" central processes. Specifically, Hebb proposed that "fear originates in the disruption of temporally and spatially organized cerebral activities" (1946, p. 274). Violation of cognitive expectancies, of course, is a large and important subset of events that disrupt "organized cerebral activities."

Currently, expectancies play a central role not only in Mandler's theory but also in Gray's (e.g., 1994) theoretical analysis of emotion. Gray postulates three emotion systems: a behavioral approach system, a fight/flight system, and a behavioral inhibition system, each of which can be described on the behavioral level, the neural level, and the cognitive level. Gray's analysis of the cognitive level, which has focused primarily on the behavioral inhibition system, importantly includes a hypothetical construct he calls "the comparator." The comparator function is a continuous monitoring of whether the current state of the world is the same as, or different from, the expected state of the world.

Neurophysiologists attempting to understand the interplay between emotional and cognitive processes in infant brain development also highlight the role of cognitive expectancies (e.g., Blakemore, 1998; Greenough, Black, & Wallace, 1987). Siegel, in fact, comments that "*The brain can be called an 'anticipation machine,' constantly scanning the environment and trying to determine what will come next*" (1999, p. 30 [emphasis in the original]).

There is extensive evidence that humans do react quickly and automatically to unexpected changes in their environment. Any unexpected disruption or interruption in the individual's customary behavioral routines, progress toward current goals and plans, and cognitive/perceptual beliefs and expectations about people and events appears to produce activation of the sympathetic nervous system (SNS; which, together with the parasympathetic nervous system, comprises the ANS). Since the work of the physiologist Walter Cannon (1929), the SNS has been viewed as a "fight or flight" emergency action system that reacts to potential danger by channeling blood supply to the muscles and brain, increasing heart rate and rate of metabolism, and raising the sugar content of the blood to provide a boost of energy – all symptoms associated with physiological arousal and the experience of emotion.

Mandler theorizes that activation of SNS arousal not only prepares the individual to *physically* respond to the changed environment but the individual's conscious perception of the internal event of SNS arousal may act as a *cognitive* "back-up" signal that alerts the individual that something is different in his or her world and thus that action may need to be taken to protect or enhance well-being. This view assumes that perceptions of environmental change may be processed by the mind and result in SNS activation and the perception of SNS symptoms before the perceptions of change in the external environment reach conscious awareness. This assumption has experimental support (e.g., Ohman & Soares, 1994; Kunst-Wilson & Zajonc, 1980); that is, people may react autonomically to stimuli they do not consciously perceive and cannot report. Thus, the perception that one is experiencing the symptoms of internal physiological arousal, symptoms that Mandler believes have priority status for representation in consciousness, may precipitate scanning of the environment to locate the cause of the arousal. In this way, if the individual is not immediately conscious of the environmental change, perception of the internal event of arousal helps ensure that changes in the environment will be noticed.

In sum, Mandler concludes that discrepancies are the major occasions for emotions to occur and that "the construction of emotion consists of the concatenation in consciousness of some cognitive evaluative schema together with the perception of visceral arousal" (1997, p. 71). Moreover, Mandler theorizes that the longer the discrepancy exists without resolution, the more intense the arousal should be and thus the more intense the emotion. Successful adaptation to the change is theorized to terminate emotional experience. Successful adaptation is marked by the individual's resumption of previously disrupted behavioral routines and progress toward his or her plans and goals, and/or by cognitive resolution of the violated expectations (e.g., by determination of their meaning, particularly their meaning for the individual's welfare, and by determination of whether action is required and, if so, what action will maximally protect or increase well-being).

Relationship infrastructure and emotion: ERM

It now can be seen why the infrastructure of a close relationship, where the two partners' activities are highly interdependent, would be an especially fertile ground for the experience of intense emotion as contrasted to less close relationships. As a relationship develops, the partners come to know each other increasingly well. "Knowing" the partner means being able to accurately predict how the partner will behave in many different situations, especially those in which the partner's behavior has positive or negative implications for the individual's own welfare. Each prediction, or expectation, about the partner's behavior guides the individual's own behavior in interaction with the partner. Knowing how their partners will behave under a variety of conditions thus allows people to plan and act in such a way as to protect and enhance their own welfare in interaction with the partner.

As the partners learn more about each other and move toward closeness by becoming increasingly dependent on each other's activities for the performance of their daily behavioral routines and the fulfillment of their plans and goals, the number and strength of their expectancies about each other increase. As a result, their opportunities for expectancy violation, and for emotional experience, also increase. When important expectancies about a close relationship partner are violated – when our partners turn out not to be the persons we thought they were – we truly are endangered. The partner has become unfamiliar and, thus, possibly unsafe. He or she has become a stranger; hence, the word "estranged" is often used to describe once-close partners. We no longer know how to act in interaction with the partner in ways that will protect and enhance our well-being. Moreover, all of our customary behaviors and plans and goals that depend on the partner's behavioral contributions may be threatened.

In brief, violation of expectancies about a close relationship partner should satisfy the conditions for the experience of emotion. Sometimes, of course, the violation does not jeopardize our well-being but, rather, it enhances it and so provides the occasion for the experience of positive emotion. For example, violation of a wife's expectation that her husband would forget their wedding anniversary for the eighteenth time by his gift of a diamond necklace and a trip to Paris should be greeted not only with surprise but with positive, rather than negative, emotion. On the other hand, the husband who has faithfully observed every previous anniversary with extravagant gifts and who delivers as expected for the eighteenth time is unlikely to precipitate as strong an emotional experience. Mild positive feeling, or even "ho-hum," is more likely this dutiful husband's reward, an observation made by many relationship therapists, who have termed this effect "reinforcement erosion": events that were initially rewarding often lose their reward power over time (e.g., Jacobson & Margolin, 1979). Of course, if the faithfully observant spouse should *fail* to perform as expected – if he unexpectedly sneaks away on a fishing trip without leaving a card, much less a gift – one suspects the wife would experience emotion.

Relationship Expectancies. As the relationship develops, then, the partners are developing expectancies about each other's habits, attitudes, personality, character, and other behavioral dispositions. Social psychologists working in the areas of person perception and cognition have been particularly interested in unraveling the processes by which people attribute dispositions to another from observing the other's behavior and noting the conditions under which it occurred. Each dispositional attribution we make to our partner represents an expectation of how he or she will behave in a variety of situations.

But many of our expectancies about our partner are not constructed through actual interaction with the partner and observance of his or her behavior. Rather than being custom-tailored to the partner's actual behavior, many of our expectancies about our partner are of the ready-made, "one size fits all," variety, and we bring them to the relationship from the start. Some of these pre-formed expectancies we immediately drape over our unsuspecting partner have their source in our past relationships. Hence, the interest relationship scholars have shown in "relationship schemas" and the history of their development (see Berscheid & Reis, 1998). For example, adults with a "secure" adult attachment style and relationship schema have been shown to have different expectations for their partner's behavior in romantic relationships than those with an "insecure" attachment style (e.g., Hazan & Shaver, 1987; Shaver, Collins, & Clark, 1996).

In addition to our own past relationship experiences, many of our pre-formed expectancies about our partner derive from our past observations of other people's relationships or from relationships we have read or heard about. Most of us have expectancies, for example, about how a husband – or wife – is supposed to look, feel, and act, or how a friend, or a coworker, or a neighbor is likely to behave under a variety of conditions. Thus, cultural norms, customs, and understandings are another source of many of our expectations about our partner's behavior.

Our partners may be aware of some of the contents of the extensive baggage of expectancies we bring to our relationships with them. In particular, they are most likely to be aware of the expectancies concerning relationships that the culture instills, for they often share such expectations. But it is unlikely that they are aware of all our expectancies, especially those that are idiosyncratic to us and to our past relationship experiences. Moreover, they are likely to remain unaware of our idiosyncratic expectancies until they inadvertently violate one of them and become the target of our emotional outburst. Such outbursts are likely to come as a surprise to them. Our bewildered partner asks, "What did I do?" But when we are experiencing emotion and the reason is not apparent to our partners, the question they should be asking us is "What did you expect?" It is likely that we expected them to do something that they failed to do or we did not expect them to do something that they did do.

It is sometimes difficult for us to answer the question, "What did you expect?" We are not always fully aware of what we expect. In fact, most of us would have a hard time articulating all the expectations we have of our relationship partners, especially when those expectations have become so entrenched that they operate outside of conscious awareness (e.g., see Fletcher & Fincham, 1991, for a discussion of "automatic" processing in the context of close relationships). Hence, our experience of emotion in relationships is not infrequently a learning experience for us as well as for our partner. It is an opportunity to get to know ourselves better, to become acquainted or reacquainted with the assumptions and expectations we hold about the world in general and our partner and the relationship in particular. That wisdom and self-knowledge is often gained from observing our own emotional reactions to events is sometimes reflected in our emotional post-mortems – often by statements prefaced with such phrases as, "I guess I thought you . . ."; "I just didn't know I wouldn't like . . . ."

In short, beneath the surface of every relationship is a web of expectancies the partners hold for each other's behavior. These expectancies allow the partners to coordinate their actions and plans to maximize their own and the other's welfare. When repeatedly confirmed, these expectancies allow interactions to run smoothly (see Snyder & Stukas, 1999). In fact, the closer and more enduring the relationship, the more likely it is that these expectancies are not only numerous but strongly held because they have been repeatedly confirmed.

Expectancies we hold about our partner and the relationship may be viewed as the emotional hostage the individual has given to the relationship – or, as Berscheid (1983) puts it, they represent the individual's "emotional investment" in the relationship because each expectancy represents potential for violation of the expectation and, thus, discrepancy detection. The greater the number of expectancies, and the more strongly they are held, the greater the potential for emotion, although that potential may never be realized during the life of a relationship because those expectancies may never be disconfirmed. In contrast, those who expect little from the partner or from the relationship have little potential to experience emotion in the relationship because holding an expectation about the partner or the relationship is a necessary condition for discrepancy detection.

Disruption of behavioral activities. Simply being in close proximity to another person much of the time gives that person the opportunity to perform actions that unexpectedly *facilitate* the achievement of our plans and goals. Such facilitation, and the resultant enhancement of our welfare, is, in fact, the *raison d'être* of most close relationships, especially romantic and marital relationships. The validity of this premise is confirmed by many studies showing that human happiness and physical and mental health are strongly associated with satisfying close relationships. The beginnings of such relationships are often marked by such intense positive emotions as "joy" and "elation" (see Baumeister & Leary, 1995), which, as Mandler notes, usually contain a strong element of happy surprise. For example, people who have fallen in love often express wonder that their world has dramatically changed, often overnight, in such a felicitous way. They say such things as "I can't believe this is happening to me!" or "It's hard to believe that someone as wonderful as you could care for a wretch like me!"

But extended close proximity and interaction with anyone not only provides the opportunity for that person to unexpectedly facilitate our aims and goals to better our life, and thus to precipitate the experience of positive emotion in our relationship with him or her, but it also gives that person the opportunity to unexpectedly *interfere* with the performance of our usual activities and with the achievement of valued goals. This would be true of virtually anyone in close physical proximity to us, whether a close relationship existed or not (hence the popular saying that "Houseguests and dead fish start to stink after three days"). Thus, most relationship scholars believe that conflict is inevitable in all relationships moving toward closeness. Some theorists, in fact, mark conflict as a relationship "stage," a period that all close relationships must pass through (e.g., Scanzoni, 1979). For this reason, many marital therapists view the probable success of a marriage to be determined not by whether the couple experiences conflict (because all do) but, rather, by whether the couple can resolve their conflicts.

Over time, if the relationship is to survive, the partners will learn to coordinate their daily activities and reconcile their individual plans and goals in such a way as to protect and enhance, rather than threaten and diminish, each other's well-being. In doing so, they are likely to develop what Berscheid (1983) terms highly "meshed interaction sequences" of behavior, or interaction routines in which each partner's influence takes the form of facilitating and augmenting the other partner's actions as the sequence or plan unfolds. In many close marital relationships, such well-meshed sequences often include shopping and preparing meals, getting the kids off to school in the morning, and entertaining guests. Sexual interactions, too, are usually highly dependent on the partner not only performing the appropriate and expected actions but performing them at the appropriate and expected time in the behavioral sequence.

If many of the individual's daily and routinely performed behavioral sequences are meshed to the partner's, and if the partner fails to perform as expected, then the individual's expectancies are violated, his or her customary performance of the sequence is disrupted, and, unless some substitute for the partner's failed actions is quickly found, arousal should occur, a negative cognitive valence should be attached to the failure, and a negative emotional experience should result. People who unexpectedly lose their long-term close relationship partners, whether through their partner's rejection of the relationship or through the partner's death, are likely to experience great disruption. Enormous "grief" – and even sometimes "anger" at the loved one who was so inconsiderate as to die and leave the individual bereft – are not unusual. In superficial relationships, however, there is much less to be disrupted and the emotional reaction to dissolution of the relationship should be less intense.

It will be recalled that Mandler theorizes that the intensity and duration of emotion is a function of the degree of disruption and its duration. In the case where the relationship is dissolved through the voluntary action of one of the partners, one can predict that the other's emotional reaction to dissolution will be a function of two variables: (1) the degree of interdependence characteristic of the relationship (i.e., the closer the relationship, the more the disruption upon dissolution); and (2) the speed with which the disrupted individual is able to find the means to resume those disrupted behavioral activities and progress toward those plans and goals and thus restore his or her well-being. The latter suggests that the intensity and duration of an individual's emotional reaction to relationship dissolution often depends on the speed with which a "substitute" partner can be found – one who can step into the role the absent partner once played in the individual's life and who can facilitate the individual as well as the former partner did.

Thus, the prediction of emotional reaction to relationship dissolution requires not only assessment of the closeness of the relationship, but also assessment of the likelihood that the individual will be able to quickly obtain an alternative partner. Many individuals who voluntarily terminate a relationship, of course, do so only after they themselves have secured an alternative partner – a third person with whom they have already established a relationship and who can provide the same facilitation, or even greater facilitation, of their welfare than their former partner did. Such individuals are unlikely to experience much negative emotion upon dissolving their previous relationship; indeed, they may experience happiness and relief if their former relationship was interfering with the further development of their new relationship.

In brief, ERM predicts that because people in close relationships are highly interdependent on each other, they have developed, whether consciously or unconsciously, many strong expectations about the partner and his or her behaviors that, when violated, provide the occasion for the experience of emotion because those interdependencies usually have implications for the individual's welfare. In contrast, people in superficial relationships, where each partner lives his or her life largely independently of the other person's activities, have fewer opportunities for expectancy violation and, even when such expectancies do exist and are violated, their consequences are likely to be much less severe in terms of threat to the individual's well-being.

Most long-term partners' expectancies are not violated, of course. As previously noted, their behaviors, plans, and goals have become well coordinated over time and there are few occasions of "discrepancy detection" in the relationship and thus little occasion for intense emotion. It is for this reason that the *current* emotional surface of a relationship may be misleading of its *potential* to cause the partners' intense emotion. A relationship may appear to be emotionally "dead" because the partners hold few expectancies about each other and those they do hold have few implications for the individual's well-being. But other relationships, especially very close relationships, may appear to be emotionally moribund because, although the partners are highly interdependent on each other, they have learned to smoothly coordinate their activities with each other and thus they never disconfirm each other's expectancies.

Berscheid describes the interdependencies characteristic of close relationships as "hidden ticking emotional bombs" because they will explode and cause great disruption when the relationship is dissolved. And all relationships dissolve. It is one of the saddest facts of the human condition that even the closest and happiest of relationships end – if not by some circumstance of fate that causes separation, then by the death of one of the partners. Upon dissolution, the individual's life circumstances will change so drastically, and his or her well-being is likely to be so threatened, that the loss of a close relationship partner is accompanied by the experience of the strongest negative emotions a human is capable of experiencing, often compromising the remaining partner's immunocompetence, and resulting in illness and even death (see Stroebe & Stroebe, 1993).

Separation from the Partner

Several investigators have examined hypotheses derived from ERM concerning the degree of emotional disruption an individual is likely to experience upon separation from the partner or dissolution of the relationship. In a prospective longitudinal study, for example, Simpson (1987) found that greater relationship closeness, as measured by the Relationship Closeness Inventory (RCI), which measures behavioral interdependence (Berscheid et al., 1989), and fewer alternative partners were associated with the experience of greater distress following relationship dissolution.

The results of a natural field experiment conducted by Attridge (1995) also confirm ERM predictions. Attridge examined the emotional reactions of women who were in serious dating relationships that had lasted for an average of one and a half years at the time of the study. Forty-two of the women experienced separation from their partner due to their own participation in an international "study abroad" program. Their emotional reactions were contrasted to 44 women who did not experience separation from their partners during the period of the study. Both the experimental "separated" couples and the control "non-separated" couples were assessed at three points: Time 1, prior to separation; Time 2, during separation; and Time 3, following separation. The assessments at Time 1 and Time 3 included Closeness (on the RCI, Berscheid et al., 1989), Relationship Longevity, Relationship Satisfaction (Hendrick, 1988), and Disruption Potential, a 5-item measure of the degree to which the partner's absence would lead to a disruption of the individual's normal activities and her likelihood of finding a substitute partner during the separation (internal reliability = .63; test-retest reliability = .69).

In accord with ERM, Attridge predicted that the closer the relationship, the greater the frequency and intensity of emotional experience upon separation. Emotion during separation was assessed by giving respondents a list of positive and negative emotions and asking them to indicate, "How frequently in the past week did you feel each emotion concerning your partner and/or the relationship?" Attridge found that neither Relationship Longevity nor Relationship Satisfaction predicted emotional experience for either Separated or Non-separated partners. For Separated partners, however, both degree of Closeness and Disruption Potential were associated with the experience of negative emotion whereas no such effect was found for Non-separated partners (see table 12.1). It should be emphasized that Closeness and Disruption Potential did not by themselves lead to emotional experience; rather, they interacted with the event of separation to produce the experience of emotion. Moreover, neither the length of the relationship nor (perhaps surprisingly to some people) the individual's satisfaction with the relationship were associated with the experience of emotion, whether the partners were separated or not.

Attridge's study confirms another ERM prediction: It will be recalled that ERM predicts that an increase in the experience of "hot" emotion, rather than mild feelings or other valenced states, should result from disruption of a close relationship. As table 12.2 illustrates, Attridge found that only emotions characterized by high arousal – that is, the more intense emotions – were significantly associated with increases in closeness for separated partners. Separated

Table 12.1   Correlations of Mean Amounts of Negative Emotion with Time 1 Relationship Closeness, Disruption Potential, Relationship Satisfaction, and Relationship Longevity as a Function of Separation Status During the Separation Period (Time 2)

Measure	Condition	
	Long-distance	*Stay-at-home*
	Negative emotion	
Relationship Closeness	.33*	.09
Disruption Potential	.39**	.08
Relationship Satisfaction	−.05	−.28
Relationship Longevity	.14	−.21

* $p < .05$.   ** $p < .01$.

Table 12.2   Correlations of Intense and Weak Emotions with Time 1 Relationship Closeness/ Disruption Potential Composite as a Function of Separation Status During the Separation Period

(Time 2) Emotion Measure	Condition	
	Long-distance	Stay-at-home
	Closeness/Disruption Potential	
"Hot" emotions		
Fear	.49*	.12
Jealousy	.53*	.14
Anger	.08	.10
Frustration	.15	.19
Passion	.40*	−.09
Joy	.47*	−.10
Excitement	−.11	−.21
Less Intense Feeling States		
Sad	.01	.07
Lonely	.15	.16
Happy	.10	.06
Needed	.15	.16
Content	.06	.02

* $p < .001$

couples who were close experienced increases in fear, jealousy, passion, and joy. However, the milder feeling states characterized by less arousal (e.g., happy, needed, content, sad, and lonely) showed no increases for anyone, not even close couples who were separated.

Emotion Spillover

Berscheid (1983) differentiates between emotion whose primary source lies *in* the relationship – by the partner's violation of the individual's expectancies, usually by unexpectedly facilitating or unexpectedly frustrating ongoing behavior sequences, plans, and goals – from emotion experienced in association with the partner but whose true source lies in an event *outside* the relationship. The partners' experiences of affective events outside the relationship have been shown to influence affective events inside the relationship. For example, relationship scholars have demonstrated that transient mood states generated by such events as watching a sad movie may influence what people remember about their relationship, what behaviors of the partner are likely to be noticed, and also, as Forgas, Levinger, and Moylan (1994) demonstrated, an individual's satisfaction with his or her partner and the relationship (satisfaction changing in such a way as to be congruent with the individual's mood at the time of the evaluation).

Emotional events whose origins are outside the relationship have great potential to create emotional storms within a close relationship, as the phrase "emotion spillover" suggests. Emotion spillover refers to an individual's experience of emotion caused by a non-relationship event (e.g., being fired from the job; falling ill) that interferes with the individual's customary interaction performance within the relationship. This, then, disrupts the partner and precipitates the partner's experience of emotion "in" the relationship (since it has been caused by the individual), which, in turn, is likely to disrupt the partner's usual interaction performance – a disruption whose effects are likely to reverberate back to the individual, further heightening that person's emotional experience.

Conger and his associates (1990) studied couples caught in the wave of farm foreclosures in the 1980s and found that economic strain not only promoted hostility in marital interaction but it reduced the frequency of supportive behaviors in the relationship – at the very time, of course, that supportive behaviors were especially needed. Job stress, too, has been shown to affect couple interaction. For example, Repetti (1989) found a significant association between an air traffic controller's exposure to job stressors and anger and aggression in the controller's family interactions.

Again, ERM predicts that emotion spillover, or the ricocheting of emotional consequences of events outside the relationship into the relationship, is more likely to occur in close relationships where the partners are highly interdependent and vulnerable to disruption than it is in less close relationships. Thus – and ironically – when an outside event produces negative emotion for an individual in a close relationship, the individual's partner may be *less* likely to remain tranquil and supportive than a superficial partner might be because the partner is likely to be experiencing emotion him- or herself; the partner's emotional state, in turn, may interfere with the partner's ability to perform as the individual expects, thus adding internal fuel to the individual's externally-generated emotional fire.

The tendency of emotion-precipitating events occurring outside the relationship to wreak disruption within a close relationship provides one more reason why close relationships, as opposed to superficial relationships, are the most frequent context for the experience of intense emotion. And there is yet another reason why close relationship partners, as contrasted to the less close, are more likely to experience intense emotion: they are more vulnerable than superficial partners are to the experience of jealousy – a highly negative emotion that has been the subject of much theory and research (see Berscheid, 1994).

Jealousy

Jealousy has been defined as ". . . the emotion that people experience when control over valued resources that flow through an attachment to another person is perceived to be in jeopardy because their partner might want or might actually give and/or receive some of these resources from a third party" (Ellis & Weinstein, 1986, p. 341). Not all individuals in such situations experience the emotion of jealousy, however, and, if they do, not all experience it with the same intensity. ERM predicts that it is individuals within close, as opposed to less close, relationships who are most likely to experience this emotion and, moreover, given high interdependence, it is those individuals who have available to them few substitute partners should the relationship dissolve who will most intensely experience jealousy when they perceive that a third party threatens the relationship.

These ERM predictions are consistent with the findings of many studies. For example, Buunk (1982) found that relationship partners who were highly dependent on their relationships expected to feel more jealousy when visualizing hypothetical third-party affairs, and White (1981) found that women's experiences of jealousy were significantly correlated with their inability to obtain an alternative relationship partner. Moreover, DeSteno and Salovey (1996) found that people were more likely to experience jealousy when a potential rival for their partner's attention was in a domain of "high self-relevance" (e.g., in areas important to the self such as the achievements shared by both self and rival). It is just this sort of rival, of course, who constitutes the greatest threat to the relationship because such persons can most easily replace the individual in facilitating the partner's interaction behaviors and current goals.

Another study that underscores the importance of the individual's ability to find a replacement partner should the third party succeed in breaking up the relationship is provided by Bringle (1995). Homosexual men, who had less exclusive relationships than the heterosexual men in this study, experienced less jealousy in their intimate relationships than did the heterosexual men. Heterosexual men may have been more dependent on their partners than the homosexual men were and they may have had fewer readily available partner substitutes. This interpretation of Bringle's finding is supported by his report that the incidence of jealousy increased in both groups between 1980 and 1992 and the increase was accompanied by an increase in the exclusiveness of both homosexuals' and heterosexuals' intimate relationships.

In sum, ERM predicts that the likelihood of an individual experiencing jealousy within a relationship is a function of three factors: the closeness of the relationship, the availability of substitute partners, and the degree to which the third party represents a threat to the continuance of the relationship.

Therapeutic Approaches to Negative Emotion in Relationships

Distressed relationships are the most common presenting problem of those who seek psychotherapy (e.g., Pinsker, Nepps, Redfield, & Winston, 1985). Distressed relationships, not surprisingly, are characterized by a great deal of negative affect and emotion (e.g., see Weiss & Heyman, 1990). Relationship therapists have long recognized the association between negative emotion and the disconfirmation of an expectancy about the partner or the relationship. Unrealistic expectations are doomed to be disconfirmed. Moreover, if the expectation is rigidly held even in the face of repeated disconfirmations, the individual is likely to chronically experience negative emotion in the relationship. Eidelson and Epstein (1982) developed the Relationship Belief Inventory to assess the degree to which relationship partners hold unrealistic beliefs and expectations about close relationships (e.g., the expectation that partners who care about each other should be able to sense each other's needs and preferences without overt communication). These investigators, as well as Fincham and Bradbury (1993), have found that holding such unrealistic beliefs is negatively associated with marital satisfaction. Moreover, Sabatelli (1988) has found that as contrasted to married partners, unmarried individuals hold significantly higher and more idealistic expectations about their prospective spouse and the relationship. Sabatelli concludes that unrealistic expectations may account for the reliable and significant drop in satisfaction in marital relationships during the first year of marriage (see Karney & Bradbury, 1995).

ERM suggests that if violated expectations are the most usual precipitating cause of intense emotion in close relationships, then the reduction of negative emotion in the relationship may be achieved primarily by two means. The first is to persuade the violating partner to bring his or her behavior in line with the individual's expectations. This is the "change the partner" approach that most people try first – with more or less success (usually less), depending on their communication, negotiation, and conflict resolution skills and the motivation and ability of the partner to change his or her behavior. This is one reason, of course, why improving communication and conflict resolution skills is a frequent objective of relationship therapy.

The second means by which the individual may reduce his or her experience of negative emotion in the relationship, however, is to change his or her own expectations to bring them in line with the partner's actual behavior. This is the "change myself (and accept the partner)" approach. Needless to say, most people find this second approach less desirable than the first because it not only requires them to change their *own* behavior but it not infrequently requires them to relinquish plans and goals they not only expected the partner *would* facilitate but believe the partner *should* facilitate. Moreover, the relinquishment of valued goals whose achievement is believed to enhance well-being should itself be accompanied by negative emotion (e.g., sadness). Thus, the task of revising our discrepant expectations to be congruent with the way the world *is* – rather than how we thought the world was or how we wish it to be – can be difficult and painful. But it may be less painful in the long run than retaining unrealistic relationship expectations that are doomed to be violated again and again and yet again, generating on each successive occasion the fresh experience of negative emotion. It should be noted that at least one individual therapy technique, Ellis's Rational-Emotive Therapy (e.g., Ellis & Dryden, 1997), directly seeks to ameliorate the negative emotions distressed individuals experience (whether in association with their interpersonal relationships or otherwise) by uncovering the individual's unrealistic expectations and directly attacking those that give rise to chronically experienced negative emotion.

With respect to distressed relationships (as opposed to distressed individuals), the traditional technique followed by many relationship therapists has been to teach partners compromise and accommodation strategies and skills to help them change those behaviors that are causing their partner to experience negative emotion and to manage their own negative emotions. For example, relationship therapists Notarius, Lashley, and Sullivan state that, "Anger is the fuel that fires relationship conflict, and its heat can either forge adaptive relationship change or melt down the foundation of the relationship" (1997, p. 219). These theorists advise their clients to "practice, practice, and practice alternative responses to anger" (1997, p. 245). Such alternative responses include replacing the "hot thoughts" that generate anger with "cool thoughts" that promote conversation and problem solving, quieting physiological arousal with relaxation techniques, and avoiding critical remarks that make the partner defensive (1997, p. 245). Unfortunately, outcome studies of relationship therapy often have been less favorable than for other kinds of therapy (see Berscheid & Reis, 1998). As a consequence, alternative approaches to traditional relationship therapy have been sought.

One promising new approach – Integrative Behavioral Couple Therapy (IBCT) – has been developed by Jacobson and Christensen (e.g., 1996), who have observed that many couples experience incompatibilities that cannot be resolved by compromise or accommodation. For example, a physical disability may preclude the husband from performing garbage and snow removal duties as his wife expects and his low intelligence may be an insurmountable obstacle to his learning to play a decent game of chess. To ameliorate negative emotion in close relationships, IBCT integrates the traditional technique intended to change both partners' behaviors with strategies that simply promote the partners' acceptance and tolerance of each other's unpleasant behaviors through coming to see those behaviors in the "larger context of the other and of their relationship together" (Christensen & Walczynski, 1997, p. 266). Jacobson and Christensen assume that a combination of change and acceptance will be more powerful than either alone (e.g., if partners receive acceptance from each other, they may be more willing to change their behavior if they possess the ability to do so). Although Jacobson and Christensen arrived at IBCT through their clinical experience and wisdom, it can be seen that their approach simultaneously utilizes both means implied by ERM for reducing negative emotion in close relationships; that is, both partners are encouraged to change their behavior to meet the other's expectations but they also are encouraged to change their own expectancies. So far, outcome studies of IBCT are showing good results in increasing marital satisfaction (see Christensen & Walczynski, 1997).

Summary

The now vast psychological literature on the subject of human emotion remains an almost impenetrable thicket to relationship scholars who hope to better understand the many emotional phenomena that occur in the context of close relationships. This chapter has sought to provide a brief reprise of the Emotion-in-Relationships Model (Berscheid, 1983), which attempts to explicate why close relationships are the most usual setting for the experience of intense emotions. In doing so, we have discussed the concept of relationship itself, the construct of closeness, the antecedents and consequences of emotional experience, and some emotional phenomena within relationships from the perspective of ERM. Given the important role that expectations about the partner and the relationship play in providing the conditions for the experience of emotion in close relationships, more research on the nature of such expectations held by different types of individuals for different types of relationships might prove fruitful for relationship scholars who seek to understand emotional phenomena within close relationships.

References

Arnsten, A. F. T. (1998). The biology of being frazzled. *Science, 280*, 1711–1712.

Attridge, M. (1995). *Reactions of romantic partners to geographic separation: A natural experiment.* Unpublished doctoral dissertation, University of Minnesota.

Baumeister, R. F., & Leary, M. R. (1995). The need to belong: Desire for interpersonal attachments as a fundamental human motivation. *Psychological Bulletin, 117*, 497–529.

Berscheid, E. (1983). Emotion. In H. H. Kelley, E. Berscheid, A. Christensen, J. H. Harvey, T. L. Huston, G. Levinger, E. McClintock, L. A. Peplau, & D. R. Peterson, *Close relationships* (pp. 110–168). New York: W. H. Freeman.

Berscheid, E. (1986). Mea culpas and lamentations: Sir Francis, Sir Isaac, and "The slow progress of soft psychology." In S. Duck & R. Gilmour (Eds.), *The emerging field of personal relationships* (pp. 267–286). Hillsdale, NJ: Erlbaum.

Berscheid, E. (1990). Contemporary vocabularies of emotion. In B. S. Moore & A. M. Isen (Eds.), *Affect and social behavior.* New York: Cambridge University Press.

Berscheid, E. (1991). The emotion-in-relationships model: Reflections and update. In W. Kessen & A. Ortony (Eds.), *Memories, thoughts, and emotions: Essays in honor of George Mandler.* Hillsdale, NJ: Erlbaum.

Berscheid, E. (1994). Interpersonal relationships. *Annual Review of Psychology, 45*, 79–129.

Berscheid, E. (1998). A social psychological view of marital dysfunction and stability. In T. N. Bradbury (Ed.), *The developmental course of marital dysfunction.* New York: Cambridge University Press.

Berscheid, E., Gangestad, S. W., & Kulakowski, D. (1984). Emotion in close relationships: Implications for relationship counseling. In S. D. Brown & R. W. Lent (Eds.), *Handbook of counseling psychology* (pp. 435–476). New York: Wiley.

Berscheid, E., & Reis, H. T. (1998). Attraction and close relationships. In D. T. Gilbert, S. T. Fiske, & G. Lindzey (Eds.), *The handbook of social psychology* (4th ed.). Boston: McGraw-Hill.

Berscheid, E., Snyder, M., & Omoto, A. (1989). The relationship closeness inventory: Assessing the closeness of interpersonal relationships. *Journal of Personality and Social Psychology, 57*, 792–807.

Blakemore, C. (1998). How the environment helps to build the brain. In B. Cartledge (Ed.), *Mind, brain, and the environment: The Linacre lectures, 1995–6* (pp. 28–56). New York: Oxford University Press.

Bringle, R. (1995). Sexual jealousy in the relationships of homosexual and heterosexual men: 1980 and 1992. *Personal Relationships, 2*, 313–325.

Buunk, B. (1982). Anticipated sexual jealousy: Its relationship to self-esteem, dependency, and reciprocity. *Personality and Social Psychology Bulletin, 8*, 310–316.

Cannon, W. B. (1929). *Bodily changes in pain, hunger, fear, and rage.* New York: Appleton.

Christensen, A., & Walczynski, P. T. (1997). Conflict and satisfaction in couples. In R. J. Sternberg & M. Hojjat (Eds.), *Satisfaction in close relationships.* New York: Guilford Press.

Clark, M. S., & Reis, H. T. (1988). Interpersonal processes in close relationships. *Annual Review of Psychology, 39*, 609–672.

Conger, R. D., Elder, G. H., Jr., Lorenz, F. O., Conger, K. J., Simons, R. L., Whitbeck, L. B., Huck, S., & Melby, J. N. (1990). Linking economic hardship to marital quality and instability. *Journal of Marriage and the Family, 52*, 643–656.

DeSteno, D., & Salovey, P. (1996). Jealousy and the characteristics of one's rival: A Self-evaluation Maintenance perspective. *Personality and Social Psychology Bulletin, 22*, 920–932.

Eidelson, R. J., & Epstein, N. (1982). Cognition and relationship maladjustment: Development of a measure of dysfunctional relationship beliefs. *Journal of Consulting and Clinical Psychology, 50*, 715–720.

Ekman, P. (Ed.). (1982). *Emotion in the human face* (2nd ed.). Cambridge, England: Cambridge University Press.

Ekman, P., & Davidson, R. J. (1994). *The nature of emotion: Fundamental questions.* New York:

Oxford University Press.

Ellis, A., & Dryden, W. (1997). *The practice of rational emotive behavior therapy* (2nd ed.). New York: Springer.

Ellis, C., & Weinstein, E. (1986). Jealousy and the social psychology of emotional experience. *Journal of Social and Personal Relationships, 3*, 337–357.

Fincham, F. D., & Bradbury, T. N. (1993). Marital satisfaction, depression, and attributions: A longitudinal analysis. *Journal of Personality and Social Psychology, 64*, 442–452.

Fletcher, G. J. O., & Fincham, F. D. (1991). Attribution processes in close relationships. In G. J. O. Fletcher & F. D. Fincham (Eds.), *Cognition in close relationships* (pp. 7–35). Hillsdale, NJ: Erlbaum.

Forgas, J. P., Levinger, G., & Moylan, S. J. (1994). Feeling good and feeling close: Affective influences on the perception of intimate relationships. *Personal Relationships, 1*, 165–184.

Gendolla, G. H. E. (1997). Surprise in the context of achievement: The role of outcome valence and importance. *Motivation & Emotion, 21*, 165–193.

Gold, P. E. (1992). Modulation of memory processing: Enhancement of memory in rodents and humans. In L. R. Squire & N. Butters (Eds.), *Neuropsychology of memory* (pp. 402–412). New York: Guilford Press.

Gray, J. A. (1994). Three fundamental emotion systems. In P. Ekman & R. J. Davidson (Eds.), *The nature of emotion: Fundamental questions* (pp. 243–247). New York: Oxford University Press.

Greenough, W. T., Black, J. E., & Wallace, C. S. (1987). Experience and brain development. *Child Development, 58*, 539–559.

Hazan, C., & Shaver, P. R. (1987). Romantic love conceptualized as an attachment process. *Journal of Personality and Social Psychology, 52*, 511–524.

Hebb, D. O. (1946). On the nature of fear. *Psychological Review, 53*, 259–276.

Hendrick, S. S. (1988). A generic measure of relationship satisfaction. *Journal of Marriage and the Family, 50*, 93–98.

Jacobson, N. S., & Christensen, A. (1996). *Integrative couple therapy: Promoting acceptance and change.* New York: Norton.

Jacobson, N. S., & Margolin, G. (1979). *Marital therapy: Strategies based on social learning and behavior exchange principles.* New York: Brunner/Mazel.

James, W. (1884). What is emotion? *Mind, 9*, 188–205.

Karney, B. R., & Bradbury, T. N. (1995). The longitudinal course of marital quality and stability: A review of theory, method, and research. *Psychological Review, 118*, 3–34.

Kelley, H. H., Berscheid, E., Christensen, A., Harvey, J. H., Huston, T. L., Levinger, G., McClintock, E., Peplau, L. A., & Peterson, D. R. (1983). *Close relationships.* New York: W. H. Freeman.

Knapp, A., & Clark, M. S. (1991). Some detrimental effects of negative mood on individuals' ability to solve resource dilemmas. *Personality & Social Psychology Bulletin, 17*, 678–688.

Kunst-Wilson, W. R., & Zajonc, R. B. (1980). Affective discrimination of stimuli that cannot be recognized. *Science, 207*, 557–558.

Lazarus, R. S. (1991). *Emotion and adaptation.* New York: Oxford University Press.

Lazarus, R. S. (1994). Appraisal: The long and short of it. In P. Ekman & R. J. Davidson (Eds.), *The nature of emotion: Fundamental questions* (pp. 208–215). New York: Oxford University Press.

Lewis, M., & Haviland, J. M. (Eds.). (1993). *Handbook of emotions.* New York: Guilford Press.

MacDowell, K., & Mandler, G. (1989). Constructions of emotion: Discrepancy, arousal, and mood. *Motivation and Emotion, 13*, 105–124.

Mandler, G. (1975). *Mind and emotion.* New York: Wiley.

Mandler, G. (1997). *Human nature explored.* New York: Oxford University Press.

Meyer, W., Reisenzein, R., & Schutzwohl, A. (1997). Toward a process analysis of emotions: The case of surprise. *Motivation and Emotion, 21*, 251–274.

Notarius, C. I., Lashley, S. L., & Sullivan, D. J. (1997). Angry at your partner?: Think again. In R. J. Sternberg & M. Hojjat (Eds.), *Satisfaction in close relationships.* New York: Guilford Press.

Oatley, K., & Johnson-Laird, P. (1987). Towards a cognitive theory of emotion. *Cognition and Emotion, 1*, 51–58.

Ohman, A., & Soares, J. J. F. (1994). "Unconscious anxiety": Phobic responses to masked stimuli. *Journal of Abnormal Psychology, 103*, 231–240.

Ortony, A., & Turner, T. J. (1990). What's basic about basic emotions? *Psychological Review, 97,* 315–331.

Osgood, C. E., Suci, G. J., & Tannenbaum, P. H. (1957). *The measurement of meaning.* Urbana: University of Illinois Press.

Panksepp, J. (1994). The clearest physiological distinctions between emotions will be found among the circuits of the brain. In P. Ekman & R. J. Davidson (Eds.), *The nature of emotion: Fundamental questions* (pp. 258–269). New York: Oxford University Press.

Pinsker, H., Nepps, P., Redfield, J., & Winston, A. (1985). Applicants for short-term dynamic psychotherapy. In A. Winston (Ed.), *Clinical and research issues in short-term dynamic psychotherapy* (pp. 104–116). Washington, DC: American Psychiatric Association.

Plutchik, R. (1980). *Emotion: A psychobioevolutionary synthesis.* New York: Harper & Row.

Plutchik, R. (1994). *The psychology and biology of emotion.* New York: HarperCollins.

Repetti, R. L. (1989). Effects of daily workload on subsequent behavior during marital interaction: The roles of social withdrawal and spouse support. *Journal of Personality and Social Psychology, 57,* 651–659.

Sabatelli, R. M. (1988). Exploring relationship satisfaction: A social exchange perspective on the interdependence between theory, research, and practice. *Family Relations, 37,* 217–222.

Scanzoni, J. (1979). Social exchange and behavioral interdependence. In R. Burgess & T. Huston (Eds.), *Social exchange in developing relationships* (pp. 61–98). New York: Academic Press.

Schachter, S., & Singer, J. E. (1962). Cognitive, social and physiological determinants of emotional state. *Psychological Review, 69,* 379–399.

Shaver, P. R., Collins, N., & Clark, C. L. (1996). Attachment styles and internal working models of self and relationship partners. In G. Fletcher & J. Fitness (Eds.), *Knowledge structures and interaction in close relationships: A social psychological approach* (pp. 25–61). Hillsdale, NJ: Erlbaum.

Siegel, D. J. (1999). *The developing mind: Toward a neurobiology of interpersonal experience.* New York: Guilford Press.

Simpson, J. (1987). The dissolution of romantic relationships: Factors involved in relationship stability and emotional distress. *Journal of Personality and Social Psychology, 53,* 683–692.

Snyder, M., & Stukas, A. A. (1999). Interpersonal processes: The interplay of cognitive, motivational, and behavioral activities in social interaction. *Annual Review of Psychology, 50,* 273–303.

Stiensmeier-Pelster, J., Martini, A., & Reisenzein, R. (1995). The role of surprise in the attribution process. *Cognition & Emotion, 9,* 5–31.

Stroebe, M. S., & Stroebe, W. (1993). The mortality of bereavement: A review. In M. S. Stroebe, W. Stroebe, & R. O. Hansson (Eds.), *Handbook of bereavement: Theory, research, and intervention* (pp. 175–195). Cambridge, England: Cambridge University Press.

Weber, A. L. (1998). Losing, leaving, and letting go: Coping with nonmarital breakups. In B. H. Spitzberg & W. R. Cupach (Eds.), *The dark side of close relationships* (pp. 267–306). Mahwah, NJ: Erlbaum.

Weiss, R. L., & Heyman, R. E. (1990). Observation of marital interaction. In F. D. Fincham & T. N. Bradbury (Eds.), *The psychology of marriage: Basic issues and applications* (pp. 87–117). New York: Guilford Press.

White, G. (1981). Some correlates of romantic jealousy. *Journal of Personality, 49,* 129–147.

Chapter Thirteen

The Status of Theory and Research on Love and Commitment

Beverley Fehr

Some of the most important issues in people's lives revolve around love and commitment. Whether entering, maintaining, or contemplating the dissolution of relationships, people struggle with questions such as whether they love their partner, or perhaps more importantly, whether they are experiencing the kind of love that is likely to lead to a satisfying, enduring, relationship. People also grapple with issues such as whether to make or break promises of commitment to relationships. The purpose of this chapter is to examine contributions that close relationships scholars have made to the understanding of love and commitment as theoretical constructs and as experienced in people's everyday lives.

In the first major section, the focus is on models of love and commitment. First, dominant theories or models of love in the social psychological literature are presented, followed by research on laypeople's conceptions of love. Theories of commitment are presented next, followed by research on laypeople's conceptions of commitment. The section ends with a discussion of the relation between love and commitment from the perspective of both experts and laypeople.

In the next major section of the chapter, the focus shifts from theories to people's *experiences* of love and commitment in close relationships. Research on levels of love reported in relationships is discussed first, followed by research on levels of commitment. Levels of love and commitment experienced in relationships are then compared to determine which construct is most prominent in people's everyday experience. The second topic in this section concerns the variable that is most frequently correlated with measures of love and commitment, namely relationship satisfaction. The strength of the relation between love and satisfaction is documented first. Parallel research on the relation between commitment and satisfaction is presented next. The final question that is addressed is: which concept is most strongly linked to satisfaction in relationships? The chapter closes with an assessment of the status of theory and research on love and commitment.

Models of Love and Commitment

Experts' models of love

Berscheid and Walster [Hatfield] (1974; see also Walster [Hatfield] & Walster, 1978) generally are credited with having developed the first social psychological model of love (see, e.g., Sprecher & Regan, 1998). They proposed a model in which love is partitioned into two major varieties, companionate love and passionate love. Companionate love is defined as "the affection and tenderness we feel for those with whom our lives are deeply intertwined" (Hatfield & Rapson, 1993, p. 9). This kind of love also is referred to as friendship love and is based on a foundation of trust, respect, honesty, caring, and commitment (Brehm, 1985). Emotions associated with this kind of love are calm, pleasant, and steady. Passionate love is defined as a "state of intense longing for union with another" (Hatfield & Rapson, 1993, p. 5). This kind of love is characterized by physiological arousal, sexual attraction, extremes of emotion, and instability.

Research on this model of love has been constrained by the absence of standard scales to measure companionate and passionate love. This situation was partially rectified by Hatfield and Sprecher (1986) who developed a measure of passionate love, the Passionate Love Scale, that has received widespread use. These theorists have not yet developed a comparable scale to assess companionate love, relying instead on single-item measures (e.g., Hatfield, Traupmann, & Sprecher, 1984; Sprecher & Regan, 1998; Traupmann & Hatfield, 1981) or, more recently, a subset of Rubin's (1970) love scale items (Sprecher & Regan, 1998). Despite the need for further scale development, as will be seen, Berscheid and Hatfield's model of love remains important and influential.

The next major theoretical contribution to the study of love was the conceptualization of love in terms of different love styles (e.g., Lee, 1973; Hendrick & Hendrick, 1986; Hendrick, Hendrick, Foote, & Slapion-Foote, 1984). Lee, a sociologist, proposed that there are six distinct styles of love. Three of these styles are considered primary: Eros (romantic, passionate love), Ludus (game-playing love) and Storge (friendship love). The remaining three styles are derived from the primary styles: Mania (possessive, dependent love) is a compound of Eros and Ludus, Pragma (pragmatic, logical love) is a compound of Storge and Ludus, and Agape (selfless, giving love) is a compound of Eros and Storge. Hendrick and Hendrick (1986) improved on early measurement attempts (Lasswell & Lasswell, 1976) and constructed the Love Attitudes Scale to assess these love styles. This scale has become the dominant measurement instrument in the love styles literature.[1]

Sternberg's (1986) triangular theory represents another milestone in the study of love. According to this model, love consists of three components: passion, intimacy, and decision/commitment. Passion refers to "the drives that lead to romance, physical attraction, sexual consummation, and related phonemena" (p. 119). The intimacy component refers to feelings of warmth, closeness, and connectedness in a relationship. The decision/commitment component entails the short-term decision that one loves one's partner as well as the longer-term commitment to maintain that love. These components have been described as the "hot," "warm," and "cold" elements of love, respectively.

Sternberg pictures these components of love as vertices of a triangle. A wide variety of relationships (both actual and ideal) can be portrayed by varying the area and shape of the love triangle. The course of a relationship over time also can be plotted in this way. In addition, an eight-item typology of love can be derived based on various combinations of these components of love. The absence of all three is labeled nonlove, whereas the presence of all three is referred to as consummate love. Romantic love is conceptualized as a combination of intimacy and passion (along with the absence of decision/commitment), and so on. Sternberg also offers a number of predictions regarding the course of love in relationships (e.g., passion declines, commitment increases). Unfortunately, attempts to test these predictions have been hampered by measurement difficulties, most notably high correlations between the three constructs (e.g., Acker & Davis, 1992; Hecht, Marston, & Larkey, 1994; Hendrick & Hendrick, 1989). Some psychometric issues have been resolved in the most recent revision of the Triangular Love Scale, although others remain (see Sternberg, 1997).

Davis and Todd (1982, 1985) took a paradigm case approach to the study of love. They formulated "ideal cases" of love and friendship relationships and developed the Relationship Rating Form as a means of comparing the fundamental characteristics or components of these relationship types. This scale consists of a measure of Global Satisfaction, along with subscales labeled Viability (acceptance, trust, respect), Intimacy (understanding, confiding), Passion (fascination, exclusivity, sexual intimacy), Care (giving, providing support), and Conflict/Ambivalence (negative feelings). Further psychometric refinement resulted in the addition of a Commitment subscale (see, e.g., Levy & Davis, 1988). According to research on this model, love relationships are characterized by greater passion and caring than are friendships (see Davis & Roberts, 1985, for a review).

A rather different approach to the conceptualization of love was taken by Aron and Aron (1986, 1997) who developed a self-expansion model of love. The central tenet of this motivational theory of love is that people enter relationships seeking to expand themselves, and that this is accomplished by incorporating aspects of the loved one's self into one's own self. Self-expansion progresses most rapidly in the early stages of relationships when partners are in the exhilarating process of developing intimacy. This theory can explain a wide variety of relational phenomena, including seemingly selfless behavior in relationships, the onset of boredom (as the other becomes more familiar, there are fewer opportunities for self-expansion), and the devastation that frequently accompanies the severing of relationship ties (e.g., Aron & Aron, 1986). Aron, Aron, and Smollan (1992) developed a pictorial measure, the Inclusion of Other in the Self scale, to assess the perceived overlap between one's self and a relationship partner. Respondents select which of seven overlapping circles (representing self and other) best portrays their relationship. The greater the overlap, the greater the commitment, satisfaction, and so on reported in the relationship (see Aron & Aron, 1997, for a review).

Finally, a developmental approach to the study of love was taken by Hazan and Shaver (1987) who applied attachment theory to the study of adult romantic relationships. According to attachment theory (Bowlby, 1969), infants develop particular ways of relating based on the availability and responsiveness of their primary caregiver. Ainsworth, Blehar, Waters, and Wall (1978) identified three primary attachment styles based on observations of infant–caregiver interactions. Secure infants experienced available, responsive caregiving and exhibited a healthy, trusting style of relating. Infants classified as anxious/ambivalent tended to receive inconsistent caregiving, including failures to respond when needed coupled with intrusiveness at other times. These infants demonstrated a pattern of anxiously seeking comfort, mingled with outbursts of anger. Finally, the caregivers of avoidant infants were generally not available or responsive. These infants tended to withdraw and not reach out for comfort, even when distressed. Hazan and Shaver (1987) proposed that these patterns of attachment may be mirrored in adult romantic relationships. They presented adults with descriptions of these three styles and found that the proportion of adults who endorsed each style was highly similar to the proportion of infants who fall into each category. Moreover, participants' descriptions of their current relationships, relationship histories, and memories of parental caregiving were consistent with the attachment style that they endorsed. Although it was initially assumed that attachment styles remained stable from infancy to adulthood, it is now generally accepted that attachment styles can and do change (see, e.g., Baldwin & Fehr, 1995; Davila, Karney, & Bradbury 1999).

In terms of theoretical refinements (Bartholomew 1990; Bartholomew & Horowitz, 1991) proposed a four-category system in which the avoidant style was subdivided into two types: dismissive and fearful. Dismissive avoidants do not acknowledge a desire for attachment, whereas fearful avoidants acknowledge such a desire, but fear the consequences of getting close to another person. Extensive factor analytic research also has established that there are two major underlying attachment dimensions, anxiety and avoidance (see, e.g., Shaver & Hazan, 1993).

With regard to measurement, Hazan and Shaver (1987) initially assessed attachment styles using a categorical measure (the Adult Attachment Questionnaire) in which participants received descriptions of the secure, anxious/ambivalent and avoidant attachment styles and were asked to choose the description that best characterized their approach to romantic relationships. Several researchers subsequently developed multi-item measures rated on continuous scales (e.g., Collins & Read, 1990; Simpson 1990). Bartholomew's attachment categories have been measured using in-depth interviews and a paper-and-pencil measure (e.g., Bartholomew and Horowitz, 1991; Scharfe & Bartholomew, 1994). Currently, the most common assessment device in attachment research is the Bartholomew and Horowitz (1991) self-report measure in which participants select which of four attachment descriptions is most applicable to them and provide a continuous rating for each style. Recently scoring procedures have been developed to enable analyses in terms of the underlying dimensions of anxiety and avoidance (e.g., Fraley, Davis, & Shaver, 1997). Although measurement instruments undoubtedly will undergo further changes and refinements, the attachment approach is likely to continue to dominate close relationships research (see, e.g., Cassidy & Shaver, 1999).

Integration of models of love.   In response to the proliferation of models of love and corresponding measurement instruments, Hendrick and Hendrick (1989) conducted a major factor analytic study that included the following scales:[2]

1.   The Passionate Love Scale (Hatfield & Sprecher, 1986) to assess the passionate component of Berscheid and Hatfield's companionate/passionate model of love.
2.   The Love Attitudes Scale (Hendrick & Hendrick, 1986) to assess the Eros, Storge, Ludus, Pragma, Mania, and Agape love styles.

3. An unpublished version of the Triangular Love Scale (provided by Sternberg) to assess passion, intimacy, and commitment.
4. The Relationship Rating Form (Davis & Todd, 1982, 1985) to assess the relationship components of Viability, Intimacy, Passion, Caring, Conflict and Satisfaction.
5. The Hazan and Shaver (1987) Adult Attachment Questionnaire to assess the secure, anxious/ambivalent, and avoidant attachment styles.

The analysis of these scales produced five factors. The first factor (accounting for the largest percentage of variance) was labeled *passionate love*. Measures that loaded on this factor included the Eros, Mania, and Agape love style scales, the Sternberg Intimacy, Passion, and Commitment scales, the Passionate Love Scale, and all of the Relationship Rating Form subscales (except for the Conflict subscale). The second factor was labeled *closeness*. Sternberg's Intimacy scale and all of the Relationship Rating Form scales (with a negative loading for the Conflict scale) loaded on this factor. In addition, the love styles of Ludus and Pragma had negative loadings. The third factor consisted of the Mania love style and the anxious/ambivalent attachment style. The secure (positive loading) and avoidant (negative loading) attachment styles loaded on the fourth factor. Finally, the fifth factor consisted of the Pragma and Storge love style scales.

The factors that emerged from these analyses were not particularly clean due to inadequacies in some of the measures (e.g., high correlations between scales purportedly measuring different constructs). Nevertheless, the findings point to a possible integration of models of love. Hendrick and Hendrick (1989) noted that their first two factors resembled passionate love and companionate love, respectively, but they resisted the conclusion that the models of love examined in their study could be subsumed by Berscheid and Hatfield's model.[3] However, there are reasons to consider such a conclusion. First, the passionate and closeness (companionate love) factors accounted for relatively large amounts of variance (32 and 14 percent, respectively) relative to the other three factors (each of which accounted for only 7 or 8 percent). Second, in contrast to the first two factors, each of the remaining factors had only two scales loading on it (in the case of Factor 4, the two "scales" were actually two single-item attachment questions). Thus, there is a basis for arguing that Berscheid and Hatfield's model provides a useful integration of extant models of love. As is discussed next, research on lay conceptions of love further supports this view.

Lay conceptions of love

The development of prototype theory (Rosch, 1973; see Mervis & Rosch, 1981 for a review), a theory of the cognitive representation of concepts, inspired research on laypeople's conceptions of a variety of concepts, including love. Prototype theory has been applied in research on behaviors of love (Buss, 1988), people's accounts of experiences of love (e.g., Fitness & Fletcher, 1993; Shaver, Schwartz, Kirson, & O'Connor, 1987), and people's conceptions of love. In this section, the focus will be on the latter.

Fehr (1988, Study 1) asked laypeople (students at the University of British Columbia) to generate features of the concept of love. Both companionate love (e.g., caring trust, respect, honesty, commitment) and passionate love (e.g., heartrate increases, think about the other all the time, sexual attraction, gazing at the other) were represented in their responses. In the next study (Study 2), a new group of participants was asked to rate these features in terms of prototypicality (the extent to which each feature was representative of the concept of love). Companionate features received the lowest ratings. Subsequent studies revealed that increases in companionate features of love were regarded as more diagnostic of increased love in a relationship than were increases in passionate features (Study 5). Conversely, decreases in companionate features were seen as more indicative of the deterioration of a love relationship than decreases in passionate features (Study 6). The lay conception of love as uncovered in these studies proved to be robust, at least across North American samples. Similar features were generated when this research was replicated on the east coast of Canada (Button & Collier, 1991) and on the west coast of the United States (Luby & Aron, 1990; see Fehr, 1993, for a review). The most prototypical features of love (i.e., those depicting companionate love) were especially likely to be reproduced across studies.

In an extension of this research, Fehr and Russell (1991; Study 1) asked lay people to list *types* of love. Again, participants listed types that represented companionate love (e.g., friendship love, maternal love, brotherly love) as well as types that represented passionate love (e.g. romantic love, passionate love, sexual love). When rated for prototypicality, companionate varieties of love received the highest ratings and passionate varieties received the lowest ratings (Fehr and Russell, 1991, Study 2). Thus, again, companionate love was seen as capturing the meaning of the concept to a greater extent than passionate love. Similarly, when Fehr (1994) conducted a cluster analysis of these kinds of love, the two main groupings that emerged portrayed companionate love (e.g., friendship, familial love, affection) and passionate love (e.g., passionate love, romantic love, sexual love).

In conclusion, research on lay conceptions of love is nicely summarized by the companionate/passionate model. Regardless of whether people are asked to list features of love, types of love, or whether ratings of types of love are subjected to cluster analytic techniques, the companionate/passionate distinction consistently emerges as a useful framework for interpreting their responses. The results of Hendrick and Hendrick's (1989) factor analytic study further suggest that Berscheid and Hatfield's model is a good candidate for integrating experts' models of love. Granted, the usefulness of the companionate/passionate model as an overarching framework is limited to other models that have taken a components, types, or love styles approach. Theories that seek to explain the motivation for entering relationships (Aron & Aron, 1986) or the developmental origins of patterns of relating in love relationships (e.g., Hazan & Shaver, 1987) are answering questions about love that falls outside of the realm of the companionate/passionate model.

Experts' models of commitment

There are two main classes of theories of commitment. One class, rooted in social exchange theory, is devoted to specifying the key predictors of commitment to a relationship. The other is concerned with delineating types of commitment. The former will be discussed first.[4]

In their formulation of interdependence theory, Thibaut and Kelley (1959; see also Kelley & Thibaut, 1979) differentiated between satisfaction and commitment in relationships. Specifically, they proposed that satisfaction in a relationship is determined by one's comparison level – the reward/cost ratio that one feels one deserves in a relationship, whereas commitment is determined by one's comparison level for alternatives – the perceived availability of attractive alternative outcomes (e.g., another partner, being alone). In making this distinction, they were able to account for situations in which people remain in unsatisfying relationships as well as situations in which satisfying relationships are abandoned. The interdependence model continues to be one of the most influential and important theories of commitment.

Rusbult (1980a, 1980b) subsequently extended this model. She began by adopting Thibaut and Kelley's proposition that people are satisfied in relationships to the extent that rewards exceed costs, and that satisfaction, in turn, predicts commitment. She also accepted Thibaut and Kelley's premise that another important predictor of commitment to a relationship is the availability of alternatives (i.e., the fewer the available alternatives, the higher the level of commitment). The unique contribution of Rusbult's model is the inclusion of a third predictor of commitment, namely the level of investments in a relationship. Investments are defined as resources (e.g., time, emotional energy, joint possessions) that cannot be recovered if the relationship dissolves. Rusbult has developed scales to measure investment model variables (see Rusbult, Martz, & Agnew, 1998, for the most recent version). This model has generated a host of empirical studies (see Rusbult et al., 1998, for a review).

Finally, Levinger (1965) developed a cohesiveness model of marital commitment. He posited that the durability of a marital relationship depends on the strength of attraction to the relationship as well as the strength of barriers preventing the partners from leaving the relationship. Sources of attraction include companionship, sexual enjoyment, socioeconomic rewards, similarity of social status, and so on. Barriers to the dissolution of marital relationships include: feelings of obligation (e.g., to dependent children, to the marital bond), moral prescriptions (e.g. religious convictions, joint church attendance), and external pressures to maintain the relationship (e.g., stigma of divorce, economic and legal costs of marital dissolution, embeddedness in a joint social network). Like Thibaut and Kelley, Levinger also proposed that marital cohesiveness is undermined when alternative sources of attraction exist. Although the cohesiveness model is frequently cited in the commitment literature, it has not received the prominence that it deserves. One reason may be that Levinger did not develop scales to measure these constructs, making it difficult to conduct empirical research. However, as discussed below, elements of this model are apparent in theories of commitment that seek to identify its types or components.

Johnson (1973, 1982, 1991), for example, has formulated a model in which commitment is partitioned into three types: personal, structural, and moral. Personal commitment refers to the feeling of "wanting to" remain in a relationship, and thus is akin to Levinger's notion of attraction. Structural commitment is based on external pressures to maintain a relationship ("have to" commitment), such as the presence of children, costs of divorce, pressure from network members to remain in the relationship, and so on. Moral commitment is defined as a sense of moral obligation to continue a relationship ("ought to" commitment) stemming from religious beliefs and personal values (e.g., beliefs that marriage should last a lifetime, vows should not be broken). Structural and moral commitment resemble the barriers in Levinger's model labeled external pressures and moral prescriptions, respectively. Johnson's model is important in highlighting the distinction between the internal and external constraints that keep people in relationships. As with Levinger's model, empirical research on Johnson's model has been hampered by the absence of standard scales to measure these types of commitment. Recently Johnson, Caughlin, and Huston (1999) have taken steps to remedy this situation by developing single-item measures of these constructs.

Similar concepts appear in more recent models of commitment (see Adams & Jones, 1999, for a review). For example, Lydon (e.g., Lydon, 1996; Lydon, Pierce, & O'Regan, 1997) differentiated between enthusiastic commitment (feelings of attraction to the partner or satisfaction with the relationship) and moral commitment (as defined by Johnson, 1991). Scales have been developed to assess these constructs in the contexts of commitment to a pregnancy (e.g., Lydon, Dunkel-Schetter, Cohan, & Pierce, 1996) and to a dating partner (Lydon et al., 1997). Stanley and Markman (1992) differentiated between personal dedication commitment and constraint commitment, and developed scales to measure these constructs.

Finally, Adams and Jones (1997) identified three dimensions of marital commitment (and developed scales to measure them) based on an integrative analysis of the marital commitment literature. The *attraction* dimension is defined as commitment based on personal dedication, attachment, love, and satisfaction. The *constraining* dimension refers to commitment based on fears of the social, emotional, and financial costs of marital dissolution. The *moral-normative* dimension involves feelings of personal responsibility to remain in a marriage as well as beliefs that marriage is an important social and religious institution. Adams and Jones note that their dimensions correspond to Johnson's typology of personal, structural, and moral commitment, respectively.

In conclusion, Levinger's cohesiveness model provides a useful framework within which other theories of commitment can be situated. Like other social exchange theorists (e.g., Thibaut & Kelley; Rusbult), Levinger regards satisfaction (attraction) and the availability of attractive alternatives as important predictors of commitment. The concept of satisfaction (conceptualized as attraction, personal commitment, or enthusiastic commitment) also surfaces in theories in which commitment is partitioned into types or components. These theories emphasize another important element of the cohesiveness model, namely the structural and moral barriers that prevent people from terminating relationships.

Lay conceptions of commitment

In a series of studies on lay conceptions of commitment, Fehr (1988, Study 1) asked laypeople to list features of the concept. Responses included features such as perseverance, responsibility, living up to one's word, caring, sacrifice, obligation, love, and so on. When rated for prototypicality (Study 2), loyalty, responsibility, living up to your word, faithfulness, and trust received the highest ratings. Features such as affection, contentment, security, and feeling trapped received the lowest ratings. This prototype structure was verified in subsequent studies. For example, prototypical features were seen as increasingly applicable to a relationship as it increased in commitment, whereas the applicability of nonprototypical features did not vary as systematically (Study 5). Violations of prototypical features were regarded as undermining commitment in a relationship to a greater extent than violations of nonprototypical features (Study 6).

In a recent extension of this research, Fehr (1999, Study 1) asked participants to list *types* of commitment. The responses included relational varieties of commitment as well as commitment to nonrelational entities (one's career, sports, a pet, one's country). The relational types could be partitioned into commitment to relationships that are close or intimate (e.g., commitment to a neighbor, commitment to relatives). These groupings were generally confirmed by a cluster analysis (Study 8). Prototypicality ratings of these types revealed that commitment to close relationships was seen as exemplifying the concept, whereas commitment to nonclose relationships and nonrelational types of commitment was considered peripheral (Study 2). Finally, in a study of dating relationships (Study 8), participants who conceptualized commitment in terms of commitment to close relationship partners reported greater satisfaction, love, and commitment compared to those who were less likely to conceptualize commitment in this way.

As with experts' theories, lay conceptions also can be interpreted in terms of Levinger's cohesiveness model (or other, similar models in which commitment is partitioned into types or components). Features of commitment such as love, caring, trust, and devotion portray attraction (or personal commitment). These features were listed most frequently in Fehr's research and were regarded as central to the concept. Features that reflect moral prescriptions (e.g., responsibility, living up to your word, being reliable, obligation, and sacrifice) also were generated frequently and received high typicality ratings. In contrast, the theme of external pressures to maintain relationships was not evident in these responses. Perhaps people are not aware of the external pressures that serve to keep them in relationships. Alternatively, they may be cognizant of such forces, but do not consider them part of the meaning of the concept.

Relation between love and commitment

Theorists have expressed a wide range of views on the relation between love and commitment. These can be summarized as follows (see Fehr, 1988):

1. Love and commitment are identical concepts. Money (1980), for example, virtually equated love and commitment in his definition of love as "the personal experience . . . of being attached or bonded to another person" (p. 218).
2. Love and commitment are largely overlapping, but partially independent. This view, espoused by Kelley (1983), has its roots in interdependence theory which posits that a person's dependence on a group is not necessarily highly correlated with his or her attraction to it (Thibaut & Kelley, 1959).
3. Love and commitment are completely independent. According to Solomon (1981), love "has nothing to do with commitment" (p. xxxiii). In his view, commitment is a promise to remain in a relationship, regardless of one's feelings (see also Rosenblatt, 1977).

4. Commitment is a component of love. As discussed earlier, in Sternberg's (1986) triangular theory, commitment is conceptualized as a component of love, along with intimacy and passion.
5. Love is a component of commitment. This view is represented by Rusbult's (1980a, 1980b) investment model in which satisfaction, conceptualized as attraction or love, is regarded as a component of commitment.

Fehr (1988, Study 1) tested which of these models corresponded most closely to laypeople's conceptions by comparing the features generated for love and commitment. Consistent with Kelley's view, there was a large degree of overlap between the features of love and commitment (e.g., trust, respect, honesty, caring). Importantly, each concept possessed unique features as well. For example, features such as friendship, sexual passion, and excitement were listed only for love; features such as perseverance, living up to your word, and obligation were listed only for commitment.

The Experience of Love and Commitment in Close Relationships

The focus so far has been on experts' and laypeople's models of love and commitment. These concepts also are important when considering people's actual relationship experiences (see, e.g., Kelley, 1983). In this section, two major issues will be addressed. The first pertains to *levels* of love and commitment experienced in romantic relationships. Questions regarding love will be framed in terms of companionate love and passionate love (based on the argument presented earlier that Berscheid and Walster's companionate/passionate model largely subsumes other models of love). One issue that has received only scant attention is whether people tend to experience only passionate love, only companionate love, or some combination of both in their romantic relationships. This issue will be examined. A related issue for commitment is whether people experience similar levels of personal, structural, and moral commitment. Finally, levels of love and commitment will be compared to determine whether one concept tends to be more salient than the other in people's subjective experience.

The other major issue to be discussed concerns the variable that is most frequently correlated with measures of love and commitment, namely relationship satisfaction. Questions to be addressed include: What is the strength of relation between measures of love (i.e., companionate and passionate love) and satisfaction? What is the strength of relation between measures of commitment and satisfaction? And, finally, are love and commitment differentially related to satisfaction?

Levels of love and commitment in relationships

Levels of love.   There has been a tacit assumption in the literature that people tend to experience passionate love *or* companionate love in relationships. For example, a common belief has been that passionate love peaks early on, and in enduring relationships, is eventually replaced by companionate love (e.g., Sternberg, 1986; Walster [Hatfield] & Walster, 1978). This implies that if asked about their experience of love at any given time, people will report primarily feelings of passionate love or companionate love (depending on the stage or length of the relationship).[5] Brehm (1985), on the other hand, suggested that these kinds of love are best conceptualized as opposite ends of the same continuum. In her view, some relationships will be situated at the two extremes, but most relationships will fall somewhere along this continuum (relationships characterized by equal amounts of passionate and companionate love would be located at the midpoint). If one accepts Brehm's premise that both companionate and passionate love can be experienced to varying degrees within the same relationship, then it becomes possible to ask whether one kind of love or the other tends to dominate over the other in people's everyday experience.

Fortunately, many researchers have administered measures of companionate and passionate love within the same investigation, thereby providing a database that can be drawn on to answer this question. However, it should be noted at the outset that the analyses to be presented here are inherently flawed. First, it is problematic to make comparisons across studies. This can be mitigated somewhat by sampling a large number of studies. If consistent patterns emerge, then one can draw conclusions with greater confidence. Therefore, the findings from a large pool of studies were examined. Second, few, if any, scales have been developed to measure companionate love per se. For the present purposes, scales such as the Storge love style scale (Hendrick & Hendrick, 1986), the Friendship-based Love Scale (Grote and Frieze, 1994), the Intimacy scale of the Relationship Rating Form (Davis & Todd, 1982, 1985) were taken as measures of companionate love. Not all close relationships researchers will agree with this assumption. However, given that no standardized measure of companionate love exists, this seemed to be a reasonable starting point for answering the questions raised concerning passionate and companionate love. Finally, it was also assumed that the various measures of passionate love assess the same construct.

Table 13.1 displays a sampling of studies that have included measures of companionate and passionate love. Given that most of the research has focused on college students' experiences of love in dating relationships, one might expect passionate love to prevail. However, as is evident from the table, people tend to report high levels of both kinds of love. When levels of companionate and passionate love are compared, conclusions about the kind of love that is most pronounced in relationships appear to depend on the measurement instruments that are used. In studies that use the Hendrick and Hendrick (1986) Love Attitudes Scale, ratings of the Eros love style (passionate love) exceed rating of the Storge love style (companionate love). (Note that in studies by Hendrick and Hendrick and by Murstein, Merighi, and Vyse, 1991, lower numbers indicate higher agreement with scale items). This pattern is reversed, however, when other measures of companionate and passionate love are considered. For example, Grote and Frieze (1994) revised Hendrick and Hendrick's Storge scale (and named it the Friendship-based Love Scale) and slightly revised the Eros scale. Ratings on the Friendship-based Love Scale are consistently higher than ratings on the Eros scale. Similarly, in studies using Sternberg's scales, Intimacy scores (companionate love) consistently surpass Passion scores. This is also the case when companionate and passionate love are measured using Aron and Westbay's (1996) Intimacy and Passion dimensions. Finally, Sprecher and Regan (1998) administered two different measures of companionate and passionate love (see table 13.1). In each case, ratings of companionate love were higher than ratings of passionate love.[6]

The studies shown in table 13.1 generally were not conducted with the intent of determining whether people report higher levels of companionate or passionate love in their relationships. Thus, in most cases, the significance of differences in ratings of these two kinds of love was not tested. Exceptions are Aron and Westbay (1996), Sprecher and Regan (1998), and Sternberg (1997), all of whom found that mean ratings of companionate love were significantly higher than mean ratings of passionate love.

In conclusion, it is apparent that people experience high levels of both companionate love and passionate love in their romantic relationships. The answer to the question of whether they experience more companionate love or passionate love is, "it depends." Specifically, it depends on how these constructs are measured. If the Hendrick and Hendrick love style scales are used, it would appear that levels of passionate love surpass levels of companionate love. However, other measures of these constructs point to the opposite conclusion.

Levels of commitment.   It is generally assumed that personal commitment will be more dominant than moral or structural commitment – at least in satisfying relationships (e.g., Lydon et al., 1997). Unfortunately, a few of the relevant studies that have been conducted report only correlational findings; mean levels of these types of commitment are not given (e.g., Johnson et al., 1999; Jones, Adams, Monroe, & Berry, 1995). However, Lydon et al. (1997) reported a mean of .33 on their moral commitment scale for participants whose dating relationships remained intact compared to −.36 for those whose relationship ended. The means on their enthusiastic commitment scale were .26 and −.18 for these two groups, respectively. Similarly, scores on Stanley and Markman's (1992) personal dedication scale exceeded those on their constraint commitment scale. Within each group, the highest ratings were assigned to the Commitment to Spouse scale (a measure of personal commitment), followed by Commitment to Marriage (moral commitment), and then Feelings of Entrapment (structural commitment). Thus, there is support for the prediction that levels of personal commitment exceed levels of either moral commitment or structural commitment. Replication of these findings would strengthen this conclusion.

Levels of love and commitment compared.   How do levels of companionate and passionate love compare with levels of commitment in relationships? Sternberg (1986) addressed this issue indirectly when making predictions about the time course of the components of his triangular theory of love. Specifically, he suggested that passion and eventually intimacy decline over time, whereas commitment increases, at least in successful relationships. Thus, from this perspective, whether love or commitment is most salient in people's experience depends on the duration of a relationship. As with research on companionate and passionate love presented earlier, studies that have assessed both love and commitment generally have not compared levels of these constructs in terms of relationship length or stage (see note 5). However, there are data available to answer the basic question of interest here, namely whether at any given time, the experience of love dominates over the experience of commitment in relationships. Stated differently, if love is conceptualized as an emotion and commitment as a cognitive construct involving the decision to remain in a relationship, the question becomes: which is more salient in everyday experience – warm (or in the case of passionate love, hot) feelings for one's partner or the "cold" awareness that one has promised to remain in this relationship for the long haul?

In studies by Sternberg (1997), ratings of intimacy (companionate love) are significantly higher than ratings of commitment, which in turn, are significantly higher than ratings of passion. (Mean commitment ratings (on a 9-point scale) were 7.06 in Study 1 and 7.20 in Study 2; see table 13.1 for intimacy and passion means). Aron and Westbay (1996, Study 5) also found that mean ratings of Sternberg's scales differed significantly from one another. In their study, intimacy received the highest ratings, followed by passion, and then commitment (Ms = 7.06, 6.37, 5.82, respectively on 8-point scales). (Hendrick and Hendrick, 1989, obtained the same pattern of means when they administered the Sternberg scale, although significance tests were not conducted.) Similar findings obtain when these constructs are assessed using Aron and Westbay's measure: M = 7.00 for the Intimacy dimension, 6.33 for the Passion dimension, and 6.08 for the Commitment dimension (all assessed on 8-point scales). These means differed significantly from one another, with the largest difference between ratings of intimacy and the other two dimensions (see Aron and Westbay, 1996, Study 5). Finally, in a study using the Relationship Rating Form (Levy & Davis, 1988), ratings were highest on the Commitment scale (M = 7.6 on a 9-point scale for women; 7.5 for men; see table 13.1 for intimacy and passion scale means). The researchers did not test whether these differences were statistically significant.

In conclusion, it is clear that people report relatively high levels of companionate love, passionate love, and commitment in their romantic relationships. When levels of these constructs are compared, companionate love (as assessed by Sternberg's scales and Aron and Westbay's dimensions) tends to receive the highest ratings. The relative placement of passionate love and commitment is less clear. In some studies, levels of passionate love exceed levels of commitment, whereas in other studies the opposite is true.

Relation between love, commitment, and satisfaction

Relation between types of love and satisfaction. Researchers generally predict that both companionate and passionate love will be positively correlated with satisfaction, rather than specifying whether one kind of love might be more strongly associated with satisfaction than another (e.g., Sternberg, 1997; Sprecher & Regan, 1998; although see Grote & Frieze, 1994). The purpose of this section is to explore whether companionate love or passionate love is most strongly linked to relationship satisfaction. Many studies have included measures of these constructs, thereby enabling comparisons of the strength of the relation between satisfaction and these kinds of love.[7]

When companionate love is measured using Hendrick and Hendrick's (1986) Storge love style scale, correlations with satisfaction are generally weak. In the studies sampled, the highest correlation reported between Storge and satisfaction was .22 (Meeks, Hendrick, & Hendrick, 1998). In most studies, correlations hover near zero or in the low teens (e.g., Bierhoff, 1991; Davis & Latty-Mann, 1987; Hendrick & Hendrick, 1988; Hendrick, Hendrick, & Adler, 1988; Jones et al., 1995; Levesque, 1993; Levy & Davis, 1988, Study 2; Morrow, Clark, & Brock, 1995; Richardson, Medvin, & Hammock, 1988). In

Table 13.1 Levels of Companionate and Passionate Love in Close Relationships

Author(s)	Participants	N			Companionate love						Passionate love					
		Total	Women	Men	Measure	(range)	Means Total	Women	Men	p <	Measure	(range)	Means Total	Women	Men	p <
Hendrick, & Hendrick (1986, Study 1)[a]	college students	807	341	466	Storge scale (LAS)	1–5		2.5	2.6	.05	Eros scale (LAS)	1–5		2.3	2.3	ns
Hendrick, & Hendrick (1986, Study 2)[a]	college students	567	368	199	Storge scale (LAS)	1–5		2.2	2.4	.05	Eros scale (LAS)	1–5		2.1	2.2	.05
Hendrick, & Hendrick (1988)[a]	college students	218	102	116	Storge scale (LAS)	1–5		2.1	2.3	ns	Eros scale (LAS)	1–5		2.2	2.3	ns
Bailey, Hendrick, & Hendrick (1987)[a]	college students	286	146	140	Storge scale (LAS)	1–5		2.21	2.30	ns	Eros scale (LAS)	1–5		2.09	2.23	ns
Hendrick, & Hendrick (1989)[a]	unmarried college students	391			Storge scale (LAS)	1–5	2.22				Eros scale (LAS)	1–5	2.19			
					Sternberg Intimacy scale	1–5	1.92				Sternberg Passion scale	1–5	2.29			
Hendrick, & Hendrick (1990)[a]	college students	1139	603	536	Storge scale (old & new versions)	1–5		2.26	2.45	.05	Eros scale (old & new versions)	1–5		2.13	2.12	ns
Hendrick, Dicke, & Hendrick (1998, Study 1)[a]	college students	1090	646	444	Storge scale (LAS)	1–5		2.31	2.58	.05	Eros scale (LAS)	1–5		2.07	2.12	ns
					Storge scale (short form)	1–5		2.48	2.76	.05	Eros scale (short form)	1–5		1.98	2.08	.05
Hendrick, et al. (1998, Study 2)[a]	college students	819	525	294	Storge scale (LAS)	1–5		2.37	2.53	.05	Eros scale (LAS)	1–5		2.04	2.08	ns
		794	510	284	Storge scale (short form)	1–5		2.48	2.71	.05	Eros scale (short form)	1–5		1.89	2.12	.05
Hendrick, et al. (1998, Study 3)[a]	college students	847	542	305	Storge scale (short form)	1–5		2.50	2.69	.05	Eros scale (short form)	1–5		1.92	2.05	.05
Murstein, Merighi, & Vyse (1991)[a]	college students – US	156	117	39	Storge scale	1–5		2.2	2.3	ns	Eros scale (LAS)	1–5		2.1	2.3	ns
	college students – France	165	50	115	Storge scale	1–5		3.0	3.0	ns	Eros scale (LAS)	1–5		2.0	2.1	ns

Study	Sample	N	N	N	Measure	Range	M	M	Sig	Measure	Range	M	M	Sig
Feeney & Noller (1990)	college students – Australia	374	212	162	Friendship factor (largely Storge items)	7–35	23.31	21.67	.05	Love Ideal factor (largely Eros items)	10–50	30.05	31.04	ns
Frazier & Esterly (1990)	college students	326	175	151	Storge scale (LAS)	1–5	3.79	3.69	ns	Eros scale (LAS)	1–5	3.64	3.60	ns
Morrow, Clark, & Brock (1995)	dating/married couples	186			Storge scale (revised)	3–15	11.24	10.55	.05	Eros scale (revised)	3–15	not reported		ns
Richardson, Medvin, & Hammock (1988)	college students	175	103	72	Storge scale (LAS)	7–35	23.43			Eros scale (LAS)	7–35	25.93		
Levesque (1993)	dating adolescents	304	177	127	Storge scale (revised)	1–6	3.10	3.57		Eros scale (revised)	1–6	4.17	4.25	ns
Sprecher, Aron, Hatfield, Cortese, Potapova, & Levitskaya (1994)	college students – US	1043	657	386	Storge scale (revised)	1–5	3.57	3.30	.01	Eros scale (revised)	1–5	3.96	3.82	ns
	college students – Japan	223	118	105	Storge scale (revised)	1–5	3.16	3.07	ns	Eros scale (revised)	1–5	3.29	3.16	ns
Levitskaya (1994)	college students – Russia	401	201	200	Storge scale (revised & translated into Russian)	1–5	3.05	3.03	ns	Eros scale (revised & translated into Russian)	1–5	3.59	3.73	ns
Grote & Frieze (1994, Study 1)	middle-aged adults	731	333	398	Friendship-based Love Scale (FBL) (revised Storge scale)	1–5	4.2	4.1	ns	Eros scale (revised)	1–5	3.7	3.8	ns
Grote & Frieze (1994, Study 2)	college students	298	220	78	FBL–6 item version	1–5	4.1	3.8	.05	Eros scale (revised)	1–5	4.0	4.0	ns
					FBL–9 item version	1–5	4.1	3.9	.05					
Grote, Frieze, & Stone (1996)	married individuals	530	217	313	FBL scale	1–5	4.4	4.2	.01	Eros scale (revised)	1–5	3.8	3.8	ns
Bookwala, Frieze, & Grote (1994)	dating women	149			FBL scale	1–5	4.36			Eros scale (revised)	1–5	4.20		
Aron & Westbay (1996, Study 5)[c]	college students	257			Intimacy dimension (self-constructed)	1–8	7.00			Passion dimension (self-constructed)	1–8	6.33		
					Sternberg Intimacy scale (revised)	1–8	7.06			Sternberg Passion scale (revised)	1–8	6.37		

Author(s)	Participants	N			Measure Companionate love	(range)	Means				Measure Passionate love	(range)	Means			
		Total	Women	Men			Total	Women	Men	p <			Total	Women	Men	p <
Sternberg (1997, Study 1)[d]	dating/married individuals	84	42	42	Sternberg Intimacy scale	1–9	7.55				Sternberg Passion scale	1–9	6.91			
Sternberg (1997, Study 2)[d]	dating/married individuals	101	51	50	Sternberg Intimacy scale	1–9	7.39				Sternberg Passion scale	1–9	6.51			
Levy & Davis (1988, Studies 1 & 2)[b]	dating/married individuals & couples	166	116	50	Intimacy scale (RRF)	1–9		7.4	6.9		Passion scale (RRF)	1–9		7.3	7.2	
		222	119	103												
Davis & Latty-Mann (1987)	dating couples	70			Intimacy scale (RRF)	1–9	6.95				Passion scale (RRF)	1–9	7.42			
Sprecher & Regan (1998)	heterosexual couples	197			Rubin's Love scale (revised)	1–9		7.73	7.53	.05	Passionate Love scale (revised)	1–9		7.21	7.05	ns
					single item	1–9		8.52	8.11	.001	single item	1–9		7.18	7.10	ns

Note: Measures

Love Attitudes Scale (LAS); Hendrick & Hendrick (1986).
Triangular Love Scale (Intimacy, Passion, Commitment subscales); see Sternberg (1997) for the most recent version.
Relationship Rating Form (RRF); Davis & Todd (1982, 1985).
Rubin's Love Scale; Rubin (1970).
Passionate Love Scale; Hatfield & Sprecher (1986).
Any scale not listed here appears in full in the article that used it.

Superscripts

[a] LAS scales were scored in a direction where 1 = strongly agree and 5 = strongly disagree. Thus participants endorsed the Eros love style slightly more that the Storge love style. In other studies using these scales, the ratings were reversed such that high numbers correspond to greater agreement with scale items.

[b] Data analyses were based on subsets of participants from Studies 1 and 2 combined.

[c] The means reported are based on ratings of actual relationships; data on participants' conceptions of love were gathered but are not reported here.

[d] The means reported are based on ratings of characteristicness (rather than importance) for relationship with lover/spouse.

contrast, correlations between passionate love (as assessed by the Eros love style scale) and satisfaction are substantially higher – generally falling in the .40 to .69 range (Bierhoff, 1991; Bookwala, Frieze & Grote, 1994; Davis & Latty-Mann, 1987; Frazier & Esterly, 1990; Grote & Frieze, 1994, Studies 1 & 2; Grote, Frieze & Stone, 1996; Hendrick & Hendrick, 1988; Hendrick, Hendrick, & Adler, 1988; Jones et al., 1995; Meeks et al., 1998; Morrow et al., 1995; Richardson et al., 1988). Thus, when companionate love and passionate love are assessed with Storge and Eros love style scales, respectively, passionate love appears to be more strongly associated with relationship satisfaction than is companionate love.

A different picture emerges, however, when other ways of measuring companionate and passionate love are considered. For example, in studies using Sternberg's scales, correlations between the Intimacy scale (companionate love) and satisfaction range from .54 (using a revised Sternberg intimacy scale; Levy & Davis, 1988) to .86 (Sternberg, 1997, Study 1), with most studies reporting correlations in the .70s (Acker & Davis, 1992; Hendrick & Hendrick, 1988; Sternberg, 1997, Study 2). Correlations between the Passion scale and measures of relationship satisfaction are slightly lower, but generally reach the .60s and .70s. Similarly, scores on both the Intimacy and Passion scales of the Relationship Rating Form (Davis & Todd, 1982, 1985) correlate strongly (in the .60s) with satisfaction (Davis & Latty-Mann, 1987; Levy & Davis, 1988).

Still other ways of assessing these kinds of love tend to produce stronger associations between companionate love and satisfaction than between passionate love and satisfaction. For example, correlations between Grote and Frieze's (1994) Friendship-based Love Scale and satisfaction range from .61 to .81 (see Bookwala et al., 1994; Grote & Frieze, 1994, Studies 1 & 2; Grote et al., 1996); correlations with passionate love (assessed with a revised Eros scale) are somewhat lower, ranging from .49 to .76. Hecht et al. (1994, Study 2) also found that companionate love (as measured by the Companionate Love Factor of their Love Ways Inventory) was more highly correlated with satisfaction than was passionate love (as measured by their Intuitive Love Factor), $rs = .50$ versus .28. Companionate love also predicted satisfaction more strongly than passionate love in a regression analysis (Hecht et al., Study 1). Finally, Sprecher and Regan (1998) obtained significantly higher correlations between companionate love (assessed mainly with Rubin's Love Scale items) and satisfaction ($rs = .54$ for women, .62 for men) than between passionate love (assessed with the Passionate Love Scale) and satisfaction ($rs = .35$ for women, .50 for men). This pattern was not replicated, however, when single items were used to assess companionate and passionate love.[8]

In conclusion, similar to the research on levels of companionate and passionate love discussed earlier, the kind of love that is most strongly linked to relationship satisfaction varies, depending on the measurement instrument that is used. If Hendrick and Hendrick's (1986) love style scales are administered, then it appears that passionate love is more strongly associated with satisfaction. If Sternberg's or Davis and Todd's Intimacy and Passion scales are used, then companionate and passionate love appear to be equally related to satisfaction, with a tendency for correlations to be slightly higher for companionate love. In studies using measures that arguably provide the most direct assessment of companionate love (e.g., Grote & Frieze's Friendship-based Love Scale; Hecht et al.'s Companionate Love Factor; Sprecher & Regan's multi-item Companionate Love Scale), correlations between companionate love and satisfaction are higher than correlations between passionate love and satisfaction.

Relation between types of commitment and satisfaction.   Commitment theorists agree that commitment based on an internal desire to remain in a relationship (i.e., personal commitment) should be more strongly linked to relationship satisfaction than commitment based on moral obligation or commitment imposed by external or structural forces. The results of the few studies that have tested this hypothesis empirically are consistent with this prediction. For example, Lydon et al. (1997) found that scores in their Enthusiastic Commitment Scale (a measure of personal commitment) were more highly correlated with satisfaction than scores on their Moral Commitment Scale (rs = .61 versus .33). Jones et al. assessed personal commitment with their Personal Dedication Scale and moral commitment with their Constraint Commitment Scale. The former was much more highly correlated with satisfaction than the latter (rs = .72 versus .31). Stanley and Markman (1992) also found that correlations between personal dedication and satisfaction were higher than correlations between constraint commitment and satisfaction. Finally, Johnson et al. (1999) constructed single-item measures of personal, moral, and structural commitment. As predicted, correlations with satisfaction were higher for personal commitment (rs = .54 for women; .40 for men) than for the other kinds of commitment (for moral commitment, rs = .09 for women; .09 for men; for structural commitment, rs = −.36 for women; −.20 for men).

In conclusion, despite the paucity of data and the variability in measures, the research conducted so far supports the prediction that personal commitment is more strongly linked to relationship satisfaction than either structural or moral commitment.

Love and commitment compared.   Earlier, it was noted that researchers tend to predict that both companionate love and passionate love will be positively correlated with relationship satisfaction, without specifying whether these correlations might differ in magnitude. The same holds true in studies that have correlated measures of love and commitment with satisfaction. Sternberg (1997), for example, simply predicted that all three subscales of the Triangular Love Scale would be positively related to relationship satisfaction. Indeed, companionate love (assessed with his Intimacy scale), passionate love, and commitment were all highly correlated with relationship satisfaction (rs = .75 to .86, Study 1; rs = .67 to .76, Study 2). Other researchers who have correlated Sternberg's scales with satisfaction also report correlations in the .60s and .70s (Acker & Davis, 1992; Hendrick & Hendrick, 1989), although these correlations were slightly lower in a study that used a revised Sternberg scale (rs = .54 to .63; Levy & Davis, 1988). When Levy and Davis administered their Relationship Rating Form, correlations with satisfaction ranged from .60 to .65 for the Intimacy and Passion scales; correlations with the Commitment scale were somewhat higher (rs = .72 for women; .82 for men).

In summary, when companionate love, passionate love, and commitment are measured with either the Triangular Love Scale or the Relationship Rating Form, all three constructs show high, positive correlations with relationship satisfaction. In approximately half of these data sets, correlations were slightly higher for intimacy than the other constructs, although it is unlikely that this difference would be statistically significant. It should be noted that the commitment subscales of the Sternberg and the Davis and Todd scales assess primarily feelings of *personal* commitment. Thus, one would expect correlations with relationship satisfaction to be high. However, the fact that companionate love, passionate love, and commitment are equally strongly linked to relationship satisfaction suggests that the construct of satisfaction is not a particularly suitable candidate for researchers wishing to establish the discriminant validity of scales that assess all three of these constructs. This issue will be discussed further in the next section.

Summary and Conclusions

Status of theories and research on love

In the past 15 years, there has been a proliferation of theories or models of love. Most of these could be considered "structural theories" in that they make claims about the structure of love as a concept (i.e., its types, components). These theories address the question, "What is love?" This is also the question addressed by research on lay conceptions of love. Theorizing and research on love styles can be seen as answering the question, "How do we love?" Berscheid and Hatfield's companionate/passionate model of love serves as a useful framework for integrating these theories as generated by both experts and laypeople.

Less common, but no less important, are theories of love that address people's motivations for entering love relationships. Aron and Aron's (1986) self-expansion theory provides an answer to the question, "Why do we love?" Attachment theories (e.g., Hazan & Shaver, 1987; Bartholomew, 1990) also seek answers to the "why" question by examining the patterns of relating that were established in people's first significant relationship, namely that with their primary caregiver. A challenging, worthwhile, next step for scholars in this area is to construct a grand theory of love, or at least an overarching framework within which the "what," "why," and "how" theories of love can be situated.

With regard to empirical research on love, it is problematic that conclusions regarding the experience of love vary, depending on how these constructs are measured. If Hendrick and Hendrick's (1986) Storge and Eros love style scales are used, then it appears that people report more passionate love than companionate love in their relationships, and that passionate love is more strongly associated with relationship satisfaction. When other scales (e.g., Aron & Westbay's, Davis & Todd's, Grote & Frieze's, Hecht et al.'s, Sternberg's) are used, the data point to the opposite conclusion, namely that levels of companionate love exceed those of passionate love, and that companionate love is equally or more strongly associated with satisfaction. These discrepancies seem to hinge primarily on the measurement of companionate love. (The various scales that were taken as measures of passionate love produced similar findings.) One problem might be the assumption adopted here that various measures of intimacy, the Storge love style scale, the Friendship-based Love Scale, and so on, all assess the construct of companionate love. However, even if one rejects this assumption, the finding that intimacy scales, for example, produce different answers to the questions raised here than the Storge scale still needs to be explained. Indeed, it is perplexing that in research on levels of love and in research on correlations between love and satisfaction, findings based on the Storge scale were opposite to those obtained using other measures, even though this scale is regarded by its creators as a measure of friendship or companionate love (see Hendrick & Hendrick, 1993, 1997). Moreover, when people's open-ended accounts of their romantic relationships are analyzed in terms of love styles, Storge is a more dominant theme (66 versus 34 percent of accounts in Study 1; 72 versus 22 percent in Study 2; Hendrick & Hendrick, 1993) than Eros. However, when these same relationships are rated on the love style scales (see Study 2), ratings of Eros once again exceed ratings of Storge. In short, it would seem worthwhile to conduct further psychometric work on the Storge scale to determine why it does not behave like other measures of companionate love.[9]

In conclusion, if one considers measures of companionate love other than the Storge scale, it would appear that companionate love is central to the experience of love in relationships. This is consistent with research on lay conceptions of love discussed earlier where companionate love was seen as representing the concept of love to a greater extent than passionate love.

Status of theories and research on commitment

Commitment theorists have sought to answer the question, "What is commitment?" by formulating structural theories in which types or components of commitment are delineated. Social exchange models address the question, "Why do people make commitments?" However, unlike the literature on love, there is a paucity of theorizing relevant to the question, "How do people make commitments?" In addition to such theoretical development, the commitment literature would benefit from attempts to integrate the theories that currently exist. As was discussed earlier, Levinger's cohesiveness model seems particularly promising for integrating both classes of experts' theories as well as research on lay conceptions.

In contrast to the literature on love, little research has been conducted on the experience of different kinds of commitment. However, the few studies that exist have produced remarkably consistent findings. Levels of personal commitment generally are higher than levels of moral or structural commitment. Personal commitment is also most strongly associated with relationship satisfaction. Regarding methodology, there has been a tendency for researchers to develop their own scales to measure these types of commitment. Given that the various scales tend to produce similar findings, this may not be particularly problematic. However, as research in this area develops, a standard set of scales may be necessary in order to make precise comparisons across studies. A factor analytic study of extant measures such as that conducted by Hendrick and Hendrick (1989) in the domain of love might be a useful first step in this regard.

Relation between love and commitment

As discussed earlier, there are a variety of views on the relation between love and commitment. According to Fehr (1988), laypeople's conception of the relation between love and commitment is most consistent with Kelley's (1983) representation of these concepts as largely overlapping but partially independent. Research on the experience of love and commitment in relationships underscores the high degree of similarity between these concepts. Although there was evidence that companionate love was more pronounced in relationships than passionate love or commitment, it should not be overlooked that in most studies, participants reported high levels of all three of these constructs. Moreover, correlations between satisfaction and these constructs were so similar that one would be hard pressed to make a case that love and commitment are distinct. In future research, it will be important to determine the extent to which these correlations reflect the inherent relatedness of these concepts as opposed to difficulties in creating measurement instruments that assess these concepts independently. To take the Triangular Love Scale as an example, the various versions of this scale have been plagued by unacceptably high intercorrelations between the intimacy, passion, and commitment subscales (see, e.g., Acker & Davis, 1992; Hecht et al., 1994; Hendrick & Hendrick, 1989; Sternberg, 1997). It also would be worthwhile to follow the lead of Lydon et al. (1997) who have responded to the problem of high correlations between commitment and satisfaction by identifying conditions (e.g. long-distance relationships) under which one would not expect strong links between these constructs.

To summarize, there is abundant evidence to support Kelley's description of love and commitment as largely overlapping. The challenge for future research will be to provide evidence in support of the other part of his description, namely that these concepts also are "partially independent."

In conclusion, the concepts of love and commitment are central in the literature on close relationships. In the last 15 years or so, impressive progress has been made in terms of theory development. Moreover, the large body of research on the experience of love (and to a lesser extent, commitment) highlights the relevance of these concepts to people's lives. This research shows that people report high levels of love and commitment in their relationships. More importantly, the higher the levels of love and commitment experienced, the greater the satisfaction with a relationship. In terms of relative importance, overall, the evidence suggests that the warmth of companionate love seems to prevail over both the heat of passion and cold cognitions about commitment to the relationship.

Notes

1. Hendrick and Hendrick also have published a short form (Hendrick, Hendrick, & Dicke, 1998) and relationship-specific version (Hendrick & Hendrick, 1990) of these scales.
2. Unfortunately, Aron et al.'s (1992) Inclusion of Other in the Self scale and Bartholomew and Horowitz's (1991) attachment scale were not published at the time of this study.
3. In their recent writings, Hendrick and Hendrick seem more accepting of such a conclusion (e.g., Hendrick & Hendrick, 1993, 1997).
4. There is another class of commitment theories in which the linking of a relationship to one's basic values and identity is seen as an important basis of commitment formation (e.g., Brickman, 1987; Lydon & Zanna, 1990). In an extension of this work, Lydon and his colleagues (e.g., Lydon, Meana, Sepinwall, Richard, & Mayman, 1999) have developed a commitment-calibration model in which commitment is conceptualized as the motivation to sustain a relationship or maintain a line of action even in the face of adversity. These models have received relatively

less attention in the close relationships literature, although recent empirical work by Lydon and his colleagues (see Lydon, 1999) is likely to be instrumental in bringing these models to the fore.

5. Apart from a few studies that have been designed specifically to address this issue, researchers who have assessed companionate and passionate love generally have not compared levels of these constructs at different lengths of relationships. Moreover, there are debates about whether it is more meaningful to compare relationships in terms of stages, rather than duration per se (e.g., Acker & Davis, 1992; Sprecher & Regan, 1998). The focus in this chapter is levels of passionate and companionate love as reported at any given time in a relationship.

6. With regard to gender differences, it has been generally reported in the literature that women's experience of love is more companionate than men's, whereas men's experience is more romantic or passionate (see, e.g., Brehm, 1985; Hendrick & Hendrick, 1995). In table 1 there is evidence that women report higher levels of companionate love in their relationships than do men, although there also are a number of cases in which this gender difference is not significant. Interestingly, the studies included in table 1 do not support the view that men experience higher levels of passionate love than do women. This is consistent with a recent trend toward the reporting of gender similarities, rather than differences, in romantic, passionate love (see, e.g., Hendrick & Hendrick, 1995).

7. A variety of satisfaction scales were used in these studies. The Relationship Assessment Scale (Hendrick, 1988), the Global Satisfaction scale of the Relationship Rating Form (Davis & Todd, 1985), and the Dyadic Adjustment Scale were the most commonly used. Researchers also frequently devised their own measure of satisfaction or simply relied on a single item (i.e., "how satisfied are you in this relationship?"). These various measures of satisfaction tended to produce similar results.

8. When single items were used, companionate love was defined for participants as caring and affection and passionate love was defined as intense longing for union with the other. For men, the correlation between satisfaction and companionate love measured in this way was .52 versus .50 for passionate love; for women these relations were reversed: .28 for companionate love; .38 for passionate love.

9. It is difficult to pinpoint why the Storge scale produces different results than the other sales that were taken as measures of companionate love. One difference between this scale and the others is that the Storge scale is worded in terms of one's general attitudes toward love and experiences in past relationships, in addition to one's current relationship experience, whereas the other scales focus only on the latter. However, if one examines the findings obtained with the relationship-specific version of the love style scales (Hendrick & Hendrick, 1990), the difference between ratings of the Storge and Eros scales is even more pronounced (in the direction of greater endorsement of Eros) than with the general version of these scales. The Storge scale does appear to be more narrowly focused on the friendship aspect of love than the other scales, which tend to measure companionate love in a more multi-faceted way (e.g., assessing trust, respect, supportiveness, warmth). However, it seems unlikely that this difference could produce findings for the Storge scale *opposite* to those obtained with other measures of companionate love. It would be useful to subject the items of the Storge scale and the other scales to factor analysis in order to determine the areas of commonality and divergence between these measures.

References

Acker, M., & Davis, M. H. (1992). Intimacy, passion and commitment in adult romantic relationships: A test of the triangular theory of love. *Journal of Social and Personal Relationships, 9*, 21–50.

Adams, J. M., & Jones, W. H. (1997). The conceptualization of marital commitment: An integrative analysis. *Journal of Personality and Social Psychology, 72*, 1177–1196.

Adams, J. M., & Jones, W. H. (1999). Interpersonal commitment in historical perspective. In J. M. Adams & W. H. Jones (Eds.), *Handbook of interpersonal commitment and stability* (pp. 3–33). New York: Kluwer Academic/Plenum.

Ainsworth, M. D. S., Blehar, M. C., Waters, E., & Wall, S. (1978). *Patterns of attachment: A psychological study of the strange situation.* Hillsdale, NJ: Erlbaum.

Aron, A., & Aron, E. N. (1986). *Love and the expansion of self: Understanding attraction and satisfaction.* Washington, DC: Harper & Row.

Aron, A., & Aron, E. N. (1997). Self-expansion motivation and including other in the self. In S. Duck (Ed.), *Handbook of personal relationships* (2nd ed., pp. 251–270). Chichester, England: Wiley.

Aron, A., Aron, E. N., & Smollan, D. (1992). Inclusion of Other in the Self Scale and the structure of interpersonal closeness. *Journal of Personality and Social Psychology, 63*, 596–612.

Aron, A., & Westbay, L. (1996). Dimensions of the prototype of love. *Journal of Personality and Social Psychology, 70*, 535–551.

Bailey, W. C., Hendrick, C., & Hendrick, S. S. (1987). Relation of sex and gender role to love, sexual attitudes, and self-esteem. *Sex Roles, 16*, 637–648.

Baldwin, M. W., & Fehr, B. (1995). On the instability of attachment style ratings. *Personal Relationships, 2*, 247–261.

Bartholomew, K. (1990). Avoidance of intimacy: An attachment perspective. *Journal of Social and Personal Relationships, 7*, 147–178.

Bartholomew, K., & Horowitz, L. M. (1991). Attachment styles among young adults: A test of a four-category model. *Journal of Personality and Social Psychology, 61*, 226–244.

Berscheid, E., & Walster, E. (1974). A little bit about love. In T. L. Huston (Ed.), *Foundations of interpersonal attraction* (pp. 355–381). New York: Academic Press.

Bierhoff, H. W. (1991). Twenty years of research on love: Theory, results, and prospects for the future. *The German Journal of Psychology, 15*, 95–117.

Bookwala, J., Frieze, I. H., & Grote, N. K. (1994). Love, aggression and satisfaction in dating relationships. *Journal of Social and Personal Relationships, 11*, 625–632.

Bowlby, J. (1969). *Attachment and loss: Vol. 1. Attachment.* New York: Basic Books.

Brehm, S. S. (1985). *Intimate relationships.* New York: Random House.

Brickman, P. (1987). Commitment. In C. B. Wortman & R. Sorrentino (Eds.), *Commitment, conflict, and Caring* (pp. 1–18). Englewood Cliffs, NJ: Prentice Hall.

Buss, D. M. (1988). The evolutionary biology of love. In R. J. Sternberg & M. L. Barnes (Eds.), *The psychology of love* (pp. 100–118). New Haven, CT: Yale University Press.

Button, C. M., and Collier, D. R. (1991, June). *A comparison of people's concepts of love and romantic love.* Paper presented at the Canadian Psychological Association conference, Calgary, Alberta.

Cassidy, J., & Shaver, P. R. (Eds.). (1999). *Handbook of attachment: Theory, research, and clinical applications.* New York: Guilford Press.

Collins, N. L., & Read, S. J. (1990). Adult attachment, working models, and relationship quality in dating couples. *Journal of Personality and Social Psychology, 58*, 644–663.

Davila, J., Karney, B. R., & Bradbury, T. N. (1999). Attachment change processes in the early years of marriage. *Journal of Personality and Social Psychology, 76*, 783–802.

Davis, K. E., & Latty-Mann, H. (1987). Love styles and relationship quality: A contribution to validation. *Journal of Social and Personal Relationships, 4*, 409–428.

Davis, K. E., & Roberts, M. K. (1985). Relationships in the real world: The descriptive psychology approach to personal relationships. In K. J. Gergen & K. E. Davis (Eds.), *The social construction of the person.* New York: Springer-Verlag.

Davis, K. E., & Todd, M. J. (1982). Friendship and love in relationships. In K. E. Davis & T. Mitchell (Eds.), *Advances in descriptive psychology* (Vol. 2, pp. 79–122). London: JAI Press.

Davis, K., & Todd, M. J. (1985). Assessing friendship: Prototypes, paradigm cases and relationship description. In S. Duck & D. Perlman (Eds.), *Understanding personal relationships: An interdisciplinary approach* (pp. 17–34). Beverly Hills, CA: Sage.

Feeney, J. A., & Noller, P. (1990). Attachment style as a predictor of adult romantic relationships. *Journal of Personality and Social Psychology, 58*, 281–291.

Fehr, B. (1988). Prototype analysis of the concepts of love and commitment. *Journal of Personality and Social Psychology, 55*, 557–579.

Fehr, B. (1993). How do I love thee? Let me consult my prototype. In S. Duck (Ed.), *Individuals in relationships* (Vol. 1, pp. 87–120). Newbury Park, CA: Sage.

Fehr, B. (1994). Prototype-based assessment of laypeople's views of love. *Personal Relationships, 1*, 309–331.

Fehr, B. (1999). Laypeople's conceptions of commitment. *Journal of Personality and Social Psychology, 76*, 90–103.

Fehr, B., & Russell, J. A. (1991). The concept of love viewed from a prototype perspective. *Journal of Personality and Social Psychology, 60*, 425–438.

Fitness, J., & Fletcher, G. J. O. (1993). Love, hate, anger, and jealousy in close relationships: A prototype and cognitive appraisal analysis. *Journal of Personality and Social Psychology, 65*, 942–958.

Fraley, R. C., Davis, K. E. & Shaver, P. R. (1997). Dismissing-avoidance and the defensive organization of emotion, cognition and behavior. In J. A. Simpson & W. S. Rholes (Eds.), *Attachment theory and close relationships* (pp. 249–279). New York: Guilford Press.

Frazier, P. A., & Esterly, E. (1990). Correlates of relationship beliefs: Gender, relationship experience and relationship satisfaction. *Journal of Social and Personal Relationships, 7*, 331–352.

Griffin, D. F., & Bartholomew, K. (1994). The metaphysics of measurement: the case of adult attachment. In D. Perlman and K. Bartholomew (Eds.), *Advances in Personal Relationships*, Vol. 5: *Attachment processes in adulthood* (pp. 17–52). London: Jessica Kingsley.

Grote, N. K., & Frieze, I. H. (1994). The measurement of friendship-based love in intimate relationships. *Personal Relationships, 1*, 275–300.

Grote, N. K., Frieze, I. H., & Stone, C. A. (1996). Children, traditionalism in the division of family work, and marital satisfaction: "What's love got to do with it?" *Personal Relationships, 5*, 211–228.

Hatfield, E., & Rapson, R. L. (1993). *Love, sex, and intimacy: Their psychology, biology, and history.* New York: HarperCollins.

Hatfield, E., & Sprecher, S. (1986). Measuring passionate love in intimate relationships. *Journal of Adolescence, 9*, 383–410.

Hatfield, E., Traupmann, J., & Sprecher, S. (1984). Older women's perceptions of their intimate relationships. *Journal of Social and Clinical Psychology, 2*, 108–124.

Hazan, C., & Shaver, P. R. (1987). Romantic love conceptualized as an attachment process. *Journal of Personality and Social Psychology, 52*, 511–524.

Hecht, M. L., Marston, P. J., & Larkey, L. K. (1994). Love ways and relationship quality in heterosexual relationships. *Journal of Social and Personal Relationships, 11*, 25–43.

Hendrick, S. S. (1985). A generic measure of relationship satisfaction. *Journal of Marriage and the Family, 50*, 93–98.

Hendrick, S. S. (1998). A generuic measure of relationship satisfaction. *Journal of Marriage and the Family, 50*, 93–98.

Hendrick, S. S., Dicke, A., & Hendrick, C. (1998). The Relationship Assessment Scale. *Journal of Social and Personal Relationships, 15*, 137–142.

Hendrick, C., & Hendrick, S. S. (1986). A theory and method of love. *Journal of Personality and Social Psychology, 50*, 392–402.

Hendrick, C., & Hendrick, S. S. (1988). Lovers wear rose colored glasses. *Journal of Social and Personal Relationships, 5*, 161–183.

Hendrick, C., & Hendrick, S. S. (1989). Research on love: Does it measure up? *Journal of Personality and Social Psychology, 56*, 784–794.

Hendrick, C., & Hendrick, S. S. (1990). A relationship specific version of the Love Attitudes Scale. *Journal of Social Behavior and Personality, 5*, 239–254.

Hendrick, C., & Hendrick, S. S. (1991). Dimensions of love: A sociobiological perspective. *Journal of Social and Clinical Psychology, 10*, 206–230.

Hendrick, S. S., & Hendrick, C. (1993). Lovers as friends. *Journal of Social and Personal Relationships*, *10*, 459–466.

Hendrick, S. S., & Hendrick, C. (1995). Gender differences and similarities in sex and love. *Personal Relationships*, *2*, 55–65.

Hendrick, S. S., & Hendrick, C. (1997). Love and satisfaction. In R. J. Sternberg & M. Hojjat (Eds.). Satisfaction in close relationships (pp. 56–78). New York: Guilford Press.

Hendrick, S. S., Hendrick, C., & Adler, N. L. (1988). Romantic relationships: Love, satisfaction, and staying together. *Journal of Personality and Social Psychology*, *54*, 980–988.

Hendrick, C., Hendrick, S. S., & Dicke, J. (1998). The Love Attitudes Scale: short form. *Journal of Social and Personal Relationships*, *15*, 147–159.

Hendrick, C., Hendrick, S. S., Foote, F. H., & Slapion-Foote, M. J. (1984). Do men and women love differently? *Journal of Social and Personal Relationships*, *1*, 177–195.

Johnson, M. P. (1973). Commitment: A conceptual structure and empirical application. *Sociological Quarterly*, *14*, 395–406.

Johnson, M. P. (1982). Social and cognitive features of the dissolution of commitment to relationships. In S. Duck (Ed.), *Personal Relationships 4: Dissolving personal relationships* (pp. 51–73). New York: Academic Press.

Johnson, M. P. (1991). Commitment to personal relationships. In W. H. Jones & D. W. Perlman (Eds.), *Advances in personal relationships* (Vol. 3, pp. 117–143). London: Jessica Kingsley.

Johnson, M. P., Caughlin, J. P., & Huston, T. L. (1999). The tripartite nature of marital commitment: Personal, moral, and structural reasons to stay married. *Journal of Marriage and the Family*, *61*, 160–177.

Jones, W. H., Adams, J. M., Monroe, P. R., & Berry, J. O. (1995). A psychometric exploration of marital satisfaction and commitment. *Journal of Social Behavior and Personality*, *10*, 923–932.

Kelley, H. H. (1983). Love and commitment. In H. H. Kelley, E. Berscheid, A. Christensen, J. H. Harvey, T. L. Huston, G. Levinger, E. McClintock, L. A. Peplau, & D. R. Peterson (Eds.), *Close relationships* (pp. 265–314). New York: W. H. Freeman.

Kelley, H. H., & Thibaut, J. W. (1979). *Interpersonal relations: A theory of interdependence*. New York: Wiley-Interscience.

Lasswell, T. E., & Lasswell, M. E. (1976). I love you but I'm not in love with you. *Journal of Marriage and Family Counseling*, *2*, 211–224.

Lee, J. A. (1973). *The colours of love*. Don Mills, Ontario: New Press.

Levesque, R. J. R. (1993). The romantic experience of adolescents in satisfying love relationships. *Journal of Youth and Adolescence*, *22*, 219–251.

Levinger, G. (1965). Marital cohesiveness and dissolution: An integrative review. *Journal of Marriage and the Family*, *27*, 19–28.

Levy, M. B., & Davis, K. E. (1988). Love styles and attachment styles compared: Their relations to each other and to various relationship characteristics. *Journal of Social and Personal Relationships*, *5*, 439–471.

Luby, V., & Aron, A. (1990, July). *A prototype structuring of love, like, and being in love*. Paper presented at the Fifth International Conference on Personal Relationships, Oxford, UK.

Lydon, J. (1996). Toward a theory of commitment. In C. Seligman, J. Olson, & M. Zanna (Eds.), *Values: The eighth Ontario symposium* (pp. 191–213). Hillsdale, NJ: Erlbaum.

Lydon, J. (1999). Commitment and adversity: A reciprocal relation. In J. M. Adams & W. H. Jones (Eds.), *Handbook of interpersonal commitment and relationship stability* (pp. 193–203). New York: Kluwer Academic/Plenum.

Lydon, J., Dunkel-Schetter, C., Cohan, C., & Pierce, T. (1996). Pregnancy decision making as a significant life event: A commitment approach. *Journal of Personality and Social Psychology*, *71*, 141–151.

Lydon, J., Meana, M., Sepinwall, D., Richard, N., & Mayman, S. (1999). The commitment calibration hypothesis: When do people devalue attractive alternatives. *Personality and Social Psychology Bulletin*, *25*, 152–161.

Lydon, J., Pierce, T., & O'Regan, S. (1997). Coping with moral commitment to long-distance dating relationships. *Journal of Personality and Social Psychology*, *73*, 104–113.

Lydon, J., & Zanna, M. (1990). Commitment in the face of adversity: A value-affirmation approach. *Journal of Personality and Social Psychology, 58*, 1040–1047.

Meeks, B. S., Hendrick, S. S., & Hendrick, C. (1998). Communication, love and relationship satisfaction. *Journal of Social and Personal Relationships, 15*, 755–773.

Mervis, C. B., & Rosch, E. (1981). Categorization of natural objects. *Annual Review of Psychology, 32*, 89–115.

Money, J. (1980). *Love and sickness*. Baltimore: Johns Hopkins University Press.

Morrow, G. D., Clark, E. M., & Brock, K. F. (1995). Individual and partner love styles: Implications for the quality of romantic involvements. *Journal of Social and Personal Relationships, 12*, 363–387.

Murstein, B. I., Merighi, J., & Vyse, S. A. (1991). Love styles in the United States and France: A cross-cultural comparison. *Journal of Social and Clinical Psychology, 10*, 37–46.

Richardson, D. R., Medvin, N., & Hammock, G. (1988). Love styles, relationship experience, and sensation seeking: A test of validity. *Personality and Individual Differences, 9*, 645–651.

Rosch, E. H. (1973). Natural categories. *Cognitive Psychology, 4*, 328–350.

Rosenblatt, P. C. (1977). Needed research on commitment in marriage. In G. Levinger & H. L. Rausch (Eds.), *Close relationships* (pp. 73–86). Amherst: University of Massachusetts Press.

Rubin, Z. (1970). Measurement of romantic love. *Journal of Personality and Social Psychology, 16*, 265–273.

Rusbult, C. E. (1980a). Commitment and satisfaction in romantic associations: A test of the investment model. *Journal of Experimental Social Psychology, 16*, 172–186.

Rusbult, C. E. (1980b). Satisfaction and commitment in friendships. *Representative Research in Social Psychology, 11*, 96–105.

Rusbult, C. E., Martz, J. M., & Agnew, C. R. (1998). The Investment Model Scale: Measuring commitment level, satisfaction level, quality of alternatives, and investment size. *Personal Relationships, 5*, 357–391.

Scharfe, E., & Bartholomew, K. (1994). Reliability and stability of adult attachment patterns. *Personal Relationships, 1*, 23–43.

Shaver, P. R., & Hazan, C. (1993). Adult romantic attachment: Theory and evidence. In D. Perlman & W. H. Jones (Eds.), *Advances in personal relationships* (Vol. 4, pp. 29–70). London: Jessica Kingsley.

Shaver, P., Schwartz, J., Kirson, D., & O'Connor, C. (1987). Emotion knowledge: Further exploration of a prototype approach. *Journal of Personality and Social Psychology, 52*, 1061–1086.

Simpson, J. A. (1990). Influence of attachment styles on romantic relationships. *Journal of Personality and Social Psychology, 59*, 971–980.

Solomon, R. C. (1981). *Love: Emotion, myth and metaphor*. Garden City, NY: Anchor Press/Doubleday.

Sprecher, S., Aron, A., Hatfield, E., Cortese, A., Potapova, E., & Levitskaya, A. (1994). Love: American style, Russian style, and Japanese style. *Personal Relationships, 1*, 349–369.

Sprecher, S., & Regan, P. C. (1998). Passionate and companionate love in courting and young married couples. *Sociological Inquiry, 68*, 163–185.

Stanley, S. M., & Markman, H. J. (1992). Assessing commitment in personal relationships. *Journal of Marriage and the Family, 54*, 595–608.

Sternberg, R. J. (1986). A triangular theory of love. *Psychological Review, 93*, 119–135.

Sternberg, R. J. (1997). Construct validation of a triangular love scale. *European Journal of Social Psychology, 27*, 313–335.

Thibaut, J. W., & Kelley, H. H. (1959). *The social psychology of groups*. New York: Wiley.

Traupmann, J., & Hatfield, E. (1981). Love and its effect on mental and physical health. In R. W. Fogel, E. Hatfield, S. B. Kiesler, & E. Shanas (Eds.), *Aging: stability and change in the family*. New York: Academic Press.

Walster, E., & Walster, G. W. (1978). *A new look at love*. Reading, MA: Addison-Wesley.

PART IV

Social Influence and Comparison

14   Interdependence in Close Relationships   359
     Caryl E. Rusbult, Ximena B. Arriaga, and Christopher R. Agnew

15   Social Comparison and Close Relationships   388
     Bram P. Buunk and Frans L. Oldersma

PART IV

Chapter Fourteen

Interdependence in Close Relationships

Caryl E. Rusbult, Ximena B. Arriaga, and Christopher R. Agnew

If we want to understand behavior in close relationships, should we examine the relationship per se or should we examine the individuals of which a relationship is composed? In explaining important phenomena, should we emphasize properties of dyads or properties of actors? Most theories of close relationships explain behavior by reference to properties that reside *within actors* – by reference to individual-level cognition (Baldwin, 1992), dispositions (Hazan & Shaver, 1994), motives (Aron & Aron, 1997), or biology (Kenrick & Trost, 1997). In contrast, interdependence theory explains behavior by reference to properties that reside *between actors* – by reference to features of interactions and relationships (Kelley & Thibaut, 1978; Thibaut & Kelley, 1959). Thus, interdependence theory provides a uniquely interpersonal analysis of relationships.

Why should we concern ourselves with interdependence? First, interdependence shapes everyday interaction. Interdependence patterns describe the opportunities and constraints that characterize interaction, defining the potential in an interaction for congeniality, contentiousness, and exploitation. Second, interdependence shapes mental events – cognition and affect reflect our attempts to understand the meaning of interdependence situations, toward identifying appropriate action in such situations. Third, interdependence shapes relationships. Interdependence properties describe the options and limitations that characterize relationships, defining the possibilities for commitment, trust, power, and conflict. And fourth, interdependence shapes the self. People develop relatively stable preferences, motives, and behavioral tendencies as a consequence of adaptation to frequently-encountered interdependence situations.

This chapter outlines the basic principles of interdependence theory. We begin by describing the manner in which individuals evaluate and select interaction partners. Following this, we discuss the nature of interaction and the importance of four key properties of

Correspondence should be addressed to Caryl Rusbult, Department of Psychology, University of North Carolina at Chapel Hill, Chapel Hill, North Carolina 27599-3270 (rusbult@unc.edu).

interdependence. Next, we describe transformation of motivation, as well as the embodiment of stable transformation tendencies in personal dispositions, relationship-specific motives, and social norms. Finally, we outline the maintenance mechanisms by which individuals manage to sustain healthy ongoing involvements, and review the manner in which relationships sometimes deteriorate and terminate.

The Evaluation and Selection of Interaction Partners

Biological and acquired needs

Unlike many theories, interdependence theory does not identify a primary need that governs human endeavors. Nevertheless, it is useful to consider the nature of the outcomes we attain in the course of everyday interaction, and to examine what we seek in long-term involvements. Humans presumably are born with a small set of survival needs, including the needs for food and shelter. Over time we develop additional needs, many of which are interpersonal. Some authors propose that the need to belong is a fundamental motive, emphasizing the implications of inadequate social bonds for physical and mental well-being (Baumeister & Leary, 1995). Others have delineated specific sources of fulfillment in ongoing relationships, identifying the needs for: (1) intimacy – sharing self-relevant information; (2) companionship – enjoying shared activities; (3) sexuality – gratifying each other's physical and sexual needs; (4) security – achieving a stable and reliable involvement; and (5) emotional involvement – belongingness, empathy, and "we-ness" (Drigotas & Rusbult, 1992). Thus, we depend on others for the fulfillment of many central needs.

Satisfaction and dependence

CL and satisfaction level.   Over the course of development we acquire expectations regarding need fulfillment. Once established, we evaluate new interactions and relationships by comparing experiences with our generalized expectations. Interdependence theory describes expectations in terms of *comparison level*, or CL (Thibaut & Kelley, 1959). CL is the standard against which we evaluate the "goodness" of interaction outcomes, and is shaped not only by direct experience but also by observing the interactions of friends and kin. Outcomes exceeding CL are experienced as satisfying, and outcomes below CL are dissatisfying. Diverse literatures reveal that satisfaction is influenced not only by the objective quality of outcomes but also by subjective standards. People are happier with close partners to the extent that the partner matches or exceeds their internal standards (Sternberg & Barnes, 1985; Wetzel & Insko, 1982). Also, research regarding nonromantic interactions reveals that when objective conditions compare unfavorably to internal standards, we experience dissatisfaction, dejection, and discontent (Crosby, 1976; Higgins, 1989).

Given that expectations are the product of experience, CL can change as a consequence of experience *within* a given relationship. For example, imagine that Mary has not experienced intense intimacy with previous romantic partners. If John discloses intimately and elicits intimate disclosure from her, Mary's CL for intimacy will rise. Over time, Mary will come to expect greater intimacy. The fact that CL rises to match current experiences has two important implications. First, given that satisfaction is greater to the extent that outcomes exceed CL, as CL rises we experience commensurately lower satisfaction – the mundane disclosure that yielded intense pleasure when Mary's CL was low will now yield reduced pleasure. Second, present and future relationships will be evaluated with a higher CL for intimacy – Mary will come to expect the level of intimacy she has experienced in her recent history (she will "take intimacy for granted").

Our earliest interaction experiences occur in infant–caregiver relationships. This initial bond produces important expectations by which later relationships are evaluated. Thus, the concept of CL shares some features with the attachment theory concept of mental model (Hazan & Shaver, 1994). However, attachment theory emphasizes the relevance of mental models to *all* adult relationships, stressing the *stability* of such expectations. Interdependence theory argues that expectations apply to *specific* sorts of interaction, suggesting that expectations are susceptible to *change*. CL not only shifts as a consequence of experience, but people also develop multiple CLs corresponding to the multiple interpersonal domains they encounter. A person may have one CL for intimacy with romantic partners, along with a different CL for companionship with tennis partners.

CL-alt and dependence level.   Typically, we experience interactions in light of the alternative circumstances in which we might find ourselves. Interdependence theory describes expectations regarding alternative interactions in terms of *comparison level for alternatives*, or CL-alt (Thibaut & Kelley, 1959). CL-alt describes the quality of the best available alternative to a relationship. What defines "best available alternative"? First, we may be aware of specific alternative interactions in which we might become involved. Second, our assessments may be influenced by the general quality of the "market" ("how favorable is the market for people of my age, gender, and orientation?"). Third, we may assess alternatives in terms of the option of independence ("could my needs be gratified by friends and kin, independent of a romantic involvement?").

CL-alt influences level of dependence, or the extent to which an individual relies uniquely on a relationship for attaining good outcomes. To the extent that the outcomes experienced with a partner exceed CL-alt the individual is increasingly dependent, or needs the partner. To the extent that outcomes are below CL-alt the individual is independent, and may abandon the partner for the best available alternative. The empirical literature reveals that dependence on a relationship is lower – and probabililty of breakup is greater – among individuals who experience poor outcomes in a relationship and regard their alternatives as attractive (Bui, Peplau, & Hill, 1996; Drigotas & Rusbult, 1992; Felmlee, Sprecher, & Bassin, 1990).

Satisfaction ("am I happy?") and dependence ("do I need this?") to some degree are independent. Figure 14.1 displays three relationships with equivalent outcomes. In Relationship A outcomes are much higher than CL and somewhat higher than CL-alt – the individual will feel very satisfied yet is only moderately dependent. In Relationship B outcomes are somewhat higher than CL and much higher than CL-alt – the individual will feel moderately satisfied yet is highly dependent. In Relationship C outcomes are lower than CL yet much higher than CL-alt. This configuration is termed *nonvoluntary dependence* – the relationship is *dis*satisfying but involves high dependence. In involvements such as Relationship C people may feel constrained, recognizing that they would incur high costs if they were to end the relationship. However, dependent individuals will not necessarily regard themselves as victims of constraint. In Relationships A and B people are unlikely to experience constraint - although they are dependent, because the relationship is satisfying, the decision to persist may be experienced as voluntary.

The importance of nonvoluntary dependence is illustrated by research regarding the decision to persist in abusive relationships. Although some researchers explain persistence with a battering partner by reference to the abused person's maladaptive dispositions (learned helplessness, low self-esteem), persistence may be governed in part by dependence. The empirical literature reveals that although an abused woman's outcomes may be poor, her alternatives – especially her economic alternatives – may be worse. Compared to women who exit abusive relationships, women who remain with their abusive partners have less job training, less work experience, and fewer employment opportunities (Rusbult & Martz, 1995; Strube, 1988). Thus, people do not necessarily remain with abusive partners because they possess maladaptive dispositions – sometimes they remain because they are dependent on their relationships and have nowhere else to go.

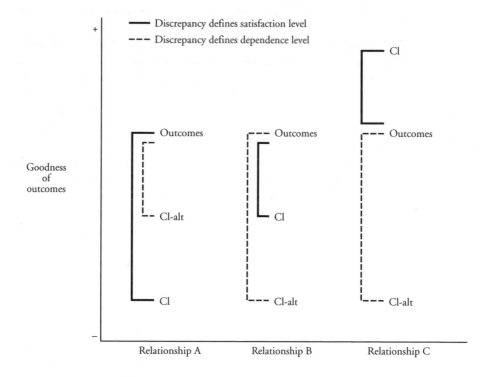

Figure 14.1   Patterns of voluntary versus nonvoluntary dependence.

Selecting interaction partners

People make choices in life. We choose to engage in some interactions but not others, and we establish some relationships but not others. To make such selections, we examine the rewards and costs of multiple interaction partners, exploring the possibilities for satisfying outcomes via direct or imagined interaction. At a given time and place, not all people are available as partners. Some people are unavailable because they are committed to monogamous involvements, some choose to make themselves unavailable (they may place greater value on other life activities), and some are unavailable due to constraints based on age or geography. Among the multiple persons who are available at a given time and place, we select as friends and lovers those persons with the highest "partner value" – those who offer the greatest opportunities for the fulfillment of important needs.

Of course, partner choice is a bilateral event. Actors cannot unilaterally choose to form relationships with specific partners – the partner must also choose to form a relationship with the actor. When people form mutually exclusive relationships, the fact of bilateral choice implies that people will pair up with targets possessing similar partner value (Kelley, 1990). How so? If everyone in the pool of available partners seeks the partner with the greatest value, those persons with the highest value will tend to pair off earliest. Among those who remain in the pool, people continue to seek partners with the greatest value, which means that those people with the next highest value will pair off next. The process of partner selection continues in such a manner until the only people available are those with relatively low value, who themselves will pair off.

Following an assortative process whereby each person seeks to form a relationship with a partner possessing the highest value, the result will be pairings in which partners offer similar "value" in terms of attractiveness, sociability, and other desirable qualities. "Value" is interchangeable in two respects (Kelley, 1990): (1) value is interchangeable within an actor – a deficiency with respect to one dimension may be compensated for by high value with respect to another dimension (Mary may have high value because she is intelligent or because she is warm); and (2) value is interchangeable within an actor–target relationship – the actor and target may provide value to each other on differing dimensions (Mary may exchange her intelligence for John's physical attractiveness).

The empirical literature supports the assertion that people with comparable value tend to form relationships. Close partners exhibit "matching" with respect to physical attractiveness, attitudes, and abilities (Byrne, 1971; Caspi & Herbener, 1990; Feingold, 1988). Is matching an inadvertent consequence of assortative mating, whereby all people seek partners with high value (cf. Kalick & Hamilton, 1986)? Does the active pursuit of partners with comparable value play any role in producing matching? Kelley (1990) identifies four complementary mechanisms by which matching may come about: (1) market principles – the more desirable an actor is, the more desirable a partner that person can attract; (2) level of aspiration – actors pursue partners who are desirable yet attainable (fear of rejection drives this phenomenon); (3) mutuality – actors anticipate that relationships involving nonmutuality will not be stable, and avoid forming such relationships (fear of desertion drives this phenomenon); and (4) equality – actors prefer relationships in which the partners' value is equal.

Interaction and Interdependence

Interaction is the elemental feature of interdependence (Thibaut & Kelley, 1959). By *interaction* we refer to the fact that people engage in behaviors that affect both their own well-being and the well-being of others. Specifically, actors simultaneously or sequentially enact behaviors with implications for their own and their partners' (1) immediate behavioral options and outcomes, as well as for (2) the future situations, options, and outcomes that are made available (or eliminated) as a consequence of their actions. Thus, the options that are available to us and the outcomes that we experience are not a sole function of our own actions. John's decision to quit his job has implications for Mary; Mary's decision to train for a marathon has implications for John. In short, and to state the obvious: No person is an island.

Interdependence theory employs the *outcome matrix* to analyze interaction (Thibaut & Kelley, 1959). The matrix is a theoretical tool, not a literal portrayal of lay cognition. (Presumably, humans do not experience interaction in terms of 2 × 2 matrices.) A specific matrix pattern may represent a class of situations with dissimilar superficial features. The importance of the matrix lies not in the specific behaviors and outcomes that are depicted, but in the pattern of outcomes the representation reveals. The columns in a matrix represent Person A's behavioral options and the rows represent Person B's options. Each cell is associated with two outcome values, representing the joint occurrence of A's behavior and B's behavior; the two values in each cell represent the impact of each joint event on each person.

Figure 14.2 represents a simple interaction for John and Mary. Neither John nor Mary has done any housecleaning for a month. Neither person likes housecleaning, but both dislike their filthy house. If both John and Mary clean the house, both enjoy the moderate pleasure of an improved environment (4 and 4). Both would prefer that the partner clean

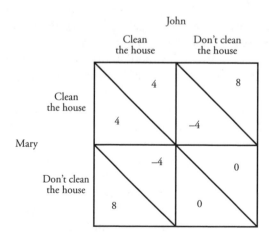

Figure 14.2   Matrix representation of interaction outcomes.

the house (8), but each is irritated by the prospect of cleaning while the partner takes a free ride (–4). The cooperative choice would be to commence cleaning. At the same time, both dislike cleaning, so each is tempted to "defect" by letting the partner do the cleaning. If both defect and pursue their direct self-interest by failing to clean, both suffer poor outcomes (0 and 0).

Of course, interaction situations frequently are more intricate than symmetrical 2 × 2 matrices: Partners may possess more than two behavioral options, each actor may possess options not shared by the partner, people may hold differing preferences for joint events, and interaction may involve more than two people. Also, the behavioral repertoires of the individuals may change over time, their preferences may change, and earlier behavioral choices may modify the range of options or the preferences attached to options in the future. The matrix is a snapshot of interaction as it exists at one time. Although this tool ignores the dynamics of action-and-reaction in ongoing relationships, the static quality of the matrix allows for a rich analysis of the abstract properties of interdependence.

Interdependence describes the strength and quality of the effects interacting people exert on one another's preferences, motives, and behavior. In what ways do people influence their own and others' outcomes? The matrix in figure 14.2 involves some *actor control* ("reflexive control") – the degree to which the actor unilaterally influences his or her personal well-being (the main effect of actor is ±2). This matrix also involves some *partner control* ("fate control") – the degree to which the partner unilaterally influences the actor's well-being (the main effect of partner is ±4). This matrix involves no *joint control* ("behavior control") – the degree to which the partners' joint actions influence the actor's well-being (the actor by partner interaction is ±0). Thus, this matrix represents a situation in which each actor's well-being is only weakly influenced by his or her own actions, but is powerfully influenced by the partner's actions. If each person pursues that which is dictated by actor control (not cleaning), both suffer poor outcomes. As we shall see, issues such as greed, fear, and trust are relevant to understanding an interaction situation such as the matrix in figure 14.2.

Key Properties of Interdependence Structure

Interdependence theory is first and foremost a theory of situations – a theory of the meaningful ways in which interactions and relationships differ (Kelley, 1997). Some properties may be present across most or all interactions encountered by a given dyad. For example, Mary may rely on John's actions for attaining good outcomes more than John relies on Mary's actions – the interpersonal arena consistently may be defined by unequal dependence. Other properties may vary dramatically from one interaction to the next for a given dyad. For example, John and Mary may have closely aligned preferences for movies, but may have disparate preferences for ways of entertaining friends.

The infinite number of possible outcome patterns across interactions can be analyzed by reference to matrices. Just as the Lewinian life space served as a tool for understanding individual experience, the matrix is a tool for understanding interpersonal experience. The numbers displayed in matrices are numeric depictions of preferences, scaled with CL-alt as the zero point. Thus, outcome values "indicate the degree to which each person is dependent on the dyad" (Kelley & Thibaut, 1978, p. 10). Given that matrices represent each person's outcomes in relation to each person's dependence, matrices depict *outcome interdependence*. Kelley and Thibaut (1978) presented a logical analysis of all possible patterns of interdependence as indicated in 2 × 2 matrices. This analysis yields a typology of situations in which interdependence patterns vary with respect to four key properties: level of dependence, mutuality of dependence, basis of dependence, and correspondence of outcomes.

Level of dependence

Level of dependence describes the degree to which each actor's well-being is influenced by the behavior of the partner, or the extent to which each person relies on the relationship to obtain outcomes better than those obtainable in the next best alternative (Kelley & Thibaut, 1978): Does John rely on Mary for attaining good outcomes, and does he therefore "need" Mary? As depicted in a matrix, dependence describes the extent to which each actor's outcomes can be influenced by the partner's unilateral actions or by the partners' joint actions. As such, actor dependence is the converse of partner power – John's dependence on Mary and Mary's power over John are two perspectives regarding a single outcome structure.

Sometimes people are dependent because alternative involvements would yield poor outcomes. Sometimes dependence is high because the costs of ending a relationship (or establishing a new one) are high. The costs of ending a relationship have been described in terms of investments in a relationship (Rusbult, 1983), termination costs (M. Johnson, 1991), and barrier forces (Levinger, 1979). Although an alternative relationship may be attractive, promising to provide outcomes that exceed both CL and the outcomes attainable in the present relationship, if the costs of ending a relationship and establishing a new one outweigh the potential for reward in the alternative relationship, the actor essentially is forced to persist in the current relationship.

Dependence exerts profound effects on interaction. To the extent that an actor is dependent on a partner, the actor is tied to the relationship and becomes increasingly unlikely to end it (Bui et al., 1996; Felmlee et al., 1990; Rusbult, 1983). Also, because dependent individuals wish to sustain their relationships, they exhibit a variety of "maintenance acts" that tend to enhance couple well-being, including constructive conflict resolution, willingness to sacrifice, and a variety of cognitive maneuvers that support the decision to persist (Rusbult, Verette, Whitney, Slovik, & Lipkus, 1991; Simpson, Gangestad, & Lerma, 1990; Van Lange, Rusbult et al., 1997). (We say more about related issues later.)

At the same time, dependence can be problematic. Dependent individuals experience distress when the continuation of a relationship is threatened, and may experience jealousy or feel threatened by the partner's good alternatives (A. Buunk, 1991; Simpson, 1987). Also, dependence sometimes takes on the properties of entrapment – once individuals commit resources to a course of action, they sometimes persist well beyond the point at which it would be rational to desist (Brockner & Rubin, 1985; Teger, 1980). Moreover, given that dependence involves relying on a partner for the fulfillment of important needs, dependence implies vulnerability. Such vulnerability can be particularly onerous for actors who are at the mercy of uncaring or malevolent partners.

Mutuality of dependence

This describes the degree to which actors exert equal effects on one another's well-being (Kelley & Thibaut, 1978). When just one person is dependent, a relationship involves *unilateral dependence*; when both are dependent a relationship involves *mutual dependence*. It is instructive to discuss this property not only in terms of symmetry of dependence, but also in terms of symmetry of power: John's power is greater than Mary's to the degree that (1) John possesses the power to provide (or not provide) Mary with outcomes of higher quality than she can provide him, (2) John has the power to provide (or not provide) Mary with outcomes of poorer quality than she can provide him, and (3) John has more attractive alternatives than Mary.

Mutuality of dependence yields benefits that parallel those accruing from balance of power. Given that mutually dependent partners possess equal control over one another's outcomes, there is reduced potential for exploitation. Research regarding the "principle of least interest" demonstrates that the partner receiving higher outcomes in a relationship tends to exhibit enhanced dependence and reduced decision-making power (Sprecher, 1985). Also, because mutually dependent partners are equally motivated to behave in such a manner as to sustain their involvement, there is less potential for disruptive emotions such as insecurity or guilt. Indeed, the empirical literature reveals that mutuality is associated with enhanced couple functioning (Drigotas, Rusbult, & Verette, 1999).

Cross-cultural, historical analyses suggest that patterns of mutuality may originate in features of the field of eligibles. Imbalanced sex ratios – circumstances where the ratio of men to women deviates from 1.0 – "dramatically influence the gender roles of men and women, shape the forms taken by relationships between men and women, and in turn produce changes in family structures and stimulate new kinds of association along gender lines" (Secord, 1983, p. 525). A high ratio of men to women is associated with valuing young women, norms of commitment, traditional division of labor, and sexual morality; a low ratio is associated with sexual libertarianism, brief liaisons, and tendencies for women to establish themselves as independent agents.

It is easy to imagine that differential dependence typically yields abuse, in that low-power persons can do little but appease high-power persons, who possess the wherewithal to use their power as they wish. Indeed, when partners' preferences are incompatible, nonmutuality produces suspicion and insecurity, abuse of power, and avoidance of interaction (Tjosvold, 1981). However, given moderate to high compatibility of preferences, nonmutual dependence activates norms of social responsibility whereby high-power persons assist low-power persons (Berkowitz & Daniels, 1963). Also, in situations of nonmutual dependence low-power partners develop tactics for encouraging formal agreements through which exploitation may be prevented (Thibaut & Gruder, 1969).

Basis of dependence

Basis of dependence describes the degree to which each actor's well-being is influenced by (1) the partner's unilateral actions versus (2) the partners' joint actions (Kelley & Thibaut,

1978): Are John's outcomes shaped largely by Mary's actions, or are his outcomes shaped by his own actions in concert with her actions? As noted earlier, the outcomes of interacting persons may reflect two types of control: partner control exists when the actor's outcomes are influenced by the partner's behavior, whereas joint control exists when the actor's outcomes are influenced by his or her own behavior in concert with the partner's behavior. If an actor's outcomes are unaffected by the partner's behavior, the actor is said to exercise high actor control, or independence.

When each person holds partner control over the other, interaction rests on "exchange," and achieving good outcomes requires establishing norms of reciprocity over an extended time period ("I'll scratch your back this time if you scratch mine next time"). Given that freeloading is a chronic problem in such situations, relationships that defy the "tit-for-tat" rule yield lower outcomes for both persons over the course of extended involvement (Axelrod, 1984). Attempts to maintain fairness often result in threats, promises, or agreements that enhance the predictability of interaction (Orbell, Van de Kragt, & Dawes, 1988). In contrast, when each person holds joint control over the other, interaction rests on "coordination," and attaining good outcomes is contingent upon both partners enacting appropriate behaviors – the partners must coordinate their actions.

Correspondence of outcomes

This describes the extent to which the partners' well-being is similarly affected across the joint behavioral events that are available to them (Kelley & Thibaut, 1978): Is that which is good (or bad) for John the same as that which is good (or bad) for Mary? Correspondence does *not* necessarily imply similarity in the desirability of discrete behaviors. Partners may have correspondent preferences involving enactment of the same behavior (John and Mary enjoy playing golf together), but they may also have correspondent preferences involving enactment of different behaviors (an agreeable division of labor wherein John cooks and Mary cleans). Correspondence of outcomes defines a continuum ranging from perfect correspondence (pure coordination) through moderate correspondence (mixed-motive), to perfect noncorrespondence (zero-sum).

Correspondence influences interaction in four respects. First, given that this property identifies the possibilities for congenial versus conflictual interaction, correspondence exerts reliable effects on cognitive and perceptual processes, determining whether interactants feel that they are working with one another or against one another, whether their relationship is experienced as congeniality or war. Relationships characterized by noncorrespondence are stormy, with partners developing suspicious, distrustful, or even hostile attitudes toward one another (Blumstein & Schwartz, 1983; Gottman, 1979; Surra & Longstreth, 1990).

Second, correspondence is relevant to ease of decision making. Decisions are easy in correspondent situations, in that the rational choice is to behave in such a manner as to maximize both one's own and a partner's outcomes ("what's good for me is good for you"). Decisions are easy in noncorrespondent situations, in that the rational choice is to pursue self-interest (partners seldom worry about whether to compete in a tennis game). Moderately correspondent situations are maximally ambiguous with respect to the appropriateness of cooperation versus competition (Blumstein & Schwartz, 1983).

Third, correspondence sets the stage for the elicitation of key motives. Given that both partners cannot achieve good outcomes in perfectly noncorrespondent situations, as correspondence decreases, competitive motives are activated; as correspondence increases, cooperative motives are activated. Situations of moderate correspondence are ambiguous, and activate a variety of motives, including (1) fear, derived from the possibililty that a partner may not cooperate, and (2) greed, derived from the temptation to compete in response to a partner's cooperation (Rapoport, 1966).

Fourth, correspondence defines opportunities for the display of important motives. It is possible for John to demonstrate his trustworthiness in relatively noncorrespondent situations, in that such situations "test" trustworthiness – if John behaves cooperatively, thereby promoting Mary's interests at the expense of his own interests, it becomes clear that he is trustworthy (Wieselquist, Rusbult, Foster, & Agnew, 1999). Interestingly, John cannot demonstrate trustworthiness in perfectly correspondent situations – in a correspondent situation John's motives remain unclear, in that the behaviors promoting Mary's interests simultaneously promote his own interests.

Temporal features of interdependence

Kelley (1984b) expanded the analysis of interdependence through the use of *transition lists*: a "set of lists, each of which specifies each person's options . . . and the consequences for each person of each combination of their respective selections among their options" (p. 960). The transition list overcomes limitations of the static outcome matrix and addresses the temporal features of interaction by specifying how current actions enlarge or constrain subsequent outcomes or options. This means of representing interdependence allows us to describe interaction in terms of both (1) patterns of outcome interdependence, and (2) changes over time in patterns. In addition to characterizing outcome control, the transition list also characterizes *transition control*, or control over movement from one interaction situation to another.

In figure 14.3, List L represents John's and Mary's initial options (A1 vs. A2 for John, B1 vs. B2 for Mary), the immediate outcomes resulting from their joint actions (actor control; +5 vs. 0 for John, +10 vs. +5 for Mary), and the future situations that will come to pass as a result of each set of actions. In List L transition control rests in Mary's hands – B2 leaves the two in the safe List L, whereas B1 moves them to the perilous List M. If Mary pursues her direct self-interest in List L by enacting B1, the partners move to a situation in which Mary's outcomes are poor (−20 or 0). In List M outcome control and transition control shift to John's hands, and rescuing Mary requires an heroic act: by enacting A3 and suffering poor outcomes (−5) John ensures that Mary does not suffer catastrophic outcomes (0 rather than −20) and restores both partners to the safe List L. Despite its simplicity, this example conveys the sophistication of the transition list representation, illustrating how earlier choices influence options and outcomes that unfold in the future, as well as how patterns of outcome control and transition control can shift over the course of extended interaction.

Parallel to the bases of outcome control, transition control differs in (1) actor control over transitions across situations, (2) partner control over transitions, and (3) joint control

List	Option sets	Option pairs	Consequences		
			Outcomes		Transition
			John	Mary	(Next List)
L	(A1/A2)	A1 and B1	+5	+10	M
	(B1/B2)	A1 and B2	+5	+5	L
		A2 and B1	0	+10	M
		A2 and B2	0	+5	L
M	(A1/A2/A3)	A1 and B3	+5	−20	M
	(B3/B4)	A1 and B4	+5	−20	M
		A2 and B3	0	−20	M
		A2 and B4	0	−20	M
		A3 and B3	−5	0	L
		A3 and B4	−5	0	L

Figure 14.3   Transition list representation of interaction outcomes and transitions across interaction situations.

over transitions. In extended involvements, behavioral choices may be based not only on the options and outcomes that presently are available, but also on the future situations that will be made available (or eliminated) as a consequence of present choices. Indeed, choices at a given time may be influenced by desire to enhance future transition control, and conflict between partners may center as much on how best to employ transition control as on how best to employ outcome control.

Transformation of Motivation

The given situation and the effective situation

Why do different people react in different ways to the same interdependence pattern? If behavior were wholly determined by the pursuit of direct self-interest, people should react identically to the same situation (barring perceptual bias, random error, and the like). The interdependence distinction between the "given situation" and the "effective situation" provides a framework in which to address this issue (Kelley & Thibaut, 1978). The *given situation* describes each person's direct, personal well-being in a specific situation – each person's "gut level," self-interested behavioral preferences based on the immediate outcomes he or she would obtain.

Behavior frequently reflects more than the pursuit of self-interested, given situation preferences. Often, behavior is shaped by broader concerns, including strategic considerations, concern for the partner's well-being, or long-term goals. Departures from given preferences result from *transformation of motivation*, a process which leads people to relinquish their direct self-interest and act on the basis of broader considerations. When people behave in accord with transformed preferences, they respond to a given pattern as if it were a different one. The *effective situation* describes the modified preferences resulting from transformation. Reconceptualized preferences in the effective situation guide actual behavior.

The transformation process may yield any of a variety of reconceptualized orientations toward a situation (Kelley & Thibaut, 1978; McClintock, 1972). The process may yield *outcome transformation* – a shift from desire to maximize own immediate self-interest (MaxOwn) toward any of several alternative orientations, including (1) pro-relationship transformations such as desire to maximize joint outcomes (MaxJoint) or desire to maximize the partner's outcomes (MaxOther), and (2) anti-social transformations such as desire to minimize the partner's outcomes (MinOther) or desire to maximize the difference between own and partner's outcomes (MaxRel). The process may also yield orientations that deal with problematic temporal features of interaction, termed *transpositional and sequential transformations* (e.g., match what the other does, tit-for-tat).

Adaptation and the acquisition of stable transformation tendencies

Specific interaction patterns initially are experienced as unique problems or opportunities. Reactions to novel situations sometimes rest on conscious thought. John may consider his options, take account of his feelings for Mary and his goals for their future, and actively decide whether to behave selfishly or benevolently ("Mary hurt me, but I'm concerned about our future, so I'll inhibit my impulse to be hostile"). Alternatively, reactions may involve little conscious thought. John may react impulsively, automatically experiencing sympathy and reacting in a benevolent manner. In either event, the unique situation has been dealt with and experience has been acquired.

Over time, some interdependence patterns will be encountered regularly. Through the process of adaptation, people develop habitual tendencies to react to specific patterns in specific ways - that is, they develop habitual transformation tendencies (Kelley, 1983b). There are three mechanisms by which experience shapes habits: (1) *retroactive selection* (selective reinforcement) – as a consequence of behaving in a specific manner in a given interaction, certain preferences, motives, and behaviors are rewarded (or punished); (2) *preemptive selection* (selective instigation) – others enact behaviors that elicit (or inhibit) specific preferences, motives, and behaviors; and (3) *situation selection* (manipulation of interaction situations) – prior actions bring about situations in which specific preferences, motives, and behaviors become more (or less) probable.

Habitual transformation tendencies are guided by *interpersonal orientations*, defined as relatively stable partner- or pattern-contingent "solutions" to interaction situations (Rusbult & Van Lange, 1996). Habitual transformation tendencies are embodied in three types of interpersonal orientation: personal dispositions (e.g., attachment style), relationship-specific motives (e.g., trust level), and social norms (e.g., the Golden Rule). Given that habitual solutions typically are specific to a given partner or pattern of interdependence, it is useful to construe interpersonal orientations as contingency rules – as rules such as "behave benevolently in noncorrespondent interactions with Mary."

The transformation process

Human intelligence is highly interpersonal – we can identify key features of interactions insofar as such features are relevant to personal well-being, recognizing that some interaction situations resemble previously encountered situations. Thus, people respond to situations as instances of general patterns rather than perceiving and responding to each situation de novo (Kelley, 1984a). The transformation process begins when the actor recognizes the given situation as either a novel situation or as a situation similar to previous interactions sharing the same structure (see figure 14.4).

If the given situation is unfamiliar, the actor may actively consider its structure and implications; if the pattern is familiar, its structure and implications may be readily apparent. Given that the successes and failures of previous interactions direct behavior in current situations, the transformation process is partially shaped simply by categorizing the situation as one pattern rather than another. The pattern perceived to exist may be one for which the solution rests on broader considerations (interpersonal orientations), or may be one for which no broader considerations are relevant.

If the perceived pattern is one for which no broader considerations are relevant, the actor will simply behave on the basis of direct self-interest (MaxOwn). No transformation occurs, and the effective situation is equivalent to the given situation – that is, outcomes in the given situation govern behavior. For example, in a highly correspondent situation with no particular coordination problems, John may simply act on the basis of direct self-interest, knowing that what is good for him is good for Mary. However, if the given situation pattern is more complex, the pattern may activate any of a variety of interpersonal

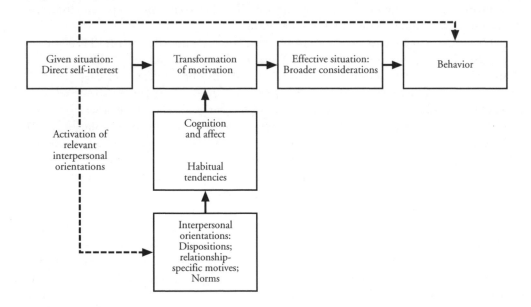

Figure 14.4   Transformation of motivation.

orientations. For example, when John and Mary are playing tennis, a disposition such as competitiveness may be activated.

The dispositions, motives, or norms that are activated in response to a specific situation influence motivation via either *cognitively- or affectively-mediated transformation* or *automatic transformation*. In the mediated case, orientations color the actor's cognition and affect. If John is highly committed, rather than experiencing indignation when Mary yells at him, he may feel concerned about Mary's well-being and form benign interpretations of her actions. These thoughts and feelings may lead him to place high value on both his own *and* Mary's well-being, yielding pro-relationship motives. Alternatively, John may automatically exhibit pro-relationship transformation, with little or no internal mediation. Assume that John and Mary have a history of strong commitment, and have encountered many noncorrespondent interactions in which each person, in turn, behaved in a benevolent and trustworthy manner. John may automatically evidence concern for Mary's well-being, and pro-relationship transformation may come about in a rather habitual and unmediated manner.

Whether the transformation process is mediated or automatic, this process produces a shift in motivation from the pursuit of direct self-interest to an alternative motive. This shift yields an effective situation that reflects the modified preferences dictated by the governing interpersonal orientation. For example, in a given situation involving noncorrespondent preferences, John's strong commitment will yield a set of effective preferences in which pro-relationship behavior takes on greater value. As a consequence, John behaves in a benevolent manner.

Habitual Transformation Tendencies

Based on repeated experience in interdependence situations, people develop relatively stable inclinations to react in a characteristic manner (Rusbult & Van Lange, 1996). Such tendencies are embodied in interpersonal orientations, which typically operate in a contingent manner, reflecting tendencies to react to specific partners in specific ways in specific situations. Thus, habitual transformation tendencies reflect the influence of important social psychological causes of behavior. In the following paragraphs we consider three classes of interpersonal orientation: personal dispositions, relationship-specific motives, and social norms.

Personal dispositions

These are actor-specific inclinations to respond to particular interdependence patterns in a particular manner (Kelley, 1983b). The characteristic ways in which actors confront situations reflect their prior histories of interdependence – that is, dispositions reflect adaptation to the interdependence situations that actors commonly confront. How so? Over the course of development different actors experience different histories, undergoing different experiences with parents and siblings, and confronting different opportunities and constraints in peer interaction. As a result of their histories actors acquire dispositions, reflected in the manner in which they approach specific interdependence patterns – they develop tendencies to perceive patterns in predictable ways, and to apply transformations to those patterns with greater or lesser probability.

It is instructive to illustrate this process using the example of attachment style (Hazan & Shaver, 1994). Recall that dependence makes one vulnerable, in that dependence reflects a partner's ability to provide one with exceptionally good *or* poor outcomes. People develop avoidant styles as a consequence of seeking intimacy and repeatedly experiencing rejection or betrayal. Accordingly, avoidant people come to regard intimacy situations as dangerous, and resolve such dilemmas by exploiting their partners or by avoiding intimacy situations. In contrast, secure people experience histories in which attempts at intimacy yield good outcomes. Accordingly, secure people perceive intimacy situations as safe, behave in a trusting manner, and create opportunities for partners to safely seek intimacy in return. Presumably, anxious-ambivalent people experience inconsistent histories and therefore behave in an erratic manner, alternating between (1) grasping at that which they most desire (intimacy, closeness) and (2) cautiously avoiding the risks of dependence.

The functioning of dispositions is also illustrated in research regarding social value orientations (Messick & McClintock, 1968; Van Lange, Agnew, Harinck, & Steemers, 1997). When given the opportunity to distribute outcomes to oneself and others, some people select options in which their own outcomes are greatest (individualism), whereas others prefer distributions of the MaxJoint (cooperation) or MaxRel (competition) variety. Social value orientations (1) influence behavior in a variety of situations, (2) are associated with distinct patterns of belief regarding others' orientations, and (3) are reflected in the probability with which specific transformations are applied to given patterns. For example, cooperators approach interaction cooperatively, and continue to do so as long as the partner cooperates. Individualists are susceptible to the temptation to exploit others' cooperation, but cooperate when doing so is advantageous. Competitors do not cooperate even when doing so would maximize their outcomes.

Dispositions are shaped in part by *behavioral confirmation* (Snyder, 1984). Interaction partners develop beliefs regarding the actor's strengths and limitations, preferences and disinclinations. During interaction, partners tend to behave in ways that are congruent with their beliefs. In so doing, partners (1) create opportunities for the actor to display some behaviors, (2) constrain interaction in such a manner as to inhibit the display of other behaviors, and (3) thereby elicit a subset of the actor's full behavioral repertoire. Over time the actor comes to behave in a manner that increasingly resembles the partner's expectations (Rosenthal & Jacobson, 1968; Snyder, Tanke, & Berscheid, 1977). In fact, actors' self-perceptions sometimes become aligned with partner expectations (Murray, Holmes, & Griffin, 1996).

The confirmation process is likely to be rather powerful in close relationships, in that close interactions involve strong, frequent, and diverse interdependence of extended duration (Kelley et al., 1983). Recent work regarding the "Michelangelo phenomenon" expands our knowledge of behavioral confirmation to the domain of close relationships by examining behavioral affirmation (Drigotas, Rusbult, Wieselquist, & Whitton, 1999). *Behavioral affirmation* describes the degree to which a partner enacts behaviors that are congruent with the actor's ideal self. When a partner holds beliefs regarding the actor that are congruent with the actor's ideal self, the partner tends to behave in a manner that elicits the actor's ideal self, which over time moves the actor closer to his or her ideal self. Both behavioral affirmation and actor movement toward the ideal self are associated with healthy couple functioning.

Once established, how do dispositions affect behavior? Although dispositions may guide behavior in an automatic manner, they frequently exert their effects by shaping interaction-relevant emotion and cognition. For example, actors who are dispositionally inclined toward perspective-taking tend to experience more benign emotions during the course of conflicted interaction, interpret their partners' actions in a more benevolent manner, and accordingly exhibit more constructive behavior (Arriaga & Rusbult, 1998; McCullough, Worthington, & Rachal, 1997). In parallel manner, competitors perceive a wide range of situations as competitive, believe that others are competitive, and interpret cooperative acts as stupid or sneaky (Kelley & Stahelski, 1970). Interestingly, because interaction partners often reciprocate the actor's behavior, actors' assumptions about partners' goals and motives frequently are confirmed (Snyder, 1984): just as competitors elicit competition and create a distrustful world for themselves, avoidant individuals elicit avoidance, and create a cold and barren world for themselves.

Relationship-specific motives

These motives are inclinations to respond to particular interdependence patterns in a particular manner with a particular partner (Holmes, 1981). In close relationships, commitment appears to be an especially important motive (M. Johnson, 1991; Levinger, 1979; Rusbult, 1983). *Commitment level* is defined in terms of affective, cognitive, and behavioral components, including: (1) psychological attachment (affective component) – John's well-being is powerfully affected by Mary, so John is vulnerable to strong, relationship-relevant emotion; (2) long-term orientation (cognitive component) – John envisions himself in the relationship for the foreseeable future, and considers the implications of current actions for the relationship's future; and (3) intent to persist (behavioral component) – John intends to continue his relationship with Mary (Arriaga & Agnew, 2000; Rusbult, 1983). Commitment increases to the extent that people are dependent on their partners – to the degree that: (1) satisfaction level is high (the actor's most important needs are gratified in the relationship); (2) quality of alternatives is poor (important needs could not be gratified elsewhere); and (3) investment size is high (important resources are linked to the relationship; Bui et al., 1996; Felmlee et al., 1990; Rusbult, 1983).

The empirical literature reveals that commitment is a powerful predictor of voluntary persistence (Rusbult, 1983). Also, strong commitment promotes pro-relationship maintenance acts such as derogation of tempting alternatives (D. Johnson & Rusbult, 1989), accommodation (Rusbult et al., 1991), and willingness to sacrifice (Van Lange, Rusbult, et al., 1997). Commitment exerts its effects by coloring emotional reactions to specific interdependence patterns (feeling affection rather than anger when a partner is neglectful) and giving rise to patterns of thought that support the decision to persist (e.g., cognitive interdependence; Agnew, Van Lange, Rusbult, & Langston, 1998). In turn, benevolent thoughts and feelings promote pro-relationship motives and behavior. (We say more about related issues later.)

The effects of commitment are particularly evident when direct self-interest is pitted against the interests of a relationship. Over the course of extended involvement partners inevitably confront situations in which personal well-being and couple well-being are at odds. Interactions of this sort are termed *diagnostic situations*, in reference to the fact that behavior in such situations is diagnostic of the actor's motives (Holmes & Rempel, 1989; such situations are also termed "strain tests"; cf. Kelley, 1983a). Commitment-inspired acts are particularly diagnostic of pro-relationship motives. Behaviors such as accommodation, sacrifice, and forgiveness provide relatively unambiguous evidence of benevolent motives – when John accommodates rather than retaliates when Mary behaves poorly, he demonstrates that he is willing to place the interests of their relationship above his own immediate interests.

How do commitment-inspired acts influence the persons with whom we are interdependent? When John departs from his direct self-interest for the good of the relationship, he conveys his concern for relationship well-being and enhances Mary's confidence in his benevolence. That is, John's actions communicate the strength of his commitment, which in turn enhances Mary's trust. *Trust* is the expectation that a partner can be relied upon to engage in pro-relationship acts and be responsive to one's needs (Holmes & Rempel, 1989). Trust includes: (1) predictability, or belief that the partner's behavior is consistent; (2) dependability, or belief that the partner can be counted on to be honest and reliable; and (3) faith, or conviction that the partner is intrinsically motivated to be caring – belief that the partner's motives go beyond instrumental bases for benevolence.

As partners develop increased trust they become more dependent on each other: increasingly satisfied, willing to forgo alternatives, and willing to invest in the relationship (Wieselquist et al., 1999). As John becomes increasingly confident of Mary's pro-relationship motives, he experiences enhanced satisfaction. In addition, he becomes more willing to make himself vulnerable by cognitively or behaviorally driving away alternatives, and becomes more willing to throw in his lot with Mary by investing in their relationship, emotionally or behaviorally. Such increased dependence yields strengthened commitment, which in turn enhances motivation to engage in pro-relationship acts.

In short, commitment and trust follow a pattern of mutual cyclical growth in which (Wieselquist et al., 1999): (1) John's dependence (high satisfaction, poor alternatives, high investments) increases his commitment; (2) John's commitment motivates him to enact pro-relationship behaviors; (3) Mary's observation of John's pro-relationship acts increases her trust; and (4) Mary's trust makes her increasingly dependent, which in turn enhances her commitment, and so on. Thus, over the course of a healthy, long-term relationship, each person's moves toward increased commitment tend to be accompanied by enhanced trust and parallel increases in commitment on the part of the partner.

Social norms

These are rule-based inclinations to respond to particular interdependence patterns in a particular manner, either with people in general ("never be the first to defect") or in a specific relationship ("never betray your best friend"). Norms are manifested in (1) regularity of behavior, (2) attempts to regain control by appealing to the norm in situations where regularity is interrupted, and (3) feelings of indignation or guilt occasioned by violations of the norm (Thibaut & Kelley, 1959).

For example, most societies develop rules regarding the expression of anger; such rules help groups avoid the chaos that would ensue if people were freely to give rein to hostile impulses. Likewise, etiquette and rules of civility regulate behavior in such a manner as to yield harmonious interaction – "good manners" are efficient solutions to everyday interaction dilemmas. For example, in the absence of normative prescriptions, Mary might feel irritated when John offers his mother the front seat of the car when driving to a restaurant. But in light of norms regarding suitable behavior toward one's elders, the potential for conflict in such situations is reduced.

Long-term partners may develop relationship-specific rules to solve interdependence problems. For example, although the temptation to become involved with alternative partners can be acute, the costs of doing so can be high. Therefore, most couples either comply with existing norms or develop their own norms to govern such behavior and minimize the negative impact of extra-relationship involvements (B. Buunk, 1987). Such norms typically specify the circumstances under which extra-relationship involvement is acceptable (marriage primacy), as well as the conditions under which such behavior is unacceptable (high visibility). Couples who violate the "ground rules" of their marriage exhibit greater jealousy regarding a spouse's infidelity.

In like manner, partners often adopt norms governing resource distribution, developing allocation rules that minimize conflict and enhance couple functioning. Thus, it is not surprising that (1) partners adhere to distribution rules such as equity, equality, or need, and that (2) people are distressed when normative standards are violated. Allocation rules frequently are relationship-specific. For example, in parent–child relationships and other communal involvements, the norms guiding behavior are need-based rather than contribution-based (Clark & Mills, 1979; Deutsch, 1975). Moreover, the rules governing allocation frequently center as much on the procedure on which allocations should be based as on the outcome distribution per se (Lind & Tyler, 1988).

Maintaining Ongoing Relationships

Over the course of extended involvement partners acquire the capacity to recognize situations that may threaten their relationship, and develop cognitive and behavioral tendencies that promote broader interaction goals. Such adaptations may reflect the influence of personal dispositions, relationship-specific motives, or broader social norms. Of particular relevance to the present chapter are the relationship maintenance mechanisms that have been shown to be promoted by strong commitment.

In addition to encouraging persistence, commitment promotes numerous *relationship maintenance mechanisms*, defined as the specific means by which partners sustain long-term, well-functioning relationships. Maintenance acts serve a positive function, helping relationships survive despite threats such as uncertainty, noncorrespondent outcomes, or tempting alternatives. At the same time, maintenance acts typically have negative implications for personal well-being, in that they involve the enactment of otherwise undesirable behaviors, the modification of existing cognitive representations, or other forms of cost or effort. Some maintenance acts involve trivial inconvenience, whereas others entail considerable cost or effort. Accordingly, it is useful to construe maintenance mechanisms as solutions to problematic situations that rest on pro-relationship transformation.

Over the past decade we have identified a handful of mechanisms by which committed people sustain long-term involvements; additional mechanisms are likely to be identified in the future. In the following pages we review: (1) behavioral maintenance acts, which involve shifts in behavior toward the goal of enhancing couple well-being; and (2) cognitive maintenance acts, which involve cognitive restructuring toward the goal of enhancing couple well-being (see figure 14.5). Although people may sometimes consciously and deliberately engage in such activities, maintenance acts may also be relatively automatic products of strong commitment.

Behavioral adaptation and relationship maintenance

Accommodative behavior.   One behavioral maintenance mechanism involves *accommodation*, defined as the inclination – when a partner enacts a potentially destructive behavior – to (1) inhibit the impulse to react destructively in turn, and (2) instead react in a constructive manner. For example, if John comes home after a stressful day and snaps at Mary, Mary would be said to have accommodated if she were to (1) inhibit her impulse to fight fire with fire by snapping back at John, and instead were to (2) swallow her irritation and begin preparing dinner, asking John how his day went.

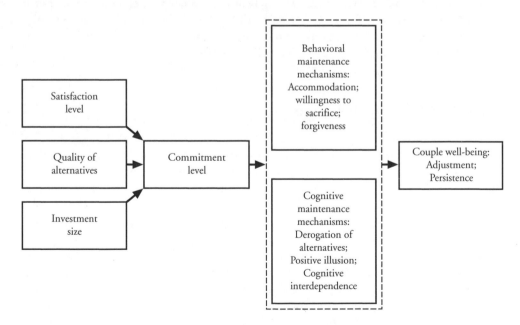

Figure 14.5   Commitment and relationship maintenance mechanisms.

The empirical literature demonstrates that partners exhibit greater accommodation to the degree that they are more committed; indeed, commitment accounts for unique variance in accommodation beyond satisfaction, alternatives, and investments (Rusbult et al., 1991). The impact of commitment on accommodation frequently is mediated by internal events such as partner perspective-taking, empathic accuracy, or the inclination to form benign attributions and experience benevolent emotions during conflict (Arriaga & Rusbult, 1998; Bissonnette, Rusbult, & Kilpatrick, 1997).

Accommodation appears to result from pro-relationship transformation (Rusbult et al., 1991; Yovetich & Rusbult, 1994). For example, when confronted with accommodative dilemmas, people given plentiful response time (time for transformation) exhibit greater inclinations to accommodate than do people given limited response time (no time for transformation). Also, partners in well-functioning relationships exhibit high levels of accommodation (Gottman, 1979; Rusbult et al., 1991). Thus, although accommodation involves personal cost, the tendency of committed individuals to accommodate clearly is beneficial to ongoing relationships.

Willingness to sacrifice.   Although partners in ongoing relationships may experience many interactions in which partner preferences are correspondent, they will inevitably be forced to confront noncorrespondent situations. John may receive a desirable job offer in Chicago, whereas Mary's most desirable offer may be in New York. When they encounter noncorrespondent situations, it becomes necessary that one or both partners exhibit *willingness to sacrifice* their direct self-interest for the good of the relationship. Sacrifice may entail forgoing behaviors that otherwise would be desirable, enacting behaviors that otherwise would not be desirable, or both.

The literature reveals that strong commitment is associated with greater willingness to sacrifice, demonstrating that commitment accounts for unique variance beyond satisfaction, alternatives, and investments (Van Lange, Rusbult, et al., 1997). Also, willingness to sacrifice is positively associated with dyadic adjustment and probability of persisting (Van Lange, Rusbult, et al., 1997). Thus, although sacrificial behavior necessitates forgoing direct self-interest, the willingness of committed individuals to sacrifice – when it becomes necessary to do so – yields clear benefits in ongoing relationships.

Forgiveness of betrayal.   One of the most serious threats to a relationship involves the experience of betrayal, or the violation of an implicit or explicit relationship-specific norm. Betrayal incidents vary in severity (telling a white lie vs. sexual infidelity), but to a greater or lesser degree such incidents yield a signature constellation of negative feelings, thoughts, and behavioral tendencies. Victims of betrayal frequently react with anger, confusion, and demands for atonement. Perpetrators often experience guilt or shame, and may show remorse or apologize for the harm they have caused. If victims continue to express outrage, perpetrators may themselves become angry and may seek to defend themselves or minimize the severity of the betrayal. Thus, the aftermath of betrayal is complex, and such incidents are difficult to resolve.

Recovery from betrayal rests on *forgiveness*, defined as the victim's willingness to forgo desire for retribution and demands for atonement, reacting in a less judgmental, more constructive manner. Complete forgiveness may be difficult, in that it rests on the resumption of pre-betrayal patterns of interaction – the victim no longer obsessively reviews the betrayal, reminds the perpetrator of the incident, demands apology, or exhibits any residue of the incident. In the case of complete forgiveness the victim experiences a "change of heart" and fully relegates the incident to the past.

Victims are more forgiving to the degree that they are more committed to their partners; the commitment–forgiveness association is evident even controlling for the recency and severity of betrayal (Rusbult, Finkel, Hannon, Kumashiro, & Childs, 2000b). Also, forgiveness appears to result from pro-relationship transformation (Rusbult, Davis, Finkel, Hannon, & Olsen, 2000a). For example, when recounting betrayal incidents, the reactions people consider enacting (given preferences) are considerably more destructive and less constructive than the reactions they actually enact (effective preferences). Moreover, forgiveness is positively associated with couple well-being (Rusbult, Davis, et al., 2000a). Thus – and parallel to pro-relationship acts such as accommodation and willingness to sacrifice – although it is a complex phenomenon that in many respects defies individuals' gut-level impulses, forgiveness is beneficial to ongoing relationships.

Cognitive adaptation and relationship maintenance

Forgoing tempting alternatives.   Tempting alternatives may threaten ongoing relationships. How do committed people deal with such threats? First, alternative partners may become more scarce over the course of an ongoing relationship. Potentially tempting alternatives may "take themselves out of the running" when they know that an individual is committed, or committed individuals may drive away alternatives by displaying conspicuous symbols of their involvement (e.g., a wedding ring; cf. Kelley, 1983a). At the same time, alternatives typically do not completely disappear – attractive alternatives continue to represent a threat to many relationships.

Research regarding *derogation of alternatives* reveals that involved individuals cognitively disparage alternative partners – they subtly minimize alternative partners' abilities or attributes ("I bet he has no sense of humor"). The tendency to derogate alternatives is greater among highly committed individuals (D. Johnson & Rusbult, 1989; Simpson et al., 1990), as is the tendency to exhibit defensive perceptual maneuvers – compared to less committed people, those with high commitment spend less time attending to tempting alternatives (Miller, 1997).

Existing evidence suggests that at least in part, derogation of alternatives is a motivated phenomenon – that is, committed individuals derogate alternatives at least in part because they "need to do so." For example, commitment interacts with threat in promoting derogation: the tendency of committed individuals to derogate alternatives is greater when the alternative is more attractive and readily available (D. Johnson & Rusbult, 1989). Although derogation of alternatives involves some opportunity loss, this type of mental restructuring would appear to have considerable adaptive value in a committed relationship.

Positive illlusion.   Individuals also develop idealized beliefs regarding their partners and relationships. In part, actors sustain idealized beliefs by translating faults into virtues, reinterpreting qualities that might otherwise be regarded in a negative light ("he slurps coffee in an adorable way"; Murray & Holmes, 1993). Interestingly, actors possess more positive beliefs regarding their partners than their partners hold regarding themselves, and the tendency to idealize one's partner is associated with increases over time in the partner's regard for self (Murray et al., 1996).

The empirical literature suggests that social comparison, too, is influenced by strong commitment. Research regarding *perceived superiority* reveals that people tend to: (1) hold a greater number of positive thoughts about their own relationships than other relationships; and (2) hold fewer negative thoughts about their own than other relationships (Van Lange & Rusbult, 1995; Rusbult, Van Lange, Wildschut, Yovetich, & Verette, 2000). In comparison to our beliefs about other relationships, we not only exhibit: (1) *perceived superiority* – perceiving a greater number of positive attributes in our own relationships than in others' relationships; but also (2) *excessive optimism* – perceiving that our relationships have rosier futures than other relationships; and (3) *unrealistic perceptions of control* – perceiving that we possess greater control over our relationships than others do (Martz et al., 1998).

Positive illusion is more pronounced among people who are highly committed (Martz et al., 1998; Rusbult et al., 2000). Also, positive illusion appears to be a motivated phenomenon. For example, emotionally threatening manipulations yield enhanced levels of perceived superiority, suggesting that committed individuals exhibit this tendency in part because they "need to do so" – because doing so reduces anxiety and doubt regarding the current involvement (Murray & Holmes, 1993; Rusbult et al., 2000). Finally, positive illusion is positively associated with dyadic adjustment and probability of persistence (Martz et al., 1998; Rusbult et al., 2000).

Cognitive interdependence. Strong commitment also produces a pro-relationship restructuring of the actor's representation of self. Cognitive interdependence involves movement from a largely individual-based internal representation of the self to a collective representation of self-and-partner. For example, compared to less committed individuals, highly committed individuals exhibit a greater rate of plural pronoun usage ("we, us, our" rather than "I, me, mine"; Agnew et al., 1998). A collectively defined representation of the self presumably promotes pro-relationship transformation. For example, MaxJoint transformation may be more probable to the extent that "we" thoughts are readily available. Thus, although cognitive interdependence involves some loss of unique, individual identity, this type of cognitive restructuring arguably is beneficial to relationships.

Deteriorating Relationships

In light of the numerous relationship maintenance mechanisms outlined above, it may seem surprising that some relationships deteriorate over time and eventually are terminated. Once partners become interdependent, what changes take place to cause some relationships to end? Many causes of termination and break-up were described in the preceding pages. Nevertheless, it may be helpful to selectively review features of interdependence that may contribute to the decline and demise of relationships.

The deterioration of a relationship may sometimes be attributable to problematic interdependence structure. Partners may unwisely enter into relationships with difficult interdependence structure, or interdependence structure may become increasingly problematic over the course of extended involvement. For example, John and Mary may marry despite the fact that John is more dependent than Mary: despite the fact that John relies on the relationship to a greater degree than Mary, and despite the fact that Mary's alternatives are superior. Or John and Mary may find that as their lives become increasingly complex – as their careers become more demanding, they bear and raise children, their parents become ill or infirm – they encounter numerous noncorrespondent interactions. Partners may feel overwhelmed by the complexities of problematic interdependence.

Also, partners do not necessarily remain consistently smitten with each other. Relationships may deteriorate because of rising expectations or declining outcomes, either of which will yield reduced satisfaction. Over the course of their marriage John or Mary may change in such a manner that they can no longer fulfill each other's most important needs. Also, if Mary enjoys uniformly good outcomes in her relationship, her CL will rise and it will become increasingly unlikely that she will experience high satisfaction (she may "take the relationship for granted"). Indeed, the empirical literature reveals that over time, the subjective costs of involvement increase and satisfaction level declines (Rusbult, 1983).

Two additional components of human psychology may contribute to deteriorating satisfaction. First, partners may experience reduced satisfaction due to satiation or declining marginal utility (Brickman, Dunkel-Schetter, & Abbey, 1987; Solomon, 1980). Over time, the once-gratifying features of a relationship may no longer possess the power to provoke strong positive affect. Second, partners may experience lower satisfaction than "objectively is warranted" due to the greater salience and potency of negative outcomes in relation to positive outcomes (Schwarz, 1990; Taylor, 1991). John and Mary may find that the bad features of their relationship – conflict, unfulfilled needs, and the like – are simply more salient than the good features. The "half-empty" portion of their relationship may dominate John's and Mary's feelings and thoughts.

Ambivalence may also be harmful to relationships. Ambivalence may raise concerns about how a relationship is likely to fare in the future, and may yield heightened negativity in interaction. Indeed, the empirical evidence reveals that ambivalence and conflict are positively associated prior to marriage, and that conflict and maintenance behaviors are negatively associated following marriage (Braiker & Kelley, 1979). Such findings suggest that ambivalence may give rise to conflict, which in turn may deplete partners' capacity to engage in pro-relationship maintenance acts.

When satisfaction declines, partners may consider alternatives to their relationship – they may actively evaluate outcomes in the current relationship, comparing their experience to that which might be available elsewhere. Even if satisfaction level remains steady, a relationship may deteriorate due to rising CL-alt – because one or both partners encounter alternatives offering outcomes superior to those obtainable in their relationship. Mary may decide that she would do better if she were to strike out on her own, or John may decide to pursue an alternative partner with whom he might enjoy a more fulfilling life. To the extent that CL-alt exceeds obtained outcomes – whether because a relationship deteriorates or because alternatives improve – partners may decide to end their relationship in order to pursue alternative involvements.

Given that pro-relationship acts such as accommodation, sacrifice, and forgiveness are influenced by commitment, when satisfaction declines and alternatives become increasingly attractive, the only force promoting maintenance acts is the third basis for commitment: high investment size. Invested resources such as shared memories, personal identity, material resources, and the like may become linked to a relationship, and may themselves motivate pro-relationship behavior. If John and Mary have not "put enough into" their relationship during the early years of involvement, they may find that when their relationship is challenged, the bank account is empty – their investment is insufficient to motivate the effort or justify the costs of needed maintenance acts.

Conclusions

What do we gain by adopting an interdependence analysis of close relationships? First, although social psychologists frequently allude to person-by-situation interactions, we devote little attention to understanding situations per se. For example, the most prominent model of couples therapy is cognitive-behavioral therapy, which emphasizes the role of poor social skills and attributional tendencies in causing marital distress. From the point of view of interdependence theory, distress may rest at least in part on the *situation* – that is, on problematic interdependence structure. To help couples achieve harmonious interaction, we should exert as much effort modifying the couple's circumstances of interdependence as we exert modifying each person's social skills and thought processes.

Second, some theories emphasize the "disappearance" of self-interest in close relationships, suggesting that with increasing closeness self-interest and partner interests become merged (Aron & Aron, 1997), or arguing that in communal relationships actors depart from their self-interest simply because the partner needs them to do so (Clark & Mills, 1979). In contrast, interdependence theory proposes that self-interest continues to make itself known in close relationships. Indeed, the fact that close partners frequently engage in positive yet personally costly acts is precisely what communicates their pro-relationship motives. The fact that we engage in positive acts, despite awareness that such behavior is antithetical to our self-interest, is precisely what makes positive behavior meaningful.

Finally, some theories of close relationships emphasize individual-level processes, explaining behavior by reference to properties that reside *within actors* – by reference to individual-level cognition, dispositions, motives, or biology. In contrast, interdependence theory explains behavior by reference to properties that reside *between actors*, highlighting the importance of interdependence structure in shaping the course of ongoing involvements. By calling attention to truly dyadic features of closeness – for example, by calling attention to the importance of dependence and the existence of noncorrespondent outcomes – interdependence theory provides the field with a much-needed *social* psychological analysis of human behavior.

References

Agnew, C. R., Van Lange, P. A. M., Rusbult, C. E., & Langston, C. A. (1998). Cognitive interdependence: Commitment and the mental representation of close relationships. *Journal of Personality and Social Psychology, 74,* 939–954.

Aron, A., & Aron, E. N. (1997). Self-expansion motivation and including other in the self. In S. Duck (Ed.), *Handbook of personal relationships: Theory, research, and interventions* (2nd ed., pp. 251–270). Chichester, England: Wiley.

Arriaga, X. B., & Agnew, C. R. (2000). *Being committed: The affective, cognitive, and conative components of relationship commitment.* Unpublished manuscript, Purdue University, West Lafayette, IN.

Arriaga, X. B., & Rusbult, C. E. (1998). Standing in my partner's shoes: Partner perspective-taking and reactions to accommodative dilemmas. *Personality and Social Psychology Bulletin, 9,* 927–948.

Axelrod, R. (1984). *The evolution of cooperation.* New York: Basic Books.

Baldwin, M. W. (1992). Relational schemas and the processing of social information. *Psychological Bulletin, 112,* 461–484.

Baumeister, R. F., & Leary, M. R. (1995). The need to belong: Desire for interpersonal attachments as a fundamental human motivation. *Psychological Bulletin, 117,* 497–529.

Berkowitz, L., & Daniels, L. R. (1963). Responsibility and dependency. *Journal of Abnormal Social Psychology, 66,* 429–436.

Bissonnette, V. L., Rusbult, C. E., & Kilpatrick, S. D. (1997). Empathic accuracy and marital conflict resolution. In W. Ickes (Ed.), *Empathic accuracy* (pp. 251–281). New York: Guilford Press.

Blumstein, P., & Schwartz, P. (1983). *American couples: Money, work, sex.* New York: William Morrow.

Braiker, H. B., & Kelley, H. H. (1979). Conflict in the development of close relationships. In R. L. Burgess & T. L. Huston (Eds.), *Social exchange in developing relationships* (pp. 135–168). New York: Academic Press.

Brickman, P., Dunkel-Schetter, C., & Abbey, A. (1987). The development of commitment. In P. Brickman (Ed.), *Commitment, conflict, and caring* (pp. 145–221). Englewood Cliffs, NJ: Prentice Hall.

Brockner, J., & Rubin, J. Z. (1985). *Entrapment in escalating conflicts: A social psychological analysis.* New York: Springer-Verlag.

Bui, K. T., Peplau, L. A., & Hill, C. T. (1996). Testing the Rusbult model of relationship commitment and stability in a 15–year study of heterosexual couples. *Personality and Social Psychology Bulletin, 22,* 1244–1257.

Buunk, A. P. (1991). Jealousy in close relationships: An exchange-theoretical perspective. In P. Salovey (Ed.), *The psychology of jealousy and envy* (pp. 148–177). New York: Guilford Press.

Buunk, B. (1987). Conditions that promote breakups as a consequence of extradyadic involvements. *Journal of Social and Clinical Psychology, 5,* 271–284.

Byrne, D. (1971). *The attraction paradigm.* New York: Academic Press.

Caspi, A., & Herbener, E. S. (1990). Continuity and change: Assortative marriage and the consistency of personality in adulthood. *Journal of Personality and Social Psychology, 58,* 250–258.

Clark, M. S., & Mills, J. (1979). Interpersonal attraction in exchange and communal relationships. *Journal of Personality and Social Psychology, 37,* 12–24.

Crosby, F. (1976). A model of egoistical relative deprivation. *Psychological Review, 83,* 85–113.

Deutsch, M. (1975). Equity, equality, and need: What determines which value will be used as the basis of distributive justice? *Journal of Social Issues, 31,* 137–149.

Drigotas, S. M., & Rusbult, C. E. (1992). Should I stay or should I go?: A dependence model of breakups. *Journal of Personality and Social Psychology, 62,* 62–87.

Drigotas, S. M., Rusbult, C. E., & Verette, J. (1999). Level of commitment, mutuality of commitment, and couple well-being. *Personal Relationships, 6,* 389–409.

Drigotas, S. M., Rusbult, C. E., Wieselquist, J., & Whitton, S. (1999). Close partner as sculptor of the ideal self: Behavioral affirmation and the Michelangelo phenomenon. *Journal of Personality and Social Psychology, 77,* 293–323.

Feingold, A. (1988). Matching for attractiveness in romantic partners and same-sex friends: A meta-analysis and theoretical critique. *Psychological Bulletin, 104,* 226–235.

Felmlee, D., Sprecher, S., & Bassin, E. (1990). The dissolution of intimate relationships: A hazard model. *Social Psychology Quarterly, 53,* 13–30.

Gottman, J. M. (1979). *Marital interaction: Experimental investigations.* New York: Academic Press.

Hazan, C., & Shaver, P. R. (1994). Attachment as an organizational framework for research on close relationships. *Psychological Inquiry, 5,* 1–22.

Higgins, E. T. (1989). Self-discrepancy theory: What patterns of self-beliefs cause people to suffer? In L. Berkowitz (Ed.), *Advances in experimental social psychology* (Vol. 22, pp. 93–136). San Diego, CA: Academic Press.

Holmes, J. G. (1981). The exchange process in close relationships: Microbehavior and macromotives. In M. J. Lerner & S. C. Lerner (Eds.), *The justice motive in social behavior* (pp. 261–284). New York: Plenum.

Holmes, J. G., & Rempel, J. K. (1989). Trust in close relationships. In C. Hendrick (Ed.), *Review of personality and social psychology* (Vol. 10, pp. 187–220). London: Sage.

Johnson, D. J., & Rusbult, C. E. (1989). Resisting temptation: Devaluation of alternative partners as a means of maintaining commitment in close relationships. *Journal of Personality and Social Psychology, 57,* 967–980.

Johnson, M. P. (1991). Commitment to personal relationships. In W. H. Jones & D. W. Perlman (Eds.), *Advances in personal relationships* (Vol. 3, pp. 117–143). London: Jessica Kingsley.

Kalick, S. M., & Hamilton, T. E., III. (1986). The matching hypothesis reexamined. *Journal of Personality and Social Psychology, 51,* 673–682.

Kelley, H. H. (1983a). Love and commitment. In H. H. Kelley, E. Berscheid, A. Christensen, J. H. Harvey, T. L. Huston, G. Levinger, E. McClintock, L. A. Peplau, & D. R. Peterson (Eds.), *Close relationships* (pp. 265–314). New York: W. H. Freeman.

Kelley, H. H. (1983b). The situational origins of human tendencies: A further reason for the formal analysis of structures. *Personality and Social Psychology Bulletin, 9,* 8–30.

Kelley, H. H. (1984a). Affect in interpersonal relations. In P. Shaver (Ed.), *Review of personality and social psychology* (Vol. 5, pp. 89–115). Newbury Park, CA: Sage.

Kelley, H. H. (1984b). The theoretical description of interdependence by means of transition lists. *Journal of Personality and Social Psychology, 47,* 956–982.

Kelley, H. H. (1990). *Interdependence in personal relationships.* Unpublished manuscript, University of California at Los Angeles.

Kelley, H. H. (1997). The "stimulus field" for interpersonal phenomena: The source of language and thought about interpersonal events. *Personality and Social Psychology Review, 1,* 140–169.

Kelley, H. H., Berscheid, E., Christensen, A., Harvey, J. H., Huston, T. L., Levinger, G., McClintock, E., Peplau, L. A., & Peterson, D. R. (Eds.). (1983). *Close relationships.* New York: W. H. Freeman.

Kelley, H. H., & Stahelski, A. J. (1970). Social interaction basis of cooperators' and competitors' beliefs about others. *Journal of Personality and Social Psychology, 16,* 66–91.

Kelley, H. H., & Thibaut, J. W. (1978). *Interpersonal relations: A theory of interdependence.* New York: Wiley.

Kenrick, D. T., & Trost, M. R. (1997). Evolutionary approaches to relationships. In S. Duck (Ed.), *Handbook of personal relationships: Theory, research, and interventions* (2nd ed., pp. 156–177). Chichester, England: Wiley.

Levinger, G. (1979). A social exchange view on the dissolution of pair relationships. In R. L. Burgess & T. L. Huston (Eds.), *Social exchange in developing relationships* (pp. 169–193). New York: Academic Press.

Lind, E. A., & Tyler, T. R. (1988). *The social psychology of procedural justice.* New York: Plenum.

Martz, J. M., Verette, J., Arriaga, X. B., Slovik, L. F., Cox, C. L., & Rusbult, C. E. (1998). Positive illusion in close relationships. *Personal Relationships, 5,* 159–181.

McClintock, C. G. (1972). Social motivation – a set of propositions. *Behavioral Science, 17,* 438–454.

McCullough, M. E., Worthington, E. L., Jr., & Rachal, K. C. (1997). Interpersonal forgiving in close relationships. *Journal of Personality and Social Psychology, 73,* 321–336.

Messick, D. M., & McClintock, C. G. (1968). Motivational bases of choice in experimental games. *Journal of Experimental Social Psychology, 4,* 1–25.

Miller, R. S. (1997). Inattentive and contented: Relationship commitment and attention to alternatives. *Journal of Personality and Social Psychology, 73,* 758–766.

Murray, S. L., & Holmes, J. G. (1993). Seeing virtues in faults: Negativity and the transformation of interpersonal narratives in close relationships. *Journal of Personality and Social Psychology, 65,* 707–722.

Murray, S. L., Holmes, J. G., & Griffin, D. W. (1996). The self-fulfilling nature of positive illusions in romantic relationships: Love is not blind, but prescient. *Journal of Personality and Social Psychology, 71,* 1155–1180.

Orbell, J. M., Van de Kragt, A. J. C., & Dawes, R. M. (1988). Explaining discussion-induced cooperation. *Journal of Personality and Social Psychology, 54,* 811–819.

Rapoport, A. (1966). *Two-person game theory.* Ann Arbor: University of Michigan Press.

Rosenthal, R., & Jacobson, L. (1968). *Pygmalion in the classroom.* New York: Holt, Rinehart, & Winston.

Rusbult, C. E. (1983). A longitudinal test of the investment model: The development (and deterioration) of satisfaction and commitment in heterosexual involvements. *Journal of Personality and Social Psychology, 45,* 101–117.

Rusbult, C. E., Davis, J. L., Finkel, E. J., Hannon, M. A., & Olsen, N. (2000a). *Forgiveness of betrayal in close relationships: Does it rest on pro-relationship transformation of motivation?* Unpublished manuscript, University of North Carolina at Chapel Hill, Chapel Hill.

Rusbult, C. E., Finkel, E. J., Hannon, M., Kumashiro, M., & Childs, N. M. (2000b). *Dealing with betrayal in close relationships.* Unpublished manuscript, University of North Carolina at Chapel Hill.

Rusbult, C. E., & Martz, J. M. (1995). Remaining in an abusive relationship: An investment model analysis of nonvoluntary commitment. *Personality and Social Psychology Bulletin, 21,* 558–571.

Rusbult, C. E., & Van Lange, P. A. M. (1996). Interdependence processes. In E. T. Higgins & A. Kruglanski (Eds.), *Social psychology: Handbook of basic principles* (pp. 564–596). New York: Guilford Press.

Rusbult, C. E., Van Lange, P. A. M., Wildschut, T., Yovetich, N. A., & Verette, J. (2000). Perceived superiority in close relationships: Why it exists and persists. *Journal of Personality and Social Psychology, 79,* 521–545.

Rusbult, C. E., Verette, J., Whitney, G. A., Slovik, L. F., & Lipkus, I. (1991). Accommodation processes in close relationships: Theory and preliminary empirical evidence. *Journal of Personality and Social Psychology, 60,* 53–78.

Schwarz, N. (1990). Feelings as information: Informational and motivational functions of affective states. In R. Sorrentino & E. T. Higgins (Eds.), *Handbook of motivation and cognition: Foundations of social behavior* (Vol. 2, pp. 527–561). New York: Guilford Press.

Secord, P. F. (1983). Imbalanced sex ratios: The social consequences. *Personality and Social Psychology Bulletin, 9,* 525–543.

Simpson, J. A. (1987). The dissolution of romantic relationships: Factors involved in relationship stability and emotional distress. *Journal of Personality and Social Psychology, 53,* 683–692.

Simpson, J. A., Gangestad, S. W., & Lerma, M. (1990). Perception of physical attractiveness: Mechanisms involved in the maintenance of romantic relationships. *Journal of Personality and Social Psychology, 59,* 1192–1201.

Snyder, M. (1984). When belief creates reality. In L. Berkowitz (Ed.), *Advances in experimental social psychology* (Vol. 18, pp. 247–305). New York: Academic Press.

Snyder, M., Tanke, E., & Berscheid, E. (1977). Social perception and interpersonal behavior: On the self-fulfilling nature of social stereotypes. *Journal of Personality and Social Psychology*, *35*, 656–666.

Solomon, R. L. (1980). The opponent-process theory of acquired motivation: The costs of pleasure and the benefits of pain. *American Psychologist*, *35*, 691–712.

Sprecher, S. (1985). Sex differences in bases of power in dating relationships. *Sex Roles*, *12*, 449–462.

Sternberg, R. J., & Barnes, M. (1985). Real and ideal others in romantic relationships: Is four a crowd? *Journal of Personality and Social Psychology*, *49*, 1586–1608.

Strube, M. J. (1988). The decision to leave an abusive relationship: Economic dependence and psychological commitment. *Psychological Bulletin*, *104*, 236–250.

Surra, C. A., & Longstreth, M. (1990). Similarity of outcomes, interdependence, and conflict in dating relationships. *Journal of Personality and Social Psychology*, *59*, 501–516.

Taylor, S. E. (1991). Asymmetrical effects of positive and negative events: The mobilization-minimization hypothesis. *Psychological Bulletin*, *110*, 67–85.

Teger, A. I. (1980). *Too much invested to quit.* New York: Pergamon.

Thibaut, J., & Gruder, C. L. (1969). Formation of contractual agreements between parties of unequal power. *Journal of Personality and Social Psychology*, *11*, 59–65.

Thibaut, J. W., & Kelley, H. H. (1959). *The social psychology of groups.* New York: Wiley.

Tjosvold, D. (1981). Unequal power relationships within a cooperative or competitive context. *Journal of Applied Social Psychology*, *11*, 137–150.

Van Lange, P. A. M., Agnew, C. R., Harinck, F., & Steemers, G. E. M. (1997). From game theory to real life: How social value orientation affects willingness to sacrifice in ongoing close relationships. *Journal of Personality and Social Psychology*, *73*, 1330–1344.

Van Lange, P. A. M., & Rusbult, C. E. (1995). My relationship is better than – and not as bad as – yours is: The perception of superiority in close relationships. *Personality and Social Psychology Bulletin*, *21*, 32–44.

Van Lange, P. A. M., Rusbult, C. E., Drigotas, S. M., Arriaga, X. B., Witcher, B., & Cox, C. (1997). Willingness to sacrifice in close relationships. *Journal of Personality and Social Psychology*, *72*, 1373–1395.

Wetzel, C. G., & Insko, C. A. (1982). The similarity-attraction relationship: Is there an ideal one? *Journal of Experimental Social Psychology*, *18*, 253–276.

Wieselquist, J., Rusbult, C. E., Foster, C. A., & Agnew, C. R. (1999). Commitment, pro-relationship behavior, and trust in close relationships. *Journal of Personality and Social Psychology*, *77*, 942–966.

Yovetich, N. A., & Rusbult, C. E. (1994). Accommodative behavior in close relationships: Exploring transformation of motivation. *Journal of Experimental Social Psychology*, *30*, 138–164.

Chapter Fifteen

Social Comparison and Close Relationships

Bram P. Buunk and Frans L. Oldersma

> Bill and Arlene Miller were a happy couple. But now and then they felt they alone among their circle had been passed by somehow, leaving Bill to attend to his book-keeping duties and Arlene occupied with secretarial chores. They talked about it sometimes, mostly in comparison with the lives of their neighbors, Harriet and Jim Stone. It seemed to the Millers that the Stones lived a fuller and brighter life. The Stones were always going out for dinner, or entertaining at home, or travelling about the country somewhere in connection with Jim's work.
>
> (From Neighbors, a story by Raymond Carver, 1976)

In *Neighbors*, Raymond Carver introduced a once happy couple that encounters the potential negative consequences of social comparison. Clearly, Bill and Arlene Miller feel bad about themselves and feel discouraged and depressed when they compare their own situation with that of the Stones. In fact, they are faced with the inferiority of their own relationship by perceiving their neighbors' relationship to be more fulfilling and satisfying than their own. The Millers' feelings illustrate in a nutshell the topic of the present chapter: they suggest that individuals may compare the state of their close relationship to that of others, and that they may draw conclusions from such comparisons about the quality of their own relationship. In addition, although many individuals may not actively seek out social comparisons, most individuals can at times hardly escape comparisons of their own intimate relationship with that of others, for instance when friends who always seemed so happy suddenly become divorced, when one hears gossip about other relationships, when one reads in magazines about the problems and joys in other relationships, or when one talks with others about mutual experiences in one's relationship.

Relating one's standing on a dimension to the standing of others on that dimension is the subject of classic and recent social comparison theory (Buunk & Gibbons, 1997; Collins, 1996; Festinger, 1954; Suls & Wills, 1991; Wood, 1989). Remarkably, despite the rapid expansion of research on social comparison in the past years, only a few studies have examined social comparison processes as they may occur with respect to the quality of intimate relationships. Nevertheless, a number of authors have pointed to the potential importance of social comparison in this context. For example, Surra and Milardo (1991) suggested that over the course of a developing relationship people engage in comparison with others in their social network to evaluate their beliefs about close relationships, the suitability of the partner, and the feelings and experiences in relationships. In a pioneering study, Titus (1980) found that many individuals sometimes made comparisons between their own relationship and that of others while talking with their friends and their friends' spouses.

The present chapter focuses upon social comparisons with regard to one's close relationship in the context of broader issues in current social comparison theory. We first examine the role of uncertainty and marital distress in fostering social comparison activity, including affiliation with similar others. Next, we discuss the affective impact of comparison with other couples, and finally, we pay attention to the way in which individuals perceive their close relationship in comparison to that of others (including the illusion of superiority), and how changing this perception may change the evaluation of one's relationship. As will become apparent, a variety of measures for assessing social comparison will be discussed.

Uncertainty, Distress, and Social Comparison

Although referred to as a "masterpiece in ambiguity" (Arrowood, 1986), Festinger's (1954) paper was the first attempt to outline a general, formal theory of social comparison processes consisting of many propositions and corollaries. As Mettee and Smith (1977) have noted, social comparison theory is a theory about "our quest to *know* ourselves, about the search for self-relevant information and how people gain self-knowledge and discover reality about themselves in the absence of objective-reality referents" (pp. 69–70). The theory maintains that people are motivated to know that their opinions are correct, and to know precisely what they are capable of doing. Festinger argued that individuals prefer to evaluate themselves employing objective and non-social standards, but when such objective information is unavailable, individuals will compare themselves with similar others to evaluate their own characteristics. Festinger emphasized the interpersonal consequences of social comparison, for example by suggesting that people will seek out the company of others similar to themselves and will try to persuade others who are dissimilar so that they become more similar to them. Although the work of Festinger was, of course, not at all concerned with close relationships, this early theorizing is clearly relevant to this domain given that close relationships occur in private settings (in large part) and that few objective standards are available to evaluate whether one's relationship is good or bad.

Festinger's (1954) work was expanded by Schachter (1959), who showed that fear, induced by the prospect of having to undergo an electric shock, evoked in most subjects the desire to wait with someone else, preferably with others also waiting to undergo the same experiment. As Schachter concluded: "Misery doesn't love just any kind of company, it loves only miserable company" (p. 24). According to Schachter: (1) emotion-producing situations often induce uncertainty because they are difficult to interpret in terms of past experience; (2) this instills a desire to compare one's emotions with others; and (3) the company of similar others is preferred as this would offer the best opportunity for such social comparison. Although there is limited evidence for Schachter's thesis that individuals under stress prefer similar others over knowledgeable others (Kulik & Mahler, 1997), and although affiliation may be at least as much fostered by other motives as by social comparison, there is some early evidence that emotional distress enhances the desire for affiliation in particular when there is uncertainty about how to interpret this distress. That is, when facing some form of threat, affiliative desires seem to be stronger when one is made uncertain about how to feel and react (e.g., Gerard, 1963; Gerard & Rabbie, 1961), when the source of one's arousal is unknown (Mills & Mintz, 1972), and when one has no information about how others have done (Singer & Shockley, 1965).

A number of studies have examined the implication of Festinger's (1954) and Schachter's (1959) theorizing that social comparison among marital couples will be fostered by distress and uncertainty, and that individuals will compare themselves with others in a similar situation. Although there may be a variety of factors instigating distress and uncertainty in one's close relationship, one important factor involves the changes in gender roles that have been occurring in Western society in the past decades. Individuals aiming for an egalitarian marriage will face more uncertainty because, in contrast to the gender-based role pattern in a traditional marital relationship, there is no standardized form or content for an egalitarian marital relationship, as well as a lack of role models for such relationships. Consequently, egalitarian partners have to develop their own rules and standards, and to discuss their mutual expectations and needs, as well as the various ways of achieving joint goals (cf. Ladewig & White, 1984; Van Yperen & Buunk, 1991), all of which may increase feelings of uncertainty about their relationship. Traditionals, on the other hand, will experience a lower level of uncertainty, as there are well-developed role models available, and as they will tend to have strong tacit agreement about their gender-based specialized and fixed roles. Research has indeed revealed that spouses with egalitarian gender-role attitudes experience more conflict about gender roles within the relationship, and that egalitarian women in particular experience dissatisfaction, because the task division often falls short of what egalitarian women expect (Fitzpatrick, 1988; Kluwer, Heesink, & Van de Vliert, 1997; Pina & Bengtson, 1993; Sillars & Kalbflesch, 1989; Steil, 2000).

In line with these assumptions, a study by Van Yperen and Buunk (1991), found that, especially among women, egalitarian sex-role beliefs were accompanied by a higher degree of uncertainty about how things are going in one's marriage and a lower level of marital satisfaction than for those with traditional sex-role beliefs. A study by Buunk, Kluwer, Schuurman, and Siero (2000) examined whether social comparisons occurred more frequently among egalitarian than among traditional women, and among those with a high as opposed to a low degree of discontent over the division of labor. It was assumed that because women trying to establish and maintain an egalitarian relationship will often experience uncertainty about what is right and appropriate in this regard, they should nevertheless often compare themselves with similar same-sex others, and such comparison tendencies should be enhanced by distress in the form of discontent. Egalitarian women (subscribers to a Dutch feminist magazine) were compared with traditional women (subscribers to a widely read Dutch, more traditional, women's magazine). The results showed that egalitarian women were more discontented with the division of labor than traditional women. This discontent was primarily related to the holding of explicit egalitarian attitudes and not to subscribership per se, and the association between such attitudes and discontent could not be explained by various demographic factors such as educational level, age, and religiosity. In line with the predictions, egalitarian women compared themselves considerably more often with other women than traditional women did, and – independent of having egalitarian versus traditional attitudes – discontent over the division of labor was associated strongly and positively with the frequency of comparison. Moreover, interestingly enough, the effect of subscribership to a feminist versus traditional magazine upon the frequency of comparison was independent of the effect of egalitarian gender-role attitudes. Probably, subscribing to a feminist magazine stems in part from a desire for social comparison. Indeed, the magazine in question contains a considerable amount of information about the experiences and opinions of other egalitarian women.

Additional findings from the Buunk et al. (2000) study testify, albeit more indirectly, to the enhanced desire for social comparison among egalitarian women and among women experiencing discontent over the division of labor. That is, we found evidence for *false consensus* effects, for the tendency to cognitively create consensual validation for one's situation by overestimating the number of others in the same situation (e.g., Marks & Miller, 1987; Spears & Manstead, 1990). Those with an unequal division of labor in their marriage estimated the percentage of women doing the major share of the household labor as higher than did women with a more equal division of labor. Although no false consensus effect was found for discontent over the division of household labor, feminist women estimated the percentage of women unhappy with the division of labor as higher than traditional women did. Because feminist women were more discontented with the task division, this effect may be interpreted as an *indirect* false consensus effect.

The role of uncertainty in fostering social comparison desires was more directly examined by Buunk, Van Yperen, Taylor, and Collins (1991) in a study which investigated the desire for affiliation, rather than comparison frequency, as a response to marital dissatisfaction and uncertainty. The sample consisted of married individuals, including couples with problematic and conflict-ridden marriages as well as couples with satisfying marriages. Although Schachter (1959) emphasized that affiliation should not include talking, and that social comparison information could be obtained by merely observing others, Schachter's evidence for the proposition that, even when talking is impossible, fearful subjects will want to affiliate was weak (Zimbardo and Formica, 1963; Kulik & Mahler, 1997). There is even evidence that giving subjects the opportunity to talk increases the affiliative tendency (Rabbie, 1963; see also Rofé, 1984). As Brickman and Bulman (1977) suggested, one of the major ways of comparing one's experiences with those of others is by engaging in a discussion of mutual viewpoints and opinions. Therefore, in the Buunk et al. (1991) study the desire for affiliation was assessed by asking individuals about their desire to talk with similar others about what was happening in their marriage. Furthermore, because such a desire concerns future behavior, assessing this desire was presumably more compatible with the interpretation that stress induces affiliative needs, compared to asking for actual affiliative patterns in the past, which could be interpreted as a cause of stress. The results showed that affiliative tendencies were enhanced in individuals facing uncertainty and dissatisfaction in their marriages, and particularly among women (Buunk et al., 1991, Study 1). Both variables (uncertainty and dissatisfaction) had independent associations with the desire for affiliation, and, in addition, there was an interaction effect, showing that stress in the form of the specific combination of marital problems *and* uncertainty was related to the strongest affiliative needs. This study thus provided one of the first direct tests outside the laboratory of Schachter's (1959) hypothesis that the desire for social comparison is dependent upon the activation of evaluative needs, i.e., that affiliation under distress is desired particularly when there is some degree of uncertainty.

Given the fact that a desire for social comparison seems particularly elevated when individuals experience distress and uncertainty in their relationship, the question arises: with *whom* do individuals under these conditions want to compare themselves and affiliate with? Do they prefer to learn more about others who are, compared to oneself, better off, equally well off, or worse off? Put in social comparison theoretical terms, do they want to make upward, lateral, or downward comparisons? Different predictions are made by various perspectives in social comparison theory. According to Schachter (1959), one would expect a preference for lateral comparisons, that is, with others experiencing the same level of distress. This is because such a group of similars would be the most appropriate comparison others. However, already in early social comparison work (e.g., Gruder, 1977; Hakmiller, 1966), it was suggested that individuals are not only interested in knowing how good they are, but also in knowing that they are doing *better* than others. This motive of *self-enhancement* received central attention in Wills's (1981, 1987) downward comparison theory which emphasizes that particularly in situations implying a decrease in well-being, individuals tend to compare themselves with others who are worse off as a way to improve their well-being. Nevertheless, although there may be some solace in the realization that others are even worse off than oneself, this does not necessarily mean that individuals facing distress want to be in the presence of such others (Gibbons & Gerrard, 1991). Indeed, Taylor and Lobel (1989) made a sharp distinction between evaluation on the one hand, and affiliation and information seeking on the other hand. They argued that when under threat, individuals will engage in self-enhancing downward evaluations to alleviate their negative feelings, but will engage in upward affiliations to obtain relevant problem-solving information to improve their situation. This notion of self-improvement was already recognized by Brickman and Bulman (1977) who emphasized that "Comparison with superior others, although painful, is more valuable than comparison with inferior others, since more useful information may be acquired by observing superior others" (p. 179). Because individuals usually have little information about what is going on in other relationships, they may, especially when they face problems in their own relationship, be interested in learning more about how couples seem able to prevent such problems, or to deal better with them (cf. Aspinwall, 1997; Collins, 1996; Lockwood & Kunda, 1997).

In the Buunk et al. (1991) study, the preferred direction of affiliation was assessed by asking subjects to indicate on a five-point scale if they wanted to talk with someone who was, in terms of the quality of his or her own marriage, worse off or better off. The results showed that the higher the level of marital dissatisfaction, the more men and women had a preference for upward affiliation. This finding supports the Taylor and Lobel (1989) prediction that among individuals facing threat, upward affiliation would dominate. Nevertheless, even among those with the highest degree of dissatisfaction only a minority preferred upward affiliation, and the majority of respondents preferred to talk with similar others, providing support for Schachter's (1959) theorizing. However, as virtually no respondent expressed a desire for downward affiliation, these data provide no direct support for Wills's (1981, 1987) downward comparison theory.

Despite these interesting results, there are several limitations of this study. First, the sample may have been subjected to a self-selection bias because individuals interested in acquiring social comparison information might have been more inclined to participate in research. Nevertheless, although the general inclination to affiliate may have been elevated in the sample, this would not affect the pattern of differential affiliation under conditions of stress. It must also be noted that considerable variation in desire for affiliation *within* the sample was found, and that those who responded were by no means uniformly interested in affiliation. A second, more serious limitation of this research is that the desire for social comparison was not assessed directly, and individuals were not asked about the motives for their affiliative desires. Such affiliative desires may not reflect social comparison needs very well, because they may be influenced by other needs, such as the seeking of companionship and emotional support. Furthermore, social comparison needs may not be expressed in affiliative desires because individuals may be reluctant to disclose their own vulnerabilities towards others, in particular others with a better marriage. To be more specific, individuals may prefer upward comparison information, provided that they can obtain this without having to discuss their own marital situation. Indeed, various experimental studies have shown that the tendency to compare upward is much stronger when the comparison can be made privately (e.g., Arrowood & Friend, 1969; Smith and Insko, 1987; Ybema & Buunk, 1993), and a number of survey studies suggest that the desire for information about similar others is more upward directed than the desire for affiliation (Buunk, 1995; Buunk et al., 1991).

The Affective and Evaluative Consequences of Social Comparison

Social comparison research has historically – as have the studies discussed thus far – focused upon the factors affecting comparison desires and preferences. Indeed, Festinger (1954) presented the individual as someone who, in search of self-knowledge, actively sought out social comparison information, and tried to influence others to meet his or her social comparison needs. However, in recent years an increasing number of theoretical approaches have emphasized the *effects* of social comparisons that are more or less forced upon the individual. Remarkably, until a decade ago this issue had been very much neglected, with the exception of early studies by, among others, Hyman (1942), Burnstein, Stotland, and Zander (1961), Mettee and Smith (1977), and Morse and Gergen (1970).

In general, research on the effects of social comparison has assumed that downward comparisons will predominantly generate positive affect by boosting self-esteem, by reducing anxiety, and by improving mood (e.g., Diener & Fujita, 1997; Gibbons, 1986; Wills, 1981; Wood, Taylor, & Lichtman, 1985), and that upward comparisons will induce negative affect by reminding oneself of one's inferiority, and by evoking envy and hostility (e.g., Marsh & Parker, 1984; Smith & Insko, 1987; Tesser, 1988). Implicit in most of these perspectives on social comparison is that individuals will primarily *contrast* themselves when comparing themselves in others (cf. Mettee & Smith, 1977), and will thus feel bad when perceiving others are doing better, and feel good when perceiving others are doing worse. However, following up on the early work by Mettee and Smith (1977), Buunk and Ybema (1997) recently argued in their *identification-contrast model* that the affective consequences of social comparison are not intrinsic to its direction, and may be opposite to what is usually assumed when individuals *identify* with the comparison targets, i.e. when they see the other's fate as their own actual or possible fate, and thus experience feelings that are concordant with those of the comparison target (see also Collins, 1996).

A first study examining these different interpretations of social comparison among marital couples was conducted by Buunk, Collins, Taylor, Van Yperen and Dakoff (1990, Study 2). In this study it was reasoned that a comparison of one's own marital relationship with a better marital relationship than one's own, provides at least two types of information: (1) that you are not as well off as everyone (contrast), and (2) that it is possible for you to be better than you are at present (identification). Those who pay attention to the positive aspects of this information (identification) should feel better as a result. Those who focus on the negative aspect (contrast) should feel worse. Conversely, comparing one's relationship with that of others who have a worse relationship than one's own, may also provide two types of information: (1) that you are not as bad off as everyone (contrast), and (2) that it is possible for you to get worse (identification). Focusing on the first aspect (contrast) should make one feel better, focusing on the second aspect (identification) should make one feel worse. In the Buunk et al. (1990) study, married respondents were asked to indicate how often they had experienced positive and negative feelings in response to upward as well as downward comparisons. The results showed that positive affect in response to downward comparison was the most frequently reported feeling, followed by, in descending order, positive feelings in response to upward comparisons, negative feelings in response to upward comparison, and negative feelings in response to downward comparisons. More importantly, those with a high level of marital distress reported more frequent negative feelings in response to upward *and* downward comparisons than those with low levels of marital distress (i.e., high levels of marital satisfaction). These findings suggest that distress in marriage is accompanied by a negative cognitive filtering of social comparison information, and that those with high levels of satisfaction tend to interpret both upward and downward comparison in a positive manner. According to Buunk and Ybema (1997), individuals characterized by high well-being (such as high marital satisfaction) will typically contrast themselves with others worse off, and identify themselves with others better off than themselves. In comparison, individuals characterized by low well-being, such as those experiencing conflicts and dissatisfaction in their marriage, will be inclined to do the reverse, i.e., contrast themselves with better-off others, and identify themselves with worse-off others. As a result, they will find it difficult to derive positive feelings from confrontation with downward as well as upward comparison targets.

Of course, a limitation of the Buunk, Collins, Taylor, Van Yperen, and Dakof (1990) study is that it assessed only the *recall* of the frequency of affect evoked by social comparison, and that the interpretation of what constituted such social comparison was left to the subjects. Moreover, the occurrence of upward and downward comparisons and the frequency of positive and negative affective responses were not assessed independently. To provide more unequivocal evidence on the affective consequences of social comparison, in a series of studies by Buunk (1998a), the responses of married individuals to vivid descriptions of other marital couples were examined. Recent experimental studies in which subjects were confronted with this type of social comparison information indicate that, unlike the findings in the Buunk et al. (1990) study, upward comparisons often generate more positive affect than downward comparisons (Aspinwall & Taylor, 1993; Collins, 1996), and that such feelings are mediated through identification with the comparison target (Ybema & Buunk, 1995). Although sometimes people may derive some benefit from identifying with downward targets through a "shared stress" mechanism ("I'm not the only one with such problems"; cf. Gibbons & Gerrard, 1991), confrontation with better-off targets may often evoke more positive feelings and identification than downward comparisons.

In addition to measuring the level of marital satisfaction, Buunk (1998a) examined the role of *attributions* for the happy or unhappy state of the target marriage in moderating the effects of social comparison. Identification and positive affect, as a consequence of upward comparisons, are more likely to be produced the more the state of the target is seen as within reach of being achieved by the subject. In general, a high degree of control by the target seems to lead to more positive affective consequences of upward comparisons (Lockwood & Kunda, 1997; Testa & Major, 1990; Ybema & Buunk, 1995). Moreover, it is easier to interpret the very happy state of another marriage as less threatening when a very high level of effort is put into it. This implies that upward comparisons will particularly evoke more positive affect than downward comparisons when the marital state of the target is attributed to the fact that the target puts a high degree of effort into his or her relationship. In this last case the happy marital situation of the target would be viewed as less threatening, and as possible for oneself, whereas the situation of a downward target putting considerable effort into the relationship would be perceived as undesirable and presenting a possibly bleak future for oneself.

To test these assumptions, marital couples were presented with a story about another marital couple representing either an upward or a downward comparison, characterized by either high or low effort. We will present here some preliminary results from these studies (Buunk, 1998a). In the first study, a computer-administered survey, upward comparisons evoked more positive affect than downward comparisons, and comparison with a downward target evoked more positive affect when the situation was attributed to high than to low effort. Upward and high-effort comparison targets instilled a higher degree of identification than downward and low-effort targets, and individuals who identified with the happily married comparison targets experienced much more positive affect than individuals who did not identify themselves with these targets. Furthermore, as predicted, identification with a downward comparison target evoked more positive affect when the unhappy marriage of the target was attributed to little effort than when it occurred despite considerable effort. Because in this study no pretest of the quality of the subjects' marriage could be included, there was no way to examine if marital quality was associated with the tendency to identify with the social comparison targets. Therefore, in the next study, before administering the experimental manipulations, an assessment was made of the marital quality of the subjects.

This second study, that included only women (Buunk & Ybema, 2000), showed that the higher the marital quality of the subjects, the more identification occurred with upward targets, who put a high degree of effort in their relationship and the less identification with downward targets in general. Moreover, identification with couples having a better marriage was strongly related to positive affect instilled by the comparisons, but identification with worse-off couples was not related to positive affect. Mediational analyses showed that those high in marital quality derived more positive effect from upward comparisons through identification with the target. In this study, in addition to the affective consequences, the evaluative consequences of social comparison were also assessed, i.e., how did these women evaluate their own relationship after being exposed to the social comparison information? It was found that downward comparisons led to a more positive relationship evaluation after being exposed to the comparison information than upward comparisons. Thus, these findings suggest a clear contrast effect: confrontation with another couple makes one less satisfied with one's own relationship when the couple is very happy, but more satisfied when the couple is quite unhappy. Furthermore, for those high in marital quality, relationship evaluation was reduced by confrontation with another couple whose marriage was good despite high effort, whereas those low in marital quality evaluated their relationship more positively after a downward comparison with another couple whose marriage was bad despite high effort. In general, this study suggested that the evaluative consequences of social comparison may be somewhat different than the affective consequences: although individuals experienced more negative effect after downward than after upward comparisons, they evaluated their own marriage as better after downward than after upward comparisons.

A question these results evoke is: are these really the result of social comparison? Do individuals indeed compare themselves with the couple in the interview fragment? Or do they just see these fragments as stories in their own right, without relating them to their own situation? Although the identification data do indicate the occurrence of a comparison process, many individuals claim that they would not compare themselves with other couples, and it has indeed been argued by various authors that individuals may be reluctant to admit social comparison (e.g., Hemphill & Lehman, 1991). The fact that individuals frequently seem hesitant to acknowledge their own social comparison activities may indicate that, because comparisons may often occur automatically, people are oblivious of the fact that they make comparisons (Brickman & Bulman, 1977). However, we would like to suggest that some individuals *do* indeed seldom engage in social comparison. Several researchers have already theorized that people may differ in their disposition to compare themselves with others (e.g., Brickman and Bulman, 1977; Hemphill & Lehman, 1991; Taylor, Buunk, Collins, & Reed, 1992; Wills, 1981). For instance, Hemphill and Lehman (1991) mentioned "the need for researchers to include measures of social comparison that acknowledge the fact that people may not wish to compare with others to an equal extent" (p. 390). Possibly, when research participants explain their difficulties with social comparison questionnaires and declare that they never compare themselves to others, this may mean that they truly lack an interest in social comparison information, and thus are indeed not disposed to frequently assess their own situation against that of others.

Recently, Gibbons and Buunk (1999) argued that the resistance of many individuals to admitting social comparisons may largely be the result of considerable individual differences in the tendency to engage in comparisons. Indeed, in a research program involving more than 20 samples, Gibbons and Buunk developed a scale to measure *social comparison orientation* that explicitly assesses individual differences in the inclination to compare one's accomplishments, one's situation, and one's experiences with those of others. Social comparison orientation was not related to social desirability, and was quite stable over time, although somewhat less stable than other personality characteristics. A high social comparison orientation seems to imply a high degree of uncertainty about the self, coupled with a strong orientation towards others. Thus, a high social comparison orientation was related to high neuroticism, low self-esteem, high anxious-ambivalent attachment style, high self-consciousness, as well as by a high communal and exchange orientation. Various studies have already shown that a social comparison orientation is positively related to the tendency to select, and to attend to social comparison information (e.g., Gibbons & Buunk, 1999; Van der Zee, Oldersma, Buunk, & Bos, 1998).

We would argue that the stories presented in the studies we described above constitute a proper social comparison only for individuals relatively high in social comparison orientation, and that individuals low in such an orientation might view the fate of the other couple more from a detached observer perspective, without relating it to their own situation. Indeed, a third study (Buunk, 1998a) that included social comparison orientation indicated that the responses particularly to upward comparison were very different for those high versus low in social comparison orientation. Although individuals high in social comparison orientation responded relatively more positively to downward comparison targets (regardless of the degree of effort exhibited by these targets), they seemed to focus in particular upon the situation of upward comparison targets, and to relate the situation of these targets to their own situation. That is, the higher the social comparison orientation, the more positive affect confrontation with the high effort couple evoked, and the less positive affect confrontation with the low effort couple evoked. Apparently, for someone high, as opposed to someone low, in comparison orientation, the idea that another couple has a happy relationship without much effort was threatening, whereas the notion that this happy state can be attained by high effort was particularly stimulating. Additional analyses showed that in this latter condition, the degree of positive affect was completely mediated by the fact that those high in social comparison orientation and marital satisfaction identified with the couple. To conclude, the original prediction that comparison with a better-off couple would evoke more positive affect when the situation of this couple was attributed to a high effort than to a low effort, was only found for those high in social comparison orientation, suggesting that various predictions in recent social comparison theory may only apply to individuals strongly inclined to compare themselves with others.

The Illusion of Superiority

Whereas the studies discussed thus far have focused upon voluntary comparisons between oneself and others, and upon the effects of social comparisons that were imposed upon the individual, social comparisons have also been assessed through *comparative ratings* (Wood, 1996). With such measures, individuals are asked to indicate how they perceive their own characteristics in comparison to, for example, those of most others, the average other, or the typical other.

Numerous studies suggest that on a variety of dimensions the majority of individuals have a more positive perception of themselves than they have in general of others (for a review, see Hoorens, 1993). For example, individuals attribute positive personality characteristics more to themselves than to others (e.g., Alicke, 1985; Brown, 1986), individuals erroneously assume that they have, compared to their peers, a lower risk of being subject to all kind of health problems, including lung cancer, diabetes, AIDS, and heart disease (Klein & Weinstein, 1997), and most professionals think that they are among the best 10 percent of people in the same profession (Meyer, 1980). Because the average person cannot be better than most others (except in extremely skewed distributions), the widespread tendency to perceive oneself as superior to most others was labeled as *illusory superiority* by Van Yperen and Buunk (1991). According to Buunk and Ybema (1997), such findings indicate that social comparison processes have in part a self-enhancing function in that individuals will try to cognitively construe their own characteristics in as positive a fashion as possible.

A series of studies suggests that such illusory superiority clearly applies to how individuals perceive their own close relationship. Buunk and Van Yperen (1991) showed that individuals perceive their own marital relationship as more equitable than the relationships of most others of their own sex. In a related vein, Buunk and Van Yperen (1989) found that married individuals felt they invested more in their marriage than most other men and women, in terms of, for example, listening and paying attention to the other, giving in when fighting, and giving up things for the other. Van Lange and Rusbult (1995) asked participants to list the positive and negative qualities that spontaneously come to mind when thinking about their own and others' relationships, and found that people hold a greater number of positive beliefs and fewer negative beliefs about their own relationships than about other relationships. Murray and Holmes (1997) found that both married and dating individuals rated their own partners' interpersonal qualities much more positively than the typical partners' qualities. In addition, it has been found that individuals think their own marriage is more satisfying than that of most others (Helgeson, 1994), believe they are above average as a spouse (Headey & Wearing, 1988), estimate their own vulnerability to divorce as lower than that of comparable others (Buunk, 1998b; Weinstein, 1980), and think their relationship has a better future than that of others (Baker & Emery, 1993; Buehler, Griffin, & Ross, 1995).

Some studies have examined to what extent the illusion of superiority occurs independently of the method used to assess the perceptions of one's own and others' relationships. This is an important issue, because, while Buunk and Van den Eijnden (1997) found that over half of the individuals felt their own relationship was better than that of "most others," one could argue that these data do not unequivocally show that there is an *illusion* of superiority as most participants may interpret "most others" as to mean "just over half of the people." In this case, slightly less than half of the participants would be right in perceiving superiority, and the finding, that about half of the participants feel their relationship is superior to that of most others, could hardly be interpreted as strong evidence for the existence of a group illusion. However, Buunk and Van den Eijnden showed that when the comparison group was – as in many other studies (Hoorens, 1993; Klein & Weinstein, 1997) – specified as the average, typical adult, perceived superiority was even stronger. Moreover, the illusion of superiority also appeared to occur when participants were asked to make separate estimates for the quality of their own relationship and that of the comparison other. Buunk and Van den Eijnden (1997, Study 4) found that virtually everyone (98 percent) rated their own relationship as at least "somewhat good," whereas only 50 percent perceived the relationship of the average, typical adult to be at least somewhat good. Nevertheless, when the comparison other is made concrete and specific, illusions of superiority become attenuated. Van Yperen and Buunk (1990) found that only 25 percent of the respondents reported that they considered their own marriage superior to that of others when they had to specify the comparison other (for example: my sister, my neighbor, my colleague, etc.), as compared to 65 percent who were asked to compare themselves with a non-specific other, i.e., a similar same-sex other.

Not only does the perception of superiority seem to be the most common human state, a perception of being better off than others is also closely related to well-being (cf. Headey & Wearing, 1988). In their well-known paper, Taylor and Brown (1988) argued that individuals who are in general happy with their situation tend to perceive their own situation as better than that of most others. This notion would apply in particular to the perception that one's relationship is superior to that of others, as such a perception may serve an important motivational function, and may contribute to a feeling of cohesion and a positive and valued social identity as a couple (cf. Hogg, 1992). A number of studies have indeed shown that individuals who perceive their relationship as superior tend to express higher levels of satisfaction and commitment in their intimate relationships. Both perceiving the input–outcome ratio in one's own marriage as superior to that of others (Buunk & Van Yperen, 1991), and feeling that one's marriage is in general better than that of most others (Buunk & Van den Eijnden, 1997), are accompanied by relatively high levels of marital satisfaction. Rusbult, Van Lange, Verette, and Yovetich (1995) found that perceived superiority was associated with higher commitment, and, assessed at an earlier time, was greater for relationships that persisted than for relationships that ended. In a similar vein, Martz et al. (1998) found positive relations between the tendency to evaluate one's own relationship more favorably than one's best friend's relationship on the one hand, and relationship satisfaction and commitment to one's own relationship on the other hand.

It has been suggested that the perception of superiority is, especially among happy couples, maintained by biased cognitive processes, including: (1) a selective focus upon the dimensions in which one's own relationship is advantaged, (2) a biased memory for negative information about other relationships and for positive events in one's own relationship, (3) the attribution of quarrels and grievances of other couples to stable characteristics of their relationship and the attribution of one's own relationship problems to transient factors, and (4) high salience of the intimacy and uniqueness of one's own relationship. Little research has examined these processes. However, there is some evidence that the illusion of superiority among happily married individuals is not associated with an overly negative view of other marriages. In fact, the literature on *false consensus* would suggest that individuals with a happy marriage would estimate the percentage of happy marriages in the population as higher than individuals with a less happy marriage (cf. Suls, Wan, & Sanders, 1988; Marks & Miller, 1987). But if happily married individuals in general feel they are better than most others, how can they at the same time assume that most others are similar to themselves? Most authors have viewed false consensus and illusory superiority as irreconcilable phenomena, and have attempted to outline the conditions under which false consensus versus illusory superiority exists (e.g., Goethals, 1986; Marks, 1984). However, in line with McFarland and Miller (1990) who suggested that both phenomena can exist simultaneously, Buunk and Van den Eijnden (1997) reasoned that individuals with a satisfying intimate relationship will not only assume that their relationship is better than that of most other people, but will also project their own situation onto others. They should dislike the perception that most relationships are in bad shape because this might be felt a threat to their own relationship ("it may happen to us too"). Buunk and Van den Eijnden showed in two independent studies that in addition to perceiving one's relationship as superior, those with a happy relationship estimated the percentage of others with such a relationship as higher than those with an unhappy relationship. In short, by simultaneously assuming that most marriages are good, but one's own is better, one may maintain an exceptionally high level of satisfaction.

Although the association between perceptions of superiority and satisfaction is a quite general phenomenon, this association seems to be moderated by a number of factors. First, there is some evidence that this association is particularly strong for women with egalitarian attitudes due to the higher uncertainty such women experience in their relationship (Van Yperen & Buunk, 1991). Apparently, in line with our earlier discussion, the marital satisfaction of women – and less so of men – aiming at an egalitarian task role division at home is particularly dependent on how they perceive their situation in comparison to that of others. Second, Buunk and Van Yperen (1989) and Buunk (2001) found that among men, the more they contributed to the relationship in comparison to others, the higher their satisfaction level. Women, however, experienced relatively little satisfaction when they felt they were contributing more to the relationship than other women. Possibly, women who provide more than other women do may feel annoyed that they are, in this sense, worse off.

In general, because women appear to discuss relationship issues more frequently with friends than men do (Titus, 1980), comparisons with other women may more directly affect women's than men's relationship satisfaction. Among men, the same study found that the more they felt they invested in their marriage as compared to other men, the more satisfied they were with their marriage. As men have fewer close relationships with friends, and talk less about their marriage with their peers than women, having a better love relationship than one's friends may evoke less negative feelings among men than among women.

Cognitive Downward Comparisons as a Way of Reducing Relationship Distress

Given the importance of the perception of superiority for relationship satisfaction, one might expect that although individuals facing relationship distress do not prefer to affiliate with others who are worse off, actively engaging in downward comparison might help them to feel better about their relationship. Indeed, this is basically what Wills's (1981, 1987) downward comparison theory assumes. According to this theory, when facing a decline in well-being, contrasting oneself with others who are doing worse will reveal one's own superiority over others, and will thus improve the way one feels about one's situation. As noted previously, Taylor and Lobel (1989) suggested that while individuals facing distress will engage in upward affiliations, they will also engage in downward evaluations, that is in focusing upon the contrast between themselves and others who are worse off.

In a more encompassing model of the cognitive adaptation employed by individuals under stress, the *selective evaluation* model, Taylor, Wood, and Lichtman (1983) proposed various cognitive strategies which people may use in an attempt to minimize their negative self-images and to reduce the threat to their well-being, including: (1) making downward comparison with worse-off others (e.g., "saying to oneself that there are others still worse off"); (2) selectively focusing on attributes that make them appear advantaged (i.e., dimensional comparison); (3) creating hypothetical worse worlds by comparing one's current situation against what could have happened; (4) construing benefit from the victimizing event; and (5) manufacturing normative standards against which victims can compare themselves in such a way as to make their own adjustment appear exceptional (see also Wills, 1981, 1987). Such selective evaluation strategies constitute active, goal-directed processes, aimed at redefining one's situation, and making it more acceptable. In particular the strategies of downward comparisons, dimensional comparisons, and self-evaluation against comparative standards involve social comparison activities, and characteristic of these strategies is their *cognitive* nature, that is, they do not necessarily involve social comparisons with actual others.

A number of studies outside the area of close relationships have provided evidence that individuals who experience some type of life stress employ cognitive downward comparison as a coping strategy in order to improve the perception of their situation. For instance, in an interview study among breast cancer patients, Wood et al. (1985) clearly demonstrated that a majority of patients made downward comparisons, that is, they evaluated their own adjustment to cancer as better relative to other women with breast cancer. Jensen and Karoly (1992) found that chronic pain patients who showed a stronger tendency to use downward comparison experienced lower levels of depression. In a sample of indiv-iduals covered by the Disablement Insurance Act, Buunk and Ybema (1995) found that people experiencing stress were more likely to engage in downward comparison, and that downward comparison positively affected individuals' evaluations of their situation one year later.

Although researchers have become increasingly interested in the role of social cognitive processes in relationships (for reviews, see Clark, Helgeson, Mickelson, & Pataki, 1994; Fletcher & Fincham, 1991; Fletcher & Fitness, 1996), experimental studies on the role of cognitive social comparison activity in the development and maintenance of relationship quality are, as far as we know, virtually non-existent. In a series of experiments (Oldersma, De Dreu, and Buunk, 1995; Buunk, Oldersma, & De Dreu, 2000), a paradigm was developed to foster an active, cognitive downward comparison process similar to that which individuals might use when faced with real-life stress. Participants were induced to explicitly describe the positive qualities of their relationship, which they considered as *better than most others*. Thus, participants were deliberately prompted to focus on the superiority of their own relationships over those of others. To test the assumption that it is specifically downward comparison that enhances relationship evaluation, and not the fact that the instruction induced increased salience of the positive features of the relationship, a no-comparison control condition was included in which participants were presented with a similar task but instead were asked to describe positive qualities of their relationship, which they considered as *good*. Cognitive downward comparison was expected to be a particularly beneficial strategy for people who experienced discontent with the relationship. Additionally, it was investigated whether downward comparison exerts a stronger positive effect on perceived relationship quality for individuals high in social comparison orientation, the individual difference variable we discussed previously.

A first laboratory experiment (Oldersma et al., 1995, 2000) showed that satisfaction and commitment were enhanced after participants were asked to engage in a cognitive downward comparison process by listing why their partner was better than other partners, as compared to when they merely were asked why their partner was good. Moreover, after engaging in the downward comparison, participants had shorter response latencies when answering questions about their relationship, suggesting that this task made the evaluation of one's relationship cognitively more accessible (cf. Fazio, 1995). Also, additional analyses showed that the difference between the two conditions was not due to the fact that in the comparison condition more qualities or more positive qualities (as rated by the participants and independent observers) were generated.

A second field experiment (Buunk et al., 2000), conducted among adult individuals of various educational backgrounds who had been in relationships lasting over 15 years on average, showed that downward comparisons improved the perceived quality of the relationship especially among people who were discontented with it. Moreover, this buffering effect of downward comparison was moderated by social comparison orientation (Gibbons & Buunk, 1999) in such a way that the downward comparisons helped in raising relationship quality only among those high in social comparison orientation. A third laboratory experiment (Oldersma & Buunk, 1997), in which individuals were asked not to engage in downward comparison of their partner, but of their *relationship*, basically replicated the findings from the second study that actively engaging in downward social comparison positively affected relationship quality especially for individuals high in social comparison orientation who reported discontent with their relationship. Moreover, when controlling for the number and positivity of qualities listed in the thought-listing task, the findings remained essentially the same, thus ruling out the possible alternative line of reasoning that the differential number and valence of qualities listed in both experimental conditions might account for the obtained effects. Additionally, participants in the downward comparison condition showed lower response latencies to the satisfaction questionnaire than those in the no-comparison conditions, thus reflecting a more accessible and favorable evaluation of the relationship in the former condition.

In sum, the findings from this research indicate that people may enhance their well-being through a cognitive downward social comparison process when they are unhappy about the relationship with their partner. The results of these three studies are consistent with Wills's downward comparison theory (1981, 1987), and selective evaluation theory proposed by Taylor et al. (1983) that would predict that when people experience relational discontent, selective evaluation through downward comparison can make individuals feel relatively better about their relationship.

Conclusion

Although little is known about how often individuals compare the state of their close relationship with that of others, in line with "classic" social comparison theory, there is evidence that individuals tend more often to affiliate with and compare themselves with others when they experience distress and uncertainty in their marriage. As Festinger's (1954) social comparison theory and subsequent research using the fear and affiliation paradigm (e.g., Gerard, 1963; Mills & Mintz, 1972) would suggest, the need for social comparison seems especially elevated among individuals who feel uncertain about the state of their own relationship. It must be noted that there is hardly any research showing whose relationships individuals actually compare their own marriage with. However, the little evidence there is suggests that, contrary to what Wills (1981) would predict, people facing relationship distress prefer upward and lateral comparisons rather than downward comparisons, and when confronted with descriptions of other marriages, individuals respond more positively to a description of happy marriages than to a description of unhappy marriages. This upward preference exists in part because individuals tend to identify with such upward comparison couples, especially when the superior state of that couple is attributed to high effort.

We have also provided preliminary evidence for the important role of individual differences in social comparison orientation, with those high in such an orientation apparently relating information about other marriages more strongly to their own situation, and thus responding more favorably to couples who are happy due to high effort, and less favorably to couples who seem to attain their happy state without much effort. In general, individuals, especially when they are satisfied with their relationship, tend to perceive their own relationship as better than that of others. At the same time, individuals estimate the percentage of happy couples as higher the happier they are themselves; thus, happy couples assume that most other couples are happy too. Consistent with the fact that having a happy relationship is intrinsically linked to perceiving superiority, we have provided preliminary experimental evidence that engaging in cognitive downward comparison can enhance relationship satisfaction, especially among those who experience discontent and are high in social comparison orientation. These findings, although of a preliminary nature, were the more noteworthy as apparently even for individuals who are involved in long-term relationships and who are dispositionally inclined to compare themselves with others, cognitive downward comparison may help in improving the evaluation of one's relationship when facing relational discontent.

In general then, and in line with Wills's (1981) downward comparison theory, the Taylor and Lobel (1989) model, and the identification contrast model (Buunk & Ybema, 1997), the research discussed in this chapter suggests that simply believing that one is relatively well off, which comes about through downward comparison, is an important step along the way to satisfactory adjustment. Hopefully, the present chapter helps in illuminating the role of social comparison in close relationships, and by putting this phenomenon in the larger context of current social comparison theory, also furthers our insight into the general role of social comparisons as related to well-being.

References

Alicke, M. D. (1985). Global self-evaluation as determined by the desirability and controllability of trait adjectives. *Journal of Personality and Social Psychology, 49*, 1621–1630.

Arrowood, A. J. (1986). Comments on "Social Comparison Theory": Psychology of the lost and found. *Personality and Social Psychology Bulletin, 12,* 279–281.

Arrowood, A. J., & Friend, R. (1969). Other factors determining the choice of comparison other. *Journal of Experimental Social Psychology, 5,* 233–239.

Aspinwall, L. G. (1997). Future-oriented aspects of social comparisons: A framework for studying health-related comparison activity. In B. P. Buunk & F. X. Gibbons (Eds.), *Health, coping, and well-being: Perspectives from social comparison theory* (pp. 125–165). Mahwah, NJ: Erlbaum.

Aspinwall, L. G., & Taylor, S. E. (1993). Effects of social comparison direction, threat, and self-esteem on affect, self-evaluation, and expected success. *Journal of Personality and Social Psychology, 64,* 708–722.

Baker, L. A., & Emery, R. E. (1993). When every relationship is above average: Perceptions and expectations of divorce at the time of marriage. *Law and Human Behavior, 17,* 439–450.

Bradbury, T. N., & Fincham, F. D. (1990). Attributions in marriage: Review and critique. *Psychological Bulletin, 107,* 3–33.

Brickman, P., & Bulman, R. (1977). Pleasure and pain in social comparison. In J. M. Suls & R. L. Miller (Eds.), *Social comparison processes: Theoretical and empirical perspectives* (pp. 149–186). Washington, DC: Hemisphere.

Brown, J. D. (1986). Evaluations of self and others: Self-enhancement biases in social judgment. *Social Cognition, 4,* 353–376.

Buehler, R., Griffin, D., & Ross, M. (1995). It's about time: Optimistic predictions in work and love. In W. Stroebe & M. Hewstone (Eds.), *European Review of Social Psychology* (Vol. 1, pp. 1–32). Chichester, England: Wiley.

Burnstein, E., Stotland, E., & Zander, A. (1961). Similarity to a model and self-evaluation. *Journal of Abnormal and Social Psychology, 62,* 257–264.

Buunk, B. P. (2001). Perceived superiority of one's own relationship and perceived prevalence of happy and unhappy relationships. *British Journal of Social Psychology, 40,* 565–574.

Buunk, B. P. (1995). Comparison direction and comparison dimension among disabled individuals: Towards a refined conceptualization of social comparison under stress. *Personality and Social Psychology Bulletin, 21,* 316–330.

Buunk, B. P. (1998a). "I don't compare, but when I look at all those other relationships": The benefits of social composition in close relationships. Invited address at the 9th International Conference on Personal Relationships, Saratoga Springs, NY.

Buunk, B. P. (1998b). Social comparison and optimism about one's relational future: Order effects in social judgment. *European Journal of Social Psychology, 28,* 777–786.

Buunk, B. P., Collins, R. L., Taylor, S. E., Van Yperen, N. W., & Dakof, G. A. (1990). The affective consequences of social comparison: Either direction has its ups and downs. *Journal of Personality and Social Psychology, 59,* 1238–1249.

Buunk, B. P., & Gibbons, F. X. (1997). *Health, coping, and well-being: Perspectives from social comparison theory.* Mahwah, NJ: Erlbaum.

Buunk, B. P., Kluwer, E. S., Schuurman, M. K., & Siero, F. W. (2000). The division of labor among egalitarian and traditional women: Differences in discontent, social comparison, and false consensus. *Journal of Applied Social Psychology, 30,* 758–778.

Buunk, B. P., Oldersma, F. L., & De Dreu, C. K. W. (2000). Downward comparison as a relationship enhancing mechanism: The moderating roles of relational discontent and individual differences in social comparison orientation. Manuscript submitted for publication.

Buunk, B. P., & Van den Eijnden, R. J. J. M. (1997). Perceived prevalence, perceived superiority, and relationship satisfaction: Most relationships are good, but ours is the best. *Personality and Social Psychology Bulletin, 23,* 219–228.

Buunk, B. P., & Van Yperen, N. W. (1989). Social comparison, equality, and relationship satisfaction: Gender differences over a ten-year period. *Social Justice Research, 3,* 157–180.

Buunk, B. P., & Van Yperen, N. W. (1991). Referential comparisons, relational comparisons, and exchange orientation: Their relation to marital satisfaction. *Personality and Social Psychology Bulletin, 17,* 709–717.

Buunk, B. P., Van Yperen, N. W., Taylor, S. E., & Collins, R. L. (1991). Social comparison and the drive upward revisited: Affiliation as a response to marital stress. *European Journal of Social Psychology, 21,* 529–546.

Buunk, B. P., & Ybema, J. F. (1995). Selective evaluation and coping with stress: Making one's situation cognitively more livable. *Journal of Applied Social Psychology, 25,* 1499–1517.

Buunk, B. P., & Ybema, J. F. (1997). Social comparison, affiliation, and coping with acute medical threats. In B. P. Buunk & F. X. Gibbons (Eds.), *Health, coping, and well-being: Perspectives from social comparison theory* (pp. 359–388). Mahwah, NJ: Erlbaum.

Buunk, B. P., & Ybema, J. F. (2000). *Feeling bad, but satisfied: The effects of upward and downward comparison with other couples upon mood and marital satisfaction.* Manuscript submitted for publication.

Carver, R. (1976). *Will you please be quiet, please?* New York: Knopf.

Clark, M. S., Helgeson, V. S., Mickelson, K., & Pataki, S. P. (1994). Some cognitive structures and processes relevant to relationship functioning. In R. S. Wyer, Jr., & T. K. Srull (Eds.), *Handbook of social cognition: Vol. 2. Applications* (2nd ed., pp. 189–238). Hillsdale, NJ: Erlbaum.

Collins, R. L. (1996). For better or worse: The impact of upward social comparison on self-evaluations. *Psychological Bulletin, 119,* 51–69.

Diener, E., & Fujita, F. (1997). Social comparisons and subjective well-being. In B. P. Buunk & F. X. Gibbons (Eds.), *Health, coping, and well-being: Perspectives from social comparison theory* (pp. 328–357). Mahwah, NJ: Erlbaum.

Fazio, R. H. (1995). Attitudes as object-evaluation associations: Determinants, consequences, and correlates of attitude accessibility. In R. E. Petty & J. A. Krosnick (Eds.), *Attitude strength: Antecedents and consequences* (pp. 247–282). Mahwah, NJ: Erlbaum.

Festinger, L. (1954). A theory of social comparison processes. *Human Relations, 7,* 117–140.

Fitzpatrick, M. A. (1988). Negotiation, problem solving and conflict in various types of marriages. In P. Noller & M. A. Fitzpatrick (Eds.), *Perspectives on marital interaction* (pp. 245–270). Philadelphia: Multilingual Matters.

Fletcher, G. J. O., & Fincham, F. D. (1991). *Cognition in close relationships.* Hillsdale, NJ: Erlbaum.

Fletcher, G. J. O., & Fitness J. (1996). *Knowledge structures and interaction in close relationships: A social psychological approach.* Mahwah, NJ: Erlbaum.

Gerard, H. B. (1963). Emotional uncertainty and social comparison. *Journal of Abnormal and Social Psychology, 66,* 568–573.

Gerard, H. B., & Rabbie, J. M. (1961). Fear and social comparison. *Journal of Abnormal and Social Psychology, 62,* 586–592.

Gibbons, F. X. (1986). Social comparison and depression: Company's effect on misery. *Journal of Personality and Social Psychology, 51,* 140–148.

Gibbons, F. X., & Buunk, B. P. (1999). Individual differences in social comparison: The development of a scale of social comparison orientation. *Journal of Personality and Social Psychology, 76,* 129–142.

Gibbons, F. X., & Gerrard, M. (1991). Downward comparisons and coping with threat. In J. M. Suls & T. A. Wills (Eds.), *Social comparison: Contemporary theory and research* (pp. 317–345). Hillsdale, NJ: Erlbaum.

Goethals, G. R. (1986). Fabricating and ignoring social reality: Self-serving estimates of consensus. In J. M. Olson, C. P. Herman, & M. P. Zanna (Eds.), *Relative deprivation and social comparison: The Ontario Symposium* (Vol. 4, pp. 135–157). Hillsdale, NJ: Erlbaum.

Gruder, C. L. (1977). Choice of comparison persons in evaluating oneself. In J. M. Suls & R. L. Miller (Eds.), *Social comparison processes: Theoretical and empirical perspectives* (pp. 21–41). Washington, DC: Hemisphere.

Hakmiller, K. L. (1966). Threat as a determinant of downward comparison. *Journal of Experimental Social Psychology, 2* (Suppl. 1), 32–39.

Headey, B., & Wearing, A. (1988). The sense of relative superiority: Central to well-being. *Social Indicators Research, 20,* 497–516.

Helgeson, V. S. (1994). The effects of self-beliefs and relationship beliefs on adjustment to a relationship stressor. *Personal Relationships, 1,* 241–258.

Hemphill, K. J., & Lehman, D. R. (1991). Social comparisosn and their affective consequences:

The importance of comparison dimension and individual variables. *Journal of Social and Clinical Psychology, 10*, 372–394.

Hogg, M. A. (1992). *The social psychology of group cohesiveness.* New York: Harvester Wheatsheaf.

Hoorens, V. (1993). Self-enhancement and superiority biases in social comparison. In W. Stroebe & M. Hewstone (Eds.), *European Review of Social Psychology* (Vol. 4, pp. 113–139). Chichester, England: Wiley.

Hyman, H. (1942). The psychology of status. *Archives of Psychology, 269.*

Jensen, M. P., & Karoly, P. (1992). Comparative self-evaluation and depressive affect among chronic pain patients: An examination of selective evaluation theory. *Cognitive Therapy and Research, 16*, 297–308.

Klein, W. M. (1997). Objective standards are not enough: Affective, self-evaluative, and behavioral responses to social comparison information. *Journal of Personality and Social Psychology, 72*, 763–774.

Klein, W. M., & Weinstein, N. D. (1997). Social comparison and unrealistic optimism about personal risk. In B. P. Buunk & F. X. Gibbons (Eds.), *Health, coping, and well-being: Perspectives from social comparison theory* (pp. 25–61). Mahwah, NJ: Erlbaum.

Kluwer, E. S., Heesink, J. A. M., & Van de Vliert, E. (1997). The marital dynamics of conflict over the division of labor. *Journal of Marriage and the Family, 59*, 635–653.

Kulik, J. A., & Mahler, H. I. M. (1997). Social comparison, affiliation, and coping with acute medical threats. In B. P. Buunk & F. X. Gibbons (Eds.), *Health, coping, and well-being: Perspectives from social comparison theory* (pp. 227–261). Mahwah, NJ: Erlbaum.

Ladewig, B. H. & White, P. N. (1984). Dual-earner marriages: The family social environment and dyadic adjustment. *Journal of Family Issues, 5*, 343–362.

Lockwood, P., & Kunda, Z. (1997). Superstars and me: Predicting the impact of role models on the self. *Journal of Personality and Social Psychology, 73*, 91–103.

Marks, G. (1984). Thinking one's abilities are unique and one's opinions are common. *Personality and Social Psychology Bulletin, 10*, 203–208.

Marks, G., & Miller, N. (1987). Ten years of research on the false consensus effect: An empirical and theoretical review. *Psychological Bulletin, 102*, 72–90.

Martz, J. M., Verette, J., Arriaga, X. B., Slovik, L. F., Cox, C. L., & Rusbult, C. E. (1998). Positive illusions in close relationships. *Personal Relationships, 5*, 159–181.

Marsh, H. W., & Parker, J. W. (1984). Determinants of student self-concept: Is it better to be a relatively large fish in a small pond even if you don't learn to swim as well? *Journal of Personality and Social Psychology, 47*, 213–231.

McFarland, C., & Miller, D. T. (1990). Judgment of self–other similarity: Just like other people, only more so. *Personality and Social Psychology Bulletin, 16*, 475–484.

Mettee, D. R., & Smith, G. (1977). Social comparison and interpersonal attraction: The case for dissimilarity. In J. M. Suls & R. L. Miller (Eds.), *Social comparison processes: Theoretical and empirical perspectives* (pp. 69–101). Washington, DC: Hemisphere.

Meyer, H. H. (1980). Self-appraisal and job performance. *Personnel Psychology, 33*, 291–295.

Mills, J., & Mintz, P. M. (1972). Effect of unexplained arousal on affiliation. *Journal of Personality and Social Psychology, 24*, 11–14.

Morse, S., & Gergen, K. J. (1970). Social comparison, self-consistency, and the concept of self. *Journal of Personality and Social Psychology, 16*, 148–156.

Murray, S. L., & Holmes, J. G. (1997). A leap of faith? Positive illusions in romantic relationships. *Personality and Social Psychology Bulletin, 23*, 586–604.

Oldersma, F. L., & Buunk, B. P. (1997). De invloed van relatieverheffende sociale vergelijking op de waargenomen kwaliteit van de relatie [The impact of relationship-enhancing social comparison on the perceived relationship quality]. In D. Daamen, A. Pruyn, W. Otten, & R. Meertens (Red.), *Sociale psychologie en haar toepassingen* (Vol. 11, pp. 77–90). Delft, The Netherlands: Eburon.

Oldersma, F. L., De Dreu, C. K. W., & Buunk, B. P. (1995). Gevolgen van zelfen partnerverheffing voor de waargenomen kwaliteit van de relatie [Consequences of self- and partner-enhancement for the perceived relationship quality]. In N. K. De Vries, C. K. W. De Dreu, N. Ellemers, & R.

Vonk (Red.), *Fundamentele sociale psychologie* (Vol. 9, pp. 153–160). Tilburg, The Netherlands: Tilburg University Press.

Pina, D. L., & Bengtson, V. L. (1993). The division of household labor and wives' happiness: Ideology, employment, and perceptions of support. *Journal of Marriage and the Family, 55*, 901–912.

Rabbie, J. M. (1963). Differential preference for companionship under threat. *Journal of Abnormal and Social Psychology, 67*, 643–648.

Rofé, Y. (1984). Stress and affiliation: A utility theory. *Psychological Review, 91*, 235–250.

Rusbult, C. E., Van Lange, P. A. M., Verette, J., & Yovetich, N. A. (1995). *Perceived superiority as a relationship maintenance mechanism.* Unpublished manuscript, University of North Carolina at Chapel Hill.

Schachter, S. (1959). *The psychology of affiliation.* Stanford, CA: Stanford University Press.

Sillars, A. L., & Kalbflesch, P. J. (1989). Implicit and explicit decision-making styles in couples. In D. Brinberg & J. Jaccard (Eds.), *Dyadic decision-making* (pp. 179–215). New York: Springer-Verlag.

Singer, J. E., & Shockley, V. L. (1965). Ability and affiliation. *Journal of Personality and Social Psychology, 1*, 95–100.

Smith, R. H., & Insko, C. A. (1987). Social comparison choice during ability evaluation: The effects of comparison publicity, performance feedback, and self-esteem. *Personality and Social Psychology Bulletin, 13*, 111–122.

Spears, R., & Manstead, A. S. R. (1990). Consensus estimation in social context. In W. Stroebe & M. Hewstone (Eds.), *European Review of Social Psychology* (Vol. 1, pp. 81–109). Chichester, England: Wiley.

Steil, J. M. (2000). Contemporary marriage: Still an unequal partnership. In C. Hendrick & S. S. Hendrick (Eds.), *Close relationships: A sourcebook* (pp. 125–138). Thousand Oaks, CA: Sage.

Suls, J., Wan, C. K., & Sanders, G. S. (1988). False consensus and false uniqueness on estimating the prevalence of health-protective behaviors. *Journal of Applied Social Psychology, 18*, 66–79.

Suls, J. M., & Wills, T. A. (1991). *Social comparison: Contemporary theory and research.* Hillsdale, NJ: Erlbaum.

Surra, C. A., & Milardo, R. M. (1991). The social psychological context of developing relationships: Interactive and psychological networks. In W. H. Jones & D. Perlman (Eds.), *Advances in personal relationships* (Vol. 3, pp. 1–36). London: Jessica Kingsley.

Taylor, S. E., & Brown, J. D. (1988). Illusion and well-being: A social psychological perspective on mental health. *Psychological Bulletin, 103*, 193–210.

Taylor, S. E., Buunk, B. P., Collins, R. L., & Reed, G. M. (1992). Social comparison and affiliation under threat. In L. Montada, S.-H. Filipp, & M. J. Lerner (Eds.), *Life crises and experiences of loss in adulthood* (pp. 213–227). Hillsdale, NJ: Erlbaum.

Taylor, S. E., & Lobel, M. (1989). Social comparison activity under threat: Downward evaluation and upward contacts. *Psychological Review, 96*, 569–575.

Taylor, S. E., Wood, J. V., & Lichtman, R. R. (1983). It could be worse: Selective evaluation as a response to victimization. *Journal of Social Issues, 39*, 19–40.

Tesser, A. (1988). Toward a self-evaluation maintenance model of social behavior. In L. Berkowitz (Ed.), *Advances in Social Psychology* (Vol 21, pp. 181–227). New York: Academic Press.

Testa, M., & Major, B. (1990). The impact of social comparisons after failure: The moderating effects of perceived control. *Basic and Applied Psychology, 11*, 205–218.

Titus, S. L. (1980). A function of friendship: Social comparisons as a frame of reference for marriage. *Human Relations, 33*, 409–431.

Van der Zee, K. I., Oldersma, F. L., Buunk, B. P., & Bos, D. A. J. (1998). Social comparison preferences among cancer patients as related to neuroticism and social comparison orientation. *Journal of Personality and Social Psychology, 75*, 801–810.

Van Lange, P. A. M., & Rusbult, C. E. (1995). My relationship is better than – and not as bad as – yours is: The perception of superiority in close relationships. *Personality and Social Psychology Bulletin, 21*, 32–44.

Van Yperen, N. W., & Buunk, B. P. (1990). A longitudinal study of equity and satisfaction in intimate relationships. *European Journal of Social Psychology, 20*, 287–309.

Van Yperen, N. W., & Buunk, B. P. (1991). Sex-role attitudes, social comparison, and satisfaction with relationships. *Social Psychology Quarterly, 54*, 169–180.

Weinstein, N. D. (1980). Unrealistic optimism about future life events. *Journal of Personality and Social Psychology, 39*, 806–820.

Wills, T. A. (1981). Downward comparison principles in social psychology. *Psychological Bulletin, 90*, 245–271.

Wills, T. A. (1987). Downward comparison as a coping mechanism. In C. R. Snyder & C. E. Ford (Eds.), *Coping with negative life events: Clinical and social psychological perspectives.* New York: Plenum.

Wood, J. V. (1989). Theory and research concerning social comparisons of personal attributes. *Psychological Bulletin, 106*, 231–248.

Wood, J. V. (1996). What is social comparison and how should we study it? *Personality and Social Psychology Bulletin, 22*, 520–537.

Wood, J. V., Taylor, S. E., & Lichtman, R. R. (1985). Social comparison in adjustment to breast cancer. *Journal of Personality and Social Psychology, 49*, 1169–1183.

Ybema, J. F., & Buunk, B. P. (1993). Aiming at the top? Upward social comparison of abilities after failure. *European Journal of Social Psychology, 23*, 627–645.

Ybema, J. F., & Buunk, B. P. (1995). Affective responses to social comparison: A study among disabled individuals. *British Journal of Social Psychology, 34*, 279–292.

Zimbardo, P., & Formica, R. (1963). Emotional comparison and self-esteem as determinants of affiliation. *Journal of Personality, 31*, 141–162.

PART V

Self and Identity

16 An Evolutionary-Psychological Approach to Self-esteem:
   Multiple Domains and Multiple Functions   411
   Lee A. Kirkpatrick and Bruce J. Ellis

17 Is Loving the Self Necessary for Loving Another? An Examination
   of Identity and Intimacy   437
   W. Keith Campbell and Roy F. Baumeister

18 The Self We Know and the Self We Show: Self-esteem,
   Self-presentation, and the Maintenance of Interpersonal Relationships   457
   Mark R. Leary

19 Self-expansion Model of Motivation and Cognition in Close
   Relationships and Beyond   478
   Arthur Aron, Elaine N. Aron, and Christina Norman

PART V

Chapter Sixteen

An Evolutionary-Psychological Approach to Self-esteem: Multiple Domains and Multiple Functions

Lee A. Kirkpatrick and Bruce J. Ellis

Evolutionary Perspectives on Self-evaluation and Self-esteem

Perhaps more ink has been devoted to the issue of *self-esteem* – loosely, the degree to which we evaluate ourselves positively or negatively – than to any other single topic in psychology. Self-esteem has been defined in a variety of ways and been analyzed into any number of constellations of dimensions, types, and subtypes. It has been recurrently implicated in phenomena of considerable psychological and social importance, from prejudice, aggression, and criminality to mood disorders, eating disorders, and other serious mental health problems. Much research focuses on perceived abilities and competence, while other research focuses on interpersonal relations, physical attractiveness, or perceived control over outcomes. Some scholars focus on defense and maintenance of self-esteem; others on its enhancement. Virtually every major psychological theory touches on the issue in some way, and the need to maintain and enhance self-esteem is widely assumed to be a fundamental human motive (Leary & Downs, 1995).

What is sorely needed is a deeper, overarching theoretical framework to bring order to this fragmented literature, to organize future research, and to provide a solid basis for applications of this knowledge in the real world. In this chapter we endeavor to show that the emerging paradigm of evolutionary psychology (Buss, 1995, 1999; Symons, 1987; Tooby & Cosmides, 1992) offers a powerful metatheoretical framework for doing so. We do not aspire, in this brief chapter, to develop a comprehensive theory of self-esteem. Our

We wish to thank David Buss, Michael Kernis, and Mark Leary for their very helpful comments on an earlier version of this chapter.

more modest goal is merely to illustrate some ways in which an evolutionary-psychological perspective is valuable in illuminating a variety of issues surrounding the topics of self-evaluation and self-esteem.

Our point of departure is sociometer theory, as developed by Leary and his colleagues (Leary & Baumeister, 2000; Leary & Downs, 1995; Leary, Tambor, Terdal, and Downs, 1995), which we review briefly in the next section. We then introduce two general sets of issues raised by an evolutionary-psychological perspective – adaptive function and do-main-specificity – and suggest some extensions and refinements of sociometer theory in light of these issues. In the final major section of the chapter, we address a sampling of prominent topics and problems in the social-psychological literature on self-esteem, and suggest some ways in which our framework may provide some unique insights, and a basis for generating testable hypotheses for empirical research, concerning these topics.

Sociometer Theory and Evolutionary Psychology

We believe that sociometer theory represents a significant advance over previous theories about the nature and origins of self-esteem. Leary and colleagues offer several important arguments that illustrate the application and utility of evolutionary-psychological thinking to social-psychological topics, and provide a general conceptualization of self-esteem that differs fundamentally from previous conceptualizations and provides a strong foundation upon which we will build in this chapter.

Leary et al. (1995) begin by noting that while theorists have long taken for granted the importance of self-esteem, and many researchers have investigated numerous causes and consequences of low and high self-esteem, few have asked the fundamental questions: (1) What exactly *is* self-esteem?, and (2) what is its *function*? (for a notable exception see Greenberg, Solomon, & Pyszczynski, 1986; Solomon, Greenberg, & Pyszczynski, 1991.) Their answer is that self-esteem is not a free-floating goal state that people are motivated to enhance and protect. Rather, it is an internal index or gauge – a "sociometer" – designed to monitor our success with respect to other adaptive goals. Leary et al. offer as an analogy the fuel gauge in an automobile, which is designed to alert the driver to refill the tank when the fuel level becomes dangerously low.

Leary et al. (1995) argue persuasively that the domain monitored by the sociometer is that of interpersonal relationships. Consistent with many other theorists such as Cooley (1902) and Rosenberg (1979), they suggest that self-esteem reflects in large part people's perceptions of how others feel about them. More specifically, they argue that the sociometer is designed to monitor one's level of *social inclusion* or *acceptance* versus *social exclusion* or *rejection*. They argue further that this sociometer represents an adaptation designed by natural selection for this purpose. A crucial adaptive problem faced by our ancestors, they maintain, was to be accepted by others as part of "the group," as rejection by the group would pose a significant threat to survival and a loss of the many well-documented benefits of group living. The sociometer is thus designed to alert one when one's level of social inclusion is dangerously low, so as to motivate corrective action to restore inclusion/acceptance to a favorable level.

We cannot overemphasize the degree to which this perspective represents a radical (and long overdue) shift from the prevailing framework underlying much past and current research on self-esteem. As summarized by Harter (1993, p. 87), "It is commonly asserted in the literature that the self-concept is a theory, a cognitive construction, and that its architecture – by evolutionary design – is extremely functional. . . . One such widely touted function is to maintain high self-esteem." From an evolutionary perspective, however, the idea that a self-system has been crafted by natural selection with the function of "maintaining high self-esteem" is dubious. It is not clear why having high self-esteem per se would have been adaptive – in the evolutionary currency of inclusive fitness – for our ancestors. Simply feeling good, for example, does not directly translate into viable offspring.[1] Moreover, there are costs to be considered as well: the effects of high self-esteem on interpersonal functioning and mental health are by no means uniformly positive (Baumeister, Smart, & Boden, 1996; Colvin, Block, & Funder, 1995; Tennen & Affleck, 1995). If perpetually high self-esteem per se were in fact universally adaptive, natural selection would have designed us simply to have it.

Another consequence of the prevailing conceptualization is that it entails the supposition that *low* self-esteem reflects some kind of maladaptation or malfunction. Harter (1993, p. 88), for example, is led to ask: "Given this functional scenario, why should the system falter, leading certain individuals to experience . . . low self-esteem?" The subtitle of the book in which her chapter appears, "The puzzle of low self-esteem," clearly illustrates this underlying assumption. From an evolutionary point of view, however, low self-esteem is no more a puzzle than is high self-esteem, and it surely does not necessarily reflect malfunctioning of an adaptive system. If you take a swig of spoiled milk and experience an unpleasant taste, has your evolved taste system malfunctioned? If you later enjoy a delicious culinary feast in a fine restaurant, is the system now working better? In both cases the system is functioning exactly as it was designed, alerting you as to which foods to avoid and which to ingest with gusto. In ancestral environments, individuals who were capable of such discriminations and differential affect died of fewer diseases and had healthier offspring; those who could not did not become our ancestors. We are not designed to enjoy the taste of all foods, or there would be no point in having a capacity to discriminate flavors.

According to Leary and colleagues, self-esteem works in a similar (though more complex) way: It is designed to monitor something about our success and failure in solving one or more adaptive problems (cf. avoiding disease-laden foods and seeking nutritious, healthful ones). The evolutionary approach then leads directly to the next questions: What adaptive problem(s) are these?, and how do self-evaluations and self-esteem help us to solve them?

Multiple Domains of Self-esteem[2]

A central premise of evolutionary psychology is that the brain/mind comprises numerous, domain-specific mechanisms (much as the remainder of the body comprises numerous, functionally distinct organs) representing evolved solutions to recurrent adaptive problems in ancestral human environments. Stated simply, qualitatively different adaptive problems require qualitatively different solutions: The brain/mind cannot be designed entirely as a general problem-solving device "because there is no such thing as a general problem," just as there are no all-purpose kitchen devices that perform all possible food-processing tasks (Symons, 1992, p. 142; also see Tooby & Cosmides, 1992, for a detailed discussion). Numerous domain-specific mechanisms are required to solve the diverse adaptive problems faced by our ancestors, from procuring food to finding suitable habitats, negotiating status hierarchies, and avoiding predators.

Likewise, interpersonal relationships of various types differ qualitatively with respect to the particular adaptive problems they pose and the solutions required to negotiate them successfully (Daly, Salmon, & Wilson, 1997). Attachment and caregiving systems guide parent–infant interactions but not sibling interactions; mechanisms of reciprocity and cheater-detection underlie social exchange relationships but not nepotistic relationships; mechanisms of sexual attraction guide mateships but not friendships. To paraphrase Symons, there can be no such thing as an all-purpose set of decision rules for guiding behavior in social relationships because there is no such thing as an all-purpose social relationship.

We therefore suggest that natural selection is likely to have fashioned numerous psychological mechanisms for monitoring functioning in distinct types of relationships. A general social-inclusion gauge alone seems unlikely to provide sufficiently detailed information about the nature of the adaptive problem to be solved, or to be very useful in guiding appropriate behavior to solve that problem. For example, a sociometer that monitors levels of inclusion and exclusion from professional work coalitions may be useful in guiding job search strategies, but not very useful in deciding whether to challenge or submit to competitors in agonistic encounters. Similarly, a sociometer that monitors levels of acceptance and rejection from romantic partners may be useful for guiding one's mate-selection strategy but not for guiding one's job-search strategy.

To return to Leary's dashboard analogy, a global sociometer designed to monitor success across all kinds of social relationships seems akin to a single, all-purpose gauge designed to monitor the engine's overall functioning. Cars do not (typically) possess such an all-purpose gauge, however; instead, they come equipped with a fuel gauge for monitoring levels of gasoline, a tachometer for monitoring engine speed in rpm, a thermometer for monitoring engine temperature, and so on. This is the case for at least two reasons. First, it is not clear how one would design an all-purpose gauge. What part of the car would it hook up to as a source of input? The only way to design such a gauge would be to first construct more specific mechanisms to tap into particular aspects of the car's functioning (engine temperature, fuel level, etc.), and then send output from these mechanisms to the global gauge. Second, and perhaps more important, a global automotive-functioning gauge would not be very useful, as it would offer little guidance for determining what needs to be done to fix the problem.[3]

Of course, the idea that global self-esteem might be carved into more specific "domains" is not new; indeed, self-esteem research has for some time evinced an increasing focus on domain-specificity (Harter, Waters, & Whitesell, 1998). Previous researchers have proposed various numbers of types or dimensions of self-esteem, such as competence or achievement, virtue or morality, power or control, and love-worthiness or acceptance by others (e.g., Coopersmith, 1967; Epstein, 1973). In most cases, multidimensionality has been inferred from factor-analytic results (Harter et al., 1998). An evolutionary perspective, in contrast to this descriptive approach, offers a strong theoretical basis for distinguishing types or dimensions of self-esteem in terms of the ways in which they operate to help solve different kinds of adaptive problems. By "carving nature at its joints," this approach is more likely to distinguish types or domains of self-esteem that correspond to real, functional differences in the operation of these mechanisms, thereby offering a more powerful heuristic for guiding empirical research.

Social inclusion

We concur with Leary et al. (1995) and numerous other self-esteem theorists with respect to the assumption that self-esteem is (largely) social in origin and reflects (largely) affect-laden perceptions of how others feel about us.[4] From an evolutionary perspective, however, we expect that several functionally distinct kinds of relationships are important for different reasons, and that domain-specific sociometers might therefore be associated with each. We will not attempt to resolve the question of exactly how many such sociometers there might be, but merely illustrate a few major categories of interpersonal relationships and the kinds of sociometers that might be associated with them.

A crucial problem of social life concerns acceptance in various forms of coalitions and alliances. This includes *macro-level* groups (i.e., one's tribe, village, community, or nation) as well as *micro-level* groups within the larger population. As suggested by Leary et al. (1995), it has always been important for humans to be "socially included" within the local population in order to obtain various benefits of group living, such as access to local resources and defense against outgroups. Self-esteem in this domain, we hypothesize, should be related to feelings of belongingness (Baumeister & Leary, 1995) and a sense of being an accepted member of one's local community or nation. It might also be correlated with such constructs as nationalism or patriotism (Schatz, Staub, & Lavine, 1998).

Within local populations, humans, like chimpanzees (Wrangham & Peterson, 1996), routinely form smaller coalitions and alliances. Inclusion in these micro-level groups affords a variety of benefits, including mutual social support, physical protection, access to external resources (e.g., food, shelter, territory), access to mating opportunities, and coalitional support in negotiating status and dominance hierarchies. Self-esteem in this domain should be reflected in feelings of being loved and/or valued by family, friends, and colleagues, and should be correlated empirically with such constructs as perceived social support, social integration, and (absence of) loneliness.

An evolutionary perspective on group affiliation highlights several types of micro-level groups that should be especially relevant to self-esteem:

Instrumental coalitions.   A special type of group relationship involves instrumental coalitions, which we define as a group of two or more individuals who coordinate their efforts to achieve shared, valued objectives. Participation in instrumental coalitions involves interdependence and subordination of individual interests to shared goals that cannot be achieved alone. Over the course of human evolutionary history, intergroup aggression and hunting of large game animals involved formation of instrumental coalitions. These coalitional activities were crucial both for obtaining animal protein and for obtaining greater sexual access to women (as a recurrent resource that flowed to the victors of war; Chagnon,

1992; Manson & Wrangham, 1991). Because group-level hunting and warfare are en-gaged in predominantly (and in most cases exclusively) by men in all human societies (Manson & Wrangham, 1991; Murdock & Provost, 1973), and because of the historical importance of these coalitional activities to male reproductive success, selection can be expected to have shaped men's affiliative psychologies to especially value participation in these kinds of groups. (See especially Tiger's, 1969, book-length treatise on the emotional satisfaction and self-validation achieved by men through participation with other men in instrumental coalitions.) Hence, we hypothesize that perceived inclusion in instrumental coalitions (such as competitive sports teams, secret societies, and gangs) will be an impor-tant facet of self-esteem, and that it should on average be more central to men's than to women's overall feelings of self-worth.

Mating relationships.   From an evolutionary perspective, no interpersonal relationships are more important than mating relationships. Attracting and retaining mates is a sine qua non of successful reproduction. It follows, therefore, that specialized sociometers should be designed to assess one's success in the "mating game." We expect that separate sociometers monitor success in short-term mating (i.e., success in achieving short-term sexual access to a variety of partners) and long-term mating (i.e., success in forming committed relation-ships with reliable and nurturant mates). According to sexual strategies theory (Buss & Schmitt, 1993), both short- and long-term mating strategies are components of both wom-en's and men's evolved psychologies, but women and men differ (on average) in the rela-tive weightings they place on short- and long-term strategies.

Because men (much more than women) can increase the number of offspring produced through short-term matings (see Trivers, 1972), selection can be expected to have shaped men's (more than women's) sexual psychology to value short-term matings; hence, we hypothesize that inclusion in short-term sexual relationships will be a more central aspect of male than female self-esteem. Conversely, because women's reproduction is limited more than men's by access to economic and nutritional resources (Clutton-Brock, 1988; Mulder, 1987), and because women in hunting-and-gathering societies depend on men to underwrite their reproduction by providing a substantial amount of the calories consumed by women and their children (Kaplan & Lancaster, 1999), selection can be expected to have shaped women's (more than men's) sexual psychology to value long-term relation-ships with reliable and investing mates. Hence, we hypothesize that inclusion in long-term mating relationships will be a more central aspect of female than male self-esteem. Consist-ent with this theorizing, Lalumiere, Seto, and Quinsey (1995) report that number of sexual partners since puberty and in the past year were negatively correlated with self-esteem among women, but positively correlated with self-esteem among men.

Family relationships.   Kin-based relationships are of great importance to humans and many other species, though they unfortunately have received scant attention from social psy-chologists (Daly et al., 1997). Whereas investment in relationships with non-kin is largely based on social exchange (i.e., mutual cooperation and reciprocity), investment in kin-based relationships is often nepotistic. That is, individuals often invest in genetic relatives (even in the absence of reciprocity) because they have a biological interest in their well-being. As specified by inclusive fitness theory (Hamilton, 1964), genes for such *altruistic* behavior can spread through a population as long as (1) they cause an organism to help close relatives to reproduce, and (2) the cost to the organism's own reproduction is offset by the reproductive benefit to those relatives (discounted by the probability that the relatives who receive the benefit have inherited the same genes from a common ancestor). Inclusive fitness theory gives deeper meaning to the expression "blood runs thicker than water" and leads one to expect that close kin are the individuals from whom one can most expect reliable support and assistance (see Buss, 1999, and Daly & Wilson, 1988, for reviews of empirical findings).

Further, inclusive fitness theory predicts that, all else being equal, individuals will allocate investment toward genetic relatives who are most able to convert that investment into current and future reproduction. This implies that investment will preferentially be directed toward younger relatives over older ones. Thus, for example, people tend to leave much more of their estates to offspring than to siblings (Smith, Kish, & Crawford, 1987), even though the average genetic relatedness is the same across these two types of relationships. These considerations lead us to hypothesize that people have specialized psychological mechanisms for monitoring inclusion in kin-based alliances, and that the functioning of these mechanisms will show predictable patterns of developmental change across the lifespan. For example, perceived levels of inclusion and support from parents should become less central to self-esteem as individuals mature from childhood to adolescence to adulthood, making the transition from being primarily receivers to primarily givers of familial investment.

Between-group competition

Feeling "included" within social groups of various types is only one source of self-esteem related to group membership, however. Many of the most important benefits of social inclusion relate to actual or potential competition *between* groups. From an evolutionary perspective, the value of being included by other people is therefore inextricably linked to the relative quality and strength of one's own group vis-à-vis other groups. We therefore expand the definition of "sociometer" to encompass both perceived levels of social inclusion (i.e., how much gas is in the tank) and the quality or social value of the people or groups who are including or excluding us (i.e., the octane of the gas).[5]

A principal adaptive function of inclusion within one's local population concerns defense against outgroups. Ongoing inter-village warfare and raiding is common between many hunter-gatherer groups (Ember, 1978; Manson & Wrangham, 1991), and of course our newspapers are filled today with reports of inter- and intra-national warfare, ethnic cleansing, and so on. High self-esteem should therefore be associated with beliefs not only about inclusion in a collective, but also the perceived quality and strength of that collective relative to competing groups. Luhtanen and Crocker (1992) have developed a measure of *collective* self-esteem designed to assess this construct, which they interpret to be the most crucial aspect of self-esteem in social identity theory (Tajfel, 1982; Tajfel & Turner, 1986). Consistent with this, we take great pride in the accomplishments of our country in the Olympic Games, in warfare, and in other international affairs.

Similarly, coalitions and alliances within populations are frequently competitive with one another, and the adaptive value of belonging to them is therefore yoked to their relative strength and quality. Some groups control important resources and confer many benefits on those who belong while other groups do not (e.g., compare being a member of the Notre Dame football team versus belonging to most other football teams). The purpose of instrumental coalitions is often to defeat competing coalitions in a zero-sum game for scarce resources (as in politics, business, and gang wars). Sociometers for monitoring the relative strength of one's coalitions and alliances would have been selected for because inclusion in larger and stronger groups afforded benefits to the individual which translated into survival and reproduction. We take pride in the accomplishments of our school basketball team, our political party, our fraternity or sorority, or the Society for Personality and Social Psychology, because our coalitions' strength is to some extent our own.

Mating relationships are also alliances, of which the principal evolutionary function is successful childrearing (Daly et al., 1997; Kirkpatrick, 1998). Within local populations, married couples are often highly competitive, intent on maintaining the best lawn or Christmas lighting on the block or otherwise "keeping up with the Joneses." Bring groups of parents together in a room and they will often spend much of the time boasting about their respective children's accomplishments in a conversational can-you-top-this game. Bumper stickers proudly announce "My child is an honor roll student at X School," one implication of which is that your child probably is not. Thus, people draw self-esteem not only from having a spouse and a satisfying marital or dating relationship, but also from the accomplishments and quality of their partnership relative to others'.

Finally, the quality and strength of one's kin-based alliances and extended family provide an important source of self-esteem. One takes great pride in being a Capulet or a Montague, a Hatfield or a McCoy, a Rockefeller or a Kennedy. Family ties and nepotism play crucial roles in politics and competition for power and prestige. Royalty, which is invariably defined along family lines, presents a clear example of strong kin-based coalitions that have succeeded at the expense of other family lines, and belonging to a royal family is undoubtedly an important source of self-esteem for those who do. Kin-based coalitions are frequently in direct competition with one another, often violently. (See Daly & Wilson, 1988, for discussion.)

Within-group competition

In addition to tracking the relative strength of one's own group vis-à-vis other groups, self-esteem should also track one's own individual position *within* various groups. As discussed in the next section, knowing where one stands relative to the competition is extremely valuable for guiding behavior in a variety of ways. Indeed, the optimal choice among alternative paths to reproductive success often differs considerably depending on one's standing relative to others. Consequently, we propose that another distinct set of sociometers is designed to assess one's local standing with respect to competition within the kinds of groups discussed above.[6]

Within local populations, interindividual competition within most social species is ongoing with respect to several overlapping dimensions. Numerous researchers have proposed that the self-esteem system in humans is related to dominance hierarchies, suggesting that self-esteem reflects an assessment of one's status, rank, or prestige relative to (mainly intrasexual) local competitors (Barkow, 1989; Gilbert, Price, & Allan, 1995). Whether based on physical size and strength, genetic lineage, quality of territory, or other factors, species ranging from crawfish (Barinaga, 1996) to chimpanzees (de Waal, 1982) display some form of dominance ranking that determines access to resources and/or mates. Human status hierarchies are clearly much more complex than, say, chickens' pecking orders, but there can be little doubt that status-striving is a universal human motive (e.g., Buss, 1999; Daly & Wilson, 1988; Symons, 1979). As discussed in the next section, self-assessments of dominance or status function to guide individuals to either challenge or submit in conflictual situations.

Other researchers have focused specifically on the adaptive problem of attracting mates, and suggested that self-esteem might reflect self-evaluations of the degree to which one is valued as a mate by members of the other sex (e.g., Dawkins, 1982; Kenrick, Groth, Trost, & Sadalla, 1993; Wright, 1994). Self-perceived *mate value* is determined by social feedback concerning one's attractiveness to the opposite sex, such as previous history of success and failure in mating, in combination with appraisals of the extant competition (Gutierres, Kenrick, & Partch, 1999). Other indicators might include feedback with respect to intrasexual competition concerning one's abilities, intelligence, and other characteristics indicative of potential mate quality. As discussed in the next section, self-assessments of mate value are important for guiding choices of mates and of mating strategies.

Within-group competition also takes place within otherwise cooperative coalitions and alliances. For example, same-sex friends or members of a group may vie for the same award, the same starting position on a baseball team, the same job opening, or the same potential mate. Likewise, dating and marital partners may compete over issues of investment and power within their relationship. Similarly, different family members often compete for access to familial resources of power and wealth (consider the ugly legal disputes that sometimes emerge over the distribution of a deceased family member's estate). And, of course, sibling rivalry over parental investment is well known in a variety of literatures, including countless ethological examples with respect to nonhuman species. As discussed in the next section, choosing the right strategies for negotiating and investing in relationships with other group members, from mates to kin to instrumental coalition partners, is contingent on self-evaluations of relative status within the group.

Global vs. specific, trait vs. state

Most previous researchers who have emphasized the domain-specificity of self-esteem have still retained the construct (and measures) of global self-worth or self-esteem, typically regarding it as a higher-order construct in a hierarchical model under which specific self-evaluations are nested (e.g., Harter et al., 1998). Our view is not inconsistent with this conceptualization, except insofar as it provides a theoretical basis for identifying the specific domains and the conditions under which each is most relevant. We suspect, however, that it is the domain-specific sociometers that generally are more functionally important in terms of guiding behavior and personality development.

However global self-esteem is sliced, its dimensions or components are invariably intercorrelated empirically. If, as we have argued, self-esteem comprises numerous domain-specific sociometers, why should this be the case? In fact, our perspective suggests several reasons to expect sociometers to be intercorrelated. First, certain characteristics are valued in the context of many different relationship domains. A man of large stature and physical strength, for example, is potentially valuable both as a mate (i.e., with respect to providing protection to mates and offspring) and as a coalitional partner (e.g., as part of a hunting or war party). Similarly, psychological traits such as kindness and loyalty are highly valued in both friends and mates. To the extent that one evinces such characteristics, then, he or she is likely to be socially accepted across a variety of relationship contexts, and consequently to experience high self-esteem across these domains.

Second, high status or inclusion in certain kinds of relationships often confers benefits with respect to other forms of status or inclusion. High status within the local population, for example, renders one desirable to others as a potential coalition partner or mate. Conversely, ties to a strong coalition (the benefits of which are resources available for social exchange) enhance one's value as a potential mate or friend. In this way success in one domain can lead to success in another, one consequence of which is that self-esteem in those respective domains will be intercorrelated. Moreover, to the extent that such interrelations among characteristics and domains were regular features of ancestral environments, it seems plausible that sociometers may themselves be interconnected within our psychological architecture. For example, to the extent that high status attained through intrasexual or inter-group competition was regularly predictive of enhanced mate value and mating opportunities – a widespread phenomenon throughout the animal world – it seems possible that (especially for men) a status sociometer might be designed to send output directly to a mate-value sociometer.

Although much of our discussion up to this point has focused implicitly on *state* self-esteem, we suggest that *trait* self-esteem is similarly domain-specific. Leary and Baumeister (2000) propose that state self-esteem reflects an (affect-laden) appraisal of one's current level of social inclusion, whereas trait self-esteem reflects an appraisal of one's *potential* or likely future level of inclusion. In other words, state self-esteem gauges current *acceptance*, whereas trait self-esteem gauges *acceptability*. We suggest that this same distinction might be applied within each of the separate self-esteem domains we propose, as will become evident in the next section.

Multiple Functions of Self-esteem

Implicit in the view that the brain/mind comprises a number of domain-specific sociometers is the assumption that these sociometers do a number of different things: sociometers evolved because they are (or were, to our distant ancestors) useful in many ways for solving adaptive problems. The fuel-gauge analogy, as well as the word "socio*meter*" itself, is somewhat misleading on this point, because gauges and meters do nothing more than display measurements.[7] Perhaps a better analogy is an engine-temperature sensor that not only sends output to a dashboard gauge, but also automatically activates an auxiliary cooling fan when a critical temperature is attained. Similarly, many older cars contained a small reserve gas tank that came online when the primary tank was detected as empty.

In this view, the dashboard gauges can be thought of as affective outputs of different sociometers. We propose that in addition to indicating the presence of specific types of problems in this way, sociometers have a second (and perhaps more important) function: to activate strategies for solving these problems. Just as temperature and fuel-level sensors function to activate different mechanical systems (e.g., cooling fans or reserve fuel tanks), we propose that different sociometers function to activate different psychological systems and processes, both at a broad level (in terms of guiding personality development) and at a more specific level (in terms of guiding day-to-day decision making and behavioral strategies). In this section we outline several of these proposed functions.

Guiding personality development

One of the basic assumptions of an evolutionary psychological perspective is that individuals have evolved to be able to function competently in a variety of different environments. According to conditional adaptation models (e.g., Belsky, Steinberg, & Draper, 1991; Mealey, 1995), what enables this flexibility and adaptation is that, as part of the inherited architecture of the brain, humans possess a repertoire of alternative developmental paths. Which strategy is "chosen" depends both on genotype and on exposure to evolutionarily relevant environmental cues during childhood.

Attachment theorists, for example, emphasize the role of early family relationships and support in the development of subsequent personality. In attachment theory, children's perceptions of inclusion and exclusion by relevant caregivers are conceptualized as their *internal working models* of attachment (Bowlby, 1969/1982). In Belsky et al.'s (1991) theory of the development of reproductive strategies, contextual stressors in early childhood are hypothesized to foster more negative and coercive (or less positive and harmonious) family relationships, which in turn are hypothesized to provoke earlier pubertal and sexual development. A key element of the theory is that the child's perception of support by family members – his or her family sociometer – influences subsequent development of differential reproductive strategies. Consistent with this, Ellis, McFadyen-Ketchum, Dodge, Pettit, and Bates (1999) found that greater warmth and positivity in the parent–child relationship, as observed in the summer prior to kindergarten, predicted later pubertal timing in daughters in the seventh grade (see also Graber, Brooks-Gunn, & Warren, 1995).

Alternative courses of personality development may also derive (in part) from self-assessment of competitive abilities (cf. Tooby & Cosmides's, 1990, discussion of "reactive heritability"). For example, many theorists have suggested that low self-esteem is a contributing factor to delinquency and criminality (e.g., Kaplan, 1980; Rosenberg, Schooler, & Schoenbach, 1989). Mealey (1995) specifically cites a perceived inability to compete for resources and mates according to conventional, socially sanctioned means as a primary causal factor in secondary sociopathy. Similarly, individual differences in self-perceived mate value may influence the development of reproductive strategies (e.g., Gangestad & Simpson, 2000; Kenrick et al., 1993). For example, men (but not women) who perceive themselves as relatively low in mate value have been found to pursue a more monogamous mating strategy, including later age of first sexual intercourse, fewer sexual partners, lower frequency of sexual intercourse, and reception of fewer sexual invitations from the opposite sex (Lalumiere et al., 1995). In sum, variations in self-perceived competitive abilities may function to channel individuals toward different life strategies that adaptively mesh with their competitive abilities.

Directly addressing a deficiency

In addition to influencing the development of personality dispositions such as sociopathy and sociosexual orientation, variations in self-esteem should also influence more immediate decision-making and behavioral choices. Leary et al. (1995) discuss only one way in which a warning message from the sociometer might be used to organize or guide behavior: consistent with the fuel-gauge analogy, they suggest that the function of an "E" reading is to alert one to the need to refill the gas tank. That is, the sociometer indicates that one has a deficiency of something (in this case, social inclusion), and the behavioral response is to redouble efforts to obtain that something. For example, a sociometer sensitive to cues that one's current mating relationship is in jeopardy should activate a number of behavioral responses for defending the relationship (or replacing it).

Although a sociometer may sometimes be useful for guiding behavior in this way, simply refilling the tank often is not an available or adaptive strategy. If people have learned from repeated rejections that members of the opposite sex do not find them attractive, then simply increasing efforts to make oneself more attractive are likely to be ineffective. Persistent attempts by a subordinate to be "socially included" by a powerful, dominant competitor could well lead to physical injury or death. Moreover, if self-esteem invariably worked this way, we should expect people with low self-esteem to work harder and persevere longer at tasks than those with high self-esteem; however, precisely the opposite pattern has been demonstrated in empirical research (e.g., Perez, 1973; Shrauger & Sorman, 1977). It is likely, therefore, that sociometers guide decision-making and behavior in other ways as well.

Guiding adaptive relationship choices

All individuals have a limited amount of investment – time, energy, resources – to budget toward various activities. Because natural selection favors individuals who make propitious decisions relative to the alternatives available to them in budgeting investment, selection should act against individuals who either (1) invest too heavily in social relationships that are substantially lower in value than they can command on the social marketplace (and thus fail to get a fair return on the value they bring to the relationships), or (2) waste investment pursuing social relationships that are higher in value than what they can realistically obtain in the social marketplace. Accordingly, we hypothesize that an important function of self-esteem is to guide individuals to approach social relationships that are of the highest quality possible, yet defensible given one's own social value (Hoop & Ellis, 1990).

For example, if a job candidate for an academic position is continually rejected by first-tier institutions, the accompanying decrement in professional self-esteem should guide the candidate to recalibrate his or her job search downward toward second- or third-tier institutions. Conversely, a plethora of job interviews and offers from lower tier institutions should boost professional self-esteem, leading the candidate to redirect his or her job search upward. Through gauging the response to his or her job applications, the candidate discovers his or her niche of acceptance and rejection on the job market. We propose that the candidate's feelings of professional self-esteem reflect his or her internal, subjective perception of this niche. These feelings function to guide job search effort toward institutions with which the candidate is well matched. Variation across candidates in feelings of professional self-esteem should make the job search process faster, more efficient, and ultimately more successful by adaptively guiding candidates toward positions that are of relatively high quality within the individual's range of affordability.

Similar self-evaluative processes should also guide approach behavior toward other types of social relationships, such as friendships and mateships (see Kenrick et al., 1993). In the mating domain, self-assessed mate value (relative to the perceived competition) provides important information for guiding partner preferences. One of us (L.K.) finds Helen Hunt particularly desirable as a potential mate, but prudently avoids wasting very much time or effort in trying to win her affections. Conversely, people (as well as close kin and friends concerned about their welfare) are clearly sensitive to the issue of choosing mates of lower value than that permitted by their own "market value." Along these lines, much evidence suggests that people typically wind up mating with partners who are similar to themselves, both in overall attractiveness (Feingold, 1988) and on a wide array of specific characteristics (Buss, 1985). Although a variety of explanations for this effect are available (see Kalick & Hamilton, 1986), several studies point explicitly to the effect of self-evaluations on mate preferences. For example, a classic study by Berscheid, Dion, Walster, and Walster (1971) showed that men's and women's minimal standards for attractiveness of a date were related to their own level of attractiveness. Similarly, Kenrick et al. (1993) and Regan (1998) showed that, at least for women, self-appraisals on mate value and other socially desirable characteristics were predictive of minimal standards acceptable in a potential mate.

Calibrating investment within ongoing relationships

Although processes of self-evaluation should generally guide individuals toward social partners with whom they are reasonably well-matched, people nonetheless sometimes become involved in "mismatched" relationships. As mentioned above, heavy investment in a social relationship that is substantially lower in value than an individual can command on the social marketplace should be selected against; however, relatively low-investment strategies in mismatched relationships may have been favored by natural selection. Consider, for example, a woman who can choose between two husbands, A and B. Her friends consider Husband A to be a "good catch" for her: he is healthy, strong, professionally successful, well-liked, and respected by his peers. Husband B, by contrast, is physically weak, has a floundering career, few friends, and is submissive to others. Even though the woman's friends think that "she could do better" than Husband B, marrying Husband A is not necessarily the best choice. In order to maintain her relationships with Husband A, she may have to devote most of her time, energy, and resources to the marriage. This heavy

investment in one domain restricts the amount of investment she can allocate to other domains, such as development of a professional career, pursuit of additional mateships, and
maintenance of friendships. In contrast, in order to maintain her relationship with Husband B, she may have to devote relatively little of her time, energy, and resources to the
marriage (while monopolizing most of Husband B's investment in return). Meanwhile, she
is able to channel most of her investment into other domains. This suggests that mating
downward in mate value could be an evolutionarily stable strategy in certain contexts.

Given these kinds of dynamics, natural selection can be expected to have designed psychological mechanisms to evaluate (1) one's own value in social relationships, (2) the value
of relationship partners, and (3) the difference between these two evaluations. We hypothesize that these assessments of relative value function to calibrate not only one's own level
of investment in ongoing relationships, but also the level of investment expected from
partners. Individuals who perceive themselves to be higher in value than their relationship
partners can be expected to invest less and expect more in return.

For example, differential levels of parental investment by mate value have been documented in both birds and humans. Burley (1986) showed that after being experimentally
manipulated to be more attractive to females, male zebra finches reduced their levels of
parental care (and achieved increased success in extra-pair matings) while their mates increased their parental care. Among the Aka pygmies of central Africa, men who hold positions of high status in the tribe (*kombeti*) only hold their infants for an average of 30
minutes per day, whereas men who lack positions of status hold their infants for an average
of 70 minutes per day (Hewlett, 1991). *Kombeti*, who are highly desired as husbands,
appear to calibrate levels of parental investment downward and then channel extra investment into additional matings (they are usually polygynous, with two or more wives). In
contrast, lower-status men with fewer resources, who are fortunate to even have one wife,
appear to calibrate levels of parental investment upward (compensating for their weaker
position by investing more time in caring for and protecting their children).

Negotiating dominance/status hierarchies

A parallel line of reasoning applies to behavioral choices regarding agonistic or competitive
relationships. In most species, very few intrasexual conflicts are resolved by actual fighting;
instead, mismatches are typically avoided because competitors are able to quickly gauge
who would likely win a fight, and the expected loser defers to the expected winner. Thus,
self-assessments of fighting ability or status – in the animal literature, *resource-holding
potential*, or *RHP* – lead individuals to back down from agonistic encounters in which they
are likely to lose (so as not to risk injury and waste energy) and to initiate such encounters
when they are likely to win (so as to take advantage of available resources and opportunities; Gilbert et al., 1995; Parker, 1974). Wenegrat (1984) has argued that RHP may be one
element of human self-esteem.

Chimpanzees, along with many other primate and non-primate species including humans, have elaborate, differentiated behavioral patterns for interacting with other individuals of higher versus lower status than themselves (de Waal, 1982). High-status
competitors are treated with deference and respect; one behaves in dominant ways toward

those below and in submissive ways toward those above (e.g., Maclay & Knipe, 1972). Although now-discredited group-selectionist theories interpreted such behaviors as designed for maintaining the social order for the good of the group or the species (e.g., Wynne-Edwards, 1986), a more defensible interpretation is that different alternative strategies are more adaptive depending on one's status within the local hierarchy. For those near the bottom an adaptive strategy is to bide one's time and hope for a change in the competitive landscape, showing deference and using strategies such as ingratiation to remain in favor with more powerful individuals (Dawkins, 1989; Wrangham & Peterson, 1996).

The ability to accurately gauge one's status within the local hierarchy, and hence the potential adaptive utility of the various behavioral strategies, is crucial for guiding appropriate dominant and submissive behavior. Low RHP, for example, leads weaker, smaller organisms to avoid directly challenging dominant competitors (and likely suffering serious injury or death in the attempt). Price, Sloman, Gardner, Gilbert, and Rhode (1994) conceptualize depression as a yielding mechanism that functions to inhibit aggressive behavior toward rivals and superiors when one's status is low.

Social psychologists have found that people adopt different *self-presentational strategies* as a function of differential self-esteem (Baumeister, Tice, & Hutton, 1989; Wolfe, Lennox, & Cutler, 1986). Those with high self-esteem (reflecting high self-perceived status) can afford to adopt riskier *acquisitive* or *enhancing* strategies in which they call attention to their strengths and abilities and portray themselves as confident and optimistic. In contrast, those with low self-esteem (reflecting low self-perceived status) tend to adopt a more self-protective self-presentational strategy in which they seek to deflect attention from themselves and approach tasks without raising others' expectations about their likelihood of success. Other researchers have shown that men possessing traits that facilitate intrasexual competitive success adopt different strategies than those who do not when competing for a date (e.g., engaging in direct comparison with and derogation of competitors; Simpson, Gangestad, Christensen, & Leck, 1999).

Summary

An evolutionary perspective on self-esteem focuses attention on the adaptive, functional value of self-evaluations – on the ways in which these evaluations are useful (or, more precisely, were useful to our ancestors) in solving adaptive problems. Because different types of interpersonal relationships differ qualitatively with respect to the particular adaptive problems they pose, a number of different sociometers serving a variety of functions – from guiding personality development to initiating submission to dominant competitors – are needed to negotiate these relationships successfully.

Implications for Some Issues in the Self-esteem Literature

We believe that an evolutionary perspective on self-esteem, and particularly the ideas of domain-specificity and adaptive functionality, offer a useful framework for reconceptualizing (and for generating empirically testable hypotheses about) a variety of major issues in the self-esteem literature. In this section we offer some illustrative examples with respect to a small sample of such issues.

Stability and contingency of self-esteem

Recent work by Kernis and his colleagues (Greenier, Kernis, & Waschull, 1995; Kernis, Cornell, Sun, Berry, & Harlow, 1993) suggests that the degree of stability in self-esteem over time, in addition to the average level of self-esteem, is an important individual-difference variable. Although level and stability are not statistically independent (i.e., stability is positively correlated with level), stability has a number of unique correlates. The two general issues on which we have focused in this paper – multiplicity of domains and multiplicity of adaptive functions – each lead to a hypothesis concerning the nature of individual differences in the stability of self-esteem.

The first possibility is that individual differences in the stability of self-esteem reflect the fact that the activity of any given sociometer varies across time. Once one has established satisfactory levels of inclusion in social groups, for example, the corresponding sociometer may go off-line until circumstances change and it is needed again (Leary & Baumeister, in press). Similarly, a mate-value sociometer should be active when one is on the "mating market," but turn off after one commits to a stable pair-bond relationship (Frank 1988; Kirkpatrick, 1998). We would therefore hypothesize that self-esteem is more stable among people currently involved in satisfying, ongoing relationships than among those who are not. We would also generally expect people in novel social environments (e.g., college freshmen) to display relatively unstable self-esteem until they have determined their position in local status and dominance hierarchies, and have established new friendships and coalitions. This perspective also helps to explain why self-esteem tends to be highly unstable during adolescence (Harter et al., 1998), a period during which we would expect many sociometers to be more or less chronically active.

The second possibility is that stable versus unstable self-esteem reflects activation of two or more distinct sociometers in different domains. A given sociometer should produce variable output to the extent that feedback about successes and failures is itself variable; such variability might be expected to differ naturally between domains. In competition with respect to status or mate value, for example, success can vary considerably across time: one might be congratulated by one's boss one day but castigated the next, or have a date invitation rejected one day but accepted the next. Inclusion in friendships and coalitions, in contrast, typically does not vary as much from day to day. This perspective could explain why Kernis et al. (1993, Study 2) unexpectedly found that people with relatively unstable (global) self-esteem were more likely than those with stable self-esteem to identify competence and physical attractiveness – but not social acceptance – as important determinants of their self-worth. People whose status-competition sociometers are highly active may be prone to less stable self-esteem, whereas those whose self-esteem hinges more upon social acceptance may evince more stable self-esteem.

Other constructs in the self-esteem literature may also be subject to similar reinterpretations. For example, although it is typically conceptualized in terms of exaggerated or unstable high self-esteem, *narcissism* "may be less a matter of having a firm conviction about one's overall goodness . . . than a matter of being emotionally invested in one's superiority" (Bushman & Baumeister, 1998, p. 220). That is, narcissism might reflect a disproportionately high level of activity of competition-related sociometers (e.g., status and dominance) relative to social-inclusion sociometers. This interpretation is consistent with other observations about narcissists, such as their high levels of hostility and aggressiveness (e.g., Bushman & Baumeister, 1998).

Social comparison and BIRGing

Another closely related issue concerns the degree to which social comparison processes are involved in the determination and maintenance of self-esteem. Since Festinger's (1954) seminal work, an enormous body of research has examined the role of social comparison in social psychological processes (e.g., Suls & Wills, 1991), including self-esteem.

Our view suggests that some sociometers are more inherently social-comparative than others. Mate value and status are by definition competitive, reflecting relative success in a zero-sum game, but inclusion in friendships or coalitions is ordinarily less so. Thus, our view provides a perspective for distinguishing among domains of self-esteem with respect to the degree to which social comparison processes are involved. In addition, it suggests that individual differences in the degree to which people are actively engaged in social comparison thinking are a function of which sociometers (domains) are currently active.

Whereas competitive domains are inherently social-comparative, the construct of *basking in reflected glory* ("BIRGing"; Cialdini et al., 1976; Tesser, Millar, & Moore, 1988) seems more clearly related to cooperative relationships such as friendships and coalitions. An individual's accomplishments indirectly benefit his or her friends and associates; a person's success is his or her partners' success, leading us to take pride in the accomplishments of our family members and coalition partners. In contrast, competitors for mating opportunities are unlikely to BIRG; in zero-sum contests, one person's success is another's failure. We think that theories such as Tesser's model of self-evaluation maintenance (Tesser, 1988; Beach & Tesser, 1995) could be extended and clarified by differentiating qualitatively different kinds of relationships and evaluations in the context of multiple, functionally distinct sociometers.

Self-enhancement

If, as we have argued, sociometers are designed to monitor our current standing with respect to particular domains in the service of guiding us toward adaptive strategic choices, one might expect them to be designed to do so as accurately as possible. However, a vast body of literature suggests that most of us have modestly inflated views of ourselves (e.g., more of us believe that we are above average than is mathematically possible) and display a variety of related "positive illusions" (Taylor & Brown, 1988). Why should a well-designed (from an evolutionary perspective) sociometer evince such a pervasive self-enhancement bias?

We believe that there may well be an inherent positive bias in the calibration of some, if not all, sociometers. As summarized by Alcock (1995; also see Haselton & Buss, 2000), our evolved psychology is designed to be adaptive, not necessarily truthful. Adaptations for information processing are biased to the extent that some kinds of errors are consistently more costly (in inclusive fitness terms) than others. A rabbit is better served by mistaking a harmless rustling of leaves caused by the wind for a predator than the other way around; ancestral rabbits that were accurate rather than paranoid did not become rabbit ancestors. Krebs and Denton (1997) suggest that many familiar social cognitive biases, from positive illusions to ingroup and outgroup biases, reflect adaptive design of these cognitive systems rather than malfunctions. Leary, Haupt, Strausser, and Chokel (1998) suggest that the self-esteem sociometer might indeed be calibrated with a built-in positive bias in this manner – "much like a fuel gauge that indicates that the gas tank is fuller than it really is" (p. 1290).

Although the adaptive advantages of accuracy were one selection pressure that shaped the evolution of sociometers, we suspect that there was another, conflicting pressure as well. Because one's value in interpersonal domains is primarily a function of how one is evaluated by others, one way to raise one's value on that dimension is by deceiving others about one's true value. The effectiveness of impression management strategies is limited by others' well-tuned abilities to detect deception in self-presentation; it is difficult to convince others of our worth if we are not so convinced ourselves. (See Zahavi & Zahavi, 1997, for a discussion of other reasons why dishonest signaling systems in general are unlikely to evolve.) Positive illusions may therefore represent a form of *self*-deception designed to enhance the effectiveness of an ongoing attempt to "induce others to overvalue us" (Krebs & Denton, 1997).

An interesting alternative perspective, offered by Leary and Baumeister (in press), likens self-esteem-enhancement to drug abuse. High self-esteem feels good by virtue of its design and, consequently, we seek out ways to experience that affective high. Much as "a drug such as cocaine may create a euphoric feeling without one's having to actually experience events that normally bring pleasure . . . [C]ognitively inflating one's self-image is a way of fooling the natural sociometer mechanism into thinking that one is a valued relational partner" (p. 24). We would add that one might alternatively fool other sociometers into thinking that one has high status, or is a desirable mate, and so forth.

According to Leary and Downs (1995, p. 129), "most behaviors that have been attributed to the need to maintain self-esteem may be parsimoniously explained in terms of the motive to avoid social exclusion." We concur, but add that many such behaviors might be explained in terms of other self-esteem domains and functions. From our perspective, self-enhancement processes represent just one aspect – and, in some sense, only a peripheral aspect – of the adaptive design of sociometers more generally.

Self-verification and depressive realism

Based on the traditional assumption that seeking high self-esteem is a fundamental motive, one might expect that self-enhancing biases would be particularly evident among people with the lowest levels of social inclusion, status, and other forms of social success; after all, it is they who presumably need it the most. We are inclined to hypothesize exactly the opposite. If sociometers are designed to motivate and organize alternative behavioral strategies as a function of status, mate value, or social inclusion, then individuals who are failing are those for whom a positive bias would be *least* adaptive. If one's social-inclusion sociometer sounds an alarm, particularly in light of its (default) positive bias, it suggests that something is seriously wrong. Fooling oneself into believing otherwise could have disastrous consequences.

Instead, the alert should motivate efforts to reappraise one's situation as accurately as possible, in order to determine if major behavioral changes or alternative strategies are called for. This analysis is consistent with research by Swann (1987) and others demonstrating that persons with low self-appraisals prefer self-verifying (consistency-enhancing) rather than self-enhancing feedback from others. Moreover, whereas self-enhancement processes may occur automatically and effortlessly, self-verification (or consistency) processes are cognitively effortful (Swann, Hixon, Stein-Seroussi, & Gilbert, 1990). Our hypothesis is that sociometers are calibrated by default to be (modestly) upwardly biased, for reasons discussed above, but that additional cognitive processes designed to deactivate these biases and to generate accurate self-appraisals are activated by low readings.

This view is also consistent with much research indicating that depressed people are "sadder but wiser," in that their views of themselves and their worlds are not biased by positive illusions and are in fact more accurate (e.g., Alloy & Abramson, 1979). Although the proximal consequences and correlates of depression appear dysfunctional in many modern circumstances, it is possible that depression involves activation of a behavioral strategy for taking time out to reassess one's situation and/or to wait for better times. If one has repeatedly experienced failure in the competition for mates, for example, an adaptive strategy would be to suspend competitive efforts temporarily and wait for a change in the competitive landscape (e.g., due to competitors weakening, dying, or moving away). The capacity to experience learned helplessness may be an adaptation designed to enable individuals to determine when they are truly helpless – that is, when continuation of one's current behavioral strategy is unlikely to lead to success with respect to a particular domain. Although it is certainly possible that at least some forms of depression are truly maladaptive, and represent some kind of malfunctioning of an otherwise adaptive system, our perspective suggests that it might be fruitful to reexamine depression in terms of a behavioral strategy activated by low self-esteem in one or more domains.

Cross-cultural differences in self-esteem processes

A common misunderstanding about evolutionary psychology is that the posited existence of species-universal psychological mechanisms seems inconsistent with the observation of cross-cultural variability in behavior. A simple illustration shows why this is not true. Human skin is designed with a callus-producing mechanism that responds to friction by toughening the skin. Although this adaptation is shared by people in all cultures, enormous variability can be observed both between people and between cultures depending on experience and environmental variability: calluses on the feet are common in cultures where people walk barefoot, but not where they typically wear shoes (Buss, 1995).

Several researchers have suggested that the emphasis on achievement, task performance, and other social-comparative dimensions as a primary basis for self-esteem is unique to modern Western cultures – specifically, *individualistic* (versus *collectivist*) cultures (Markus & Kitayama, 1991; Triandis, Bontempo, Villareal, Asai, & Lucca, 1988). In collectivist cultures, it is argued, self-esteem is more closely related to matters concerning one's acceptance within the group or society rather than to interindividual competition. Our perspective suggests a way to conceptualize this difference in terms of the particular sociometers that are regularly activated within the local environment (cf. the callus analogy). In environments in which success depends on integration within the local group, or strong coalitional relationships, coalition-related sociometers are likely to be regularly or chronically activated, whereas a sociometer designed to monitor status and rank might remain quiescent; the reverse is true in cultures in which success in most domains depends on competition rather than cooperation.

Another view is suggested by Leary and Baumeister (2000), who suggest that contemporary Westerners' (especially Americans') obsession with self-esteem may be a consequence of the relative (and evolutionarily novel) instability of social relationships in modern society. When people move away from their families, change jobs, and get divorced at high rates, they repeatedly find themselves in new contexts in which they must reassess or rebuild their relative standing and interpersonal relationships.

Implications for intervention

In recent years, the idea that low self-esteem lies at the heart of a variety of personal and societal problems has become popular among legislators and the general public, and has led to interventions designed to boost the self-esteem of schoolchildren as a prevention strategy (e.g., California Task Force to Promote Self-esteem and Personal and Social Responsibility, 1990). The perspective on self-esteem we have outlined in this chapter suggests at least two ways in which such a strategy could be severely misguided.

Our view (like Leary's) of self-esteem as a functional, dynamic system that monitors one's degree of success in particular domains, rather than as an end in itself, suggests that manipulating self-esteem is like treating symptoms without treating their underlying cause. Interventions designed to manipulate self-esteem directly are akin to counseling drivers to feel better about the fact that their car is overheating, rather than stopping and adding water to the radiator. (See Leary, 1999, for a general discussion of implications of the sociometer model for clinical and counseling psychology.)

Second, our view (unlike Leary's) further suggests that interventions are likely to fail unless they are directed toward the relevant domain of self-esteem. For example, individuals who feel a lack of coalitional inclusion may remain unaffected by attempts to manipulate their feelings of (or actual) accomplishment and competence – and vice versa. Adding water to the radiator will not be very helpful if the gas tank is empty. Our perspective suggests that intervention strategies must first identify the domain of self-esteem in which an individual is at risk, determine the conditions that are leading to negative self-evaluations within this domain, and then target intervention strategies accordingly. Again, however, effective interventions are likely to be those that work toward fixing the underlying causes of the problems, not the gauges that simply monitor them.

Conclusion

Sociometer theory represents a significant advance in self-esteem research, and opens the door to a dynamic view of self-esteem processes based on evolutionary psychology. As Leary and colleagues have argued, self-esteem reflects the operation of adaptation(s) designed to monitor success and failure in negotiating interpersonal relations. We have offered an extension of the model, based on evolutionary psychology, and attempted to illustrate just a few of the ways in which a functional, domain-specific view of sociometers might inform research on long-standing issues in the self-esteem literature.

With respect to the structure of self-esteem, an evolutionary approach offers a way of potentially "carving nature at its joints." That is, it should be possible to identify components or dimensions of self-esteem that parallel the actual design of our species-general cognitive architecture, rather than simply reflecting the conscious self-reflections of contemporary Western college students. We believe this approach offers a promising basis for constructing better self-esteem measures and for generating hypotheses about the antecedents and consequences of varying levels of self-esteem within specific domains.

From an evolutionary perspective, function is inextricably tied to structure. Following Leary et al. (1995), an evolutionary approach shifts attention away from the problem of enhancing, maintaining, and restoring self-esteem per se, and toward the interpersonal relationships and problems that sociometers are designed to monitor. It shifts attention away from the gauges in the dashboard of the car and toward the engine, transmission, and auxiliary components that actually determine automotive functioning. Such an approach is not only theoretically rich and inherently interesting, but has clear implications for practice and intervention.

We wish to emphasize once again that this chapter is intended as no more than a general framework for guiding research and generating testable hypotheses. Future research may well show that there are many more (or at least different) sociometers than we have suggested here. We have no doubt that many more adaptive functions of such sociometers remain to be identified, and that many other current issues in the self-esteem literature can be usefully reexamined from this perspective. We are equally confident that a functional, evolutionary approach has enormous heuristic value for guiding and generating exciting new research on self-esteem in social psychology and the many other disciplines within which the construct of self-esteem plays an important role.

Notes

1. Even though happy people may on average live slightly longer or suffer fewer medical problems, such effects typically are not evident until well beyond the primary reproductive years.
2. We acknowledge that many researchers might prefer to use a term such as *self-evaluation* rather than *self-esteem* in referring to distinct domains. However, we prefer to follow Leary and Baumeister (in press) in defining self-esteem in terms of affectively laden appraisals of one's own value.
3. Actually, many modern automobiles do in fact come equipped with a kind of general warning

light, labeled simply "engine" or something equally cryptic, which is activated by an on-board computer that internally monitors a variety of specific aspects of engine functioning. The reason for this design, we presume, is that the kinds of engine problems that would activate it are those that drivers would be unable to repair without a mechanic. Although the computer monitors many domains of engine functioning, in this case they all have just one functional solution for the average driver: Bring the car to a mechanic – i.e., someone with the experience and knowledge required to solve the problem. Human infants are designed in a similar manner: they respond to all kinds of discomfort and cues of potential danger with attachment behaviors intended to increase proximity to a primary caregiver (Bowlby, 1969/1982). Adults, however, have much more differentiated strategic and behavioral repertoires, and we suspect that their brains/minds are designed to implement a diverse collection of adaptive strategies for dealing with different problems.

4. Another major source of self-esteem recognized by most theorists involves self-perceived competence and abilities or self-efficacy (Bandura, 1977) – self-evaluations that are not inherently social in nature. Given space limitations, we have chosen to focus our discussion only on interpersonal relationships. We hope it will be evident, however, that the theoretical approach adopted in this chapter could be applied to self-evaluations of skills and competencies in a similar manner. To some extent this analysis would resemble that of Harter (1993), in which the importance of self-perceived competencies derives in large part from their anticipated impact on the evaluations of important others – with different competencies linked to different classes of relationships.

5. We thank Mark Leary for suggesting the analogy of octane versus fuel level. We also note that Leary's own preference is to reserve the term "sociometer" for the latter (personal communication, July 1999). We think, however, that *socio-meter* aptly describes many of the other facets of self-esteem discussed in this paper as well.

6. Leary and Baumeister (2000) argue instead that the role of dominance in self-esteem is in the service of social inclusion; that is, status "is sometimes a criterion for inclusion" and "has implications for one's relational value" (p. 19). We address the interrelatedness of sociometers later in the chapter, but simply note here that status/dominance and inclusion/acceptance are often quite independent. For example, it may be "lonely at the top" because intense status-striving can undermine social inclusion.

7. We thank Don Forsyth for bringing this point to our attention.

References

Alcock, J. E. (1995). The belief engine. *Skeptical Inquirer, 19*(3), 14–18.

Alloy, L. B., & Abramson, L. Y. (1979). Judgment of contingency in depressed and nondepressed students: Sadder but wiser? *Journal of Experimental Psychology, 108*, 441–485.

Bandura, A. (1977). Self-efficacy: Toward a unifying theory of behavioral change. *Psychological Review, 84*, 191–215.

Barinaga, M. (1996). Social status sculpts activity of crayfish neurons. *Science, 171*, 290–291.

Barkow, J. H. (1989). *Darwin, sex, and status: Biological approaches to mind and culture.* Toronto: University of Toronto Press.

Baumeister, R. F., & Leary, M. R. (1995). The need to belong: Desire for interpersonal attachments as a fundamental human motivation. *Psychological Bulletin, 117*, 497–529.

Baumeister, R. F., Smart, L., & Boden, J. M. (1996). Relation of threatened egotism to violence and aggression: The dark side of self-esteem. *Psychological Review, 103*, 5–33.

Baumeister, R. F., Tice, D. M., & Hutton, D. G. (1989). Self-presentational motivations and personality differences in self-esteem. *Journal of Personality, 57*, 547–579.

Beach, S. R. H., & Tesser, A. (1995). Self-esteem and the extended self-evaluation maintenance model: The self in social context. In M. H. Kernis (Ed.), *Efficacy, agency, and self-esteem* (pp. 145–170). New York: Plenum.

Belsky, J., Steinberg, L., & Draper, P. (1991). Childhood experience, interpersonal development, and reproductive strategies: An evolutionary theory of socialization. *Child Development, 62,* 647–670.

Berscheid, E., Dion, K., Walster, E., & Walster, G. W. (1971). Physical attractiveness and dating choice: A test of the matching hypothesis. *Journal of Experimental Social Psychology, 1,* 173–189.

Bowlby, J. (1969/1982). *Attachment and loss: Vol. 1. Attachment.* New York: Basic Books. (Original work published 1969)

Burley, N. (1986). Sexual selection for aesthetic traits in species with biparental care. *American Naturalist, 127,* 415–445.

Bushman, B. J., & Baumeister, R. F. (1998). Threatened egotism, narcissism, self-esteem, and direct and displaced aggression: Does self-love or self-hate lead to violence? *Journal of Personality and Social Psychology, 75,* 219–229.

Buss, D. M. (1985). Human mate selection. *American Scientist, 73,* 47–51.

Buss, D. M. (1995). Evolutionary psychology: A new paradigm for psychological science. *Psychological Inquiry, 6,* 1–30.

Buss, D. M. (1999). *Evolutionary psychology: The new science of the mind.* Boston: Allyn & Bacon.

Buss, D. M., & Schmitt, D. P. (1993). Sexual strategies theory: An evolutionary perspective on human mating. *Psychological Review, 100,* 204–232.

California Task Force to Promote Self-esteem and Personal and Social Responsibility (1990). *Toward a state of self-esteem.* Sacramento: California State Department of Education.

Chagnon, N. A. (1992). *Yanomamo: The last days of Eden.* San Diego, CA: Harcourt Brace Jovanovich.

Cialdini, R. B., Borden, R. J., Thorne, A., Walker, M. R., Freeman, S., & Sloan, L. R. (1976). Basking in reflected glory: Three (football) field studies. *Journal of Personality and Social Psychology, 34,* 366–375.

Clutton-Brock, T. H. (Ed.) (1988). *Reproductive success: Studies of selection and adaptation in contrasting breeding systems.* Chicago: University of Chicago Press.

Colvin, C. R., Block, J., & Funder, D. C., (1995). Overly positive self-evaluations and personality: Negative implications for mental health. *Journal of Personality and Social Psychology, 68,* 1152–1162.

Cooley, C. H. (1902). *Human nature and the social order.* New York: Scribner's.

Coopersmith, S. (1967). *The antecedents of self-esteem.* San Francisco: W. H. Freeman.

Daly, M., Salmon, C., & Wilson, M. (1997). Kinship: The conceptual hole in psychological studies of social cognition and close relationships. In J. A. Simpson & D. T. Kenrick (Eds.), *Evolutionary social psychology* (pp. 265–296). Mahwah, NJ: Erlbaum.

Daly, M., & Wilson, M. (1988). *Homicide.* New York: Aldine de Gruyter.

Dawkins, R. (1982). *The extended phenotype.* San Francisco: W. H. Freeman.

Dawkins, R. (1989). *The selfish gene* (new ed.). Oxford: Oxford University Press.

de Waal, F. (1982). *Chimpanzee politics: Power and sex among apes.* Baltimore: Johns Hopkins University Press.

Ellis, B. J., McFadyen-Ketchum, S., Dodge, K. A., Pettit, G. S., & Bates, J. E. (1999). Quality of early family relationships and individual differences in the timing of pubertal maturation in girls: A longitudinal test of an evolutionary model. *Journal of Personality and Social Psychology, 77,* 387–401.

Ember, C. R. (1978). Myths about hunter-gatherers. *Ethnology, 27,* 239–448.

Epstein, S. (1973). The self-concept revisited: Or a theory of a theory. *American Psychologist, 28,* 404–416.

Feingold, A. (1988). Matching for attractiveness in romantic partners and same-sex friends: A meta-analysis and theoretical critique. *Psychological Bulletin, 104,* 226–235.

Festinger, L. (1954). A theory of social-comparison processes. *Human Relations, 7,* 117–140.

Frank, R. H. (1988). *Passions within reason: The strategic role of the emotions.* New York: Norton.

Gangestad, S. W., & Simpson, J. A. (2000). The evolution of human mating: trade-offs and strategic pluralism. *Behavioral and Brain Sciences, 23,* 573.

Gilbert, P., Price, J., & Allan, S. (1995). Social comparison, social attractiveness, and evolution: How might they be related? *New Ideas in Psychology, 13,* 149–165.

Graber, J. A., Brooks-Gunn, J., & Warren, M. P. (1995). The antecedents of menarcheal age: Heredity, family environment, and stressful life events. *Child Development, 66,* 346–359.

Greenberg, J., Solomon, S., & Pyszczynski, T. (1986). The causes and consequences of a need for self-esteem: A terror management theory. In R. F. Baumeister (Ed.), *Public self and private self* (pp. 189–212). New York: Springer-Verlag.

Greenier, K. D., Kernis, M. H., & Waschull, S. B. (1995). Not all high (or low) self-esteem people are the same: Theory and research on stability of self-esteem. In M. H. Kernis (Ed.), *Efficacy, agency, and self-esteem* (pp. 51–71). New York: Plenum.

Gutierres, S. E., Kenrick, D. T., & Partch, J. J. (1999). Beauty, dominance, and the mating game: Contrast effects in self-assessment reflect gender differences in mate selection. *Personal and Social Psychology Bulletin, 25,* 1126–1134.

Hamilton, W. D. (1964). The evolution of social behavior. *Journal of Theoretical Biology, 7,* 1–52.

Harter, S. (1993). Causes and consequences of low self-esteem in children and adolescents. In R. F. Baumeister (Ed.), *Self-esteem: The puzzle of low self-regard* (pp. 87–116). New York: Plenum.

Harter, S., Waters, P., & Whitesell, N. R. (1998). Relational self-worth: Differences in perceived worth as a person across interpersonal contexts among adolescents. *Child Development, 69,* 756–766.

Haselton, M. G., & Buss, D. M. (2000). Biases in cross-sex mindreading: Errors in design or errors by design? *Journal of Personality and Social Psychology, 78,* 81–91.

Hewlett, B. S. (1991). *Intimate fathers: The nature and context of Aka pygmy paternal infant care.* Ann Arbor: University of Michigan Press.

Hoop, D. K., & Ellis, B. J. (1990). *An evolutionary approach to cognitive concepts in personality.* Unpublished manuscript, University of Michigan.

Kalick, S. M., & Hamilton, T. E. (1986). The matching hypothesis reexamined. *Journal of Personality and Social Psychology, 51,* 673–682.

Kaplan, H. B. (1980). *Deviant behavior in defense of self.* New York: Academic Press.

Kaplan, H. S., & Lancaster, J. B. (1999, April). The evolution of human life course and male parental investment. In J. B. Lancaster (Chair), *Evolutionary and cross-cultural perspectives on male parental investment.* Symposium conducted at the biennial meeting of the Society for Research in Child Development, Albuquerque, NM.

Kenrick, D. T., Groth, G. E., Trost, M. R., & Sadalla, E. K. (1993). Integrating evolutionary and social exchange perspectives on relationships: Effects of gender, self-appraisal, and involvement level on mate selection criteria. *Journal of Personality and Social Psychology, 64,* 951–969.

Kernis, M. H., Cornell, D. P., Sun, C., Berry, A., & Harlow, T. (1993). There's more to self-esteem than whether it is high or low: The importance of stability of self-esteem. *Journal of Personality and Social Psychology, 65,* 1190–1204.

Kirkpatrick, L. A. (1998). Evolution, pair-bonding, and reproductive strategies: A reconceptualization of adult attachment. In J. A. Simpson & W. S. Rholes (Eds.), *Attachment theory and close relationships* (pp. 353–393). New York: Guilford Press.

Krebs, D. L., & Denton, K. (1997). Social illusions and self-deception: The evolution of biases in person perception. In J. A. Simpson & D. T. Kenrick (Eds.), *Evolutionary social psychology* (pp. 21–47). Mahwah, NJ: Erlbaum.

Lalumiere, M. L., Seto, M. C., & Quinsey, V. L. (1995). *Self-perceived mating success and the mating choices of human males and females.* Unpublished manuscript, Queen's University at Kingston, Ontario, Canada.

Leary, M. R. (1999). The social and psychological importance of self-esteem. In R. M. Kowalski & M. R. Leary (Eds.), *The social psychology of emotional and behavioral problems* (pp. 197–221). Washington, DC: APA Books.

Leary, M. R., & Baumeister, R. F. (2000). The nature and function of self-esteem: Sociometer theory. In M. Zanna (Ed.), *Advances in experimental social psychology* (*Vol. 32*, pp. 1–62). San Diego, CA: Academic Press.

Leary, M. R., & Downs, D. L. (1995). Interpersonal functions of the self-esteem motive: The self-esteem system as a sociometer. In M. H. Kernis (Ed.), *Efficacy, agency, and self-esteem* (pp. 123–144). New York: Plenum.

Leary, M. R., Haupt, A. L., Strausser, K. S., & Chokel, J. T. (1998). Calibrating the sociometer: The relationship between interpersonal appraisals and state self-esteem. *Journal of Personality and Social Psychology, 74*, 1290–1299.

Leary, M. R., Tambor, E. S., Terdal, S. K., & Downs, D. L. (1995). Self-esteem as an interpersonal monitor: The sociometer hypothesis. *Journal of Personality and Social Psychology, 68*, 518–530.

Luhtanen, R., & Crocker, J. (1992). A collective self-esteem scale: Self-evaluation of one's social identity. *Personality and Social Psychology Bulletin, 18*, 302–318.

Maclay, G., & Knipe, H. (1972). *The dominant man.* New York: Delta.

Manson, J. H., & Wrangham, R. W. (1991). Intergroup aggression in chimpanzees and humans. *Current Anthropology, 32*, 369–390.

Markus, H. R., & Kitayama, S. (1991). Culture and the self: Implications for cognition, emotion, and motivation. *Psychological Review, 98*, 224–253.

Mealey, L. (1995). The sociobiology of sociopathy: An integrated evolutionary model. *Behavioral and Brain Sciences, 18*, 523–599.

Mulder, M. B. (1987). Resources and reproductive success in women with an example from the Kipsigis of Kenya. *Journal of Zoology, London, 213*, 489–505.

Murdock, G. P., & Provost, C. (1973). Factors in the division of labor by sex: A cross-cultural analysis. *Ethnology, 12*, 203–235.

Parker, G. A. (1974). Assessment strategy and the evolution of fighting behavior. *Journal of Theoretical Biology, 47*, 223–243.

Perez, R. C. (1973). The effect of experimentally-induced failure, self-esteem, and sex on cognitive differentiation. *Journal of Abnormal Psychology, 81*, 74–79.

Price, J. S., Sloman, R., Gardner, R., Gilbert, P., & Rhode, P. (1994). The social competition hypothesis of depression. *British Journal of Psychiatry, 164*, 309–315.

Regan, P. C. (1998). Minimum mate selection standards as a function of perceived mate value, relationship context, and gender. *Journal of Psychology & Human Sexuality, 10*, 53–73.

Rosenberg, M. (1979). *Conceiving the self.* New York: Basic Books.

Rosenberg, M., Schooler, C., & Schoenbach, C. (1989). Self-esteem and adolescent problems: Modeling reciprocal effects. *American Sociological Review, 54*, 1004–1018.

Schatz, R. T., Staub, E., & Lavine, H. (1999). On the varieties of national attachment: Blind versus constructive patriotism. *Political Psychology, 20*, 151–174.

Shrauger, J. S., & Sorman, P. B. (1977). Self-evaluations, initial success and failure, and improvement as determinants of persistence. *Journal of Consulting and Clinical Psychology, 45*, 784–795.

Simpson, J. A., Gangestad, S. W., Christensen, P. N., & Leck, K. (1999). Fluctuating asymmetry, sociosexuality, and intrasexual competitive tactics. *Journal of Personality and Social Psychology, 76*, 159–172.

Smith, M. S., Kish, B. J., & Crawford, C. B. (1987). Inheritance of wealth as human kin investment. *Ethology and Sociobiology, 8*, 171–182.

Solomon, S., Greenberg, J., & Pyszczynski, T. (1991). A terror management theory of social behavior: On the psychological functions of self-esteem and cultural worldviews. In M. P. Zanna (Ed.), *Advances in Experimental Social Psychology* (Vol. 24, pp. 93–159). San Diego: Academic Press.

Suls, J., & Wills, T. A. (Eds.). (1991). *Social comparison: Contemporary theory and research.* Hillsdale, NJ: Erlbaum.

Swann, W. B., Hixon, J. G., Stein-Seroussi, A., & Gilbert, D. T. (1990). The fleeting gleam of praise: Cognitive processes underlying behavioral reactions to self-relevant feedback. *Journal of Personality and Social Psychology, 59*, 17–26.

Swann, W. B. (1987). Identity negotiation: Where two roads meet. *Journal of Personality and Social Psychology, 53*, 1038–1051.

Symons, D. (1979). *The evolution of human sexuality*. New York: Oxford University Press.

Symons, D. (1987). If we're all Darwinians, what's the fuss about? In C. Crawford, D. Krebs, & M. Smith (Eds.), *Sociobiology and psychology* (pp. 121–145). Hillsdale, NJ: Erlbaum.

Symons, D. (1992). On the use and misuse of Darwinism in the study of human behavior. In J. H. Barkow, L. Cosmides, & J. Tooby (Eds.), *The adapted mind* (pp. 137–159). New York: Oxford University Press.

Tajfel, H. (1982). Social psychology of intergroup relations. *Annual Review of Psychology, 33*, 1–39.

Tajfel, H., & Turner, J. C. (1986). The social identity theory of intergroup behavior. In S. Worchel & W. Austin (Eds.), *Psychology of intergroup relations* (2nd ed., pp. 7–24). Chicago: Nelson-Hall.

Taylor, S. E., & Brown, J. D. (1988). Illusion and well-being: A social psychological perspective on mental health. *Psychological Bulletin, 103*, 193–210.

Tennen, H., & Affleck, G. (1995). The puzzles of self-esteem: A clinical perspective. In M. H. Kernis (Ed.), *Efficacy, agency, and self-esteem* (pp. 241–262). New York: Plenum.

Tesser, A. (1988). Toward a self-evaluation maintenance model of social behavior. In L. Berkowitz (Ed.), *Advances in experimental social psychology* (Vol. 21, pp. 181–227). New York: Academic Press.181–227.

Tesser, A., Millar, M., & Moore, J. (1988). Some affective consequences of social comparison and reflection processes: The pain and pleasure of being close. *Journal of Social and Personality Psychology, 54*, 49–61.

Tiger, L. (1969). *Men in groups*. New York: Random House.

Tooby, J., & Cosmides, L. (1990). On the universality of human nature and the uniqueness of the individual: The role of genetics and adaptation. *Journal of Personality, 58*, 17–67.

Tooby, J., & Cosmides, L. (1992). The psychological foundations of culture. In J. H. Barkow, L. Cosmides, & J. Tooby (Eds.), *The adapted mind* (pp. 19–136). New York: Oxford University Press.

Triandis, H. C., Bontempo, R., Villareal, M. J., Asai, M., & Lucca, N. (1988). Individualism and collectivism: Cross-cultural perspectives on self-ingroup relations. *Journal of Personality and Social Psychology, 54*, 323–338.

Trivers, R. L. (1972). Parental investment and sexual selection. In R. B. Campbell (Ed.), *Sexual selection and the descent of man: 1871–1971* (pp. 136–179). Chicago: Aldine.

Wenegrat, B. (1984). *Sociobiology and mental disorder: A new view*. Menlo Park, CA: Addison-Wesley.

Wolfe, R. N., Lennox, R. D., & Cutler, B. L. (1986). Getting along and getting ahead: Empirical support for a theory of protective and acquisitive self-presentation. *Journal of Personality and Social Psychology, 50*, 356–361.

Wrangham, R., & Peterson, D. (1996). *Demonic males: Apes and the origins of human violence*. Boston: Houghton Mifflin.

Wright, R. (1994). *The moral animal: The new science of evolutionary psychology*. New York: Pantheon.

Wynne-Edwards, V. C. (1986). *Evolution through group selection*. Oxford: Blackwell Scientific.

Zahavi, A., & Zahavi, A. (1997). *The handicap principle*. New York: Oxford University Press.

Chapter Seventeen

Is Loving the Self Necessary for Loving Another? An Examination of Identity and Intimacy

W. Keith Campbell and Roy F. Baumeister

In this chapter, we examine one important facet of the relation between identity and intimacy. Our review of this broad literature is guided by an effort to assess the popular belief that self-love is necessary for loving another. We begin by addressing some of the possible sources of this belief, including the work of Erikson, Maslow, and Rogers, as well as the influence of what has come to be called the "self-esteem movement. " We then address several specific questions: Does self-love result in love for others? Does self-love lead others to love the self ? Does loving others result in self-love? Finally, does being loved lead to self-love?

Neither "self-love" nor "loving others" are well defined psychological constructs. Therefore, in our review, we strive to be inclusive rather than exclusive in our use of these terms (although there are certainly variants of both terms that we did not examine or uncover). Our conceptualization of self-love focuses primarily on two constructs, self-esteem and narcissism. We also examine related constructs, such as social dominance and positive self-beliefs, as well as dependency and depression. Our conceptualization of loving others includes a range of relationship variables including love styles, attraction, commitment, and relationship maintenance behaviors.

Why Popular Culture has it that Self-love Is a Prerequisite for Loving Others

The notion that self-love is a necessary precursor to loving others appears to be widely accepted in popular culture. One has only to look on the shelves of any large bookstore or on the Internet to see a large selection of individuals and organizations promoting the importance of achieving self-love. Titles of books and cassette courses include *Learning how to love yourself*, and *How to love yourself: Cherishing the incredible miracle that you are*

(Cruse, 1987; Hay, 1992). At the same time, it is difficult to find individuals or organizations promoting the importance of humility for loving others or maintaining relationships. (Certain religious organizations may be an example of the latter, but their messages are arguably drowned out by the groups promoting self-love. In addition, several religious or quasi-religious groups proudly promote the virtue of self-love.)

Where did the belief that self-love is crucial for loving others come from? We review several possibilities. One is that this view stems from a misreading of the work of Erik Erikson. In his theory of psychosocial development, Erikson postulated that a sense of identity had to be established before intimacy with another could be achieved (Erikson, 1950). In Erikson's scheme, the task of establishing identity arose primarily in the teen and early young adult years. These years were spent wrestling with a crisis between achieving a solid sense of self and being trapped in a state of role confusion. If this early identity crisis was resolved appropriately, the young adult years became a time to experience intimacy. (What Erikson had in mind when he used the term *intimacy* was likely heterosexual marriage, although other stable sexual relationships would probably be evidence of similarly successful resolutions to the question of intimacy.) As Erikson put it, the crisis became one of intimacy versus isolation.

In general, some research has supported Erikson's speculations regarding the importance of achieving identity before the establishment of intimacy. Longitudinal data have shown that the establishment of identity in the teen years predicts stable intimate relationships in the young adult years, both in terms of marital status and marital stability (Kahn, Zimmerman, Csikszentmihalyi, & Getzels, 1985). These findings, however, do not unequivocally support the notion that self-love is a necessary precursor to loving others. Although a clear sense of self or identity is associated with a degree of high self-esteem (J. D. Campbell et al., 1996), stable self-views do not necessarily imply self-love. Certainly, a stable view of the self is more central to Erikson's conceptualization of identity than a positively valenced view of the self.

Two other highly influential psychological thinkers, Rogers (1961) and Maslow (1962), may have also inadvertently played a role in focusing society on the importance of self-love. These authors emphasized the importance of living up to one's ideals, even becoming self-actualized. This self-actualization was, of course, presumed to have beneficial effects on interpersonal relationships. Conversely, the positive regard of others was presumed to be a helpful first step toward self-actualization. Indeed, Rogers's model of psychotherapy rested on the therapist's ability to have unconditional positive regard for the client, as well as an accurate, empathic stance toward the client. Furthermore, it is clear that self-actualization and self-love are not the same thing, although people may have interpreted them as such. Self-actualization includes an accurate view of self, and an acceptance of the failings, problems, and shortcomings that the self contains. Self-actualization is more closely related to self-acceptance than self-love, but some of this detail may have been lost in the popularization of Rogers's work.

In addition to sharing many insights into self-actualization with Rogers, Maslow spoke of deficiency or "D" love – that is, love for which the goal is to correct for failings or deficits in the self. This concept clearly indicates that Maslow felt that self-love was not necessary for love of others. Deficit love could be based on precisely a lack of self-love, for example, if someone full of self-doubts and insecurities latched on to someone else to provide support and shore up the sense of self. Alternatively, it is plausible that individuals with inflated self-opinions would engage in loving to overcome deficits in the self. For example, a man with no job, bad looks, and weak interpersonal skills, who, at the same time, thinks he is a winner in the game of life, might seek out relational partners who would confirm his inflated self-views. Maslow also spoke of self-actualized ("B") love. Self-actualized love is evidenced not by self-love but by acceptance of one's own and others' faults, psychological non-defensiveness, spontaneity, and honesty.

Furthermore, the theoretical relationship between loving self and loving others can be inferred from Maslow's (1968) hierarchy of needs, in which he explained that people first address the most urgent, basic needs and only move on to higher needs when the basic ones are satisfied. In Maslow's hierarchy, belongingness needs are more basic to human functioning than self-esteem needs and self-actualization. Thus, in his theory, receiving love is a prerequisite for self-love, rather than the other way around. In sum, it would be a misreading of Maslow's views to propose that self-love leads to loving others.

The final source for the view that self-love may be necessary for the love of others is what is popularly called the "self-esteem movement." This is a general term for a group of movements, efforts, or attempts that stress the importance of self-esteem for success in a host of domains. The most visible emblem of this movement was the California Task Force to Promote Self-esteem and Personal and Social Responsibility. The California Task Force was signed into law by Governor George Deukmejian in 1986, and the driving force behind the legislation was Assemblyman John Vasconcellos. (Not coincidentally, Vasconcellos was strongly influenced by the work of Carl Rogers and had undergone client-centered therapy in the 1960s.) According to the California Task Force, self-esteem is important, perhaps necessary, for staying off welfare, succeeding in school, and resisting the temptations of premarital sex and drugs (Mecca, Smelser, & Vasconcellos, 1989). Indeed, self-esteem improvement has become an integral component of several efforts to cure social ills. Certainly, the ideas of the self-esteem movement have spread far into popular culture. This movement may help account for the belief that self-love is necessary for intimate relationships. (To be fair, the goal of the California Task Force was arguably noble and explicitly *not* designed as a strategy for promoting narcissism. Furthermore, the Task Force did make an effort to garner scientific evidence to support their views. Apparently, some of this has gotten lost in the dissemination and popularization of these ideas.) If feeling good about oneself is good for keeping a job, staying off drugs, and staying in school, it might also be good for staying in relationships.

Today, popular books on self-esteem often appear to consider it a truism that self-love is necessary for loving others. Nathaniel Branden, one of the most prolific promoters of self-esteem, notes that "it is not difficult to see the importance of self-esteem to success in romantic relationships" and makes explicit reference to the phrase "If you do not love yourself, you will be unable to love others" (Branden, 1994, pp. 7–8). Lesser known authors echo this point. As one author notes in a description of his book, *Loving is becoming intimate with your real self,* "You may well have noticed that people who love themselves find it easy to love others and to accept love from others" (Dolan, 1999). In the present chapter we will attempt to examine systematically the link between self-love and the love of others to see if this is actually the case.

Does Loving the Self Promote Loving Others?

We turn now from popular beliefs and theoretical speculations to actual research findings. As any experienced researcher might expect, the empirical links between self-love and loving others are far more complex and dubious than popular wisdom holds.

Self-esteem

The first step in our analysis is to examine the literature on the association between self-esteem and loving others. The popular view would predict that high self-esteem would be related to love for others. This, however, does not always appear to be the case. In an early look at this question, Dion and Dion (1975) found that low self-esteem was associated with more intense experiences of love as well as more unrequited love. (High self-esteem was associated with more frequent love experiences, but only when the favorable views of self were coupled with low defensiveness. There was no main effect of self-esteem on frequency of love.) Hendrick and Hendrick (1986) found that low self-esteem was associated with more manic love, although high self-esteem was associated with greater passionate love. Manic love is evidenced by obsession with the love object and experiencing bouts of both intense joy and intense sorrow in the relationship (Hendrick & Hendrick, 1986, 1990; Lee, 1973). This intense love experience, which in the past has been called "lovesickness" or being "sick of love," has also been reported in the clinical literature as related to low self-esteem (Moss, 1995).

Other studies have likewise linked low rather than high self-esteem to some kinds of love. In one study, women who were self-identified as "loving too much" reported self-esteem that was lower than published norms (Petrie, Giordano, & Roberts, 1992). Meanwhile, research conceptualizing love more broadly as acceptance for others has found little evidence that high self-esteem predicts love. Using a German sample, Schuetz (2000) found no relationship between self-esteem and acceptance for others. Overall, it seems, there is little evidence that self-esteem promotes loving others. Indeed, low self-esteem may be predictive of certain experiences of love.

Self-esteem may play a role in maintaining intimacy, however. Relational fidelity, for example, may be associated with high self-esteem, although evidence for any causal relationship (in either direction) is lacking (Sheppard, Nelson, & Andreoli-Mathie, 1995). Likewise, self-esteem may act as a buffer that partially shields the self from relationship stressors, such as inequity (Longmore & DeMaris, 1997) and childbirth (Terry, 1991). Put another way, romantic relationships may be affected by problems from both inside and outside of the relationship. To the extent that possessing self-esteem helps the individual cope with these negative events, self-esteem will be beneficial to the relationship. Furthermore, low self-esteem may damage romantic relationships in other ways. Low-self-esteem individuals may develop a pattern of emotional neediness in relationships. They find it difficult to fathom that someone could care about them all that much. (Not surprisingly, if you do not like yourself, you tend to assume that others will not like you.) Researchers have found that individuals low in self-esteem (at least when also depressed) constantly seek reassurance from close others (Joiner, Alfano, & Metalsky, 1992). This pattern of behavior, however, may not aid in the longevity of the relationship. On the contrary, it might impair or shorten it.

Still, it is far from clear whether self-esteem has any consistent effect on duration or maintenance of relationships. One study of marital interactions yielded a negative relationship between narcissistic grandiosity (and instability) and positive interactions with the spouse, suggesting that some forms of self-love are detrimental to good relationship maintenance. This effect was especially noticeable when participants discussed ego-threatening topics (Schuetz, 1998). Self-acceptance, however, did predict liking for and positive interactions with the spouse. Self-esteem may also be implicated in violent or aggressive responses to self-esteem threat (Baumeister, Smart, & Boden, 1996). Such threats, for example, may include jealousy stemming from one's partner's desire to leave the romantic relationship. This violence may serve some purpose in maintaining a relationship but may also seriously damage any benefits gained from it. Finally, high self-esteem may be associated with exit behaviors in response to relationship conflict (Rusbult, Morrow, & Johnson, 1987). In other words, people with favorable opinions of themselves are more likely to respond to relationship conflict by doing things that might end the relationship, possibly because they begin looking for alternative partners. This may be good for the self but detrimental to the relationship. Of course, it is possible that leaving a bad relationship may lead to a better future relationship. For example, research has noted that a lack of alternatives often leads individuals to remain in abusive relationships, whereas the presence of alternatives helps them exit (Rusbult & Martz, 1995). Still, these findings confirm that self-love can prove detrimental to relationships, contrary to the simple view that self-love breeds love for others.

Narcissists

We now turn our attention to the classic symbol of self-love in Western culture: Narcissus, the hopelessly attractive character in Greek mythology who refused the romantic offers of others and fell in love with himself. This classic image of self-love has been adapted theoretically to describe a modern personality pattern called *narcissism*. Narcissism is a personality variable that includes highly positive evaluations of self vis-à-vis others. These positive beliefs are maintained by intrapersonal strategies (e.g., fantasies of power [Raskin & Novacek, 1991], self-serving biases [Rhodewalt & Morf, 1998]) as well as interpersonal strategies) (e.g., admiration-seeking [Buss & Chiodo, 1991], social dominance [Bradlee & Emmons, 1992]). Narcissism, as one may guess, has several implications for relational functioning.

If self-love is a prerequisite for intimacy, then narcissists, the true paragons of self-love, ought to have the greatest intimate connections with others. This simple theoretical prediction, however, is contradicted by the data. Narcissists have been noted by both clinicians and social/personality psychologists to be deficient in the domain of intimacy. The formula looks something like this: self-love leads to more self-love, but detracts from other-love – when other-love is defined as caring, concern, empathy, or intimacy. This formula goes back to some of the earliest clinical reports. For example, Nacke noted a paraphilia (which he named after Narcissus) that involved kissing or touching the self (Nacke, 1899; cited in Freud, 1914/1957). Even Freud, in his introductory work on narcissism, noted two types of individuals, those of the "anaclitic" (attachment) type and those of the "narcissistic" type. The anaclitic type directs love outward toward objects (i.e., experiences intimacy). The narcissistic type, on the other hand, directs love inward to the self. For the narcissist, the object of intimacy becomes: "(a) what he himself is (i.e., himself), (b) what he himself was, (c) what he himself would like to be, (d) someone who was once part of himself" (Freud, 1914/1957, p. 90). In a later work, Freud expanded his definition of self-love to include self-sufficiency and self-preservation. Narcissists are concerned with protecting and maintaining the self (Freud, 1931/1950).

These observations are amplified in the social and personality psychology literature on the trait of narcissism. Narcissists (i.e., people who score high on the trait scale of narcissism) have high self-esteem (Raskin, Novacek, & Hogan, 1991a, 1991b) and think about themselves often (Emmons, 1987; Raskin & Shaw, 1988). They see themselves as superior (Gabriel, Critelli, and Ee, 1994) and unique (Emmons, 1984) individuals. Their self-love is associated with less need for intimacy and greater need for power (Carroll, 1987), less agreeableness and greater hostility (Rhodewalt & Morf, 1995), less communion and more agency (Bradlee & Emmons, 1992), reduced empathy and perspective taking (Watson, Grisham, Trotter, & Biderman, 1984), and (when conceptualized as inflated self-views) greater conflict in discussion (Colvin, Block, & Funder, 1995), as compared with other people. Clearly, narcissistic self-love does not seem to improve the capacity to love others; rather, it seems to impair it.

In fact, it appears that narcissists use intimate relationships to bolster or increase their own self-love. Put another way, narcissists use relationships as a forum for self-regulation – specifically, regulating the positivity of the self. This interpersonal self-regulation can take several forms. Narcissists take credit from (and even derogate) fellow group members (Gosling, John, Craik, & Robins, 1998; John & Robins, 1994) and close or similar others (W. K. Campbell, Reeder, Sedikides, & Elliot, 2000; Farwell & Wohlwend-Lloyd, 1998; Morf and Rhodewalt, 1993) in achievement settings. Narcissists report that they are smarter and more attractive than other college students (Gabriel et al., 1994) and criticize others who tell them differently (Kernis & Sun, 1994). They show off to others as part of an effort to feel grandiose or important (Buss & Chiodo, 1991; Raskin et al., 1991a, 1991b). When they date, they are attracted to other wonderful people to whom they feel similar and who make them feel important by association (W. K. Campbell, 1999). Indeed, these strategies are evident in narcissists' love styles. Narcissists report being game-playing and pragmatic (but not selfless) in romantic relationships – there is little correlation between narcissism and other love styles (W. K. Campbell & Foster, 1999). (Similar experiences of love have also been reported by individuals who are high in psychological individualism, especially when it contains placing self-interest above other-interest; Dion & Dion, 1991.) Taken together, these interpersonal self-regulatory strategies may temporarily help prop up a narcissist's sense of self-worth, but this effect is likely not to last indefinitely. Narcissists' quest for self-love actually turns off other individuals (Paulhus, 1998). It appears that not only does self-love not increase love for others but it actually decreases others' love for the self. We shall return to this point later in the chapter.

Is there any benefit of narcissism for maintaining romantic relationships? The data available so far have not shown any such benefits. It is conceivable that there are some potential benefits of narcissism to maintaining relationships. Narcissists tend to think they are better than other people (e.g., Gabriel et al., 1994). If this perceived superiority on the part of narcissists extends into their interpersonal relationships, it may increase the longevity of the relationship. Specifically, individuals who believe that their relationships are superior to others' express more commitment (Buunk & van der Eijnden, 1997; Van Lange & Rusbult, 1995), and so if narcissists hold these relationship superiority beliefs, they may also experience increased commitment. On the other hand, narcissists presumably regard themselves as exceptionally attractive to other people in general, and so they may have inflated confidence about their ability to replace a partner who does not fully satisfy them.

Echoes

It appears that self-love as defined by narcissism does not predict intimacy. So what about the opposite of narcissism? If one reflects on the story of Narcissus, there was, at least in some of the tellings, another important character, Echo. Echo was desperately in love with Narcissus, so much so that she repeated every word that he said. Hence, even if narcissism is detrimental to love, maybe "echoism" promotes love. This has intuitive appeal, although the myth tells us otherwise. Echo may have been willing to experience love, but she did not win a healthy relationship with Narcissus. How do modern research findings square with this bit of mythological wisdom?

First, we can look in the clinical literature for an analogue to echoism. One likely candidate is the dependent personality disorder. Individuals diagnosed with dependent personality disorder will go to great lengths to maintain intimate relationships. One of the criteria for the disorder is engaging in unpleasant behaviors for the sake of the relationship, up to and including suffering serious abuse. Dependent individuals will also refrain from expressing disagreement or conflict in the relationship. If the relationship does end, they will quickly seek out another one to take its place (American Psychiatric Association, 1994). In short, these clinically diagnosed "echoes" are likely to maintain relationships at great cost to the self. These relationships, however, may exhibit certain negative characteristics (e.g., abuse) and, although they may not last, they will certainly be replaced quickly.

Is there evidence that being an echo may help maintain a relationship? The answer seems to be a qualified "yes." Several (although not all) of the relationship maintenance mechanisms identified by researchers support this contention. Individuals who are willing to make sacrifices for the sake of their relationship – for example, giving up a favorite hobby or job – are likely to display greater commitment and longer lasting relationships (Van Lange et al., 1997). In fact, accommodation in relationship conflict – for example, not escalating a conflict that one's partner starts – is usually related to commitment and may lead to relationship endurance. Furthermore, as noted earlier, high-self-esteem individuals may be more likely to respond to conflicts with strategies that are detrimental to the relationship (Rusbult et al., 1987).

Summary

We have reviewed several lines of research examining whether loving one's self (as evidenced by self-esteem and narcissism) predicts intimacy or love. The answer to this question is clearly more complicated than popular sentiment would suggest. Self-esteem does not promote love, especially manic love, but a healthy degree of self-esteem may function to maintain ongoing relationships, at least in certain situations (e.g., when problems outside the relationship impact the relationship). Similarly, narcissism does not seem to promote intimacy or love (except when love involves game-playing and pragmatism). Furthermore, narcissism does not appear to bode well for relationship maintenance. The complement to narcissism, which we call echoism, does appear to be related to relationship maintenance. These relationships, however, may not always be healthy or lasting. Taken together, the evidence indicates that loving the self is not a prerequisite for loving others and may even detract from it.

Does Loving the Self Prompt Others to Love the Self?

In this section we address the effect of self-love on the love received from others. Does loving the self lead others to love the self? Put another way: Do people generally tend to love people who love themselves?

There are some obvious reasons to think that self-love is an attractive characteristic in a potential romantic partner. It seems intuitively plausible that individuals who are self-assured and ambitious inspire confidence and may make good leaders. It is difficult, for example, to think of a successful or popular United States president who did not have a strong sense of confidence in his beliefs and his ability to make those beliefs a reality. Reagan's popularity rested in large part on his optimistic forecasts regarding the future of America and the world – a future that could supposedly be realized if his policies were implemented. Similarly, Clinton has been called the "Comeback Kid" for his ability to confidently overcome multiple threats to his presidency.

In the realm of romantic relationships, self-confidence, success, and esteem are arguably desirable traits in a potential partner. The attractive heroines and heroes of popular culture are not, in general, weak of will. Sharon Stone and Harrison Ford are attractive, in part, because the characters they play are strong and self-confident. Few people are romantically attracted to emotionally needy individuals (W. K. Campbell, 1999). Even Freud suggested that narcissism is an attractive quality in a potential romantic partner, although his reasoning behind this statement was somewhat complicated (see discussion of the ego ideal below).

We find additional evidence for this desire to be with confident and assured individuals in the depression literature (see Segrin & Dillard, 1992, for a review). Depression, a component of which is low self-esteem, does not bode well for relationships, romantic or otherwise. Depressed people are not fun to be around, and they drive relationship partners away. Indeed, in situations where the other cannot escape the depressive's cone of gloom, the other may well find himself or herself becoming fed up or worse. College roommates of depressed individuals, for example, are likely to increasingly dislike those depressed individuals over the course of a semester (Joiner, Alfanso, & Metalsky, 1993). Furthermore, the roommates of depressed individuals may themselves become depressed (Joiner et al., 1992). Of course, depressives may love others as much as or more than anyone else (although there is some evidence that depressives experience a reduction in sex-drive). The point is that depressives are not necessarily loved in return.

Can we therefore conclude that people who love themselves are loved by others? The answer may not be as simple as it seems upon first glance. There is a host of research suggesting that self-love may be at best a mixed blessing in a potential leader, romantic partner, or friend. In fact, self-love may be seriously undesirable.

Confidence may be an important quality of leaders, but a good dose of humility may add to a leader's appeal. A popular leader can show humility in several ways. A leader may be well served by having a sense of humor, especially self-deprecating humor. A leader who makes small slip-ups or other minor mistakes may also be popular. For example, a confident leader who garbles her words, and then makes a joke out of it, or a leader who slips on his way out of a famous golfer's house and can laugh about it, may gain in popular appeal. This so called "pratfall effect" (Aronson, Willerman, & Floyd, 1966) may operate in several ways. First, a leader who makes a small mistake now and again may reassure the public that he is just like everyone else, and can thus be trusted to work for the "people." Imagine if Dan Quayle, after his famous mishap over the word "potato," had laughed at himself and said he should have paid more attention to his teachers in school. This incident might have actually have helped him politically, even winning over part of the teachers' vote to the Republicans. Second, the ability to laugh at oneself may imply that the self-confident leader is not rigid and defensive. This implies that the leader will act reasonably and appropriately in response to threats, rather than on the basis of emotional impulses. It is hard to imagine a Mussolini or a Stalin laughing at himself. Clearly, laughing at oneself does not necessarily imply a serious lack of self-love but may imply a healthy dose of humility.

In the realm of romantic relationships, self-love is also not always attractive. When people talk about themselves chronically (as narcissists are prone to do; Raskin & Shaw, 1988), we may get the sense that they are not interested in or concerned about the well-being of anyone but themselves (and this may well be the case). Researchers have tested some of these ideas in the laboratory. In one study, actors were videotaped playing the role of narcissists. When this tape was shown to subjects, the narcissists were not seen as attractive. In fact, they were rated as less attractive than controls (Carroll, Corning, Morgan, & Stevens, 1991). The clinical literature suggests that narcissists themselves may be aware of the negative influence of talking too much about the self. Narcissists, it seems, often use charm or flattery, rather than or in addition to self promotion, to get others romantically attracted to them (Masterson, 1988). To the outside observer the narcissist may look slippery, slimy, or otherwise snake-like, but this strategy often may work.

A second line of research on romantic attraction has argued that social dominance, a personal quality strongly related to self-love (correlations with narcissism range from .76 [Raskin, Novacek, & Hogan, 1991a], to .36 [Raskin & Terry, 1988]), is ultimately not as important as agreeableness in winning the attraction of others (Cunningham, Druen, & Barbee, 1997). We may like self-confident, socially dominant, or narcissistic traits in others, but it is perhaps more important to be nice, kind, and caring.

Summary

Where inconsistency exists, it may be wise to look for a moderator variable. In this case, such a variable may be relationship duration. It is possible that self-love is an important facilitator in the initial stages of a relationship, but may become detrimental as the relationships proceeds (Paulhus, 1998; Tice, Butler, Muraven, & Stillwell, 1995). We may like self-confident leaders or romantic partners to start with, but being in the presence of excessive self-love may be exasperating after a time. One of the authors, for example, spent an amusing evening at a restaurant listening to a young male regale loudly a potential romantic partner with stories of his ice-climbing adventures. A typical statement used by the suitor was: "Ice-climbing is not for everyone: it takes a certain verve." After three minutes, the author was admiring; after thirty minutes he was ready to take a piton to the story-teller. The target of the story-teller's affection, on the other hand, appeared impressed. Still, one wonders how many dinners she could endure where ice-climbing was the only topic of conversation.

Does Loving Others Promote Self-love?

The next step in our effort to identify the link between self-love and other-love is to address the question: Does loving others in a close relationship promote loving the self? Alternatively, does loving others in a close relationship actually lead to a decrease in self-love? An examination of the literature suggests that the answer to both questions may be "yes." Intimacy can promote positive self-views, but it can also temper those positive self-views. This conclusion will likely not come as a surprise to the lay reader. Individuals commonly report that increased self-esteem is a major benefit of entering romantic relationships – and, indeed, a possible outcome of being in love (Aron, Paris, & Aron, 1995) – but also that loss of self-esteem is an important potential cost of romantic involvement (Sedikides, Oliver, & Campbell, 1994; also Baumeister, Wotman, & Stillwell, 1993).

Loving others can help

How might intimacy with close others lead to a more positive identity? We discuss four pathways. First, there seems to be a communication gap between close others that can leave both parties feeling good about themselves. Close partners find it difficult to tell us the truth about ourselves (Felson, 1993). They would rather talk about our positive than negative traits (Blumberg, 1972) even to the point of distortion (Manis, Cornell, & Moore, 1974). They also may refrain from judging us (at least to our face; Goffman, 1959), and may even flatter us (Jones, 1973). Finally, intimate others feel driven to stay mum about the bad news in our lives (Tesser & Rosen, 1975).

Intimate others may also buffer us from the effects of bad news (Cohen & Wills, 1985). Close relationships are often where we turn to cope with life's grimmer aspects. Such social support from close others may help us feel good about our lives and ourselves (Cohen & Hoberman, 1983; Major, Testa, & Bylsma, 1991).

Close relationships can also help us to love ourselves in somewhat less noble ways. One of these involves leaching esteem from a close other who does well (at least in a non-self-relevant domain; Tesser, 1988) or is physically attractive (Sigall & Gould, 1977). If one dates a famous celebrity, for example, one might start to think that one is a pretty impressive person in one's own right. This process has been called identification (A. Freud, 1936; Tajfel & Turner, 1986), reflection (Tesser, 1988), and, most poetically, basking in reflected glory (Cialdini et al., 1976).

An interesting version of this process of identification was noted by Freud (1922/1959) and further elaborated by Reik (1944). According to Freud, the experience of love, specifically manic or euphoric love, was the result of the lover projecting his or her ideal self ("ego ideal") onto the object of affection. According to Freud, the result of this projection was twofold. First, the target of affection becomes idealized. Second, the lover feels the pleasure of having the psychological tension normally produced by the ideal self alleviated. In other words, the lover feels as if he or she has reached her ideal self simply by perceiving the love object. Freud described this state as the experience of mania. (To understand this experience, one might recall the early stages of an infatuation where the worries and complexities of the working world vanish and consciousness is filled with images of the loved one.) Although this theory is somewhat fanciful, there are several findings that can be seen as supportive. Researchers have noted that individuals in romantic relationships report feeling closer to their ideal selves (i.e., diminished actual/ideal self-discrepancy; W. K. Campbell, Sedikides, & Bosson, 1994). Similarly, the seeking of the ideal self has been implicated in attraction (Karp, Jackson, & Lester, 1970; LaPrelle, Hoyle, Insko, & Bernthal, 1990), and low-self-esteem individuals may report enhanced attraction to targets of affection (Mathes & Moore, 1985). Additionally, idealization of a relationship partner is related to a more satisfying relationship and to enhanced self-views (Murray, Holmes, & Griffin, 1996a, 1996b).

Finally, when we cannot gain esteem from identifying with a close other's success, we can get it from favorable comparisons in the moments when they fail. This is especially true if we are the ones who outperform them. As noted by Tesser (1988), self-evaluation is particularly enhanced when a close other is outdone in a highly self-relevant domain.

Loving others can also hurt

One of the important consequences of intimacy with others is sharing. We share with those we love, and the things we share include resources, successes, positive evaluations, and, indeed, ourselves. One consequence of this sharing is that it can, under certain circumstances, bound or attenuate self-love.

An important aspect of any intimate relationship is sharing resources. This sharing may even occur without explicit or implicit reciprocity (Clark, 1984). When seeking out rewards, relationship partners may engage in a strategy by which they strive to maximize the outcomes for both individuals (Rusbult & Arriaga, 1997). For example, two lovers may share a helping of dessert, rather than one keeping this reward for himself or herself. This strategy is clearly important in maintaining relationships, but will, at least at times, lead to negative individual-level outcomes.

This sharing becomes especially relevant to self-love or self-esteem when the resources shared are highly diagnostic of important self attributes. This can be seen clearly in a study of the self-serving bias as evidenced by close and non-close others (Campbell, Sedikides, Reeder, & Elliot, 2000; Sedikides, Campbell, Reeder, & Elliot, 1998). To describe briefly this research: two strangers are brought into the laboratory and asked to perform an interdependent task. In this case, the task is a dyadic test of creativity in which both partners are asked to come up with multiple uses for a brick and a candle. The strangers are then given bogus success or failure feedback at the dyadic level, that is, they are told that they performed well or poorly as a dyad. Each dyad member is then asked to attribute responsibility privately to the self or to the partner for the task outcome. In the case of strangers, what one finds is evidence of the self-serving bias. Individuals take credit for success and blame their partners for failure, thus maintaining positive self beliefs. A rather different picture emerges, however, when the partners are not strangers but close others. In this instance, individuals refrain from showing the self-serving bias. Instead, they share credit with their partners for successes and failures. Put another way, the close relationship acts as a buffer that suppresses self-enhancement or self-love.

A similar pattern of findings is evident in research on positive evaluations. The majority of individuals, for example, report that they are better than the average other on a host of positive traits (Alicke, 1985; Dunning & Cohen, 1992). This is a robust self-enhancement effect and can be seen clearly, for example, by asking a classroom of students to report how they compare to the average citizen on the trait of "modesty." Still, the above-average effect, despite its strength, can be reduced. One way of doing this is to ask individuals to compare themselves not to the average citizen, but instead compare themselves to a specific college student or a friend (Alicke, Klotz, Breitenbecher, Yurak, & Vredenburg, 1995). Put another way, the positivity of self-evaluations drops to the extent that the comparison group involves close others. The extension of positive evaluations of the self into the realm of close others has been demonstrated repeatedly (e.g., Brown, 1986; Taylor & Koivumaki, 1976).

The message here is that loving others involves the incorporation of the others by the self. This sharing of self, in many cases, may inhibit opportunities for self-love. This idea is not a new one. Freud (1914/1957) suggested that there was a limited store of lust ("libido") and the lust that was connected to the representation of others ("objects") became unavailable for connection to the self. James (1890) also noted the social nature of the self, and our dependence on close others' successes and failures for our own feelings of self-worth. Finally, Heider (1958) noted that affection for the other ("sentiment relation") can lead to an assumed sharing of attitudes with the other.

More recently, researchers have proposed that the self expands to incorporate the other in love relationships. Furthermore, the extent of the incorporation has important cognitive consequences (for a review, see Aron & Aron, 1997). Relationship closeness may even lead close others to protect each other's self-concepts (Beach & Tesser, 1995). Finally, a similar process can be seen in the groups literature. Individuals feel that the group is an important aspect of the self-concept, therefore group outcomes influence the self and individual outcomes are shared with the group (Turner, Oakes, Haslam, & McGarty, 1994).

It is also essential to consider the common experience of unrequited love, which is to say, loving someone who fails to reciprocate that love. Reports of these experiences agree that unrequited love is generally a blow to self-esteem – sometimes minor and transient, but at other times powerful and lasting (Baumeister et al., 1993). A central reason appears to be that romantic rejection commonly carries a strong implicit message that the rejected person was not good or desirable enough to be a suitable partner for the rejecter, and this negative evaluation is hard for the rejected lover to dismiss.

Summary

It appears that loving others can increase the love of the self. The channels for this process include receiving skewed communications from loved others that protect or enhance the self, associating with idealized close others, and outperforming loved others. Intimacy with another may, however, also constrain self-love. The basic model for this is sharing. People not only share resources in close relationships, but also successful outcomes, positive evaluations, and, more generally, their self-concepts. The issue can be looked at this way: If a person loves someone worse off than him- or herself, he or she may increase in self-love via downward comparison and social support, but lose self-love via identification and sharing. If the person loves someone better off than him- or herself, he or she may decrease in self-love via upward comparisons, but gain self-love via identification, sharing and social support. If the person loves someone equal to him- or herself, he or she may end up with little gain in self-love, except via distorted feedback and social support. In sum, the gain in self-love offered by loving others depends strongly on the extent to which various processes occur.

Does Being Loved Lead to Self-love?

Our final question is whether receiving love boosts self-love The answer of "yes" seems obvious. One of the oldest ideas in study of the self is that self-evaluation flows from the evaluations of others. This idea was put forth memorably by Cooley (1902), who spoke of the "looking glass self." Insofar as self and self-evaluation are shaped by the appraisals of others, one may conclude that if appraisals are positive (i.e., if others love the self) then self-appraisals will become similarly positive (i.e., self-love).

Unfortunately, the evidence for the influence of the appraisals of others on the self is somewhat tempered by several factors. The self, to a large extent, seems to perceive positivity in the appraisals of others – regardless of whether this positivity actually exists (Felson, 1993). In other words, individuals selectively interpret information in a way that makes them feel good. For example, we have all witnessed the young male whose amorous advances are turned down, yet who still manages to feel he is attractive: "She really likes me. She's just playing hard to get, etc. . . . "

At the same time, some individuals have dismal self-opinions that cannot be swayed by the opinions of others. This phenomenon has baffled researchers since at least the time of Freud. Why is it that individuals who have negative self-views simply change those views when reliable others tell them that the negative views are incorrect? Clinical examples include the self-loathing exhibited by depressives and the distorted body images displayed by anorexics. More common, perhaps, is the example of a friend who bemoans being a bad parent or professional. Although he or she may clearly be successful in both domains, we will be unable to convince him otherwise. In fact, this friend may be uncomfortable with the positive feedback and actually want to refrain from discussing the issue again. Researchers have actually found evidence for such phenomena in individuals with very low self-esteem. Such individuals may prefer to associate with people who evaluate them poorly rather than positively (Swann, 1983).

The affection of others, however, may be an especially powerful force in shaping self-evaluation during childhood. This is likely because the immaturity of the self in early stages of development leaves it wide open to outside influence. This process has been noted by object relations theorists (Greenberg & Mitchell, 1983) and well documented by researchers on attachment theory (Ainsworth, Blehar, Waters, & Wall, 1978). To provide a brief summary, individual representations of self and other emerge out of the early interactions with the primary caregiver. Where the primary caregiver provides a constant source of support and a "secure base" for environmental exploration, high self-esteem is likely to result. Where this security is absent, a positive sense of self is less likely to result (Bartholomew & Horowitz, 1991; Griffin & Bartholomew, 1994).

In short, the opinions of others likely do matter. However, these appraisals are shaped strongly by preexisting self-evaluations. For this reason, the strength of outside appraisals in shaping the self is likely to be strongest in infancy and to wane gradually across the lifespan. Still, there may be specific instances in adulthood where the positive appraisals of intimate or loving others play an important role in modifying self-beliefs. We describe several of these below.

One such instance would be the change in self-discrepancy that may occur in the context of romantic relationships. Researchers have noted that, in the context of romantic relationships, individuals often will see themselves as more like, or more similar to, their ideal selves (W. K. Campbell et al., 1994). How does this transition occur? One explanation for the process involves the mechanism of behavioral confirmation. A three-step version of this process, termed the "Michelangelo Phenomenon," has been tested (Drigotas, Rusbult, Wieselquist, & Whitton, 1999). In the first step, the loving other (O) expects the self (P) to act in a manner consistent with P's ideal self. Second, P behaves in a manner consistent with O's expectations, and therefore consistent with P's ideal self. Third, P notes cognitively the reduction in the distance between the actual and ideal self (i.e., feels reduced self-discrepancy). Take the following example. Craig's ideal self is humorous. At the same time, his romantic partner, Kerry, expects him to be humorous and laughs at or otherwise encourages his jokes. The result is that Craig becomes more humorous, perceives himself as more humorous, and therefore feels closer to his ideal self. A similar process has been examined by Ruvolo and Brennan (1997). Although the findings were qualified somewhat by gender, these researchers found that being loved and being supported in romantic relationships is associated with growth toward the ideal self.

The appraisals we do receive from loving others may be more positive than reality may support. People who love us may see us in a light that is more favorable than that in which we may view ourselves. Indeed, Murray, et al. (1996a, 1996b) have found evidence that these idealized appraisals actually lead to better functioning in romantic relationships. Specifically, idealization correlates positively with relationship satisfaction and persistence, and negatively with relationship conflict. Furthermore, these idealized appraisals from others may lead to more positive self-appraisals.

Are there cases where being loved would actually decrease self-love? Some have argued that in highly committed relationships (i.e., marriage) – although not in dating relationships – individuals actually strive for and receive accurate rather than flattering self-appraisals (Swann, De La Rhonde, Hixon, 1994; Swann, Hixon, & De La Rhonde, 1992). This phenomenon may exemplify a preference on the part of marriage partners for predictability in their lives over self-esteem.

Another special case may involve unrequited feelings of love. That is, the experience of being loved by someone whom you do not love. While these situations are painful for the lover, they can also have consequences for the object of affection. For example, the love object may experience intense feelings of guilt and confusion that may be damaging to self-evaluation (Baumeister et al., 1993). Similarly, being loved may not enhance self-evaluations if the admirer is considered unworthy (W. K. Campbell, 1999). It might feel good to be loved by a "10," but the affections of a "2" may leave us feeling nothing or even a little negative.

Summary

Being loved may often lead to self-love. However, there are certain important qualifications to this seemingly obvious statement. First, the influence of an other's love on the self is strongly influenced by existing levels of self-evaluation. If you hate yourself to begin with, the love of others will have a hard time changing your self-evaluation Being loved is also likely to have a minimal (and possibly negative) effect on self-love when (1) the love from the other is not reciprocated, (2) the other is a loser, or, (3) you have low self-esteem and the other is your spouse.

Summary and Conclusion

Despite popular belief that loving oneself is a prerequisite for loving others, the actual connections between loving self and loving others are complex, inconsistent, and often weak. Although a healthy self-esteem may sometimes be advantageous to preserving relationships, self-esteem is often unrelated to relationship outcomes, and some forms of self-love (especially narcissism) seem largely detrimental. Loving oneself is clearly not a prerequisite and only occasionally helpful for loving others.

By the same token, loving oneself does not necessarily increase one's chances of attracting the love of others. Confidence may be appealing, especially in terms of initial attraction, but self-love in general may be a source of trouble and instability in long-term relationships. Highly egotistical people may have the highest levels of self-love but they are certainly not the most liked and loved by others – indeed, such traits of extreme self-love are often disliked by others.

The processes of giving and receiving love may provide a boost to self-love under favorable circumstances, and these seem to represent the strongest link between loving self and loving others. They reverse the widespread view that self-love comes first: rather, it appears that giving and receiving love contribute to loving the self. Even these relationships break down under unfavorable circumstances, however. In particular, loving someone who fails to reciprocate that love can provide a devastating blow to self-esteem that can last for months or conceivably even years. More generally, love can entail sacrifices to the self, and these too can be damaging to the self and self-love. Loving someone is thus a potentially useful strategy for boosting self-love but one that carries a significant risk of backfiring.

Just as it was wrong to assert that loving oneself leads to loving others, it would be wrong to insist that loving self and loving others are completely unrelated, orthogonal phenomena. Recent empirical findings have demolished the sweeping, positive generalizations and begun to replace them with narrowly focused, specific effects, which may operate independently of each other, either as potentially additive phenomena or confined to separate, non-overlapping situations. Given this present state of knowledge, the relationships between self-love and loving others make a promising topic for creative research and empirically based theoretical advances.

References

Ainsworth, M. D. S., Blehar, M. C., Waters, E., & Wall, S. (1978). *Patterns of attachment*. Hillsdale, NJ: Erlbaum.

Alicke, M. D. (1985). Global self-evaluations as determined by the desirability and controllability of trait adjectives. *Journal of Personality and Social Psychology, 49*, 1621–1630.

Alicke, M. D., Klotz, M. L., Breitenbecher, D. L., Yurak, T. J., & Vredenburg, D. S. (1995). Personal contact, individuation, and the better-than-average-effect. *Journal of Personality and Social Psychology. 68*, 804-825.

American Psychiatric Association (1994). *Diagnostic and statistical manual of mental disorders* (4th ed.). Washington, DC: Author.

Aron, A., & Aron, E. N. (1997). Self-expansion motivation and including other in the self. In S. Duck (Ed.), *Handbook of personal relationships: Theory, research and intervention* (2nd ed., pp. 251–270). Chichester, England: Wiley.

Aron, A., Paris, M., & Aron, E. N. (1995). Falling in love: Prospective studies in self-concept change. *Journal of Personality and Social Psychology, 69*, 1102–1112.

Aronson, E., Willerman, B., & Floyd, J. (1966). The effect of a pratfall on increasing interpersonal attractiveness. *Psychonomic Science, 4*, 227–228.

Bartholomew, K., & Horowitz, L. M. (1991). Attachment styles among young adults: A test of a four category model. *Journal of Personality and Social Psychology, 61*, 226–244.

Baumeister, R. F., Smart, L., & Boden, J. M. (1996). Relation of threatened egotism to violence and aggression: The dark side of high self-esteem. *Psychological Review, 103*, 5–33.

Baumeister, R. F., Wotman, L., & Stillwell, A. M. (1993). Unrequited love: On heartbreak, anger, guilt, scriptlessness, and humiliations. *Journal of Personality and Social Psychology, 64*, 377–394.

Beach, S. R. H., & Tesser, A. (1995). Self-esteem and the extended self-evaluation maintenance model: The self in social context. In M. Kernis (ed.), *Efficacy, agency, and self-esteem* (pp. 145–170). New York: Plenum.

Blumberg, H. H. (1972). Communication of interpersonal evaluations. *Journal of Personality and Social Psychology, 23*, 157–162.

Bradlee, P. M., & Emmons, R. A. (1992). Locating narcissism within the interpersonal circumplex and the five-factor model. *Personality and Individual Differences, 13*, 821–830.

Branden, N. (1994). *The six pillars of self-esteem*. New York: Bantam.

Brown, J. D. (1986). Evaluations of self and others: Self-enhancement biases in social judgments. *Social Cognition, 4*, 353–376.

Buss, D. M., & Chiodo, L. M. (1991). Narcissistic acts in everyday life. *Journal of Personality, 59*, 179–215.

Buunk, B. P., & van der Eijnden, R. J. J. M. (1997). Perceived prevalence, perceived superiority, and relationship satisfaction: Most relationships are good, but ours is the best. *Personality and Social Psychology Bulletin, 23*, 219–228.

Campbell, J. D., Trapnell, P. D., Heine, S. J., Katz, I. M., Lavallee, L. F., & Lehman, D. R. (1996). Self-concept clarity: Measurement, personality correlates, and cultural boundaries. *Journal of Personality and Social Psychology, 70*, 141–156.

Campbell, W. K. (1999). *Narcissism and romantic attraction. Journal of Personality and Social Psychology, 77*, 1254–1270.

Campbell, W. K., & Foster, C. A. (1999). *Narcissism and love.* Unpublished manuscript, Case Western Reserve University.

Campbell, W. K., Reeder, G. D., Sedikides, C., & Elliot, A. T. (2000). *Narcissism and comparative self-enhancement strategies. Journal of Research in Personality, 34*, 329–347.

Campbell, W. K., Sedikides, C., & Bosson, J. (1994). Romantic involvement, self-discrepancy, and psychological well-being: A preliminary investigation. *Personal Relationships, 1*, 399–404.

Campbell, W. K., Sedikides, C., Reeder, G. D., & Elliot, A. J. (2000). Among friends?: An examination of friendship and the self-serving bias. *British Journal of Social Psychology, 39*, 229–239.

Carroll, L. (1987). A study of narcissism, affiliation, intimacy, and power motives among students in business administration. *Psychological Reports, 61*, 355–358.

Carroll, L., Corning, A. F., Morgan, R. R., & Stevens, D. M. (1991). Perceived acceptance, psychological functioning, and sex role orientation of narcissistic persons. *Journal of Social Behavior and Personality, 6*, 943–954.

Cialdini, R. B., Borden, R. J., Thorne, A., Walker, M. R., Freeman, S., & Sloan, L. R. (1976). Basking in reflected glory: Three (football) field studies. *Journal of Personality and Social Psychology, 34*, 366–375.

Clark, M. S. (1984). Record keeping in two types of relationships. *Journal of Personality and Social Psychology, 47*, 549–557.

Cohen, S., & Hoberman, H. (1983). Positive events and social supports as buffers of life change stress. *Journal of Applied Social Psychology, 13*, 99–125.

Cohen, S., & Wills, T. A. (1985). Stress, social support, and the buffering hypothesis. *Psychological Bulletin, 98*, 310–357.

Colvin, C. R., Block, J., & Funder, D. C. (1995). Overly positive self-evaluations and personality: Negative implications for mental health. *Journal of Personality and Social Psychology, 68*, 1152–1162.

Cooley, C. H. (1902). *Human nature and the social order.* New York: Scribner's.

Cruse, S. W. (1987). *Learning how to love yourself.* New Jersey: Health Communications.

Cunningham, M. R., Druen, P. B., & Barbee, A. P. (1997). Angels, mentors and friends: Trade-offs among evolutionary, social, and individual variables in physical appearance. In J. A. Simpson & D. T. Kendrick (Eds.), *Evolutionary social psychology* (pp. 109–140). Hillsdale, NJ: Erlbaum.

Dion, K. D., & Dion, K. L. (1991). Psychological individualism and romantic love. *Journal of Social Behavior and Personality, 6*, 17–33.

Dion, K. K., & Dion, K. C. (1975). Self-esteem and romantic love. *Journal of Personality, 43*, 39–57.

Dolan, A. (1999). *Loving is becoming intimate with your real self.* New York: First Books.

Drigotas, S. M., Rusbult, C. E., Wieselguest, J., & Whitton, S. W. (1999). Close partner as sculptor of the ideal self: Behavioral affirmation and the Michelangelo phenomenon. *Journal of Personality and Social Psychology, 77*, 293–323.

Dunning, D., & Cohen, G. L. (1992). Egocentric definitions of traits and abilities in social judgment. *Journal of Personality and Social Psychology, 63*, 341–355.

Emmons, R. A. (1984). Factor analysis and construct validity of the Narcissistic Personality Inventory. *Journal of Personality Assessment, 48*, 291–300.

Emmons, R. A. (1987). Narcissism: Theory and measurement. *Journal of Personality and Social Psychology, 52*, 11–17.

Erikson, E. H. (1950). *Childhood and society*. New York: Norton.

Farwell, L., & Wohlwend-Lloyd, R. (1998). Narcissistic processes: Optimistic expectations, favorable self-evaluations, and self-enhancing attributions. *Journal of Personality, 66*, 65–83.

Felson, R. B. (1993). The (somewhat) social self: How others effect self-appraisals. In J. Suls (Ed.), *Psychological perspectives on the self* (Vol. 4, pp. 1–26). Hillsdale, NJ: Erlbaum.

Freud, A. (1936). *The ego and the mechanisms of defense* (Rev. ed.). In *The Writings of Anna Freud* (Vol. 2). New York: International Universities Press.

Freud, S. (1957). On narcissism: An introduction. In J. Strachey (Ed. and Trans.), *The standard edition of the complete psychological works of Sigmund Freud* (Vol. 14, pp. 67–104). London: Hogarth Press. (Original work published 1914)

Freud, S. (1950). Libidinal types. In J. Strachey (Ed. and Trans.), *The standard edition of the complete psychological works of Sigmund Freud* (Vol. 21, pp. 217–220). London: Hogarth Press. (Original work published 1931)

Freud, S. (1959). *Group psychology and the analysis of the ego* (Trans. J. Strachey). New York: Norton. (Original work published 1922)

Gabriel, M. T., Critelli, J. W., & Ee, J. S. (1994). Narcissistic illusions in self-evaluations of intelligence and attractiveness. *Journal of Personality, 62*, 143–155.

Goffman, E. (1959). *The presentation of self in everyday life*. New York: Doubleday.

Gosling, S. D., John, O. P., Craik, K. H., & Robins, R. W. (1998). Do people know how they behave? Self-reported act frequencies compared with on-line codings by observers. *Journal of Personality and Social Psychology, 74*, 1337–1349.

Greenberg, J. R., & Mitchell, S. A. (1983). *Object relations in psychoanalytic theory*. Cambridge, MA: Harvard University Press.

Griffin, D. W., & Bartholomew, K. (1994). Models of the self and other: Fundamental dimensions underlying measures of adult attachment. *Journal of Personality and Social Psychology, 67*, 430–445.

Hay, L. L. (1992). *How to love yourself: Cherishing the incredible miracle that you are*. Carlsbad, CA: Hay House.

Heider, F. (1958). *The psychology of interpersonal relations*. New York: Wiley.

Hendrick, C., & Hendrick, S. S. (1986). A theory and method of love. *Journal of Personality and Social Psychology, 50*, 392–402.

Hendrick, C. & Hendrick, S. S. (1990). A relationship specific version of the Love Attitudes Scale. *Journal of Social Behavior and Personality, 5*, 239–254.

James, W. (1890). *The principles of psychology* (Vol. 1). New York: Henry Holt.

John, O. P., & Robins, R. W. (1994). Accuracy and bias in self-perception: Individual differences in self-enhancement and the role of narcissism. *Journal of Personality and Social Psychology, 66*, 206–219.

Joiner, T. E., Alfano, M. S., & Metalsky, G. I. (1992). When depression breeds contempt: Reassurance seeking, self-esteem, and rejection of depressed college students by their roommates. *Journal of Abnormal Psychology, 101*, 165–173.

Joiner, T. E., Alfano, M. S., & Metalsky, G. I. (1993). Caught in the crossfire: Self-consistency, self-enhancement and the response of others. *Journal of Social and Clinical Psychology, 12*, 113–134.

Jones, S. C. (1973). Self and interpersonal evaluations: Esteem theories versus consistency theories. *Psychological Bulletin, 79*, 185–199.

Kahn, S., Zimmerman, G., Csikszentmihalyi, M., & Getzels, J. W. (1985). Relations between identity in young adulthood and intimacy at midlife. *Journal of Personality and Social Psychology, 49*, 1316–1322.

Karp, E. S., Jackson, J. G., & Lester, D. (1970). Ideal-self fulfillment in mate selection. A corollary to the complementary need theory of mate selection. *Journal of Marriage and the Family, 32*, 269–272.

Kernis, M. H., & Sun, C. (1994). Narcissism and reactions to interpersonal feedback. *Journal of Research in Personality, 28*, 4–13.

LaPrelle, J., Hoyle, R. H., Insko, C. A., & Bernthal, P. (1990). Interpersonal attraction and descriptions of the traits of others: Ideal similarity, self-similarity, and liking. *Journal of Research in Personality, 24*, 216–240.

Lee, J. A. (1973). *The colors of love: An exploration of the ways of loving.* Don Mills, Ontario: New Press.

Longmore, M. A., & DeMaris, A. (1997). Perceived inequity and depression in intimate relationships: The moderating effect of self-esteem. *Social Psychology Quarterly, 60,* 172–184.

Major, B., Testa, M., & Bylsma, W. H. (1991). Response to upward and downward comparisons: The impact of esteem relevance and perceived control. In J. Suls & T. A. Wills (Eds.), *Social comparison: Contemporary theory and research* (pp. 237–260). Hillsdale, NJ: Erlbaum.

Manis, M., Cornell, S. D., & Moore, J. C. (1974). The transmission of attitude-relevant information through a communication chain. *Journal of Personality and Social Psychology, 30,* 81–94.

Maslow, A. H. (1962). *Toward a psychology of being.* Princeton, NJ: Van Nostrand.

Maslow, A. H. (1968). *Toward a psychology of being* (2nd ed.). Princeton, NJ: Van Nostrand.

Masterson, J. F. (1988). *The search for the real self.* New York: Free Press.

Mathes, E., & Moore, C. (1985). Reik's complementary theory of romantic love. *Journal of Social Psychology, 125,* 321–327.

Mecca, A. M., Smelser, N. J., & Vasconcellos, J. (1989). *The social importance of self-esteem.* Berkeley: University of California Press.

Morf, C. C., & Rhodewalt, F. (1993). Narcissism and self-evaluation maintenance: Explorations in object relations. *Personality and Social Psychology Bulletin, 19,* 668–676.

Moss, E. (1995). Treating the love-sick patient. *Israel Journal of Psychiatry and Related Sciences, 32,* 167–173.

Murray, S. L., Holmes, J. G., & Griffin, D. W. (1996a). The benefit of positive illusions: Idealization and the construction of satisfaction in close relationships. *Journal of Personality and Social Psychology, 70,* 79–98.

Murray, S. L., Holmes, J. G., & Griffin, D. W. (1996b). The self-fulfilling nature of positive illusions in romantic relationships: Love is not blind, but prescient. *Journal of Personality and Social Psychology, 71,* 1155–1180.

Paulhus, D. L. (1998). Interpersonal and intrapsychic adaptiveness of trait self-enhancement: A mixed blessing? *Journal of Personality and Social Psychology, 74,* 1197–1208.

Petrie, J., Giordano, J. A., & Roberts, C. S. (1992). Characteristics of women who love too much. *Affilia, 7,* 7–20.

Raskin, R. N., & Novacek, J. (1991). Narcissism and the use of fantasy. *Journal of Clinical Psychology, 47,* 490–499.

Raskin, R. N., Novacek, J., & Hogan, R. (1991a). Narcissism, self-esteem, and defensive self-enhancement. *Journal of Personality, 59,* 19–38.

Raskin, R. N., Novacek, J., & Hogan, R. (1991b). Narcissistic self-esteem management. *Journal of Personality and Social Psychology, 60,* 911–918.

Raskin, R. N., & Shaw, R. (1988). Narcissism and the use of personal pronouns. *Journal of Personality, 56,* 393–404.

Raskin, R. N., & Terry, H. (1988). A principal components analysis of the Narcissistic Personality Inventory and further evidence of its construct validity. *Journal of Personality and Social Psychology, 54,* 890–902.

Reik, T. (1944). *A psychologist looks at love.* New York: Farrar & Rinehart.

Rhodewalt, F., & Morf, C. C. (1995). Self and interpersonal correlates of the narcissistic personality inventory. *Journal of Research in Personality, 29,* 1–23.

Rhodewalt, F., & Morf, C. C. (1998). On self-aggrandizement and anger: A temporal analysis of narcissism and affective reactions. *Journal of Personality and Social Psychology Bulletin, 74,* 672–685.

Rogers, C. (1961). *On becoming a person.* Boston: Houghton Mifflin.

Rusbult, C. E., & Arriaga, X. B. (1997). Interdependence theory. In S. Duck (Ed.), *Handbook of personal relationships: Theory, research and intervention* (2nd ed., pp. 221–250). Chichester, England: Wiley.

Rusbult, C. E., & Martz, J. M. (1995). Remaining in an abusive relationship: An investment model analysis of nonvoluntary commitment. *Personality and Social Psychology Bulletin, 21,* 558–571.

Rusbult, C. E., Morrow, G. D., & Johnson, D. J. (1987). Self-esteem and problem-solving behaviour in close relationships. *British Journal of Social Psychology, 26,* 293–303.

Ruvolo, A. P., & Brennan, C. J. (1997). What's love got to do with it? Close relationships and perceived growth. *Personality and Social Psychology Bulletin, 23*, 814–823.

Schuetz, A. (2000). Self-esteem and interpersonal strategies. In J. P. Forgas, K. D. Williams, & L. Wheeler (Eds.), *The social mind: Cognitive and motivational aspects of interpersonal behavior*, 157–176. New York: Cambridge University Press.

Schuetz, A. (1998). Coping with threats to self-esteem: The differing patterns of subjects with high versus low self-esteem in first person accounts. *European Journal of Personality, 12*, 169–186.

Schuetz, A., & Tice, D. T. (1997). Associative and competitive indirect self-enhancement in close relationships moderated by trait self-esteem. *European Journal of Social Psychology, 27*, 257–273.

Sedikides, C., Campbell, W. K., Reeder, G. D., & Elliot, A. J. (1998). The self-serving bias in relational context. *Journal of Personality and Social Psychology, 74*, 378–386.

Sedikides, C., Oliver, M. B., & Campbell, W. K. (1994). Perceived benefits and costs of romantic relationships for women and men: Implications for exchange theory. *Personal Relationships, 1*, 5–21.

Segrin, C., & Dillard, J. P. (1992). The interactional theory of depression A meta-analysis of the research literature. *Journal of Social and Clinical Psychology, 11*, 43–70.

Sheppard, V. J., Nelson, E. S., & Andreoli-Mathie, V. (1995). Dating relationships and infidelity: Attitudes and behavior. *Journal of Sex and Marital Therapy, 21*, 202–212.

Sigall, H., & Gould, R. (1977). The effects of self-esteem and evaluator demandingness on effort expenditure. *Journal of Personality and Social Psychology, 35*, 12–20.

Swann, W. B., Jr. (1983). Self-verification: Bringing social reality into harmony with the self. In J. Suls & A. G. Greenwald (Eds.), *Psychological perspectives on the self* (Vol. 2, pp. 33–66). Hillsdale, NJ: Erlbaum.

Swann, W. B., De La Rhonde, C., & Hixon, J. G. (1994). Authenticity and positivity strivings in marriage and courtship. *Journal of Personality and Social Psychology, 66*, 857–869.

Swann, W. B., Hixon, J. G., & De La Rhonde, C. (1992). Embracing the bitter "truth": Negative self-concepts and marital commitment. *Psychological Science, 3*, 118–121.

Tajfel, H., & Turner, J. C. (1986). The social identity theory of intergroup behavior. In S. Worchel & W. G. Austin (Eds.), *Psychology of Intergroup Relations* (2nd ed., pp. 7–24). Chicago: Nelson-Hall.

Taylor, S. E., & Koivumaki, J. H. (1976). The perception of self and others: Self-enhancement biases in social judgments. *Journal of Personality and Social Psychology, 33*, 403–408.

Terry, D. J. (1991). Stress, coping, and adaptation to new parenthood. *Journal of Social and Personal Relationships, 8*, 527–547.

Tesser, A. (1988). Toward a self-evaluation maintenance model of social behavior. In L. Berkowitz (Ed.), *Advances in experimental social psychology* (Vol. 21, pp. 181–227). New York: Academic Press.

Tesser, A., & Rosen, S. (1975). The reluctance to transmit bad news. In L. Berkowitz (Ed.), *Advances in experimental social psychology* (Vol. pp. 193–232). New York: Academic Press.

Tice, D. M. (1993). Self-concept change and self-presentation: The looking glass self is also a magnifying glass. *Journal of Personality and Social Psychology, 63*, 435–451.

Tice, D. M., Butler, J. L., Muraven, M. B., & Stillwell, A. M. (1995). When modesty prevails: Differential favorability of self-presentation to friends and strangers. *Journal of Personality and Social Psychology, 69*, 1120–1138.

Turner, J. C., Oakes, P. J., Haslam, A., & McGarty, C. (1994). Self and collective: Cognition and social context. *Personality and Social Psychology Bulletin, 20*, 454–463.

Van Lange, P. A. M., & Rusbult, C. E. (1995). My relationship is better than – and not as bad as – yours is: The perception of superiority in close relationships. *Personality and Social Psychology Bulletin, 21*, 32–44.

Van Lange, P. A. M., Rusbult, C. E., Drigotas, S. M., Arriaga, X. B., Witcher, B. S., & Cox, C. L. (1997). Willingness to sacrifice in close relationships. *Journal of Personality and Social Psychology, 72*, 32–44.

Watson, P. J., Grisham, S. O., Trotter, M. V., & Biderman, M. D. (1984). Narcissism and empathy: Validity evidence for the narcissistic personality inventory. *Journal of Personality Assessment, 45*, 159–162.

Chapter Eighteen

The Self We Know and the Self We Show: Self-esteem, Self-presentation, and the Maintenance of Interpersonal Relationships

Mark R. Leary

As the capacity for self-reflection evolved among the prehistoric people from whom modern human beings descended, they presumably became aware that other individuals did not always see them the way that they saw themselves. This realization was a benchmark in human social life because it involved the emergence of a private sense of self that the individual knew was not accessible to others and created the possibility that people could purposefully convey images of themselves that were inconsistent with how they knew themselves to be. Many other animals engage in displays that, in one sense, do not jibe with how they really are (fluffing hair or feathers to appear larger, for example), and chimpanzees have been observed to deceive other chimps and their human caretakers (de Waal, 1986). But other animals' efforts at self-presentation pale in comparison to those of human beings, limited by their meager ability to self-reflect (Gallup, 1977; Gallup & Suarez, 1986). Only in human beings do we see deliberate efforts to convey a public image to other people, an image that may or may not mesh with the individual's private view of him- or herself.

Following James's (1890) seminal descriptions of various public and private aspects of the self, two traditions emerged in the study of the self, one focusing primarily on the private, subjective self and the other on the social, public self. Early theorists and researchers interested in the private self explored how people develop a sense of self, the factors that determine the nature of people's self-concepts, the psychological motives that affect their self-views, and the emotional and behavioral implications of how people perceive themselves (Cooley, 1902; Lecky, 1945; Mead, 1934; Rogers, 1959; Rosenberg, 1965; Wylie, 1961).

Interest in the public or social self was spurred by developments in sociology, particularly those that emerged from the symbolic interactionist and dramaturgical perspectives. Goffman (1959), for example, championed a purely public characterization of the self, proposing that the only true self was the public one. In discussing the link between the self and self-presentation, Goffman wrote: "A correctly staged and performed scene leads the audience to impute a self to a performed character, but this imputation – this self – is a *product* of a scene that comes off and is not a *cause* of it" (p. 252, italics in original). He cautioned that the self should not be regarded as an internal, organic thing but rather as the dramatic effect of a person's public presentation. When social psychologists began to explore the dynamics of self-presentation (e.g., E. E. Jones, 1964; Jones, Gergen, & Jones, 1963), they adopted a view of the self that drew from both the psychological and sociological traditions. They assumed the existence of a private psychological self, but saw as one of its functions the management of a public identity.

Although early symbolic interactionists had discussed the interplay between the self as known to the individual and the self as seen by others (Cooley, 1902; Mead, 1934), psychological theory and research on the private vs. public aspects of the self were, for the most part, pursued separately for many years. Researchers who were interested in the inner workings of the self did not deny that private psychological processes affect people's public persona and vice versa, but they were interested primarily in the intrapsychic aspects of the self. In contrast, researchers interested in the public self did not ignore ways in which the public, social self was influenced by the private, psychological self, but they were interested primarily in the interpersonal factors that affect the kinds of public selves that people present to others, and the private self took a back seat.

Since the 1980s, however, much has been written about the relationship between the private and public aspects of the self (e.g., Baumeister, 1982a, 1986; Carver & Scheier, 1981; Greenwald, 1982; Greenwald & Breckler, 1985; Leary & Baumeister, 2000; Schlenker, 1985, 1986), but it is not my intention to review this extensive literature here. Rather, my interest in this chapter is on one particular motivational feature of the private and public selves.

Private and Public Self-enhancement

The self is not only a cognitive structure that permits self-reflection and organizes information about oneself but has motivational features as well. Three self-motives have attracted the most attention: self-consistency (the motive to maintain, if not verify, one's existing view of oneself), self-evaluation (or self-assessment; the motive to see oneself accurately), and self-enhancement (the motive to maintain a positive image of oneself) (see Hoyle, Kernis, Leary, & Baldwin, 1999; Sedikides, 1993). Of these, our interest in this chapter is in self-enhancement. Researchers in both traditions have posited the existence of a fundamental self-enhancement motive that prompts people to construe themselves in favorable, socially desirable ways. These two enhancement motives – one involving the private self and one involving the public self – have been regarded as separate, but I will make the case that they are aspects of a single process.

Private self-enhancement: the self-esteem motive

Most psychologists accept the assumption that people are motivated to maintain a positive evaluation of themselves. Greenwald (1980) provided perhaps the most vivid characterization of the self-esteem motive, which he compared to a totalitarian political regime. Just as a totalitarian government suppresses information and rewrites history to preserve a particular desired image of the government, the "totalitarian ego" distorts the facts about oneself and rewrites one's memory of personal history to maintain one's own positive evaluation. Some writers have suggested that people not only want to feel good about themselves but *need* to do so, elevating self-esteem from something people merely like to have to something that they require in order to function optimally.

The assumption that people have a motive (or need) for self-esteem has guided a great deal of research. The self-esteem motive has been used to explain a variety of behaviors, including self-serving attributions, self-affirmation, self-handicapping, rationalization, social comparison, derogation of outgroups, and defensive pessimism (for reviews, see Blaine & Crocker, 1993; Hoyle et al., 1999, chap. 7). Furthermore, deficiencies in self-esteem have been blamed for problems as diverse as depression, unwanted pregnancies, drug abuse, illiteracy, and child abuse (Branden, 1994; Mecca, Smelser, & Vasconcellos, 1989).

Public self-enhancement: self-presentation

Theorists interested in the public self have posited an analogous motive to self-esteem, suggesting that people are typically motivated to be evaluated positively by others. Given that being regarded favorably by other people is a prerequisite for many positive outcomes in life – respect, friendship, romantic relationships, job success, and so on – it is not surprising that people are generally motivated to be perceived positively and to pursue others' approval.

The primary way in which people seek social approval and its attendant benefits is through conveying particular images of themselves to others – that is, through *self-presentation* or *impression management* (Baumeister, 1982a; Leary & Kowalski, 1990; Schlenker, 1980). People are highly motivated to project positive, socially desirable impressions of themselves, and are quite versatile in how they do so. Through what they say about themselves, the attitudes they express, their explanations of their behavior, their physical appearance, the people with whom they associate, their possessions, and other means, people convey impressions that they think will lead to desired reactions from other people (Leary, 1995; Schlenker, 1980).

Although people usually want to make "good" impressions and to be evaluated favorably, in some instances they believe that their interests will be best served by projecting an undesirable impression that carries a high probability of being evaluated negatively. For example, people may want to be seen as emotionally unstable to reduce the demands that other people place on them, or as threatening and hostile in order to coerce other people to behave in certain ways (Jones & Pittman, 1982; Shepperd & Kwavnick, 1999). In such cases, people are willing to sacrifice others' positive evaluations and good will in order to obtain other goals. Although people sometimes resort to undesirable self-presentations, the predominant self-presentational motive is clearly self-enhancement (Jones & Pittman, 1982).

Integrating private and public enhancement

Thus, a self-enhancement motive has been postulated with reference to both the private self that is known only to the individual and the public self that is shown to other people. Several efforts have been made to provide overarching conceptual frameworks that encompass both the private and public selves (e.g., Baumeister & Tice, 1986; Greenwald, 1982; Greenwald & Breckler, 1985; Scheier & Carver, 1983; Schlenker, 1985, 1986), but none of them explicitly addresses the common self-enhancement process that is the focus of this chapter.[1] Before examining the common link between private and public self-enhancement, it is necessary to address two fundamental issues that underlie our understanding of these processes – one involving the distinction between the private and the public self, and the other involving the function of private self-enhancement.

The private and public self.   Although many psychologists have drawn a distinction between the public and private selves, strictly speaking, there is in actuality only one self, and it is private. The term "self" has been used in many ways over the years to refer to a variety of thoughts, behaviors, beliefs, abilities, motives, and other psychological processes. However, at the most fundamental level, the self is the cognitive apparatus that permits self-reflexive thought – the cognitive structures and associated processes that permit people to take themselves as an object of their own thought and to think consciously about themselves. Most other animals apparently do not possess the neural substrate that underlies this cognitive apparatus for, with the exception of certain great apes, other taxa do not appear to be capable of self-reflection (Gallup & Suarez, 1986). As a literary or theoretical device, we sometimes find it useful to talk about the private and public selves as different types of self, and I am not disputing these uses of the terms. Yet, if we think critically about what the psychological self really is, we see that it resides in the cognitive-affective apparatus of the individual and that all self-processes involve self-reflection – that is, the private self.

The term "public self" has been used to refer to three distinct entities: the image that an individual conveys to other people (including the person's reputation and roles), the individual's beliefs about his or her public image (i.e., how the individual thinks he or she is perceived by others), and the impressions that other people actually hold of the person. Whichever of these we may mean when we refer to the public self, we are referring to a very different concept than the private psychological self that permits people to think about and deliberately control these public impressions. Unless we endorse Goffman's (1959) radical dramaturgical view of the self described earlier, what we commonly call the public self is not a "self" at all, but rather behaviors from which other people and the individual him- or herself draw inferences about the person's characteristics, motives, feelings, roles, and other attributes. Depending on whether we're talking about the person's beliefs about his or her public image or about others' impressions, this so called public self resides either within the individual's own private sense of self or in others' minds, respectively. In either case, it is not a "self" in the true sense of the term. The importance of this point is not merely semantic. How we explain the relationship between the so-called private and public selves – particularly, how we account for the relationship between self-esteem and self-presentation – depends heavily on how we conceptualize these constructs.[2]

The function of self-esteem. A second issue that is fundamental to understanding private and public self-enhancement involves the function of the self-esteem motive. The fact that people want *other individuals* to view them positively seems easy to explain: good things come to those who make good impressions. But why are people so concerned with their own *self*-evaluations? What benefits, if any, does trying to maintain one's self-esteem confer?

As noted, most researchers have implicitly assumed that people simply "need" self-esteem for its own sake, but most have not considered why this should be so. Theorists who have considered the function of self-esteem have tended to arrive at one of three general conclusions. First, some writers have argued that people seek self-esteem because high self-esteem promotes effective living by enhancing people's ability to cope with threats (e.g., Bednar, Wells, & Peterson, 1989), bolstering self-confidence (Branden, 1994), or promoting psychological well-being (Greenberg et al., 1992; Taylor & Brown, 1988). However, several facts raise questions about these explanations of self-esteem: (1) high self-esteem is not always associated with better coping than low self-esteem (Baumeister, Heatherton, & Tice, 1993; Baumeister, Smart, & Boden, 1996); (2) although self-efficacy beliefs facilitate coping, a causal role of self-esteem per se in behavior has not been established (Dawes, 1994; Leary, 1999); and (3) positive illusions about oneself are as likely to be maladaptive as adaptive (Asendorpf & Ostendorf, 1998; Colvin & Block, 1994; Colvin, Block, & Funder, 1995).

A second line of thought suggests that self-esteem is integrity of the self. For example, Deci and Ryan (1995) proposed that people possess true self-esteem when they behave in ways that are consistent with their true selves (as opposed to behaving for extrinsic reasons), a contemporary version of the humanistic perspective that ties self-esteem to authenticity (Rogers, 1959). Steele and his colleagues have offered a similar approach, suggesting that the self-system functions to maintain self-integrity – the person's perception of moral and adaptive adequacy (Steele, 1988; Steele, Spencer, & Lynch, 1993; Spencer, Josephs, & Steele, 1993). However, it remains unclear precisely what tangible benefits people derive from behaving congruently or seeing themselves as morally adequate.

A third approach suggests that people do not pursue self-esteem for its own sake but rather use subjective feelings of self-esteem as an indicator of some other desired social commodity, such as dominance (Barkow, 1980) or social acceptance (Leary & Downs, 1995). This approach is particularly useful for our purposes because it provides a direct link between self-esteem and self-presentation by conceptualizing self-esteem as a gauge of interpersonal effectiveness, thus showing why private feelings of self-esteem are related to public self-presentations.

Sociometer Theory

In particular, sociometer theory (Leary, 1999; Leary & Baumeister, 2000; Leary & Downs, 1995) provides a framework for thinking about the nature of private and public self-enhancement. According to sociometer theory, human beings possess a psychological mechanism – a *sociometer* – that monitors the quality of their interpersonal relationships, specifically the degree to which other people value having relationships with them. As a gauge of relational evaluation – the degree to which other people regard their relationship with the individual to be important, close, or valuable – the sociometer operates more or less continuously outside of focal awareness, alerting the individual through affective signals when cues indicating possible relational devaluation are detected. Thus, people do not devote constant attention to the task of monitoring other people's responses, yet they become quickly attuned to indications that others may be feeling negatively about them.

Although one may accept the existence of such a monitor without adopting any particular perspective on where such a mechanism might have come from, I personally favor an evolutionary perspective on this question. Although being accepted by other people remains important for our well-being today, in the ancestral environment in which human evolution occurred, social acceptance would have been literally vital (Baumeister & Leary, 1995). Individuals who, for whatever reason, did not develop mutually supportive relationships with other people and who were not valued as members of the social group would have found themselves in dire straits. In extreme cases, they might have been ostracized or abandoned on the African plains, likely to fall victim to predators, injury, or starvation. In less extreme cases, they would have been relegated to the social periphery of the group, with limited access to mates, food, childcare, and other types of assistance. Thus, it was essential that each individual behave in ways that found favor with others in the group and that led others to value having relationships with them. In light of the importance of being accepted, it was also essential for them to keep track of how well they were doing in terms of social acceptance by other individuals.

Tooby and Cosmides (1996) made a very similar point. They suggested that a primary task faced by our prehistoric ancestors was to insure that they had relationships with those who would help them when they needed it. As Tooby and Cosmides observed, "if you are a hunter-gatherer with few or no individuals who are deeply engaged in your welfare, then you are extremely vulnerable to the volatility of events – a hostage to fortune" (p. 135). Thus, natural selection would have favored adaptations that kept individuals attuned to their social value and motivated them to be valued and accepted by others.

Two features of the sociometer are particularly relevant to the present discussion. First, as noted, when cues that are relevant to low relational evaluation are detected, the person is alerted by negative affect (Leary, Tambor, Terdal, & Downs, 1995; Leary, Haupt, Strausser, & Chokel, 1998). Thus, the sociometer resembles other systems that alert individuals when events threaten their well-being through unpleasant feelings, thereby prompting a conscious appraisal of the event's meaning. In the case of threats to relational value, the appraisal will focus on one's social acceptability. According to sociometer theory, this affect-tinged self-appraisal is what we typically call self-esteem. One might imagine that other social animals also have a mechanism for detecting social threats, but for an organism without the capacity for self-relevant thought, the affective warnings would not be accompanied by a self-relevant appraisal. Thus, although the affective aspect of the process may be present, the animal could not be said to have self-esteem per se.

Second, when activated by cues that connote that one is not being adequately valued as a social participant or relational partner, the sociometer prompts the individual to behave in ways that will restore his or her relational value in other people's eyes (Leary & Downs, 1995). In large part, the resulting behaviors are self-presentational efforts to show other people that the individual possesses characteristics, beliefs, motives, and abilities that are valued by others. Thus, in addition to signaling low relational evaluation through lowered self-esteem, the sociometer motivates self-presentational behavior when decrements in relational evaluation are detected. The sociometer/self-esteem system monitors relational value and motivates remedial behavior when needed, and self-presentation is the behavioral means of enhancing the person's relational value in others' eyes.

Sociometer theory provides a very different perspective on the nature of self-enhancement than the view that has prevailed for over 100 years. As noted, most theorists have assumed that people need self-esteem because it is important for its own sake or because it somehow enhances psychological well-being. From the standpoint of sociometer theory, self-esteem is important because it serves as a gauge of relational evaluation – or, more concretely, acceptance and rejection. People do not seek self-esteem for its own sake but rather use feelings of self-esteem as an indicator of the degree to which they are valued (Leary & Baumeister, 2000).

State and Trait Self-esteem

People's evaluations of themselves fluctuate over time as the sociometer detects changes in relational evaluation. Researchers use the term *state self-esteem* to refer to an individual's feelings about him- or herself at a particular moment in time. Consistent with sociometer theory, research shows that state self-esteem is strongly tied to how valued and accepted the individual feels at a given moment (Haupt & Leary, 1997; Leary et al., 1998; Leary, Tambor, et al., 1995).

However, these changes in state self-esteem occur against a backdrop of *trait self-esteem* – the person's general or average level of self-esteem across situations and time. From the standpoint of sociometer theory, trait self-esteem may be regarded as the resting point of the sociometer's gauge in the absence of incoming social information relevant to relational evaluation. Trait self-esteem is the result of the person's assumptions (most of which are implicit) regarding the degree to which he or she possesses characteristics that other people value and, thus, the extent to which other people tend to regard their relationships with him or her as important, close, or valuable. Research supports the idea that trait self-esteem reflects people's general beliefs about their relational value, social desirability, and includability (Leary, Tambor et al., 1995, Study 5).

The question then arises of whether people are motivated to maintain their state self-esteem, their trait self-esteem, or both. From the standpoint of sociometer theory, the answer is either "neither" or "both," depending on how one views the question. The answer is "neither" in the sense that, as we have seen, people are not actually motivated to maintain their self-esteem at all. Rather, they are motivated to be valued and accepted, and self-esteem is simply the psychological gauge that they use to monitor their social inclusion.

However, if we concede that people may be said, in a loose sense, to want to keep their self-esteem high (in the same way that a driver does not want a car's fuel gauge to fall to Empty), the answer is that people seek both state and trait self-esteem. That is, they desire for others to value them in the present context (state self-esteem) as well as in the long run (trait self-esteem). Just as financial investors monitor both the daily fluctuations in the stock market and long-term trends, the sociometer monitors momentary changes in relational evaluation as well as one's ongoing potential for social acceptance and rejection.

Incidentally, sociometer theory helps to explain why most people who are classified as "low" in trait self-esteem (by virtue of having a score in the lower third or lower half of the distribution of self-esteem scores) do not actually have low self-esteem in an objective sense. When their responses are examined closely, one finds that most people at the lower end of the distributions of self-esteem scores do not endorse highly negative self-statements. Rather, they express neutral, ambivalent, or mixed opinions about themselves. (Put differently, the statistical median of all self-esteem scales is always above the conceptual midpoint [i.e., neutral feelings about oneself], and often far above it; Baumeister, Tice, & Hutton, 1989). Presumably, people who are high in trait self-esteem experience a greater proportion of experiences that connote high relational evaluation than people with low trait self-esteem. However, lows are not necessarily rejected by other people; rather, they simply perceive a lower degree of relational appreciation than highs. Given that most people are valued by at least some individuals, we should rarely find people with bona fide low self-esteem, and those whose self-esteem is truly low should show psychopathological symptoms consistent with widespread rejection (Leary, Schreindorfer, & Haupt, 1995).

Moderating Effects of Self-esteem on Self-presentation

Sociometer theory provides an overarching framework for thinking about private and public self-enhancement and helps to explain why self-esteem and self-presentation are reciprocally related. Self-esteem – as an indicator of relational evaluation – is associated both with the degree to which people are motivated to obtain acceptance and the ways in which they try to do so. At the same time, by affecting real and anticipated relational evaluation, self-presentation feeds back to affect subjective self-esteem. After first examining the role of self-esteem in self-presentation, I will turn to the effects of self-presentation on self-esteem.

Self-esteem, need for approval and impression-motivation

A consistent finding is that self-esteem – whether measured as a state or a trait – is inversely related to the degree to which people are concerned about others' impressions of them. Compared to people who score high on measures of trait self-esteem, people who are low in trait self-esteem are more concerned with how they are viewed by others, have a stronger desire to obtain approval and to avoid disapproval, and are more motivated to be perceived favorably (S. C. Jones, 1973; Shrauger, 1975; Watson & Friend, 1969). Furthermore, people whose state self-esteem is lowered by failure, rejection, or other events become more highly motivated to obtain others' approval and will engage in self-presentational behaviors that will attain it (Apsler, 1975; Baumeister & Jones, 1978; Miller & Schlenker,

1978; Modigliani, 1971; Schneider, 1969; Walster, 1965).

Sociometer theory provides a clear explanation for the inverse relationship between self-esteem and approval motivation. Given that self-esteem reflects perceived relational evaluation, lower self-esteem is associated with feeling insufficiently valued, thereby naturally inducing a desire to increase one's relational value. Along these lines, Tooby and Cosmides (1996) suggested that evolutionary adaptations may be designed "to respond to signs of waning affection by increasing the desire to be liked, and mobilizing changes that will bring it about" (p. 139). Whether one accepts the evolutionary underpinnings, it is clear that lowered self-esteem is associated with an increased desire for approval and acceptance.

One exception to this general pattern involves the fact that, although their overall desire for approval increases after rejection, people are sometimes less interested in being accepted by those who have rejected them than they were previously, and they may even retrospectively minimize the degree to which they say that they wanted the rejector to accept them in the first place (Leary, Tambor, et al., 1995). On the surface, this sour grapes rationalization may seem to work against the person being socially accepted. However, such a tactic may be functional in disengaging rejected individuals from pursuing acceptance by those who do not adequately value them, thereby freeing them to seek relational appreciation in more promising places.

Along these lines, evidence suggests that events that cause people to feel inadequately valued in one interpersonal context increase their motivation to pursue acceptance in other, unrelated contexts and relationships. For example, people who embarrass themselves in front of one audience may subsequently go out of their way to project a more favorable image of themselves to other audiences (Apsler, 1975).

Self-presentational strategies

As we have seen, low self-esteem is related to the motivation to seek approval through impression-management, presumably because low self-esteem signals low relational evaluation. In addition, once people are motivated to manage their impressions, self-esteem is related to the self-presentational strategies they prefer. Although everyone desires both to make favorable impressions and to avoid making unfavorable impressions, the relative strength of these self-presentational orientations differs across situations and among individuals. Based on a comprehensive review of the empirical evidence, Baumeister et al. (1989) concluded that low- and high-self-esteem people tend to adopt different self-presentational styles. Specifically, people with high self-esteem tend to strive to make a positive impression (what Arkin, 1981, labeled acquisitive self-presentation), whereas those with low self-esteem try to prevent others from developing negative impressions of them (protective self-presentation).[3]

In line with Baumeister et al.'s (1989) conclusions, Schlenker, Weigold, and Hallam (1990) found that participants with high self-esteem were more egotistical (i.e., acquisitive) when they were particularly concerned about another person's evaluations, whereas participants with low self-esteem were less egotistical. Along the same lines, Tice (1991; Tice & Baumeister, 1990) found evidence that trait self-esteem moderates the use of enhancing and protective self-handicapping strategies. Her studies showed that people with high self-esteem self-handicap when doing so allows them to make favorable impressions, whereas people with low self-esteem are prone to self-handicap to avoid making negative impressions. Furthermore, she found that participants who were low vs. high in self-esteem explicitly reported having different reasons for self-handicapping. Low-self-esteem people indicated that they self-handicapped to diffuse the implications of failure, whereas high-self-esteem people indicated that they self-handicapped when it allowed them to look better following success. Similarly, when enhancing and protective self-presentational styles were measured as individual difference variables, trait self-esteem correlated positively with the self-enhancing style but negatively with self-protection (Wolfe, Lennox, & Cutler, 1986).

The fact that people with lower self-esteem are not as self-enhancing as those with higher self-esteem does not reflect the fact that people who have low self-esteem do not desire approval or want other people to evaluate them negatively, as was once assumed (e.g., Aronson & Mettee, 1968; Maracek & Mettee, 1972). As noted earlier, they desire approval and acceptance as much as, if not more than people with high self-esteem (S. C. Jones, 1973; Shrauger, 1975; Swann, Griffin, Predmore, & Gaines, 1987). Nonetheless, their efforts to impression-manage tend to be cautious, prudent, noncommital, or evasive, particularly when self-presentational failure may have negative repercussions (Baumeister et al., 1989; Tice, 1993).

Sociometer theory provides a straightforward interpretation of this pattern. People who believe that others do not habitually value them – people who score low in trait self-esteem – feel less secure in their relationships and experience their social bonds as more tenuous. As a result, they believe that they cannot afford to take self-presentational risks that, if unsuccessful, will leave them with lower relational value than before. Thus, they may settle for a neutral or minimally acceptable image that will at least insure that they will not be rejected and that might even promote acceptance (although perhaps not as much as if they successfully self-aggrandized). Just as a person with little money cannot afford to lose it in risky investments (no matter how large the potential payoff), people with low self-esteem seem unwilling to risk whatever relational value they have by trying to be perceived more positively. On top of that, a history of low relational evaluation leads people with low self-esteem to believe that they do not possess characteristics that readily draw other people to them. As a result, they are less likely than high-self-esteem people to believe that they can successfully present themselves in highly positive ways (Baumeister, 1982b).

In contrast, people with high self-esteem already feel accepted and, certain that they are the kind of people whom others value, are not greatly concerned about being rejected in the long run. However, they often seek the benefits of even greater acceptance and are willing to invest some of their interpersonal capital in seeking it. Thus, people with high self-esteem are particularly self-aggrandizing when they have something to gain by being egotistical (Schlenker et al., 1990; Schneider & Turkat, 1975).

One empirical finding that is particularly relevant to sociometer theory involves the fact that the relationship between behavior and self-esteem is moderated by the degree to which the situation is public (i.e., open to observation by other people) or private (Archibald & Cohen, 1971; Baumeister, 1982a; Schlenker et al., 1990; Tice & Baumeister, 1990). The general pattern is that people with high self-esteem are more self-enhancing in public than their private self-reports suggest they really see themselves, whereas people with low self-esteem are more self-effacing in public than they are in private (see Baumeister et al., 1989 for a review).

If self-esteem were only a private, intrapsychic self-evaluation – as has typically been assumed – there is no clear reason why it should typically moderate behavior differently in public than in private (see, however, Tetlock & Manstead, 1985). However, if one accepts the premise that self-esteem reflects something about the perceived security of one's inter-personal relationships, the effects of publicness are easily explained. This is not to say that self-serving biases never occur in private; they sometimes do. However, the frequency and intensity of self-serving responses are clearly lower in private than in public.

Effects of Self-presentation on Self-esteem

As noted, much self-presentation is in the service of enhancing one's relational value in other people's eyes. To the extent that people are successful in projecting images that increase their relational value, their self-esteem should increase correspondingly. Under some circumstances, self-presentational behaviors may influence self-esteem even in the absence of interpersonal feedback if the person believes that his or her relational value will be enhanced.

Little research has been conducted on the effects of self-presentation on people's private thoughts and feelings about themselves, but the available evidence clearly shows that pre-senting images of oneself to other people affects the presenter's self-perceptions and self-esteem. Most relevant to the present chapter, presenting oneself in a positive fashion generally leads to changes in state self-esteem. In a series of studies, Jones, Rhodewalt, Berglas, and Skelton (1981) found that participants who were induced to present themselves positively to another person – either because they were explicitly instructed to do so or because they observed other self-enhancing people (people tend to match the positivity of others' self-presentations) – subsequently showed higher state self-esteem than participants who were induced to be less self-enhancing. Similar effects of self-presentation on self-esteem have been found by Schlenker and Trudeau (1990) and McKillop, Berzonsky, and Schlenker (1992).

Kowalski and Leary (1990) found that the effects of self-presentation on state self-esteem were more pronounced for participants who were low than high in trait self-esteem. Not only did presenting themselves positively (presenting images of being psychologically adjusted) raise the self-esteem of participants who were low in trait self-esteem, but after presenting themselves favorably, the state self-esteem of participants low in trait self-esteem was as high as that of participants high in trait self-esteem. One explanation of this finding is that the inducement to present themselves positively may have overridden low-self-esteem participants' cautious, protective self-presentational style (Arkin, 1981; Baumeister et al., 1989). By eliciting more favorable self-presentations, the experiment may have led low-self-esteem participants to perceive an increase in their relational value, thereby raising their state self-esteem. Participants who were high in trait self-esteem were accustomed to conveying positive impressions of themselves, so being induced to project a positive image in the context of the study had no notable effect on their subsequent self-esteem.

   This explanation may help to account for why low self-esteem is chronic and difficult for people to change. Perceiving low relational value lowers self-esteem and leads to a cautious, protective self-presentational style. Protective self-presentations rarely make a truly positive impression (although they may stave off a negative one), so perceived relational value and self-esteem remain low. If people who are low in trait self-esteem rarely take the self-presentational risks that will lead others to value them more highly, their self-esteem is unlikely to increase. Incidentally, many clinical interventions that have been designed to increase self-esteem include features that indirectly enhance the positivity of the individual's public image, such as social skills training and help with physical appearance (Leary, 1999; Mruk, 1995).

   In an important contribution to our understanding of the effects of self-presentation on the private self, Tice (1992) found that participants' private self-views were affected more strongly when they engaged in identity-relevant behaviors in public than in private. In fact, Tice concluded that her results "cast doubt on whether people will internalize their behavior (i.e., alter their self-concepts to fit their recent behavior) in the absence of an interpersonal context and self-presentational concerns" (p. 449). Although her studies did not measure self-esteem per se, one might expect – both on the basis of Tice's research and sociometer theory – that public self-presentations would likewise affect self-esteem more strongly than either private self-thoughts or behaviors that are performed when one is alone. Consistent with this reasoning, McKillop et al. (1992) found that participants who described themselves positively subsequently showed an increase in state self-esteem when they presented themselves in a face-to-face interview, but not when they described themselves in a written interview or on an anonymous questionnaire. Importantly, this effect was obtained only for participants whose identities were based heavily on their social roles and relationships (i.e., those who were high in social identity).

   The effects of self-presentation on state self-esteem appear to occur via at least three routes. First, to the extent that the person's self-presentational behavior actually affects the degree to which other people value and accept him or her – for better or for worse – state self-esteem should change accordingly. Conveying images that lead to approval, approbation, and acceptance will raise state self-esteem, and conveying images that lead to disapproval, ridicule, and rejection will lower it. Given that people typically try to be regarded positively, most successful self-presentations will be accompanied by increased relational evaluation and state self-esteem. Along these lines, Gergen (1965) showed that, when another person explicitly agreed with participants' favorable self-presentations, participants showed an increase in state self-esteem over the course of the experiment.

   Second, even without receiving feedback from others, people can anticipate the effects of their self-presentations on others' reactions and experience corresponding changes in state self-esteem. Thus, knowing that we made a good impression makes us feel better about ourselves without anyone having to indicate their approval or acceptance explicitly. Likewise, embarrassments and other self-presentational predicaments lower state self-esteem even if we only imagine other people's reactions (Miller, 1996).

   The notion that *imagined* social reactions affect self-esteem may seem to run counter to sociometer theory. If self-esteem is an internal gauge of others' feelings about the individual, why should it be affected by how the person imagines others will react? The answer is that, in order to prevent the individual from jeopardizing his or her relational ties, the self-esteem/sociometer system must alert the individual whenever he or she behaves in ways that may lower relational evaluation or even when he or she contemplates such actions, whether or not explicit social feedback is received. As the symbolic interactionists noted, one function of the self is to allow people to think about themselves from the perspectives of other people (Cooley, 1902; Mead, 1934). This ability to take the role of other people in thinking about ourselves allows us to imagine how they are feeling about us and helps us behave accordingly, and the sociometer must be responsive to these imaginings.

A third process by which self-presentation may affect self-esteem involves what Jones et al. (1981) called biased scanning. Presenting oneself in a particular way may prime thoughts about oneself that are associated with the projected image, temporarily changing how the individual feels about him- or herself. According to this explanation, which was first used to explain the effects of role-playing on attitude change (Janis & Gilmore, 1965), behaving in a particular way leads certain aspects of the self to become more or less salient. Because people typically try to present positive rather than negative images of themselves, self-presentations usually make people think about their desirable attributes, thereby moving people's self-esteem upward.

Although positive self-presentations generally raise self-esteem, a reversal of this effect may occur under special circumstances. The person who is trying to make a favorable impression is faced with two tasks: conveying positive self-relevant information and concealing (or at least downplaying) negative information. According to ironic processes theory (Wegner, 1994), trying to suppress an undesired thought sometimes makes that thought more cognitively accessible. Thus, when people wish to conceal unflattering information about themselves, negatively-tainted self-thoughts become cognitively available, which may lead to diminished self-esteem in spite of a positive projected impression under certain conditions.

To test this hypothesis, Smart and Wegner (1994) asked participants to make either a good or a bad impression, or gave participants no self-presentational instructions. Before publicly answering each of a series of questions about themselves, participants were asked to memorize either a one-digit number (low cognitive load) or a five-digit number (high cognitive load). After completing the self-presentation task, participants' state self-esteem was measured. For participants who were under low cognitive load, self-esteem was higher when they presented themselves positively rather than negatively, replicating previous research (Jones et al., 1981; Kowalski & Leary, 1990). However, participants who were under a high cognitive load showed an inverse relationship between the positivity of their impressions and their subsequent self-esteem. Apparently, presenting a positive impression of oneself under high cognitive load makes information relevant to one's negative characteristics more salient and lowers self-esteem.

Private Self-enhancement and Self-deception

Our discussion of self-esteem and self-presentation motives would not be complete without considering the question of whether people are "taken in" by their own overly positive self-beliefs and self-presentational behaviors. The topic of self-deception has fueled much controversy within psychology for many years, and I make no pretense at resolving the issues here. Rather, I simply wish to raise several questions about the nature of self-deception and offer some thoughts.

The concept of self-deception presents a paradox because it implies that the private self is split into a part that knows the truth about oneself and a part that does not know, and that the knowing part actively misleads the other one. Disassociation of this nature undoubtedly occurs in certain cases of psychopathology, but whether it is a normal component of psychological functioning is unclear.

The prevailing view, both in psychology and the popular culture, seems to be that a certain degree of self-deception is normal, if not psychologically beneficial. Many writers have touted the advantages of self-deception, suggesting that self-enhancing illusions enhance behavioral efficacy and psychological well-being (see Martin, 1985; Taylor & Brown, 1988). However, whatever its occasional benefits, self-deception would seem to be generally maladaptive. Effective coping requires a reasonably accurate assessment of one's personal capabilities and characteristics relative to the challenges one confronts (Bandura, 1997). A pervasive self-enhancing bias that exaggerates one's physical, intellectual, or interpersonal abilities would appear to be a recipe for chronic disaster, and it is difficult to understand how an ostensibly universal motive for deceptive self-enhancement could have arisen as a fundamental feature of human nature. Without denying occasional advantages of mild self-deception (Baumeister, 1989), I find it difficult to reconcile the general disadvantages of self-deception with the pervasive idea that people are inherently disposed to privately self-enhance.

These arguments notwithstanding, empirical research does seem to demonstrate a wide array of self-serving biases in how people perceive themselves, make attributions about their good and bad behaviors, compare themselves to others, evaluate the groups to which they belong, and so on (e.g., Blaine & Crocker, 1993; Greenwald, 1980). These biases have typically been interpreted as efforts to maintain private self-esteem and as evidence for a certain degree of self-deception. After all, if the self-enhancing person does not *believe* his or her self-serving judgments – that is, if he or she is not truly self-deceived – those egotistical beliefs would not maintain self-esteem.

However, three issues call into question the idea that people are as self-aggrandizingly deluded as they often appear in psychological research. First, although most psychologists have emphasized the human tendency toward private self-enhancement and self-serving illusions, a moment's thought will reveal that people are as often self-deprecating as they are self-aggrandizing. People often underestimate their abilities and other desirable characteristics, expect the worst in situations in which they will be evaluated, and react strongly to seemingly trivial failures, slights, and personal shortcomings. Whatever self-enhancing biases people exhibit are counterbalanced by equally self-deprecating ones, yet we do not view these negative biases as examples of "unflattering self-deception."

Second, in most studies of self-serving biases, participants' responses are not fully private, opening the possibility that their self-enhancing reactions reflect public self-presentations rather than privately-held self-beliefs. Some studies make no effort to convince participants that their answers are anonymous, and in others, participants may well have doubted the researcher's claim that no one – the researcher included – would be able to identify their answers. As a result, participants have a clear self-presentational stake in conveying certain impressions of themselves, and whatever self-enhancing biases their responses show may well be self-presentational rather than self-deceptive. This is a difficult, though not insurmountable methodological problem that limits our ability to infer that experimental results are due to self-deception rather than self-presentation (Leary, 1993, Tetlock & Manstead, 1985).

Third, as noted above, self-enhancing reactions are highly dependent upon the social context, and particularly on who will ostensibly see participants' responses (Kolditz & Arkin, 1982; Leary, Barnes, Griebel, Mason, & McCormack, 1987; Schlenker et al., 1990). This fact alone argues against true self-deception which, with a few exceptions (Aronson, 1968; Tetlock & Manstead, 1985), should occur regardless of who else might see a person's answers. Even more convincing is the fact that self-serving biases often disappear or reverse when participants assume that the others will disapprove of self-enhancing claims (Miller & Schlenker, 1985).

I am not suggesting that self-deception never occurs. However, conceptual, logical, and empirical considerations strongly suggest that much of what has been interpreted as private self-enhancement for the purpose of preserving self-esteem is better interpreted as public self-enhancement for the purpose of presenting desired images. These self-serving behaviors undoubtedly affect self-esteem, but they do so by affecting real, imagined, or anticipated relational evaluation rather than through private self-delusion.[4]

Conclusions

Self-esteem and self-presentation have been studied by psychologists and other behavioral scientists for many years. As a result, we know a great deal about these constructs, and both have been used to explain a wide array of cognitive, affective, and behavioral phenomena. For both, the fundamental process of interest involves a strong proclivity toward self-enhancement. In the case of self-esteem, people seem strongly motivated to maintain favorable images of and to feel good about themselves; in the case of self-presentation, people are pervasively motivated to make good impressions on other people. The central thesis of this chapter is that underlying superficial differences between private and public self-enhancement is a common process that helps the individual monitor and respond to interpersonal events that have implications for the degree to which he or she is valued and accepted vs. devalued and rejected by other people. Private self-esteem lies at the heart of the system that monitors relational value (i.e., the sociometer), and public self-presentation serves as a primary means of maintaining and enhancing one's relational value to other people.

Having examined the connections between self-esteem and self-presentation, and their joint role in maintaining one's relational value, a reasonable question is whether this is all there is to self-esteem and self-presentation. Is self-esteem only part of an interpersonal monitoring system, or does it do other things? Is self-presentation only a means of maintaining relational value, or does it have other functions?

The second question is the easier of the two to answer. People clearly engage in self-presentational behaviors for many reasons other than to be accepted. Although people engage in self-presentation to increase their relational value and promote social acceptance, they also impression-manage to influence other people for many other reasons. By conveying particular images of themselves, people can obtain assistance from other people, induce others' compliance, improve their financial well-being, avoid unpleasant tasks, perform social roles more effectively, inflict distress on others, and achieve other personal and interpersonal goals (Baumeister, 1982a; Jones & Pittman, 1982; Leary, 1995; Leary & Kowalski, 1990; Schlenker, 1980). So, although self-presentation is centrally involved in maintaining one's connections with other people, it serves other goals as well.

The first question – whether self-esteem involves more than the subjective output from the sociometer – is less easy to answer. A strong case can be made that most documented antecedents, consequences, and concomitants of self-esteem can be explained in terms of their role in the maintenance of relational value (Leary & Baumeister, 2000; Leary & Downs, 1995; Leary, Schreindorfer, & Haupt, 1995; Leary, Tambor, et al., 1995). Virtually all events that affect self-esteem have potential implications for the degree to which people are socially valued and accepted, and their effects can be explained by sociometer theory. However, the fact that these events have implications for relational evaluation does not imply that their effects on self-esteem are necessarily mediated by perceived relational value nor that they owe their effects to processes associated with the sociometer. Perhaps the safest conclusion at present is that much of what we know about self-esteem and about the self-esteem motive can be explained in terms of sociometer theory, but whether the theory can account for all features of self-esteem remains an open question.

Much early theorizing about self-esteem and self-presentation explicitly considered how they relate to the give-and-take of social life. In particular, the symbolic interactionists tied both the private self and public self-presentation directly to people's relationships with one another (Cooley, 1902; Goffman, 1959; Mead, 1934). Yet, until recently, psychologists have tended to regard self-esteem and self-presentation as independent constructs, treating self-esteem purely as an intrapsychic entity and self-presentation solely as a means of projecting impressions in social interactions. As we have seen, however, both the self we know and the self we show are involved in perhaps the most important interpersonal task that a social species must face – insuring acceptance by other members of its own kind.

Notes

1. Schlenker's (1985, 1986) self-identification theory perhaps comes closest. This theory subsumes both private self-thoughts and public self-presentations within the broader construct of "self-identification" – the process of showing oneself to be a particular type of person. Schlenker proposed that self-identification may occur with respect to three kinds of audiences: other people with whom we interact, imagined audiences, and ourselves. He discussed similarities and differences in the ways in which people identify themselves to these three audiences, but did not explicitly address the relationship between self-esteem and self-presentation that is our focus in this chapter.

2. I am not arguing here against the distinction between private and public *self-consciousness* proposed by Fenigstein, Scheier, and Buss (1975). When they are self-aware, people may focus their attention on either private, unobservable aspects of themselves (e.g., sensations, thoughts, motives, emotions) or on public, observable aspects (e.g., their physical appearance, overt

behavior, or speech), and focusing attention on private versus public aspects of oneself moderates how people respond to events (Carver & Scheier, 1987; Fenigstein, 1987). However, whether people are focused on private or on public aspects of themselves, the processes involved in both private and public self-awareness occur in the private self.

3. Baumeister et al. (1989) took the argument a step further to suggest that self-report measures of self-esteem are, at least in part, measuring people's willingness to make enhancing claims about themselves. People who are willing to present themselves very positively will endorse "high self-esteem" items on such scales and, thus, score higher in self-esteem than those who are reluctant to self-enhance. Accordingly, scores on commonly used self-esteem scales may reflect, in part, individual differences in self-presentation

4. Trivers (1985) suggested another benefit of self-deception with direct implications for self-presentation. People will be more convincing in projecting highly favorable impressions of themselves if they believe that their self-presentations are accurate and honest than if they know they are contrived. Thus, self-deception may enhance people's ability to make positive impressions. Trivers may be correct, but his view seems to argue for a very selective form of self-deception that is engaged primarily when the individual is making impressions but disengaged when the individual needs to know the truth about his or her characteristics in order to respond effectively to the environment.

References

Apsler, R. (1975). Effects of embarrassment on behavior toward others. *Journal of Personality and Social Psychology, 32*, 145–153.

Archibald, W. R., & Cohen, R. L. (1971). Self-presentation, embarrassment, and face-work as a function of self-evaluation, conditions of self-presentation, and feedback from others. *Journal of Personality and Social Psychology, 29*, 287–297.

Arkin, R. M. (1981). Self-presentational styles. In J. T. Tedeschi (Ed.), *Impression management theory and social psychological research* (pp. 311–323). New York: Academic Press.

Aronson, E. (1968). Dissonance theory: Progress and problems. In R. P. Abelson, E. Aronson, W. J. McGuire, T. M. Newcomb, M. J. Rosenberg, & P. H. Tannenbaum (Eds.), *Cognitive consistency theories: A sourcebook* (pp. 5–27). Skokie, IL: Rand McNally.

Aronson, E., & Mettee, D. (1968). Dishonest behavior as a function of differential levels of induced self-esteem. *Journal of Personality and Social Psychology, 9*, 121–127.

Asendorpf, J. B., & Ostendorf, F. (1998). Is self-enhancement healthy? Conceptual, psychometric, and empirical analysis. *Journal of Personality and Social Psychology, 74*, 955–966.

Bandura, A. (1997). *Self-efficacy: The exercise of control.* New York: Freeman.

Barkow, J. H. (1980). Prestige and self-esteem: A biosocial interpretation. In D. R Omark, F. F. Strayer, & D. G. Freedman (Eds.), *Dominance relations: An ethological view of human conflict and social interaction* (pp. 319–332). New York: Garland STPM Press.

Baumeister, R. F. (1982a). A self-presentational view of social phenomena. *Psychological Bulletin, 91*, 3–26.

Baumeister, R. F. (1982b). Self-esteem, self-presentation, and future interaction: A dilemma of reputation. *Journal of Personality, 50*, 29–45.

Baumeister, R. F. (Ed.). (1986). *Public self and private self.* New York: Springer-Verlag.

Baumeister, R. F. (1989). The optimal margin of illusion. *Journal of Social and Clinical Psychology, 8*, 176–189.

Baumeister, R. F., Heatherton, T. F., & Tice, D. M. (1993). When ego threats lead to self-regulation failure: The negative consequences of high self-esteem. *Journal of Personality and Social Psychology, 64*, 141–156.

Baumeister, R. F., & Jones, E. E. (1978). When self-presentation is constrained by the target's knowledge: Consistency and compensation. *Journal of Personality and Social Psychology, 36,* 608–618.

Baumeister, R. F., & Leary, M. R. (1995). The need to belong: Desire for interpersonal attachments as a fundamental human motivation. *Psychological Bulletin, 17,* 497–529.

Baumeister, R. F., Smart, L., & Boden, J. M. (1996). Relation of threatened egotism to violence and aggression: The dark side of high self-esteem. *Psychological Review, 103,* 5–33.

Baumeister, R. F., & Tice, D. M. (1986). Four selves, two motives, and a substitute process self-regulation model. In R. F. Baumeister (Ed.), *Public self and private self* (pp. 63–74). New York: Springer-Verlag.

Baumeister, R. F., Tice, D. M., & Hutton, D. G. (1989). Self-presentational motivations and personality differences in self-esteem. *Journal of Personality, 57,* 547–579.

Bednar, R. L., Wells, M. G., & Peterson, S. R. (1989). *Self-esteem: Paradoxes and innovations in clinical theory and practice.* Washington, DC: American Psychological Association.

Blaine, B., & Crocker, J. (1993). Self-esteem and self-serving biases in reactions to positive and negative events: An integrative review. In R. F. Baumeister (Ed.), *Self-esteem: The puzzle of low self-regard* (pp. 55–85). New York: Plenum.

Branden, N. (1994). *The six pillars of self-esteem.* New York: Bantam.

Carver, C. S., & Scheier, M. F. (1981). *Attention and self-regulation: A control-theory approach to human behavior.* New York: Springer-Verlag.

Carver, C. S., & Scheier, M. F. (1987). The blind men and the elephant: Examination of the public-private literature gives rise to a faulty perception. *Journal of Personality, 55,* 525–541.

Colvin, C. R., & Block, J. (1994). Do positive illusions foster mental health? An examination of the Taylor and Brown formulation. *Psychological Bulletin, 116,* 3–20.

Colvin, C. R., Block, J., & Funder, D. C. (1995) Overly positive self-evaluations and personality: Negative implications for mental health. *Journal of Personality and Social Psychology, 68,* 1152–1162.

Cooley, C. H. (1902). *Human nature and the social order.* New York: Scribner's.

Dawes, R. (1994). *House of cards: Psychology and psychotherapy built on myth.* New York: Free Press.

Deci, E. L., & Ryan, R. M. (1995). Human autonomy: The basis for true self-esteem. In M. H. Kernis (Ed.), *Efficacy, agency, and self-esteem* (pp. 31–71). New York: Plenum.

de Waal, F. B. M. (1986). Deception in the natural communication of chimpanzees. In R. W. Mitchell & N. S. Thompson (Eds.), *Deception: Perspectives on human and nonhuman deceit* (pp. 221–266). Albany: State University of New York Press.

Fenigstein, A. (1987). On the nature of public and private self-consciousness. *Journal of Personality, 55,* 543–554.

Fenigstein, A., Scheier, M. F., & Buss, A. H. (1975). Public and private self-consciousness: Assessment and theory. *Journal of Consulting and Clinical Psychology, 43,* 522–527.

Gallup, G. G., Jr. (1977). Self-recognition in primates: A comparative approach to the bidirectional properties of consciousness. *American Psychologist, 32,* 329–338.

Gallup, G. G., Jr., & Suarez, S. D. (1986). Self-awareness and the emergence of mind in humans and other primates. In J. Suls & A G. Greenwald (Eds.), *Psychological perspectives on the self* (Vol. 3, pp 3–26). Hillsdale, NJ: Erlbaum.

Gergen, K. J. (1965). The effects of interaction goals and personalistic feedback on the presentation of self. *Journal of Personality and Social Psychology, 1,* 413–424.

Goffman, E. (1959). *The presentation of self in everyday life.* Garden City, NY: Doubleday Anchor.

Greenberg, J., Pyszcynski T., Solomon, S., Rosenblatt, A., Burling, J., Lyon, D., Simon, L., & Pinel, E. (1992). Why do people need self-esteem? Converging evidence that self-esteem serves an anxiety-buffering function. *Journal of Personality and Social Psychology, 63,* 913–922.

Greenwald, A. G. (1980). The totalitarian ego: Fabrication and revision of personal history. *American Psychologist, 35,* 603–613.

Greenwald, A. G. (1982). Ego task analysis: An integration of research on ego-involvement and awareness. In A. H. Hastorf & A. M. Isen (Eds.), *Cognitive social psychology* (pp. 109–147). New York: Elsevier North Holland.

Greenwald, A. G., & Breckler, S. (1985). To whom is the self presented? In B. R. Schlenker (Ed.), *The self and social life* (pp. 126–145). New York: McGraw-Hill.

Haupt, A, & Leary, M. R. (1997). The appeal of worthless groups: Moderating effects of trait self-esteem. *Group Dynamics: Theory, Research, and Practice, 1*, 124–132.

Hoyle, R. H., Kernis, M. H., Leary, M. R., & Baldwin, M. W. (1999). *Selfhood: Identity, esteem, regulation.* Boulder, CO: Westview Press.

James, W. (1890). *The principles of psychology.* New York: Holt.

Janis, I. L., & Gilmore, J. B. (1965). The influence of incentive conditions on the success of role playing in modifying attitudes. *Journal of Personality and Social Psychology, 1*, 17–27.

Jones, E. E. (1964). *Ingratiation.* New York: Appleton-Century-Crofts.

Jones, E. E., Gergen, K. J., & Jones, R. G. (1963). Tactics of ingratiation among leaders and subordinates in a status hierarchy. *Psychological Monographs, 77* (Whole No. 566).

Jones, E. E., & Pittman, T. (1982). Toward a general theory of strategic self-presentation. In J. Suls (Ed.), *Psychological perspectives on the self* (Vol. 1, pp. 231–262). Hillsdale, NJ: Erlbaum.

Jones, E. E., Rhodewalt, F., Berglas, S., & Skelton, J. A. (1981). Effects of strategic self-presentation on subsequent self-esteem. *Journal of Personality and Social Psychology, 41*, 407–421.

Jones, S. C. (1973). Self- and interpersonal evaluations: Esteem theories vs. consistency theories. *Psychological Bulletin, 79*, 185–199.

Kolditz, T. A., & Arkin, R. M. (1982). An impression management interpretation of the self-handicapping strategy. *Journal of Personality and Social Psychology, 43*, 492–502.

Kowalski R. M., & Leary, M. R. (1990). Strategic self-presentation and the avoidance of aversive events. Antecedents and consequences of self-enhancement and self-depreciation. *Journal of Experimental Social Psychology, 26*, 322–336.

Leary, M. R. (1993). The interplay of private self-processes and interpersonal factors in self-presentation. In J. Suls (Ed.), *Psychological perspectives on the self* (Vol. 4, pp. 127–155). Hillsdale, NJ: Erlbaum.

Leary, M. R. (1995). *Self-presentation: Impression management and interpersonal behavior.* Boulder, CO: Westview Press.

Leary, M. R. (1999). The social and psychological importance of self-esteem. In R. M. Kowalski & M. R. Leary (Eds.), *The social psychology of emotional and behavioral problems: Interfaces of social and clinical psychology* (pp. 197–221). Washington, DC: American Psychological Association.

Leary, M. R., Barnes, B. D., Griebel, C., Mason, E., & McCormack, D., Jr. (1987). The impact of conjoint threats to social- and self-esteem on evaluation apprehension. *Social Psychology Quarterly, 50*, 304–311.

Leary, M. R., & Baumeister, R. F. (2000). The nature and function of self-esteem: Sociometer theory. *Advances in Experimental Social Psychology, 32*, 1–62.

Leary, M. R., & Downs, D. L. (1995). Interpersonal functions of the self-esteem motive: The self-esteem system as a sociometer. In M. Kernis (Ed.), *Efficacy, agency, and self-esteem* (pp. 123–144). New York: Plenum.

Leary, M. R., Haupt, A., Strausser, K., & Chokel, J. (1998). Calibrating the sociometer: The relationship between interpersonal appraisals and state self-esteem. *Journal of Personality and Social Psychology, 74*, 1290–1299.

Leary, M. R., & Kowalski, R. M. (1990). Impression management: A literature review and two-factor model. *Psychological Bulletin, 107*, 34–47.

Leary, M. R., Schreindorfer, L. S., & Haupt, A. L. (1995). The role of self-esteem in emotional and behavioral problems: Why is low self-esteem dysfunctional? *Journal of Social and Clinical Psychology, 14*, 297–314.

Leary, M. R., Tambor, E. S., Terdal, S. K., & Downs, D. L. (1995). Self-esteem as an interpersonal monitor: The sociometer hypothesis. *Journal of Personality and Social Psychology, 68*, 518–530.

Lecky, P. (1945). *Self-consistency: A theory of personality.* New York: Island Press.

Maracek, J., & Mettee, D. (1972). Avoidance of continued success as a function of self-esteem, level of esteem certainty, and responsibility for success. *Journal of Personality and Social Psychology, 22*, 98–107.

Martin, M. W. (1985). General introduction. In M. W. Martin (Ed.), *Self-deception and self-under-*

standing (pp. 1–27). Lawrence: University of Kansas Press.

McKillop, K. J., Jr., Berzonsky, M. D., & Schlenker, B. R. (1992). The impact of self-presentation on self-beliefs: Effects of social identity and self-presentational context. *Journal of Personality, 60,* 789–808.

Mead, G. H. (1934). *Mind, self, and society.* Chicago: University of Chicago Press.

Mecca, A. M., Smelser, N. J., & Vasconcellos, J. (Eds.). (1989). *The social importance of self-esteem.* Berkeley: University of California Press.

Miller, R. S. (1996). *Embarrassment Poise and peril in everyday life.* New York: Guilford.

Miller, R. S., & Schlenker, B. R. (1978). *Self-presentation as affected by a valid or invalid past performance.* Paper presented at the meeting of the American Psychological Association, Toronto.

Miller, R. S., & Schlenker, B. R. (1985). Egotism in group members: Public and private attributions of responsibility for group performance. *Social Psychology Quarterly, 48,* 85–89.

Modigliani, A. (1971). Embarrassment, facework, and eye contact: Testing a theory of embarrassment. *Journal of Personality and Social Psychology, 17,* 15–24.

Mruk, C. (1995). *Self-esteem: Research, theory, and practice.* New York: Springer.

Rogers, C. (1959). A theory of therapy, personality, and interpersonal relationships, as developed in the client-centered framework. In S. Koch (Ed.), *Psychology: A study of a science* (Vol. 3, pp. 184–256). New York: McGraw-Hill.

Rosenberg, M. (1965). *Society and the adolescent self image.* Princeton, NJ: Princeton University Press.

Scheier, M. F., & Carver, C. S. (1983). Two sides of the self: One for you and one for me. In J. Suls (Ed.), *Psychological perspectives on the self* (Vol. 1, pp. 123–157). Hillsdale: Erlbaum.

Schlenker, B. R. (1980). *Impression management: The self-concept, social identity, and interpersonal relations.* Monterey, CA: Brooks/Cole.

Schlenker, B. R. (1985). Identity and self-identification. In B. R. Schlenker (Ed.), *The self and social life* (pp. 65–99). New York: McGraw-Hill.

Schlenker, B. R. (1986). Self-identification: Toward an integration of the private and public self. In R. F. Baumeister (Ed.), *Public self and private self* (pp. 21–62). New York: Springer-Verlag.

Schlenker, B. R., & Trudeau, J. V. (1990). Impact of self-presentation on private self-beliefs: Effects of prior self-beliefs and misattribution. *Journal of Personality and Social Psychology, 58,* 22–32.

Schlenker, B. R., Weigold, M. F., & Hallam, J. R. (1990). Self-serving attributions in social context: Effects of self-esteem and social pressure. *Journal of Personality and Social Psychology, 58,* 855–863.

Schneider, D. J. (1969). Tactical self-presentation after success and failure. *Journal of Personality and Social Psychology, 13,* 262–268.

Schneider, D. J., & Turkat, D. (1975). Self-presentation following success or failure: Defensive self-esteem models. *Journal of Personality, 43,* 127–135.

Sedikides, C. (1993). Assessment, enhancement, and verification determinants of the self-evaluation process. *Journal of Personality and Social Psychology, 65,* 317–338.

Shepperd, J. A., & Kwavnick K. D. (1999). Maladaptive image maintenance. In R. M. Kowalski & M. R. Leary (Eds.), *The social psychology of emotional and behavioral problems* (pp. 249–277). Washington, DC: American Psychological Association.

Shrauger, J. (1975). Responses to evaluation as a function of initial self-perceptions. *Psychological Bulletin, 82,* 581–596.

Smart, L., & Wegner, D. M. (1994, July). *The ironic effects of self-presentation on self-esteem.* Paper presented at the meeting of the American Psychological Society, Washington, DC.

Spencer, S. J., Josephs, R. A., & Steele, C. M. (1993). Low self-esteem: The uphill struggle for self-integrity. In R. F. Baumeister (Ed.), *Self-esteem: The puzzle of low self-regard.* New York: Plenum.

Steele, C. M. (1988). The psychology of self-affirmation: Sustaining the integrity of the self. In L. Berkowitz (Ed.), *Advances in experimental social psychology* (Vol. 21, pp. 261–302). San Diego, CA: Academic Press.

Steele, C. M., Spencer, S. J., & Lynch, M. (1993). Self-image resilience and dissonance: The role of affirmation processes. *Journal of Personality and Social Psychology, 64,* 885–896.

Swann, W. B., Jr., Griffin, J. J., Predmore, S. C., & Gaines, B. (1987). The cognitive affective crossfire: When self-consistency confronts self-enhancement. *Journal of Personality and Social Psychology, 52*, 881–889.

Taylor, S. E., & Brown, J. D. (1988). Illusion and well-being: A social psychological perspective on mental health. *Psychological Bulletin, 103*, 193–210.

Tetlock, P. E., & Manstead, A. S. R. (1985). Impression management vs. intrapsychic explanations in social psychology: A useful dichotomy? *Psychological Review, 92*, 59–77.

Tice, D. M. (1991). Esteem protection or enhancement? Self-handicapping motives and attributions differ by trait self-esteem. *Journal of Personality and Social Psychology, 60*, 711–725.

Tice, D. M. (1992). Self-concept change and self-presentation: The looking glass self is also a magnifying glass. *Journal of Personality and Social Psychology, 63*, 435–451.

Tice, D. M. (1993). The social motivations of people with low self-esteem. In R. F. Baumeister (Ed.), *Self-esteem: The puzzle of low self-regard* (pp. 37–53). New York: Plenum.

Tice, D. M., & Baumeister, R. F. (1990). Self-esteem, self-handicapping, and self-presentation: The strategy of inadequate practice. *Journal of Personality, 58*, 443–464.

Tooby, J., & Cosmides, L. (1996). Friendship and the banker's paradox: Other pathways to the evolution of adaptations for altruism. *Proceedings of the British Academy, 88*, 119–143.

Trivers, R. (1985). *Social evolution*. Menlo Park, CA: Benjamin/Cummings.

Walster, E. (1965). The effect of self-esteem on romantic liking. *Journal of Personality and Social Psychology, 1*, 184–197.

Watson, D., & Friend, R. (1969). Measurement of social-evaluative anxiety. *Journal of Consulting and Clinical Psychology, 33*, 448–457.

Wegner, D. M. (1994). Ironic processes of mental control. *Psychological Review, 101*, 34–52.

Wolfe, R. N., Lennox, R. D., & Cutler, B. L. (1986). Getting along and getting ahead: Empirical support for a theory of protective and acquisitive self-presentation. *Journal of Personality and Social Psychology, 50*, 356–361.

Wylie, R. C. (1961). *The self-concept: A critical review of pertinent research literature*. Lincoln: University of Nebraska Press.

Chapter Nineteen

Self-expansion Model of Motivation and Cognition in Close Relationships and Beyond

Arthur Aron, Elaine N. Aron, and Christina Norman

The self-expansion model proposes that a central human motivation is self-expansion and that one way people seek such expansion is through close relationships in which each includes the other in the self (Aron & Aron, 1986, 1996, 1997). In this chapter we first examine the motivational aspect of the model (what is meant by self-expansion motivation) and the research it has generated in the close relationship area. The second section examines the inclusion-of-other-in-the-self aspect of the model and the research it has generated in the close relationship area. A final section considers recent extensions of the inclusion-of-other-in-the-self notion to social psychology topics beyond the direct study of close relationships, including empathy and helping and intergroup relations.

Self-expansion Motivation

The first overarching principle of the self-expansion model is that people seek to expand the self in the sense that they seek to enhance their potential efficacy by increasing the physical and social resources, perspectives, and identities that facilitate achievement of any goal that might arise.[1] (For a recent elaboration of the motivational aspect of the model, see Aron, Norman, & Aron, 1998.) The emphasis here is not on a motivation for the actual achievement of goals, but on a motivation to attain the resources to be able to achieve goals. Probably for humans the most important resource for achieving goals is knowledge.[2] Other kinds of resources are also relevant, such as social status and community, possessions and wealth, and physical strength and health.

The idea for the proposed motivation emerged in part from R. W. White's (1959) classic argument that there is a biologically based fundamental drive for efficacy or competence that is comparable to such drives as hunger and thirst and is centered in the nervous system. However, White emphasized the satisfaction arising from acting effectively, while we would, as just noted, emphasize the satisfaction arising from knowing that one has the potential to act effectively. The present view was also developed taking into account self-efficacy models of motivation (for a review, see Gecas, 1989). However, our view is somewhat different from Bandura's (1977), the most widely cited self-efficacy theory. Bandura emphasizes the role of self-efficacy expectancy (the perceived likelihood that self will be able to achieve a particular goal) as a mediator of the motivational process of selecting a goal or energizing oneself with regard to a particular goal, rather than our view that something like self-efficacy expectancy (in a general sense) is a goal in its own right. Yet another long-standing motivational view that influenced the development of the self-expansion model is the idea of intrinsic motivation (e.g., Deci & Ryan, 1987), the value associated with the *process* of achieving a goal, as opposed to extrinsic motivation, the value of the goal itself. However, we hold that both intrinsic and extrinsic motives can be directed, ultimately, to self-expansion. Finally, the intrinsic motivation idea is in a sense allied with phenomenological views, such as Maslow's (1970), that the ultimate motivation is to actualize the full potential of the self. However, the self-expansion model lays out the processes involved in a much more precise way, and there are major differences. For example, Maslow argued that self-actualization does not come into play until more "basic" motives like hunger and safety are satisfied, while the self-expansion model posits that self-expansion can play a major role at any point, even, for example, when one is hungry or in danger.

There are also important links with current work in the social psychology of motivation, most of which focuses on the processes involved in attaining goals and the influence of goals on cognitive processes (e.g., Higgins & Sorrentino, 1990). Where social psychology has focused on the selection of goals, it has tended to emphasize how we combine values with expectancies, leaving unspecified the question of what makes something of value. In contrast, the self-expansion model specifically proposes that what makes a potential goal of value is the extent to which it facilitates self-expansion.

There has been some speculation in recent years in mainstream social psychology that is relevant to this issue of what makes something of value, focusing on various self-oriented motives (Sedikides & Strube, 1995). In this context, Taylor, Neter, and Wayment (1995) proposed a self-related motive that they labeled "self-improvement," that is roughly comparable to self-expansion. Taylor et al. conducted a series of studies in which participants reported using quite different sources of information when satisfying self-improvement motives than when satisfying other self-motives such as self-verification (the desire to have confirmed what you believe you are) or self-enhancement (the desire to see yourself in the most positive light).

Our motivational model can also be understood in the context of some of the major current relationship theories. For example, interdependence theory (Kelley & Thibaut, 1978; Rusbult & Arriaga, 1997) focuses on the ways in which expected benefits and costs guide behavior in relationships. What the self-expansion model adds is a specification of what counts as an expected benefit or cost. Similarly, self-expansion motivation is at least in principle intimately linked with attachment models (e.g., Bowlby, 1969; Shaver & Hazan, 1993). The core of attachment theory is a dialectical process in which an infant naturally explores the environment, but regularly monitors and periodically returns to the caregiver as a source of safety. The focus of most attachment work has been on the sense of safety provided by caregivers and relationship partners. The exploration motivation, which is the foundation of the process to begin with, has been largely ignored. We think that self-expansion processes describe this aspect of attachment very well. Indeed, we have argued elsewhere (Aron, Aron, & Allen, 1998) that one can construe attachment styles as arising from early experiences of consistent support in self-expansion (secures), consistent failure to support self-expansion (avoidants), or inconsistent support and failure (anxious/ ambivalents).

Research generated by the motivational aspect of the model

Self-expansion from developing a relationship.   One implication of the proposed self-expansion motivation in the relationship area is that developing a relationship expands the self. In this regard, Sedikides (personal communication, October, 1992) collected self-descriptions of participants who were or were not currently in a close relationship. These self-descriptions were analyzed for number of different domains of the self they included. Consistent with this prediction (based on the self-expansion model), he found that the self-descriptions of those in relationships included terms representing significantly more domains of the self.

Following up on this idea, in a longitudinal study, Aron, Paris, and Aron (1995) tested 325 students five times, once every two and a half weeks over a ten-week period. At each testing the participants listed as many self-descriptive words or phrases as came to mind during a three-minute period in response to the question, "Who are you today?" and answered a number of other questions which included items indicating whether the participant had fallen in love since the last testing. As predicted, there was a significantly greater increase in diversity of self-content domains in the self-descriptions from before to after falling in love. (This was found when comparing this increase to the average changes from before to after other testing sessions for those who fell in love, and when comparing this increase to the typical testing-to-testing changes for participants who did not fall in love.) In a sense, there was a literal expansion of self. A second study, with a new sample of 529 participants, administered scales measuring self-efficacy and self-esteem every two and a half weeks. As predicted, there was a significantly greater increase in these variables from before to after falling in love. (Again, this was found when comparing the increase to the average changes from before to after other testing sessions for those who fell in love, and when comparing this increase to the typical testing-to-testing changes for those who did not fall in love.) In both of these studies, the effects on the self were maintained when measures of mood change were controlled statistically.

Self-expansion process as a motivator.   Another key implication of the motivational aspect of the model that has generated a number of studies is based on the idea that the process of rapid expansion is affectively positive, that rapid self-expansion produces strong positive affect (so long as the rate of expansion is not so great as to be stressful). Because this rapid expansion is pleasurable, in addition to a desire to be expanded (to possess high levels of potential efficacy), a key motivator is the desire to experience the process of expanding, to feel oneself increasing rapidly in potential self-efficacy. This notion is similar to Carver and Scheier's (1990) self-regulatory process in which people monitor the rate at which they are making progress towards goals and experience positive affect when the perceived rate exceeds an acceptable or desired rate. Indeed, they argue further that accelerations in the rate cause feelings of exhilaration. Our notion of being motivated to experience the expanding process is also similar to Pyszczynski, Greenberg, and Solomon's (1997) "Self-expansive" motivational system (one of their three main motivations). Expansive activities are motivating because of the pleasure that "engagement [in them] provides" (p. 6).

Some support for this process-motivation aspect of the model comes from the research on the arousal-attraction effect. As we have detailed elsewhere (e.g., Aron, Norman, & Aron, 1998), this aspect of the self-expansion model suggests what may be an important mechanism driving the arousal-attraction effect, best known from the Dutton and Aron (1974) suspension-bridge study, the basic results of which are now well replicated (for a review, see Foster, Witcher, Campbell, & Green, 1998). The idea is that because arousal often co-occurs with rapid self-expansion, when a potential relationship partner is associated with arousal, the partner is positively valued because of the link with rapid self-expansion.

Other support for this self-expansion process-motivation idea comes from research on unreciprocated love. Based on the self-expansion model, Aron, Aron, and Allen (1998) developed and provided empirical support for a mini-theory of unreciprocated love that proposes three motivational factors: (1) high levels of desirability (the extent to which self believes a relationship with the beloved would expand the self), (2) greater-than-zero levels of probability that a relationship (and hence self-expansion) is possible, and (3) opportunity to experience the expanding process associated with the falling in and being in love (even if it is not reciprocated). Regarding this third factor, falling and being in love may itself be desirable by permitting the individual to experience the process of expanding the self through enacting the culturally scripted role of the lover (and thus experiencing a dramatically different life perspective) and redirecting attention and resources to a single very important goal (and thus experiencing a rapid increase in apparent energy). While in principle these three motivational factors might also have been derived from other theoretical models, the self-expansion model's focus on the benefits of rapid expansion is more likely to bring such ideas to mind – particularly ideas like that of the third factor.

The major line of work developed directly from the principle of the self-expansion process as a motivator and, supporting that view, is a set of studies focusing on a predicted increase in satisfaction in long-term relationships from joint participation in self-expanding activities. This work emerged from a consideration of the well-documented typical decline in relationship satisfaction after the "honeymoon period" in a romantic relationship, a lowered average level which is also maintained over subsequent years (e.g., Tucker & Aron, 1993). When two people first enter a relationship, typically there appears to be an initial, exhilarating period in which the couple spends hours talking, engaging in intense risk-taking and self-disclosure. From the perspective of the self-expansion model, this initial exhilarating period is one in which the partners are expanding their selves at a rapid rate by virtue of the intense exchange in which they are rapidly including in the self perspectives and identities of the other. Once the two know each other fairly well, opportunities for further rapid expansion of this sort inevitably decrease. When rapid expansion occurs there is a high degree of satisfaction; when expansion is slow or nonexistent, there is little emotion, or perhaps boredom. If slow expansion follows a period of rapid expansion, the loss of enjoyable emotion may be disappointing and attributed to the particular relationship. There has been surprisingly little previous theorizing about the reasons for the decline in marital satisfaction, other than fairly general allusions to habituation-type processes (e.g., Huesmann, 1980; Jacobson & Margolin, 1979; Plutchik, 1967). The self-expansion model adds to a simple habituation idea by specifying what about the other and the relationship becomes decreasingly novel (the loss of new information to be included in the self) and, most important from the current perspective, by specifying why habituation leads to dissatisfaction (the decline in the highly desired rapid rate of self-expansion, in this case associated with the relationship). Thus the model provides a more precise and motivationally based explanation for the role of habituation in relationships.

Basically, our notion is that if self-expanding activities create positive affect, then when couples engage in such activities *together*, this positive affect should become associated with both the behaviors involved in that activity and also the behavior of staying near the other and any other behaviors that maintain the relationship. (The point is, the self-expansion model contributes an explanation for why certain kinds of activities would be especially rewarding: they arise as a result of or are associated with the process of expanding the self.) What distinguishes an activity that is self-expanding? We think novelty is the key aspect. Participating in a novel activity expands the self by providing new information and experiences. However, arousal is also relevant. Novelty is arousing (Berlyne, 1960) so that through life experience, arousal is likely to be associated with novelty, and hence with self-expansion. In terms of how self-expanding activities are recognized, we have assumed that the most likely ordinary-language label is "exciting," since this term covers both arousal and novelty (and as noted in the research below, it is precisely novel and/or arousing activities that couples label as exciting).

There is substantial evidence that, in general, time spent together is correlated with marital satisfaction (e.g., L. K. White, 1983) and some evidence from these studies that the correlation is strongest for intense activities. There are also some survey data focusing directly on the link of "exciting" activities and satisfaction. Aron, Norman, Aron, McKenna, and Heyman (2000, Studies 1 & 2), in both a newspaper questionnaire study and a telephone survey, found strong correlations between the two variables, even after partialing out measures of relationship-relevant socially desirable response bias. Additional analyses in these studies suggested that boredom with the relationship is a key mediator of this association.

In a field experiment to test this idea (Reissman, Aron, & Bergen, 1993), volunteer married couples were randomly assigned to spend one and a half hours each week for ten weeks engaging together in either "exciting" or "pleasant" (but not particularly exciting) activities selected from an individually prepared list of activities both spouses had rated above the midpoint on the scale corresponding to their condition. As predicted, change in marital satisfaction was significantly greater for exciting-condition than pleasant-condition couples. (Change in marital satisfaction was intermediate for a third group of couples who had been randomly assigned to a no-activity control condition.)

We have also conducted three experiments in order to establish a laboratory paradigm in which we could test crucial points of the theory under highly controlled conditions (Aron et al., 2000 Studies 3–5). In these experiments couples came to our lab for what they believed was an assessment session involving questionnaires and being videotaped interacting. Indeed, when they came, that is what happened – they completed some questionnaires, participated together in a task that was videotaped, and then completed some more questionnaires. However, from our perspective, the questionnaires before the task served as a pretest, those after as a posttest, and the task itself was experimentally manipulated so that some couples engaged in a self-expanding activity (one that was novel and arousing) and those in the control condition, in a more mundane activity. (In the expanding activity the couple was tied together on one side at the wrists and ankles and then took part in a task in which they crawled together on mats for 12 meters, climbing over a barrier at one point, while pushing a foam cylinder with their heads. This was a timed task such that the couple received a prize if they beat a time limit and the situation was rigged so that they almost make it in the prize-winning time the first two tries and then just barely make it on the third try. In the mundane condition one partner slowly crawled to the middle of the mat and back, then the other partner did the same, then the first partner repeated this, and so on.)

The first study employing this paradigm, in which participants were mainly student dating couples, found, as predicted, a significantly greater increase in relationship satisfaction for the expanding-condition couples. The second study replicated the first experiment's results with married couples recruited from the community. It also included a no-activity condition in which, it turned out, the increase in satisfaction was less than even in the mundane-activity condition. Thus, the difference between the expanding-activity and mundane-activity conditions is clearly due to increased satisfaction in the expanding condition and not decreased satisfaction in the mundane condition. A third experiment, also with couples recruited from the community, included a short videotaped discussion of a standardized topic (e.g., plan a trip together), before and after the interaction task. This study again replicated the basic finding of greater increases in satisfaction for the expanding activity group on the usual questionnaire ratings. More importantly, this study found the same effect on measures based on blind coding of the videotaped interactions using standard rating protocols for statements made during the interaction. Specifically, from before to after the activity, couples in the expanding-activity condition, compared to couples in the mundane-activity condition, showed significantly greater increases in positive and supportive statements and decreases in hostile statements. Preliminary results of two additional experiments (Aron, Aron, & Norman, 1999) demonstrated that the effect cannot be accounted for by arousal alone, that the sense of expansion mediates the effect, and that the effect requires that the partner be salient during the expanding activity.

Summary

We described the desire to expand the self as a core motive. The goal is to acquire social and material resources, perspectives, and identities that enhance one's ability to accomplish goals. The basic idea is linked to long-standing models of competence motivation, self-efficacy, intrinsic motivation, and theories of self-actualization. While social cognition approaches have generally focused on how goals lead to behavior rather than on what goals we select, work in the area of self-evaluation is an exception, and within that domain

Taylor et al. (1995) have proposed that self-improvement, an idea much like self-expansion, may be an important motive. The self-expansion motive is also, of course, specifically relevant to major relationship theories, in that it specifies one basis for evaluating ultimate benefits and costs in interdependence approaches, and it seems to describe well the exploratory motive that plays an important, though mainly implicit, role in attachment theories. The motivational aspect of the self-expansion model has generated a number of studies in the relationship area. One such line of work has shown that entering a new relationship (operationalized as falling in love) expands the self in the sense that one's spontaneous self-description increases in diversity and in the sense of an increase in perceived self-efficacy. Other studies have focused on the implication of the model that rapid self-expansion creates positive affect and thus people are motivated to experience rapid self-expansion in order to experience this positive affect – an idea consistent with a proposal by Carver and Scheier (1990) that strong positive affect is associated with rapid progress toward goals. This motivation suggests a major mechanism driving the arousal-attraction effect, provides a motivational explanation for the maintenance of unreciprocated love, and offers a way to understand the decline in relationship satisfaction after the early relationship stages as well as a means of minimizing or reversing that decline (by having couples participate together in expanding activities).

Including Other in the Self

Having postulated a general motivation to expand the self, we also proposed that the desire to enter and maintain a particular relationship can be seen as one, especially satisfying, useful, and human, means to this self-expansion – cognitively, the self is expanded through including the other in the self, a process which in a close relationship becomes mutual, so that each person is including the other in his or her self. (For fuller reviews of the inclusion-of-other-in-the-self aspect of the self-expansion model, see Aron & Aron, 1986, 1996.) That is, people seek relationships in order to gain what they anticipate as self-expansion. When faced with a potential relationship, one compares one's self as it is prior to the relationship – lacking the other's perspectives, resources, and identities – to the self as prospectively imagined after it has entered the relationship, a self now with access both to the self's own perspectives and so forth *plus* the other's perspectives and so forth. Metaphorically, I will have the use of all my house plus gain the use of yours. Thus before one enters a relationship, the motive of self-expansion may seem to have a decidedly self-centered air to it. But after entering, the effect of including each other in each other's self is an overlapping of selves. Now I must protect and maintain my house *and* your house, as *both* are "mine" (as both are now "yours"). This post-inclusion, larger self creates (and explains) the sometimes remarkably unselfish nature of close relationships.

The notion that in a relationship each is included in each other's self is consistent with a wide variety of social psychological ideas about relationships. For example, Reis and Shaver (1988) identified intimacy as mainly a process of an escalating reciprocity of self-disclosure in which each individual feels his or her innermost self validated, understood, and cared for by the other. Indeed, perhaps the most prominent idea in social psychology directly related to the present theme is the "unit relation," a fundamental concept in Heider's (1958) cognitive account of interpersonal relations. This idea is also related to Ickes, Tooke, Stinson, Baker, and Bissonnette's (1988) idea of "intersubjectivity" – which Ickes and his colleagues made vivid by citing Merleau-Ponty's (1945) description of a close relationship as a "double being" and Schutz's (1970) reference to two people "living in each other's subjective contexts of meaning" (p. 167).

Several currently active lines of theory-based social psychology research focus on closely related themes. For example, in a series of experimental and correlational studies, Tesser (1988) has shown that a relationship partner's achievement, so long as it is not in a domain that threatens the self by creating a negative social comparison, is "reflected" by the self (i.e., the self feels pride in the achievement as if it were the self's). Another relevant line of work focuses on what is called "fraternal relative deprivation" (Runciman, 1966), in which the relative disadvantage of the group to which the self belongs affects the self as if it were the self's own deprivation. Yet another example is work arising from social identity theory (Tajfel & Turner, 1979) which posits that one's identity is structured from membership in social groups.

In the field of marketing, Belk (1988) has proposed a notion of ownership in which "we regard our possessions as part of ourselves" (p. 139), an idea that has been the subject of considerable theoretical discussion and several studies. For example, Sivadas and Machleit (1994) found that items measuring an object's "incorporation into self" (items such as "helps me achieve my identity" and "is part of who I am") form a separate factor from items assessing the object's importance or relevance to the self. Ahuvia (1993) has attempted to integrate Belk's self-extension approach with the self-expansion model and has proposed that processes hypothesized in the domain of personal relationships also apply to relations to physical objects and experiences. In an interview study, Ahuvia showed that people sometimes describe their "love" of things in much the same way as they describe their love of relationship partners, that they often consider this "real" love, and that they treat these love objects as very much a part of their identity. At the same time, as with human relationships, there is often a sense of autonomous value to the object, even a sense of being controlled by or at the mercy of it. These ideas about including the owned object in the self are also related to the notion of relationship, as each "possessing" the other (e.g., Reik, 1944).

In the relationship domain, Agnew, Van Lange, Rusbult, and Langston (1998) have explicitly linked the inclusion-of-other-in-the-self model with interdependence, describing it as "cognitive interdependence – a mental state characterized by a pluralistic, collective representation of self-in-relationship" (p. 939). Cialdini, Brown, Lewis, Luce, and Neuberg (1997) have linked the model to evolutionary theories of relationships, suggesting that interpersonal closeness, experienced as including other in the self, may be how we recognize those with whom we share genes (a kind of literal, physical self-other inclusion) in the interest of knowing with whom one should share resources to enhance collective fitness. Finally, although there has been no explicit work on the possible link, we think that there may be a close connection between self-other inclusion and communal relationships (e.g., Clark & Mills, 1979, 1993). That is, we see including other in the self as the foundation for spontaneously being concerned with the others' needs (since other's needs are my needs) and thus both directly facilitating communal motivation (attention to and acting on other's needs) and having possibly functioned historically to help create a social norm of communal orientation in close relationships.

The notion of relationship as an overlap of selves has been popular more generally among psychologists and sociologists, starting at least with James (1890/1948). For example, Bakan (1966) wrote about "communion" in the context of his expansion on Buber's (1937) "I–Thou" relationship. Jung (1925/1959) emphasized the role of relationship partners as providing or developing otherwise unavailable aspects of the psyche, so leading to greater wholeness. Maslow took it for granted that "beloved people can be incorporated into the self" (1967, p. 103). And from a symbolic interactionist perspective, McCall (1974) described "attachment" as "incorporation of . . . [the other's] actions and reactions . . . into the content of one's various conceptions of the self" (p. 219).

Research generated by the inclusion-of-other-in-the-self aspect of the model

One line of relevant research focuses on the extent to which people *view* relationships as connected or overlapping selves. Sedikides, Olsen, and Reis (1993) found that people spontaneously cluster information about other people in terms of their relationships with each other, grouping the people together on recall tasks based on their relationships. This suggests that cognitive representations of other individuals are in a sense overlapped or at least tied together as a function of these others being perceived as being in close relationships with each other. Focusing on the issue of the perceived overlap of one's self with a relationship partner, Aron, Aron, and Smollan (1992) asked participants to describe their closest relationship using the Inclusion of Other in the Self (IOS) Scale (see figure 19.1), which consists of a series of overlapping circles from which one selects the pair that best describes one's relationship with a particular person. The scale appears to have levels of reliability, as well as of discriminant, convergent, and predictive validity, that match or exceed other

Please circle the picture below which best describes your relationship.

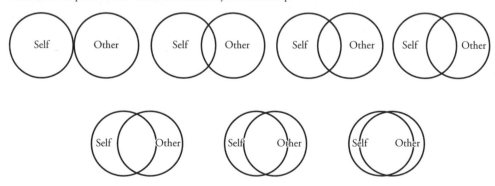

Figure 19.1   The Inclusion of Other in the Self (IOS) Scale (Aron, Aron, & Smollan, 1992). Respondents are instructed to select the picture that best describes their relationship.

measures of closeness—measures which are typically more complex and lengthy. (For example, the correlation between a score on this test and whether the participant remained in a romantic relationship three months later was .46.) Further, most measures of closeness seem to fall into one of two factors: they measure either *feelings of closeness* or *behaviors associated with closeness*. The IOS Scale, however, loads, to some extent, on both of these factors. This suggests that the Scale may be tapping the core meaning of closeness and not merely a particular aspect of it. The point of all this is that this measure may be so successful because the metaphor of overlapping circles representing self and other corresponds to the reality of how people process information about relationships.

Agnew et al. (1998), in a study of dating couples, found that scores on the IOS Scale correlated highly with a variety of relationship measures, such as satisfaction, commitment, investment in the relationship, and centrality of the relationship. Most interesting, the IOS Scale correlated moderately with proportion of first-person plural pronouns ("we" and "us") the dating partners used when speaking about their relationship, a finding that Agnew et al. took as an indication of what they called "cognitive interdependence." Cross et al. (1997) found that IOS Scale ratings of close others correlated with what they called "interdependent self-construal" (an example item is "When I feel close to someone, I typically think of their triumphs as if they are my own"). In another study, Loving and Agnew (1998) found that the overall IOS Scale correlated significantly with reported self-partner overlap in specific areas of personal, physical, work, and social lives, with personal and social being most important. The IOS Scale has also been used in a wide variety of relationships studies along with other relationship measures where its performance is generally similar to those other measures. In one example Aron, Melinat, Aron, Vallone, and Bator (1997) found that IOS Scale scores were greater after an experimental task involving gradual self-disclosure and relationship building activities, as compared to a small-talk control group. In another example, Knee (1998) conducted a longitudinal study in which couples with initial high IOS Scale scores were more likely to stay together if the two of them believed in relationship destiny, but couples with low initial IOS Scale scores were more likely to stay together if the partners did not believe in relationship destiny. In the third section of the paper we describe several studies that have used the IOS Scale successfully in areas of social psychology other than close relationships. We should also mention that Tropp and Wright (2000) have developed (and demonstrated the reliability and validity of) a version of the IOS Scale that assesses overlap of self and ingroup; Uleman, Rhee, Bardoliwalla, Semin, & Toyama (2000) have applied the Tropp and Wright version of the IOS Scale successfully in a series of cross-cultural studies; and Perreault and Bourhis (1999) successfully used a similar adaptation of the Scale in their research on ingroup identification.

Finally, regarding the principle behind the IOS Scale, we should note that even before it was developed (and unknown to the IOS Scale authors), Pipp, Shaver, Jennings, Lamborn, and Fischer (1985) had used overlapping-circle diagrams as part of a closeness measure. They had adolescents draw a picture of two circles, one representing the self and one a parent, "in relation to each other as you believe best illustrates your relationship with that parent . . . " (p. 993). Among other findings, Pipp et al. reported that perceived closeness and the amount of overlap of the circles were both strongly related to scale ratings of love and friendship.

Several studies have focused more directly on the underlying cognitive mechanisms of including other in the self. One set of such studies was based on the well-established differences in actor versus observer perspectives in attributional processes (Jones & Nisbett, 1971). In the context of the self-expansion model, to the extent a particular person is included in the self, the difference between self's and that particular person's perspective should be reduced. Several studies support this conclusion. Nisbett, Caputo, Legant, and Marecek (1973, Study 3) found that the longer people had been in a relationship with a close friend, the less willing they were to make dispositional attributions about the friend. Similarly, Goldberg (1981) found that participants made fewer dispositional attributions for people they have spent more time with, compared to people they have spent less time with. Other research has followed this same theme of examining actor-observer differences in attribution but using different approaches. Prentice (1990) had participants describe each of several persons, describing each such person in each of three different, relatively important specific situations. She found least overlap across situations for descriptions of self, next least for familiar others, and most for unfamiliar others. This finding suggests that people are making situational attributions for self and those close to self but regard less familiar others in terms that are not differentiated by situation. Using yet another approach, Sande, Goethals, and Radloff (1988) found that self, and then liked friends, and then disliked friends, were progressively less likely to be attributed *both* poles of pairs of opposite traits (e.g., "serious-carefree"). The point here is that for self – and those liked by self – behaviors can vary according to the situation, even to the extent of representing opposites. But for those distant from self, a single-sided trait description (i.e., a dispositional attribution) is quite adequate. Aron, Aron, Tudor, and Nelson (1991, introduction to Study 2) replicated Sande et al.'s procedure, but compared different degrees of *closeness* (as opposed to liking vs. disliking). They found choices of both traits were most frequent for self, next for best friend, and least for a friendly acquaintance.

Yet another approach relevant to including the other's perspective in the self is based on an adaptation of a research paradigm developed by Lord (1980, 1987). Lord presented participants with a series of concrete nouns, for each of which they were instructed to form as vivid and interesting a mental image as possible of a target person *interacting* with whatever the noun referred to. The target person was sometimes self and sometimes someone else, such as Johnny Carson. On a free recall task afterwards, Lord found *fewer* nouns were recalled which were imaged with self than which were imaged with the other target person. He interpreted these results in terms of a figure–ground difference between one's experience of self and other when acting in the world. Because self, being ground, is less vivid than other, imaging things interacting with the self is less enhancing to memory than imaging them interacting with someone other than self. In this light, Aron et al. suggested that if the other is included in the self, other should become more like ground and less like figure – that is, more like the self. Based on this reasoning, Aron, Aron, et al. (1991, Experiment 2) replicated Lord's procedures, again using as target persons self and a prominent entertainment personality, but also added a third target, a close other, the participant's mother. Consistent with predictions, recall was greatest for nouns imaged with the entertainment personality and much less for both those imaged with self and those imaged with mother. This result was also replicated in a new sample, substituting friend of mother for the entertainment personality (to deal with the possibility that entertainment personalities are simply especially vivid images). In the replication, participants were also asked to rate their similarity, closeness, and familiarity with their mother. Also, consistent with the model's closeness emphasis, the difference in recall for nouns imaged with mother's friend minus recall for nouns imaged with mother (presumably indicating the degree to which other is included in the self) correlated .56 with ratings of closeness to mother, but only .13 with similarity, and only .16 with familiarity.

Another influential general body of research in social cognition has focused on the unique role of self-representations, going back to the pioneering articles by Markus (1977) and Rogers, Kuiper, and Kirker (1977), and what has become known as the self-reference effect (that information processing and memory is enhanced for information related to the self). If, in a close relationship, each includes other in the self, then any advantage for self-relevant information over other-relevant information should be lessened when other is in a close relationship with self – a pattern supported by several studies (for a review, see Symons & Johnson, 1997). In one such study, Bower and Gilligan (1979) found little difference in incidental memory for trait adjectives which participants had earlier judged for their relevance to their own life or their mother's life. In another study, Keenan and Baillet (1980) had participants indicate whether trait adjectives were true of a particular person. The persons were self, best friend, parent, friend, teacher, favorite TV character, and the US president. They found a clear linear trend from self through president of increasing time to make the decisions and fewer adjectives recognized later. Similarly, Prentice (1990) showed that both the content and organization of self-descriptions and other-descriptions tended to follow a pattern in which familiar others were intermediate between self and unfamiliar others.

Why is there this continuum from self to close others to strangers? We have argued that it is because the knowledge structures of a close other actually share elements (or activation potentials) with the knowledge structures of the self. Thus we hypothesized that self and close-other traits may actually be confused or interfere with each other. To test this idea, Aron, Aron, et al. (1991, Experiment 3) had married participants first rate 90 trait adjectives for their descriptiveness of themselves and their spouse. After a distracting intermediate task, they made a series of "me" – "not-me" reaction time choices to these traits. The prediction was that there would be the most confusion – and thus longer response latencies – for trait words that were different for self and spouse. (The confusion is hypothesized to arise because one is asked here to rate these traits as true or false for *self*; but if other is part of self, when self and other differ on a trait, the difference is a discrepancy between two parts of "self.") The results were as predicted: longer response times when the trait was different between self and spouse. The same pattern was obtained in a follow-up study. Also, in the follow-up study, participants completed the IOS Scale, which correlated significantly with the difference between the average response time to spouse-different words minus the average response time to spouse-similar words. Aron and Fraley (1999) and Smith, Coates, and Walling (1999) independently replicated the significant association of the reaction time measure with the IOS Scale in samples of individuals in romantic relationships; Aron and Fraley also tested for and found significant correlations of the reaction time measure with Sande et al.'s (1988) attribution measure, self-report measures of love and commitment, and change in self–reported closeness over a three–month period.

Finally, Omoto and Gunn (1994) found a self-other confusion effect for episodic memory. In their study, participants paired with friends versus participants paired with strangers were more likely to mix up whether they or their partner had earlier solved particular anagram tasks. Although the focus of their study was on other issues, these data would seem to suggest that in a personal relationship identities are sufficiently intermixed that we can actually confuse biographical memories of self and other.

Summary

A key proposal of the self-expansion model is that participants in a close relationship include each other in their selves in the sense that other's perspectives, resources, and identities are to some extent one's own. This idea is consistent with a number of ideas in social psychology and in psychology more generally, as well as having direct links with some major relationship models including interdependence theory ("cognitive interdependence"), evolutionary psychology (from the perspective of inclusive fitness), and the communal-exchange norm model (communal orientation). One line of research has shown that a Venn-diagram metaphor of self and other as overlapping circles (the IOS Scale) is a remarkably effective measure of emotional and behavioral interpersonal closeness, suggesting that this metaphor may capture how people spontaneously process information about relationships. Various nonobvious cognitive procedures have also been employed to demonstrate the role of inclusion of other in the self. These include studies showing that in a close relationship (vs. a less close relationship) there is less difference in self–other perspectives in attributions and in imaging tasks, differences in response time and memory for material related to self and other are reduced, characteristics of other interfere with self-relevant processing to a greater extent (suggesting that there is overlap in semantically based cognitive structures representing self and other), and there are self–other confusions in episodic memories.

Implications of Including Other in the Self for Other Social Psychology Topics

This final section considers recent extensions of the inclusion-of-other-in-the-self notion to two major social psychology topics beyond the direct study of close relationships – empathy and helping, and intergroup relations.[3]

Empathy and helping

An implication of our including-other-in-the-self notion is that when other is part of the self, helping other is helping self. That is, since whatever is given to other is to some extent given to self, then from the psychological perspective, giving to other is selfish, egoistic. Yet at the same time, there need be no direct benefit to self's welfare whatsoever for the process to work. Thus, from an external observer's perspective, the motivation is entirely unselfish, purely altruistic. Several studies lend support to the basic idea that in a close relationship there is less distinction between own and other's outcomes. Aron, Aron, et al. (1991, Study 1 and first and second replications) found that in a money allocation game, participants distributed money about equally to self and close others but they distributed more to themselves when other was a stranger or acquaintance; further, this result was robust over conditions in which real money was involved and participants believed that the other person would not be able to know one's allocations. MacKay, McFarland, and Buehler (1998) found that false feedback about a relationship partner's performance affected own mood only when the partner was a close relationship partner. Beach et al. (1998) supported an "extended" version of Tesser's self-esteem maintenance model in which, for example, participants' affective reaction to success or failure of their partner outperforming the self was impacted by whether or not the performance was in a domain believed to be important to the partner. (In a parallel fashion, De La Ronde & Swann, 1998, demonstrated an extended version of Swann's self-verification model, such that when married participants were given feedback inconsistent with their view of their partner, they attempted to restore the original view even when it was negative.) Finally, Medvene (2000) found the usual equity effect of greatest satisfaction for those who are neither under- nor overbenefited in a romantic relationship, but this pattern was much weaker for those who scored high on the IOS scale. That is, for couples who reported high levels of including other in the self, over- and underbenefit did not much affect their satisfaction – presumably because if other is included in the self, a benefit to other *is* a benefit to self.

Furthermore, we think that even in relatively transitory relationships people often include others in the self to some slight extent – that inclusion of other in the self is the essence of relationshipness (Aron & Aron, 1993). Indeed, one may be especially likely to include another person in the self if one becomes aware that this person is in need, because this awareness increases the other person's saliency and because recognizing another's need is associated with close relationships (Clark, Mills, & Corcoran, 1989). Finally, a number of studies by Batson and his colleagues have shown that empathy can be a key mediator between perceived need and helping: "the more empathy felt for a person in need, the more altruistic motivation to have that need reduced" (Batson, 1991, p. 87). But what *is* empathy? One interpretation (though not Batson's) is that empathy means feeling spontaneously what the other feels. In our terms, empathy means the other's feelings are my feelings, the other's need is my need. That is, we see empathy as a subset of including other in the self. If becoming aware of a person in need produces empathy, then becoming aware of a person in need produces including other in the self. Thus, Wegner (1980) suggested that empathy may "stem in part from a basic confusion between ourselves and others" (p. 133), which he proposed may arise from an initial lack of differentiation between self and caregiver in infancy (Hoffman, 1976). Davis, Conklin, Smith, and Luce (1996), explicitly linking their thinking with the self-expansion model, emphasized the importance of taking the perspective of the other, in which "the mental processes associated with perspective taking cause an observer's thoughts and feelings about a target to become, in some sense, more 'selflike'" (pp. 713–714).

In a study conducted by Cialdini et al. (1997), participants responded to a variety of scenarios involving a person in need. The finding was that the extent to which a person indicated they would help the other was mediated by measures of both empathic feeling and including other in the self; however, when they included both in the equation, empathic feeling dropped out and the measure of including other in the self turned out to be the key mediator. However, Batson et al. (1997) challenged Cialdini et al.'s conclusions, arguing that self–other overlap may account for some cases of altruism (particularly in close relationships), but altruism can exist independently of this effect (particularly when it is towards strangers). Their study used a standard perspective-taking empathy manipulation – participants attended to a video of a supposed person in need under instructions either to listen objectively or to imagine how the person in need feels – and then provided the participant an opportunity to help the person in need. Results were that differences across conditions in helping remained, even after controlling for measures of including other in the self. This controversy continued in two subsequent commentaries (Batson, 1997; Neuberg, Cialdini, Brown, Luce, & Sagarin, 1997).

Regardless of the precise eventual outcome of this controversy, it would still be consistent with including other in the self being at least one route to enhanced empathy. Davis et al.'s (1996) experiment would seem to be consistent with this view. In two experiments using a standard perspective-taking manipulation, participants in the high-empathy condition were more likely to attribute self-descriptive traits to the empathy target. Addressing the role of including other in the self more directly, Aron, Fraley, and Cialdini (2000) conducted three experiments using standard perspective-taking manipulations, in each case finding (1) a significant effect on the standard empathic feeling measure, and (2) that this effect was partially or totally mediated by the IOS Scale.

In sum, the idea of including other in the self and several supportive studies suggest that in a close relationship other's outcomes are to some extent self's outcomes, possibly explaining the apparently unselfish behavior sometimes found in such relationships. We also suggested that there may even be some degree of including other in the self with strangers, particularly when the stranger is in need so that the person is salient and the context of needs (and hence a communal relationship) is primed. Studies by Cialdini et al. (1997) support this view; however Batson et al. (1997) have challenged whether including other in the self can fully account for empathy with strangers. Other studies focusing just on empathy (a presumed mediator of helping) suggest that it is facilitated by including other in the self.

Extensions to intergroup relations

What does including other in the self have to do with intergroup relations? One possibility is a link with Allport's (1954) "contact hypothesis," the idea that under appropriate conditions (such as equal status), contact with a member of an outgroup can lead to reduced prejudice toward that outgroup. Some recent research (Pettigrew, 1997, 1998), however, suggests that such contact is only effective in reducing prejudice when the other is in a close relationship (such as a friendship) with self. In this light, we have suggested that a key mechanism driving this effect is inclusion in the self of the outgroup member – and hence also of the outgroup member's group membership.

In a questionnaire study conducted by McLaughlin-Volpe, Aron, Wright, and Reis (2000, Study 1), respondents indicated their prejudice towards and relationships with members of each of three different ethnic outgroups. Differences between outgroups in the number of friends one had or the amount of interaction with members of those outgroups did not predict parallel differences in prejudice toward those outgroups. However, differences among outgroups in the extent to which one included in the self a friend in that outgroup did significantly predict parallel differences in prejudice – the greater the inclusion of the outgroup friend in the self, the less prejudice was found for that outgroup. In another series of studies conducted by these authors, instead of ethnic outgroups, they used students at rival US universities as the outgroup – USC for UCLA and vice versa, Texas for Texas A&M. This provided outgroups about which participants would probably be willing to admit to having negative attitudes. The findings were the same as before. *Amount* of outgroup contact was not associated with prejudice. However, as long as the participant had interacted with at least one outgroup member, the degree of inclusion of this outgroup member in the self was associated with less prejudice. In a final study, 100 students kept records over a one-week period of every social interaction lasting ten minutes or longer (this was a version of the Rochester Interaction Record method; Reis & Wheeler, 1991). That is, they carried around little booklets and as soon as possible after each such interaction they would record in the booklet their answers to a short series of questions about the interaction, notably including the initials of the interaction partners and completing the IOS scale for felt closeness during the interaction. At the end of the week, participants were given some prejudice measures towards each of the major ethnic groups at their university and also, based on the initials on each record, indicated the ethnicity of each interaction partner. During the study itself, participants had no way to know the study had anything whatsoever to do with inter-ethnic interaction. The results, quite consistent with everything we have reported before, were that number of interactions with outgroup individuals had little relation to prejudice, but there was a clear association between prejudice and including outgroup interaction partners in the self. In the most important analysis, we found that differences among ethnic groups, in the extent to which one included members of a particular ethnic group in the self, predicted parallel differences in prejudice towards those ethnic groups – of course in the direction of the more inclusion of other in the self, the less prejudice. Two additional results that were found over the three studies are of particular interest. First, structural equation modeling analyses using instrument variables suggested that there were unique causal paths in both directions – that including other in the self led to reduced prejudice and that reduced prejudice also led to including other in the self (though the effect of inclusion on prejudice was bigger and more consistent). Second, in each study there was a significant interaction in predicting prejudice between number of interactions and inclusion of other in the self. When inclusion of other in the self was high, the more interactions, the less prejudice. However, when inclusion of other in the self was low, with more interactions, there was either no relation to prejudice or actually *higher* levels of prejudice.

The self-expansion model has also generated a new theoretical idea that goes beyond the contact hypothesis, taking it one step further. Specifically, we reasoned that under some conditions direct contact with an outgroup member may not be necessary. It may be enough simply to be aware that someone *else* in the ingroup has an outgroup friend. This possible impact of knowledge of an ingroup member's outgroup friendship is what we have labeled the *extended contact hypothesis* (Wright, Aron, McLaughlin-Volpe, & Ropp, 1997). That is, we reasoned as follows. Ordinarily, in self's conception of the world, my ingroup is part of myself and outgroups are not part of myself. Thus, I spontaneously treat ingroup members, to some extent, like myself, including feeling empathy with their troubles, taking pride in their successes, generously sharing resources with them, and so forth. Outgroup members, because they are not part of myself, receive none of these advantages. Literally, I could not care less about them.

However, we argue, this changes when someone who is in the ingroup, and thus part of myself, is known to have an outgroup person as part of that person's self. In this case, the outgroup friend – and hence to some extent the outgroup itself – becomes part of myself. The effect is that, to some extent, I begin to see members of that group as part of myself. Thus my ingroup–outgroup distinctions are directly undermined, as are negative attitudes I may have held toward the outgroup.

This logic rests on two key assumptions. First, it assumes that an ingroup member is part of the self. This idea is supported in studies conducted by Smith and his colleagues (Smith et al., 1999; Smith & Henry, 1996) and by Tropp and Wright (2000), employing a version of the reaction time procedure from one of the relationship studies we described earlier (e.g., Aron, Aron et al., 1991, Experiment 3) in which participants were slower at deciding whether a trait was true or false of themselves when the trait was not equally true or false of a close relationship partner. In these studies, this same pattern was found when the trait was not equally true or false of their ingroup (but the same pattern was not found for whether the trait was not equally true or false for an outgroup). The authors interpret these studies as demonstrating that individuals spontaneously include ingroup members, but not outgroup members, in the self.

Second, our logic assumes that we spontaneously group together persons we perceive as friends. In support of this idea, as noted earlier, Sedikides et al. (1993), using a procedure involving clustering of recall, found that observers treat partners in a close relationship as a single cognitive unit in a manner that Sedikides et al. explicitly associate with self–other overlap. Putting these various findings together leads to the following: In an observed ingroup–outgroup friendship, the ingroup member is part of myself, the outgroup member is part of that ingroup member's self, and hence part of myself. Presuming that the outgroup member's group membership is part of what I have included of that outgroup member in myself, then to some extent the outgroup is part of myself.

Having come up with the extended contact idea and having identified at least one plausible mechanism, the initial question was whether the phenomenon exists. In that regard, Wright et al. (1997) conducted two questionnaire surveys involving prejudice toward actual ethnic outgroups, plus a laboratory-constructed intergroup conflict study modeled after the Sherif Robber's Cave studies, and a minimal-group experiment. In the questionnaire studies participants indicated, for each of three ethnic outgroups, how many people they knew of their own ethnic group who had a friend in that outgroup. Participants were also asked about their own direct friendships with individuals in each of the three ethnic outgroups. As expected from the extended contact hypothesis, knowing ingroup members who have friends in a particular ethnic outgroup was significantly associated with having relatively less prejudice towards that ethnic outgroup – even after controlling for direct friendships with members of that ethnic outgroup. These studies were important because they show the predicted association in a real-world setting involving actual prejudice towards actual ethnic outgroups. Moreover, that these findings hold up even after controlling for direct outgroup friendships lends support to the hypothesized causal direction of this association from extended contact to reduced prejudice. Nevertheless, an unambiguous case for a causal interpretation of this association required an experimental manipulation of the hypothesized independent variable, knowledge that an ingroup member has an outgroup friend.

Wright et al.'s (1997, Study 3) first study involving such a manipulation utilized a laboratory-constructed intergroup conflict procedure, inspired by Sherif's Robber's Cave studies (Sherif, Harvey, White, Hood, & Sherif, 1961) and the series of similarly constructed experiments with adults from industrial organizations by Blake and Mouton (see Blake, Shepard, & Mouton, 1964, for a review). Wright et al. actually conducted four such studies, each involving the construction of an intergroup conflict, between two interacting seven-person groups. In each day-long experiment, they first introduced activities designed to induce strong intergroup conflict, and then, later in the day, systematically introduced an intervention involving the creation of cross-group friendships (Aron, Melinat, et al., 1997) for a small subset of the group members. The results were clear (and even with only four replications, significant): the first two testings (both preintervention) showed an increase in outgroup prejudice, but the third testing (postintervention) showed a decrease.

These findings are nevertheless limited in that there was no control group that did not get the intervention. (As did Sherif and his colleagues before them, Wright et al. considered it impractically costly to conduct a series of control experiments in which there were no interventions.) Thus, it remained possible that the obtained effects could be due to time-related factors (or factors associated with repeated testing) unrelated to the experimental intervention. Therefore, the next study (Wright et al., 1997, Study 4) was designed to test the causal direction of the extended contact hypothesis, employing a true experimental design. This was accomplished by employing a modified "minimal group procedure" (Turner, 1978). Numerous experiments using this paradigm have demonstrated that mere categorization of participants can lead to discrimination in favor of the ingroup on attitude measures, evaluations, and on the allocation of resources (see Brewer, 1979; Mullen, Brown, & Smith, 1992, for reviews). Following typical procedures in this kind of research, participants were told that they were divided into groups based on their performance on an object estimation task. The researchers then arranged for participants to observe an ingroup and an outgroup member – actually confederates – interacting in the solution of a puzzle task. The behavior of the confederates when they arrived to do the puzzle task suggested that their existing relationship was that of warm friends, unacquainted strangers, or disliked acquaintances. For example, in the friendly condition, when the ingroup and outgroup member met they expressed delight at seeing an old friend and hugged; in the neutral condition they showed no sign of any previous acquaintance; and in the hostile condition they showed signs of displeasure about being paired with this person, implying they had a long-standing hostile relationship. The result was that those who observed what they believed was an ingroup member having a close outgroup friend showed less outgroup bias over several measures, compared to those who observed an ingroup member have either no relationship or a hostile relationship with an outgroup member.

In sum, the self-expansion model predicts that forming a relationship with an outgroup person, or even becoming aware that someone in your ingroup has a friendship with an outgroup person, should reduce prejudice towards that outgroup. The logic is that when one's own friend is of the outgroup, as part of including this friend in the self, one includes the friend's group identity, thus undermining ingroup–outgroup distinctiveness and negative feelings toward the outgroup (if the outgroup is part of me, and I value myself, then it would be inconsistent to devalue the outgroup). This logic is extended to knowledge that an ingroup person has an outgroup friend because when I include ingroup members in the self, I also include to some extent the identities I perceive them to include in their self. Several studies generated by these ideas yielded supportive results.

Summary

In this section we have examined implications of the inclusion-of-other-in-the-self idea for areas of social psychology beyond close relationships, including empathy and helping, and intergroup relations. In addition to the direct importance of this work for these particular areas, this research is also important as an illustration of the potential for advancing knowledge from work that crosses subarea boundaries within social psychology – in this case between close relationships and prosocial behavior and between close relationships and intergroup relations. As Mackie and Smith (1998) said, "the very exercise of considering the continuities between the topics [of different areas of social psychology] . . . offers some suggestion as to the kinds of underlying principles or processes that we think would be central to . . . an integrated theory" (p. 520), noting also that one result of such work is that "wheels invented in one domain need not be reinvented in another" (p. 521).

Conclusions

We understand the self-expansion model as a conceptual framework that sensitizes researchers to variables and patterns that might otherwise be missed. We believe that the various theoretical insights and research programs that have been generated by this model (as summarized in this chapter) support the utility of this conceptual framework as a heuristic of this kind. However, we do not see the conceptual framework as a precise theory from which highly specific predictions can be formally derived. We see it, rather, as a stimulus for the development of precise theories, a platform for viewing relationships and relationship-linked phenomena that turns one in directions that would not otherwise be considered. Further, the developing body of research around this perspective both shapes the overall conceptual framework and provides a set of methods and concepts that we believe offer considerable promise for furthering understanding of cognition and motivation in close relationships, and beyond.

Acknowledgment

The preparation of this paper and several of the studies reported here were supported by grants from the National Science Foundation.

Notes

1. We have also discussed (Aron & Aron, 1986; Aron, Norman, & Aron, 1998) three other major aspects of the self-expansion model that are of some importance, but we do not discuss them in this chapter (other than in this note) because we are only beginning to conduct systematic studies of them. One of these aspects is that, along with the desire to expand the self, we hypothesize an equally strong desire to integrate expansion experiences and make sense of them, a desire for wholeness or coherence which sometimes preempts the desire for expansion until it is satisfied to some degree. Expansion and integration are seen as two steps in a general pattern of movement toward self-expansion. Second, we have argued that if expansion proceeds at a rate faster than it can be integrated, this will be stressful. That is, too rapid expansion is distressing and thus aversive. A final major aspect of the motivational angle of the model that has not yet received much research attention is the suggestion that there are individual specialties or preferences for modes of expansion. Further, these may change over the course of a day or a lifetime. Thus, some individuals at some times may seek expansion through creative work, at other times through relationships, at other times through physical development, and so forth.
2. Sorrentino, Raynor, Zubek, and Short (1990) argue for two basic sources of value in determining goals: information value and affective value. The former is akin to our notion of knowledge.
3. There has also been some preliminary work extending the model to persuasion and attitude change (Steele, 1999; Steele & Aron, 2000) and to the role of relationship cognition in logical processing (Dorrity, 2000). However, in the interest of space, the focus of this section is on the two areas in which the most research has been done.

References

Agnew, C. R., Van Lange, P. A. M., Rusbult, C. E., & Langston, C. A. (1998). Cognitive interdependence: Commitment and the mental representation of close relationships. *Journal of Personality and Social Psychology, 74*, 939–954.

Ahuvia, A. (1993). *I love it! Towards a unifying theory of love across diverse love objects.* Unpublished PhD dissertation, Northwestern University.

Allport, G. (1954). *The nature of prejudice.* Reading, MA: Addison-Wesley.

Aron, A., & Aron, E. N. (1986). *Love as the expansion of self: Understanding attraction and satisfaction.* New York: Hemisphere.

Aron, A., & Aron, E. N. (1993). Relationship as a region of the life space. *Personal Relationship Issues, 1*, 22–24.

Aron, A., & Aron, E. N. (1996). Self and self-expansion in relationships. In G. J. O. Fletcher & J. Fitness (Eds.), *Knowledge structures in close relationships: A social psychological approach* (pp. 325–344). Mahwah, NJ: Erlbaum.

Aron, A., & Aron, E. N. (1997). Self-expansion motivation and including other in the self. In W. Ickes (Section Ed.) & S. Duck (Ed.), *Handbook of personal relationships* (2nd ed., Vol. 1, pp. 251–270). London: Wiley.

Aron, A., Aron, E. N., & Allen, J. (1998). Motivations for unrequited love. *Personality and Social Psychology Bulletin, 24*, 787–796.

Aron, A., Aron, E. N., & Norman, C. (1999, August). Relationship effects of participating together in novel and arousing activities. In A. Aron (Chair), *Making relationships work – new ideas from the social psychology laboratory.* Symposium conducted at the American Psychological Association, Boston.

Aron, A., Aron, E. N., & Smollan, D. (1992). Inclusion of Other in the Self Scale and the structure of interpersonal closeness. *Journal of Personality and Social Psychology, 63*, 596–612.

Aron, A., Aron, E. N., Tudor, M., & Nelson, G. (1991). Close relationships as including other in the self. *Journal of Personality and Social Psychology, 60,* 241–253.

Aron, A., & Fraley, B. (1999). Relationship closeness as including other in the self: Cognitive underpinnings and measures. *Social Cognition, 17,* 140–160.

Aron, A., Fraley, B., & Cialdini, R. (2000). *Empathy as including other in the self.* Manuscript in preparation.

Aron, A., Melinat, E., Aron, E. N., Vallone, R., & Bator, R. (1997). The experimental generation of interpersonal closeness: A procedure and some preliminary findings. *Personality and Social Psychology Bulletin, 23,* 363–377.

Aron, A., Norman, C. C., & Aron, E. N. (1998). The self-expansion model and motivation. *Representative Research in Social Psychology, 22,* 1–13.

Aron, A., Norman, C. C., Aron, E. N., McKenna, C., & Heyman, R. (2000). Couple's shared participation in novel and arousing activities and experienced relationship quality. *Journal of Personality and Social Psychology, 78,* 273–283.

Aron, A., Paris, M., & Aron, E. N. (1995). Falling in love: Prospective studies of self-concept change. *Journal of Personality and Social Psychology, 69,* 1102–1112.

Bakan, D. (1966). *The duality of human existence: Isolation and commitment in Western man.* Boston: Beacon Press.

Bandura, A. (1977). Self-efficacy: Toward a unifying theory of behavioral change. *Psychological Review, 84,* 191–215.

Batson, C. D. (1991). *The altruism question: Toward a social-psychological answer.* Hillsdale, NJ: Erlbaum.

Batson, C. D. (1997). Self–other merging and the empathy-altruism hypothesis: Reply to Neuberg et al. (1997). *Journal of Personality and Social Psychology, 73,* 517–522.

Batson, C. D., Sager, K., Garst, E., Kang, M., Rubchinsky, K., & Dawson, K. (1997). Is empathy-induced helping due to self–other merging? *Journal of Personality and Social Psychology, 73,* 495–509.

Beach, S. R., Tesser, A., Fincham, F. D., Jones, D. J., Johnson, D., & Whitaker, D. J. (1998). Pleasure and pain in doing well, together: An investigation of performance-related affect in close relationships. *Journal of Personality and Social Psychology, 74,* 923–938.

Belk, R. W. (1988). Possessions and the extended self. *Journal of Consumer Research, 15,* 139–168.

Berlyne, D. E. (1960). *Conflict, arousal, and curiosity.* New York: McGraw-Hill.

Blake, R. R., Shepard, H. A., & Mouton, J. S. (1964). *Managing intergroup conflicts in industry.* Houston, TX: Gulf.

Bower, G. H., & Gilligan, S. G. (1979). Remembering information related to one's self. *Journal of Research in Personality, 13,* 420–432.

Bowlby, J. (1969). *Attachment and loss: Vol. 1. Attachment.* New York: Basic Books.

Brewer, M. B. (1979). In-group bias in the minimal intergroup situation: A cognitive-motivational analysis. *Psychological Bulletin, 86,* 307–324.

Buber, M. (1937). *I and thou.* New York: Scribner's.

Carver, C., & Scheier, M. (1990). Principles of self-regulation, action, and emotion. In E. T. Higgins & R. M. Sorrentino (Eds.), *Handbook of motivation and cognition: Foundations of social behavior* (Vol. 2). New York: Guilford Press.

Cialdini, R. B., Brown, S. L., Lewis, B. P., Luce, C., & Neuberg, S. L. (1997). Reinterpreting the empathy-altruism relationships: When one into one equals oneness. *Journal of Personality and Social Psychology, 73,* 481–494.

Clark, M. S., & Mills, J. (1979). Interpersonal attraction in exchange and communal relationships. *Journal of Personality and Social Psychology, 37,* 12–24.

Clark, M. S., & Mills, J. (1993). The difference between communal and exchange relationships: What it is and is not. *Personality and Social Psychology Bulletin, 19,* 684–691.

Clark, M. S., Mills, J., & Corcoran, D. (1989). Keeping track of needs and inputs of friends and strangers. *Personality and Social Psychology Bulletin, 15,* 533–542.

Cross, S. E., Morris, M. L., Brunscheen, S., Frederick, K., McGregor, A., Meyer, G., & Proulx, B. (1997, August). *The interdependent self-construal and descriptions of close relationships.* Paper presented at the American Psychological Association Convention, Chicago.

Davis, M. H., Conklin, L., Smith, A., & Luce, C. (1996). Effect of perspective taking on the cognitive representation of persons: A merging of self and other. *Journal of Personality and Social Psychology, 70,* 713–726.

Deci, E. L., & Ryan, R. (1987). The support of autonomy and the control of behavior. *Journal of Personality and Social Psychology, 53,* 1024–1037.

De La Ronde, C., & Swann, W. B., Jr. (1998). Partner verification: Restoring shattered images of our intimates. *Journal of Personality and Social Psychology, 75,* 374–382.

Dorrity, K. (2000). *Social logic.* Manuscript under review.

Dutton, D. G., & Aron, A. (1974). Some evidence for heightened sexual attraction under conditions of high anxiety. *Journal of Personality and Social Psychology, 30,* 510–517.

Foster, C. A., Witcher, B. S., Campbell, W. K., & Green, J. D. (1998). Arousal and attraction: Evidence for automatic and controlled processes. *Journal of Personality and Social Psychology, 74,* 86–101.

Gecas, V. (1989). Social psychology of self-efficacy. *American Sociological Review, 15,* 291–316.

Goldberg, L. R. (1981). Unconfounding situational attributions from uncertain, neutral, and ambiguous ones: A psychometric analysis of descriptions of oneself and various types of others. *Journal of Personality and Social Psychology, 41,* 517–552.

Heider, F. (1958). *The psychology of interpersonal relations.* New York: Wiley.

Higgins, E. T., & Sorrentino, R. M. (1990)., *Handbook of motivation and cognition: Foundations of social behavior.* New York: Guilford Press.

Hoffman, M. L. (1976). Empathy, role taking, guilt, and development of altruistic motives. In T. Lickona (Ed.), *Moral development and behavior.* New York: Holt.

Huesmann, L. R. (1980). Toward a predictive model of romantic behavior. In K. S. Pope et al. (Eds.), On love and loving (pp. 152–171). San Francisco: Jossey-Bass.

Ickes, W., Tooke, W., Stinson, L., Baker, V., & Bissonnette, V. (1988). Naturalistic social cognition: Intersubjectivity in same-sex dyads. *Journal of Nonverbal Behavior, 12,* 58–84.

Jacobson, N. S., & Margolin, G. (1979). *Marital therapy: Strategies based on social learning and behavior exchange principles.* New York: Brunner/Mazel.

James, W. (1948). *Psychology.* Cleveland, OH: Fine Editions Press. (Original work published 1890)

Jones, E. E., & Nisbett, R. (1971). The actor and the observer: Divergent perceptions of the causes of behavior. In E. E. Jones, D. Kanouse, H. Kelley, R. Nisbett, S. Valins, & B. Weiner (Eds.), *Attribution: Perceiving the causes of behavior* (pp. 79–94). Morristown, NJ: General Learning Press.

Jung, C. G. (1959). Marriage as a psychological relationship. In V. S. DeLaszlo (Ed.), *The basic writings of C. G. Jung* (R. F. C. Hull, Trans., pp. 531–544). New York: Modern Library. (Original work published 1925)

Keenan, J. M., & Baillet, S. D. (1980). Memory for personally and socially significant events. In R. S. Nickerson (Ed.), *Attention and performance* (Vol. 8, pp. 652–669). Hillsdale, NJ: Erlbaum.

Kelley, H. H., & Thibaut, J. W. (1978). *Interpersonal relationships: A theory of interdependence.* New York: Wiley.

Knee, C. R. (1998). Implicit theories of relationships: Assessment and prediction of romantic relationship initiation, coping, and longevity. *Journal of Personality and Social Psychology, 74,* 360–370.

Lord, C. G. (1980). Schemas and images as memory aids: Two modes of processing social information. *Journal of Personality and Social Psychology, 38,* 257–269.

Lord, C. G. (1987). Imagining self and others: Reply to Brown, Keenan, and Potts. *Journal of Personality and Social Psychology, 53,* 445–450.

Loving, T. J., & Agnew, C. R. (1998, June). *Examining components of the "self" in self-other inclusion.* Paper presented at the International Conference on Personal Relationships, Saratoga Springs, NY.

MacKay, L., McFarland, C., & Buehler, R. (1998, August). *Affective reactions to performances in close relationships.* Paper presented at the American Psychological Association, San Francisco.

Mackie, D. M., & Smith, E. R. (1998). Intergroup relations: Insights from a theoretically integrative approach. *Psychological Review, 105,* 499–529.

Markus, H. (1977). Self-schemata and processing information about the self. *Journal of Personality and Social Psychology, 35,* 63–78.

Maslow, A. H. (1967). A theory of metamotivation: The biological rooting of the value-life. *Journal of Humanistic Psychology, 7,* 93–127.

Maslow, A. H. (1970). *Motivation and personality*. New York: Harper & Row.

McCall, G. J. (1974). A symbolic interactionist approach to attraction. In T. L. Huston (Ed.), *Foundations of interpersonal attraction* (pp. 217–231). New York: Academic Press.

McLaughlin-Volpe, Aron, A., Wright, S. C., & Reis, H. T. (2000). *Intergroup social interactions and intergroup prejudice: Quantity versus quality*. Manuscript under review.

Medvene, L. J., Teal, C. R. & Slavich, S. (2000). 'Including the other self: Implications for judgments of equity and satisfaction in close relationships'. *Journal of Social and Clinical Psychology, 19*, 396–419.

Merleau-Ponty, M. (1945). *Phénoménologie de la perception*. Paris: Gallimard.

Mullen, B., Brown, R., & Smith, C. (1992). Ingroup bias as a function of salience, relevance, and status: An integration. *European Journal of Social Psychology, 22*, 103–122.

Neuberg, S. L., Cialdini, R. B., Brown, S. L., Luce, C., & Sagarin, B. J. (1997). Does empathy lead to anything more than superficial helping? Comment on Batson (1997). *Journal of Personality and Social Psychology, 73*, 510–516.

Nisbett, R. E., Caputo, C., Legant, P., & Marecek, J. (1973). Behavior as seen by the actor and as seen by the observer. *Journal of Personality and Social Psychology, 27*, 154–164.

Omoto, A. M., & Gunn, D. O. (1994, May). *The effect of relationship closeness on encoding and recall for relationship-irrelevant information*. Paper presented at the May Meeting of the International Network on Personal Relationships, Iowa City, IA.

Perreault, S., & Bourhis, R. Y. (1999). Ethnocentrism, social identification, and discrimination. *Personality and Social Psychology Bulletin, 25*, 92–103.

Pettigrew, T. F. (1997). Generalized intergroup effects on prejudice. *Personality and Social Psychology Bulletin, 23*, 173–185.

Pettigrew, T. F. (1998). Intergroup contact theory. *Annual Review of Psychology, 49*, 65–85.

Pipp, S., Shaver, P., Jennings, S., Lamborn, S., & Fischer, K. W. (1985). Adolescents' theories about the development of their relationships with parents. *Journal of Personality and Social Psychology, 48*, 991–1001.

Plutchik, R. (1967). Marriage as dynamic equilibrium: Implications for research. In H. L. Silverman (Ed.), *Marital counseling: Psychology, ideology, science* (pp. 347–367). Springfield, IL: Charles C. Thomas.

Prentice, D. A. (1990). Familiarity and differences in self- and other-representations. *Journal of Personality and Social Psychology, 59*, 369–383.

Pyszczynski, T. A., Greenberg, J., & Solomon, S. (1997). Why do we need what we need? A terror management perspective on the roots of human social motivation. *Psychological Inquiry, 8*, 1–20.

Reik, T. (1944). *A psychologist looks at love*. New York: Farrar & Reinhart.

Reis, H. T., & Shaver, P. (1988). Intimacy as interpersonal process. In S. Duck (Ed.), *Handbook of personal relationships: Theory, research and interventions* (pp. 367–389). Chichester, England: Wiley.

Reis, H. T., & Wheeler, L. (1991). Studying social interaction with the Rochester Interaction Record. In M. P. Zanna (Ed.), *Advances in experimental social psychology* (Vol. 24, pp. 269–318). San Diego, CA: Academic Press.

Reissman, C., Aron, A., & Bergen, M. R. (1993). Shared activities and marital satisfaction: Causal direction and self-expansion versus boredom. *Journal of Social and Personal Relationships, 10*, 243–254.

Rogers, T. B., Kuiper, N. A., & Kirker, W. S. (1977). Self-reference and the encoding of personal information. *Journal of Personality and Social Psychology, 35*, 677–688.

Runciman, W. G. (1966). *Relative deprivation and social justice*. Berkeley: University of California Press.

Rusbult, C., & Arriaga, X. (1997). Interdependence theory. In W. Ickes (Section Ed.) & S. Duck (Ed.), *Handbook of personal relationships* (2nd ed., Vol. 1, pp. 221–250). London: Wiley.

Sande, G. N., Goethals, G. R., & Radloff, C. E. (1988). Perceiving one's own traits and others': The multifaceted self. *Journal of Personality and Social Psychology, 54*, 13–20.

Schutz, A. (1970). *On phenomenology and social relations*. Chicago: Chicago University Press.

Sedikides, C., Olsen, N., & Reis, H. T. (1993). Relationships as natural categories. *Journal of Personality and Social Psychology, 64*, 71–82.

Sedikides, C., & Strube, M. J. (1995). The multiply motivated self. *Personality and Social Psychology Bulletin, 21*, 1330–1335.

Shaver, P. R., & Hazan, C. (1993). Adult romantic attachment: Theory and evidence. In D. Perlman & W. Jones (Eds.), *Advances in personal relationships* (Vol. 4, pp. 29–70). London: Jessica Kingsley.

Sherif, M., Harvey, O. J., White, B. J., Hood, W. R., & Sherif, C. W. (1961). *Intergroup conflict and cooperation: The Robbers Cave experiment.* Norman, OK: University of Oklahoma Book Exchange.

Sivadas, E., & Machleit, K. A. (1994). A scale to determine the extent of object incorporation in the extended self. *American Marketing Association, 5*, 143–149.

Smith, E., Coats, S., & Walling, D. (1999). Overlapping mental representations of self, in-group, and partner: Further response time evidence and a connectionist model. *Personality and Social Psychology Bulletin, 25*, 873–882.

Smith, E., & Henry, S. (1996). An in-group becomes part of the self: Response time evaluation. *Personality and Social Psychology Bulletin, 22*, 635–642.

Sorrentino, R. M., Raynor, J. O., Zubek, J. M., & Short, J. C. (1990). Personality functioning and change: Informational and affective influences on cognitive, moral, and social development. In E. T. Higgins & R. M. Sorrentino (Eds.), *Handbook of motivation and cognition: Foundations of social behavior* (Vol. 2, pp. 193–228). New York: Guilford Press.

Steele, J. L. (1999). *Cognitive mechanisms of attitude change in close relationships.* Doctoral dissertation, State University of New York at Stony Brook.

Steele, J. L., & Aron, A. (2000). *Do you believe what I believe? Attitude change in close relationships.* Manuscript under review.

Symons, C. S., & Johnson, B. T. (1997). The Self-reference effect in memory: A meta-analysis. *Psychological Bulletin, 121*, 371–394.

Tajfel, H., & Turner, J. C. (1979). An integrative theory of intergroup conflict. In W. G. Austin & S. Worchel (Eds.), *The social psychology of intergroup relations* (pp. 33–47). Monterey, CA: Brooks/Cole.

Taylor, S. E., Neter, E., & Wayment, H. A. (1995). Self-evaluative processes. *Personality and Social Psychology Bulletin, 21*, 1278–1287.

Tesser, A. (1988). Toward a self-evaluation maintenance model of social behavior. In L. Berkowitz (Ed.), *Advances in experimental social psychology* (Vol. 11, pp. 288–338). San Diego, CA: Academic Press.

Tropp, L. R., & Wright, S. C. (2000). *Ingroup identification as the inclusion of ingroup in the self.* Manuscript under review.

Tucker, P., & Aron, A. (1993). Passionate love and marital satisfaction at key transition points in the family life cycle. *Journal of Social and Clinical Psychology, 12*, 135–147.

Turner, J. C. (1978). Social categorization and social discrimination in the minimal group paradigm. In H. Tajfel (Ed.), *Differentiation between social groups: Studies in the social psychology of intergroup relations* (pp. 101–140). London: Academic Press.

Uleman, J. S., Rhee, E., Bardoliwalla, N., Semin, G., & Togama, M. (2000). The relational self: Closeness to ingroups depends on who they are, culture and types of closeness. *Asian Journal of Social Psychology, 3*, 1–17.

Wegner, D. M. (1980). The self in prosocial action. In D. M. Wegner & R. R. Vallacher (Eds.), *The self in social psychology* (pp. 131–157). New York: Oxford University Press.

White, L. K. (1983). Determinants of spousal interaction: Marital structure or marital happiness. *Journal of Marriage and the Family, 45*, 511–519.

White, R. W. (1959). Motivation reconsidered: The concept of confidence. *Psychological Review, 66*, 297–333.

Wright, S. C., Aron, A., McLaughlin-Volpe, T., & Ropp, S. A. (1997). The extended contact effect: Knowledge of cross group friendships and prejudice. *Journal of Personality and Social Psychology, 73*, 73–90.

PART VI

Methods

20   A Statistical Framework for Modeling Homogeneity and
Interdependence in Groups   505
Richard Gonzalez and Dale Griffin

PART VII

Chapter Twenty

A Statistical Framework for Modeling Homogeneity and Interdependence in Groups

Richard Gonzalez and Dale Griffin

Social behavior can be explained at many different levels. Some questions elicit explanations at the "group" level (e.g., Why are Canadians so reserved?). Other questions elicit explanations at the "individual" level (e.g., Why is Jim Carrey, a Canadian, so wild and crazy?). And other questions seem to elicit explanations at multiple levels of explanation: Why do people obey the law? What makes a marriage last? What makes a family dysfunctional? How do social norms shape an individual's behavior? These and many other central questions in social psychology require analysis at multiple levels – an individual level, a group level, and possibly higher social levels as well (Doise, 1986).

Social psychology is the study of the "individual within the group." In this chapter, we present a framework for conceptualizing and analyzing social behavior as a joint function of individual and group-level forces. The chapter is organized into three sections. The first section discusses several areas of research in social psychology that have focused on group-level phenomena. From that review we extract a necessary feature for group-level phenomena – homogeneity among members of a group. The second section discusses how to conceptualize, measure, and analyze (theoretically as well as statistically) this necessary feature. The intraclass correlation will serve as a conceptual and statistical building block. The final section extends the framework to include interdependent processes, processes that are at a "higher level" than individual processes but are not group-level processes in that they do not require homogeneity. Our goal in this chapter is to present a framework for conceptualizing multi-level social psychological processes, a framework that leads naturally into a data-analytic strategy.

This research was partially supported by a grant from the National Science Foundation (Gonzalez). We thank Bill Ickes and David Kenny for their helpful discussion and suggestions. Correspondence about this article may be addressed to either author: Richard Gonzalez, Department of Psychology, University of Michigan, Ann Arbor, MI 48109, or Dale Griffin, Marketing Division, Faculty of Commerce and Business Administration, University of British Columbia, 2053 Main Hall, Vancouver, BC, Canada, V6T 1Z2. Electronic mail may be sent to either gonzo@umich. edu (Gonzalez) or dale.griffin@commerce.ubc.ca (Griffin).

The Individual and the Group

> There are therefore Agents in Nature able to make the Particles of Bodies stick to-
> gether by very strong Attraction. And it is the Business of Experimental Philosophy
> to find them out.
>
> (Isaac Newton, 1717)

The question of what attracts "particles" to each other and binds them together has been a central problem in science. Over a century ago, chemists used the concept of cohesiveness: "by cohesive attraction . . . we mean that force which binds together the particles of a body" (Daubeny, 1850), e.g., the force that binds together atoms to form a molecule. Modern chemists now favor the term bond over cohesive attraction, and several types of bonds have been identified (e.g., covalent, ionic, hydrogen). Chemists attempt to understand the behavior of a molecule, an aggregate entity, from the behavior of individual atoms and the bonds between those atoms. Chemists also acknowledge the existence of the aggregate entity (e.g., molecules, proteins) and consider the aggregate worthy of study in its own right.

Social psychology has been concerned with forces that bind individuals to create an aggregate, or a group. Since the very founding of the discipline, social psychologists have been at odds about how to allocate priority to the different levels of analysis. Should the behavior of individuals be used to explain group processes? Should group processes be used to explain the behavior of individuals? The individual or the group – which is the independent variable and which is the dependent variable? What "holds" individuals together in a group? What are the predictors of cohesiveness? Is the group more than the sum of its parts? These are deep questions which, for the most part, remain unanswered. Much as Isaac Newton called for scientists of the day to study attraction between particles, Floyd Allport (1924, 1962) identified the issue of individuals and groups as the "master problem of social psychology."

Some theorists such as George Herbert Mead placed explanatory priority on the group – the group provides the context against which the behavior of individuals can be understood. Mead wrote, '. . . the behavior of an individual can be understood only in terms of the behavior of the whole social group of which he is a member, since his individual acts are involved in larger, social acts which go beyond himself and which implicate the other members of that group" (1934, pp. 6–7). Similarly, Durkheim, in his influential sociological treatise (1974, English translation), also placed explanatory priority on the group and Comte placed priority on the family. See Turner and Killian (1957) and Milgram and Toch (1969) for reviews; see Coleman (1990) for a contemporary theory.

Other theorists, such as Floyd Allport, placed explanatory priority on the individual. "All theories which partake of the group fallacy have the unfortunate consequence of diverting attention from the true focus of cause and effect, namely, the behavior mechanisms of the individual" (Allport, 1933, p. 9). When a group-level process is translated into a theory, he argued, the concept needs to be defined in terms of an aggregation of individuals in a way that does not produce a tautology or a personification of the group. "There is no psychology of groups which is not essentially and entirely a psychology of individuals" (Allport, 1933, p. 4).

We agree that individual-level psychology must mediate all group processes, but argue that individual-level explanations are not sufficient. We believe that it is possible to study both levels simultaneously, and that interesting social psychological questions can be asked at each level (see also Kenny & La Voie, 1985). That is, as well as asking questions at the individual level (e.g., does an infant's babbling behavior correlate with the infant's attachment?), we can and should ask questions at higher group levels, such as the levels of the dyad, family, or team (e.g., does a mother–infant dyad that jointly exhibits high emotional expressivity tend to be a dyad that jointly exhibits high behavioral responsivity?).

Emergent processes that operate at higher levels of analysis occur in other areas of psychological research. For example, in connectionist modeling prototypes can be conceptualized as constructs that emerge through the pattern of weights – a higher-level construct built from lower-level processes (e.g., Rumelhart & McClelland, 1986). In evolutionary models, there has also been utility in thinking about separate processes at different levels of analysis (e.g., Wilson & Sober, 1994).

Many social psychologists who study interaction tend to strip away "non-independent" interdependent processes from their experiments and data analysis. For instance, to make studies easier to manage, an investigator examining heterosexual dating couples may focus only on the female partner. To return to the analogy with chemistry, one of our colleagues once criticized our focus on multi-levels of analysis. He claimed that if a chemist is interested in studying salt, she studies sodium chloride, but if she is interested in studying sodium, she studies sodium in isolation. There is a sense in which this critique makes exactly our point. If the chemist interested in sodium can only observe sodium in the context of salt, then the understanding of sodium is qualified by the presence of the element chlorine. Rather than eliminating the effects of chlorine, it is possible to learn much more about sodium by also studying how it interacts with chlorine. The connection to the study of dating couples, and the costs of only studying one partner of the dating couple, should be immediate. Does it make sense to study, for instance, dating relationships by examining only the behavior of one individual, even though the behavior of that individual is confounded with that of the partner as well as with any synergistic effects that may result from the interaction of both individuals?

While there is certainly useful information to be gained by studying an individual in the group, there is additional information that can be extracted at the higher level of the group. We suggest that a complete understanding of dating, for instance, requires an assessment of both individuals as well as of the couple, and by extension we claim that any study purporting to be about social interaction must examine both individual-level and group-level processes.

In previous work, we identified four common errors that occur in social psychological research involving multiple levels of analysis (Gonzalez & Griffin, 1997). These errors are: (1) the *assumed independence error* where the analyst ignores the interdependency between interacting individuals, (2) the *deletion error* where only one individual in a social group is studied (this was described in the two previous paragraphs), (3) the *levels of analysis* error where measures such as dyad or group means are used to denote a supra-individual process, and (4) the *cross-level generalization error* where inferences about one level of analysis are made from analyses at a different level (e.g., Robinson, 1950).

This last error has received renewed interest through the work of King (1997), who has developed a technique to infer bounds on individual-level parameters when only aggregate group-level data are available. However, even with the new developments in statistical procedures, researchers should be careful of inferring processes at one level of analysis from processes observed at a different level. To illustrate, we turn to an example given by Asch (1952, p. 175). He referred to the workings of a firefighting "bucket brigade" to illustrate emergent property of the group. The efficiency of a bucket brigade working well together to extinguish a fire far exceeds the capacity of a similar number of individuals working alone. In Asch's words, "the final accomplishment is more than, and different from, the sum of the individual effort." A cross-level generalization would lead to a faulty inference when, for example, a researcher incorrectly infers the properties of an effective bucket brigade from the properties that make an individual effective at putting out a fire.

Examples of multiple levels and interdependence in social psychological research

We offer several examples of social psychological research questions that can be modeled within a multi-level, interdependent approach. Our intention is to provide examples of the kinds of theoretical problems that can be addressed with the present framework, so the list should not be viewed as exhaustive.

One research question involves whether dyads or groups have "personalities" or "minds" of their own (e.g., Le Bon, 1903). Are these group personalities unique and separate from the individual members' own personalities? This notion of a group mind was attacked decades ago with the reasoning that groups are made up of individuals and thus "the whole is equal to the sum of its parts" (Allport, 1962). Even Allport, who criticized the notion of the group mind, acknowledged that aggregates can be perceived as having personalities, such as "the spirit of a meeting," but, as discussed earlier, he placed explanatory priority on the individuals making up the aggregate. Allport notwithstanding, the notion that there is psychological reality to group-level constructs is becoming popular again as seen in the following (partial) list of research topics: socially-shared cognition (Resnick, Levine, & Teasley, 1991); relationship awareness (Acitelli, 1993); culture and mind (Markus, Kitayama, & Heiman, 1996); group cohesiveness (Bollen & Hoyle, 1990; Cota, Evans, Dion, Kilik, & Longman, 1995; Hogg, 1993; Mullen & Copper, 1994); and social norms (Miller & Prentice, 1996).

We present below a data-analytic approach that is consistent with Allport's critique because group-level processes are modeled as latent (unmeasured) variables underlying individual-level measurements (hence, "made up" of individuals). Moreover, there is a sense in which the group-level effect is orthogonal to the individual-level effect allowing for a decomposition of individual- and group-level much like sums of squares in an ANOVA (analysis of variance). In this sense, the framework is also consistent with the synergistic arguments of Durkheim (1974), Lewin (1940), and others, that the group is "more than the sum of its parts," or perhaps more appropriately, the group is *different from* the sum of its parts.

Recently, we have seen an increase in research on the "group-level" topic of "entitativity" (e.g., Hamilton & Sherman, 1996; McConnell, Sherman, & Hamilton, 1997). Entitativity is a term coined by Campbell (1958) to denote the perception of group structure. The data-analytic framework we present permits a comparison of the subjective estimates of entitativity of the type assessed by McConnell et al. with a more "objective" statistical estimate, permitting studies of accuracy and calibration of entitativity judgments. Frey and Smith (1993) conducted an analogous study comparing the perception of interdependence with objective estimates based on Kenny's social relations model.

The study of cohesiveness has recently received new momentum. Bollen and Hoyle (1990) suggested group members perceive cohesiveness along two dimensions: "sense of belonging" and "feelings of morale." Clearly, for a group to be called "cohesive" its members should have a high "sense of belonging" and all members should have a high "feeling of morale" in relation to the group. Cohesiveness appears to be related to several variables measuring group process and function (e.g., Shaw, 1971). However, the measurement of cohesiveness (both perceived and actual) has been debated and some claim that it has not been well-defined (see, for example, Bollen & Hoyle, 1990, as well as Cota et al., 1995). Some investigators have attempted to sidestep the measurement issue by manipulating cohesiveness (e.g., Festinger, Gerard, Hymovitch, Kelley, & Raven, 1952; Schachter, Ellertson, McBride, & Gregory, 1951), but the measurement problem still exists whenever manipulation checks are attempted.

The work on "intersubjective" social cognition (Ickes & Gonzalez, 1994) is also relevant. Much of the research in social cognition has focused on the cognitive mechanisms of individuals devoid of social interaction. Extending social cognition to social interaction, and separating the effects of the individual and group influences, would lead to a new set of empirical phenomena to observe and understand. This work may have implications for topics such as group decision making and majority/minority influence, as well as specific theories such as Aron and Aron's self-expansion theory (e.g., Aron, Paris, & Aron, 1995), Williams's (1997) recent work on social ostracism, and in the social psychology of organizations (e.g., Allmendinger & Hackman, 1996; Schriesheim, 1995).

Another relevant research problem involves misperceptions related to different levels of analysis – a process may operate at one level but the social perceiver is using another level to make inferences. For example, in a study of how managers at a manufacturing facility make decisions about salary raises, Markham (1988) found evidence for a group-level correlation between pay increase and performance evaluation of the workgroup (that is, higher-performing work groups received higher joint pay awards), but no evidence emerged for an individual-level correlation (higher-performing individuals within a work team were not differentially rewarded). As Markham suggested, the manager may view their raise decisions as fair because they were based on group-based merit. However, the individuals within the work team were not privy to the group-level analysis (i.e., performance observations and talk around the water cooler may be primarily with members of one's own workgroup). The individuals have better information about performance variability within the workgroup than across workgroups, so the individuals may have a difficult time making the connection between merit and raise, which could lead to misunderstandings between management and labor. Studying questions such as these could open new theoretical problems regarding the accuracy of group perceptions.

Related observations can be made about other aggregates and levels of analysis: aggregates of cues, behavior versus genetic levels, and aggregates of variables. For example, the "lens model" has seen renewed interest in the judgment and decision-making literature (e.g., Gigone & Hastie, 1997) as well as the accuracy literature in personality (e.g., Funder, 1995). Without getting into details, this model attempts to capture judgment in the context of noisy cues. The fundamental equations of the lens model are related to the decomposition of individual- and group-level effects (see Castellan's, 1973, derivation of the lens model). Thus, the present framework can be extended to models in the judgment literature whose parameters are commonly estimated without reference to any statistical theory. The pairwise approach described below provides standard errors for those parameters (hence confidence intervals and statistical tests).

Another example is in behavioral genetics, where there is an interest in separating genetic and environmental effects of particular behaviors. For instance, is a trait (whether it be physical, behavioral, or psychological) related to another trait at a genetic level, an environmental level, or both. It turns out that some of the estimators we present below have counterparts in the behavioral genetics literature (such as measures of "familial resemblance"), and one of our contributions is to give standard errors for those estimators. Indeed, we use a method initially developed by Elston (1975) to derive standard errors for genetic correlations. Interest in behavioral genetics (and also the related, though not identical, area of evolutionary psychology) has grown recently among social psychologists. The present techniques will be useful in addressing the theoretical and empirical issues that may emerge as those areas gain popularity. By replacing the terms *genetic* and *environmental* with "method" effects and "trait" effects, the same model applies to problems in personality measurement using the multi-trait multi-method matrix (see Kenny, 1976). Dependence of the type seen in diary studies can also be modeled by the pairwise multilevel approach.

These are but a few research problems that could benefit from using the techniques reviewed in this chapter. What may be more important, though, are the new theoretical questions that could emerge once researchers have new tools in their common tool chest. As one of our colleagues noted, "Invention is the mother of necessity."

A Necessary Property of Group-level Phenomena: Homogeneity

The list of research examples given above highlights a necessary feature of group-level phenomena: *homogeneity*. By homogeneity we mean similarity in the thoughts, behavior, or affect of interacting individuals. The two individuals in a married couple can be homogeneous in their ratings of satisfaction of the marriage (e.g., both partners rate satisfaction as high or both rate as low). Members of a workgroup can be homogeneous in their level of respect for each other (e.g., all members of the workgroup share a common level of respect). Of course, the specific variables on which homogeneity is defined depend on the particular application. The general point is that similarity on each variable of interest is required in order to examine group-level processes. Deal, Wampler, and Halverson (1992) made an analogous observation that the perception of shared values, shared goals, and shared perspectives are critical for the existence of group-level processes in marital relationships. Similarly, Klein, Dansereau, and Hall (1994) argued that in organizational psychology homogeneity of group members is a "prerequisite" for group level processes to be invoked. Other terms besides homogeneity that could be used to convey the same notion are *concordance* and *uniformity*.

Cartwright and Zander (1956, pp. 305–318) make the case that homogeneity is not sufficient for group-level phenomena because, for instance, a group goal may fail to emerge even when individuals share similar goals. For example, ". . . the members of a committee might each individually want to get home after a long day of meetings, but it would not seem useful to assert that the committee had a goal of going home" (p. 309). Within our framework, however, we want to study the case where individuals share goals and compare that, say, to groups where individuals do not share the same goal. We will model the shared goal as a latent variable that can then be related to other variables; we do not need to equate the shared goal (as indexed by the similarity of the individuals' goals) with the concept of the "group goal." It is this step that avoids the problem that Allport raised. Cartwright and Zander provide another example to suggest that homogeneity may not be necessary at all. Three boys successfully construct a lemonade stand (group goal) but the individual goals differ: one boy wants to earn money to buy a baseball glove, another wants to use his new carpentry tools, and a third simply wants to be included because the other two rarely allow him to play with them. We agree with their analysis that this example illustrates the power of interdependence in social interaction and, thus, that not all social interaction requires notions of group-level phenomena (however, we still argue that group-level phenomena require homogeneity). Below we generalize the framework to include the concept of interdependence, which according to Cartwright and Zander is "a more promising basis for a definition of a group goal" (p. 313).

Notions of homogeneity appear in several treatments of group behavior. Homans (1950), as well as Simon's (1957) mathematical model of the Homans framework, defines "activity within the group" in terms of homogeneity of behavior. Lewin (1935) in his cross-cultural comparison of Germany and the United States referred to differences in homogeneity of behavior. In the study of language and communication, a quintessential social act, the concept of homogeneity is also invoked. At minimum, there must be a shared sense of meaning in order for communication to occur (e.g., Clark, 1996; Quine, 1960). Homogeneity was also central to classic theories of crowd and mob behavior (McDougall, 1920; Milgram & Toch, 1969).

There are several mechanisms through which homogeneity of group members can develop. It could develop through self-selection because people may be attracted to groups whose members are similar to them (e.g., Byrne, 1997; Hinde, 1997). Homogeneity could also be achieved through social norms exerting pressure leading to a "convergence process" (e.g., Newcomb, 1961; Newcomb, Turner, & Converse, 1965; Sherif, 1936), through contagion processes in which information is propagated through group members (e.g., Coleman, 1964; Le Bon, 1903; McDougall, 1920), or through cohesiveness and communication (Back, 1950; Festinger & Thibaut, 1950; Festinger, Schachter and Back, 1950). Common goals can exert pressure to homogeneity (e.g., Asch's discussion of the bucket brigade) as can the perception of common fate (e.g., Campbell, 1958). The mechanism by which homogeneity is achieved is of interest in its own right (e.g., studies by Festinger, his colleagues and students; see, e.g., Cartwright and Zander, 1956), and is in the spirit of understanding the development of group processes. Here we are concerned with the measurement of homogeneity, rather than its development. Further, we want to be consistent with Allport's (1924) mandate that group-level processes be explainable by individual-level variables, even if the process cannot be explained by reference to a single individual. The specific measure of homogeneity we consider below takes individual-level measurements as the building block, and thus is consistent with Allport's mandate. Curiously, Allport speculated that homogeneity may lead an observer to falsely perceive a group mind (Allport, 1924).

We now turn to a statistical framework, the *multi-level pairwise approach*, that both measures homogeneity and builds upon homogeneity as a necessary feature of group-level process. The multi-level part of the approach provides a clear statistical criterion for indexing group- and individual-level effects. The pairwise part of the approach offers two types of goods: it provides parameters that measure homogeneity and it provides statistical corrections for nonindependence of data. We first present an introduction to the pairwise approach and review the intraclass correlation, which serves as the building block for the rest of the model. We then show how to use the pairwise model to assess multiple levels simultaneously. The intraclass correlation will serve as the basis for a latent-variable approach to model group-level processes independently from individual-level process. We will then show how the pairwise approach can be extended to include regression models that tackle the issue of interdependence.

A Statistical Implementation of Homogeneity: The Pairwise Approach

Social interaction presents statistical problems because data from individuals within an aggregate are not independent. As Kenny said, nonindependence is the "very stuff" that makes up social interaction and should be modeled rather than ignored or treated as a nuisance. The pairwise approach presented here deals with nonindependence in two ways: the multi-level or latent variable version models interdependence directly so that individuals are "nested" within higher levels of analysis and individual effects are estimated separately from other levels, such as group levels; the regression version accounts for the nonindependence in the estimation and testing of the relevant parameters, but does not model the hierarchical nature of the data. (Note, however, that the two versions can be combined into more general models, as we discuss near the end of this chapter.) By formalizing the concepts in terms of statistical parameters we hope to clarify the issues, and thus avoid another of Allport's critiques: that writers of group-level phenomena "speak in a babble of tongues" (Allport, 1933, p. 13).

Currently, there are several pockets of methodological research on the statistical problem of nonindependence but there has been relatively little interaction between them. It is possible to handle some of the problems created by nonindependence through structural equations modeling (e.g., Bollen, 1989), by modeling individual scores as a function of an underlying group-level latent variable. It is also possible to handle quite complex problems created by nonindependence (e.g., multiple measures on multiple individuals over multiple times) through hierarchical linear modeling (e.g., Bryk & Raudenbush, 1992), by creating linear models at the lowest levels of analysis (e.g., a regression analysis between variables measured on a single individual over multiple times). The parameters are then entered from the low-level analysis into a higher-level linear model. Sometimes special "tricks" are needed to alter the existing models in just the right way to handle specific problems of nonindependence, but these tricks are not widely known and sometimes difficult to implement (e.g., Kaplan & Elliott, 1997; Longford & Muthen, 1992; McArdle & Hamagami, 1996; Muthen, 1994). When there is overlap between the pairwise approach and either structural equations modeling or hierarchical equations modeling, both lead to identical parameter estimates when maximum likelihood estimation is used and all groups have equal sizes.

We will relate the parameters of the pairwise model to substantive constructs in social psychology, and will label the parameters of the model with theoretically meaningful terms. To the typical researcher, our efforts, and those of colleagues such as David Kenny, may appear to be about correct ways to analyze data in the presence of nonindependence. While we certainly are interested in "correct" data-analytic techniques, we are more interested in finding new ways of mining social science data to address psychological questions about social interaction. We view the statistics of nonindependence as an opportunity to study social processes rather than as additional constraints placed on researchers.

Another advantage of the pairwise approach is that it is accessible to researchers from varied backgrounds. One of our goals has been to express the parameters of the statistical estimation in terms that are familiar to researchers (e.g., a Pearson-type correlation, a regression slope) and do the "dirty work" behind the scenes through the standard error, statistical significance test, and the confidence interval. Most of our techniques involve standard estimators and computations that can be performed using widely available computer software (even spreadsheets). Thus, a benefit of the pairwise approach is that researchers can concentrate on their "substantive" domains of interest rather than esoteric statistical procedures and programs.

There has been recent interest in comparing gay/lesbian relationships to heterosexual relationships (e.g., Kurdek, 1997b, for relationship commitment; Kurdek, 1997a, for distress after separation). These comparisons involve delicate statistical issues because they compare dyads whose members are exchangeable (same sex) with dyads whose members are distinguishable (opposite sex). The approach in this chapter extends other models (e.g., Kenny, 1996; Kraemer & Jacklin, 1979) and presents a simple way to analyze these complicated designs.

There are other modeling approaches that investigators have pursued. One approach is to model the social interaction over time as a dynamic process (Coleman, 1964, 1990; Simon, 1957; Stasser, Kerr, & Davis, 1980; Suppes & Atkinson, 1960; Thomas & Malone, 1979; Thomas & Martin, 1976). Another approach is to model the structural properties of the interaction using concepts from graph theory and network analysis (e.g., Harary, Norman, & Cartwright, 1965; Wasserman & Faust, 1994). For a general review of some of these models see Abelson (1967).

Kenny and associates (e.g., Kenny & La Voie, 1984) have worked on round-robin models where, for example, an individual interacts with every other individual. This design feature differs from the present one because we consider the case where group members interact only with group members (e.g., a husband and wife interact with each other, not with other husbands and wives in the sample) and all possible dyads within a group need not interact (e.g., data from a family of five can be collected without requiring family members to interact in various combinations of dyads or triads).

A few social psychologists have used "independence as the null hypothesis" in the sense that if individuals in a group behave differently than a simple probabilistic model based on independence (i.e., non-independence of interacting individuals), then it is assumed that there is some higher-level psychological process that needs to be explained. The simple chance model has usually been of the type that accounts for the "probability of at least one person" exhibiting the behavior. This "independence as null hypothesis" approach has been used in the bystander intervention literature (Latane & Darley, 1969) and in recent work on group discussion (e.g., Stasser & Titus, 1985; see Larson, 1997, for an extension). The limitation of this approach is that even though it identifies situations where nonindependence might be present, it does not model the type nor the degree of nonindependence.

The intraclass correlation: The building block for measures of homogeneity, multiple-levels, and interdependence

The framework we use is the pairwise correlation, which dates back to Pearson (1901; see also Fisher, 1925). The intraclass correlation is simple, even basic, but it serves as the basis of virtually all statistical models designed to capture nonindependence. The intraclass indexes the absolute similarity of scores; in contrast, the more familiar interclass or Pearson correlation indexes the relative similarity of scores around the group mean.

In the pairwise approach, the structure of nonindependence is built directly into the organization of the data matrix, and common estimators are computed on the reorganized data matrix with appropriate corrections to the standard error. The pairwise correlation is so named because each possible within-group pair of scores is used to compute the correlation. For example, with individuals Adam and Amos in the first dyad, there are two possible pairings: Adam in column 1 and Amos in column 2; or Amos in column 1 and Adam in column 2. This coding is represented symbolically in table 20.1. Thus with $N = 3$ dyads, each column contains $2N = 6$ scores because each individual is represented in both columns. The two columns (i.e., variables X and X') are then correlated using the usual product–moment correlation. This correlation is denoted $r_{xx'}$, and is called the _pairwise intraclass correlation_. It is an estimate of the intraclass correlation of one person's score with his or her partner's score. The pairwise intraclass correlation is the maximum likelihood estimate of the intraclass correlation and therefore is endowed with the usual properties of maximum likelihood estimators (such as consistency).[1] For theoretical development of the exchangeable case, formulas, and examples see Griffin and Gonzalez (1995).

The correlation $r_{xx'}$ indexes the absolute similarity between two exchangeable partners in a dyad. This can be seen in a simple scatterplot of X against X'. On this plot each dyad is represented twice, once as the point (X_i, X_i') and again as the point (X_i', X_i). We draw line segments between points from the same dyad. These line segments will be bisected by the identity line and will have a slope of -1. The summed squared length of these line segments is inversely proportional to $r_{xx'}$; it is in this sense that the pairwise intraclass is a measure of homogeneity between dyad members – the longer the line segment for a pair, the less similar are the two scores. Note that when the two individuals in the dyad perfectly

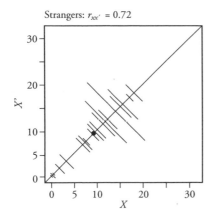
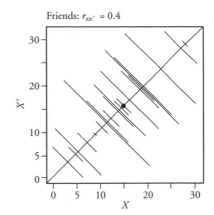

Figure 20.1   Graphical display of the pairwise intraclass correlation. Data are from Stinson and Ickes (1992) and represent the frequency of smiles and laughter for same-sex dyads where both members are either friends or strangers. The point on the identity line represents the mean frequency for strangers and the mean frequency for friends; the length of the line segments is related to the similarity in the within-dyad scores.

agree, then the line segments will have length 0 (i.e., all points will be on the identity line), and the pairwise intraclass correlation $r_{xx'}$ will equal 1. An analogous plot was proposed in the context of calibration and resolution of judgment (Liberman & Tversky, 1993).

Two examples of these plots appear in figure 20.1. The data, from Stinson and Ickes (1992), are the frequency of smiles and laughter between dyad members, separately for dyads consisting of strangers and dyads consisting of friends. For dyads of strangers the pairwise intraclass $r_{xx'}$ was .72 whereas for dyads of friends $r_{xx'}$ was .40. The plot highlights an interesting difference in interaction between friends and strangers. It appears that the interaction pattern between strangers involves matching each other's frequency of smiling to a higher degree than for dyads of friends. That is, for strangers both partners' frequency of smiling was more similar than the frequency of smiling between friends. For friends, the interaction pattern consisted of pairs where one partner smiled relatively much more than the other. This matching difference was independent of the mean level of smiling. The closed circle on the identity line represents the mean frequency of smiles. Dyads of friends had a higher frequency of smiles than dyads of strangers, yet dyads of strangers had a higher degree of matching (as indexed by the pairwise intraclass). Simply reporting mean differences between friends and strangers misses an interesting part of the interaction involving the matching process.

It is important to remember that the correlation $r_{xx'}$ is computed over $2N$ pairs. Because the correlation $r_{xx'}$ is based on $2N$ pairs rather than on N dyads as in the usual case, the test of significance must be adjusted. The sample value $r_{xx'}$ can be tested against the null hypothesis $\rho_{xx'} = 0$ using the asymptotic test,[2]

$$Z = r_{xx'} \sqrt{N} \qquad (1)$$

Table 20.1   Symbolic representation for the pairwise data setup in the exchangeable case

Dyad	Variable	
	X	X′
1	X_{11}	X_{12}
	X_{12}	X_{11}
2	X_{21}	X_{22}
	X_{22}	X_{21}
3	X_{31}	X_{32}
	X_{32}	X_{31}
4	X_{41}	X_{42}
	X_{42}	X_{41}

Note. The first subscript represents the dyad and the second subscript represents the individual. Categorization of individuals as 1 or 2 is arbitrary.

where N is the number of dyads and Z follows a standardized normal distributed.

The pairwise intraclass correlation indexes the similarity of individuals within dyads, and is closely related to other estimators of the intraclass correlation such as the ANOVA estimator (Fisher, 1925; Haggard, 1958). However, the pairwise method has several important advantages in the present situation. Most important, it is calculated in the same manner as the usual Pearson correlation: the two "reverse-coded" columns are correlated in the usual manner, thus offering ease of computation, flexibility in the use of existing computer packages, and an intuitive link to general correlational methods. It also has certain statistical properties that make it ideal to serve as the basis for more complicated statistics of interdependence (e.g., it is the maximum likelihood estimator of the intraclass correlation on groups of equal size). Moreover, the pairwise method used to compute the intraclass correlation within a single variable can be used to compute the "cross intraclass correlation" across different variables, an important index discussed below. Thus, the pairwise approach can extend to multivariate situations.

The previous example on dyads (table 20.1) was defined implicitly on dyads where the members are "exchangeable"; that is, there is no a priori way to classify an individual in a dyad. Examples of exchangeable dyads include gay couples, same-sex roommates, and identical twins. However, examples of distinguishable dyads (such as heterosexual couples where individuals within a dyad can be classified by sex) also occur. The calculation of the *partial pairwise intraclass correlation* in the distinguishable case follows the same general pattern. In the distinguishable case the pairwise correlation model requires one extra piece of information: a grouping code indexing the dyad member. This extra information is needed because each dyad member is distinguishable according to some theoretically meaningful variable, which is indexed by the grouping code. One simply computes the usual partial correlation between the two reversed columns, i.e., partialing out the variable of the grouping code. This partial correlation is the maximum likelihood estimator of the pairwise intraclass correlation for the distinguishable case. For the theoretical background underlying the distinguishable case, relevant formulae, computational examples, and extensions to a structural equations modeling framework, see Gonzalez and Griffin (1999).

The intraclass correlation can also measure divergent processes in a dyad, which would be indicated by a negative intraclass correlation. A negative intraclass correlation is interpretable in dyads but becomes difficult to interpret in groups of three more because then the intraclass correlation is asymmetric.

Extensions to groups

For simplicity we will focus much of the discussion in this chapter on dyads, but the framework can easily be extended to groups of any size. Here we show how to extend the pairwise approach to situations where all groups are of size k. The direct extension is to perform the pairwise coding for all possible combinations of dyads. For instance, in a group of size 3 with members denoted A, B, and C, the possible combinations are AB, AC, BA, BC, CA, and CB. For each of the six combinations, data from the person coded on the left (e.g., A in AB) is entered into column X and data from the person coded on the right (e.g., B in AB) is entered into column X'. Thus, for groups of size 3 columns X and X' will contain $6N$ data points, where N is the number of groups. The Pearson correlation between columns X and X' is the pairwise intraclass correlation for the exchangeable case.

Obviously, with large groups the pairwise framework becomes cumbersome because of the many combinations that need to be coded, but it still maintains its interpretational simplicity. A computational shortcut to the pairwise framework for groups is given by using a traditional analysis of variance source table. Compute a one-way ANOVA using the grouping code as the single factor (e.g., if there are 20 groups of size 4, then there will be 20 cells in the ANOVA, each cell having four observations). Denote the sum of squares between groups as SSB, the sum of squares within groups as SSW, and the corresponding mean square terms as MSB and MSW, respectively. The exchangeable pairwise intraclass correlation is identical to

$$r_{xx'} = \frac{(k-1)\text{SSB} - \text{SSW}}{(k-1)(\text{SSB} + \text{SSW})} \tag{2}$$

where k is the group size (Haggard, 1958). Contrast this definition of the pairwise with the ANOVA-based intraclass correlation (e.g., Shrout & Fleiss, 1979), which is

$$r_{xx'} = \frac{\text{MSB} - \text{MSW}}{\text{MSB} + (k-1)\text{MSW}} \tag{3}$$

where k is the group size. For a comparison of these two different formulations of the intraclass correlation, see Gonzalez and Griffin (1999). The setup is similar for the distinguishable case: include a second factor indexing each member of the group and compute the source table for the two-way ANOVA.

Extensions of the intraclass correlation with closed-form expressions (either in pairwise or ANOVA-based formulations) are not straightforward for situations where the size of the groups varies within the same study. For example, a study on families may have some families of size 3, some of size 4, etc. For preliminary treatments of this problem see Karlin, Cameron, and Williams (1981), and Donner (1986).

Another way to express the intraclass correlation is in terms of a random effects linear model. For the exchangeable case each observation is modeled as an additive function of the grand mean, a group effect and error, where the group effect and the error term each are random variables. The variances of each of these two random variables (V_g and V_e respectively) leads to the intraclass correlation through the simple formula

$$\frac{V_g}{V_g + V_e} \tag{4}$$

With equal size groups, if one uses maximum likelihood to estimate these variance components, then the resulting intraclass correlation is identical to equation (2) (the pairwise estimate); if one uses restricted maximum likelihood to estimate the variance components, then the resulting intraclass correlation identical to equation (3) (the ANOVA estimate). This random effects formulation can be extended to more complicated situations involving nested factors and can include cases with unequal group sizes. This general framework is called hierarchical linear modeling and there are now several commercial computer packages available (e.g., Bryk & Raudenbush, 1992).

Levels of Analysis

We now apply the pairwise framework to address different levels of analysis present in dyad research. A researcher studying dyads can ask questions at the level of the individual, of the dyad, or of both (Kenny & La Voie, 1985). For instance, a researcher can ask the question: Do *individuals* who gesture more also verbalize more? A researcher can also ask the question: Are *dyads* where both individuals gesture more also the dyads where both individuals verbalize more? These two questions differ in their level of analysis: individuals or dyads.

Both levels of analysis can be informative, and focusing on only one level is wasteful of information that might be important for testing theory because psychological theory usually refers to both levels. Further, there may be situations where the direction of the relationship between two variables differs in sign across the two levels. For instance, imagine that trust and satisfaction scales are taken from married couples. Each partner answers both scales so there are a total of four observations per couple: two trust scores and two satisfaction scores. It is plausible that the correlation between trust and satisfaction at the dyad level is positive (more trusting dyads are more satisfied with the relationship) whereas at the individual level the correlation between trust and satisfaction could be negative (the individual within a dyad who is relatively more trusting could be relatively less satisfied because his or her trust is not reciprocated). Thus, one may find correlations of different signs at the different levels of analysis for the same data. Such patterns are interesting from the perspective of both theory development and theory testing, and a complete theory of dyadic interaction should address both levels of analysis.

The problem of separating the individual-level analysis from the dyad-level analysis has troubled methodologists for a long time. Robinson (1950) pointed out that the correlation between two aggregated variables (e.g., mean educational attainment and mean income correlated *across* states) is not equivalent to the correlation between the same two variables measured on individuals (e.g., educational attainment and average income *within* a state). The erroneous generalization from one level to another has been termed the "ecological correlation fallacy" (Hauser, 1974; Robinson, 1950; Schwartz, 1994; Susser, 1994a, 1994b). A similar problem arises in cultural psychology: "[a]n ecological fallacy is committed when a researcher uses a culture-level correlation to interpret individual behavior . . . [a] reverse ecological fallacy is committed when researchers construct cultural or ecological indices based upon individual-level measurements (Kim, Triandis, Kagitcibasi, Choi, & Yoon, 1994, p. 4). The need for statistical techniques that permit analysis at different levels ("multi-level analysis") has led to a cottage industry of different viewpoints and statistical programs (see Bock, 1989; Bryk & Raudenbush, 1992; Goldstein, 1987; Goldstein & McDonald, 1988; Kreft, de Leeuw, & van der Leeden, 1994).

The pairwise correlation can be extended to handle analyses at different levels. Figure 20.3 shows a simple latent variable model for the exchangeable dyadic design. In this model, each measured variable is coded in a pairwise fashion so that the variables X and X' (and, by the same logic, Y and Y') are identical except for order. There are four unique correlations on these six variables because $r_{xy} = r_{x'y'}$ and $r_{xy'} = r_{x'y}$ (these correlations are depicted in figure 20.2).

The variance of a given observed variable is assumed to result from two different latent sources: a dyadic component representing the portion of that variable that is shared and an individual component representing the portion of that variable that is not shared, or is unique, between dyadic partners. Here shared variance within a variable refers to homogeneity and is indexed by the intraclass correlation. As figure 20.3 illustrates, there are two levels at which the variables X and Y can be correlated: (1) the shared dyadic variance of X and Y can be related through the dyadic correlation r_d, and (2) the unique individual variance of X and Y can be related through the individual-level correlation r_i. The model depicted in figure 20.3 permits simultaneous estimation and testing of r_d and r_i.

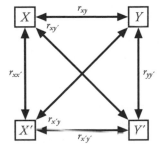

Figure 20.2   All possible pairwise correlations between variables X, Y, and their corresponding "reverse codes." Note that in the exchangeable case $r_{xy} = r_{x'y'}$ and $r_{xy'} = r_{x'y}$.

The individual-level correlation r_i and the latent dyad-level correlation r_d can be computed directly from the four pairwise correlations as follows:

$$r_i = \frac{r_{xy} - r_{xy'}}{\sqrt{1 - r_{xx'}}\sqrt{1 - r_{yy'}}} \qquad (5)$$

and

$$r_d = \frac{r_{xy'}}{\sqrt{r_{xx'}}\,\sqrt{r_{yy'}}} \qquad (6)$$

These values are maximum likelihood estimates for the case of equal group sizes, such as dyads. The numerator of the individual-level correlation r_i is the difference between the observed correlation r_{xy}, which combines dyad-level and individual-level effects, and the cross intraclass correlation $r_{xy'}$, which contains only dyad-level effects. Thus r_i is a measure of the individual-level relation uncontaminated by dyad-level effects. The numerator of the dyad-level correlation r_d is simply the pairwise cross intraclass correlation $r_{xy'}$, and in this model corresponds to the direct measure of the dyad-level relations. The denominators, too, are conceptually straightforward: they correct the scale of the correlations for the fact that only "part" of each observed variable is being correlated. When the individual components of variables X and Y are correlated, the denominator adjusts for the proportions of variance in the observed X and Y that correspond to the *non-shared* effects ($\sqrt{1 - r_{xx'}}$ and $\sqrt{1 - r_{yy'}}$, respectively). Similarly, when the *dyadic* components of the variables X and Y are correlated, the denominator adjusts for the proportions of variance in the observed X and Y that correspond to the shared dyadic effects ($\sqrt{r_{xx'}}$ and $\sqrt{r_{yy'}}$, respectively). Note that r_d can be interpreted as $r_{xy'}$ that has been disattenuated (i.e., divided by the geometric mean of the intraclass correlations representing the proportion of dyadic variance). Thus, if one of the intraclasses is negative, then r_d is not defined and the present latent variable model will not apply. The latent variable correlation r_d is equivalent to the maximum likelihood group-level correlation suggested by Gollob (1991). Kenny and La Voie (1985) proposed an analogous model based on ANOVA rather than maximum likelihood estimators.

For the special case of exchangeable dyads, r_i can be computed either by equation (5) or equivalently by correlating the deviation scores on X and on Y. That is, the dyad mean on X is subtracted from each X score and the dyad mean on Y is subtracted from each Y score, and then the $2N$ deviations on X are correlated with the $2N$ deviations on Y. For dyads, equation (5) and the deviation method yield identical values for r_i. The correlation r_i can be tested using the usual Pearson correlation table (or the associated t-test formula) with $N - 1$ degrees of freedom (Kenny & La Voie, 1985).

When either of the intraclass correlations $r_{xx'}$ or $r_{yy'}$ (or both) are small, r_d will tend be large and may even exceed 1.0. Because the dyadic model is based on the assumption of dyadic similarity, the model should only be tested when *both* intraclass correlations are significantly positive.[3] In psychological terms, the dyadic model should only be applied when there is homogeneity within each variable, which translates into positive intraclass correlations. The latent variable correlation r_d may be interpretable when both intraclass correlations are negative, but adjustments would have to be made to deal with the asym-

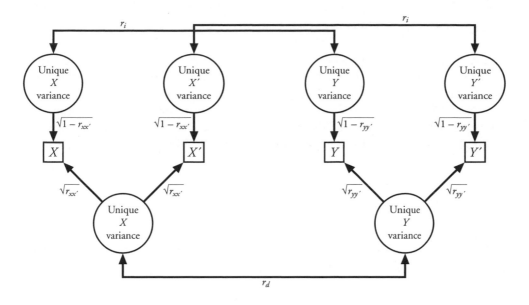

Figure 20.3 A latent variable model separating individual-level (unique) and dyad-level (shared) effects.

metry of negative intraclass correlations. In general, the practice of restricting the application of this model to cases when both intraclass correlations are significantly positive should reduce the occurrence of out-of-bounds values for r_d (see also Kenny & La Voie, 1985).

A significance test for r_d is reported in Griffin and Gonzalez (1995). Under the null hypothesis that population $\rho_d = 0$, the standard error of r_d is

$$\sqrt{\frac{1 + r_{xx'}r_{yy'} + r_{xy}^2}{2Nr_{xx'}r_{yy'}}} \tag{7}$$

Interestingly, the p-value associated with r_d is identical to the p-value associated with $r_{xy'}$. Therefore, when both intraclass correlations are significant, implying significant dyad-level variance (homogeneity) in both X and Y, we recommend interpreting $r_{xy'}$ as the raw-score version of r_d because r_d is a disattenuated version of $r_{xy'}$. For computational details, theoretical background and numerical examples, see Griffin and Gonzalez (1995); for extensions of the latent variable model to the distinguishable case, see Gonzalez and Griffin (1999).

Extensions to groups: The latent variable model

When groups consist of three or more individuals and all groups are of equal size, then the computation of the individual-level and group-level correlations proceeds in a manner similar to that described for the group intraclass (equation (2)). One computes the SSB and SSW separately for variable X and for variable Y. In addition, one must compute cross-product sum of squares SSB_{xy} and SSW_{xy} where subscripts denote variables (see Kenny & La Vole, 1985, for computational details). The individual-level r_i is equivalent to

$$\frac{SSW_{xy}}{\sqrt{SSW_x \, SSW_y}} \tag{8}$$

This is also identical to the ANOVA-based r_i given in Kenny and La Voie (1985). The pairwise cross intraclass correlation $r_{xy'}$ is

$$\frac{SSB_{xy} - \dfrac{SSW_{xy}}{k-1}}{\sqrt{SSB_x \, SSB_y}} \tag{9}$$

where k is the group size. The group version of the group-level r_d, which we denote r_g, is equation (6) where one plugs in the group versions of $r_{xy'}$ (equation (9)), $r_{xx'}$ (equation (2)), and $r_{yy'}$ (equation (2)).

The mean-level correlation.   It may appear that the correlation between the means for each dyad on the two variables should yield an estimate of the dyad-level correlation. Contrary to this intuition, the "mean-level" correlation (denoted r_m) reflects both individual and dyad-level processes (under the model in figure 3); it can best be thought of as a "total" correlation. The correlation between dyad means can be expressed as a function of pairwise correlations:

$$r_m = \frac{r_{xy} + r_{xy'}}{\sqrt{1 + r_{xx'}} \sqrt{1 + r_{yy'}}} \tag{10}$$

The mean-level correlation r_m should not be used as an index of dyad-level relations because it can be significantly positive or negative even when the dyad-level correlation r_d = 0. According to the model in figure 20.3, a positive dyad-level correlation exists only when the tendency for *both* dyad members to be high on X is matched by the tendency for *both* dyad members to be high on Y. However, this is only one of several circumstances that can lead to a positive value of r_m. For example, a positive mean-level correlation will result when the tendency of one member to be extremely high on X is matched with the tendency of that same member to be extremely high on Y, which is an individual-level effect.

A Regression Model for Separating Actor and Partner Effects

We presented above a latent variable dyadic design that decomposed the relationship between two pairwise coded variables into dyadic-level and individual-level relations. However, this particular decomposition is only one of a number of possible models that can be applied in this situation (Kenny, 1996). Another useful way to model social interaction within a dyad is as a combination of two paths linking X and Y: an actor effect, which represents the extent to which a dyad member (the "actor") standing on variable X determines that actor's standing on variable Y, and a partner effect, which represents the extent to which the partner's standing on X determines the actor's standing on Y. We now turn to an example of this actor–partner model, which models interdependence directly without the hierarchy of group and individual effects.

In the Stinson and Ickes example, we might ask: "What predicts an individual's verbalization frequency?" An individual actor's speech frequency might be influenced by the joint effect of the individual's own gazes and his or her partner's gazes. Following the structural model illustrated in figure 20.4 leads to the interpretation of the (semi-partial) pairwise r_{xy} as the "actor correlation" and the (semi-partial) pairwise $r_{xy'}$ as the "partner correlation." To obtain the actor and partner effects in the exchangeable case, it is necessary to partial out the shared component of the actor and partner variance – which means partialling out $r_{xx'}$, the pairwise intraclass correlation on X. The comparison of this model (depicted in figure 20.4) with the decomposition presented earlier in this chapter (figure 20.4) illustrates the importance of a theoretical model in guiding and formulating how an analysis should be conducted. Under different models the same correlations r_{xy} and $r_{xy'}$ carry different interpretations and can be modeled differently.

Thibaut and Kelley (1959; see also Kelley & Thibaut, 1978; Kelley, 1979) proposed a theory of close relationships focusing in particular on interdependence between individuals. The model begins with an economic approach in that it assumes each person in the relationship maximizes "outcomes." Some of these outcomes are under the control of the

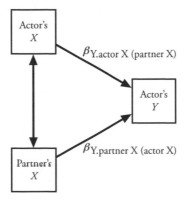

Figure 20.4   Representation of the actor–partner regression model.

individual actor, some are under the control of the partner, and some are under the joint control of the actor and the partner. A particular outcome may be a result of any combination of these three influences. The theory also introduced additional mechanisms such as attributions and goals, and these mechanisms influence the process by which the outcomes are maximized. For instance, an individual may have a "maximize other" goal where he is trying to maximize his partner's outcomes and neglect his own, or a "maximize joint" goal where she is trying to maximize the sum of both her outcomes and her partner's outcomes. The theory attempts to model which situations are subject to different types of outcome influences and outcome goals, and an extension of their model uses a "transition list" structure to model sequential aspects of interdependence (Kelley, 1984). See Rusbult and Van Lange (1996) for a recent review.

Empirical tests of the Kelley and Thibaut model have been limited in part because it is not clear how one would analyze data that emerge from research that brings interdependence into the laboratory, nor is it clear how to implement their analogy to game-theoretic payoff matrices with the typical variables used in social psychological research (see Hinde, 1979, for a similar point). The analytic techniques reviewed in this chapter permit tests for which responses are, and which responses are not, interdependent in dyadic and group interaction. The techniques implement the Kelley and Thibaut framework in a way that allows an investigator to categorize different types of interdependence. By adding the X by X' interaction term to the regression in figure 20.4, it is possible to build a regression model that includes terms for the actor's control, the partner's control, and the joint control. One advantage of the present extension is that it is not necessary to stay within the framework of "outcome matrices" as Kelley and Thibaut did. Instead, a researcher can ask whether an individual's Y variable is a function of her X variable, her partner's X variable, and some suitably defined interaction term (there are several ways of conceptualizing this interaction, see, e.g., Kenny, 1996). We note that Kelley and Thibaut (1978) proposed an "index of correspondence" to measure the similarity of payoffs; this index is identical to the pairwise intraclass correlation.

Some examples of the types of research questions that can be addressed within the Kelley and Thibaut framework include: Does a person's trust of the partner relate to the partner's satisfaction in the relationship? Does a person's trust of the partner relate to her own satisfaction? Does the joint level of both members' trust relate to a given individual's satisfaction? A priori knowledge of the "outcome matrix" would not be needed because the proposed technique estimates (from data) the various sources of influence. Thus, theories that make specific predictions about which behaviors and which outcomes should be interdependent (such as the theory of Kelley and Thibaut) can be tested. These techniques will help our understanding of conflict in relationships (e.g., Holmes & Murray, 1996), aid in understanding applied problems such as identifying the relationship patterns that predict divorce, and could be extended to the study of conflict within and between larger groups.

Necessary properties revisited

Earlier in the chapter we argued that a necessary property of group-level phenomena is homogeneity. The multilevel model is somewhat restrictive because in order to model a higher level (e.g., group) there must be homogeneity at the lower level (e.g., individual). There is a different way to conceptualize social interaction that does not involve multiple levels, hence does not require homogeneity. This alternative model involves the concept of interdependence.

Kurt Lewin, writing 16 years after Allport's critique of the group mind, argued that "a group can be characterized as a 'dynamic whole'; this means that a change in the state of any subpart changes the state of any other subpart" (1940, p. 68). The degree to which individuals influence each other, i.e., a change in one subpart leading to a change in another subpart, is what we refer to as *interdependence*. Interdependence occurs when the actions and feeling of one individual influence the actions and feelings of another. Indeed, the subjective feeling of "closeness" may be dictated, in part, by how much interdependence there is between the individuals. This interdependence need not occur face-to-face as illustrated by the Yogi Berra quip: "We have a good time together, even when we're not together."

Thibaut & Kelley (1959) had a more specific operationalization of interdependence involving three components: how an actor influences his/her own behavior, how an actor influences his/her partner, and how the actions of the pair as a joint entity influence the actor. This operationalization can be implemented in a regression-like model, which we do below in a manner that preserves the statistical nonindependence of the data. Related terminology, though emphasizing different features of interaction, was used by Newcomb, Turner, and Converse (1965) when they distinguished three types of interpersonal influence: unilateral effects, reciprocal effects, and mutual adaptation. Kenny & La Voie (1984) used the terms *actor effect*, *partner effect*, and *relationship effect*. Allport (1924) used the term *circular reaction* for the iterative process where one person influences another, who in turn influences the first person, who in turn . . ..

McDougall (1920), in his classic but underappreciated work on collective psychology, recognized the two necessary conditions of homogeneity and interdependence.

> The essential conditions of collective mental action are, then, a common object of mental activity, a common mode of feeling in regard to it, and some degree of reciprocal influence between the members of the group.   (p. 23)

He argued that without these conditions, an aggregate of individuals is merely that – an aggregation. In order for an aggregate to acquire emergent properties (such as a "group spirit" or a "national character," issues McDougall was concerned with), homogeneity (a common object and a common mode) and interdependence (reciprocal influence) must be in place.

Note that homogeneity and interdependence are logically independent concepts. For example, individuals in an aggregate could influence each other by their "mere" presence (see Zajonc's, 1980, review of social facilitation), demonstrating interdependence, but the behaviors need not be homogeneous. Likewise, group members may exhibit homogeneity in their behavior because of common fate (a common third variable) and not be interdependent. Even though the two concepts are logically independent, in real world groups the two are probably positively correlated (in ordinal language, high homogeneity goes with high interdependence).

Statistical implementations of interdependence

The actor–partner regression model (introduced in a more general form by Kenny, 1995) can be estimated on dyads with the pairwise method. The dependent variable of interest (Y) is regressed on the X and X' columns, using a standard regression program on the pairwise data setup we have used throughout this chapter (where each column contains $2N$ data points). Either the raw or the standardized regression coefficients can be read from the program output and tested for significance (see Griffin and Gonzalez, 1998, for proper tests of significance). Like the tests for the pairwise model given earlier, the significance tests for the actor and partner regression coefficients are made up of the four pairwise correlations: $r_{xx'}$, $r_{yy'}$, r_{xy}, and $r_{xy'}$. We will not go through the computational details here, but simply present examples and discuss their interpretation. Technical details as well as a generalized model that includes an interaction term that permits estimation of the Thibaut & Kelley (1959) concepts of reflexive control, fate control, and behavioral control are given in Griffin and Gonzalez (1998).

It is instructive to express these raw score regression coefficients in terms of pairwise correlations. The actor regression coefficient is given by

$$\frac{s_y(r_{xy} - r_{xy'}r_{xx'})}{s_x(1 - r_{xx'}^2)} \tag{11}$$

where s_y and s_x are the standard deviations of the criterion variable and the predictor variable, respectively. This formula produces a value that is identical to the coefficient produced by standard regression programs. The regression coefficient for the partner effect has the same form with the role of r_{xy} and $r_{xy'}$ interchanged. Under the null hypothesis that the population $\beta = 0$, the variance for the actor regression slope is

$$V(\beta_{\text{actor}}) = \frac{s_y^2(r_{xx'}^2 \; r_{xy'}^2 - r_{xx'}r_{yy'} + 1 - r_{xy}^2)}{2Ns_x^2(1 - r_{xx'}^2)} \tag{12}$$

The test of significance for the actor effect is computed with a Z test using $\frac{\beta}{\sqrt{V(\beta)}}$. The test for the partner effect is analogous, except that r_{xy} appears in equation (12) in place of $r_{xy'}$.

For the Stinson and Ickes data that we have been using throughout this chapter, the actor correlation r_{xy} between gaze and verbalization was .386. In the context of the model shown in figure 20.4, the standardized regression coefficient was 0.173 ($Z = 0.97$). This standardized regression coefficient is interpreted as the influence on an actor's frequency of verbalization given one standard deviation change on the actor's frequency of gaze, holding constant the partner's frequency of gaze. In this case, the actor effect was not statistically significant. Similarly, the partner correlation $r_{xy'}$ between gaze and verbalization was 0.471. The standardized regression coefficient was 0.372 ($Z = 2.09$). In other words, the influence on the actor's frequency of verbalization given one standard deviation change on the partner's frequency of gaze, holding constant the actor's frequency of gaze, was statistically significant. The partner's gaze frequency was a more powerful predictor of the actor's verbalization frequency than the actor's own gaze frequency. For one possible theoretical

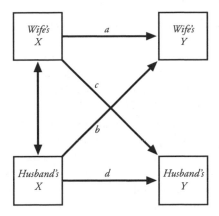

Figure 20.5 Representation of the actor–partner regression model for testing differences in regression coefficients between two classes.

analysis of these results, see Duncan and Fiske (1977).

A more complicated form of the actor–partner regression model is used for analyzing data from distinguishable dyads because when there are two different types of dyad members it is usually of interest to examine whether the actor effects and the partner effects vary across the two types of individuals. For example, consider the model presented in figure 5, adapted from Murray, Holmes, and Griffin's (1996) study of married couples. In this model, a woman's image of her partner is determined by two causes: her own self-image (the "projection" path labeled *a*, which is an actor effect) and her partner's self-reported self-image (the "matching" path labeled *b*, which is a partner effect). A man's image of his partner is similarly determined by an actor effect *d* and a partner effect *c*.

In such a model it is of central interest to test whether the actor (projection) paths are equal across sexes, or whether the partner (matching) paths are equal across sexes. This can be most easily done using structural equation modeling, as in the Murray et al. (1996) study, where the fit of the model under equality constraints is compared to the model where the constraints are not imposed. If both the actor and the partner effects are equal across the two classes, then *a* and *d* can be pooled and *b* and *c* can be pooled. In a simple model such as this, the pooled structural equation model is essentially equivalent to carrying out the pairwise regression model adjusted for distinguishable dyads because there the parameters are also averaged across the two types of people. The structural modeling approach can be extended to estimate much more complex models, as illustrated in the Murray et al. paper.

In the Murray et al. example, the tests revealed that both the actor and partner effects were equal across husbands and wives. Furthermore, both the actor and partner effects were significant and almost equal in magnitude (standardized regression coefficients = 0.315 and 0.304, respectively).

Connections between the latent variable model and the regression model

While the latent variable and regression models appear to have different necessary properties (homogeneity and interdependence), it is instructive to examine special cases of the two models that are equivalent (up to a linear transformation). Consider the special case of the exchangeable actor–partner model. The model has two βs that model the observed r_{xy} and $r_{xy'}$ correlations. Standard regression arguments show that this can be formalized as a matrix of coefficients A multiplying a vector of unknowns (the βs) leading to the vector of correlations r_{xy} and $r_{xy'}$ (Edwards, 1985). Similarly, the exchangeable latent variable model with two variables can represent the same two observed correlations so there is a matrix of coefficients B multiplying a vector of unknowns (r_i and r_d) leading to the vector of correlations r_{xy} and $r_{xy'}$. It can be shown that the vector of βs is linearly related to the vector of parameters from the latent variable. Thus, the special case implementations of these two models are identical up to a linear transformation. The two models diverge, however, in more complicated situations such as the addition of statistical interaction terms in the regression model or the freeing of equality constraints.

Moreover, it is possible to merge the two models into a more general model. Gonzalez and Griffin (1997) showed that for three or more variables one can compute separate matrices of individual-level correlations and dyad-level correlations. These matrices can then be entered into a standard regression package, and regression equations can be tested after appropriate adjustment to the statistical tests. These regressions are interpreted differently than the actor–partner regressions of the type depicted in figure 20.4. The actor–partner models are simple bivariate regressions, and are used to answer whether an actor's score on an outcome variable is predicted by that actor's score on a predictor variable and by his or her partner's score on the predictor variable. These models provide estimates and significance tests that are corrected for interdependence, but they do not specifically model the interdependence itself. The dyadic-level regressions, in contrast, can be bivariate or multiple regressions, but they explicitly model the interdependence within dyads and answer questions at a different level of analysis. Finally, the individual-level regressions may be bivariate or multiple regressions, and they answer whether the unique or unshared qualities of an individual on the outcome variable are determined by some combination of his or her unique qualities on the predictor variables. For more details, examples, and sample computer code see Gonzalez and Griffin (1997).

Summary and Conclusion

This chapter sketched the general pairwise model. This model provides a framework for dealing with issues of nonindependence as they arise in social psychological studies. Such a framework is useful for at least three reasons. First, it will supply the researcher with a tool to handle different types of problems. Our hope is that the technique will be used not only as a data analysis tool but also as a vehicle to translate psychological theory into testable models. For instance, we showed how some of the theoretical statements made by Kelley and Thibaut could be translated into a regression model within the context of the pairwise approach leading to a direct way to test hypotheses in data.

Second, it will provide the empirical researcher with an intuitive understanding of why treating nonindependence correctly is important. This should not be undervalued. A new statistical technique that is not understood by the users, the empirical researchers in the "trenches," will not have much impact. Empirical researchers need to have both a clear understanding of why a new technique is needed (or is useful in their research), should have a relatively simple way of implementing the new technique, and should be familiar with how to interpret the results of the analyses. The advantage of the pairwise approach is that it is relatively easy to use (e.g., it uses parameter estimates that are familiar to the researcher, such as a Pearson correlation or a regression slope), it can illustrate why nonindependence in data requires special care (as illustrated above for the case of why the correlation between group means can be misleading), and it can provide a stepping stone to more complicated and more general techniques such as structural equations modeling and hierarchical linear modeling.

Third, it will provide the teacher of methodology and data analysis a way of showing how techniques that appear different on the surface are actually related. At present, students interested in dealing with nonindependent data must learn a battery of techniques such as SEM and HLM. Implementation of some tests presented here would require complicated SEM or HLM tricks (Kaplan & Elliott, 1997; Muthen, 1994). We hope that the simplicity of the pairwise model (and its generality) will be a welcome change in the classroom.

For these reasons, we see much value in the pairwise approach. We believe that such a simple yet general tool will be useful to researchers. The technique not only helps the analyst tackle thorny problems but also forces him or her to come to terms with the details of the data. The Introduction outlined a few theoretical questions that can be addressed with the techniques proposed here. However, more exciting opportunities may be the new theoretical questions that, we hope, will emerge once social psychological researchers begin dealing with different levels of analysis and tackling nonindependence.

We see the pairwise approach as offering one way to implement Allport's call to study the "master problem of social psychology. What *are* social phenomena if they are not the behaviors of individuals? Or, if social realities *are* entirely composed of individual actions, is there some way of describing and aggregating the latter, not before realized, that will hold the key to the statement of both realities simultaneously and without personification, tautology, or hypostatizied agency?" (Allport, 1962, italics in original).

Notes

1. There are additional uses of the intraclass correlation. For instance, it appears in reliability theory and can be used where a measure of similarity between two scores is needed.
2. To simplify matters in this chapter, we have chosen to present large sample asymptotic significance tests. We present a null hypothesis testing approach rather than a confidence interval approach, but the latter will also be developed. Deriving analytic results for confidence intervals over correlations has not been an easy problem. Fortunately, there have been recent advances in the variance components literature for deriving confidence intervals that are applicable to the pairwise models (e.g., Donner & Eliasziw, 1988).

3.   This restriction is well known in the structural equations modeling (SEM) literature. Note that the application of the SEM model in the case of exchangeable dyads is not straightforward because it is not clear how to compute the observed covariance matrix – one does not know which individual to put in column 1 and which individual to put in column 2 when computing the input covariance matrix. Implementing the exchangeable case in SEM models involves some "tricks" such as setting some equality constraints. However, in the distinguishable case the SEM implementation is relatively straightforward (Gonzalez & Griffin, 1999).

References

Abelson, R. P. (1967). Mathematical models in social psychology. In L. Berkowitz (Ed.), *Advances in experimental social psychology* (Vol. 3, pp. 1–54). New York: Academic Press.

Acitelli, L. K. (1993). You, me, and us: Perspectives on relationship awareness. In S. Duck (Ed.), *Understanding: relationship processes: Vol. 1. Individuals in relationships* (pp. 144–174). Newbury Park, CA: Sage.

Allmendinger, J., & Hackman, R. (1996). Organizations in changing environments: The case of East German symphony orchestras. *Administrative Science Quarterly, 41*, 337–369.

Allport, F. H. (1924). The group fallacy in relation to social science. *Journal of Abnormal and Social Psychology, 19*, 60–73.

Allport, F. H. (1933). *Institutional behavior: Essays toward a re-interpretation of contemporary social organization*. Chapel Hill: University of North Carolina Press.

Allport, F. H. (1962). A structuronomic conception of behavior: Individual and collective. *Journal of Abnormal and Social Psychology, 64*, 3–30.

Aron, A., Paris, M., & Aron, E. M. (1995). Falling in love: Prospective studies of self-concept change. *Journal of Personality and Social Psychology, 69*, 1102–1112.

Asch, S. E. (1952). *Social psychology*. New York: Prentice Hall.

Back, K. W. (1950). The exertion of influence through social communication. In L. Festinger (Ed.), *Theory and experiment in social communication* (pp. 21–36). Ann Arbor, MI: Research Center for Group Dynamics.

Bock, R. D. (1989). *Multilevel analysis of educational data*. San Diego, CA: Academic Press.

Bollen, K. A. (1989). *Structural equations with latent variables*. New York: John Wiley.

Bollen, K. A., & Hoyle, R. H. (1990). Perceived cohesion: A conceptual and empirical examination. *Social Forces, 69*, 479–504.

Bryk, A. S., & Raudenbush, S. W. (1992). *Hierarchical linear models: Applications and data analysis methods*. Newbury Park, CA: Sage.

Byrne, D. (1997). An overview (and underview) of research and theory within the attraction paradigm. *Journal of Social & Personal Relationships, 14*, 417–431.

Campbell, D. T. (1958). Common fate, similarity, and other indices of the status of aggregates of persons as social entities. *Behavioral Science, 3*, 14–25.

Cartwright, D., & Zander, A. (1956). *Group dynamics: Research and theory* (2nd ed.). Evanston, IL: Row, Peterson.

Castellan, N. J. (1973). Comments on the "lens model" equation and the analysis of multiple cue judgment tasks. *Psychometrika, 38*, 87–100.

Clark, H. H. (1996). *Using language*. Cambridge, England: Cambridge University Press.

Coleman, J. S. (1964). *Introduction to mathematical sociology*. London: Free Press.

Coleman, J. S. (1990). *Foundations of social theory*. Cambridge, MA: Harvard University Press.

Cota, A. A., Evans, C. R., Dion, K. L., Kilik, L., & Longman, R. S. (1995). The structure of group cohesion. *Personality and Social Psychology Bulletin, 21*, 572–580.

Daubeny, C. (1850). *An introduction to the atomic theory* (2nd ed.). Oxford: Oxford University Press.

Deal, J. E., Wampler, K. S., & Halverson, C. F. (1992). The importance of similarity in the marital relationship. *Family Process, 31*, 369–382.

Doise, W. (1986). *Levels of explanation in social psychology*. New York: Cambridge University Press.

Donner, A. (1986). A review of inference procedures of the intraclass correlation coefficient in the one-way random effects model. *International Statistical Review, 54*, 67–82.

Donner, A., & Eliasziw, M. (1988). Confidence interval construction for parent–offspring correlations. *Biometrics, 44*, 727–737.

Duncan, S., & Fiske, D. W. (1977). *Face-to-face interaction: Research, methods, and theory*. Hillsdale, NJ: Erlbaum.

Durkheim, E. (1974). *Sociology and philosophy*. New York: Free Press.

Edwards, A. L. (1985). *Multiple regression and the analysis of variance* (2nd ed.). New York: W. H. Freeman.

Elston, R. C. (1975). On the correlation between correlations. *Biometrika, 62*, 133–140.

Festinger, L., Gerard, H., Hymovitch, B., Kelley, H. H., & Raven, B. (1952). The influence process in the presence of extreme deviates. *Human Relations, 5*, 327–346.

Festinger, L., Schachter, S., & Back, K. (1950). *Social pressures in informal groups: A study of human factors in housing*. Stanford, CA: Stanford University Press.

Festinger, L., & Thibaut, J. (1950). Interpersonal communication in small groups. In L. Festinger (Ed.), *Theory and experiment in social communication* (pp. 37–50). Ann Arbor, MI: Research Center for Group Dynamics.

Fisher, R. A. (1925). *Statistical methods for research workers*. Edinburgh, UK: Oliver & Boyd.

Frey, K. P., & Smith, E. R. (1993). Beyond the actor's traits: Forming impressions of actors, targets, and relationships from social behaviors. *Journal of Personality and Social Psychology, 65*, 486–493.

Funder, D. C. (1995). On the accuracy of personality judgment: A realistic approach. *Psychological Review, 102*, 652–670.

Gigone, D., & Hastie, R. (1997). Proper analysis of the accuracy of group judgments. *Psychological Bulletin, 121*, 149–167.

Goldstein, H. (1987). *Multilevel models in educational and social research*. New York: Oxford University Press.

Goldstein, H., & McDonald, R. P. (1988). A general model for the analysis of multilevel data. *Psychometrika, 53*, 455–467.

Gollob, H. F. (1991). Methods for estimating individual- and group-level correlations. *Journal of Personality and Social Psychology, 60*, 376–381.

Gonzalez, R., & Griffin, D. (1997). On the statistics of interdependence: Treating dyadic data with respect. In S. Duck (Ed.), *Handbook of personal relationships* (2nd ed., pp. 271–302). New York: John Wiley.

Gonzalez, R., & Griffin, D. (1999). *Analyses on group data*. University of Michigan and University of Sussex.

Gonzalez, R., & Griffin, D. (1999). The correlational analysis of dyad-level data in the distinguishable case. *Personal Relationships, 6*, 449–469.

Griffin, D., & Gonzalez, R. (1995). The correlational analysis of dyad-level data: Models for the exchangeable case. *Psychological Bulletin, 118*, 430–439.

Griffin, D., & Gonzalez, R. (1998). *Regression models in dyadic research*. University of Sussex and University of Washington.

Haggard, E. A. (1958). *Intraclass correlation and the analysis of variance*. New York: Dryden Press.

Hamilton, D. L., & Sherman, S. J. (1996). Perceiving persons and groups. *Psychological Review, 103*, 336–355.

Harary, F., Norman, R. Z., & Cartwright, D. (1965). *Structural models: An introduction to the theory of directed graphs*. New York: Wiley.

Hauser, R. M. (1974). Contextual analysis revisited. *Sociological Methods and Research, 2*, 365–375.

Hinde, R. A. (1979). *Towards understanding relationships*. London: Academic Press.

Hinde, R. A. (1997). *Relationships: A dialectical perspective*. East Sussex, UK: Psychology Press.

Hogg, M. A. (1993). Group cohesiveness: A critical review and some new directions. In W. Stroebe & M. Hewstone (Eds.), *European review of social psychology* (Vol. 4, pp. 85–111). Chichester: Wiley.

Holmes, J. G., & Murray, S. L. (1996). Conflict in close relationships. In E. T. Higgins & A. W. Kruglanski (Eds.), *Social psychology: Handbook of basic principles* (pp. 622–654). Newbury Park, CA: Guilford Press.

Homans, G. C. (1950). *The human group*. New York: Harpers.

Ickes, B., & Gonzalez, R. (1994). *Social* cognition and social cognition: From the subjective to the intersubjective. *Small Group Research, 25*, 294–315.

Kaplan, D., & Elliott P. R. (1997). A didactic example of multilevel structural equation modeling applicable to the study of organizations. *Structural Equation Modeling, 4*, 1–24.

Karlin, S., Cameron, E. C., Williams. P. T. (1981). Sibling and parent–offspring correlation estimation with variable family size. *Proceedings of the National Academy of Science, 78*, 2664–2668.

Kelley, H. H. (1979). *Personal relationships: Their structure and processes*. Hillsdale, NJ: Erlbaum.

Kelley, H. H. (1984). The theoretical description of interdependence by means of transition lists. *Journal of Personality and Social Psychology, 47*, 956–82.

Kelley, H. H., & Thibaut, J. W. (1978). *Interpersonal relations: A theory of interdependence*. New York: Wiley.

Kenny, D. A. (1976). An empirical application of confirmatory factor analysis to the multitrait-multimethod matrix. *Journal of Experimental Social Psychology, 12*, 247–252.

Kenny, D. A. (1995). Design issues in dyadic research. *Review of Personality and Social Psychology, 11*, 164–184.

Kenny, D. A. (1996). Models of non-independence in dyadic research. *Journal of Social and Personal Relationships, 13*, 279–294.

Kenny, D. A., & La Voie, L. (1984). The social relations model. In L. Berkowitz (Ed.), *Advances in experimental social psychology* (Vol. 18, pp. 141–182). Orlando, FL: Academic Press.

Kenny, D. A., & La Vole, L. (1985). Separating individual and group effects. *Journal of Personality and Social Psychology, 48*, 339–348.

Kim, U., Triandis, H. C., Kagitcibasi, C., Choi, S.-C., & Yoon, G. (1994). *Individualism and collectivism: Theory, method, and applications*. London: Sage.

King, G. (1997). *A solution to the ecological inference problem*. Princeton, NJ: Princeton University Press.

Klein, K. J., Dansereau, F., & Hall, R. J. (1994). Levels issues in theory development, data collection, and analysis. *Academy of Management Review, 19*, 195–229.

Kraemer, H. C., & Jacklin, C. N. (1979). Statistical analysis of dyadic social behavior. *Psychological Bulletin, 86*, 217–224.

Kreft, I., de Leeuw, J., & van der Leeden, R. (1994). Review of five multilevel analysis programs: Bmdp-5v, genmod, hlm, ml3 varcl. *American Statistician, 48*, 324–335.

Kurdek, L. A. (1997a). Adjustment to relationship dissolution in gay, lesbian, and heterosexual partners. *Personal Relationships, 4*, 145–161.

Kurdek, L. A. (1997b). Relation between neuroticism and dimensions of relationship commitment: Evidence from gay, lesbian, and heterosexual couples. *Journal of Family Psychology, 11*, 109–124.

Larson, J. R. (1997). Modeling the entry of shared and unshared information into group discussion: A review and BASIC language computer program. *Small Group Research, 28*, 454–479.

Latane, B., & Darley, J. M. (1969). Bystander "apathy." *American Scientist, 57*, 244–268.

Le Bon, G. (1903). *The crowd*. New York: Unwin.

Lewin, K. (1935). Some social-psychological differences between the United States and Germany. *Character and Personality, 4*, 265.

Lewin, K. (1940). The background of conflict in marriage. In M. Jung (Ed.), *Modern marriage* (pp. 52–69). New York: F. S. Crofts.

Liberman, V., & Tversky, A. (1993). On the evaluation of probability judgments: Calibration, resolution, and monotonicity. *Psychological Bulletin, 114*, 162–173.

Longford, N. T., & Muthen, B. O. (1992). Factor analysis for clustered observations. *Psychometrika, 57*, 581–597.

Markham, S. E. (1988). Pay-for-performance dilemma revisited: Empirical example of the importance of group effects. *Journal of Applied Psychology, 73*, 172–180.

Markus, H. R., Kitayama, S., & Heiman, R. J. (1996). Culture and "basic" psychological principles.

In E. T. Higgins & A. W. Kruglanski (Eds.), *Social psychology: Handbook of basic principles* (pp. 857–913). Newbury Park, CA: Guilford Press.

McArdle, J. J., & Hamagami, F. (1996). Multilevel models from a multiple group structural equation perspective. In G. A. Marcoulides & R. E. Schumacker (Eds.), *Advanced structural equation modeling: Issues and techniques* (pp. 89–124). Hillsdale, NJ: Erlbaum.

McConnell, A. R., Sherman, S. J., & Hamilton, D. L. (1997). Target entitativity: Implications for information processing about individual and group targets. *Journal of Personality and Social Psychology, 72,* 750–762.

McDougall, W. (1920). *The group mind.* London: Cambridge University Press.

Mead, G. H. (1934). *Mind, self, and society.* Chicago: University of Chicago Press.

Milgram, S., & Toch, H. (1969). Collective behavior: Crowds and social movements. In G. Lindzey & E. Aronson (Eds.), *Handbook of social psychology* (2nd ed., Vol. 4, pp. 507–610). Reading, MA: Addison-Wesley.

Miller, D. T., & Prentice, D. A. (1996). The construction of social norms and standards. In E. T. Higgins & A. W. Kruglanski (Eds.), *Social psychology: Handbook of basic principles* (pp. 799–829). Newbury Park, CA: Guilford Press.

Mullen, B., & Copper, C. (1994). The relation between group cohesiveness and performance: An integration. *Psychological Bulletin, 115,* 210–227.

Murray, S. L., Holmes, J. G., & Griffin, D. W. (1996). The benefits of positive illusion: Idealization and the construction of satisfaction in close relationships. *Journal of Personality and Social Psychology, 70,* 79–98.

Muthen, B. O. (1994). Multilevel covariance structure analysis. *Sociological Methods & Research, 22,* 376–398.

Newcomb, T. M. (1961). *The acquaintance process.* New York: Holt, Rinehart, & Winston.

Newcomb, T. M., Turner, R. H., & Converse, P. E. (1965). *Social psychology: The study of human interaction.* New York: Holt, Rinehart, & Winston.

Pearson, K. (1901). Mathematical contributions to the theory of evolution ix. On the principle of homotyposis and its relation to heredity, to the variability of the individual, and to that of the race. *Philosophical Transactions of the Royal Society of London, Series A, 197,* 285–379.

Quine, W. (1960). *Word & object.* Cambridge MA: MIT Press.

Resnick, L. B., Levine, J. M., & Teasley, S. D. (1991). *Perspectives on socially shared cognition.* Washington, DC: American Psychological Association.

Robinson, W. S. (1950). Ecological correlations and the behavior of individuals. *American Sociological Review, 15,* 351–357.

Rumelhart, D. E., & McClelland, J. L. (1986). Pdp models and general issues in cognitive science. In *Parallel distributed processing: Explorations in the microstructure of cognition: Vol. 1: Foundations* (pp. 110–149). Cambridge, MA: MIT Press.

Rusbult, C. E., & Van Lange, P. A. (1996). Interdependence processes. In E. T. Higgins & A. W. Kruglanski (Eds.), *Social psychology: Handbook of basic principles* (pp. 564–596). Newbury Park, CA: Guilford Press.

Schachter, S., Ellertson, N., McBride, D., & Gregory, D. (1951). An experimental study of cohesiveness and productivity. *Human Relations, 4,* 229–238.

Schriesheim, C. A. (1995). Multivariate and moderated within- and between-entity analysis (waba) using hierarchical linear multiple regression. *Leadership Quarterly, 6,* 1–18.

Schwartz, S. (1994). The fallacy of the ecological fallacy: The potential misuse of a concept and the consequences. *American Journal of Public Health, 84,* 819–824.

Shaw, M. E. (1971). *Group dynamics: The psychology of small group behavior.* New York: McGraw-Hill.

Sherif, M. (1936). *The psychology of norms.* New York: Harper & Row.

Shrout, P. E., & Fleiss, J. L. (1979). Intraclass correlations: Uses in assessing rater reliability. *Psychological Bulletin, 86,* 420–428.

Simon, H. A. (1957). *Models of man.* New York: Wiley.

Stasser, G., Kerr, N., & Davis, J. (1980). Influence processes in decision-making groups: A modeling approach. In P. B. Paulus (Ed.), *Psychology of group influence* (pp. 431–477). Hillsdale, NJ: Erlbaum.

Stasser, G., & Titus, W. (1985). Pooling of unshared information in group decision making: Biased information sampling during discussion. *Journal of Personality and Social Psychology, 48*, 1467–1478.

Stinson, L., & Ickes, W. (1992). Empathic accuracy in the interactions of male friends versus male strangers. *Journal of Personality and Social Psychology, 62*, 787–797.

Suppes P., & Atkinson, R. C. (1960). *Markov learning models for multiperson interactions.* Stanford, CA: Stanford University Press.

Susser, M. (1994a). The logic in ecological: 1. the logic of analysis. *American Journal of Public Health, 84*, 825–829.

Susser, M. (1994b). The logic in ecological: 2. the logic of design. *American Journal of Public Health, 84*, 830–835.

Thibaut, J. W., & Kelley, H. H. (1959). *The social psychology of groups.* New York: Wiley.

Thomas, E. A. C., & Malone, T. W. (1979). On the dynamics of two-person interactions. *Psychological Review, 86*, 331–360.

Thomas, E. A. C., & Martin, J. A. (1976). Analyses of parent–infant interaction. *Psychological Bulletin, 83*, 141–156.

Turner, R. H., & Killian, L. M. (1957). *Collective behavior.* Englewood Cliffs, NJ: Prentice Hall.

Wasserman, S., & Faust, K. (1994). *Social network analysis: Methods and applications.* Cambridge, UK: Cambridge University Press.

Williams, K. D. (1997). Social ostracism. In R. M. Kowalski (Ed.), *Aversive interpersonal behaviors* (pp. 133–170). New York: Plenum.

Wilson, D. S., & Sober, E. (1994). Reintroducing group selection to the human behavioral sciences. *Behavioral and Brain Sciences, 17*, 585–654.

Zajonc, R. B. (1980). Feeling and thinking: Preferences need no inferences. *American Psychologist, 35*, 151–175.

PART VII

Applications

21 Attachment Style and Affect Regulation: Implications for Coping with
    Stress and Mental Health   537
    Mario Mikulincer and Victor Florian

22 Marital Therapy and Social Psychology: Will We Choose Explicit
    Partnership or Cryptomnesia?   558
    Steven R. H. Beach and Frank D. Fincham

Chapter Twenty-One

Attachment Style and Affect Regulation: Implications for Coping with Stress and Mental Health

Mario Mikulincer and Victor Florian

In contemporary social psychology, a wealth of theoretical and empirical work has been carried out in understanding the ways in which people regulate emotional distress, cope with stressful events, and maintain an adequate level of mental health. In this context, Bowlby's (1969, 1973, 1980) attachment theory appears to provide one of the best frameworks for examining individual differences and psychological processes related to the broad issue of affect regulation. In this chapter, we present our conceptualization of the attachment system as a psychoevolutionary affect regulation device and our view of adult attachment style as a basic source of individual differences in the use of specific regulatory strategies. Then we review the existing body of empirical knowledge, examining (1) the contribution of adult attachment style to the process of coping with stressful events and the management of negative emotions, and (2) the implications of attachment-style differences in affect regulation for mental health and psychopathology.

A Brief Introduction to Attachment Theory and Research

Bowlby's theory (1969, 1973) is based on three tenets. First, human infants are born with a repertoire of behaviors aimed at maintaining proximity to other persons, who help them to survive and provide a "secure base" for exploring the environment. Second, proximity maintenance also depends on the availability and responsivity of other persons to one's attachment needs. Third, experiences with significant others are internalized into mental working models of the world and the self and generalized to new relationships. Bowlby

(1988) suggested that these models are the building blocks of a person's attachment style – stable patterns of relational cognitions, emotions, and behaviors.

Following Bowlby's premises, Ainsworth, Blehar, Waters, and Wall (1978) delineated three prototypical attachment styles in infancy (secure, avoidant, and anxious-ambivalent), and Hazan and Shaver (1987) constructed a self-report scale tapping these styles in adulthood. Hazan and Shaver defined the secure style by comfort with closeness and confidence in others' responses; the avoidant style by insecurity in others' intentions and preference for distance; and the anxious-ambivalent style by insecurity in others' responses and a strong desire for intimacy. While secure people perceive others as a "secure base," avoidant and anxious-ambivalent people have serious doubts about others' responses in times of need.

Using self-reports of adult attachment style, extensive research has shown theoretically congruent attachment-style differences in the experience of love (e.g., Feeney & Noller, 1990; Kirkpatrick & Davis, 1994), marital relationships (e.g., Kobak & Hazan, 1991), self disclosure (Mikulincer & Nachshon, 1991), self-image (Mikulincer, 1995), and social perception (Collins, 1996). In this context, there is also evidence on the links between attachment style, affect regulation, and mental health. This is the main focus of the current chapter.

Attachment as an Affect Regulation System

Although Bowlby's theory mainly deals with developmental and interpersonal issues, the association between the attachment system, affect regulation, and mental health is one of the basic pillars of this theoretical framework. According to Bowlby (1969), attachment-related behaviors are organized around a psychoevolutionary affect regulation system. Attachment figures function as a haven of safety to which people can retreat for comfort and reassurance in times of stress. These figures also act as an "auxiliary ego" in managing distress and as a "secure base" from which people can develop their personality in an approving atmosphere. On this basis, proximity to significant others can be seen as an inborn affect regulation device, which allows people to manage distress with the assistance of others.

The affect regulation function of the attachment system is also highlighted by the fact that attachment theory was formulated in order to understand animal and human reactions to two major life stressors, loss and separation (Bowlby, 1969, 1973, 1980). Overall, Bowlby (1973) proposed that the attachment system functions as a protective mechanism, which is activated when the individual experiences distress. In his view, the goal of attachment responses is to maintain proximity to a significant other, who may assist the person in the process of managing distress and may promote a sense of well-being and security.

The link between the activation of the attachment system and distress arousal led Bowlby to suggest that basic emotions are constructed around attachment experiences. In his terms, the activation of the attachment system usually goes together with anxiety and anger, which are adaptive signals that something is going wrong and some coping action should be taken (Bowlby, 1973). Moreover, the deactivation of this system following distress management may elicit relief, positive feelings, and gratitude toward significant others. If, however, the significant others fail to manage distress, anxiety and anger may become chronic and may lead to a sense of helplessness and detachment. Furthermore, attachment relationships may become by themselves an additional source of distress (Bowlby, 1973, 1988).

On this basis, one can claim that attachment experiences play a major role in determining the habitual affective tone of a person's inner world. On the one hand, interactions with significant others who are available and responsive to one's attachment needs may lead to the experience of more and longer episodes of positive affect, the development of positive feelings toward the world and the self, and the appraisal of anxiety and anger as valued signals for restoring well being. On the other hand, interactions with unavailable and rejecting others may elicit chronic distress, dysfunctional experiences of anxiety and anger, and may create problems around attachment themes.

Bowlby's premises also imply that attachment experiences may be viewed as a major source of individual differences in the way people regulate distress and cope with life adversities. Interactions with available and responsive others may signal that the inborn attachment system is an effective method of affect regulation and may lead people to continue to rely on this system when facing distress and other life problems. In contrast, when people perceive significant others as unavailable and unresponsive, they may learn that inborn attachment behaviors fail to bring the expected relief and that other defensive strategies should be developed and employed. According to Bowlby (1988), these strategies replace the original attachment system. However, they lack the backing of a secure base and the hope that one can rely on the support of significant others.

On this basis, we claim that a basic component of a person's attachment style is the habitual regulatory strategies he or she employs in coping with different sources of distress. The basic hypothesis here is that people differing in attachment style would differ in the strategies of affect regulation they employ while facing stress. These strategies would shape the management of negative emotions and coping with life stressors, and would have meaningful repercussions on the individual's mental health.

The positive attachment experiences of secure persons may create the basis for the formation of a salutatory pattern of reality appraisal. These persons may find out that distress is manageable and external obstacles can be overcome. Moreover, they may learn about the good intentions of others in times of need and about the control they can exert over the course and outcomes of external events. In this way, secure persons could develop optimistic beliefs regarding distress management, a sense of trust in others' responses, and a sense of self-efficacy in dealing with distress (Shaver & Hazan, 1993).

The experience of significant others as a "secure base" also may set the basis for the construction of effective distress management strategies (Mikulincer & Florian, 1998). First, secure persons may find out that acknowledgment and display of distress elicit positive responses from significant others. Second, they learn that their own active responses are instrumental means for bringing relief and managing distress. Third, they may become aware that seeking for the support of others is an effective way of coping. In this way, secure persons would be prone to regulate affect through the basic guidelines of the attachment system: acknowledgment and display of distress, engagement in instrumental actions, and support seeking (Kobak, Cole, Ferenz, & Fleming, 1993; Kobak & Sceery, 1988; Mikulincer & Florian, 1998; Rholes, Simpson, & Grich-Stevens, 1998).

Another important aspect of secure attachment is the construction of reality-tuned affect regulation strategies. Secure people's belief in their skills for dealing with stress may lead them to open themselves to new, even threatening, information (Mikulincer, 1997), and then to develop suitable strategies for dealing with environmental demands. Moreover, their experience of attachment figures as approving may allow them to revise erroneous beliefs without fear of criticism or rejection (Mikulincer, 1997). In this way, secure people could avoid cognitive entrapments derived from the inability to revise these beliefs.

In the case of insecure attachment, the negative and painful experiences with significant others may hinder the normal activation of the attachment system and lead to the adoption of less effective ways of affect regulation (Bowlby, 1988). However, although both insecure types may hold a negative appraisal of reality (Collins, 1996; Collins & Read, 1990), they seem to differ in the ways they manage distress (Kobak et al., 1993; Mikulincer & Florian, 1998; Shaver & Hazan, 1993). In fact, Ainsworth's attachment typology already implies the existence of two antagonistic coping responses. On the one hand, people characterized by the avoidant style appear to adopt a "flight" response in dealing with the unavailability of significant others. On the another hand, people characterized by the anxious-ambivalent style seem to "fight" to elicit others' love, compassion, and support.

The "flight" response of avoidant persons seems to have two facets (Kobak et al., 1993; Mikulincer, 1998; Mikulincer, Orbach, & Iavnieli, 1998). One includes defensive attempts to "deactivate" the attachment system in order to avoid confrontation with attachment related distress (Fraley & Shaver, 1997). These attempts include cognitive and behavioral distancing from others' lack of involvement and interdependence in close relationships, and denial of attachment needs. The second facet consists of compulsive attempts to attain self-reliance (Bowlby, 1973, 1988). Due to the deactivation of the attachment system, avoidant persons may remain without a "secure base." As a result, they may search for comfort within their selves and may believe that they can rely only on themselves in times of need. This facet also involves pursuit of autonomy, control, and individuality as well as avoidance of situations in which they would need others' help.

In our terms, the way avoidant persons deal with attachment insecurity would be generalized to the management of other sources of distress. Their tendency to detach from negative attachment figures would, in general, result in behavioral and cognitive distancing from distress-related cues (Kobak et al., 1993; Mikulincer & Florian, 1998). Moreover, their pursuit of self-reliance may lead them to suppress personal imperfections and weaknesses as a way of preventing the recognition that their own self is a source of distress (Mikulincer, 1998a). As a result, avoidant people would restrict awareness of self-aspects that they do not want to possess, suppress bad thoughts and emotions, inhibit displays of distress, repress painful memories, and attempt to escape from any confrontation with life problems (Mikulincer & Florian, 1998; Shaver & Hazan, 1993).

The way anxious-ambivalent people deal with insecurity implies an "hyperactivation" of the attachment system (Kobak et al., 1993). They attempt to minimize distance from distressing attachment figures and to maximize the "secure base" they can obtain (Mikulincer et al., 1998). This is a "fight" strategy aimed at eliciting others' positive affect and responses via clinging, controlling, and hypervigilant responses. The problem with this strategy is that it may create excessive anxious focus on attachment-related distress and may lead to preoccupation with relationships, anxious demands for proximity, conflictual feelings toward others, fear of rejection, and inability to leave frustrating partners (Brennan & Shaver, 1995; Hazan & Shaver, 1987; Shaver & Hazan, 1993).

In our terms, anxious-ambivalent persons' excessive focus on attachment-related distress would result, in general, in a hyperactivation of distress-related cues. This hyperactivation may lead people to direct attention to distress in a hypervigilant manner, to mentally ruminate on its causes and meanings, and to deliberate on related negative thoughts, memories, and emotions. As a result, anxious-ambivalent persons would have free access to negative emotions and thoughts, would be unable or unwilling to suppress these negative inner experiences, and therefore might become overwhelmed with negative feelings about the self and the world (Mikulincer, 1998).

According to the above reasoning, secure attachment can be viewed as an inner psychological resource and a resilience factor, which may foster a constructive attitude toward life and buffer the psychological distress resulting from the encounter with stressful events. In contrast, insecure attachment can be viewed as a risk factor, which may increase a person's vulnerability while facing stress and may obstruct the development of the inner resources necessary for coping with life stressors and maintaining psychological well-being.

With regard to anxious-ambivalent persons, their regulatory strategies may lead to an exaggeration of the appraisal of adversities as irreversible and uncontrollable and may impair the ability to control the arousal and spreading of distress throughout the cognitive system. As a result, anxious-ambivalent persons may experience an endless and uncontrollable flow of negative affect, which, in turn, may lead to cognitive disorganization and fragmentation and may, in certain cases, culminate in psychopathology (Shaver & Hazan, 1993). In the case of avoidant persons, their regulatory strategies may emphasize the need to rely exclusively on oneself and the maintenance of distance from attachment and distress cues. Although these strategies may reduce overt expressions of distress, they may be unable in the long run to mitigate internalized sources of insecurity and may be shattered upon confrontation with severe and persistent problems.

In the rest of this chapter, we review data on (1) the way attachment-related regulatory strategies are manifested in the process of coping with life stressors as well as in the management of emotions, and (2) the repercussions of these strategies on mental health. Most of the reviewed studies have assessed attachment style via self-report scales (e.g., Hazan & Shaver's Adult Attachment Scale), which have been developed within a personality and social psychology context and tap current attachment to significant others. However, there are some studies that have used the Adult Attachment Interview (Main, Kaplan, & Cassidy, 1985), which is derived from a developmental perspective and taps a person's state of mind regarding attachment to parents. Importantly, despite these conceptual and methodological differences, similar and coherent patterns of associations between attachment style, coping, and mental health were found in studies using either self-report scales or the Adult Attachment Interview.

Adult Attachment Style and Coping with Life Stressors

In this section, we present empirical data on attachment-style differences in the process of coping with life stressors. Although this process has been analyzed from a wide variety of theoretical and empirical perspectives, Lazarus and Folkman's (1984) theoretical framework has become during the last decade the most prominent model for conceptualizing coping and stress. In this model, coping responses are sorted into the following four categories: problem-focused coping, emotion-focused coping, distancing coping, and support seeking.

(1)   Problem-focused coping attempts to channel resources to solve the stress-inducing problem. It consists of a vast array of cognitive and behavioral maneuvers aimed at making changes in the environment and eliminating the external sources of stress. For example, Carver, Scheier, and Weintraub (1989) mentioned four basic problem-focused coping strategies: (1) active coping – procedures to remove obstacles from one's goals; (2) planning – thinking about action strategies and about how to solve the problem; (3) suppression of competing activities – disengagement from other goals and activities that may divert resources away from problem solving; and (4) restraint – holding back actions and avoiding premature decisions. There is extensive evidence that problem-focused coping has beneficial adaptive outcomes (e.g., Epstein & Meier, 1989; McCrae & Costa, 1986).

(2)   Emotion-focused coping attempts to ease inner tension without trying to solve the distress-eliciting problem. It consists of cognitive strategies aimed at understanding and alleviating distress, such as self-preoccupation, self-criticism, mental rumination on distress-related feelings and thoughts, affect amplification, overt displays of distress, and wishful thinking. There is extensive evidence documenting the negative adaptive outcomes of emotion-focused coping, mainly when the stressful situation can be ended by problem-focused responses (e.g., McCrae & Costa, 1984; Mikulincer, 1994). Although emotion-focused coping may help in maintaining emotional balance, an adaptive response still requires active attempts to solve the problem.

(3)   Distancing coping seems to encompass two types of strategies. First, cognitive maneuvers aimed at preventing the intrusion of threatening thoughts into consciousness, such as suppression of painful emotions and thoughts and repression of painful memories (e.g., Carver et al., 1989; Lazarus & Folkman, 1984). Second, behavioral disengagement from the stressful situation by either withdrawing problem-focused efforts or consuming drugs and alcohol (e.g., Carver et al., 1989; Stone & Neale, 1984). Although distancing coping strategies may initially have beneficial adaptive outcomes, in the long run they may have detrimental adaptive effects (Lazarus, 1983; Roth & Cohen, 1986).

(4)   Support seeking consists of responses aimed at maintaining or restoring proximity to a significant other who can help us in coping with stress. According to Lazarus and Folkman (1984), this coping category includes the seeking of love, reassurance, and affection; the search for information, advice, and/or feedback; and the seeking of material aid and services. There is extensive evidence on the positive adaptive outcomes of support seeking (Lazarus & Folkman, 1984).

In examining the above four categories of coping responses, Folkman and Lazarus (1985) developed a self-report scale – the Ways of Coping Checklist, which has been used in hundred of studies around the world. This scale includes items assessing problem-focused coping (e.g., "I try to analyze the problem in order to understand it better"), emotion-focused coping (e.g., "I wish I could change how I feel," "I criticize myself"), distancing coping (e.g., "I try to forget the whole thing"), and support seeking (e.g., "I talk to someone to find out more about the situation"), which can be tailored to specific stressful events. In all the studies we review below, a person's coping responses were assessed through the Ways of Coping Checklist.

In integrating Lazarus and Folkman's (1984) ways of coping with our analysis of attachment-related regulatory strategies, one can easily predict how these strategies would be manifested in the way people cope with life adversities. Secure persons' constructive and optimistic attitude toward life problems would lead them to try to remove the source of stress by employing problem-focused coping strategies and/or by seeking the support of relevant others. Whereas avoidant persons' deactivating strategy would lead them to rely on cognitive and behavioral distancing ways of coping, anxious-ambivalent persons' hyperactivating strategy would lead them to ruminate on their emotional state and then to adopt emotion-focused ways of coping. Moreover, one can predict that the two insecure styles would be reluctant to seek support due to their basic mistrust of others' intentions and responses (Collins, 1996; Shaver & Hazan, 1993). In examining these predictions, we would review studies which have been conducted on three major life areas: coping with military and war-related stressors, coping with pregnancy and motherhood, and coping with separation and loss.

Ways of coping with military and war-related stress

Three major studies have examined the role of attachment style in explaining coping responses to military and war-related stressful events. One study dealt with the reactions of young adults to the stressful experience of Iraqi Scud missile attacks on Israeli cities during the Gulf War (Mikulincer, Florian, & Weller, 1993). Some 140 Israeli university students who lived in cities that either were or were not attacked by missiles were approached two weeks after the end of the Gulf War. They completed the adult attachment style scale (Hazan & Shaver, 1987) and the Ways of Coping Checklist (Folkman & Lazarus, 1985), which was adapted to ways of coping with the missile attacks.

The findings supported the hypothesis that attachment style is a useful construct for explaining individual differences in coping with the missile attack. Secure persons reported having sought more support from relevant others during the missile attacks than insecure persons. Anxious-ambivalent persons were found to report heightened reliance on emotion-focused coping (e.g., ruminating on their own distress, wondering why this happened to them), whereas avoidant persons were found to report heightened reliance on distancing coping (e.g., dismissing the immediate threat, avoiding thinking about their own distress or about the implications of the missile attack).

In another relevant study, Mikulincer and Florian (1995) examined the reactions of young Israeli recruits undergoing a four-month combat training. One should be aware that soldiers who undergo combat training are exposed to stressful experiences, such as long periods of physical exercise and short periods of sleep. Ninety-two young Israeli recruits completed the adult attachment style scale (Hazan & Shaver, 1987) at the beginning of the training. Four months later (one week before ending this training), they completed Folkman and Lazarus's (1985) appraisal and coping measures regarding their current experiences.

The findings partially replicated Mikulincer et al.'s (1993) findings. As expected, anxious-ambivalent soldiers reported more emotion-focused strategies than secure soldiers, and avoidant soldiers reported more distancing coping. However, both secure and anxious-ambivalent persons reported seeking more support than avoidant persons. It may be that anxious-ambivalent persons seek support mainly when they are in intensive inter-actions with peers who experience the same stress, like combat training. In this case, the sharing of stress with their peers may allow anxious-ambivalent soldiers to talk freely about their worries without feeling any fear of being misunderstood, criticized, or rejected, and, then, to seek social support. In fact, one of the reasons that inhibits anxious-ambivalent persons from support seeking is the fear that others would discover and criticize their helplessness.

The findings also revealed attachment-style differences in the cognitive appraisal of combat training. In line with their basic optimistic attitude, secure soldiers appraised the training in more challenging terms, and appraised themselves as capable of coping with it. In con-trast, anxious-ambivalent soldiers appraised the training in more threatening terms and reported a sense of personal inadequacy in dealing with it. This pessimistic pattern may reflect the hyperactivation of the distress cues that anxious-ambivalent soldiers encounter during the combat training. Quite interestingly, avoidant soldiers also appraised the train-ing in threatening terms, but revealed a sense of personal adequacy in dealing with it. This pattern of appraisal may reflect two conflictual facets of avoidant persons' way of affect regulation: their basic insecurity and the compensatory belief in their own self-reliance and personal strength.

In a more recent study, Solomon, Ginzburg, Mikulincer, Neria, and Ohry (1998) ex-amined the association between attachment style of ex-prisoners of war (POWs) and their retrospective accounts of the experience of captivity. Some 164 Israeli ex-POWs of the Yom Kippur War were interviewed 18 years after the war about their personal recollection of the captivity period and completed the adult attachment style scale (Hazan & Shaver, 1987). A content analysis of the ex-POWs' retrospective accounts revealed interesting dif-ferences among attachment styles. Compared to insecure ex-POWs, secure ex-POWs re-ported lower levels of suffering, less helplessness, they felt less abandoned and less hostile toward the army, and relied on more active coping strategies. It is important to note that secure ex-POWs reported having dealt with the helpless nature of captivity by recruiting positive memories or imaginary encounters with others, which may have created a sense of security and served as positive coping models.

The negative experience of insecure ex-POWs seemed to reflect their habitual regula-tory strategies. The suffering of anxious-ambivalent ex-POWs was mainly characterized by feelings of abandonment and loss of control, which may reflect their preoccupation with rejection. The negative experience of avoidant ex-POWs was characterized by hostile feel-ings and reactions toward the army, which can be viewed as a manifestation of their basic mistrust toward non-supportive others.

Ways of coping with pregnancy and motherhood

In the process of becoming a mother, women are exposed to pleasant and challenging experiences together with episodes of worries, anxieties, and uncertainties. In this subsection, we review a series of recent studies dealing with the possible impact of women's attachment style on the ways of coping with several aspects of their motherhood.

A study conducted by Mikulincer and Florian (1999) focused on the process of coping with pregnancy-related stress. In this study, a sample of first-time pregnant Israeli women (N = 30), previously classified according to their attachment style, were followed up during the first, second, and third trimesters of pregnancy. In each one of the trimesters, women answered a self-report scale on their attachment to the fetus (Cranley, 1981) and completed the Ways of Coping Checklist (Folkman & Lazarus, 1985), which was adapted to pregnancy-related problems. The findings indicated that anxious-ambivalent women reported having relied on more emotion-focused coping in dealing with pregnancy-related stress than avoidant and secure women. In addition, avoidant women were found to rely on more distancing coping than secure women, whereas secure women were found to seek more support than other women. It is worth noting that these differences were replicated in the three stages of pregnancy. This finding emphasizes the stable nature of the ways by which each attachment style coped with the demands of pregnancy.

The psychological literature has documented the demands and pressures that the delivery of a newborn may impose on the mother's well-being (e.g., Power & Parke, 1984; Terry, 1991). In a recent chapter, Mikulincer and Florian (1998) cited a study of 80 healthy young women who delivered their first child 2–3 months before the study. All the women completed the adult attachment style scale (Hazan & Shaver, 1987) and Lazarus and Folkman's (1984) appraisal scale, tapping the way they appraised motherhood, and the Ways of Coping Checklist (Folkman & Lazarus, 1985), tapping the strategies they used to deal with motherhood-related tasks. Again, results were in line with the hypothesized strategies of affect regulation that characterize each attachment style. Specifically, secure women appraised the task of being a mother in less threatening terms than anxious-ambivalent women, and reported having used more problem-focused strategies in coping with motherhood tasks. However, the findings did not support the hypothesis that secure persons are more likely to seek support than insecure persons. Interestingly, this is one of the few studies that failed to find the expected attachment-style differences in support seeking. One can only speculate that secure women in Mikulincer and Florian's (1998) study were so engaged in problem-focused activities that they did not feel any urge to seek support and help.

At this point, one may wonder how mothers differing in attachment style react to the birth of an infant who suffers from a physical, life-threatening illness. In an attempt to provide some initial empirical answers to this question, Berant (1998) designed a field study examining the association between the attachment style of mothers of infants with congenital heart disease (CHD) and the pattern of cognitive appraisal and coping with the task of motherhood. In this study, three groups were approached around three months after the birth of an infant: (1) a group of 46 mothers of healthy infants, (2) a group of 53 mothers of infants who had been diagnosed by physicians two weeks previously as suffering from mild CHD, and (3) a group of 47 mothers of infants who had been diagnosed two weeks before as suffering from severe, life-threatening CHD. All the mothers completed the adult attachment style scale (Hazan & Shaver, 1987) and Folkman & Lazarus's (1985) scales tapping appraisal of and coping with motherhood-related tasks.

Whereas the findings regarding cognitive appraisal in the control group were similar to those reported by Mikulincer and Florian (1998), attachment-style differences in appraisal were somewhat different in the two other groups. Among mothers of infants with mild CHD, secure and avoidant mothers appraised motherhood tasks in less threatening terms and themselves as having more control over these tasks than anxious-ambivalent mothers. However, among mothers of infants with severe CHD, only those with secure attachment still viewed their condition as manageable and themselves as capable of coping with it. Both avoidant and anxious-ambivalent mothers appraised their plight as more threatening and viewed themselves as less able to deal with it.

It seems that secure mothers could maintain a positive appraisal even after encountering a severe stressful situation, maintaining a sense of mastery in dealing with the special demands imposed by motherhood. In contrast, anxious-ambivalent mothers showed a basic negative appraisal of their motherhood even when the infant's health condition was not severe. Interestingly, avoidant mothers seem to be the most affected by the infant's medical condition: while they showed a positive appraisal of their motherhood when their infant suffered from mild CHD, they revealed a more pessimistic appraisal when their infant was diagnosed as having a severe, life-threatening problem.

The findings also showed that the three attachment groups differed in the ways in which they coped with motherhood tasks and that these differences depended on the infant's health condition. Secure mothers of both healthy infants and infants having mild CHD tended to rely on support-seeking strategies in coping with motherhood tasks. However, when their infant had severe CHD, secure mothers tended to cope with these tasks by relying on both support-seeking and distancing strategies (e.g., mental suppression of painful thoughts and feelings about the infant's CHD, engagement in distracting thoughts unrelated to the infant's health). The findings are in line with the hypothesis that support seeking is the basic regulatory strategy of secure attachment. They also imply that secure mothers can flexibly employ distancing coping whenever thoughts about the stressful condition can impair functioning and well-being, as in the case of a real threat to the infant's life.

It may be that the suppression of painful thoughts and feelings about the infant's CHD, which was found to be positively associated with the mother's mental health (Berant, 1998), might have provided a moratorium until mothers could grasp the meaning of their predicament. Moreover, this coping strategy may prevent secure mothers from being occupied or preoccupied with pessimistic and distressing thoughts, and, then, may allow them to maintain a positive appraisal of motherhood. As a result, the overwhelming demands of the infant's illness may not discourage secure mothers. Rather, they may be able to mobilize internal and external resources for caring for the baby without feeling any interfering intrusion of negative thoughts.

With regard to anxious-ambivalent mothers, their ways of coping directly reflected their hyperactivating regulatory strategies. In all the three research groups, these mothers reported heightened reliance on emotion-focused strategies and tended to mentally ruminate on their condition regardless of the objective health status of their infants. With regard to avoidant mothers, their habitual deactivating regulatory strategies were only manifested when infants were healthy or had mild CHD. In these cases, they reported heightened reliance on distancing strategies. However, the reported frequency of these strategies was reduced when avoidant mothers had to face an infant's severe health condition. Here, these mothers, like anxious-ambivalent mothers, reported heightened reliance on emotion-focused coping strategies.

The above findings may reflect the fragile nature of the "pseudo-safe" world of avoidant persons. Their habitual confident appraisal of coping abilities and their reliance on distancing coping seems to be sufficient when dealing with daily hassles or minor stressors. However, when facing uncontrollable and persisting stressors, this facade may fade out and the basic insecurity of avoidant persons may become overtly manifested, leading to pessimistic appraisals and the adoption of more ineffective ways of coping.

Ways of coping with interpersonal loss

In the third volume of his classic trilogy, Bowlby (1980) suggested that when people feel that their attachment figures are lost, they may experience an upsurge of attachment needs and their regulatory strategies may be activated in order to adjust to the painful condition. The above ideas were recently examined by Unger (1998), who interviewed 93 middle-aged women who had lost their husband two to five years before. These women filled out the adult attachment style scale (Hazan & Shaver, 1987) and Folkman and Lazarus's (1985) scales tapping cognitive appraisal and coping with widowhood. Findings indicated that secure attachment was significantly related to higher appraisal of one's ability to deal with widowhood and more frequent reliance on problem-focused coping and distancing strategies. Anxious-ambivalent attachment was significantly related to higher appraisal of widowhood in threatening terms, lower appraisal of one's ability to deal with it, and more frequent reliance on emotion-focused coping strategies. The avoidant style was significantly related only to a more frequent reliance on emotion-focused strategies.

It is worth noting that the above pattern of findings is quite similar to that found by Berant (1998). It may be that when facing a severe real-life crisis related to the potential or actual loss of a loved person (e.g., child, spouse), both problem-solving and distancing strategies serve as protective mechanisms, which allow the securely attached person to maintain an adequate level of functioning despite the traumatic circumstances. In contrast, it seems that when encountering a potential or actual loss, avoidant persons' habitual use of repression and suppression is impaired, and they may be driven to focus on their own negative emotions like anxious-ambivalent persons.

The above attachment-style differences also have been found in the emotional and cognitive reactions to another life crisis related to separation and loss – divorce (Birnbaum, Orr, Mikulincer, & Florian, 1997). A sample of 123 Israeli individuals who were involved in a long process of divorce were interviewed in the waiting rooms of the rabbinic divorce court. They filled out the adult attachment style scale (Hazan & Shaver, 1987) and reported on how they appraised and coped with the stressful experience of the divorce. As expected, secure persons appraised themselves as more capable of coping with the divorce and appraised this crisis in less threatening terms than anxious-ambivalent persons. Moreover, anxious-ambivalent persons reported more social withdrawal and more self-defeating thoughts in coping with divorce than secure persons. However, unexpectedly, avoidant persons tended to resemble anxious-ambivalent persons in the way they appraised and coped with the divorce crisis. Specifically, they appraised divorce in more threatening terms and reported more self-defeating thoughts and social withdrawal in coping with it than secure persons.

Secure persons, who handle separations constructively and learn that separation is a solvable episode, seem to react to the reconstruction of this experience as it reappears in the process of divorce with their habitual optimistic and constructive attitudes. In contrast, anxious ambivalent persons tended to appraise divorce as a threat and themselves as being unable to deal with the crisis, and tended to rely on their habitual hyperactivating strategies. Interestingly, the observed reactions of avoidant persons imply that their habitual deactivating strategies prove to be again ineffective in dealing with separation and loss. Divorce may reactivate early unresolved separations from attachment figures and lead to a flood of overwhelming negative feelings, which avoidant persons fail to repress.

Summary

The reviewed data clearly indicate that people varying in attachment style differ in the way they habitually cope with acute and chronic life stressors. Moreover, findings show that these differences seem to be a direct manifestation of the hypothesized regulatory strategies that characterize each attachment style. Findings also indicate that whereas secure and anxious-ambivalent persons' strategies seem to be stable across different levels of stress intensity, avoidant persons' strategies seem to fade under severe stressful circumstances. In these conditions, avoidant persons resemble anxious-ambivalent persons in their reliance on emotion-focused coping. Findings also provide initial evidence about the flexibility and richness of secure persons' ways of coping under severe and persistent stressful events.

Adult Attachment Style and the Management of Negative Emotions

Another hypothesis derived from our conceptualization of attachment-related regulatory strategies is that attachment style would be related to the way people process emotions. On the one hand, secure people would acknowledge negative emotions without being overwhelmed by them and show easy accessibility and well-elaborated processing of them. On the another hand, avoidant people would repress negative emotions and show low accessibility and poor processing of them. For anxious-ambivalent persons, their tendency to ruminate mentally on negative emotional states may prevent the use of repression and increase the chronic accessibility of emotional states as well as the likelihood of experiencing different emotions together. This coping strategy may facilitate the creation of associative links between distinct emotions in the semantic memory network, so that the arousal of one emotion could easily activate other associated emotions. As a result, anxious-ambivalent persons' experience of one particular emotion would be automatically followed by the activation of other emotional states.

In examining the above ideas, Mikulincer and Orbach (1995) conducted a study on the processing of negative emotional memories. Participants completed the adult attachment style scale (Hazan & Shaver, 1987), the Crowne-Marlowe social desirability scale tapping defensiveness and the Taylor Anxiety Scale. People also were asked to recall early experiences in which they felt anger, sadness, anxiety, and happiness, and the time for retrieving a memory was taken as a measure of cognitive accessibility. Then people rated the intensity of dominant and nondominant emotions in each recalled event.

The findings fit the above hypothesis. Avoidant and secure persons scored higher in defensiveness than anxious-ambivalent persons, and the two insecure groups scored higher in anxiety than secure people. That is, while anxious-ambivalent people hyperactivated anxiety and failed to defend themselves against it, avoidant people repress negative thoughts but failed to reduce anxiety, and secure persons were able to defend themselves with minimal anxiety. In the memory task, avoidant people showed the lowest accessibility (highest reaction time) to sadness and anxiety memories, anxious-ambivalent people showed the highest, and secure people were in between them. In addition, anxious-ambivalent people were rated as having experienced stronger emotions in sadness and anxiety memories than avoidant persons. As expected, avoidant persons had difficulties in accessing negative memories and those recalled were characterized by emotional shallowness. In contrast, due to the hyperactivation of distress cues, anxious-ambivalent people had easy accessibility to negative memories and to their related emotions.

The emotional architecture of secure persons' memories indicated a highly differentiated pattern: they rated dominant emotions (sadness in a sad memory) as highly intense and nondominant emotions (anger in a sad memory) as far less intense. These persons may acknowledge distress while controlling for its spreading to other emotions. Anxious-ambivalent people revealed a non-differentiated emotional architecture: They rated both dominant and non-dominant emotions as highly intense. These persons seem to be unable or unwilling to limit the spreading of distress to other emotions. In contrast, avoidant people rated both dominant and nondominant emotions as far less intense than secure persons. As expected, avoidant people inhibited the processing of negative memories and the spreading of the dominant emotional tone.

Following the same line of research, Mikulincer (1998b) conducted two studies dealing with the experience of anger. In Study 1, participants completed the adult attachment style scale (Hazan & Shaver, 1987) and the Multidimensional Anger Inventory (Siegel, 1986) tapping anger-proneness, hostility, mental rumination over anger feelings (anger-in), and overt expression of anger (anger-out). They also completed the Experience of Anger Scale (Averill, 1982). People recalled an anger event and reported the control they exerted over anger as well as goals (constructive, malevolent), responses (adaptive, escapist, aggressive), and emotions they felt in that episode (positive, negative).

Findings indicated that anxious-ambivalent persons scored higher in anger proneness, anger-in, and displaced aggression than other persons; avoidant persons reported higher hostility and more escapist responses; and secure persons scored higher in anger-out, constructive goals, adaptive responses, and positive affect. Moreover, secure and avoidant people reported more anger control than anxious-ambivalent persons.

In Study 2, participants were exposed to hypothetical anger-eliciting scenarios differing in the intentions of a romantic partner: hostile, ambiguous, non-hostile. Then they rated their anger feelings and the extent to which partners were hostile. In addition, data were collected on changes in heart rate (a sign of physiological arousal).

Overall, anxious-ambivalent persons reported more anger than other persons, and anxious-ambivalent and avoidant people showed higher heart rate changes and higher hostility attributions than secure people. However, while avoidant persons showed relatively high hostility attributions and low anger in the three scenarios, secure persons reacted with more hostility attribution and anger to the hostile scene than to the other scenes. Anxious-ambivalent persons reacted with more hostility attribution and anger to hostile and ambiguous scenes.

Taken as a whole, secure persons' experience of anger fits the guidelines of the attachment system: they acknowledged physiological signs of anger, adopted constructive goals aimed at repairing the relationship with the anger instigator, engaged in adaptive problem-solving actions, expressed anger outward in a controlled and non-hostile way, and experienced positive affect. In addition, they tended to attribute hostility to another person only when there were clear contextual cues. That is, for these persons, anger arousal seems to depend on a rational analysis of the situation and it seems to be a trigger for adaptive and constructive actions.

The anger experience of anxious-ambivalent people may result from their hyperactivating strategy: they tended to report high levels of anger-proneness and to react with strong anger feelings. This strategy also was manifested in the tendency of anxious-ambivalent persons to ruminate on anger feelings, to allow uncontrollable access to anger and negative affect, and to appraise ambiguous stimuli as hostile. As a result, anger may become an interfering emotion, which may overwhelm the cognitive system and draw resources away from adaptive actions.

Avoidant persons' deactivating strategy seems to produce dissociated anger. While avoidant persons did not report intense anger, they still revealed intense physiological signs of anger, intense hostility, and an undifferentiated tendency to attribute hostility to other persons. A dissociated attitude was also manifested in avoidant persons' tendency to enact escapist responses, which diffuse the conscious experience of anger feelings without solving the problem that elicited the anger. These attempts may leave avoidant persons unaware of their own anger, full of paranoid suspicions and hostile feelings, and unable to reduce tension.

Adult Attachment Style, Mental Health, and Psychopathology

Bowlby (1973, 1988) has emphasized the important role of the attachment system for the normal and abnormal development of personality and social behavior. Fitting these ideas, several studies have reported consistent associations between adult attachment style and mental health (e.g., Brennan, Shaver, & Tobey, 1991; Brennan & Shaver, 1995; Mickelson, Kessler, & Shaver, 1997). In all these studies, secure attachment seems to be a crucial inner resource that facilitates adjustment and well-being, whereas insecure attachment seems to act as a risk factor for the development of distress and maladjustment. In this section, we review empirical data that examine the various facets of the attachment–mental health association.

Adult attachment style and psychological well-being

In a series of studies conducted in our laboratory, we have assessed the association between attachment style and mental health in different populations (Berant, 1998; Birnbaum et al., 1997; Mikulincer & Florian, 1998, 1999; Unger, 1998). In all these studies, we have employed a well-validated measure of mental health: the Mental Health Inventory (MHI, Veit & Ware, 1983). This scale taps two separate, but related, facets of mental health (psychological well-being and psychological distress), and possesses a robust psychometric basis (Veit & Ware, 1983). Specifically, it includes 14 items tapping psychological well-being (e.g., life satisfaction, engagement in enjoyable activities) and 24 which tap psychological distress (e.g., sadness, nervousness).

Without exception, all the above studies have shown that secure attachment is positively associated with well-being and negatively related to distress. In contrast, anxious-ambivalent attachment reveals an inverse relationship with well-being and a positive association with distress. These associations have been found both in so-called "normal" community samples and in samples of people who were under stressful conditions that demanded immediate readjustment (e.g., divorce, the birth of an infant suffering from CHD, widowhood). They have been also found in both cross-sectional and longitudinal prospective designs.

Avoidant attachment seemed to have differential associations with mental health, depending on the presence of stressful circumstances. Most of the above studies have found no significant association between avoidant attachment and mental health in community samples. However, under stressful circumstances, avoidant attachment has been found to be inversely related to well-being and positively associated with distress. In one longitudinal study assessing the mental health of mothers whose babies were born with severe CHD (Berant, 1998), avoidant attachment (measured immediately following the diagnosis of the dysfunction) was more strongly related to high psychological distress (measured one year later) than anxious-ambivalent attachment.

The above pattern of findings seems to be in line with previously reviewed findings on avoidant persons' ways of coping with stressful events. In normal circumstances, the deactivation strategy of these people seems to help them to maintain adequate levels of well-being. However, under persistent stressful conditions, this strategy seems to collapse and avoidant persons tend to reveal similar patterns of coping and distress to anxious-ambivalent persons.

Two studies also provide initial support for the hypothesis that attachment-style differences in mental health may result from the activation of habitual regulatory strategies (Berant, 1998; Birnbaum et al., 1997). In these studies, structural analyses have shown that the association between attachment styles and mental health under stressful circumstances was mediated by cognitive appraisal and ways of coping. Specifically, security in attachment was associated with less distress and more well-being via the high appraisal of one's ability to cope with the stressor and a tendency to rely on support seeking. Avoidant attachment was associated with more distress via the appraisal of the stressful circumstance in threatening terms and reliance on more emotion-focused coping. Anxious-ambivalent attachment was related to more distress via the low appraisal of one's abilities to cope with the stressor and reliance on more emotion-focused coping.

Adult attachment style and affective disorders

Several studies have documented a consistent pattern of relationship between attachment style and depressive symptomatology. In a series of studies, Kobak and his colleagues (Cole-

Detke & Kobak, 1996; Kobak & Ferenz-Gillies, 1995; Kobak, Sudler, & Gamble, 1991) assessed attachment styles and regulatory strategies, using the Adult Attachment Interview (Main et al., 1985), and measured depressive symptoms in adolescents. Findings indicated that anxious-ambivalent attachment was positively associated with the report of depressive symptoms. This was replicated in cross-sectional and prospective analyses. Accordingly, the more the adolescent relied on hyperactivation strategies of affect regulation, the more depressive symptoms they tended to report. Findings also indicated that depressive symptoms in adolescence were positively related to cognitive and behavioral aspects of the anxious-ambivalent style, such as appraisal of mothers as unavailable, expressions of anger toward parents, exaggerated processing of attachment-related worries, and lack of autonomy in communication patterns with mothers (Cole-Detke & Kobak, 1996; Kobak & Ferenz-Gillies, 1995).

Another group of studies conceptually replicated the association described above between anxious-ambivalent attachment and depression in adult samples and using self-report scales of attachment styles (Brennan & Shaver, 1995; Carnelley, Pietromonaco, & Jaffe, 1994; Roberts, Gotlib, & Kassel, 1996; Kennedy, Malowney, & McIntosh, 1996; Mikulincer et al., 1993; Pearson, Cohn, Cowan, & Cowan, 1994). Moreover, some of these studies have provided evidence about the mediating factors that may underlie this association. For example, Roberts et al. (1996) found that dysfunctional attitudes (negative conceptions of the self, world, and future) and low self-esteem seem to mediate between insecure attachment and depressive symptomatology. Accordingly, Kennedy et al. (1996) found that the association between anxious-ambivalent attachment style and depression also appears to be mediated by mental rumination on negative thoughts and memories.

It is worth noting that most of the studies have not found significant association between avoidant attachment and depressive symptomatology. However, one study, which differentiated between two kinds of depression, made some interesting findings about such an association (Zuroff & Fitzpatrick, 1995). Specifically, whereas anxious-ambivalent attachment was positively related to anaclitic depression (overdependence, lack of autonomy), avoidant attachment was positively related to self-critical depression (perfectionism, self-punishment, self-criticism). That is, avoidant attachment appears to be related to depressive symptoms of perfectionism and unachievable standards. This conclusion is in line with Mikulincer's (1995) finding that avoidant persons showed high levels of discrepancies between the way they perceive themselves and their self-standards.

Adult attachment style and severe psychopathology

Insecure styles also seem to be related to severe types of psychopathology, such as personality disorders – rigid and maladaptive patterns of relating to other people, situations, and events (Halgin & Whitbourne, 1994). In a recent study, Tweed and Dutton (1996) found positive correlations between self-reports of anxious-ambivalent attachment style and high scores in scales tapping the following personality disorders:

1.   borderline personality disorder (extreme fluctuations in mood, unstable interpersonal relationships, and negative self-image);

2. paranoid personality disorder (suspiciousness about others' intentions and fear of being persecuted or harassed);
3. passive-aggressive personality disorder (angry feelings that are expressed indirectly rather than openly);
4. avoidant personality disorder (fear of being involved in close relationships and terror of being publicly embarrassed);
5. antisocial personality disorder (lack of regard for social norms and rules); and
6. schizotypical personality disorder (indifference to social relationships and a very limited range of emotional expression).

Following the same line of research, Williams and Schill (1993, 1994) found a positive relationship between self-reports of anxious-ambivalent attachment and cognitive and behavioral signs of self-defeating personality disorder (a tendency to avoid gratification, to undermine one's interests, and to choose suffering). Lamentably, these studies did not provide any data on the psychological mechanisms that underlie the associations between anxious-ambivalent attachment style and personality disorders. However, one can see that basic facets of this style (mood fluctuations, negative self-image, worries about rejection and abandonment, mistrust of others' intentions) are also the definitional components of the above personality disorders.

Additional studies have found that avoidant attachment style was positively related to both dissociative disorders (Ogawa, Sroufe, Weinfield, Carlson, & Egeland, 1997) and eating disorders (Cole-Detke & Kobak, 1996). These findings may reflect avoidant persons' deactivation strategy, which may lead to fragmentation of the self (Mikulincer, 1995) and the expression of overwhelming distress through more somatic symptomatology (Mikulincer et al., 1993).

It is important to note that studies that were conducted on clinical hospitalized samples have found a very similar pattern of findings. In these cases, the two types of insecure attachment have been found to be positively related to the severity of borderline and schizophrenic symptoms (Fonagy et al., 1996; Patrick, Hobson, Castle, & Howard, 1994; Wilson & Constanzo, 1996). In addition, Fonagy et al. (1996) found a high frequency of random fluctuations between anxious-ambivalent and avoidant styles, unresolved conflicts around attachment themes, and memories of childhood abuse. All these cognitive responses have been conceptualized by Main et al. (1985) as signs of a disorganized attachment style and severe psychopathology.

Concluding Remarks

An overall look at the reviewed studies indicates the importance of adult attachment style as a key factor in coping with life stressors, managing negative emotions, and maintaining an adequate level of mental health. Specifically, secure persons seem to be characterized by optimistic and constructive regulatory strategies, which have been manifested in reliance on problem solving and support seeking as well as in the maintenance of an adequate level of mental health even in stressful circumstances. Avoidant persons seem to be characterized by deactivating strategies, which have been manifested in reliance on distancing coping, repression, and dissociation as well as in the failure to maintain well-being in times of stress. Anxious-ambivalent persons seem to be characterized by hyperactivating strategies, which have been found to be manifested in reliance on emotion-focused coping and ruminative thinking, inability to control the flow of negative emotions, and failure to maintain psychological well-being even in the absence of any recognizable stressful event.

The findings reviewed above clearly indicate that secure attachment seems to serve as a resilience factor that, even in times of stress, prevents the development of psychopathology and maintains high levels of well-being. In our terms, this adaptational advantage seems to result from three major sources. The first is secure people's optimistic attitude toward life, their basic trust of the world, and their tendency to seek support from others in times of need (Collins & Read, 1990). The second source may be the positive view secure persons have of themselves, their ability to organize experiences into differentiated self-schemata, and the coherence of their self-structure (Mikulincer, 1995). The third possible source of resilience might be secure persons' open, flexible, and positive attitude toward information processing – high tolerance for unpredictability, disorder, and ambiguity, reluctance to endorse rigid beliefs, and a tendency to integrate new evidence within cognitive structures when making social judgments (Mikulincer, 1997).

In contrast, the two insecure attachment styles seem to be a risk factor for poor mental health and sometimes for the development of psychopathology. For anxious-ambivalent persons, there is a danger that their hyperactivating strategies could culminate in chronic emotional overwhelming and mental disorganization and lead to poor mental health even during regular life circumstances. For avoidant persons, their deactivating strategies may put them at risk mainly when they encounter severe and persistent life stressors. In fact, avoidant persons may have the required abilities to endure minor hassles and stressors and to maintain a certain level of mental health in everyday life.

The studies reviewed above are only a first step in delineating attachment-related strategies of affect regulation. Research should examine how these strategies affect non-attachment behaviors and processes of attention, memory, reasoning, and language. In fact, an affect regulation approach expands attachment research beyond dyadic relationships and highlights the central role the attachment system may play in explaining individual differences in broad areas of adult life.

Research should also deal with questions that an affect regulation approach arises. First, why do negative attachment experiences evolve into deactivating strategies in some cases and into hyperactivating strategies in others? In this context, studies should adopt a multifactorial approach and examine the contribution of temperamental factors, family dynamic dimensions, parental personality, and other relationships within and out of the family of origin to adult attachment style. Second, research should examine the effectiveness of attachment-related strategies, to reveal those conditions in which deactivating or hyperactivating strategies are effective in maintaining mental health, and to explore the mechanisms that underlie secure persons' strategies (e.g., cognitive flexibility, emotional intelligence). Third, research should attempt to deal with other typologies of adult attachment, such as Bartholomew and Horowitz's (1991) distinction of dismissing and fearful avoidance. In our terms, the dismissing type may reflect the habitual way by which avoidant people regulate affect, whereas the fearful type may reflect the failure of this defensive armour due to extreme negative attachment history or current stressful events.

Finally, our conceptualization of attachment-related strategies of affect regulation has important implications for attachment-centered psychotherapy. In our terms, psychotherapy has two main tasks: (1) to work through negative attachment history and ineffective strategies of affect regulation, and (2) to provide patients with a "secure base" that may allow them to rediscover the basic guidelines of the attachment system and to heighten confidence in their biological potential for adaptation. In this context, patients should recover the sense of hope and faith implicit in the attachment system. In fact, infants' automatic activation of attachment behavior upon signals of distress implies the existence of a basic hope that there will be someone who will respond to our cry for help. Maybe this hope is the basic human potential that, after being fulfilled through positive experiences with responsive caregivers and consolidated in secure attachment, allows us to confront life's adversities and develop our unique personality.

References

Ainsworth, M. D. S., Blehar, M. C., Waters, E., & Wall, S. (1978). *Patterns of attachment: A psychological study of the strange situation*. Hillsdale, NJ: Erlbaum.

Averill, J. R. (1982). *Anger and aggression: An essay on emotion*. New York: Springer-Verlag.

Bartholomew, K., & Horowitz, L. M. (1991). Attachment styles among young adults: A test of a four category model. *Journal of Personality and Social Psychology, 61*, 226–244.

Berant, E. (1998). *The contribution of adult attachment style to women's coping and adjustment with the birth of a child with cardiac problems*. Unpublished PhD dissertation. Bar-Ilan University.

Birnbaum, G., Orr, I., Mikulincer, M., & Florian, V. (1997). When marriage breaks up: Does attachment style contribute to coping and mental health? *Journal of Social and Personal Relationships, 14*, 643–654.

Bowlby, J. (1969). *Attachment and loss: Attachment*. New York: Basic Books.

Bowlby, J. (1973). *Attachment and loss: Separation, anxiety and anger*. New York: Basic Books.

Bowlby, J. (1980). *Attachment and loss: Sadness and depression*. New York: Basic Books.

Bowlby, J. (1988). *A secure base: Clinical applications of attachment theory*. London: Routledge.

Brennan, K. A., & Shaver, P. R. (1995). Dimensions of adult attachment, affect regulation, and romantic relationship functioning. *Personality and Social Psychology Bulletin, 21*, 267–283.

Brennan, K. A., Shaver, P. R., & Tobey, A. E. (1991). Attachment styles, gender, and parental problem drinking. *Journal of Social and Personal Relationships, 8*, 451–466.

Carnelley, K. B., Pietromonaco, P. R., & Jaffe, K. (1994). Depression, working models of others, and relationship functioning. *Journal of Personality and Social Psychology, 66*, 127–140.

Carver, C. S., Scheier, M. F., & Weintraub, J. K. (1989). Assessing coping strategies: A theoretically-based approach. *Journal of Personality and Social Psychology, 56*, 267–283.

Cole-Detke, H., & Kobak, R. (1996). Attachment processes in eating disorder and depression. *Journal of Consulting and Clinical Psychology, 64*, 282–290.

Collins, N. L. (1996). Working models of attachment: Implications for explanation, emotion, and behavior. *Journal of Personality and Social Psychology, 71*, 810–832.

Collins, N. L., & Read, S. J. (1990). Adult attachment, working models, and relationship quality in dating couples. *Journal of Personality and Social Psychology, 58*, 644–663.

Cranley, M. S. (1981). Development of a tool for the measurement of maternal attachment during pregnancy. *Nursing Research, 30*, 281–284.

Epstein, S., & Meier, P. (1989). Constructive thinking: A broad coping variable with specific components. *Journal of Personality and Social Psychology, 57*, 332–350.

Feeney, J. A., & Noller, P. (1990). Attachment style as a predictor of adult romantic relationships. *Journal of Personality and Social Psychology, 58*, 281–291.

Folkman, S., & Lazarus, R. S. (1985). If it changes it must be a process: Study of emotion and coping during three stages of a college examination. *Journal of Personality and Social Psychology, 48*, 150–170.

Fonagy, P., Leigh, T., Steele, M., Steele, H., Kennedy, R., Mattoon, G., Target, M., & Gerber, A. (1996). The relationship of attachment status, psychiatric classification, and response to psychotherapy. *Journal of Consulting and Clinical Psychology, 64*, 22–31.

Fraley, R. C., & Shaver, P. R. (1997). Adult attachment and the suppression of unwanted thoughts. *Journal of Personality and Social Psychology, 73*, 1080–1091.

Halgin, R. P., & Whitbourne, S. K. (1994). *Abnormal psychology.* Fort Worth, TX: Harcourt Brace.

Hazan, C., & Shaver, P. (1987). Romantic love conceptualized as an attachment process. *Journal of Personality and Social Psychology, 52*, 511–524.

Kennedy, J. H., Malowney, C. L., & McIntosh, W. D. (1996). *Relationships among attachment style, rumination, self-esteem, and depressive affect.* Poster presented at the annual meeting of the American Psychological Association, Toronto, Canada.

Kirkpatrick, L. A., & Davis, K. E. (1994). Attachment style, gender, and relationship stability: A longitudinal analysis. *Journal of Personality and Social Psychology, 66*, 502–512.

Kobak, R. R., Cole, H. E., Ferenz, G. R., & Fleming, W. S. (1993). Attachment and emotion regulation during mother teen problem solving: A control theory analysis. *Child Development 64*, 231–245.

Kobak, R., & Ferenz-Gillies, R. (1995). Emotion regulation and depressive symptoms during adolescence: A functionalist perspective. *Development and Psychopathology, 7*, 183–192.

Kobak, R. R., & Hazan, C. (1991). Attachment in marriage: Effects of security and accuracy of working models. *Journal of Personality and Social Psychology, 60*, 861–869.

Kobak, R. R., & Sceery, A. (1988). Attachment in late adolescence: Working models, affect regulation, and representations of self and others. *Child Development, 59*, 135–146.

Kobak, R. R., Sudler, N., & Gamble, W. (1991). Attachment and depressive symptoms during adolescence: A developmental pathways analysis. *Development and Psychopathology, 3*, 461–474.

Lazarus, R. S. (1983). The costs and benefits of denial. In Breznitz, S. (Ed.), *The denial of stress* (pp. 1–30). New York: International Universities Press.

Lazarus, R. S., & Folkman, S. (1984). *Stress, appraisal, and coping.* New York: Springer.

Main, M., Kaplan, N., & Cassidy, J. (1985). Security in infancy, childhood, and adulthood: A move to level of representation. *Monographs of the Society for Research in Child Development, 50*, 66–104.

McCrae, R. R., & Costa, R. T. (1986). Personality, coping, and coping-effectiveness in an adult sample. *Journal of Personality, 54*, 385–405.

Mickelson, K. D., Kessler, R. C., & Shaver, P. R. (1997). Adult attachment in a nationally representative sample. *Journal of Personality and Social Psychology, 73*, 1092–1106.

Mikulincer, M. (1994). *Human learned helplessness: A coping paradigm.* New York: Plenum.

Mikulincer, M. (1995). Attachment style and the mental representation of the self. *Journal of Personality and Social Psychology, 69*, 1203–1215.

Mikulincer, M. (1997). Adult attachment style and information processing: Individual differences in curiosity and cognitive closure. *Journal of Personality and Social Psychology, 72*, 1217–1230.

Mikulincer, M. (1998a). Adult attachment style and affect regulation: Strategic variations in self-appraisals. *Journal of Personality and Social Psychology, 75*, 420–435.

Mikulincer, M. (1998b). Adult attachment style and individual differences in functional versus dysfunctional experiences of anger. *Journal of Personality and Social Psychology, 74*, 513–524.

Mikulincer, M., & Florian, V. (1995). Appraisal of and coping with a real life stressful situation: The contribution of attachment styles. *Personality and Social Psychology Bulletin, 21*, 406–414.

Mikulincer, M., & Florian, V. (1998). The relationship between adult attachment styles and emotional and cognitive reactions to stressful events. In J. A. Simpson & W. S. Rholes (Eds.), *Attachment theory and close relationships* (pp. 143–165). New York: Guilford Press.

Mikulincer, M., & Florian, V. (1999). Maternal–fetal bonding, coping strategies, and mental health during pregnancy: The contribution of attachment style. *Journal of Social and Clinical Psychology,*

18, 255–276.

Mikulincer, M., Florian, V., & Weller, A. (1993). Attachment styles, coping strategies, and post-traumatic psychological distress: The impact of the Gulf War in Israel. *Journal of Personality and Social Psychology, 64*, 817–826.

Mikulincer, M., & Nachshon, O. (1991). Attachment styles and patterns of self disclosure. *Journal of Personality and Social Psychology, 61*, 321–331.

Mikulincer, M., & Orbach, I. (1995). Attachment styles and repressive defensiveness: The accessibility and architecture of affective memories. *Journal of Personality and Social Psychology, 68*, 917–925.

Mikulincer, M., Orbach, I., & Iavnieli, D. (1998). Adult attachment style and affect regulation: Strategic variations in subjective self-other similarity. *Journal of Personality and Social Psychology, 75*, 436–448.

Ogawa, J. R., Sroufe, A., Weinfield, N. S., Carlson, E. A., & Egeland, B. (1997). Development and the fragmented self: Longitudinal study of dissociative symptomatology in a nonclinical sample. *Development and Psychopathology, 9*, 855–879.

Patrick, M., Hobson, R. P., Castle, D., & Howard, R. (1994). Personality disorder and the mental representation of early social experience. *Development and Psychopathology, 6*, 375–388.

Pearson, J. L., Cohn, D. A., Cowan, P. A., & Cowan, C. P. (1994). Earned and continuous security in adult attachment: Relation to depressive symptomatology and parenting style. *Development and Psychopathology, 6*, 359–373.

Power, T. G., & Parke, R. D. (1984). Social network factors and the transition to parenthood. *Sex Roles, 10*, 949–972.

Rholes, W. S., Simpson, J. A., & Grich-Stevens, J. (1998). Attachment orientations, social support, and conflict resolution in close relationships. In J. A. Simpson & W. S. Rholes (Eds.), *Attachment theory and close relationships* (pp. 166–188). New York: Guilford Press.

Roberts, J. E., Gotlib, I. H., & Kassel, J. D. (1996). Adult attachment security and symptoms of depression: The mediating roles of dysfunctional attitudes and low self-esteem. *Journal of Personality and Social Psychology, 70*, 310–320.

Roth, S., & Cohen, L. J. (1986). Approach, avoidance, and coping with stress. *American Psychologist, 41*, 813–819.

Shaver, P. R., & Hazan, C. (1993). Adult romantic attachment: Theory and evidence. In D. Perlman & W. Jones (Eds.), *Advances in personal relationships* (Vol. 4, pp. 29–70). London: Jessica Kingsley.

Siegel, J. M. (1986). The multidimensional anger inventory. *Journal of Personality and Social Psychology, 51*, 191–200.

Solomon, Z., Ginzburg, K., Mikulincer, M., Neria, Y., & Ohry, U. (1998). Attachment style and long-term adjustment to captivity in war. *European Journal of Personality, 12*, 271–285.

Stone, A. A., & Neale, J. M. (1984). New measure of daily coping: Development and preliminary results. *Journal of Personality and Social Psychology, 46*, 892–906.

Terry, D. J. (1991). Stress, coping, and adaptation to new parenthood. *Journal of Social and Personal Relationships, 8*, 527–547.

Tweed, R. G., & Dutton, D. G. (1996). *The relationship of attachment style to the axis II Personality Disorders*. Poster presented at the annual meeting of the American Psychological Association, Toronto, Canada.

Unger, L. (1998). *Personality and adjustment to widowhood*. Unpublished PhD dissertation. Bar-Ilan University

Veit, C. T., & Ware, J. E. (1983). The structure of psychological stress and well-being in general populations. *Journal of Consulting and Clinical Psychology, 51*, 730–742.

Williams, D., & Schill, T. (1993). Attachment histories for people with characteristics of self defeating personality. *Psychological Reports, 73*, 1232–1234.

Williams, D., & Schill, T. (1994). Adult attachment, love styles, and self defeating personality characteristics. *Psychological Reports, 75*, 31–34.

Wilson, J. S., & Constanzo, P. R. (1996). A preliminary study of attachment, attention, and schizotypy in early adulthood. *Journal of Personality and Social Psychology, 15*, 231–260.

Zuroff, D. C., & Fitzpatrick, D. K. (1995). Depressive personality styles: Implications for adult attachment. *Personality and Individual Differences, 18*, 253–265.

Chapter Twenty-Two

Marital Therapy and Social Psychology: Will We Choose Explicit Partnership or Cryptomnesia?

Steven R. H. Beach and Frank D. Fincham

How can social psychological research contribute to the development of increasingly powerful marital therapies? This question is of interest to both social psychologists and clinical researchers. The natural partnership between social and clinical psychology has a long history (cf. Morton Prince and Floyd Allport's establishment of *Journal of Abnormal and Social Psychology* in 1921) and has been remarked on many times (e.g., Brehm, 1976; Kanfer & Schefft, 1988; Snyder & Forsyth, 1991 among many others). However, in the marital area it is a partnership that has been strained for several years by the view of many marital therapy researchers that theory may be irrelevant to the advancement of treatment efficacy. At the same time, the partnership may be strained to the extent that social psychological researchers have not kept up with recent changes in the marital area, leading their commentary to miss the mark in some cases. Because the partnership between social psychology and marital therapy research is one that neither side can afford to abandon, it is prudent to examine carefully the view that theory is irrelevant to clinical progress, and to provide updated information about current developments in the field of marital therapy.

Agenda and Rationale

The chapter begins by situating our discussion in a broader literature on the interface between social and clinical psychology. We then consider the role of social psychology in

We would like to express our appreciation to Richard Marsh and Benjamin Karney for helpful suggestions regarding this chapter. Work on the chapter was supported, in part, by a grant from the National Science Foundation award to Steven R. H. Beach and by a grant from the Templeton Foundation awarded to Frank Fincham and Steven R. H. Beach.

the origins and development of Behavioral Marital Therapy (BMT). In doing so, we identify developments that led to some of its more prominent offspring (e.g., Integrative Couple Therapy (ICT), Jacobson & Christensen, 1996; Cognitive-Behavioral Marital Therapy (CBMT), Baucom & Epstein, 1990; Prevention and Relationship Enhancement Program (PREP), Markman, Stanley, & Blumberg, 1994). However, because Integrative Couple Therapy is the most recent development, and because it may be of particular interest to social psychologists, we emphasize ICT in our historical discussion. Next, we turn to the phenomenon of cryptomnesia or unconscious plagiarism (Marsh, Landau, & Hicks, 1996) to explain the phenomenology of clinical innovation and the perplexingly common view that basic research and theory do not help applied researchers and clinicians. Finally, in looking towards the future, we examine how two different perspectives, attachment theory and goal theory, might facilitate interplay between social psychology and marital therapy.

We utilize the literature on marital therapy to inform our discussion of the interplay between clinical practice and social psychology because marital relationships provide a prototype of close relationships for which therapies are available and relatively well developed. Accordingly, a focus on marital therapy allows for full exploration of the social–clinical interface in an arena well studied by both subdisciplines.

Before turning to our task, we need to address the question of whether focusing on BMT and its offspring is overly restrictive given the basic equivalence in outcome of several approaches to marital therapy (see Baucom, Shoham, Mueser, Daiuto, & Stickle, 1998). However, limiting our focus to BMT and recent developments has several advantages. First, BMT's relatively clear boundaries allow more precise discussion of historical events. Second, because BMT has grown up in an academic environment, the citation trail within the field, while far from perfect, provides a foundation for speculation about the origin of ideas and the timeline for advances. Finally, a careful case study of BMT is ideal for our purposes because the debate over the role of theory has been raised explicitly by several BMT leaders (e.g., Jacobson's preface to Jacobson & Christensen, 1996, p. viii; Markman, Notarius, Stephen, & Smith, 1981).

Accordingly, we can use the special case of BMT and its offspring to provide for social psychologists a window on the historical and psychological processes that lead clinical psychologists to engage in rhetorical practices that have baffled social psychologists over the years. To the extent that this "anthropological" examination is successful, it should accomplish two important goals. First, it should demonstrate to social psychologists that they have an important role to play in the continuing development of marital therapy and alert them to particular areas of potential interest. Second, it should demonstrate the need to be skeptical in evaluating the self-reports of marital therapy researchers when they claim independence from social psychology. At the same time, we hope this examination may help marital therapy researchers reclaim a theoretical foundation for their research. Parenthetically, we believe there is considerable opportunity for positive bi-directional influence between social psychological research and research on marital therapy. We focus on one direction of influence, that from social psychology to marital therapy, because this aspect of the relationship has not been well documented in the past. As a result, the literature on marital therapy is awash with mythological accounts that may be destructive of future progress in the marital area.

The Broader Social–Clinical Interface

Even among clinical researchers who view basic research as a source of creative inspiration, there may be limited enthusiasm for a continuing interface between basic and applied research once a set of techniques has been generated. As a consequence, there are many possible positions regarding the appropriate relationship between basic research on personal relationships and the development of increasingly powerful marital therapies. For example, one common position in the broader clinical literature is that good theory may lead to innovation, but that the subsequent process of refining and developing the intervention for purposes of dissemination is better viewed as a-theoretical (see the Agras & Berkowitz, 1980, model).

The shedding of theoretical underpinnings can be viewed as necessary and important in that a transition from "theory-laden" to "theory-independent" intervention allows for the emergence of a technically "eclectic" approach to psychotherapy (see Beutler & Consoli, 1992). This position therefore implies a split between basic and applied research as a therapeutic intervention matures. It further suggests that this split should not be alarming. Indeed, recent writings on the relationship between outcome research and clinical practice (e.g., Nathan & Gorman, 1998; see also Barlow & Hofmann, 1997), show that variants of this view have become normative within the field of behavior therapy and are closely tied to the movement to disseminate empirically supported treatment (see Chambless & Hollon, 1998).

Some variants of the Agras and Berkowitz (1980) model even suggest a destructive role for theory should it be retained too long. For example, it has been argued that theory may sometimes be problematic in that it blocks openness to the results of outcome research and so may interfere with the dissemination of effective therapies (Goldfried, 1980). In particular, rigid adherence to theory has been viewed as being responsible for the resistance of therapists to new and better forms of therapy. This view suggests that after an intervention is well specified, one should rapidly eschew theory.

Perry London (1972), the first to propose technical eclecticism, argued that the first issue for applied researchers was not theoretical but rather factual, "do they [the interventions] work? On whom? When? The how and why come later." From this perspective, theory development is always secondary to the identification of effective therapies, and the identification of effective therapy can be done a-theoretically. Indeed, the recently adopted standards for "Empirically Supported Therapy" (Chambless & Hollon, 1998) make no mention of the viability of the theoretical underpinnings of an approach. Accordingly, the current standard for empirically supported intervention appears to assume a clean break between the context of discovery and the context of application. There is no emphasis on the need to examine or support the theoretical underpinnings of a particular intervention approach as part of the empirical validation process.

The Agras and Berkowitz (1980) model also posits that careful "clinical observation" may represent an alternative to basic research and theory development. This has typically been viewed as an innocuous recognition of the important role of active clinician-researchers in generating new techniques (e.g., Beck and Ellis in the development of cognitive therapy; or Stuart, Weiss, Greenberg, Wile in the marital area). However, an emphasis on the role of clinical observation in generating clinical advances becomes anti-theoretical if it is taken to imply that such clinical observations are "a-theoretical." That is, if most, or even many of the innovations we now view as clinical advances resulted when persons, isolated from developments in basic research, reacted to the clinical processes they saw in front of them, this could suggest that basic research in social psychology is irrelevant to clinical advancement.

Comment

No doubt many social psychologists view with some bemusement the assertion that a technique can be divorced from its theoretical underpinnings, or the claim that clinicians can open themselves to "reality" uninfluenced by theoretical preconceptions. However, such assertions, at least in their milder forms, are not at all uncommon among clinical researchers and are entertained as well by many in the marital area. Accordingly, it is important to examine closely such claims and correct them to the extent that correction is warranted. To do so, in the next section we examine sources of change in technique in behavioral marital therapy over the last three decades of the twentieth century.

The Role of Social Psychology in the Origins and Development of BMT

Behavioral Marital Therapy, like other forms of behavior therapy, has its roots in the psychology laboratory. However, in the case of BMT, it was not simply the rat lab of Skinner or the dog kennel of Pavlov that have been cited as the inspiration.

Social psychological roots

Among other influences (e.g., Blau, 1964; Homans, 1961), BMT therapists also credited a small volume published in 1959 by Thibaut and Kelley, *The social psychology of groups*. Awareness of Thibaut and Kelley's theoretical framework was ubiquitous, and all early behavioral marital texts cite Thibaut and Kelley's (1959) and/or Kelley's (1979) work (e.g., Gottman, et al., 1976a; Jacobson & Margolin, 1979; Stuart, 1980). Clearly, most early BMT researchers were familiar with some variant of interdependence and social exchange theory and viewed it, along with social learning principles more generally, as providing a framework within which to understand marital satisfaction and commitment.

Reading Thibaut and Kelley (1959) today remains both interesting and instructive. Most concepts used by BMT researchers and therapists can be found in this volume. In particular, enhancing satisfaction by increasing rewards minus costs relative to some comparison level is discussed (pp. 21–24). The concept of the behavioral repertoire as skills to be taught is explicated (p. 20, pp. 38–39). The potential importance of communication and communication training (p. 73) and the value of brainstorming in problem solving discussions (pp. 263–270) are dealt with. Even developments commonly attributed to later sources are presaged by Thibaut and Kelley. For example, the potential importance of idiographic analysis of dyadic interaction and the need to examine sequences of observed interaction are discussed (p. 10, pp. 18–19). The likely impact of inferences about partner behavior and factors that could influence perception of partner behavior (later called filters by Gottman et al., 1976a, and then elaborated by attribution researchers and incorporated into cognitive marital therapy) were discussed (pp. 73–77). Anticipating the structure of the Prevention and Relationship Enhancement Program (PREP), it was suggested that a general discussion, emphasizing participation by all parties, might be an important pre-liminary step to effective problem-solving discussion (pp. 261–263). Anticipating a goal-theoretic analysis of marital conflict (Fincham & Beach, 1999), a goal framework was alluded to as a way of understanding the organization of individual and dyadic behavior.

Notwithstanding the above observations, over a decade passed between the publication of Thibaut and Kelley (1959) and the emergence of BMT in its mature form. By the mid-1970s BMT emphasized the instigation of positive behavior between spouses (e.g., Gottman et al.'s, 1976a, "up deck"; Weiss Patterson, and Hops's, 1973, Love days). Communica-tion training had been formalized (e.g., Gottman et al., 1976a), and it was commonly held that the behavioral repertoire of distressed couples might be lacking important "skills" that could be taught as a way of interrupting coercive cycles (e.g., Weiss, Patterson, & Hops,1973). Thus, it appears that on the basis of theory (including social psychological theory), and in interaction with clinical creativity but well before randomized clinical out-come trials of BMT began in earnest (e.g., Crowe, 1978; Turkewitz & O'Leary, 1976; Jacobson, 1977, etc.), BMT had reached a mature form. Outcome research served, prima-rily, as a check on the generalizability of various techniques (e.g., O'Leary & Turkewitz, 1978), and not as a stimulus to innovation. Indeed, positive outcome results were typically characterized as supporting the broad strategies of change proposed as important by behavioral marital therapists rather than the specific procedures used in a given investiga-tion. In sum, BMT owes much of its current form to the theory and basic science of the 1950s and 1960s, and particularly to the social psychology of that period.

The importance of a unifying framework

A key factor in the remarkable progress made during the early 1970s was the presence of a shared framework or paradigm. A unifying theoretical framework was important both in allowing couple interactions to be described and in allowing possible points of therapeutic intervention to be identified. A strong shared theoretical framework also allowed topographically dissimilar interventions based on the use of token exchange (e.g., Stuart, 1969) or quid pro quo contracts between spouses (e.g., Azrin, Naster, & Jones 1973) to be viewed as having conceptual continuity with later BMT outcome research that used neither technique. Thus, the shared framework influenced even the perceived strength of the cumu-lative support for BMT. But, most importantly, it was the existence of this conceptual frame-work that stimulated a group of creative, applied researchers to think along similar lines, see similar processes, discuss the implications of these processes, and view as reasonable a certain set of possible interventions. Accordingly, social psychological theory appears to have been important in enabling the emergence of BMT as a recognizable form of therapy.

Comment. It should not be surprising that traditional BMT, and by extension CBMT, ICT, and PREP, owe their existence to a basic science foundation. BMT arose in the context of the behavioral movement in clinical psychology. At its best, this movement represented a pragmatically motivated attempt to tie applied clinical intervention to basic experimental psychology. To ensure the ongoing transfer of basic research into clinical applications, those establishing early behavioral training programs decided to house them within psychology departments. They believed that a close connection was necessary in order to facilitate the incorporation of the evolving scientific base into ongoing clinical applications (see Davison, 1998). We explore this theme in more detail as we discuss the importance of cryptomnesia for clinical advances. In the present context, it suffices to note that the founders of behavior therapy self-consciously encouraged the ongoing transfer of ideas, values, and developments from the experimental lab to clinical application. In brief, BMT grew up looking to experimental psychology for inspiration at many levels and so it was quite natural, within that context, to extrapolate from the social psychology lab to the marital therapy hour.

The development of an intellectual crisis

Given its initial development, BMT seemed destined to become the poster child for the social–clinical interface. Yet, by the mid-1970s there was a growing sentiment that innovation in the marital area would be largely driven by the efforts of marital researchers and that it was unlikely that further clinical advancement would result from attention to basic research. How then did BMT lose its theoretical grounding? We turn to consider several factors that might provide an answer to this question.

Outcome studies? Early BMT outcome studies were often portrayed as rather striking in their demonstration of effectiveness (e.g., Hahlweg & Markman, 1988). In addition, early studies using techniques that were more closely tied to the interdependence framework produced slightly better outcomes than did later outcome studies that utilized more "sophisticated" versions of BMT (Jacobson et al., 1984; Christensen & Heavey, 1999). If anything, the outcome research available in the early 1980s seemed to argue against innovation. Indeed, the strong showing of outcome studies maintained considerable stability in the field, and was often used as a persuasive tool in favor of adopting BMT as an approach for dealing with marital problems (Jacobson & Margolin, 1979; Stuart, 1980). Accordingly, it is hard to find evidence that outcome results brought into question the theoretical underpinnings of the field.

Intellectual rigidity? Was it, then, their strong adherence to interdependence and social learning theory that led behavioral marital therapists to turn away from social psychology as the field of social psychology further emphasized cognitive accounts of behavior with the emergence of social cognition? Stated differently, did clinicians cling to the past and allow new developments to pass them by? This is also not supported by the data. The BMT field was clearly open to the idea of cognitive interventions and cognitive processes relatively early in its development (cf. Gottman et al., 1976a; O'Leary & Turkewitz, 1978).

While early cognitive theorizing in the marital area was simplistic, this feature simply reflected the social psychology of the 1950s and 1960s. In addition, these early theorists and researchers made no claim to have all the answers, often suggested the potential for continuing advances in the enhancement of outcome, and explicitly called for more data.

Inability to tolerate ambiguity?   So, what was responsible for the emergence of an increasingly a-theoretical stance in the marital area? One influence must be the broader clinical psychology context we discussed earlier. This broader context readily supported a shift toward a-theoretical, technical eclecticism. At the same time, the desire among clinical psychologists to find some a-theoretical foundation for claims of therapeutic efficacy may be fueled, in part, by the needs of clinicians and marital therapy researchers to feel confident about the applied aspects of their work. Because therapists are attempting to influence the lives of others, it may be more comfortable to base their prescriptions and suggestions on something perceived as more "solid" and "factual" than the shifting sands of theory. That particular outcome results cannot really be considered "more solid" or "factual" than well-tested theoretical propositions need not diminish the allure of this position. Certainly, marital therapists are as vulnerable to the allure of "facts" as clinical psychologists (and psychiatrists) in general.

Critical tests of theory.   In our view, however, the more important source of the intellectual shift was a series of studies that were conducted by marital researchers to test the theoretical underpinnings of their treatment approach. In particular, in research designed to test key aspects of interdependence theory it was found that "skill level" or "the behavioral repertoire" as measured with strangers did not differentiate satisfied and dissatisfied couples (Vincent, Weiss, & Birchler, 1975). Similarly, performance on prisoner's dilemma games failed to discriminate distressed and non-distressed couples (e.g., Speer, 1972), but observed interaction did (e.g., Birchler, Weiss, & Vincent, 1975). These studies falsified claims that BMT was useful to the extent that it expanded the "behavioral repertoire" of couples, thereby opening them to the "natural contingencies" that would then maintain their more positive behavior with each other. Because the skills were typically already established in the behavioral repertoire of distressed couples, something else was keeping the natural contingencies from working with these couples. In addition, these investigations seemed to call into question the utility of methods drawn from social psychology and to highlight the need for new methods of studying patterns of interaction.

Around the same time, it was also shown that greater reciprocity of positive behavior did not predict greater satisfaction as was predicted by interdependence theory (Gottman, Notarius, Markman, et al., 1976). That is, direct, immediate application of reinforcing contingencies in response to the spouse's positive behavior did not reliably predict a better marriage. In their 1976 book, *A couple's guide to communication*, Gottman, Notarius, Gonso, and Marman noted that "Although non-distressed couples may seem to be reciprocating positive codes more often than distressed couples, that may only be an artifact of the higher probability of positive codes in non-distressed couples." As numerous replications have shown, these early findings were correctly interpreted as disconfirming key elements of the Thibaut and Kelley framework. Indeed, they fed back into the social psychology literature and led to significant conceptual advances (e.g., Kelley et al., 1983a; Clark & Mills, 1979).

But these developments were yet to come. In the mid 1970s what seemed clear to behavioral marital researchers was that key theoretical assumptions and predictions of the Thibaut and Kelley (1959) model were not true. Further, some of the basic research methods of the time appeared inadequate for investigating "real world" marital behavior.

Thus, by the mid- to late 1970s the theoretical underpinnings of BMT were under siege by prominent behavioral marital researchers (for a similar account of the details but a different interpretation, see Baucom, Epstein, Rankin, & Burnett, 1996). Studies had been conducted with the expectation that they would support the theoretical underpinnings of BMT, but the results were opposite to expectations and were stunningly conclusive. In effect, BMT researchers found themselves without a unifying theoretical framework. Rather than repair or extend the framework that inspired BMT, leaders in the area called for careful description and an inductive approach to science. Dust bowl empiricism therefore triumphed over a theory-driven approach to scientific advancement. However, it was not a rejection of theory per se. Theory was simply put on long-term hold (see Gottman, 1998, for a recent call for integrative theory in the marital area). As we shall see below, inevitably theory will be reintroduced. The only question is whether it will be reintroduced knowingly and explicitly, or implicitly in the form of cryptomnesia.

Comment

It is worth digressing at this point to note the potential for mutual enrichment between marital therapy research on the one hand and social psychological research on the other. It took clinical marital researchers, interested in applied issues, to frame pivotal tests of interdependence theory. Without the applied focus of behavioral marital researchers, it is hard to know how long we might have waited before game-theoretic tests with undergraduate subjects would have led to similar conclusions. This example demonstrates well the need for social psychologists to move beyond the examination of convenient undergraduate samples in the laboratory to adequately test social psychological theories, a need that received extensive discussion by social psychologists in the 1980s (e.g., Sommer, 1982).

Without such research it was all too easy for marital researchers to attribute the problems encountered with interdependence theory (Thibaut & Kelley, 1959) to social psychologists' preoccupation with theories of convenience samples and with prisoner's dilemma games (see Gottman et al., 1976a). Because this preoccupation was viewed as stable and as precluding further fruitful exchange, BMT researchers determined that they would need to create their own basic, observational literature pertaining to marital interaction (again, see Gottman et al., 1976a). They therefore began documenting observed differences between distressed and non-distressed couples. Because they believed that starting with theory had misled the field, they determined to engage the work a-theoretically. This time theory would be formed only after careful observation. The strength of this new agenda is exemplified by Markman's comment several years later that "a solid data base is a prerequisite to theory development [and] can best be accomplished by descriptive studies which focus on observable behavior" (Markman et al. 1981, p. 236). Indeed, this a-theoretical, descriptive agenda remains strong today. On the positive side, the commitment to careful observation has led to many of the methodological advances in the marital area over the past 20 years, and much of the data linking marital behavior to longitudinal outcomes (see Bradbury, 1998; but see Glenn, 1998, for a cautionary note).

The emergence of a-theoretical BMT

At the same time that a literature on marital interaction was being created through inductive procedures, BMT researchers found themselves saddled with an unanticipated paradox. They had a technology that worked, and that has continued to work over many replications for the past 20 years (Baucom et al., 1998; Christensen & Heavey, 1999), but whose theoretical underpinnings had been called into question. A broadly shared enthusiasm in the field for the great inductive enterprise was sufficient to maintain some intellectual momentum. However, by its very nature such a process could not be expected to yield dramatic results overnight and it led to a shift in the focus of BMT research away from theory development and toward methodological and measurement issues. Indeed, the most creative thinkers in the area devoted themselves to untangling the nuances of observational methodology.

At the same time, the limitations of an a-theoretical approach to intervention became apparent as marital researchers noticed the difficulty they had in describing goals for therapy and conveying overall strategies of therapy without making reference to theoretical constructs. To compound the problem, there were no new theoretical constructs being offered to account for the efficacy of BMT techniques. In the face of a relative theoretical vacuum left by the demise of the Thibaut and Kelley (1959) framework, clinicians and clinical researchers continued to describe BMT in terms that had already been discredited on theoretical grounds (see for example the descriptions of BMT provided in Jacobson & Margolin, 1979; Stuart, 1980, or more recently in Christensen & Heavey, 1999). Widespread discomfort with framing interventions in terms of a discredited theory, rather than discomfort with the outcome results obtained, is the more plausible explanation for the round of innovation in BMT that began in the late 1970s and early 1980s. For some sense of this discomfort one may examine Jacobson and Margolin (1979, pp. 14–17) or, more recently, Gottman (1998, p. 190).

The collapse of a-theoretical BMT

Oddly, and perhaps perversely from the perspective of doctrinaire behaviorists, in the late 1970s and early 1980s, behavioral marital therapists began borrowing widely from non-behavioral approaches. Often they borrowed from approaches with no outcome data supporting the efficacy of the approach. During this period one can discern efforts to find a new integrative theory, albeit not theory drawn from the empirical, social psychological literature. Instead BMT researchers turned to other therapeutic traditions for possible inspiration. Systems theory concepts were an early favorite of those looking for a more inclusive theoretical framework (e.g., Weiss, 1978). Cognitive therapy also emerged as providing a possible inclusive framework (e.g., Baucom & Epstein, 1990). However, neither of these potential organizing frameworks proved sufficiently unifying or powerful to galvanize the field as a whole. Instead, BMT researchers adopted a technique-oriented approach to innovation, borrowing techniques or "modules" of therapy from distinct forms of marital therapy in the hopes of enhancing therapeutic outcomes (e.g., Baucom, Sayers, & Sher, 1990). This approach also fostered the view that BMT was a collection of techniques applied in a modular format (see Jacobson & Christensen, 1996, for a similar characterization). Of course, in the absence of theory, the pull of a modular, technique-driven approach to marital therapy is nearly irresistible. In line with the modular view of marital therapy, a series of outcome investigations were conducted in which topography rather than function guided the differentiation of component interventions (see Baucom et al., 1998).

During this period outcome research began to play an increasingly important, albeit negative, intellectual role. Precisely because there was no theoretical standard by which to evaluate the potential value of innovations, BMT researchers increasingly turned to outcome research for vindication of their new composite therapies. Accordingly, when none of the new approaches was able to demonstrate significantly enhanced impact on marital satisfaction (Baucom et al., 1998), this was interpreted as failure and stagnation. As it became clear that the various clinical innovations were not translating into more powerful treatments, researchers in the field became increasingly dissatisfied both with traditional BMT and with its alternatives (see also Gottman, 1998). Arguably, however, outcome research is an overly blunt instrument with which to determine the "potential" of a particular technique or approach. Rather, due to overlap in goals and strategies of intervention across approaches, outcome research in the marital area may be biased toward "null" results for comparisons between active treatments. In addition, two interventions could appear equally effective in an outcome study despite one approach having greater potential to become more powerful with relatively minor modifications. Accordingly, outcome research alone may be a particularly problematic foundation for the identification of "promising" technical innovations.

Notwithstanding the increasing dissatisfaction with the BMT framework, there were significant achievements during the 1980s and early 1990s in the application of traditional BMT to various problems. For example, this period saw the successful application of BMT to the treatment of alcoholism (Epstein & McCrady, 1998; O'Farrell, Choquette, Cutter, Brown, & McCourt, 1993), depression (Beach, Fincham, & Katz, 1998), divorce prevention (Sayers, Kohn, & Heavey, 1998), and violence (O'Leary, Heyman, & Neidig, 1999). However, there were modest achievements, at best, in the generation of a more powerful theoretical framework to guide marital intervention. In addition, because no theoretical structure guided BMT outcome research, there was little opportunity for theory-driven outcome research of the sort that could potentially guide clinical innovation (see Beach, 1991; Borkovec & Castonguay, 1998; Whisman & Snyder, 1997). In brief, in the absence of a robust theoretical framework, openness to innovation proved insufficient to avoid stagnation.

Comment. While the field of behavioral marital therapy was *Waiting for Godot* in the form of an ultimate, inductively derived answer about the nature of marital interaction, the once-thriving applied tradition of BMT was approaching intellectual collapse. In retrospect, more rapid applied progress might have been prompted by theory-focused efforts to amend or replace the social psychological theory that had initially informed BMT.

The ascendance of the field of personal relationships

A development with the potential to enhance the rocky relationship between (social psychological) theory and marital application began in the early 1980s. Concurrent with resurgent interest in the general social–clinical psychology interface (e.g., Harvey, 1983), a new dialogue began, broad enough to include BMT researchers, social psychologists, developmental psychologists, and persons in the closely related fields of communication, cognitive science, and sociology. An important intellectual product of this emerging dialogue was the volume, *Close Relationships* (Kelley et al., 1983a). In the 1980s and early 1990s the dialogue expanded exponentially and the field of personal relationship research was progressing. The dialogue spawned a number of important developments and new developments continue to emerge. Among these continuing developments are the integration of the attachment and social cognition literatures (Shaver, Collins, & Clark,1996; Baldwin et al., 1996), and the introduction of goal theory into characterization of marital conflict (Fincham & Beach, 1999), two areas to which we return later in the chapter.

Movement toward a new integrative framework

A further important development was the emergence of social cognition as an area of interest within social psychology. Although a burgeoning social cognition literature failed to transform clinical technique in marital therapy during the 1980s (but see Baucom & Epstein, 1990, and Fincham, Fernandes, & Humphreys, 1993, for evidence of some impact), it was incorporated wholeheartedly into the new "personal relationships" movement. As a result, this movement occasioned the emergence of a broader and more flexible framework for understanding and describing interaction. To be attractive to the field of marital therapy, social psychological theory needed to be wedded to a wide-ranging framework that could describe a variety of dyadic behaviors and could allow for the possibility of multiple influences. Even if it was not really a theory, and even if it did not directly incorporate all the available and potentially useful mid-level theories, such a framework might provide a springboard for a new round of creative clinical innovation.

In their 1983 book, Kelley et al. provided such a preliminary framework, but by the early 1980s relatively few applied marital researchers were looking at developments in social psychology. Among applied researchers, most of the attention devoted to basic processes focused rather narrowly either on understanding the role of attributional processes in marriage (see Bradbury & Fincham, 1990; Fletcher & Fincham, 1991), or on the description of marital interaction (see Gottman, 1998; Fincham & Beach, 1999). Kelley et al. however, presented a new framework for understanding and examining personal relationships. This new framework dealt with many of the problems left unanswered in the earlier Thibaut and Kelley (1959) volume. In addition, the framework highlighted the importance of "patterning" in dyadic relationships (p. 47), causal connectedness between partners leading to positive (and negative) feedback loops (p. 58), and the resulting emergence of stable interaction patterns. As was the case for Thibaut and Kelley, the framework provided is not so much a particular theory as it is an organizing scheme capable of accommodating many different mid-level theories and perhaps allowing for their integration.

One behavioral marital therapy researcher who was listening to the discussion of the new framework (and indeed participating in the dialogue) was Andy Christensen. Interestingly, around this same time, his clinical work began to shift profoundly. These shifts led eventually to Christensen's co-creation of Integrative Couple Therapy (ICT) with Jacobson. From the standpoint of the current discussion, it is particular interesting to examine ICT and the Kelley et al. (1983a) framework to see if there are any points of connection. Indeed, there are several. For example, Kelley et al.'s discussion of positive feedback loops appears to be a direct conceptual precursor of the "polarization process" discussed in ICT. "Polarization" is described in ICT as the process by which a focus on change may lead to an increase in the perceived discrepancy between the partners' positions. Hence, through polarization a relatively small area of disagreement may grow to be an area of perceived incompatibility. Likewise, Kelley et al.'s discussion of the way in which stable interaction patterns develop and are maintained appears to be the direct intellectual precursor of the ICT discussion of the "mutual trap." The "mutual trap" is described in ICT as the feeling of entrapment experienced by both partners in distressed couples that results from their perceiving that they must continue doing exactly what they are already doing despite the realization that it does not appear to help. Finally, Kelley et al.'s analysis of patterning in relationships appears to be a precursor of the identification of the couple "theme" in ICT. The "theme" is described in ICT as the underlying structure of the couple's interaction that ties together what may appear to be disparate areas of conflict. Thus, although the techniques of ICT are not directly given by theory, they appear to be built upon and constrained by the framework provided in the Kelley et al. (1983a) book. Parenthetically, it may be that placing ICT back into the Kelley et al. framework could prove useful in generating interesting marital therapy process questions.

Implications for the interrelationship of BMT, ICT and social psychological research

There is a relationship between the techniques ultimately generated by applied researchers and the framework that guided their thinking. In addition, we would argue that techniques are typically more useful when wedded to a theoretical context and that innovation is likely to be more sustained when the links between theory and technique are explicitly recognized. Thus, we do not mean to detract from the creativity displayed in the clinical innovation process by highlighting links to underlying theory. Rather, we hope that this exercise will help sustain clinical innovation and prevent a return to the doldrums of BMT in the 1980s. It may also highlight for social psychologists potential areas in which their research may have direct implications for understanding marital therapy, or for the identification of boundary conditions on the effectiveness of marital intervention.

As may be apparent already, while applauding much about ICT, the assertion that it owes little to basic psychological science, and to social psychology in particular, seems to us jarringly incorrect. In addition, the assertion (Jacobson & Christensen, 1996, p. viii) that one might be better off by eschewing theory, and opening up instead to the "natural contingencies" operating in the therapy session, seems potentially misleading. We would suggest that this type of assertion come with a warning label: "Try this only if you have strong implicit theories at work." In particular, we would argue that BMT and ICT are healthier with explicit theory than without, and that modern social psychology and the emerging field of personal relationships is an excellent place to look for relevant theoretical advances.

What are the consequences of failing to acknowledge the theoretical foundation of BMT and its various offshoots, including ICT? First, failure to acknowledge the theoretical ground upon which a set of techniques rests undermines the important activity of process research. If we have not acknowledged the basic processes that inform the techniques being proposed, we are in a poorer position to capture these processes in process research. Hence, we are likely to conduct sub-optimal variants of outcome research, condemning outcome research to be used as a mere persuasive device rather than as a truly informative experiment (for extended discussion, see Beach, 1991; Borkovec & Castonguay, 1998).

Second, recent developments in BMT and in the field of close relationships give rise to the hope that BMT may once again be able to claim a coherent and explicit theoretical foundation. This was the situation during the early 1970s, arguably the time of fastest growth and development for BMT. After the apparent collapse of that theoretical foundation in the early 1980s BMT moved increasingly toward the modular and technique-oriented approach rightly criticized by Jacobson and Christensen (1996). Technique-oriented approaches are vulnerable to decreasing fidelity as they are copied and variants proliferate. Without a coherent nomological network to steer development and to provide a context within which to detect and correct errors, a technique-oriented system is doomed to accumulate fatal errors during the replication process. Much like an organism with no autoimmune system to identify defective cells, an approach without a theoretical foundation has no way to catch and correct problematic drift in technique. Indeed, as Snyder and Forsyth (1991) point out, without theoretical grounding it is impossible even to gauge the range of applicability of one's techniques.

Finally, in addition to the problem of limiting the clinical potential of BMT and ICT, failure to acknowledge the theoretical grounding of ICT has the additional unfortunate side effect of inappropriately devaluing the generative heuristic power of new work coming from social, developmental, and personal relationship perspectives. Indeed, there is considerable new basic research that suggests the potential for further development of the power of BMT or ICT (cf. Fincham & Beach, 1999). It would be unfortunate, and probably wrong, to think that BMT and ICT have reached their zenith in terms of their power (efficacy) or their accessibility (effectiveness) for distressed couples (see Gottman, 1998, for a similar view). To the extent that we recognize basic research and theory as the engine of innovation, we will be more likely to tap this resource appropriately.

In view of such observations, one is left to wonder why the contributions of social psychologists are underestimated in the BMT literature. When the facts do not support the importance of "outcome research" in stimulating clinical innovation and appear to point to a critical role for "theory," why do so many bright and creative individuals appear to think otherwise?

Understanding the Problem of Cryptomnesia

In this section we discuss several factors that bear upon the underestimation of social psychology's contribution to the development of marital therapy. We grapple with the question of how marital therapy researchers come to view their intervention packages as "new" and uninfluenced by basic research. We use the term "cryptomnesia," or literally "theft of ideas," to refer to this phenomenon, not to suggest that marital therapy researchers are blameworthy, but rather to highlight the continuity of their behavior with that of other persons who are asked to be creative. The term "cryptomnesia" has appeared in the basic cognitive psychology literature recently and seems to capture many of the processes of interest rather well.

Figure versus ground

The simple distinction between figure and ground is useful for understanding cryptomnesia in its simplest form: the under-citation of work that is known to be logically prior to one's own. To illustrate in a neutral context, we first discuss the way in which therapists in private practice may under-credit marital therapy researchers and highlight the similarity of this behavior to that of academic psychologists who under-credit basic research. In this context we also discuss whether an increased focus on process research, by itself, would reverse the tendency toward under-citation.

Marital therapists in practice. It is relatively common for behaviorally trained marital therapists in private practice settings to indicate that they are "eclectic" in their practice and that they do not follow any particular treatment package, or to suggest that they have created their own treatment approach over the years. However, if asked to describe what they do in therapy these same individuals may describe the use of techniques that have a strong resemblance to those described in various treatment manuals. Marital therapists in clinical practice appear to emphasize the differences and overlook the similarities between their favorite techniques and those appearing in various marital therapy manuals, leading perhaps to an underestimate of the extent to which manualized approaches have influenced their work. Perhaps marital therapists overlook the influence of treatment manuals on their practice for the same reason that marital researchers overlook the influence of basic research on their innovations. In each case the problem may be one of figure versus ground.

For the marital therapist, the goal that structures their attention and activity is what to do with a particular couple presenting for therapy. What to do "on average," or what works "in general," is not the pivotal issue and may not even seem to be a very compelling issue to therapists working with couples. Rather, the compelling issue for clinicians in practice remains "what treatment, by whom, is most effective for this individual with that specific problem, under which set of circumstances" (Paul, 1969). The goal of deciding what to do with this particular couple makes the tailoring of treatment the "figure" for clinicians and makes the broad set of techniques and guidelines for couples in general the "background." That is, clinicians are likely to think of themselves as having creatively combined techniques from across sources and as having developed a novel intervention that fits "this particular couple" even if their overall strategy is consistent with a treatment manual. In this view, clinicians are led to underestimate the extent to which the existence of treatment manuals has influenced their work because the techniques from treatment manuals provide only the "background" for their choices. In just the same way, marital therapy researchers may be led to underestimate the extent to which theory or findings from basic research have influenced them.

Marital researchers designing new treatment packages.   Academic marital researchers may have as their goal the development of new treatment packages that influence positive couple outcomes on average. This goal focuses attention on whether a particular approach works, on average, and for whom, but draws attention away from how distressed couples change, or why therapy produces its benefits. It also leads to attempts to standardize treatments, increase fidelity to manuals, and provide comparisons to alternative treatments. Alternatively stated, the context of treatment design and outcome evaluation focuses attention on accounting for the most variance possible, not on cleanly explicating the various processes that may be contributing to the power of the intervention. Indeed, hypothesized mechanisms of change may be viewed as important only insofar as they are conveyed to clients as part of the rationale for treatment, i.e., to the extent that they become embedded in the intervention itself. Because the truth value of assertions about mechanisms seems relatively unimportant in this context, marital therapy researchers may feel little pressure to cite the relevant basic literature. A focus on "what works" to the exclusion of "how things work" may therefore obscure the relationship between basic research and therapeutic innovation.

Marital therapy process researchers. One way to increase attention on mechanisms of change by behavioral marital therapy researchers is greater encouragement of technique-oriented and processes-oriented research (cf. Goldfried & Wolfe, 1996; Whisman & Snyder, 1997). Such an approach focuses attention on understanding the way important aspects of therapeutic intervention work to produce change. Measures designed to capture the process of change in marital therapy might be more likely to have a theoretical component and to reflect the content of the basic literature on personal relationships. However, it would not be surprising if there continued to be a focus on variance accounted for, rather than clean tests of theoretical propositions. In turn, the potential for under-citing the basic literature, and perhaps underestimating its heuristic importance, might remain high even if marital therapy researchers became more attentive to therapy processes issues.

Consider the hypothetical example of a researcher examining the effect of BMT on the occurrence of benign attributions among distressed spouses. Assume that BMT is found to render attributions for partner behavior more benign, and it is found that the occurrence of benign attributions at the end of therapy is associated with greater positive change in satisfaction. This would be of great interest to marital therapists, and is a prediction that comes directly from the literature on responsibility attributions in close relationships. However, in the clinical literature the investigation would most probably not be discussed as a test of an attributional model of change in marital therapy, but rather as an attempt to determine the relative importance of attending to dysfunctional attributions or changing negative behavior in producing positive marital outcomes. This presentation of the study would prompt attention to variance accounted for in the dependent variable, and pit topographically distinct aspects of marital change against each other to see which one better accounted for variance in change. At best, this type of presentation would tend to obscure any discussion of mediation. At worst it would preempt any discussion of theoretically specified mechanisms. Thus, while process investigations have the potential to help tie applied results to a more basic set of results, in practice "mediational" issues are unlikely to be addressed (as has been the case for the example relating to attributions, see Fincham; Beach, & Bradbury, 1990), and applied researchers may still be prone to underestimate the relevance and importance of basic research.

In sum, practicing clinicians and clinical researchers share at least one reason to under-credit the influence of others doing more basic work. It is common to view as figure those things that are the focus of one's own creative efforts. Those aspects that are shared or logically prior to one's own creative efforts recede into the background, while those aspects that are different or are novel are emphasized and become figure. Thus, the work of others working in the same area on the same problem at the same level of abstraction is likely to be well cited. However, the work of others doing pertinent work that is more basic may be under-cited.

Cryptomnesia proper

A second, less conscious reason, for under-citation of basic research may be the common tendency to overlook ways in which one's work has borrowed from a template or used the work of others as an outline (Marsh et al., 1996). As highlighted in a series of interesting studies, there is a pervasive tendency to steal the ideas of others and not realize the theft. This practice of cryptomnesia or unconscious plagiarism is extremely common. In one study, when people were asked to draw "novel" alien creatures and were given examples that others had drawn "just to get the creative process going," there was an overwhelming tendency to incorporate those aspects of the examples that were consistent. So, for example, if all the sample aliens had four legs, the newly generated aliens were far more likely to have four legs. The plagiarism occurred despite warnings and admonitions. In addition, the plagiarism did not appear to result from laziness. Even though the examples constrained the shape of the creatures, they did not decrease the volume of new alien creatures that were generated (Marsh et al., 1996).

Apparently, there is a strong tendency to pick up ideas that are "in the air" and run with them. The new creations that result are viewed as purely novel and not in need of attribution to anyone else. Thus, it may be relatively easy for psychologists in the marital area to come in contact with many ideas about interpersonal, cognitive, and developmental processes, and abstract from this intellectual milieu a template about processes that may be important in guiding and structuring couple interactions. However, as is highlighted by the Marsh et al. (1996) data, marital researchers may never conclude that they have an intellectual debt to those who informed their work in important ways.

Contextual embeddedness

Under-citation of influences from the social psychology literature relative to influences from other marital therapy literature may also result from differences in the way information from these two sources are represented in memory. Given a focus on differentiating one's work from that of other applied researchers, as well as the direct relevance of the comments of such individuals for one's own work, one might expect that suggestions made by other marital therapy researchers would be embedded in a rich network of relevant information. In contrast, information from social or developmental psychology might be encoded in a less rich semantic network. If so, there could be considerably greater difficulty in generating cues for accurate source monitoring in the latter case than in the former case, leading to the expectation of more errors of source monitoring in relation to social and developmental literatures (cf. Johnson & Raye, 1981), and so greater under-citation.

From partnership to cryptomnesia and back again

As a result of these three factors – figure-ground, cryptomnesia, and contextual embeddedness – there is the potential to profoundly underestimate the impact of social and developmental psychology on the marital therapy literature. Even if the basic literature had a considerable number of direct and indirect effects on the generation of new techniques, there might still be few direct citations.

Ironically, cryptomnesia and an exaggerated sense of one's own unique contribution may tend to degrade the quality of the creative process over time for both clinicians and researchers. In particular, as the theoretical "ground" for the creative process recedes and so is less chronically accessible, it may exert less influence on creative decision making. In place of explicit theory, other less reliable influences will come to carry more weight. Thus, over time, the failure to remember and consider the foundation of one's creative activity should lead to poorer quality innovations. Equally as problematic, the shared framework offered by theory and basic research that allows clinicians, clinical researchers, and basic researchers to share observations and see the relevance of one domain for the other is eroded by the process of cryptomnesia. It therefore seems important for the long-term health of marital therapy that the tendency to under-recognize the impact of theory be reversed. Accordingly, although we suspect that the three processes outlined above can never be eradicated, it is important to mitigate their worst effects. One way to do this is to return to the initial, explicit partnership that existed between social psychology and BMT. Such a partnership would explicitly acknowledge the contributions and the need for communication between social psychologists, marital therapy researchers, and marital therapists.

In the 1960s such a three-way connection was forged by the presence of common framework that facilitated communication and interchange. Indeed, we suspect a common intellectual framework is essential for the partnership in that it makes sensible the exchanges between social psychologists and those working at different levels of abstraction and application. The identification of a robust framework that can support such a three-way interchange is therefore key to stimulating a new period of creativity and development in marital therapy. While we do not suggest that such a framework is already available, there are signs that such a framework is possible. We therefore identify two areas that exemplify the potential for renewed synergy between social psychology and behavioral marital therapy in the future.

A Look Toward the Future

If a comprehensive framework can be advanced that builds on the Kelley et al. (1983b) framework and incorporates recent developments in the study of personal relationships, it may generate the level of sustained enthusiasm within the marital therapy area necessary to re-ignite a period of rapid applied progress. Past success suggests that such a framework need not be a fully fledged theory or provide a complete integration of relevant mid-level theories in order to stimulate applied creativity and progress. As happened in the late 1960s and early 1970s, a shared paradigm can allow strong collaboration and implicit coordination of effort across labs and geographic regions.

Toward a broader framework for understanding "close relationships"

Below we provide a very brief sketch of attachment and goal theory as potential components of a broader framework for the study of dyadic conflict and marital distress, and articulate some of their current and potential connections to marital therapy. Before doing so, we need to make a brief observation about the central construct of marital/relationship quality and the utility of a "vulnerability-stress-adaptation" model (Karney & Bradbury, 1995).

In our view, it is important to conceptualize the construct of marital satisfaction in terms that are consistent with recent developments in research on the structure of attitudes and emotions (Cacioppo, Gardner & Berntson, 1997; Russell & Carroll, 1999). Specifically, conceptualizing marital/relationship quality in terms of evaluative judgments (see Fincham & Bradbury, 1987) that vary along positive and negative dimensions (Fincham & Linfield, 1997) helps ensure conceptual clarity as well as reclaim the close connection with social psychology sought in this section (see also Fincham, Beach, & Kemp-Fincham, 1997).

We also find it useful to have a "meta-framework" for thinking about change processes in marital satisfaction. Karney and Bradbury (1995) offer such a "meta-framework" that identifies the potential importance of enduring vulnerabilities, life events, the various coping responses couples make or fail to make, and the impact of both the context and the dyadic response on changes in marital quality and marital stability. The suggestions that follow are meant to identify processes that may explicate particular pathways within such a broad framework.

Attachment

Because attachment theory appears to have been particularly influential in the development of ICT, and because it provides an important link to social psychology, we elaborate several aspects of its utility for marital therapy. It should be noted, however, that extensive and well-crafted discussions of the relevance of attachment theory for marital therapy, albeit with a different focus, can be found elsewhere (e.g., Kobak, Ruckdeschel, & Hazan, 1994; Whiffen & Johnson, 1998). In addition, excellent discussions of the integration of attachment theory with the broader social cognition and adaptation literatures are also available (e.g., Shaver et al., 1996).

Attachment theory has made its way into behavioral marital therapy both through the influence of attachment-inspired approaches to marital therapy (e.g., Kobak et al., 1994; Greenberg & Johnson, 1988) and indirectly through the influence of ego-analytic writers (e.g., Wile, 1981, 1995). Its contribution to behavioral marital therapy has been directly acknowledged by some BMT researchers (e.g., Notarius, Lashley, & Sullivan, 1997) and indirectly acknowledged through the citation of those who themselves cite attachment theory (e.g., Jacobson & Christensen, 1996). Nonetheless, its contribution tends to be underestimated.

In our view, the contribution of the attachment literature to the evolution of BMT has been both dramatic and profound. The attachment literature suggests that behavioral marital therapists should look for a universal mechanism, activated by the perception that the partner is psychologically or physically unavailable or unresponsive, that has as its goal the reinstatement of a sense of "felt security" (Sroufe & Waters, 1977). At the same time, it suggests that this universal mechanism could take different forms for different individuals (Rholes, Simpson, & Stevens, 1998). It also introduces into behavioral marital therapy the notion that attachment-related emotions may be masked, or entirely deactivated, or hyperactivated, leading to interesting marital dilemmas and sources of confusion and mis-understanding within marital dyads. For example, the attachment perspective suggests that anger may sometimes be prompted by feelings of hurt and vulnerability. But rather than clearly signaling a need for nurturance, the angry response may be misunderstood by the partner and lead to further unavailability and defensiveness. Thus attachment models have introduced the idea that couple problems are not the result of "skill deficits," but rather may be understood as resulting from a positive feedback loop triggered by unac-knowledged or masked feelings of neediness.

In addition, by emphasizing working models, the attachment literature also focuses at-tention on the human capacity for future-oriented simulation and so the potential for strong affective reactions to events that "might" happen, or implications for possible future selves. Thus, attachment accounts lend themselves to elaboration in social-cognitive terms. Attachment-like accounts have been incorporated into marital therapy as a vehicle for "formulating the couples problem" (Jacobson & Christensen, 1996, p. 46), and for help-ing couples understand their problems in a non-blaming manner (Notarius et al., 1997). Attachment explanations are particularly good in this regard in that they suggest a way of construing marital difficulties that renders them understandable to partners while indicat-ing that symptoms of marital distress may be adaptive and constructive at base (see also Emotion Focused Therapy; Greenberg & Johnson, 1988).

Likewise, the implications for therapists are clear. If concerns about partner availability result in masked signals that are interpreted by the partner as signs of unavailability, this may be the source of a vicious cycle maintaining marital discord. Later forms of BMT such as ICT (Jacobson & Christensen, 1996) and PREP (Markman et al., 1994), highlight the central importance of perceiving the partner to be available and interested. Indeed, Markman et al. label lack of acceptance "the mother of all hidden agendas." Thus, the notion that perceived lack of availability or acceptance may result in misunderstanding and extreme forms of dysfunctional interaction is explicitly included in both these newer versions of BMT. Further, this attachment-like idea entirely supplants the previous notion that miscommunication is the result of not knowing how to implement certain communication skills. Accordingly, in recent BMT writings, one might conclude that attachment theory has become the de facto theoretical foundation for communication training as well as for the instigation of positive behavior. It has become a favorite vehicle for reattribution training with distressed couples as well, supplanting to some degree the cognitive-behavioral movement in BMT (e.g., Notarius et al., 1997).

The mere presence of attachment ideas, and the discussion of those ideas, appears to have led to changes in the way BMT researchers think about the process of therapy. In turn, this changed conceptualization seems to have led to changes in the types of techniques proposed in innovative treatment packages. Thus, exposure to ideas from attachment theory has led to changes in the way BMT researchers apply the interventions retained from previous variants of BMT. In particular, rather than focusing on problem-solving communication per se, behavioral marital therapists now focus on the "theme" of the conflict, hidden agendas are likely to be viewed in attachment terms, the critical importance of expressed commitment to the relationship receives greater attention, and the power of the simple act of attentive listening (Markman et al.,1994) has received a new emphasis. In turn this has led behavioral marital therapy researchers to take a new and closer look at the role of supportive interactions between partners (e.g., Carels & Baucom, 1999; Pasch & Bradbury, 1998). We believe that greater recognition of the impact of attachment research on marital therapy and its incorporation into a broader framework for close relationships will have further salutary effects. In particular, making explicit the ongoing incorporation of attachment theory into BMT should allow assumptions that are currently implicit to be explicated clearly and so be better tested. In addition, making attachment influences explicit should highlight possible additional innovations, and should allow BMT (or BCT) researchers to take advantage of ongoing developments in research on adult attachment (e.g., Simpson & Rholes, 1998).

Goals

As important as attachment theory has been for recent changes in BMT, it may be viewed as only a specific instance of goal theory. In attachment theory, many behaviors are made sensible by reference to the goal of maintaining felt security and a comfortable level of proximity/distance. However, even a cursory examination of the social psychological literature suggests that a variety of goals impinge directly or indirectly on couple interaction and have the potential to affect satisfaction or distress. For example, self-evaluation maintenance goals (e.g., Beach et al., 1996; 1998a), belongingness goals (Baumeister & Leary, 1995), self-verification and self-enhancement goals (e.g., Katz & Beach, 1997; Murray & Holmes, 1996; Murray, Holmes, & Griffin, 1996; Snyder & Stukas, 1999), communal relationship goals (Clark & Mills, 1979), and identity and personal growth goals (Aron &

Aron, 1996; Ryan, Sheldon, Kasser, & Deci, 1996), among others, may influence behavior in relationships. Adopting a framework that allows for the interaction of multiple goal systems could therefore be particularly useful for guiding the study of marital interaction and stimulating innovative marital interventions. However, developing a framework that can readily incorporate a range of goals will probably need to go beyond a reliance on attachment theory.

Recent work on goal-directed behavior provides insights into the nature and organization of goals, important characteristics of goals, and the impact of goal orientation on behavior (see Austin & Vancouver, 1996; Gollwitzer & Bargh, 1996). We have argued elsewhere (Fincham & Beach, 1999) that a goal-theoretic perspective has the potential to provide an overarching framework for understanding marriage. Dunning (1999) similarly points to the importance of studying goals to "break open the black box implicit in social cognitive work" and "in exploring how people manage their relations with loved ones" (p. 8). We begin by considering whether such a perspective adds anything new to the marital literature.

A potentially serious obstacle to adopting a broad, goal framework in the marital area is that use of the goal construct remains largely unacknowledged both in work on marriage and in work on personal relationships (see Berscheid, 1994, for a similar lament). Thus, despite frequent, indirect references to goals, there is relatively little in the way of direct guidance on the effect of goals on marital interaction. Also, there is little guidance on how to understand the interplay of multiple goals. This is unfortunate, as a number of heuristic and conceptual advantages follow from making explicit our implicit reliance on the goal construct.

Five premises capture much of the promise of a goal framework for marital therapy. First, all behavior is goal-directed (discrepancies between current and desired states drive behavior to reduce the difference through such processes as test-operate-test-exit cycles; Miller, Galanter, & Pribram,1960). In marital therapy, this premise highlights the importance of identifying the goal that problem behavior serves. This allows alternative, non-problematic ways of meeting the goal to be generated.

Second, spouses don't always know what the goal is even for their own behavior (goals can be latent or implicit as well as consciously experienced). For marital therapy, this premise highlights the potentially limited value of self-report. In the same vein, it should be noted that some goals may emerge in a situation rather than being well formed in advance. In such circumstances, it may not be possible for spouses to self-report all goals that will ultimately influence their interaction because some of the goals will not be elicited until after the interaction is under way.

Third, goals vary widely (from internal set points to complex, cognitively represented outcomes) and cannot be understood in isolation from each other or the dynamics of the larger goal system in which they are embedded (establishing, planning, striving towards, and revising goals; see Austin & Vancouver, 1996). In the marital context, this underscores the importance of allowing for multiple goal influences on behavior. In addition, goal theory provides a theoretically informed way of understanding the potential interaction of contextual effects and enduring vulnerabilities on coping and adaptation in marriage, as well as the way in which such effects could result in shifts in marital satisfaction and stability (cf. Karney & Bradbury, 1995).

Fourth, affect results from moving toward or away from goals, with avoidance goals generating negative affect as discrepancies are reduced, and approach goals generating positive affect as discrepancies are reduced (Carver & Scheier, 1999). In the marital context, this premise suggests different emotional experiences for defensive versus collaborative goals and suggests that affect will be directed toward the partner primarily when the partner is perceived as facilitative or obstructive with regard to active goals. Accordingly, this premise suggests the hypothesis that satisfaction with the partner may vary somewhat as a function of the dimension primed prior to asking for satisfaction ratings and the role of the partner vis-à-vis that dimension (see Fincham & Beach, 1999). Perhaps more importantly, this premise also suggests that careful attention to affective reactions may illuminate unspoken goals or unstated evaluations of partner behavior as facilitative or obstructive.

Therapeutic implications. As noted above, goal theory lends itself to the generation of novel hypotheses about therapeutic processes. Carver and Scheier (1999), for example, point out that it is not merely the degree to which individuals meet their goals that influences affective reactions. Instead, the direction, velocity, and acceleration of movement toward goals is related to magnitude of positive feelings. As a result, goal theory suggests that structuring therapy so that it provides frequent, and concrete feedback about improvement on various goals may help increase positive feelings about therapy and about the partner, even if initial goals have not been met. In a similar vein, it is likely that a focus on concrete goals may be associated with more positive affect in marital therapy (Emmons & Kaiser, 1996).

Importantly, if the partner is viewed as thwarting valued goals, this could lead to ruminative thought regarding the blocked goal (Tesser, Martin, & Cornell, 1996). This should lead to more thinking about the partner and about the thwarted goal. Internal rehearsal of one's own arguments and one's own view of the problem will commonly prove polarizing (Tesser, 1976), and lead to feelings of powerlessness to change (Vanzetti, Notarius & NeeSmith,1992). Such a pattern may be among the most undesirable consequences of traditional behavioral marital therapy with its strong focus on change and its implicit tendency to encourage partners to locate needed changes in the spouse rather than in the self (see Jacobson & Christensen, 1996), and suggests additional possible changes in therapeutic format.

New marital therapies. A marital therapy approach tied to a self-regulatory, goal-setting, framework has been suggested by Halford (1998). Reasoning that couples are likely to experience the greatest sense of control over changes in their own behavior, Halford, Sanders, and Behrens (1994) proposed an emphasis on individual, self-directed change by partners entering marital therapy. This approach emphasizes helping each partner identify ways in which they can begin to address relationship problems without any requirement or expectation that the partner change (see also Coyne & Benazon, 2001, for a similar suggestion about marital therapy in the context of depression). Halford et al. (1994) highlight five different types of goals that may follow from adopting this approach. First, partners may be encouraged to think of new ways to communicate their concerns. Second, the partners may be encouraged to consider ways of making their spouse's behavior less stressful to them even if their partner continues engaging in the behavior. Third, the partners may be encouraged to generate ways of meeting needs that do not require the spouse. Fourth, the partners may consider ways to dissolve their current relationship. And fifth, the partners may decide to uphold the status quo in their relationship. In all cases, the goal of Self-Regulation Couples Therapy (SRCT) is to assist both partners to identify their problems in a way that leads to the formulation of individual goals to address the problem area (Weiss & Halford, 1996).

The self-regulatory approach to marital therapy has the advantages of potentially short-ening the course of marital therapy (e.g., Halford, Osgarby, & Kelly, 1996) and of being considerably more flexible in format than traditional BMT. At the same time, this innova-tive approach illustrates the potential for social psychological theory to guide the elabora-tion and development of an emerging form of marital therapy.

In sum, the assumptions of goal theory outlined earlier provide a vehicle for integrating attachment and self-regulation perspectives within a single framework. In addition, goal theory would appear to be compatible with an emphasis on understanding key contextual and developmental issues in marriage such as the effect of stressors and enduring vulnerabilities (Karney & Bradbury, 1995). Wedded to other considerations highlighted in the Kelley et al. (1983a) framework, the result might be a framework sufficiently flexible to accommodate ongoing developments in broad areas of social psychology such as the psychology of self and the rapidly developing area of social cognition. At the same time, such a framework has the potential to be sufficiently specific to speak to practical issues that are central in such applications as ICT and SRCT. Because work on the goal frame-work is already quite advanced (e.g., Austin & Vancouver, 1996), and because the Kelley et al. framework has already inspired clinical innovation, it seems possible that a new clini-cally informative framework may be close to becoming a reality. In combination with a new willingness by marital therapy researchers to be explicit about their theoretical com-mitments, such a framework seems promising indeed.

Conclusion

Behavioral Marital Therapy (BMT) has changed dramatically over the 1980s and 1990s. It changed from a vibrant, theory-driven enterprise to a stagnant, outcome-study driven en-terprise characterized by a focus on the topography rather than the function of marital interventions. Happily, it now appears to be moving back toward recognition of the im-portance of a unifying framework. At the same time, the most recent innovations (Integra-tive Couples Therapy [ICT] and Self-Regulation Couples Therapy, [SRCT]) appear to have clear links to thriving areas of investigation of interest to social psychologists. We propose that with appropriate input from social psychologists, ICT and SRCT could help stimulate a return to explicit partnership between social psychologists and marital therapy researchers. ICT appears to take a number of technical developments and use the Kelley et al. (1983a) framework to integrate them into a cohesive pattern. At the same time, changes introduced in both PREP and ICT are understandable as responses to developments in the basic attachment literature, even if these influences are somewhat under-cited. Conversely, SRCT is explicitly tied to the self-regulatory framework of Karoly (1993), and this provides a direct route to the consideration of the broader literature on goals. In both cases, the dialogue between marital therapy researchers and social psychologists seems full of promise.

Epilogue

The absence of theoretical development during the 1980s, and the concomitant stagnation of BMT, appears to have resulted from a considered decision to avoid theory, rather being the result of some inevitable split between behavioral marital therapy and its social psychological roots. Because behavioral marital therapy researchers believed that the documentation of couple behavior was necessary before clinically useful theory building could occur, they quit looking to developments in social psychology as a source of creative inspiration. However, there is now an opportunity for a renewed dialogue between behavioral marital therapy researchers and social psychologists.

A new integrative framework that may incorporate many potentially useful mid-level theories appears within reach. To realize this potential it is important for marital therapy researchers to acknowledge more fully the role of basic research in inspiring creative leaps in technique. Likewise, it will be important for social psychologists to look past the shroud of cryptomnesia and see the opportunity to comment on the many interesting processes that unfold in the context of marital therapy. Such commentary, if it is to be credible, may require social psychologists to do research with samples other than undergraduate students, to learn more about clinical phenomena, and to be receptive to input from sources other than the social psychological literature. Likewise, such a dialogue requires greater willingness on the part of marital therapy researchers and marital therapists to examine the social psychological literature and not require that every theoretical proposition be tested on married couples before it is considered potentially relevant to understanding marital dynamics. If social psychologists and clinical psychologists interested in marital therapy each carry out even a small part of this prescription, the first decade of the new century is likely to be an exceptionally exciting period for marital research.

References

Agras, W. S., and Berkowitz, R. (1980). Clinical research and behavior therapy: Halfway there? *Behavior Therapy, 11*, 472–487.

Aron, A., and Aron, E. N. (1996). Self and self-expansion in relationships. In G. J. O. Fletcher and J. Fitness (Eds.), *Knowledge structures in close relationships* (pp. 324–344). Mahwah, NJ: Erlbaum.

Austin, J. T., & Vancouver, J. B. (1996). Goal constructs in psychology: Structure, process, and content. *Psychological Bulletin, 120*, 338–375.

Azrin, N., Naster, B., & Jones, R. (1973). Reciprocity counseling: A rapid learning-based procedure for marital counseling. *Behavior Research and Therapy, 11*, 365–382.

Baldwin, M. W., Keelan, J., Patrick, R., Fehr, B., Enns, V., & Koh-Rangarajoo, E. (1996). Social-cognitive conceptualization of attachment working models: Availability and accessibility effects. *Journal of Personality and Social Psychology, 71*, 94–109.

Barlow, D. H., & Hofmann, S. G. (1997). Efficacy and the dissemination of psychological treatments. In D. M. Clark & C. G. Fairburn (Eds.), *Science and practice of cognitive behaviour therapy.* (pp. 95–117). Oxford: Oxford University Press.

Baucom, D. H., & Epstein, N. (1990). *Cognitive behavioral marital therapy.* New York: Brunner/ Mazel.

Baucom, D. H., Epstein, N., Rankin, L. A., & Burnett, C. K. (1996). Understanding and treating marital distress from a cognitive-behavioral orientation. In K. S. Dobson & K. D. Craig (Eds.), *Advances in cognitive-behavioral therapy.* (pp. 210–236). Thousand Oaks, CA: Sage.

Baucom, D. H., Sayers, S., & Sher, T. G. (1990). Supplementing behavioral marital therapy with cognitive restructuring and emotional expressiveness training: An outcome investigation. *Journal of Consulting and Clinical Psychology, 58,* 636–645.

Baucom, D. H., Shoham, V., Mueser, K. T., Daiuto, A. D., & Stickle, T. R. (1998). Empirically supported couple and family interventions for marital distress and adult mental health problems. *Journal of Consulting and Clinical Psychology, 66,* 53–88.

Baumeister, R. F., & Leary, M. R. (1995). The need to belong: Desire for interpersonal attachments as a fundamental human motivation. *Psychological Bulletin, 117,* 497–529.

Beach, S. R. H. (1991). Social cognition and the relationship repair process: Toward better outcome in marital therapy. In G. J. O. Flecher & F. D. Fincham (Eds.), *Cognition in close relationships* (pp. 307–328). Hillsdale, NJ: Erlbaum.

Beach, S. R. H., Fincham, F. D., & Katz, J. (1998). Marital therapy in the treatment of depression: Toward a third generation of therapy and research. *Clinical Psychology Review, 18,* 635–661.

Beach, S. R. H., Tesser, A., Fincham, F. D., Jones, D. J., Johnson, D., & Whitaker, D. J. (1998a). Pleasure and pain in doing well, together: An investigation of performance related affect in close relationships. *Journal of Personality and Social Psychology, 74,* 923–938.

Beach, S. R. H., Tesser, A., Mendolia, M., Anderson, P., Crelia, R., Whitaker, D. G., & Fincham, F. D. (1996). Self-evaluation maintenance in marriage: Toward a perfomance ecology of the marital relationship. *Journal of Family Psychology, 10,* 379–396.

Berscheid, E. (1994). Interpersonal relationships. *Annual Review of Psychology, 45,* 79–129.

Beutler, L. E., & Consoli, A. J. (1992). Systemic Eclectic Psychotherapy. In J. C. Norcross and M. R. Goldfried (Eds.), *Handbook of psychotherapy integration* (pp. 264–299). New York: Basic Books.

Birchler, G. R., Weiss, R. L., & Vincent, J. P. (1975). A multimethod analysis of social reinforcement exchange between maritally distressed and nondistressed spouse and stranger dyads. *Journal of Personality and Social Psychology, 31,* 349–360.

Blau, P. M. (1964). *Exchange and power in social life.* New York: Wiley.

Borkovec, T. D., & Castonguay, L. G. (1998). What is the scientific meaning of empirically supported therapy? *Journal of Consulting and Clinical Psychology, 66,* 136–142.

Bradbury, T. N. (1998). *The developmental course of marital dysfunction.* Cambridge, UK: Cambridge University Press.

Bradbury, T. N., & Fincham, F. D. (1990). Attributions in marriage: Review and critique. *Psychological Bulletin, 107,* 3–33.

Brehm, S. S. (1976). *The application of social psychology to clinical practice.* Washington, DC: Hemisphere.

Cacioppo, J. T., Gardner, W. L., & Berntson, G. G. (1997). Beyond bipolar conceptualizations and measures: The case of attitudes and evaluative space. *Personality and Social Psychology Review, 1,* 3–25.

Carels, R. A., & Baucom, D. H. (1999). Support in marriage: Factors associated with on-line perceptions of support helpfulness. *Journal of Family Psychology, 13,* 131–144.

Carver, C. S., & Scheier, M. F. (1999). Themes and issues in the self-regulation of behavior. In R. S. Wyer, Jr. (Ed.). *Perspectives on behavioral self-regulation: Advances in social cognition, Vol. XII.* (pp. 1–105). Mahwah, NJ, US: Lawrence Erlbaum Associates, Inc.

Chambless, D. L., & Hollon, S. D. (1998). Defining empirically supported therapies. *Journal of Consulting and Clinical Psychology, 66,* 7–18.

Christensen, A., & Heavey, C. L. (1999). Interventions for couples. *Annual Review of Psychology, 50,* 165–190.

Clark, M. S., & Mills, J. (1979). Interpersonal attraction in exchange and communal relationships.

Journal of Personality and Social Psychology, 37, 12–24.

Coyne, J. C., & Benazon, N. R. (2001). Not agent blue: Effects of marital functioning on depression and implications for treatment. In S. R. H. Beach (Ed.). *Marital and family processes in depression: A scientific foundation for clinical practice.* (pp. 25–43). Washington, DC, US: American Psychological Association.

Crowe, M. J. (1978). Conjoint marital therapy: A controlled outcome study. *Psychological Medicine, 8,* 623–636.

Davison, G. (1998). Being bolder with the boulder model: The challenge of education and training in empirically supported treatments. *Journal of Consulting and Clinical Psychology, 66,* 163–167.

Dunning, D. (1999). Postcards from the edge: Notes on social psychology, the story so far. *Contemporary Psychology, 44,* 6–8.

Emmons, R. A., & Kaiser, H. A. (1996). Goal orientation and emotional well-being: Linking goals and affect through the self. In L. Martin & A. Tesser (Eds.), *Striving and feeling: Interactions among goals, affect, and self-regulation* (pp. 79–98). Mahwah, NJ: Erlbaum.

Epstein, E. E., & McCrady, B. S. (1998). Behavioral couples treatment and drug use disorders: Current status and innovations. *Clinical Psychology Review, 18,* 689–711.

Fincham, F. D., & Beach, S. R. H. (1999). Conflict in marriage: Implications for working with couples. *Annual Review of Psychology, 50,* 47–77.

Fincham, F. D., & Beach, S. R. H. (1999). Marriage in the new Millennium: Is there a place for social cognition in marital research? *Journal of Social and Personal Relationships, 16,* 685–704.

Fincham, F. D., Beach, S. R. H., & Bradbury, T. N. (1990). Purging concepts from the study of marriage and marital therapy. *Journal of Family Psychology, 4,* 195–201.

Fincham, F. D., Beach, S. R. H., & Kemp-Fincham, S. I. (1997). Marital quality: A new theoretical perspective. In R. J. Sternberg & M. Hojjat (Eds.), *Satisfaction in close relationships* (pp. 275–304). New York: Guilford Press.

Fincham, F. D., & Bradbury, T. N. (1987). The assessment of marital quality: A reevaluation. *Journal of Marriage and the Family, 49,* 797–809.

Fincham, F. D., Fernandes, L. O. L., & Humphreys, K. (1993). *Communicating in relationships.* Champaign, Il: Research Press.

Fincham, F. D., & Linfield, K. J. (1997). A new look at marital quality: Can spouses feel positive and negative about their marriage? *Journal of Family Psychology, 11,* 489–502.

Fletcher, G. J. O. & Fincham, F. D. (Eds.) (1991). *Cognition in close relationships.* Hillsdale, NJ: Erlbaum.

Glenn, N. D. (1998). Problems and prospects in longitudinal research on marriage: A sociologist's perspective. In T. N. Bradbury (Ed.), *The developmental course of marital dysfunction.* (pp. 427–440). Cambridge, UK: Cambridge University Press.

Goldfried, M. R. (1980). Toward the delineation of therapeutic change principles. *American Psychologist, 35,* 991–999.

Goldfried, M. R., and Wolfe, B. E. (1996). Psychotherapy practice and research: Repairing a strained alliance. *American Psychologist, 51,* 1007–1015.

Gollwitzer, P. M., & Bargh, J. A. (Eds.). (1996). *The psychology of action.* New York: Guilford Press.

Gottman, J. M. (1998). Psychology and the study of marital processes. *Annual Review of Psychology, 49,* 169–197.

Gottman, J. M., Notarius, C., Gonso, J., & Marman, H. (1976a). *A couple's guide to communication.* Champaign, Il: Research Press.

Gottman, J. M., Notarius, C., Markman, H., Yoppi, B., & Rubin, M. R. (1976b). Behavior exchange theory and marital decision making. *Journal of Personality and Social Psychology, 34,* 14–23.

Greenberg, L. S., & Johnson, S. M. (1988). *Emotionally focused therapy for couples.* New York: Guilford Press.

Hahlweg, K., & Markman, H. J. (1988). Effectiveness of behavioral marital therapy: Empirical status of behavioral techniques in preventing and alleviating marital distress. *Journal of Consulting and Clinical Psychology, 56,* 440–447.

Halford, W. K. (1998). The ongoing evolution of behavioral couples therapy: Retrospect and prospect. *Clinical Psychology Review, 18,* 613–634.

Halford, W. K., Sanders, M. R., & Behrens, B. C. (1994). Self-regulation in behavioral couples therapy. *Behavior Therapy, 25,* 431–452.

Halford, W. K., Osgarby, S., & Kelly, A. (1996). Brief behavioral couples therapy: A preliminary evaluation. *Behavioural and Cognitive Psychotherapy, 24,* 263–273.

Harvey, J. (1983). The founding of the *Journal of Social and Clinical Psychology. Journal of Social and Clinical Psychology, 1,* 1–3.

Homans, G. C. (1961). *Social behavior: Its elementary forms.* New York: Harcourt, Brace, & World.

Jacobson, N. S. (1977). Problem solving and contingency contracting in the treatment of marital discord. *Journal of Consulting and Clinical Psychology, 46,* 442–452.

Jacobson, N. S., & Christensen, A. (1996). *Integrative couple therapy: Promoting acceptance and change.* New York: Norton.

Jacobson, N. S., Follette, W. C., Revenstorf, D., Baucom, D. H., Hahlweg, K., & Margolin, G. (1984). Variability in outcome and clinical significance of behavioral marital therapy: A reanalysis of outcome data. *Journal of Consulting and Clinical Psychology, 52,* 497–504.

Jacobson, N. S., & Margolin, G. (1979). *Marital therapy.* New York: Brunner/Mazel.

Johnson, M. K., & Raye, C. L. (1981). Reality monitoring. *Psychological Review, 88,* 67–85.

Kanfer, F. H., & Schefft, B. K. (1988). *Guiding the process of therapeutic change.* Champaign IL: Research Press.

Karney, B. R., & Bradbury, T. N. (1995). The longitudinal course of marital quality and stability: A review of theory, method, and research. *Psychological Bulletin, 118,* 3–34.

Karoly, P. (1993). Mechanisms of self-regulation: A systems view. *Annual Review of Psychology, 44,* 175–184.

Katz, J., & Beach, S. R. H. (1997). Self-verification and depressive symptoms in marriage and courtship: A multiple pathway model. *Journal of Marriage and the Family, 59,* 903–914.

Kelley, H. H. (1979). *Personal relationships.* Hillsdale, NJ: Erlbaum.

Kelley, H. H., Berscheid, E., Christensen, A., Harvey, J. H., Huston, T. L., Levinger, G., McClintock, E., Peplau, L. A., & Peterson, D. R. (1983a). *Close relationships.* New York: Freeman.

Kelley, H. H., Berscheid, E., Christensen, A., Harvey, J. H., Huston, T. L., Levinger, G., McClintock, E., Peplau, L. A., & Peterson, D. R. (1983b). Analyzing close relationships. In Kelley, H. H., Berscheid, E., Christensen, A., Harvey, J. H., Huston, T. L., Levinger, G., McClintock, E., Peplau, L. A., & Peterson, D. R. (Eds.), *Close relationships* (pp. 20–67). New York: Freeman

Kelley, H. H., & Thibaut, J. W. (1978). *Interpersonal relations: A theory of interdependence.* New York: Wiley.

Kobak, R., Ruckdeschel, K., & Hazan, C. (1994). From symptom to signal: An attachment view of emotion in marital therapy. In S. M. Johnson & L. S. Greenberg (Eds.), *The heart of the matter.* (pp. 46–71). New York: Brunner/Mazel.

London, P. (1972). The end of ideology in behavior modification. *American Psychologist, 27,* 913–920.

Markman, H. J., Notarius, C. I., Stephen, T., & Smith, T. (1981). Behavioral observation systems for couples: The current status. In E. Filsinger & R. Lewis (Eds.), *Assessing marriage: New behavioral approaches* (pp. 234–262). Beverly Hills, CA: Sage.

Markman, H. J., Stanley, S., & Blumberg, S. L. (1994). *Fighting for your marriage.* San Fancisco: Jossey-Bass.

Marsh, R. L., Landau, J. D., & Hicks, J. L. (1996). How examples may (and may not) constrain creativity. *Memory and Cognition, 24,* 669–680.

Miller, G. E., Galanter, E., & Pribram, K. H. (1960). *Plans and the structure of behavior.* New York: Holt.

Murray, S. L., & Holmes, J. G. (1996). The construction of relationship realities. In G. J. O. Fletcher & J. Fitness (Eds.), *Knowledge structures in close relationships* (pp. 91–120). Mahwah, NJ: Erlbaum.

Murray, S. L., Holmes, J. G., & Griffin, D. W. (1996). The benefits of positive illusions: Idealization and the construction of satisfaction in close relationships. *Journal of Personality and Social Psychology, 71,* 1155–1180.

Nathan, P. E., & Gorman, J. M. (1998). *A guide to treatments that work.* Oxford: Oxford University

Press.

Notarius, C. I., Lashley, S. L., & Sullivan, D. J. (1997). Angry at your partner? Think again. In R. J. Sternberg & M. Hojjat (Eds.), *Satisfaction in close relationships* (pp. 219–248). New York: Guilford Press.

O'Farrell, T. J., Choquette, K. A., Cutter, H. S. G., Brown, E. D., & McCourt, W. F. (1993). Behavioral marital therapy with and without additional couples relapse prevention sessions for alcoholics and their wives. *Journal of Studies on Alcohol, 54*, 652–666.

O'Leary, K. D. & Turkewitz, H. (1978). Marital therapy from a behavioral perspective. In T. J. Paolino & B. S. McCrady (Eds.), *Marriage and marital therapy* (pp. 240–297). New York: Brunner/ Mazel.

O'Leary, K. D., Heyman, R. E., & Neidig, P. (1999). Treatment of wife abuse: A comparison of gender specific and conjoint approaches. *Behavior Therapy, 30*, 475–505.

Pasch, L. A., & Bradbury, T. N. (1998). Social support, conflict, and the development of marital dysfunction. *Journal of Consulting and Clinical Psychology, 66*, 219–230.

Paul, G. L. (1969). Behavior modification research: Design and tactics. In C. M. Franks (Ed.), *Behavior therapy: Appraisal and status*. New York: McGraw-Hill.

Rholes, W. S., Simpson, J. A., & Stevens, J. G. (1998). Attachment orientations, social support, and conflict resolution in close relationships. In J. A. Simpson, & W. S. Rholes (Eds.), *Attachment theory and close relationships* (pp. 166–188). New York: Guilford Press.

Russell, J. A., & Carroll, J. M. (1999). On the bipolarity of positive and negative affect. *Psychological Bulletin, 125*, 3–30.

Ryan R. M., Sheldon, K. M., Kasser, T., & Deci, E. (1996). All goals are not created equal: An organismic perspective on the nature of goals and their regulation. In P. M. Gollwitzer & J. A. Bargh (Eds.), *Psychology of action: Linking cognition and motivation to behavior* (pp. 7–26). New York: Guilford Press.

Sayers, S. L., Kohn, C. S., & Heavey, C. (1998). Prevention of Marital Dysfunction: Behavioral approaches and beyond. *Clinical Psychology Review, 18*, 713–745.

Shaver, P. R., Collins, N., & Clark, C. L. (1996). Attachment styles and internal working models of self and relationship patterns. In G. J. O. Fletcher and J. Fitness (Eds.), *Knowledge structures in close relationships* (pp. 25–62). Mahwah, NJ: Erlbaum.

Simpson, J. A., & Rholes, W.S. (1998). *Attachment theory and close relationships*. New York: Guilford Press.

Snyder, C. R., & Forsyth, D. R. (1991). *Social and clinical psychology united*. In C. R. Snyder & D. R. Forsyth (Eds.), *Handbook of social and clinical psychology* (pp. 3–17). New York: Pergamon.

Snyder, M., & Stukas, A. A. (1999). Interpersonal processes: The interplay of cognitive, motivational, and behavioral activities in social interaction. *Annual Review of Psychology, 50*, 273–304.

Sommer, R. (1982). The district attorney's dilemma: Experimental games and the real world of plea bargaining. *American Psychologist, 37*, 526–532.

Speer, D. C. (1972). Marital dysfunctionality and two person non-zero-sum game behavior. *Journal of Personality and Social Psychology, 21*, 18–24.

Sroufe, L. A., & Waters, E. (1977). Attachment as an organizational construct. *Child Development, 48*, 1184–1199.

Stuart, R. B. (1969). Operant interpersonal treatment for marital discord. *Journal of Consulting and Clinical Psychology, 33*, 675–682.

Stuart, R. B. (1980). *Helping couples change: A social learning approach to marital therapy*. New York: Guilford Press.

Tesser, A. (1976). Thought and reality constraints as determinants of attitude polarization. *Journal of Research in Personality, 10*, 183–194.

Tesser, A., Martin, L. L., & Cornell, D. P. (1996). On the substitutability of self-protective mechanisms. In P. M. Gollwitzer & J. A. Bargh (Eds.), *The psychology of action: Linking cognition and motivation to behavior*. New York: Guilford Press.

Thibaut, J., & Kelley, H. H. (1959). *The social psychology of groups*. New York: Wiley.

Turkewitz, H., & O'Leary, K. D. (1976, December). *Communication and behavioral marital therapy: An outcome study*. Paper presented at the Annual Meeting of the Association for the Advancement of Behavior Therapy. New York.

Vanzetti, N. A., Notarius, C. I., & NeeSmith, D. (1992). Specific and generalized expectancies in marital interaction. *Journal of Family Psychology, 6,* 171–183.

Vincent, J. P., Weiss, R. L., & Birchler, G. R. (1975). Dyadic problem solving as a function of marital distress and spousal vs. stranger interactions. *Behavior Therapy, 6,* 475–487.

Weiss, R. L. (1978). The conceptualization of marriage from a behavioral perspective. In T. J. Paolino, Jr. and B. S. McCrady (Eds.), *Marriage and marital therapy: Psychoanalytic, behavioral and systems theory perspectives* (pp. 165–239). New York: Brunner/Mazel.

Weiss, R. L., & Halford, W. K. (1996). Managing marital therapy: Helping partners change. In V. Van Hasselt & M. Hersen (Eds.), *Sourcebook of psychological treatment manuals for adult disorders* (pp. 312–341). New York: Plenum.

Weiss, R. L., Patterson, G. R., & Hops, H. (1973). A framework for conceptualizing marital conflict: A technology for altering it, some data for evaluating it. In L. D. Handy & E. L. Mash (Eds.), *Behavior change: Methodology, concepts and practice* (pp. 309–342). Champaign, IL: Research Press.

Whiffen, V. E., & Johnson, S. M. (1998). An attachment framework for the treatment of childbearing depression. *Clinical Psychology: Science and Practice, 5,* 478–493.

Whisman, M. A., & Snyder, D. K. (1997). Evaluating and improving the efficacy of conjoint marital therapy. In W. K. Halford & H. J. Markman (Eds.), *Clinical handbook of marriage and couples intervention* (pp. 679–693). New York: Wiley.

Wile, D. B. (1981). *Couples therapy: A nontraditional approach.* New York: Wiley.

Wile, D. B. (1995). The ego-analytic approach to couple therapy. In N. S. Jacobson & A. S. Gurman (Eds.), *Clinical handbook of couple therapy* (pp. 91–120). New York: Guilford Press.

Subject Index

abusive relationships, 132, 148–9, 567
  attributions in, 9, 13
  dependence in, 362, 367, 441, 443
  see also exploitation
acceptance, 420, 461, 577
  of self, 438, 439
  see also social inclusion
accessibility
  of behavior, 67
  of cognitions, 23, 43–5, 52, 69, 72, 77, 94,
    101, 402
  of emotions, 548–9
accommodation, 231, 375, 376, 378–9, 443
accuracy
  and self, 438, 470, 510
  costs of, 94, 230, 232, 235, 240, 246, 247,
    428
  of group, 208, 509
accuracy motives, 92, 458
  individual differences in, 235, 240–2, 245,
    429
  situational influences on, 49–50, 94–6, 102,
    229–30, 238, 451
actor–partner model, 523–8
actual–ideal discrepancies, 88, 91–6, 98–9,
    101–2, 447, 450
  consequences of, 38–40, 98, 552

adolescence, 146, 148, 167, 426, 552
affect *see* emotion
affiliation motives, 390–3, 403, 416
age differences, 167, 169, 179, 197, 417, 450
agency, 180, 442
aggression, 129–53, 415, 418
  and self-esteem, 411, 427, 441
  defined, 130–2, 136, 137
  goals in, 130–2, 153, 459
  see also abusive relationships
alcohol, 151, 284, 542
alcoholism, 567
alexithemia, 280–2, 299
alternatives *see* comparison level for
    alternatives; flexibility; partner
    alternatives; relationship alternatives
altruism, 162–3, 170, 283, 301, 416–17
  in helping, 166, 170–3, 175, 177–8, 181–2,
    186, 490–2
  reciprocal, 143, 177
ambiguity
  and attributions, 37, 149, 210, 215
  and empathic accuracy, 239, 241, 244
  and interactions, 42, 164, 185, 197, 368–9
  in cognitive bias, 95, 207, 208, 209, 390–2,
    400, 403
  of fairness, 208, 209

ambivalence, 241, 284, 300, 382
amygdala, 313
anaclicticism, 441–2, 552
anger, 255, 283
    associated emotions, 132, 263, 286
    expression of, 256, 257, 258, 266
    generation of, 17, 140, 168, 260, 286, 320,
        379, 576
    outcomes of, 140, 142, 168, 217–18, 326
    regulation of, 117, 149, 287, 326–7, 377,
        538–9, 549–50
anxiety
    expression of, 266, 269
    in empathic accuracy, 235, 241–6
    regulation of, 288, 381, 393, 538–9, 549
    see also attachment (styles); social anxiety
Aristotle, 313
aroma, 164
arousal *see* physiological arousal
aspirations, 204, 208, 363
    see also hope
associative networks, 113, 132, 548
    see also knowledge structures (integration of)
astronomy, 289, 295
attachment
    and behavior, 78–80, 414
    and cognitive response, 72–6, 242, 397,
        540–2, 544–7, 552
    and emotion, 76–8, 254, 265–7, 269, 272,
        538–55, 576
    and therapy, 575–6, 580
    in adult close relationships, 62, 64–80, 318,
        333–4, 349, 361, 371, 374, 375, 537
    measuring, 62–3, 68, 334, 335, 507, 538,
        541, 554
    styles, 60, 62–3, 70, 333–4, 374, 480,
        538–55
    theory, 60–2, 333–4, 421, 450, 479–80,
        537–41, 555
    see also working models
attention, 163–4, 315, 380
    selective, 48, 72–3, 77, 95, 139, 382, 397,
        399, 401
attentive listening, 577
attitudes, 469, 552, 575
    vs ability, 284, 301
    see also beliefs, values
attractiveness
    and self-esteem, 411, 422, 442, 444–7

influence of, 36, 91, 92, 96, 147, 165, 167,
    232–3, 380, 423
attribution hypothesis, 6, 8
attributions
    and behavior, 10–12, 18, 78, 165, 168, 170
    dysfunctional, 12, 573
    in negotiations, 209–12, 214–16
    measuring, 6, 8, 12–13, 21–2
    style, 15, 20, 21, 75
    see also disposition/situation attributions
authenticity, 461
authoritarianism, 197
automatic mechanisms
    in behavior, 72, 142, 371, 373, 375
    in cognition, 22, 95, 118, 316, 318, 396
autonomic nervous system, 311–13, 315, 316
    see also physiological arousal
auxiliary ego, 538
avoidance/escape, 234–5, 239, 241, 246, 287,
    288
awe, 286

basking in reflective glory, 427, 447
behavior
    and working models, 36, 71–2, 78–9
    interdependence in, 310–11
    regulated/inhibited, 88, 101–2, 134, 138,
        144–51, 313, 315, 374, 378, 425
behavioral confirmation, 374, 375, 439
    see also self-fulfilling prophecies
behavioral contrast, 526
behavioral decision theory, 196, 199–201,
    209, 219
behavioral genetics, 510
behavioral marital therapy (BMT), 559,
    561–70, 574, 575, 577, 580–1
behavioral repertoire, 561, 562, 564
behaviorism, trends in, 6, 34, 563
beliefs, 36, 41–2
    about emotion, 299, 539
    about relationships, 34–5, 37, 64, 89, 265,
        266, 269, 337, 398
    and behavior, 138, 169, 206, 210
    changing/maintaining, 32, 40, 46, 50, 52,
        374, 540
    in relationship satisfaction, 35–8, 43, 326
    unrealistic, 35, 325–6
belongingness, 173, 360, 415, 485, 509, 577
betrayal, 379

between-spouse differences *see* self-partner
  differences
blame, 6, 13, 210, 214
boredom, 312, 313, 333, 482
brainstorming, 561
business relationships, 255, 270
business schools, 196, 199
bystander intervention model, 163–4, 178,
  514
  see also altruism; helping

California Task Force to Promote Self-esteem
  and Personal and Social Responsibility,
  439
career achievement, 66, 181, 213, 218, 300
caretaker–child relationships *see* parent–child
  relationships
central nervous system, 313
character education, 301
charitable donations, motives for, 179, 181,
  183
chemistry, 506, 507
children
  in close relationships, 94, 337, 418
  in coping, 545–7
client-centered therapy, 438, 439
clinical psychology
  and attachment, 553, 555
  and self-esteem, 430, 440, 445, 449, 468
  and social psychology, 4–6, 16–18, 558–81
closeness, 317, 319, 485, 525
  defined, 256, 309, 310–11
  degrees of, 320–1, 324–5, 488–9, 491, 495
  measuring, 335, 487
  see also interdependence
coercion, 203, 459, 562
coercive tactics *see* aggression
cognition
  and emotion, 8–9, 17, 88, 185, 218, 279,
    280, 282, 284, 288, 296, 299, 311–27,
    342–3, 351, 375, 401, 445, 541, 542
  in study of close relationships, 14, 46, 51–2,
    485
  shared, 231–2, 508, 525
  structure of, 33, 312
cognitive behavioral therapy, 383, 560, 566
  marital, 559, 562
cognitive complexity, 41–3, 46, 197
cognitive disorganization/fragmentation, 541,

553, 554
cognitive interdependence, 375, 381, 485, 487
cognitive learning model, 167
cognitive processes
  defined, 46
  in relationship satisfaction, 35–40, 42–3,
    44, 47–9, 337, 360, 578
  relational aspects of, 310, 366, 375
cognitive science, 568
cohesiveness, 399, 506, 508, 509, 511
  model of commitment, 337–9, 350
commitment, 175, 181, 200, 215
  see also relationship commitment
communal/interpersonal orientation, 271,
  371–7, 397
  individual differences in, 180, 254, 265,
    267–71
communal relationships
  and motives, 165, 175–6, 260, 485–6, 577
  defined, 255–7, 261
  strength of, 256, 257, 270
  see also closeness; relationship *categories*
communication, 198, 207, 445, 446, 511,
    552, 579
  for social comparisons, 388, 389, 391
  theory, 568
  training for, 561, 562, 577
  see also disclosure; emotional expression
companionate love *see* passionate *vs*
  companionate love
comparator, 316
comparison level
  as relationship standard, 35, 87, 337,
    360–2, 366
  changes to, 361, 382
  in therapy, 561
comparison level for alternatives, 87, 337,
    361–2, 365, 382
  see also partner alternatives; relationship
    alternatives
compartmentalization, 115, 117–18
competitiveness, 197, 217, 374, 375, 417–22,
    427
competitor
  perceptions of, 198–200, 209–10, 212,
    214–15, 217
  responses to, 152, 325, 414, 424–5, 429
computational theories, 135–7, 142, 152
confirmation bias, 210, 449

conflict, 5, 108, 211, 218–19, 382, 441, 524, 562
  and cognitive bias, 93–4, 109, 111, 208, 215, 216, 394
  attributions in, 9–11, 15, 17, 19, 78, 210, 212, 379, 399
  avoiding, 67, 234–5, 443
  interdependence in, 319, 359, 368
  themes in, 569, 577
conflict resolution, 234, 238, 398, 443
  evolution in, 133, 140
  in relationship quality, 319, 366
  poor strategies for, 11, 148, 153
  see also problem-solving
connectionist modeling, 507
consciousness, arousal in, 313, 316
consistency motives, 32, 73–4, 120, 215, 458, 461, 479, 491
construal, 75–6, 198–9, 210–12, 487
contact hypothesis *see* extended contact hypothesis
contagion processes, 511
contextual embeddedness, 574
contingency rules, 371
  see also decision-making
control
  in interactions, 66, 198, 199, 213, 365, 368–70, 376–7
  measuring, 526
  theory, 91
controllability, 165, 168, 197, 198, 244, 262, 395, 411, 579
  illusions of, 213–15
convergence, 511
conviction, 108–21
cooperation, 204, 213, 374, 375
coping strategies, 401, 542, 555
  and self-enhancement, 93, 115, 212, 215, 216, 401, 470
  emotion in, 286, 288, 300, 312
  in relationships, 37, 38, 575, 578
  individual differences in, 67, 93, 270, 461, 539–48, 551, 553–4
cost–reward analysis
  of aggression, 145–6
  of helping, 162, 165–7, 171–3, 175, 180, 182–3
  in close relationships, 245, 337, 363, 366, 479

counselors, emotional intelligence of, 297
creativity
  emotion in, 284–5, 296, 297
  in therapy, 574, 575
criminality, 411, 421
cross-cultural comparisons
  aggression, 133, 146, 149–51, 417
  groups, 198, 511
  helping, 163–5, 174, 176, 179
  relationship cognitions, 8, 367
  self, 424, 429–30, 487
  universal factors in, 133, 150, 168, 176, 177, 185, 416, 419, 429
cross-level generalization error, 507–8
cross-sectional research, 33, 40, 98
cross-species comparisons
  emotion, 315, 538
  groups/status, 131, 133, 142–3, 415, 419, 420, 424–5
  kin behavior, 177, 424
  learning, 145
  self, 457, 460
crowd behavior, 511
  see also bystander intervention model
cryptomnesia, 559, 563, 565, 571–5, 581
cultural psychology, 519
culture, 134, 139, 140, 143–4, 150–1, 508
  see also cross-cultural comparisons; norms

danger zones, 234, 236, 239, 246
decision games, 177, 207, 211, 213–14, 564, 565
decision-making
  biases in, 200, 215, 216, 509
  evolutionary rules in, 137, 139, 140, 141, 149, 153, 414, 421
  in helping, 163, 171
  mediating influences on, 145, 149, 150, 152, 218
  relationships in, 204, 367, 368, 574
  see also behavioral decision theory
default hierarchy, 68
defense mechanisms, 239
defensiveness, 203, 296, 327, 549, 576
deficiency love, 438
deficiency perception, 422
denial, 112, 239
dependency regulation hypothesis, 120
dependent personality disorder, 443

depression
  and self, 93, 401, 429, 444–5, 449, 459,
    552
  and therapy, 4, 567, 579
  conceptualized, 34, 425, 429, 551–2
  emotional intelligence in, 287, 288, 296,
    299, 300
  in attribution research, 4, 8–10
derogation, 48, 95, 113, 214–15, 375, 380,
    425, 442, 459
description/prescription, 199–201, 203, 217,
    219
desensitization, 146–7
detachment, 539
development algorithms, 138
developmental psychology, 568, 570, 573, 574
diagnostic situations, 376
diagnosticity bias, 50
disclosure, 288–9, 481, 484, 487
  see also emotional expression
discrepancy detection, 314–16, 319, 321
disengagement
  behavioral, 542
  moral, 150
disgust, 257
disposition/situation attributions, 3, 174, 210,
    214
  in close relationships, 5, 38, 95, 112–13,
    317–18, 488
dissociative disorders, 553
distancing, 542–7
distress
  and attachment, 538–42, 551, 555
  and empathy, 229–31, 233–5, 239, 246
  and relationships, 321, 366, 377
  cognitive influences on, 6, 11, 118, 325,
    383, 390, 392, 394, 400–3
  expression of, 267, 269–70, 539, 540
  in others, 164, 167–71, 472
divorce, 32, 94, 109, 337, 398, 524, 547–8,
    551, 567
  see also relationship dissolution
domain specificity, 413–14, 420
  in attributions, 13, 23
  in self-esteem, 412, 414–15, 419–21, 426,
    428, 430
dominance
  hierarchies, 415, 419, 426
  seeking, 441, 445, 461

downward comparisons, 392–7, 400–3
  in partner selection, 423–4, 449, 451
drug abuse, 428, 439, 459, 542
dyadic adjustment, 230–1, 379, 381
dyadic interaction, 101–2, 202–3, 515–17
  approach to analysis of, 515–28, 562, 568
  in interdependence theory, 359, 365, 383
  in therapy, 326–7, 575
  need to analyze, 14–15, 39, 238, 253, 507,
    518

eating disorders, 449, 553
echoism, 443
ecological correlation fallacy, 519
education, 179, 301, 439
effort, 174, 395–6, 397, 403
egalitarian relationships
  cognition in, 19, 390–1, 398, 400
  in relationship quality, 363, 367, 449
ego analysis *see* psychodynamic theory
egocentrism/egoism *see* self-interest
embarrassment, 465, 468
emergency, 163, 179, 183
emotion, 261–3, 285–6, 311–13, 367, 575
  and love, 319, 332, 342–3, 351
  and social comparisons, 389–403
  appraisal of, 168, 280–4, 287, 296, 299,
    300, 311, 320, 539
  functions of, 217, 254, 261, 264, 279, 284,
    285, 462, 538
  in aggression, 132, 139–42
  in helping, 164, 165, 167–75, 178, 183–5,
    260, 262, 289
  in negotiations, 216–19
  in working models, 63, 64, 76–8
  intensity of, 256, 265, 270, 287, 308, 309,
    320, 324, 332, 542, 549, 553, 554; *see
    also* "hot" emotions
  links/blends, 286, 308, 312, 319, 379,
    548–9
  managing in others, 218, 280, 286, 289
  regulation, 76, 117, 149, 280, 286–9, 296,
    326, 327, 537–55
  spillover, 308, 323–4
  understanding of, 285–9, 296, 308, 313,
    318
emotional awareness, 282, 295
emotional expression, 16–18, 258, 259, 312,
    313, 318

emotional expression *cont'd*
   appropriateness of, 259–61, 270–1
   functions of, 263, 264, 271–3
   in emotional intelligence, 280, 283, 284,
      300
   individual differences in, 254, 265–71
   needs in, 254, 255, 261, 271–3
   of partner, 114, 116, 117
   relationship differences in, 254–61, 264–5,
      270–1, 273
   response to, 11, 255, 258–61, 265
emotional infidelity, 236
emotional intelligence, 279–301
   defined, 279, 280, 289
   measuring, 281–4, 289–301
emotion-focused coping, 542–8, 551
emotion-focused therapy, 576
emotion-in-relationship model, 308, 314,
   317–27
empathic joy, 171–2, 261, 262, 289
empathy, 130, 183, 215, 283, 284, 360, 491
   accuracy of, 229–47, 283, 284, 300, 379,
      438
   and emotion, 261–4, 271, 272, 283, 375,
      491
   in helping, 168–73, 184, 491–2
   individual differences in, 180, 186, 231,
      235, 240–1, 284, 296, 375, 442
   inheritance of, 176–7, 182, 185
"empty-shell" marriage, 235, 310
enactive learning, 145–6
entitativity, 508
entrapment, 366, 569
environmental problems, attributions for, 214,
   215
envy, 393
   see also jealousy
equality of distribution, 201–2, 207, 209, 211,
   217, 377
   see also egalitarian relationships
equity, 174, 176, 201–2, 207, 377
ethnicity
   and behavior differences, 166, 179, 197
   in interactions, 492–3
   see also cross-cultural comparisons
evaluations
   changes to, 32–3, 95, 98, 107
   global, 34, 41, 45–52
   integration of, 34, 114, 116–19, 121

   standards for, 87, 91, 98–100, 396, 401–2
   see also social evaluation; standards/ideals
evolutionary perspectives, 129–53, 462, 507
   aggression, 129–53, 415, 418
   close relationships, 91, 94, 101, 359, 485,
      538, 554–5
   emotion, 279, 312, 314
   prosocial behavior, 168, 176–8, 184, 416–17
   self-esteem, 411–31, 465
exchange orientation, 397
exchange relationships, 255, 258, 261, 368,
   371, 414, 416
excitement, 340, 482
exclusiveness, 325
expectations, 36, 72–3, 174, 175, 327
   and experience, 37–8, 69–70, 317, 319, 321
   emotion in, 285, 299–300, 315–21, 325–7
   unrealistic, 89, 325–6
   violated, 315–21, 326–7
experimental psychology, 143, 203, 208, 217,
   234, 561, 563
   see also methodology, research
expertise, 198, 208
exploitation, 203, 207, 255, 367, 374
exploration, 479–80, 537
extended contact hypothesis, 492–6
extroversion, 288, 299

face saving *see* status/power (motives)
facial expression, 114, 142, 170, 283, 284, 515
fairness, 166, 174–6, 205–9, 368
false consensus effect, 391, 399–400
false polarization effect, 209–10
family, 416–19, 506, 507, 513–14, 518
   see also communal relationships; parent–
      child relationships
fantasies of power, 441
fate, shared perception of, 511, 525
fear, 145, 146, 257, 269, 554–5
   antecedents of, 315, 323, 369
   motives in, 285, 389, 391, 403
feature positive bias, 15
feedback loops, 568, 569, 576
fight/flight, 140, 315, 316, 540
filters, 149, 394, 562
flattery, 445, 446
flexibility
   in biological-based behavior, 130, 133, 136,
      149, 152, 178, 184–5, 421

in coping, 546, 548, 554
in ideals, 92, 98–100, 102
food provision, 415, 416
forgiveness, 176, 376, 379–80
fraternal relative deprivation, 485
friendships, 262, 419
and love, 332, 340
and support, 180, 183, 256
in negotiations, 203, 204
in social comparisons, 388, 389, 399, 400
fundamental attribution error, 210
see also disposition/situation attributions
future
emotion in anticipating, 285, 576
predictions of, 109, 213, 398, 444
see also optimism

gambling, 213
game theory, 143, 198, 199, 203, 209, 524,
565
gender differences, 527
behavior, 148, 180, 181, 183, 197
cognition, 11, 18–19, 39, 43, 400
emotion, 266, 283, 295, 297
relationship perceptions, 231, 236, 242,
416, 421–3
gender roles, 180, 367, 390–1, 416, 424
genetic influences, 138, 149, 177–8
see also evolutionary perspectives
goal theory, 562, 568, 577–80
goal-directed behavior, 57, 578
goals, 72–3, 478, 511
and attachment, 66, 69, 77
and emotion, 263, 481, 484, 579
in close relationships, 23–4, 89, 94, 101,
319–20, 326, 378, 415, 524, 577–80
in helping, 163, 170, 175, 181
long- *vs* short-term, 141, 217, 218, 370
multiple, 243, 578
government, use of force by, 141, 151
see also leadership
greed, 365, 369
grief, 320
group
adaptivity of, 131, 415–17
mind/personality, 508, 512, 525
vs individual analysis, 505–10, 529
see also belongingness: ingroup; outgroup
group-selectionist theory, 425

guilt, 150, 257, 262–4, 367
generation of, 286, 379, 451
in helping, 165, 168–70, 174, 185
Gulf War, 543

habituation, 238, 371, 373, 482
happiness, 257, 285, 319, 320
response to, 255, 258
harm, 130, 131, 137, 141–2, 168, 186
hedonism, 167
helping, 162–86, 490–2
helplessness, 539, 544
see also learned helplessness
hierarchical legitimacy, 198
see also dominance
hierarchical linear modeling, 512–13, 518, 529
homicide motives, 140–1
homogeneity, 510–18, 524–5
see also similarity
honesty, 213, 301
hope, 286, 555
hostile aggression, 131–2, 137
hostility, 324, 393, 427, 442, 483, 544
in attributions, 23, 148–9, 210, 549–50
"hot" emotions, 218, 313–17, 322–4, 327
human uniqueness, 133, 142–4
humanistic theory, 86, 461
humility, 438, 445
humor, 89, 113, 284, 445, 450
hunger, 132, 479
hunting, 415–16
Huxley, Thomas, 94
hypertension, 282
hypervigilance, 242, 244, 246

"I–Thou" relationships, 486
ideal self, 444, 447
see also actual–ideal discrepancies
ideal standards model, 87–103
ideals *see* standards/ideals
identical twin studies, 177
identification-contrast model, 394–7, 403
identity, 437–52, 485, 577
see also social identity
"if–then" cognitions, 65, 79
illusory superiority, 398–400
see also positive illusions; relationship
enhancement motives; self-enhancement
motives

imaging, 488–9
immunological functioning, emotion in, 282, 288, 321
impasse, 207–8, 216
impression formation, 36, 113, 258, 289
impression management, 428, 459, 471–2
    see also self-presentation
impulse, 132, 219
inclusive fitness theory, 416–17
independence, 368, 514
individualism, 442
inductivism, 564, 566
information availability, 200, 206, 208, 209
    see also ambiguity
information processing, 72–6, 136–7, 139, 145, 285, 554
    emotion in, 77–9, 244, 246, 272, 279–82, 285, 373, 394, 548–9
    in negotiations, 197–8, 200, 210
    in-depth, 96, 102, 244, 552
    of imperfect information, 41, 139, 147, 148
    motives in, 46–51, 92–6, 102, 110, 208–9, 373, 428, 469
    self in, 489, 492
information sharing, 203, 215
ingroup, 487, 494–6, 524
    see also belongingness; social inclusion
insight, 107, 110–12, 284
instrumental coalitions, 415–16, 418, 420
insult, 150–1
integrative couple therapy (ICT), 10, 327, 559, 569–70, 575–7, 580
intelligence, 120, 213, 372
    types of, 296, 297, 301
    see also emotional intelligence
interactionism, 179, 184, 270–1
interactions, 112, 364
    and attributions, 11, 15
    approach to studying, 512–28, 562, 564, 568, 573
    interdependence in, 309–10, 319, 320, 359–83, 511, 523–4
    stability of, 368, 568, 569
    see also dyadic interactions
interdependence, 174, 233, 310, 317, 373–5, 525
    in emotion, 253, 310, 317, 320–1, 324–5
    inequalities in, 310, 365, 367, 382
    levels of, 361, 366

relationship consequences of, 108, 359, 374, 381–3
interdependence theory, 35, 87, 337, 339, 359–83, 479, 561, 563–5
inter-hemispheric transfer, 281
international relations, 214, 216, 417
interpersonal attraction
    cognition in, 45, 48, 447
    consequences of, 165, 174, 232
    emotion in, 258–60, 267, 271–3, 444
    see also mate value; similarity
interpersonal orientation *see* communal/ interpersonal orientation
intersubjectivity, 485
inter-temporal integration, 203–5, 210, 211
intimacy, 21, 66, 360, 399, 438
    as component of love, 332, 333, 342, 343, 348, 349, 351, 441
    as standard/ideal, 91, 95–7, 361
    defined, 332, 484
    see also attachment
investment, in relationship, 102, 243, 319, 337, 376, 398, 422–4, 487
    and interdependence, 366, 375, 383
ironic processes theory, 469
irrationality, 196, 199–200, 203, 205, 235, 366

jealousy, 116, 235, 286, 308, 323–5, 366, 377, 441
job search strategies, 414, 422–3
Journal of Abnormal and Social Psychology, 558
joy, 319, 323
    see also empathic joy
judgment, study of, 509–10
just-world beliefs, 176, 215

kindness, 176, 420, 445
knowledge, as resource, 478
knowledge structures
    and content, 52, 64, 74, 115–16
    influencing cognitions, 23, 34, 40–6, 113
    integration of, 41–2, 113–19, 121, 152, 280, 420, 554
    self in 65, 486, 489, 554

labeling, of emotion, 288–9, 299, 300
labor divisions, 364–5, 367, 368, 390–1
    see also gender roles

language learning, 138
language use
  and cooperation, 211
  and emotion, 286, 288–9, 295, 312
  in close relationships, 381, 487
  in research, 20, 36, 131, 273, 513
leadership, 289, 444, 445
learned helplessness, 6, 20, 362, 429
lens model, 509–10
life satisfaction, 283, 288
limbic system, 177, 185
loneliness, 415
long-distance relationships, 38, 321–3
longitudinal studies, need for, 40, 42, 46, 52
long-term relationships
  accuracy in, 49, 231–2, 245, 451
  cognition in, 79, 92, 373, 375, 377
  emotion in, 308, 319, 321, 340–1
  requirements for, 37, 94, 229, 378–81
  social comparisons in, 402
love, 332–6, 340–2, 349, 441, 538
  and commitment, 332, 339–40, 342–3,
    350–1
  and self, 415, 437–52
  costs/benefits of, 446–50, 452
  lay views of, 75, 89–90, 107, 308, 331,
    335–6, 446, 485
  measuring, 332–5, 341, 347, 349–51
  styles, 332, 335, 349–50, 442
  unrequited, 440, 448, 451, 452, 481
loyalty, 420
luck, 315
lust, 448

Machiavellianism, 197
maintenance acts, 377–81, 443
  motives in, 36, 37, 94, 102, 366, 375–6,
    382–3
management training, 301
manic love, 440, 444, 447
marital adjustment, 36, 230–2
marital dissolution *see* divorce; relationship
  dissolution
marital relationships, 326, 338, 559
  see also relationship *categories*
mass media, 139, 144, 146–8, 163
  see also popular culture
mate selection *see* partner selection strategies
mate value, 416, 419–21, 423–4, 426

meaning, 316, 359, 511
memory, 132, 548
  and attachment, 63–4, 540, 548–9, 553
  and emotion, 77, 285, 313–14, 548–9
  biases, 32, 49, 73–4, 95, 206, 209, 399
  self in, 488, 489
mental health *see* psychological health
mental models, 4, 117, 121, 144
  see also knowledge structures
mental set, 285
methodology, 505–39
  clinical observation as, 560, 564–6
  for cognition research, 35–6, 41, 65, 67, 80,
    115, 470–1
  see also experimental psychology; research
Michelangelo phenomenon, 374–5, 450
mistakes, 196, 214, 445
modeling, 144, 167
  see also social learning
modesty, 448
monitoring, 232, 242, 245, 279, 287–8, 299,
  300, 462
monogamy, 421–2
morality, 130, 301, 367
  and obligation, 337–9, 348
  in decision-making, 165, 167, 177
motherhood, coping with, 544–7
  see also parent–child relationships
motivated construal *see* relationship-
  enhancement motives
motivated inaccuracy, 229–30, 232–3, 239,
  241, 244, 246
motives
  intrinsic/extrinsic, 479
  transforming, 371–3, 376, 379, 381
multi-level pairwise approach, 510, 512–22,
  529

naïve psychology, 6
  see also love (lay views of); relationship
    success
narcissism, 427, 439, 441–5, 451
neediness, 440, 444, 576
needs
  and emotion, 253–65, 272, 273
  and relationships, 360, 366, 375, 393
  hierarchy, 439, 479
  in distribution, 202, 205
  in volunteering, 175, 181

needs *cont'd*
    self-esteem in, 411, 428, 442
negative state relief model, 168–70
negotiation, 196–220, 415
negotiators
    individual differences in, 197–9, 211
    relationships among, 201–5, 217
nepotism, 414, 416
neuromodulators, 313
neurophysiology
    aggression, 133, 142
    computational theories, 136, 142
    emotion, 312, 313, 315–16
    helping, 177, 185
    learning, 145
    self-reflection, 460
neuroticism, 287, 299, 397
newly weds, 32, 111, 232, 245, 481
Newton, Isaac, 506
nonverbal perception, 283
nonvoluntary dependence, 362
norms, 401, 508, 511
    aggression, 147, 149–51
    close relationships, 261, 265, 271, 318, 338,
        377, 481
    gender role, 180, 390
    helping, 164, 168, 173–6, 185
    interdependence, 367, 371, 376–7, 379
nostalgia, 286
novelty, 72, 314–15, 482–3, 573

observational learning, 144–6, 360
operant conditioning, 167
optimism, 20, 111, 215, 299
    unrealistic, 213, 381
organizations, 509–11
    and emotion, 260, 301
    interactions in, 182, 184, 198, 201, 204–5,
        216, 495
ostracism, 509
outcome matrix, 364–6, 524
outcome research, 562, 563, 567, 570
outgroup, 150, 417–18, 492–6, 524
ownership, 485

paraphilia, 441
parent–child relationships
    abuse in, 148–9, 459
    and attachment, 61, 64, 69–70, 167, 333–4,

        361, 414, 421, 552
    and self, 417, 424, 450, 491
    asymmetries in, 18–19, 257, 261, 310, 377
    in learning, 148, 153, 167
partisanship, 208, 209, 210
partner
    and control, 92, 326, 327, 365, 368, 568
    attributions for, 5, 38, 46, 70, 75, 119, 562,
        568, 572–3
    availability, 576–7
    death of, 320, 321
    expectancies of, 317–21, 374
    ideals for, 89–91, 95, 96, 100, 110, 380–1,
        447, 527
    matching ideals, 38, 93, 99, 110, 112, 118,
        119, 121, 360, 375, 381
    see also self–partner differences
partner alternatives, 320, 321, 325, 382, 441
partner selection strategies, 91, 95, 100, 363,
        414, 419, 421–3, 425, 445
    in negotiations, 204–5
    long- *vs* short-term, 91, 416
passion, 323, 332
    as component of love, 332, 333, 340, 342,
        343, 351
    as ideal, 86, 90, 91, 96–7, 308
passionate *vs* companionate love, 97, 335, 336,
        340–9, 351
    defined, 332
patterning, 9, 15, 568, 569
peacemaking, 133
perception
    and cognition, 2, 44, 72
    figure *vs* ground, 488, 571–4
    of others, 34, 283, 538
    of patterns, 372
    of threat, 137, 139, 540, 544
    see also information processing
perfectionism, 552
performance standards, 200
persistence, 375, 379, 381
personal growth, 180, 577
personality
    components of, 20, 60, 283, 421
    development of, 421–2, 550, 555
    disorders, 443, 552–3
    in behavior, 197–8, 243
    measuring, 510
    perceptions of, 37, 198, 398, 488

see also self; self-partner differences
persuasion, 167, 289
physical exercise, 170, 288
physical health
  and emotion, 282, 288, 300
  and positive illusions, 212, 213, 216, 398
  and relationship satisfaction, 319
physical illness, coping with, 267, 401, 545–6, 551
physiological arousal
  in cognitive appraisal, 169–70, 185, 272, 279, 311, 549–50
  in identifying emotion, 280, 282, 311–16, 320
  influencing behavior, 140, 166, 167–70
  interpersonal aspects of, 310, 332, 390, 481–3
  regulating, 287, 289, 299, 327
polarization, 569, 579
politics, 214, 418, 445
popular culture
  emotion in, 279, 289, 298, 300, 301, 323
  for social comparisons, 388, 391
  self in, 437–40, 444, 470
  see also mass media
positive illusions, defined, 109, 212
  see also relationship-enhancement motives; self-enhancement motives; standards/ideals
power *see* status/power
pratfall effect, 445
preferences, 312, 359, 365, 368, 370–1
prefrontal cortex, 313
pregnancy, 338, 459, 545
prejudice, 492–6
  see also partisanship
Prevention and Relationship Enhancement Program (PREP), 559, 562, 576–7, 580
pride, 174, 417–18, 427, 485
  see also basking in reflective glory
primate studies *see* cross-species comparisons
priming, 118, 139, 152–3, 469, 492
  experimental, 23, 45, 65, 66, 67, 69, 74, 153
principle of least interest, 367
prisoners of war, 544
problem-focused coping, 542–3, 545, 547
problem-solving
  cognition in, 11, 37, 207, 211, 212, 215, 392

developing skills for, 148, 153, 301
  emotion in, 284–5, 297, 313, 314
  individual differences in, 42–3, 67, 77–8
  in therapy, 561, 562, 576, 580
professionals, self-perceptions of, 398, 422–3
prosocial behavior, 150, 162
  disposition for, 165, 171, 172, 178–84, 186, 374
  see also altruism; helping
prototypes, 335, 507
  commitment, 338–9
  emotion, 268–9
  love, 90, 335–6
proximity
  in relationships, 319, 540, 577
  maintenance, 537
psychodynamic theory, 86, 576
psychological health
  attachment, 538–41, 546, 550–4
  emotion, 288, 298, 299, 300
  relationship satisfaction, 319
  self-enhancement, 212, 215, 470
  self-esteem, 411, 413, 421, 461, 464
psychopathology, attachment in, 422, 541, 552–4
public self, defined, 460
  see also self-presentation
public/private context, 14, 175, 206, 208, 234, 466, 468, 470–1
punishment motives, 143, 145–6, 148, 150, 176, 207

quid pro quo contracts, 562

random effects linear model, 518
rational emotive therapy, 34, 326
rationalization, 48–9, 51, 166, 239, 459, 465
reciprocation, 9, 120, 202, 261, 273, 368, 414, 447, 484, 564
  norms for, 174–6, 368
reinforcement erosion, 317
rejection
  anticipating, 37, 121, 363, 540
  impact of, 92, 99–100, 119–21, 320
  self-esteem in, 412, 422, 448–9, 464, 465
relational efficacy, 38, 109, 111, 381, 579
relationship
  defined, 309–10
  motives for, 319, 336, 337, 339, 348, 349

relationship alternatives, 235, 337, 338,
    361–2, 367, 375, 376, 380
    see also comparison level for alternatives;
    partner alternatives
relationship commitment
    and perceived superiority, 399, 402, 443
    consequences of, 375–9, 443
    and empathic accuracy, 231
    in therapy, 561, 577
    interdependence in, 359, 373, 375, 487
    levels of, 343, 375
    measuring, 337–8, 350–1, 513
    motives in, 94, 102, 108, 111, 121, 337–8
    types of, 337–9, 342, 348, 350
relationship dissolution
    barriers to, 337, 362, 366, 441, 540
    cognition in, 10, 49, 93, 109, 361, 382–3
    decisions about, 96, 101, 102, 381–3, 441,
        580
    emotion in, 245, 309, 320, 321, 325, 333,
        513
relationship ideals, 89–91, 96, 109, 381
    and reality, 109–10, 112, 114, 118, 121,
        389, 401
relationship quality, 20, 90–1
    influence of past on, 244, 318, 360, 372
    see also relationship satisfaction; relationship
        stability
relationship satisfaction
    and attributions, 5–6, 8–11, 14, 15, 21, 34,
        44, 46, 395–6, 403, 572
    and commitment, 338, 348–51, 376
    and dependence, 361–2, 375–6
    and emotion, 271–2, 284, 287, 300
    and evaluation, 23, 42, 93, 110–12, 121,
        337, 360, 390–1, 394, 395, 398–403,
        447
    and love, 343–9, 351
    and therapy, 327, 482, 561, 564, 567
    conceptualized, 338, 349, 575
    decline in, 32–3, 39, 107, 111, 230, 326,
        382, 481–2
    empathic accuracy in, 230, 234, 236, 238,
        240
    self in, 426, 487, 491
relationship stability
    and accuracy/ideals, 50, 93, 95, 102, 107,
        111, 113, 116–19, 229, 233, 236,
        238–40

antecedents of, 32, 438, 443, 575, 578
    threats to, 230, 244, 247, 430
relationship success, lay views of, 90–1, 439,
    451
relationship therapy, 5, 10, 17–18, 319,
    325–7, 383, 558–81
relationship types
    and responsibility, 254, 255, 261
    consistency across, 18
    distinguishing among, 5, 333, 339, 414
    in helping, 168, 171, 175, 177
    in negotiations, 203–4
    self-enhancement in, 448
    study of, 13, 70, 257, 513, 564
relationship-enhancement motives, 47–9, 51,
    93–4, 102, 108–21, 375, 381, 398–400,
    402
religion, 180, 438
reproductive success, 91, 101, 413, 416, 418
research
    basic *vs* applied, 559–61, 570–4, 581
    fragmentation of, 4, 12, 51, 273, 411, 458,
        512
resource-holding potential, 424–5
resources, 447–8, 478
    and emotion, 217, 254
    in power/competition, 198, 416, 418, 419
    investment alternatives for, 422, 424
    rules for distributing, 201–2, 255, 377, 414,
        491
response latency, 44, 45, 65, 67, 402
responsibility
    attributions of, 6, 11, 13, 15, 19–20
    for others' needs, 253–65
    in helping, 163, 164, 165, 168, 174, 176,
        182
    social, 174, 183
retribution/revenge, 142–3, 149, 207
    forgoing, 379
rewards
    external, 167, 174, 175
    immediacy of, 218
    see also cost–reward analysis
risk, perceptions of, 200, 215
risk-taking, 197, 466, 481
role models, 144, 147, 167, 390
    see also modeling; social learning
romantic love, 333
royalty, 418

ruminative thinking, 118, 210, 287–8, 300, 542–3, 548, 552, 579

sadness, 268–9, 323, 326, 549
  and cognition, 169, 170, 172–3, 260, 285
  expression of, 257, 266, 269
  response to, 255, 258–62, 267–8
satiation, 382
satisficing, 137, 204
schema, 315, 554
  relational, 61, 69, 70, 73–4, 79, 318
  -triggered affect, 77
  see also knowledge structures; working models
security/safety, as need, 360, 480, 481
  see also attachment (styles)
selective attention *see* attention
selective evaluation model, 401
self
  adjustments to, 319–20, 326, 359, 378, 381, 401, 403, 448, 579–80
  and attachment, 61, 65, 74, 540, 542, 553, 554
  defined, 460
  development of, 450, 457, 486
  domains in, 74, 88, 480, 491
  functions of, 458, 469
  in attributions, 15, 19, 457, 459, 470, 488
  motives in, 457, 458
  see also actual–ideal discrepancies
self-actualization, 438–9, 479
self-awareness, 208, 397
self-concept, 42, 413, 538
  fairness in, 166, 208–9
  in helping, 166, 171, 174, 175, 184, 185, 262
  in view of partner/relationship, 21, 88, 91, 93, 100, 109, 527
  protecting, 440, 442, 448
  see also self-discrepancy theory
self-critical depression, 552
self-deception, 469–71
self-defense, 150–2
self-discrepancy theory, 88–9, 91
  vs relationship discrepancy, 100–1
self-efficacy, 100, 182–3, 539, 544, 551
  and emotional intelligence, 287, 289, 295
  in close relationships, 10, 36–7, 478–9, 481
  theory, 479

see also relational efficacy
self-enhancement motives, 47–8, 52, 212–16, 389, 392, 397–8, 438–9, 447–8, 458–72, 479, 577
  adaptivity of, 93, 212, 215–16, 427–8, 470
  and reality, 213, 215, 450, 464, 470
  and self-esteem, 114, 120, 168, 181, 186, 425, 441, 448, 459, 461, 466–7
  individual differences in 44–5, 51, 94
self-esteem, 411–31, 437–52, 457–72
  and behavior, 168, 197, 362, 422–5, 429, 459, 465–6
  and beliefs/ideals, 88, 100, 113–15, 119–21
  collective, 417
  defined, 411, 412, 420
  dimensions of, 414–15, 420, 431, 463–4
  emotion in, 286, 288, 415, 462
  functions of, 412, 422, 425, 429, 430, 439, 440, 459, 462–3, 465, 472
  harm to, 230, 239, 448, 452
  interventions for, 430, 439, 468
  measuring, 419, 431
  stability of, 426–7, 450–1, 463, 467–8
self-evaluation maintenance
  goals, 577
  model, 427, 491
  see also evaluations
self-expansion model, 333, 349, 448, 478–96
  measurement in, 486–7, 490, 509
self-fulfilling prophecies, 36, 37, 39, 112, 243, 244–6
  see also behavioral confirmation; consistency motives
self-handicapping, 459, 465–6
self-improvement motives, 392, 479, 484
self-interest
  in helping, 163, 167, 169–73, 175, 181, 186, 262, 490
  in interactions, 368–70, 372–3, 379, 383
  in negotiations, 200, 205–9
self-knowledge, 115, 318, 389, 393
self–other overlap, 76, 173, 484–90
self–partner differences, 327, 365, 423–4, 569
  cognition, 14–15, 19, 39–40, 93, 102, 111, 231, 234, 236, 238, 309
  empathic accuracy, 240, 245, 246
  investment, 102, 243
  personality, 108, 109, 111, 113
self-presentation, 457–72

self-presentation *cont'd*
  strategies, 425, 428, 465–7
self-reference effect, 489
self-reflection, 457, 460
self-regulation couples therapy, 580
self-reliance, 540, 541, 544
self-report
  limitations of, 35–6, 65, 284, 297, 301, 578
  vs behavior, 35, 289, 295
self-verification *see* consistency motives
semantic memory network, 548, 574
sentiment override, 9, 11, 34
sex ratios, 367
sexual attraction, 332, 414
sexual infidelity, 152, 236, 325, 377, 440
sexual interactions, 97, 102, 320, 337, 360
sexual libertarianism, 367
sexual orientation, 325, 513
sexual strategies theory, 416
shame, 286, 287
siblings, 414, 419
signaling systems, 428
similarity, perceived
  in empathy/helping, 165–6, 186, 262
  in interpersonal attraction, 363, 423, 442
  in learning/memory, 74, 144, 147, 167
  in social comparisons, 389, 392, 403
  see also homogeneity
sinister attribution error, 210
situation
  aggression, 136, 139, 146–7, 151–3
  helping, 163–4, 178–9, 184–6
  interdependence theory, 365, 370, 383
  negotiations, 197–9, 210
  see also construal; disposition/situation
    attributions; public/private context
social anxiety, 287, 288, 296, 299
social cognition, 3, 32, 65, 401, 509
  and attachment, 80, 568, 576
  and close relationships, 14, 22–4, 75–6,
    568, 580
  and negotiations, 196, 199, 217, 219
social comparisons, 47–8, 109, 110, 381,
    388–403, 485
  and self-esteem, 76, 212, 393, 397, 418–19,
    427, 447, 459, 470
  see also derogation; downward comparisons;
    upward comparisons
social competence, 19, 283, 389, 468

social evaluation
  and self-esteem, 449–51, 459, 464–9, 472
  and support, 165, 167, 171, 178, 544
  real *vs* imagined, 468–9
  see also social inclusion
social exchange theory, 336, 338, 350, 561
social facilitation, 525
social identity, 165, 175, 399
  and self, 417, 458, 468, 485
social inclusion, adaptivity of, 412, 414, 415,
    417, 420, 427, 462
social justice, 174, 176
social learning
  and relationships, 318, 561
  of aggression, 129–31, 133, 140, 144–9,
    153
  of helping, 166–7, 173, 185
social networks, 201, 204–5, 337, 389
  in coping, 283, 289
social psychology
  and evolutionary models, 129–30, 134–7,
    142, 176, 510
  and marital attribution theory, 4, 6, 18–20
  and negotiation research, 196, 199, 219
  see also clinical psychology
social tactics, 131, 132, 139, 140, 144, 153
social utility, 201, 207–8
Society for Personality and Social Psychology,
    418
socioeconomic variables, 179, 337, 362
socioemotional learning, 301
sociology, 86, 506, 568
sociometer theory, 100, 412–31, 461–72
sociosexual orientation, 97, 422
somatic symptoms, 287, 553
sports, 416, 417–18
spouse *see* partner
standards/ideals
  impact of, 38–40, 93, 107–12, 121, 326,
    375, 402
  maintaining/changing, 92, 95, 112–13,
    116–17, 121
status/power
  and inclusion, 415, 422, 426
  in relationship attributions, 18–19, 91, 96,
    99
  interdependence in, 359, 366, 367
  motives, 140–2, 145–6, 151, 152, 175, 176,
    337, 419, 424–5

stimulus overload, 164
strangers, 202, 203, 317, 448, 490
  and emotional expression, 256, 261, 515
  see also relationship types
stress
  motivating affiliation, 164, 390–2
  shared, 395, 544
stressors
  and close relationships, 37, 38, 67, 76, 79,
    324, 382, 440
  response to, 164, 287, 538–48
  see also coping strategies
structural equations modeling, 513, 517, 527,
  529
stubbornness, 113, 117
students, in research, 12, 565, 581
submissiveness, 424–5
superstitious behavior, 213
supportive behavior, 261, 324, 483, 577
support-seeking, 258, 261, 542
  and self-esteem, 415, 421, 440–1, 446,
    449
  individual differences in, 76, 265, 269–70,
    538, 539, 543–6, 551, 554
surprise, 315, 319
survival needs, 360, 412–14, 462, 479
symbolic interactionism, 457–8, 460, 469,
  472, 486
symbolic models, 130, 136
sympathetic nervous system, 316
sympathy, 168, 170, 171
systems theory, 566

taste, 413
technical eclecticism, 560, 564
technology, 133, 139, 147–8, 152
temporal comparisons, 49, 182
theory, in applied settings, 558–70, 580–1
token exchange, 562
totalitarianism, 459
transition lists, 369
triangular theory of love, 332–3, 340, 342

trust, 114, 261, 359, 365, 369, 371, 376, 518,
  524
  and attachment, 66, 539, 554
"two-component" theory of emotion, 311

ultimatum bargaining, 207, 217–18
uncertainty *see* ambiguity
unconscious plagiarism *see* cryptomnesia
unit relation, 485, 494
upward comparisons, 392–7, 403, 449
urban–rural comparisons, 163–4

values, 36, 38–40, 46, 181–2, 312
  social, 174, 176, 374
verbalization, 518, 523, 526
victim
  in aggression, 131, 149, 150
  in helping, 165–6, 170, 172–4, 176, 185–6
  response of, 379–80, 401
violence *see* abusive relationships; aggression
volunteering motives, 174, 175, 179–83
vulnerability
  and close relationships, 108, 366, 578, 580
  and emotion, 261, 576
vulnerability–stress–adaptation model, 575

war, 216, 415–17, 543–4
warmth, 75, 96, 99, 117, 296, 421
Watergate, 214
weapons, 133, 152–3
widowhood, coping with, 547, 551
willingness to sacrifice, 366, 375, 376, 379, 443
wish-fulfillment, 10
withdrawing, 270, 547–8
working models, 36, 40, 60–80, 421, 537
  priming, 45, 65, 66, 67, 69, 74
  see also attachment

"yes, but . . ." refutations, 114, 115, 117, 118
Yom Kippur War, 544

zero-sum game, 418, 427

Author Index

Abelson, R. P., 115, 513
Abramson, L. Y., 6, 15, 34, 93, 429
Acitelli, L. K., 40, 508
Acker, M., 333, 347, 348, 351, 352n
Adams, A. A., 211
Adams, J. M., 338
Aderman, D., 263
Affleck, G., 413
Afifi, W. A., 38
Agnew, C. R., 375, 381, 485, 487
Agras, W. S., 560
Ahuvia, A., 485
Ainsworth, M. D. S., 62, 333, 450, 538, 540
Akerlof, G., 203
Akert, R. M., 283
Albert, S., 49
Alcock, J. E., 138, 177, 428
Aldous, J., 234
Alfert, E., 147
Alicke, M. D., 122n, 398, 448
Alioto, J. T., 147
Allard, L. M., 66, 67, 70, 75, 77, 78, 119
Allen, D. R., 230
Allen, N., 181
Allison, S. T., 215
Allmendinger, J., 509
Alloy, L. B., 93, 429

Allport, F. H., 506, 508, 511, 512, 525, 529
Allport, G., 492
Allred, K., 217
Amato, P. R., 162
American Psychiatric Association, 443
Ammazzalorso, H., 253
Andersen, S. M., 74, 77, 114
Anderson, C. A., 151, 153
Anderson, J. C., 181
Anderson, K. B., 154
Apfel, R. J., 280
Apsler, R., 464, 465
Arbib, M. A., 145
Archer, D., 283
Archer, R. L., 171
Archibald, W. R., 466
Arias, I., 13
Arkin, R. M., 465, 467, 471
Armor, D. A., 115
Arnsten, A. F. T., 313
Aron, A., 89, 90, 333, 336, 341, 342, 343, 345, 349, 351n, 359, 383, 446, 448, 478, 480, 481, 482, 483, 484, 486, 487, 488, 489, 491, 492, 494, 497n, 509, 577
Aron, E. N., 333, 336, 349, 359, 383, 448, 478, 484, 491, 497n, 578
Aronson, E., 49, 445, 466, 471

Arriaga, X. B., 245, 375, 379, 447, 479
Arrowood, A. J., 389, 393
Asch, S. E., 34, 117, 263, 508, 511
Asendorpf, J. B., 461
Ashmore, R., 180
Aspinwall, L. G., 392, 395
Atkin, C., 147
Atkinson, R. C., 513
Attridge, M., 102, 321, 322
Austin, J. T., 24, 578, 580
Austin, W., 202
Averill, J. R., 290, 296, 549
Axelrod, R., 368
Axelrod, S., 198
Azrin, N., 562

Babcock, L., 205, 206, 207, 208, 209
Back, K. W., 511
Bagarozzi, D. A., 6
Bagby, R. M., 281
Bailey, W. C., 344
Baillet, S. D., 489
Bakan, D., 486
Baker, L. A., 398
Baker, W. E., 201, 204
Baldwin, M. W., 36, 41, 45, 63, 65, 68, 69,
    70, 79, 89, 119, 120, 334, 359, 568
Bandura, A., 129, 144, 145, 147, 150, 432n,
    470, 479
Banikiotes, P. G., 230
Bargh, J. A., 72, 73, 79, 578
Barinaga, M., 419
Barkow, J. H., 129, 419, 461
Barlow, D. H., 560
Barnes, M. L., 89, 360
Bar-On, R., 292, 298
Baron, R. A., 130, 131, 142, 164, 209, 217
Baron, R. M., 21
Baron, R. S., 77
Barrett, L. F., 255, 256, 266
Barrowclough, C., 17
Barry, B., 197, 216, 217
Barry, W. A., 231
Barsalou, L. W., 90
Bar-Tal, D., 167
Bartholomew, K., 62, 66, 68, 70, 81n, 265,
    334, 349, 450, 554
Bassili, J. N., 22
Batson, C. D., 162, 163, 168, 170, 171, 172,

173, 174, 177, 186, 262, 272, 283, 491,
    492
Baucom, D. H., 4, 7, 12, 14, 15, 33, 35, 36,
    38, 39, 46, 48, 51, 559, 565, 566, 567, 568,
    577
Baum, A., 77
Baumeister, R. F., 95, 115, 117, 120, 168,
    263, 264, 319, 360, 412, 413, 415, 425,
    427, 428, 430, 431n, 432n, 441, 446, 448,
    451, 458, 459, 460, 461, 462, 463, 464,
    465, 466, 467, 470, 472, 473n, 577
Bauserman, S. A., 8
Bazerman, M. H., 197, 198, 200, 201, 202,
    203, 204, 207, 208, 213, 214, 215, 216,
    217, 218
Beach, S. R. H., 19, 22, 23, 24, 45, 427, 448,
    491, 562, 567, 568, 570, 577, 578, 579
Bebbington, P., 16
Beck, G. D., 230, 231
Bednar, R. L., 461
Beer, J. S., 69
Belk, R. W., 485
Bell, D. E., 199
Bell, F. A., 164
Bellah, R. N., 179
Belsky, J., 421
Bem, D. J., 262
Benazon, N., 579
Bengston, V. L., 175, 390
Ben-Yoav, O., 204, 205
Bera, S., 36
Berant, E., 545, 546, 547, 550, 551
Berger, C. R., 33, 234
Berger, P., 14
Berkowitz, L., 51, 130, 131, 132, 142, 147,
    152, 162, 174, 175, 367
Berkowitz, R., 560
Berlin, L. J., 242
Berlyne, D. E., 482
Bernet, M., 293, 299
Berscheid, E., 5, 18, 22, 24, 33, 77, 86, 97,
    103, 120, 253, 308, 309, 310, 311, 313,
    318, 319, 320, 321, 322, 323, 324, 327,
    332, 335, 336, 340, 349, 423, 578
Bersoff, D. M., 176, 185
Betancourt, H., 209
Beutler, L. E., 560
Bierhofft, H. W., 343, 347
Bies, R. J., 209

Birchler, G. R., 34, 564
Birnbaum, G., 547, 550, 551
Bissonnette, V. L., 238, 245, 379
Blaine, B., 459, 470
Blair, I., 209
Blake, R. R., 495
Blakemore, C., 316
Blau, P. M., 561
Block, J., 93, 109, 461
Blount, S., 207, 211
Blumberg, H. H., 446
Blumstein, P., 368
Bock, R. D., 519
Boden, J. M., 117
Bogen, J. E., 281
Bollen, K. A., 508, 509, 512
Bookwala, J., 345, 347
Borgida, E., 163
Borkovec, T. D., 567, 570
Bosson, J. K., 66
Bottom, W. P., 211
Boucher, J. D., 283
Bourhis, R. Y., 487
Bower, G. H., 77, 489
Bowers, K. S., 295
Bowlby, J., 60, 61, 62, 71, 79, 80n, 100, 242,
    243, 333, 421, 432n, 479, 537, 538, 539,
    540, 547, 550
Boyd, R., 143
Bradbury, T. N., 5, 7, 8, 9, 10, 11, 12, 13, 14,
    15, 19, 20, 22, 33, 34, 35, 36, 37, 42, 46,
    51, 75, 77, 112, 209, 326, 566, 568, 575,
    577, 578, 580
Bradlee, P. M., 441, 442
Braiker, H. B., 5, 108, 382
Branden, N., 439, 459, 461
Breckler, S., 458, 460
Breedlove, J., 95, 234
Brehm, S. S., 107, 108, 332, 341, 352n, 558
Brennan, C. J., 450
Brennan, K. A., 62, 66, 70, 81n, 540, 550,
    552
Bresler, C., 265
Bretherton, I., 60, 61, 68, 81n
Brewer, M. B., 495
Brewin, C. R., 17, 18
Brickman, P., 107, 108, 351n, 382, 391, 392,
    394, 396
Bringle, R., 325

Brissette, I., 257, 266, 269
Brockner, J., 366
Brodt, S. E., 216
Brown, B. R., 196, 197, 201
Brown, G. W., 16
Brown, J., 149
Brown, J. D., 93, 109, 122n, 212, 215, 398,
    399, 427, 448, 461, 470
Brown, R. C., 149
Bruner, J. S., 43
Bryk, A. S., 512, 518, 519
Buber, M., 486
Buchanan, G. M., 21
Buck, R., 130, 140, 254, 264, 282, 283
Buehler, R., 117, 398
Bugental, D. B., 18
Bui, K. T., 361, 366, 375
Bulman, R., 391, 392, 394, 396
Bumpass, L., 32
Burgess, E. W., 41
Burgoon, J. K., 38, 39
Burley, N., 424
Burnstein, E., 177, 393
Bushman, B. J., 151, 427
Buss, D. M., 91, 92, 130, 135, 140, 146, 152,
    153, 176, 177, 236, 335, 411, 416, 417,
    419, 423, 428, 429, 441
Button, C. M., 336
Buunk, A. P., 366
Buunk, B. P., 47, 95, 113, 325, 377, 388, 390,
    391, 392, 393, 394, 395, 396, 397, 398,
    399, 400, 401, 402, 403, 443
Byrne, C. A., 13
Byrne, D., 165, 262, 363, 511

Cacioppo, J. T., 575
Cadoret, R. J., 149
Cairns, K. J., 95
California Task Force to Promote Self-esteem
    and Personal and Social Responsibility, 430
Callero, P., 167, 175, 179
Camerer, C., 206, 207
Campbell, D. T., 508, 511
Campbell, J. D., 438
Campbell, L. J., 91, 95, 98, 100, 101
Campbell, R. J., 283
Campbell, W. K., 442, 444, 447, 448, 450,
    451
Campos, J., 133

Cannon, W., 316
Canon, L. K., 163
Cantor, J. R., 263
Cantril, H., 210
Carels, R. A., 577
Carlo, G., 183
Carlson, G. E., 283
Carlson, M., 169
Carlson, N. R., 177
Carnelley, K. B., 552
Carnevale, P. J. D., 175, 197, 217
Carroll, J. M., 575
Carroll, J. S., 198, 200, 215
Carroll, L., 442, 445
Cartwright, D., 511
Carver, C. S., 49, 91, 458, 460, 472n, 481, 484, 542, 579
Carver, R., 388
Caspi, A., 363
Cassidy, J., 242, 334
Castellan, N. J., 510
Castonguay, L. G., 567, 570
Castro-Martin, T., 32
Catanzaro, S. J., 287, 294, 300
Cecil-Pigo, E. F., 202
Chagnon, N. A., 146, 415
Chaiken, S., 113, 114, 284
Chambless, D. L., 560
Chambre, S. M., 175
Chapman, D. I., 201, 203, 204
Charng, H. W., 162, 174, 175, 184
Chartrand, T. L., 72
Cherlin, A. J., 32
Chiodo, L. M., 441
Chlopan, B. E., 283
Chorost, A. F., 112
Chrisman, K., 201, 202
Christensen, A., 10, 34, 230, 327, 559, 563, 566, 567, 569, 570, 576, 579
Cialdini, R. B., 168, 169, 170, 171, 172, 173, 427, 447, 485, 491, 492
Clark, C. L., 65
Clark, H. H., 511
Clark, L., 254
Clark, M. S., 79, 107, 165, 169, 175, 201, 202, 254, 255, 256, 257, 258, 259, 261, 262, 265, 266, 267, 269, 274n, 309, 314, 377, 383, 401, 447, 485, 491, 564, 577
Clary, E. G., 167, 174, 181

Cline, V. B., 147
Clore, G. L., 284
Clutton-Brock, T. H., 143, 416
Cohen, C. E., 72
Cohen, D., 150, 151
Cohen, G. L., 448
Cohen, J., 301
Cohen, L. J., 542
Cohen, R. L., 466
Cohen, S., 265, 446
Coie, J. D., 131, 132, 149
Coke, J. S., 283
Colby, A., 165, 182
Cole, S. W., 74
Cole-Detke, H., 551, 552, 553
Coleman, J. S., 506, 511, 513
Collier, D. R., 336
Collins, N. L., 23, 60, 63, 64, 66, 67, 68, 69, 70, 71, 75, 76, 77, 78, 119, 334, 538, 540, 543, 554
Collins, R. L., 267, 388, 392, 395
Colvin, C. R., 93, 109, 413, 442, 461
Comstock, G., 147
Conger, R. D., 324
Consoli, A. J., 560
Constanzo, P. R., 553
Cook, M., 145
Cooley, C. H., 88, 412, 449, 457, 458, 469, 472
Coombs, R. H., 49
Cooper, R. K., 301
Coopersmith, S., 414
Copper, C., 508
Corsini, R. J., 230, 231
Cosmides, L., 135, 136, 139, 411, 414, 421, 462, 465
Costa, R. T., 542
Cota, A. A., 508, 509
Coyne, J. C., 579
Craiger, J. P., 183
Cranley, M. S., 545
Crary, W. G., 95
Crittenden, P. M., 68, 81n
Crocker, J., 95, 186, 213, 417, 459, 470
Crockett, W. H., 41
Crosby, F., 360
Cross, S. E., 487
Crouse, B., 42
Crowe, M. J., 562

Crowell, J. A., 68, 70, 81*n*
Crowley, M., 180
Cruse, S. W., 438
Cummings, E. M., 148, 149
Cunningham, M. R., 168, 177, 445
Curtis, R. C., 273
Cutrona, C. A., 265

Daly, M., 137, 140, 141, 142, 151, 414, 416,
    417, 418, 419
Damon, W., 165, 182
Daniels, L. R., 174, 175, 367
Darley, J. M., 163, 164, 514
Darwin, C., 130, 279
Daubeny, C., 506
Daubman, K. A., 285
Davey, A., 13, 15
Davidson, G. N. S., 10
Davidson, M. N., 217
Davidson, R. J., 133, 154*n*, 253, 308, 311
Davies, B., 272
Davies, M., 289, 298, 300
Davies, P. T., 148, 149
Davila, J., 40, 334
Davis, K. E., 3, 4, 5, 18, 245, 333, 335, 341,
    343, 346, 347, 348, 349, 352*n*, 538
Davis, M. H., 177, 182, 183, 333, 347, 348,
    351, 352*n*, 491, 492
Davison, G., 563
Dawes, R., 461
Dawkins, R., 140, 144, 419, 425
De Dreu, C. K. W., 207, 208, 209
De Harpport, T., 201, 203, 211
De la Ronde, C., 49, 491
De Maris, A., 440
De Steno, D., 325
De Waal, F. B. M., 133, 419, 424, 457
Deal, J. E., 510
Deaux, K., 175, 182
Deci, E. L., 479
Denton, K., 428
Denton, W. H., 43
Deutsch, M., 201, 377
Devine, P. E., 51
Dewaraja, R., 282
Di Girolamo, G. J., 139
Di Paula, A., 267
Diekmann, K. A., 200, 205, 207, 208, 209,
    214

Diener, E., 393
Dillard, J. P., 444
Dion, K., 440, 442
Dix, T. H., 18
Dodge, K. A., 131, 132, 133, 140, 149
Doherty, W. J., 37
Doise, W., 505
Dolan, A., 439
Donner, A., 518, 529*n*
Donnerstein, E., 146, 170
Doré, F., 283
Dorrity, K., 497*n*
Dovidio, J. F., 164, 165, 166, 168, 169, 170,
    173, 174, 178
Downey, G., 37, 120
Downs, D. L., 411, 412, 428, 461, 462, 472
Drapkin, I., 141
Drews, J. L., 198
Drigotas, S. M., 108, 360, 361, 367, 374, 450
Drolet, A., 207, 208
Druckman, D., 196, 198
Dryden, W., 326
Duncan, S., 527
Duncker, K., 285
Dunn, J., 149
Dunning, D., 52, 95, 448, 578
Durkheim, E., 506, 508
Dutton, D. G., 166, 481, 552
Dweck, C. S., 37
Dye, M. L., 13
Dymond, R. F., 230, 283, 284

Eagly, A. H., 180
Easterbrook, J. A., 284
Eckhard, C. I., 13
Edelmann, R. J., 166
Edwards, A. L., 528
Egeland, B., 62
Eidelson, R. J., 34, 35, 39, 325
Eisenberg, N., 167, 168, 170, 180, 182
Ekman, P., 133, 154*n*, 253, 283, 308, 311,
    312
Elias, M. J., 301
Eliasziw, M., 529*n*
Ellard, J. H., 176
Elliott, P. R., 513, 529
Ellis, A., 34, 326
Ellis, B. J., 137, 140, 154*n*, 421, 422
Ellis, C., 324

Ellis, H. C., 79
Elston, R. C., 510
Ember, C. R., 417
Emery, R. E., 398
Emmons, R. A., 284, 294, 300, 441, 442, 579
Epstein, E. E., 567
Epstein, N., 14, 34, 35, 39, 51, 283, 284, 325, 559, 566, 568
Epstein, S., 414, 542
EQ Japan Inc., 293, 298
Erikson, E. H., 437, 438
Esterly, E., 345, 347
Evans, M. G., 103*n*
Eysenck, M. W., 77

Fabes, R. A., 167, 168, 169, 170, 180
Fadiga, L., 145
Falbo, T., 14
Farber, E., 62
Farwell, L., 442
Faust, K., 513
Fazio, R. H., 15, 44, 45, 72, 113, 402
Feeney, J. A., 64, 67, 71, 75, 76, 266, 271, 272, 345, 538
Fehr, B., 45, 89, 90, 334, 335, 336, 338, 339, 340, 350
Fei, J., 120
Feingold, A., 363, 423
Feldman, S., 37, 120
Felmlee, D., 361, 366, 375
Felson, R. B., 130, 131, 134, 140, 142, 446, 449
Fenigstein, A., 472*n*
Ferenz-Gillies, R., 552
Ferguson, L. R., 230
Festinger, L., 388, 389, 393, 403, 509, 511
Fichten, C., 4
Fincham, F. D., 4, 5, 6, 7, 8, 9, 10, 11, 12, 13, 14, 15, 18, 19, 20, 21, 22, 23, 24, 33, 34, 35, 36, 37, 44, 46, 52, 72, 75, 77, 112, 209, 318, 326, 401, 562, 568, 570, 573, 575, 578, 579
Finkelstein, M. A., 175, 181, 183
Fischer, D. H., 150
Fisher, R., 217
Fisher, R. A., 514, 516
Fiske, A., 178
Fiske, D. W., 527
Fiske, S. T., 77, 81*n*

Fitness, J., 33, 72, 75, 258, 335, 401
Fitzpatrick, D., 552
Fitzpatrick, M. A., 390
Fleiss, J. L., 517
Fletcher, G. J. O., 9, 11, 12, 14, 22, 33, 34, 35, 36, 38, 41, 45, 72, 75, 87, 89, 90, 91, 96, 98, 108, 129, 139, 238, 245, 318, 335, 401, 568
Florian, V., 539, 540, 543, 545, 546, 551
Folkman, S., 78, 267, 541, 542, 543, 545, 547
Fonagy, P., 553
Forgas, J. P., 77, 169, 209, 217, 244, 246, 323
Formica, R., 391
Forsyth, D. R., 558, 570
Foshee, V. A., 148
Foster, C. A., 176, 481
Fraley, B., 489
Fraley, R. C., 62, 67, 73, 74, 76, 334, 540
Francis, M. E., 288
Frank, R. H., 141, 142, 426
Frazier, P. A., 345, 347
Freud, A., 447
Freud, S., 86, 441, 442, 447, 448
Frey, D. L., 174
Frey, K. P., 509
Fridlund, A. J., 254
Friedland, N., 209
Friedlander, L., 282
Friedman, R. A., 197, 210
Friend, R., 393, 464
Friesen, W. V., 283
Frieze, I. H., 341, 343, 345, 347, 349
Frijda, N. H., 254, 263, 264
Frisch, M. B., 181
Fritzsche, B. A., 165, 183
Fry, W. R., 203
Fujita, F., 393
Fultz, J., 171
Funder, D. C., 109, 510

Gabriel, M. T., 442
Gaertner, S. L., 166, 170, 174
Gallistel, C. R., 145
Gallup, G. G., 457, 460
Galper, J., 179, 180
Gangestad, S. W., 91, 421
Gaschke, Y. K., 287
Geary, D. C., 134, 138
Gecas, V., 479

Geen R. G., 129, 131, 136, 147
Geher, G., 290, 296
Gendolla, G. H. E., 315
George, C., 68, 70
Gerard, H. B., 390, 403
Gerard, M., 181
Gergen, K. J., 178, 393, 468
Gerrard, M., 392, 395
Gibbons, F. X., 388, 392, 393, 395, 396, 397, 402
Giddings, C. W., 6
Gigerenzer, G., 137
Gigone, D., 510
Gilbert, D. T., 186
Gilbert, P., 419, 424
Gilkey, R. W., 204
Gilligan, S. G., 77, 489
Gilmore, J. B., 469
Ginsburg, B., 130
Giuliano, T. A., 287, 288, 294, 299
Glenn, N. D., 566
Goethals, G. R., 399
Goffman, E., 289, 446, 457, 458, 460, 472
Gold, P. E., 314
Goldberg, L. R., 488
Goldfried, M. R., 560, 572
Goldman, S. L., 282, 287, 288
Goldstein, D. G., 137
Goldstein, H., 519
Goleman, D., 279, 289, 292, 298, 301
Gollob, H. F., 520
Gollwitzer, P. M., 94, 578
Gonzalez, R., 507, 509, 514, 517, 521, 526, 528, 530n
Goodnow, J. J., 18
Goranson, R., 175
Gordis, E. B., 149
Gorman, J. M., 560
Gosling, S. D., 442
Gotay, C. C., 265
Gottman, J. M., 9, 17, 112, 230, 287, 368, 379, 561, 562, 563, 564, 565, 566, 567, 568, 570
Gould, R., 447
Gouldner, A., 149, 174, 175
Graber, J. A., 421
Graesser, A. C., 73
Gray, J. A., 315
Gray, J. P., 130

Graziano, W. G., 182
Green, L. R., 132, 139
Greenberg, J. R., 202, 208, 209, 412, 450, 461
Greenberg, L. S., 576
Greenberg, M. A., 288
Greener, S. M., 294, 299
Greenhalgh, L., 201, 203, 204, 217
Greenier, K. D., 426
Greenough, W. T., 316
Greenwald, A. G., 65, 122n, 215, 458, 459, 460, 470
Greenwood, G., 287, 300
Greer, S., 266
Grieger, R., 34
Griffin, D., 507, 514, 517, 521, 526, 528, 530n
Griffin, D. W., 450
Grote, N. K., 107, 261, 341, 343, 345, 347, 349
Grube, J. A., 175
Gruder, C. L., 367, 392
Grusec, J. E., 18, 167
Guerra, N. G., 146, 149, 150
Gunn, D. O., 489
Gustafson, R., 137
Guthrie, D. M., 230
Gutierres, S. E., 419
Guttentag, M., 100

Hackman, R., 509
Haggard, E. A., 516, 517
Hahlweg, K., 563
Hakmiller, K. L., 392
Halford, W. K., 579, 580
Halgin, R. P., 552
Hall, H. V., 153
Hall, J. A., 95, 283
Halpern, J. J., 201, 203, 204
Hamagani, F., 513
Hamilton, D. L., 508
Hamilton, T. E., 363, 423
Hamilton, W. D., 416
Hannah, M. E., 175
Hanson, E., 285
Harary, F., 513
Harter, S., 413, 414, 419, 426, 432n
Hartshorne, H., 178
Harvey, J., 568
Harvey, J. H., 5, 6, 7, 25, 46

Haselton, M. G., 428
Hassebrauck, M., 90
Hastie, R., 73, 216, 510
Hastorf, A. H., 210
Hatfield, E., 332, 334, 335, 336, 346, 349
Haupt, A., 463
Hauser, R. M., 519
Haviland, J. M., 311
Hay, L. L., 438
Hayden, T., 210
Hazan, C., 40, 62, 64, 66, 70, 265, 266, 318,
    333, 334, 335, 336, 349, 359, 361, 374,
    479, 538, 539, 540, 541, 543, 544, 545,
    547, 548, 549
Headey, B., 398, 399
Heavey, C. L., 563, 565
Hebb, D. O., 315
Hecht, M. L., 333, 347, 349, 351
Hedge, A., 164
Heider, F., 3, 5, 6, 18, 448, 485
Heinold, W. D., 164
Helgeson, V. S., 38, 109, 398
Hemphill, K. J., 396
Henderson, V. L., 37
Hendrick, C., 35, 322, 332, 333, 334, 335,
    336, 341, 343, 344, 346, 347, 348, 349,
    350, 351, 351n, 352n, 440
Henrich, R., 143
Henry, L., 494
Herbener, E. S., 363
Hermann, M. G., 197
Hewlett, B. S., 424
Hewstone, M. R. H., 4
Heyman, R. E., 9, 11, 325
Hicks, D. J., 147
Higgins, E. T., 23, 36, 43, 72, 73, 87, 88, 91,
    360, 479
Hill, R., 86
Hinde, R. A., 5, 511, 524
Hiraiwa-Hasegawa, M., 141
Hoberman, H. M., 265, 446
Hoffman, M. L., 168, 170, 491
Hofmann, S. G., 560
Hogan, R., 283, 284
Hogg, M. A., 399, 508
Hollon, S. D., 560
Holmes, J. G., 32, 48, 72, 93, 95, 108, 109,
    110, 111, 112, 113, 114, 115, 117, 119,
    120, 122n, 375, 376, 381, 398, 524, 577

Holtzworth-Munroe, A., 6, 9, 13, 14, 21
Homans, G. C., 511, 561
Hooley, J. M., 16, 17, 19
Hoop, D. K., 422
Hoorens, V., 398
Hoover, C. W., 174
Hoover-Dempsey, K. V., 260
Hoppe, K. D., 281
Horesh, N., 74
Horneffer, K. J., 15, 21
Hornstein, H. A., 168
Horowitz, L. M., 62, 66, 68, 70, 265, 334,
    450, 554
Horvath, A. O., 10
Hotaling, G. T., 148
Howard, J. A., 174, 182
Hoyle, R. H., 458, 459, 508, 509
Hrebec, D., 210
Huesmann, L. R., 132, 145, 147, 150, 482
Humphrey, N. K., 131
Huston, A. C., 146
Huston, T. L., 107, 111, 112, 162
Hutchinson, G., 13
Hyman, H., 393

Ickes, B., 509
Ickes, W., 230, 232, 233, 236, 240, 243, 245,
    284, 485, 515, 523
Independent Sector, 179, 180, 181
Infrasca, R., 282
Insko, C. A., 360, 393
Isen, A. M., 79, 167, 217, 284, 285

Jacklin, C. N., 513
Jacobson, L., 374
Jacobson, N. S., 5, 6, 10, 14, 19, 21, 34, 51,
    317, 327, 482, 559, 561, 562, 563, 566,
    567, 569, 570, 576, 579
James, W., 88, 313, 314, 448, 457, 486
Janis, I., 214
Janis, I. L., 218, 469
Janoff-Bulman, R., 230
Jaspars, J. M., 6, 15
Jehn, K. A., 201, 204
Jensen, M. P., 401
John, O. P., 442
Johnson, B. T., 489
Johnson, D. F., 198
Johnson, D. J., 48, 95, 108, 113, 375, 380

Johnson, D. R., 49
Johnson, E. J., 285
Johnson, M. K., 147, 574
Johnson, M. P., 337, 338, 342, 348, 366, 375
Johnson, S. M., 576
Johnson, T. E., 209
Johnson-Laird, P., 312
Joiner, T. E., 18, 441, 444
Jones, E. E., 3, 4, 5, 18, 458, 459, 464, 467, 469, 472, 488
Jones, J. J., 254
Jones, S. C., 446, 464, 466
Jones, W. H., 338, 342, 343, 347
Josephson, W. L., 147
Jung, C. G., 486

Kagan, N., 283
Kahn, A., 175
Kahn, M., 230, 236
Kahn, S., 438
Kahneman, D., 200
Kaiser, H. A., 579
Kalbflesch, P. J., 390
Kalick, S. M., 363, 423
Kanfer, F. H., 558
Kaplan, D., 513, 529
Kaplan, H. B., 416, 421
Karlin, S., 518
Karney, B. R., 9, 10, 15, 20, 22, 33, 42, 49, 51, 326, 575, 578, 580
Karoly, P., 401, 580
Karp, E. S., 447
Katz, J., 13, 577
Katz, M., 230
Kauhanen, J., 282
Keenan, J. M., 489
Kelley, H. H., 3, 4, 5, 6, 15, 18, 35, 38, 39, 48, 51, 78, 87, 108, 120, 198, 210, 211, 245, 310, 337, 338, 339, 340, 351, 359, 360, 361, 363, 364, 365, 366, 367, 368, 370, 371, 372, 373, 374, 375, 376, 377, 380, 382, 479, 523, 524, 525, 526, 528, 561, 562, 564, 565, 566, 568, 569, 575, 580
Kelln, B. R. C., 176
Kellner, H., 14
Kelly, C., 111
Kelly, G., 42

Keltner, D., 209, 210, 216, 217
Kennedy, J. E., 552
Kenny, D. A., 21, 40, 273, 507, 510, 512, 513, 518, 520, 521, 522, 523, 525, 526
Kenrick, D. T., 92, 169, 176, 177, 359, 419, 421, 423
Kernis, M. H., 119, 426, 442
Kerr, W. A., 284
Kessler, R. C., 283
Ketelaar, T., 137, 154n
Kette, G., 209
Kihlstrom, J. F., 69, 77, 79
Killian, L. M., 506
Kilpatrick, S. D., 231, 232
Kim, H., 77
Kim, U., 519
King, G., 56
King, J., 507
King, L. A., 284, 294, 300
Kininmonth, L., 12, 35, 38, 90
Kinney, R. F., 94
Kirkpatrick, L. A., 40, 245, 418, 426, 538
Kirouac, G., 283
Kitayama, S., 430
Klein, B., 206
Klein, K. J., 510
Klein, W. M., 398
Kling, K. C., 118
Klohnen, E. C., 36
Kluwer, E. S., 390
Knapp, A., 314
Knee, C. R., 22, 35, 37, 487
Knight, J. A., 5
Knipe, H., 425
Knudson, R. A., 230
Kobak, R. R., 67, 70, 76, 242, 538, 539, 540, 551, 552, 553, 576
Kogan, N., 197, 198
Koivumaki, J. H., 5, 448
Kolditz, T. A., 471
Kooiman, D. G., 280
Korte, C., 164
Kotlar, S. L., 231
Kowalski, R. M., 459, 467, 469, 472
Kraemer, H. C., 513
Kramer, R. M., 210, 213, 214, 216, 217
Krebs, D. L., 163, 262, 283, 428
Kreft, I., 519
Kring, A. M., 217

Kuipers, L., 16
Kulik, J. A., 390, 391
Kunda, Z., 32, 46, 109, 113, 117, 215, 392, 395
Kunkel, D., 146
Kunst-Wilson, W. R., 316
Kurdek, L. A., 35, 36, 513
Kursh, C. O., 234
Kwavnick, K. D., 459
Kyle, S. O., 14

La Prelle, J., 447
La Voie, L., 273, 507, 513, 518, 520, 521, 522, 525
Ladewig, B. H., 390
Laing, R. D., 230
Laird, J. D., 265
Lalumiere, M. L., 416, 422
Lambert, A. J., 95
Lamm, H., 198
Lancaster, J. B., 416
Landau, M. O., 169
Landau, S. F., 141
Lane, R. D., 281, 282, 290, 295
Langer, E., 213
Langer, E. J., 49
Lanzetta, J. T., 170
Larrick, R. P., 211
Larson, J. R., 514
Lasswell, M. E., 332
Latané, B., 163, 164, 514
Latty-Mann, H., 343, 346, 347
Lax, D. A., 199
Lazarus, R. S., 78, 147, 286, 308, 312, 541, 542, 543, 545, 547
Le Bon, G., 508, 511
Le Doux, J., 140, 142
Le Page, A., 152
Lea, S. E. G., 176
Leary, M. R., 100, 119, 254, 319, 359, 411, 412, 413, 414, 415, 422, 426, 428, 430, 431, 431n, 432n, 458, 459, 461, 462, 463, 464, 465, 467, 468, 469, 471, 472, 577
Lecky, P., 457
Lee, J. A., 332, 440
Leff, J., 16
Lehman, D. R., 396
Lemerise, E. A., 133, 140
Lennon, R., 180

Lennox, V. L., 166
Leonard, K. E., 8, 15
Lerner, M. J., 174, 176
Leung, C. C., 147
Levenson, R. W., 254
Levesque, R. J. R., 343, 345
Levine, R. V., 163
Levinger, G., 95, 337, 338, 366, 375
Levy, M. B., 333, 343, 346, 347, 348
Lewicki, R. J., 197, 234
Lewin, K., 210, 508, 511, 525
Lewis, M., 311
Leyens, J. P., 147
Liberman, V., 515
Licht, D. M., 17, 19
Lichtenberg, J. W., 42
Lickona, T., 301
Lind, E. A., 377
Linden, W., 281
Linder, D., 49
Linfield, K. J., 20, 575
Linville, P. W., 42
Linz, D., 147
Lipsey, M. W., 151
Liss, M. B., 147
Lobel, M., 392, 400, 403
Locke, H. J., 36
Lockwood, P., 392, 395
Loewenstein, G., 201, 205, 206, 207, 209, 216, 217, 218
London, P., 560
Longford, N. T., 513
Longmore, M. A., 440
Longstreth, M., 368
Lord, C. G., 488
Lord, R. G., 209
Lore, R. S., 133
Loving, T. J., 487
Luby, V., 336
Luckey, E. B., 230
Luhtanen, R., 417
Lumley, M. A., 282
Lussier, Y., 13
Lydon, J. E., 48, 338, 342, 348, 351, 351n, 352n
Lykken, D. T., 108

Ma, H., 174
Macaulay, J. R., 162

MacDowell, K., 315
Machleit, K. A., 485
MacKay, L., 491
Mackie, D. M., 496
Maclay, G., 425
MacLean, P. D., 177
Madden, M. E., 230
Mahler, H. I. M., 390, 391
Main, M., 60, 61, 62, 66, 81, 541, 552, 553
Major, B., 95, 186, 395, 446
Malamuth, E., 134
Malamuth, N. M., 134, 138, 140, 148
Malone, T. W., 513
Malouff, J., 297
Mandler, G., 312, 313, 314, 315, 316
Manis, M., 446
Mannix, E. A., 202, 205
Manson, J. H., 416, 417
Manstead, A. S. R., 391, 467, 471
Manucia, G. K., 169
Maracek, J., 466
March, J. G., 204
Margolin, G., 5, 6, 19, 317, 482, 561, 563, 566
Mari, J., 17
Markham, S. E., 509
Markman, H. J., 338, 342, 348, 559, 563, 565, 576, 577
Marks, E., 170
Marks, G., 95, 391, 399
Markus, H. R., 44, 72, 430, 489, 508
Marsh, H. W., 393
Marsh, R. L., 559, 573
Martin, J. (Miss Manners), 260
Martin, J. A., 513
Martin, L. L., 272
Martin, M. W., 470
Martin, R., 42, 72
Martin, R. W., 42
Martz, J. M., 108, 362, 381, 399, 441
Marwell, G., 176, 182, 198
Maslow, A. H., 86, 437, 438, 439, 479, 486
Masterton, J. F., 445
Mathes, E., 447
Mathews, K. E., 163
May, J. G., 198
May, M. A., 178
Mayer, J. D., 279, 280, 281, 283, 285, 287, 290, 296, 297, 298, 301

Maynard-Smith, J., 140
McArdle, J. J., 513
McCall, G. J., 486
McClelland, J. L., 507
McClintock, C. G., 371, 374
McConnell, A. R., 508, 509
McCrady, B. S., 567
McCrae, R. R., 542
McCullough, M. E., 375
McDonald, R. P., 519
McDougall, W., 511, 525
McFarland, C., 117, 399
McGuire, A. M., 162
McGuire, W., 118
McKillop, K. J. Jr, 467, 468
McLaughlin-Volpe, 492
McMillen, D. L., 164
Mead, G. H., 457, 458, 469, 472, 506
Mealey, L., 421
Mearns, J., 294, 300
Mecca, A. M., 439, 459
Medvene, L., 491
Meeks, B. S., 343, 347
Mehrabian, A., 283
Meier, P., 542
Merleau-Ponty, M., 485
Mervis, C. B., 335
Messick, D. M., 201, 205, 207, 208, 209, 212, 374
Metalsky, G. I., 15
Mettee, D. R., 389, 393, 394, 466
Metts, S., 35, 38
Meyer, H. H., 398
Meyer, W., 315
Michela, J. L., 15
Mickelson, K. D., 550
Midili, A. R., 184
Midlarsky, E., 175
Mikulincer, M., 64, 65, 66, 67, 73, 74, 76, 242, 244, 538, 539, 540, 541, 542, 543, 545, 546, 548, 549, 551, 552, 553, 554
Milardo, R. M., 389
Milgram, S., 164, 506, 511
Miller, D. T., 213, 399, 508
Miller, F. D., 23
Miller, G. E., 11, 578
Miller, J. B., 74, 77
Miller, J. G., 176, 185
Miller, K., 273

Miller, N., 169, 391, 399
Miller, P., 167, 170
Miller, R. S., 32, 39, 48, 113, 254, 380, 464, 468, 471
Miller, S. A., 18
Mills, J., 175, 255, 256, 263, 272, 377, 383, 403, 485, 564, 577
Mills, P., 390
Mineka, S., 145
Mintz, P. M., 390, 403
Mischel, W., 95, 178, 210
Mitchell, S. A., 450
Modigliani, A., 464
Moghaddam, F. M., 165, 177
Molm, L. D., 131
Money, J., 339
Moore, C., 447
Moore, D., 34
Moore, L., 181
Morf, C. C., 441, 442
Morgan, W., 201, 202
Morris, K. A., 66
Morris, M. W., 198, 210, 213, 214
Morrow, G. D., 343, 347
Morse, S., 393
Moss, E., 440
Mowrer, O. H., 279
Mruk, C., 468
Mueller, C. W., 170
Mulder, M. B., 416
Mullen, B., 495, 508
Mullin, C. R., 147
Munholland, K. A., 81*n*
Munton, A. G., 22
Murdock, G. P., 416
Murnigham, J. K., 198, 205, 207, 212, 217
Murray, D. W., 18
Murray, S. L., 32, 39, 48, 93, 95, 100, 108, 109, 110, 111, 112, 113, 114, 115, 117, 118, 119, 120, 122*n*, 374, 381, 398, 447, 450, 524, 527, 577
Murstein, B. I., 109, 230, 231, 341, 344
Muthen, B. O., 513, 529

Nachson, O., 67, 538
Nagin, D., 153
Najarian, B., 298
Nakamura, G. V., 7
Nathan, P. E., 560

Navran, L., 230
Nazby, W., 149
Neale, J. M., 542
Neale, M. A., 197, 200, 207, 208, 216
Negrao, M., 184
Neimeyer, G. J., 42, 230
Nelson, D., 262
Nemiah, J. C., 281
Nesse, R. M., 139, 140
Neuberg, S. L., 173, 492
Newcomb, T. M., 262, 511
Newman, H. M., 13, 49
Newman, L. S., 115
Newmark, C. S., 230
Nezlek, J. B., 119
Nies, D. C., 34
Nisbett, R. E., 32, 150, 151, 197, 198, 211, 488
Noirot, M., 74, 77
Nolen-Hoeksema, S., 287
Noller, P., 64, 230, 231, 236, 345, 538
Nordby, G., 282
Northcraft, G. B., 200, 211
Norton, R., 272
Notarius, C. I., 326, 576, 577
Novacek, J., 441
Nunley, E. P., 290, 296

Oatley, K., 312
Ochs, J., 207
O'Connor, K. M., 211, 218
O'Farrell, T. J., 567
Ogawa, J. R., 553
Ognibene, T. C., 67
Ohman, A., 316
Okun, 217
Oldersma, F. L., 401, 402
O'Leary, K. D., 34, 562, 563, 567
O'Leary, S. G., 18
Oleson, K. C., 171
Oliner, P., 165, 167, 182, 183, 184
Oliver, R. L., 216
Olson, C., 207, 208
Omoto, A. M., 181, 489
Orbach, I., 64, 548
Orbell, J. M., 368
Orenstein, L., 181
Organ, D. W., 176
Ortony, A., 286, 312

Orvis, B. R., 4, 5, 14
Osgood, C. E., 312
Oskamp, S., 210
Ostendorf, F., 461
Osti, R. M. A., 282
Otten, C. A., 164, 165, 180, 183
Owens, G., 68, 70

Paese, P. W., 211
Paik, H., 147
Pakaslahti, L., 153
Palfai, T. P., 284, 285
Panksepp, J., 133, 312
Papageorgis, D., 118
Pape, K. T., 13
Parke, R. D., 545
Parker, G. A., 143, 424
Parker, J. W., 393
Parry, D., 234
Pasch, L. A., 577
Passer, M. W., 5, 12
Patrick, M., 553
Paul, G. L., 571
Paulhus, D. L., 442, 446
Pavelchak, M. A., 77
Pearce, P. L., 162, 175
Pearson, J. L., 552
Pearson, K., 514
Pelham, B. W., 50, 113, 114
Pennebaker, J. W., 258, 288
Penner, L. A., 165, 175, 179, 181, 182, 183,
    184
Perez, R. C., 422
Perreault, S., 487
Perry, D. G., 146, 147
Perry, L. C., 147
Perry, P., 287
Peterson, C., 20, 21
Peterson, D., 415, 425
Petrie, J., 440
Pettigrew, T. F., 492
Petty, R. E., 125
Pham, L. B., 37
Picus, S., 147
Pierce, G. R., 75
Piliavin, J. A., 162, 164, 165, 166, 167, 169,
    174, 175, 178, 179, 180, 184
Pillutla, M. M., 207, 217
Pina, D. L., 390

Pinker, S., 135, 136, 152
Pinkley, R. L., 198, 211, 212
Pinsker, H., 325
Pipp, S., 487
Pittman, T., 459, 472
Pleban, R., 3
Plutchik, R., 311, 312, 482
Polzer, J. T., 201, 202, 215
Porterfield, A. L., 230
Posner, M. I., 139
Power, T. G., 545
Prentice, D. A., 488, 489, 508
Pretzer, J., 12
Price, J. S., 425
Priest, G., 206
Provost, C., 416
Pruitt, D. G., 196, 197, 203, 204, 205, 208
Puccio, C., 210
Pysczynski, T. A., 95, 481

Quigley, B. M., 131
Quine, W., 511

Rabbie, J. M., 390, 391
Rabow, J., 163
Radvansky, J. A., 147
Raiffa, H., 199, 200
Rapaport, A., 369
Rapson, R. L., 332
Raskin, R. N., 441, 442, 445
Raudenbush, S. W., 512, 518, 519
Rausch, H. L., 41, 234
Raven, B. H., 131, 140
Raviv, A., 167
Raye, C. L., 574
Read, S. J., 51, 60, 63, 68, 69, 70, 71, 76, 77,
    78, 334, 540, 554
Reddy, R. D., 174, 182
Regan, D. T., 210
Regan, P. C., 89, 92, 100, 332, 341, 342, 343,
    346, 347, 352*n*, 423
Reik, T., 447, 485
Reis, H. T., 5, 22, 309, 318, 327, 484, 493
Reissman, C., 482
Reivich, K., 21
Rempel, J. K., 72, 75, 108, 114, 120, 376
Rempel, J. R., 113
Repetti, R. L., 149, 324
Resnick, L. B., 508

Rhodewalt, F., 441, 442
Rholes, W. S., 243, 539, 576, 577
Richardson, D. C., 3
Richardson, D. R., 130, 132, 139, 142, 343, 345, 347
Richerson, P., 143
Riley, H. C., 216
Rime, B., 258
Rioux, S., 182, 184
Riskind, J. H., 265
Rizzolatti, G., 145
Roberts, J. E., 120, 552
Roberts, M. K., 333
Robins, R. W., 442
Robinson, R. J., 209, 210, 216
Robinson, W. S., 507, 519
Rochill, C. M., 294, 299
Rodin, J., 214, 286
Rofé, Y., 391
Roger, D., 298
Rogers, C. R., 86, 88, 437, 438, 439, 457, 461
Rogers, T. B., 489
Roloff, M. E., 33
Rosch, E. H., 335
Rosen, S., 446
Rosenberg, M., 412, 421, 457
Rosenblatt, P. C., 339
Rosenhan, D., 167
Rosenthal, R., 283, 374
Roskos-Ewoldsen, D. R., 72
Ross, L., 32, 197, 198, 200, 208, 210, 211
Ross, M., 23, 50, 51, 213
Roth, A. E., 204, 205, 207
Roth, S., 542
Rotondo, J. L., 37
Rotter, J. B., 283
Rousseau, J. J., 129
Rubin, J. Z., 196, 197, 201, 210, 366
Rubin, Z., 332, 346, 347
Rule, B. G., 209
Rumelhart, D. E., 507
Runciman, W. G., 485
Rusbult, C. E., 47, 48, 89, 95, 108, 109, 113, 176, 245, 337, 338, 340, 360, 361, 362, 366, 371, 373, 375, 379, 380, 381, 382, 398, 399, 441, 443, 447, 479, 524
Rushton, J. P., 177, 181, 183
Russell, D. W., 265
Russell, J. A., 89, 90, 336, 575

Ruvolo, A. P., 37, 39, 450
Ruzzene, M., 230, 231, 236
Ryan, K., 176
Ryan, R. M., 461, 479, 578
Ryback, D., 301

Sabatelli, R. M., 202, 326
Sabourin, S., 8, 12
Sacco, W. P., 18
Sagi, A., 170
Salovey, P., 164, 167, 168, 214, 279, 280, 281, 282, 284, 285, 286, 287, 288, 293, 296, 297, 298, 299, 325
Samuels, S. M., 211
Samuelson, W. F., 200
Sande, G. N., 488, 489
Sanitioso, R., 32, 95
Sarason, I. G., 77, 267
Savage, L. J., 213
Savin-Williams, R. C., 182
Sawaf, A., 301
Sawyer, J., 201, 202
Sayers, S. L., 12, 567
Scanzoni, J., 319
Sceery, A., 67, 70, 76, 242, 539
Schachter, S., 311, 312, 313, 389, 390, 391, 392, 509
Schaller, M., 169, 171, 172
Schank, R. C., 115
Scharfe, E., 334
Schatz, R. T., 415
Schefft, B. K., 558
Scheier, M. F., 49, 91, 458, 460, 472n, 481, 484, 579
Schelling, T. C., 218
Schill, T., 553
Schlenker, B. R., 19, 458, 459, 460, 464, 465, 466, 467, 471, 472, 472n
Schmitt, D. P., 91, 92, 416
Schmitt, D. R., 176, 198
Schneider, D. J., 464, 466
Schoeninger, D., 201, 203
Schriesheim, C. A., 509
Schroder, H. M., 41
Schroeder, D. A., 162, 173, 179
Schuetz, A., 440, 441
Schultz, L., 133
Schutte, N. S., 292, 297
Schutz, A., 485

Schwartz, G. E., 282
Schwartz, P., 368
Schwartz, S., 519
Schwartz, S. H., 173, 174, 182
Schwarz, N., 284, 382
Scott, C. K., 22
Scott, J. P., 254
Scott, M. D., 230, 231, 234
Scott, W. A., 41
Sebenius, J. K., 199
Secord, P. F., 100, 367
Sedikides, C., 95, 446, 448, 458, 479, 480, 486, 494
Segal, N. L., 177
Segall, M. H., 133
Segrin, C., 444
Seligman, M. E. P., 21, 34, 215
Senchak, M., 8, 15
Sentis, K. P., 201, 205, 207, 208, 209
Shackelford, T. K., 146, 152
Shafir, E., 213
Shah, P. P., 201, 204
Shaver, K. G., 6, 19
Shaver, P. R., 36, 62, 63, 64, 65, 66, 67, 74, 76, 265, 266, 269, 318, 333, 334, 335, 336, 349, 359, 361, 374, 479, 538, 539, 540, 541, 543, 544, 545, 547, 548, 549, 550, 552, 568, 576
Shaw, M. E., 509
Shaw, R., 442, 445
Shefrin, H. M., 218
Shennum, W. A., 18
Sheppard, V. J., 440
Shepperd, J. A., 459
Sherif, M., 495, 511
Sherman, S. J., 508
Shimanoff, S. B., 261
Shockley, V. L., 390
Shotland, R. L., 162, 164
Showers, C., 42, 113, 114, 115, 118
Showronski, J. J., 95
Shrauger, J. S., 422, 464, 466
Shrout, P. E., 517
Sibicky, M. E., 172, 183, 186
Sicoly, F., 208
Siegel, J. M., 549
Sifneos, P. E., 280
Sigall, H., 447
Silk, J. B., 142, 143

Sillars, A. L., 51, 230, 231, 233, 234, 236, 243, 390
Sills, D. L., 175
Silvera, D. H., 186
Silverberg, J., 130
Simmons, C. H., 176
Simon, H. A., 177, 204, 254, 263, 511, 513
Simpson, J. A., 48, 67, 91, 94, 95, 112, 113, 119, 230, 232, 233, 235, 236, 240, 242, 243, 244, 245, 269, 321, 334, 366, 380, 421, 425, 577
Sinclair, L., 120
Singer, J. E., 311, 312, 390
Singh, G. K., 94
Sividas, E., 485
Skitka, L. J., 176
Slaby, R. G., 146
Slep, A. M. S., 18
Smart, L., 469
Smith, E., 489, 494
Smith, E. R., 3, 23, 24, 496, 509
Smith, G., 389, 393, 394
Smith, J., 44
Smith, J. E., 209
Smith, K. D., 172
Smith, L., 146
Smith, M. S., 417
Smith, R. H., 393
Smith, S. M., 125
Smuts, B., 142
Snyder, C. R., 570, 577
Snyder, D. K., 6, 7, 8, 567, 572
Snyder, M., 36, 174, 181, 210, 319, 374, 375, 558
Soares, J. J. F., 316
Sober, E., 162, 177, 507
Solomon, J., 68
Solomon, R. C., 339
Solomon, R. L., 382
Solomon, S., 412
Solomon, Z., 544
Sommer, R., 565
Sommers, S., 261
Sondak, H., 201, 202, 204, 205
Sorman, P. B., 422
Sorrentino, R. M., 479, 497*n*
Spanier, G. B., 93
Spears, R., 391
Speer, D. C., 564

Spencer, S. J., 461
Speroff, B. J., 284
Sprecher, S., 35, 49, 332, 334, 341, 342, 343, 345, 346, 347, 352n, 367
Sroufe, L. A., 61, 576
Srull, T. K., 41, 72, 73
Stahelski, A. J., 375
Stanley, S. M., 338, 342, 348
Stark, B. E., 175, 182
Stasser, G., 513, 514
Staub, E., 167, 182
Steele, C. M., 93, 121, 461
Steele, J. L., 497n
Steil, J. M., 390
Steiner, C., 287
Stephan, W., 95
Sterling, B., 170
Sternberg, C. R., 133
Sternberg, R. J., 89, 332, 333, 340, 341, 342, 343, 346n, 347, 348, 349, 351, 360
Stillinger, C., 200
Stinson, L., 240, 245, 515, 523
Stone, A. A., 288, 542
Stoner, P., 272
Strange, J. J., 147
Streiner, D. L., 17
Stretton, M. S., 282
Stroebe, M. S., 289, 321
Strube, M. J., 362, 479
Stryker, S., 175
Stuart, R. B., 561, 562, 563, 566
Stuckert, R., 230, 231
Stukas, A. A., 175, 319, 577
Suarez, S. D., 457, 460
Suedfeld, P., 42
Sugarman, D. B., 148
Suls, J., 388, 399, 427
Sun, C., 442
Suppes, P., 513
Surra, C. A., 368, 389
Susser, M., 519
Swann, W. B., 49, 50, 113, 114, 210, 429, 450, 451, 466, 491
Swinkels, A., 287, 288, 294, 299
Symons, C. S., 489
Symons, D., 411, 414, 419

Tajfel, H., 417, 447, 485
Tangney, J. P., 36, 89, 286

Taraban, C. B., 255, 256, 258, 266, 267
Taylor, B. A., 230
Taylor, G. J., 281
Taylor, K. L., 47
Taylor, S. E., 5, 37, 81n, 93, 95, 109, 115, 122n, 212, 213, 215, 382, 392, 395, 396, 399, 400, 401, 402, 403, 427, 448, 461, 470, 479, 484
Tedeschi, J. T., 130, 131, 134, 140, 142, 149
Teger, A. I., 366
Tellegen, A., 108
Tenbrunsel, A. E., 204, 205, 214
Tennen, H., 413
Terry, D. J., 440, 445, 545
Tesser, A., 19, 73, 393, 427, 446, 447, 448, 485, 579
Testa, M., 395
Tetlock, P. E., 41, 42, 114, 467, 471
Tett, R., 291, 297
Thagard, P., 51, 113
Thaler, R., 218
Thayer, R. E., 288
Thibaut, J. W., 35, 48, 51, 87, 199, 211, 245, 337, 338, 339, 359, 360, 361, 364, 366, 367, 368, 370, 371, 377, 479, 511, 523, 524, 525, 526, 529, 561, 562, 564, 565, 566, 568
Thoits, P., 283
Thomas, E. A. C., 513
Thomas, G., 11, 34, 36, 41, 89, 91, 109, 174, 231, 232, 238, 245
Thomas-Knowles, C., 290, 296
Thompson, J. S., 6, 7, 8
Thompson, L., 197, 200, 201, 202, 203, 205, 206, 207, 208, 209, 210, 211, 216, 217
Thorndyke, E. L., 34
Tice, D. M., 446, 460, 465, 466, 468
Tice, T., 175
Tidwell, M. O., 244
Tiger, L., 416
Tillman, P., 182, 184
Titus, S. L., 389, 400
Titus, W., 514
Tjosvold, D., 367
Toch, H., 506, 511
Todd, M. J., 333, 335, 341, 346, 349, 352n
Tomkins, S. S., 280
Tooby, J., 135, 136, 139, 411, 414, 421, 462, 465

Traupmann, J., 332
Tremblay, R. E., 129, 133, 153
Triandis, H. C., 430
Trivers, R. L., 143, 177, 416, 473
Tropp, L. R., 487, 494
Trost, M. R., 359
Trudeau, J. V., 467
Tucker, P., 481
Turkat, D., 466
Turkewitz, H., 562, 563
Turner, C. W., 147, 152, 153
Turner, J. C., 417, 447, 448, 485, 495
Turner, R. H., 506
Turner, T. J., 312
Tversky, A., 200, 213, 285, 515
Tweed, R. G., 552
Tyler, T., 216
Tyler, T. R., 377
Tyndall, L. W., 42

Uleman, J. S., 487
Unger, L., 547, 551
Unger, R. K., 180
Ury, W., 217
Utne, M. K., 202

Vaillant, C. O., 49
Vallacher, R. R., 5
Valley, K. L., 201, 203, 204, 205
Van den Eijnden, R. J. J. M., 47, 398, 399, 400, 443
Van der Zee, K. E., 397
Van Lange, P. A. M., 47, 95, 108, 109, 366, 371, 373, 374, 375, 379, 381, 398, 443, 524
Van Yperen, A. L., 107, 111, 263
Vancouver, J. B., 24, 578, 580
Vangelisti, A. L., 107, 111, 263
Vanzetti, N. A., 38, 579
Vaughan, K. B., 170
Vaughn, C., 16
Veit, C. T., 551
Venardos, C., 230
Veroff, J., 39
Vidmar, N., 198
Vincent, J. P., 564
Vorauer, J. D., 23, 50, 51

Wade-Benzoni, K. A., 205, 207, 214, 215

Wagner, H. L., 283
Wagner, K. D., 18
Walczynski, P. T., 327
Wallace, A., 230
Wallace, K. M., 36
Waller, N. G., 62
Waller, W., 86
Walster, E. H., 86, 97, 103, 174, 176, 205, 332, 340, 341, 464
Walster, G. W., 332, 341
Walters, A. E., 197
Walton, M. D., 166
Walton, R. E., 201
Ward, A., 211
Ware, J. E., 551
Wasielewski, P. L., 289
Wasserman, S., 513
Waters, E., 61, 576
Watson, C., 197
Watson, D., 254, 464
Watson, M., 266
Watson, P. J., 442
Watzlawick, P., 234
Wearing, A., 398, 399
Weber, A. L., 14, 309
Webley, P., 176
Wedell, D. H., 95
Wegner, D. M., 469, 491
Wehmer, F., 282
Weiner, B., 4, 6, 17, 19, 20, 78, 168, 174
Weinstein, E., 324
Weinstein, N. D., 47, 398
Weisinger, H., 301
Weismann, R. X., 179
Weiss, R. L., 9, 11, 34, 44, 325, 562, 566, 580
Wenegrat, B., 424
Westbay, L., 89, 90, 341, 342, 343, 345, 349
Wetzel, C. G., 360
Wheeler, L., 493
Whiffen, V. E., 576
Whisman, M. A., 567, 572
Whitaker, L. C., 153
Whitbourne, S. K., 552
White, G., 325
White, L. K., 482
White, P. N., 390
White, R. W., 478, 479
Wichman, H., 198
Widom, C. S., 148

Wieselquist, J., 369, 376
Wile, D. B., 576
Williams, D., 553
Williams, K. D., 509
Williamson, G. M., 165, 169, 262, 274n
Wills, T. A., 34, 95, 388, 392, 393, 396, 400, 401, 402, 403, 427, 446
Wilson, D. S., 177, 507
Wilson, J. P., 164
Wilson, J. S., 553
Wilson, M., 137, 140, 141, 142, 146, 151, 153, 417, 418, 419
Wispé, L. G., 163, 283
Wohlwend-Lloyd, R., 442
Wolfe, B. E., 572
Wolfe, R. N., 425, 466
Wood, J. V., 47, 388, 393, 397, 401
Wood, W., 201, 203
Wrangham, R., 415, 416, 417, 425
Wright, J., 4
Wright, R., 100, 419
Wright, S. C., 487, 493, 494, 495
Wyer, R. S., 41, 72, 73, 147

Wylie, R. C., 457
Wynne-Edwards, V. C., 425

Yates, S., 113, 114
Ybema, J. F., 393, 394, 395, 398, 401, 403
Yeung, R. R., 288
Yinon, Y., 169
Yousif, Y. H., 164
Yovetich, N. A., 379

Zahavi, A., 428
Zahn-Waxler, C., 177
Zaidi, L. Y., 148
Zajonc, R. B., 185, 316, 525
Zander, A., 511
Zanna, M. P., 113
Zarate, M. A., 23
Zeitlin, S. B., 281
Zillmann, D., 263
Zimbardo, P., 391
Zukier, H., 117
Zuroff, D. C., 552

VERMONT COLLEGE LiBRARY

0 0036 00002801

DATE DUE

SE 28 '06			

Please remember that this is a library book,
and that it belongs only temporarily to each
person who uses it. Be considerate. Do
not write in this, or any, library book.